The Handbook of Homeland Security

The Handbook of Homeland Security is a convenient, one-stop reference and guide to the latest regulations and developments in all things relevant to the homeland security and defense domain.

The book is divided into five parts and addresses such critical areas as countering terrorism, critical infrastructure protection, information and cybersecurity, military and private sector support for homeland security, risk assessment, and preparedness for all-hazards and evolving threats. In total, more than 100 chapters outline the latest developments in homeland security policies, directives, and mandates as well as emergent threats and topical considerations for the Department of Homeland Security (DHS) and its stakeholders.

The diverse array of chapter topics covered—contributed to by dozens of top experts in the field—provides a useful and important resource for any student, professional, researcher, policy-maker, or library in understanding the domestic initiatives of public-sector homeland security entities and their responsibilities in the current global environment.

The Handbook of Homeland Security

Edited by

Scott N. Romaniuk
Martin Scott Catino
C. Augustus Martin

CRC Press
Taylor & Francis Group
Boca Raton New York London

CRC Press is an imprint of the
Taylor & Francis Group, an informa business

Front cover image: Volodymyr Kyrylyuk/Shutterstock

First edition published 2023
by CRC Press
2385 NW Executive Center Drive, Suite 320, Boca Raton FL 33431

and by CRC Press
4 Park Square, Milton Park, Abingdon, Oxon, OX14 4RN

CRC Press is an imprint of Taylor & Francis Group, LLC

Library of Congress Cataloging-in-Publication Data
Names: Martin, Gus, editor. | Romaniuk, Scott N., 1979- editor. | Catino, Martin Scott, author.
Title: The handbook of homeland security / edited by Scott N. Romaniuk, C. Augustus "Gus" Martin and Martin Scott Catino.
Identifiers: LCCN 2022046524 (print) | LCCN 2022046525 (ebook) | ISBN 9781138501720 (hardback) | ISBN 9781032362632 (paperback) | ISBN 9781315144511 (ebook)
Subjects: LCSH: United States. Department of Homeland Security. | Terrorism--Prevention--United States. | Computer security--United States.
Classification: LCC HV6432.4 .H34 2023 (print) | LCC HV6432.4 (ebook) |
DDC 353.30973--dc23/eng/20230201
LC record available at https://lccn.loc.gov/2022046524
LC ebook record available at https://lccn.loc.gov/2022046525

ISBN: 978-1-138-50172-0 (hbk)
ISBN: 978-1-032-36263-2 (pbk)
ISBN: 978-1-315-14451-1 (ebk)

DOI: 10.4324/9781315144511

Typeset in Garamond
by SPi Technologies India Pvt Ltd (Straive)

Contents

About the Editors xiii
List of Contributors xvii
Introduction xxi

PART I DEPARTMENT OF HOMELAND SECURITY (DHS) AND CRITICAL INFRASTRUCTURE
JOHN M. CALLAHAN

1 **Blackouts and Brownouts or Power Outages** 3
MILA DEMCHYK SAVAGE

2 **Body Scanners** 9
AARON COOLEY

3 **Bureau of Alcohol, Tobacco, Firearms, and Explosives** 13
DARREN E. TROMBLAY

4 **Central Intelligence Agency (CIA) and the Intelligence Community** 19
SUZETTE A. HAUGHTON AND SCOTT N. ROMANIUK

5 **Critical Infrastructure and Key Resources** 25
MILA DEMCHYK SAVAGE

6 **Critical Manufacturing Sector** 31
CARL A. MARRARA

7 **Department of Homeland Security (DHS)** 39
SUZETTE A. HAUGHTON AND SCOTT N. ROMANIUK

8 **Domestic Nuclear Detection Office (DNDO)** 45
DARREN E. TROMBLAY

9 **Emergency Response Task Forces to Address Physical and Cyber Threats** 53
THOMAS J. BECK

10 Energy (Power) Security and Grids **59**
MILA DEMCHYK SAVAGE

11 Federal Aviation Administration (FAA) **65**
WILLIAM R. PATTERSON

12 Federal Bureau of Investigation **71**
DARREN E. TROMBLAY

13 Immigration and Customs Enforcement (ICE) **79**
LORA HADZHIDIMOVA

14 Industrial Resilience **87**
MILA DEMCHYK SAVAGE

15 National Domestic Preparedness Office **93**
DARREN E. TROMBLAY

16 National Protection and Programs Directorate **99**
DARREN E. TROMBLAY

17 Partnership for Peace Consortium **107**
HUSO HASANOVIC

18 Protecting Critical Infrastructure and Key Resources **111**
RUSSELL RICHARDSON JR.

19 Riots and Rioting **117**
LORA HADZHIDIMOVA

20 Secure Border Initiative **125**
MARGARET SEYMOUR AND SCOTT N. ROMANIUK

21 Smuggling **129**
WILLIAM R. PATTERSON

22 The Bureau of Alcohol, Tobacco, Firearms, and Explosives (ATF) **137**
WILLIAM R. PATTERSON

23 The National Biosurveillance Integration Center (NBIC) **147**
WAYNE LESPERANCE

24 The National Emergency Management Association (NEMA) **153**
JAMES VALIQUET

PART II CYBERSECURITY, TERRORISM, AND ASYMMETRIC THREATS

ZOHA WASEEM

25 Advanced Persistent Threats (APTs) 163
ANWAR OUASSINI AND MICHAEL HUNTER

26 Chain of Custody 167
GARY LEIGH

27 Conficker Worm 173
GORDON ALLEY-YOUNG

28 Cryptocurrencies 181
SCOTT N. ROMANIUK AND RONALD LORENZO

29 Cyber Security and Social Media 187
AARON T. WALTER

30 Cyber Security Operations: Tactics, Techniques, and Procedures 197
GARY LEIGH

31 Cyberattacks 205
CHAD PATRICK OSORIO

32 Cybercrime, National Security, and Internet Governance 211
SCOTT N. ROMANIUK AND PRIYANKA HATTIANGADY

33 Cybersecurity 231
DARREN E. TROMBLAY

34 Cyberweapons 237
GARY LEIGH

35 Distributed Denial-of-Service (DDoS) Threats and Attacks 243
MOSTAFA AMINI

36 Government Communications Headquarters (GCHQ) 249
MADELAINE PREEDY

37 Hackers and Hacktivism 255
MARY MANJIKIAN

38 Internet of Things (IoT) 263
SCOTT N. ROMANIUK AND RONALD LORENZO

39 Malware 267
GARY LEIGH

40 **National Security Agency (NSA): From the Cold War to Post-9/11** 273
JÁNOS KEMÉNY AND SCOTT N. ROMANIUK

41 **Social Engineering** 283
CHAD PATRICK OSORIO

42 **Stuxnet** 289
DOMINIKA DZIWISZ

43 **Swatting** 295
SCOTT N. ROMANIUK AND RONALD LORENZO

44 **Third Department of the People's Liberation Army General Staff Headquarters (3PLA)** 301
ANWAR OUASSINI AND BRYNN DAO

45 **US Cyber Command (USCYBERCOM)** 305
DOMINIKA DZIWISZ AND SCOTT N. ROMANIUK

PART III TERRORISM AND ASYMMETRIC THREATS
ZOHA WASEEM

46 **Al Qaeda in the Islamic Maghreb (AQIM)** 317
TAVIS D. JULES

47 **Al Qaeda** 325
RAPHAËL LEDUC

48 **Ansar Allah** 335
ROBERT FORSTER AND HAMISH KINNEAR

49 **Basque Separatists** 345
NELL BENNETT

50 **Car Bombs** 351
RAPHAËL LEDUC

51 **Chemical and Biological Weapons (CBW)** 361
JAMES REVILL AND GIOVANNA FERRIANI MADUREIRA PONTES

52 **Foreign Terrorist Fighters (FTF)** 369
NELL BENNETT AND SCOTT N. ROMANIUK

53 **Hezbollah** 379
MARIAM FARIDA

54 **Hijackings** 387
EUGENIO LILLI

55 **Improvised Explosive Devices (IEDs)** 393
JADE HUTCHINSON

56 **Irish Republican Army (IRA)** 403
GLEN M. E. DUERR

57 **Lone Actor Terrorism** 411
RAPHAEL D. MARCUS

58 **Nationalists** 421
GLEN M. E. DUERR

59 **Right-Wing Extremism** 429
JADE HUTCHINSON

60 **State-Sponsored Terrorism** 441
TAVIS D. JULES

61 **Suicide Bombers** 451
CHARLIE WINTER

62 **Target Hardening** 457
ZOHA WASEEM

63 **Terrorism Copycat Effects** 467
NIKITA KOHLI

64 **Urban Warfare** 477
UMER KHAN AND SCOTT N. ROMANIUK

PART IV UNITED STATES (US) DOMESTIC AND BORDER SECURITY
ERIKA CORNELIUS SMITH AND SUZETTE A. HAUGHTON

65 **Active Shootings on College and University Campuses** 491
ALLISON MCDOWELL-SMITH

66 **Barrio Azteca (Los Aztecas) Mexican-American Gang** 497
RÉJEANNE M. LACROIX

67 **Beltrán-Leyva Organization (BLO)** 505
RÉJEANNE M. LACROIX

68 Border Patrols and National Entry Points 513
JASON R. JOLICOEUR

69 Civil Liberties and Homeland Security 525
SUZETTE A. HAUGHTON AND SCOTT N. ROMANIUK

70 Disaster Management and Assistance (DMA) 533
ALEX D. COLVIN AND ANGELA N. BULLOCK

71 Domestic Security 543
NABIL OUASSINI

72 Gangs and Law Enforcement in the United States 549
TAMARRA SMITH

73 Improvised Explosive Devices (IEDs) 559
BOYD P. BROWN III

74 Kidnappings 569
MEGAN LAMARE

75 La Familia Michoacana (LFM) Mexican Drug Cartel 575
ASHLEY CORCORAN

76 Law Enforcement and Legal Foundations of Homeland Security 581
NICHOLAS J. BARNES

77 Los Zetas Mexican Drug Cartel 587
RYAN ROBERTS

78 Mara Salvatrucha (MS-13) International Criminal Gang 591
RYAN ROBERTS AND SCOTT N. ROMANIUK

79 Maritime Domain Awareness (MDA) 595
ALLISON MCDOWELL-SMITH

80 Militias 601
RÉJEANNE M. LACROIX

81 National Preparedness for Natural and Human-Caused Hazards 611
STEPHEN WILLIAMS AND SCOTT N. ROMANIUK

82 Passive Surveillance 617
LEONARD J. SAMBOROWSKI

83 Radicalization Prevention and Response (RPR) 625
DAVID PARKER, DAVID CHAPOT AND JONATHAN DAVIS

84 Screening 637
CHELSEA A. BROWN

85 The Evolution and Future of SWAT 641
BOYD P. BROWN III

86 The National Security Strategy (NSS) of the United States 649
RÉJEANNE M. LACROIX

87 The Sinaloa-Tijuana Complex 657
CLIFFORD GRIFFIN

88 United States Citizenship and Immigration Services (USCIS) 669
MAX CRUMLEY-EFFINGER

89 United States–Mexico Border Fence 675
GORDON ALLEY-YOUNG

PART V EMERGENCY PLANNING AND PREPAREDNESS AND HEALTH SECURITY
FRANCIS GRICE

90 Agroterrorism 687
FRANCIS GRICE AND LYRA HOUGHTON

91 Anthrax 697
PÉTER MARTON

92 Disaster Impact on Minorities 707
PATRICE NATALIE DELEVANTE

93 Earthquakes and US National Security 713
ARUNDHATI BHATTACHARYYA AND SCOTT N. ROMANIUK

94 Emergency Management and Response 721
CLIFFORD E. GRIFFIN

95 Homeland Security and the Arctic 731
JAMES ROGERS

96 Legal Frameworks of Interstate Disaster Management 739
MST MARZINA BEGUM AND MD NURUL MOMEN

97 Nuclear Threats **747**
DAVID ANDREW OMONA

98 Ricin **759**
PÉTER MARTON

99 Sarin **765**
PÉTER MARTON

100 Smallpox **773**
PÉTER MARTON

101 Suspicious Packages **781**
JÁNOS KEMÉNY

102 Urban Search and Rescue (SAR) **787**
SCOTT R. DIMARCO AND SCOTT N. ROMANIUK

Index **793**

About the Editors

Primary Editors

Scott N. Romaniuk is a visiting fellow at the International Centre for Policing and Security at the University of South Wales in the UK. He is also a non-resident expert at the Taiwan Center for Security Studies and a senior Research Fellow at the Centre for Studies of South and South-East Asian Societies at Kazi Nazrul University in West Bengal, India. He is also a 2022 Newton International Fellow of the British Academy and the Royal Society.

Martin Scott Catino is a US Fulbright Scholar and Program Director of Graduate Military Operations at Liberty University Online. He served in the United States, Bahrain, Iraq, Afghanistan, and the UAE in various research, supervisory, and advising posts for diverse entities, including the Department of Defense, FBI, and private security programs. His research on civil unrest, terrorism, and insurgency has involved field studies around the world as well as numerous publications in scholarly and industry journals. He has achieved the following awards: two US Fulbright Scholarships; US State Department Visiting Scholar to Saudi Arabia; US Visiting Scholar to Beijing University; and the Sasakawa Visiting Scholarship. His most recent scholarship includes: "Origins of Cyber-Warfare" in The Palgrave Encyclopedia of Global Security Studies, 2019; "Teddy Bears for Terrorists: President Theodore Roosevelt and America's First War on Terrorism," paper presented at the South Carolina Historical Association Annual Conference, Columbia, South Carolina, 2018; "The US Home Front: Drug Cartels and Security along the US-Mexico Border: Routledge": The Future of US Warfare. January 15, 2017; "Diving for Pearls: Shia Insurgency and Counterterrorism Measures in Bahrain": The Palgrave Handbook of Global Counterterrorism Policy, January 2, 2017; and "Assessing Iranian Security Capabilities: The Case of the Green Movement Protests, 2009–2011" in Mohammed Aman, ed., *The Middle East: New Order or Disorder*, Washington: 2016. Email: mscottcat1@yahoo.com

C. Augustus Martin is founding Director of the School of Public Service and Justice at California State University, Dominguez Hills. He is also a Professor of Criminal Justice Administration, where he teaches courses on terrorism and extremism, criminal law, and the criminal justice system. He has served as Associate Vice President for Human Resources Management, Acting Associate Dean of the College of Business Administration and Public Policy, Associate Vice President for Faculty Affairs, and Chair of the Department of Public Administration. He began his academic career as a member of the faculty of the Graduate School of Public and International Affairs, University of Pittsburgh, where he was an Administration of Justice professor. His current research and professional interests are terrorism and extremism, homeland security, and the administration of justice. Dr. Martin is author of instructional books and chapters on the subjects of terrorism and homeland security, including *Understanding Homeland Security* (SAGE Publications, 2023); *Essentials of Terrorism: Concepts and Controversies* (2022); *Understanding Terrorism: Challenges, Perspectives, and Issues* (2021); *Terrorism: An International Perspective* (with Fynnwin Prager; 2019); *The SAGE Encyclopedia of Terrorism*, Second Edition (2011); *Terrorism and Homeland Security* (2011); and *The New Era of Terrorism: Selected Readings* (2004). He is also the author of *Juvenile Justice: Process and Systems* (2005). Prior to joining academia, Dr. Martin served as Managing Attorney for the Fair Housing Partnership of Greater Pittsburgh. He was also Special Counsel to the Attorney General of the US Virgin Islands on the island of St. Thomas. Prior to serving as Special Counsel, he was a "floor" Legislative Assistant to Congressman Charles B. Rangel of New York. Dr. Martin received his A.B. degree from Harvard College, J.D. from Duquesne University Thomas R. Kline School of Law, and Ph.D. from the Graduate School of Public and International Affairs at the University of Pittsburgh. Email: gmartin@csudh.edu

Subject Editors

Department of Homeland Security (DHS) and Critical Infrastructure

John M. Callahan has served as the Dean of the School of Graduate and Professional Studies since September 2019. He continues to serve as the Director for Combined Online Military Programs in International Relations, Homeland Security, and Public Policy for New England College and has taught there since 2010. He received a PhD in International Studies from Old Dominion University in 2015. His research focus is on foreign policy decision-making, framing, and strategic communication. He is a Co-Convenor for the Political Science Association of the UK German Studies Group, focusing on the rise of populism in Europe. Dr. Callahan served as Deputy Spokesman at the Office of the Director of National Intelligence, helping the Director, Ambassador John Negroponte, to communicate key messages of intelligence reform to the American people. Prior to this, John was honored to be selected by the Department of Defense and the Department of State to serve as a Public Affairs Officer at the American Embassy in Baghdad, Iraq. From 2000 to 2004, John served as a government relations and public affairs officer for several well-known US student leadership organizations. He has served on the Board of Directors of the International Ambassador Club since 2018. Email: jcallahan@nec.edu

United States (US) Domestic and Border Security

Erika Cornelius Smith is the Director of Alumni Relations and Engagement for Marietta College. Previously, she held appointment as the Robert E. Stansky Distinguished Professor and tenured Associate Professor of International Business and Political Science, as well as chair of the International Business and Civic Leadership programs. As a graduate instructor at Purdue University, Erika has taught courses on US politics and political parties for the Political Science department, introductory courses in the Women's Studies program, and US history courses for the History department. Additionally, she taught US and World History courses at Indiana University Southeast and Ivy Tech Community College of Indiana. Her research interests include women's citizenship and political activism through transnational social organizations, civic bodies, and educational institutions in the early 20th century. Email: erika.smith@nichols.edu

Suzette A. Haughton is a Senior Lecturer at the Department of Government, The University of the West Indies, Mona Campus, Kingston, Jamaica. She obtained her PhD from the Department of War Studies, King's College London, and lectures on International Security Issues. Her research spans security threats affecting the Americas. Email: suzette.haughton@uwimona.edu.jm

Cybersecurity, Terrorism, and Asymmetric Threats

Zoha Waseem is a postdoctoral research fellow at the Institute for Global City Policing, University College London, and Co-coordinator for the Urban Violence Research Network. She holds a PhD from the School of Security Studies, King's College London. She specializes in policing, terrorism and counterterrorism, urban security, police culture, and institutional reform in South Asia, UK, and beyond. Email: z.waseem@ucl.ac.uk

Emergency Planning and Preparedness and Health Security

Francis Grice is Assistant Professor of Political Science and International Studies at McDaniel College in Maryland, US. He holds a PhD in Defence Studies from King's College London (2014) and specializes in Asian Security Studies and International Relations. Recent books include *The Myth of Mao Zedong and Modern Insurgency* (2018), *The Palgrave Handbook of Global Counterterrorism Policy* (with Scott N. Romaniuk, Daniela Irrera, and Stewart Webb, 2017), and *The Future of US Warfare* (with Scott N. Romaniuk, 2017). Email: fgrice@mcdaniel.edu

Contributors

Gordon Alley-Young
Kingsborough Community College – City University of New York
Brooklyn, New York, United States

Mostafa Amini
Harvard University Medical School
Cambridge, Massachusetts, United States

Nicholas J. Barnes
Brown University
Providence, Rhode Island, United States

Thomas J. Beck
New England College
Henniker, New Hampshire, United States

Mst Marzina Begum
University of Rajshahi
Rajshahi, Bangladesh

Nell Bennett
Macquarie University
Sydney, New South Wales, Australia

Arundhati Bhattacharyya
University of Burdwan
Purba Bardhaman, India

Boyd P. Brown III
Nichols College
Dudley, Massachusetts, United States

Chelsea A. Brown
Prairie View A&M University
Prairie View, Texas, United States

Angela N. Bullock
University of the District of Columbia
Washington, DC, United States

David Chapot
Local Authority Counter-Radicalization Practitioner
United Kingdom

Alex D. Colvin
Texas Woman's University
Denton, Texas, United States

Aaron Cooley
New England College
Henniker, New Hampshire, United States

Ashley Corcoran
Nichols College
Dudley, Massachusetts, United States

Max Crumley-Effinger
Loyola University Chicago
Chicago, Illinois, United States

Brynn Dao
Delaware State University
Dover, Delaware, United States

Jonathan Davis
Former Counter-Radicalization Practitioner
United Kingdom

Patrice Natalie Delevante
Independent Researcher
United States

Mila Demchyk Savage
Old Dominion University
Norfolk, Virginia, United States

Scott R. DiMarco
Mansfield University of Pennsylvania
Mansfield, Pennsylvania, United States

Glen M. E. Duerr
Cedarville University
Cedarville, Ohio, United States

Dominika Dziwisz
Jagiellonian University
Kraków, Poland

Mariam Farida
Macquarie University
Sydney, New South Wales, Australia

Robert Forster
University of Edinburgh
Edinburgh, Scotland, United Kingdom

Francis Grice
McDaniel College
Westminster, Maryland, United States

Clifford E. Griffin
North Carolina State University
Raleigh, North Caroline, United States

Lora Hadzhidimova
Old Dominion University
Norfolk, Virginia, United States

Huso Hasanovic
Old Dominion University
Norfolk, Virginia, United States

Priyanka Hattiangady
Independent Researcher
India

Suzette A. Haughton
The University of the West Indies
Kingston, Jamaica

Lyra Houghton
McDaniel College
Westminster, Maryland, United States

Michael Hunter
Delaware State University
Dover, Delaware, United States

Jade Hutchinson
Macquarie University
Sydney, New South Wales, Australia

Jason R. Jolicoeur
Washburn University
Topeka, Kansas, United States

Tavis D. Jules
Loyola University Chicago
Chicago, Illinois, United States

János Kemény
National University of Public Service
Budapest, Hungary

Umer Khan
University of Buckingham
Buckingham, England, United Kingdom

Hamish Kinnear
Independent Researcher
United Kingdom

Nikita Kohli
Center for Land Warfare Studies
New Delhi, India

Réjeanne M. Lacroix
University of Leicester
Leicester, England, United Kingdom

Megan LaMare
Nichols College
Dudley, Massachusetts, United States

Raphaël Leduc
The Graduate Institute of International and Development Studies
Geneva, Switzerland

Gary Leigh
Charles Darwin University
Darwin, Northern Territory, Australia

Wayne Lesperance
New England College
Henniker, New Hampshire, United States

Eugenio Lilli
University College Dublin
Dublin, Ireland

Ronald Lorenzo
Prairie View A&M University
Prairie View, Texas, United States

Mary Manjikian
Regent University
Virginia Beach, Virginia, United States

Raphael D. Marcus
King's College London,
London, England, United Kingdom

Carl A. Marrara
New England College
Henniker, New Hampshire, United States

Péter Marton
Corvinus University of Budapest
Budapest, Hungary

Allison McDowell-Smith
Nichols College
Dudley, Massachusetts, United States

Md Nurul Momen
University of Rajshahi
Rajshahi, Bangladesh

David Andrew Omona
Uganda Christian University
Mukono Town, Uganda

Chad Patrick Osorio
University of Negros Occidental-Recoletos
Bacolod, Philippines

Anwar Ouassini
Delaware State University
Dover, Delaware, United States

Nabil Ouassini
Prairie View A&M University
Prairie View, Texas, United States

David Parker
Aarhus University
Aarhus, Denmark

William R. Patterson
Independent Researcher
United States

Giovanna Ferriani Madureira Pontes
University of Sussex
Brighton, England, United Kingdom

Madelaine Preedy
Queen Mary University of London
London, England, United Kingdom

James Revill
University of Sussex
Brighton, England, United Kingdom

Russell Richardson Jr.
New England College
Henniker, New Hampshire, United States

Ryan Roberts
Old Dominion University
Norfolk, Virginia, United States

James Rogers
University of Southern Denmark
Odense, Denmark

Leonard J. Samborowski
Nichols College
Dudley, Massachusetts, United States

Margaret Seymour
Old Dominion University
Norfolk, Virginia, United States

Tamarra Smith
Lone Star College
The Woodlands, Texas, United States

Darren E. Tromblay
George Washington University
Washington, DC, United States

James Valiquet
New England College
Henniker, New Hampshire, United States

Aaron T. Walter
University of Ss. Cyril & Methodius, Slovakia & Masaryk University
Brno, The Czech Republic

Zoha Waseem
King's College London
London, England, United Kingdom

Stephen Williams
AH Community Builders, United States Army, Harris Country Sheriff's Department
Houton, Texas, United States

Charlie Winter
King's College London
London, England, United Kingdom

Introduction

Homeland Security: Concepts, Actors, Threats

Scott N. Romaniuk, Martin Scott Catino, and C. Augustus Martin

> The United States, through a concerted national effort that galvanizes the strengths and capabilities of federal, state, local, and tribal governments; the private and nonprofit sectors; and regions, communities, and individual citizens – along with our partners in the international community – will work to achieve a secure homeland that sustains our way of life as a free, prosperous, and welcoming America.
>
> National Strategy for Homeland Security,
> Homeland Security Council (2007: 13)

Immediately following the 9/11 attacks against the United States homeland, the White House, in conjunction with several principal government bodies, including the executive branch and the US Congress, undertook unprecedented measures to ensure that the country would be secure from many of the pre-existing threats in the world in addition to new and emerging, and future, threats. In less than 2 weeks following al-Qaeda's deadly terrorist attacks, Pennsylvania Governor Tom Ridge was appointed the first Director of the Department of Homeland Security (DHS), which became a fully fledged independent Cabinet-level department on March 1, 2003 (Thessin, 2003). DHS integrated 22 different US federal departments and agencies in a cohesive unit and employed approximately 250,000 personnel (Homeland Security, 2021). It embodied the vision that US security would ultimately require and entail a long-term strategic vision based on cohesion, unity, and whole-of-government operational capacities.

This vision of deep and broad security for the United States, however, has predated the establishment of DHS, as violent non-state actors (VNSAs) and manifold threats striking at and against the United States, its citizens, its territories, and its various resources has persisted at home and abroad for decades. However, despite the blatantly violent acts alongside more discreet warning signs of materializing threats toward the United States, obstacles and attitudes served as impediments to the formulation of what have been considered necessary safeguards. Despite the immense expenditures associated with strengthening US homeland security since 9/11, questions of whether the United States and its citizens are safe or safer, and how the relative material and non-material costs compare to the benefits of the United States' sweeping security measures, have been repeatedly raised. Many of the costs have been overlooked or brushed aside on the basis of immediate hysteria and fear stemming from the 9/11 attacks and the general need to defend the homeland as a priority above all other matters.

DHS released its (FY) 2020 Budget request to the US Congress on March 18, 2019, in which the Cabinet outlined its plan to invest US$51.7 billion across a spectrum of strategies, measures, and resources, with the aim of defending and safeguarding the nation's borders, among a plethora of initiatives and activities (Department of Homeland Security, 2021). In 2001, the US federal government spent $17.1 billion on homeland security (Department of Homeland Security, 2021). That number increased steadily over previous years. The enormous injections of funds over the course of two decades illustrate the ongoing security policy priorities of three administrations and their presidents and have elevated the total homeland security spending since 2001 to approximately $635.9 billion (Department of Homeland Security, 2021). While these figures represent the immediate financial costs involved in DHS operations and solutions to threats to US national security, they fail to capture the social and economic costs related to the business of securing the homeland through an all-hazards approach – one that tends to accentuate threats and consequences of terrorism.

One of the most popular topics in scholarship and among professions in the United States and in many countries around the world, homeland security is widely studied and practiced in comparative contexts. This topic has attracted a great deal of attention since the events of September 1, 2001, but the issues encompassed under this umbrella term predate 9/11, particularly in the United States and throughout the "Western" world. A growing number of security and defense issues are intricately related to the concept of homeland security and affect hundreds of millions of individuals and their lifestyles around the world, in positive and negative ways.

The Handbook of Homeland Security allows readers to engage with a diverse range of concepts, issues, and practices within the general milieu of homeland security, understanding their evolution, roles, and impacts across overlapping fields. This new volume introduces readers to homeland security topics not covered in other volumes. We address the broad and expansive area of homeland security politics in an interdisciplinary and comparative manner, with a special focus on the United States and its citizens. This volume is organized around four distinctive but interrelated themes of US homeland security, forming the overarching structure of this book:

- Department of Homeland Security and Critical Infrastructure
- United States and Domestic Border Security
- Cybersecurity, Terrorism, and Asymmetric Threats
- Emergency Planning and Preparedness and Health Security

Within each section, readers are presented with articles on key issues guided by keywords and supplemented with additional reading material and resources. The volume's themes or subject areas have been overseen by scholars with specializations in the fields, and each chapter peer-reviewed and updated over the many months that this volume has been in the making.

Homeland security, as a general topic, is inherently interdisciplinary and continues to cross fields of scholarly investigation as we approach it from diverse methodological, epistemological, and ontological positions. The frequently polemical nature of the field of homeland security, in which deeply discordant discourses and assertions have been produced and proliferated in response to issues in the United States, include past issues and those that continue to unfold today., There are also sundry dimensions of homeland security that will likely emerge in the coming years and decades.

In addition to serving as an authoritative reference source on the subject matter, this volume sheds light on the controversial issues related to the US homeland, its people, and security. Homeland security issues are addressed in the context of past and present – events that are critical today – world affairs not exclusively in the United States, but rather events emerging and taking shape around the world and that share either a direct or indirect relationship with US homeland affairs and management. With that in mind, this volume seeks to re-introduce the field of study and practice to a much broader and even global audience through US and non-US perspectives. It is through this methodology that we can establish a pluralistic and valuable contribution to the existing literature while contributing to ongoing discussions and exchanges around this vast field.

Experts, both scholars and practitioners across many fields, for an immense audience range, have authored the chapters in this volume. We seek to connect with individuals considered beginners in the field of study, and those working and living beyond academia. We also seek to connect with a general readership – individuals who have a keen interest in some, many, or all aspects of homeland security. This volume will serve as a critical textbook and resource for those interested in homeland security, criminal justice, national security and defense, foreign policy, and intelligence.

References

Department of Homeland Security. (2019, March 18). *"President's fiscal year 2020 budget fortifies DHS operations, supports frontline personnel, secures our borders & confronts emerging"*. https://www.dhs.gov/news/2019/03/18/president-s-fiscal-year-2020-budget#:~:text=Nielsen%20released%20the%20details%20of,Disaster%20Relief%20Fund%20(DRF).

Department of Homeland Security. (2021). "*DHS budget*". https://www.dhs.gov/dhs-budget

Homeland Security. (2021). "*About DHS*". https://www.dhs.gov/about-dhs

National Strategy for Homeland Security. (2007, October). Washington, DC: Department of Homeland Security. https://www.dhs.gov/xlibrary/assets/nat_strat_homelandsecurity_2007.pdf

Thessin, J. (2003). Department of homeland security. *Harvard Journal on Legislation*, *40*(2): 513–536.

I

DEPARTMENT OF HOMELAND SECURITY (DHS) AND CRITICAL INFRASTRUCTURE

John M. Callahan
New England College, Henniker, NH, United States

Chapter 1

Blackouts and Brownouts or Power Outages

Mila Demchyk Savage
Old Dominion University, Virginia, United States

Contents

Introduction 3
Power Outages: Threats, Causes, and Factors 4
Power Outages and Their Complexity 5
Blackouts 5
Brownouts 6
Dropout 6
Load Shedding 6
Minimizing Electrical Power Disruptions 6
Conclusion 7
Further Reading 7
References 7

Introduction

Modern society has come to depend on reliable electricity as an essential resource for nearly all aspects of modern life, including national security and economic enterprise (UCPSOTF, 2004). For example, most critical assets of the Department of Defense (DOD) are vulnerable to disruptions in electrical power supplies, but DOD lacks sufficient information to determine the full extent of the risks and vulnerabilities these assets face. All 34 of these most critical assets require electricity continuously to support their military missions, and 31 of them rely on commercial power grids, which the Defense Science Board Task Force on DOD Energy Strategy has characterized as increasingly fragile and vulnerable (GAO-10-147, 2015). Thus, assuring that electric

DOI: 10.4324/9781315144511-2

power is reliable, accessible, sustainable, and affordable is a national security imperative (GAO-10-147, 2015).

Interruptions in electricity services vary by frequency and duration throughout the country across the many electric distribution systems that serve roughly 145 million customers in the United States. Although some distribution customers have backup generators that provide auxiliary power, most customers are simply without electricity when outages occur (United States Energy Information Administration [EIA] website).

Electricity failures can be caused by numerous threats, such as direct physical attacks or cyberattacks, severe weather and other natural disasters, imperfections of the conventional grid, and human errors.

Since 2000, the number of reported power outages in the United States kept steadily rising. In 2000, there were an average of 2.5 grid disruption events a month; in 2017, the average was 12.5 disruption events a month (Electric Disturbance Events Annual Summaries, DOE, n.d.).

Advancing legislation on federal, state, and local levels; changing grid structure by decreasing the country's reliance on large regional power plants; and switching to the smart grid would help minimize power outages as well as would positively impact the country's national and homeland security.

Power Outages: Threats, Causes, and Factors

The current U.S. electric grid's overreliance on aging twentieth-century technology—based on centralized power generation and interconnected distribution architecture—makes it susceptible to a wide variety of threats (GAO-10-147, 2015). Electricity failures can be caused by intentional or unintentional threats.

Intentional threats include direct physical attacks or cyberattacks. Between 2011 and 2014, electric utilities reported 362 targeted attacks that caused outages or other power disruptions. Of those, 14 were cyberattacks, and the rest were physical in nature (Tett, 2015). While there are not many incidents of physical attacks recorded, several of them took place recently. One of them happened in 2013, when the Pacific Gas and Electric (PG&E) Metcalf Transmission Substation located outside San Jose, CA, was the target of a sophisticated sniper attack. The Metcalf Substation supplies power to Silicon Valley, an American landmark of innovation. During the attack, gunmen fired on and disabled 17 transformers, causing $15 million worth of damage (GAO-10-147, 2015).

Unintentional outages are primarily caused by severe weather and other natural disasters, imperfections of the conventional grid, and human error. Electric grids are currently designed for limited resilience to naturally occurring incidents such as tornadoes, hurricanes, ice storms, and earthquakes (Chopade & Bikdash, 2016). While the impact due to natural incidents is self-explanatory, the one caused by the flaws of the existing system of electricity generation and distribution requires some clarification. Electricity must be consumed as soon as it is produced, and consumers have grown accustomed to the on-demand availability of electricity. Currently, this combination requires utility companies to generate enough supply to meet the electrical demand at any given moment. Because the exact demand is unknown, utility companies generate more electricity than is needed to compensate for the unexpected rise in consumption and achieve this level of service. This system of supply and demand results in waste when demand is overestimated and rolling blackouts when demand is underestimated (Flick et al., 2010).

The Northeast blackout of 2003 illustrates how imperfections of the existing system, combined with human errors, could lead to large-scale consequences. It started as a local blackout in Ohio and cascaded into the collapse of the entire electric grid. Based on the analysis of the investigation team, the initial blackout was caused by deficiencies in specific practices, equipment, and human decisions by various organizations that affected conditions and outcomes. For example, insufficient reactive power was an issue in the blackout, but it was not a cause in itself. Rather, deficiencies in corporate policies, lack of adherence to industry policies, and inadequate management of reactive power and voltage caused the blackout (UCPSOTF, 2004).

An aging power delivery infrastructure is another major cause of unintentional outages. The majority of equipment in the area of an electric utility is more than 40 years old (Willis, 2017). One of the most recent examples, when the difficulty in maintaining aging energy infrastructure has also resulted in the power outage, is a fire in Boston Back Bay transformers on March 2012, which caused widespread power outages and compelled authorities to close subway stations, block roads, and conduct evacuations. Other age-related failures occur with uncomfortable regularity, from small rural towns to megacities (GAO-10-147, 2015).

Power Outages and Their Complexity

Based on their complexity, power outages can be divided into several categories: dropout, brownout, blackout, and load shedding (Flick et al., 2010).

Blackouts

Grid blackouts are one of the power outages' categories accompanied by a complete failure of electrical power supply. In recent years, the frequent large-scale blackouts around the world have shown the vulnerability of interconnected power systems. Scientists and engineers have worked together to identify the reasons for major large-scale blackouts; yet, in many cases, convincing analytical results are still missing, and electrical accidents occur continuously (Mei et al., 2011).

Large-scale unintentional blackouts are usually associated with a higher level of consequences compared to other categories. They have immediate costs to the economy and place the country's security at risk (GAO-10-147, 2015). For example, the Northeast blackout of 2003 impacted over 50 million people across eight American states and the Canadian province of Ontario. The loss of 61,800 MW in power took up to 4 days to restore, disrupting manufacturing and virtually all public services, including shutting down 19 nuclear generators at 10 plants and costing between 10 and 10 billion U.S. dollars (UCPSOTF, 2004).

Brownouts

The grid can be disrupted by numerous factors. One of them is a drop in voltage from a power supply, which does not result in a complete cutoff of electricity but leads to brownouts. Visually, this phenomenon appears as lighting becoming less bright and that is how the term originated. Consequences of brownouts can differ from the poor performance of equipment to incorrect operations.

Dropout

This refers to a loss of power that has a short duration, on a timescale of seconds, and is usually fixed quickly.

Load Shedding

The term load shedding refers to a deliberate reduction or a complete shutdown of the available power to sections of the grid, generally to prevent the failure of the entire system when, for example, the demand strains the capacity of the system.

Minimizing Electrical Power Disruptions

A power grid failure can lead to serious consequences, which include financial loss, decreased public safety, disruption of economic activities, poor performance of equipment, and incorrect operations. Frequently occurring electricity outages illustrate low reliability of the grid and signal that there are barriers to the efficient use of electricity in the country. Thus, it is important to look at ways of minimizing power outages.

- First, since a stable electricity supply is a matter of national security, coordinated actions of federal, state, and local governments are important. Creating advanced policies and incentives for public and private investments as well as data collection and research would lead to modernizing and designing a reliable and secure grid.
- Second, building a 'smarter' power grid that automatically responds to problems could reduce the rising number of debilitating blackouts (Schewe, 2017). The smart grid adds two-way digital communication technology to devices associated with the grid. It can connect consumers and producers, allowing consumers to have a greater input on demand signals associated with price or capacity fluctuation (GAO-10-147, 2015). The smart grid will also be able to incorporate conventional and unconventional sources of energy into one system.
- Third, changing the grid structure through increasing electrical energy that is generated closer to the user is important. Reducing the country's reliance on large regional power plants would positively impact the country's national and homeland security.

Conclusion

Reliable electricity underpins every facet of life in the United States. Without it, American homes, businesses, and national security engines would grind to a halt (GAO-10-147, 2015). The current U.S. system of generating and supplying electrical power is not capable of responding to the country's needs adequately. Numerous factors lead to the increasing number of power outages across the country, which negatively impacts all aspects of modern life, including the country's national and homeland security. To minimize grid failures and, thus, to ensure the country's stability, a number of actions on federal, state, and local levels are required to support switching to the smart grid and restructuring the electrical power network.

Further Reading

Flick, T., Morehouse, J., & Veltsos, C. *Securing the Smart Grid: Next Generation Power Grid Security*. Burlington: Syngress, 2010.

Lee, W. H. *Aging Power Delivery Infrastructures*. Boca Raton: CRC Press, 2017.

Sørensen, B. *Energy Intermittency*. Boca Raton: CRC Press, 2014.

References

Chopade, P., & Bikdash, M. New centrality measures for assessing smart grid vulnerabilities and predicting brownouts and blackouts. *International Journal of Critical Infrastructure Protection*, March 2016, Vol. 12, pp. 29–45.

Electric disturbance events annual summaries, DOE. https://www.oe.netl.doe.gov/OE417_annual_summary.aspx

Flick, T., Morehouse, J., & Veltsos, C. *Securing the Smart Grid: Next Generation Power Grid Security*. Burlington, MA: Syngress, 2010.

GAO-10-147. Defense critical infrastructure actions needed to improve the identification and management of electrical power risks and vulnerabilities to DOD critical assets: report to congressional committees. United States. Government Accountability Office, 2015. https://www.gao.gov/assets/300/297162.pdf

Lee, Willis H. *Aging Power Delivery Infrastructures*. Boca Raton: CRC Press, 2017.

Mei, S. *Power Grid Complexity*. New York: Springer, 2011. http://ebookcentral.proquest.com/lib/odu/detail.action?docID=884872

National Security and Assured U. S. Electrical Power. CNA Military Advisory Board's report, November *CNA Military Advisory Board's Report*, November 2015. https://www.cna.org/CNA_files/PDF/National-Security-Assured-Electrical-Power.pdf

Schewe, P. F. *Preventing blackouts: building a smarter power grid*, August 14, 2017. https://www.scientificamerican.com/article/preventing-blackouts-power-grid/

Tett, G. Will cyber attacks switch off the lights? *FT Magazine*, April 24, 2015. http://www.ft.com/cms/s/0/ed59e166-e92d-11e4-a71a-00144feab7de.html

UCPSOTF. *Final Report on the August 14, 2003 Blackout in the United States and Canada: Causes and Recommendations*. U. S.-Canada Power System Outage Task Force, 2004. https://reports.energy.gov/BlackoutFinal-Web.pdf

Chapter 2

Body Scanners

Aaron Cooley
New England College, Henniker, New Hampshire, United States

Contents

Introduction 9
Further Reading 11
References 11

Introduction

Body scanners are machines that allow security personnel to review persons entering a facility or mode of transportation to search for prohibited and dangerous items. In the past decade, they have increasingly been used at airports in countries all over the globe to facilitate quicker, more thorough, and less invasive searches of travelers. Backscatter and millimeter wave devices are the two primary types of body scanners that have come to replace outdated metal detectors and standard x-ray machines. This increased use in the United States is part of the hardening of security in public and private spaces since the attack on September 11, 2001 (9/11). (L3 Security and Detection Systems. https://www.tsa.gov/travel/security-screening).

It is likely body scanners will continue to increase their ability to detect items and substances along with providing greater accuracy in the results they produce. Furthermore, body scanners would seem on track to become more ubiquitous in all public and private venues for work, entertainment, and civil engagement as concerns about safety and preventing harm continue in the public mindset. Accordingly, they continue to be a prevalent tool in protecting spaces to lessen the risk to those entering these secured areas. However, there remain several relevant issues in terms of the effectiveness of the technology and possible health concerns from exposure to the scans. (TSA Security Screening. https://www.tsa.gov/travel/security-screening).

DOI: 10.4324/9781315144511-3

The remainder of the entry will discuss these issues after a brief discussion of the technology used by the main types of scanners.

The reduction in the use of old-style x-ray machines came with the evolution of the technology used by backscatter x-ray machines. The backscatter machines began to be used more widely in the late 2000s. What makes the backscatter an innovation from previous models is that it evaluates the radiation that is mirrored by the body being scanned. The view of the person being scanned is two-dimensional. The images can be very detailed to the point that questions began to be raised about the legality of using them. Legal critics in the United States asserted they could be violative of the Fourth Amendment in terms of unreasonable searches of individuals. The machines were growing in use until several public incidents pushed lawmakers to require new software to be used on the machines to obscure the clear and realistic images of individuals being scanned with more generic human bodies. However, there were issues in the implementation of the software and newer machines were not considered to be adequate. Given this result, there was a move away from them to a greater use of millimeter wave scanners at the points of entry to facilities and transportation hubs.

The millimeter wave scanners use a different technology to create images without x-rays. Instead, they use fine radio waves that make passes around the individual, which then reflect waves back to sensors to produce a picture of the subject. The newest forms of the technology avoid many of the issues around privacy concerns by using general outlines of the human form with contraband items highlighted on them. Similarly, the software used on the machines are derived from automatic target recognition which can be used to produce a judgment about allowing access to enter or determining that the person needs further screening without creating a revealing image.

With the movement to address the privacy concerns about the capturing of images that provide extremely detailed views of the bodies of individuals being scanned, additional policy attention has been directed at the accuracy of the machines and possibilities of false-positive readings from the scanners. In particular, there have been questions about being able to locate firearms on individuals who are being scanned. Additionally, there have been questions about conditions that make accurate scanning more difficult such as excessive clothing or perspiration on subjects that can impact imaging.

On another front, the adoption of millimeter wave scanners has lessened the threat of health hazards from repeated scanning during entry to events and during travel. The backscatter x-ray machines posed more of a problem in this area. Backscatter x-ray machines created more concerns for health researchers about the levels of radiation and repeated exposures. However, even though the millimeter wave technology has so far been deemed to be safe, many people still opt for, and instead choose, a pat-down screening over the body scanner. Opting for this more physically invasive screening demonstrates that members of the public still have reservations about the health consequences of scanning technology.

Overall, the use of body scanners has become a taken-for-granted part of entering secure buildings and transportation centers. As the public seeks more security in public and private settings, the use of the machines will likely continue. If the price of them is reduced or more resources are put toward securing facilities, then these scanners may even begin to be used in schools and hospitals. It remains to be seen if the public will see this expansion of body scanners' use as a benefit to security or an intrusion on privacy rights.

Further Reading

Accardo, J. & Chadhry, M. A. (2014). Radiation exposure and privacy concerns surrounding full-body scanners in airports, *Journal of Radiation Research and Applied Sciences*, 7(2): 198–200.

Accardo, J., & Chaudhry, A. (2014). Radiation exposure and privacy concerns surrounding full-body scanners in airports. *Journal of Radiation Research and Applied* Sciences, 7(2), 198–200.

Mironenko, O. (2011). Body scanners versus privacy and data protection. *Computer Law & Security Review*, *27*(3), 232–244.

References

L3 Security and Detection Systems. https://www.tsa.gov/travel/security-screening

TSA Security Screening. https://www.tsa.gov/travel/security-screening

Chapter 3

Bureau of Alcohol, Tobacco, Firearms, and Explosives

Darren E. Tromblay
George Washington University, Washington, DC, United States

Contents

Introduction 13
Further Reading 16
References 17

Introduction

The Bureau of Alcohol, Tobacco, Firearms, and Explosives (usually still referred to as ATF) is an awkward organization. It has enforcement responsibilities – premised on the use of specific items for criminal activities – which often put it in direct conflict with agencies responsible for disrupting the actors who are using those items in furtherance of illicit activity. This cross-cutting role should position the ATF to complement other US government agencies by enhancing their work through the contribution of subject-matter expertise, but the reality seems to more often be a devolution into turf wars. The ATF's dysfunctional relationship with the broader US domestic national security enterprise – at both the federal and sub-federal levels – is exacerbated by the organization's internal organizational deficiencies.

ATF can trace the lineage of its functions through approximately two centuries of US history. (ATF, n.d. *Timeline*. http://www.atf.gov/content/about/our-history/timeline.) However, it came into existence only in 1972 – under the auspices of the Department of the Treasury – when it supplanted the Alcohol, Tobacco, and Firearms Division of the Internal Revenue Service (US House of Representatives, 1982). It remained part of Treasury until 2002, when a provision of the Homeland Security Act transferred it to the Department of Justice and formally added "explosives" to its

DOI: 10.4324/97813151445`1-4

name (Parson & Gerney, 2015). At present, ATF consists of eight offices, under the supervision of a Deputy Director, who reports to the Bureau's Director (ATF, 2014). Of those offices, the two of greatest significance for intelligence in the domestic environment are the Office of Strategic Intelligence and Information and the Office of Field Operations.

Organizationally, the ATF has a field-oriented culture. Early in its operations, it was organized along divisional line, with homogenous skill groups structured vertically into functional entities (alcohol, tobacco, firearms, explosives, and state and local assistance), with Assistant Directors at its Washington, DC, headquarters (HQ) directing their field-based functional counterparts (US House of Representatives, 1982). However, decentralization began to occur in 1979, when the ATF reorganized and created Regional Directors of Investigations in four locations, throughout the United States (US Senate, 1979). By the early 1980s, the ATF had shifted from being headquarters-directed to a headquarters-monitored organization that focused on localized law enforcement issues (US House of Representatives, 1982). This created an organization which turned field divisions into autonomous fiefdoms in which the Special Agents in charge functioned independently, with limited accountability to the ATF's executive leadership (Parson & Gerney, 2015). Following debacles such as the Fast and Furious firearms trafficking investigation, ATF HQ attempted to exert more oversight by establishing a "monitored case program" in 2011. Ironically, the initial delegation of authority to the field was done in an effort to strengthen management capability and ensure that personnel were operating within the constraints of policy guidelines and good law enforcement practices (US House of Representatives, 1979).

Although it is primarily domestic in nature, ATF does have a limited international aspect to its mission. Through its international Programs Branch, ATF stations a small number of Country Attaches abroad (GAO. Combating Terrorism, 2003a). ATF also assists foreign law enforcement authorities operationally via its International Incident Response Team – created in 1993 – which deploys to address explosives and fire incidents (GAO. Combating Terrorism. 2003b). Additionally, ATF provides training to foreign law enforcement officials on firearms and explosives topics such as tracing and post-blast investigations (GAO, 1997).

ATF's mission, in the context of the broader national security community, has been ill-defined. Early in its existence, ATF directed its investigative emphasis toward problems of special concern to the Federal government. Starting, in 1980, however, the ATF implemented its Crime Impact Program (CIP). The CIP originated with the ATF's mandate to assist state and local law enforcement and focused on the issues which fell to ATF jurisdiction by virtue of exceeding state and local capabilities (US House of Representatives, 1981). Contemporaneously, the ATF began to focus on crimes of violence and de-emphasize tobacco-related offenses (although these would re-emerge as an area of interest following the attacks of September 11, 2001) (US House of Representatives, 1981). In 2012, ATF replaced CIP with the Frontline Business Model, which assessed criminal threats, prioritized and conducted investigations, and evaluated the extent to which its efforts reduced violent crimes (GAO, 2014). Consistent with this emphasis on violent crime, senior ATF officials indicated interest, as of 2012, in changing ATF's name to the Violent Crimes Bureau (Perez, 2012).

Beyond assistance to non-federal law enforcement, the ATF has attempted, over multiple decades, to carve out a role in several of the national security problems du jour. An early example of this, which has remained relatively consistent, is the international trafficking of firearms. Starting with a 1974 project called "Guns to Mexico", the ATF attempted to combat the illicit transport of firearms across the southwest border (US House of Representatives, 1982). "Project Gunrunner", which the ATF initiated in 2005, is a more recent iteration of the effort to disrupt trafficking (Parson & Gerney, 2015). Unfortunately, the focus on firearms trafficking led ATF personnel to engage in efforts such as Fast and Furious, which lost track of hundreds of firearms (and was exacerbated, in its ineptitude, by the lack of meaningful HQ oversight) (GAO, 2014).

During the 1980s, the ATF became involved with the United States' war on drugs. Through its Achilles Program, the ATF targeted violent criminals through the establishment of 20 task forces comprised of ATF agents and sub-federal law enforcement officers (GAO, 1993). The premise of Achilles was that the illegal possession of firearms was often the "Achilles heel" of individuals involved with narcotics activity (GAO, 1993). Enforcement of these firearms violations – under the authorities of the Comprehensive Crime Control Act of 1984 – could help to disrupt narcotics activity (GAO, 1993).

The ATF also became involved with counterterrorism efforts. (GAO. Combating Terrorism, 2003a). As early as 1981, the ATF was dedicating personnel to monitor terrorist and extremist matters (US House of Representatives, 1981) (The Federal Bureau of Investigation [FBI], by comparison, did not elevate terrorism to a national priority until the following year.). During the 1990s, the ATF participated in the investigations of the 1993 World Trade Center bombing and the 1995 bombing of the Alfred P. Murrah Federal Building in Oklahoma City (GAO, 2007). It was also a member of the Interagency Intelligence Committee on Terrorism, which operated under the oversight of the CIA Counterterrorist Center's Community Counterterrorism Board (GAO, 1997). However, inherent to these actions was the potential for conflict with the Federal Bureau of Investigation. ATF agents were angered by the FBI's claiming of success for solving the 1993 World Trade Center bombing, as it had been an ATF agent who had found the essential part that identified the van which the bombers had used (Cavanagh & Teasley, 1993). Furthermore, both agencies duplicated capabilities, such as critical incident response components (GAO, 1993).

Following the attacks of September 11, the ATF continued to work in the field of counterterrorism. The ATF received explicit direction to investigate acts of "domestic terrorism" as part of its move to the Department of Justice (Markon, 2008). However, this also created an impression, within ATF, that no one wanted to hear about the bureau unless the work pertained to national security (Parson & Gerney, 2015). In addition to its explosives and firearms expertise, ATF brought its authority for tobacco-related crimes to bear in disrupting terrorists' use of bootlegged cigarette-derived financing (Krouse, 2011). According to ATF officials, Hizballah, HAMAS, and al-Qaeda have all been involved with cigarette-related activities (GAO. Terrorist Financing. 2003b). (GAO. Combating Terrorism, 2003a).

The FBI's exertion of primacy in counterterrorism work prompted the post-September 11 ATF to refocus its energies against gangs (a form of terrorists in their own right). To justify its participation in anti-gang efforts (an area that the FBI addresses via its Safe Streets Task Forces, which it initiated in 1992), ATF has emphasized the nexus between violent gangs and their use of firearms in criminal activity (Parson

& Gerney, 2015). This is not an entirely new area for the ATF, which had previously sought to lead efforts in establishing a Gang Intelligence Network in the early 1990s (US House of Representatives, 1992).

Because its mandate overlaps with other agencies' missions, the ATF has repeatedly found itself at odds with its ostensible federal law enforcement partners. (GAO, 1999). Historically, this tension has been most apparent in ATF–FBI relations. In 2002, an FBI memo denigrated ATF agents as being poorly trained and lacking strategic vision (Markon, 2008). The two agencies also engaged in a highly publicized disagreement about their competing repositories of bomb data (US Department of Justice, 2009). Coordination between the ATF and FBI was so dismal that on one occasion the ATF inadvertently purchased counterfeit cigarettes from the FBI because both agencies were running parallel investigations of tobacco smuggling (Markon, 2008). ATF responsibilities also overlap with Department of Homeland Security (DHS) components. For instance, Immigration and Customs Enforcement (ICE) accused the ATF of taking information which ICE had shared and using it in furtherance of ATF's own investigations (GAO, 2009).

The ATF's ill-fitting status has led to repeated considerations of realignment. In the early 1980s, Congress considered a proposal by the Department of the Treasury to merge ATF with the US Secret Service (which was also under the auspices of Treasury) (US Senate, 1982). This proposal highlighted a fundamental problem with ATF: its functions lacked a commonality of purpose (US Senate, 1982). Then, in 1993, a review of government functions, led by Vice President Al Gore, recommended the merger of ATF, as well as Drug Enforcement Administration (DEA), into the FBI (Parson & Gerney, 2015). There was also discussion about whether ATF would have been an appropriate fit for incorporation into DHS (the same legislation which produced DHS instead moved ATF to Justice) (Relyea, 2002).

ATF, as an investigatory agency, currently creates unnecessary complications in the domestic setting. The FBI and DHS/ICE currently focus on the threat actors who engage in trafficking the illicit commodities around which ATF's identity revolves. Folding ATF, or at least portions of it, into the FBI is not a bad idea. The FBI, as currently structured, has elements, such as the WMD Directorate (WMDD), which are repositories of expertise that facilitate the FBI's work. ATF's functions, distributed across the FBI, would complement WMDD and the Laboratory Division. The other resolution to the current situation would be for the FBI to cede its violent crimes mission to the ATF, freeing up FBI resources to focus on the FBI's post-9/11 consolidation around an intelligence mission.

Further Reading

Azrael, D., Hepburn, L., Hemenway, D. & Miller, M. (2017). "The Stock and Flow of U. S. Firearms: Results from the 2015 National Firearms Survey," *Journal of the Social Sciences*, *3*(5): 38–57.

Gramlich, J. & Schaeffer, K. (2019, October 22). "*7 Facts about Guns in the U.S.*," *PEW Research Center*. https://www.pewresearch.org/fact-tank/2019/10/22/facts-about-guns-in-united-states/

Parker, K., Horowitz, J., Igielnik, R., Oliphant, B. & Brown, A. (2017, June 22). "The Demographics of Gun Ownership – Gun Ownership is Most Common Among Men, Whites," *America's Complex Relationship With Guns: An In-depth Look at the Attitudes and Experiences of U. S. Adults*. Washington, DC: Pew Research Center (US Politics & Policy). pewsocialtrends.org/2017/06/22/the-demographics-of-gun-ownership/

References

ATF. (n.d.). *Timeline*. http://www.atf.gov/content/about/our-history/timeline

Cavanagh, S & Teasley, D. (1993). *U.S. Bureau of Alcohol, Tobacco, and Firearms. CRS Report for Congress*. Washington, DC: Congressional Research Service.

GAO. (1993). *Firearms and Explosives: Information and Observations on ATF Law Enforcement Operations*. Washington, DC: General Accounting Office.

GAO. (1997). *Combating Terrorism: Federal Agencies' Efforts to Implement National Policy and Strategy*. Washington, DC: General Accounting Office.

GAO. (1999). *Combating Terrorism: Issues to Be Resolved to Improve Counterterrorism Operations*. Washington, DC: General Accounting Office.

GAO. (2003a). *Combating Terrorism: Interagency Framework and Agency Programs to Address the Overseas Threat*. Washington, DC: General Accounting Office.

GAO. (2003b). *Terrorist Financing: U.S. Agencies Should Systematically Assess Terrorists' Use of Alternative Financing Mechanisms*. Washington, DC: General Accounting Office.

GAO. (2007). *Combating Terrorism: Law Enforcement Agencies Lack Directives to Assist Foreign Nations to Identify, Disrupt, and Prosecute Terrorists*. Washington, DC: Government Accountability Office.

GAO. (2009). *Firearms Trafficking: U.S. Efforts to Combat Arms Trafficking to Mexico Face Planning and Coordination Challenges*. Washington, DC: Government Accountability Office.

GAO. (2014). *Bureau of Alcohol, Tobacco, Firearms, and Explosives: Enhancing Data Collection Improve Management of Investigations*. Washington, DC: General Accounting Office.

Krouse, W. J. (2011). *The Bureau of Alcohol, Tobacco, Firearms and Explosives (ATF): Budget and Operations*. Washington, DC: Congressional Research Service.

Markon, J. (2008, May 10). FBI, ATF Battle for Control of Cases. *Washington Post*.

Parson, C & Gerney, A. (2015). *The Bureau and the Bureau. A Review of the Bureau of Alcohol, Tobacco, Firearms, and Explosives and a Proposal to Merge it with the Federal Bureau of Investigation*. Washington, DC: Center for American Progress.

Perez, E. (2012, August 14). U.S. News Firearms Bureau Struggles to Define Its Role, Wall Street Journal.

Relyea, H.C. (2002). *Homeland Security: Department Organization and Management*. Washington, DC: Congressional Research Service.

US Department of Justice. (2009). *Department of Justice. Explosives Investigation Coordination between the Federal Bureau of Investigation and the Bureau of Alcohol, Tobacco, Firearms, and Explosives*. Washington, DC: US Department of Justice.

US House of Representatives. (1981). *Dismantling of the Bureau of Alcohol, Tobacco, and Firearms, Before the Subcommittee on Crime of the Committee on the Judiciary, House of Representatives. 97th Congress*. Washington, DC: US House of Representatives.

US House of Representatives (1982). *Enforcement Efforts of the Bureau of Alcohol, Tobacco and Firearms, Before the Subcommittee on Crime of the Committee on the Judiciary, House of Representatives. 97th Congress*. Washington, DC: US House of Representatives.

US House of Representatives. (1992). *Bureau of Alcohol, Tobacco, and Firearms' Proposal for a Gang Information Network*. Washington, DC: US House of Representatives.

US Senate. (1979). *Oversight Hearings on Bureau of Alcohol, Tobacco and Firearms, Before a Subcommittee of the Committee on Appropriations, United States Senate. 96th Congress*. Pt 2. Washington, DC: US Senate.

US Senate. (1982). *Proposed Disolution [Sic] of Bureau of Alcohol, Tobacco, and Firearms, Before a Subcommittee of the Committee on Appropriations, United States Senate. 97th Congress*. Washington, DC: US Senate.

Chapter 4

Central Intelligence Agency (CIA) and the Intelligence Community

Suzette A. Haughton

The University of the West Indies, Kingston, Jamaica

Scott N. Romaniuk

University of South Wales, Caerleon, United Kingdom

Contents

Introduction and Genesis of the Central Intelligence Agency 19
The CIA 21
The National Security Council 21
CIA and Intelligence Community 22
The 2004 Changes to the Law 23
Conclusion 23
Further Reading 23
References 23

Introduction and Genesis of the Central Intelligence Agency

The Central Intelligence Agency (CIA) is an important USA government agency with a national security mandate to collect intelligence globally. This chapter explains the establishment and role of the CIA within the wider USA's intelligence community.

There were four agencies involved in intelligence which heralded the establishment of the CIA. These agencies were the Office of the Coordinator of Information

DOI: 10.4324/9781315144511-5

(COI), Office of Strategic Service (OSS), Strategic Services Unit (SSU), and Central Intelligence Group (CIG).

Established on July 11, 1941, the COI was designed to gather strategic and economic intelligence during World War II. It lasted less than one year, only for 337 days, because World War II had come to an end. However, this agency managed to coordinate the intelligence gathered from the USA's Department of State, the army, the navy, and the Federal Bureau of Investigations (FBI) and was able to disseminate this intelligence in an organized and coordinated way to USA's President Franklin D. Roosevelt. The COI engaged in collaborations with other countries such as Britain. For instance, it liaised with the British intelligence agencies to obtain training and information. It was adequately staffed and funded to execute its tasks. It had a USD 10 million budget and 600 staff complement.

Strategically, the COI was moved under the umbrella of the Joint Chiefs of Staff (JCS) to better align its resources and expertise with the military. However, a part of the staff and elements of the COI was redirected, on instructions of the President, to the Office of War Information (OWI). The part of the COI that was moved to the JCS became known as the OSS.

The OSS was therefore created on June 13, 1942 and it operated for just over 3 years. It became the collection and analysis arm of the JCS on strategic information. However, it also carried out paramilitary operations in Europe, North Africa, China, India, and Burma. Despite its strategic intelligence collection and analysis role, the OSS was not allowed to get involved in domestic counter intelligence as other agencies such as the Navy was very protective of this role. Likewise, a USA Presidential decree obtained by the US Department of State and the armed forces effectively blocked the OSS from decoding World War II's intelligence intercepts. Despite these challenges, the OSS managed to establish a counterintelligence clandestine foreign capability through engaging diplomatic, non-official connections as well as the military.

Like its predecessor, the OSS was properly staffed. It had a staff complement of 13,000 drawn from the USA's army and air force, the navy, marines, or coast guards as well as from civilians. Almost half of the OSS staff, including males and females, carried out duties overseas. The change in the USA Presidency and the new leadership headed by President Truman felt there was no great need for a peacetime intelligence agency and so the OSS was closed on October 1, 1945. However, some of the departments were preserved and transferred to other areas. The USA Department of State took on the Research and Analysis Branch and the War Department took over the Counter Intelligence Branch as well as the Secret Intelligence Branch. The War Intelligence Branch became known as the Strategic Services Unit (SSU).

To ensure continuity, the birth of the SSU on October 1945 saw this unit undertaking the operation of the foreign posts formerly held by the OSS. Considered a temporary solution, the SSU lasted for 1 year and 5 months after its establishment. Hence, by January 1946, the Central Intelligence Group (CIG) was established. The full operations, resources, personnel, and capabilities of the SSU were transferred under the ambit of the CIG.

The CIG had a dual role of coordinating the intelligence received from varying government agencies as well as collecting and producing the group's intelligence. It also conducted independent research and engaged in the collection of covert foreign intelligence. The CIG reported to the National Intelligence Authority. This authority comprised of a representative of the USA President, the Secretary of State, the Secretary of War, and the Secretary of the Navy. Although it played a vital role in disseminating warnings of covert foreign activities to the USA, it was constrained by the USA Department of State and the armed forces. To obtain greater autonomy, the CIG emerged into an independent agency named the Central Intelligence Agency (CIA).

The CIA

The 1947 National Security Act legally established the CIA. This act was signed by the USA's President Harry Truman on July 26, 1947. The CIA began to operate on September 18, 1947 and remains USA's foreign intelligence agency.

Four broad developments resulted from the passage of the National Security Act. These are:

- Merging of three departments under the authority of the Secretary of Defense. These were the Department of War, the Department of the Navy, and the National Military Establishment. By doing this, the act reorganized the USA foreign policy, armed forces, and the intelligence community, therefore restructuring the foreign policy and military departments in the USA government.
- Providing greater autonomy for the USA Air Force by making it a distinct service. In this regard, the act created the Department of Defense and the United States Air Force.
- Protecting the Marine Corp by placing it under the Department of the Navy but as an autonomous service.
- Creating two important bodies in the USA national security and intelligence architecture. These bodies were the National Security Council and the CIA.

The National Security Council

Section 110 (a) of the 1947 National Security Act establishes the National Security Council and mandates that the USA President is to preside over the council's meetings. It also stipulates that the function of the council is to advise the President on matters of integration concerning domestic, foreign, and military policies in order to facilitate better coordination between agencies and departments of government. This section orders that the President should be one of the persons on the council. Other members appointed to the council are the:

- Secretary of State and the Secretary of Defense through Section 202
- Secretary of the Army through Section 205
- Secretary of the Navy and the Secretary of the Air Force through Section 207
- Chairman of the National Security Reserve Board as well as other officers named by the President on an ad hoc basis through Section 103
- Secretaries of the executive departments as well as the Chairman of the Munitions Board through Section 213
- Chairman of the Research and Development Board through Section 214

Section 110 (b) elaborates the duty of the council as to:

- Assess the actual and military power of the USA in an attempt to make recommendations to the USA President on this matter.
- Consider national security policies of similarity to government agencies and departments and to make recommendations to the President on these matters.

CIA and Intelligence Community

Section 102 of the 1947 National Security Act establishes the CIA. It also places the CIA under the National Security Council and stipulates that this agency should be headed by the Director of Central Intelligence (DCI). The President of the USA is also mandated through Section 102 to appoint the DCI from either the armed forces or from the civilian population. The President's appointment must be done based on the advice and consent of the USA Senate. However, if a commissioned officer from the armed force is appointed to the post of Director, this person in performing his duties is not subjected to the supervision, control, restriction, or prohibition of the military to which he or she was formerly employed. Likewise, this Director is not empowered to exercise any supervision, control, powers, or functions over the Department of the Army, Department of the Navy, Department of the Air Force, or any of their affiliated units or divisions.

Section 102 (c) allows the Director of the CIA the power to terminate the employment of any employee of the agency once he deems it in the interest of the USA. However, this termination does not bar the individual from seeking employment in other areas of the Government once authorized by the USA Civil Service Commission.

Under the direction of the National Security Council, the coordinating duty of the CIA is stipulated through Section 102 (d) of the act. These are to:

- Advice the National Security Council (NSC) on national security matters concerning intelligence activities of government departments and agencies
- Make recommendations to the NSC in an effort to coordinate intelligence activities across government departments and agencies
- Utilize existing agencies and facilities to evaluate national security intelligence and to disseminate this intelligence within the Government. Notwithstanding:
  - The agency must not have any policing, subpoena, law enforcement, or internal security functions.
  - The Director of the CIA has responsibility to protect intelligence sources and methods from unauthorized disclosure.
  - The departments and other agencies of the government must continue with the collection, evaluation, and dissemination of departmental intelligence.
- Perform added services to the NSC as determined by the NSC, either based on an ad hoc basis or those determined to be more efficiently performed centrally.

Finally, on the recommendation of the NSC and the President, the DCI may request to inspect the intelligence of the departments and agencies of the government. In this regard, upon the written request of the DCI, the Director of the Federal Bureau of Investigations (FBI) must make available to the DCI the FBI's intelligence for correlation, evaluation, and dissemination as may be deemed crucial to national security.

The 2004 Changes to the Law

The 2004 Intelligence Reform and Terrorism Prevention Act made changes to the 1947 National Security Act. These changes had implications for USA's intelligence community. The CIA was restructured and the posts of DCI and Deputy Director of Central Intelligence were discarded. The Director of Central Intelligence Agency (D-CIA) was created as stipulated through Section 104(A) of the Intelligence Reform and Terrorism Prevention Act.

The 2004 Act also created a new position called Director of National Intelligence (DNI). The DNI was charged with the responsibility of the administration of the Intelligence community as well as the National Counterterrorism Center (NCTC).

Conclusion

The CIA is responsible for providing the USA government with foreign intelligence. The establishment of the CIA is rooted in a long history of intelligence departments and agencies during the post-World War II era. The 1947 National Security Act established the CIA, and the 2004 Intelligence Reform and Terrorism Prevention Act reformed the CIA. The CIA continues to collect, evaluate, and disseminate foreign intelligence to the USA government and in this regard plays a central role in the security and protection of USA's homeland.

Further Reading

London, D. (2020, February 10). "The CIA in the age of trump," *Just Security*. https://www.justsecurity.org/68539/the-cia-in-the-age-of-trump/

Lowenthal, M. M. (2012). *The U.S. Intelligence Community: An Annotated Bibliography*. Abingdon: Routledge.

Zegart, A. B. (2006). "September 11 and the adaptation failure of U.S. intelligence agencies," *International Security*, *29*(4): 78–111.

References

Byman, D (2014), The intelligence war of terrorism *Journal Intelligence and National Security*, 29: 837–863.

Central Intelligence Agency (CIA), Accessed on: https://www.cia.gov/about-cia/history-of-the-cia

Intelligence Reform and Terrorism Prevention Act of 2004, 17 December 2004, *Public Law 108-458, 108th Congress, 118 STAT. 3638*. Accessed on: https://www.dni.gov/files/documents/IRTPA%202004.pdf

Jervis, R (2013), Why intelligence and policy makers clash, *Political Science Quarterly*, 25 (2): 185–204.

Marrin, S (2011), The 9 11 terrorist attacks: a failure of policy not strategic intelligence analysis, *Journal Intelligence and National Security*, 26(2–3): 182–202.

Thornton, J (2009), *The US Intelligence Community and Foreign Policy: Getting Analysis Right*, The Brookings Institution, Washington, DC.

The National Security Act of 1947, 26 July 1947. *Public Law 253, 80th Congress, Chapter 343, 1st Section, S. 758*. Accessed on: http://global.oup.com/us/companion.websites/9780195385168/resources/chapter10/nsa/nsa.pdf

Chapter 5

Critical Infrastructure and Key Resources

Mila Demchyk Savage
Old Dominion University, Norfolk, VA, United States

Contents

Introduction 25
Defining Critical Infrastructure and Key Resources 26
Resilience vs. Protection 27
National Infrastructure Protection Plan 27
CIKR Collaboration 28
Conclusion 28
Further Reading 28
References 29

Introduction

Our national well-being relies upon secure and resilient critical infrastructure – those assets, systems, and networks that underpin American society (NIPP 2013). As of today, 16 infrastructure sectors with their assets, systems, and networks, whether physical or virtual, are defined as critical. A complete destruction or even a partial damage of one of these sectors would negatively affect national security, economy, public safety, and other areas.

The Department of Homeland Security (DHS) is playing a key role in identifying, prioritizing, and coordinating the overall national effort for enhancing the protection of critical infrastructure and key resources. The department encourages continuous collaborative actions to ensure that resources are applied in the most effective

DOI: 10.4324/9781315144511-6

and efficient manner to reduce vulnerability, deter threats, and minimize the consequences of attacks and other incidents.

Defining Critical Infrastructure and Key Resources

Critical infrastructure (CI) covers the structures and functions that modern societies require to operate continuously. Failures in these infrastructures may cause substantial undesired consequences in other services due to the high degree of interconnectivity of services. Therefore, the continuous operation of these services is essential, even during severe failure situations (Seppänen et al., 2016 A46). The term 'CI' is defined as systems and assets, whether physical or virtual, so vital to the United States that the incapacity or destruction of such systems and assets would have a debilitating impact on security, national economic security, national public health or safety, or any combination of those matters (Section 1016(e) of the USA PATRIOT Act of 2001 (42 U.S.C. 5195c(e)). The term 'Key Resources' (KR) is defined as publicly or privately controlled resources essential to the minimal operations of the economy and government (6 U.S. Code § 101, section 2(9) of the Homeland Security Act of 2002 (6 U.S.C. 101(9)).

After 9/11, a key role in managing CI and KR (together – CIKR) was granted to DHS and its Secretary. The initial task of the department was to identify, prioritize, and coordinate the overall national effort for enhancing the protection of CIKR of the United States. The Secretary of Homeland Security is entitled to periodically evaluate the need for and approve changes to CI sectors and shall consult with the Assistant to the President for Homeland Security and Counterterrorism before changing a critical infrastructure sector or a designated sector-specific agency (SSA) for that sector (Homeland Security Presidential Directive 7, 2003).

Today, in the United States, 16 infrastructure sectors with their assets, systems, and networks, whether physical or virtual, are defined as critical. Each sector has an associated SSA responsible for overseeing it (PPD-21 2013). SSAs coordinate CIKR efforts within their sectors to deter threats, mitigate vulnerabilities, and minimize the consequences of manmade and natural incidents (CIKR Support Annex 2008). For example, the Department of Energy is responsible for all aspects related to securing a steady energy supply to the nation by collecting and analyzing the data, coordinating actions of key actors of the energy market, supporting the nation's transition to the smart grid, etc.

The 16 sectors and SSAs are as follows (PPD-21 2013):

- chemical – DHS;
- commercial facilities – DHS;
- communications – DHS;
- critical manufacturing – DHS;
- dams – DHS;
- defense industrial base – Department of Defense (DOD);
- emergency services – DHS;
- energy – Department of Energy;

- financial services – Department of Treasury; food and agriculture – U.S. Department of Agriculture and Department of Health and Human Services;
- government facilities – DHS and General Services Administration;
- healthcare and public health – Department of Health and Human Services;
- information technology – DHS;
- nuclear reactors, materials. and waste – DHS;
- transportation systems – DHS and Department of Transportation;
- water and wastewater system – Environmental Protection Agency.

A complete destruction or even a partial damage of one of these sectors would negatively affect national security, economy, public safety, and other areas.

Resilience vs. Protection

From the moment of its creation, DHS has made CI a priority. Recent years brought a shift in emphasis from CI protection to that of resilience. This development reflects the acknowledgment that complete protection can never be guaranteed, and that achieving the desired level of protection is not cost-effective as a rule in relation to the actual threats (Pursiainen, 2018).

The key criteria illustrating the evolution of the approach to managing CIKR is an elevated role of security and resilience in CI homeland security planning efforts (NIPP 2013). After 9/11, the concept of CI protection became a new catchword in the United States (Moteff et al., 2003). Events following the day of 9/11, like the financial crisis of 2008 or the Northeast blackout of 2003, illustrated that a terror attack is not the only source of threat to national security and the country's overall stable functioning. Besides acts of terror, evolving threats to CI include extreme weather, accidents or technical failures, cyber threats, and pandemics (NIPP 2013). Thus, policies initially focused on the identification and protection of key resources have evolved to include an all-hazards approach to CI security and resilience across 16 sectors (Smith, 2014).

National Infrastructure Protection Plan

Initiated by PPD-21, National Infrastructure Protection Plan (NIPP) is a central document unifying national efforts related to CIKR protection. It provides a coordinated approach, making sure that resources are applied in the most effective and efficient manner to reduce vulnerability, deter threats, and minimize the consequences of attacks and other incidents.

NIPP 2013 identifies nation's vision as such, where physical and cyber CI remain secure and resilient, with vulnerabilities reduced, consequences minimized, threats identified and disrupted, and response and recovery hastened. The document specifies that the vision and mission depend on the achievement of goals that represent the strategic direction on which CI activities should be focused over the next several years. Thus, NIPP is an evolving plan, which depends on a rapidly changing external environment. Besides establishing a vision, mission, and goals that are supported by a set of core tenets, NIPP calls to action and describes a national unity of effort to achieve CI security and resilience.

CIKR Collaboration

Addressing CIKR-related prevention, protection, preparedness, response, and recovery requires cooperation and collaboration between and among CIKR entities. A primary objective of this collaborative effort between the private-sector owners and operators; state, tribal, and local governments; nongovernmental organizations; and the Federal government is to ensure that resources are applied where they offer the most benefit for mitigating risk, deterring threats, and minimizing the consequences of incidents (CIKR Support Annex, 2008).

On the national level, organizational structures provide formal and informal mechanisms for public- and private-sector coordination, situational awareness, impact assessments, and information sharing with regard to CIKR-related concerns on a sector-by-sector and/or a cross-sector basis (CIKR Support Annex, 2008). The national structure includes numerous actors, among them are National Operations Center, National Response Coordination Center, National Infrastructure Coordinating Center, Federal Emergency Operations Centers, and United States Computer Emergency Readiness Team.

While the government plays a crucial role in managing CIKR, voluntary collaboration between private-sector owners and operators (including their partner associations, vendors, and others) and their government counterparts has been and will remain the primary mechanism for advancing collective action toward national CI security and resilience (NIPP 2013).

Conclusion

Secure and resilient infrastructure is a basis of national well-being. Thus, efforts to enhance the protection of CIKR are important. Since its formation, DHS has been playing a key role in ensuring that resources are applied in the most effective and efficient manner to reduce vulnerability, deter threats, and minimize the consequences of attacks and other incidents.

The concept of CI resilience is gradually replacing the original CI protection, with the latter focusing on protective measures and resilience as opposed to focusing on the whole cycle of a crisis, emphasizing the impossibility of safeguarding against all threats (Pursiainen, 2018).

Further Reading

Baggett, R. K. & Simpkins, B. K. (2018). *Homeland Security and Critical Infrastructure Protection*. Santa Barbara: Praeger.

Ellis, J. W. (2014). *Fundamentals of Homeland Security*. An Operations Perspective. Springfield.

Gheorghe, A. V., Vamanu, D. V., Katina, P. F., & Pulfer, P. (2018). *Critical Infrastructures, Key Resources, Key Assets: Risk, Vulnerability, Resilience, Fragility, and Perception Governance*. Cham: Springer.

References

CIKR – 1. *Critical Infrastructure and Key Resources Support Annex*. January 2008. https://www.fema.gov/pdf/emergency/nrf/nrf-support-cikr.pdf

HSPD – 7. Homeland Security Presidential Directive 7: Critical Infrastructure Identification, Prioritization, and Protection. December 17, 2003. https://www.dhs.gov/homeland-security-presidential-directive-7

Moteff, J., Copeland, C., & Fischer, J. 2003. Critical infrastructures: What makes an infrastructure critical? Report for Congress, Received through the CRS Web, Order Code RL31556, *The Library of Congress*.

NIPP 2013. https://www.dhs.gov/sites/default/files/publications/national-infrastructure-protection-plan-2013-508.pdf

PPD-21. *Presidential Policy Directive -- Critical Infrastructure Security and Resilience*. February 12, 2013. https://obamawhitehouse.archives.gov/the-press-office/2013/02/12/presidential-policy-directive-critical-infrastructure-security-and-resil

Pursiainen, C. Critical Infrastructure resilience: A Nordic model in the making? *International Journal of Disaster Risk Reduction*, 2018, 27, 632–641.

Smith, K. Designing flexible curricula to enhance critical infrastructure security and resilience. *International Journal of Critical Infrastructure Protection*, 2014, 7, 1.

Seppänen, H., Virrantaus, K., Kauppinen, T., et al. 125 Improving critical infrastructure resilience by identifying vulnerable interconnections. *Injury Prevention* 2016, 22: A46–A47.

Section 1016(e) of the USA PATRIOT Act of 2001 (42 U.S.C. 5195c(e)). https://www.law.cornell.edu/uscode/text/42/5195c

6 U.S. Code § 101, section 2(9) of the Homeland Security Act of 2002 (6 U.S.C. 101(9). https://www.law.cornell.edu/uscode/text/6/101

Chapter 6

Critical Manufacturing Sector

Carl A. Marrara
New England College, Henniker, NH, United States

Contents

Introduction 31
About the Critical Manufacturing Sector 32
History 33
Current Programs/Plan 34
Goals and Advancement 36
Further Reading 37
References 37

Introduction

The Critical Manufacturing Sector is a key component to the overall infrastructure of the United States. Responsible for the production of goods and resources that are essential to the safety, security, and stability of the nation, the Critical Manufacturing Sector requires a plan that is a collaborative product among the private sector, federal government, state governments, local governments, territorial governments, and nongovernmental organizations. The Department of Homeland Security labels the Critical Manufacturing Sector as a critical infrastructure sector; it recognizes that this spans across several sector categories. The goal of the Department of Homeland Security is to improve security and resilience to outside threats and to enhance incident response and recovery within the Critical Manufacturing Sector.

Currently, the government bodies that contribute to the coordination, writing, and implementation of these sector-specific plans are the Critical Manufacturing Sector Coordinating Council, Government Coordinating Council, and the U.S. Department of Homeland Security. The most recent comprehensive plan written was the 2015 dated "Critical Manufacturing Sector-Specific Plan, An Annex to the NIPP 2013," as published by the Department of Homeland Security. (NIPP 2013)

DOI: 10.4324/9781315144511-7

One member of the council reported in a recent personal interview that, "The DHS Critical Manufacturing Sector really is a vibrant sector overall with a lot of key information exchanged between the government and the critical manufacturing industry partners" (Confidential 2018).

There is constant exchange of information and collaboration of best practices between the various councils, individual manufacturers, and government agencies. The agencies, councils, and government bodies meet twice a year at a minimum with other meetings occurring as needed across different industries and disciplines.

About the Critical Manufacturing Sector

The Critical Manufacturing Sector is responsible for the production of goods and resources that are essential to the safety, security, and stability of the nation. The sector creates products that are essential to the energy, transportation, and defense industries of the United States. This includes manufacturers of machines that could be used in a period of conflict or emergency, but also those manufacturers that contribute to the supply chains and distribution networks that produce component parts of the essential finished goods. Companies participating in the original charter included manufacturers of weapons, aerospace, automotive, pharmaceuticals, information technology, general electronics, metals, and all the various component parts that are needed to create those finished products. The major categories of manufacturers that comprise the Critical Manufacturing Sector are primary metals manufacturing, machinery manufacturing, electrical equipment and appliance manufacturing, and transportation equipment manufacturing.

When the Critical Manufacturing Sector Coordinating Council of manufacturing companies was first established in 2008, there were 11 manufacturing companies that comprised the council (U.S. Department of Homeland Security, 2008). As of July 2017, there were 57 active manufacturing companies among industry clusters ranging from Alexion Pharmaceuticals, Inc., to The Boeing Company, to GrayGlass, to ITT Corporation, to the United States Steel Corporation (U.S. Department of Homeland Security, 2017b). The sector and the council are highly diversified but necessary in the Critical Manufacturing Sector of the United States.

According to a 2017 study conducted by the Aerospace Industries Association, it was estimated that in 2016 the aerospace and defense industry supported 2.4 million jobs, generated $872 billion in sales, with $146 billion representing exports (Aerospace Industries Association, 2017). According to an IHS Markit Economics report from 2015, defense industry manufacturing supported 1.8 percent of the total nominal gross domestic product in the United States and also represented approximately 2 percent of the nation's employment base and 13 percent of the nation's manufacturing employment base (IHS Markit Economics & Aerospace Industries Association, 2016).

However, the economic activity of the Critical Manufacturing Sector upholds the stability and functionality of the overall manufacturing sector in the United States. According to 2016 studies commissioned by the National Association of Manufacturers, manufacturers contributed $2.25 trillion to the U.S. economy in 2016, accounting for 11.7 percent of gross domestic product. This activity sustained nearly 12.5 million manufacturing workers in the United States, representing 8.5 percent of the workforce (National Association of Manufacturers, 2018).

History

Established in 2008, the Critical Manufacturing Sector was recognized by the Department of Homeland Security. This was announced via a public notice authored by R. James Caverly, the director of the partnership and outreach division of the Office of Infrastructure Protection within the Department of Homeland Security on September 17, 2008. In the notice it stated:

> …that the Secretary, Department of Homeland Security (DHS), has designated the DHS Office of Infrastructure Protection (IP) as the Sector-Specific Agency (SSA) for the Critical Manufacturing Sector under the National Infrastructure Protection Plan (NIPP). IP will now move forward with the organization and coordination processes identified in the NIPP for establishing a new critical infrastructure and key resources (CIKR) sector. These initial steps will include establishing Government and Sector Coordinating Councils, which will begin the process of full integration into the CIKR Sector Partnership, implementation of the NIPP Risk Management Framework and development of the Critical Manufacturing Sector Specific Plan.
>
> (U.S. Department of Homeland Security, 2008)

In a corresponding press release by the Department of Homeland Security, then Secretary Michael Chertoff stated:

> Because of the unique operating and supply-chain challenges faced by manufacturers, we determined that a new sector council would best address the needs of companies that did not fit precisely within the original 17 sector structure. Critical manufacturers are important members of our national team that will help us develop plans and exchange information in order to achieve our common security goals in this vital sector.
>
> (U.S. Department of Homeland Security, 2008)

In the same release, the private sector was represented by Richard A. Douglas, global security chief for the United States Steel Corporation. He stated:

> U.S. manufacturers are responsible for creating essential products, contributing billions of dollars to the economy and providing over one million American jobs. We are grateful for DHS' recognition and look forward to working together in strengthening the manufacturing sector's ability to be prepared and resilient against the threats of terrorism and all-hazard emergencies.
>
> (U.S. Department of Homeland Security, 2008)

The original sector-specific plan was released in 2010. Coordination and collaboration were necessary as the Critical Manufacturing Sector Coordinating Council and the Government Coordinating Council forged the details of this first plan in 2010. The "National Infrastructure Protection Plan (NIPP) 2013: Partnering for Critical Infrastructure Security and Resilience" incorporated plans from the Critical Manufacturing Sector.

Prior to the publishing of the updated plan in 2015, the coordination letter from council chairs reported the following major accomplishments:

- Gathered wide private sector input for the National Strategy for Global Supply Chain Security.
- Developed supply chain resilience workshops to improve information exchange in support of the National Strategy.
- Developed a Business Continuity Plan Suite designed to help small- and mid-size businesses develop robust continuity plans and improve resilience along sector and cross-sector supply chains.
- Developed tabletop exercises specifically aligned with the emergency response plans of Sector Coordinating Council members, creating opportunities for stakeholders to discuss supply chain disruption and resilience practices, facility access control, and issues with disgruntled employees.
- Established the Global Crisis Response System to serve as a small community discussion forum in the event of an overseas crisis.

(U.S. Department of Homeland Security, 2015)

While many of the tenants of the 2013 National Infrastructure Protection Plan (NIPP) document were applicable to the Critical Manufacturing Sector, this plan was later updated in 2015 with the "Critical Manufacturing Sector-Specific Plan Update: An Annex to the NIPP 2013." This is the most recent and comprehensive document that serves as the foundation for the sector, private industry councils, and government agencies.

Current Programs/Plan

The Critical Manufacturing Sector-Specific Plan accounts for five significant risks that could drastically compromise operations. These risks include natural disasters and extreme weather, supply chain disruptions, global political and social implications, deliberate attacks and terrorism, and cyberattacks.

These dependencies, interdependencies, and overlapping sector relationships are crucial to the Critical Manufacturing Sector for many reasons. For example, all manufacturers consume more than 30 percent of the nation's energy consumption in the process of creating finished goods. According to the U.S. Energy Information Administration, industrial users consumed 31.5 quadrillion BTU of energy in 2014 or 32 percent of the total (National Association of Manufacturers, 2018). Should there be a disaster, deliberate attack, or major energy infrastructure malfunction, the Critical Manufacturing Sector would be greatly impacted.

Likewise, manufacturers rely on information technology to modernize plants to enhance efficiency, reduce redundancy, and expedite processes. "The internet of things" is a term/phrase that is often used in manufacturing so that firms can maximize productivity. Often, the success of the manufacturing sector in the United States is due to the enhanced efficiency of operations here, and this asset of the sector has been identified as a risk to the Critical Manufacturing Sector. The National Association of Manufacturers estimates that the, "…output per hour for all workers in the manufacturing sector has increased by more than 2.5 times since 1987" (National Association of Manufacturers, 2018). However, the "internet of things" is all controlled through information technology. Likewise, many of the vendors of materials and industrial services are also connected to manufacturing firms they service. If and when these webs of communication are interrupted, chaos could ensue. Therefore, it has been a recent focus of the Critical Manufacturing Sector to plan for this emergency situation should a need arise.

Though there are other overlapping industry relationships, the third major dependency is in the transportation infrastructure sector. There are three major components of transportation and transportation infrastructure as it pertains to manufacturers. First is the creation of transportation manufacturing goods such as automobiles, aircraft, or other vehicles. Second is the production of transportation infrastructure goods and inputs such as metal beams, cement structure, and other necessary components of road, bridge, lock, port, and rail development. And last is the dependency of these transportation systems to move raw materials to manufacturers for processing as well as moving those finished goods to market or for final use (U.S. Department of Homeland Security, 2017). As stated in a 2016 Homeland Security "Infrastructure System Overview: Critical Manufacturing" analysis, "Transportation Systems Sector regarding the transportation of materials by land, water, and air. Harm to the Transportation Systems Sector has the potential to hinder the movement of materials and products and cause cascading effects throughout the Critical Manufacturing Sector and its customers" (U.S. Department of Homeland Security, 2017).

Though these are just three examples of the most major dependencies, interdependencies, and overlapping sector relationships, others do exist in the areas identified by the Department of Homeland Security such as the chemical sector, defense industrial base sector, emergency services sector, and water and wastewater systems sector.

Regarding risk management and national preparedness, information sharing and sector communication and collaboration are paramount. Because of this, the NIPP 2013 Critical Infrastructure Management Framework follows a precise process. First, the element of critical infrastructure is identified as physical, cyber, or human, though often these elements are woven together. Regardless of their identity, the same process is followed. Goals and objectives are set, infrastructure is identified, assessments and risk analyzation occurs, risk management strategies are implemented, and the effectiveness of those activities is then measured. During every step of this process, information is shared between all parties be they private industry, government coordinating councils, or the Department of Homeland Security (U.S. Department of Homeland Security, 2017).

While the manufacturing industry itself remains a focus, those sector independencies that manufacturers rely so heavily upon are also of constant concern. These sectors include energy, water, and natural resources; communications and information technology; transportation and infrastructure systems; and chemical processing. Any goals in the protection of the Critical Manufacturing Sector must take into account these vital sector interdependencies. Mitigating the risks of these crucial complimentary industries remains a focus of the Critical Manufacturing Sector.

A majority of the current programs and plans can be found in the foundational documents of the 2013 NIPP and the 2015 Annex to the 2013 NIPP. In addition to these main documents, the Department of Homeland Security has the following resources available to the public: private sector clearance programs; a business continuity planning suite that includes trainings, plans, and exercises; Critical Manufacturing Roadshow; regional outreach programs; and the Critical Manufacturing Sector Cybersecurity Framework Implementation Guidance program.

Goals and Advancement

The Department of Homeland Security identified four key operating characteristics that affect nearly all Critical Manufacturing Sector contributors. The first is that, "most manufacturing enterprises are integrated into complex, interdependent global supply chains." The second stated, "an uninterrupted supply of energy and water is needed for high-temperature and power-intensive operations." The third stated, "geographic concentration localizes expertise and reduces logistics cost." The fourth stated, "the sector's global networks demand constant monitoring to anticipate and mitigate disruptions" (U.S. Department of Homeland Security, 2017). The goal of the Critical Manufacturing Sector is to ensure that these four key operating characteristics are protected so that the sector itself can function as properly and effectively as possible, regardless of the mitigating circumstances faced.

Most important to the success of any and all programs and initiatives is the cooperation, collaboration, and shared mission of the Critical Manufacturing Sector Coordinating Council and the Government Coordinating Council.

To measure the success of the current programs and to identify where more effort is needed, the councils established a table of measurements and goals. The top goal of the councils to strengthen the sector is to, "improve information-sharing processes and promote continuous learning through exercises, incidents, and planning to strengthen sector and cross-sector partnerships." The second goal is to, "identify and access sector-specific threats, vulnerabilities, and consequences of inaction to raise sector risk awareness and information risk management." The third goal is to, "develop strategies to reduce risks to the Critical Manufacturing Sector assets from human, physical, and cyber threats without hindering economic viability." And the last major goal of the sector is to, "support research and development, advance planning and risk mitigation, coordinated response, and repaid recovery to ensure resilient operation of critical services" (U.S. Department of Homeland Security, 2017).

These overarching goals have been paired with six top priorities. The first priority being to, "evaluate supply chain resilience and interdependencies with other critical infrastructure sectors and collaborate across sectors on risk management." The second priority is to, "increase active engagement with Critical Manufacturing Sector partners to strengthen collaboration information sharing across member companies." The third priority is to, "work with public-private and cross-sector partners to share timely, relevant, and actionable information." The fourth priority is to, "work with sector partners to characterize the Critical Manufacturing Sector profile of cyber and physical risks and raise risk awareness, particularly at executive levels." The fifth priority is to, "improve Critical Manufacturing Sector cybersecurity knowledge, tolls, capabilities, and practices to secure critical cyber assets." And lastly to, "participate in cross-sector training and exercises to improve response and recovery capabilities to cascading disruptions" (U.S. Department of Homeland Security, 2017).

In all programs, the Critical Manufacturing Sector partners will work to measure the effectiveness of programs and efforts by asking three simple questions. The first, "was the information received current and relevant?" The second, "will the information inform decision-making?" And the last, "will participants share the information within their organization?" (U.S. Department of Homeland Security, 2017)

As stated in the interview with a private coordinating council member, only with constant measurements of effectiveness can programs continue to serve this "vibrant sector with 'key information' exchanged between government and the critical manufacturing industry partners"…" (Confidential, 2018).

Further Reading

Cybersecurity & Infrastructure Security Agency (CISA). (2014, June 27). "*Critical Manufacturing Sector Resources*." https://www.dhs.gov/critical-manufacturing-sector-resources

Miller, E. (2016, June). "Terrorist Attacks Targeting Critical Infrastructure in the United States, 1970–2015." *College Park*, United States. start.umd.edu/pubs/DHS_I%26A_GTD_Targeting%20Critical%20Infrastructure%20in%20the%20US_June2016.pdf

Tal, J. (2018, September 20). "America's critical infrastructure: threats, vulnerabilities and solutions," *Security Info Watch*. securityinfowatch.com/access-identity/access-control/article/12427447/americas-critical-infrastructure-threats-vulnerabilities-and-solutions

References

Aerospace Industries Association. (2017, June 15). 2015 Economic Impact Study of the U.S. *Aerospace & Defense Industry*. Retrieved March 28, 2018, from https://www.aia-aerospace.org/report/2017-facts-figures/

Confidential. (2018, March 23). Interview with Critical Manufacturing Sector Coordinating Council Member [Telephone interview].

IHS Economics, & Aerospace Industries Association. (2016, April 20). *2015 Economic Impact Study of the U.S. Aerospace & Defense Industry*. Retrieved March 28, 2018, from https://www.aia-aerospace.org/report/aerospace-and-defense-an-economic-impact-analysis/

National Association of Manufacturers. (2018). *Top 20 Facts About Manufacturing*. Retrieved March 27, 2018, from http://www.nam.org/Newsroom/Top-20-Facts-About-Manufacturing/

NIPP 2013. *Partnering for Critical Infrastructure Resilience (U.S. Department of Homeland Security, Trans.). (2013, February)*. Retrieved March 27, 2018, from https://www.dhs.gov/sites/default/files/publications/NIPP2013_Partnering-for-Critical-Infrastructure-Security-and-Resilience_508_0.pdf

Schreiber, T. D. (2015, March 11). *Critical Manufacturing Sector Government Coordinating Council Charter*. Washington, DC: Office of Infrastructure Protection.

U.S. Department of Homeland Security. (2017a, June 7). *Critical Manufacturing Sector-Specific Plan: An Annex to the NIPP 2013*. Retrieved March 28, 2018, from https://www.dhs.gov/sites/default/files/publications/nipp-ssp-critical-manufacturing-2015-508.pdf

U.S. Department of Homeland Security. (2017b, July 10). *Critical Manufacturing Sector: Council Charters and Membership*. Retrieved March 28, 2018, from https://www.dhs.gov/critical-manufacturing-sector-council-charters-membership

U.S. Department of Homeland Security, Homeland Security Department Documents and Publications. (2008, September 5). *DHS Recognizes Critical Manufacturing Sector as Key New Private Sector Security Partner [Press release]*. Retrieved March 27, 2018.

Chapter 7

Department of Homeland Security (DHS)

Suzette A. Haughton
The University of the West Indies, Kingston, Jamaica

Scott N. Romaniuk
International Centre for Policing and Security, University of South Wales, Caerleon, United Kingdom

Contents

Introduction 39
Establishment 40
Roles 41
DHS and Other Security Entities 43
Conclusion 43
Further Reading 44
References 44

Introduction

The Department of Homeland Security (DHS) aims to protect US citizens and the nation from security threats. It was created to prevent terrorist attacks, reduce instances of terrorism, mitigate the damage from terrorist attacks, and facilitate recovery. It also undertakes recovery efforts in natural disasters and other emergencies. This chapter addresses the establishment and role of the DHS. It also explores cooperation with other similar agencies to the DHS.

DOI: 10.4324/9781315144511-8

Establishment

The DHS falls under the US Federal government and has the role of maintaining US national security and public safety. The following sections discuss its establishment and roles.

The 2002 Homeland Security Act established the DHS. Created on November 25, 2002, in response to September 11, 2001 terrorist attacks on the US, the DHS aimed to establish a single Federal Government Agency to consolidate the activities of homeland security agencies across the US. Section 101 of the Homeland Security Act established the DHS as an executive department of the US in accordance with Title 5 of the US Code, which addresses government organizations and employees (US Homeland Security Act 2002).

Section 102 of the Act stipulates that the DHS must be headed by a Secretary of Homeland Security. This Secretary is appointed by the President upon consent and advice of the Senate. The Secretary of Homeland Security is therefore empowered to direct and exercise authority as well as control over the DHS. In carrying out its role, Section 102 (3) (f) authorizes the Secretary to appoint a Special Assistant. This Special Assistant is charged with the responsibility of:

- Communicating with the private sector to foster the DHS mission in protecting the US homeland
- Advising the Secretary about the DHS policies, regulations, processes, and actions on the private sector
- Interfacing with other relevant governmental federal agencies to determine the DHS impact on the private sector

The appointments of other officers to the DHS are stipulated through Section 103 of the Act. In this regard, upon consent and advice of the Senate, the US President may appoint the following persons:

- Deputy Secretary of Homeland Security to operate as the Secretary's first Assistant
- Under Secretary for Informational Analysis and Infrastructure protection
- Under Secretary for Science and Technology
- Under Secretary for Border and Transportation Security
- Under Secretary for Emergency Preparedness and Response
- Director of the Bureau of Citizenship and Immigration Services
- Under Secretary for Management
- Chief Legal Officer

There should be no more than 12 Assistant Secretaries. Additionally, to further assist the Secretary, the President must appoint a Director of Secret Service, Chief Information Officer, Chief Human Capital Officer, Chief Financial Officer, and Officer for Civil Rights and Civil Liberties. (US Department of Homeland Security, n.d.).

Roles

The roles of the DHS are stipulated through Sections 101 (1) and (2) of the Homeland Security Act. (US Homeland Security Act 2002). These are to:

- Prevent, reduce, or minimize terrorist attacks from happening on US soil, and if they happen, minimize the damage resulting from such attacks. The DHS is also charged with the responsibility to assist in recovery from terrorist attacks.
- Investigate and prosecute terrorism. The primary responsibility for investigating and prosecuting terrorism, however, rests with the Federal, state, and local law enforcement agencies.
- Act as a focal point to plan and organize in matters concerning natural and man-made crises and emergencies.
- Monitor relationships between terrorism and drug trafficking.
- Contribute to illegal drug interdiction efforts.

The DHS in providing protection for the US public and in maintaining national security has itemized 20 specific topics forming the cornerstone of its work. These are:

- **Academic Engagement** – The DHS has established the Office of Academic Engagement (OAE) to maintain relationships and liaise with the academic community on matters relating to the DHS core areas of disaster response, national security issues, and matters of public safety.
- **Border Security** – The DHS has deployed personnel, technology, and resource to watch US borders in an effort to make them safer from the exploits of criminals. Hence, it protects US borders from the smuggling of weapons, trafficking of illicit drugs, movement of contraband, and from human or migrant trafficking. As a key border security initiative, the DHS partnered with the US Department of State to create the Western Hemisphere Travel Initiative (WHTI). Haughton (2017) noted that the WHTI is an important border security mechanism which requires US citizens and permanent residents to travel on their passports or on WHTI compliant documentations. Such documentations verify the identity and citizenship of all persons who are entering US zones of sovereignty.
- **Citizenship and Immigration Services** – The DHS in cooperation with US Citizenship and Immigration Services grants citizenships, permanent resident cards, and eligibility documentation for persons who are eligible for citizenship, permanent residence, and for individuals who have the right to work in the US.
- **Civil Rights and Civil Liberties** – In protecting the US from security threats, the DHS is concerned about individual liberty, fairness, and equality under the law. Hence, the DHS works with the Office for Civil Rights and Civil Liberties (CRCL) to implement civil rights and liberties in the department's policies. It also addresses civil rights and liberties complaints and promotes workforce diversity in the DHS human resources management.

- **Critical Infrastructure Security** – The US critical infrastructure sectors are chemical, commercial facilities, critical manufacture, dams, defense industrial base, emergency services, energy, financial services, food and agriculture, government facilities, healthcare and public health, information technology, nuclear reactors, materials and waste, transport systems, and waste and water systems. These 16 critical infrastructure sectors are central to the DHS work as the destruction of any of these sectors will have severe implications on the security of the US. Hence, the DHS works with varying stakeholders, inclusive of the private sector and state governments across the US, to enhance the critical infrastructures' security operability and resilience.
- **Cybersecurity** – The DHS collaborates with other relevant agencies to carry out cybercrime investigations. It also engages in the recruitment and training of technical experts to investigate cybercrime cases.
- **Disasters** – The DHS works in collaboration with the Federal government's Emergency Management and Preparedness Agency (FEMA) in establishing a National Preparedness System aimed at preventing, responding to, and recovering from disasters and acts of terrorism.
- **Economic Security** – The movement of people, goods, capital, and services in and out of the US is central to US economic security. The DHS works in identifying threats to US economic security. In this regard, it tracks and investigates terrorist financing, intellectual property rights theft, immigration and citizenship document fraud, as well as social security benefit frauds.
- **Election Security** – A resilient election system is central to electoral security and to democracy. As a part of the government facilities critical infrastructure, the DHS has created the election infrastructure in 2017. Through its National Protection and Program Directorate, the DHS has provided services for state and local officials in an effort to minimize cyber or physical risk to their electoral systems.
- **Emergency Communications** – To strengthen US preparedness against threats and emergencies, effective emergency communication is required. In this regard, through the Office of Emergency Communication, the DHS supports first responders and government officials to execute their communication tasks during crisis situations or emergencies.
- **Homeland Security Enterprise** – The DHS is considered to be part of a homeland security enterprise involving 22 federal agencies and is ranked as the third largest federal department. The incorporation of so many federal agencies in the role of the DHS has informed its goal, which is "one DHS, one enterprise, a shared vision, with integrated results-based operation."
- **Human Trafficking** – Human trafficking involves the exploitation of human beings through forced labor or forced commercial sexual activities. The DHS is the agency responsible for investigating human trafficking. It arrests human traffickers and provides support for human trafficking victims. It also processes immigration relief by granting special visas referred to as T and U visas for victims of human trafficking.
- **Immigration Enforcement** – The DHS is actively involved in immigration enforcement. Through the January 2017 Presidential Executive Orders, the DHS is given additional resources to strengthen its border security role and

to enforce immigration laws. This immigration enforcement is resulting in the deportation of persons who have violated US immigration laws and who are deemed a threat to the state's security.

- **International Engagements** – The DHS collaborates with international partners to strengthen US economic as well as physical security.
- **Law Enforcement Partnerships** – The first level of security buffer rests with the state, local, tribal, and territorial partners. In this regard, the DHS works closely with law enforcers at the state, local, and tribal levels in an attempt to decentralize resources from Washington DC into those levels.
- **Preventing Terrorism** – The DHS's core responsibility is to protect the US from terrorist acts.
- **Privacy** – The DHS Privacy Office is responsible for determining the privacy impacts of the department's programs, systems, and initiatives.
- **Resilience** – The DHS remains adaptable to changing security environment so as to respond to acts of terrorism, cyber-attacks, pandemics, and natural disasters.
- **Science and Technology** – The Science and Technology Directorate of the DHS was created in 2003 in order to provide tools, technologies, and knowledge solutions to meet the needs of the entire homeland security enterprise. It partners with US government agencies, international governments, businesses, and the academic community to test options that assist the US to respond to hazards and threats.
- **Transportation Security** – To ensure the legal movement of people and commerce, the DHS Transportation Security Administration secures the US transport system by working closely with law enforcement and the intelligence community. In this regard, it uses a risk-based strategy to provide security on all modes of transportation, such as land, air, and sea.

DHS and Other Security Entities

Section 102 of the Homeland Security Act empowers the Secretary of the Homeland Security to enter into agreements with other governmental executive agencies. It empowers the Secretary to take steps to ensure that the information systems and databases of the DHS are compatible with other relevant governmental databases. The act also allows the Secretary to coordinate, through the Office of State and Local Coordination, with the private sector, state and local government personnel, and agencies in order to plan and distribute warnings and information to the public as well as to other governmental agencies and authorities. Finally, upon the direction of the US President, the DHS Secretary may be required to attend meetings of the National Security Council, and therefore, the Secretary engages with representatives from other governmental agencies and departments.

Conclusion

The US DHS is a federal department created through the 2002 Homeland Security Act. Although only in operation for 16 years, it has emerged as a critical department in the protection of US national security and public safety.

Further Reading

Martin, G. (2019). *Understanding Homeland Security* (3rd ed.). Thousand Oaks: Sage Publications.

Nemeth, C. P. (2016). *Homeland Security: An Introduction to Principles and Practices* (3rd ed.). Boca Raton: CRC Press.

Ramsay, J. D. & Kiltz, L. A. (2014). *Critical Issues in Homeland Security: A Casebook*. Abingdon: Routledge.

References

Haughton, S. (2017). Border Security and Cooperative Initiatives to Counter Illicit Drug Trafficking: The Case of Jamaica and the USA, in *Developing Next Generation Counter Measures for Homeland Security Threat Prevention* by M. Dawson, D. R. Kisku, P. Gupta, J. K. Sing, W. Li eds., pp. 104–119, Hershey, PA: IGI Global.

US Department of Homeland Security, Accessed on: https://www.dhs.gov/topics

US Homeland Security Act, Public Law 107–296, November 25, 2002, Proceedings of the 107th Congress, 116 Stat., 2135. Accessed on: https://www.dhs.gov/sites/default/files/publications/hr_5005_enr.pdf

Chapter 8

Domestic Nuclear Detection Office (DNDO)

Darren E. Tromblay
George Washington University, Washington, DC, United States

Contents

Introduction 45
The History of Concern About a Potential, Unconventional Nuclear Attack on US Soil 46
Creation of DNDO 47
Global Nuclear Detection Architecture 47
Research and Development 48
Intelligence Analysis and Information Sharing 49
Dismantlement of the DNDO 50
Conclusion 50
Further Reading 51
References 51

Introduction

The Domestic Nuclear Detection Office (DNDO) was a relatively short-lived component of the Department of Homeland Security (DHS). DNDO was created to address a longstanding concern about an unconventional nuclear attack on US soil. Since the early 1950s, the US intelligence community (IC) had indicated varying degrees of concern that a hostile power could attack the homeland with a nuclear weapon. These fears took on new life after the September 11 attacks demonstrated the United States' vulnerability to asymmetrical tactics. Through the DNDO, the US government attempts to facilitate research, information sharing, and preparedness efforts to mitigate one potential threat. Unfortunately, DNDO never fulfilled its mission and the

DOI: 10.4324/9781315144511-9

DHS' Countering of Weapons of Mass Destruction (CWMD) Office ultimately subsumed DNDO's functions.

The History of Concern About a Potential, Unconventional Nuclear Attack on US Soil

The Cold War competition between the United States and the Soviet Union ushered in concerns that Moscow might attempt to deliver a weapon of mass destruction through clandestine, rather than traditional, means. In 1949, the Soviets had detonated their first nuclear weapon – thanks to espionage against the Manhattan project – which caught Washington off-guard. In 1951, the Central Intelligence Agency (CIA) published a National Intelligence Estimate (NIE) which assessed that the Soviet Union might use part of its atomic stockpile in a clandestine attack against the United States through means including smuggling the device into the United States; bringing a weapon piecemeal into the United States, where Soviet operatives would then assemble it; and even bringing a weapon in among the household effects of Soviet diplomatic representatives (Central Intelligence Agency [CIA] 1951; Federal Bureau of Investigation [FBI], 1951). As the Cold War progressed, the agency's concerns encompassed the Peoples' Republic of China (PRC) after that country acquired a nuclear capability. Even though China lacked diplomatic establishments in the United States, the CIA suggested that the Chinese could introduce agents under the guise of bona fide immigrants (CIA, 1968).

Contemporaneous with these early assessments, the Federal Bureau of Investigation (FBI) was attempting to follow up on a lead, which suggested that a foreign power had smuggled an atomic device into the United States. An investigation, which began in 1951, predicated on information from Sao Paulo, Brazil, attempted to determine whether the Soviets had placed an atom bomb in the New York consulate of an unknown country, to be detonated at a time that Moscow deemed expedient (Federal Bureau of Investigation [FBI], 1951). As part of this intelligence effort, the FBI tried to determine through US Customs whether any suspiciously heavy packages, under diplomatic seal, entered the United States and also sought information from the Atomic Energy Commission about the physical characteristics of a disassembled atomic weapon (FBI, 1951). In 1952, the FBI placed the case in a closed status but also set forth instructions to periodically solicit information from sources who had knowledge of Soviet and Soviet satellite consulates and forward the information to the FBI Headquarters under the caption "Smuggling of Atomic Bombs and parts Thereof and Other Weapons of Mass Destruction into the United States" (FBI, 1952).

More than half of a century after the beginning of the atomic age, the United States was still looking for the best approach to dealing with nuclear threats. Following the September 11, 2001 terrorist attacks on the United States, the possibility of an unconventional nuclear/radiological – not much different than the earlier concerns about smuggling of nuclear device – attack was still a concern. The 2002 capture of Jose Padilla, who was exploring a plan to build and detonate a dirty bomb in the United States on behalf of al-Qaeda, highlighted the real potential for a nuclear/radiological attack (US Department of Justice [DoJ] 2002). (Ashcroft, 2002). DHS's Customs and Border Protection (CBP) took responsibility, in 2002, for the deployment of radiation detection equipment at US ports of entry (Government Accountability Office [GAO], 2008). This was a continuation of an effort with which Customs had been involved with since the late 1990s (US Senate, 2006).

Creation of DNDO

DHS announced the establishment of the new DNDO, in April 2005, to coordinate US efforts at developing improved radiation detection technologies. This office was part of then-DHS Secretary Chertoff's DHS Second Stage Review, which implemented a number of organizational changes in the department (Bea, 2005). The SAFE Port Act of 2006 codified the office's existence. DNDO was the lead agency, within DHS, for integration of efforts to combat the threat of nuclear attack and was DHS's representative for all interagency activities to coordinate the nuclear defense posture of the US government. The DNDO Director was a Presidential appointee, and the office was staffed with personnel from the Departments of Defense (DoD), Energy (DOE), and State (DoS); the FBI; the Nuclear Regulatory Commission (NRC); and multiple DHS components, including the Science and Technology Directorate (DHS S&T), CBP, Transportation Security Administration (TSA), and the US Coast Guard (USCG). DNDO did not have a role as a collector of intelligence (US House of Representatives, 2008). Instead, its functions were facilitation of other agencies' collection of radiological/nuclear measures and signatures intelligence (MASINT) and to share information with federal and sub-federal (e.g. state and local) agencies. Although DNDO was not a collector in its own right, it had a role in driving operations by other agencies. DNDO was supposed to interact with the IC, as a developer of intelligence requirements (US House of Representatives, 2008). Consistent with this, the CIA indicated that it would accept collection requirements from DNDO (GAO, 2006).

Global Nuclear Detection Architecture

One of DNDO's core missions was the development of a Global Nuclear Detection Architecture (GNDA). However, while the SAFE Port Act mandated the establishment of the GNDA, it did not define the term (GAO, 2006). As defined by DHS, the GNDA was a multilayered system of detection technologies, programs, and guidelines designed to enhance the nation's ability to prevent a radiological or nuclear attack. Through the GNDA, the DNDO attempted to identify vulnerabilities and gaps in the nation's nuclear detection capabilities and then use these identified gaps, in existing capabilities, as the starting points for developing a list of detection priorities. DNDO conceptualized the GNDA as a multilayered system of exterior, border, and interior components. Exterior elements were the initiatives conducted at sea and in foreign territory; border elements focused on detecting and interdicting radiological or nuclear material at land, sea, and air ports of entry as well as at the borders in between these ports of entry; interior programs were those within the United States (Department of Homeland Security [DHS], 2007).

Development of the GNDA was a troubled process. In 2006, the DNDO completed an analysis of the current worldwide nuclear detection programs, identifying

72 programs across the US government that focused on radiological and nuclear management (DHS, 2007). However, by 2010, the actual defense plan – as opposed to an analysis of existing elements – remained incomplete (US House of Representatives, 2010). The approach that DNDO had adopted was flawed in multiple ways. It looked at the GNDA through a static optic, which did not reflect physical reality and did take into account the dynamic role of intelligence which might help to identify threats (US House of Representatives, 2011). Furthermore, the GNDA relied too much on unproven technologies, while, at the same time, it failed to take existing assets of law enforcement and intelligence agencies into account (US House of Representatives, 2010). In 2010, DNDO returned to the drawing board and re-designed the GNDA as intelligence-informed architecture that could respond to information that might become available (US House of Representatives, 2011). In December 2010, a GNDA strategic plan was released, and in April 2012, a GNDA implementation plan for domestic aspects was issued (GAO, 2012). Unfortunately, even the reworked GNDA fell short of expectations as it did not clearly identify priorities, determine necessary funding, or establish monitoring mechanisms to assess progress.

Research and Development

The DNDO's role in research and development (R&D) was supposed to complement the development of a GNDA. Gaps identified in the GNDA would provide direction to efforts directed at reducing those vulnerabilities. DNDO, at the time of its creation, subsumed DHS S&T's radiological/nuclear programs as well as the associated staff (GAO, 2012). Three directorates, within DNDO, focused on technological R&D. The Transformational and Applied Research Directorate focused on long-term R&D to address architectural and technical challenges that did not have near-term solutions. DNDO's Systems Engineering and Evaluation Directorate was responsible for establishing performance requirements and specifications and for assessing commercial off-the-shelf systems and next-generation technologies. Finally, the Production, Acquisition, and Development Directorate attempted to handle the development, production, procurement, and deployment of current and next-generation nuclear detection systems (DHS, 2008). This final directorate's functions became sources of significant embarrassment for DNDO.

The development of nuclear detection technology proved to be an area DNDO would experience high-profile mismanagement. The Radiation Portal Monitor Program – which DNDO had taken over from CBP and on which it continued to collaborate with CBP – put an early focus on devices known as advanced spectroscopic portals (ASPs). Although DHS had completed a cost–benefit analysis of the technology in May 2006, the Government Accountability Office (GAO) cast doubts on the results of that analysis when, in October 2006, GAO reported that the analysis was methodologically flawed (GAO, 2007a). In an especially egregious misstep, the DNDO conducted numerous preliminary runs of nearly all the materials that the ASPs were supposed to detect and then allowed the ASP contractors to collect test data and adjust their systems to identify the materials (GAO, 2007b). This defeated the objective of developing a system to scan for unknown and potentially deadly contraband. When DNDO finally began field testing the ASPs at ports, in 2009, the monitors registered an unacceptably high number of false alarms and also experienced a critical failure, during which the scanner simply shut down without notifying the operator (GAO, 2009). Not surprisingly, DNDO announced, in early 2010, that it had ceased pursuing the ASP as a primary scanning technology (US Senate, 2010).

The cargo advanced automated radiography system (CAARS) was another large-scale DNDO gaffe. The DNDO began working on the CAARS program, in 2005, as a means for CBP to automatically detect and identify highly shielded nuclear material at US ports of entry. In 2006, DNDO awarded a contract for research, development, acquisition, and deployment of CAARS. However, DNDO seems to have planned the acquisition and deployment of CAARS machines with no understanding of CBP logistical requirements. Only after completing several years' worth of work on CAARS did DNDO learn that CBP did not want the machines for the simple reason that they would not fit in the primary inspection lanes and would, consequently, slow down the flow of commerce and produce significant delays (GAO, 2010).

Intelligence Analysis and Information Sharing

DNDO's role of interfacing with interagency and non-US government customers meant that it had to establish an information sharing apparatus. The Joint Analysis Center (JAC) was the DNDO's 24/7 information hub (US House of Representatives, 2008). It included detailees from the FBI, the DOE, and the US Coast Guard (USCG) (US House of Representatives, 2013). In addition to sharing of informational and database resources with – among others – the IC; fusion centers; FBI Joint Terrorism Task Forces; and state, local, and tribal law enforcement agencies, the JAC provided technical support for federal and non-federal agencies, with the resolution of radiological and nuclear detection alarms. Through the technical reachback (TRB) program, DNDO – via the JAC – provided 24/7 regional and national-level expertise to resolve alarms promptly and accurately. The DNDO's Nuclear Assessment Program – also facilitated through the JAC – was a DOE initiative, before being incorporated into DNDO, which provided assessments of illicit nuclear trafficking events and of nuclear threat communication credibility (US House of Representatives, 2008).

In addition to JAC-associated functions, the DNDO also conducted analytic work through its Red Teaming and Net Assessments Directorate. Red Teams (which look at problems from an adversary's perspective) evaluated deployed systems and operations, including tactics, techniques, and procedures, in an as-close-to realistic environment as possible (US House of Representatives, 2014; DHS, 2008). Analytical red teaming used openly available information to develop realistic courses of action, while operational red teaming implemented those courses of action. The DNDO red teaming process tested the GNDA by using only the information to which terrorist adversaries would have access (US House of Representatives, 2008). DNDO partnered with DHS components, including CBP, TSA, USCG, and US Secret Service, as well as state and local agencies, in these activities (US House of Representatives, 2014). The directorate conducted net assessments to validate the Red Team results and evaluate the effectiveness of technologies, operational protocols, and procedures (DHS, 2008). Related to red teaming was the development of threat scenarios – in conjunction with DHS's Office of Intelligence and Analysis – to develop a more robust GNDA (US House of Representatives, 2011a; US House of Representatives, 2011b; US House of Representatives, 2007).

A subset of analysis is the exploitation of MASINT information. The National Technical Nuclear Forensics Center (NTNFC) was the primary DNDO entity for this specialized task. It was established in 2006 to serve as the national capability provider for nuclear forensics on pre-detonation nuclear and radiological materials (US House of Representatives, 2007; US House of Representatives, 2007). This forensics function was the primary NTNFC R&D focus. Furthermore, NTNFC was responsible for implementing national-level integration, centralized planning, exercising, evaluation, and stewardship across the full spectrum of US government nuclear forensics capabilities, from pre- to post-detonation (US House of Representatives, 2008). In addition to working with US government agencies, the NTNFC provides Nuclear Forensics Awareness Outreach training to state and local law enforcement officials as well as to foreign allies (US House of Representatives, 2008).

Dismantlement of the DNDO

As the DNDO stumbled in its key missions and drew scrutiny, worried overseers began to reduce the office's scope of responsibilities, until a new office finally subsumed DNDO's functions entirely. In 2011, a US Senate committee strongly endorsed transferring radiological and nuclear R&D back to DHS's Directorate of Science and Technology (the same Directorate from which DNDO had acquired these components several years earlier) (Lake, 2011). The DNDO's R&D activities also shifted from government-sponsored development of material solutions to an emphasis on existing, commercially available capabilities (US House of Representatives, 2017). Congress went even further when it directed the DHS Secretary to provide a plan, in 2014, for consolidation of DNDO and the Department's Office of Health Affairs into an Office of Weapons of Mass Destruction Defense (Painter, 2013). In 2016, DHS identified a Chemical, Biological, Radiological, Nuclear, and Explosives (CBRNE) Office as the primary entity of the US government to further develop, acquire, and support the deployment of an enhanced system for detection and reporting on attempts to import, possess, store, transport, develop, or use an unauthorized nuclear explosive device, fissile material, or radiological material in the United States (US House of Representatives, 2016). Then, in 2017, Kirstjen Nielsen, the then-newly confirmed DHS Secretary described DHS's CWMD Office as the entity which would "elevate and streamline DHS efforts to prevent terrorists and other national security threat actors from using harmful agents, such as chemical, biological, radiological, and nuclear material and devices." The Director of the new office would be James F. McDonnell, who had previously headed the DNDO (Miroff, 2017).

Conclusion

The United States has been cognizant of the potential for a hostile state- or non-state-inflicted nuclear event on domestic soil for multiple decades. DNDO was designed to facilitate both the development of countermeasures and information sharing. Despite this relatively limited mission, DNDO's short history is littered with failed initiatives.

Consistent themes in these missteps were the failure of DNDO – as a service provider – to understand its customers (e.g. CBP) and DNDO's failure to provide sufficient leadership – indicated by its failure to demand results from the private sector and by its inability to develop a GNDA that reflected awareness of partners' capabilities and gaps.

Further Reading

Avey, P. C. (2019). *Tempting Fate: Why Nonnuclear States Confront Nuclear Opponents*. Ithaca: Cornell University Press.

Richardt, A., Hülseweh, B. Niemeyer, B. & Sabath, F. (2013). *CBRN Protection: Managing the Threat of Chemical, Biological, Radioactive and Nuclear Weapons*. Hoboken: Wiley-VCH.

Wilson, W. (2014). *5 Myths About Nuclear Weapons*. New York: Mariner Books.

References

Ashcroft, John. (2002). *Transcript of the Attorney General John Ashcroft Regarding the Transfer of Abdullah al Muhajir (Born Jose Padilla) to the Department of Defense as an Enemy Combatant*. Washington, DC: US Department of Justice.

Bea, Keith. (2005). *Organization and Mission of the Emergency Preparedness and Response Directorate: Issues and Options for the 109th Congress*. Washington, DC: Congressional Research Service.

CIA. (1951). *National Intelligence Estimate. Soviet Capabilities for Clandestine Attack against the US with Weapons of Mass Destruction and the Vulnerability of the US to Such Attack: mid 1951 to mid 1952*. Washington, DC: Central Intelligence Agency.

CIA. (1968). *National Intelligence Estimate. Number 4-68. 18 June 1968*. Washington, DC: Central Intelligence Agency.

DHS. (2007). *DHS' Domestic Nuclear Detection Office Progress in Integrating Detection Capabilities and Response Protocols*. Washington, DC: US Department of Homeland Security.

DHS. (2008). *Domestic Nuclear Detection Office (DNDO) DNDO Overview. Summer 2008*. Washington, DC: Department of Homeland Security.

DHS. (2014). *Protecting the Homeland from Nuclear and Radiological Threats, Before the Subcommittee on Cybsersecurity, Infrastructure Protection, and Security Technologies of the Committee on Homeland Security, House of Representatives, 113th Congress*. Washington, DC: US Department of Homeland Security.

FBI. (1951). *105-14562. Atomic Bomb in Unknown Consulate, New York City, Internal Security - R. November 7, 1951*. Washington, DC: Federal Bureau of Investigation.

FBI. (1952). *105-14562. Director FBI to SAC, New York. Atomic Bomb in Unknown Consulate, New York City, Internal Security – R.* Washington, DC: Federal Bureau of Investigation.

GAO. (2006). *Combating Nuclear Smuggling: DHS Has Made Progress Deploying Radiation Detection Equipment at US Ports of Entry but Concerns Remain*. Washington, DC: Government Accountability Office.

GAO. (2007a). *Combating Nuclear Smuggling: DNDO Has Not Yet Collected Most of the National Laboratories' Test Results on Radiation Portal Monitors in Support of DNDOs Testing and Development Program*. Washington, DC: Government Accountability Office.

GAO. (2007b). *Combating Nuclear Smuggling: Additional Actions Needed to Ensure Adequate Testing of Next Generation Radiation Detection Equipment*. Washington, DC: Government Accountability Office.

GAO. (2008). *Combating Nuclear Smuggling: DHS's Program to Procure and Deploy Advanced Radiation Detection Portal Monitors Is Likely to Exceed the Department's Previous Cost Estimates*. Washington, DC: Government Accountability Office.

GAO. (2009). *Combating Nuclear Smuggling: Recent Testing Raises Issues about the Potential Effectiveness of Advanced Radiation Detection Portal*. Washington, DC: Government Accountability Office.

GAO. (2010). *Combating Nuclear Smuggling: Inadequate Communication and Oversight Hampered DHS Efforts to Develop an Advanced Radiography System to Detect Nuclear Materials*. Washington, DC: Government Accountability Office.

GAO. (2012). *Combating Nuclear Smuggling: DHS Has Developed Plans for Its Global Nuclear Detection Architecture, but Challenges Remain in Deploying Equipment*. Washington, DC: Government Accountability Office.

Lake, Jennifer E. (2011). *Homeland Security Department: FY2011 Appropriations*. Washington, DC: Congressional Research Service.

Miroff, Nick. (2017). "New anti-terrorism office to focus on countering weapons of mass destruction". *Washington Post*.

Painter, William L. (2013). *Department of Homeland Security: FY2013 Appropriations*. Washington, DC: Congressional Research Service.

Shea, Dana. (2008). *The Global Nuclear Detection Architecture: Issues for Congress*. Washington, DC: Congressional Research Service.

US House of Representatives. (2007). *H 2631. The Nuclear Forensics and Attribution Act. Before the Subcommittee on Emerging Threats, Cybersecurity, and Science and Technology of the Committee on Homeland Security. House of Representatives. 110th Congress*. Washington, DC: US House of Representatives.

US House of Representatives. (2008). *Department of Homeland Security Appropriations for 2009, Before a Subcommittee of the Committee on Appropriations, House of Representatives 110th Congress. Pt. 1B (2008)*. Washington, DC: U.S House of Representatives.

US House of Representatives. (2011a). *Overview of Science and Technology Research and Development Programs and Priorities at the Department of Homeland Security, Before the Subcommittee on Technology and Innovation, Committee on Science, Space, and Technology, House of Representatives, 112th Congress*. Washington, DC: US House of Representatives.

US House of Representatives. (2011b). *The Last Line of Defense: Federal, State, and Local Efforts to Prevent Nuclear and Radiological Terrorism within the United States, Before the Subcommittee on Cybersecurity, Infrastructure Protection, and Security Technologies of the Committee on Homeland Security, House of representatives, 112th Congress*. Washington, DC: US House of Representatives.

US House of Representatives. (2013). *Counterterrorism Efforts to Combat a Chemical, Biological, Radiological, and Nuclear (CBRN) Attack on the Homeland. Before the Subcommittee on Counterterrorism and Intelligence of the Committee on Homeland Security, House of Representatives, 113th Congress*. Washington, DC: US House of Representatives.

US House of Representatives. (2017). *Department of Homeland Security Appropriations for 2018, Before a Subcommittee of the Committee on Appropriations House of Representatives, 115th Congress. Pt 1C*. Washington, DC: US House of Representatives.

US Senate. (2006). *Detecting Smuggled Nuclear Weapons. Before the Subcommittee on Terrorism, Technology, and Homeland Security, of the Committee on the Judiciary*. Washington, DC: US Senate.

US Senate. (2010). *Nuclear Terrorism: Strengthening Our Domestic Defenses, Before the Committee on Homeland Security and Governmental Affairs, United states Senate. 111th Congress S Doc. 111-1096 Pts I and II*. Washington, DC: US Senate.

Chapter 9

Emergency Response Task Forces to Address Physical and Cyber Threats

Thomas J. Beck
New England College, Henniker, NH, United States

Contents

Introduction 53
Further Reading 57
References 57

Introduction

Over the past two decades, the United States has seen a number of watershed events that have led to significant changes in the way emergencies are handled. On September 11, 2001, the world witnessed a terror attack – the magnitude of which had never been seen before. Four passenger airliners had been hijacked and used as improvised guided missiles to bring down the World Trade Center and strike the pentagon. By the time the dust had settled in New York, Washington DC, and Pennsylvania, 2,996 people were killed, more than 6,000 were injured, and billions of dollars were lost in infrastructure alone (Institute for the Analysis of Global Security, 2004). Four years later, when Hurricane Katrina ravaged the gulf coast and devastated New Orleans, as the flooding and lack of services persisted, many in New Orleans found themselves trapped without adequate food, clean water, or services. When the waters receded and the damage was surveyed, Katrina was the worst in recorded history, costing an estimated $125 billion dollars (National Oceanic and Atmospheric Administration, 2018) and claiming 1,833 lives (Ramsay and Kiltz, 2014). Just in

DOI: 10.4324/9781315144511-10

2017, the United States and its territories saw three hurricanes that ranked in the top 10 of most destructive storms (NOAA, 2018). The improved preparedness and responsiveness of national and regional assets, as compared with Hurricane Katrina, saved countless lives during Hurricane Harvey. Early bureaucratic action, along with rapidly deployable, flexible Urban Search and Rescue (US&R) Task Forces, and sanctioning of volunteer rescue forces were major contributing factors that resulted in far less loss of life when compared with Hurricane Katrina. Continuing and proliferating the Task Force model in conjunction with citizen volunteers may be the formula for success to cyberthreats as well as physical threats.

There will always be a need for an immediate response when a serious incident occurs. Whether it is a bombing or shooting at a public event, a super storm, or an advanced persistent threat (APT) on our cyber infrastructure, there will always be a need for flexible, adaptable, and rapidly responsive capabilities to come to the aid of those in the affected areas. The most commonly thought of response task force are the ones we see during large-scale disasters. In these cases, such as Hurricane Katrina, Hurricane Harvey, and the 9/11 terror attacks, the local emergency responders were quickly overwhelmed and knew they would require support from the state and federal government. Often, we see responders from the task forces of the National US&R System. This framework of task forces provides greater regional and national response during a catastrophic national disaster. These task forces, such as Texas Task Force-1 (TX-TF-1), are self-sustaining, rapidly deploying capabilities from 28 locations all over the country (Federal Emergency Management Agency, 2015).

TX-TF-1 was organized in 1997 and became a full member of the National US&R System in June 2001 and currently has over 600 members from jurisdictions across the state and has the capability to deploy Type 1, 2, 3, and 4 US&R teams (Federal Emergency Management Agency (FEMA), 2018) (Texas Task Force 1 Urban Search and Rescue, 2016). Furthermore, the nature of the task force allows for the flexibility and scalability of the team deployment in order to meet the mission needs. TX-TF-1 has the ability to respond within 4 hours, be self-sufficient for up to 72 hours, and conduct US&R, wide area search, water rescue, helicopter rescue, or in the case of a smaller event, a mission ready package (MRP) that can provide scaled down capabilities (TX-TF-1, 2016). TX-TF-1 has been deployed in support of numerous natural and manmade disasters across the country. During Harvey, the National US&R team forces became overwhelmed. In this instance, we saw ordinary citizens with limited or no experience in rescue self-deploy on an unprecedented scale.

Hurricane Harvey was the first major hurricane to make landfall in the United States in over a decade. Though at its height it reached a peak of a category 4 storm with sustained winds of 130 mph, most of the damage from the storm came as a result of massive flooding in and around the Houston area. As the storm stalled for days in southeast Texas, the rainfall totals broke records (Samenow, 2016). As more and more people became trapped by the flood waters, regular citizens from Texas, Louisiana, and other surrounding states formed make shift search and rescue teams, referred to by the media as the "Texas Navy" or "Cajun Navy." Unlike Hurricane Katrina, where similar good Samaritans were seen as a potential liability and sent away, this time they were permitted to help pull people from the flood waters and escort them to safety (Phillipps, 2017). While this response was ad hoc in nature, ordinary citizens are being called upon more often to prepare their communities to be more resilient and provide greater capability to the response after a disaster. This is not completely foreign to FEMA.

The idea of using individuals with lower levels of training to perform less dangerous rescues and provide basic first aid is manifest in the FEMA program called The Community Emergency Response Team (CERT). CERT is a program that educates volunteers about disaster preparedness for the hazards that may impact their area and trains them in basic disaster response skills, such as fire safety, light search and rescue, team organization, and disaster medical operations (Department of Homeland Security, 2018). CERT offers a consistent, nationwide approach to volunteer training and organization that professional responders can rely on during disaster situations, which allows the high-demand, low-density, highly skilled professionals to focus on more complex tasks. Through CERT, greater capability to prepare for, respond to, and recover from disasters is built and enhanced. According to Ready.gov, there are over 2,700 local CERT programs nationwide, with more than 600,000 individuals trained since CERT became a national program (DHS, 2018). This type of grassroots, crowdsourcing-like approach to disaster response can be effective, especially when paired with highly skilled professionals included in the National US&R System and led by well-organized local and state emergency managers. This model proved itself to be functional during the response to Hurricane Harvey and was part of the reason the loss of life was considerably less than Hurricane Katrina, despite what is estimated to be equal economic damage of the two storms. We will continue to see disasters in the country and will need to continually refine the nation's response capabilities.

Major disasters that require a robust local, regional, and federal response task force will inevitably strike the United States again. There are numerous fault lines that run through the country, and a major earthquake similar to or bigger than the 1994 Northridge Earthquake will occur somewhere in the country eventually. Another major hurricane will strike the gulf coast or eastern seaboard. Terrorists affiliated with or inspired by violent extremist organizations (VEOs) will attack the United States as a lone wolf bomber or gunman. These are familiar threats and hazards that the nation is most prepared to respond to. Nationally, there are teams of trained professionals and volunteers available and ready to respond to these disasters. Can we take a similar model of a flexible professional response capabilities and grass roots local initiatives and apply it to emerging threats from the virtual world?

In May 2017, the National Cyberspace and Communications Integrations Center (NCCIC), a DHS-led cyber watch and warning center, issued a report disclosing that it has become aware of an emerging sophisticated campaign that uses multiple malware implants to place these sophisticated malware implants on critical systems. According to the report, victims have been IT service providers, where credential compromises could potentially be leveraged to access customer environments. Depending on the defensive mitigations in place, the threat actor could possibly gain full access to networks and data in a way that appears legitimate to existing monitoring tools (National Cybersecurity and Communications Integration Center, 2017). As the information age continues its exponential growth and our lives become more and more interconnected, we become more and more vulnerable as a nation to a devastating cyberattack. Cybercrimes and cyberattacks will continue to proliferate as our world becomes more and more dependent upon interconnected devices.

Cybercrimes and cyberattacks can come via any number and combination of APTs. APTs generally use a variety of attack tools and methodologies such as port scanning, social engineering, phishing, spear phishing, vishing, smishing, vulnerability exploitation, and other resources in the hacker's tool kit (Ramsay and Kiltz, 2014). These attacks can come from all over the globe and a number of sources with three general motivations. (1) cyber-criminals motivated by monetary gain; (2) nation-states motivated by the political economic, military, or other strategic advantage gained through espionage and intelligence gathering; (3) hacktivists or terrorists motivated by politics or ideology (Ramsay and Kiltz, 2014). In 2016, Bankrate.com research poll stated that as many as 41 million Americans have already had their identity stolen (Dickler, 2016). The United States' use of Stuxtnet to cripple the Iranian nuclear program is a prime example of a nation using a cyberattack to gain strategic advantage. Also, China has on more than one occasion used a variety of APTs to steal U.S. company's intellectual property to the cost of hundreds of millions of dollars to U.S. businesses (Goodman, 2016). Hacker groups like "anonymous" have attacked various cyber networks of nations or organizations that offended their own ideological beliefs (Goodman, 2016). The Islamic State in Iraq and Syria has demonstrated an ability to utilize the cyber domain to recruit and inspire attacks in the physical world. As their physical caliphate has all but vanished over the last two years, it is not unreasonable to expect they will use the World Wide Web to launch the next major attack against the U.S. Homeland. A Princeton University research group found that most Internet experts feel that a devastating cyberattack will occur within the next 10 years, possibly affecting business, utilities, banking, communication, and other Internet-dependent components of society (Bullock et al., 2013). The United States and DHS should ensure that they are prepared to prevent and respond to a cyberattack in the same manner they would to a natural disaster or more traditional "physical" terror attack.

Under the all-hazards approach to emergency management, the response to cyber incidents would have the same basic framework as seen with any of the disasters manifesting from the physical world. And rightfully so, as many of the effects of a cyberattack could be manifested in the physical domain. As Ted Koppel points out in his book "Lights Out," an attack on the Supervisory Control and Data Acquisition (SCADA) system could knock out power to a large portion of the country, causing a catastrophic disaster for an entire region (Koppel, 2015). An attack on the transportation cyber infrastructure could paralyze the nation and result in multiple incidents across the country. As demonstrated by the response to disasters such as hurricanes, the capability to quickly respond via established FEMA-certified task forces, local first responders and local and state emergency managers. DHS and the U.S. government should apply this model to cybersecurity and cyber-response.

Excerpts from the White House Cyber Policy Review of May 2010 point out that the federal government is not organized to address the growing problem now or in the future (Bullock et al., 2013). Responsibilities for cybersecurity are distributed across a wide array of federal departments and agencies (Bullock et al., 2013). To fix this problem, the government should consider consolidating national cybersecurity assets into DHS and create professional Cybersecurity Incident Response Teams (CSIRT) throughout the nation with the responsibility to identify and mitigate vulnerabilities in our critical infrastructure and key resources and identify and respond to cyberattacks. Similar to the FEMA US&R teams, these task forces could surge their capability throughout the nation as more serious APTs emerge. Additionally, the government could explore crowd-sourcing as a non-traditional means to solving the ever-evolving problem of cybersecurity and cyber-response. Crowd-sourcing is defined by Merriam-Webster as "the practice of obtaining needed services, ideas, or content by soliciting contributions from a large group of people and especially from the online community rather than from traditional employees or suppliers." Similar to the "Cajun Navy" of Hurricane Harvey, citizens of the U.S. could be called into service in the case of a potential catastrophic cyberattack. These concepts should be explored by DHS to refine the existing National Cyber Incident Response Plan, support the NCCIC and U.S. Computer Emergency Readiness Team, and consolidate overlapping authorities from other government agencies.

In the future, threats to the security of our nation will come from not only natural, manmade, and terrorist threats in the physical world but also the virtual world as well. As FEMA has developed, flexible, redundant, and responsive rescue capabilities through the National US&R System, so too should the DHS build responsive, redundant, and flexible professional CSIRTs to respond to threats from cyberspace. Furthermore, it should look for innovative means to quickly call the public at large into service to provide additional cybersecurity in times of crisis. The threats from cyberspace will only grow overtime, and the nation needs to be ready with cutting-edge, creative, flexible, and powerful response capabilities.

Further Reading

Buchanan, B. (2020). *The Hacker and the State: Cyber Attacks and the New Normal of Geopolitics*. Cambridge: Harvard University Press.

Caravelli, J. & Jones, N. (2019). *Cyber Security: Threats and Responses for Government and Business*. Santa Barbara: Praeger.

Lawson, S. T. (2019). *Cybersecurity Discourse in the United States: Cyber-Doom Rhetoric and Beyond*. Abingdon: Routledge.

References

Bullock, J., Haddow, G.D., Coppola, D.P., (2013). *Homeland Security: The Essentials*. Waltham, MA: Elsevier.

Department of Homeland Security, (2018). *Community Emergency Response Team*. https://www.ready.gov/community-emergency-response-team

Dickler, J. (2016). *41 Million Americans Have Had Their Identities Stolen*, https://www.cnbc.com/2016/10/10/41-million-americans-have-had-their-identities-stolen.html

Federal Emergency Management Agency (FEMA), (2015). *Fact Sheet: National Urban Search and Rescue Response System*. https://www.fema.gov/media-library-data/1440617086863-f6489d2de59dddeba8bebc9b4d419009/USAR_July_2015.pdf

Federal Emergency Management Agency (FEMA), (2018). *Texas Task Force Joins National US&R System (Press release)*. https://www.fema.gov/news-release/2000/07/25/texas-task-force-joins-national-urban-search-and-rescue-system

Goodman, M. (2016). *Future Crimes: Inside the Digital Underground and the Battle for Our Connected World*: New York, Anchor Books.

Institute for the Analysis of Global Security (IAGS), (2004). http://www.iags.org/costof911.html

Koppel T., (2015). *Lights Out: A Cyberattack, A Nation Unprepared, Surviving the Aftermath*: New York, Crown Publishing Group.

National Cybersecurity and Communications Integration Center (2017). *Intrusions Affecting Multiple Victims Across Multiple Sectors. (Incident Report)*. https://www.us-cert.gov/sites/default/files/publications/IR-ALERT-MED-17-093-01C-Intrusions_Affecting_Multiple_Victims_Across_Multiple_Sectors.pdf

National Oceanic and Atmospheric Administration (NOAA) National Hurricane Center, "*Costliest U.S. tropical cyclones tables updated*" January 26, 2018. https://www.nhc.noaa.gov/news/UpdatedCostliest.pdf

Phillipps, D. (2017). *Seven Hard Lessons Federal Responders to Harvey Learned From Katrina*. https://www.nytimes.com/2017/09/07/us/hurricane-harvey-katrina-federal-responders.html

Ramsay, J. D. & Kiltz, L., (2014). *Critical Issues in Homeland Security. A Casebook*. Boulder, CO: Westview Press.

Samenow J., (2016). *60 Inches of Rainfall from Hurricane Harvey in Texas*, Shattering U.S. Storm Records. https://www.washingtonpost.com/news/capital-weather-gang/wp/2017/08/29/harvey-marks-the-most-extreme-rain-event-in-u-s-history/?utm_term=.a57607226114

Texas Task Force 1 Urban Search and Rescue, (2016). https://texastaskforce1.org/

Chapter 10

Energy (Power) Security and Grids

Mila Demchyk Savage
Old Dominion University, Norfolk, VA, United States

Contents

Introduction 59
What Is an Energy or Power Grid? 60
Legislation 60
Grid Reliability and Smart Grids 61
Grid Resilience 62
Grid Security 62
Energy Security and Adequacy of Energy Sources 62
Microgrids 63
Conclusion 63
Further Reading 64
References 64

Introduction

Commercial manufacturing of light bulbs at the intersection of the 19th and 20th centuries began a new era of society's electrification. Humankind's excitement from having an access to electricity kept evolving over the last century. Rapid urbanization, endless technological breakthroughs, and increased levels of consumption intensified society's dependency on electricity. Despite this trend, a large part of the world's population takes access to electricity for granted nowadays.

Historically, growth in economic activity had tended to be coupled with increases in electricity use as populations grow and generate more goods and services. More

DOI: 10.4324/9781315144511-11

recently, this relationship has been decoupling in many countries. This trend can be explained by many factors. One of them is the shift of developed countries from manufacturing, which heavily relies upon electricity, toward service-based and advanced manufacturing economies, which require less electricity. The relationship of gross domestic product (GDP) and electricity growth rates (2011–2015) illustrates that the United States is a good example of this trend (U.S. Energy Information Administration [EIA] website).

Despite a weak link between growth in economic activities and electricity use, the American society heavily depends on electricity. In fact, steady electrical power supply is considered to be a matter of national security. The Generation, transmission, and distribution of electricity are parts of one network called the grid. Today, the U.S. infrastructure responsible for a steady supply of electrical power is outdated and requires an upgrade to accommodate society's daily needs.

Switching from the conventional grid to the smart grid is one of the main U.S. long-term strategies to ensure a steady electrical supply. Thus, making sure that the grid is reliable, resilient, and secure is a multidimensional task requiring federal, state, and local levels of action.

What Is an Energy or Power Grid?

An energy grid is a complex network of transmission and distribution lines, substations, transformers, and more designed for generating, transporting, and delivering electrical power to millions of end-use customers in the United States. Traditionally, electricity is generated at a station by converting nonrenewable sources of energy such as gas, oil, and nuclear. Among less common means driving electromechanical generators at plants are wind or flowing water. In brief, after being generated, electricity is moved by high-voltage transmission lines from power plants to power companies' distribution systems. Then, power is being distributed by lower voltage transmission lines to a final consumer.

In the United States, the electric power grid consists of over 200,000 miles of high-voltage transmission lines interspersed with hundreds of large electric power transformers (Parformak, 2014). Current America's power grid includes three interconnections or smaller grids: The Eastern, The Western, and The Texas one.

As the world's population keeps growing, so does the energy consumption. According to the U.S. EIA, total energy consumption by all end-use sectors (commercial, residential, transportation, and industrial) between 1950 and 2016 kept steadily increasing (U.S. EIA website). Therefore, a steady electricity supply through the network is crucial for the economic health of any nation and is dependent on numerous factors. Among them are grid's technical reliance and resilience, network's security, energy security, and adequacy of energy sources.

Legislation

The Department of Energy (DOE) is a primary government agency, which plays a critical role in developing national energy policies, including the one related to the smart grid (Department of Energy, n.d.). There are several organizations within DOE executing specific functions. For example, the U.S. EIA is a principal agency responsible for collecting, analyzing, and disseminating energy information.

Among recent laws directly impacting grid upgrade are Energy and Independence Security Act of 2007 and American Recovery and Reinvestment Act of 2009. Energy and Independence Security Act of 2007 reflected the official policy of the federal government to modernize the electricity grid and established a smart grid framework (Energy Interdependence and Security Act of 2007). In response to the Great Recession during the late 2000s and early 2010s, The American Recovery and Reinvestment Act of 2009 allocated an extensive funding for the Office of Electricity and Energy to modernize the nation's electrical grid and to fund a smart electricity grid (The American Recovery and Reinvestment Act of 2009).

A grid's proper functioning largely depends on upgrading its aging infrastructure. The American policy supporting the modernization of the nation's electricity transmission and distribution system is stated in the Title 42 of the United States Code. The policy aims to maintain a reliable and secure electricity infrastructure that can meet future demand growth and to achieve numerous goals, which together characterize a smart grid. Some of those goals are increased use of digital information and technology; dynamic optimization of grid operations and resources, with full cyber-security; and deployment of "smart" technologies (real-time, automated, interactive technologies that optimize the physical operation of appliances and consumer devices) for metering, communications concerning grid operations and status, etc. (42 U.S. Code § 17381, n.d.).

Grid Reliability and Smart Grids

Since its introduction by Thomas Edison in 1882, a commercial electric lighting and power industry has been trying to remain technically reliable and resilient. A highly reliable electrical network is the one with fewer and shorter interruptions in power supply. Although these reliability problems tend to occur on a local scale, they can lead to more widespread problems that affect larger areas (Flick et al., 2010).

Due to the size and scale of the U.S. grid, it would be virtually impossible to keep its' functioning completely uninterrupted. The current electrical infrastructure in the United States is not up to the task of powering America's future. The system is outdated, which leads to reoccurring blackouts and brownouts. While there are numerous ideas about modernizing conventional grids, the most prominent of them is a smart grid (Flick et al., 2010). One of its defining features is the ability to support more distributed power generation options by utilizing local renewable resources. Utilization of smart technologies would make the grid economic, more environmental friendly, and reliable as never before.

Briefly, in order to be smart, the grid must have the digital technology allowing mutual communication between suppliers and consumers as well as the sensing along the transmission lines. The exact day of smart grid's full implementation does not exist because shifting from the conventional system to the upgraded one is a permanent process of constantly perfecting technologies, installing new equipment, and testing systems.

Grid Resilience

A resilient grid is the one better prepared to recover from disruptions of different natures. Adverse events like severe weather conditions evoked the grid resilience study, particularly, because they are the leading cause of power outages in the United States and cost billions to the American economy annually (Economic Benefits of Increasing Electric Grid Resilience To Weather Outages, n.d.). The goal of the grid resilience increase is to minimize the loss of grid functionality caused by adverse events.

The assessment of grid resilience must include both potential impact and grid's capability. The determinants of the impact are the extreme weather events, grid exposure, and the grid vulnerability or fragility, whereas determinants of the grid's capability are physical durability of the grid, its operational versatility, and the grid rehabilitation capacity (Fauzan Hanif, 2017). Due to obvious reasons, such adverse events like severe weather are beyond humankind's control. However, the rest of them can be impacted by applying enhancement methods, which would result in an increased resilience of the grid.

Grid Security

With globalization on the rise, grid security became another key concern related to a steady energy supply. While the smart grid's major challenges would be related to protecting users' privacy, securing networks, and withstanding cyber threats, the conventional grid has its own weak spots. One of them is the difficulty to protect substations against coordinated acts of terror. There is widespread agreement among state and federal government officials, utilities, and manufacturers that high-voltage transformers in the United States are vulnerable to terrorist attack, and that such an attack potentially could have catastrophic consequences (Parformak, 2014). A targeted use of a conventional weapon could be fatal to the nation's power grid. Furthermore, an electromagnetic pulse, produced by a nuclear bomb explosion, can destroy, damage, or cause the malfunction of electronic systems by overloading their circuits. If successfully employed, the explosion could lead to a partial- or a full-grid destruction. On a positive note, a coordinated action is a high-difficulty task, which diminishes the chances of the attack's occurrence. Developing effective security regulations on federal, state, and local levels would improve the grid's physical and cyber perspectives as well as increase its reliability.

Energy Security and Adequacy of Energy Sources

Energy security can be defined as the ability to access energy sources at an affordable price. Today, primary sources of power for generating electricity are conventional (oil, natural gas, coal, and nuclear). To some extent, this makes domestic consumers sensitive to market prices of natural resources, particularly, when it comes to oil. First of all, America uses more oil than any country. And second, oil's price is defined by the common market. In 2016, for example, the energy production, 39% of which belongs to electric power, in the United States accounted for: natural gas – 33%, petroleum – 28%, coal – 17%, nuclear – 10%, and renewable – 12% (U.S. EIA website).

As non-conventional types of energy sources become available, such as solar, wind, biomass, and hydropower, new suggestions for advancing the smart grid appear. One of them is to integrate renewable and nonrenewable energy sources with the distributed power generation link (Islam et al., 2014). Diversification of energy sources is necessary for the future economic growth of any nation. This would increase the country's energy security as well as will secure a steady supply of distributed electricity. Therefore, being able to incorporate renewable sources of energy and plug them into the grid is important. Unfortunately, renewable resources have problems of their own, including localization and continuity. This results in the inability of the current electric grid to properly accommodate renewable energy sources (***Securing the smart grid***).

It is important to consider the concept of energy security when switching to the smart grid and pursuing the integration of renewable energy sources into the national grid. A slight change in costs for both utility companies and consumers might affect the usual consumption behavior of the end user.

Microgrids

As part of the future implementation of smart energy grid, it is important to demonstrate regional and micro energy grids with renewable energy as distributed generation (Hossam, 2016). Implementing localized microgrids is a way to enhance all factors positively impacting the national grid's healthy functioning: grid's technical reliance and resilience, network security, and energy security and adequacy of energy sources.

Microgrids are normally connected to the more traditional electric grid but can disconnect to operate autonomously. Microgrids use advanced smart grid technologies and the integration of distributed energy resources such as backup generators, solar panels, and storage. Because they can operate independently of the grid during outages, microgrids are typically used to provide reliable power during extreme weather events (Department of Energy, n.d.).

Conclusion

The U.S. power grid is a complex network generating, transmitting, and distributing electricity across the country to a final consumer. A steady energy supply through the network is crucial for the economic health of any nation and is dependent on numerous factors. Among them are grid's technical reliance and resilience, network's security, and energy security and adequacy of energy sources. Since the current American electrical system is outdated, the grid requires substantial improvement. Implementing the smart grid is one of the ways to satisfy the country's current and future needs.

Further Reading

Flick, T., Morehouse, J., & Veltsos, C. *Securing the Smart Grid: Next Generation Power Grid Security* (Burlington, MA: Syngress, 2010).
Duffield, J. *Fuels Paradise: Seeking Energy Security in Europe, Japan, and the United States* (Johns Hopkins University Press, 2015).
Anne-Marie, S. *The Chessboard and the Web: Strategies of Connection in a Networked World* (Yale University Press, 2017).

References

Flick, T, Morehouse, J, & Christophe Veltsos. *Securing the Smart Grid: Next Generation Power Grid Security* (Burlington, MA: Syngress, 2010).
Gabbar, H. *Smart Energy Grid Engineering* (Academic Press; 1st edition (November 7, 2016).
Jufri, F. H., Jun-Sung, K., & Jung, J. Analysis of determinants of the impact and the grid capability to evaluate and improve grid resilience from extreme weather events, *Energies*. 10, 11, (2017): 1779.
Department of Energy. www.energy.gov
Economic Benefits of Increasing Electric Grid Resilience To Weather Outages. https://energy.gov/downloads/economic-benefits-increasing-electric-grid-resilience-weather-outages
Energy Interdependence and Security Act of 2007. https://www.gpo.gov/fdsys/pkg/PLAW-110publ140/pdf/PLAW-110publ140.pdf
Islam, MA, Hasanuzzaman, M, Rahim, Nasrudin Abd, Nahar, A, & Hosenuzzaman, M. Global renewable energy-based electricity generation and smart grid system for energy security. *The Scientific World Journal*, 2014.
International Energy Agency (IEA). World Energy Investment Outlook: 2003 Insights, OECD/IEA, Paris, France, 2003. www.IEA.gov
Parformak, P. W. *Physical Security of the U.S. Power Grid: High-Voltage Transformer Substations, Congressional research Service*. June 17, 2014. https://fas.org/sgp/crs/homesec/R43604.pdf
The American Recovery and Reinvestment Act of 2009. https://www.gpo.gov/fdsys/pkg/BILLS-111hr1enr/pdf/BILLS-111hr1enxr.pdf
42 U.S. Code § 17381. n.d. http://uscode.house.gov/view.xhtml?path=/prelim@title42/chapter152&edition=prelim

Chapter 11

Federal Aviation Administration (FAA)

William R. Patterson
Independent Researcher, United States

Contents

Introduction 65
History 66
The Evolution of Aviation Security, 1961–2001 66
9/11 and Its Aftermath 67
UAVs 69
Conclusion 70
Further Reading 70
References 70

Introduction

The Federal Aviation Administration (FAA) is an agency within the United States Department of Transportation. It is responsible for regulating all U.S. civil aviation activities, including the management of air traffic in U.S. airspace. The organization's stated mission is "to provide the safest, most efficient aerospace system in the world" (FAA Website, 2018). The FAA is a key organization involved in homeland security due to the pervasive threat of hijackings, most devastatingly demonstrated during the attacks perpetrated by the international terrorist group Al-Qaeda against the World Trade Center in New York and the Pentagon in Washington, DC, on September 11, 2001. Although the management of airport and general aviation security now falls under the purview of the Transportation Security Administration (TSA), the FAA's responsibilities include reacting to scenarios involving hijacked aircraft, as well as the establishment of other regulations and guidelines crucial to homeland security,

DOI: 10.4324/9781315144511-12

such as the rules governing operation of unmanned aerial vehicles (UAVs). Additional responsibilities include issuing and enforcing various regulations pertaining to aircraft, airports, independent air carriers, pilots, training requirements, and commercial space launches.

History

The history of commercial air regulation began with the Aeronautics Branch of the Department of Commerce, formed as a result of the Air Commerce Act of 1926 signed by President Calvin Coolidge. The new Aeronautics Branch was tasked with facilitating safe and efficient air commerce through licensing pilots, establishing air traffic rules, certifying aircraft, and assisting with air navigation and air traffic control. In 1934, the Aeronautics Branch was renamed the Bureau of Air Commerce. This was replaced in 1938 by the Civil Aeronautics Authority (CAA) which itself split into two separate organizations in 1940: the Civil Aeronautics Administration, under the Department of Commerce and the Civil Aeronautics Board, which was independent. The Federal Aviation Agency, the direct forerunner of the FAA, and the Civil Aeronautics Board, were established as independent entities in 1958 following passage of the Federal Aviation Act. The FAA reached its current form, as the Federal Aviation Administration (rather than agency) under the Department of Transportation in 1966 with the passage of the Department of Transportation Act signed by President Lyndon B. Johnson.

The Evolution of Aviation Security, 1961–2001

In 1961, the first hijackings of aircraft in the United States caught the FAA largely by surprise. Prior to being directly faced with it, the substantial risk of violent attacks against civil aviation had gone unrecognized and security measures were few to non-existent. The first plane to be hijacked occurred in May 1961 when a passenger flight bound for Key West, Florida, was instead forced to fly to Cuba after a passenger took control of the aircraft. This event was followed in short order by other hijacking incidents.

The immediate response was to employ armed border patrolmen from the U.S. Immigration and Naturalization Service on civilian flights. These were later replaced, in 1962, with FAA safety inspectors who were made special U.S. deputy marshals and served as armed guards aboard flights when specifically requested to do so by airlines or by the Federal Bureau of Investigation (FBI). An additional step was the passage of an amendment to the Federal Aviation Act of 1958, making the hijacking of aircraft a federal crime. This amendment also made it illegal to interfere with a flight crew or to carry a weapon aboard a passenger aircraft (Krauss 2008, pp. 15–16).

Additional hijackings in 1969 led to the development of a profiling system to identify potential hijackers before allowing them to board an aircraft. The system was based on demonstrated behavioral characteristics of previous attackers. The FAA also developed a magnetometer to detect weapons during screening before boarding which became universally mandatory by 1972 (Krauss 2008, p. 19). According to William Waugh, Jr., "In the early 1960s, airports and aircraft were 'soft targets.' Security measures put into place to prevent hijackings and armed attacks may well have reduced the number of incidents." Waugh also points to other factors, such as international conventions and agreements, as playing an important role in reducing the number of hijacking incidents (Waugh, p. 308).

In 1973, air carriers were mandated to conduct inspections of all carry-on luggage and subject all passengers to metal detectors, or a physical pat down if detectors were not available, prior to boarding. The area in which passengers were prohibited from carrying weapons was expanded from the aircraft itself to all areas beyond the designated checkpoint in 1979. This was enacted to protect terminals as well as aircraft. Despite these additional measures, hijackings continued to occur throughout the 1980s as Middle East-based terrorism was on the rise.

Bombings replaced hijackings as the greatest perceived threat to aviation with the downing of Pan American World Airways Flight 103 over Lockerbie, Scotland, in December 1988. The destruction of Flight 103 resulted in the deaths of all 259 persons aboard and 11 people on the ground. In reaction, the FAA imposed rules on U.S. carriers in Europe and the Middle East, requiring the searching or X-raying of all checked baggage, random checks of both passengers and baggage, and the matching of passengers and baggage to prevent unattended baggage from making its way on to aircraft (Krauss 2008, p. 77). The FAA also began funding explosive detection devices in high-volume airports, starting with Kennedy airport in New York.

The FAA continued its focus on flights originating from abroad by posting civil aviation security liaison officers overseas and starting, in 1991, to require foreign carriers entering or leaving U.S. airports to provide a similar level of security as that provided in U.S. airports. Though screening was an important element of airline security, it was focused primarily on baggage and preventing the placement of bombs on aircraft. The FAA's approach to security was primarily reactive, updating its methods in the wake of various attacks. The focus would change again in the aftermath of the attacks on New York and Washington, DC, on September 11, 2001. As Waugh pointed out, "The bombing of PanAm Flight 103 in 1988 focused attention on the need for baggage screening, and the hijackings that culminated in the attacks on the World Trade Center and Pentagon focused attention on the need for greater passenger screening" (Waugh, p. 308).

9/11 and Its Aftermath

In the late 1990s, in response to increased incidents of bombings, the FAA initiated a program known as CAPPS, the Computer-Assisted Passenger Prescreening System, designed to identify passengers with a high-risk profile who should undergo further security measures. This system successfully highlighted a number of the individuals who would hijack the aircraft used in the attacks of September 11, 2001, as they were boarding their planes. Unfortunately, their identification by the system resulted only in either their bags being checked for explosives or being held off of their planes until the owners were confirmed to be aboard. This was to prevent terrorists from checking bags containing bombs and then not boarding the target aircraft. In this case, the focus on bombings failed to protect aircraft from terrorists with other plans in mind.

The FAA played an intimate part in the tragedy that unfolded with the hijackings of American 11, American 77, United 175, and United 93 on 9/11. FAA air traffic controllers heard some of the attacks happen in real time, and FAA managers and leaders made crucial decisions as events were unfolding. As the true magnitude of the catastrophe became clear, FAA employees at all levels worked, though not always successfully, to prevent more attacks, notify proper authorities, and clear other aircraft from the skies.

The FAA became aware that there was a problem aboard American 11 at 8:25 AM when one of the terrorists aboard the aircraft relayed a message to the passengers through the overhead system, which was also heard by air traffic controllers. At 8:47, controllers began to worry about United 175 when it changed beacon codes twice, deviated from its predetermined course, and failed to respond to communications. The report composed by the 9/11 Commission noted that "United 175 was hijacked between 8:42 and 8:46, and awareness of that hijacking began to spread after 8:51. American 77 was hijacked between 8:51 and 8:54. By 9:00, FAA and airline officials began to comprehend that attackers were going after multiple aircraft" (Kean and Hamilton, 2004, p. 10). Flight 11 barreled into the North Tower of the World Trade Center at 8:46. Flight 175 struck the South Tower of the World Trade Center at 9:03. Flight 77 crashed into the Pentagon in Washington, DC, at 9:37. And at 10:02, after the passengers rebelled against the flight's hijackers, United 93 crashed nose-first into an empty field in Shanksville, PA.

The 9/11 Commission Report faulted the FAA for failure to quickly relay critical information regarding the hijackings to airlines and to provide sufficiently timely information to the North American Aerospace Defense Command (NORAD). NORAD is tasked with protecting the airspace of North America from any threat, internal or external. Prior to 9/11, there was a protocol in place for FAA to notify NORAD in the event of a hijacking, but it proved to be inadequate in the face of the events that transpired on that day.

The first notification the FAA made to NORAD about any of the hijackings occurred at 8:37 after air traffic controllers realized, a little over 10 minutes earlier, that American 11 had been hijacked. Boston Center disregarded the normal chain-of-command and notified NORAD's Northeast Air Defense Sector (NEADS) directly that American 11 had been hijacked. According to the 9/11 Report, "this was the first notification received by the military—at any level—that American 11 had been hijacked" (Kean and Hamilton, 2004, p. 20). Flight 11 struck the North Tower less than 10 minutes later. The FAA notified NEADS of the hijacking of United 175 at 9:03, at nearly the same time that it crashed into the South Tower. The FAA failed to intentionally notify NORAD of the fact that American 77 was missing, but relayed the information to NEADS by chance at 9:34. FAA notified NEADS at 9:36 that an unidentified aircraft was approaching Washington, DC. American 77 crashed into the Pentagon only 3 minutes later. The FAA never notified the military of the hijacking of Flight 93 (Kean and Hamilton, 2004, p. 28).

The FAA did notify the White House when FAA officials detected Flight 77 approaching Washington, DC. Although the president was not in residence, the Secret Service ushered Vice President Dick Cheney from his office at 9:32 and took him to the underground bunker beneath the White House. Transportation Secretary Norman Mineta soon joined him, at which time he patched into a communications line with the FAA Operations Center for immediate updates (Freni, 2003, pp. 33–34).

One major, and unprecedented, action taken by the FAA on 9/11 was a complete grounding of all aircraft in U.S. airspace. At 9:42, FAA leadership gave the order to air traffic controllers to instruct all aircraft to land at the nearest airport. Never in the history of American aviation had such an order been issued. The 9/11 Commission notes that "The air traffic control system handled it with great skill, as about 4,500 commercial and general aviation aircraft soon landed without incident" (Kean and Hamilton, 2004, p. 29). On September 12, at the order of Secretary Mineta, grounded commercial flights were allowed to fly to their initially intended destinations, but only with the original passengers and after thorough security scrutiny. Secretary Mineta announced the resumption of normal commercial traffic the following day, September 13, though it would take considerable time to get flights back on their normal patterns and routines.

In the aftermath of 9/11, the FAA took several immediate regulatory security steps. First, it required that 6,000 passenger planes have hardened cockpit doors by April 09, 2003. Foreign air carriers arriving or departing from the United States were also required to have hardened cockpit doors. These doors are required to be locked and access to the cockpit tightly controlled. One cost–benefit analysis comparing the level of expected risk reduction with anticipated cost found that hardened cockpits provide higher risk reduction at a lower cost than does the presence of Federal Air Marshal Service officers aboard flights (Stewart and Mueller, 2008). Additionally, the FAA discontinued curbside check-in and off-airport check-in. Only ticketed passengers were to be permitted past airport screeners, and vehicles parked outside of terminals were to be more strictly monitored. The air marshal program was expanded and certain flight paths, particularly around the Washington, DC, area, were put off-limits.

Within 2 months of the 9/11 attacks, the U.S. Congress had passed, and President George W. Bush signed the Aviation and Transportation Security Act which transferred much of the FAA's security responsibilities to the newly formed TSA. With this legislation, the FAA continued to be responsible for controlling air traffic, regulating aircraft manufacturing, operation, and maintenance, and for certifying airports and pilots. For the first time in American history, a federal workforce, the TSA, was made responsible for screening passengers and baggage at airports and for overall air cargo and airport security. The FAA remained responsible for aviation security until February 13, 2002, by which time the TSA had been set up and was able to assume its functions.

UAVs

UAVs are a crucial consideration for homeland security as they offer both opportunity and danger. UAVs offer opportunity as they can potentially be used in defensive homeland security operations, such as border monitoring and terrorist surveillance. They present a danger, however, in that they could be used in various methods of attack against civilian and military targets. The FAA is faced with striking an appropriate regulating balance of permitting UAVs to serve positive purposes for homeland security and military operations, as well as civilian commercial and personal applications, while also protecting the public from their possible abuse as weapons. The FAA continues to work with various commercial and government entities, including the military, to establish effective and appropriate regulations regarding these aircraft.

Conclusion

The FAA remains dedicated to its mission of facilitating the safest and most efficient air travel in the world. Although its role in airport security has largely been ceded to the TSA, it remains the sole government entity responsible for general aviation safety, for air traffic control, and for a variety of regulatory duties. Looking to the future, the FAA has instituted the Next Generation Air Transportation (NextGen) System which, according to an FAA document, will strive to "enhance economic growth and create jobs, expand system flexibility and deliver greater capacity, tailor services to customer needs, integrate capabilities to ensure national defense, promote aviation safety and environmental stewardship, and retain U.S. leadership and economic competitiveness in global aviation" (Krauss 2008, p. 159). The FAA is also stepping into the fairly new realms of UAVs and commercial space craft, both of which it must regulate for safety and security without smothering their potential commercial and operational applications. The FAA remains a crucial organization to America's commercial well-being, aviation safety, and homeland security.

Further Reading

Elias, B. (2010). *Airport and Aviation Security: U. S. Policy and Strategy in the Age of Global Terrorism*, Boca Raton: CRC Press.

Geilen, D. & Morrison, W. G. (2015). "Aviation Security: Costing, Pricing, Finance and Performance," *Journal of Air Transport Management*, *48*: 1–12.

Israelsen, R. G. (2013). "Applying the Fourth Amendment's National Security Exception to Airport Security and the TSA," *Journal of Air Law and Commerce*, *78*(3): 501–539.

References

Federal Aviation Administration Webpage, "About," https://www.faa.gov/about/mission, Accessed 14 July 2018.

Freni, P. S., *Ground Stop: An Inside Look at the Federal Aviation Administration on September 11, 2001*, New York: iUniverse, 2003.

Kean, T. H., and Hamilton, L, National Commission on Terrorist Attacks upon the United States, *the 9/11 Commission Report: Final Report of the National Commission on Terrorist Attacks upon the United States*, Washington, DC: National Commission on Terrorist Attacks upon the United States, 2004.

Krauss, T, *The Federal Aviation Administration: A Historical Perspective, 1903–2008*, Washington, DC: U. S. Department of Transportation, Federal Aviation Administration, 2008.

Stewart, M. G. and Mueller, J. "A Risk and Cost-Benefit Assessment of United States Aviation Security Measures," *Journal of Transportation Security*, 1, 3, 2008, 143–159.

Waugh, W. L., Jr., "Securing Mass Transit: A Challenge for Homeland Security," *Review of Policy Research*, 21, 3, 2004, 307–316.

Chapter 12

Federal Bureau of Investigation

Darren E. Tromblay
George Washington University, Washington, DC, United States

Contents

Introduction 71
Further Reading 76
References 76

Introduction

The Federal Bureau of Investigation (FBI) is the United States' primary intelligence service within the domestic setting. It has evolved via aggregation rather than architecture. In addition to its intelligence (including investigative) missions, the bureau conducts a wide variety of services for federal, state, and local intelligence and law enforcement partners. The FBI has not evolved in a vacuum, and the growth of a more complex ecosystem of players in the domestic security space raises new questions about how to ensure that the FBI remains effectively and efficiently integrated into this larger enterprise.

Currently, the FBI is postured to address threat actors in three general categories, which are represented at the FBI headquarters (FBIHQ) by its Counterterrorism Division (CTD), Counterintelligence Division (CD), and Criminal Investigative Division (CID). In addition, the Bureau's Directorate of Intelligence (DI), Weapons of Mass Destruction Directorate (WMDD), and Cyber Division (CyD) contain expertise applicable to its CTD, CD, and CID missions. All of these functions are similar in their reactive nature – a legacy of the FBI's law enforcement origins.

The bureau has no definitive, legislative charter. It owes its existence to 1871 legislation which authorizes the Department of Justice to use investigators for the

DOI: 10.4324/9781315144511-13

"detection and prosecution of crimes against the United States" (US Senate. 1975). Attempts to develop a charter for the FBI began belatedly, more than a century later, but did not come to fruition (US Senate. FBI Charter Act. 1979b). The bureau's activities fall under the purview of the Department of Justice (DoJ) and, hence, the Attorney General (AG). However, although multiple AGs provided direction to the FBI, the first formal set of AG guidelines date only to 1976 (US Department of Justice. The Federal Bureau of Investigation's Compliance with the Attorney General's Investigative Guidelines. 2005a; US Senate. Impact of Attorney General's Guidelines for Domestic Security Investigations. 1983a; Department of Justice. 2008). The FBI has, in turn, interpreted the AG guidelines and produced its Domestic Investigations and Operations Guide.

In its first decades, the bureau (originally called simply the "Bureau of Investigation") – initially using special agents (SAs) with backgrounds in the US Secret Service – focused on antirust and political corruption. Although these issues do not conjure up the national security concerns associated with foreign state and non-state threats, they nonetheless imperil the nation's well-being by undercutting the integrity of the government. The FBI (renamed in 1935) became firmly responsible for combating foreign state and non-state actors in 1939, at the direction of President Franklin D. Roosevelt (FDR).

The FBI pre-dates the formation of the modern US intelligence community (IC) and has been a member of the IC since the community's outset. In 1939, FDR created the Interdepartmental Intelligence Conference (IIC) – arguably a prototype IC – for which then-FBI Director J. Edgar Hoover served as chairman *ex officio*. With the passage of the National Security Act of 1947, the FBI became a member of the new IC, with formal responsibility for domestic security.

In addition to the missions described above, the FBI was a pioneer in the field of information sharing with federal, state, and local intelligence and law enforcement partners. The bureau established its famous fingerprint Identification Division in 1924; in 1967, the FBI launched the National Crime Information Center (NCIC); and the bureau consolidated these two entities under the Criminal Justice Information Services (CJIS) Division (the FBI's largest division) in 1992 (US House of Representatives. 1992). Additionally, the FBI has provided guidance to US law enforcement, through a number of initiatives, including the National Academy program – a multiple week course of study, at the FBI Academy, for law enforcement officers – which began in 1934. The FBI also has a distinct leadership role within the IC as the agency responsible for the Director of National Intelligence's National Representative Program (Intelligence and National Security Alliance. 2016). In this capacity, the heads of FBI offices oversee 12 geographic regions, where the FBI executives work with IC partners, operating within the 12 respective domestic regions to develop a coordinated intelligence enterprise (US Senate. 2015).

Organizationally, the FBI is divided between headquarters (HQ) and field offices (FOs). HQ coordinates the bureau's operational activities (e.g. intelligence collection) via the aforementioned divisions. Intelligence analysis at HQ is the responsibility of the DI – part of the Intelligence Branch (IB) which was created in 2014 (Previously, the DI was part of the National Security Branch [NSB], which also included CTD, CD, and WMDD.). The IB is the element within the FBI that serves as the bureau's representative to the IC. Overlap between HQ programs is facilitated by entities such as the Counterproliferation Center – which brings together CD and WMDD components – as well as fusion cells that integrate analysts into operational components (Federal Bureau of Investigation. 2016). The FBI has historically been a "field-oriented organization" (US Senate. Appropriations for Fiscal Year 1980, 1979a). However, following 9/11, then-Director Robert Mueller III centralized the direction of counterterrorism and counterintelligence cases at HQ (US Senate. 2002; US House of Representatives. 2003). In retrospect, this was an ill-considered approach, given that a number of the bureau's share of pre-9/11 gaffes had occurred not at the field – which presciently produced the "Phoenix memo" warning – but at the HQ. For instance, one well-documented incident involved an analyst failing to facilitate the sharing of crucial information (US Department of Justice. 2004; Wright. 2006).

FOs are structured to align with the FBI's functional missions. Squads are specifically responsible for investigating activities (e.g. espionage, organized crime, etc.) (GAO. 1976). In 2003, as the FBI attempted to better-institutionalize its, in reality, longstanding, intelligence mission, it created Field Intelligence Groups (FIGs) in each of its 56 FOs. These were stand-alone entities comprised largely of intelligence analysts, linguists, and surveillance specialists. Additionally, the FBI assigned SAs to the FIGs, as part of human intelligence (HUMINT) squads. Unlike traditional squads, FIG SAs were not investigators but, instead, were supposed to develop sources capable of reporting against intelligence requirements (US House of Representatives. 2010; Cumming & Masse. 2005). A revamp of FOs' intelligence structure, less than a decade later, rearranged resources by establishing a Central Strategic Coordinating Component – which consisted of domain management, collection management, and reports – in addition to tactically oriented intelligence analysts (9/11 Review Commission. 2015; US Senate. 2012).

Beyond its FOs – and FO satellite offices known as resident agencies (RAs) – the FBI also has more than 50 foreign liaison offices, known as Legal Attaches (Legats). The origin of the Legats was actually in World War II, and when they were established, they were the coordinators, located within US embassies, for clandestine intelligence collection conducted abroad by the FBI's Special Intelligence Service (SIS), which was ultimately incorporated into the CIA. However, the bureau continued to maintain an overt presence to work with foreign law enforcement and intelligence counterparts.

The bureau has extensive experience in a number of intelligence collection disciplines. It is, at its heart, a HUMINT agency focused on identifying and recruiting informants – now called confidential human sources (CHSs) – and conducting interviews of witnesses. In fact, its aptitude for interviewing made it the natural home for the interagency High Value Detainee Interrogation Group (HIG), which the administration of President Barack Obama established in 2009 (Watkins. 2017). The FBI also has a long history in the field of electronic surveillance (e.g. wiretaps, microphones), which falls under the discipline of signals intelligence (SIGINT) and is authorized, in law, via the Omnibus Crime Control and Safe Streets Act of 1968 and the Foreign Intelligence Surveillance Act of 1978. Through its aviation program, which dates to the 1970s, the bureau also collects imagery intelligence (IMINT) (US Senate. 1977). Finally, the FBI – although it does not often phrase the issue as such – is well established in measures and signatures intelligence (MASINT), which describes much of the FBI's forensic work. The specialized discipline is consistent with Hoover's emphasis on a scientific approach to law enforcement, which has continued to be an FBI strength. A scientific orientation is particularly apparent in the Laboratory Division, which dates to 1932; the psychological research of National Center for the Analysis of Violent Crime; and in the collection activities of the bureau's evidence response teams (US Senate. 1971).

Where the FBI has been less successful is in the field of analysis. Prior to 9/11, the concept of intelligence analysis equated – according to the FBI's descriptions – to data entry and manipulation (US Senate. Appropriations for 1980. 1979a). The limited aptitude required for this work meant that multiple positions were filled by individuals who lacked college educations (US Department of Justice. 2004). To the FBI's credit, it attempted to improve standards in 1996 and 1999, but these efforts proved to be too little too late, considering the descriptions that both the Congressional Joint Inquiry into the 9/11 attacks and the 9/11 Commission provided (US Department of Justice. 2004; Cumming. 2004; 9/11 Commission. n.d.). Following 9/11, the bureau made a concerted push to hire well-qualified personnel. However, as these new hires encountered the inadequate pre-9/11 analytic culture, an unfortunate paradigm emerged. According to the DoJ's Office of the Inspector General (IG), newer analysts, particularly those with graduate degrees, were the most likely to leave the FBI within two years of being hired (Cumming. 2005). Furthermore, potentially attesting to the low standards that the pre-9/11 analysts had established for "analytic" work, was the IG's finding that "the higher the level of education an intelligence analyst reported, the more likely that analyst was dissatisfied with his or her work assignments" (US Department of Justice. The Federal Bureau of Investigation's Efforts to Hire, Train, and Retain Intelligence Analysts. 2005a).

Because the FBI was, throughout much of the 20th century, the default agency for security-related responsibilities not explicitly assigned to other government components, it accumulated elements of what would now be called a "first-responder" mission. For instance, in 1940, the bureau established a Disaster Squad, which was responsible for deploying to mass fatality incidents (US Senate. 1961). In 1983, the FBI formed its Hostage Rescue Team (HRT) (US Senate. FBI Oversight and Authorization. 1983b). During the 1990s, the FBI became responsible for the National Domestic Preparedness Office (NDPO) and the National Infrastructure Protection Center (NIPC) (US Senate. Domestic Preparedness in the Next Millennium. 1999a; US Senate. Office of Justice Programs Oversight; Examining the OJP Reorganization Plan. 1999b; US House of Representatives. 1998). Both the NDPO and the NIPC were transferred to the Department of Homeland Security (DHS) at the time of that department's creation.

Due to the nature of its evolution, the bureau has found itself in an awkward position as of the early 21st century. By default, the FBI has found itself cast as the United States' primary domestic intelligence service (Rosenbach & Peritz. 2009; US House of Representatives. 2005). According to the AG's guidelines, its duties include not only reactive functions but also the collection of information with foreign intelligence value (Tromblay. 2015). The potential for collection of positive foreign intelligence is present within the United States, and the bureau has been successful in, from time to time, exploiting these opportunities. One need only look at the SOLO operation, which provided significant intelligence about the Sino–Soviet split, for an example of this (Barron. 1996). Despite the recognition that these opportunities exist, the FBI has never found a way to systematize the collection of such information. Instead, post-9/11 reforms which committed the bureau to a more intelligence-centric approach have given way to the culture of responsive investigations only after a threat actor has become evident. Nowhere is this clearer than in the FBI's Threat Review and Prioritization (TRP) process. TRP has actually discouraged pursuing opportunities to develop foreign intelligence – despite the fact that such information can provide US policymakers with an informational advantage (Tromblay. 2015).

Additionally, the FBI has never found a way to develop a cohesive corporate culture. Mueller, who fought to keep policymakers from splitting the FBI following 9/11, nevertheless conceptually split it, describing it as having a bifurcated mission of "intelligence" and "law enforcement" (US House of Representatives. 2004). To be fair, the problem long predated Mueller, as indicated by the discussions of the FBI charter, which would have actually created two charters – one for counterintelligence and one for the bureau's other missions – and thereby given a single organization a split identity (US Senate. 1980). Mueller, at a time when real discussion of how to reform intelligence in the domestic setting was taking place, chose to plead for keeping the FBI intact and to gild the FBI's reactive culture with intelligence terminology (US House of Representatives. 2003). Mueller is a man of integrity but his post-9/11 fight to keep the FBI unified discouraged discussion of the hard truth that perhaps the bureau was spread too thin and that its very diverse – and sometimes competing – missions should not exist under the same roof.

The domestically oriented US intelligence architecture has changed fundamentally since the formation of the FBI. Multiple bureau missions now overlap with DHS, as well as with other agencies, including the Drug Enforcement Administration (DEA) and the Bureau of Alcohol, Tobacco, Firearms, and Explosives (ATF). If there is not an American political will to create yet another new agency, then serious thought should be afforded to where missions fit best among existing agencies. For instance, it would make sense for DHS – which has the bailiwick for coordinating with the network of state and local fusion centers – to assume responsibility for the FBI's CJIS, which would complement the fusion center network's information-sharing mission. Similarly, HRT is not bureau-specific in its mission – the subjects of multiple investigative agencies are capable of taking hostages – and consequently, along with other FBI first-responder functions, it should be moved to DHS.

Throughout the 20th century, the FBI, by default, not only carried out law enforcement and intelligence functions but also pioneered a variety of national security-related missions. However, it is anchored to a culture of reactivity, despite expectations that it will not only respond to threats but also collect information of foreign intelligence value. Despite Mueller's protestations, there is no reason to keep all of the FBI's current functions within one agency. Other entities, notably DHS, have emerged and provide natural fits for a variety of functions. Movement of components such as CJIS and HRT – as examples – would help the bureau become a more cohesive organization, capable of greater efficiency and effectiveness in the mission sets with which it is entrusted.

Further Reading

Kessler, R. (2016). *The Bureau: The Secret History of the FBI.* New York: St. Martin's Press.
Weiner, T. (2012). *Enemies: A History of the FBI.* New York: Random House.
Zegart, A. B. (2007). *Spying Blind: The CIA, the FBI, and the Origins of 9/11.* Princeton: Princeton University Press.

References

9/11 Commission. (n.d.). *Law Enforcement, Counterterrorism, and Intelligence Collection in the United States Prior to 9/11. Staff Statement No. 9, 9/11 Commission.* http://govinfo.library.unt.edu/911/staff_statements/staff_statement_9.pdf
9/11 Review Commission. (2015). *The FBI: Protecting the Homeland in the 21st Century.*
Barron J. (1996). *Operation SOLO.* Washington, DC: Regnery.
Cumming. A. (2004). *FBI Intelligence Reform Since September 11, 2001: Issues and Options for Congress.* Washington, DC: Congressional Research Service.
Cumming A. (2005). *Intelligence Reform Implementation at the Federal Bureau of Investigation: Issues and Options for Congress.* Washington, DC: Congressional Research Service.
Cumming A. & Masse T. (2005). *Intelligence Reform Implementation at the Federal Bureau of Investigation: Issues and Options for Congress.* Washington, DC. Congressional Research Service.
Federal Bureau of Investigation (2016). *FY2017 Authorization and Budget Request to Congress.* Washington, DC: Federal Bureau of Investigation.
General Accounting Office. (1976). *FBI Domestic Intelligence Operations - Their Purpose and Scope: Issues that Need to Be Resolved.* Washington, DC: General Accounting Office.
Intelligence and National Security Alliance. (2016). *Protecting the Homeland: Intelligence Integration 15 Years after 9/11.* Arlington, VA: Intelligence and National Security Alliance.
Rosenbach E. & Peritz A. J. (2009). *Domestic Intelligence. Belfer Center for Science and International Affairs.* Cambridge, MA: Harvard Kennedy School.
Tromblay D. E. (2015). The Threat Review and Prioritization Trap: How the F.B.I.'s New Threat Review and Prioritization process compounds the Bureau's oldest problems. *Intelligence and National Security.* http://dx.doi.org/10.1080/02684527.2015.1105496
US Department of Justice (2004). *A Review of the FBI's Handling of Intelligence Information Related to the September 11 Attacks.* Washington, DC: US Department of Justice.
US Department of Justice. (2005a). *The Federal Bureau of Investigation's Compliance with the Attorney General's Investigative Guidelines.* Washington, DC: US Department of Justice.
US Department of Justice. (2005b). *The Federal Bureau of Investigation's Efforts to Hire, Train, and Retain Intelligence Analysts.* Washington, DC: US Department of Justice.
US Department of Justice. (2008). *The Attorney General's Guidelines for Domestic FBI Operations.* Washington, DC: US Department of Justice.
US House of Representatives. (1992). *FBI Oversight and Authorization, Fiscal Year, 1993. Before the Subcommittee on Civil and Constitutional Rights of the Committee on the Judiciary, House of Representatives. 102nd Congress.* Washington, DC: US House of Representatives.
US House of Representatives. (1998). *Departments of Commerce, Justice, and State, the Judiciary, and Related Agencies Appropriations for 1999, Before a Subcommittee of the Committee on Appropriations, House of Representatives, 105th Congress Pt. 6.* Washington, DC: US House of Representatives.
US House of Representatives. (2003). *Departments of Commerce, Justice, and State, the Judiciary, and Related Agencies appropriations for 2004, Before a Subcommittee*

of the Committee on Appropriations, House of Representatives, 108th Congress Pt 10. Washington, DC: US House of Representatives.

US House of Representatives. (2004). *Departments of Commerce, Justice, and State, the Judiciary, and Related Agencies Appropriations for 2005, Before a Committee of the Committee on Appropriations, House of Representatives. 108th Congress Pt 10.* Washington, DC: US House of Representatives.

US House of Representatives. (2005). *Science, the Departments of State, Justice, and Commerce, and Related Agencies Appropriations for 2006, Before a Subcommittee of the Committee on Appropriations, House of Representatives. 109th Congress Pt. 2.* Washington, DC: US House of Representatives.

US House of Representatives. (2010). *Commerce, Justice, Science, and Related Agencies Appropriations for 2011, Before a Subcommittee of the Committee on Appropriations, House of Representatives, 111th Congress Pt 1A.* Washington, DC: US House of Representatives.

US Senate. (1961). *Departments of State, Justice, the Judiciary, and Related Agencies Appropriations, 1962, Before the Subcommittee of the Committee on Appropriations, United States Senate. 87th Congress* Washington, DC: US Senate.

US Senate. (1971). *Departments of State, Justice, and Commerce, the Judiciary, and Related Agencies Appropriations for Fiscal Year 1972, Before a Subcommittee of the Committee on Appropriations. United States Senate.* Washington, DC: US Senate.

US Senate. (1975). *Intelligence Activities. Senate Resolution 21. Before the Select Committee to Study Governmental Operations with Respect to Intelligence Activities, United States Senate. 94th Congress.* Vol. 6. Washington, DC: US Senate.

US Senate. (1977). *Departments of State, Justice, and Commerce, the Judiciary, and Related Agencies Appropriations for Fiscal Year 1978, Before a Subcommittee of the Committee on Appropriations, United States Senate. 95th Congress Pt 6.* Washington, DC: US Senate.

US Senate. (1979a). *Departments of State, Justice, and Commerce, the Judiciary, and Related Agencies Appropriations for Fiscal Year 1980, Before a Subcommittee of the Committee on Appropriations, United States Senate, 96th Congress.* Washington, DC: US Senate.

US Senate. (1979b). *FBI Charter Act of 1979, S. 1612, Hearings before the Committee on the Judiciary, United States Senate, 96th Congress Pt. 1.* Washington, DC: US Senate.

US Senate. (1980). *FBI Charter Act of 1979, S 1612, Hearings before the Committee on the Judiciary, United States Senate, 96th Congress Pt. 2.* Washington, DC: US Senate.

US Senate. (1983a). *Impact of Attorney General's Guidelines for Domestic Security Investigations (The Levi Guidelines). Report of the Chairman of the Subcommittee on Security and Terrorism. Committee on the Judiciary, United States Senate. 98th Congress. S. Doc.* 98–134. Washington, DC: US Senate.

US Senate. (1983b). *FBI Oversight and Authorization, Before the Subcommittee on Security and Terrorism of the Committee on the Judiciary, United States Senate. 98th Congress.* Washington, DC: US Senate.

US Senate. (1999a). *Domestic Preparedness in the Next Millennium. Before the Subcommittee on Youth Violence and the Subcommittee on Technology, Terrorism, and Government Information of the Committee on the Judiciary, United States Senate. 106th Congress. S. Doc.* 106–424. Washington, DC: US Senate.

US Senate. (1999b). *Office of Justice Programs Oversight; Examining the OJP Reorganization Plan, Before the Subcommittee on Youth Violence of the Committee on the Judiciary, United States Senate. 106th Congress.* Washington, DC: US Senate.

US Senate. (2002). *Reforming the FBI in the 21st Century. Before the Committee on the Judiciary. United States Senate. 107th Congress. S. Doc. 107–971.* Washington, DC: US Senate.

US Senate. (2012). *Ten Years after 9/11 - 2011, Before the Committee on Homeland Security and Governmental Affairs, United States Senate. 112th Congress.* Washington, DC: US Senate.

US Senate. (2015). *Commerce, Justice, Science, and Related Agencies Appropriations for Fiscal Year 2015, Before a Subcommittee of the Committee on Appropriations, United States Senate. 113th Congress.* Washington, DC: US Senate.

US Senate & US House of Representatives. (2002). *Joint Inquiry into Intelligence Community Activities before and after the Terrorist Attacks of September 11, 2001, Before the Select Committee on Intelligence. U.S. Senate. And the Permanent Select Committee on Intelligence, House of Representatives. S Doc. 107–1086.* Vol II. Washington, DC: US Senate and US House of Representatives.

Watkins, A. (2017, December 5). *Elite Terrorist Interrogation Team Withers Under Trump.* Politico.

Wright, L. (2006, July 10). *The Agent.* New Yorker.

Chapter 13

Immigration and Customs Enforcement (ICE)

Lora Hadzhidimova
Old Dominion University, Norfolk, VA, United States

Contents

Introduction: General Structure and Budget 79
Functions of the Units 80
Challenges and Concerns 82
Conclusion 83
Further Reading 84
References 84

Introduction: General Structure and Budget

The Immigration and Customs Enforcement (ICE) agency is a government agency that was established in 2003 as part of the U.S. Department of Homeland Security. It united two previous agencies – the U.S. Customs Service (USCS) and the Immigration and Naturalization Service (INS). The budget of ICE approximates $6 billion per year, divided between its five branches – Homeland Security Investigations (HSI), Enforcement and Removal Operations (ERO), Office of the Principal Legal Advisor (OPLA), the Management and Administration unit, and the Office of Professional Responsibility. The proposed budget for 2018 includes improvements in fields such as border security, technology, equipment, assets, and personnel. Some funds are also designated for the signed in January 2017 Executive Order *Border Security and Immigration Enforcement Improvements* (EO 13767) and Executive Order EO 13780 – *Protecting the Nation from Foreign Terrorist Entry into the United States* (Department of Homeland Security, 2017).

DOI: 10.4324/9781315144511-14

Functions of the Units

ICE's main functions are related to enforcement of border, immigration, trade, and security-related laws intended to ensure and maintain public safety and order. The responsibilities of the ERO unit include determining non-U.S. residents who are subject to removal, and detaining and deporting them, as needed. It is divided into six operational units – *Field Operations* that manage and supervise the work of 24 field offices; *Enforcement*, responsible for the actions undertaken by authorities for detention of illegally residing in the U.S. aliens; *Custody Management* handling the procedures during the detention; *Removal*, responsible for the physical acts of deportation and the proper coordination with foreign governments; *ICE Health Service Corps* that supervise the health needs of the detainees; and *Operation Support* that plays the role of the administrative apparatus of ERO, assuring proper financial, budgetary, human resources, and organizational functioning of the entire unit.

ERO also supports a directory that tracks the location of detainees that have already been assigned an "Alien Registration Number." Individuals under the age of 18 are not registered through the system as well as persons who have been already deported. Visits to the detention facilities, located in 30 states, are allowed when arranged with the responsible authorities. In addition to this, the Detention Reporting and Information Line receives inquiries for violence, abuse, serious mental and physical health issues of the detainees, and their parental rights and provides general information about individuals who are detained. In order for ICE to provide transparency and publicity of its work, detainees, relatives, and acquaintances of detainees, non-governmental organizations (NGOs), attorneys, counselors, and the public could obtain information about detained aliens.

Under the Delegation of Immigration Authority Section 287(g) Immigration and Nationality Act, the Executive Associate Director of ERO could sign an agreement with a federal, state, or local structure to delegate certain prerogatives that are within the pool of ICE's responsibilities to ensure public safety and efficacy of the law enforcement investigations and procedures. The officers who undertake the duties and the functions of ERO should respond to the following qualifying criteria: U.S. citizenship, completed background check, no disciplinary procedures pending or completed against the official, and accumulated experience in the job position.

The HSI division executes a large range of functions primarily oriented to ensure that the movement of goods and people across the U.S. border will be in accordance with the border and customs laws. In this aspect, HIS conducts operations both in the United States and abroad to achieve the aforementioned goals. The unit also consists of eight sub-divisions – *Domestic Operations, International Operations, the National Intellectual Property Rights Coordination Center, Information Management, Investigative Programs, Mission Support, National Security Investigations*, and *Office of Intelligence*.

The Domestic Operations unit supervises and conducts investigations in its 26 domestic offices located in East, Central, and West branches.

The International Operations collaborates with foreign jurisdictions in an effort to establish control over the movement of goods and individuals across the U.S. borders. It has two components – *International Operations East* and *International Operations West*. The first one covers operations executed in Europe, Africa, the

Middle East, Asia, and the Pacific, as each center in these geographical regions has a separate command. The second one includes campaigns in non-U.S. North-American states, Central America, South America, and the Caribbean. The specific nature of the efforts abroad requires reporting both to the HSI central leadership and to the U.S. ambassadors in the respective countries.

The National Intellectual Property Rights Coordination Center conducts operations related to protecting the market from goods that do not fulfill the intellectual property requirements of the U.S. laws for merchandise, distributed both in the physical and/or in the online space.

The Information Management unit works to collect and disseminate information for HSI cases. It is responsible for sharing the data across different offices in the Homeland Security Department. In addition, it looks to incorporate effective technological solutions to investigations and to increase the overall reliability of the conducted statistical analyses.

The Investigative Programs aim to enforce national security through various traditional and cyber operations. Special designated teams combat drug-cartels and drug smuggling across the U.S. border, the profits made from it, and any other financial benefits that resulted from contraband and/or other illicit activities. Furthermore, the Investigative Programs unit oversees a forensic laboratory equipped to examine fingerprints and handwritten documents in order to bolster HSI's investigation efforts.

The Mission Support division within HSI serves as a mechanism ensuring proper financial, budgetary, logistics, policy, and human resources planning as well as advising to U.S. officials fulfilling duties as diplomatic representatives abroad.

National Security Investigations reveal a quite diverse range of responsibilities. This subdivision serves as a counter-terrorist unit that seeks to prevent violent groups from obtaining weapons of mass destruction (WMD) of a different kind – chemical, biological, or any U.S. technology that could support the construction of such. This entity also handles the actions related to war criminals and individuals accused of violations of human rights and genocide. Another task that the National Security Investigations have is to maintain the Student and Exchange Visitor Information System (SEVIS) that collects data for every non-U.S. degree student that seeks a degree or non-degree qualification from eligible American education institutions.

The Office of Intelligence's main task is to share completed reports of cases and/or the information collected in regard to the cases within HSI. The data pertains to traditional and cyber-crimes committed both in the United States and abroad, including terrorism, identity thefts, frauds, money laundering, smuggling, intellectual property violations, and others.

The Management and Administration division does not have independent operational functions but provides overall leadership and supervision of other units. In addition, it is responsible for a wide range of administrative duties such as managing budget and finance, information systems, hiring processes, facilities, and equipment. The access to the information that this office collects and maintains for operations of its branches is free to the public and guaranteed by the Freedom of Information Act. Individuals can obtain information upon written request to the agency. The U.S. Congress constitutes three exceptions to this rule. They all pertain to national security interests and law enforcement units: (1) cases of criminal investigations in which disclosure of information could create obstacles for the operations, (2) cases of criminal law enforcement in which the identity of an informant has not been disclosed officially, and (3) FBI's classified records of cases of international terrorism and international intelligence gathering (FOIA, 2018).

The Office of Professional Responsibility is accountable for the integrity of the conducted operations and their compliance with laws and professional ethics. It investigates two types of misconduct. First, alleged "violations of state or federal criminal law," and second, allegations that "undermine the agency's ability to perform its mission" (ICE, 2018). A signal for misconduct could be sent via telephone, e-mail, and mail and could come from a government agency, inmates, or the public.

The OPLA consists of attorneys and administrative employees who initiate, lead, and supervise the proceedings for the removal of people for whom there are no legal grounds for staying in the United States and violated its federal or state laws. Four sub-divisions within the OPLA execute various functions in regard to leadership and management ("Chief of Staff"), legal services ("Enforcement and Litigation"), distributing legal counsel to local law enforcement ("Field Legal Operations"), and providing expert advice in various categories of law – commercial, administrative, government information, labor, and employment ("General Law"). OPLA's attorneys defend actions of ICE's employees in front of the federal jurisdictions and work alongside the Department of Justice in litigations against illegally residing in the U.S. aliens who are subjects of removal.

Challenges and Concerns

Two of the biggest concerns related to ICE are related to the detention of immigrants, the conditions in which they reside, their rights and needs, especially of vulnerable groups, and some challenges that question the overall effectiveness of the agency. It is reported that detainees express heightened levels of stress because of potential deportation, lack of access to health care, and lack of transparency, fairness, and objectivity in the cooperation between local law enforcement and ICE (Hacker et al., 2011). If the medical staff discovers a condition or a disease after an examination of an immigrant, they receive treatment by the Division of Immigrant Health Services (DIHS). However, the treatment is very often incomplete due to the deportation of the patient (Schneider and Lobato, 2007).

Even more problematic are cases of detention related to vulnerable groups such as children and victims of trafficking. Children of undocumented immigrants suffer a large number of consequences after their parents' detention, particularly in cases of single parenting. The act of detention usually entails a significant emotional burden for adolescents' psyche and other unpleasant consequences of financial character, for instance. If deportation follows, the children either leave with their parents to their respective countries of origin or could remain in foster care, in case they are U.S. citizens themselves. If they become part of the foster care system, the parents are not permitted to visit them in the upcoming 3–10 years (McLeigh, 2010). The toll that detention of immigrant parents takes on their children often finds expression in increased anxiety, depression, and even aggressive behaviors (Phillips and Gleeson, 2007).

Another vulnerable population is the victims of human trafficking. They are a group under the special protection of the Victims of Trafficking and Violence Protection Act of 2000. The act itself is criticized for its limited resources to protect victims of all forms of human trafficking, regardless of the severity of the case (Chacón, 2010). In addition, law enforcement officers encounter significant difficulties in recognizing and proving that a certain undocumented immigrant has fallen victim of human trafficking (Clawson and Dutch, 2016).

Another set of challenges that ICE encounters refer to the overall effectiveness of the policies that the agency follows. One of the main questions raised in this regard is if programs and measures adopted and executed by ICE, whose ultimate goal is to decrease the crime rates in the United States, are productive. The success of two similar programs that ICE supports – the Delegation of Immigration Authority Section 287(g), part of the Immigration and Nationality Act, and the Secure Communities program – is a subject of comparison and assessment in the literature. The latter is characterized as an improved continuation of the former.

While in the first case, local enforcement units cooperate and partner with ICE on a voluntary basis, in the second case, federal structures directly constitute a mandatory collaboration. Regardless of their discrepancies, both initiatives exemplify a delegation of functions from federal structures (ICE) to local law enforcement units. The effectiveness of the collaboration depends largely on the resources that local agencies have and the financial incentives for them. Counties that have contracts with private detention facilities or enter an Intergovernmental Service Agreement (IGSA) are found to be positively correlated with higher number of deportations (Jaeger, 2016). Regardless, a study reveals that the overall crime rates have not been influenced by the number of detained immigrants as part of the Secure Communities program (Miles and Cox, 2014). Another negative side of the joint campaign points to the fact that both programs "can generate incentives for officers to arrest people primarily on the suspicion that they are unauthorized immigrants, knowing that they will be screened through the program and likely placed in removal proceedings" (Capps et al., 2011).

The forms of collaboration between federal and local structures often lead to racial profiling, as a result of an insufficient or absent training of the local law enforcement officers whose responsibilities are to apply federal immigration policies (Briggs, 2014). Furthermore, such practices could engender mistrust between the community and the law enforcement. They could also lead to fear of reporting crimes to the authorities by undocumented immigrants who could take the role of either the victim or the witness.

Conclusion

The ICE is a complex structure with many divisions and sub-divisions. It is governed in accordance with the main political principles outlined by the President's administration. It seeks to incorporate multilateral initiatives that involve both local and federal agencies and the public and the private sector. Some of these campaigns become a subject of criticism. Others merely demonstrate the challenges that ICE faces in the execution of their duties. It is mostly the ethics of the campaigns and the procedures that ICE undertakes that are placed under scrutiny. In particular, in the center of the debates about ICE's success and morality stand the concerns of immigrants' health, the wellbeing of the children whose parents are detained undocumented aliens, racial profiling practices, and the motivations behind entering into public–private partnerships that aim to provide more detention facilities. ICE's functions and programs raise many questions that stand on the borderline between the struggle for equality and human and civil rights, on one hand, and border control, security policies, and community safety, on the other.

Further Reading

Brown, D. L. (2012). An invitation to profile: Arizona v. United States. *International Journal of Discrimination and the Law, 12*(2), 117–127.

Fryberg, S. A., Stephens, N. M., Covarrubias, R., Markus, H. R., Carter, E. D., Laiduc, G. A., & Salido, A. J. (2012). How the media frames the immigration debate: The critical role of location and politics. *Analyses of Social Issues and Public Policy, 12*(1), 96–112.

Khashu, A. (2009). *The role of local police: Striking a balance between immigration enforcement and civil liberties* (Vol. 11). Washington, DC: Police Foundation.

References

Briggs, C. (2014). The reasonableness of a race-based suspicion: The fourth amendment and the costs and benefits of racial profiling in immigration enforcement. *Southern California Law Review*, 88, 379.

Capps, R., Rosenblum, M. R., Rodriguez, C., & Chishti, M. (2011). *Delegation and divergence: A study of 287 (g) state and local immigration enforcement.* Washington, DC: Migration Policy Institute, 20.

Chacón, J. M. (2010). Tensions and trade-offs: Protecting trafficking victims in the era of immigration enforcement. *University of Pennsylvania Law Review, 158*(6), 1609–1653.

Clawson, H. J., & Dutch, N. (2016). *Identifying victims of human trafficking: Inherent challenges and promising strategies for the field.* US Department of Health and Human Services Office of the Assistant Secretary for Planning and Evaluation.

Coon, M. (2017). Local immigration enforcement and arrests of the hispanic population. *Journal on Migration & Human Security*, 5, 645.

Department of Homeland Security (2017, June 13). Written testimony of CBP for a House Appropriations Subcommittee on Homeland Security hearing titled "Immigration and Customs Enforcement & Customs and Border Protection FY18 Budget Request". Retrieved February 09, 2018, from https://www.dhs.gov/news/2017/06/13/written-testimony-cbp-house-appropriations-subcommittee-homeland-security-hearing

FOIA.gov (Freedom of Information Act), (2018). Retrieved January 28, 2018, from https://www.foia.gov/index.html

Hacker, K., Chu, J., Leung, C., Marra, R., Pirie, A., Brahimi, M., ... Marlin, R. P. (2011). The impact of immigration and customs enforcement on immigrant health: Perceptions of immigrants in Everett, Massachusetts, USA. *Social Science & Medicine, 73*(4), 586–594.

ICE (Immigration and Customs Enforcement), (2018). Retrieved January 28, 2018, from https://www.ice.gov/

Jaeger, J. (2016). Securing communities or profits? The effect of federal-local partnerships on immigration enforcement. *State Politics & Policy Quarterly*, 16(3), 362–386.

McLeigh, J. D. (2010). How do immigration and customs enforcement (ICE) practices affect the mental health of children? *American Journal of Orthopsychiatry*, 80(1), 96.

Miles, T. J., & Cox, A. B. (2014). Does immigration enforcement reduce crime? Evidence from secure communities. *The Journal of Law and Economics*, 57(4), 937–973.
Phillips, S. D., & Gleeson, J. P. (2007). What we know now that we didn't know then about the criminal justice system's involvement in families with whom child welfare agencies have contact. Center for Social Policy and Research.
Schneider, D. L., & Lobato, M. N. (2007). Tuberculosis control among people in US immigration and customs enforcement custody. *American Journal of Preventive Medicine*, 33(1), 9–14.

Chapter 14

Industrial Resilience

Mila Demchyk Savage
Old Dominion University, Norfolk, VA, United States

Contents

Introduction 87
Defining Industrial Resilience 88
Evaluating Industrial Resilience 88
How Long Could It Withstand an Incident without Significant Reduction of Capabilities? 89
Abilities to Absorb the Impact of an Undesirable Event and to Adapt through Self-Recovery 89
Recovery Time and Cost After Being Impacted by an Incident 89
Increasing Industrial Resilience 90
Conclusion 90
Further Reading 91
References 91

Introduction

Increased interconnectedness, technological advancement, changing weather conditions, and growing population are just a few factors contributing to the fact that the world is constantly changing. This tendency impacts the nature of threats, which means that there is a need for continuous adjustment. Therefore, the concept of protection is being replaced by resilience. Resilience applied to industrial activities is an important aspect of national well-being. The ability to withstand an incident, absorb the impact, and recover quickly is particularly important in regard to industries related to the critical infrastructure (CI) and key resources. Building a resilient infrastructure is a strategic approach requiring evaluation, planning, and financial input. When preparing for possible threats, it is important to consider a combination of incidents and not just the potential impact from an individual event.

DOI: 10.4324/9781315144511-15

Defining Industrial Resilience

In general, a resilient industry can be described as an ability of a system to maintain efficient supply and production flows under disruptions as well as to recover from the impact of undesirable events quickly. The time of disruption and rate of service decline would depend on the nature of the event, the design of the system, and the mode with which the system is operated (Willis and Loa, 2015). Resilience is a response to routinely caused man-made and natural potentially destabilizing or disruptive events, as well as non-routine risks – disturbances with small likelihood and large impacts (GCIE-2016).

Due to individual specifics, each industry would have a different approach to addressing potential threats and increasing its own resilience. For example, factors like energy security, switching to the smart grid, maintenance of the Strategic Petroleum Reserve, and diversification of energy sources would be important in increasing the resilience of the energy industry. Meanwhile, the financial system would require a different set of tools to increase its resilience, Which include reliable capital and liquidity, improved market discipline, enhanced transparency of business practices, and adjustment of monetary and fiscal policies.

Usually, resilience is built around the most common individual threats to industrial stability: a natural disaster, industrial accident, or terrorist attack. However, preparing for possible threats also requires a consideration of a combination of incidents, not just the potential impact from an individual event. Fukushima Daiichi Nuclear Disaster is a good illustration that correlated risks and system interdependencies need to be carefully considered when evaluating resilience (Langeland et al., 2016). In brief, all powerlines from the grid to the power plant were destroyed due to the earthquake in 2011, which prevented the reactors from cooling. The possibility of using the backup diesel generators was cut off by the subsequent tsunami while the backup batteries providing a third level of redundancy were destroyed by the flooding from the tsunami. This resulted in leaks that released a significant amount of radiation (Langeland et al., 2016).

High resilience of key industries is particularly important for the national well-being and security. Key industries derive from the list of CI sectors and their sector-specific agencies (PPD-21, 2013).

Evaluating Industrial Resilience

Resilience evaluation is the overall activities of modeling and analysis of the CI system aimed to evaluate the ability to prevent, absorb, adapt, and recover from a disruptive event, either natural or man-made (GCIE-2016).

In order to have a general reference document applied to all CI sectors, the Guidelines for Critical Infrastructures Resilience Evaluation document was created. The document provides practical hints on how to evaluate the concept of resilience in the domain of CI. The guidelines were intended to be used and customized to draft sector-specific similar documents. The guidelines moved on from the concept of protection toward a resilience status (GCIE-2016). While every system has its own ways of measuring resilience by using specific industrial standards, several aspects can be applied to any system when evaluating its resilience.

How Long Could It Withstand an Incident without Significant Reduction of Capabilities?

It is crucial for industries, particularly those related to the CI and key resources, to maintain regular operations after being threatened. Therefore, standards are created to set up requirements followed by the members of a certain industry. Promoting resilience has a high cost, which is not always seen as a justified one, because it has no visible output except in the event of a disaster (GCIE-2016). Even though it is crucial to meet industry goals, occasional disruptions illustrate that not all of them are followed. For example, research assessing the application of the Utility Resilience Index related to the water sector (Morley, 2012b) found that many utilities have not heeded the lessons of the past. Nearly 25% of those surveyed would be unable to sustain critical operations for more than 48 h. For perspective, that 25% collectively represents 6.4 million customers who could have compromised water service if they are affected by an event like derecho (Morley, 2012a).

Abilities to Absorb the Impact of an Undesirable Event and to Adapt through Self-Recovery

The financial crisis of 2008 is an illustration of low resilience. The ability of the financial system to absorb the shock of the crisis was unsatisfactory despite efforts of the Treasury Department and Federal Reserve to rescue the situation. Furthermore, the financial system was not able to recover on its own. To avoid a collapse of the system, bailouts of financial institutions and fiscal and monetary policies' adjustments had to be applied. While evaluating a system's ability to absorb and adapt, it is important to consider how seriously a performance disruption or a reduction of capabilities of one industry would impact other industries, national security, and the overall well-being of the United States.

A reduction in capabilities would represent in many cases a significant safety hazard. Some examples of hazardous organizations include air-traffic control and nuclear power plants. Air-traffic control has a low tolerance for collision and as such may prioritize collision avoidance over, for example, cost-cutting measures or timeliness. Similarly, a nuclear power plant may prioritize measures that mitigate the risk of a meltdown, even if this significantly increases operations costs. Complex, integrated systems are often a hallmark of hazardous industries, compounding the challenge of developing means of avoiding disruption and degradation (Langeland et al., 2016). Because a reduction in capabilities of some industries may represent a safety hazard and lead to the increase of operational costs, resilience and sustainable development are often viewed as closely connected concepts.

Recovery Time and Cost After Being Impacted by an Incident

The state of a system depends on how it was designed and how it is operated. These choices influence whether and how service is degraded during a disruption, how quickly it recovers, and how completely it recovers. For example, an electricity grid system that is designed with more redundancy, operated with more contingencies for backup, and designed with recovery in mind might experience a lesser and briefer disruption and, if so, would be more resilient than a system that has less redundancy, has fewer backups, and is more difficult to rebuild (Willis and Loa, 2015).

Increasing Industrial Resilience

Industrial resilience can be increased in many ways. One of them is updating policies and revisiting industrial standards. Resilience has become a distinct policy objective for sustainable and equitable development (Bousquet et al., 2016).

Another way of impacting industrial resilience in a positive way is through applying active cyber-defense techniques. As the world gets more technologically advanced, it is important to develop and apply resilience strategies for industrial control systems that employ an active defense technique to reduce, if not eliminate, the likelihood of a common cause failure induced by a cyber-attack (Chaves et al., 2017). Essentially, security should be designed into a system, not bolted on after the fact. Firewalls, intrusion detection systems, and anti-virus software are common passive defense techniques. Although they may be effective, architectures and passive defense techniques are inadequate to keep out sophisticated and well-resourced attackers. Active defense begins after an attacker is inside a network. Active defense is accomplished by identifying the attack, developing an understanding of the attacker, and having the flexibility to respond to the attack (Lee, 2015).

When it comes to the relationship between economic resilience and industry diversity, one of the findings suggests that while counties with higher industry diversity tended to experience higher unemployment rates when the national economy was doing well, they had relatively lower unemployment rates when the national economy experienced employment shocks (Brown, 2017).

Social, economic, and ecological resilience play an important role when it comes to the American well-being. For instance, it is hard to expect communities to be resilient when many of them are already in disarray. When the city is not resilient, one cannot expect any organization operating there to be resilient (for instance, the city of New Orleans during Katrina Hurricane) (GCIE-2016).

In resilience thinking, development issues for human well-being, for people and planet, are framed in a context of understanding and governing complex social–ecological dynamics for sustainability as part of a dynamic biosphere. Such approach suggests to continue to develop with ever-changing environments (Folke, 2016).

Conclusion

A resilient industry can be described as an ability of a system to maintain efficient supply and production flows under disruptions as well as to recover from the impact of undesirable events quickly. Due to individual specifics, each industry would have a different approach in addressing potential threats and increasing its own resilience. Common threats to industrial stability are natural disasters, industrial accidents, and terrorist attacks. However, preparing for possible threats also requires a consideration of a combination of incidents. Since applying a resilient strategy is costly, it is important to make a prior evaluation by looking at a system's ability to prevent, absorb, adapt, and recover from a disruptive event. Furthermore, a continuous work on increasing resilience is vital for some industries like finance and energy. Among ways positively impacting industrial resilience are updated policies, revisited industrial standards, applied active cyber-defense techniques, and industrial diversification.

Further Reading

Gheorghe, Adrian V., Vamanu, Dan V., Katina, Polinpapilinho F., Pulfer, Poland Critical Infrastructures, Key Resources, *Key Assets: Risk, Vulnerability, Resilience, Fragility, and Perception Governance* (New York: Springer International Publishing, 2018).

Rieger, C., Ray, I., Zhu, Q., Haney, M. A. (eds). (2019). *Industrial Control Systems Security and Resiliency: Practice and Theory*. Cham: Springer.

Zhu, Junming, Ruth, Matthias. Exploring the resilience of industrial ecosystems. *Journal of Environmental Management*, 15 June 2013, Vol. 122, pp. 65–75

References

Bousquet, F. Aurélie Botta, Luca Alinovi, Olivier Barreteau, Deborah Bossio, Katrina Brown, Patrick Caron, Philippe Cury, Marco d'Errico, Fabrice DeClerck, Hélène Dessard, Elin Enfors Kautsky, Christo Fabricius, Carl Folke, Louise Fortmann, Bernard Hubert, Danièle Magda, Raphael Mathevet, Richard B. Norgaard, Allyson Quinlan and Charles Staver. Resilience and development: mobilizing for transformation. *Ecology and Society*. Vol. 21, No. 3 (Sep 2016).

Chaves, Andrew, Rice, Mason, Dunlap, Stephen, Pecarina, John Improving the cyber resilience of industrial control systems. *International Journal of Critical Infrastructure Protection*, June 2017, Vol.17, pp. 30–48.

Folke, Carl. *Resilience; Source: Ecology and Society*, Resilience Alliance Inc., Vol. 21, No. 4 (Dec 2016).

Guidelines for Critical Infrastructures Resilience Evaluation – 2016. http://www.infrastrutture critiche.it/new/media-files/2016/04/Guidelines_Critical_Infrastructures_Resilience_Evaluation.pdf

Langeland, Krista S., Langeland, David Manheim, Gary McLeod and George Nacouzi. *How Civil Institutions Build Resilience Organizational Practices Derived from Academic Literature and Case Studies*, RAND Corporation; 2016).

Lee, R. *The Sliding Scale of Cyber Security, InfoSec Reading Room*, SANS Institute, Bethesda, Maryland, 2015. www.sans.org/reading-room/whitepapers/analyst/sliding-scale-cyber-security-36240.

Morley, K.M. A Lesson in Resilience from Derecho. *Journal (American Water Works Association)*, Vol. 104, No. 9 (September 2012a), pp. 20–23.

Morley, K.M. Evaluating Resilience in the Water Sector: Application of the Utility Resilience Index (URI). Doctoral dissertation, George Mason University, 2012b.

PPD-21. Presidential Policy Directive – Critical Infrastructure Security and Resilience. February 12, 2013. https://obamawhitehouse.archives.gov/the-press-office/2013/02/12/presidential-policy-directive-critical-infrastructure-security-and-resil

Willis, Henry H. and Loa, Kathleen. *Measuring the Resilience of Energy Distribution Systems*, RAND Corporation, 2015.

Chapter 15

National Domestic Preparedness Office

Darren E. Tromblay
George Washington University, Washington, DC, United States

Contents

Introduction 93
Further Reading 96
References 97

Introduction

The National Domestic Preparedness Office (NDPO) was an interagency body – under the leadership of the Federal Bureau of Investigation (FBI) – which had a role in coordinating federal and sub-federal contingency planning for an incident involving weapons of mass destruction (WMD). NDPO's first-responder-centric mission was an ambitious undertaking but an awkward fit for the bureau, which was an agency with expertise in the collection of information, the disruption of threats, and crisis management but no substantial legacy in pre-event preparedness. The creation of the Department of Homeland Security (DHS) provided a more appropriate setting for NDPO's mission.

NDPO's origins are in the second half of the 1990s – following the 1993 World Trade Center and 1995 Oklahoma City bombings – when the United States was attempting to develop a counterterrorism strategy. After soliciting input from more than 200 state and local officials – who represented the disciplines that would most likely be involved with responding to a terrorist event – Attorney General (AG) Janet Reno learned that these officials saw a critical need for a central point, within the federal government, for response coordination (US House of Representatives, 1999). These officials – in the presence of the AG, the Director of the Federal Emergency

DOI: 10.4324/9781315144511-16

Management Agency (FEMA), and the Secretary of Defense – strongly recommended the coordination and integration of all the federal programs responsible for rating state and local agencies' terrorism preparedness (US House of Representatives, 1999).

The AG, in response to these concerns and in consultation with the National Security Council and other US government (USG) agencies, proposed the NDPO. At the direction of the AG – as part of the Five Year Interagency Counterterrorism and Technology Crime Plan – the FBI became the lead agency for this new office, which began functioning in 1998 (US Senate, 1999a). The bureau was already responsible for counterterrorism investigations and the NDPO was assigned in the context of this existing mission (US Senate, 1999b).

Federal and sub-federal entities would all have input to the NDPO's functioning. As the chair of the USG Cabinet-level Domestic Preparedness Leadership Group (DPLG), the AG would provide oversight for the NDPO (National Domestic Preparedness Office, 2001). (The DPLG included the Secretaries of Defense, Energy, and Health and Human Services; the Directors of FEMA and the FBI; the Administrator of the Environmental Protection Agency [EPA]; and the National Security Council's [NSC's] National Coordinator for Security, Infrastructure Protection, and Counterterrorism.) (National Domestic Preparedness Office, 2001). A State and Local Advisory Group (SLAG) would provide input, on strategy and implementation, from the sub-federal audience that had driven the creation of the NDPO (National Domestic Preparedness Office, 2001). Creation of the SLAG was the result of stakeholders' articulated desire for formal representation by state and local agencies to guide the development and delivery of more effective federal programs (US House of Representatives, 1999).

The NDPO was a platform for facilitating readiness, as opposed to having an operational role in responding to crises. Preparedness programs under the auspices of the NDPO covered six broad areas, including planning, training, exercises, equipment, information sharing, and public health and medical assistance (US House of Representative, 2001). A significant portion of the NDPO's mission was serving as a liaison between sub-federal agencies and the USG entities responsible for programs in the six broad areas. This included not only providing ready-made guidance but also ensuring that appropriate federal representatives were involved with state and local planning efforts (National Domestic Preparedness Office, 2001). Additionally, the NDPO would help to bridge the federal/sub-federal gap by facilitating the distribution of the USG's Interagency Domestic Terrorism Concept of Operations Plan (US House of Representatives, 1999). However – consistent with its operational role – the NDPO did not produce intelligence, preempt terrorist attacks, directly respond to terrorist attacks, or conduct investigations (Bea, Krouse, Morgan, Morrisey, & Redhead, 2003; National Domestic Preparedness Office, 2001).

Although it was not supposed to produce intelligence about WMD, interfacing with intelligence components was a part of NDPO's mission. The planning document, *Blueprint for the National Domestic Preparedness Office*, stated that the NDPO would coordinate with an analytical team from substantive units – including those within the International Terrorism Section, the Domestic Terrorism Section, and the National Infrastructure Protection Center – within the FBI to ensure that domestic preparedness information was properly compiled, sanitized, and uniformly disseminated, via Special Bulletins, law enforcement channels, or directly to appropriate personnel (2001). The NDPO was also supposed to disseminate knowledge through training activities and ensure that training curriculum incorporated "lessons learned" (GAO, 2000).

The creation of the NDPO was not *sui generis*. Instead, it incorporated some existing capabilities. The Department of Defense (DoD), in 1996, had become responsible for training first responders and had also developed a standardized equipment list (SEL) of commercially available WMD equipment which had passed DoD safety tests (National Domestic Preparedness Office, 2001). The DoD transferred, via a formal memorandum of understanding, most aspects of its domestic preparedness program to NDPO (US Senate, 1999). The NDPO planned to continue DoD's initiative to establish and maintain a compendium of federal training courses available to emergency responders (US House of Representatives, 1999). DoD remained engaged on the topic of equipment and – in conjunction with the FBI – organized the Interagency Board for Equipment Standardization and Interoperability (co-chaired by the DoD and the FBI) which maintained and updated the DoD-established SEL. The Interagency Board was an advisory body to the NDPO (GAO, 1999). The DoD continued to provide a full-time liaison officer to assist with staffing the NDPO (US House of Representatives, 2001).

In addition to the DoD, the NDPO drew on the competencies of other federal and non-federal agencies. Through the NDPO, the Department of Energy (DoE) served as the principal source of information about WMD-related nuclear and radiological preparedness issues (National Domestic Preparedness Office, 2001). The Environmental Protection Agency (EPA) supported federal counterterrorism programs by using and building upon the established hazardous materials response structure and mechanism at the federal, state, and local levels (National Domestic Preparedness Office, 2001). A liaison from the Department of Health and Human Services (HHS) – which was the lead for upgrading national public health capability to counter biological and chemical terrorism – was also part of the NDPO (National Domestic Preparedness Office, 2001). Under guidance from HHS and the Public Health Service, NDPO would coordinate efforts to support metropolitan medical response systems and pharmaceutical stockpiling systems (US House of Representatives, 1999). Other federal participants in the NDPO included FEMA, the Nuclear Regulatory Commission, and the US Coast Guard (US Senate, 2006). In addition to the federal officials, one-third of the NDPO would consist of state and local experts (US House of Representatives. Domestic Preparedness for the Next Millennium, 1999: US House of Representatives. Combating Terrorism, 1999).

The NDPO had to establish a structure to facilitate the transfer of knowledge to its sub-federal customers. According to the Blueprint for the National Domestic Preparedness Office, the AG and the Director of FEMA would ask state governors to designate a single point of contact, within the states and territories, who would have direct contact with the NDPO and function as a state-level link to federal efforts (National Domestic Preparedness Office, 2001). In conjunction with these state-level appointees, NDPO would communicate with city and community officials (National Domestic Preparedness Office, 2001). Additionally, the FBI, working with the other agencies represented within the NDPO, would assist state and local planners in developing threat and risk assessments and providing assistance with the development of integrated domestic preparedness plans at the state and local levels (Blueprint for the National Domestic Preparedness Office, 2001).

Even before September 11, 2001, the NDPO was already the subject of criticism. In May 2001, FEMA, in arguing for an Office of National Preparedness, assessed that the NDPO lacked sufficient authority, resources, interagency support, and historic ties to the state and local responder communities to fully integrate the consequence management, preparedness, and response efforts (US House of Representatives, 2001). In a similar vein, James Clapper Jr., the Vice-Chairman of the Advisory Panel to Assess Domestic Response Capabilities for Terrorism Involving Weapons of Mass Destruction stated that "[a]ttempts to create a Federal focal point for coordination with State and local officials – such as the National Domestic Preparedness Office – have been only partially successful" (US Senate, 2001).

The creation of DHS ended the FBI's leadership of the NDPO. Even before September 11, the US Commission on National Security in the 21st century had recommended the creation of a "National Homeland Security Agency," to which the NDPO should be transferred (US Senate, 2001). When President George W. Bush submitted his proposal for the creation of DHS, it included the NDPO as well as the FBI's National Infrastructure Protection Center, both of which were ultimately relocated by the legislation – inspired in part by the NHSA concept – which created DHS (CRS, 2005). NDPO became subordinate to FEMA (which had previously helped to create – and subsequently criticize – the NDPO infrastructure) (Bea, K, 2003).

The NDPO's brief history has significant implications for how one looks at the United States' domestic national security apparatus. First, it was a pioneering effort to simultaneously bridge the gap between intelligence agencies (e.g., the FBI) and relevant non-intelligence agencies (e.g., HHS), as well as incorporate sub-federal actors (i.e., state and local agencies). A second consideration is how functions are aligned with agencies. The FBI, although highly accomplished in many areas, was not the right home for the NDPO – the bureau lacked expertise in almost all of the NDPO's functions (and had difficulties with information sharing, an essential competency for the NDPO). Assignment of the NDPO to the FBI is one episode in a trend that has historically done a disservice to the FBI. Throughout the 20th century, the bureau – because it was the catch-all for functions not explicitly assigned to other agencies – accumulated a wide variety of disparate, sometimes competing missions. The NDPO example is a reminder that when the USG identifies the need for a new capability, it is in the national interest to ensure that the capability enhances, rather than undermines, an agency's strengths.

Further Reading

de Jong-Chen, J. & O'Brien, B. (2017, November). "*A Comparative Study: The Approach to Critical Infrastructure Protection in the U.S., E.U., and China*," The Wilson Center, Washington, DC. wilsoncenter.org/sites/default/files/media/documents/publication/approach_to_critical_infrastructure_protection.pdf

Ferraiolo, H. (2018). "Codes for the Identification of Federal and Federally-Assisted Organizations," NIST Special Publication 800-87, Revision 2. https://doi.org/10.6028/NIST.SP.800-87r2

Fry-Pierce, C. C. & Lenze, P. E., Jr. (2011). "Bioterrorism and U.S. domestic preparedness: bureaucratic fragmentation and American vulnerability," *Journal of Homeland Security and Emergency Management*, *8*(1): 39.

References

Bea, K. (2003). *Congressional Research Service. Homeland Security: Department Organization and Management – Legislative Phase*. Washington, DC: Congressional Research Service.

Bea, K. Krouse, W. Morgan, D. Morrisey, W. Redhead, C. S. (2003). *Emergency Preparedness and Response Directorate of the Department of Homeland Security*. Washington, DC: Congressional Research Service.

CRS. (2005). *Organization and Mission of the Emergency Preparedness and Response Directorate: Issue and Options for the 109th Congress*. Washington, DC: Congressional Research Service.

GAO. (1999). *Combating Terrorism: Analysis of Potential Emergency Response Equipment and Sustainment Costs*. Washington, DC: General Accounting Office.

GAO. (2000). *Combating Terrorism: Issues in Managing Counterterrorist Programs*. Washington, DC: General Accounting Office.

National Domestic Preparedness Office. (2001). Blueprint for the national domestic preparedness office. http://oai.dtic.mil/oai/oai?verb=getRecord&metadataPrefix=html&identifier=ADA395255

US House of Representatives. (1999). *Combating Terrorism: Proposed Transfer of the Domestic Preparedness Program*. Washington, DC: US House of Representatives.

US House of Representatives. (2001). *H R. 525, the Preparedness against Domestic Terrorism Act*. Washington, DC: US House of Representatives.

US Senate. (1999a). *Domestic Preparedness in the Next Millennium*. Washington, DC: US Senate.

US Senate. (1999b). *Office of Justice Programs Oversight; Examining the OJP Reorganization Plan*. Washington, DC: US Senate.

US Senate. (2001a). *Domestic Response Capabilities for Terrorism Involving Weapons of Mass Destruction*. Washington, DC: US Senate.

US Senate. (2001b). *Strategies for Homeland Defense. A Compilation by the Committee on Foreign Relations United States Senate*. Washington, DC: US Senate.

Chapter 16

National Protection and Programs Directorate

Darren E. Tromblay
George Washington University, Washington, DC, United States

Contents

Introduction 99
Further Reading 103
References 104

Introduction

Maintaining awareness of infrastructure security has been a core mission of the Department of Homeland Security (DHS) since the creation of the department in 2002. The National Protection and Programs Directorate (NPPD) consolidated multiple aspects of this mission by bringing evolving knowledge of physical and cyber vulnerabilities, as well as efforts to address these vulnerabilities, under a single organizational umbrella. As with much of DHS, NPPD adds value to the domestic security enterprise through information sharing with federal, sub-federal, and private sector entities.

DHS created the NPPD, in 2007, out of multiple pre-existing DHS components. NPPD was the successor to the DHS Preparedness Directorate, which, itself, replaced the Emergency Preparedness and Response Directorate (one of DHS' original directorates, which began operations in 2003) (Government Accountability Office. National Protection and Programs Directorate. 2015; Bea. 2005; US Congress. Department of Homeland Security Appropriations for 2005. 2004). As of 2016, DHS was in the process of reorganizing NPPD to position the directorate in furtherance of effecting greater unity of effort (achieving "unity of effort" was an objective of then-DHS Secretary Jeh Johnson) (Government Accountability Office. Critical Infrastructure

DOI: 10.4324/9781315144511-17

Protection. 2016). The reorganization was intended to better integrate NPPD by revising a legacy structure that had created a programmatic divide between physical and cybersecurity resilience efforts (US Congress. Examining the Mission, Structure, and Reorganization Effort of the National Protection and Programs Directorate. 2015).

Per DHS's designation, NPPD is the lead component for government-wide critical infrastructure security and resilience (Government Accountability Office. 2014). NPPD's constituent elements are the Federal Protective Service (FPS), the Office of Biometric Identity Management (OBIM), the Office of Cyber and Infrastructure Analysis (OCIA), the Office of Cybersecurity and Communications (CS&C), and the Office of Infrastructure Protection (OIP). The NPPD is responsible for developing and ensuring the implementation of the National Infrastructure Protection Plan (NIPP), which establishes the framework for integrating the United States' critical infrastructure protection and resilience initiatives into a combined enterprise (US Congress. 2009; US Congress. Appropriations for 2012. 2012a).

NPPD's OIP traces its lineage to the creation of DHS. OIP – which leads and coordinates national programs and policies on critical infrastructure issues, including implementation of the NIPP – began as part of the Information Analysis and Infrastructure Protection (IAIP) Directorate, which DHS dismantled in 2005 (Relyea & Hogue. 2006; Government Accountability Office. 2014). DHS then transferred OIP to the Preparedness Directorate. OIP contains the Infrastructure Information Collection Division, which is responsible for DHS' gathering and management of information regarding infrastructure data and ensures that this data is available to homeland security partners (Department of Homeland Security. Infrastructure information collection division. n.d.-b). The Infrastructure Security Compliance Division, of OIP, is responsible for implementing the Chemical Facility Anti-Terrorism Standards (CFATS) – which regulates security at high-risk chemical facilities (Department of Homeland Security. Information security compliance division. n.d.-c). In the course of executing its NIPP responsibilities, which include coordinating the implementation of the NIPP across the 16 critical infrastructure sectors, OIP provides guidance to asset owners and operators on protective measures to assist in enhancing the security of infrastructure as well as assisting state, local, tribal, territorial, and private sector partners develop capabilities to mitigate vulnerabilities and identifiable risks to assets (Government Accountability Office. 2014).

Because a significant amount of the United States' critical infrastructure resides in private sector hands, DHS must work closely with industry, a function which OIP facilitates. OIP's Protective Security Coordination Division (PSCD) engages in both strategic coordination and support to field operations in furtherance of curbing risk to critical infrastructure and key resources (CI/KR) from man-made or natural disasters (Department of Homeland Security. Protective security coordination division. n.d.-d). The Protective Security Advisor (PSA) Program – which began in 2004 – is a significant PSCD component and is responsible for much of the OIP's field effort (Government Accountability Office. 2010; US Congress. Appropriations for 2012. 2012a). PSAs serve as a link between DHS infrastructure partners and state, local, tribal, and territorial organizations, conducting vulnerability and security assessments directed at identifying security gaps and vulnerabilities in components of critical infrastructure (Government Accountability Office. 2010). This information, developed by PSAs, helps to inform the national risk picture (Government Accountability

Office. 2010). In addition to informing the strategic picture, PSAs also share vulnerability information and insights about protective measures with local partners as well as asset owners and operators (Government Accountability Office. 2010). OIP's Sector Outreach and Programs Division (SOPD) builds capacities among critical infrastructure partners via voluntary partnerships through which SOPD provides tools, resources, and partnerships (Department of Homeland Security. Sector outreach and programs division n.d.-e) SOPD incorporated the former OIP Partnership and Outreach Division, which worked with public and private partners to coordinate efforts directed at establishing and operating councils dedicated to protecting CI/KR and helping to strengthen CI/KR-related incident response.

NPPD has significant responsibilities in the field of cyber security (Government Accountability Office. 2010). (DHS cybersecurity functions – including US-Computer Emergency Readiness Team (US-CERT) – can be traced to the IAIP Directorate's National Cyber Security Division (Government Accountability Office. 2005.). The OCIA fulfills functions including the integrated analysis of critical infrastructure and identifying critical infrastructure where cyber incidents could have catastrophic impacts on public health and safety, the economy, and national security. OCIA was previously known as the Infrastructure Analysis and Strategy Division (IASD) within OIP but became an independent office under the NPPD in 2014 (Department of Homeland Security. n.d.-a). The IASD was responsible for managing the National Critical Infrastructure Prioritization Program (NCIPP) – established in 2006 – which used a tiered approach to identify nationally significant infrastructure, based on the consequence associated with a disruption of the identified infrastructure element (Government Accountability Office. 2013).

The NPPD Office of CS&C is also essential to protecting the US communications infrastructure. Its mission is assuring the security, resilience, and reliability of the nation's cyber and communications infrastructure (Government Accountability Office. 2015). It is responsible for securing Federal executive branch civilian government networks, providing technical expertise, analysis, and warnings to the private sector and critical infrastructure owners and operators, raising cybersecurity awareness among the general public, coordinating the national response to cyber emergencies, and planning for and providing national security and emergency preparedness communications to the federal government and other stakeholders (US Congress. Appropriations for 2012. 2012a). CS&C engages critical infrastructure owners and operators with a suite of voluntary vulnerability assessments to assist with securing those owners' and operators' cyber systems (Government Accountability Office. Critical infrastructure protection. 2017a). Furthermore, the CS&C National Cybersecurity Assessment and Technical Services team provides cybersecurity scanning and testing services that identify vulnerabilities within stakeholder networks, furnishes risk analysis, and provides recommendations for remediation (Government Accountability Office. Critical infrastructure protection. 2017a).

Under the CS&C is the National Cybersecurity and Communications Integration Center (NCCIC) (Department of Homeland Security. 2017). The NCCIC is the federal government's 24/7 hub for sharing cybersecurity information, provision of technical assistance, and response to security incidents (Department of Homeland Security. 2017). As of 2015, it handled 100,000 cyber incident detections and more than 850 requests for assistance, from the private sector, per month (US Congress. Department of Homeland Security Appropriations for 2016. 2015b). DHS developed NCCIC in 2009 and, in 2014, the National Cybersecurity Protection Act statutorily established the Center within DHS (Government Accountability Office. Cybersecurity. 2017b). NCCIC contains four branches: the United States Computer Emergency Readiness Team (US-CERT), which leads efforts to improve the US cybersecurity posture, coordinate cyber information sharing, and proactively manage cyber risks to entities in both the government and private sector; the Industrial Control Systems Cyber Emergency Response Team (ICS-CERT), which is responsible for reducing risks to the United States' critical infrastructure by strengthening control systems' security and resilience through public–private partnerships; the National Coordinating Center for Communications, which assists the government, private industry, and international partners with sharing and analyzing threat information about, assess the operating status of, and understand the risk posture of, the communications infrastructure; and Operations and Integration, which plans, coordinates, and integrates capabilities to synchronize analysis, information sharing, and incident response efforts across NCCIC's branches and activities (Government Accountability Office. Cybersecurity. 2017b).

CS&C is also home to the Office of Emergency Communications (OEC) and the National Communications System (NCS) (US Senate. Ten years after 9/11 – 2011. 2012c). OEC, which dates to 2007, supports and promotes communications used by emergency responders and government officials. The office leads the United States' operable and interoperable public safety and national security and emergency preparedness (NS/EP) communications efforts. OEC provides training, coordination, tools, and guidance to help its federal, state, local, tribal, territorial, and industry partners develop their emergency communications capabilities (Department of Homeland Security. Emergency Communications Division. n.d.-a). Originally part of the Department of Defense (DoD), NCS manages partnerships between government and industry entities to assist decision-makers with understanding risks to the communications sector (US Senate. Ten years after 9/11 – 2011. 2012c).

The NPPD's OBIM facilitates collection and sharing of information about individuals to appropriate federal, state, and local government officials, in furtherance of determining whether those individuals pose a threat to the United States. OBIM, which was formed in 2013, replaced the US Visitor and Immigration Status Indicator Technology (US-VISIT) program (Department of Homeland Security. n.d.-a). US-VISIT had facilitated the collection, storage, and sharing of biometric and biographic identity information on foreign visitors seeking entry into the United States and immigration benefits, as well as on US citizens who were applying for access to government sites, programs, and critical infrastructure (US Senate. 2011). The creation of OBIM followed consideration, in 2012, of transferring US-VISIT from NPPD to Customs and Border Protection (CBP) and Immigration and Customs Enforcement (ICE) (US Congress. Appropriations for 2013. 2012b).

Finally, NPPD includes the FPS. Originally part of the General Services Administration, FPS is responsible for protecting and executing law enforcement functions at federal facilities (Government Accountability Office. 2015). Additionally, FPS provides police emergency and special security services during out-of-the-ordinary events, including natural disasters and major civil disturbances (Lake. 2003). FPS was originally part of DHS' Border and Transportation Security Directorate (Krouse. 2003).

NPPD does not operate in a vacuum but, instead, interfaces with a variety of DHS, federal government, and state and local entities to implement its mission. The 2016 NPPD reorganization was intended to achieve greater integration within the department by leveraging expertise, skills, information, and relationships throughout DHS (Government Accountability Office. 2016). One of NPPD's most significant partners within the department is the Office of Intelligence and Analysis (OI&A), originally part of the IAIP Directorate (Government Accountability Office. Critical infrastructure protection. 2017a). OI&A develops threat-related analytic products for each of the 16 critical infrastructure sectors (Government Accountability Office. Critical infrastructure protection. 2017a). The Homeland Threat Division of OI&A participates in biweekly briefings, hosted by the NPPD's OIP, for critical infrastructure owners and operators (Government Accountability Office. Critical infrastructure protection. 2017a). In fiscal year 2010, an NPPD-led initiative with ten state and local fusion centers sought to enhance engagement with critical infrastructure private sector stakeholders and build out information-sharing capabilities (US Senate. 2011). OIP also planned to place 15 infrastructure security specialists in state and local fusion centers to develop state and regional critical infrastructure risk management and resiliency plans and to collaborate with fusion center personnel to support national-level critical infrastructure strategic analysis and decision-making (US Congress. Appropriations for 2012. 2012a). The NCCIC hosts multiple federal partners from the defense, law enforcement, and intelligence sectors (US Congress. Appropriations for 2012. 2012a). Furthermore, NPPD's assignment of Cyber Mission Integration Analysts – who can "reach back" to the NCCIC, to the DHS/DoD Joint Coordination Element at Fort Meade – provides an additional venue for integration (US Senate. 2011).

The creation of NPPD and the ongoing internal reorganization of the directorate's components has formed a unified approach to infrastructure protection, by aligning awareness of physical and cyber vulnerabilities. NPPD complements its responsibility for vigilance through initiatives – such as US-CERT and the PSA program – to mitigate vulnerabilities. The outliers in the NPPD's coherent structure are OEC, NCS, and OBIM, which provide platforms for information sharing, rather than infrastructure-focused functions. Although their presence is not fundamentally disruptive, future reorganizations could enhance NPPD's organizational identity by re-assigning these elements to DHS components where they might benefit from greater synergy.

Further Reading

Donahue, T. (n.d.). "The Worst Possible Day U.S. Telecommunications and Huawei," *PRISM*, *8*(3): 14–35. https://ndupress.ndu.edu/Portals/68/Documents/prism/prism_8-3/prism_8-3_Donahue_14-35.pdf

Taylor, F. X. (2019, April 2). "*PERSPECTIVE: Post-9/11 Counterterrorism Is Right Model for Infrastructure Cybersecurity,*" *Government Technology & Services Coalition's Homeland Security Today*. hstoday.us/subject-matter-areas/infrastructure-security/perspective-9-11-counterterrorism-response-should-be-model-for-critical-infrastructure-cybersecurity/

The White House. (2019, May 15). "*Executive Order on Securing the Information and Communications Technology and Services Supply Chain.*" whitehouse.gov/presidential-actions/executive-order-securing-information-communications-technology-services-supply-chain/

References

Bea, K. (2005). *Organization and mission of the emergency preparedness and response directorate: issue and options for the 109th congress*. Washington, DC: Congressional Research Service.

Department of Homeland Security (2017). *Biennial report on DHS' implementation of the cybersecurity act of 2015*. Washington, DC: Author.

Department of Homeland Security (n.d.-a). Emergency communications division. https://www.cisa.gov/emergency-communications-division.

Department of Homeland Security (n.d.-b). Infrastructure information collection division. https://www.cisa.gov/iicd.

Department of Homeland Security (n.d.-c). Information security compliance division. https://www.cisa.gov/iscd.

Department of Homeland Security (n.d.-d). Protective security coordination division. https://www.cisa.gov/protective-security-coordination-division.

Department of Homeland Security (n.d.-e). Sector outreach and programs division. https://www.cisa.gov/sopd.

Government Accountability Office (2005). *Critical infrastructure protection: department of homeland security faces challenges in fulfilling cybersecurity responsibilities*. Washington, DC: Government Accountability Office.

Government Accountability Office (2010). *Critical infrastructure protection: DHS efforts to assess and promote resiliency but program management could be strengthened*. Washington, DC: Government Accountability Office.

Government Accountability Office (2013). *Critical infrastructure protection: DHS list of priority assets needs to be validated and reported to congress*. Washington, DC: Government Accountability Office.

Government Accountability Office (2014). *Critical infrastructure protection: DHS action needed to enhance integration and coordination of vulnerability assessment efforts*. Washington, DC: Government Accountability Office.

Government Accountability Office (2015). *National protection and programs directorate: factors to consider when reorganizing*. Washington, DC: Government Accountability Office.

Government Accountability Office (2016). *Critical infrastructure protection: DHS has made progress in enhancing critical infrastructure assessments, but additional improvements are needed*. Washington, DC: Government Accountability Office.

Government Accountability Office (2017a). *Critical infrastructure protection: DHS risk assessments inform owner and operator protection efforts and departmental strategic planning*. Washington, DC: Government Accountability Office.

Government Accountability Office (2017b). *Cybersecurity: DHS's national integration center generally performs required functions but needs to evaluate its activities more completely*. Washington, DC: Government Accountability Office.

Krouse, W. E. (2003). *Department of homeland security: consolidation of border and transportation security agencies*. Washington, DC: Congressional Research Service.

Lake, J. E. (2003). *Department of homeland security: consolidation of border and transportation security agencies*. Washington, DC: Congressional Research Service.

US Senate (2004). *Department of homeland security appropriations for 2005*. Washington, DC: US Senate.

US Senate (2009). *The homeland security department's budget submission for fiscal year 2010*. Washington, DC: US Senate.

US Senate (2012a). *Department of homeland security, appropriations for 2012*. Washington, DC: US Senate.

US Senate (2012b). *Department of Homeland Security Appropriations for 2013*. Washington, DC: US Senate.

US Senate (2015a). *Examining the mission, structure, and reorganization effort of the national protection and programs directorate*. Washington, DC: US Senate.

US Senate (2015b). *Department of Homeland Security Appropriations for 2016*. Washington, DC: US Senate.

US Senate (2011). *The Homeland Security Department's Budget Submission for Fiscal Year 2012*. Washington, DC: US Senate.

US Senate (2012c). Ten Years after 9/11 – 2011. Washington, DC: US Senate.

Relyea, H. C. & Hogue, H. B. (2006). *Department of homeland security reorganization: The 2SR initiative*. Washington, DC: Congressional Research Service.

Chapter 17

Partnership for Peace Consortium

Huso Hasanovic
Old Dominion University, Washington, DC, United States

Contents

Introduction 107
Expanded Scope of PFP 108
Conclusion 109
Further Reading 109
References 110

Introduction

This chapter discusses foundational beginnings of North Atlantic Treaty Organization's (NATO) Partnership for Peace (PFP) program and its saliency in Euro-Atlantic relations and broader global security environment. NATO members have an agreement of collective defense in case of an external attack as well as promoting peaceful conflict prevention through democratic principles. Nonmembers can still have a relationship with NATO through programs such as the PFP. PFP program is an organization within NATO tasked with building relations and cooperation among NATO and its Euro-Atlantic partner countries. Currently, there are 21 countries that participate in this individualized program where states have the option to choose their level of cooperation and information sharing with NATO.

Some of the main agendas of establishing PFP include empowering participants' relationships with NATO; building critical enablers of peace, progress, and cooperation; increasing stability; eliminating threats of peace; and enhancing security relations between NATO and nonmember states located in the Euro-Atlantic region. Peace activities usually encompass numerous international relations and endeavors.

DOI: 10.4324/9781315144511-18

These activities include civil–military relations, education training, defense policy and planning, defense reform, disaster planning, environmental reforms, and military training (NATO framework for Partnership for Peace Program, accessed 2018). Some countries choose to strengthen their relations with NATO through individual partnership action plans (IPAPs). These action plans are usually meant to coordinate various cooperation mechanisms with NATO providing country-specific advice and are reviewed periodically. PFP and IPAP agreements usually encompass joint military training exercises and military professionalization endeavors.

Expanded Scope of PFP

Aside from the cooperation through military drills and crisis-response training offered to nonmembers, NATO also offers educational opportunities for outsiders. Founded during the 1999 NATO Summit, Partnership for Peace Consortium (PfPc) is an international security cooperation organization that provides a forum to leading defense and security institutions to share and discuss meaningful practices and expertise in the area of defense and security. To date, the PfPc has over 800 participant think-tanks and institutions from all over the globe. Aside from holding regular conferences and presenting on security issues, the PfPc also publishes a quarterly journal *Connections* and provides policy recommendations via its international network of defense education and defense institution building experts.

The many offshoots of NATO allow it to promote its democratic ideals and manifest themselves into many aspects of security considerations. Nonmember states as well as private institutions have many avenues and connections through which they can enjoy a reciprocal relationship with NATO. Solidifying these relationships is key to stabilizing the alliance and its influence in world affairs (Goldgeier, 2010). Indeed, the PFP initiative has also gone global in scope. The alliance created a Mediterranean Dialogue and the Istanbul Cooperation Initiative to encourage prospective bilateral cooperation with Mediterranean and Middle Eastern countries, respectively.

Growing literature has also pointed to the consequential effects of NATO membership, including democratization. In addition to betterment of one's security position externally, states are affected by this improved security position on the homefront. A fundamental precondition for democratization is the establishment of a security regime, particularly one guaranteed by the international community (Barany, 2004). Making such connections between guaranteed security and democratization can also lead us to speculate about economic affects as well. While the literature is inconclusive, there are reasons for one to believe that greater security guarantees will induce more foreign direct investment and private spending.

Fundamental changes have occurred to the security environment since the end of the Cold War and even more so with the advent of non-traditional threats in nonstate actors. These changes have warranted the global outlook of partnerships for the alliance (Krahmann, 2003). Countries in the PFP program realize numerous benefits to partnership in an increasingly interconnected and dangerous security environment where trust building and information sharing can prevent and deter major attacks. Several PFP member states have recently joined the NATO alliance fully. Most of these new entities are from the former Soviet Union and Balkan region.

The main aspiration of newest members of the alliance is state security and, thus, protection from external attacks provided by the most resourceful security alliance in NATO. While this condition is important to understand, growing literature has also pointed to the power of ideas and socialization effects of liberal norms across Europe and beyond (Schimmelfennig 2000). This literature argues that Western communities transmit their norms to other parts of Europe and beyond, reflecting the socializing power of powerful institutions. The emergence of subsequent institutions facilitates trust and multiplies institutional building among the many nonmember states.

Other scholars have noted the "Europeanization" of foreign policymaking across the continent with increasingly convergent and coordinated national policies (Wong and Hill, 2011). Efforts like the PFP suggest the willingness of states to join binding commitments for the overall improvement of their security position. Even Russia, conventionally against NATO expansion, is a member of the PFP program. The various programs offered by the alliance have been able to win the trust of other nonmember states, because states have come to believe that peace is the primary driver of a nation's economic development and political and social well-being. Thus, some states view full-fledged NATO membership as potentially detrimental to their security and choose to opt for a less binding and more inclusive structure such as PFP. This alternative option has served the interests of the global community well because it falls short of NATO expansion while at the same time increasing cooperation and trust among states. At its core, full-fledged NATO membership is a security alliance with a hierarchy of decision-making. While the United States contributes the most to NATO's budget as of this writing, intra-European politics have historically entangled America's commitments beyond reproach (Ireland, 1981).

Conclusion

While many scholars have questioned the need for NATO in a post-Cold war world and outright called for its dissolution, it has stood the test of time to mold into something that goes beyond a traditional security alliance. The growing institutionalism of the post-Cold war era may have attributed to the adoption of various linkages between nonmember states and NATO. States join institutions such as the PFP program and other nonstate actors participate in the PfPc, where ideas and expertise are shared in order to maximize macrolevel security. The first 1991 pivot away from traditional alliance toward a strategic concept for NATO has proven to be influential in establishing cooperating networks around the world both in the private sector and at the state level. It is likely that we are going to continue to see convergence on security matters among Euro-Atlantic states and their peripheries. Flexible and more efficient security partnerships may be the wave of the future, especially if current avenues of dialogue prove successful.

Further Reading

Larres, Klaus. "North Atlantic Treaty Organization." In DeConde, Alexander, Richard Dean Burns, and Fredrik Logevall, eds. *Encyclopedia of American Foreign Relations: Studies of the Principal Movements and Ideas*, Scribners 2002: 573–593.

Van Ham, Peter. "EU, NATO, OSCE: Interaction, Cooperation, and Confrontation. In *European Security in Transition*, pp. 31–46. Routledge, 2016.
Whitfield, K. (2012) "North Atlantic Treaty Organization." The Wiley-Blackwell Encyclopedia of Globalization.

References

Barany, Zoltan D. "NATO's Peaceful Advance." *Journal of Democracy* 15, no. 1 (2004): 63–76.
Goldgeier, James M. *The Future of NATO*. No. 51. Council on Foreign Relations, 2010.
Ireland, Timothy P. *Creating the Entangling Alliance: The Origins of the North Atlantic Treaty Organization*. No. 50. Greenwood Pub Group, 1981.
Krahmann, Elke. "Conceptualizing security governance." *Cooperation and Conflict* 38, no. 1 (2003): 5–26.
NATO Article V https://www.nato.int/cps/ua/natohq/topics_110496.htm
NATO Partnership for Peace program https://www.nato.int/cps/su/natohq/topics_50349.htm
Schimmelfennig, Frank. "International socialization in the new Europe: Rational action in an institutional environment." *European Journal of International Relations* 6, no. 1 (2000): 109–139.
Wong, Reuben, and Christopher Hill, eds. *National and European Foreign Policy: Towards Europeanization*. Vol. 74. Routledge, 2012.

Chapter 18

Protecting Critical Infrastructure and Key Resources

Russell Richardson Jr.
New England College, Henniker, NH, United States

Contents

Introduction 111
Further Reading 116
References 116

Introduction

It has been determined that the national critical infrastructure and key resources (CIKR) is a key target for those who wish to disrupt or destroy the American way of life. The physical and virtual vulnerabilities inherent within national resources and each sector, coupled with each sector's reliance on one another, render the nation's CIKR unusually susceptible to the threats posed by natural hazards, radicalized individuals ("lone wolves"), and organized terrorist groups. Like a house of cards, our nation's CIKR could possibly collapse upon itself when effectively interrupted if not properly protected. With that said, the Homeland Security Enterprise (HSE) must work together to keep CIKR safe. Even though determining who protects the many, interdependent sectors that comprise critical infrastructure can be confusing; the government, private sector, and public sector are all responsible for protecting CIKR as directed by national legislation.

The HSE is a conglomeration of entities, systems, and resources, a "whole community approach", which participates in a concerted effort to protect American citizens,

DOI: 10.4324/9781315144511-19

critical infrastructure, and national interest. "This enterprise extends far beyond DHS and the many departments and agencies that contribute to our homeland security mission" (U.S. Department of Homeland Security, 2018, par. 1). The responsibility of ensuring homeland security via protecting CIKR can extend as far up as international alliances and all the way down to each individual citizen. "An effective, unified [CIKR protection effort] requires layered, mutually supporting capabilities. The [Whole community] should understand their respective roles and responsibilities and how to complement each other" (U.S. DEPARTMENT OF HOMELAND SECURITY, 2016, p. 8). While some of the CIKR protection responsibilities of the HSE or whole community overlap, particular "bodies of persons" within the whole community retain specific roles and responsibilities of protecting the various sectors that comprise CIKR. Those particular bodies can be separated into three groups: the government, the private sector, and the public sector. The first group to be discussed is the government and the roles and responsibilities it possesses toward protecting CIKR.

When discussing the roles and responsibilities of the government during a crisis or CIKR protection, it must be made clear that government exists at many different levels and consists of hundreds of different sub-organizations that are in charge of the daily operations that support the functioning and protection of infrastructure and society. State, regional (county), local, tribal, and territorial are examples of the various levels of government that must pay close attention to the role they play in protecting CIKR within their area of responsibility. "[The] implementation of the CIKR protection mission requires the cooperation of, and coordination between, Federal departments and agencies; State, Local, tribal, and territorial governments; regional coalitions; private sector owners and operators; and international partners" (Guide to CIKR, 2008a, p. 1). The officials at each of these levels must understand how their level of government is nested within the overall HSE plan to protect CIKR. Due to the complex rules and relationships of the tribal and territorial levels of government, this essay will only focus on the role of local, state, and federal levels of government and their responsibilities as they pertain to protecting CIKR. The local level of government plays an extremely crucial role in CIKR protection.

No matter the disaster, it usually takes place at the local level and initially affects CIKR in varying degrees based on the severity of the interruption. This is due to the local level being the area where the "rubber meets the road". In other words, the local level is where the sectors within critical infrastructure are physically located (dams, commercial/government facilities, nuclear facilities, monuments), where manufacturing takes place (food, chemical, water processing), where operations are conducted (banking, IT, communications, energy), where resources are present (people, water, land), where goods are transported (road, rail, air platforms), and where services are rendered (shipping, health care, emergency services). Due to the close proximity to and direct control of sectors and resources, the local-level government (mayors, councilmen, emergency managers) takes on a more engaged and active role in CIKR protection and is directly responsible for enabling and achieving the protection of CIKR. This mission is accomplished in a variety of ways at the local level.

"Local Governments provide front line leadership for local law enforcement, fire, public safety, environmental response, public health, and emergency medical services for all manner of hazards and emergencies" (Bullock et al., 2013, p. 13). Frontline leadership refers to the actions taken by local-level leaders to reduce the effect of disasters and ensure the infrastructure and resources are safe and functioning properly. It is leadership at the local level in conjunction with guidance and coordination with the private sector and other governmental levels for planning, funding, and resources that facilitate the implementation of policies and procedures, hiring and training of first responders, emplacement of tangible and virtual assets, and public sector disaster prevention and preparedness efforts that enhance the protection of CIKR. The next higher governmental level that best supports the local level is the state level.

The state level of government plays a major support and coordination role during the protection of CIKR within the emergency management arena. "State governments are responsible for establishing partnerships, facilitating coordinated information sharing, and enabling planning and preparedness for CIKR protection within their jurisdiction" (Bullock et al., 2013, p. 173). The state level acts as a conduit between the local and federal levels of government as well as the private sector. The state level links key authorities and capabilities based throughout the governmental levels, and HSE and is prepared to provide the response/recovery assistance required when a disaster exceeds the local-level ability. One unique aspect of the state level of government is how closely it resembles the local level of government. According to David G. Kamien (2012), CEO of Mind-Alliance Systems, "[emergency management] responsibilities of State and Local governments are shared or may even overlap" (p. 594). This is evidenced as both levels of government share similar focuses on CIKR protection outlined by the National Infrastructure Protection Plan (NIPP). An example of this similarity includes, but is not limited to, both levels developing an approach to CIKR identification, mitigation planning, security information sharing, and documenting lessons learned. Two distinct state-level responsibilities are (1) identifying local-level deficiencies and providing response and protection to cover them and (2) formally requesting federal support for situations that exceed local and/or state response capacity. The federal level of government has an important role in CIKR protection as well.

At the federal level, CIKR protection is of the utmost importance as it supports the national objective of protecting citizens, securing the homeland, and preserving national interest at home and abroad. "CIKR protection and restoration mission [is] a vital component of the [Federal], unified approach to domestic incident management" (CIKR Support Annex, 2008b, p. CIKR-2). This level is composed of a myriad of departments, committees, and key positions that are (1) in a constant state of fluctuation and (2) instrumental in ensuring national security and fostering resiliency. The role of the federal level of government in CIKR protection is to provide the national guidance, organizational structure, and resource support required by the local/state levels, private sector, and public sector to ensure the defense and functioning of infrastructure sectors. In order to fulfill the federal level's role, and in response to the horrific events of 9/11, the Department of Homeland Security (DHS) was established in November 2002.

The DHS would be the focal point for emergency management/CIKR protection and restoration efforts by developing policies, coordinating interagency efforts, tasking interagency entities, and procuring funding and resources at the federal level. The DHS CIKR Support Annex (2008b), "charges the Secretary of Homeland Security with responsibility for coordinating the overall national effort to enhance the protection of the CIKR of the United States" (p. CIKR-2). The Federal Emergency Management Agency (FEMA), Transportation Security Administration (TSA), U.S. Customs & Border Protection (CBP), and the U.S. Coast Guard (USCG) are all examples of subordinate DHS agencies that contribute to the national effort of protecting CIKR at the federal level.

Interestingly enough, the federal level has mandated that no federal support will be provided to local, state, or private sector entities unless formally requested. According to David G. Kamien (2012), "the federal government has distinct powers and responsibilities that may be used only to supplement state and local capabilities, and must await a request from state and local governments before it can step in" (p. 594). This forces the local and state levels to employ their emergency management/CIKR protection plans and assets while reducing the doubling of efforts and waste of manpower and resources. The responsibilities and actions of the various government levels to ensure the protection of CIKR can serve as an example for the private sector as they work toward defending their CIKR interests.

The private sector is a body of persons that do not fall directly under the umbrella of a specific level of government but is larger and more organized than the public sector. "Private sector entities include large, medium, and small businesses; commerce, private cultural and educational institutions; and industry; as well as public/private partnerships that have been established specifically for emergency management purposes" (U.S. DEPARTMENT OF HOMELAND SECURITY, 2016, p. 10). These entities play an extremely important role in CIKR protection as they "develop protective programs and measures to ensure that systems and assets, whether physical or virtual, are secure from and resilient to cascading, disruptive impacts" (Bullock et al., 2013, p. 14). Private sector owners are most often the experts in specific infrastructure sectors and can best describe the requirements to protect their specific areas of expertise.

The private sector shoulders most of the responsibility of protecting national CIKR due to the intimate relationship and possession it maintains of this complex system. "The Department of Homeland Security (DHS) indicates that the majority of the nation's critical infrastructure is owned by the private sector" (Peppers, 2013, p. 1). The private sector provides CIKR protection by sharing critical information, conducting strenuous vulnerability/threat/risk assessments, and implementing the physical and virtual barriers necessary to ensure the continuation of CIKR functions. However, the private sector cannot maintain CIKR protection indefinitely and must coordinate with the DHS and various levels of government to ensure CIKR protection deficiencies are fulfilled. The Private-Sector Office, under the DHS sub-component Office of Policy, works to synchronize the efforts of the private sector and the levels of government to ensure CIKR remains protected and resistant to attacks. The private sector and the various levels of government also work with the public sector to protect CIKR.

The public sector can be considered a key resource as people are what's needed to operate, monitor, and protect critical infrastructure. The public sector's attention during CIKR protection is more internally focused. The U.S. DEPARTMENT OF HOMELAND SECURITY (2016: p. 8) supports this idea with the following:

> Although not formally part of emergency management operations, individuals, families, households [and Communities] play an important role

> in emergency preparedness, and response. By reducing hazards in and around homes…individuals reduce potential emergency response requirements. Individuals, families, and households should also prepare emergency supply kits and emergency plans, so they can take care of themselves and their neighbors until assistance arrives. Individuals can also contribute to the preparedness and resilience of their households and communities by volunteering with emergency organizations.

When internal elements of the public sector (individuals, families, households, and communities) focus on their own emergency preparedness, they simultaneously enhance CIKR. "Communities can serve as vital partners and resources for law enforcement to detect and prevent events such as attacks by individual lone-wolf actors" (Kamien, 2012, p. 643). Being aware of their surroundings at the public sector level and sharing their observations with the local level and private sector is a method of security that adds to CIKR protection by preventing and deterring attacks. Another method of security that applies to all levels of government, private sector, and public sector and significantly adds to protecting infrastructure and resources is the development, implementation, reinforcement, and refinement of laws that protect CIKR.

Many attempts by U.S. Presidents to safeguard infrastructure can be found in several pieces of past and present legislation. Presidential Decision Directive (PDD) 63: Protecting America's Critical Infrastructure, directed in 1998 by President Clinton, was a key piece of past CIKR protection as it specifically identified vulnerabilities, clarified roles and responsibilities, and delegated specific tasks which laid the ground work for follow-on CIKR plans and directives. Following on the heels of PPD-63, the events of 9/11 occurred and horrifically solidified the need to protect CIKR as key sectors of infrastructure were infiltrated and attacked. The 9/11 Commission Report (2004), a ten-member committee charged with reviewing the circumstances surrounding the terrorist attacks on September 11, 2001, recommended that, "The DHS…regularly assess the types of threats the country faces to determine…the adequacy of the government's plans – and the progress against those plans – to protect America's critical infrastructure" (p. 428).

This was the catalyst behind many of the integral, legislative actions that the DHS based their CIKR protection focus on such as Homeland Security Presidential Directive (HSPD) 7. "HSPD-7 provides the overarching approach for integrating the Nation's many CIKR protection initiatives into a single national effort" (NIPP, 2006, p. i). This particular HSPD was the basis for the development of the NIPP which meets the national requirements directed in the HSPD-7. The NIPP was the federal level's initiative to further communicate national CIKR protection goals, establish vulnerability/threat/risk assessment guidance, designate roles and responsibilities between the HSE, promote information sharing, and allocate funding and resources. Various updates to NIPP have been published and continue to enhance CIKR protection efforts. While many more guides, annexes, directives, and policies exist to address safeguarding CIKR, the PPD-63, 9/11 Commission Report, HSPD-7, and NIPP have been some of the most instrumental legislation developed in support of the national infrastructure resiliency and restoration plan.

The government, private sector, and public sector are all entities with designated roles and responsibilities within the HSE to safeguard CIKR. They contribute directly to the protection of the nation's CIKR by adhering to specific legislation (PPD-63, 9/11 Commission Report, HSPD-7, NIPP) that outlines how the HSE will work together and accomplish its mission. The duties charged, relationships built, and policies implemented within the HSE regarding the protection of CIKR seems to be effective and will need to be constantly reviewed and redefined in order to continue providing crucial infrastructure safety, security, and resiliency.

Further Reading

Auerswald, P, Branscomb, L. M., La Porte, T. M. & Michel-Kerjan, E. (2005). "The Challenge of Protecting Critical Infrastructure," *Issues in Science and Technology*, *22*(1): 77–83.

Bennett, B. T. (2018). *Understanding, Assessing, and Responding to Terrorism: Protecting Critical Infrastructure and Personnel* (2nd ed). Hoboken: John Wiley & Sons, Inc.

Lewis, T. G. (2020). *Critical Infrastructure Protection in Homeland Security: Defending a Networked Nation* (3rd ed.). Hoboken: John Wiley & Sons, Inc.

References

Bullock, J. A., Coppola, D., & Haddow, G. D., (2013). *Introduction to homeland security*. Burlington, MA: Butterworth-Heinemann.

Kamien, D., (2 Ed.). (2012). *The mcgraw-hill homeland security handbook: Strategic guidance for a coordinated approach to effective security and emergency management*. New York, NY: McGraw-Hill.

National Commission on Terrorist Attacks. (2004). *The 9/11 commission report*. http://govinfo.library.unt.edu/911/report/911Report.pdf.

Peppers, S. (2013). Entrepreneurial Security: A Free-Market Model for National Economic Security. *Homeland Security Affairs*, 91–112. https://eds.a.ebscohost.com/ehost/pdfviewer/pdfviewer?vid=4&sid=da237580-d471-4601-9960-6dd49aaca844%40sessionmgr4007

U. S. Department of Homeland Security. (2006). *National infrastructure protection plan*. Washington DC: Government Printing Office. https://www.dhs.gov/NRF

U. S. Department of Homeland Security. (2008a). *A guide to critical infrastructure and key resources protection at the state, regional, local, tribal, and territorial level*. Washington, DC: Government Printing Office. https://www.dhs.gov/xlibrary/assets/nipp_srtltt_guide.pdf

U. S. Department of Homeland Security. (2008b). *Critical infrastructure and key resources support annex*. Washington, DC: Government Printing Office. https://www.fema.gov/media-library-data/20130726-1914-25045-7032/nrf_support_annex_cikr_20130505.pdf

U. S. Department of Homeland Security. (2016). *National response framework (3rd edition)*. Washington, DC: Government Printing Office. https://www.dhs.gov/NRF

U. S. Department of Homeland Security. (2018). *Strengthening the homeland security enterprise*. Washington, DC: Government Printing Office. https://www.dhs.gov/strengthening-homeland-security-enterprise

Chapter 19

Riots and Rioting

Lora Hadzhidimova
Old Dominion University, Washington, DC, United States

Contents

Introduction 117
Definition 118
Types of Riots and Rioting 119
Participants in Riots 121
Reasons for Riot and Rioting 122
Conclusion 122
Further Reading 122
References 123

Introduction

Riots and rioting are social phenomena with a very long history. While it is not clear when they occurred for the first time, these forms of public disorder could be traced to the times of ancient Rome and ancient Greece. In this historical period, they were an expression of anger against people in power or their decision, ethnic and/or religious groups, or even related to sporting events. At the time, there was no established definition or laws for rioting, but it was clear that the public order was disturbed, and that a measure or even series of measures had to be undertaken to limit the future emergence of riots and their consequences. Frequently in the past, riots resulted in bloodshed, loss of life, and significant property damage. As civil laws increased in number and in efficiency, citizens received rights allowing them to peacefully influence the political apparatus and riots remained an even more unaccepted form of showing disagreement with an institution or an issue.

In modern times, dictatorships severely punish any attempt for obstructing the established order. The laws imposed by authoritarian regimes are quite often

DOI: 10.4324/9781315144511-20

ambiguous, thus, giving the regime freedom to decide when and how to punish disobedience. In contemporary democracies, rioting becomes penalized much less harshly than in the past. Nowadays, anger toward the governing elites and toward issues of importance still exists and with that, riots as well. Sometimes, they are preceded by unsuccessful endeavors to lawfully initiate a desired change in the status quo, and when they fail, in many cases, rioting takes place. Not small in number are also the cases in which riots happen instantaneously, instead of attempts for a peaceful resolution of a conflict or disagreement. Even though legislatures in ancient and medieval times were not as elaborate a mechanism for social control as they are now, riots and rioting in the 21st century are not a rare phenomenon. On the contrary, they are not only occurring often, but in current times, they are even much more complicated by the existence of multiple forces – the struggle for public order and safety, on one hand, and the desire for expressing a certain civic position, on the other.

Definition

Riots and rioting are forms of unlawful behavior, frustration, anger, or any other emotional reaction against institutional structure or person in regard to a social, health, environmental, or political problem. It includes a certain number of people, typically more than three participants, as jurisdictions vary in this, who demonstrate their dissatisfaction or strong affect in a forbidden-by-the-law manner, including but not only limited to violence. They are usually an expression of a perceived loss of control and the struggle to regain it (Brass, 2016).

Riots show some similarities with protests, uprisings, and revolts, but they reveal important differences when compared in depth. In terms of legislation, a clearly stated difference between the aforementioned notions is often not made. National courts typically accept a few practical criteria that distinguish them, although it has to be mentioned that judiciaries across the world could have a quite diverse understanding of the topic. First, the right to protest is one of the most central tenets of democracy implicated by Rousseau's theory of the social contract (Rousseau, 1920). It is a lawful measure that citizens of a particular state could undertake as a sign of disagreement with a political structure or a decision that this structure or its representative has or has not taken. Quite often, even protests have to be specifically allowed by the local authorities in order to take place. Some states do not permit protests or any public gatherings that include more than a certain number of people. Many states with non-democratic regimes do not permit protests. In such cases, it is not rare that the lack of an option for protests engenders other forms of demonstrating social dissatisfaction such as riots and uprisings. Unlike protests, riots do not include any form of organization of the participants, they do not have a common goal that is desired by the group and are not permitted by the law.

Riots do not have ambitions to overthrow the regime as opposed to uprisings and revolutions. While all the other types of civil unrests are directed toward the government or require the latter to enact changes, in riots, quite often the public dissatisfaction is directed toward another social group, rather than to a government structure. Also, riots may or may not include violence as they could merely take the expression of destroying public property which is an unlawful but non-violent act. The World Health Organization (WHO) defines violence as "intentional use of physical force or power, threatened or actual, against oneself, another person, or against a group or community, that either results in or has a high likelihood of resulting in injury, death, psychological harm, maldevelopment or deprivation" (WHO, 2002). Thus, if the definition of riots includes only acts of violence, then it will not account for public disorder caused by property crimes and only violent crimes.

Riots also differ from uprisings/rebellions as well. In cases of uprisings and rebellions, which are frequently encountered in the literature and in the mass media as synonyms, an organized group of people has specific demands from the ruling elite. If the ultimate goal of the uprising/rebellion is to overthrow the existing political regime, then they will flow into another category – the one of revolts/revolutions. Quite often, all of these terms are used interchangeably. The reasons for this are related either to a misunderstanding of what the concepts incorporate or to the practical obstacles in identifying the intent of the collective intent that could lead to different conclusions about the type of the observed civic unrest. The events during the Arab Spring are a useful example in this regard. The words describing them vary from protests, through riots and uprisings, to revolts. While this seems controversial, it is to a large extent corresponding with the different goals that the participants pursued. In some states, the overthrow of the regime was desired as an end goal after the realization that reforms will not be achieved, such as in Tunisia, Egypt, and Libya, while in Iraq and Jordan, reforms and replacement of government figures were sought, instead of changing the entire regime. In third countries, like Syria, protests shifted to a rebellion against the regime of Bashar al-Assad (Lesch and Haas, 2012).

In all of the mentioned forms of civil unrests, it is possible that riots have taken place at some point. Another example in this regard is how the Arab Spring itself began. In the town of Sidi Bouzid, Tunisia, a young vendor named Mohamed Bouazizi set himself on fire in front of the governor's office. His desperation of the poverty, unemployment, humiliation, and abuse by the side of the government was allegedly among the reasons that led to his decision. No specific political agenda was pursued by this violent act, but it was rather an impulsively expressed dissatisfaction with the status quo. However, it was an event disrupting the public order and it was probably intended as one. Therefore, according to the definition above and the features that distinguish the types of civil unrests, while clearly unusual, this case could be perceived as an example of rioting.

Types of Riots and Rioting

There are two types of riots based on the issue that triggers the escalation of emotions. First, the riots could be in response to frustrations caused by an action of the government, and second, by actions of non-governmental structures in the private sector, mostly companies. In the past, the most widespread type of riots was the one that expresses disagreement with the ruling elite or with a particular position or policy but nowadays both categories frequently merge. This type of riots is still the predominant phenomenon in present days because even issues directly related to the private sector are situated in a broader, political context for which government officials are considered responsible. An instance in this regard is the Ford Hunger March in Detroit. The high unemployment in the United States during the Great Depression led to approximately 15 million people losing their jobs, especially in the previously profitable sector of the automobile industry (Baskin, 1972). The protestors intended to hand their demands to the Ford company in Detroit but instead Ford security officers and the local police opened fire against the demonstrators and the rioting began.

Another distinction divides the riots into two groups according to where they occur – in the public space or in a special setting, such as in the military or in prisons. While most of the riots occur in public and thus are disrupting the public order, some other riots violate a special set of rules inherent for some untraditional settings. In order for a form of public disorder to be characterized as a "riot", the latter has to include committing a crime which makes the entire act of rioting punishable.

Different crimes involve different punishments as they could vary significantly across criminal codes. Regardless, unless they involve inflicting death or a severe physical injury, it is unlikely that rioters will receive sentences as serious as in cases in which members of the military are involved as participants. Mainly because the military personnel are supposed to ensure public order, this particular form of disobedience is considered endangering public safety much more than civil unrests. Riots in the military are thus punishable much more severely than if the rioters were civilians. Mutiny, for instance, could have the meaning of either rioting or rebelling, depending on the concrete context of the offense, but in any way, it will imply insubordination and even in democratic countries could be punishable by death.

Another setting where riots could take the form of disobedience to specific rules is in prisons. The disruption of order in these cases is expressed in violations against established behavioral norms and are directed toward the authority that supervises the structure – prison administrators, prison guards, and other prison employees. Therefore, prison riots are frequently punished by separate laws different from the ones for non-inmates. Riots both in prisons and in the military are unique categories mostly because the acts of resistance confront rules of very high significance for the society that are imposed to create and maintain order. Consequently, the constituted punishments for prison riots are designed for special groups of the population that commit violations in regard to their role in the social structure. Such violations threaten the authority to which rioters are subordinated, and hence, they are punished more severely than other citizens because both military and prison structures are assigned a vital role in ensuring the public order in a society.

In addition to the above mentioned distinction, there are two more types of rioting based on the environment in which the harm is inflicted: physical rioting and cyber-rioting. So far, riots and rioting were placed in the context of a physical environment where they cause disruptions of the public order. In the new digital era, perceptions of riots and rioting include not only traditional crimes and disorder. Cybercrimes are a new category in legislatures, technology, engineering, and even the social sciences, and as such, they should be taken into consideration when discussing forms of civil unrests.

As outlined previously, riots include a number of people without a prior organization that disrupt the public order by committing violent and/or property crimes. However, they do not share a common goal and participants in them may have different motivations for committing the acts. Thus, the definition could accommodate cyber behavior as well, namely when a particular group of hackers engages in sabotaging public or private computer systems or use malware. Both social and political issues could be among the reasons for the cyber-rioting. A series of cyberattacks on the Church of Scientology's websites illustrates how rioting in the online space occurs. What triggered the cyber campaign launched initially by the Anonymous was the church's attempt to limit the distribution of a video, circulating in the web-space, that was intended to be shown exclusively to members of the church during a special event. In fact, many of the cyber-riots are related mainly to the right of access to information when the latter is limited or denied by governmental or non-governmental organizations. However, cyber-rioting occurs as a result of political reactions as well. An example in this regard is the cyber actions undertaken by Russian hackers to replace content in Estonian webpages with pro-Russian slogans – a form of retaliation for the demolition of a Soviet monument in Estonia's capital, Tallinn. The cyber-riots were surrounded by physical unrests as well.

Participants in Riots

While in other forms of social unrests, the presence of leaders is sometimes crucial, in the case of riots, leaders are absent. Instead, some inferences could be made about the participants in riots. In the past, privileged groups of the population become the core of riots against underprivileged ones. Destruction of property and infliction of physical injuries to Jews and other immigrant groups were a common occurrence in the medieval and in the modern world history. Riots that have their roots in racial and ethnic tensions are usually a reflection of the fact that "the subordinate group is regarded as an undesirable competitor for services, goods, control of market, and the allocation of occupations" (Dahlke, 1952). After the Civil War was over, African-Americans obtained a new social status but remained to a large extent an underprivileged group and a target of numerous acts of rioting, many of which were committed by the Ku Klux Klan. The driving force between the acts of violence that the members of this movement committed was frustration, anger, and hatred rather than a specific political appeal. In more recent times, it is much more common for underprivileged groups to participate in riots since democratic laws in most countries constituted a wide range of civil and economic rights based on equality between races, ethnicities, genders, and age.

When underprivileged groups consider that the rights declared by the state are not applied in practice, they protest. Often, they fail to achieve their demands through protests as this could cause frustration that rapidly transforms otherwise peaceful protests into riots. Examples include food riots triggered by an increase of food prices in Mauritania, Senegal, Egypt, Yemen, Tunisia, and Venezuela (Bush, 2010). Among the most frequent participants in riots are groups that hold traditionally strong views on certain political and social questions regarding immigration, religion, gender, and economic and environmental issues.

Since riots are not organized and do not have a common goal that the rioters agreed upon, participants could be quite diverse, and their actions could be driven by multiple factors. A large-scale study of riots in England conducted by the Riots

Communities and Victims Panel (2002), revealed five groups of individuals participating in riots. First, rioters who have criminal past. Second, people inclined to use violence and to commit more serious offenses. Third, individuals who came to the place of the riots to loot. Fourth, participants who joined the riots because of feelings of extreme excitement and other overwhelming emotions. Five, people who were just observing the riots but not committing crimes.

Reasons for Riot and Rioting

Among the most interesting questions about riots is the one pertaining to the reasons for the demonstrated aggression. Research shows that factors such as education, the presence/absence of parental role-model and its quality, self-control, unemployment, age, and level of maturity could affect persons' inclination for violence, especially young people's (Riots Communities and Victims Panel, 2002). These elements could become an important explanation for reactions in the context of different socio-political situations: in cases of natural disasters, food shortages, epidemics, and in such where strong reactions are produced as a consequence of environmental, religious, ethnic and economic and social issues, and even from festive events (Marx, 1970).

A combination of both individual and situational features could lead to strong emotions that take the expression of violent behavior. The state and its reaction to riots could also contribute to the presence or the lack of riots in the future. In some cases, expectations for the government to punish rioters severely or not to punish them at all thus encouraging violence could also determine the likelihood of future civil unrests (Wilkinson, 2009).

Conclusion

What are riots and rioting in brief? They are an expression of anger from undesired social and political circumstances. They stand on the borderline between protests and uprisings. They are a violation of the legal and institutional norms of the environment in which they occur. They could be observed both in the physical and the cyberspace. They could be a result of numerous issues and could depend to a large extent on the states' response to them. Therefore, if states succeed to maintain a balance between social and political tensions in society, and the means for social control, then uprisings, revolts, and riots will merely take the form of peaceful protests – constitutionally established and enforced by the public mechanism for influence in every democratic regime.

Further Reading

Cohen, J. (2002). Christian theology and anti-jewish violence in the middle ages: connections and disjunctions. In *Religious Violence between Christians and Jews* (pp. 44–60). Palgrave Macmillan UK.

Kelley, R. D., & Lewis, E. (Eds.). (2000). *To make our world a new: A history of African Americans*. Oxford University Press.
Klier, J. D., & Lambroza, S. (Eds.). (2004). *Pogroms: Anti-Jewish violence in modern Russian history*. Cambridge University Press.

References

Baskin, A. (1972). The Ford hunger march—1932. *Labor History, 13*(3), 331–360.
Brass, P. R. (Ed.). (2016). *Riots and Pogroms*. Springer.
Bush, R. (2010). Food riots: Poverty, power and protest. *Journal of Agrarian Change, 10*(1), 119–129.
Dahlke, H. O. (1952). Race and minority riots-A study in the typology of violence. *Social Forces*, 30:4, 419–425.
Lesch, D., & Haas, M. (Eds.). (2012). *The Arab Spring: Change and Resistance in the Middle East*. Westview Press.
Marx, G. T. (1970). Issueless riots. *The Annals of the American Academy of Political and Social Science, 391*(1), 21–33.
Riots Communities and Victims Panel (2002). After the riots: the final report of the Riots Communities and Victims Panel. http://webarchive.nationalarchives.gov.uk/20121003200027/; http://riotspanel.independent.gov.uk/wp-content/uploads/2012/03/Riots-Panel-Final-Report1.pdf
Rousseau, J. J. (1920). *The Social Contract: & Discourses* (No. 660). JM Dent & Sons.
Wilkinson, S. I. (2009). Riots. *Annual Review of Political Science, 12*, 329–343.
World Health Organization. (2002). *World Report on Violence and Health*. http://www.who.int/violence_injury_prevention/violence/world_report/en/summary_en.pdf

Chapter 20

Secure Border Initiative

Margaret Seymour
Old Dominion University, Washington, DC, United States

Scott N. Romaniuk
China Institute, University of Alberta, Edmonton, Canada

Contents

Launch 125
SBInet 126
Project 28 126
Program Cancellation 126
Further Reading 127
References 127

Launch

The Secure Border Initiative was announced by Department of Homeland Security (DHS) Secretary Michael Chertoff on November 2, 2005. The program was meant to decrease illegal immigration along the southern and northern borders of the United States, bringing both under complete control of the United States by 2010, and organized the four major organizations tasked with border security: (1) Customs and Border Protection (CBP), (2) Immigration and Customs Enforcement (ICE), (3) US Citizenship and Immigration Services (USCIS), and (4) U.S. Coast Guard (USCG).

The initiative sought to improve border security, increase enforcement of laws, and implement a temporary worker program. The program ended the "catch and release" policies of undocumented immigrants from countries other than Mexico, expanded deportation authorities and capacities, and generally increased immigration enforcement in the interior of the United States (American Immigration Council, 20).

DOI: 10.4324/9781315144511-21

The primary goal of the initiative, however, was the implementation of "tactical infrastructure" along the border through the SBInet program.

SBInet

A major component was SBInet, under the authority of the US CBP. The SBInet program was tasked with developing and implementing a hybrid border protection composed of physical (fencing) and technological security (radars, sensors, and communication devices) (GAO, 2007). Boeing was awarded the contract consisting of eight task orders. Those orders are as follows: SBI Program Management at $136 million (September 2006), Project 28 Prototype at $20 million (October 2006), Physical fencing at $122 million (January 2007), Fence Development Laboratory at $700,000 (March 2007), SBInet design at $69 million (August 2007), Project 28 maintenance support at $8 million (December 2007), Command, control, communications, intelligence, and common operating picture (COP) at $65 million (December 2007), and supply chain management solution at $733 million (January 2008) (Lipowicz, 2008).

Project 28

Project 28, a $20.6 million project awarded to Boeing, was intended to be the first segment of the SBInet technology. The project included covering 28 miles of border in Sasabe, Arizona, and required Boeing to provide mobile radar towers, a COP capability, and vehicle-mounted secure laptop terminals integrated with the COP for field agents. The delivery of assets was completed by the intended deadline, but the network was delayed by problems with software integration in addition to delays in the emplacement of physical security features (American Immigration Council, 2010). According to a government affairs office report in 2007, the program was delayed and over budget (GAO, 2007). By the following year, public reports disclosed that Boeing had received over $1 billion toward an estimated $30 billion project (Lipowicz, 2008). An additional review of the program plans in 2008 found that the proposed plans met seven, partially met seven, and failed to meet one of the 15 legislative conditions set by congress (Lipowicz, 2008).

In 2009, the prototype system implemented in Sasabe as part of Project 28 was refined and improved. Construction of the revamped system began in the desert south and west of Tucson, AZ. In the areas where SBInet was emplaced, software glitches often prevented agents from receiving real-time information about possible movements. Wind, rain, and terrain further hindered the network's effectiveness (Wood, 2009). Nonetheless, by 2009, the system had assisted in more than 5,000 apprehensions and detected six tons of smuggled marijuana (Wood, 2009).

Program Cancellation

By 2010, the program had continued to fall below expectations and DHS Secretary Janet Napolitano reallocated $50 million of stimulus funds from the SBInet program to purchase commercial technology to secure the border, stating that, "the system of sensors and cameras along the Southwest border known as SBInet has be plagued with cost overruns and missed deadlines" (Ahlers, 2010, DHS, 2010).

Aside from critiques on missed deadlines and excessive cost, the SBI program faces scrutiny from a policy perspective, with some reports arguing that the program was destined to fail as it wasn't implemented in conjunction with immigration reform (American Immigration Council, 2010). Ultimately, in 2011, Secretary Napolitano canceled the program after 5 years of implementation along 53 miles in two areas of Afghanistan (CNN, 2011). Costing $1 billion by its end, Secretary Napolitano argued that the program did not meet current standards for viability and cost-effectiveness (Preston, 2011).

Further Reading

Ackleson, J. (2003). "Directions in Border Security Research," *The Social Science Journal*, *40*(4): 573–581.

Ackleson, J. (2004). "Constructing Security on the U.S-Mexico Border," *Political Geography*, *24*(2): 165–184.

Doty, R. L. (2007). "States of Exception on the Mexico-U.S. Border: Security, 'Decisions,' and Civilian Border Patrols," *International Political Sociology*, *1*(2): 113–137.

References

Ahlers, M. (2010). "Secure Border Initiative to Undergo Overhaul" *CNN*. March 17, 2010. Retrieved May 1, 2018 from http://edition.cnn.com/2010/US/03/16/us.border.security.initiative/index.html

CNN Wire Staff. (2011). "Homeland Security Chief Cancels Costly Virtual Border Fence." *CNN Wire* Retrieved May 1, 2018 from http://edition.cnn.com/2011/US/01/14/border.virtual.fence/index.html

Lipowicz, A. (2008). "GAO: SBI So Far Nets Boeing More than $1B." *Washington Technology*. June 30, 2008. Retrieved May 1, 2018 from https://washingtontechnology.com/articles/2008/06/30/gao-sbi-so-far-nets-boeing-more-than-1b.aspx.

U. S. Department of Homeland Security. (2010). "*Press Release: Statement by Homeland Security Secretary Janet Napolitano*," March 16, 2010.

U. S. Government Accountability Office. (2007). "*Observations on Selected Aspects of SBInet Program Implementation*." October 24, 2007. Retrieved May 1, 2018 from https://www.gao.gov/assets/120/118258.pdf

Wood, D. B. (2009). "Reboot for 'Virtual' Border Fence." *Christian Science Monitor*. May 15, 2009. Retrieved May 1, 2018 from https://www.csmonitor.com/USA/2009/0515/p02s01-usgn.html

Chapter 21

Smuggling

William R. Patterson
Independent Researcher, United States

Contents

Introduction 129
Multifaceted Threats to Human and State Security 130
Drugs 130
Nuclear Materials 131
Sanctions Busting 132
People Smuggling/Human Trafficking 133
Conclusion 134
Further Reading 135
References 135

Introduction

Smuggling is the illicit transport of materials or persons across legally constituted borders or boundaries. A wide variety of goods can be smuggled, from tobacco products to nuclear material, to human beings. The motives for smuggling are equally diverse. Some people smuggle to avoid taxation, this is especially the case with tobacco and alcohol, while others smuggle because the item itself is illegal, as with drugs or nuclear material. States may engage in smuggling in order to avoid internationally applied sanctions or to obfuscate clandestine activities, such as the development of weapons programs. Human smugglers typically seek to benefit financially either by profiting from the facilitation of illegal migration or through the exploitation of the people within their power as either sex workers or underpaid laborers.

Smuggling adversely impacts both human security and state security in a variety of ways, depending upon the particular form under consideration. The illicit gains amassed by narcotics smuggling, for example, can fuel insurgencies, like that in

DOI: 10.4324/9781315144511-22

Afghanistan, or power transnational criminal organizations such as those prevalent in Mexico. The smuggling of nuclear weapons-related materials presents obvious threats to international security if that material ends up in the hands of rogue states or terrorist organizations. The avoidance of taxation by the smuggling of commodities such as tobacco and alcohol threatens states with the loss of important revenue, which could be used for a variety of expenditures directly related either to security or provision of the public good. Human trafficking potentially increases the threat of terrorism or crime, or in the case of labor exploitation, whether sexual or otherwise, directly threatens the well-being of those being smuggled, along with their loved ones.

States have sought to combat smuggling in numerous ways, including the institution of both domestic and international laws, the establishment of international institutions and organizations, and on some occasions, through the direct application of force. These measures have met with varying levels of success and failure. Overly strict anti-smuggling protocols and enforcement activities can exact unacceptable costs on licit trade and economic activity, so any actions taken against smuggling must be weighed against the cost of their enactment. It is unlikely that any measure or combination of measures will be able to completely eliminate the multifaceted problem of smuggling, but rationally planned and implemented strategies may serve to reduce the magnitude of the problem and ameliorate some of the greatest threats posed by it.

Multifaceted Threats to Human and State Security

The remainder of this entry will focus on particular types of smuggling, the threats they present to both human and state security, and the international measures taken to combat them. The particular issues presented here are by no means exhaustive but are meant to detail the global security concerns that arise from smuggling within particular contexts.

Drugs

Often the first thing that comes to mind when people think of smuggling is drugs, specifically illegal drugs as defined by various domestic laws and international drug control conventions. This is largely because these drugs are, generally speaking, illegal by their very nature and therefore any transportation of them across borders involves smuggling. The non-governmental organization (NGO) Global Financial Integrity estimated in a 2017 report that the annual illicit proceeds from drug trafficking was somewhere between $426 billion and $652 billion US dollars (USD).

In addition to the costs to human health and security, in terms of deaths and disabilities resulting from overdoses, the increased spread of contagious diseases such as HIV/AIDS and Hepatitis C, and lost economic productivity, the massive illicit drug market has clear global security implications. According to the World Drug Report 2017, produced by the United Nations Office on Drugs and Crime (UNODC), transnational criminal organizations (TCOs) derive from between one-fifth to one-third of their total revenues from drug sales. (United Nations Office on Drugs and

Crime, 2018). This income allows these groups to flourish and to diversify into other criminal activities. The danger presented by these types of groups is most clearly displayed in Mexico, where an estimated 150,000 people have been killed and close to 30,000 more have gone missing in the drug war since 2006.

The income from illicit drug smuggling has also fueled insurgent groups around the world. In Colombia, the Revolutionary Armed Forces of Colombia (FARC) bankrolled its decades-long violent opposition to the government, often in the form of terrorist attacks, largely through the illicit drug trade. The same has been true in Afghanistan, where the UNODC estimated that non-State armed groups, such as the Taliban, generated approximately $150 million from the cultivation and trafficking of opiates in 2016 alone. (United Nations Office on Drugs and Crime, 2018).

Due to the international scope of the problem that drug smuggling presents, the efforts of individual states, while necessary, have proven to be insufficient to deal with it. By its very nature, smuggling is a cross-border activity and therefore necessitates a multilateral response. In recognition of this reality, a variety of bilateral, regional, and international institutions and organizations have been developed. The Merida Initiative is an example of a bilateral cooperative arrangement between the United States and Mexico. The Initiative, among other things, involves the provision of financial aid from the United States to improve the capacity of law enforcement, justice, and anti-corruption institutions in Mexico. In Europe, the European Union has developed an EU Drugs Strategy and Action Plan, and Europol, a Europe-wide law enforcement agency, aids in the coordination of law enforcement efforts against drug trafficking that cross national borders. At the international level, the UNODC serves as a clearinghouse of information crucial to understanding the extent of the problem in global terms. There are a plethora of other bilateral, regional, and international organizations, both government and non-governmental, that seek to address this issue. While these institutions have not ended the problem of drug smuggling, and are not likely to in the future, they offer states the opportunity to share information and resources and the ability to mount joint operations and initiatives directed at the problem.

Nuclear Materials

Though much smaller in scope than drug smuggling, the trafficking of nuclear materials and technologies is potentially much more dangerous. Such materials falling into the hands of terrorists could result in catastrophic attacks against civilian populations and when possessed by rogue states, such as North Korea, Iran, or Syria, could be used either for international blackmail or in actual warfare. The Treaty on the Non-Proliferation of Nuclear Weapons, commonly known as the Non-Proliferation Treaty (NPT), first signed in 1968 with an effective timeline of 25 years and then extended indefinitely in 1995, was designed to limit nuclear weapons to those already in possession of them and obligated nuclear weapon states to make good faith efforts toward their complete eradication. The International Atomic Energy Agency (IAEA) was formed in 1957 to advance the peaceful use of nuclear energy while preventing its conversion to military usage. It is the IAEA that is often responsible for inspections of nuclear facilities to ensure compliance with the NPT and other accords.

The magnitude of the problem appears to be small in terms of actual smuggling activity. As researcher Rensselaer Lee has put it, "The true dimensions of the nuclear smuggling business and its implications for international stability and relationships are somewhat ambiguous. Little fissile material of significance and no nuclear warheads appear to circulate in the black market; buyers are elusive; and arrest and seizure statistics provide little evidence participation in the market by rogue states, terrorists, and major transnational criminal syndicates" (Lee, 2006). Lee goes on to say, however, that these appearances may be deceiving as we may not have knowledge of successful smuggling efforts. Furthermore, we do know that such smuggling has been attempted on at least a few additional occasions. Even the successful smuggling of a small amount of nuclear material in a single instance could have major effects. An amount of nuclear material insufficient to make a bomb or other weapon could still potentially be mixed with more conventional explosives, thereby making a dirty bomb. Such dirty bombs do not explode with the power of a nuclear detonation, but they do have the potential to spread radiological materials and thereby greatly enhance the deadliness of an otherwise conventional explosion.

There are two types of smuggling in nuclear materials and technologies: one by individuals or non-state criminal organizations and the other by states themselves. Nuclear smuggling carried out by individuals generally involves theft by people working in nuclear facilities or by others who have access to those facilities (Zaitseva and Hand, 2003). Most of the worry regarding this type of nuclear smuggling focuses on Russia. Fortunately, this activity appears to be rare, but not unheard of. Rensselaer points to a case in 1998 when a plot by employees of a nuclear facility in Chelyabinsk, Russia, to steal highly enriched uranium (HEU) was foiled by Russian law enforcement authorities as an example. The most likely customers for such materials would be either rogue states with ambitions of nuclear power status or terrorist organizations, two of which, Al Qaeda and the Japanese cult Aum Shinrikyo, which notoriously attacked a Japanese subway system with sarin gas, are known to have considered the possibility of obtaining a nuclear device for use as a weapon of terror.

The second type of nuclear smuggling involves state actors. It remains unclear if the A.Q. Khan network, named for Abdul Qadeer Khan, the Pakistani nuclear scientist who directed it, was state-sponsored. Known as "The Father of the Bomb" in Pakistan, Khan was instrumental in Pakistan's own acquisition of nuclear weapons, in contravention of the Non-Proliferation Treaty (NPT). Pakistan continues to deny that the government had any knowledge of Khan's international smuggling activities and Khan was arrested and placed under house arrest in 2004. Some see it as unlikely, however, that his activities could have gone on so extensively and for such a long time without at least tacit approval from the government. According to scholar Molly MacCalman (2016), Khan's smuggling activities spanned nearly two decades and his network involved businesses and accomplices in more than 20 countries. Whether Khan worked alone or with the backing of the Pakistani government, he was likely responsible for the illicit provision of crucial elements to the nuclear programs in North Korea, Libya, and Iran. These states then are responsible as customers in this illicit market.

Sanctions Busting

One reason that states engage in smuggling is to avoid sanctions imposed by international bodies, such as the United Nations (UN). These sanctions are generally imposed as either punishment or deterrence, or both, for some type of internationally prohibited activity and involve restrictions on normally allowable imports and exports. One commodity frequently targeted for sanctioning is oil. Attempts by states to limit the effectiveness of sanctions through smuggling are known as "sanctions busting."

A recent example of sanctions busting involved the Democratic People's Republic of Korea (commonly referred to as North Korea). Over a number of years, the UN placed North Korea under a variety of economic sanctions in an attempt to deter the country from advancing its nuclear program. In December 2017, in the face of repeated nuclear tests, the UN levied sanctions against North Korea that included reducing the amount of refined fuel that it could import by 89%. North Korea was later discovered to be smuggling fuel into the country in violation of those sanctions.

A report issued by the UN further revealed that the North Koreans had generated $270 million in revenues through the smuggling of commodities from which they had been banned or restricted from exporting. The report concluded that "Lax enforcement of the sanctions regime coupled with the country's evolving evasion techniques are undermining the goals of the resolutions that the Democratic People's Republic of Korea abandon all weapons of mass destruction and cease all related programs and activities" (United Nations General Assembly, 2017).

Sanctions busting has serious implications for global security as it diminishes the effectiveness of coercive options short of war. The failure of sanctions to achieve desired outcomes may lead to force being seen as the only available option.

People Smuggling/Human Trafficking

INTERPOL defines people smuggling as "the procurement, for financial or material gain, of the illegal entry into a state of which that person is neither a citizen nor a permanent resident." (INTERPOL, n.d.). This is distinct from human trafficking in that "the individuals who pay a smuggler in order to gain illegal entry to a country do so voluntarily whereas the victims of human trafficking are often duped or forced into entering another country." Both people smuggling and human trafficking often involve the production of false documents, such as passports or other identification paperwork, the use of concealment devices within vehicles, or the exploitation of insecure border areas. In the case of human trafficking, once the victims have reached the country of destination, their passports are usually confiscated by the trafficker, they are often controlled through violence and manipulation, and are frequently forced into becoming sex workers or menial laborers with little or no monetary remuneration.

People smuggling and human trafficking usually involve the movement of people from relatively poor, war-torn, or otherwise unstable countries to wealthier and more stable countries. Illicit migrations from Africa or Asia to Europe and from Latin America to the United States are primary examples. The people involved are often motivated by desperation in the face of poverty or violence to seek new lives in more prosperous countries. The traffickers take advantage of that desperation for their own personal benefit. A report by the International Organization for Migration (IOM) notes that "Limited opportunities for safe and regular migration drives would-be migrants into the hands of smugglers, feeding an unscrupulous trade that threatens the lives of desperate people" (Brian and Laczko, 2014). At the time the report was issued in 2014, the IOM estimated that 40,000 such migrants had died since the year 2000, although the report conceded that the estimate was likely low due to the fact that much of this illegal migration occurs in remote and dangerous areas, such as in deserts and across seas, where the bodies of the deceased are less likely to be discovered.

In addition to the danger posed directly to the people being smuggled/trafficked, this activity victimizes states to the extent that their sovereignty is eroded by the undermining of their immigration policies and poses potential danger in terms of economic harms (in terms of job competition and wage reduction as well as the provision of social services), criminality, and terrorism. By circumventing the state's ability to prevent the migration of criminal or terrorist actors, there is a possibility that criminals and terrorists will infiltrate the state through people smuggling. A study published in the journal *Terrorism and Political Violence* in 2006 examined the immigration status of 373 charged, convicted, or killed terrorists in North America and Western Europe and determined that 6% entered the country in which the event took place illegally.

In terms of criminality, a review of the empirical literature conducted by scholars Matthew T. Lee and Ramiro Martinez, Jr. found that in overall terms immigration has actually had a downward pressure on crime, at least in the United States (Lee and Martinez, 2009). Undocumented immigration in particular, however, is still problematic in terms of criminality, at least in some circumstances. Criminal gangs, such as Mara-Salvatrucha-13 (MS-13), are pointed to as being heavily dominated by undocumented immigrants. In fact, legal scholar Kris Kobach notes that 90% of MS-13's membership is composed of illegal immigrants and that the Latin Kings gang specifically targets illegal immigrants for recruitment (Kobach, 2008). How substantially illegal immigration affects overall crime rates, however, remains controversial. A 2016 study conducted by David Green in the United States found only a weak correlation between undocumented immigrants and overall violent crime that did not reach standard levels of statistical significance (Green, 2016). The same study did find a statistically significant, though still weak, correlation between undocumented immigrants and drug arrests.

Conclusion

Smuggling is a serious transnational problem with the potential to undermine global security in myriad ways and negatively impact the lives of human beings around the world. Although this entry has focused on a few examples of smuggling, there are many more. Almost anything that is illegal or regulated can be, and has been, smuggled. Diamond smuggling in Africa has fueled crime and conflict throughout the continent; the smuggling of natural resources, such as timber and wildlife, has negatively impacted the environment and had pernicious economic effects on numerous developing countries; and the trafficking of small arms has increased violence around the globe.

International smuggling has been facilitated by globalization and the massive increase in global trade that it has entailed. Smugglers have been able to capitalize on the enormous size and speed of legal international trade to hide their own illicit activities. Money laundering has grown hand-in-hand with smuggling, and indeed, most smuggling activities would collapse without the ability to launder the ill-gotten proceeds to avoid scrutiny.

States have reacted to various forms of smuggling in a variety of ways. These include the passage of domestic legislation aimed at the problem, the formation of bilateral agreements and cooperative efforts, and the establishment of regional and global international institutions with the purpose of collating information and coordinating law enforcement and other responses. In the face of these efforts, however, smuggling in many of its forms has continued to grow and represents an increasing threat not only to individual lives but also to global security writ large. Smuggling is a global challenge that will continue to demand national and international action for the foreseeable future.

Further Reading

Andreas, Peter, "Criminalizing Consequences of Sanctions: Embargo Busting and Its Legacy," *International Studies Quarterly*, Vol. 49, 2005, pp. 335–360.

Chestnut, Sheena, "Illicit Activity and Proliferation," *International Security*, Vol. 32 Issue 1, (Summer 2007), pp. 80–111.

Thachuk, Kimberly, ed., *Transnational Threats: Smuggling and Trafficking in Arms, Drugs, and Human Life*, Westport, CT: Praeger Security International, 2007.

References

Brian, Tara and Frank Laczko (eds.), *Fatal Journeys: Tracking Lives Lost During Migration*, International Organization for Migration, 2014.

Channing, May, "Transnational Crime and the Developing World," *Global Financial Integrity*, March 27, 2017. http://www.gfintegrity.org/report/transnational-crime-and-the-developing-world/. Accessed on 19 February 2018.

Green, David, "The Trump Hypothesis: Testing Immigrant Populations as a Determinant of Violent and Drug-Related Crime in the United States," *Social Science Quarterly*, Vol. 97, No. 3, September 2016, pp. 506–524.

INTERPOL, "People Smuggling," https://www.interpol.int/Crime-areas/Trafficking-in-human-beings/People-smuggling

Kobach, Kris W., "Reinforcing the Rule of Law: What States Can and Should Do to Reduce Illegal Immigration," *Georgetown Immigration Law Journal*, Vol. 22, 2008, pp. 459–483.

Lee, Matthew T. and Ramiro Martinez, Jr., "Immigration Reduces Crime: An Emerging Scholarly Consensus," *Immigration, Crime, and Justice (Sociology of Crime, Law, and Deviance Vol. 13)*, 2009: Emerald Group Publishing Limited, pp. 3–16.

Lee, Rensselaer, "Nuclear Smuggling, Rogue States and Terrorists," *China and Eurasia Forum Quarterly*, Vol. 4, No. 2, 2006, pp. 25–32.

Leiken, Robert S. and Steven Brooke, "The Quantitative Analysis of Terrorism and Immigration: An Initial Exploration," *Terrorism and Political Violence*, Vol. 18, Issue 4, 2006, pp. 503–521.

MacCalman, Molly, "A.Q. Khan Nuclear Smuggling Network," *Journal of Strategic Security*, Vol. 9, No. 1, 2016, pp. 104–118.

United Nations General Assemby, S/2017,742, 05 September 2017, http://www.un.org/ga/search/view_doc.asp?symbol=S/2017/742 on 02/11/2018

United Nations Office on Drugs and Crime, "World Drug Report 2017," https://www.unodc.org/wdr2017/index.html Accessed on 19 February 2018.

Zaitseva, Lyudmila and Kevin Hand, "Nuclear Smuggling Chains," *American Behavioral Scientist*, Vol. 46, Issue 6, February 2003, pp. 822–844.

Chapter 22

The Bureau of Alcohol, Tobacco, Firearms, and Explosives (ATF)

William R. Patterson
Independent Researcher, United States

Contents

Introduction 138
Historical Overview 138
Enforcement Responsibilities 139
 Alcohol 139
 Tobacco 139
 Firearms 140
 Explosives 141
 Arson 142
Significant and Controversial Historical Events 142
 Ruby Ridge 142
 Waco, Texas 143
 The Oklahoma City Bombing 143
Operation Fast and Furious 144
Conclusion 144
Further Reading 145
References 145

DOI: 10.4324/9781315144511-23

Introduction

The Bureau of Alcohol, Tobacco, Firearms, and Explosives (ATF) is a federal law enforcement agency under the umbrella of the U.S. Department of Justice. As of 2015, the ATF had 5,026 employees, 2,618 of whom were special agents, and had a total operating budget of $1,201,000. The ATF's mission, as stated on its website, is "to protect communities from violent criminals, criminal organizations, the illegal use and trafficking of firearms, the illegal use and storage of explosives, acts of arson and bombings, acts of terrorism, and the illegal diversion of alcohol and tobacco products." (ATF Website, 2018).

Historical Overview

It was only in 2003, pursuant to Title IX of the Homeland Security Act of 2002, that the ATF was permanently incorporated into the Department of Justice. Prior to that, except for a brief time in 1930, it was a part of the Department of the Treasury. Throughout its history, the ATF (and its forerunners) has gone through a variety of changes and iterations. Although the organization's origins are traced to various beginnings (some trace its history all the way back to the passage of the Domestic Tax on Alcohol and Tobacco Act of 1791), its most clear and direct roots stem from Prohibition. In 1920, the Prohibition Unit, later reorganized and renamed the Bureau of Prohibition in 1927, was created under the Bureau of Internal Revenue, itself under the Department of the Treasury. The unit was formed for the purpose of enforcing the Volstead Act, more formally known as the National Prohibition Act of 1919, and the 18th Amendment, which banned the production, sale, and transportation of alcohol. The enforcement officers of this unit were often referred to colloquially as "Dry Agents."

The Bureau of Prohibition was transferred to the Department of Justice in 1930 as the violence associated with the enforcement of Prohibition laws escalated. It was during this era that the organization's most famous crime fighter, Eliot Ness, was active in taking down the likes of Al Capone. When Prohibition ended in 1933, the Prohibition Unit briefly became the Alcohol Beverage Unit within the Federal Bureau of Investigation (FBI) before being transferred back to the Department of the Treasury as the Alcohol Tax Unit (ATU). Though Prohibition was over and it was again legal to produce, transport, and sell alcohol, this renewed business required regulation and tax collection, which fell under the purview of the ATU.

The responsibilities of the ATU were soon expanded to include enforcement of the National Firearms Act of 1934 and the Federal Firearms Act of 1938. In the wake of the assassinations of President John F. Kennedy, his brother Robert Kennedy, and Martin Luther King, Jr. in quick succession in the 1960s, the Gun Control Act of 1968 was passed. The ATU was again reorganized and rebranded as the Alcohol and Tobacco Tax Division (ATTD) and given responsibility for the enforcement of the Gun Control Act in addition to its previously assigned duties. In 1972, the Bureau of Alcohol, Tobacco, and Firearms itself was born. The functions of the ATTD were removed from the Internal Revenue Service and transferred to the ATF as a newly formed and independent organ of the Department of the Treasury. Finally, in 2002, the word Explosives was appended to the agency's name.

Enforcement Responsibilities

Alcohol

Alcohol is the A in ATF and goes back to the very beginnings of the agency's history. It was the regulation and taxation of alcohol that ATF's forerunner organizations were tasked with undertaking. Since 2003, however, the regulation of alcohol, particularly in regard to its manufacture and taxation, has been moved to the newly created Alcohol and Tobacco Tax and Trade Bureau which is housed within the Department of the Treasury. As a result, the ATF has refocused its own efforts on the connection between illicit alcohol sales and organized crime. The ATF website notes that its Alcohol and Tobacco Enforcement Programs seeks "…to target, identify, and dismantle criminal enterprises with ties to violent crime, that traffic illicit liquor or contraband tobacco in interstate commerce; seize and deny their access to assets and funds; and prevent their encroachment into the legitimate alcohol and tobacco industry." (ATF Website, 2018). In other words, as it regards alcohol, the ATF has become a law enforcement, rather than both a law enforcement and regulatory, agency. Its primary targets are violent criminal organizations that seek to profit from and evade taxation through the interstate smuggling of alcohol.

Tobacco

As with alcohol, the ATF's regulatory role regarding cigarettes has been largely, though not entirely, eclipsed by its focus on the investigation of illicit trafficking in accordance with the Contraband Cigarette Act of 1978 and the Prevent All Cigarette Trafficking Act (PACT) of 2009. As with illicit alcohol sales, a primary goal of ATF's tobacco enforcement efforts revolves around denying criminal and terrorist organizations the ability to profit from such activity. Because cigarettes are so highly taxed, they are one of the most smuggled commodities in the world (Shelley and Melzer, 2008). In the United States, where tobacco taxes differ among states, there is profit incentive to smuggle cigarettes from low-tax states to high-tax states where the smugglers can sell them at a profit but still below the local price.

The potential profits to be made by tobacco smuggling have not gone unnoticed by criminal organizations. According to William Billingslea, a Senior Intelligence Analyst with ATF, the agency has "…found that Russian, Armenian, Ukrainian, Chinese, Taiwanese, and Middle Eastern (mainly Pakistani, Lebanese, and Syrian) organized crime groups are highly involved in the trafficking of contraband and counterfeit cigarettes and counterfeit tax stamps for profit" (2004). And in at least two cases, tobacco smuggling within the United States has been used by Hezbollah, a Lebanese terrorist organization, to garner funding for its terrorist activities. The cells were illegally smuggling cigarettes from North Carolina, where they are lightly taxed, to Michigan, where they are more heavily taxed. The proceeds of this activity were used to support the organization's activities in Lebanon and to purchase dual-use equipment. Although the total profit realized by the group from this smuggling activity is unknown, it is estimated to have been between $1.5 and $2.5 million by the time the ring was discovered and dismantled (Shelley and Melzer, 2008).

Firearms

More than anything else, the enforcement of firearms-related laws has become the defining mission of the ATF. The first federal legislation regarding firearms was the National Firearms Act of 1934. This act focused on the regulation and taxation of machine guns, sawed-off shotguns, and silencers, which were being used primarily by gangsters involved in illicit alcohol production, transport, and sale. Since it was the ATU that was investigating the underlying alcohol-related offenses and was most often coming in contact with those gangsters, it was ATU that was given primary responsibility for enforcing the act. The ATU was also tasked with enforcing the Federal Firearms Act, passed in 1938. This act regulated the interstate transportation of firearms and ammunition and required licensing of manufacturers, dealers, and importers who were engaged in interstate commerce. It placed restrictions on ownership by certain convicted felons, fugitives, and persons under indictment. The act also imposed regulations on firearms manufacturers and importers regarding requisite markings on firearms and record-keeping procedures (Zimring, 1975).

Passage of the Gun Control Act in 1968 solidified ATF's (at that time known as the ATTD) role in enforcing firearms laws. This law prohibited the shipment of firearms between states by anyone other than a licensed dealer, importer, manufacturer, or collector. It also established that the businesses of manufacturing and dealing of firearms required a federal license. The act also prohibited possession of firearms by minors, convicted felons, users of illegal drugs, and those adjudicated to be mentally ill. Dealers were prohibited from selling guns to residents of other states and were required to obtain identification from buyers proving their state of residence. The act also limited or prohibited the importation of certain types of firearms (Zimring, 1975). In addition to firearms, the bill also introduced regulations on explosives.

This law had a major impact on the ATTD and was the greatest impetus toward its rebirth as the ATF. William Vizzard notes that between 1968, when the bill was passed, and 1972, when the ATTD became the ATF, the law enforcement element of the organization doubled and firearms, rather than alcohol, became its main focus. As Vizzard put it, "Among all the forces that would shape the future ATF, the Gun Control Act was distinctly, the most important. From the moment it was passed, things were never the same" (Vizzard, 1997).

The Gun Control Act of 1968 was amended by the Brady Handgun Violence Prevention Act of 1993, often referred to as the Brady Bill. This law requires that all Federal Firearms Licensees conduct background checks on those to whom they transfer firearms. In order to accomplish this, the Attorney General was tasked with establishing the National Instant Criminal Background Check System (NICS), which is run by the FBI. Another major bill was aimed not at enhancing the ATF's ability to enforce gun laws but to constrain or limit them. The Firearms Owners' Protection Act of 1986 limited ATF's regulatory powers in two ways. The first was that it limited ATF audits of dealers to once annually. The second was that it prohibited the establishment and maintenance of a firearms registry. This bill also banned the possession of fully automatic machine guns manufactured after May 19, 1986.

The enforcement of the federal firearms laws created by the above legislation has become the predominant function of the ATF. Though these laws apply to everyone, the ATF focuses its efforts where they will have the most impact on reducing violent crime. According to its website, "ATF recognizes the role that firearms play in violent crimes and pursues an integrated regulatory and enforcement strategy. Investigative priorities focus on armed violent offenders and career criminals, narcotics traffickers, narco-terrorists, violent gangs, and domestic and international arms traffickers." (ATF Website, 2018). By prioritizing investigations targeting the most dangerous offenders, the ATF seeks to have the biggest impact on reducing gun violence while reducing the perception of some gun rights advocates that the organization is a danger to the freedom of law-abiding citizens to possess firearms.

In addition to its own investigations, the ATF works to assist local law enforcement agencies in their efforts to combat firearms-related crimes. One way they do this is through the establishment of ATF Task Forces, which develop partnerships with other federal and local agencies. Another is with its eTrace system. With this internet-based system, law enforcement officers from any jurisdiction can enter in the particulars of a firearm (make, model, serial number, etc.) and ATF traces its origins through the manufacturer, to the retailer, and then to the original purchaser. This assists the ATF, and local law enforcement agencies, in determining how criminals came into possession of firearms and also helps detect patterns that are indicative of trafficking.

Though the enforcement of federal firearms laws was tasked to ATF's forerunner agencies, mainly due to the prevalence of gun violence around Prohibition enforcement, this element of its mission has become the organization's primary *raison d'etre.* This is demonstrated by the massive disparity in the types of cases investigated by the ATF on an annual basis. In the year 2016, for example, the ATF initiated criminal investigations into more than 30,000 firearms-related cases and less than 4,000 investigations in all other areas (explosives, alcohol/tobacco, and arson) combined.

Explosives

ATF first gained jurisdiction over explosives cases pursuant to the Gun Control Act of 1968, which went beyond firearms regulations and included regulations on explosives. Bombs, missiles, artillery, land mines, and various other explosive devices were required to be registered and their transfer between persons was taxed. ATF's role in explosives regulation and enforcement activity was expanded with the Explosives Control Act passed in 1970 as part of the Organized Crime Control Act. This legislation assigned joint jurisdiction to both the ATF and the FBI. The ATF also enforces the Safe Explosives Act which requires federal licensing to use or possess certain explosives. According to the ATF website, "Explosive materials are any chemical compound, mixture, or device, the primary or common purpose of which is to function by explosion. The term includes, but is not limited to, dynamite and other high explosives, black powder, pellet powder, initiating explosives, detonators, safety fuses, squibs, detonating cord, igniter cord, and igniters." (ATF Website, 2018).

ATF's role in explosives investigations was highlighted in 1985 when it was the lead agency responsible for investigating a string of abortion clinic bombings. The investigation resulted in the arrest and conviction of three suspects involved in highly publicized abortion clinic bombings in the Washington, DC, area. This success brought nationwide attention to the agency and solidified its reputation as being the premier law enforcement agency for the investigation of this type of crime (Vizzard, 1997).

Arson

The ATF used its jurisdiction over explosives cases to expand into the investigation of commercial arson. Arson is defined as the intentional damage of property through the use of fire. Title XI of the Organized Crime Control Act of 1970 gives ATF jurisdiction over cases involving the destruction of any business involved in interstate commerce by means of explosives. Given that most accelerants used to commit arsons are also technically considered explosive materials, the ATF has acquired jurisdiction over commercial arsons. The Anti-Arson Act, 1982 further clarified ATF jurisdiction over this crime.

As the recognized leader in arsons investigations, the ATF has developed elite training courses in this field. ATF runs a Fire Research Laboratory and a Certified Fire Investigator School. To become a Certified Fire Investigator (CFI) requires passing a rigorous two-year course which includes fire scene examination and fire dynamics. Additionally, ATF offers a variety of Arson and Explosives Training programs available to other federal and local agencies. The ATF is also engaged in data accumulation and maintains BATS, the Bomb Arson Tracking System. This system collates arson- and explosives-related data and makes that data available to investigative agencies around the country.

Significant and Controversial Historical Events

Ruby Ridge

During the 1980s, white supremacist and anti-government groups began drawing the attention of law enforcement due to large increases in their membership and involvement in criminal activity. In 1987, while investigating one such group called the Aryan Nation, an ATF informant came in contact with a man named Randy Weaver who was a dedicated Christian Identity and anti-government advocate. Weaver sold two illegal shotguns to the informant and a warrant was obtained for his arrest. ATF agents were able to arrest Weaver in 1990 on charges related to the sale. Weaver posted bond but then failed to appear in court.

Weaver's failure to appear resulted in the case being handed over to the U.S. Marshal's Service to secure his re-arrest. After numerous attempts to convince Weaver to turn himself in, deputy marshals began surveilling his secluded home in Idaho in an effort to recapture him. During this surveillance, Weavers' dog scented the officers and began following them. Randy Weaver's 14-year-old son Sammy and one of his friends, both armed, also began following the marshals. The details of how the following events unfolded remain in dispute, but one of the deputy marshals shot Weavers' dog, Sammy's friend Kevin Harris shot and killed Deputy Marshal William Degan, and one of the deputy marshals shot and killed Sammy Weaver.

These events resulted in nearly a week-long standoff between federal law enforcement agents and the remaining members of the Weaver family at their home in Ruby Ridge. Kevin Harris and Randy Weaver were both injured by gunfire during the course of the siege, and Randy's wife Vicki was inadvertently killed while an FBI sniper was shooting at Harris. Both Randy Weaver and Harris eventually surrendered and were later acquitted of all charges, other than a conviction against Weaver for failing to appear at his scheduled court hearing. The government eventually paid Weaver a $3.1 million settlement subsequent to a law suit (Vizzard, 1997).

Though ATF was not involved in any of the shootings or in the siege of Weaver's Ruby Ridge residence, the fact that they initiated the charges which led to the stand-off resulted in substantial anti-ATF sentiment among some quarters, particularly among the sorts of anti-government groups of which Weaver was a member.

Waco, Texas

The events that transpired in 1993 near Waco, Texas, were among the most tragic in law enforcement history, and certainly, the most tragic in ATF history. The ATF had been investigating a group calling itself the Branch Davidians who were led by an individual who had assumed the name David Koresh (his actual name was Vernon Wayne Howell) for various firearms and explosives crimes related to an arsenal of weapons that the group was stock-piling. The ATF secured a warrant for Koresh's arrest and attempted to serve the warrant on February 28, 1993, by raiding the Branch Davidian Mount Carmel Compound where the group had secluded itself.

The results were immediately disastrous. A shooting match erupted in which four ATF agents were killed and 28 were injured. Four Branch Davidians were injured and six were killed (five during the raid and one later). Koresh himself was injured but remained in control of the compound. The ATF subsequently surrendered jurisdiction over the situation to the FBI which initiated a siege of the compound that lasted 51 days. The FBI eventually moved in on the compound and a fire, started by the Branch Davidians themselves, along with the intentional suicides of some of the occupants, resulted in the deaths of 76 people. Among the dead were a large number of children and Koresh himself. Thirty-five Branch Davidians left the compound during the course of the siege and nine escaped after the fires were started during the final raid. In the aftermath of the event, nine surviving Branch Davidians were convicted of manslaughter and various weapons-related charges.

Though ATF played only a minor support role in the siege and final assault on the compound, it was heavily criticized for its planning of the initial raid. This event further inflamed the sentiments of anti-government radicals and would lead directly to another, even greater, tragedy: the bombing of the Alfred P. Murrah Federal Building in Oklahoma City, Oklahoma.

The Oklahoma City Bombing

Timothy McVeigh, an anti-government activist and U.S. Army veteran, was motivated in large part by anger over both the Ruby Ridge and Waco incidents. McVeigh was assisted in the planning and preparation phases of the attack by Terry Nichols and in the initial stages by Michael Fortier, who would later testify against both McVeigh and Nichols. The bombing was carried out on April 19, 1995 – the second-year anniversary of the final raid at the Branch Davidian compound. The primary criteria for target selection were that the target is a federal office building that housed at least two federal law enforcement agencies from among the ATF, the FBI, or the Drug Enforcement Administration (DEA). The Alfred P. Murrah building housed offices for both the ATF and the DEA, as well as the Secret Service and other federal agencies and departments.

McVeigh and Nichols manufactured a massive bomb out of fertilizer, fuel, and other chemicals which McVeigh loaded into a truck, parked alongside the building, and detonated. The explosion resulted in the deaths of 168 people, 19 of whom were children. Nearly 700 people were injured. Buildings and vehicles were damaged in a large radius around the building, causing hundreds of millions of dollars in damage. McVeigh, Nichols, and Fortier were all convicted for their roles in the attack. McVeigh was executed. Nichols was convicted of multiple life terms, and Fortier, after cooperating with authorities, was fined $75,000 and sentenced to 12 years in prison, of which he served ten before being released into the Witness Protection Program. In 1997, the Oklahoma City National Memorial and Museum was established to honor the victims of the attack.

Operation Fast and Furious

One of ATF's primary goals is to target firearms traffickers, both domestically between states and across U.S. borders. Gun smuggling across the U.S.–Mexico border to notoriously violent Mexican drug cartels and transnational criminal organizations has been an increasingly visible problem. One estimate dealing with the years 2010–2012 found that slightly more than 2% of all gun sales in the United States, totaling around 200,000 firearms, were for the purpose of trafficking to Mexico (McDougal, et al., 2015). In an effort to combat this problem, the ATF developed Project Gunrunner and its offshoot Operation Fast and Furious.

Operation Fast and Furious began in September 2009 with the purpose of identifying the end receivers of firearms trafficked into Mexico. In typical sting operations, ATF officers would arrest the person making an actual straw purchase – a purchase intended not for the purchaser him/herself but for someone else who directed the purchase and to whom the firearm would be trafficked – at, or shortly after, the time of purchase. The concept of Operation Fast and Furious was to allow the trafficked firearms to go further up the chain so that those who were actually directing the trafficking, rather than those who merely carried it out at the lowest level, could be identified and prosecuted.

In pursuit of that objective, ATF officers allowed firearms to be illegally purchased and trafficked without stopping the transport of the firearms or arresting the low-level traffickers. These officers hoped to be able to keep track of the firearms through the use of informants, wiretaps, surveillance, and even GPS devices implanted on the weapons themselves. Those methods failed in many instances and the ATF lost track of some of the 2,000 firearms that were allowed to be transported to Mexico. Many began to be recovered at crime scenes, including several at the murder scene of a Border Patrol agent in Arizona. The failed operation turned into a scandal that engulfed the agency in Congressional investigations for years (Young, 2012).

Conclusion

The ATF's name, mission, and parent organization have all varied throughout the organization's controversial, but important, history. Developed to combat illegal alcohol production and sales during the Prohibition era, the ATF's mission today is most focused on firearms-related crimes, but also engaged in investigations of explosives cases, arsons, and tobacco smuggling. Despite controversial episodes in its history, the ATF provides vital law enforcement expertise in its areas of responsibility and plays a crucial role in safeguarding the American homeland.

Further Reading

Bureau of Alcohol, Tobacco, Firearms and Explosives, *Federal Firearm Regulations Reference Guide*, 2017.

Garrett, Terence M., "The Waco, Texas, ATF Raid and Challenger Launch Decision: Management, Judgment, and the Knowledge Analytic," *American Review of Public Administration*, Vol. 31, No. 1, 2001, pp. 66–86.

Moore, James, *Very Special Agents*, Urbana and Chicago: University of Illinois Press, 2001.

References

ATF Website, www.atf.gov, downloaded on 24 February 2018.

Billingslea, William, "Illicit Cigarette Trafficking and the Funding of Terrorism," *The Police Chief*, Vol. 71, No. 2, February 2004.

McDougal, Topher L., David A. Shirk, Robert Muggah and John H. Patterson, "The Way of the Gun: Estimating Firearms Trafficking across the US-Mexico Border," *Journal of Economic Geography*, Vol. 15, Issue 2, 2015, pp. 297–327.

Shelley, Louise I. and Sharon A. Melzer, "The Nexus of Organized Crime and Terrorism: Two Case Studies in Cigarette Smuggling," *International Journal of Comparative and Applied Criminal Justice*, Vol. 32, Issue 1, Spring 2008.

Vizzard, William J. *In the Cross Fire: A Political History of the Bureau of Alcohol, Tobacco and Firearms*. Boulder, CO: Lynne Rienner Publishers, 1997.

Young, Stewart M., "Going Nowhere Fast (or Furious): The Nonexistent U.S. Firearms Trafficking Statute and the Rise of Mexican Drug Cartel Violence," *University of Michigan Journal of Law Reform*, Vol. 46, Issue 1, 2012, pp. 1–67. https://mjlr.org/category/print/volume-46/ Accessed 27 February 2018.

Zimring, Frank E., "Firearms and Federal Law: The Gun Control Act of 1968," *The Journal of Legal Studies*, Vol. 4, 1975, pp. 133–198.

Chapter 23

The National Biosurveillance Integration Center (NBIC)

Wayne Lesperance

New England College, Henniker, NH, United States

Contents

Introduction 147
Origins of the NBIC 148
The NBIC at Work 148
National Health Challenges 148
External Requests for Support 149
NBIC's Outreach 150
Future Considerations 150
Further Reading 150
References 151

Introduction

In December 2017, Department of Homeland Security (DHS) Secretary Kirstjen Nielsen established the Countering Weapons of Mass Destruction (CWMD) Office. Within this new organizational structure, the functionality of the former National Biosurveillance Integration Center (NBIC) can be found. The new CWMD Office incorporated the former Nuclear Detection Office and a majority of the Office of Health Affairs along with other functions within the DHS.

The December 2017 reorganization plucked the NBIC from the Office of Health Affairs and positioned its work more prominently alongside other, complimentary threats associated with Weapons of Mass Destruction. Such reorganization reflects a change in emphasis from naturally occurring diseases and illnesses such as the

DOI: 10.4324/9781315144511-24

EBOLA virus and ZIKA to weaponized threats from hostile powers and groups. Such an approach is more in line with the current administration's focus on external threats.

Origins of the NBIC

The NBIC was created as a result of 9/11 Commission Act of August 3, 2007. Organizationally part of the broader DHS, the organization was housed under the Office of Health Affairs.

The NBIC's mission as described in the Act was to, "… disseminate alerts and other information to Member Agencies and, in coordination with (and where possible through) Member Agencies, to agencies of State, local, and tribal governments, as appropriate, to enhance the ability of such agencies to respond to a biological event of national concern" (Public Law 110-53, 2007: 121 Stat. 375).

Functionally, the NBIC had two primary areas of operational interest. First, the Center served as the chief agency responsible for national biosurveillance. In this role, it was tasked with maintaining situational awareness of all threats, naturally occurring and human made, of a biological nature. The second area of interest was to collaborate with the broader national security community to "acquire, integrate, analyze, and disseminate information pertaining to emerging biological events and their impact on US interests" (Bennett, n.d.: 4).

In November 2012, the DHS issued its National Biosurveillance Integration Center Strategic Plan. This strategic plan reflected the wisdom of the National Biosurveillance Integration System, an interagency community of biological threat professionals and organizations. The strategic plan identified the following goals and objectives which remained the focus of the organization throughout its existence:

- Build and maintain enduring processes to support interagency collaboration and operations through the NBIS and other partnerships.
- Enhance federal government ability to rapidly identify, characterize, localize, and track a biological event of national concern.
- Enhance federal government ability to disseminate alerts and other information to partners and stakeholders.
- Mature and strengthen NBIC into a world-class biosurveillance analysis and integration organization (The White House, 2012).

In each of these strategic goals, the NBIC serves as an integrating force on a variety of levels, including within the DHS, among agencies of the federal government, between federal and state and local agencies, among private sector groups and non-profits focused on potential biological threats, and the public at large.

The NBIC at Work

National Health Challenges

Two contemporary examples of the NBIC at work can be found in April 2013 with a call for an NBIC response to the H7N9 Avian Influenza Virus and the MERS-CoV

Middle East Respiratory Syndrome Coronavirus. In both cases, the NBIC was tasked with coordinating interagency resources of the US Federal Government along with state and local resources and relevant nonprofit partners in response to growing concerns about both illnesses associated with the viruses mentioned above.

In practice, this tasking meant that NBIC would do the following:

- Monitored developments of infection both in the United States and abroad.
- Established and host weekly interagency calls.
- Coordinated interagency activities, including significant efforts from the Centers for Disease Control and Prevention (CDC) and the United States Department of Agriculture (USDA).
- Coordinated distribution of reports to the Association of State and Territorial Health Officials (ASTHO) and the National Association of County and City Health Officials (NACCHO) with the CDC Influenza Coordination Unit and the CDC National Center for Immunization and Respiratory Diseases.

As part of its work, the NBIC worked with its partners to develop coordination opportunities for future H7N9 and MERS-CoV issues such as:

- Established operating protocols through relationships with USDA Animal and Plant Health Inspection Service (APHIS) and National Security Staff (NSS).
- Appointed a full-time liaison from the Department of Interior National Wildlife Health Center (NWHC).
- Surveillance of Department of Veterans Affairs data through part-time VA liaison.

External Requests for Support

The work of the NBIC is not limited to interagency responses to national health and security concerns. Two examples of external requests for NBIC products are also available. First, in 2014, the organizers of Superbowl XLVIII in partnership with the New Jersey Department of Health requested a comprehensive assessment of national and international disease events with potential impact on Superbowl participants.

Second, consistent with the experience the Superbowl organizers had with the NBIC, a separate request was submitted on behalf of the Little League World Series organizing group. Working through the Pennsylvania Department of Health, Little League requested ongoing reporting that focused on, "up-to-date information on disease acuity that may pose risk to the PA community" (Bennett, n.d.: 9).

Other examples of this sort of partnership with external groups exist as well. For example, the NBIC was asked to develop a report, similar to the ones produced for the Superbowl and Little League World Series, for the Biennial International Amateur Athletic Federation (IAAF). In all cases, the NBIC served as an integrator of activities between and among agencies at all levels of government and worked directly with private and public sectors all in the effort to promote awareness of biological and health risks in the two communities above.

NBIC's Outreach

The day-to-day operations of NBIC created a routinized set of outreach efforts with agencies, non-profits, private sector groups, and other partners. Among the various forms of outreach were the following:

- The ongoing administration of monitoring lists to nearly 1,000 partners across the United States.
- The distribution, via the DHS, of biosurveillance reports to DHS partners nationally and in the territories.
- Hosting of weekly interagency conference calls to facilitate communication and updates on biosurveillance.
- As needed, information was gathered and disseminated agency to leadership to support their decision making.
- The activation of agency protocols to assemble relevant partners in response to biological challenges.

In sum, the NBIC was uniquely positioned to support interagency needs in the face of potential biological threats. The Center served its partners to provide general information, supported proactivity, coordinated responses, and led the DHS's efforts to maintain robust biosurveillance.

Future Considerations

As mentioned earlier, in late 2017, Homeland Security Secretary Nielsen reorganized the structure of DHS which had a direct impact on the Biosurveillance Integration Center. The CWMD Office, which emerged as a support component within the DHS, assumed the responsibilities of biosurveillance formerly held by the NBIC. And with that restructuring, the work of the Center came to an end in its former structure and now continues through the broader efforts of the CWMD.

Further Reading

Department of Defense (DoS). (2014, June). "*Department of Defense Strategy for Countering Weapons of Mass Destruction*." https://archive.defense.gov/pubs/DoD_Strategy_for_Countering_Weapons_of_Mass_Destruction_dated_June_2014.pdf

Joint Chiefs of Staff (JCOS). (2019, November 27). "*Joint Countering Weapons of Mass Destruction*," *Joint Publication 3–40*. https://www.jcs.mil/Portals/36/Documents/Doctrine/pubs/jp3_40.pdf

Nuzzo, J. B. (2017). "Improving Biosurveillance Systems to Enable Situational Awareness During Public Health Emergencies," *Health Security*, *15*(1): 17–19. ncbi.nlm.nih.gov/pmc/articles/PMC5314963/

References

Bennett, S. (n.d.). "National Biosurveillance Integration Center: Operations and Development". https://cdn.ymaws.com/www.cste.org/resource/resmgr/DisasterEpi/Bennett_NBIC.pdf

Public Law 110-53, IMPLEMENTING RECOMMENDATIONS OF THE 9/11 COMMISSION ACT OF 2007. (August 3, 2007). https://www.gpo.gov/fdsys/pkg/PLAW-110publ53/pdf/PLAW-110publ53.pdf

The White House. (2012, July 31). "National Strategy for Biosurveillance." https://obamawhitehouse.archives.gov/sites/default/files/National_Strategy_for_Biosurveillance_July_2012.pdf

Chapter 24

The National Emergency Management Association (NEMA)

James Valiquet
New England College, Henniker, NH, United States

Contents

Introduction 153
Conclusion 160
Further Reading 160
References 160

Introduction

This chapter describes the formation of a non-profit association (NPA) that was formed to bring a consolidated voice on behalf of the Emergency Management Directors across the nation.

The National Emergency Management Association (NEMA) is a 501 (c) 3 NPA. It is made up of Emergency Managers from the 50 states and eight US Territories, as well as the District of Columbia. These members constitute the voting members of the association. As a non-profit, it would be classified as a non-governmental organization (NGO). The association collectively serves as a resource of information, assistance, and policy recommendations ensuring the progressive improvement and advancement of emergency management.

The association is a resource for all Emergency Management Personnel at all levels of government from the President and Congress to the local Emergency Management Directors.

DOI: 10.4324/9781315144511-25

Membership varies and is made of many different categories from the directors, Homeland Security representatives, private sector representatives, and concerned citizens. Due to their common goals, in 1990, NEMA became an affiliate organization with The Council of State Governments (CSG). NEMA also works in concert with the National Governors Association and the International Association of Emergency Managers.

NEMA Goals (1):

1. Strengthen the relationship with Congress and federal agencies
2. Develop strategic partnerships with key organizations and individuals who impact emergency management
3. Tackle emergency management issues through our pro-active committees
4. Hold two national conferences annually that bring together the most knowledgeable speakers and emergency management professionals from around the country
5. Serve as an information-sharing and support network for state directors and senior staff
6. Offer professional development and training so that emergency management professionals may continue honing their skills

Many associations are formed by individuals with common goals and concerns. Emergency managers united to form a collective voice with the legislative and executive branches of government. NEMA is recognized as a source of expertise in emergency management. The terror attacks of 9/11 shocked the United States, and most of the world, into the new reality that there are groups of people in the world capable of devastating acts of violence. Acts so erratic and so heinous that we had never conceived them possible. President George W. Bush issued a Presidential Declaration, which resulted in the establishment of the Department of Homeland Security.

> Following the attacks of 9/11 NEMA established National Homeland Security Consortium which included key state and local organizations, elected officials, the private sector, and others with roles and responsibilities for homeland security prevention, preparedness, response, and recovery activities.
>
> (Bullock, 2013: page 92)

The consortium began addressing infrastructure issues. One of the key issues facing the country at the time was interoperability and communications. There needed to be a re-farming of frequencies so units responding could communicate with each other. Also, there needed to be a better understanding of how responding units were going to work with each other. National Incident Management System (NIMS) was developed out of this effort. For state, local, and private sector responders to be qualified for certain grants, their responding personnel must train in the NIMS and the "Incident Command" system. Fire departments have been doing this for years. Law Enforcement has started to adapt to the system. It has been very difficult for Law Enforcement to adapt to the "Incident Command System". Except in large communities and jurisdictions, Law Enforcement response varies by number, but a "routine" response maybe a single officer to a response of three or four; there has been a definite improvement especially in team responses, for example, Special Operating Units or Special Weapons and Tactics (SWAT) teams.

NEMA also publishes a 5-year Strategic Plan that it uses to promote and improve its relationship with the legislature, the executive branch, and its mission performance.

The current Strategic Plan is for the fiscal year 2017–2020 and states:

> The NEMA Strategic Plan for Fiscal Year 2017–2020 outlines a reasonable and practical framework that enables the association to further promote our vision as the national leader in advancing the emergency management profession and programs.
>
> (NEMA Strategic Plan 2017–2020: Wendy Smith-Reeve, NEMA President 2016–2017)

In the Executive Summary of the NEMA Strategic Plan, three goals are noted:

Goal 1: Strengthen the nation's emergency management system.

- Support the professionalization of emergency management
  Objective – Increase opportunities for training, professional development, and information exchange to advance leadership, innovation, and model practices in states.
- Promote and administer the Emergency Management Assistance Compact (EMAC) to help strengthen state capabilities
  Objective – Increase the number of states that are EMAC Ready and also the number that participates in international mutual aid.
- Promote, sustain, and enhance the Emergency Management Accreditation Program (EMAP)
  Objective – Work collaboratively with EMAP to seek incentives for jurisdictions, thereby increasing the number of jurisdictions seeking accreditation.

Goal 2: Enhance emergency management information sharing and support.

- Ensure that NEMA has an impact on national policy, program, and legislative issues
  Objective – The majority of state directors are conducting legislative visits and are actively engaged through NEMA on national policy and legislative issues.
- Provide informational resources to help state leaders better understand emergency management
  Objective – NEMA will annually produce information and educational materials and publications for state leaders.
- Facilitate direct assistance between states
  Objective – States will have access to technical assistance and an information clearinghouse through the NEMA website.
- Provide opportunities for the exchange of information on emerging trends and practices and solutions
  Objective – Increased information exchange for NEMA members

Goal 3: Facilitate partnerships to advance emergency management through innovative programs and policies.

- Enhance and promote the value of NEMA to its members
  Objective – Performance and satisfaction ratings will increase through the annual membership services survey.

- Provide opportunities for enhanced private sector engagement with NEMA
  Objective – Increased opportunities for the involvement of private sector members in NEMA and annual needs and satisfaction surveys.
- Leverage the CSG resources to build internal capacity and external influence
  Objective – The return on investment with CSG demonstrates quality services and support and opportunities for the advancement of emergency management.
- Facilitate emergency management policy development and implementation through collaborative partnerships
  Objective – Identify at least one state policy need and identify partnerships to address it.

NEMA's Action Plan to accomplish the above is outlined in the Strategic Plan appendix and states:

Objective 1.1.

- Develop a process to identify, develop, and promote national Emergency Management (EM) leaders
- Develop and institutionalize a training program for new state directors
- Develop robust information-sharing groups for state personnel
- Identify and share model practices for states to become more self-reliant for EM and disaster assistance funding

Objective 1.2.

- Support implementation of the EMAC Strategic Plan and provide regular review and update
- Identify, share, and promote EMAC and mutual aid model practices with states and mutual aid stakeholders
- Develop methodology and data to quantify the value of EMAC and measure in ways that help to promote the Compact and build support
- Support international cross-border mutual aid initiatives

Objective 1.3.

- Work collaboratively with EMAP to seek incentives for jurisdictions to achieve accreditation.
- Ensure NEMA representatives to the EMAP Commission are well positioned to carry forward ideas to advance the program and encourage jurisdictions to achieve accreditation.

Objective 2.1.

- Ensure NEMA's continued recognition and credibility with Congress and staff as an information and technical assistance resource through regular briefings, information sharing, and responsiveness to requests for input.
- Pro-actively identify issues that need to be addressed through legislation, regulation, or policy and develop recommendations for Congress and the Federal government.

- Emphasize and demonstrate with the membership the importance and value of their legislative visits, regular information sharing with congressional offices, and comments on proposed legislation.

Objective 2.2.

- Provide information and educational materials for state leaders, including, but not limited to, governors, governors' transition teams, state legislators, and members of Congress
- Continue to collect and share state data that informs, builds, and maintains support for EM

Objective 2.3.

- Identify areas of excellence and innovation in states and those that would be willing to provide expertise or technical assistance to other states when requested.
- Collect and share lessons learned, after action reports, and other data garnered from state/regional/national exercises, audits, and other events that would provide helpful information for states and post to the NEMA website.

Objective 2.4.

- Develop, deliver, and evaluate a webinar series for members focused on issue-specific emerging practices and solutions.
- Develop external partnerships to help analyze emerging trends, consider how they are going to impact the profession, and convey that information to states in timely and actionable ways.

Objective 3.1.

- Identify, develop, and promote opportunities for member engagement.
- Examine the role and process of NEMA committees, subcommittees, and work groups annually and make changes as needed to ensure effectiveness.
- Explore opportunities for attracting new members, retaining current members, and expanding partnerships with other organizations.
- Develop, implement, and evaluate an annual marketing plan for NEMA.
- Ensure the ongoing financial viability of NEMA through regular analysis of the changing fiscal environment, revenue and expenditures, investments, grants, and investments with CSG.
- Benchmark to other influential national organizations and incorporate best practices.

Objective 3.2.

- Empower the Private Sector Committee to:
  - Provide analysis and recommendations on national EM policy, legislation, emerging initiatives, and academic research that affect the relationship between public and private sectors.

  - Create, discover, collect, and share national "smart/emerging" practices in public–private relationships that are applicable to state EM missions. Promote emerging practices that are mutually beneficial to the public and private sectors, such as emerging technology, innovative services, and partnerships.
  - Provide appropriate private sector subject matter expertise on committees and issue-specific work groups.
  - Deploy appropriate subject matter expert liaisons to meetings and events, as requested, to provide technical assistance to state EM agencies.
- Regularly assess the needs and interests of private sector members and determine how NEMA can address them.

Objective 3.3.

- Position NEMA to provide articles for national publications, speakers at national and regional conferences, and a seat on CSG committees in order to expand knowledge of EM to broader state government community.
- Ensure the NEMA–CSG relationship remains mutually beneficial and cost-effective through ongoing evaluation of needs and services provided. Ensure ongoing and transparent communication between organization leaders and senior staff.

Objective 3.4.

- Solicit and analyze state policy needs.
- Promote initiatives with national organizations to advance EM.

While NEMA has a 5-year Strategic Plan, it is reviewed and updated on an annual basis. It appears that NEMA has recognized, whether it is in dealing with the legislature or when dealing with emergencies, that there is strength in numbers.

Trina Sheets, the Executive Director of NEMA, has been with NEMA for 24 years and majored in public communication. She advised the membership is divided on the issue of Federal Emergency Management Agency's (FEMA's) position in Department of Homeland Security (DHS). The Post Katrina Reform Act authorized the director of FEMA to redirect FEMA's focus on all-hazards. She indicated that NEMA had no responsibilities tied to Homeland Security and FEMA's responsibilities have now shifted. (Interview Trina Sheets Executive Director, NEMA n.d.) Major events, both manmade and natural, have driven reactions from different administrations. President Jimmy Carter founded FEMA in 1979, and it started as an all-hazard federal agency responsible for assistance to state, local, and tribal governments during times of disaster. President Ronald Reagan directed FEMA to focus on the threat of nuclear attack. President Bill Clinton directed FEMA focus back to the all-hazards approach. After 9/11, President George W. Bush created the DHS and FEMA was moved into DHS with its new focus now on terrorism. This was very discouraging to many of the senior Emergency Managers in FEMA. Many in turn left, leaving FEMA focused on terrorism and now short on experienced personnel in emergency management. This was a perfect storm. In 2005, in the aftermath of Hurricane Katrina, FEMA was unable to mitigate, prepare, respond, and assist in the recovery in a timely and effective manner. This resulted in NEMA and others pushing for FEMA's return to its prior status and focus on all-hazards approach.

Sheets believes that FEMA can do its primary mission if it can stay focused on the all-hazards approach to disaster preparation. As for communication, she feels that DHS has come a long way with communications, within the department, with the establishment of the Office of Public Affairs.

Membership in NEMA is made up of the 50 state emergency directors from each state along with the eight territories and District of Columbia. There are 450–500 members from the private sector, police and fire organizations, and individuals who make up the membership of NEMA.

In an interview with Director Perry Plummer, Department of Homeland Security and Emergency Preparedness for the State of New Hampshire, he stated that part of his duties is to serve as one of the TRI-Chairs for the Homeland Security Consortium. (Interview Director Perry Plummer, n.d.). He represents NEMA as one of the three chairs currently on the Homeland Security Consortium. The Chairs represent NEMA, the private sector, and the public. The private sector is represented by a member from the National Chamber of Commerce, and a Captain from the Michigan State Police represents the public sector. The consortium meets twice a year.

Plummer advises that there are plenty of processes in place in the FEMA approach to handling emergencies. The inherent problem is the bureaucracy surrounding the process. FEMA is so huge and the "Oversight of checks and balances drags out aid when it is most needed". As an example, he feels that the legislature should create laws regulating that insurance companies require flood insurance for every home owner. This would be a small amount for each residence, but the funding would be there to allow the benefits to be immediate. There is an elderly woman whose residence is located on a hill and had never been affected by water damage. With the recent rains and climate changes, her home was damaged by flooding water and she has not been able to get any assistance. The residence is outside of the flood plain and she was not required to have flood insurance. Next door to this lady, during the same storm, a tree fell on a car, and after an hour with the claims agent, the check was in the mail. This he points out is the difference between bureaucracy and the private sector.

One of Plummer's major concerns is that flooding emergencies are high risk based not only on their frequency but serious damage. These events are "bankrupting FEMA". If insurance companies could lessen this demand on FEMA by spreading the costs while improving response and recovery, this would allow FEMA to concentrate on Catastrophic Disasters.

Another area of concern is the large number of prohibitions preventing Department of Defense (DOD) from assisting civilian authorities. We can activate our Nation Guardsmen but we the state or local governments must rent the equipment. One example is the Town of Hampton was looking for the necessary equipment to assist first responders during the flooding today along the beach (March 2, 2018). The personnel could respond but the truck would cost $1,000.00 a day because it is a federal asset. The second example is during the relief in Porto Rico; the Governor and others collected food and other supplies that were donated. The problem was getting the supplies where they were needed. The National Guard has aircraft capable of flying cargo to Porto Rico. In fact, the aircrafts were flying training missions during the same time period when needed. Because flying food to Porto Rico was an assignment change from the training mission, the state would have to pay $1,000.00 an hour for the aircraft.

DHS is an immense department with its own communication and sharing issues, FEMA is a revolving door with constant focus changes, and DOD should be given greater latitude to assist and be a force multiplier in times of a Presidential Declaration.

Conclusion

The formation of NEMA was to collectively bring together experienced Emergency Management Directors so that they could bring a collective voice before the decision makers in Washington. Over the years, they have continued to push for an all-hazard theory for mitigation, preparation, response, and recovery, the essential point being money. It is apparent that NEMA has been found to be a formidable group of expert, experienced, and informed personnel with the wellbeing of the nation and its citizens at heart. As a 501(c)3 IRS organization, they cannot normally lobby. They can spend up to 20% of their assets on lobbying. But, NEMA is so respected that the legislature, in most cases, seeks out their input, asking them for advice on a regular basis.

Further Reading

Anderson, A. I., Compton, D. & Mason, T. (2004). "Managing in a Dangerous World – The National Incident Management System," *Engineering Management Journal, 16*(4): 3–9.

Coen, M. A. & Zimmerman, E. A. (2020, March 21). "What a National Emergency Means for FEMA During COVID-19 Crisis," *Government Technology & Services Coalition's Homeland Security Today*. hstoday.us/subject-matter-areas/emergency-preparedness/what-a-national-emergency-means-for-fema-during-covid-19-crisis/

Walsh, D. W., Christen, H. T., Callsen, C. E., Miller, G. T., Maniscalco, P. M., Lord, G. C. & Dolan, N. J. (2012). *National Incident Management System: Principles and Practice* (2nd ed.). Sudbury: Jones & Bartlett Learning.

References

Bullock, J. (2013). *Homeland Security: The Essentials*. New York: Elsevier.

Interview Director Perry Plummer, *Department Homeland Security and Emergency Management State of NH*.

Interview Trina Sheets Executive Director, *NEMA*.

NEMA Strategic Plan, 2017–2020. Wendy Smith-Reeve, NEMA President 2016–2017.

CYBERSECURITY, TERRORISM, AND ASYMMETRIC THREATS

11

Zoha Waseem
King's College London, London, United Kingdom

Chapter 25

Advanced Persistent Threats (APTs)

Anwar Ouassini and Michael Hunter
Delaware State University, Dover, DE, United States

Contents

Introduction 163
Further Reading 165
References 165

Introduction

The rapid development of cybertechnologies has allowed both state and non-state actors to produce sophisticated and advanced cybercapabilities. As a result, one of the emerging developments drawing increased attention for both National and Homeland Security personnel is advanced persistent threats (APTs). APTs are cyber-based attacks launched against governmental institutions, multinational corporations, and financial institutions to obtain strategic political and economic benefits and gain access to critical intelligence (Ghafir & Prenosil, 2014). Unlike traditional cyberattacks, APTs are designed with dedicated governmental resources and the highest level of technological know-how. The sophistication of APT attacks enables the actor to "pursue its objectives repeatedly over an extended period; adapt to defenders' efforts to resist it; and is determined to maintain the level of interaction needed to execute its objectives" (Chen et al., 2014, P. 64). This stealth approach (Siddiqi & Ghani, 2016) allows APTs to make frequent use of unknown security holes in variegated commercial and government infrastructures to avoid suspicion while making it challenging to actively detect and counter (Ghafir & Prenosil, 2014; Siddiqi & Ghani, 2016). Perhaps the element that separates APTs from other traditional cyberattacks is their ability to go undetected for extended periods occupying a host system for months to years on

DOI: 10.4324/9781315144511-27

end (Chen et al., 2014; Siddiqi & Ghani, 2016). This makes APT attacks extremely worrisome for the would-be victim especially if the strike is a coordinated, longitudinal incursion or various strikes during the period of occupation (Ask et al., 2013).

While there are several APT attack methods noted by cybersecurity scholars (Siddiqi & Ghani, 2016), most follow a general pattern. The first includes the exploration or reconnaissance stage where the source actor gathers intelligence while seeking a loophole to have access to the intended target's system (Siddiqi & Ghani, 2016, p. 47). This intelligence gathering is important because it generates the plan of action leading to the actual "break-in". This can be through phishing techniques utilizing email attachments and website links from known persons to breach the internal networks of the intended system. Once the source actor has access, they install backdoor malware to conduct successive incursions on the target network to capture the intended data. Once the attack is successful, they leave the network through several established escape routes to encrypt the forensic pathways to discovery (Siddiqi & Ghani, 2016, p. 47).

Beginning in 2009, one of the most lethal APT attacks was unleashed using two digital certificates and dozens of encrypted code blocks moving from computer to computer across the globe eluding detection with one intended target, the nuclear installations in Iran (Zetter, 2011).

The Stuxnet worm was composed using multiple languages, was nearly 500 kilobytes in size, and was initiated manually with a USB stick (Kushner, 2013). Stuxnet utilized vulnerabilities in Microsoft Windows computers to move laterally across cybernetworks in multiple national contexts, infecting more than 100,000 computers (Goodins, 2017). Once the worm 'broke into' Iranian nuclear installations, it destroyed a large number of centrifuges and reprogrammed their systems by "sending damage-inducing instructions to the electro-mechanical equipment the PC controlled" while sending encrypted "false feedback to the main controller" (McAfee, 2020). The Stuxnet incursion was designed to act in stealth to elude detection as the developers intended that outsiders view the worm as having multiple global targets when in reality, it was designed specifically to disable and destroy Iranian nuclear installations. The sophistication of the Stuxnet attack necessitated a lot of resources and technological know-how in what many experts suggest was a joint cyberintelligence operation between the United States and Israel. Both nations have neither claimed nor denied their involvement.

The threat of APTs on critical infrastructure is a major national and homeland security concern and necessitates countermeasures that are holistic and multilayered (Chen et al., 2014). This includes ensuring that organizations and governments can shore up their defenses at every stage of the attack. Consequently, this requires awareness training programs to understand the differences between an APT attack and a regular cyberattack. This training would allow organizations to be aware of viruses that are seeking undetected and unknown loopholes within their respective network (Chen et al., 2014). Moreover, the use of traditional and advanced malware protection, event anomaly protection, and data loss prevention can mitigate the possibilities of an APT having access to its intended target (Chen et al., 2014). Finally, Chen et al. call for an intelligence-driven defense, a "strategy that leverage(s) the knowledge about adversaries, and adapt defense based on the fathered intelligence" (2014, p. 70). This will produce alternative and creative countermeasures based on the adversary's aims to equip an organization with the tools to recognize intrusion attempts and techniques.

Understanding the attack methods of APTs will be critical to mitigate and protect against any future attacks. This requires the APT paradigm to become more ingrained in cybersecurity studies as the sophistication and expansion of these methods will shape the future of international relations, cyberwarfare, and political and economic stability.

Further Reading

Chen, P., Desmet, L., & Huygens, C. (2014). A study on advanced persistent threats. In *IFIP International Conference on Communications and Multimedia Security* (pp. 63–72).

Rot, A., & Olszewski, B. (2017). Advanced persistent threats attacks in cyberspace. Threats, vulnerabilities, methods of protection. *FedCSIS Position Papers* (pp. 113–117).

Siddiqi, M.A., & Ghani, N. (2016). Critical Anlaysis on Advanced Persistent Threats. *International Journal of Computer Applications*, 141 (13), 46–50.

References

Ask, M., Bondarenko, P., Rekdal, J. E., Nordbø, A., Bloemerus, P., & Piatkivskyi, D. (2013). Advanced Persistent Threat (APT) beyond the hype. *Project Report in IMT4582 Network Security at GjoviK University College, 2013.*

Chen, P., Desmet, L., & Huygens, C. (2014). A study on advanced persistent threats. In *IFIP International Conference on Communications and Multimedia Security* (pp. 63–72).

Ghafir, I., & Prenosil, V. (2014). Advanced persistent threat attack detection: an overview. *International Journal of Advancements in Computer Networks and Its Security*, *4*(4), 50–54.

Goodins, D. (2017). Windows bug used to spread Stuxnet remains world's most exploited. Retrieved February 22, 2020, https://arstechnica.com/information-technology/2017/04/windows-bug-used-to-spread-stuxnet-remains-worlds-most-exploited/

Kushner, D. (2013). The Real Story of Stuxnet. *IEEE Spectrum* 53 (3), 48. Retrieved February 22, 2020, https://spectrum.ieee.org/telecom/security/the-real-story-of-stuxnet

McAfee (2020). What is Stuxnet. Retrieved February 22, 2020, https://www.mcafee.com/enterprise/en-us/security-awareness/ransomware/what-is-stuxnet.html

Rot, A., & Olszewski, B. (2017). Advanced persistent threats attacks in cyberspace. Threats, vulnerabilities, methods of protection. *FedCSIS Position Papers* (pp. 113–117).

Siddiqi, M.A., & Ghani, N. (2016). Critical Anlaysis on Advanced Persistent Threats. *International Journal of Computer Applications*, 141 (13), 46–50.

Wang, Y., Wang, Y., Liu, J., & Huang, Z. (2014). A network gene-based framework for detecting advanced persistent threats. *2014 Ninth International Conference on P2P, Parallel, Grid, Cloud and Internet Computing* (pp. 97–102).

Wang, X., Zheng, K., Niu, X., Wu, B., & Wu, C. (2016). Detection of command and control in advanced persistent threat based on independent access. *2016 IEEE International Conference on Communications (ICC)* (pp. 1–6).

Zetter, K. (2011). How Digital Detectives Deciphered Stuxnet, the Most Menacing Malware in History. Retrieved February 22, 2020, https://www.wired.com/2011/07/how-digital-detectives-deciphered-stuxnet/

Chapter 26

Chain of Custody

Gary Leigh
Charles Darwin University, Darwin, Australia

Content

Further Reading 171
References 171

The chain of custody for cybersecurity operations may appear rather simple but it is certainly worthy of attention. The chain of custody is a process that is enacted by those involved in a cybersecurity undertaking, and it is considered the foundation of sound digital forensics (Casey, 2011, pp. 21). The process has the primary purpose of preserving the integrity of digital artifacts for many potential uses. Although the following refers to chain of custody in a cyber security setting, the judicial requirements for a sound chain of custody apply broadly in the realm of homeland security today.

The most common, primary use of the chain of custody concerns the complete, true, and veritable recount of the acquisition, utilization, and handling of digital evidence in a cybersecurity proceeding. This is most common surrounding digital evidence for legal purposes rather than departmental business. It applies to those involved in the immediate acquisition of evidence as well as those involved in the lifecycle of the evidence from curation to long-term storage which can be known as sentencing. It may further extend to anyone involved in cybersecurity who may create a piece of evidence that could be later used in court, forensically or for departmental business as they are now involved in the process.

The Computer Security Resource Center (CSRC, 2020) and the National Institute of Standards and Technology (NIST, 2020) define the chain of custody as:

> A process that tracks the movement of evidence through its collection, safeguarding, and analysis lifecycle by documenting each person who handled the evidence, the date/time it was collected or transferred, and the purpose for the transfer.

DOI: 10.4324/9781315144511-28

Careful consideration should be given by homeland security practitioners and those involved in the chain of custody of digital evidence. The term is a well-known legal protocol in stereotyped criminal investigations and prosecution for non-computer-related offenses. Commonly, it can be thought of as the cliché of a forensic investigation into a homicide or recounting the order of operations of a terrorist plot with chronological and authenticated evidence presented to a security committee. Due to the immaterial nature of digital evidence, it is especially important to consider the NIST definition as it applies to best practices in security operations.

Advances in technology and sophistication of criminal cyber activity mean that the chain of custody is becoming increasingly complex. This is pertinent when considering the ability to authenticate the digital evidence as well as determine its admissibility in legal proceedings (Goodison et al., 2015). From the intelligence or strategic perspective alone, the chain of custody is paramount in ensuring the preservation of the authenticity of the evidence. The custodianship of the digital evidence is no small feat depending on the importance of the evidence. These matters tend to additionally conform to sound legal and regulatory instrumentation as well. Security efforts surrounding the integrity of the chain of custody are an additional concern as only the highest standard of evidence custodianship can ensure no tampering for the truth of the evidence to be of ethical use. This extends even beyond a successful prosecution into records keeping as well as from the initial sourcing of the evidence.

Precisely how the digital evidence is seized, curated, or created and subsequently stored, accessed, and utilized must be documented to fulfill the needs of the chain of custody process. Depending on the importance of the evidence or the intricacies of its forensic properties and sensitivity, a high degree of expertise is generally required. That said, an awareness of the chain of custody is important as it is unknown when one might become involved in a matter that becomes evidence. Even routine cybersecurity operations, if not properly documented and evidenced, may incite potential interference in the chain of custody. Awareness of the chain of custody further improves the process as we are aware of the chain of custody's importance for the integrity, confidentiality, and accessibility of such evidence.

There is currently no universally accepted standard in this process, as there is a trifecta of legal instrumentation, digital systems, and human involvement, including policy and procedure. This is further complicated by the complexity and distinctive nature of each country's unique legal systems and distinct computer systems and modus operandi for forensic work in the digital domain. The issue is posing a great challenge for transnational cases of cybercrime and can hamper interdepartmental cooperation (Smith, 2004).

Advances in technology mean that there are numerous evolving ways to validate that a chain of custody of digital evidence is sound. This speaks to the central issue of the chain of custody: how, "the moment of capturing the proof has been cited as the most critical moment in the chain of custody" (Marques-Arpa & Serra-Ruiz, 2016, pp. 274). If this is the case, when considering the acquisition of an original piece of evidence that must be forensically validated, there are a few aspects to cover. One is the legislative and compliance requirements of the acquiring agency. Another is the sophistication of the evidence item in question, is it a simple e-mail? Lost file? Or an encrypted hard disk? Or a fleeting self-destructing message by which its acquisition could potentially break another law, making it inadmissible? Was access to the device with the evidence even lawful? This adds to the potential quagmire of digital evidence in cyber operations needing to be not only forensically proven but also operationally acceptable. The advent of big data, encryption, and distributed storage further complicate not only evidence sourcing but the complete process of the chain of custody.

The National Institute of Justice (Novak et al., 2018) has a stance that factors into the chain of custody. They denote a three-step process that broadly identifies the importance but also the difficulty in the cyber domain of:

- Seizure of the media from which the digital artifact originates and its preservation;
- The creation of the forensic image and data of the media suitable for examination within a legal context; and
- Analysis of both the original media and the forensic data of said media.

Despite how clear this may appear, the actual tradecraft of digital forensics introduces yet again further complexity. It is worth noting that during the practice of digital evidence integrity and protection, multiple additional layers of protection are added to the digital artifact of evidence. Each of these introduces more people into the process and heightens the chances for evidence tampering or spoilage, despite the attempt being for the purposes of assuring evidence validity and truth. These layers of protection are deeply technical and pervasive, going beyond the surface layer of what the actual evidence is. If even one fault is found in the preservation and integrity of forensic measures, it may cascade into a negative effect on the overall integrity of the chain of custody and insight undue scrutiny.

For example, a log data of a network breach and data exfiltration would be considered forensically sound and admissible only if several conditions are met. As there is no universal standard, the conditions may range from having the original evidence item in question preserved; possession of forensically complete proof of its originality; the authenticity of the forensics itself; and proof no tampering has occurred. Effectively, a complete account of the chain of custody surrounding said evidence item is needed, and it must be forensically sound. This would be a catalog of the evidence's complete journey from its discovery to its presentation to its audience be it judicial, departmental, or otherwise. It is worth noting that the seizure, handling, forensics, and use of evidence must all be within the bounds of the judicial practice of being admissible evidence depending on the circumstances of needing such cybersecurity-related evidence. Certain operational requirements may also be apparent depending on the acting agency or the nature of the operation, which requires digital evidence and the chain of custody to prove its applicability.

This circles back to the importance of the chain of custody. As the *Journal of Digital Forensics, Security and Law* states:

> If integrity of the evidence presented in court could not be proved then it becomes inadmissible. If there is even a doubt that the evidence could have been tampered with then its integrity becomes questionable.
>
> **(Shahm et al., 2017, pp. 121)**

Due to the immaterial nature of digital evidence, it is a fair suggestion that the requirements for a demonstrable success of a chain of custody process involving digital evidence are different to that of a traditional chain of custody scenario (Gayed et al., 2015). Careful attention to detail must be undertaken from all involved in the process as well as the requisite level of technological expertise to account for the authenticity of evidence. A non-exhaustive account of this entails that the security department and personnel involved, the judiciary, and forensic counterparts have the right levels of technological maturity and capability to act on and accept such evidence. The debate is ongoing as to precisely how and what constitutes a minimum level of secure storage, access, and the technology infrastructure underpinning the digital forensics and legal process. Arguments range from utilizing proof from a blockchain to securely transmitting evidence on encrypted satellite channels or relying on expert testimony.

This is precisely why having a holistic approach to not only digital forensics but also security operations and eventual prosecution or governmental action is required. The chain of custody simply forms part of the broader activity involved in cybersecurity operations. There is now the open debate about how to continuously improve in this space, as both evidence articles from non-computer-based crime and cybercriminal activity continue to produce greater data amounts and custody requirements. This leads to considering not only the human aspects of evidence procurement, handling, and use but also the technology that enables this activity. Thinking in terms of an information lifecycle approach enables those involved in the chain of custody to accept that throughout, "the entire lifecycle of digital evidence, there are threats that can affect its [the digital evidence's] integrity and thus in the end, [affect] the court's decision" (Ćosić & Ćosić, 2012, pp. 128).

Lifecycle approaches may appear academic, but they share commonalities with the Department of Homeland Security's (DHS's) own recommended practices, which continue to evolve. Consider DHS National Cyber Security Division, Control Systems Security Program, which goes to great lengths to articulate that, "the goal of cyber forensics is to support the elements of troubleshooting, monitoring, recovery, and the protection of sensitive data. Moreover, in the event of a crime being committed, cyber forensics is also the approach to collecting, analyzing, and archiving data as evidence in a court of law" (Department of Homeland Security, 2008, pp. 3).

Such cyber forensic plans and control systems may be the corporate speak of the homeland security nexus in the United States, but it is most certainly the type of systemized and framework-based thinking needed. There are great challenges to incorporating yesterday's legacy systems and data and tomorrow's emerging digital toolkit that enables cybercrime and defenses. The chain of custody is that valuable process that forms part of the lynchpin of integrity for classified and sensitive operations. It is perhaps due to the sensitivity of these operations and the complexity of cyber operations themselves that more tradecraft on the technicalities and techniques of acquiring and preserving evidence is not more abundant.

In summary, the chain of custody is an important part of any security operation. Its importance in cyber security, cybercrime investigation, and as a requirement to support general evidence-based investigation cannot be understated. The chain of custody may be simply known as having the proof that evidence has changed hands and how, but as it stands, may also be as complex as it is important in homeland security.

Further Reading

Giannelli, P. C. (1983). "Chain of Custody and the Handling of Real Evidence," *American Criminal Law Review*, *20*(4): 527–568.

Giova, G. (2011). "Improving Chain of Custody in Forensic Investigation of Electronic Digital Systems," *International Journal of Computer Science and Network Security*, *11*(1): 1–9.

Hayes, D. R. (2020). *A Practical Guide to Digital Forensics Investigations*. Pearson IT Certification.

References

Casey, E. (2011). *Digital Evidence and Computer Crime: Forensic Science, Computers, and the Internet* (3rd. ed.). Academic Press.

Ćosić, J. and Ćosić, Z. (2012). "Chain of Custody and Life Cycle of Digital Evidence," *Journal of Computer Technology and Applications*, 126–129. https://www.researchgate.net/publication/279175015_Chain_of_custody_and_life_cycle_of_digital_evidence

Department of Homeland Security, National Cyber Security Division. (2008). Recommended Practice: *Creating Cyber Forensics Plans for Control Systems*. CISA. Department of Homeland Security. https://www.us-cert.gov/sites/default/files/recommended_practices/Forensics_RP.pdf

Gayed, T.F., Lounis, H., and Bari, M. (2015). "Digital Chain of Custody: State of the Art," *International Journal of Computer Applications*, *114*(5): 1–9. https://www.semanticscholar.org/paper/Digital-Chain-of-Custody%3A-State-of-the-Art-Gayed-Lounis/315e09a433afbb4b446e6fe1bb890bd5ba9617e4

Goodison, E., Davis. R., and Jackson, B. (2015). Digital Evidence and the U.S. Criminal Justice System: *Identifying Technology and Other Needs to More Effectively Acquire and Utilize Digital Evidence*. RAND Corporation. https://www.rand.org/pubs/research_reports/RR890.html

Marques-Arpa, T. and Serra-Ruiz, J. (2016). "PRS Signal in Acquiring Evidence of Digital Chain of Custody," *International Conference for Internet Technology and Secured Transactions*, (11): 273–278. https://ieeexplore.ieee.org/document/7856711

National Institute of Standards and Technology & Computer Security Resource Center. (2020). Glossary: *Chain of Custody*. US Government. https://csrc.nist.gov/glossary/term/chain-of-custody

Novak, M., Grier, J., and Gonzales, D. (2018). "*New Approaches to Digital Evidence Acquisition and Analysis*," National Institute of Justice. https://nij.ojp.gov/topics/articles/new-approaches-digital-evidence-acquisition-and-analysis

Shahm M., Saleem, S., and Roha, Z. (2017). "Protecting Digital Evidence Integrity and Preserving Chain of Custody," *Journal of Digital Forensics, Security and Law*: *12*(2), 121–130. https://doi.org/10.15394/jdfsl.2017.1478

Smith, R. (2004). "Impediments to the successful investigation of transnational high-tech crime. Australian Institute of Criminology." Australian Government. https://www.aic.gov.au/publications/tandi/tandi285

Chapter 27

Conficker Worm

Gordon Alley-Young
Kingsborough Community College – City University of New York, New York, NY, United States

Contents

Introduction 173
Presumed Origins of Conficker 174
Variations of Conficker 175
Conficker's Creator(s) and Fighting Conficker 176
Moving Forward: Positive and Negative Outcomes of Conficker 177
Further Reading 178
References 179

Introduction

Conficker worm is a malware that was deployed in late 2008 to take over personal computers remotely and turn them into networks of computers that can be controlled remotely. It followed a design to take advantage of vulnerabilities inherent within the Microsoft Windows operating system with users who were slow to (or who did not) upload software fixes. The malware avoids detection by general users and would subsequently infect other computers at an alarming rate. Conficker was believed to be financially motivated as infected computers' users would, in many cases, have their computer and related file functions effectively hijacked. As a result, pop-up messages would demand ransoms for unlocking the computer and its contents and threaten to destroy the machine and its contents if ransom demands were not met. The worm was to be used to steal information from users, damage computers, erase data, violate privacy, shut down computer-based services, and/or extort money from infected users.

DOI: 10.4324/9781315144511-29

Conficker was particularly hard to fight because it was originally believed to be an experimental piece of software that was accidentally released. However, when Conficker released updated versions aimed at circumventing efforts to fight its earlier versions, this suggested to experts that it had been created and released intentionally. To date, the creator of Conficker has not been discovered, though security experts alternately suspect a wealthy multinational criminal network and/or a state-sponsored cybercrime operation based in Eastern Europe or Asia to be behind the effort; however, neither has been conclusively proven. Some experts argue that the Conficker worm ushered in a new era of organized cybercrime using worms and malware.

Presumed Origins of Conficker

Late in November 2008, a new piece of malicious software or malware that would come to be called the Conficker worm was released. Some security experts cite November 20, 2008 as its release date but given that experts do not know what time zone the virus started and the undetectable nature of the worm, this might not be accurate. With Conficker's release, a domino effect was started as infected computers infecting other computers created a botnet (i.e., a network of malware-infected computers controlled by another person(s)). The new worm was first detected by what is called a network telescope (e.g., millions of fake internet addresses used to find suspicious activity online). Conficker was found in honeypots (i.e., unprotected computers used to attract computer malware) and in honeynets (i.e., networks of honeypot computers). Initially, Conficker was named Downadup and Kido. The name Conficker comes from the fact that the worm tried to access a fake security website named trafficconverter.biz (e.g., using con and er from converter); in addition, the interfix in the name (i.e., ficker) is German slang for the English F-word expletive. The worm's name is credited to Microsoft security experts. Prior to Conficker, the last significant worm outbreak is believed to be the Sasser worm in 2004 designed by then 18-year-old German computer science student Sven Jaschan. Microsoft used a $250,000 ransom to find Jaschan successfully, but the same approach when used to find Conficker's originator(s) proved unsuccessful.

Computer worms like Conficker, along with Trojans and viruses, are examples of malware (i.e., malicious software) that can infect (i.e., be downloaded, often unknowingly by the user) a computer. A Trojan, named after the Trojan horse, pretends to be something else (e.g., free PDF reading or word processing software available online) in order to get users to download it into a computer. A virus attacks a computer soon after entering a hole in its operating system. A worm enters a computer like a virus but it does not attack the computer; instead, it spreads rapidly, often unknown to the individual computer users, until a remote control center sends the worms coded instructions on what operations it will carry out on the computers where it resides. Despite these distinctions, some computer security experts argue the differences are more sematic and think of all three collectively as malware to be fought, dismantled, and defended against.

The success of Conficker worm is due to both its ability to go unnoticed and the speed with which it is able to spread. At about 35 kilobytes (i.e., smaller than a 2,000-word document), Conficker was designed to be missed in the average home computer that can have as much as 200 gigabytes of storage. Conficker exploited computers with Port 445 enabled (i.e., often used for sharing files and print functions) in Microsoft's operating systems. Microsoft learned of the vulnerability in late 2008, and on October 23, 2008, it issued a critical security bulletin and a patch to repair the hole. Experts argue that the bulletin may have alerted hackers to exploit the vulnerability with Conficker. Once discovered, the worm began generating 250 random domain names a day across five top-level domains (e.g.,.com,.edu, and .uk). Conficker's first version operated according to the host computer's clock and when it hit the desired time, it would generate the domain names that it would then take over for purposes of communicating (i.e., getting its instructions) from the command center. Conficker's controller only had to register one of the addresses, for about $10, and wait for the worm to contact it, and then he/she could issue instructions that the worm would carry out. Defeating Conficker requires knowing the numbers to purchase, block, or shut down those addresses before Conficker could communicate.

Computer security workers would set computer clocks ahead of the desired time and then use the generated domain information to buy and close the domains and then dispose of Conficker's communication in a sinkhole. A sinkhole is a place where information is lost permanently, so computer security/coding experts and scientists working to protect computer users use sinkholes for positive ends, although computer code hackers who work for criminal, terrorist, and/or anarchical purposes also use sinkholes to destroy data or to threaten to destroy data and thus wreak havoc. Given the vast spread, Conficker's creator(s) likely wanted to slow down and prevent total eradication of the worm by security experts by making it timely and expensive (i.e., purchasing domains) to fight, thus making it unlikely that Conficker would ever be completely eradicated. In response to attempts to fight it, Conficker adapted and instead set a schedule for domain name generation by the time on company home pages (e.g., Google, Yahoo, and msn.com).

Variations of Conficker

Experts originally speculated that Conficker was a computer lab exercise that was accidental. However, on December 29, 2008, a new version of Conficker was first noticed in computers and was dubbed Conficker B. Some cite that by January 2009 Conficker had affected 20 million computers, including those used by the French Navy, the UK's Defense Ministry, and the Greater Manchester Police, and ironically, US television investigative program 60 Minutes' computers were hit just as they were working on a story about Conficker. The impact of Conficker B created a crisis situation for British hospitals that could not access computerized patient records and had to go back to pen-and-paper forms of record keeping temporarily until the issue could be resolved. The new version of the worm accounted for the fact that certain domain registries were being monitored because of the original Conficker worm, so Conficker B expanded the number of domains it worked on, increased the number of domain names it generated, and would keep trying to find a domain it could use to connect to its control center for months or even years.

Other innovations in Conficker B included peer-to-peer communications, meaning Conficker B no longer needed Port 445 or a USB drive but instead spread directly to every machine with which it interacted. Similarly, instructions now no longer required communication with a control center but were delivered computer to computer. With computers no longer calling a control center for instructions, it became less clear how many computers were affected. Conficker B used portable devices like a USB flash drive combined with Windows' Autorun feature to spread itself, meaning if users disabled Windows Autorun, then an installed USB could allow the worm access to the computer.

Conficker C appeared in March 2009; the experts fighting the worm immediately noticed that the new worm's code could potentially generate 50,000 domain names every day. Conficker C was scheduled to begin generating names starting on April 1. The irony was not lost on experts that April 1st is April fool's day. Conficker C also had the potential to contact and reinfect computers infected with previous strains of the worm. Experts consider that this innovation was meant to exhaust the time and resources of volunteer experts working to fight Conficker.

Conficker's Creator(s) and Fighting Conficker

Conficker's creators are yet unknown but are believed to have considerable skill due to its complex encryption code. Given that Conficker's code initially appeared to be unbreakable, some experts suspected that they were either facing sophisticated cyber criminals, potentially an organization funded or working under the auspices of a nation-state. Computer security experts and police have yet to track, find, and stop the worm's creator(s), and Conficker is believed to have been designed to avoid detection by all except advanced computer experts. Conficker's patient zero computer (i.e., the first infected) and its exact origin date and time are not known, though experts argue it was likely a computer under the control of the hacker(s). Motivations for releasing a worm are diverse: it could be to distribute malware to worm-infected computers as a way to steal private or secure information for the purposes of blackmail and/or ransom or to perpetuate credit card or banking fraud. Worm creators may only create the worm-infected botnet and then sell access to it to a criminal enterprise. Experts argue that advancements in computer encryption technology and the creation of Bitcoin (i.e., the untraceable digital currency) have facilitated cybercrimes and helped to ensure that its perpetrators would not be caught. When financial gain is not a motivation, a nation-state and/or a government agency might use cyberattacks as part of their modern defense arsenal (i.e., to cripple an enemy's infrastructure and/or for espionage).

Early in the fight against Conficker, experts noted that the worm was designed to bypass computers using Ukrainian keyboards, thus implicating Ukraine as Conficker's country of origin. Others argue that Russia is the country of origin and that creator(s) are using the Ukrainian keyboard clue to deflect attention from Russia as part of the ongoing cyber war between the two countries. Russia's extensive involvement in organized cybercrime is cited as evidence for this claim. Others look more generally at Eastern Europe due to the region's high percentage of computer scientists. In 2009, experts turned their eyes further east to China as in that year, cell/mobile phone users experienced a virus that once it infected a user's phone, then it spreads to everyone in that user's contact list, and it perpetuated a spam on infected phones. It's believed to be the first virus spread by text message, and its spread reminded experts of Conficker, though the two phenomena have not been conclusively linked. While experts continue to try and root out the originator(s) of Conficker, computer laws are incredibly diverse across countries and, therefore, bringing those who perpetrate crimes using computer worms to justice could be very difficult or even impossible, based on the legal jurisdiction.

Fighting Conficker and similar threats have taken a two-pronged approach of defense (i.e., preventing the spread) and aggression (i.e., attempting to destroy the worm and bring those who use it to harm others to justice). The US combines these two operations under the National Security Administration. France uses two separate agencies to deal with cyber defense and aggression when dealing with Conficker. Many countries came up with plans to work with internet providers to help rid users' computers of the Conficker worm. Countries like Finland monitored the problem and other Scandinavian countries like Norway and Sweden did not have working groups dedicated to fighting Conficker but they managed to somewhat control the worm's spread. In 2009, in response to Conficker and other computer security issues, the US Department of Homeland Security under President Barrack Obama said it would hire a thousand advanced experts in computer security over a period of 3 years, but experts questioned whether there was an adequate supply of these experts to bring this plan to fruition.

Conficker will block an infected computer from reaching security websites, so users can try contacting computer security websites to detect an infection. Solutions for fighting Conficker and future worms in the same vein are multifaceted. On the level of the individual, experts suggest that the computer security industry makes it easier for people to fix their computers by themselves. On the macro level, education of computer security experts is suggested to encourage them that they have to commit a mindset of fighting worms like Conficker like they are an enduring battle and not a quick gunfight and encourage them to be vigilant against all malware, dangerous or not, as many as 10% of computers affected by Conficker were compromised by other malware. Businesses are urged to protect, monitor, and segment all of their data (i.e., a segmented computer network is split up into smaller subnetworks). A non-segmented network makes it easier for a cyber-attacker to infect the entire network from a single entry point. The example of Conficker has led computer security experts to consider using the tricks of malware creators by creating fixer worms that would infect computers worldwide to patch and cure them of their malware infections. In 2003, such a worm named Waledac was used on computers infected with the malware worm Blaster. Fixer worms, though well-intentioned, might require a reboot or cause the computer to shut down and restart at an inappropriate time, thus causing data loss and network failures. Generally, security experts urge computer users not to click on any unknown attachments, to always use strong and unique passwords, and to keep a continually updated data backup to protect themselves against worms and other malware.

Moving Forward: Positive and Negative Outcomes of Conficker

One positive outcome of Conficker is that it has increased awareness of worms and the damage they can cause among computers used by public and security experts alike. An additional benefit is that Conficker brought computing experts together both across the globe and in the private and public sectors in a spirit of cooperation to fight the worm when in the past it was difficult to successfully unite this community around a common effort on such a large scale. In February 2009, the so-called Conficker Cabal was formalized under the singular leadership, initially by a Microsoft program manager, and became known professionally as the Conficker Working Group.

As Conficker operates by randomly generating and buying up internet domains (new names for website pages) at increasingly accelerated rates with each new variation of the worm and then using those domains as bases to communicate with its creator(s). Knowing that Conficker operates this way, Microsoft had initially tried to buy up all the domains generated/used by Conficker but even with its vast financial resources, it could not keep up with Conficker's ability to generate domains. Recognizing the work of the Conficker Cabal/Conficker Working Group, The Internet Corporation for Assigned Names and Numbers (ICANN) agreed to waive domain registration fees for working group members and informed over 100 top-level country internet domain registrars that the Conficker worm would try to automatically register names with them.

Post-Conficker did not see an explosion in the use of worms, but the worms that emerged were in some cases more sophisticated. For example, the Stuxnet worm emerged in 2011 and perhaps learning from how Conficker was captured and studied in order to fight its spread, the Stuxnet worm was programmed to self-destruct to avoid capture and analysis. Gabi Ashkenazi, the Chief of General Staff of the Israel Defense Forces (2007–2011), claimed he created Stuxnet. Stuxnet was used by the Anonymous Group to reveal personal records and information and to mount attacks against the FBI's and NATO's websites, in some cases claiming to access its secure information. Also in 2011, the Mirai worm targeted webcams and routers primarily and thus seriously compromised computer users' privacy when communicating in the vicinity of their computers. Criminals using Mirai would threaten to make users' private chats and information public unless ransoms were paid (i.e., this is called doxware). Conversely, a less effective worm emerged in 2017 and was named WannaCry. This worm, when studied, exposed a badly hidden kill switch that could destroy the worm. WannaCry was argued by experts to have been sponsored by the North Korean government. By 2015, despite 7 years of effort in fighting the worm internationally, an estimated 1 million computers remained infected worldwide. This led computer researchers in the Netherlands to argue that individuals whose computers remain infected with the Conficker worm might be forever infected.

Further Reading

Sanders, A. D. (2010). Conficker: Lessons in secure software and system design. *Information Security Journal: A Global Perspective*, *19*(2), 95–99.

Talbot, D. (2010). Moore's outlaws. *Technology Review*, *113*(4), 36–43.

Zhang, C., Zhou, S., & Chain, B. M. (2015). Hybrid epidemics--a case study on computer worm conficker. *PLoS One*, *10*(5), e0127478.

References

Bowden, M. (2010). The enemy within. *Atlantic Monthly*, *305*(5), 72–83.

Giles, J. (2009). Conficker: the inside story. *New Scientist Archive*, *202*(2712), 36–39.

Hern, A. (2017, December 30). WannaCry, Petya, NotPetya: How ransomware hit the big time in 2017. Retrieved from *The Guardian: US Edition* at https://www.theguardian.com/technology/2017/dec/30/wannacry-petya-notpetya-ransomware

Hiller, J. S. (2015, March). Civil cyberconflict: Microsoft, cybercrime, and botnets. *Santa Clara High Technology Law Journal*, *31*(2), 163–188.

Kirk, J. (2015, August). Cleaning up botnets takes years, if ever, to complete. *PC World* (08131384), 1.

Kerner, S. M. (2016, June). Ransomware Goes After Manufacturing. *Eweek*, *9*.

Larkin, E. (2009). The Conficker Worm: A Potential Threat to PCs. *Pcworld*, *27*(5), 37.

Moyer, M. (2009). Pulling up worms. The Conficker worm exposes computer flaws, fixes and fiends. *Scientific American*, *300*(6), 30.

Westrup, H. (2010). Worm Infestation. *Current Science*, *96*(2), 6–7.

Chapter 28

Cryptocurrencies

Scott N. Romaniuk
International Centre for Policing and Security, University of South Wales, Caerleon, United Kingdom

Ronald Lorenzo
Prairie View A&M University, Prairie View, TX, United States

Contents

Introduction 181
Precursors to Cryptocurrencies 182
Invention of Cryptocurrencies 182
Incorporation into Markets 183
Legality and Criminal Activity 183
Risk and Terrorism Issues 184
Conclusion 184
Further Reading 185
References 185

Introduction

Cryptocurrencies are digital forms of currency or cash that are exchanged on the World Wide Web. Cryptocurrencies are a form of technology that uses encrypted coding and decentralized networks in order to facilitate the global transaction of money. Unlike cash issued by national governments, cryptocurrencies are not legal tender, operate beyond the limit of government regulation, and have a value that is not backed by any national bank. The technological novelty of cryptocurrencies, along with their supranational properties, have raised concerns about their vulnerability to hacking, use for illegitimate purposes, and financial volatility.

DOI: 10.4324/9781315144511-30

Precursors to Cryptocurrencies

Prior to the invention of cryptocurrencies, private sector companies made attempts at creating digital forms of cash. These companies tried to establish digital cash payment systems based on a trusted third-party model. This is similar to a credit card payment model by which one party exchanges credit for a good or service offered by a second party who recognizes the value of the credit as backed by a third party. Companies such as Flooz, Beenz, and Digicash in the 1990s were early third-party backers of digital cash on the Internet but failed for various reasons (Berman, 2018). Early third-party backers of digital cash failed for reasons of financial problems, fraud, or poor management (Berman, 2018). Digital cash under the model of trusted third parties depended on the success and existence of a third party in order to exist.

Invention of Cryptocurrencies

The first cryptocurrency, Bitcoin, was invented by a hacker or collective of hackers using the moniker of Satoshi Nakamoto. Unlike digital cash that is backed by a trusted third party, Bitcoin established the basic template for cryptocurrencies by foregoing the backing by third parties. Bitcoin as a currency operates by treating cash as information that is exchanged between parties. In the case of Bitcoin, cash transactions are seen as information that is exchanged between two parties who are incorporated into a peer-to-peer network. All transactions within the network are publicly recorded by a technology known as a blockchain. A blockchain is a public record that is shared by all users of the network to ensure that money cannot be spent more than one time per transaction.

To receive cryptocurrency, a user needs a virtual wallet with a public number known to everyone in the network. Someone making a payment deposits the money to the publicly numbered virtual wallet using a private key. At that point, the transaction is broadcast throughout the network and becomes valid when a third computer, known as a Bitcoin miner, is able to solve a mathematically complex puzzle associated with the cryptographic nature of the transaction. At that point, the Bitcoin miner earns a small percentage of the transaction for his or her efforts in legitimizing the transaction in the network's blockchain. However, the miner earns a transaction by unlocking cryptocurrency within the network, not by taking a percentage of the transaction. Transactions are semi-anonymous since the virtual wallet numbers are publicly known but their owners can try to remain anonymous.

Unlike forms of currencies backed by national banks or governments, which can manage their currencies by creating more cash, cryptocurrencies such as Bitcoins place a limit on the number of Bitcoins in existence. The Bitcoin blockchain has 17 million Bitcoins in circulation, with an additional 4 million Bitcoins that can be unlocked by miners. After miners unlock all 21 million Bitcoins, the supply of Bitcoins will be exhausted. The limited number of Bitcoins means that the value of a single Bitcoin fluctuates, making it possible for the cryptocurrency itself to be an object of financial speculation.

Incorporation into Markets

As of February 2018, there are over 1,300 different cryptocurrencies in existence in addition to Bitcoin; other cryptocurrencies have names such as Ethereum and Monero (Siripurapu, 2021; Cointelegraph n.d.). The estimated value of all cryptocurrencies in 2018 is estimated at $500 billion USD (Siripurapu, 2021). As of 2018, over 13,000 online and offline retailers accept cryptocurrencies for payments, including major companies such as Microsoft, Apple Computers, Dish Network, and Overstock.com (Coinmap n.d.). Cryptocurrency can be used to purchase pizzas, pay for online dating sites, and make limited tuition payments for some colleges in Europe and in the United States such as the European School of Management and Technology in Berlin and King's College in New York (IBT). Users of Bitcoin and other currencies can spend their money indirectly at major retailers by using the cryptocurrency to purchase gift cards valued in US dollars.

Cryptocurrencies are volatile investments. From January 2017 to November 2017, the value of a Bitcoin increased from around $800 to around $8,000 (Statista 2021). Because of their volatility, cryptocurrencies have attracted speculators. In addition to volatility, cryptocurrencies face the possibilities of being criminalized in certain countries and also of being hacked (Cointelegraph, n.d.).

Another economic activity associated with cryptocurrency is mining. Miners earn a reward for facilitating transactions by solving ever-increasing mathematical puzzles for the blockchain. As the number of transactions increases, so does the complexity of the puzzles as well as their potential reward, often in the form of that cryptocurrency. Early miners of cryptocurrencies such as Bitcoin and Ethereum could use consumer-grade technology to mine Bitcoins. Mining currencies that are widely in use now, such as Bitcoin and Ethereum, entail investment in sophisticated technology beyond the financial reach of the average individual.

Legality and Criminal Activity

Countries mostly recognize the legality and legitimate uses of cryptocurrencies. A few countries such as Venezuela, Bolivia, Namibia, Kyrgyzstan, and Iceland have banned the use of cryptocurrencies by their citizens and institutions (Bajpai, 2021). China banned the use of cryptocurrency transactions among banks and other financial institutions, although it allows individuals to buy and sell cryptocurrencies (Bajpai, 2021). Different countries recognize the legality of cryptocurrencies, but because of their novelty, treat them differently. Depending on the country, cryptocurrencies are treated as either currencies, properties, or financial services in regard to existing laws. Mexico treats cryptocurrencies as currencies for the sake of enforcing money laundering laws (Berman 2018). Japan recognizes cryptocurrencies and cryptocurrency exchanges as innovations in technology and finance (Graham, 2017). The United States recognizes cryptocurrencies as properties, not as currencies, and subjects them to capital gains under its tax laws (Bajpai, 2021).

Early adopters of cryptocurrencies such as Bitcoin included criminals who used the cryptocurrencies for illegal activity online, mostly in purchasing narcotics, in anonymized online marketplaces known as the dark web (Siripurapu, 2021). In 2013, the United States Federal Bureau of Investigation and the Drug Enforcement Agency shut down Silk Road, a dark web marketplace, and arrested its founder, Ross Ulbricht (Siripurapu, 2021). The US government estimates that cryptocurrencies were used to buy and sell over $200 million in illegal goods and services on Silk Road (Siripurapu, 2021).

Ransomware used to take over personal, private sector, and private sector computers often ask for payment in cryptocurrency. The City of Atlanta was a victim of such an attack which asked for $50,000 million in payments, which the city did not pay, choosing instead to use $2.6 million in emergency spending to circumvent the ransomware instead (Newman, 2018).

Other criminal uses of cryptocurrencies include using the technology for laundering money and for drug trafficking (Siripurapu, 2021). Drug cartels find different levels of success in moving large amounts of money depending on the sophistication of the government they are trying to evade.

Risk and Terrorism Issues

Since at least 2014, Islamic terrorist sites and their supporters have encouraged the use of cryptocurrencies to fund groups such as Al-Qaeda and the so-called Islamic State (Bin Mohamad Hasbi, and Mahzam 2018). Cryptocurrencies have been used to fund terrorist attacks in Europe and Asia. Terrorist groups used Bitcoin and other cryptocurrencies to carry out the 2015 Charlie Hebdo attacks in France and the 2016 Jakarta attacks in Indonesia (Bin Mohamad Hasbi and Mahzam 2018). In the United States, supporters of the so-called Islamic State have been arrested for their attempts to transfer money using Bitcoin and other cryptocurrencies.

Mainstream institutions in the Islamic world, such as the Grand Mufti of Egypt, and the governments of Saudi Arabia and Turkey have condemned the use of cryptocurrencies. Mainstream Islamic religious authorities liken the use of cryptocurrencies to gambling and money laundering (Bin Mohamad Hasbi and Mahzam 2018). Secular authorities have condemned the use of the currency for its semi-anonymous quality, associating it with criminal activity.

Conclusion

Cryptocurrencies are a new technology that make possible transnational financial transactions and create new financial markets. A minority of cryptocurrency transactions are used for criminal and terroristic activities. The very nature of cryptocurrencies that make transactions public makes it difficult for criminals to use cryptocurrencies with impunity. The virtual wallet of cryptocurrencies can be matched to individuals and groups.

Like most emerging technology, there is a "cat and mouse" game between law enforcement agencies and criminals. Criminals have turned to ever more anonymous forms of cryptocurrencies, called altcurrencies, that add layers of anonymity to cryptocurrency transactions. Law enforcement agencies continue to learn more about cryptocurrency in order to develop forensic tools for unmasking criminal users. There is always the potential for terrorist groups to use cryptocurrencies in the commission of an attack, particularly in funding attacks or transferring funds. However, the real potential for terrorism may be in terrorist groups hacking blockchains and attempting to bring down multibillion cryptocurrency markets.

Further Reading

Narayanan, A., Bonneau, J., Felten, E., Miller, A., and Goldfeder, S. (2016). *Bitcoin and Cryptocurrency Technologies: A Comprehensive Introduction*. Princeton University Press.

Vigna, P. and Casey, M. J. (2016). *The Age of Cryptocurrency: How Bitcoin and the Blockchain Are Challenging the Global Economic Order*. Picador.

Werbach, K. (2018). *The Blockchain and the New Architecture of Trust*. The MIT Press.

References

Bajpai, P. (2021, August 25). "Countries Where Bitcoin Is Legal and Illegal", *Investopedia*. https://www.investopedia.com/articles/forex/041515/countries-where-bitcoin-legal-illegal.asp

Berman, A. (2018, September 13). "Mexican State Bank Announces Stricter Rules for Crypto Exchanges", *Cointelgraph*. https://cointelegraph.com/news/mexican-state-bank-announces-stricter-rules-for-crypto-exchanges

Coinmap. (n.d.). https://coinmap.org/#/world/54.82600800/-92.72460938/3

Cointelgraph. https://cointelegraph.com/bitcoin-for-beginners/what-are-cryptocurrencies#historyfinancing/#.W7u_PWNN7IV

Graham, L. (2017, September 29). "As China cracks down, Japan is fast becoming the powerhouse of the bitcoin market", *CNBC*. https://www.cnbc.com/2017/09/29/bitcoin-exchanges-officially-recognized-by-japan.html

Hasbi, Bin Mohamad, A. H. Mahzam. (2018, April 30). "CO18075 | Cryptocurrencies: Potential For Terror Financing?", S. Rajaratnam School of International Studies. https://www.rsis.edu.sg/rsis-publication/icpvtr/co18075-cryptocurrencies-potential-for-terror-

Newman, L. H. (2018, April 23). "Atlanta Spent $2.6M to Recover From a $52,000 Ransomware Scare", *WIRED*. https://www.wired.com/story/atlanta-spent-26m-recover-from-ransomware-scare/

Siripurapu, A. (2021, September 24). "Cryptocurrencies, Digital Dollars, and the Future of Money", *Council on Foreign Relations*. https://www.cfr.org/backgrounder/cryptocurrencies-and-national-security

Statista. (2021). "Bitcoin (BTC) price per day from October 2013 to December 9, 2021". statista.com/statistics/326707/bitcoin-price-index/

Chapter 29

Cyber Security and Social Media

Aaron T. Walter

University of Ss. Cyril & Methodius, Slovakia & Masaryk University, Brno, The Czech Republic

Contents

Introduction 187
Trust, Not Verified 189
Cybersecurity and Personal SM 189
Balance of Power between State and Personal Use of SM 191
Conclusion 194
Further Reading 195
References 195

Introduction

Online websites popularly known as Facebook, Twitter, Myspace, along with email, messaging, and other digital platforms are used regularly to advertise and communicate, so as to make purchases or gather socially online in countries throughout the world. Social media connects you with friends, family, business associates, and even total strangers. What you put out on social media may end up being circulated around the World Wide Web before you know it. It is estimated that there will be about 2.77 billion users on social media in 2019 (Statista 2019). The Statista database company also estimated that in 2018, there were approximately 243 million users of various social networks in the United States (Statista 2020). This number has been steadily increasing each year by roughly three million people. By 2023, some 257 million

DOI: 10.4324/9781315144511-31

people in the United States will be using some form of social media. Vitak (2008) reported that there are several reasons why people use a social networking site: most popular is to meet strangers and become friends. Through social networking sites, users can keep their interpersonal relationships with their friends. and users can send private messages and can use chatrooms and other methods of communication.

Nowadays, online social networks involve people from the entire world, of any age and with any kind of education. They also helped to increase computer usage among categories that previously showed little interest in it (Stroud, 2008). The compilation of the most popular social networks worldwide by active users (October, 2018) prepared by Statista gives a clear picture of the number of active users – in millions – with Facebook ruling supreme. With over 2 billion active users, Facebook holds the majority market share. Google's YouTube is second with Facebook-owned WhatsApp and Messenger. Facebook's Instagram platform has fewer than half of the visits of Facebook.

Following from this, the predominantly APAC-favored platforms are next, with QQ, We Chat, and Qzone all with over 600 million active users. As thousands of new social media users log on every week, the numbers relating to the flow of information on Facebook become ever more staggering. In one minute of Facebook, 243,055 photos are uploaded by users, 100,000 friends are requested, 13,888 apps are installed, 3,298,611 items are shared, 50,000 links are posted, and 15,277,777 like and share buttons are viewed on other websites (Ahmad, 2014). Furthermore, most social network users share a large amount of their private information in their social network space. This information ranges from demographic information, contact information, comments, images, videos, etc. Bicen and Cavus (2010) report in their study that the use and exchange of knowledge on the Internet are popular among university students.

Besides the social element, the expanded use of social media (SM) has facilitated the economic growth of corporations through their technological development of commercial products from which communication and digital communities thrived, and one can make the argument that the theme of SM's geopolitical and economic influence also brings the promise of global democracy, despite the countless challenges that threaten and present degrees of danger in actual democratic distribution.

Nowadays, SM is the primary medium where citizens can assemble socially and the disenfranchised organize politically. Market and constituent use of data derived from SM platforms do benefit a capitalist democracy within certain limits for example by the active participation, readied knowledge, and consent of those whom the State governs. The power of SM is readily observed. In brief, understanding the local significance and national significance of this interconnectedness is to contrast SM in the context of its benefits, when traditional media such as radio, television, newspapers, and even landline phones have a limited, communication use. Moreover, webpages only provide a one-way communication between those who post and those who read said webpages. Similarly, while the use of webpages, landline phones, billboards radio, and television has not been abandoned, it is the evolution of messaging or iMessaging for Apple products or messaging on smartphones where communication has developed both a two-way and one-way function. SM provides an additional tool to use. The result, however, is a high level of trust and a large amount of sensitive data. That trust is not always valid is of increasing concern (Benson, et al. 2015). With such sensitive data, it is necessary to verify.

Trust, Not Verified

Social networks have become a large pool of sensitive data. Easy to access, widely used, and outside of enterprise control, SM sites are gold mines for malicious actors. Moreover, social network users tend to have a high level of trust toward other social network users. They tend to accept friend requests easily and trust items that friends send to them (Gunatilaka, 2011). Summarized by *Social Media Today* (2013), in an example, a socialbot built an extended social network of one million people, successfully friending 3,055 individuals from a total of 8,570 invites sent. In other words, this resulted in a mind-boggling 35% acceptance rate. Once the socialbot made some friends, it in turn targeted those friends' friends. As the bot's network grew, so did its friend-acceptance rate. Additionally, the bot collected 250 GB of personal data, including 35% of all the personally identifiable information found on friend pages and 24% from extended friend-of-friend networks.

According to Christie Terrill, information that people post "can be used to craft a targeted phishing email containing a malicious link," which raises the probability that people will take the bait. (Terrill, 2017). To avoid personal complacency, SM providers are working hard to bolster their security features to make users feel safer and counter ever-increasing cyber threats, though do not rely on safeguards too heavily. Individually, one should not click on suspicious links, nor should a person accept friend requests from people not known because there are hackers working to move past defenses. There are a variety of entry points for hackers to invade digital spaces because of the variety of SM platforms commonly used with not only Twitter and Facebook notable but also Instagram, Tumblr, and LinkedIn. With the intersection of the Internet and mobile devices, data is more widely available than it was in the past, especially in marketing. Therefore, this has given hackers more outlets in which they can obtain sensitive information, even an unsecured network in a coffee shop.

Cybersecurity and Personal SM

There are several ways that individuals can offer personal cybersecurity to protect themselves through SM to prevent SM sites to sabotage. The first is not to provide too much information. Simply, do not leave a trail of breadcrumbs for SM hackers. Whether personally or via a company, avoid sharing information like your date of birth, schools attended, as well as names and pictures of family. Those are enough for most identity thieves to break into your accounts or even apply for credit cards using your personal info. Facebook, by design, breaks these precautions. However, being selective as to what to share in the biography section is important. Therefore, trust is important, yet within the online domain, it is unpredictable on the grounds that the online world is characterized as frail.

By utilizing social networking sites (Van Eecke, and Truyens 2010), people open themselves to different sorts of dangers that have the regular impact of breaking their privacy, most commonly collected and used in phishing or spear phishing campaigns. Malware is most common. Malware on SM according to Steve Durbin (2016), Managing Director at Information Security Forum, is

> from a hacker standpoint, is easy access. The social media is an environment where people are not guarded in what personal information is shared. People readily engage with a third party. This is a prime opportunity to gather information from people in the form of spear phishing to social engineering to push out malware.

Most malware hides inside emails and download links; they can also be spread through SM via shortened URLs or even hidden inside SM ads.

According to the NopSec report,

> Twitter is becoming one of the top platforms for security researchers and attackers looking to disseminate proof-of-concept exploits. Vulnerabilities associated with active malware are tweeted nine times more than vulnerabilities with just a public exploit and 18 times more than all other vulnerabilities.
>
> (Zurkus 2016)

Likewise, while SM and online dating apps are extremely convenient since they allow you to find a partner online in no time, one of the most common problems of online dating is catfishing, where your partner fakes their identity, whereby personal and financial information is gathered about the person. Accessing your SM accounts using your mobile phone can be done with just one tap, which is great, as long as you are the only person using your phone. Therefore, protecting a phone with a strong password is highly recommended. Additional precautions can ensure safe use of social networks.

1. Clearing browser history: Different kinds of browsers where usernames and passwords are kept saved are available to hackers. Avoid this security concern by clearing the browser history.
2. Two-factor verification: Using two-factor verification, a text code on a person's registered mobile number, is considered by many SM websites as an effective verification method to prevent unknown access to accounts.
3. Updating privacy settings: The use of privacy settings is very much important where hiding contact information such as email, date of birth, and mobile number helps avoid hacking personal SM accounts.
4. Avoid clicking ads on SM: SM is full of ads. The users always click different kinds of ads as these ads are very attractive.
5. Avoid using third-party apps: Using third-party apps is common today where a user downloads an app, and when opened, the person must sign in with SM accounts. This sign in via the individual SM accounts shares personal information from the SM account with the app. The app uses that information to access

the individual account but is also capable of sharing contents. Avoid these security issues by not using personal SM information to sign in to an app.

6. Minimizing the use of virtual private networks: Virtual private networks usually works as key loggers. What personal information is input in the system is stored by the virtual private network app.
7. Using different and strong passwords: To be on the safer side of SM, it is recommended to always use a different password for online accounts instead of common passwords. SM websites always recommend using a strong password where the password consists of numbers and letters and special characters.
8. Do not trust a message: Hackers often break into accounts and send messages that appear as if from your friends or family. Suspected fraudulent messages should be checked using an alternate method.

All of this should not discourage a person from using SM. SM is an immensely powerful tool when used correctly. But an individual should think about their actions online and take responsibility for personal cybersecurity. Cybersecurity and state interaction is of great importance in this new decade of the twenty-first century as democratic principles of privacy, civil liberties, and SM use are fought over and protected.

Balance of Power between State and Personal Use of SM

SM has strengthened the State's surveillance and unintentionally reinforced the power of the electorate in western societies and proven its use as an additional tool to strengthen checks and balances against the questionable actions of traditional, democratic governments because we value the right to privacy legitimized through our historical freedoms. It has also given a political tool of expression to those government systems globally that possess a desire to embrace democratic reforms and capitalist, democratic policies and customs. "Understanding social media critically means (…) to engage with the different forms of sociality on the Internet in the context of society" (Fuchs 2014, p. 6). Fuchs' broad definition of what SM comprise also guides this entry; the underlying sentiment that has also been driving much of the digital peacebuilding agenda is outlined well by Clay Shirky:

> As the communications landscape gets denser, more complex, and more participatory, the networked population is gaining greater access to information, more opportunities to engage in public speech, and an enhanced ability to undertake collective action. In the political arena (…) these increased freedoms can help loosely coordinated public's demand change.
>
> (Shirky 2011, p. 29)

The transformative potential of this Internet-powered networked society can be envisioned in similar ways to other parts of society that have also been digitally disrupted: "New media accelerates and reinforces various facets of peacebuilding and protest activities, from effective counter knowledge production to coordinating protest" (Firchow et al. 2017, p. 18). This sort of imbalance is unacceptable to our democracy because the threat to a nation's security should not be the sole factor that justifies the indiscriminate use of metadata for surveillance purposes. If a nation of citizens allows this surveillance to exist unchecked, then it challenges not only our understanding of a democratic, open society but the very foundations and ideals of a democratic state. Most notably and interestingly, Alexander Hamilton makes an observation with relation to the war between the states. In the Federalist Paper 8, titled The Consequences of Hostilities Between the States, Hamilton (1787) relates:

> Safety from external danger is the most powerful director of national conduct. Even the ardent love of liberty will, after a time, give way to its dictates. The violent destruction of life and property incident to war, the continual effort and alarm attendant on a state of continual danger, will compel nations the most attached to liberty to resort for repose and security to institutions which have a tendency to destroy their civil and political rights. To be more safe, they at length become willing to run the risk of being less free.

Moreover, SM has strengthened the State's surveillance and unintentionally reinforced the power of the electorate in western societies and proven its use as an additional tool to strengthen checks and balances against the questionable actions of traditional, democratic governments, because the right to privacy legitimized through historical freedoms is highly valued. It has also given a political tool of expression to those government systems globally that possess a desire to embrace democratic reforms and capitalist, democratic policies and customs. Therefore, SM can be an immensely useful tool that brings interconnectedness with both rewards and risks. Arguably, one should not presume that there is a correlation between the use of SM as a surveillance tool and the eventual movement of government and nation-states to totalitarian regimes.

The civil war in Syria is a focal point for the complexities around SM use to instigate conflict as well as to support information from the frontlines or advocacy through information and communications technology (ICT). The communication of the so-called Islamic State relied heavily on SM, creating new media platforms diametrically opposed to liberal peacebuilding ideals and practices. As Lynch et al. conclude in their report for USIP:

> The growth and complexity of the Arabic language Twitterverse highlight the importance of avoiding research designs that look only at English language social media; a more sophisticated understanding of the structural biases in social media and the difficult challenges posed by activist curation.
>
> (2014, pp. 28–29)

Each stakeholder involved in the conflict is able to communicate, amplify, or mobilize through SM, creating a complex web of (mis)information that will persist for a long time after the war is officially declared over. Some of the initial gains of SM to contribute to social change have been pulled bad, and an "ICT4Bad," rather than ICT4D, infrastructure has been built up by various governments, organizations, and regimes to protect itself against the power of Internet-based transformations. In terms of building peace and democracy, new areas of "politicizing surveillance" will once again change the landscape of SM use as a "whole system of exploitation and oppression" (Duncan 2018, p. 173) and challenge previous approaches to using digital tools for social change. Currently, the potential of SM to support peacebuilding is under tremendous pressure from global corporations, governments investing in surveillance technologies, and societal trends that are often opposed to foundations of building peace, achieving compromises, or creating cohesive visions for future development.

The promise of social media-enabled "revolutions" that led to peaceful social change was eventually met with the realities of governments, elites, and powerful groups not only suppressing and blocking SM but also using them against activists, ordinary citizens, or marginalized groups. Similar to developments at the end of the twentieth century when "civil society" was seen as the solution for peacebuilding, ICT, SM, and digital platforms face similar political or economic constraints that fall short of building positive peace.

> While technology opens up apparently new opportunities it is worth bearing in mind old questions of epistemology and positionality (…). A key part of the equation is editorial intervention and the decision to filter, parse and phrase information in particular ways – all subjective activities involving judgement calls.
>
> (MacGinty 2017, p. 9)

At the same time, it is again the individual. What a person shares online is important, not only by sharing opinions online, but also other intimate details via shopping and communication. The marketing of products to the consumer through the use of SM platforms on commercial websites, or even when asked for personal information like ZIP codes and mobile phone numbers while shopping online, exposes an imbalance between how widespread availability of personal information is not entirely acceptable in a democracy.

What precisely then is the national interest of the State in the context of cybersecurity and civil liberties? Embedded liberal paradigm of government protection and citizen free speech. The speed, comprehensiveness, and double-edged nature of this data-driven social change has caught both governments and citizens out-of-step. Governments may use SM for its crowdsource information about citizens. Thus, although the promise of social media-enabled "revolutions" possibly leading to peaceful social change continues, this has been met with the realities of governments, elites, and powerful groups suppressing and blocking SM. This has been observed worse in non-traditional democracies, where cybersecurity was not guaranteed and instead used against activists, ordinary citizens, and even marginalized groups. Government protection and citizen free speech are arguably more acute in western democracy where consent and balance are sought.

Michel Foucault illustrated how society utilizes power, by underscoring the essential understanding that social control in a society is inherent in the individual. The individual as a subject is free. Therefore, the existence of an individual in the power relationship exercising both recalcitrance against oppression and intransigence in the pursuit of freedom of choice shows a balance between the governed and those who govern (Felluga, 2011). The author's, Michael Williams, interpretation of political authority through Thomas Hobbes promotes the understanding that,

> the extraordinarily powerful, evocative and metaphorical language of Leviathan recognizes the construction of rational political order requires an affective element if it was to be effective. Logic alone was insufficient to this task. Nor were the coercive powers of the sovereign alone sufficient to construct and maintain such a political order.
>
> (Williams, 2005)

Hobbes, he asserts, does not believe in the simple existence and power of the sovereign adequate to ensure a stable political order. Precisely because SM is in the hands of the individual and has a decentralized nature to power out of government (sovereign) control, consent for power and distribution is needed. Moreover, the consent of the governed is essential in maintaining order in a society, and consent is essential because the governed feel that their consent has been obtained justly. SM only provides a record of the event and a communications medium to express political dissent, but the underlying philosophy that is adequately validated by consent is not to destroy society but to make it better for the governed and those who govern to exist legitimately. Therefore, the notion of consent juxtaposed with the State's right to security and secrecy has brought forward a need to promote and preserve privacy and the *balance* between the civil needs of the citizens within an open society against the State's national/international and security needs to maintain order.

In recent decades, the threat to privacy by western democratic governments has been revealed. A prime example of this is through the activities of the National Security Agency (NSA) of the United States and justified legally by an interpreted section of the Patriot Act. Congressional deference to the executive branch of the US government has forever been altered. Yet, the use of SM to protect citizens is present and has had its success preventing terror attacks or tracking and bringing to justice criminals. In sum, through SM platforms, a balance to promote an open society against an overreliance on security and surveillance is connected with citizenry consent either through the vote, the right to redress the government, or a free press.

Conclusion

This brief chapter examined the role of SM in daily interactions and the tradeoffs between web activity for pleasure or business and the potential threats to security for the State. The challenges to an open, democratic society remain to strike a balance between the civil liberties of the citizenry and the national interest of the State and to protect its self-interest, as well as the lives of its citizens and the continual flow of economic commerce and personal enjoyment. By utilizing SM, people open themselves to different sorts of dangers that have the regular impact of breaking their privacy. Interestingly, enough individual privacy concerns are very feeble in the social networking sites and the users' endeavors to make the appropriate changes to their SM privacy is substantially lower than other modes of security operations. At the same time, SM has strengthened the State's surveillance and also unintentionally reinforced the power of the electorate in western societies, while also proving its use as an additional tool to strengthen checks and balances against the questionable actions of traditional, democratic governments. It has also given a political tool of expression to those government systems globally that possess a desire to embrace democratic reforms and capitalist, democratic policies and customs.

Further Reading

Erbschloe, M. (2017). *Social Media Warfare: Equal Weapons for All*. Boca Raton: CRC Press.

Gupta, R. & Brooks, H. (2013). *Using Social Media for Global Security*. Indianapolis: Wiley.

Wall, D. S. (2014). *Policing Cybercrime: Networked and Social Media Technologies and the Challenges for Policing*. Abingdon: Routledge.

References

Ahmad I. (2014). What Happens in Just one Minute on Facebook? *Social media today*. https://goo.gl/1rqAR8

Benson, V., Saridakis, G., Tennakoon, H. & Ezingeard, J. N. (August 2015). The role of security notices and online consumer behaviour: An empirical study of social networking users, *International Journal of Human Computer Studies*, *80*, 36–44.

Bicen, H. & Cavus, N. (2010). The Most Preferred Social Network Sites by Students. *Procedia Social and Behavioural Sciences*, *2*(2), 5864–5869.

Duggan, M., Greenwood, S. & Perrin, A. (2016, November 11). Social Media Update 2016. Pew Research Center. https://www.pewresearch.org/internet/wp-content/uploads/sites/9/2016/11/PI_2016.11.11_Social-Media-Update_FINAL.pdf

Duncan, J. (2018). Taking the spy machine south: Communications surveillance in Sub-Saharan Africa, in B. Mutsvairo (ed.), *The Palgrave handbook of media and communication research in Africa* (pp. 153–176). London: Palgrave Macmillan.

Felluga, D. (2011). Modules on Foucault: Panoptic and Carceral Society, Introductory Guide to Critical Theory. http://www.purdue.edu/guidetotheory/newhistoricism/modules/foucaultcarceral.html

Fuchs, C. (2014). *Social media: a critical introduction*. London: Sage.

Firchow, P., Martin-Shields, C., Omer, A. & MacGinty, R. (2017). PeaceTech: The liminal spaces of digital technology in peacebuilding, *International Studies Perspectives*, *18*(1), 4–42.

Gunatilaka D. (2011). A Survey of Privacy and Security Issues in Social Networks, Washington University. https://goo.gl/JfbUp2

Hamilton, A. (November, 1787). Federalist No. 8: The Consequences of Hostilities Between the States. http://thomas.loc.gov/home/histdox/fed_08.html

Lynch, M., Freelon, D. & Aday, S. (2014). Blogs and bullets III: Syria's socially mediated civil war (Peaceworks No. 91). United States Institute of Peace, Washington, DC.

MacGinty, R. (2017). Peacekeeping and data. *International Peacekeeping*, *24*(5), 695–705.

Risher, M. (2013, February 10). The Asocial Network: How Hackers Use Social Networks To Destroy Your Online Life. https://www.socialmediatoday.com/content/asocial-network-how-hackers-use-social-networks-destroy-your-online-life

Shirky, C. (2011). The political power of social media: Technology, the public sphere, and political change, *Foreign Affairs*, *90*(1), 28–41.

Terrill, C. (2017, April 28). What You Need To Know Now About Cybersecurity and Social Media. *Forbes*. https://www.forbes.com/sites/christieterrill/2017/04/28/what-you-need-to-know-now-about-cybersecurity-and-social-media/#42864e883a16

Statista (2019). 'Number of social network users worldwide from 2010 to 2021'. https://www.statista.com/statistics/278414/number-of-worldwide-social-network-users/

Statista (2020). 'Number of social network users in the United States from 2017 to 2023'. statista.com/statistics/278409/number-of-social-network-users-in-the-united-states/

Stroud D. (2008). Social networking: An age-neutral commodity—Social networking becomes a mature web application *Journal of Direct, Data and Digital Marketing Practice*, *9*(3), 278–292.

Van Eecke, P. & Truyens, T. (2010). Privacy and social networks, *Computer Law & Security Review*, *26*(5), 535–546.

Vitak, J. M. (2008). *Facebook Friends: How Online identities Impact Offline Relations*. Washington, DC. https://goo.gl/R4WdWd

Williams, M. (2005). *The Realist Tradition and the Limits of International Relations*. Cambridge: Cambridge University Press.

Zurkus, K. (August 29, 2016). Social media, the gateway for malware. *CSO Online*. https://www.csoonline.com/article/3106292/social-media-the-gateway-for-malware.html

Chapter 30

Cyber Security Operations: Tactics, Techniques, and Procedures

Gary Leigh
Charles Darwin University, Darwin, NT, Australia

Content

Further Reading 202
References 202

This chapter reviews the intricate nature of cyber security operations for their tactics, techniques, and procedures. There is a tremendous amount of variety for potential cyber operations due to the realities of crafting operations, their purposes, and their resources. The way of appreciating cyber security operations is by understanding how these operations are in fact a culmination of various components. Tactics, techniques, and procedures (TTPs) are one of these components and feature evidently in all types of cyber operations (Cybersecurity and Infrastructure Security Agency, 2020).

The National Institute of Standards and Technology's Computer Security Resource Center (2020) defines TTPs as:

> The behavior of an actor. A tactic is the highest-level description of this behavior, while techniques give a more detailed description of behavior in the context of a tactic, and procedures an even lower-level, highly detailed description in the context of a technique.

There is a great degree of overlap across TTPs and other concepts. Some of these concepts can be simply viewed with a meta-view, which is to say – cyber operations

DOI: 10.4324/9781315144511-32

are just that, cyber operations. TTPs simply form a part of it. Other concepts that overlap include terms that reflect the function of an aspect of a cyber operation. For example, threat hunting, threat intelligence, and adversarial modeling are all functions that help cyber operations understand the adversary and risk involved in the operation. If viewing cyber operations from a functional view, which is to understand a cyber operation by the functions it is composed of or outcomes to achieve, we begin to have a more holistic approach to knowing where TTPs fit into the picture.

This view can go so far as to cover functions such as, but not limited to:

- Intelligence gathering and open source intelligence work
- Disinformation and deception campaigns
- Red, blue, and purple teaming
- Penetration testing
- Offensive and defense engagement (from seizure to warfare)
- Exploit, general tooling development and reverse engineering
- Infrastructure engineering and data preservation
- Cryptographic operations
- Signals and telemetry, including data transmission or lack thereof
- Computer engineering and architecture design.

These are all functions that share a common language that is readily accepted by U.S. cyber practitioners. And without doubt, there are even more operations and functions that cyber security operations fulfill that are not mentioned here. Those who are already familiar with TTPs may not be satisfied with such a wide list. The physical, human, governance, and strategic aspects are not to be ignored either; however, there are numerous frameworks that exist that incorporate and address these aspects for the purposes of cyber security modeling. It is worth reinforcing that TTPs must be taken at face value for each of these terms are generally present in all aspects of cyber security operations. It is only when using a specific TTPs framework such as MITRE ATT&CK that stricter codified language should be used. More discussion on frameworks follows later in this chapter.

A granular focus on TTPs without strategic context is not very useful. When the Federal Bureau of Investigation (FBI) can report the United States suffering over 10 billion dollars in losses from cybercrime between 2015 and 2019 alone (Federal Bureau of Investigation, 2019, p 5), how can Homeland Security cyber operations assist when only considering the hacking and not the wider strategy in motion? This is especially pertinent when considering the actionable aspects of the third pillar of the Department of Homeland Security's Cyber Security Strategy (2018). The third pillar being, "Threat Reduction" by means of targeting transnational criminal groups and disrupting their operations. Without an analytical and granular view that can account for the role of TTPs, planning cyber operations is potentially weaker due to the absence of sound technical substance. This is no different from when a cyber operation is solely strategically focused and does not incorporate the ever-evolving realm of TTPs by adversaries. Such thinking also applies to improving our own TTPs as guardians of U.S. interests in cyberspace.

This touches on the operations of our adversaries, threat actors, and agents. However, here we will refer to them as adversaries. Adversaries have come to be synonymous with TTPs. This is simply due to how TTPs help cyber defenders with attribution of who is doing what against the United States. As such, there is a tendency to use TTPs as a way of knowing the enemy is the enemy. And if this is the case, it applies vice versa, that adversaries can know it is us on the defense and therefore we cannot ignore TTPs as an area of focus for strategic outcomes.

The National Cyber Security Center (2017), which is part of the British Government Communications Headquarters (GCHQ) lists some TTPs and identifiers of cybercriminal organizations below:

- Malware design and varying degree of sophistication in hacking approaches
- Their order of operations and scope that match what operatives they may have
- Nature of victims and target systems
- Certain, traceable but difficult monetization strategies and use of the online black market for resources
- Patterns of attack.

For Homeland Security professionals, it is not uncommon to apply both computer science and computer security lenses to understand our vulnerabilities. By identifying how our information systems come together, how people come together, and how cyber security tooling and operations come together, we can gain a more complete view of our cyber security architecture. When such approaches are taken, a business analyst might speak in terms of processes and process improvement. A military perspective might speak to a culmination of these things as doctrine or strategy. A terrorist or state-sponsored cyber actor might view this as tradecraft. Despite how we view our systems, and at what levels we view them, semantics and nomenclature can sometimes make interoperability more difficult. However, the essence of these components that support or inform cyber operation will have a series of TTPs to some degree.

The definitive work on this approach to thinking of cyber operations, threat modeling, and TTPs for Homeland Security purposes is from the Homeland Security Systems Engineering & Development Institute (HSSEDI). HSSEDI is in fact a federally funded research and development center, which operates in conjunction with MITRE and the Department of Homeland Security. This strategic partnership allows the HSSEDI, "to serve as its primary systems engineering resource and to meet DHS-wide demand for rapid access to deep technical expertise" (MITRE, 2020d). The HSSEDI framework document titled, *Cyber Threat Modelling: Survey, Assessment and Representative Framework* (2018) explores risk management frameworks and threat modeling approaches with exceptional detail and is considered mandatory reading for advanced understanding of this field.

An additional resource that is considered the gold standard in understanding TTPs in cyber security is the MITRE ATT&CK framework. This framework is a knowledge base of TTPs sourced from real-world cyber security adversaries and is applied globally. The framework is exceptionally detailed and rapidly evolving. As a way of providing a taxonomy of all this information, the ATT&CK framework has a matrix which comprises of the following:

- Initial access
- Execution

- Persistence
- Privilege escalation
- Defense evasion
- Credential access
- Discovery
- Lateral movement
- Collection
- Command and control
- Exfiltration
- Impact.

Another perspective on cyber operations and TTPs is Lockheed Martin's (2020) own "cyber kill chain." The kill chain explores operations concerning computer network attacks and computer network espionage. (Lockheed Martin Corporation, 2020). The kill chain has seven stages which are:

- Reconnaissance
- Weaponization
- Delivery
- Exploitation
- Installation
- Command and control (c2)
- Actions on objectives.

The kill chain is an excellent foundation for analyzing TTPs. Moreover, the kill chain's stages can map across to courses of action. These courses of action are part of Lockheed Martin's approach. Naturally, depending on the cyber operation and agency involved, there will be other courses of action to be taken. The courses of action capture the response to each stage and include (Lockheed Martin Corporation et al., 2011, p. 5):

- Detection
- Denial
- Disruption
- Degradation
- Deception
- Destruction.

For those familiar with the National Security Agency (NSA) and perhaps defense approaches to TTPs, the NSA's Central Security Service's Technical Cyber Threat Framework offers its own taxonomy for threat analysis as well.

As this chapter on TTPs has discussed how nomenclature can be a burden to understanding the elements of a cyber operation, the NSA framework is here to put this to rest. The framework is, "designed to standardize how NSA characterizes and categorizes adversary activity by using a common technical lexicon that is operating system independent and closely aligned with industry definitions. This common technical cyber lexicon supports sharing, product development, operational planning, and knowledge driven operations across the Intelligence Community" (NSA, 2018, p. 2).

This framework features some of the following attributes which are useful for operational purposes (NSA, 2018, p. 5):

- Administration (planning, resource development, research)
- Preparation (reconnaissance and staging)
- Engagement (delivery, exploitation)
- Presence (execution, privilege escalation, lateral movement, persistence)
- Effect (monitoring, exfiltration, modify, deny, destroy)
- Ongoing process (command and control, evasion).

Putting this type of information to use is not exclusively for Homeland and National Security actors though. Some of these frameworks come from private enterprise and research institutions that form part of the United States' overall cyber capability. Advances to thwart adversaries can draw from this body of knowledge to utilize TTPs and is exemplified by the MIT-IBM Watson AI Lab. Here, combined artificial intelligence, machine learning, and neural networks focus on "acting as the adversary" to "figure out how the attacks are learning to evade detection, which will help us to craft better detectors" (O'Reilly, et al. 2018).

These frameworks have many uses, despite how they have been concisely laid out here. The frameworks become rapidly powerful as they are incorporated into cyber operations to help with intelligence and strategy. In this chapter, we base our thinking in terms of functions to understand operations. In the spirit of this, the function that the MIT-IBM AI Lab is undertaking, which is adversary modeling and defense, is empowered by these frameworks. MITRE (2020b) also offers similarly applied threat modeling for cyber operators known as "adversary emulation plans." These plans are an effective way for cyber operators to model operations based on the ATT&CK framework as well as up-to-date publicly available information sourced from advanced persistent threat (APT) actors.

These APTs are a common industry-based terminology in the world of cyber security. Essentially APTs are categorizations of adversarial activity that can be grouped together based on known TTPs. A commonly cited APT is APT38, also known as the Lazarus Group. APT38 is best known for global attack WannaCry, which affected over 150 countries (MITRE, 2019). Cyber security industry leader FireEye (2018) has an extensive report on APT38 and note many of the TTPs. Some of which include patterns of behavior, unique malware identifiers, and a traceable history of operations. This again reinforces how TTPs, threat modeling, and cyber security frameworks can empower U.S. cyber operations.

How can we culminate this together to have an actionable approach to cyber security on a Homeland level? There is no higher level that best embodies this than Homeland Security's own Cyber Storm Exercises. To date, there has been six Cyber Storm Exercises, each one growing greater in scale and complexity and demonstrating U.S. prowess with cyber security (Austin, 2019). The *Cyber Storm V: After Action Report* details how, "Cyber Storm (CS), the Department's capstone national-level cyber exercise series, provides the framework for 12 of the most extensive government-sponsored cybersecurity exercises of its kind" (Department of Homeland Security,

2016, p. 1). Furthermore, how "CS V adversaries incorporated real world threat elements and had the resources, capabilities, and intent to carry out sophisticated and pervasive attacks" (Department of Homeland Security, 2016, p. 6).

To concluded, TTPs form a vital part of not only our own cyber operations, but that of our adversaries as well. It is becoming even more integral that we understand the concept today as cyber adversaries grow more sophisticated and criminal action more damaging to the United States.

Further Reading

Bodeau, D. J., McCollum, C. D., & Fox, D. B. (2018, April 7). "*Cyber threat modeling: survey, assessment, and representative framework*," Homeland Security Systems Engineering and Development Institute. mitre.org/sites/default/files/publications/pr_18-1174-ngci-cyber-threat-modeling.pdf

Cybersecurity and Infrastructure Security Agency (CISA). (n.d.). https://www.cisa.gov/sites/default/files/publications/CyberStormV_AfterActionReport_2016vFinal-%20508%20Compliant%20v2.pdf

Galinec, D. (2018). "Cybersecurity and cyber defence: national level strategic approach," *Journal for Control, Measurement, Electronics, Computing and Communications*, *58*(3): 273–286.

References

Austin, G. (2019). *Cyber discussion paper #6: Civil defence gaps under cyber blitzkrieg*. https://www.unsw.adfa.edu.au/unsw-canberra-cyber/sites/accs/files/pdf/Discussion-Paper-6-Cyber-blitzkrieg_0.pdf

Cybersecurity and Infrastructure Security Agency. (2020). *Tactics, techniques, and procedures (TTPs)*. https://csrc.nist.gov/glossary/term/Tactics-Techniques-and-Procedures

Department of homeland Security. (2016). *Cyber storm V: After action report*. https://www.cisa.gov/sites/default/files/publications/CyberStormV_AfterActionReport_2016vFinal-%20508%20Compliant%20v2.pdf

Department of Homeland Security. (2018). *U. S. Department of Homeland Security: Cybersecurity strategy*. https://www.dhs.gov/sites/default/files/publications/DHS-Cybersecurity-Strategy_1.pdf

Federal Bureau of Investigation. (2019). *2019 internet crime report*. https://pdf.ic3.gov/2019_IC3Report.pdf

FireEye. (2018). *Special report, APT38: Unusual suspects*. https://content.fireeye.com/apt/rpt-apt38

FireEye. (2020). *Advanced persistent threat groups*. https://www.fireeye.com/current-threats/apt-groups.html

HSSEDI, Bodeau, D., McCollum, C., & Fox, D. (2018) *cyber threat modelling: Survey, assessment, and responsive framework*. https://www.mitre.org/sites/default/files/publications/pr_18-1174-ngci-cyber-threat-modeling.pdf

Lockheed Martin Corporation. Amin, R., Cloppert, M., & Hutchins, E. (2011). *Intelligence-driven computer network defense informed by analysis of adversary campaigns and intrusion kill chains*. https://www.lockheedmartin.com/content/dam/lockheed-martin/rms/documents/cyber/LM-White-Paper-Intel-Driven-Defense.pdf

Lockheed Martin Corporation. (2020). *The cyber skill chain.* https://www.lockheedmartin.com/en-us/capabilities/cyber/cyber-kill-chain.html
MITRE. (2020a). *ATT&CK matrix for enterprise.* https://attack.mitre.org/
MITRE. (2020b). *Adversary emulation plans.* https://attack.mitre.org/resources/adversary-emulation-plans/
MITRE. (2020c). *Corporate overview.* https://www.mitre.org/about/corporate-overview
MITRE. (2020d). *Who we are: The HSSEDI difference?* https://www.mitre.org/centers/homeland-security-systems-engineering-and-development-institute/who-we-are/the-hssedi
National Cyber Security Centre. (2017). *Cyber crime: Understanding the business model.* https://www.sbs.ox.ac.uk/cybersecurity-capacity/system/files/Cyber%20crime%20-%20understabnding%20the%20online%20business%20model.pdf
National Security Agency & Central Security Service. (2018). *Technical cyber threat framework v2.* https://media.defense.gov/2019/Jul/16/2002158108/-1/-1/0/CTR_NSA-CSS-TECHNICAL-CYBER-THREAT-FRAMEWORK_V2.PDF
O'Reilly, U., Hember, E., Huang, A., & Al-Dujaili, A. (2018). *Adversarial deep learning for robust detection of binary encoded malware.* MIT & IBM. https://arxiv.org/pdf/1801.02950.pdf

Chapter 31

Cyberattacks

Chad Patrick Osorio

University of Negros Occidental-Recoletos, Bacolod, Philippines

Contents

Introduction 205
Common Types of Cyberattacks 206
Federal and State Laws Regarding Cyberattacks 208
Conclusion 209
Further Reading 209
References 210

Introduction

Cyberattacks are a series of techniques committed through cyberspace with the goal of bypassing security protocols and accessing restricted information or damaging both online and offline infrastructures of the target entity. These intrusive modus operandi can be done through internal and external networks as well as through the Internet (Ponemon Institute, 2019). Individuals who conduct these attacks are more commonly known as 'hackers'.

There are many reasons for committing cyberattacks (Rutherford, 2017). Often, hackers commit these attacks to gain information they can use for intellectual property and identity theft, unauthorized transfer of funds, and blackmail. They can also prevent the use of the victim's operating systems, effectively rendering the latter's processing units infirm if they are not paid ransom. Hackers can also install clandestine software which allows them to monitor both online and real-world activities of the target as well as take control of the latter's computer and enable them to infect other operating systems within its expanded network. In the real world, these cyberattacks are akin to trespassing, vandalism, robbery, and blackmail and are thus referred to as cybercrimes.

DOI: 10.4324/9781315144511-33

However, not all cyberattacks exhibit absolute criminal intent. Some of them have been launched as a means for political statement and social activism, whose perpetrators are called 'hacktivists' (Maxwell, 2010). In the international front, both state and non-state parties utilize hackers to forward their political aims, including espionage and destruction of property. These cyberattacks may potentially serve as a prelude, a complement, or an alternative to modern warfare.

Cyberattacks pose an increasing concern for homeland security. As of 2019, the United States remains one of the most affected countries in the world, topping the list with the highest average annual cost of cybercrime (Ponemon Institute, 2019). The FBI Cyber Division (2018) estimates a total loss exceeding US$2.7 billion. These attacks result in consequences within and outside the sphere of business and government, including disruption of services, information loss, damage to equipment, and loss of revenue.

Common Types of Cyberattacks

There are various cyberattacks which rely on purely technological means of infiltrating the target's information system.

One of the simplest cyberattacks is the **password attack**, where hackers attempt to gain access into the files of another individual or entry into a protected network by trying to guess the security code. This can be done through a **dictionary attack**, manually inputting universally common passwords to test which works, or the more complex **brute force**, which uses software to generate passwords from a set of characters and test their viability through repeated log-in attempts (Shankdhar, 2019).

Some cyberattacks primarily seek to undermine websites and network databases. **SQL injections** utilize structured query language (SQL), a type of programming language useful for handling structured data. Inserting arbitrary SQL codes into web-based application database query can grant a certain measure of control to the hacker attempting to infiltrate the information system, especially if the database inputs are not sanitized – meaning, they are not checked for harmful code (Porup, 2018).

Malware, an amalgam from the words 'malicious' and 'software', is a broad category of software designed to infect and damage target computers and systems (Cisco, 2018). There are many types; the most common known as viruses, worms, trojans, and bots. **Viruses**, which are usually attached to an infected file, remain dormant until a particular program is activated, upon which the virus implements its programming and wreaks havoc on the system. **Worms**, on the other hand, require no host file. Once within the system, they can replicate and propagate within information networks without active assistance from human agents. **Trojans**, true to the concept of the Trojan Horse after which they have been named, are seemingly legitimate software downloaded by human agents. Being non-self-replicating, they activate upon download and program execution. **Bots** are automated, self-propagating malware which open backdoors within the system and connect back to command and control servers, ultimately allowing the latter to remotely control the actions of the former.

These different types of malware have varying purposes. **Spyware** allows the perpetrator of the cyberattack to closely and clandestinely watch the online and offline activities of the infected computer, including recording video and audio, accessing files, and logging keystrokes. These information allow the harvesting of sensitive information from the target's information networks. **Ransomware** shuts down the functions of the infected computer, either fully or partially; promising to restore them to full working condition, perpetrators demand payment of expiation. Computers infected by bots can also be turned into **botnets**, which allow the perpetrator of the cyberattack to remotely control the infected hosts as a network, coordinating massive attacks on other information systems.

There are a number of other **attack vectors** used to deliver malware to the target information system (Sumo Logic, n.d.). For example, the use of websites to spread malware is a well-known technique for cyberattack perpetrators. **DNS tunneling** utilizes the domain name system to do so, a trusted protocol which translates website URLs into internet protocol (IP) addresses. DNS is not primarily intended for data transfers and therefore is usually allowed movement through the firewall. Cybercriminals take advantage of this fact by creating 'tunnels' to access private data within the network, disguised as DNS to bypass security (Paloalto Cyberpedia, n.d.). **Cross-site scripting** involves the insertion of a malicious code into the webpage, which infects the computers of the visitors to the site (Kaspersky Encyclopedia, n.d.).

Other attack vectors sometimes need no active participation from the target. An example is the **drive-by exploit**, which takes advantage of the outdated security status of existing apps, operating systems, or web browsers to directly download malicious code into the target computer (Kaspersky Encyclopedia, n.d.). Such security flaws may have always existed, but can be newly discovered. If such fact is utilized by cybercriminals, the attack would then thus be known as a **zero-day vulnerability exploit**, referring to the number of days that the developers have to fix the security system before attackers can exploit it (i.e., zero).

Man-in-the-middle (MITM) attacks are those where the hackers insert themselves in the middle of an information exchange online. DuPaul (n.d.) characterizes it as a form of data traffic interception, which can be used to eavesdrop into private conversations to be used to the advantage of the perpetrator. The hacker may also intercept the message from one party and enter into the exchange pretending to be that party, in order to facilitate fraud. **Birthday attacks** are a form of MITM which replaces the original message with the perpetrator's own message by fooling the hash algorithm to falsely confirm the veracity of the sender.

Some attacks are coordinated, which means that rather than just relying on one computer, it utilizes an entire network to launch a series of attempts at breaching security systems. A good example is the **denial-of-service** (DOS) attack, which overwhelms the target's information system, network resources, or service infrastructure to the point that legitimate users cannot access them (Department of Homeland Security, 2019). There are many ways of doing this, which might include a single computer sending repeated requests, a network of hackers, or the use of botnets. In the latter two cases, it is then known as a **distributed denial-of-service** (DDOS) attack. In **Smurf attacks**, the perpetrator sends broadcast packets to a considerable number of hosts but using the IP address of the target. The goal is to inundate the target machine's IP address with the hosts' responses. A **TCP/SYN flood** will send a transmission control protocol (TCP) request to the target system but will not complete the connection, keeping a fraction of the system's resources occupied to wait for its response. Similarly repeated requests will saturate the system's ability to respond to legitimate queries.

IP fragmentation attacks target the fragmentation and reassembly process of information sent through the network (Imperva Learning Center, n.d.). One variant, called the **teardrop attack**, disrupts the reassembly process of the recipient, rendering them unable to process data packets and ultimately overwhelms its servers. The **ping of death attack**, on the other hand, would send irregularly sized fragmented data packets to the recipient; once assembled, however, its sheer size can overwhelm the target system. (Ping of Death, n.d.).

Particular infrastructures may be vulnerable to DOS attacks. For example, **telephony denial-of-service** (TDoS), as the name suggests, overwhelms telephone systems by occupying all telephone lines and prevents incoming and outgoing calls (Center for Internet Security, 2017).

Finally, **advanced persistent treatments** (APTs) are a combination of several malicious computer programs closely coordinated to override the security of an information system. They are considered advanced because of the nature of the attacks and the higher level of technological sophistication required to carry out the breach attempt (Higgins, 2016). They allow hackers to infiltrate an information system undetected for particular periods of time.

The aforementioned list of cyberattacks is not exhaustive, there are a number of variations on how these security attempts may be carried out, each with varying terms. At the same time, because security technology is constantly upgraded and it is more difficult to identify and take advantage of vulnerabilities in the technical aspect of the cyberworld, many perpetrators of cyberattacks also rely on the vulnerabilities of the human psyche. This series of techniques is called **social engineering** and includes such modus operandi as phishing, baiting, and scareware.

Federal and State Laws Regarding Cyberattacks

Because the United States is a known target for cyberattacks, which may include domestic and international threats, there are a number of laws in the United States which seek to provide security measures to prevent the damage associated with cyberattacks as well as deal with the consequences thereof.

These include the **Counterfeit Access Device and Computer Fraud and Abuse Act of 1984**, together with its amendment, the **Electronic Communications Privacy Act of 1986 (ECPA)**, which prohibits the access of computer and network systems for those without proper authorization or beyond the scope of their authority. The **Homeland Security Act of 2002 (HSA)** granted the Department of Homeland Security (DHS) the mandate to strengthen not only security for the homeland and critical infrastructure, but deemed to include cyberspace as well. This is supported by the **Cyber Security Research and Development Act of 2002**, which required the National Science Foundation (NSF) and the National Institute of Standards and Technology (NIST) to delve deeper into cybersecurity research. In addition, the mandate granted the NIST under the **Computer Security Act of 1987** to develop a general security framework and establish set standards for federal information network systems.

Laws against systematic cyberattacks may also pertain to the corporate sphere. For example, the Gramm-Leach-Bliley Act, otherwise known as the **Financial Modernization Act of 1999**, requires full disclosure from companies on how they safely keep their clients' personal and financial information private. This includes cybermeasures to protect such data from hackers. On the other hand, the relatively more recent **Cybersecurity Information Sharing Act of 2015** allows the US government and private companies to share data traffic and information about cyberthreats, thus enabling cooperation to promote security in cyberspace.

As regards cyberterrorism, the foremost federal law is the Uniting and Strengthening America by Providing Appropriate Tools Required to Intercept and Obstruct Terrorism Act, commonly known as the **USA PATRIOT Act of 2001**. This particular legal measure expanded penalties for the use of cyberattacks with the goal of terrorism, including actions that lead to threats against personal safety, loss of public data, or damage to infrastructures. At the same time, it established forensic laboratories specifically trained for computer-related criminal and terrorist activities.

There are a number of proposed amendments to the existing general legal framework for national cybersecurity but are still undergoing intensive discussion at the level of the legislative. At the same time, individual states have passed and are implementing laws against cyberattacks. At present, 31 states have enacted legislation related to cybersecurity (National Conference of State Legislatures, 2019).

Conclusion

Fischer (2014) notes that the US government recognizes the grave threat of cyberattacks to homeland security. That being the case, it has forwarded legislative measures to ensure that the different agencies of the state are mandated to conduct trainings for increasing the knowledge platform with the advocacy of strengthening cybersafety. At the same time, it also recognizes the importance of creating ad hoc committees and task forces dedicated solely to investigating and improving security in cyberspace. This is necessary because of the varying needs of each agency, foremost the level of privacy that its services require for operations and the type of data it handles for its public clients.

In the near future, it is imperative for all actors within the public and private sphere to work hand in hand, delve into newer and more secure technologies for government data files and information networks, and commit to similar other actions in order to provide a united front to foil attempts at cyberattacks and promote security within and outside homeland information systems.

Further Reading

Hathaway, O. A. and Crootof, R. (2012). The Law of Cyber-Attack. In *Faculty Scholarship Series* (Paper 3852). Retrieved from https://digitalcommons.law.yale.edu/fss_papers/3852/

National Conference of State Legislatures. (2019, October 25). *Cybersecurity Legislation 2019.* Retrieved from http://www.ncsl.org/research/telecommunications-and-information-technology/cybersecurity-legislation-2019.aspx

References

Attack Vector. (n.d.) In *DevOps Glossary*. Retrieved from https://www.sumologic.com/glossary/attack-vector/

Center for Internet Security (2017, March). *Telephony Denial of Service Attacks*. Retrieved from https://www.cisecurity.org/white-papers/cis-primer-telephony-denial-of-service-attacks/

Cross-site scripting (n.d.) In *Kaspersky Encyclopedia*. Retrieved from https://encyclopedia.kaspersky.com/glossary/cross-site-scripting-xss/

Department of Homeland Security. (2019, November 20). Understanding Denial-of-Service Attacks. Retrieved from https://www.us-cert.gov/ncas/tips/ST04-015

DuPaul, N. (n.d.) Man In The Middle (MITM) Attack. In *Appsec Knowledge Base*. Retrieved from https://www.veracode.com/security/man-middle-attack

Federal Bureau of Investigation Internet Crime Complaint Center. (2018). *Internet Crime Report*. Washington, D.C.: Author.

Fischer, E.A. (2014, December 12). *Federal Laws Relating to Cybersecurity: Overview of Major Issues, Current Laws, and Proposed Legislation*. Washington, D.C.: Congressional Research Service.

Hacktivist. (n.d.). In *Macmillan Dictionary*. Retrieved from https://www.macmillandictionary.com/buzzword/entries/hacktivist.html

Higgins, D. (2016, July 6). The growing challenge of Advanced Persistent Threats. *CSO Online*. Retrieved from https://www.csoonline.com/article/3501517/the-growing-challenge-of-advanced-persistent-threats.html

IP Fragmentation Attack. (n.d.) In *Imperva Learning Center*. Retrieved from https://www.imperva.com/learn/application-security/ip-fragmentation-attack-teardrop/

Patel, S. (1999). Over the Air Service Provision. In S. Tavares & H. Meijer *Selected Areas in Cryptography: 5th Annual International Workshop* (pp. 174–189). Ontario: Springer.

Ping of Death (n.d.) In *Imperva Learning Center*. Retrieved from https://www.imperva.com/learn/application-security/ping-of-death/

Ponemon Institute LLC. (2019). *The Cost of Cybercrime* (9th Ed.). Traverse City, MI: Accenture.

Porup, J.M. (2018, October 2). What is SQL injection? How SQLi attacks work and how to prevent them. *CSO Online*. Retrieved from https://www.csoonline.com/article/3257429/what-is-sql-injection-how-sqli-attacks-work-and-how-to-prevent-them.html

Rutherford, S. (2017, March 6). Why Do Hackers Commit Cyber-Attacks?. *FICO Blog*. Retrieved from https://www.fico.com/blogs/why-do-hackers-commit-cyber-attacks

Shankdhar, P. (2019, February 12). Popular Tools for Brute-force Attacks. *Infosec Institute*. Retrieved from https://resources.infosecinstitute.com/popular-tools-for-brute-force-attacks/#gref

What is a Drive-By Download? (n.d.) In *Kaspersky Resource Center*. Retrieved from https://www.kaspersky.com/resource-center/definitions/drive-by-download

What is DNS Tunneling? (n.d.) In *Paloalto Cyberpedia*. Retrieved from https://www.paloaltonetworks.com/cyberpedia/what-is-dns-tunneling

Chapter 32

Cybercrime, National Security, and Internet Governance

Scott N. Romaniuk
International Centre for Policing and Security, University of South Wales, Caerleon, United Kingdom

Priyanka Hattiangady
Independent Researcher, India

Contents

Introduction 212
Cybercrime as a Transnational Problem 212
The Cost of Cyberattacks and Cybercrime 213
Definition and Difficulties in Defining High-Tech Crime/Cybercrime 214
Dominant Approaches to Address Cybercrime 215
High-Tech Crime, Cyber Attacks, and US Vulnerability 217
Economic Losses due to Data Theft and Identity Theft in US Enterprises 218
Threats and Vulnerabilities to Democratic Political Discourse 218
High-Tech/Cybercrime and US Presidential Elections 218
The Transnational Nature of Cybercrime 219
US Cybersecurity Policy Framework 220
Evolving International Law in Cyberspace 222
Toward the Responsible Behavior of States in the Cyber World 224
Conclusion 226
Further Reading 226
Notes 226
References 227

DOI: 10.4324/9781315144511-34

Introduction

While cybercrime has been rising as computer networks become central to the realms of commercial and business activities, governance, and defense throughout the world, cybercrime has existed for around 50 years. However, the sheer scale of cybercrime, with trillions of security incidents and millions of attacks made against personal and public computer systems each year, has whisked scores of nations into a state of alarm. More than half the populations of developing countries are now dependent on the Internet to manage their daily affairs. There exists a positive correlation between digitization of economies and states' gross domestic product (GDP) per capita income growth (see Brynjolfsson and Saunders 2009).

The World Bank estimates that on average a 10% increase in broadband economic penetration can increase the GDPs of low and middle-income countries by 1.38% (Minges 2015). The benefits accruing from the digitization of the economy, however, can remain limited due to the exponential increase in high-tech crime (also referred to as cybercrime or computer crime). As such, cyber regulations and governance have assumed a prominent position in both national and international debates as a necessity for any country. Today, international law related to high-tech and cybercrime is still in a relatively nascent stage of development. There is, nonetheless, a growing body of treaties and declarations among countries at both the regional and international levels that seek to address high-tech and cybercrime; yet, these have proven decidedly inadequate or slow in addressing issues and threats that appear to develop markedly quicker.

We begin with a brief exploration of cybercrime and its impacts from a financial-cost perspective. We then provide a functional definition of "high-tech" cybercrime before turning our attention to dominant approaches in addressing cybercrime. This is followed by an exploration of responses to the persistence of high-tech crime actors within the context of the United States and US vulnerability. We then look into the economic impacts of cybercrime and challenges that persist in the political domain before addressing the transnational character and nature of cybercrimes. In the latter sections, we explore the US response in the form of policy against cyber threats and developments in the area of international law to address the challenges and problems of cyberspace. Finally, we look at behavior and states in the cyber realm.

Cybercrime as a Transnational Problem

Over the past several years, cybercrime has become a transnational issue, recognized as such by state and non-state actors (NSAs) due to the ability of either individuals or groups engaging in varying degrees and scales of fraud, hacking of public and private websites and accounts, identity theft on an individual or larger scale, scamming and computer virus contamination (here one can appropriately refer to phishing, malware, and spyware), in addition to espionage, and state-sanctioned or supported cyberattacks to further states' foreign policy objectives and economic interests. In 2000, the three most prevalent types of cybercrime included, in ascending order, unauthorized access of information by "insiders," general abuse of the Internet and Internet privileges by employees, and the spreading of viruses.

Five further, though significantly less prevalent, types of cybercrime included in ascending order are financial fraud, sabotaging data and/or networks, theft of proprietary information, system penetration from the outside, and denial of service (Johnston 2000). The World Economic Forum (WEF, 2019) noted that, via advanced and sophisticated, and scalable instruments, cybercriminals have posed a serious threat to private individuals, companies, and state governments, with more than two billion data records stolen in 2017 and more than 4.5 billion records breached during the first half of 2018.

The Cost of Cyberattacks and Cybercrime

Described as a "crippling cost," it is estimated that criminal activity in the cyber realm costs the global economy approximately US$445 billion per year, and for the 2019–2023 period, the total global value of cybercrime is estimated to be in the area of US$5.2 trillion (World Economic Forum 2019). The former figure represents an underground economy of roughly US$114 billion. For the United States, the wide coverage of cybercrime impacts numerous industries. As illustrated in Table 32.1,

Table 32.1 Average Cost of Cyberattacks (Per Organization) Across Industries

Industry	*2017 Cost*	*2018 Cost*	*% Change*
Banking	$16.6M	$18.4M	+11%
Utilities	$15.1M	$17.8M	+18%
Software	$14.5M	$16M	+11%
Automotive	$10.5M	$15.8M	+47%
Insurance	$12.9M	$15.8M	+22%
High-tech	$12.9M	$14.7M	+14%
Capital markets	$10.6M	$13.9M	+32%
Energy	$13.2M	$13.8M	+4%
US Federal	$10.4M	$13.7M	+32%
Consumer goods	$8.1M	$11.9M	+47%
Health	$12.9M	$11.8M	−8%
Retail	$9M	$11.4M	+26%
Life sciences	$5.9M	$10.9M	+86%
Media	$7.6M	$9.2M	+22%
Travel	$4.6M	$8.2M	+77%
Public sector	$6.6M	$7.9M	+20%

Source: World Economic Forum (2019).

organizations across multiple critical industries have increased by nearly 70% over the past 5 years with the banking industry shown to be the most affected.

It is well organized, employs expert hackers, and operates like any legitimate economy (Paganini 2019). The cybercrime economy exists somewhat openly, with many web-based forums and other websites in existence where cybercriminals list tools and display stolen information for sale and discuss future plans and projects for subsequent criminal activity aimed at the acquisition of highly sensitive and valuable data. As such, cybercrime economy can be aptly referred to as a thriving domain, even during a time when legitimate enterprises are struggling to survive while also spending copious amount of money to safeguard their systems. We identify three of the most important issues related to high-tech or cybercrime: (a) challenges posed by high-tech crime to the United States and state policy toward them, (b) whether governance of these transnational networks should be regulated within the United Nations (UN) or outside, and (c) current issues and events.

Definition and Difficulties in Defining High-Tech Crime/Cybercrime

The term "high-tech crime" refers to criminal acts that use, in some cases, new, electronic, and digitally based technology, such as the Internet, to gain control over a computer system/mobile device with the intent to steal valuable information or damage data stored in order to further illegal objectives such as financial fraud, violation of intellectual property, stealing identities, among other aims (a more comprehensive list of criminal intend and aims was noted previously). As noted, these crimes are also referred as cybercrime, depending upon the area in which they are being committed. While high-tech and cybercriminals use various malware tools, ranging from banking trojans to ransomware, and phishing to stage their attacks, attacks of this nature have not only been committed by NSAs, including terrorist organization, but also state actors (Europol 2020).

Since 2006, Russia and China have been identified as the top two cybercrime perpetrators. Cyber threats have also been shown to originate in Eastern Europe, notably Poland, Ukraine, and Belarus, as well as Romania, Brazil, Nigeria, Vietnam, Indonesia, South Korea, and the United States. In each of the aforesaid countries, cybercrime and attacks have been perpetrated by independent criminal actors and government organization. However, in some cases, government organizations have been far more active in committing cybercrime than individuals and if or when individuals have been involved, many cases exist in which government support has been offered. For example, Russia-linked hacker groups like Darkside, REvil, and Nobelium have launched successful cyberattacks against the United States and its interests. Darkside is best known for its attack on the US fuel pipeline known as the "Colonial Pipeline." REvil perpetrated a remarkable cyberattack against meat supplier JBS, which paid a heavy ransom of US$11 million in 2021. Nobelium hacked SolarWinds in 2020, which compromised nearly 100 US companies, including Microsoft (*The Moscow Times*, 2021). Thus, unfortunately cybercrime is not a simple and unambiguous single act that can be easily addressed by a single state authority or a multinational organization. Rather, it can be categorized in various ways depending upon types of offenses, objective(s), and the modus operandi. One point of congruence among states, however, is the existing agreement as to what can be considered a computer-related crime. We address this at a later point in the article with reference to the Convention on Cybercrime (2001), otherwise known and referred to as The Budapest Convention on Cybercrime.

Dominant Approaches to Address Cybercrime

Within the realm of cyberspace, a point of consonance can be identified with respect to the defense of cyber networks, whereby states and cross-national organization mutually subscribe to the view that cyber defense capabilities are much costlier than acquiring offensive capabilities. Often time, both states and NSAs infiltrate the cyber-networks of their adversaries with the aim of undermining the benefits accruing to the latter. In 1998, the German Aerospace Center-led satellite X-ray telescope known as ROSAT was the target of a cyberattack by Russia, which resulted in a defunct DEM 560 million piece of equipment making an uncontrolled re-entry into the atmosphere (United Nations Office for Disarmament Affairs, UNODA 2015). Governance and dominance of these transnational networks have become contentious and the ROSAT incident spawned extensive review of satellite hacking. Although hacking a satellite is far more complicated than hacking someone's personal mobile, such operations remain real possibilities.

The insertion of code into a targeted operating system represents another cyber offensive capability. The United States, like Russia and China, has been implanting logical bombs in the cybernetworks of other countries. Logical bombs, which "switch on" a malicious function, are frequently employed alongside various viruses, worms, and trojan horses in order to optimize their intended impact on targeted systems. When switched on, logic bombs have the ability to destroy critical infrastructure that thousands, hundreds of thousands, and even millions of people rely on, such as water supply networks, nuclear power stations, hospital and medical services, vital economic apparatuses, and space research programs. In 2012, then US Secretary of Defense, Leon Panetta, termed this type of situation a "cyber Pearl Harbor" vis-à-vis the United States, but one that is entirely applicable to other countries as well (DoS 2012).

In 2010, the United States employed Stuxnet, the world's digital weapon to attack Iran's Natanz uranium enrichment plant (fuel enrichment plant, FEP), which is the country's primary enrichment facility. Stuxnet destroyed 984 uranium enriching centrifuges, thus substantially reducing the efficiency of Iran's nuclear power station (Langner 2011; Zetter 2014). Referred to as the world's first digital weapon, Stuxnet was a completely different form of cyber weapon than anything seen previously. Unlike conventional cyber weapons such as viruses or worms, Stuxnet was successful in evading the digital realm and eventually causing serious physical damage to computer equipment. The accomplishment of Stuxnet, of which the primary mode of delivery was a simple flash drive, was the result of intricate planning that entailed a cyber offensive against multiple computers across four companies, each of which held a role in processing and control and a connection to Natanz (Langner 2011; Zetter 2014).

There have been two dominant, though competing approaches, put into practice in an effort to address cybercrime via cyberattacks. One has been advocated by the United States and other Western countries while the other has been emphasized by China, Russia, Japan, and a myriad of less-developed countries (LDCs).

The US approach to cyber governance is primarily security driven. It focuses on limiting high-tech crime in the economic realm, such as data theft, along with the prevention of cyberattacks on government departments and critical infrastructure. It further seeks to maintain its pre-eminent position in cyberspace. At the international level, the United States has demonstrated across administrations a preference for the multi-stakeholder approach in cyber governance outside of the UN system in order to avoid the politicization of technical functions. Russia and China's approach toward high-tech crime, on the other hand, is unsurprisingly entirely state-centric, wherein the state regulates every aspect of Internet governance (i.e., in the case of Russia and China, one might prefer to use the word "management" or "control"), including the flow of information within their respective societies (Sacks n.d.).

Russia and China's respective cybersecurity policies are driven by a substantial angst over US domination of the current global cyberspace beyond the manner in which US private entities such as the California-based Internet Corporation for Assigned Names and Numbers (ICANN) and Internet Assigned Numbers Authority (IANA) operate. Russia and China have demonstrated their desire to see substantial changes in present cyber governance structures at the international level. Both advocate for a more multilateral approach to cyber governance or governance within the UN system of cyberspace as an essential trajectory through which the circumvention of US hegemony can be achieved. Hjortdal (2011: 6), a researcher associated with CHINA-SEC, Centre for Military Studies at the University of Copenhagen (during the time of publication), asserts that China's development of "the most extensive and aggressive cyber warfare capability in the world" stems from "the fact that authoritative Chinese writings on the subject present cyber warfare as an obvious asymmetric instrument for balancing overwhelming (mainly U.S.) power, especially in case of open conflict." China's cybersecurity strategy is multi-dimensional, composed of the internal and external. China's external strategy was first spelled out by President Xi Jinping in his statements at the 2015 World on Information Technology in April 2016 (Chuanying 2016).

Until recently, the Internet Engineering Task Force (IETF) and the IANA, under the supervision of the US Department of Commerce's National Telecommunications and Information Administration (NTIA), performed vital technical functions essential for the maintenance of transnational networks. In 1998, various functions of the IANA were transferred to ICANN by means of a memorandum of an understanding between ICANN and the US government. In the wake of the Snowden revelation and amid the backdrop of NET-Mundial's global gathering on the future of Internet governance in March 2014, the Obama administration announced the transition of oversight of these important functions to a multi-stakeholder community by 2015. Since October 1, 2016, ICANN oversees these important technical functions.

Russia, China, Japan, the European Union (EU), and many LDCs currently experience issues with ICANN with respect to its decision-making procedure, administration of vital Internet functions, and limited participation of states in the day-to-day functions of ICANN. Many countries, most notably Russia and China, have advocated for the coordination of root systems under the International Telecommunication Union (ITU) rather than ICANN. Thus, Russia and China have been promoting a cyber arm control approach modeled on the negotiated Chemical Weapons Convention, Biological Weapons Convention in the sphere of cyberspace. The arms control approach to cyberspace was first raised in 1996 with the advent of the commercialization of the Internet in the UN system. In 2017, a military delegation from the United States and Russia have also met in Moscow to discuss this subject, but no agreement could be reached (Ó Siochrú 2004: 31; Markoff and Kramer 2009).

High-Tech Crime, Cyber Attacks, and US Vulnerability

The Internet was developed in the United States as a medium to facilitate data exchange between scientists and researchers with the key aim of promoting innovation and the boosting of technology. It was not originally designed with the security of cyber networks in mind. These networks were primarily developed as public–private partnership ventures. In these ventures, the security of physical infrastructure was always the responsibility of private entities, while the government played a subsidiary role. Over the years, policy-making concerning these cyber networks in the United States was divided into three main categories: (1) classified, (2) government networks, and (3) private networks. Classified networks are considered the most secure. However, currently, even classified cyber networks of the US government can be easily infringed by hackers.

As part of its portfolio of vulnerabilities and cybersecurity failures, the US government has been shown to have a great deal of work to do in the area of cyberspace in terms of defensive measures and capacities. The Government of Accountability Office's (GAO) February 2017 report presented an array of US government weaknesses when it comes to safeguarding federal data and information systems. In 2015, the Office of Personal Management (OPM) was the target of an attack by Chinese hackers that resulted in the theft of 22 million personal records. Previously, in 2016, the US government shared the news that US government agencies reported more than 30,000 cases of information security breach. The Center for Strategic and International Studies (CSIS) website provides a comprehensive, 43-page list of significant cyber incidents between 2006 and (December) 2019 (CSIS 2001).

One of the most recent attacks against the United States was perpetrated by Chinese hackers that resulted in the cyber theft of data of an estimated 145 million US citizens. Attorney General William Barr referred to the Equifax attack as a sweeping campaign against the United States in an effort to steal an immeasurable amount of data from the United States, stating that, "[u]nfortunately, the Equifax hack fits a disturbing and unacceptable pattern of state-sponsored computer intrusions and thefts by China and its citizens that have targeted personally identifiable information, trade secrets and other confidential information" (NPR 2020). On February 9, 2020, the Department of Justice (DoJ) announced charges against four individuals with the Chinese military and faced nine counts, which included conspiracy to commit computer fraud and conspiracy to commit economic espionage.

Economic Losses due to Data Theft and Identity Theft in US Enterprises

Information theft has cost many US enterprises billions of dollars in losses annually. General Keith Alexander, head of US National Security Agency (NSA) and United States Cyber Command (USCYBERCOM), which we discuss at a later point in this chapter, argues that the cost of intellectual property (IP) theft from US companies stands at approximately US$250 billion annually and, in the context of China, has resulted in the greatest transfer of wealth (McChesney 2004: 7; Kshetri 2014). Since the early 2000s, cyber espionage has profoundly strained US–China relations. Although every country engages in espionage in some form, China has been referred to as the most active player in cyber espionage, ahead of Russia, employing the practice for the economic benefit of its domestic companies and state-owned enterprises (SOEs).

According to a 2017 Symantec report, the United States tops the list for both the number of breaches by a country and within the country, followed by the United Kingdom, Canada, Australia, and India. In terms of identities stolen, again the United States, followed by France, Russia, Canada, and Taiwan, was the most affected country. The service sector has been identified as the most affected by data breaches in which finance, insurance, real estate, and health services occupy the top position. It is worth noting that the financial sector spends three times more on cyber security than non-financial institutions throughout the world (Symantec 2017).

Threats and Vulnerabilities to Democratic Political Discourse

According to the Computational Propaganda Research Project (COMPROP) at the Oxford Internet Institute (OII), University of Oxford, the use of social media by political parties for public opinion manipulation is rampant. A dozen researchers for nine countries comprised the COMPROP team that conducted interviews with 65 experts and subsequently analyzed tens of millions of posts across seven social media platforms during elections, political crises, and national security incidents. Case studies analyzed qualitative, quantitative, and computational evidence from 2015 to 2017 and included the United States, China, Russia, Canada, Taiwan, Brazil, Germany, Poland, and Ukraine (Wooley and Howard 2017). Exiled activist Sam Rainsy, from Cambodia, filed a case in the Courts of California against Facebook. He had alleged that Cambodian Prime Minister, Hun Sen, purchased fake Facebook "likes" as part of a larger effort to justify his authoritarian rule and human right abuses and influence the elections in Cambodia (Smith 2018).[1]

High-Tech/Cybercrime and US Presidential Elections

During the 2016 US presidential election, the email account of the chairperson of Hillary Clinton's campaign, John Podesta, was hacked. These emails were subsequently leaked in an attempt to influence the outcome of the US elections. A joint investigation launched by the US intelligence community concluded that two groups, namely Fritillary and Swallowtail, linked to Russia's intelligence services were partly involved in infringing on the email account of the campaign head of the Democratic Party.[2] During the final week of the elections, voter turnout was re-calculated, leading to the conclusion that Donald Trump could win if he focused on Wisconsin, Pennsylvania, and Michigan even after losing the popular vote in the US elections. They used Facebook to feature so-called "dark posts" or targeted ads (on Facebook, these are known as "unpublished posts") to send newsfeeds depending upon user's insecurities and lifestyle behavior to influence voters' thinking (Winston 2016).

Some non-profit media organizations, such as National Public Radio (NPR), have suggested that that Trump and his campaign team could not have won the election without journalist and media manipulation and the use of fake news on platforms like Facebook (see Gunther, Nisbet and Beck 2018; Kurtzleben 2018; Polletta and Callahan 2018). That is, Trump's victory would not have been possible if the average US citizen did not rely on social media like Facebook and online news as opposed to traditional media for election news (Allcott and Gentzkow 2017: 211).[3] The period was also marked by a proliferation of news websites with far-right inclinations such as Breitbart (Allcott and Gentzkow 2017: 214). These websites flourished on the anxiety of the average US voter. Social media platform such as Facebook relays content among users with no significant third-party filters, fact checking, or editorial judgment. In 2000, the growth of online news resulted in an extensive array of opinion and viewpoints, facilitating likeminded citizens' formation of eco-chambers, in which groups of people would be insulated from contrary perspective. According to independent fact-checking website, PolitiFact, only 4% of Trump's statements during the election were indeed true.

The Transnational Nature of Cybercrime

A well-organized, underground cybercrime economy employs expert hackers and operates like any legitimate economy. The costs of dealing with such crime are mostly paid by large organizations, such as banks, while both prevention and damage control require larger investments in cybersecurity (Deutsch 2019; Paganini, 2019). According to the 2014 report by CSIS, "Net Losses: Estimating the Global Cost of Cybercrime," the United States is the most vulnerable and affected country due to cybercrime, noting further that countries considered to be "richer" are more affected given the concentration of strategic and critical industries in these countries being digitized.

State-sponsored bank heists have become a major issue and serious challenge. Russia, North Korea, and Iran have been identified as the three most active countries in hacking financial institutions. NSA Deputy Director, George C. Barnes, remarked in March 2018 that, "nation-states are robbing banks and they are doing it with computers." China remains more active in economic espionage and for over a long period has carried out denial of service attacks on leading US banks (Symantec Report 2017).

North Korea employs offenses committed against banks and financial institutions to fund its nuclear program and circumvent international sanctions imposed on its dictatorial regime. In 2017, North Korean hackers have been targeting at least three South Korean cryptocurrency exchanges. By using Bitcoin, cybercriminals have been successful in circumventing international sanctions. They targeted developing countries, such as Bangladesh, Vietnam, and Ecuador, all of which are known to have low cybersecurity expertise. In Russia, where a close and complex relationship between state and organized crime has been observed, advanced cybercriminals who have breached cyber security in financial sectors around the world are provided criminal sanctuary and remain out of reach of Western authorities or the capacities of multinational organizations seeking to apprehend and prosecute such criminals.

US Cybersecurity Policy Framework

The cybersecurity policy framework of the current US administration, as echoed in the strategic papers of the Department of Defense (DoD) and various Executive Orders (EOs) of the President of the United States (POTUS), explicates the following priorities of its cybersecurity strategy:

- Protecting the country's critical infrastructure from cyber threats
- Improving the government's ability to identify and report cyber incidents so that it can respond in a timely manner
- Engaging with international partners to promote Internet freedom and build support for an open, interoperable, secure, and reliable cyberspace
- Securing federal networks by setting clear security targets and holding agencies accountable for meeting those targets
- Shaping a cyber-savvy workforce and moving beyond passwords in partnership with the private sector
- Emphasis on securing partnership between public and private actors rather than making cyber defense purely a government function

(The White House 2016)

Strategic papers from DoD, the Department of Homeland Security (DHS), the Federal Bureau of Investigation (FBI), and the EOs of POTUS, as well as those in several prominent policy positions in the United States and in various international fora, provide critical acumen for the objectives, priorities, and policies of the US government in the realm of cybersecurity. Some of the more notable or important documents include the National Strategy to Secure Cyberspace, Presidential Policy Directives – Signal Intelligence Activities, 2014, policy statements on critical infrastructure, EO 13636 – Improving Critical Infrastructure Cyber-Security, Directives on National Security Strategy, International Strategy for Cyberspace, 2011, and the National Institute of Standards and Technology (NIST) Cybersecurity Framework, 2013.

The 2011 International Strategy for Cyberspace (The White House 2011) discusses the protection and furtherance of the United Nations Declaration of Human Rights (UNDHR), the International Covenant on Civil and Political Rights (ICCPR) from the Office of the United Nations High Commissioner for Human Rights (OHCHR), and principles of the World Trade Organization (WTO) in the realm of cyberspace. The document stands for the free flow of information and protection of IP rights and further asserts the right to self-defense (The White House 2011). The strategy papers of DoD and DHS mention a layered-approach in the realm of human rights protection (DHS 2018: 5).

The current US cybersecurity policy is primarily a culmination of efforts from the administration of George W. Bush to that of Barack Obama and extended into the Trump administration. US Director of National Intelligence (DNI), Joseph Maguire, pointed to cyberattacks as the most important strategic threat to the United States ahead of international terrorism after the terrorist attacks on the World Trade Center on September 11, 2001 (DoD 2018; The White House 2018). It was under the Bush–Cheney–Rumsfeld administration that DHS was created as a nodal contact for the federal government and industry to report incidents of cyber theft. DHS was responsible for creating a comprehensive national plan to secure key resources and critical infrastructure for the US homeland from cyberattacks beyond US borders.

As early as 1972, DoD had warned about the vulnerabilities of cyber networks (UC Cyber Command, USCYBERCOM n.d.). The post-Cold War period presented a manifold increase in vulnerabilities and attacks on computer networks. As a result of radically changed political order, rapidly developing threats, and nascent technologies that presented the double-edged sword of opportunity and vulnerability, the United States established its Cyber Command in 2009 (Ferdinando 2018; USCYBERCOM n.d.). This command is one of ten unified within DoD. On May 4, 2018, USCYBERCOM was elevated to the status of a unified independent combatant. During the Obama administration, DoD prepared a manual in which the Cyber Command structure is to operate without any cyber network at its disposal to deal with lawlessness and panic brought about as a result of a cyberattack or series of attacks against the US homeland.

From the very beginning, the US government had a strong disinclination to directly intervene on behalf of its economic entities even in the event of major cyber financial fraud. Even during 2014, Sony was hacked by a group that referred to itself as the Guardians of Peace, who were widely believed to be working with or alongside the North Korean regime, and earlier during the federal agency breaches of 2014–2015,the Obama administration routinely ducked away from any kind of direct intervention as it implied the probability of high costs both in the realm of defense and diplomacy. The US government additionally feared widespread protest from the general public as its intervention would have inevitably given rise to inspecting every piece of data flowing into and out of the country (Knake 2016).

In addition to the aforementioned routine, the US government has done remarkably well in upholding its right to indulge in cyber electronic espionage under the guise of protecting and furthering its own national interests. In fact, the United States marks a distinction between espionage for the purpose of protecting its own national interests and commercial espionage, deeming the latter as less acceptable than the former (Brown and Yung 2017). This dichotomy though seems quite irrelevant given that the NSA has habitually engaged in spying on a number of financial institutions such as the World Bank and the International Monetary Fund (IMF) (Brown and Yung 2017). In a draft NSA Signals Intelligence Directive, the agency prepared policies that would grant it the powers to spy on its allies at any time (Brown and Yung 2017). In the past, the US government instructed software firms to install "backdoors" in their encryption so as to allow access to data if the government considered a need to protect its national interests (The Economist 2017). Awareness about the NSA's plans to maintain built-in access to data raised a chorus of criticism resulting in statements by former NSA director, Mike Rogers, who publicly defended their need, reasoning that in addition to a lack of harm to privacy, the "backdoors" would present neither danger to any encryption nor harm international markets in which US technology products compete. In 2013, the Snowden revelation exposed the massive surveillance structure of the NSA's interception of the Brazilian president's private communications and spying on millions of Brazilians, who had stored their private data in the networks of US companies such as Facebook and Google (Lieberthal and Singer 2012; Kshetri 2014).

Evolving International Law in Cyberspace

During the early 1990s, multilateral organizations such as the ITU and the United Nations Educational, Scientific and Cultural Organization (UNESCO) were gradually losing their power to regulate the telecommunications and information sectors to bodies like ICANN and the WTO, both of which constantly attracted the suspicions of Russia, China, Japan, and LDCs. ICANN favored US and Western multinationals in the telecommunications sectors (see Hills 2007). Third-world countries thus demanded equity and more say in telecommunications regulations, including Internet governance, and subsequently formulated their demands in the form of the New Information and Communication World Order (NWICO or NWIO). Demands presented within the formulation were met with an icy response when the United States and United Kingdom withdrew from UNESCO in protest (McChesney and Schiller 2003: 5). This initial period in the domain of cyberspace was marked by a general lack of interest by the US and Western actors to evolve norms related to responsible state practice in cyberspace within the UN system.

The First Committee (otherwise known as Committee on Disarmament and International Security) of the United Nations General Assembly (UNGA) has been the locus of deep debate on cybersecurity since 1998 when Russia introduced its draft resolution, "Developments in the field of information and telecommunications in the context of international security" to the UNGA. The draft was effortlessly adopted as Resolution 53/70 (UNODA 2015). The resolution garnered near non-existent support by the United States and Western countries as any multilateral arrangement within or outside the UN was unacceptable to them. During the 2003 and 2005 UN World Summits on the Information Society (WSIS) held in Geneva and Tunis, high-level political officers of the EU criticized the multi-stakeholder model of the United States on the grounds that relaxed cyber regulations along with the absence of virtual accountability on data privacy requirements by American companies like Facebook and Google (Thimm and Schaller, 2014).

More substantial work began at the UN in 2003, when Russia proposed constituting a Group of Governmental Experts (GGE) consisting of professionals in the realm of cyber security from permanent members of the United Nations Security Council (UNSC) to examine "the existing and potential threats from the cybersphere and possible cooperative measures to address them" (United Nations 2003: 2). However, during the first and second GGE, consensus could not be achieved because countries were unable to agree on many cyber issues. The United States, through the course of discussion and critical exchange, vehemently resisted the resolution since it gave dictatorial regimes immense power to control the flow of data and information within their societies (Observer Research Foundation 2014).

In 2003, at the regional level, the Convention on Cybercrime or the Budapest Convention on Cybercrime (ETS No 185) is "the first international treaty on crimes committed via the Internet and other computer networks, dealing particularly with infringements of copyright, computer-related fraud, child pornography and violations of network security" (Council of Europe 2020). The primary aim is the establishment of an international standard for a "common criminal policy" for the protection of society. To facilitate this, the Council of Europe's Cybercrime Convention Committee has actively sought to find solutions that would enable greater criminal justice accessibility to data and evidence. Privacy concerns remain at the core of community concerns and while much effort is put into the language of cyber law and the protection of private citizens' information, the prevalence of searches, wiretappings, and surveillance has increased. Thus, while the legal language and general discourse surrounding societal protection against cybercrime appear to be concrete and in the best interest of those wanting and indeed needing protection, it sometimes does not make sense to over inhibit authorities from accessing the very domains that they are to safeguard.

The problem is an implicit tension and incongruence in the need, objectives, and permissibility for authorities tasked with the protection of individuals and society. The general assumption is that while criminals seek to people and broader society in the realm of cyberspace, government authorities seek only to protect with good intention and without over-stepping their legal boundaries and engaging in unethical or illegal activities of their own. On a cross-national level, states have argued against the Budapest Convention due to their concerns over ceding national sovereignty to foreign authority. As such, governments have questioned the essence of Article 32b, which accommodates cross-border access to potentially sensitive data that could compromise the public and national security of a given nation. Such is the case with India, and other observer states, who are not yet ready or willing to adjust their image of their respective digital nations by joining the treaty.

In addition to India, both China and South Korea, which according to recent Symantec Internet Security Threat Reports (ISTR) occupy high-ranking position in the list of cybersecurity breaches, are yet to sign on the treaty. Interestingly, the Korean National Police have organized the International Symposium on Cybercrime Response (ISCR) and uses the symposium as a conduit for dialogue between Korean authorities and representatives of the EU. Although Asia accounts for approximately 56% of the world's population and some Asian counties have become hotbeds of cybercrime, the treaty has not been ratified by any Asian country. In another region of the world, while Brazil has been called the hacking capital of the world, it too is yet to even become a signatory of the treaty. In Europe, Russia has neither signed nor ratified the treaty, as the Putin regime interprets the treaty as blatantly compromising Russia's sovereignty. For the United States, two important reservations can be noted: first, the treaty violates the principles of human rights and privacy; second, US administrations have generally remained uncomfortable with the idea of assisting other countries with enforcing their laws due to the lack of a "dual criminality" provision.

Russia's 2007 cyberattack on Estonia marked a watershed in international relations and validated to the world how a state can launch a cyber offensive to advance its foreign policy objectives. In 2008, Russia launched another cyberattack, this time on Georgia, which were followed up with a 2010 cyber offensive on the US NASDAQ stock exchange. As mentioned, the United States and Israel Stuxnet was used against Iran's Natanz nuclear facility. These developments made states aware that in the near future, cyber wars are imminent and might escalate into full-fledged armed conflict or war. The combination of these events and concerns reveals that while there is a growing exigency to evolve international norms in cyberspace and promote responsible state practices in this domain, there remains a potentially hidden danger in allowing states greater access to the digital realm of national security.

Toward the Responsible Behavior of States in the Cyber World

In 2011, Russia, China, Tajikistan, and Uzbekistan, all part of the Shanghai Cooperation Organization (SCO), established, for the first time, the principles of responsible behavior of states within the realm of both information and cybersecurity. In the 2011 draft, signatories are restricted from using information and communications technologies (ICTs), "including networks, to carry out hostile activities or acts of aggression and pose threats to international peace and security, hamper political, social, cultural norms and ethos of a society" (CCDCOE n.d.). Both Russia and China regard their national segments of the Internet as parts of "sovereign domains" and insisted that they be afforded a greater degree of control over distributed content and infrastructure (Observer Research Foundation 2014). This perspective found little support with the United States and other Western countries.

During the 2012 International Conference on International Telecommunication (WCIT-12) in Dubai, issues of cyber governance assumed center stage. It was an important conference since the general rules of telecommunications were last updated in 1988, prior to the commercialization and development of the Internet (Congress.gov n.d.). Once again, negotiations faltered on numerous issues, including efforts by Russian delegates to create a greater role for the ITU in the domain of Internet governance.

A notable achievement of 2013 was the third GGE report, adopted in the UNGA, in which groups of governmental experts at the UN level recognized that international law, including the principles of the law of state responsibility, fully apply to state behavior in cyberspace (United Nations Institute for Disarmament Research 2013). This accord can be seen as a major step forward for the legal framework as one of universal acceptance, as an initial piece in a very large and complex puzzle. A second point of significance is the responsibility that falls on the state, namely that a given state bears the responsibility for the actions and activities of its own NSAs. Third, this thrust forward enshrined states' agreement that they are required to comply with the prohibition of the use of force, full respect for the territorial sovereignty and independence of other nations, and principle for settling disputes by peaceful means. Finally, Article 51 of the UN Charter, the right to self-defense, including the use of force, will apply in the case of a cyberattack, if such an event reached the level of an armed attack. However, the adopted resolution did not specify circumstances in which a cyberattack reaches such a level that it may be interpreted as an "armed attack" and responded to as such.

On December 27, 2013, the UNGA unanimously adopted Resolution 68/243, in which it took note of the outcome of the 2012/2013 GGE and requested the Secretary General to establish a new GGE that would report to the UNGA in 2015. The fourth GGE report reiterated the significance of the principle of non-interference in the internal affairs of other countries via ICTs and the use of ICTs for peaceful purpose. Moreover, the report underscored the significance of norms and confidence building measures (CBMs) and capacity building goals among states at the regional level and the role of the UN in evolving dialogue on the security of ICTs in their use by states, and in developing common and harmonizing understandings of the application of international law and norms and rules and principles for responsible state behavior (UNODA 2020).

Beyond the UN, in 2013, the North Atlantic Treaty Organization's (NATO) Cooperative Cyber Defence Centre of Excellence (CCDCOE) developed the *Tallinn Manual*, which serves as a code of conduct for cyberwarfare developed amid Russia's cyberattacks (some alleged) against European nations. This is a strong example of soft international law and lays out circumstances in which the law of war would apply. The second Tallinn Manual, known as *Tallinn 2.0*, postulates the application of international law to cyberspace in times of peace.

In 2014, due to Russia's interference in Ukraine and eventual annexation of Crimea, sanctions were imposed by the EU, the United States, and Canada and were followed by an array of others. Despite having a crippling effect on the Russian economy, collectively these sanctions facilitated US–Russia bilateral dialogue by pressuring Russia to reconcile its differences in the realm of cyberspace (NATO 2015). The process began in 2013, at the Group of Eight summit in Scotland, and Presidents Obama and Putin signed a number of CBMs. It is comprised of three types of cyber-specific communications:

> [...] a channel between computer emergency response teams (CERTs) from the two countries to discuss malware stemming from each other's territory, a link between nuclear risk reductions centers for cyberincidents of national security importance, and a telephone hotline between the White House and the Kremlin for major cyberincidents.
>
> (Wolter 2013)

The success of previous efforts paved the way for further positive developments, notably the creation of a bilateral working group dealing with the challenges and opportunities associated with cybersecurity and as a means of dialogue between the two parties for positively treating any tension, confusion, and misperceptions of the other. More specifically, the forum sought to ease any hostility surrounding any accusation that might arise over largescale "cyberintrusions for the purposes of military and economic intelligence" (Wolter 2013).

The year 2015 also marked a period of strengthening of relations between China and Russia. Sharing a common view in the realm of cyber governance both signed non-aggression pact and arrived at a mutual understanding on various issues of cyberspace (Gabuv 2015). The key element of this pact is a shared strategic interest of cyber sovereignty as opposed to the United States' position of cyber freedom (Wei 2016). In its 2012 white paper, China presented its concept of cyber sovereignty (网络主权) as part of its Internet governance that became a foundation of the Chinese

Communist Party's (CCP's) state management (ChinaFile 2015; Wei 2016). Echoed at the Wuzhen World Internet Conference in December the following year, China maintained its stance that "Internet sovereignty" relates to a clearly defined space of governance in which the government retains the right to manage what flows in and out of the country, not only in the physical, but in the virtual realm as well. As an appendage of a sovereign state territory, government has the legal right to decide what information, knowledge, and wisdom (i.e., values and principles, even social norms and practices) are expressed, disseminated, and flourished within the virtual domain of a particular sovereign state. Thus, the virtual world itself features borders, fences, and walls as can any country with physical features. For China, this is an intricate governance instrument through which the CCP can ensure the "Chinese dream" (中国梦). In tandem with the principles of sovereign nations, Internet freedom does not accommodate foreign interference. Such is the practice in China and Russia, with efforts by the governments of both those countries to restrict and exclude non-state activities and initiatives, such as those undertaken by ICANN, that either run counter to state-level moral codes or outright defy and contest variegated forms of state power.

Conclusion

Although a vast majority of future netizens will emerge from developing countries, particularly Asia, the United States continues to dominate cyberspace even though China boasts twice as many users as the United States. In 2014, US companies held 27% of the global ICT market. The country remains the second-largest user of the Internet overall, home to eight of the ten largest information companies in the world (see Nye, Jr. 2014; Centre for International Governance Innovation 2017). The United States, moreover, continues to guide cybersecurity policy due to its influence over ICANN, and while Washington announced in 2014 that it intends to relax its supervision of ICANN and the IANA, broad acceptance of the US multi-stakeholder model can be viewed as an exertion of its influence by other means that has been met by stringent opposition by major contenders of US power and hegemony.

Further Reading

Buchanan, B. (2020). *The Hacker and the State: Cyber Attacks and the New Normal of Geopolitics*. Harvard University Press.

Cheng, D. (2016). *Cyber Dragon: Inside China's Information Warfare and Cyber Operations*. Praeger.

Romaniuk, S. N. and Manjikian, M. (eds.). (2021). *Routledge Companion to Global Cyber-Security Strategy*. Routledge.

Notes

1 For details see, Smith (2018), "How Facebook Became 'Tool of Dictators' in Asia's Teetering Democracies," available at: https://www.telegraph.co.uk/news/2018/05/30/facebook-became-tool-dictators-asias-teetering-democracies/

2 According to Symantec's 2017 report, Fritillary is previously known to have targeted high-profile individuals and organizations in the government, international policy, and research institutes in EU and the US while Swallowtail primarily targets military, government, embassy, and defense contractors and personnel in Eastern European countries. In September 2017, Swallowtail was also implicated in the leak of medical records stolen from the World Anti-Doping Agency (WADA), and the publishing of stolen data to prove that athletes had been breaking anti-doping rules.

3 Social media platforms such as Facebook relays content among users with no significant third-party filters, fact checking, or editorial judgment. According to Allcott and Gentzkow (2017: 211), "[i]n 2000, the growth of online news resulted in great diversity of viewpoints making it easier for likeminded citizens to form eco-chambers where they will be insulated from the contrary perspective."

References

Allcott, H. and Gentzkow, M. (2017). "Social Media and Fake News in the 2016 Election," *Journal of Economic Perspectives*, *31*(2): 211–236.

Brown, G. and Yung, C. D. (2017, January 19). "Evaluating the US-China Cybersecurity Agreement, Part 1: The US Approach to Cyberspace," *The Diplomat*. https://thediplomat.com/2017/01/evaluating-the-us-china-cybersecurity-agreement-part-1-the-us-approach-to-cyberspace/

Brynjolfsson, E. and Saunders, A. (2009). *Wired for Innovation: How Information Technology Is Reshaping the Economy*. Cambridge, MIT Press.

Centre for International Governance Innovation. (2017, January 17). "Who Runs the Internet? The Global Multi-Stakeholder Model of Internet Governance." https://www.jstor.org/stable/resrep05243

Chuanying, L. (2016, May 24). "China's Emerging Cyberspace Strategy," *The Diplomat*. https://thediplomat.com/2016/05/chinas-emerging-cyberspace-strategy/

Congress.gov. (n.d.). "H.R.4992 - Telecommunications Accessibility Enhancement Act of 1988 – 100th Congress (1987–1988)." https://www.congress.gov/bill/100th-congress/house-bill/4992

Center for Strategic and International Studies. (2001, August). "Significant Cyber Incidents Since 2006." https://csis-prod.s3.amazonaws.com/s3fs-public/200108_Significant_Cyber_Events_List.pdf?aj4_VlDq2hSan2U8O5mS29Iurq3G1QKa

Center for Strategic and International Studies. (2014). "Net Losses: Estimating the Global Cost of Cybercrime." https://csis-prod.s3.amazonaws.com/s3fs-public/legacy_files/files/attachments/140609_rp_economic_impact_cybercrime_report.pdf

Deutsch, A. L. (2019, May 17). "Watch Out for These Top Internet Scams," *Investopedia*. https://www.investopedia.com/articles/personal-finance/040115/watch-out-these-top-internet-scams.asp#ixzz5HTSi97OH

Europol. (2020). "High-Tech Crime." https://www.europol.europa.eu/crime-areas-and-trends/crime-areas/cybercrime/high-tech-crime

Ferdinando, L. (2018, May 3). "Cybercom to Elevate to Combatant Command," *DOD News*. https://www.defense.gov/Explore/News/Article/Article/1511959/cybercom-to-elevate-to-combatant-command/

Gabuv, A. (2015, December 16). "How China and Russia see the Internet," *World Economic Forum*. https://www.weforum.org/agenda/2015/12/how-china-and-russia-see-the-internet/

Gunther, R., Nisbet, E. C. and Beck, P. (2018, February 15). "Trump May Owe His 2016 Victory to 'Fake News,' New Study Suggests," *The Conversation*. http://theconversation.com/trump-may-owe-his-2016-victory-to-fake-news-new-study-suggests-91538

Hills, J. (2007). *Telecommunications and Empire*. Urbana and Chicago: University of Illinois Press.
Hjortdal, M. (2011). "China's Use of Cyber Warfare: Espionage Meets Strategic Deterrence," *Journal of Strategic Security*, *4*(2): 1–24. https://thediplomat.com/2017/01/evaluating-the-us-china-cybersecurity-agreement-part-1-the-us-approach-to-cyberspace/
Johnston, M. (2000, June 16). "Cybercrime is on the Rise," TechRepublic. https://www.techrepublic.com/article/cybercrime-is-on-the-rise/
Knake, R. (2016, May 6). "Obama's Cyberdoctrine: Digital Security and the Private Sector," *Foreign Affairs*. https://www.foreignaffairs.com/articles/united-states/2016-05-06/obamas-cyber doctrine
Kshetri, N. (2014). "Cybersecurity and International Relations: The U.S. Engagement with China and Russia," Prepared for FLACSO-ISA 2014, University of Buenos Aires, School of Economics, Buenos Aires, Argentina, July 23–25. http://web.isanet.org/Web/Conferences/FLACSO-ISA%20BuenosAires%202014/Archive/6f9b6b91-0f33-4956-89fc-f9a9cde89caf.pdf
Kurtzleben, D. (2018, April 11). "Did Fake News on Facebook Help Elect Trump? Here's What We Know," *National Public Radio*. https://www.npr.org/2018/04/11/601323233/6-facts-we-know-about-fake-news-in-the-2016-election
Langner, R. (2011). "Stuxnet: Dissecting a Cyberwarfare Weapon," *IEEE Privacy and Security*, *9*(3): 49–51.
Lieberthal, K. and Singer, P. W. (2012, February). "Cybersecurity and U.S.-China Relations – 网络安全与美中关系," Brookings Institution, Washington, DC. brookings.edu/wp-content/uploads/2016/06/0223_cybersecurity_china_us_lieberthal_singer_pdf_english.pdf
Markoff, J. and Kramer, A. E. (2009, June 27). "U.S. and Russia Differ on a Treaty for Cyberspace," *The New York Times*. nytimes.com/2009/06/28/world/28cyber.html
McChesney, R. (2004). "The Political Economy of International Communications," in Z. Nain and P. Thomas (eds.), *Who Owns the Media? Global Trends and Local Responses* (pp. 3–22). London: Zed Books.
McChesney, R. W. and Schiller, D. (2003, November). "The Political Economy of International Communications: Foundations for the Emerging Global Debate about Media Ownership and Regulation," Technology, Business and Society Programme Paper Number 11, United Nations Research Institute for Social Development, Geneva Switzerland. http://www.unrisd.org/unrisd/website/document.nsf/(httpPublications)/C9DCBA6C7DB78C2AC1256BDF0049A774?OpenDocument
Minges, M. (2015, January). "Exploring the Relationship Between Broadband and Economic Growth," World Development Report 2016. http://pubdocs.worldbank.org/en/391452529895999/WDR16-BP-Exploring-the-Relationship-between-Broadband-and-Economic-Growth-Minges.pdf
North Atlantic Treaty Organization. (2015, July 13). "Sanctions after Crimea: Have they Worked?" https://www.nato.int/docu/review/articles/2015/07/13/sanctions-after-crimea-have-they-worked/index.html
National Public Radio. (2020, February 10). "Chinese Hackers Charged In Alleged Cyber-Theft Of 145 Million Americans' Data." https://www.npr.org/2020/02/10/804501991/chinese-hackers-charged-in-alleged-cyber-theft-of-145-million-americans-data
Nye, Jr., J. S. (2014, May). "The Regime Complex for Managing Global Cyber Activities," Chatham House, Global Commission on Internet Governance, Paper Series No. 1. https://www.cigionline.org/sites/default/files/gcig_paper_no1.pdf
InfoSec Institute. https://resources.infosecinstitute.com/cybercrime-and-the-underground-market/#gref
Ó Siochrú, S. (2004). "Global Institutions and the Democratisation of the Media," in Z. Nain and P. Thomas (eds.), *Who Owns the Media? Global Trends and Local Responses* (pp. 23–42). London: Zed Books.

Observer Research Foundation. (2014, February 1). "The UN and Cyberspace Governance." https://www.orfonline.org/article/the-un-and-cyberspace-governance/

Paganini, P. (2019, August 30). "Cybercrime and the Underground Market [Updated 2019]."

Polletta, F. and Callahan, J. (2018). "Deep Stories, Nostalgia Narratives, and Fake News: Storytelling in the Trump Era," in J. L. Mast and J. C. Alexander (eds.), *Politics of Meaning/ Meaning of Politics: Cultural Sociology of the 2016 U.S. Presidential Election* (pp. 55–73). Abingdon: Palgrave Macmillan.

Reuters. (2014, June). "Cyber Crime Costs Global Economy $445 Billion a Year: Report." https://www.reuters.com/article/us-cybersecurity-mcafee-csis/cyber-crime-costs-global-economy-445-billion-a-year-report-idUSKBN0EK0SV20140609

Robel, D. (2007). "International Cybercrime Treaty: Looking Beyond Ratification," SANS Institute. https://www.sans.org/reading-room/whitepapers/incident/international-cybercrime-treaty-ratification-1756

Sacks, S. (n.d.). "China's Emerging Cyber Governance System," Center for Strategic and International Studies. https://www.csis.org/chinas-emerging-cyber-governance-system%20

Symantec. (2017, April). "Internet Security Threat Report." https://www.symantec.com/content/dam/symantec/docs/reports/istr-22-2017-en.pdf

The Economist. (2017, May 13). "A large-scale cyber-attack highlights the structural dilemma of the NSA." https://www.economist.com/science-and-technology/2017/05/13/a-large-scale-cyber-attack-highlights-the-structural-dilemma-of-the-nsa

The Moscow Times. (2021, July 13). "Russia-Linked Hacking Groups Targeting the U.S.: What You Need to Know." themoscowtimes.com/2021/07/13/russia-linked-hacking-groups-targeting-the-us-what-you-need-to-know-a74505

The White House. (2011, May). "International Strategy for Cyberspace." https://obamawhitehouse.archives.gov/sites/default/files/rss_viewer/internationalstrategy_cyberspace.pdf

The White House. (2016, February 9). "FACT SHEET: Cybersecurity National Action Plan." https://obamawhitehouse.archives.gov/the-press-office/2016/02/09/fact-sheet-cybersecurity-national-action-plan

The White House. (2018, September). "National Cyber Security Strategy of the United States of America." https://www.whitehouse.gov/wp-content/uploads/2018/09/National-Cyber-Strategy.pdf

Thimm, J. and Schaller, C. (2014, October 22). "Internet Governance and the ITU: Maintaining the Multistakeholder Approach: The German Perspective," Council on Foreign Relations. https://www.cfr.org/report/internet-governance-and-itu-maintaining-multistakeholder-approach

United Nations Institute for Disarmament Research. (2013, June 24). "Group of Governmental Experts on Developments in the Field of Information and Telecommunications in the Context of International Security." https://www.unidir.org/files/medias/pdfs/developments-in-the-field-of-information-and-telecommunications-in-the-context-of-international-security-2012-2013-a-68-98-eng-0-518.pdf

United Nations Institute for Disarmament Research. (2015, July). "Developments in the field of information and telecommunications in the context of international security." https://www.un.org/disarmament/ict-security/

United Nations Office for Disarmament Affairs. (2020, January). "Fact Sheet – Developments in the Field of Information and Telecommunications in the Context of International Security." https://unoda-web.s3.amazonaws.com/wp-content/uploads/2020/01/Information-Security-Fact-Sheet-Jan2020.pdf

United Nations. (2003, December 18). "Resolution adopted by the General Assembly on 8 December 2003." http://undocs.org/A/RES/58/32

United States Cyber Command. (n.d.). "U.S. Cyber Command History." https://www.cybercom.mil/About/History/

United States Department of Defense. (2018). "Summary – Department of Defense Cyber Strategy." https://media.defense.gov/2018/Sep/18/2002041658/-1/-1/1/CYBER_STRATEGY_SUMMARY_FINAL.PDF

United States Department of State. (2012, October 21). "New Transcript – Remarks by Secretary Panetta on Cybersecurity to the Business Executives for National Security, New York City." https://archive.defense.gov/transcripts/transcript.aspx?transcriptid=5136

United States Departments of Homeland Security. (2018, May 15). "U.S. Department of Homeland Security Cybersecurity Strategy." https://www.dhs.gov/sites/default/files/publications/DHS-Cybersecurity-Strategy_0.pdf

Wei, Y. (2016, June 21). "China-Russia Cybersecurity Cooperation: Working Towards Cyber-Sovereignty." https://jsis.washington.edu/news/china-russia-cybersecurity-cooperation-working-towards-cyber-sovereignty/

Winston, J. (2016, November 18). "How the Trump Campaign Built an Identity Database and Used Facebook Ads to Win the Election," *Medium*. https://medium.com/startup-grind/how-the-trump-campaign-built-an-identity-database-and-used-facebook-ads-to-win-the-election-4ff7d24269ac

Wooley, S. C. and Howard, P. N. (eds.). (2017, November). "Computational Propaganda Worldwide: Executive Summary," *Working Paper 2017.11., Project on Computational Propaganda*, Oxford, UK. http://comprop.oii.ox.ac.uk/research/working-papers/computational-propaganda-worldwide-executive-summary/

Wolter, D. (2013). "The UN Takes a Big Step Forward on Cybersecurity," Arms Control Association, Washington, DC. https://www.armscontrol.org/act/2013-09/un-takes-big-step-forward-cybersecurity

World Economic Forum. (2019a, March 4). "Here are the Biggest Cybercrime Trends of 2019." https://www.weforum.org/agenda/2019/03/here-are-the-biggest-cybercrime-trends-of-2019/

World Economic Forum. (2019b, November 7). "This is the Crippling Cost of Cybercrime on Corporations." https://www.weforum.org/agenda/2019/11/cost-cybercrime-cybersecurity/

Zetter, M. (2014November 3). "An Unprecedented Look at Stuxnet, the World's First Digital Weapon," *Wired*. https://www.wired.com/2014/11/countdown-to-zero-day-stuxnet/

Chapter 33

Cybersecurity

Darren E. Tromblay

George Washington University, Washington, DC, United States

Contents

Introduction 231
Further Reading 234
References 234

Introduction

US cybersecurity efforts have gone through several phases. Operationally, they have evolved from single-agency-driven investigations to interagency initiatives. Furthermore, cybersecurity efforts have expanded, from primarily federal efforts to also include non-federal governments (e.g., state and local authorities) as well as the private sector. The United States' perception of the threats that can be perpetrated within cyberspace has broadened as well, from computer-facilitated fraud to attacks on US infrastructure by state and non-state actors.

The FBI recognized, in the mid-1970s, how computers could lead to new permutations of crime. In 1975, then-FBI Director, Clarence Kelley explained that it was necessary for Bureau personnel to become more familiar with computer frauds, and by the late 1970s, the FBI academy was training agents on aspects of investigating computer fraud (US House of Representatives, 1975). The FBI's understanding of how cyber-enabled actors could impact US security evolved through the 1990s, until it was formalized in 1998, with the FBI's addition of "Targeting the National Information Infrastructure" to its foreign counterintelligence National Security Threat List (US Senate, 1998).

Agencies' understanding of their responsibilities for the emerging cyber environment evolved along with their awareness of the changing environment's implications for security. Starting in 1984, the National Security Agency became responsible for

DOI: 10.4324/9781315144511-35

the oversight of federal computer systems (a role which subsequently shrank to the monitoring of national security networks) (Boys, 2018). In 1984, the US Secret Service (USSS) received authority to investigate certain cybercrimes, a function consistent with the USSS's financial security bailiwick (US Senate, 1985). In 1989, a USSS–FBI memorandum of understanding gave the FBI jurisdiction for computer crimes in traditional Bureau investigative areas (US House of Representatives, 1992). The FBI established its first dedicated computer fraud squad in 1992 (US House of Representatives, 1992). (As of 2011, each of the FBI's 56 field offices had established a cyber squad (US Department of Justice, 2011)). Meanwhile, in 1995, the USSS established its first Electronic Crimes Task Force (US Senate, 2001). This has caused the FBI consternation, as indicated by then-Director James Comey's statement that it made no sense for both the USSS and the FBI to both have cyber task forces (US House of Representatives, Oversight of the Federal Bureau of Investigation, 2015c).

Securing cyberspace introduced a new problem for agencies, such as the FBI, which had traditionally divided operational responsibilities by geographic jurisdictions. In an effort to overcome this, the FBI established the Computer Investigations and Infrastructure Threat Assessment Center (CITAC), in 1996, at the FBI headquarters (US House of Representatives, 1998). CITAC, as a parochial FBI entity, proved to be inadequate, since threats in cyberspace crossed interagency jurisdictions. To remedy this, the Bureau established the interagency-staffed National Infrastructure Protection Center (NIPC) in 1998 (US Senate, 1998). However, the FBI, an agency which focused on collection, found that it was ill-suited to run an entity which focused on preparedness, and NIPC became part of the Department of Homeland Security (DHS) (also the home to the USSS) when Congress established DHS in 2002 (Wall Street Journal, 2002).

Both the FBI and DHS have significant responsibilities in the field of cybersecurity. DHS has the mission of monitoring network security and initially established the National Cyber-security Division under its Information Analysis and Infrastructure Protection Directorate (IAIP) (GAO, 2005). DHS cybersecurity responsibilities have gone through several reorganizations and are now under the auspices of the National Protection and Programs Directorate (NPPD). In 2002, the FBI created its cyber division, which differs from DHS in that the FBI's mission is to investigate intrusions to determine criminal, terrorist, and nation-state actor identities and disrupt these threats (US House of Representatives. Appropriations for 2016, 2015). (One does wonder why the FBI has a cyber division alongside of its counterterrorism, counterintelligence, and criminal investigative divisions, since cyber is not an actor or activity to be investigated, but, rather, an environment in which threats operate.)

As the FBI learned, via its experience with CITAC, effective cybersecurity cannot be performed in a silo. Both DHS and the FBI have established platforms for interagency collaboration. The FBI is the lead agency for the National Cyber Investigative Joint Task Force (NCIJTF), which synthesizes a common operating picture of hostile cyber intrusion activity and coordinates operational initiatives (US House of Representatives, 2014). DHS's NPPD leads the National Cybersecurity and Communications Integration Center (NCICC), which is the US government's 24/7 hub for cybersecurity information sharing, incident response, and coordination (US House of Representatives. Worldwide Threats and Homeland Security Challenges. 2015d). The NCICC's US Cyber Emergency Response Team (US-CERT) is responsible for identifying compromises of the US federal government's civilian networks (US House of Representatives, 2016). The US Department of Defense's [DoD's] Cyber Command is responsible for the security of DoD networks (US Cyber Command, 2016).

In 2015, the Office of the Director of National Intelligence established the Cyber Threat Integration Center (CTIIC). The CTIIC's multifaceted mission includes provision of integrated all-source analysis of intelligence related to foreign cyber threats or to cyber incidents that affect US national interests. Additionally, the center provides support to federal cyber centers by providing access to intelligence necessary to carry out those centers' respective missions (Office of the Director of National Intelligence, 2018).

Private-sector networks are equally important to national security and multiple agencies have initiated efforts to engage industry on cyber matters. The FBI's Infragard program, which began as a project of the Cleveland field office, became a Bureau-wide program as part of the NIPC and transferred to the cyber division when NIPC migrated to DHS (US House of Representatives, 1998; Tromblay, 2018). Infragard was formed to facilitate collaboration between the FBI and subject matter experts from local industry and academia, on issues including cybersecurity (Federal Bureau of Investigation, n.d.). The NPPD's regionally based cybersecurity advisers function as the link between critical infrastructure owners and operators, community leadership, and other NPPD programs (US House of Representatives, 2016). DHS's US-CERT also engages with the private sector to provide assistance with assessment of threats and vulnerabilities (Department of Homeland Security, 2012).

Unfortunately, federal engagement of industry on cybersecurity has encountered multiple, persistent difficulties. For instance, most of the alerts issued by the NIPC's Watch and Warning Unit pertained to attacks that were already under way (GAO, 2001). Furthermore, information seemed to move in only one direction. According to the CEO of the national cyber forensics and training alliance, the FBI would accept unclassified information from the private sector and then classify it, which prevented the Bureau from then sharing it with other entities in the private sector (US Department of Justice, 2015). It is not only FBI entities that have been targets of criticism. As of 2015, DHS' US-CERT program did not provide information as quickly as private-sector cyber-analysis companies (US Senate, 2015). The federal government, writ large, may lack the nimbleness to interface effectively with private-sector counterparts on fast-moving cyber-related issues.

Cybersecurity is no longer strictly the domain of the federal government. The FBI, for instance, has integrated state and local partners into the cyber task forces in each of its 56 field offices (US House of Representatives, 2014). State and local governments have also taken the lead on cybersecurity issues in their areas of responsibility. The Multi-State Information Sharing and Analysis Center seeks to "improve the overall cybersecurity posture of the nation's state, local, tribal and territorial governments through focused cyber threat prevention, protection, response, and recovery" (Center for Internet Security, n.d.). Furthermore, New Jersey established its own cybersecurity and communications integration cell (US House of Representatives. Mission, Structure, and Reorganization. 2015b).

Increasingly, the federal government seems to be lagging behind private-sector cybersecurity consultants in identifying significant cyber threats. In 2015,

ThreatConnect, a US defense contractor linked the hack of Anthem, a US health insurance company, to China (Nakashima, 2015). During the same year, the information technology firm CyTech accidentally discovered the breach of 21 million federal employees' personal data during a product demonstration for the office of personnel management (Paletta, 2015). Also, in 2015, FireEye Inc. determined, through forensic analysis, that Chinese hackers may have accessed US military technology when they hacked into systems of the engineering department at Pennsylvania State University (Grossman, 2015). Although the Federal Bureau of Investigation brought the university's attention to the fact that a hack had occurred, the university had to resort to assistance from the private sector to identify the fact that US government information may have been compromised (Dilanian, 2012). In 2016, Crowdstrike discovered the infamous, Russian-sponsored FANCY BEAR and COZY BEAR hacks of the democratic national committee (Alperovitch, 2016).

Cybersecurity has proven to be a thorny problem for US authorities. Development of an approach to counter threats to the cyber area of responsibility has progressed from individual agency operations to interagency collaboration. The picture is complicated by the fact that private industry – rather than the US government – controls a significant portion of the networks that are vulnerable to state and non-state actors' attacks. Finally, other actors, including state and local governments, as well as private industry, are taking an increasing prominent role in securing US. networks – even as the US government has experienced difficulty in developing cooperative relationships with key stakeholders.

Further Reading

Jasper, S. E. (2016). "U.S. Cyber threat intelligence sharing frameworks," *International Journal of Intelligence and Counter Intelligence*, 30(1): 53–65.

Romaniuk, S. N. and Manjikian, M. (eds.). (2021). *Routledge Companion to Global Cyber-Security Strategy*. London, UK: Routledge.

Warner, M. (2012). "Cybersecurity: a pre-history," *Intelligence and National Security*, 27(5): 781–799.

References

Alperovitch, D. (2016). *Bears in the Midst: Intrusions into the Democratic National Committee*. Crowdstrike. https://www.crowdstrike.com

Boys, J.D. (2018). The Clinton administration's development and implementation of cybersecurity strategy (1993–2001). *Intelligence and National Security*, *33*(5), 755–770.

Center for Internet Security. (n.d.). https://www.cisecurity.org/ms-isac/

Dilanian, K. (2012, December 4). Cyber security gets confrontational. *Los Angeles Times*.

GAO. (2001). *Critical Infrastructure Protection: Significant Challenges in Developing National Capabilities*. Washington, DC: General Accounting Office.

GAO. (2005). *Critical Infrastructure Protection: Department of Homeland Security Faces Challenges in Fulfilling Cybersecurity Responsibilities*. Washington, DC: Government Accountability Office.

Grossman, A. (2015, May 20). US. Charges six Chinese with economic espionage. *Wall Street Journal.*
Nakashima, E. (2015, February 27). Security firm finds link between China and Anthem Hack. *Washington Post.*
Office of the Director of National Intelligence. (2018). *Cyber threat intelligence integration center.* https://www.dni.gov/index.php/ctiic-who-we-are. (Accessed February 19, 2018).
Paletta, D. (2015, June 15). Cybersecurity firm says it found spyware on government network in April. *Wall Street Journal.*
Tromblay, D. E. (2018). *Protecting Partners or Preserving Fiefdoms? How to Reform Counterintelligence Outreach to Industry.* Washington, DC: Information Technology and Innovation Foundation.
US Cyber Command. (2016). http://www.stratcom.mil/Media/Factsheets/Factsheet-View/Article/960492/us-cyber-command-uscybercom/
US Department of Justice. (2011). *The Federal Bureau of Investigation's Ability to Address the National Security Cyber Intrusion Threat.* Washington, DC: US Department of Justice.
US Department of Justice. (2015). *Audit of the Federal Bureau of Investigation's Implementation of Its Next Generation Cyber Initiative.* Washington, DC: US Department of Justice.
US House of Representatives. (1975). *Departments of State, Justice, and Commerce, the Judiciary, and Related Agencies Appropriations for 1976.* Washington, DC: US House of Representatives.
US House of Representatives. (1992). *Departments of Commerce, Justice, and State, the Judiciary, and Related Agencies Appropriations for 1993.* Washington, DC: US House of Representatives.
US House of Representatives. (1998). *Departments of Commerce, Justice, and State, the Judiciary, and Related Agencies Appropriations for 1999.* Washington, DC: US House of Representatives.
US House of Representatives. (2009). *Commerce, Justice, Science, and Related Agencies Appropriations for 2009.* Washington, DC: US House of Representatives.
US House of Representatives. (2012). *Department of Homeland Security, Appropriations for 2012.* Washington, DC: US House of Representatives.
US House of Representatives. (2014). *Worldwide Threats to the Homeland.* Washington, DC: US House of Representatives.
US House of Representatives. (2015a). *Commerce, Justice, Science, and Related Agencies Appropriations for 2016.* Washington, DC: US House of Representatives.
US House of Representatives. (2015b). *Examining the Mission, Structure, and Reorganization Effort of the National Protection and Programs Directorate.* Washington, DC: US House of Representatives.
US House of Representatives. (2015c). *Oversight of the Federal Bureau of Investigation.* Washington, DC: US House of Representatives.
US House of Representatives. (2015d). *Worldwide Threats and Homeland Security Challenges.* Washington, DC: US House of Representatives.
US House of Representatives. (2016). *Department of Homeland Security Appropriations for 2017.* Washington, DC: US House of Representatives.
US Senate. (1985). *FBI Oversight and Budget Authorization for Fiscal Year 1986.* Washington, DC: US Senate Homeland Security and Government Affairs Committee.
US Senate. (1998). *Current and Projected National Security Threats to the United States.* Washington, DC: US Senate Homeland Security and Government Affairs Committee.
US Senate. (2001). *Improving Our Ability to Fight Cybercrime: Oversight of the National Infrastructure Protection Center.* Washington, DC: US Senate Homeland Security and Government Affairs Committee.

US Senate. (2015). *A Review of the Department of Homeland Security's Missions and Performance*. Washington, DC: US Senate Homeland Security and Government Affairs Committee.

Wall Street Journal. (2002. March 21). US. Charges six Chinese with economic espionage. *Wall Street Journal*.

Chapter 34

Cyberweapons

Gary Leigh
Charles Darwin University, Darwin, NT, Australia

Contents

Introduction 237
Definitions of Cyber Weapons Today 238
Debates on Cyber Weapons 239
The Homeland Security Considerations 241
Further Reading 241
References 242

Introduction

Cyber weapons are becoming more prolific on the world stage as they feature in cyber warfare operations. Their modern publicity stems from their unconventional nature and how alien it appears that the right computer programing can have real-felt geopolitical effects. Perhaps no better example is the malware worm Stuxnet, which brought to light US efforts to curb nuclear proliferation in the Middle East. But what of other types of cyber weapons? Do botnets, denial of service attacks, storage wipers, and data exfiltration and espionage tools count as cyber weapons too?

To better equip Homeland Security professionals and those with an interest of cyber weaponry from a Homeland Security perspective, this chapter will seek to cover the contentious issue of cyber weapons. The conceptual domain of cyber weapons is fascinating as it is still not mature, nor has there been a true consensus reached across the world. Efforts have been taken, however, to create pathways between pre-existing legal doctrines and the emerging influence of cyber warfare. The *Tallinn Manual 2.0 on the International Law Applicable to Cyber Operations* (2017) is at the pinnacle of this effort and should be considered mandatory for review in this field.

The potential of cyber weapons as a form of armament, as a field of engineering, as a field for national strategy, or even as a humble academic pursuit continues to

DOI: 10.4324/9781315144511-36

grow in importance. The potentially disturbing reality of this is that as we take our time to understand the phenomena of cyber weaponry, there is a platitude of actors actively developing such things with interests that do not align with the US or its principles.

This chapter provides a cursory overview of cyber weapons in three parts. The first part shall cover the definitions of cyber weapons. Here, the nuance and contention of such phenomena will be shown. The second part will review some of the debates that surround cyber weapons as they are known today. The third and final part explores cyber weapons for Homeland Security considerations.

Definitions of Cyber Weapons Today

No discussion on cyber weapons can be complete without a working definition. However, the definition of what constitutes a cyber weapon is contentious today. This is despite the urge for a common-sense approach to cyber weapons being akin to a weaponized computer system. It will become clear, however, that a nuanced definition is of utmost importance. This is because these definitions factor into not only normative and operational understandings of cyber weapons but also the legal instruments that act as the foundation for Homeland Security.

A well-accepted definition of cyber weapons is as follows:

> a cyber-weapon is seen as a subset of weapons more generally: as computer code that is used, or designed to be used, with the aim of threatening or causing physical, functional, or mental harm to structures, systems or living beings
>
> (Rid and McBurney 2012: 7)

Despite the merits of this definition, it is open to criticism. In the words of the authors, they note, "most weapons analogies break down even more quickly today than they did four years ago. Serious research and wider public debate would be best served if we all stop using the hackneyed moniker 'cyber weapons' entirely" (Biller and Schmitt 2019: 224). This is largely due to how rapidly evolving the field of malware is and the advancements not only in cyber operations but also in the world of technology, which legal instruments tend to follow.

There are other definitions that take a different stance. The research from the Stockton Center for International Law at the U.S. Naval College offers a deep dive into the legal considerations of the definition. The work titled, *the Classification of Cyber Capabilities and Operations as Weapons, Means, or Methods of Warfare* considers the Tallinn Manual on the International Law Applicable to Cyber Warfare for its legal working definitions on an international level:

> For the Tallinn 2.0 experts, a "cyber means of warfare" encompasses "cyber weapons and their associated cyber systems," including "any cyber device, material, instrument, mechanism, equipment, or software used, designed, or intended to be used to conduct a cyber-attack".
>
> (Biller and Schmitt 2019: 109)

Building on this are the sound conceptions that in order to classify a digital artifact as a cyber weapon, it needs to be used in a "warfare-like manner" (Herr and Rosenzweig 2016: 302). To interrogate this notion further, a cyber artifact that could be used in a warfare-like manner would require weapon-like attributes. These attributes should contain "three component parts – a Propagation method, an Exploit, and a Payload" (Herr and Rosenzweig 2016: 302). This is a sound determination due to the multifaceted nature of technology and its uses.

However, despite the propagation method, how exactly a system can be exploited and what the payload or negative effect may be – "the effectiveness of a cyber weapon is a very strong function of the target's characteristics" (Lin and Zegart 2018: 7). What this means is that an assembly of cyber tools, which can be configured and utilized like a weapon, can suddenly no longer be a weapon due to a change in target characteristics (Lin and Zegart 2018: 7). Therefore, having a multifaceted definition of a cyber weapon is useful for policy-makers and Homeland Security practitioners alike to avoid misunderstandings.

A profiling framework on cyber weapons was created as an outcome of the *International Conference on Cyber Conflict* held in Washington (Maathuis et al. 2016). The framework suggests identifying potential cyber weapons against a range of classification criteria. These can include: offensive or defensive purposes, use count such as one-time use or ongoing, sophistication of the device or code, and the scale being unitary to global. Each of these definitions is important to having a holistic understanding of the cyber weapon phenomena.

Debates on Cyber Weapons

With the stage set for how we can understand what cyber weapons may or may not be, let us review some of the debates surrounding cyber weapons as they apply to Homeland Security. One of the most contentious debates as it stands is the actual legal conduct of cyber operations. This is especially important for Homeland Security professionals. The boundaries between operating within a US jurisdiction and having information travel overseas is one consideration. Another consideration is the legality of curbing or interacting with foreign computer systems.

Why might this be the case? As it stands, Homeland Security must protect the interior against cyber threats and preserve critical infrastructure. The nature of a cyber threat in the form of a cyber weapon is difficult to forecast. Cyber weapons development is multifaceted due to the unknown potential for how dangerous they could be in terms of second- and third-order effects. When considering the examples of definitions given earlier, it may be entirely possible that a Homeland Security cyber defender may be on the precipice of discovering a potential cyber weapon of mass destruction – or even a component of it.

This may seem unlikely, but the conduction of self-defense, retaliation, escalation, maneuvers, and so on is in legislative flux. The norms and protocols that need to be followed in the never-ending cyberattack space continue to evolve despite the flux. Homeland Security professionals must move forward and succeed in their operations despite this. Even though the US has been involved in serious cyber activity for over 10 years, "under current legal regimes...none meet the requirement of self-defense against an armed attack under Article 51 of the UN Charter, and even if they did, the response would need to be proportionate to the attack under the Law of Armed Conflict. So, to date, no cyber weapons have been used that could be called weapons of mass destruction" (Carr 2013: 36). It is debatable if the US has conducted itself disproportionately to the threat it faces today.

How exactly the legal debate has evolved over the over years is beyond the scope of this chapter. But it does go to demonstrate that cyber weapons can be viewed as not being in the same class as weapons of mass destruction despite the potential being there. Nevertheless, the argument made in the *Bulletin of the Atomic Scientists* illuminates a wider debate – is the lack of legislative jurisprudence in this domain a hamstring in the defense of the US or has it been an enabler to gain a competitive advantage? After all, Homeland Security can achieve close alignment with the States it protects as well as international partners.

In addition to this, the acquisition of cyber weapons is hotly debated today. Due to the recency of cyber weapons, the norms of arms procurement are not mature. For those good and bad actors seeking US technologies, it has been argued that the US must bolster its export controls and be a leader in this space. This could see limits placed on suppliers of digital products that may be combined or altered or used as weapons via regulatory requirements. Whatever path the US takes to ensure minimal spread of unnecessary or disadvantageous cyber weapons to US interests, Homeland Security will have a role in the active use and defense of cyber weapons into the future. This said, by considering the definition of cyber weapons that stipulate that there must be a propagation method, exploit, and payload, it becomes easier to create the relevant policy and for government to stop proliferation unduly (Herr and Rosenzweig 2016: 318–319).

So far, the debates have focused on the legal evolution of cyber weapons and the reality that the US has a role to play in curbing the procurement of cyber weapons. But this glances over an important reality of the national fabric that underpins the US as a nation. That is, the ability for ordinary citizens and corporates to defend themselves – not just the government. This conjures the notion that perhaps the citizens themselves have the right to bare cyber arms.

The debate has on the one hand offered a word from the Supreme court, noting, "that only weapons that are not "dangerous and unusual" are permissible," moreover that, "the next question is what would constitute a dangerous and unusual cyber weapon that would preclude ownership—including placement on computers—by citizens" (Kallberg 2019: 71–76). As it stands today, "the current Second Amendment doctrine would not exclude cyber arms unless these arms are of no military value or not suitable for military use or require no intent to be dangerous for the general population."

This ties-in the current issue of the market for procuring malware and the notorious 0-day exploit. The 0-day exploit means a cyberattack, malware, or weapon for which there is no readily apparent defense (Stockton and Golabek-Goldman 2013). It is argued that, "the United States and the international community are enabling O-day exploit market to flourish, which empowers terrorist organizations and rogue states to purchase cyber weaponry" (Stockton and Golabek-Goldman 2013: 265). Therefore, it may seem that as much as the US is part of the solution, it also creates its own issues with the introduction of cyber weapons.

The Homeland Security Considerations

The terminology of cyber weapon might not be a common vernacular in Homeland Security official documentation for public use – but it does not preclude Homeland Security professionals potentially being involved with cyber weapons. We can see by the definitions used here that cyber weapons are indeed multifaceted, and that depending on the right legal circumstances and operations, cyber weapons may become a routine part of the arsenal.

What this speaks to is something not yet touched on, which is the notion of the rules of engagement and tactics, techniques, and procedures of cyber operations in the Homeland Security realm. After all, for adversaries, small states, and allies, the potential cyber weapon uses range from warfighting, coercion, deterrence, and defense diplomacy (Hughes and Colarik 2016: 21). Semantics dictate that depending on the adversary, these uses of cyber weapons will change. The nature of this change, and that this change forms part of the fog of cyberwar and crime, means policy-making and operational planning become more difficult. Cyber defense and offense is one thing but being able to determine whom your adversary may be is another. Classic tradecraft would suggest identifying adversaries by their weapons, and thus the task of "attribution of a hostile act in cyberspace" needs to "draw on multiple sources of information, both historical and collected in the wake of the hostile act in question" (Robert Kehler et al., 2017: 74).

For the Homeland Security Professional operating in cyber operations, it is important to reflect on how, "the rules and strategy relating to the use of any cyber weapon are still being determined…will rules and strategies follow those of an existing class of weapons, will they be a hybrid of old and new, or completely new?" (Peterson 2013: 124). Being able to determine if cyber weapons are in use, or what precisely is the cyber activity that is being witnessed speaks to being able to "navigate ambiguous intent due to the intelligence gathering nature as well as advanced tactics to throw off true intentions" (Robert Kehler et al., 2017). As the threats are ever persistent, new tools and weapons will need to be made, so understanding how we define cyber weapons will be crucial.

In summary, this chapter has encouraged thought into the nature of cyber weapons. How we know them, who may have them, and what they need them to do, when does a tool become a weapon? This said, to conclude, consider the German malware *Bundestrojaner*. This tool "was used domestically, by a law-enforcement agency – that is federal or state police – and was designed to enforce the laws and to maintain the state's legitimate monopoly of force through the use of arms" (Rid and McBurney 2012: 11). Because of this, *Bundestrojaner* was not considered a weapon, mainly due to it being a state-sponsored software for intelligence purposes, rather than causing harm.

Further Reading

Givens, A. D., Busch, N. E., and Bersin, A. D. (2018). "Going Global: The International Dimensions of U.S. Homeland Security Policy," *Journal of Strategic Security*, *11*(3): 1–34.

Rid, T. and McBurney, P. (2012). "Cyber-Weapons," *The RUSI Journal*, *157*(1): 6–13.

Tropeano, R. (2019). *Tallinn Manual 2.0 on the International Law Applicable to Cyber Operations*. National Security Archive. https://nsarchive.gwu.edu/news/cyber-vault/2019-04-24/tallinn-manual-20-international-law-applicable-cyber-operations

References

Biller, T. and Schmitt, M. (2019). "Classification of Cyber Capabilities and Operations as Weapons, Means, or Methods of Warfare." https://digital-commons.usnwc.edu/cgi/viewcontent.cgi?article=2462&context=ils

Maathuis, C., Pieters, W. and Den Berg, J. V. (2016). "Cyber Weapons: A Profiling Framework," *International Conference on Cyber Conflict (CyCon US)*, Washington, DC. https://ieeexplore.ieee.org/document/7836621/

Carr, J. (2013). "The Misunderstood Acronym: Why Cyber Weapons Aren't WMD," *Bulletin of Atomic Scientists, 69*(5): 32–37.

Peterson, D. (2013). "Offensive Cyber weapons: Construction, Development, and Employment," *Journal of Strategic Studies, 36*(1): 120–124.

Dewar, R. (2018). "Cyberweapons: Capability, Intent and Context in Cyberdefense." https://css.ethz.ch/content/dam/ethz/special-interest/gess/cis/center-for-securities-studies/pdfs/Cyber-Reports-2017-06.PDF

Herr, T. and Rosenzweig, P. (2016). "Cyber weapons and Export Control: Incorporating Dual Use with the PrEP Model," *Journal of National Security Law & Policy, 8*(301): 300–319. https://jnslp.com/wp-content/uploads/2016/04/Cyber-Weapons-and-Export-Control_2.pdf

Hughes, D. and Colarik, A. (2016). "Cyber weapons into Small States," *Joint Force Quarterly, 83* (4): 19–26. https://ndupress.ndu.edu/Portals/68/Documents/jfq/jfq-83/jfq-83_19-26_Hughes-Colarik.pdf

Kallberg, J. (2019). The Second Amendment and Cyber weapons: Constitutional Relevance of Digital Gun Rights. *IEEE Technology and Society Magazine*, 38(2), 71–77. https://doi.org/10.1109/MTS.2019.2913073

Lin, H. and Zegart, A. (eds.). (2018). *Bytes, Bombs, and Spies: The Strategic Dimensions of Offensive Cyber Operations*. Washington, D.C.: Brookings Institution Press.

Rid, T. and McBurney, P. (2012). "Cyber-Weapons," *The RUSI Journal, 157*(1): 6–13.

Robert Kehler, C., Lin, H. and Sulmeyer, M. (2017). Rules of engagement for cyberspace operations: a view from the USA," *Journal of Cybersecurity, 3*(1). https://doi.org/10.1093/cybsec/tyx003

Stockton, P. N. and Golabek-Goldman, M. (2013). "Curbing the Market for Cyber weapons," *Yale Law & Policy Review, 32*(1): 239–266. https://digitalcommons.law.yale.edu/ylpr/vol32/iss1/11/

Chapter 35

Distributed Denial-of-Service (DDoS) Threats and Attacks

Mostafa Amini
Harvard University Medical School, Cambridge, MA, United States

Contents

Introduction 243
Further Reading 246
References 246

Introduction

Cybersecurity in the United States has become a national security priority in recent years. While it has always been at the forefront of government policy, the rapid rise of external threats to key American institutional processes has brought cybersecurity concerns to the mainstream (Ohlin, 2017). One reason that perhaps explains this recent convergence is the rapid development in technological innovation, which has facilitated more advanced methods of exploiting potential gaps in the American security architecture. Foreign influences on American elections are especially relevant, considering the main battleground being social media platforms (Berghel, 2017; Ouassini and Amini, 2018). Examples of targets can include IT systems, personal data, or data associated with national institutions.

Common types of cybersecurity threats can range from simple techniques, including password exploitations, social engineering, and phishing attempts (Das et al., 2019) to more elaborate techniques, including man-in-the-middle (MITM) attacks (Kang et al., 2018), SQL injections (Boyd and Keromytis, 2004), and denial-of-service (DoS) attacks (Hui et al., 2017). This chapter will briefly discuss the concept of DoS threats, and more specifically, *distributed* denial-of-service (DDoS) threats. It will provide a brief discussion on the role of DDoS in the national American landscape

DOI: 10.4324/9781315144511-37

viz-a-viz national security strategy and infrastructure. Finally, we will quickly evaluate innovative techniques in the detection and prevention of DDoS attempts utilizing artificial intelligence and machine learning techniques.

At the highest level, a DoS attack is simply an attempt by an actor to exploit, prevent, or disrupt a specific service, with the potential of affecting internal stakeholders, external users, or both. A DDoS attains the aforementioned objective – with the potential for greater impact and magnitude – by using an array of resources *in tandem* (Reiher et al., n.d.; *Understanding Denial-of-Service Attacks | CISA*, n.d.). The multi-phased "recruitment" process in DDoS consists of procuring numerous agents or slave machines through automated scanning techniques, after which security weaknesses are found and exploited. The agent machines are then masked via spoofing of the source from which data is transmitted to prevent the identification of the source machine (Mahjabin et al., 2017; Reiher et al., n.d.).

A series of different approaches exists under the DDoS umbrella. An example of two traditional methods are referred to as the "Ping of Death" and "IP fragmentation" – also referred to as "teardrop" – attacks. Under the former approach, a constant stream of protocol-specific data, or packets, is over-transmitted to a target system, overloading network traffic, consuming resources, and thus leading to the disabling of the system (Yihunie et al., 2018). The latter "IP fragmentation" approach simply seeks to somewhat perplex the receiving target by transmitting fragmented and otherwise "deformed" packets (Kim and Kim, 2006). An example of a more contemporary method of DDoS is the utilization of botnets, the commonly used tactic of procuring – or infecting – multiple systems to launch largescale DDoS attacks, as mentioned above (Amirshahi and Ahangari, 2015). The rise of the "Internet of Things" (IoT) – a term referring to the ubiquitous nature of data connectivity via internet-enabled household objects – adds layers of complexity to botnets, where DDoS vulnerability now extends beyond traditional computer systems (Nogueira, 2016).

The role that the Department of Homeland Security (DHS) plays in counteracting cybersecurity, and DDoS in particular, is fairly large in scope. Progenitors of DDoS attacks come from a diverse assortment of actors, whether it be terrorist organizations, nation-state institutions, adversarial countries, or independent hackers (Urcuyo, 2016). Due to the dynamic nature of potential aggressors, DHS similarly has comprehensive cybersecurity strategies that contain an amalgam of perspectives on prevention, responsiveness, recovery, and innovation (Jaikaran, n.d.). The tactical coordination against DDoS attacks consists of a few key components: the coordination with major US industries, companies, and sectors to establish guidelines and policies on DDoS attacks; the active, direct regulation and scanning of government network architecture and other security mechanisms to detect or prevent DDoS attacks; the exchange of data and information within the federal government, local state governments, or private entities; the research and development of innovative methods to counteract DDoS threats; and the actual enforcement of US law and prosecution of offenders who execute DDoS-related crimes (Maughan et al., 2015).

The aforementioned goals are carried out by the main cybersecurity arm nested under the DHS, the Cybersecurity and Infrastructure Security Agency (CISA), established recently in 2018 and enabled by the Cybersecurity and Infrastructure Security

Agency Act of 2018 (Gilbert-Bonner, 2018). Key elements of innovation take place under the umbrella of the Science and Technology Directorate (S&T). Nested under CISA, the National Cybersecurity and Communications Integration Center (NCCIC) plays the pivotal role of a centralized entity which pulls together important intelligence figures and resources to analyze security threats, facilitate the transmission of data and knowledge on potential threats, rapidly respond to cybersecurity attacks, and perform continuous risk assessments (Jasper, 2017). With the goal of being a bridge between federal and non-federal resources, NCCIC works with people across 13 federal departments and 16 private organizations (Jasper, 2017).

The frequency and magnitude by which international actors deploy DDoS attacks on the United States progressively increase year-by-year. In 2018, for the first time, a 1.7 Tbps DDoS attack took place, marking a 273% increase in the global maximum attack size (*New world record DDoS attack hits 1.7Tbps days after landmark GitHub outage | ZDNet*, n.d.). The end of 2019 saw an increase in DDoS botnet activity, with the highest occurrence being 17.53% of total DDoS attacks on a given day. The top 3 countries with the highest number of botnet servers were the United States, the Netherlands, and China. The top 3 countries for DDoS origin were China, the United States, and Hong Kong, with an unexpected appearance by South Africa in the top 5 countries (*DDoS report Q3 2019*, n.d.). Another alarming trend is the increased usage of IoT devices in facilitating DDoS attacks, with 17% of DDoS attacks exploiting compromised IoT devices in 2018 (NETSCOUT's 14th Annual Worldwide Infrastructure Security Report).

The impact of DDoS attacks on US infrastructure is substantial. It has the potential to disrupt major institutions and core infrastructure, including financial institutions, public utilities like the electric grid, private companies, and vital daily services and affect the distribution of vital public information. Notable attacks include the record-breaking 1.3 Tbps DDoS attack on GitHub (*New world record DDoS attack hits 1.7Tbps days after landmark GitHub outage | ZDNet*, n.d.) and largescale attack on six financial institutions, including J.P. Morgan and Bank of America (Sidel, 2014).

To prevent future attacks, the United States is taking both a proactive and responsive approach to the problem of DDoS on the US infrastructure. The United States has renewed strategic efforts to further strengthen the protection of data and network systems, including the empowerment of DHS in continuing to secure federal, individual agency, and contractor networks. In collaboration with academic institutions, an array of tools and services have also been implemented, including IP identification tools, the capacity to handle higher bandwidth from potential threats, a centralized emergency response system in the face of DDoS attack impact, and tools to measure the efficacy of source address validation (*DDoS Attacks A Cyberthreat and Possible Solutions*, n.d.).

Amid increasingly complex techniques to bypass technological and infrastructural defenses against DDoS attacks, there have been recent attempts to utilize machine learning algorithms, a form of artificial intelligence (AI) applications, to further mitigate and prevent the success of DDoS attacks. Two examples which we will briefly mention are "Bayesian networks" and "neural networks". Put simply, Bayesian networks provide a probabilistic in the process of deriving an association between variables. One example of using Bayesian networks in combating DDoS is using a "classifier" approach, where an algorithm is used to evaluate the integrity of incoming packets and identify other historical trends in the anomalous transmission of data. An advantage of such a method is its real-time processing, whereas a disadvantage is its limitation on only User Datagram (UDP) and Transmission Control (TCP) protocols.

Finally, neural networks are a category of algorithms that refer to a type of mathematical model that seeks to simulate the behavior of neurons. Although much less complex than the actual function of the brain, neural networks contain a combination of multiple layers, weights, and learning the values of parameters via "training" datasets (Koupaee and Wang, 2018). One manifestation of neural networks to detect incoming DDoS attacks is NLP neural networks, where a detection system scans social media networks. The idea is that by using public data, social activity can be a measurement of a given service and can determine if anomalies exist. One major drawback of this method is that it's limited in the scope of attacks it can detect (Chambers et al., 2018; Khalaf et al., 2019).

Further Reading

Amirshahi, B., and Ahangari, A. (2015). HF-Blocker: Detection of Distributed Denial of Service Attacks Based On Botnets. *Journal of Advances in Computer Engineering and Technology, 1*(3), 39–45.

Chambers, N., Fry, B., and McMasters, J. (2018). Detecting Denial-of-Service Attacks from Social Media Text: Applying NLP to Computer Security. *Proceedings of the 2018 Conference of the North American Chapter of the Association for Computational Linguistics: Human Language Technologies, Volume 1 (Long Papers)*, 1626–1635. https://doi.org/10.18653/v1/N18-1147

DDoS Attacks A Cyberthreat and Possible Solutions. (n.d.). https://www.isaca.org/resources/isaca-journal/past-issues/2013/ddos-attacks-a-cyberthreat-and-possible-solutions

Mahjabin, T., Xiao, Y., Sun, G., and Jiang, W. (2017). A survey of distributed denial-of-service attack, prevention, and mitigation techniques. *International Journal of Distributed Sensor Networks, 13*(12). https://doi.org/10.1177/1550147717741463

References

Amirshahi, B. and Ahangari, A. (2015). "HF-Blocker: Detection of Distributed Denial of Service Attacks Based On Botnets," *Journal of Advances in Computer Engineering and Technology, 1*(3): 39–45.

Berghel, H. (2017). "Oh, What a Tangled Web: Russian Hacking, Fake News, and the 2016 US Presidential Election," *Computer, 50*(9): 87–91. https://doi.org/10.1109/MC.2017.3571054

Boyd, S. W., and Keromytis, A. D. (2004). "SQLrand: Preventing SQL Injection Attacks," in M. Jakobsson, M. Yung, and J. Zhou (eds.), *Applied Cryptography and Network Security* (vol. 3089, pp. 292–302). Springer. https://doi.org/10.1007/978-3-540-24852-1_21

Chambers, N., Fry, B., and McMasters, J. (2018). "Detecting Denial-of-Service Attacks from Social Media Text: Applying NLP to Computer Security," *Proceedings of the 2018 Conference of the North American Chapter of the Association for Computational Linguistics: Human Language Technologies, Volume 1 (Long Papers)*: 1626–1635. https://doi.org/10.18653/v1/N18-1147

Das, S., Kim, A., Tingle, Z., and Nippert-Eng, C. (2019). "All About Phishing: Exploring User Research through a Systematic Literature Review," *ArXiv:1908.05897 [Cs]*. http://arxiv.org/abs/1908.05897

DDoS Attacks A Cyberthreat and Possible Solutions. (n.d.). https://www.isaca.org/resources/isaca-journal/past-issues/2013/ddos-attacks-a-cyberthreat-and-possible-solutions

DDoS report Q3 2019. (n.d.). https://securelist.com/ddos-report-q3-2019/94958/

Gilbert-Bonner, P. (2018). *DHS Structure and Strategy of the Cybersecurity and Infrastructure Security Agency (CISA)*.

Hui, K.-L., Kim, S. H., and Wang, Q.-H (2017). "Cybercrime Deterrence and International Legislation: Evidence from Distributed Denial of Service Attacks," *MIS Quarterly*, *41*(2): 497–523.

Jaikaran, C. (n.d.). *DHS's Cybersecurity Mission—An Overview*. 2.

Jasper, S. E. (2017). "U.S. Cyber Threat Intelligence Sharing Frameworks," *International Journal of Intelligence and CounterIntelligence*, *30*(1): 53–65. https://doi.org/10.1080/08850607.2016.1230701

Kang, J. J., Fahd, K., and Venkatraman, S. (2018). "Trusted Time-Based Verification Model for Automatic Man-in-the-Middle Attack Detection in Cybersecurity," *Cryptography*, *2*(4): 38. https://doi.org/10.3390/cryptography2040038

Khalaf, B. A., Mostafa, S. A., Mustapha, A., Mohammed, M. A., and Abduallah, W. M. (2019). "Comprehensive Review of Artificial Intelligence and Statistical Approaches in Distributed Denial of Service Attack and Defense Methods," *IEEE Access*, *7*: 51691–51713. https://doi.org/10.1109/ACCESS.2019.2908998

Kim, B.-R., and Kim, K.-C. (2006). "Improved Technique of IP Address Fragmentation Strategies for DoS Attack Traceback," in D. Grigoriev, J. Harrison, and E. A. Hirsch (eds.), *Computer Science – Theory and Applications* (pp. 427–437). Springer. https://doi.org/10.1007/11753728_43

Koupaee, M., and Wang, W. Y (2018). "Analyzing and Interpreting Convolutional Neural Networks in NLP," *ArXiv:1810.09312 [Cs, Stat]*. http://arxiv.org/abs/1810.09312

Mahjabin, T., Xiao, Y., Sun, G., and Jiang, W. (2017). "A survey of Distributed Denial-of-Service Attack, Prevention, and Mitigation Techniques," *International Journal of Distributed Sensor Networks*, *13*(12). https://doi.org/10.1177/1550147717741463

Maughan, D., Balenson, D., Lindqvist, U., and Tudor, Z. (2015). "Government-Funded R D to Drive Cybersecurity Technologies," *IT Professional*, *17*(4): 62–65. https://doi.org/10.1109/MITP.2015.70

New world record DDoS attack hits 1.7Tbps days after landmark GitHub outage | ZDNet. (n.d.). https://www.zdnet.com/article/new-world-record-ddos-attack-hits-1-7tbps-days-after-landmark-github-outage/

Nogueira, M. (2016). "Anticipating Moves to Prevent Botnet Generated DDoS Flooding Attacks," *ArXiv:1611.09983 [Cs]*. http://arxiv.org/abs/1611.09983

Ohlin, J. D. (2017). "*Did Russian Cyber-Interference in the 2016 Election Violate International Law?*" [Preprint]. LawArXiv. https://doi.org/10.31228/osf.io/3vuzf

Ouassini, A., and Amini, M. (2018). "The Pershing Myth: Trump, Islamophobic Tweets, and the Construction of Public Memory," *Journal of Social Science Research*, *12*(1): 2499–2504. https://doi.org/10.24297/jssr.v12i1.6794

Reiher, P., Profile, S., Mirkovic, J., and Reiher, P. (n.d.). *A Taxonomy of DDoS Attack*.

Sidel, E. G. A. R. (2014, August 28). "J.P. Morgan Working Closely With Law Enforcement on Cyberattack," *Wall Street Journal*. https://www.wsj.com/articles/j-p-morgan-not-seeing-unusual-fraud-regarding-reports-of-hacking-1409227168

Understanding Denial-of-Service Attacks | CISA. (n.d.). https://www.us-cert.gov/ncas/tips/ST04-015

Urcuyo, M. S. (2016). "From Internet Trolls to Seasoned Hackers: Protecting Our Financial Interests from Distributed-Denial-of-Service Attacks," *Rutgers Computer & Technology Law Journal*, *42*(2): 299–330. Gale OneFile: LegalTrac.

Yihunie, F., Abdelfattah, E., and Odeh, A. (2018). "Analysis of ping of death DoS and DDoS attacks," *2018 IEEE Long Island Systems, Applications and Technology Conference (LISAT)*: 1–4. https://doi.org/10.1109/LISAT.2018.8378010

Chapter 36

Government Communications Headquarters (GCHQ)

Madelaine Preedy
Queen Mary University of London, London, United Kingdom

Contents

Introduction 249
The History of GCHQ and the Anglo-American Intelligence Relationship 250
The Effects of 9/11 251
Twenty-First-Century Issues for GCHQ 252
Further Reading 253
References 253

Introduction

Government Communications Headquarters (GCHQ) is a British intelligence agency that monitors signal intelligence (SIGNIT) (see Signals Intelligence Agencies). GCHQ gathers information by deploying intercepting technologies to read satellite, terrestrial, radio, and microwave communications. It is agreed that for most of the 20th century, intelligence agencies exist within a clandestine environment (Aldrich, 2013). The inner workings of intelligence agencies continue to remain a lacuna. Most of what we have learnt about GCHQ in the 21st century has been due to document leaks and whistle-blowers (see Wikileaks for an example of how whistle-blowers release information). GGCHQ is often dubbed as the UK's most secret organisation, and since its introduction, the British government has consistently maintained an aura of secrecy around it. The introduction of the Intelligence Services Act (1994) was the first official acknowledgement of GCHQ within the Parliament. As this chapter demonstrates, GCHQ has played a significant role in British history, especially during

DOI: 10.4324/9781315144511-38

the Second World War. However, at times, its importance has been questioned. GCHQ is now faced with extensive challenges as a result of technological transformations.

The History of GCHQ and the Anglo-American Intelligence Relationship

Formed 100 years ago, on November 1, 1919, GCHQ was formally known as the Government Code and Cypher School (GC&CS). It was founded in response to the successes of code breaking during the First World War. As its ostensive function was merely defensive, GC&CS was mainly used to protect cyphers and codes used across different government departments. In addition, its more clandestine task was attacking communications used by foreign powers. The development of GC&CS began in the inter-war period and the significance of its activities only became apparent during the Second World War.

Most fascinating is the breaking of the infamous Enigma at GC&CS. From 1940, cryptographers were working on intercepting and decrypting the supposedly impenetrable Enigma. The Enigma was a device used to protect communications; it was extensively used by Nazi Germany throughout the Second World War. The purpose of the Enigma machine was to encrypt communications by scrambling the 26 letters of the alphabet to produce a coded word. General Dwight D. Eisenhower (Supreme Commander of the Allied Expeditionary Force) believed that the cryptographers at GC&CS 'saved thousands of British and American lives and, in no small way, contributed to the speed with which the enemy was routed and eventually forced to surrender' (Moran, 2012, pp. 254). Hitherto the cracking of the Enigma code was inconceivable. By 1943, the GC&CS were reading 3000 enemy communications a day. Reportedly, some of the decryption that occurred in the GC&CS was so rapid that communications from the Eastern Front reached Britain, before they reached Nazi Germany (Hinsley, 1993). Evidently, the work of GC&CS was deemed essential in protecting Britain during the war, an ethos transported to the subsequent GCHQ.

During the Second World War, the Anglo-American intelligence relationship strengthened. In a joint mission, both the UK and the USA read the traffic of allies and enemies alike. The UK was tasked with reading the communications traffic of European states, for example, France and Germany, while the USA read South American and Japanese traffic. The SIGNIT attack on Japan that was carried out by the US provided the UK with evidence to suggest future relationships would be robust and powerful (Andrew, 1996, pp. 162–163). This further fuelled this newly formed relationship between the USA and the UK. While the USA could offer resources such as constantly evolving technology, the UK were able to offer strategic land as the UK possessed remote outposts close to enemy states where listening stations could be based. For example, Cyprus is situated in a strategic location ideal for US interception of communications from the Middle East. The UKUSA Agreement gradually evolved after a series of overlapping pacts were agreed upon by both the UK and the USA. This global multilateral alliance resulted from many overlapping agreements which are mutually beneficial through sharing intelligence. Lowenthal (2014) argues that this agreement represents a globalised Western intelligence service. At various points throughout its history, the UKUSA alliance has expanded to encompass Australia,

Canada, and New Zealand as secondary parties. This SIGNIT and security network is also known as the 'Five Eyes'.

After the Second World War, in 1946, the GC&CS formally changed its name to GCHQ (Rudner, 2004, pp. 572). Despite the influence of GCHQ in the war effort, it has not been discussed in much detail in the post war years (Aldrich, 2011, pp. 2). As this chapter discusses below, GCHQ faces increasing criticisms surrounding its secrecy, particularly in relation to civilian privacy. Consequently, in 2017, GCHQ announced it was commissioning its first authorised history, in celebration of its centenary year, providing a selective insight into the inner workings of the intelligence agency.

Providing further evidence for a robust and resilient relationship is the creation of Echelon, through GCHQ and the National Security Agency (NSA). Echelon is an intelligence programme designed to monitor the flow and content of signals and intercepts roughly 5 billion communications a day. It has the ability to monitor virtually all types of electronic (public and private) communications in almost every county (Smith, 2003, pp. 318–319).

The Effects of 9/11

Throughout the 20th century, Western states have had a turbulent relationship with their respective intelligence agencies. The end of the Cold War bought with it the idea that it would result in a new peaceful era of history; consequently, the funding for GCHQ was drastically cut, which is incomprehensible in today's security climate. The threat of Communism to Western states was soon overtaken by new ideas about the spread of liberal democracies, influenced by Fukuyama's 'End of History and the Last Man' (Fukuyama, 1992). For example, 1991 bought with it a decline in political tensions, particularly in the Middle East. Yasser Arafat agreed to meet with Israel for the first time, dramatically easing pressures on the states involved. Ostensibly, the need for intelligence to ensure state security was deemed to be decreasing.

It is undeniable that 9/11 resulted in significant political, economic, and social ramifications; it overturned this period of peacefulness. Since the terror attack, intelligence agencies across the globe have increasingly been placed in the spotlight concerning intelligence failures. Criticisms towards intelligence agencies after 9/11 mainly stemmed from them being under-staffed and under-funded. In the wake of 9/11, Western states in particular pumped large sums of money into intelligence agencies, in particular GCHQ and the NSA. Aldrich (2009, pp. 889) referred to this as a 'diet and binge' approach that was adapted by states. Across the globe, the threat of terrorism grew and the work of the intelligence agencies became increasingly important once again. For example, research conducted by the Global Terrorist Database shows in 2000 the number of fatal terror attacks (580) was lower than in 1979 (832). After 9/11, the number of attacks rose again, hitting a 10-year high in 2007 (3,300) (LaFree, 2010). In September 2001, 18 days after the terror attack, the UN passed Security Council Resolution 1373, which declared that states should ensure that 'terrorist acts are established as serious criminal offences in domestic laws and regulations and that the seriousness of such acts is duly reflected in sentences served.' Given that as a peacekeeping organisation, the United Nations (UN) traditionally avoids intelligence agencies, passing this resolution highlighted how grave the threat of terrorism was perceived, thusdemonstrating the developing need for the intelligence agencies to counteract this (Aldrich, 2011, pp. 511).

Twenty-First-Century Issues for GCHQ

Today, GCHQ faces a plethora of challenges and threats which seemingly threaten its existence on a daily basis. The growing literature suggests that technological advancements and the omnipresence of the internet have affected many aspects of GCHQ. The type of communications being analysed has changed, as well as sharing of the intelligence that has been gathered. GCHQ, like many intelligence agencies across the globe, is arguably unable to deal with the huge mass of communication that occur on a daily basis. In 2003, GCHQ moved to a new headquarters in retaliation to post-9/11 criticisms and the struggle to cope with the increasing presence of the internet and therefore the need for more staff. At the time, it cost an estimated £335 million to build (Norton-Taylor, 2003). However, it is often reported that by the time the GCHQ personnel had moved into their new HQ, they had already outgrown it. Since then, the monitoring of traffic flow also proves to be an ever-increasing challenge, despite the support of Echelon.

The increasing threat of cybersecurity within the UK has issued GCHQ with a new type of threat to Britain's security. In 2010, GCHQ announced it identified cybersecurity as a Tier 1 threat, equal to terrorism, war, and natural disaster (2010 National Security Strategy). The borderless world that technology has facilitated highlights different threats for GCHQ to protect against. For example, the increasing volume and intricacy of financial and commercial transactions which fall within the realm of cyber security. According to the Office for National Statistics, 1.83% of adults have been a victim of a computer misuse crime, compared to 0.8% who had been a victim of theft (ONS, 2019). Fundamentally, GCHQ is moving away from the more 'traditional' monitoring of signal intelligence to focus on these new challenges.

GCHQ, like many intelligence agencies situated in democratic states, is facing increasing issues surrounding privacy and civil liberties. Edward Snowden's revelations in 2013 not only ignited debates surrounding civilian privacy, but also demonstrated the full extent of the relationship between GCHQ and the NSA. For example, of the 1.5 million documents that Snowden leaked, 60,000 refer to GCHQ, highlighting the closeness of the two security organisations (Lashmar 2015). Snowden's revelations further fuelled discussion surrounding how intelligence is shared, as it is no longer the case that intelligence is held amongst specialised government agencies. Private companies can now access data and intelligence gathered by GCHQ and other intelligence agencies, including data from social media. One recent book coined the phrase 'surveillance capitalism'. This phrase is used to describe the role intelligence agencies, such as GCHQ, play in the purchase and exchange of intelligence (see Zuboff, 2019).

Social media intelligence (SOCMINT) is a seemingly new problem that GCHQ is dealing with. The use of SIGNIT continues to decline as social media becomes ever more favoured as a means of communication. Intelligence agencies are increasingly finding it difficult to cope with the amounts of communication that occur at any given time (Omand, 2017). As Echelon cannot replace human judgement, the increasing use of social media highlights issues of how information is selected and extracted as intelligence.

As GCHQ celebrates its centenary year, it is easy to overlook the achievements of GCHQ and its predecessor organisation. Although many of them will remain unknown to the general public, the cracking of the Enigma and the interception of communications throughout the Second World War have often been described as shortening the war by up to 2 years (Hinsley, 1993). However, this should not take attention away from the challenges GCHQ faces today. Tasked with tracking almost all private and public communications throughout Britain and beyond, GCHQ will have to evolve in order to continue successfully in an era of rapid technological change. Perhaps, the publication of its first authorised history may provide an answer to these ever-growing controversies.

Further Reading

Aldrich, R. (2011). *GCHQ: the Uncensored Story of Britain's Most Secret Intelligence Agency.* London, Harper Collins Publishers.

Ferris, J. (2020). *Behind the Enigma: The Authorized History of GCHQ Britain's Secret Cyber Intelligence Agency.* Bloomsbury Publishing.

Omand, D. (2017). Social Media Intelligence. In Dover, R., Dylan, H. and Goodman, M. (Eds.) *The Palgrave Handbook of Secuirty, Risk and Intelligence.* London. Palgrave Macmillan UK.

References

Aldrich, R. (2011). *GCHQ: the Uncensored Story of Britain's Most Secret Intelligence Agency.* London, Harper Collins Publishers.

Aldrich, R. J. (2009). Beyond the vigilant state: globalisation and intelligence. *Review of International Studies, 35*(4), 889–902.

Aldrich, R. J. (2013). Counting the cost of intelligence: the Treasury, National Service and GCHQ. *The English Historical Review, 128*(532), 596–627.

Andrew, C. (1996). *For the President's Eyes Only: secret Intelligence and the American Presidency from Washington to Bush.* London: Harper Perennial.

Barrett, D. (2013, July 10). One Surveillance camera for every 11 people in Britain, says CCTV survey. The Telegraph. https://www.telegraph.co.uk/technology/10172298/One-surveillance-camera-for-every-11-people-in-Britain-says-CCTV-survey.html

Fukuyama, F. (1992). *End of History and the Last Man.* New York: Free Press.

Hinsley, F. (1993). *Codebreakers: the inside story of Bletchley Park.* Oxford: Oxford University Press.

Jackson, P. (2010). On Uncertainty and the limits of intelligence. In Johnson, L. (Ed.) *The Oxford Handbook of National Security Intelligence.* Oxford: Oxford University Press.

LaFree, G. (2010). The global terrorism database (GTD) accomplishments and challenges. *Perspectives on Terrorism, 4*(1), 24–46.

Lashmar, P. (2015). Spies and journalists: Towards an ethical framework? *Ethical Space: The International Journal of Communication Ethics, 12*(3/4), 4–14.

Lowenthal, P. (2014). *Intelligence: From Secrets to Policy.* Washington: CQ Press.

Matei, F. C., & Bruneau, T. (2011). Intelligence reform in new democracies: factors supporting or arresting progress. *Democratization*, *18*(3), 602–630.

Moran, C. (2012). *Classified: Secrecy and the State in Modern Britain*. Cambridge: Cambridge University Press.

Norton-Taylor, R. (2003). The Doughnut, the less secretive weapon in the fight against international terrorism. *The Guardian*. https://www.theguardian.com/uk/2003/jun/10/terrorism.Whitehall.

Office for National Statistics. (2019). Crime in England and Wales; year ending June 2019. https://www.ons.gov.uk/peoplepopulationandcommunity/crimeandjustice/bulletins/crimeinenglandandwales/yearendingjune2019

Rudner, M. (2004). Britain betwixt and between: UK SIGINT alliance strategy's transatlantic and European connections. *Intelligence & National Security*, *19*(4), 571–609.

Smith, M. (2003). *The Spying Game: The Secret History of British Espionage*. London: Politico.

Zuboff, S. (2019). *The Age of Surveillance Capitalism: The Fight Future and the New Frontier of Power*. London: Profile Books.

Chapter 37

Hackers and Hacktivism

Mary Manjikian
Regent University, Virginia Beach, VA, United States

Contents

Introduction: What Is Hacking? 255
Classifying the Hacker 256
Architecture of the Internet Creates a Haven for Hackers 258
Specific Types of Cyberweapons 261
State Awareness of Vulnerabilities 261
Further Reading 262
References 262

Introduction: What Is Hacking?

"Hackers" have been present since the earliest incarnations of the internet, which began as a Department of Defense project known as the Advanced Research Projects Agency Network (ARPANET) in the 1960s. Originally, the term hacker referred to an amateur computer hobbyist who worked on his own. Hacking refers to the modification of a system or piece of software, so that it can be used for other than its original intended use. Hacking or cracking also refers to "digital breaking and entering" or practices by which individuals seek to bypass security controls in order to access others' computer systems without permission (Manjikian, 2017).

Since the internet itself developed before systems which subsequently came to regulate the space, hackers operated in a quasi-legal space throughout the early 1980s, until the adoption of the United States Computer Fraud and Abuse Act (CFFA) in 1986. While the actions of hackers – including breaking into the files of corporations and government entities – might have been seen as a violation of norms regarding private property, hackers themselves either did not accept these norms or did

DOI: 10.4324/9781315144511-39

not see these conventional norms (such as the notion of private property) as having any applicability to the world of cyberspace which they regarded as libertarian and unregulated (Brown, 2011).

Instead, these original hobbyists often "hacked" in order to learn more about new computer systems or to show off or compete against other hackers. They were said to abide by their own "hacker code" which prized qualities such as transparency (sometimes expressed through the slogan "information wants to be free") and sharing technologies through the use of open source code, rather than conforming to traditional notions of private property. Today, groups like Anonymous and Wikileaks claim to be upholding these hacker values, like transparency, in making information, such as classified government information, available to the public (Manjikian, forthcoming).

However, these original attempts at hacking into computer systems were often neither criminal or malicious in intent nor were they a type of warfare carried out on behalf of either governments or nongovernmental organizations. Instead, many of these so-called "white-hat hackers" claimed to be contributing to the global order through policing and helping to secure the internet commons. Indeed, advances to corporate security have often come about due to the actions of hackers who have identified bugs and vulnerabilities within existing computer systems and then notified their targets of the vulnerabilities once found, so that these systems can be patched and made stronger. Furthermore, today, white-hat practitioners in the field of computer forensics may "hack" on behalf of law enforcement agencies or intelligence services, breaking and entering into the computers and files of those suspected of having committed crimes.

Classifying the Hacker

However, in addition to white-hat hacking activities, there exist today a much larger variety of black hat hacking activities – to include criminal hacking activities such as identity theft as well as state-run, state-sponsored, or independent activities to include attacks on critical infrastructure belonging to nations, individuals, or corporations.

Tavani (2004, 121) defines specific types of criminal hacking to include cyber vandalism, cyber trespass, computer fraud, and cyber terrorism. Brey refers to another class of hacking activity which can be considered not as criminal activity, but rather as a type of information warfare (Brey, 2007). Here, he refers to tools such as using information media to spread propaganda, disrupting and hijacking enemy communications infrastructure, as well as hacking into computer systems which control vital infrastructure.

Hacking is thus a tactic or set of tactics which can be utilized as a tool for criminal activity or for military operations in either kinetic or information warfare activities. Hackers may work for states – through working in a national Cybercommand which augments a nation's conventional military forces – for nonstate actors like Islamic State of Iraq and the Levant (ISIS), or for corporations.

Today, hacking as well as hacking-back (responding to an unauthorized incursion into one's computer systems with an attack in kind) can become a tool within the strategy of information warfare, in which a state or nonstate actor may seek to own another's information space through affecting a target's access to information or sending out and creating new information which appears to come from the original target. Such attacks form a vital part of many nations' strategies of active cyber defense.

But hackers may also engage in industrial espionage through stealing another corporation's or nation's technological secrets, or they may engage in disinformation campaigns aimed at sowing rumors in order to destabilize another state. Here, political doxing refers to the practice of finding unsavory information about a politician or other figure and then releasing that information to the general public in order to defame the individual. They may utilize hacking as an adjunct to traditional military activities as Russia did, for example, in shutting down Ukraine's power grid during the Russian invasion of Crimea. They may carry out attacks on a nation's critical infrastructure, including its power sources, its hospitals, its transportation infrastructure, or its dams and rivers. Hackers may aim to destroy equipment, or they may temporarily hold information or equipment hostage, through utilizing ransomware, until their target pays a fee to the attackers or meets a political demand.

Finally, some hackers may work on behalf of an organization and view themselves as a type of vigilante group which seeks to preserve the information commons of the internet through identifying and ejecting those unsavory actors (like ISIS) who they see as "polluting" the infosphere. Here, Brey refers to so-called "hacktivists" as "electronic political activists" (Brey, 2007).

Today, hackers may engage in industrial espionage through stealing another corporation's or nation's technological secrets, or they may engage in disinformation campaigns aimed at sowing rumors in order to destabilize another state. Here, political doxing refers to the practice of finding unsavory information about a politician or other figure and then releasing that information to the general public in order to defame the individual.

Hackers may include individuals or groups acting upon their own volition often in support of a particular cause (such as the members of Anonymous). They may include contractors or agents who are loosely affiliated with a government or organization (such as the Russian citizens who worked as trolls to interfere in the US Presidential election through contracts with the Internet Research Agency), or they may include official government members of an organization such as the US Cyber Command. Hackers may thus work as volunteers, unpaid vigilantes or activists, or as contracted or official salaried employees.

Within the United States Department of Defense community, as well as within international bodies such as the United Nations, analysts have debated whether and under what circumstances a hacking attack might be construed and punished as an act of war. The North Atlantic Treaty Organization (NATO) has stated that in principle, Article Five of its charter (which authorizes the alliance as a whole to respond in reaction to an attack on any of its members) could be invoked in response to a cyberattack on a NATO member (Lynch, 2018).

In addition, in the aftermath of the 2016 United States Presidential election, scholars debated whether Russian interference in the US Presidential election – through the release of information which was hacked and stolen from the United States Democratic National Committee – constituted a violation of America's state sovereignty and an act of war. Michael Schmitt, the lead author on NATO's Tallinn Manual, which spelled out the applicability of international law to the cyber arena, noted that the Tallinn Manual had been drafted prior to the 2016 events, so therefore no definitive rendering could be given. He noted that while the 2016 hack might not rise to the level of an "act of war", there was a vigorous debate among the scholars who worked on the manual about whether such interference constituted an "internationally wrongful act" – which would in turn open Russia up to the possibility of international legal countermeasures (Waterman, 2017).

Table 37.1 illustrates various sub-types of hacking along with historical examples of each type.

Architecture of the Internet Creates a Haven for Hackers

Hackers who wish to create malicious activity are aided by three technological facets of the internet which make it easy to engage in activities like phishing (sending e-mail communications to a target which when opened route the user to a phony website where they are encouraged to enter personal information like credit card numbers), spoofing (using a phony Internet Protocaol (IP) address to make it appear that a communication or attack is coming from a different originating address), and trolling (engaging in social media activities in order to stir up doubt and uncertainty through violating social norms online or disseminating false information). In particular, the existence of multiple routes by which information can travel on the internet due to its networked rather than linear nature, as well as the fact that packets of information are encoded with their end address but not with their originating address, leads to what is referred to as the attribution problem. In short, it is not always easy to tell where an attack on one's system originated, nor who was responsible for the attack. Secondly, it is relatively easy and cheap to create so-called cyberweapons (including worms, Trojans, and viruses) or to carry out cyberattacks such as a dedicated denial of service attack – in comparison to the resources and funds required to create conventional weapons. For this reason, hacking and related activities are regarded as a type of asymmetric warfare, in which a smaller actor (such as a terrorist group) may actually have the advantage over a larger, well-funded actor (like a national government), since smaller groups can quickly change tactics and strategies, leveraging skills to make up for a shortage of conventional resources like funds. Finally, the speed at which activities can occur over the internet means that a successful "hack" can be quickly planned and carried out in contrast to a conventional military campaign which might require years of planning (Manjikian, 2010).

For this reason, some analysts today suggest that hacking today is a type of covert activity which is better compared to the sorts of operations carried out by intelligence operatives, rather than an official type of state activity such as a declared act of conventional war (Valeriano and Manness, 2015).

In addition, in situations where analysts have used computer forensics to identify the code within a cyberweapon as emanating from a particular country due either to its signature or the language of the comments, they have still often not been able to directly implicate another state as the creator of the code. Because anyone can write code anywhere, the code is often traced to a collective which may have an unofficial relationship with a foreign government, or which may serve as a contractor, or even a group of patriotic volunteers – but cannot be definitely said to have been created by the government itself. Today, analysts speak about the Russian hacker collective

Table 37.1 Types of Hacking

Type of Activity	*Definition*	*Activities*	*Example*
Cybervandalism	Using programs to disrupt or alter computer networks or to corrupt data (Tavani, 2004)	Changing photos or slogans on websites, or changing the appearance or messaging of a social media account	Attempts by Anonymous in 2016 to embarrass ISIS members by altering their Twitter accounts to support causes like gay rights
Cybertrespass	Using information technology to gain unauthorized access to computer systems or password-protected sites		Incursions into the Department of Defense computers at the Pentagon by hackers in DATES --
Computer fraud	The use of deception to impersonate a person or corporate entity for the purposes of collecting, altering, or misrepresenting data	Spoofing, phishing	In 2016, hackers accessed the computers of Bangladesh's central bank and used it to make 81 million dollars of electronic payments to themselves
Cyber terrorism	The carrying out of politically motivated hacking operations intended to cause harm by states, individuals, or nonstate actors	Targeting SCADA (Supervisory Control and Data Acquisition) systems in critical infrastructure, such as energy, power, water, and transportation	Although such attacks have not yet occurred, American security analysts fear that enemy states or groups could alter software to affect food and water safety, or to affect the information which air traffic controllers receive when landing planes
Cyber warfare	"actions by a nation-state to penetrate another nation's computers or networks for the purposes of causing damage or disruption" (Richard Clarke)		Attempts in 2005 to damage Iran's nuclear program through introduction of the Stuxnet worm into SCADA systems
Information warfare	An extension of ordinary warfare in which combatants use information and attacks on information systems as tools of warfare (Brey, 2007)	Creating fake troll accounts on Twitter, using robot accounts to "spam" Twitter with key propaganda messages; using dedicated denial of service attacks to shut down access to websites	October 2016 denial of service attack against the internet service provider Dyn left many Americans on the East coast without internet access

(Continued)

Table 37.1 (Continued) Types of Hacking

Type of Activity	*Definition*	*Activities*	*Example*
Election hacking	The interference in a nation's sovereign affairs through attempting to alter electoral outcomes by changing data or voter profiles	Tampering with voting machines, voter registration rolls	A US congressional commission in the Fall of 2018 found evidence that Russian hackers had placed fake election ads on Facebook in support of American Presidential candidates. Many Americans viewed these ads.
Doxing/political doxing	Releasing potentially damaging personal and private information to the public	Release of private e-mails of celebrities and Hollywood producers Release of high-ranking political names associated with Ashley Madison accounts (website for the conduct of extramarital affairs)	Sony Hacks
Ransomware attacks	The commission of extortion through attacking a system with software which encrypts data, making it unusable and inaccessible to the host, until demands are met	Utilizing programs which hold data hostage until demands are met (monetary or political)	2016 hack against Hollywood Presbyterian Medical Center
Hacktivism	Political activism carried on in the territory of the internet	Patrolling and ejecting unsavory political actors, aiding democracy activists in scaling firewalls and evading censorship and surveillance, conducting transparency activities through the release of documents	Anonymous' campaign against ISIS Twitter accounts Activities of Wikileaks Democracy activists in Belarus or Arab Spring

Source: Author.

Fancy Bear and the Chinese collective Putter Panda, as well as groups like Russia's Internet Research Agency, which produced much of the social media disruption and disinformation associated with the American Presidential election in 2016. Such groups are said to be agents of state-sponsored cyberwarfare or cyberterrorism, but the legal and normative framework for regulating such actions is still in its infancy.

Specific Types of Cyberweapons

In the years since the development of the ARPANET, those in the field of cybersecurity have seen the advent of various classes of cyberweapons. Such weapons include ransomware, which can be used to encrypt a target's files until a ransom is paid, usually in bitcoin or a related cryptocurrency; backdoor Trojans, which give programmers remote access and control of a target's computer; zero-day exploits, which can be loaded on a computer system and then activated later in response to a particular event or command; and dedicated denial of service attacks, which can shut down a target's computer through making multiple simultaneous attempts to access it.

Regulating the creation and dissemination of cyberweapons is particularly difficult since, like chemical or biological weapons, cyberweapons are often dual-use technologies. That is, the user can control how a piece of code is ultimately used and whether it is used for benevolent or malicious purposes. For this reason, in summer 2017, the United Nations attempted to modify the existing Wassenaar Arrangement, which requires states to abide by export restrictions in relation to chemical and biological materials, to include cyber code as well. The Wassenaar Arrangement requires that those who produce materials which might potentially have harmful military uses be aware of the dangers associated with their products and take steps to assure that they do not fall into the wrong hands. While the attempt was ultimately defeated, this event shows that cyberweapons, like other types of weapons, can be used both defensively by states and aggressively by nonstate actors, including terrorists and cyber terrorists.

State Awareness of Vulnerabilities

States have been aware of the vulnerabilities created due to hacking and have responded by establishing Computer Emergency Response Teams (CERTs). The United States CERT was formed in 1993 and subsequently other states have followed suit, establishing their own national and regional CERTS. A key facet of the CERT model is that private actors cooperate closely with state actors, since a majority of the sites which might be targeted by hackers for national security reasons are privately held and managed utilities, such as internet service providers, electrical companies, or heating companies. Private actors have also led the way in responding to hacking, with groups like Microsoft coordinating so-called botnet takedowns, actions in which bots created to carry out dedicated denial of service (DDoS) attacks have been targeted for removal from the internet by the coordinated efforts of many actors.

Due to variations in the types of activities classified as "hacking", today analysts are more likely to speak about regulating hacking, rather than outlawing hacking.

In the future, the Law of Armed Conflict may be amended and modified to include specific provisions, for example, about what types of hacking and what sorts of targets might be considered ethical within the conduct of either a cyberwar or a conventional war with cyber elements.

Further Reading

Goodman, M. 2015. Future Crimes. New York: Doubleday.

Manjikian, M. 2017. *Cybersecurity Ethics: An Introduction*. New York: Routledge.

Schneier, B. 2017. "The Security of our Election Systems." Schneier on Security blog. Available at: https://www.schneier.com/blog/archives/2016/07/the_security_of_11.html

References

Brey, P. (2007). "Ethical Aspects of Information Security and Privacy," in *Security, Privacy and Trust in Modern Data Management*, M. Petkovic and W. Jonker, eds., Springer Berlin Heidelberg, pp. 21–36.

Brown, J.J. "Exploits, Ethics and the Little Old Lady Problem," Clinamen Blog. 2011. http://clinamen.jamesjbrownjr.net/2011/07/01/exploits-ethics-and-the

Lynch, J. "Cyber Ambiguity: NATO's Digital Defense in Doubt amid Unstable Alliances" July 10, 2018. Available at https://www.defensenews.com/international/2018/07/09/cyber-ambiguity-natos-digital-defense-in-doubt-amid-unstable-alliances/

Tavani, H. 2004. *Ethics and Technology; Ethical Issues in an Age of information and communication technology*.

Manjikian, M. 2010. "From Global Village to Virtual Battlefield: The Colonization of Cyberspace and the Extension of Realpolitik." *International Studies Quarterly* 54(2): 281–301.

Manjikian, M. 2017. *Cybersecurity Ethics: AN Introduction*. New York: Routledge.

Manjikian, M. Forthcoming. *Cyber Politics and Policies*. New York: Sage.

Valeriano, B. and Manness, R. 2015. *Cyber War versus Cyber Realities Cyber Conflict in the International System*. New York: Oxford University Press.

Waterman, S. 2017. "Tallinn Manual 2.0 clarifies cyber rules in peace, conflict short of war." Cyberscoop. Available at https://www.cyberscoop.com/tallinn-manual-2-0/

Chapter 38

Internet of Things (IoT)

Scott N. Romaniuk
International Centre for Policing and Security, University of South Wales, Caerleon, United Kingdom

Ronald Lorenzo
Prairie View A&M University, Prairie View, TX, United States

Contents

Introduction 263
The History of Things 264
Conclusion 264
Further Reading 265
References 265

Introduction

Internet of things (IoT) consists of millions of existing devices that are connected to the Internet, which collects and distributes data. IoT refers to devices that are not personal computers or smartphones but nevertheless connect to the Internet, collect, and share data. These can include consumer products such as watches that record the number of steps we take, security systems in homes, or wireless tollway technology that allows motorists to drive without having to stop to pay tolls. Technologies that comprise IoT give the consumer the benefits of efficiency and convenience. IoT also has the potential of endangering freedoms, exposing individuals' vulnerabilities to untrusted third parties, and loss of privacy.

DOI: 10.4324/9781315144511-40

The History of Things

Kevin Ashton, a computer sensor expert, coined the term "Internet of Things" in 1999 (Smithsonian). IoT refers to the change in the human and computer environment by which computers are less dependent on humans to input information; machines with sensors collect data without the need of human operators (Smithsonian). The term was first used to describe the process by which products in a supply chain can be tracked with RFID (radio frequency identification) chips (DeNisco Rayome, 2018). RFID chips are inexpensive chips that are powered by radio signals which can be coded with unique identification codes (DeNisco Rayome, 2018). At its core, IoT is an extension of the RFID chip: any item that can communicate information with a wireless network is part of IoT (Morgan, 2014).

In a residential home, IoT may comprise bathroom scales connected to the home's Wi-Fi network, cable television, devices that reorder commonly used household goods such as detergents, toys with cameras, and a home security system. These devices make life more convenient for consumers, but as devices connected to the Internet, they become devices that collect and record the habits and activities that take place within the home: when people come and go, how much weight people have gained or lost recently, and what are the preferences when it comes to entertainment. Information on the habits and activities within households becomes a product that can be sold between companies or shared with government agencies because data becomes a monetized commodity. Malicious users of data such as hackers can also steal or use data for illicit purposes.

Thanks in part to the inexpensive and widespread availability of wireless connectivity, an increasing number of consumer and industrial items now comprise the IoT. Not only refrigerators and coffee machines that connect to the Internet are part of the IoT but also industrial objects such as jet planes and the engines of the planes themselves (Morgan, 2014). In 2018, IoT was estimated to number about 8.4 billion units of items connected to the Internet (Ranger, 2020). Forecasters estimate that the IoT will more than double and comprise more than 25 billion items connected to the Internet (Statista, 2021). IoT is expected to dominate industrial sectors in hardware, software, infrastructure, security, and connectivity.

Conclusion

IoT technology is now being used by virtually everyone in the world, with human dependency on IoT constantly growing. Trillions of devices all around the world are connected to an ever-expanding IoT system, enabling new functions and engagements while producing potential challenges for society at all levels. The benefits of IoT range from minor, everyday practices in the bathroom or kitchen to macro functions comprising whole societies, seen when wireless technology transforms cities of the past into "Smart Cities" of today and tomorrow. Productivity and management benefits result from well-connected devices and correct digital infrastructure and setup. However, the benefits may cohabitate alongside concerns like complex systems that can be prone to problems or failure, privacy and security of data protection (insecure communications and storage), and increased unemployment (due to automation) across societies. Despite its advantages, these challenges already seem to be insurmountable ones in the present day.

Further Reading

Bloomberg, J. (2014, July 7). "7 Reasons Why the Internet of Things is Doomed", *Wired.* https://www.wired.com/insights/2014/07/7-reasons-internet-things-doomed/

Greengard, S. (2021). *The Internet of Things.* The MIT Press.

Tian, J. and Chen, S. (2020, December 7). "Internet of Things (IoT) in China: State and Future Directions". https://www.chinatechblog.org/blog/internet-of-things-iot-in-china-state-and-future-directions

References

Burgess, M. (2018, February 16). "What is the Internet of Things? WIRED Explains". *WIRED.* https://www.wired.co.uk/article/internet-of-things-what-is-explained-iot

Columbus, L. (2017, December 10). "Roundup Of Internet Of Things Forecasts", *Forbes.* https://www.forbes.com/sites/louiscolumbus/2017/12/10/2017-roundup-of-internet-of-things-forecasts/#48568eb91480

Gabbai, A. (2015, January). "Kevin Ashton Describes "the Internet of Things"", *Smithsonian Magazine.* https://www.smithsonianmag.com/innovation/kevin-ashton-describes-the-internet-of-things-180953749/

Greenfield, A. (2017, June 6). "Rise of the machines: who is the 'internet of things' good for?", *The Guardian.* https://www.theguardian.com/technology/2017/jun/06/internet-of-things-smart-home-smart-city

Morgan, J. (2014, May 13). "A Simple Explanation Of 'The Internet Of Things'", *Forbes.* https://www.forbes.com/sites/jacobmorgan/2014/05/13/simple-explanation-internet-things-that-anyone-can-understand/#cee3f71d0919

Notopoulos, K. (2012, February 3). "Somebody's watching: how a simple exploit lets strangers tap into private security cameras", *The Verge.* https://www.theverge.com/2012/2/3/2767453/trendnet-ip-camera-exploit-4chan

Ranger, S. (2020, February 3). "What is the IoT? Everything you need to know about the Internet of Things right now," *ZDNet.* https://www.zdnet.com/article/what-is-the-internet-of-things-everything-you-need-to-know-about-the-iot-right-now/

DeNisco Rayome, A. (2018, July 27). "How the term 'Internet of Things' was invented," *TechRepublic.* https://www.techrepublic.com/article/how-the-term-internet-of-things-was-invented/

Statista. (2021). "Internet of Things (IoT) connected devices installed base worldwide from 2015 to 2025". https://www.statista.com/statistics/471264/iot-number-of-connected-devices-worldwide/

Chapter 39

Malware

Gary Leigh
Charles Darwin University, Darwin, NT, Australia

Content

Further Reading 271
References 271

The field of malware in cybersecurity and Homeland Security is exceptionally large. Its intersection with the Homeland Security community grows more important with each day. Such claims cannot be considered egregious or novel as they are fact. Moscow-based cybersecurity company, Kaspersky (2017) reports openly that 360,000 approximate new malicious files are found daily. Kaspersky's antimalware U.S. counterpart, Malwarebytes (2020) builds on this rising trend by providing a global perspective by which North America (NORAM) accounted for 48% of global detections of malware alone. The number of attack groups using destructive malware has grown by 25% in 2019, targeting on average 55 organizations each (Symantec, 2019). Setting the stage this way makes it obvious that Homeland Security professionals must be attuned to the realities and roles that malware plays today.

Malware, antivirus, and cyber defenses are a rapidly evolving field. The American machinery of government that underpins the U.S. response to cyberattacks is also constantly evolving. This section may not have the most current formulation of the American response, but it endeavors to lay the foundations for understanding malware and the Homeland Security response well into the future.

With this said, in terms of understanding malware, the best approach to take is to create and analyze segments to arrive at actionable moments. For example, consider Microsoft's community-driven approach. At the time of this writing, nearly 5 million devices have had encounters as detected by Microsoft Security Intelligence (2020) in a 30-day period. The education sector being the hardest hit, accounting for 65% of these malware encounters. Largescale numbers however should not warrant

DOI: 10.4324/9781315144511-41

unnecessary concern. After all, a fair analysis would dictate that 5 million affected computer devices are not the same as 5 million affected Americans requiring attention from the Federal Emergency Management Agency (FEMA). But even organizations like FEMA (2019, p. 2) that can support the 2.3 million survivors of natural disasters in 2017 have been compromised by failing to safeguard those affected people's personal information.

Before we can truly dissect the nuances of malware, a working definition should be used to base the discussion. The National Institute of Standards and Technology's Computer Security Resource Center (2020) has a working definition that stipulates that malware is:

> Software or firmware intended to perform an unauthorized process that will have adverse impact on the confidentiality, integrity, or availability of an information system. A virus, worm, Trojan horse, or other code-based entity that infects a host. Spyware and some forms of adware are also examples of malicious code.

The common thread with many working definitions is that they encompass the digital side of the physical technology. They further reinforce the primary tenants of information security surrounding confidentiality, integrity, and availability. Lastly, the distinction is made that malware, or as it is commonly referred to, malicious software, interacts with a computer system typically against one's intention. This is to say that a computer, mobile device, or critical infrastructure system that is physically designed to work against one's intentions is not necessarily the same as a computerized device that has the software element to do so. This is the most common manifestation of a compromised supply chain whereby a device fundamentally no longer works as it was intended to by the procurer.

Microsoft's (2019) official documentation on malware and other threats is a veritable source that outlines some of the major families of malware. The list is non-exhaustive but includes coin miners, exploits and exploit kits, macro malware, phishing, ransomware, rootkits, supply chain attacks, tech support scams, Trojans, unwanted software, and worms. It may be readily apparent that some of these are not precisely malware, but most certainly each of them will involve malware as the core piece of malicious software that will create an undesired effect.

Furthermore, the list does not include viruses, which despite being able to fall into the family of malware has an addendum added to the definition. For Microsoft (2019), a malware can be known as a virus, "from a technical viewpoint… what makes a virus a virus is that it spreads itself." If a distinction on malware can be made in the form of a virus, what other subcategorizations are available? For Homeland Security purposes, having such a broad, all-encompassing definition of malware as being malicious software that creates a security incident is useful. There are, however, times where more granularity is required without expounding the deep technical details.

If more granularity is sought, the combination of American industry partners and the ongoing enhancement of the protective machinery of government has the answer. Since 2018, Homeland Security has evolved in its approach to cybersecurity affairs. With the signing of the Cybersecurity and Infrastructure Security Agency

Act of 2018, the Cyber Security and Infrastructure Agency (CISA) was created. The U.S. Department of Homeland Security (2020) views CISA as building the, "capacity to defend against cyber-attacks and works with the federal government to provide cybersecurity tools, incident response services and assessment capabilities to safeguard the '.gov' networks that support the essential operations of partner departments and agencies."

In CISA's own words, improving America's national cyber security posture requires several key mission priorities. This includes federal network protection, comprehensive cyber protection, infrastructure resilience and field operations, and lastly, emergency communications. These five key mission priorities may seem few, but they stretch across ten defined regions in alignment with existing FEMA offices (CISA, 2020). Even though official reporting is not readily available on how effective CISA has been since inception, past indications are promising for future expectations. CISA's creation included integrating the elite cybersecurity center known as the National Cybersecurity and Communications Integration Center (NCCIC). The NCCIC might not have the notoriety of the National Security Agency (NSA); however, in 2017 alone, they officially reported matching beyond 700,00 threats, discovering over 200,000 new federal vulnerabilities, and provided onsite cyber deployments to approximately 30 U.S. government and private sector clientele.

When a sophisticated, adversarial cyber security attack takes place that requires Homeland Security intervention, it seems obvious after the fact that Homeland Security's agencies were the required agency partner. However, this is not always the case. The United States. has some of the most advanced and intricate – but equally as capable – federal resources at its disposal. The National Cyber Incident Response Plan (2016) that encompasses responding to attacks by which malware is certainly present articulates the following. Firstly, the guiding principles that reinforce government unity in all action to thwart cyber threats. Secondly, how exactly the plan works side by side with the National Preparedness System. This system designates the wider preparedness efforts needed to deal with today's cyber challenges. Thirdly, the National Cyber Incident Response Plan outlines the role of the Department of Justice (DOJ) and the Department of Homeland Security. It does all of this to canvas the roles and responsibilities of state governments and municipalities to coordinate cyber incident severity and disasters. Without such a sophisticated framework, coordinating a response that yields the appropriate level of response capability would make the United States less agile as a cyber defender.

Interdepartmental meshing creates a cohesive unit response. This is precisely how the United States can react so swiftly to a variety of cyber incidents outside of responding to just malware. The Government Accountability Office (GAO, 2005) further outlines a threat table that factors into who and what adversaries may be employing malware as part of the cyber operations against the United States. The list is non-exhaustive and despite its age is still relevant. The threat table outlines a series of potential sources of malware utilizing actors that stand to benefit from compromising the U.S. cyber security. These include:

- Bot-network operators
- Criminal groups
- Foreign intelligence services

- Hackers
- Insiders
- Phishers
- Spammers
- Spyware authors
- Terrorists

This is an interesting list and truly reinforces the multifaceted role Homeland Security plays in fighting against cyberattacks. With such a wide variety of actors, which could either be at home or abroad, it is clear a multiagency approach is required. The Congressional Research Service (2017) authored a report for Congress on cybersecurity issues and challenges that offers a lay of the land for federal agency roles in cybersecurity. On the one hand, the Department of Homeland Security must coordinate government response internally and see to it that critical infrastructure protection is fulfilled. Defending against malware that may impede the United States' ability to have full command of its interior becomes obvious at this point. On the other hand, this malware and the aforenoted list of malware wielding actors that prey on Homeland America are often abroad. Therefore, despite how technology has brought the world closer together, it has not done so without risks. Responding to these risks by having the Department of Defense and the NSA defending the perimeter and acting abroad, and Homeland Security securing the Homeland is part of U.S. national response to cyber activity.

Now that it is clear what malware is, who may be wielding it, and how Homeland Security is geared to respond to the threats, we can turn our eye toward developments in malware for Homeland Security purposes. Perhaps, the largest development for Homeland Security practitioner purposes is captured in the report from 2016 titled *Malware Trends* by the Industrial Control Systems Emergency Response Team (ICS-CERT) and the Advanced Analytical Laboratory. The report's language identifies the "state of the battlefield" and articulates three alarming developments. The first development surrounds the innovation of malware accessibility, known as malware-as-a-service. The second is that malware is becoming increasingly destructive and more persistent. Persistence means that the malware is more survivable and difficult to eradicate or detect. Finally, the report discusses the problems of ransomware and the sharing of code bases, which are providing insight on which actors are attacking the U.S. and creating the malware that is used for their attacks.

To illustrate the point that malware is evolving, and interdepartmental efforts are critical to the cyber defense of the Homeland, no better example is available than a series of malware that originate from North Korea. This example again demonstrates that national boundaries are permeable in the world of cybersecurity. The CISA's National Cyber Awareness System (2020) has an advanced technical repository of analysis reports which are publicly available that outline developments as they occur.

The U.S. government's official position on the cyber activity undertaken by the government of North Korea against the American Homeland is a strong one. For governmental and Homeland Security purposes at the time of writing, the malware developments and utilization by North Korean actors against the United States is known as HIDDEN COBRA. This is the same family of cyber activity responsible for

WannaCry, one of the world's most infamous ransomware attacks. An intergovernmental effort has been undertaken from as far back as 2017 according to publicly available records. On February 14, 2020, CISA, the Federal Bureau of Investigation (FBI), and the Department of Defense (DoD) have disclosed and updated the following seven malware varieties. The North Korean Trojan: HOPLIGHT, for example, has a family of 20 malicious executables; each of these branches can be traced back to a cyberattack. Notable HIDDEN COBRA malware are:

- Malware Analysis Report (10265965-1.v1) – North Korean Trojan: BISTROMATH
- Malware Analysis Report (10265965-2.v1) – North Korean Trojan: SLICKSHOES
- Malware Analysis Report (10265965-3.v1) – North Korean Trojan: CROWDEDFLOUNDER
- Malware Analysis Report (10271944-1.v1) – North Korean Trojan: HOTCROISSANT
- Malware Analysis Report (10271944-2.v1) – North Korean Trojan: ARTFULPIE
- Malware Analysis Report (10271944-3.v1) – North Korean Trojan: BUFFETLINE
- Malware Analysis Report (10135536-8.v3) – North Korean Trojan: HOPLIGHT

In summary, cyber threats are ever evolving. Malware is an integral part of these cyber threats, and there exists a range of potential actors working to undermine U.S. security. America's own collective effort to neutralize any effort to disrupt national prosperity and Homeland Security is not to be underestimated when considering the fleet of capable departmental agencies and units in Homeland Security alone. Cohesive effort is being undertaken to forewarn and forearm Americans and her allies through intergovernmental unity on the issue of cybersecurity and malware. As it stands, malware is responsible for an alarming chunk of U.S. economic losses and must be dealt with. The Council of Economic Advisors from the Executive Office of the President of the United States has declared that in 2016 malicious cyber activity cost the U.S. economy over 100 billion dollars alone.

Further Reading

Lewis, T. D. (2020). *Critical Infrastructure Protection in the Homeland Security: Defending a Networked Nation*. Hoboken: Wiley.

Raiyn, J. (2014). "A Survey of Cyber Attack Detection Strategies," *International Journal of Security and Its Applications*, *8*(1): 247–256.

Yan, P. and Yan, Z. (2018). "A Survey on Dynamic Mobile Malware Detection," *Software Quality Journal*, *26*: 891–919.

References

Cybersecurity and Infrastructure Security Agency. (2020a). Analysis Reports: National Cyber Awareness System. Retrieved from https://www.us-cert.gov/ncas/analysis-reports

Cybersecurity and Infrastructure Security Agency. (2020b). Cyber Threat Source Description. Retrieved from https://www.us-cert.gov/ics/content/cyber-threat-source-descriptions

Cybersecurity and Infrastructure Security Agency. (2020c). Cybersecurity and infrastructure security agency's regional offices. Retrieved from https://www.cisa.gov/cisa-regional-offices

Cybersecurity and Infrastructure Security Agency. (2020d). North Korean Malicious Cyber Activity. Retrieved from https://www.us-cert.gov/northkorea

Department of Homeland Security. (2016). *National Cyber Incident Response Plan*. Retrieved from https://www.us-cert.gov/sites/default/files/ncirp/National_Cyber_Incident_Response_Plan.pdf

Department of Homeland Security. (2020). Cybersecurity. Retrieved from https://www.dhs.gov/topic/cybersecurity

Fisher, E. (2017). *Congressional Research Service, In Focus: Cyber Security Issues and Challenges*. (9). Retrieved from Congressional Research Service website: https://crsreports.congress.gov/product/pdf/IF/IF10001

Industrial Control Systems Emergency Response Team & Advanced Analytical Laboratory. (2016). Malware Trends. Retrieved from https://www.us-cert.gov/sites/default/files/documents/NCCIC_ICS-CERT_AAL_Malware_Trends_Paper_S508C.pdf

Kaspersky Labs. (2017). Kaspersky Lab detects 360,000 new malicious files daily – up 11.5% from 2016. Retrieved from https://www.kaspersky.com/about/press-releases/2017_kaspersky-lab-detects-360000-new-malicious-files-daily

Malwarebytes. (2020). *2020 State of Malware Report*. (February 2020). Retrieved from https://resources.Malwarebytes.com/files/2020/02/2020_State-of-Malware-Report.pdf

Microsoft. (2019). Understanding Malware & Other Threats. Retrieved from https://docs.microsoft.com/en-us/windows/security/threat-protection/intelligence/understanding-Malware

Microsoft. (2020). Global Threat Activity. Retrieved from https://www.microsoft.com/en-us/wdsi/threats

Microsoft & Moir, R. (2019). Defining Malware: FAQ. Retrieved from https://docs.microsoft.com/en-us/previous-versions/tn-archive/dd632948(v=technet.10)?redirectedfrom=MSDN

National Cyber Security and Communications Integration Center. (2017). *NCCIC Year in Review 2017: Operation Cyber Guardian*. Retrieved from https://www.us-cert.gov/sites/default/files/publications/NCCIC_Year_in_Review_2017_Final.pdf

National Institute of Standards and Technology & Computer Security Resource Center. (2020). Glossary: *Chain of Custody*. US Government. https://csrc.nist.gov/glossary/term/Malware

Office of Inspector General. (2019). *Management Alert – FEMA Did Not Safeguard Disaster Survivors' Sensitive Personally Identifiable Information (REDACTED)*. Retrieved from https://www.oig.dhs.gov/sites/default/files/assets/2019-03/OIG-19-32-Mar19.pdf

Symantec. (2019). *Internet Security Threat Report*. (Volume 24, February 2019). Retrieved from https://www.symantec.com/content/dam/symantec/docs/reports/istr-24-2019-en.pdf

The Council of Economic Advisors. (2018). *The Cost of Malicious Cyber Activity to the U.S. Economy*. Executive Office of the President of the United States. Retrieved from https://www.whitehouse.gov/wp-content/uploads/2018/03/The-Cost-of-Malicious-Cyber-Activity-to-the-U.S.-Economy.pdf

Chapter 40

National Security Agency (NSA): From the Cold War to Post-9/11

János Kemény

Strategic Defense Research Institute of the József Eötvös Research Center at the National University of Public Service, Budapest, Hungary

Scott N. Romaniuk

International Centre for Policing and Security, University of South Wales, Caerleon, United Kingdom

Contents

Introduction 274
The Collection Authority of the NSA 274
Early History 274
Early Success: The Venona Project 275
NSA's Role in Selected Major Cold War Crises 275
The Cuban Missile Crisis 276
The Vietnam War 276
Establishment of the Central Security Service 276
Incidents in the Cold War Involving NSA Intelligence Collection Platforms 277
Controversies during from the 1950s until the 1970s 277
The NSA in the 1980s 278
The NSA after the Cold War and before 9/11 278
The NSA's Role after 9/11 and Its Controversies 279
The NSA and US Cyber Command 279
Conclusion 279
Further Reading 280
References 280

DOI: 10.4324/9781315144511-42

Introduction

The National Security Agency (NSA) is one of the primer intelligence-gathering agencies of the US Intelligence Community. Its mission is twofold: it is the lead agency to provide Information Security for the US government, and it is tasked with breaking the cyphers of foreign entities. In short, the NSA has cryptology at the core of its mission (Federation of American Scientists undated). Regarding its collection focus, this centers on signals intelligence (SIGINT), which is defined by the Department of Defense's JP 1-02 as "a category of intelligence comprising either individually or in combination all communications intelligence, electronic intelligence, and foreign instrumentation signals intelligence, however transmitted" (JP 1-02 2016, p. 217). To be able to achieve its mission, the NSA has a great foreign language analysis capability and has high-capacity computer systems to process the collected data. It operates in the continental United States as well as at selected sites on the territory of countries allied with the United States (FAS undated). With the development in information technology, its mission was widened to include gathering information on communication forms through the internet and other means. Although the role of the NSA is focused on gathering SIGINT from foreign sources, in different historical periods, there were notable exceptions to this practice which caused controversy.

The Collection Authority of the NSA

Currently, the intelligence collection activities of the NSA are based on two key documents: the Foreign Intelligence Surveillance Act (FISA) of 1978 and Executive Order (EO) 12333. FISA regulates intelligence collection in regard to citizens and non-citizens on the territory of the United States as well as US citizens outside of the US territory. Non-citizens outside the territory of the United States can be targeted for information collection, and EO 12333 regulates this type of activity. The NSA is authorized by the directive to utilize communication networks around the world. As the United States is an important communications hub for the whole world, and methods such as metadata collection can include information related to US citizens, careful consideration is sometimes required to find the right balance. FISA Courts are tasked with maintaining this between the need to collect foreign intelligence and information on potential threats and the defense of the civil liberties of US citizens (NSA 2013, pp. 2–6).

Early History

The history of SIGINT gathering and cryptanalysis goes back to the early 20th century, but the immediate predecessor of the NSA was established in 1949 as a result of the National Security Act of 1947. On May 20, 1949, the Secretary of Defense created the Armed Forces Security Agency (AFSA), which centralized the functions of all communications intelligence and security under AFSA and placed it under the direct control of the Joint Chiefs of Staff (JCS). The new agency proved to be controversial, as civilian agencies as well as the Air Force and the Navy opposed its establishment for different reasons. AFSA wasn't able to end duplications in capabilities and focus, and this led to a bureaucratic quagmire, which in turn had serious implications on operational capabilities. This was brought to light during the early stages of the Korean War (Burns 2009, p. 59).

The result of this was the creation of a committee, which abolished the AFSA and created the NSA in 1952. The memorandum creating the new agency was classified, and thus, the creation of the NSA was itself a secret for some years (Johnson 1995a-1, p. 35).

The agency started its move to its current headquarters to Fort Meade, Maryland, in 1957. The location was a compromise between security and accessibility to other partners as well as a need to centralize the operations of the agency. The facilities at Fort Meade were however not large enough to house the entire needs of the NSA, and the Communications Security Organization only moved in 1968 (NSA 2012, pp. 15–16).

Early Success: The Venona Project

One of the best-known operations of the NSA was the Venona Project. The United States was able to record Soviet diplomatic communications during World War II to and from the United States. Although the project started already in 1943, it ran until 1980 (Benson undated, p. 5).

The success of Venona had multiple sources, which partially originated in World War II and were aided by Soviet defectors, but needed a concentrated, high-intensity effort in order to decrypt the coded messages. The first breakthrough occurred in the late 1940s and helped to unmask Soviet spying efforts in the United States. The information won through Venona provided important leads to identify people working for Soviet intelligence inside the nuclear program of the United States and also provided important leads on member of the spy ring now commonly known as the Cambridge Five. It also provided important insight into the Soviet intelligence services' (the KGB and GRU) thinking and modus operandi (Johnson 1995a-2, pp. 161–167).

NSA's Role in Selected Major Cold War Crises

The NSA as the main SIGINT agency had played important roles in crises and wars during this period. It was able to provide important information to decision makers in many crucial moments; other times, it was able to corroborate information gleaned through other means by other members of the Intelligence Community. Also, sometimes, it was proved unable to forecast major changes, and using sea born collection platforms also caused its own political problems in a few cases.

The first big test was the crises of 1956 (the Arab–Israeli War and the Hungarian Revolution, just to mention the well-known crises). We have selected two major Cold War crises to illustrate the difficult role of the NSA.

The Cuban Missile Crisis

The crisis that developed due to Soviet missile sites being established on Cuban territory was a failure, as prior to the reconnaissance flight no information gleaned through SIGINT indicated the Soviet efforts. Prior to the crisis, the NSA was able provide some information on the manifests of the Soviet ships traveling to Cuba and was able to point to the increasingly military nature of the trade relationship, as well as indication of modern Soviet arms (air defense weaponry and Soviet built aircraft) and the presence of Soviet advisers. During the Missile Crisis, the NSA was able to provide updates on the readiness of Soviet army units as well as the movement of supplies and people to Cuba. The NSA was also able to provide some information on the command arrangements, but Soviet communications security made the task more difficult (Johnson 1995b, pp. 317, 323 and 332).

The Vietnam War

The Vietnam War has produced mixed results from the perspective of the NSA. The NSA was the lead agency in Vietnam on the field of SIGINT, but the effort remained decentralized, because of organizational problems. Also, the information originating from the SIGINT effort was not able to provide a perspective into the strategic thinking of the leadership of the Democratic Republic of Vietnam (DRV). It was however suitable to support allied military operations and provided important insight into the infiltration efforts of the DRV. The Vietnam War had important lessons from the technical and organizational perspective and on the topic of cooperation with host nation as well (Hanyok 2002, pp. 461–464).

Establishment of the Central Security Service

During the Vietnam War, an already difficult relationship with the JCS became even tenser over the control of cryptology. The NSA intended to centralize all related tasks, while the JCS wanted to keep some specialized information collection areas out of NSA control. The conflict was solved by the Nixon Administration, as it, based on the work of a committee led by James Schlesinger, decided on centralizing the cryptologic effort in 1971. There was initial confusion on how the new structure would be established and what it would control. At the end, the new organization called Central Security Service (CSS) placed electronic warfare tasks under the NSA/CSS command, and the Director of the NSA got authority on things like research and development, logistics, etc. However, tactical SIGINT capabilities remained with the branches of the US armed forces. The new concept wasn't thorough as any side imagined, partially, because presidential interest for the final details was not there. Also, the build-up of the CSS was slower than anticipated, (Johnson 1998, pp. 59–61, 63 and 65), but the CSS remains an integral part of the NSA until today.

Incidents in the Cold War Involving NSA Intelligence Collection Platforms

The NSA, like other intelligence agencies, uses mobile platforms for information collection, sometimes in cooperation with other partners. For example, the NSA in cooperation with the US Navy operated vessels for SIGINT purposes in 1960s, designated as Technical Research Ships (TRSs) (Johnson 1995b, p. 315). During the late 1960s, the attack on two TRSs became well known: the attack on the USS Liberty during the 1967 Arab–Israeli War, which was conducted by Israel and caused severe losses to the crew, and the attack on the trawler named Pueblo in 1968, which was lost to North Korea.

In the case of the Liberty, the subsequent inquiry pointed out communication problems, which made a timely course correction for the Liberty impossible, and the order to change course was received by the ship only after the attack. The attack killed 34 crew members, among them a civilian NSA linguist. According to official sources, the Israeli side made multiple identification errors, believing the ship was Egyptian and initiated an air strike, later a torpedo boat attacked the Liberty (Johnson 1995b, pp. 433 and 437). The incident caused much controversy diplomatically, and had long-term reverberations, and also among surviving members of the crew.

The Pueblo incident took place at another Cold War hotspot in 1968: near the territorial waters of North Korea. In January 1968, after a short chase, the North Koreans boarded the ship, capturing the crew and much of the SIGINT material on board, because of unsuccessful emergency destruction process. One crew member was killed during the chase, and the rest of the crew was captured and held in captivity. The North Koreans forced members of the crew to make televised appearances, in which they were forced to talk about their work. The Pueblo incident also had serious consequences on the US side, highlighting problems in the cooperation between the Navy and the NSA (Johnson 1995b, pp. 443, 445 and 450).

Controversies during from the 1950s until the 1970s

In the early history of the NSA and its predecessors, the issue of foreign intelligence and law enforcement relevant information wasn't strictly divided. During World War I, cable companies provided information, but this practice was terminated in the 1920s, and in 1934, the practice was outlawed. During World War II, the cooperation was restored, but with reservations, as the existing legislation made things more difficult. However, during and after World War II, the practice remained, named Project Shamrock, but no new legislation was approved. Until the 1950s, law enforcement relevant information gathered during SIGINT activities was passed on to the concerned agencies. The practice was later formalized on some issues, such as travel to Cuba after the embargo, and later included prominent peace activists during the Vietnam War. In 1965, the Secret Service initiated the creation of a watchlist, which contained people, who in the opinion of the Secret Service could pose a danger to the US President. Out of this practice, the "Minaret Program" (or "Project Minaret") was born, and the list was broadened due to the domestic upheaval in the late 1960s. According to an official history of the agency, the practices of the "Minaret Program" were probably not considered to be legal by the employees of the NSA, but the program continued until 1973, when the attorney general initiated a review and asked the NSA to stop the program until it was completed (Johnson 1998, pp. 84–85).

The NSA in the 1980s

This decade brought new challenges for the NSA, as for all of the Intelligence Community. New threats, like terrorism, became part of the mission already in the 1970s. The spread of international terrorism and the intensification of the War on Drugs in the Reagan years set out new challenges, but old ones were still there as well. There were other, older problems, like the debate over ownership of some assets with other parts of the US military. The NSA also needed to support military operations, but there is only limited information about the NSA's role in supporting US military operations in Grenada and Panama (Johnson 1999, pp. 345 and 371). The 1980s brought a widening of the operational scope of the NSA. In 1984, the agency was tasked with computer security, thanks to a presidential directive (FAS undated).

The 1980s also brought problems for the NSA, as one former employee, Ronald Pelton, was convicted of spying for the Soviet Union. Reportedly, he met Soviet intelligence officers in the United States as well as in Austria. Pelton was convicted and received three life sentences plus 10 years in prison. This case was not the only one which hit the US cryptologic community in the 1980s. The other very damaging case was that of John Walker, who worked at the US Navy as a communications and crypto technician and not only provided materials since 1968 to the Soviets himself but also managed to recruit others (Johnson 1999, pp. 412, 414, 420 and 422).

The NSA after the Cold War and before 9/11

After the collapse of the Eastern Bloc, US outlook on the world, and thus, collection priorities changed. The 1990s brought some classic intelligence problems, like the Iraq War and its aftermath in 1991, but increasingly new, often non-state actors emerged, which posed threats to US security. The post-Cold War political environment, however, meant that the NSA and other members of the Intelligence Community had to contend with budget cuts (NSA 2012, pp. 83–84). At the same time, the 1990s saw the beginning of the revolution in information technology, which made the information security and intelligence collection tasks of the agency more difficult. Intelligence consumers had an increasing need for SIGINT information, which motivated some changes in the organization (NSA 2012, pp. 87–89).

The 1990s also saw a different approach to public relations: in order to demystify the NSA, the leadership assisted the making of a documentary about the agency (NSA 2012, p. 87).

In 2001, a decision was made to rely on contractor support to keep the agency's systems operating (NSA 2012, p. 97).

Internationally, the role of the NSA and its operations came into the foreground, with allegations that the agency with the help of its partners was running a program codenamed "ECHELON", which captured satellite communication and with pre-designated search words analyzed the captured traffic. This information had especially in Europe a high resonance, where the European Parliament started an investigation into US intelligence-gathering measures (Richelson 2013).

The NSA's Role after 9/11 and Its Controversies

With the 9/11 attacks, the need for intelligence related to counterterrorism rose significantly, and with the start of the wars in Afghanistan and Iraq, the need for SIGINT support for the US armed forces also increased drastically. Most of these activities remain classified, thus not much information can be added about the exact nature of the NSA's role.

The NSA's role in the domestic counterterrorism effort also increased. The agency received new presidential authorizations for collection, which later caused concern, when these were reported by the news media. The US press reported in 2006 that the NSA was collecting information on calls in the United States and to and from the United States with the help of telecommunication companies in the United States. During later revelations, and especially after the information provided by Edward Snowden, several codenamed collection programs were publicized. This caused public backlash not only in the United States but also in Europe, because there were indications that the security of facilities of foreign governments was also penetrated by the NSA (Richelson 2013).

The NSA and US Cyber Command

There is a close relationship between the NSA and US Cyber Command (USCYBERCOM). The first commander of USCYBERCOM, named in 2010 to the position, was Lieutenant General Keith B. Alexander, who was Director of the NSA since 2005 and remained in this position after assuming command at USCYBERCOM (NSI undated).

The physical infrastructure of the two organizations is co-located in Fort Meade, because their close cooperation is important from a technical and legal perspective. The nature, extent, and other details of the cooperation are classified, but thanks to Freedom of Information Act requests, some details became known about it. According to this information, the NSA is supporting the offensive and the defensive cyber operations of US Cyber Command, shares some of its infrastructure and personnel, and assists in the training of USCYBERCOM personnel (Pomerleau 2019).

Conclusion

As the primer of SIGINT and Communications Security (COMSEC), the NSA/CSS has a very important role in the US Intelligence Community, and its tasks have increased, as have the number of fields in which it has to operate, such as cyberspace. Like any other member of the Intelligence Community, it had to contend with a changing strategic landscape, budgetary problems, as well as problems unique to the field of SIGINT, which itself was profoundly changed by technological development. The COMSEC mission aspect of the NSA's mission is also vital, as without secure communication, it is impossible to think of operational security in any field.

Achieving the objectives set for the NSA was not without danger for its workforce. According to the official publication of the NSA, from 1952 until 2012, there were 170 people, whom the NSA acknowledges, who have died in the line of duty (NSA 2012, p. 85). At the same time, a recurring problem for the agency (and for other members of the Intelligence Community) was the issue of striking a balance between the needs formulated by intelligence consumers, the threat environment, and civil liberties. As the listed examples have shown, this was indeed a difficult balancing act for the NSA and for the intelligence consumers formulating their demands as well.

Further Reading

Aid, M. M. (2001). "The National Security Agency and the Cold War," *Intelligence & National Security*, 16(1): 27–66.

Aid, M. M. (2009). The Secret Sentry: The Untold History of the National Security Agency, New York: Bloomsbury Press.

Cheney-Lippold, J. (2016). "*Jus Algoritmi*: How the National Security Agency Remade Citizenship," *International Journal of Communication*, 10: 1721–1742.

References

Benson, Robert L.: The Venona Story, Center for Cryptologic History National Security Agency, undated, https://www.nsa.gov/Portals/70/documents/about/cryptologic-heritage/historical-figures-publications/publications/coldwar/venona_story.pdf

Burns, Thomas L.: The Origins of the National Security Agency 1940–1952, Center for Cryptologic History, National Security Agency, 1990 in: The Secret Sentry Declassified: Declassified Documents Reveal the Inner Workings and Intelligence Gathering Operations of the National Security Agency, National Security Archive Electronic Briefing Book No. 278, June 19, 2009 https://nsarchive2.gwu.edu/NSAEBB/NSAEBB278/02.PDF

Federation of American Scientists: National Security Agency, undated, https://fas.org/irp/nsa/oldind.html

Hanyok, Robert J.: Spartans in Darkness: American SIGINT and the Indochina War, 1945–1975, Center for Cryptologic History, National Security Agency, 2002 https://fas.org/irp/nsa/spartans/spartans.pdf

Johnson, Thomas R. (1995a): American Cryptology during the Cold War, 1945–1989: Book I: The Struggle for Centralization 1945–1960, National Security Agency: Center for Cryptologic History, 1995 in: "Disreputable if Not Outright Illegal": The National Security Agency versus Martin Luther King, Muhammad Ali, Art Buchwald, Frank Church, et al., National Security Archive Electronic Briefing Book No. 441, September 25, 2013; the book is available in two parts: A-1: https://nsarchive2.gwu.edu/NSAEBB/NSAEBB260/nsa-1.pdf; A-2: https://nsarchive2.gwu.edu/NSAEBB/NSAEBB260/NSA-2.pdf

Johnson, Thomas R. (1995b): American Cryptology during the Cold War, 1945–1989 Book II: Centralization Wins, 1960–1972. Center for Cryptologic History, National Security Agency, 1995. in: "Disreputable if Not Outright Illegal": The National Security Agency versus Martin Luther King, Muhammad Ali, Art Buchwald, Frank Church, et al., National Security Archive Electronic Briefing Book No. 441, https://nsarchive2.gwu.edu/NSAEBB/NSAEBB441/docs/doc%203%202008-021%20Burr%20Release%20Document%201-%20Part%20C.pdf

Johnson, Thomas R.: American Cryptology during the Cold War, 1945–1989: Book III: Retrenchment and Reform, 1972–1980, National Security Agency: Center for Cryptologic History, 1998 in: "Disreputable if Not Outright Illegal": The National Security Agency versus Martin Luther King, Muhammad Ali, Art Buchwald, Frank Church, et al., National Security Archive Electronic Briefing Book No. 441, September 25, 2013 https://nsarchive2.gwu.edu/NSAEBB/NSAEBB260/nsa-5.pdf

Johnson, Thomas R.: American Cryptology during the Cold War, 1945–1989 Book IV. Cryptologic Rebirth, 1981–1989, National Security Agency, 1999. in: The 1983 War Scare: "The Last Paroxysm" of the Cold War Part I, National Security Archive Electronic Briefing Book No. 426, 2013 https://nsarchive2.gwu.edu/NSAEBB/NSAEBB426/docs/2.American%20Cryptology%20During%20the%20Cold%20War%201945-1989%20Book%20IV%20Cryptologic%20Rebirth%201981-1989-1999.pdf

JP 1-02: Joint Publication 1-02: Department of Defense Dictionary of Military and Associated Terms, Department of Defense, as amended through 15 February 2016 https://fas.org/irp/doddir/dod/jp1_02.pdf

National Security Agency: 60 Years of Defending Our Nation, 2012 https://www.nsa.gov/Portals/70/documents/about/cryptologic-heritage/historical-figures-publications/nsa-60th/NSA-60th-Anniversary.pdf?ver=2018-08-07-102513-607

National Security Agency: Missions, Authorities, Oversight and Partnerships, 2013 in: National Security Archive Electronic Briefing Book No. 436, 2013 https://nsarchive2.gwu.edu/NSAEBB/NSAEBB436/docs/EBB-114.pdf

NSI: General (Ret.) Keith Alexander, National Security Institute at George Mason University's Antonin Scalia Law School, undated. https://nationalsecurity.gmu.edu/general-ret-keith-alexander/

Pomerleau, Mark: New documents provide details on NSA relationship with Cyber Command, *Fifth Domain*, May 3, 2019 https://www.fifthdomain.com/dod/2019/05/03/new-documents-provide-details-regarding-nsa-support-to-cyber-command/

Richelson, Jeffrey T. (ed.): The Snowden Affair Web Resource Documents the Latest Firestorm over the National Security Agency National Security Archive Electronic Briefing Book No. 436, September 4, 2013. https://nsarchive2.gwu.edu/NSAEBB/NSAEBB436/

U.S. Cyber Command History undated, https://www.cybercom.mil/About/History/

Chapter 41

Social Engineering

Chad Patrick Osorio

University of Negros Occidental-Recoletos, Bacolod, Philippines

Contents

Introduction 283
Types of Social Engineering 283
The Process of Social Engineering 285
Conclusion 287
Further Reading 287
References 287

Introduction

Social engineering may be defined as a series of deception techniques intended to mislead unwary users into transmitting sensitive information to the perpetrators or allowing the latter access to restricted areas, unwittingly acting against the interest of their own privacy. Rather than relying on software error, these techniques focus on the vulnerabilities of the human psyche, which form an integral aspect of cybersecurity assurance (Evans, Maglaras, He & Janicke, 2016). Social engineering is often employed by hackers and cybercriminals in order to open links to infected sites, introduce malware into computer systems, and grant access to private and sensitive information. Social engineering primarily takes advantage of human psychology instead of technical hacking methods in order to do so (Fruhlinger, 2019). Oftentimes, however, a combination of these techniques is used in cyberattacks.

Types of Social Engineering

Generally, the myriad social engineering techniques rely on three general aspects of human behavior: social norms and relationships of trust, threat of negative

DOI: 10.4324/9781315144511-43

consequences, and promise of reward. The first group relies on creating a relationship based on trust, or utilizing an existing one, in order to gain access to confidential information and restricted areas. **Phishing** is the most common and comes in many different forms. It involves the use of false information in order for people to reveal sensitive or personal data (Federal Trade Commission, 2019). In many cases, they are aspects of **pretexting**, such as when the perpetrator pretends to be a co-employee, a person of authority, or within the circle of trust of the target person (European Union Agency for Cybersecurity, n.d.).

Angler phishing refers to faux customer service accounts asking for personal information under the pretense of providing better service or responding to client queries. Targets are usually acquired through social media, where unassuming customers post private details which can be used to deceive them. **Spear phishing** targets specific individuals, enterprises, and organizations. Oftentimes, a significant amount of research is made before making first contact, in order to provide a foolproof narrative with which to deceive the target (Swinhoe, 2019). One of its primary methods is the **business email compromise (BEC)**, where the target is made to believe that it is a senior member of the staff, or otherwise a superior in the organizational hierarchy, who is requesting the desired confidential information. Because employees are trained to respond to authority, this method can be quite effective.

Whaling is another type of spear phishing, but instead of targeting employees, it targets the upper echelon of management, including the leaders of the organization and members of the board (Swinhoe, 2019). These can be faux messages from important business partners, consultants, or even among their peers. Because these high-valued targets and the purported message senders are often observed and studied well ahead of time, the messages they receive are often convincingly crafted. Because of the strong relationship of trust and authority within these circles, gaining a foothold into these interactions under disguise can yield to the illegal harvest of confidential information only available to individuals in their position.

The types of phishing can also be done through a variety of methods. According to Aharoni (2019), a **watering hole** is oftentimes a trusted website which has been hacked to facilitate the downloading of malicious software in the site visitor's computer. The software will then automatically or upon command be made to monitor the log and usage of the infected computer, access sensitive data, and even control the functions of the computer remotely. Watering holes can either be generic, meaning its intended target is the general public to facilitate the spread of botnets, or in many cases, much more specific. This means, for example, to gain access to the computers of nuclear scientists, hackers may choose to infect a website that nuclear scientists often visit, including those on toxic research wastes.

Not all types of phishing require the use of computers to gain sensitive information or launch attacks, they may take the form of primarily physical actions outside the virtual world. These include **vishing** (voice phishing) and **smishing** (SMS phishing). In many cases, these aforementioned methods similarly require research and pretexting.

Piggybacking, or **tailgating**, uses deceptive means to gain access to restricted areas. Perpetrators pretend to be deliverymen or co-workers asking legitimate employees to hold the door (Strawbridge, 2018). This allows them to bypass security systems requiring the use of keys and access cards. The psychology behind this type of deception relies on common courtesy and social norms.

Tabnabbing refers to the practice of using unattended browsers to insert malicious content, taking advantage of people's manufactured sense of security (Magid, 2010).

Other types of methods similarly use aspects of human psychology to gain the trust of their victims. For example, using the threat of negative consequences, **scareware** fools individuals into downloading potentially harmful 'security' software, or otherwise purchase useless applications and services. Often, scareware comes in the form of pop-ups, warning of fake security threats, and offering better protection. Instead, it actually facilitates malware infection.

On the other side of the coin are social engineering techniques which promise great rewards, taking advantage of human want and greed. These include **baiting**, which requires offering the target with a specific desirable item which makes it difficult to refuse (European Union Agency for Cybersecurity, n.d.). Online, these can be in the form of purported free downloads of pirated movies or music, which later on turns out to contain malware. Offline, a good example is a USB enticingly labeled 'Organizational Salary Chart.xls', which prompts the curiosity of the employee to insert it to the computer, not knowing that the USB itself is actually infected. **Quid pro quo** is a subtype of baiting, offering a reward in exchange for something seemingly insignificant, such as the maternal maiden name, the last four digits of one's social security number, or three digits printed on the back of one's credit card (European Union Agency for Cybersecurity, n.d.).

Other aspects of baiting include **honey traps**, promising romantic or sexual favors in exchange for access to information. In **419 scams**, also known as the Nigerian Prince or advanced fee scams, perpetrators falsely undertake to pay the victim a large amount of money in exchange for advanced payment under the pretense of assistance (Newman, 2018).

It is important to keep in mind that while many of these social engineering techniques are used in conducting cyberattacks, many if not all of them have offline and online aspects. For example, **diversion theft** deals with misdelivered goods, which can be done through techniques both online and offline. The same can be said for pretexting and phishing.

At the same time, it is equally important to remember that not all types of deceptive techniques are a means unto themselves; in a lot of cases, they are only preliminary steps in order to gain more information before launching much more serious attacks in cyberspace and in the real world.

The Process of Social Engineering

There are many aspects of psychology which can be used to understand the topic of social engineering. Those referencing the macro include social psychology, which looks at the quality of interactions between humans; cross-cultural psychology, which seeks to understand the role of culture in human behavior; and criminal psychology, which studies how socially deviant individuals think and behave as a collective. Looking at these situations through the micro lens requires an understanding of personality psychology, the variance on how different humans will react to the same situation; cognitive psychology, which discusses how humans process information; and finally, behaviorism, a platform for understanding reward and punishment.

When looking at social engineering techniques and why they are successful, it is necessary to have an understanding of the basic concepts in these aspects of psychology. After all, perpetrators of social engineering tactics rely on a combination of these mental frameworks and behavioral models in order to facilitate fraud.

Social engineering primarily relies on two types of misrepresentation: *suggestio falsi* and *suggestion veri* (Grazioli, Jamal & Johnson, 2006). The first one is a set of falsehood, which through delivery is presumed by the target to be true. The second type presents an incomplete truth, which the target usually inaccurately perceives. It relies on flaws in Gestalt heuristics, mental shortcuts which lead the target into assuming a different conclusion than what is real and factual. In all cases, these misrepresentations are geared toward earning the trust of the victim. This is why in greater social science literature pioneered by the studies of Cressey (1973), the perpetrators of social engineering tactics are often called 'trust violators'.

Skinner (2014) described trust not merely as a psychological state but as a process. It consists of three stages: the evaluation of the trustworthiness and integrity of the other person; the decision to trust; and the risk-taking act to demonstrate one's trust.

Once trust has been gained through either, or both, of the two types of misrepresentation, the next step is usually a call to action, the risk-taking part of the trust process. It can be as simple as clicking a link or downloading and opening an attachment infected with malware. However, in many instances, it can go as far as sending considerable amounts of money to strangers or the revelation of private and sensitive information with the active participation of the victim of the social engineering tactics.

Social engineers utilize a variety of shortcuts to bypass the trust process. This includes assuming the identity of a person with whom the target shares a relationship of trust. This is common in both pretexting and whaling, where perpetrators masquerade as trusted contacts in order to gain the confidence of employees and high-ranking officials in the organization. The trust relationship does not have to be a deeply personal one; it can be merely professional. For example, in a multitude of phishing tactics, victims easily reveal sensitive information to social engineers pretending to be phone bankers and IT personnel.

Authority can also substitute for a personal relationship built on trust. BEC tactics involve pretending to be and name-dropping high-ranking members of the organization in order to fool individuals into granting them access or giving them information otherwise not available to the general public.

At the same time, there are a number of well-documented persuasion techniques which seek to influence and manipulate others, with both online and offline methods to fool victims (Cialdini, 2007). For example, acting confidently is a hallmark for social engineers, whether in person or not (Goodchild, 2009). This is particularly useful when attempting to gain entry into publicly inaccessible spaces, as in the case of piggybacking or tailgaiting. Individuals are more likely to hold the door open for people who exude confidence and act as if they belong in the building, rather than for those who stick out.

Using the concept of reciprocation is also a common tactic of social engineers. More than just bridging a trust relationship, giving small gifts encourages the feeling of the need for reciprocation in the recipient (Goodchild, 2009). This is particularly useful in gaining information, or even unauthorized entry, in quid pro quo tactics, which can be a prelude to other social engineering activities, including eavesdropping and tabnabbing.

Finally, emotions are powerful gateways to nudging people into action. This is the mental framework upon which baiting and scareware operate: the reward and punishment centers of the brain are activated by these situational stimuli. Coupling this with economic, non-emotional benefits is a potent method to persuade people to act accordingly. This is seen in pleas for help in the Nigerian Prince scams, where victims are motivated to act both by the feeling of helping someone else and at the same time for personal gain.

Conclusion

In the past few years, the United States has become a hotbed of cyberattacks. Many of them target the government and large corporations, but because these data breaches affect the safety and security of US citizens, this has become an urgent matter for homeland security. It is important to look at this from the social engineering perspective because according to the Human Factor Report (2019), 99% of perpetrators use these deception techniques into tricking individuals to download malicious software, thereby facilitating more sophisticated cyberattacks in the foreseeable future.

Gaining deeper insights into mental processes and human behavior, termed the weakest link in the security chain, is an effective way of providing counter-measures against cyber trust violators. Only by understanding these can we diffuse social engineering tactics and create a more secure environment, both real and virtual.

Further Reading

Fruhlinger, J. (2019, September 25). Social Engineering Explained: How Criminals Exploit Human Behaviour. *CSO Online*. Retrieved from https://www.csoonline.com/article/2124681/what-is-social-engineering.html

Ramamoorti, S. (2008). The Psychology and Sociology of Fraud: Integrating the Behavioral Sciences Component into Fraud and Forensic Accounting Curricula. *Issues in Accounting Education*, *23* (4), pages 521–533.

Skinner, D., Dietz, G., & Weibel, A. (2014). The Dark Side of Trust: When Trust Becomes a 'Poisoned Chalice'. *Organization*, *21* (2), pages 206–224.

References

Aharoni, E. (2019, January 2). Watering Hole Attack: "Don't Drink the Water". *Cymulate*. Retrieved from https://blog.cymulate.com/watering-hole-attack-dont-drink-water

Cialdini, R. B. (2007). *Influence: The Psychology of Persuasion*. New York, NY: HarperCollins.

Cressey, D. (1973). *Other People's Money: A Study in the Social Psychology of Embezzlement*. Mont-clair, NJ: Patterson Smith.
Evans, M., Maglaras, L.A., He, Y., and Janicke, H. (2016, October 20). Human Behaviour as an Aspect of Cybersecurity Assurance. *Security and Communication Networks 9* (17), 4667–4679.
Goodchild, J. (2009, July 22). Mind Games: How Social Engineers Win Your Confidence. *CSO Online*. Retrieved from https://www.csoonline.com/article/2124219/mind-games--how-social-engineers-win-your-confidence.html?page=4
Grazioli, S., Jamal, K. & Johnson, P. E. (2006). A Cognitive Approach to Fraud Detection. *Journal of Forensic Accounting* 7 (1), pages 65–88.
Federal Trade Commission. (2019). How to Recognize and Avoid Phishing Scams. In *Consumer Information*. Retrieved from https://www.consumer.ftc.gov/articles/how-recognize-and-avoid-phishing-scams
Fruhlinger, J. (2019, September 25). Social Engineering Explained: How Criminals Exploit Human Behaviour. *CSO Online*. Retrieved from https://www.csoonline.com/article/2124681/what-is-social-engineering.html
Magid, L. (2010, June 11). Tabnabbing: Like Phishing Within Browser. *CNET*. Retrieved from https://www.cnet.com/news/tabnabbing-like-phishing-within-browser-podcast/
Newman, L.H. (2018, May 3). Nigerian Email Scammers Are More Effective Than Ever. *Wired*. Retrieved from https://www.wired.com/story/nigerian-email-scammers-more-effective-than-ever/
Proofpoint (2019). The Human Factor Report. Retrieved from https://www.proofpoint.com/us/resources/threat-reports/human-factor
Skinner, D., Dietz, G., & Weibel, A. (2014). The Dark Side of Trust: When Trust Becomes a 'Poisoned Chalice'. *Organization, 21* (2), pages 206–224.
Strawbridge, Geraldine. (2018, August 20). The Dangers of Tailgating in the Workplace. *Metacompliance*. Retrieved from https://www.metacompliance.com/blog/the-dangers-of-tailgating-in-the-workplace/
Swinhoe, D. (2019, January 21). What is Spear Phishing? Why Targeted Email Attacks are So Difficult to Stop. *CSO Online*. Retrieved from https://www.csoonline.com/article/3334617/what-is-spear-phishing-why-targeted-email-attacks-are-so-difficult-to-stop.html
European Union Agency for Cybersecurity. (n.d.) What is "Social Engineering"? Retrieved from https://www.enisa.europa.eu/topics/csirts-in-europe/glossary/what-is-social-engineering

Chapter 42

Stuxnet

Dominika Dziwisz
Jagiellonian University, Kraków, Poland

Contents

Introduction 289
Stuxnet and Cyber War 290
Implications for the Future 291
Conclusion 292
Further Reading 293
References 293

Introduction

In 2006, President George W. Bush might have been considering two obvious options for responding to Iran's nuclear plans: either let Iran make an atomic bomb or don't allow that and start a war (Sanger 2012, p. 191). However, due to advancements in computer technology, there was a third possibility. The Department of Defense began to seriously consider the use of cyber weapons against enemy's critical infrastructure facilities. "It was an entirely new territory for the Defense Department, which for the first time in decades was thinking about a weapon's system it didn't know how to build" (Sanger 2012, p.192). Therefore, it is likely, but still unacknowledged, that plans for a cyberattack arose at the end of George W. Bush's second term.

There is no definitive evidence of the source of the Stuxnet worm attack on Iranian nuclear installations, which was detected in June 2010. Although the White House has never issued an official statement, it is suspected, and there is sizable, though uncertain, evidence that this advanced cyber weapon was created in American–Israeli cooperation. In any event, both countries have never denied the claims that they were involved with Stuxnet's development (De Falco, 2012). In May 2011, the U.S. Deputy Defense Secretary William Lynn, when directly asked if the United States

DOI: 10.4324/9781315144511-44

was involved in the development of Stuxnet, answered evasively that "this is not something that we're going to be able to answer at this point" (Lee, 2011 after: De Falco, 2012). Regardless of which country was involved in the construction of the Stuxnet, the fact that it required the resources of a nation (Langner, 2010) suggests a new approach to using cyberattacks to achieve national goals. This was a significant event because for the first time in history a computer program was used to attack the critical infrastructure elements of a hostile state.

Stuxnet and Cyber War

Stuxnet, a malicious computer worm, first uncovered in 2010, has been called "the world's first digital weapon" (Zetter), one of "the most complex threats ever analyzed" (Falliere, Murchu, Chien, 2011, p. 2) and "the one of the most sophisticated and unusual pieces of software ever created" (McMillan, 2010). The worm was attacking Iran's uranium enrichment program for over a year and later spread out of control and infected computers outside of Iran. Although Stuxnet has attacked over 60,000 computers, of which more than half were in Iran, but also in India, Indonesia, China, Azerbaijan, South Korea, the United States of America, Great Britain, Australia, Finland, and Germany (Farwell, Rohozinski, 2011, p. 23), the real target of the attack was Iran's nuclear installations. Stuxnet caused malfunction of Iran's uranium enrichment centrifuges by manipulating the frequency of the converters, which affected the speed of the engine. Detecting infection of one or more system components can be more difficult than detecting damage to the entire system. In the case of Stuxnet, the failure was only discovered after a few days. The Natanz nuclear facility was temporarily shut down, and Iran's attempt to obtain enough highly enriched uranium to build a nuclear weapon was delayed.

Stuxnet was the first known computer program to spy on and reprogram industrial installations. The purpose of the worm's attack was not the common theft of money or personal data, but an assault on a strategically important physical target. Its complexity and the political motive of the attack also indicate that it was not carried out by a terrorist group, but by a country that has taken enormous measures to sabotage the Iranian nuclear industry. Mainly due to the attribution of the organization of the attack to some country, Stuxnet is often analyzed in the category of war, not terrorism. This opinion is expressed by the German expert Ralph Langner, who was the first to recognize the offensive features of the program:

> The attack combines an awful lot of skills – just think about the multiple zero-day vulnerabilities, the stolen certificates etc. This was assembled by a highly qualified team of experts, involving some with specific control system expertise. This is not some hacker sitting in the basement of his parents' house. To me, it seems that the resources needed to stage this attack point to a nation state.
>
> (Langner, 2010)

A similar view is held by Martin C. Libicki from RAND Corporation, who claims that: "when you look at the nature of this worm and how much work has been put into constructing it, you can see that only two countries could do it: the USA and Israel" (Dziwisz, 2015).

The theory that Stuxnet was built in American–Israeli cooperation is the most popular. This is mainly due to the fact that:

- Iran suffered the most in the attack, and it seems that Iran nuclear facilities were the main target.
- Israel felt threatened by Iran's growing nuclear program (De Falco, 2012).
- In 2007, Israel launched a cyberattack on the modern Syrian anti-aircraft defense system. Israeli hackers took control of the system, and a few minutes later, bombed the Al-Kibar Syrian nuclear reactor. Hackers made the fighters that attacked the nuclear installations built in Syrian–North Korean cooperation invisible on the monitor screen (Clarke, Knake, 2011).
- According to McAfee estimations, the USA and Israel are, respectively, the first and fourth countries in the world regarding cyber warfare capabilities (McAfee, 2020 after: De Falco, 2012).
- Stuxnet's code construction is also indicative of Israeli involvement. "Israel has its own *style points* – they used not one, but two stolen certificates, four zero-day vulnerabilities, and entered hints in the code." That is why some, like Martin Libicki, say that Stuxnet was mostly an Israeli project (Dziwisz, 2015, p. 117).

Stuxnet is one of the most serious computer attacks revealed to this day. However, there are many more examples of successful cyberattacks. Most go undetected because they are not always associated with immediately crashing computer systems. Their effects may be delayed. Hackers employed in special cyber-military units and state intelligence services place delayed ignition bombs in the computer systems of other countries – "logic bombs" – and install "backdoors." These pieces of code remain dormant on enemy computers. At any time, they can be used to take control of a banking, energy, or communications system (Clarke and Knake, 2011, pp. 41, 42). This creates a new dangerous dimension of instability, because the border between war and peace is blurring.

Implications for the Future

Over the past years, there has been a great deal of discussion about the Stuxnet worm and the consequences of its use. The Stuxnet implementation and its proven effectiveness are worrisome for several reasons.

First, when analyzing the scale, goals, and complexity of the entire cyberattack campaign, it is certain that Stuxnet is an example of a state-sponsored effort to conduct hostile activity in cyberspace against an enemy country. Compared to the earliest cyberattacks, today's cyberspace operations are the result of a thoroughly planned and careful penetration of the attacked networks so as to find the best access point. It is unlikely that such a large-scale intelligence operation would be organized by a group of independent hackers. The characteristics of the Stuxnet attack indicate that it was prepared by professionals who are able to properly compile information, set priorities for action, and divide tasks between various groups of operators, intelligence analysts, and malware coders. Presumably, this intelligence network consists of uniformed military, officers of civilian agencies, and world-class hackers.

This leads to a second conclusion that Stuxnet ends the debate about whether such a malicious attack is even possible (Porche, Sollinger, McKay, 2011, p. 8). It was the first major case of a cyberattack being used to cause physical damage across international boundaries. Consequently, Stuxnet-based (e.g., Duqu, 2011; Flame, 2012; Havex, 2013; Industroyer, 2016) and newer, even more sophisticated cyber weapons are clearly a threat to a range of critical infrastructure elements, including power production, electrical grids, and defense.

Third, even if it is assumed that the decision to use Stuxnet was guided by good intentions, that is, to prevent a larger, physical conflict, it cannot be considered a "good standard." If that were the case, "in the conflict with Taiwan or in the dispute over the South China Sea, the Chinese could use similar methods to stop the US from intervening," commented Jason Healey (Dziwisz, 2015, p. 326). In other words, the Stuxnet attack possibly changed the accepted norms of cyberspace behavior.

Fourth, despite the lack of definitive evidence of the source of the Stuxnet attack, it is commonly attributed to the United States. Therefore, Stuxnet's unmasking caused a wave of criticism of US cyber security policy. On the one hand, Barack Obama declared that the United States would not attack first, and on the other hand, everything indicates that he allowed hostile activity to be conducted in cyberspace. Since the detection of the Stuxnet attack, every decision regarding cyberspace has been very cautious. However, noble declarations do not always go hand in hand with real actions. The dual nature of US policy: assurance of a coalition for common goals, but preparation for secret action, did not meet the expectations of world opinion, which was particularly noticeable given that Barack Obama had been awarded the Nobel Peace Prize.

Conclusion

Stuxnet was the first piece of undeniable proof of how powerful and effective cyber weapons might be. It became evident that weaponized software can cause real damage in the physical world. Therefore, it has come to be permanently included in the arsenal of states' offensive capabilities. Stuxnet was also a kind of a wake-up call for governments to enhance their cybersecurity by raising awareness of the fact that even air-gapped (physically isolated) networks are at risk. States need to develop plans or processes for responding to cyberattacks such as Stuxnet as well as create cybersecurity norms to comply with standards, ensuring a minimum level of security in networked equipment.

Stuxnet worm is proof that cyber war is no longer a scenario of the future, and that what has been called the future for a long time is already happening (Klimburg 2017; Clarke and Knake, 2011). That is why special military cyber units and state intelligence services are testing a new battlefield. Undoubtedly, cyberattacks like Stuxnet share many traits with war in its classical meaning. Regardless of which country or coalition of countries was involved in the creation of Stuxnet, it was a successful demonstration of power.

Scott N. Romaniuk, International Centre for Policing and Security, University of South Wales, United Kingdom.

Further Reading

Porche III I. R., Sollinger J. M., McKay S., *A Cyberworm that Knows no Boundaries*, Santa Monica, CA: RAND National Defense Research Institute, 2011.

Sanger D. E., *Confront and Conceal. Obama's Secret Wars and Surprising Use of American Power*, New York: Random House Group, 2012.

Zetter K., *Countdown to Zero Day: Stuxnet and the Launch of the World's First Digital Weapon*, New York: Broadway Books 2015.

References

Clarke R. A., Knake R., *Cyber War. The Next Threat to National Security and What to Do About It*, HarperCollins e-books, 2011.

Correspondent Melissa Lee in the documentary "CodeWars: America's Cyber Threat", 05.15.2011, https://www.cnbc.com/code-wars/, 12.27.2019.

De Falco M., *Stuxnet Facts Report. A Technical and Strategic Analysis*, NATO Cooperative Cyber Defence Centre of Excellence, Tallinn 2012, https://ccdcoe.org/uploads/2018/10/Falco2012_StuxnetFactsReport.pdf, 01.03.2020.

Dziwisz D., *Stany Zjednoczone a międzynarodowe bezpieczeństwo cybernetyczne*, Sowa, Kraków, 2015.

Falliere N., Murchu L. O., Chien E., *W32. Stuxnet Dossier*, White paper, Symantec Corp., Security Response, http://www.symantec.com/content/en/us/enterprise/media/security_response/whitepapers/w32_stuxnet_dossier.pdf, February 2011, 01.02.2020.

Farwell J. P., Rohozinski R., Stuxnet and the Future of Cyber War. *Survival*, vol. 53, no. 1, 2011.

Klimburg A., *The Darkening Web. The War for Cyberspace*, Penguin Press, New York, 2017.

Langner R., *Stuxnet Logbook, Sep 16 2010, 1200 hours MESZ*, 09.16.2010, https://www.langner.com/2010/09/stuxnet-logbook-sep-16-2010-1200-hours-mesz/, 01.02.2020.

McAfee, *Virtual Criminology Report 2009 - Virtually Here: The Age of Cyber Warfare*, http://www.mcafee.com/us/resources/reports/rp-virtual-criminology-report-2009.pdf, 01.02.2020.

Porche III I. R., Sollinger J. M., McKay S., *A Cyberworm that Knows no Boundaries*, Santa Monica, CA: RAND National Defense Research Institute, 2011.

Sanger D. E., *Confront and Conceal. Obama's Secret Wars and Surprising Use of American Power*, New York: Crown Publishers, 2012.

Chapter 43

Swatting

Scott N. Romaniuk
International Centre for Policing and Security, University of South Wales, Caerleon, United Kingdom

Ronald Lorenzo
Prairie View A&M University, Prairie View, TX, United States

Contents

Introduction 295
Background to Swatting 296
Motivations for Swatting 297
Legal Responses to Swatting 297
Conclusion 298
Further Reading 298
References 298

Introduction

Swatting is a form of social engineering by which law enforcement agencies are tricked into deploying their SWAT (Special Weapons and Tactics) teams unnecessarily as the result of a malicious hoax. Swatting is a phone activity carried out by phreaks who hack the telephone network to place calls from phone numbers other than their own, which is a technique known as spoofing. Usually, phreaks will spoof the phone number of a residence to place a call to emergency service numbers such as 911 or directly to law enforcement. The phreaks will then provoke the police into thinking that the resident of the address is in a situation calling for a SWAT resolution. Phreaks are motivated to commit acts of swatting out of revenge against another phreak or hacker, for "lulz" ("for fun"), boredom, or as a rite of passage among certain hacker groups. Celebrities are frequent targets for swatting, and news coverage of celebrity

DOI: 10.4324/9781315144511-45

swatting may be a motivating factor. News media rarely cover swatting events against non-celebrities, making it harder for phreaks to ascertain if the swatting phone call succeeded in manipulating the police. Swatting is a dangerous phreak activity since it wastes police resources as well as endangers the lives of police officers and the general public.

Background to Swatting

Swatting as a lethal prank is an extreme extension and evolution of earlier pranks. Except for the element of deadly force, it is fundamentally similar to pranks where addresses receive deliveries for items, such as pizzas, that were not authentically ordered.

Swatting follows a similar social structure of pranking evident in historical pranks such as the Berners Street Hoax of 1810. That prank was perpetrated by a young writer, Theodore Hook, who placed a bet that he could make a random address in London the most talked about address for a week (Boese, 2015). Hook had sent out hundreds of letters summoning delivery services to arrive at the home of an unsuspecting person at 54 Berners Street (Boese, 2015). First to arrive on that day were the chimney sweeps, followed by wine porters, barbers, bakers, the Lord Mayor of London, the Archbishop of Canterbury, the Governor of the Bank of England, the Chairman of the East India Company, The Lord Chief Justice, dentists, doctors, lawyers, brewers, opticians, piano sellers, auctioneers, grocers, and undertakers (Boese, 2015). The prank resulted in fist fights among the various merchants summoned and resulted in a traffic gridlock affecting central London for hours until the police could restore order later that evening (Boese, 2015). The Berners Street Hoax was facilitated by the efficient postal system of London, which allowed Hook to engineer the prank in several days.

Telephones allow pranksters to engineer and execute hoaxes instantly. The oldest known prank call variation of the Berners Street Hoax was in 1884, just 8 years after the invention of the telephone (*The Atlantic*, 2016). Made during the winter, the prank followed the social structure of the Berners Street Hoax: it summoned a service to an address that did not request it. A mortuary delivered a coffin to a house under the impression that someone had passed away.

Swatting more recently has connections to the 1970s phone phreak culture (FBI, 2008). Phone phreaks, or hackers of the telephone network, learned that they could get free long-distance calls by manipulating the phone lines. Early phone phreaks learned that by playing a tone at 2600 hz into the phone line, they could fool the phone system into believing the caller had hung up the phone (Telephone Museum, 2021). Once this happened, the phreaks could enter dial tones to access a telephone switch, or computer that routes phone calls, and hijack it into dialing long-distance calls for free. Phone phreaking, starting in 1970s and continuing into the present day, is a communal activity by a deviant subculture. Phreaking involves pranks and practical jokes – often with a tone of cruelty – on innocent parties.

The term 'swatting' itself was coined by the Federal Bureau of Investigation (FBI, 2008). Celebrities are often the target of swatting calls, and SWAT teams have been hoaxed into responding to the present or former addresses of actors and musicians, including Tom Cruise, Miley Cyrus, Justin Bieber, Chris Brown, and Ashton Kutcher (Harlow, 2012; McCartney, 2013).

Motivations for Swatting

Phreaks make swatting phone calls for similar reasons that they make prank calls in general. Prank calling is usually a group activity, even when it is done by an individual (Dresser, 1973). Individuals make audio recordings of their phone calls or broadcast them on the Internet to turn solitary prank calling into a group activity. As a group activity, the prank call serves as an act of group solidarity and makes the active prank caller the center of the group's attention (Dresser, 1973). Prank calls also are a form of rebellion in which groups release hostility and frustration with what is perceived as little risk of retaliation (Dresser, 1973).

As a group activity, individuals make swatting calls that will have a high profile. For this reason, phreaks have swatted political bloggers, pundits, and politicians, including Georgia Senator Saxby Chambliss (Stahl, 2015). Non-political but high-profile targets of swatting include celebrities, whose high profile almost ensure news and tabloid coverage of swatting incidents (Stahl, 2015). Online gamers also are targets for swatting. Using social media platforms such as Twitch, online gamers often broadcast live video feeds, which make SWAT team raids into their homes visible to sometimes tens of thousands of viewers (Stahl, 2015).

Petty revenge can also motivate incidents of swatting, both of which seem to be elements of online video game culture. The fatal shooting of a Kansas man in December 2017 was the first documented case of a death resulting in a swatting incident (Statt, 2017). The incident was the result of two online video gamers arguing over a wager amounting to $1.50, with one of the gamers swatting what he believed to be the address of the other gamer (Statt, 2017). Police in Wichita Kansas arrived at an address belonging to neither of the gamers and shot Andrew Finch, a 28-year-old father of two children (Statt, 2017).

Legal Responses to Swatting

The FBI estimates that 400 swatting calls take place annually, and swatting is treated as a public safety issue (Statt, 2017). Hoax calls waste police resources, and the FBI estimates that the average swatting hoax call costs law enforcement around $10,000 (McCartney, 2013).

Charges for swatting vary across jurisdictions (McCartney, 2013). Charges can range from making a false emergency call, which is a misdemeanor, to interstate wire fraud charges, a felony (McCartney, 2013). Punishments can range from fines starting at $2,500 to $80,000 and imprisonment from a mandatory minimum of 13 months to 11 years (Stahl, 2015; Statt, 2017). Many phreaks who make swatting calls are minors (McCartney, 2013).

The technically complex nature of the phone calls complicates investigations and prosecutions of these types of calls. A single swatting phone call can involve up to 40 police jurisdictions, several states, and several federal agencies (FBI, 2008).

The prosecution and investigation of swatting phone calls are complicated even further when the calls are determined to originate outside of the United States (McCartney, 2013). Swatting is an expensive crime to investigate.

Responses to swatting have come in two forms. The Seattle Police Department has pioneered a program for residents to preregister as potential swatting victims, intended for online gamers and public figures in mind (Lane, 2018). Police will still respond to emergency calls but dispatchers will alert them if there is a possibility that they are responding to a swatting call (Lane, 2018).

A second response to swatting has been in calls for the passage of state and national legislation to increase punishments and to make criminals liable for the monetary costs of emergency services (McCartney). Proposed federal legislation would increase the penalty for swatting to 20 years imprisonment (Kwch.com, 2018).

Conclusion

Law enforcement agencies treat swatting as a public safety issue. As a deviant phone activity, swatting is a dangerous variation of established social structures in hoax phone calls. Swatting calls are technically complex, making them difficult but not impossible to investigate and prosecute. Swatting can be potentially lethal, and it wastes emergency resources that otherwise could be directed to legitimate needs. Most swatting calls seem to be driven by egotistical motivations on the part of callers, and most swatting calls in the United States seem to be domestic in origin. A minority of swatting calls are political in nature by targeting activists, pundits, or politicians. In response to the quantity of swatting calls that take place, in addition to their potentially lethal outcomes, legislatures have introduced legislation to increase punishments for this type of criminal phone activity.

Further Reading

Grimes, R. A. (2017). *Hacking the Hacker: Learn From the Experts Who Take Down Hackers* (1st edition). Wiley.

Lapsley, P. (2014). *Exploding the Phone*. Grove Press.

Pollard, J. (2011). *Secret Britain: The Hidden Bits of Our History*. Hodder.

References

Boese, A. (2015). "The Berners Street Hoax". http://hoaxes.org/archive/permalink/the_berners_street_hoax/

Dresser, N. (1973, June 1). "Telephone Pranks", *New York Folklore Quarterly*, *29*(2): 121–130. https://search.proquest.com/openview/e51d543d53ab1de14e3e0c604125a0b9/1?pq-origsite=gscholar

Harlow, J. (2012, December 2). "Swat Teams fly into Hoax at Stars' Homes", *The Times*. thetimes.co.uk/article/swat-teams-fly-into-hoax-at-stars-homes-wnnf5lr275p

Kwch.com. (2018, March 8). "Congressman Estes introduces federal legislation to combat 'swatting'". https://www.kwch.com/content/news/Congressman-Estes-introduces-federal-legislation-to-combat-swatting-476247783.html

Lane, R. (2018, October 2). "Seattle Police Launch Opt-In Registry System to Help Prevent Swatting", *PCGamer*. https://www.pcgamer.com/seattle-police-launch-opt-in-registry-system-to-help-prevent-swatting/

McCartney, A. (2013, January 26). "Lawmakers to call for stiffer penalties to stop swatting'", *Police1*. https://www.police1.com/legal/articles/lawmakers-to-call-for-stiffer-penalties-to-stop-swatting-kBEu1N5vD4My3uDr/

Stahl, J. (2015, March 11). "A Brief History of Swatting, the Criminal Hoax that Just Befell Lil Wayne". http://www.slate.com/blogs/the_slatest/2015/03/11/lil_wayne_swatted_a_brief_history_of_swatting_the_dangerous_internet_hoax.html

Statt, N. (2017, December 29). "Swatting over Call of Duty game results in deadly police shooting of Kansas man", *The Verge*. https://www.theverge.com/2017/12/29/16830626/call-of-duty-swatting-prank-kansas-man-dead-police-shooting

The Atlantic. (2016, April). "The Long Life (and Slow Death?) of the Prank Phone Call". https://www.theatlantic.com/technology/archive/2016/04/the-life-and-death-of-the-prank-phone-call/476340/

The Federal Bureau of Investigation (FBI). (2008, February 4). "Don't Make the Call The New Phenomenon of 'Swatting'". https://archives.fbi.gov/archives/news/stories/2008/february/swatting020408

The Telephone Museum. (2021). "Cap'n Crunch Bo'sun Whistle". https://telephone-museum.org/telephone-collections/capn-crunch-bosun-whistle/

Chapter 44

Third Department of the People's Liberation Army General Staff Headquarters (3PLA)

Anwar Ouassini and Brynn Dao
Delaware State University, Dover, DE, United States

Contents

Introduction 301
Further Reading 303
References 303

Introduction

Once an army composed of peasants, the People's Liberation Army of China (PLA) has made major strides toward becoming a formidable force in cyberwarfare and intelligence. Beginning in 1978, Deng Xiaoping, known as the "Architect of Modern China," initiated what is now known as the modernization of the PLA (Jian, 2018). Building on what Xiaoping started, in 2007, the PLA moved toward its third modernization program to enhance its capabilities to combat future cyberwars (Finkelstein, 2007). This shift toward weaponizing information and internet technologies developed from three pillars that set the framework for the PLA's modernization efforts in the post-Mao era (Finkelstein, 2007). First, the PLA has moved toward localizing the production of weapons systems and scientific research, effectively seeking to end their dependency on third parties (Finkelstein, 2007). Second, the PLA has revamped its educational institutions and intensified the screening process for its

DOI: 10.4324/9781315144511-46

military (Finkelstein, 2007). Finally, they have pursued access to alternative technologies to be at the forefront of the changing dynamics of "informationized" warfare in the twenty-first century. The modernization of the PLA has given the 3PLA (General Staff Department, Third Department of the People's Liberation Army) the primary responsibility of developing its military cyber forces while ensuring that it focuses on cyberwarfare, intelligence, and cyber operations (USCC, 2016, p. 290).

The 3PLA mandate initially pursued political and commercial espionage with nearly 100,000 hackers and signals intelligence troops (Gertz, 2016). The NSA has estimated that the hackers under the control of the 3PLA have conducted thousands of cyberattacks seeking defense and commercial-related industrial secrets while protecting the PLA's and CCP'S (Chinese Communist Party) cybersecurity infrastructure (Gertz, 2016). In 2013, the Shanghai-based 3PLA Unit 61398 targeted several American commercial sector facilities and stole sensitive data, including business and manufacturing procedures, white papers, and systems designs with "more than 1,600 network computers penetrated, compromising 600,000 user accounts and causing over $100 million in damage to rebuild networks" (Gertz, 2018). Furthermore, the

> extent of the cybercrimes documented in the indictment illuminate the likelihood that China Inc. uses cyber-penetrations to enrich both the state and individual Chinese Communist Party members with privileged financial and commodities market information to the tune of trillions, not billions, of dollars.
>
> (Gertz, 2014)

In response, the United States Department of Justice (DOJ) announced an indictment of five 3PLA officers for economic espionage, trade secret thefts, identity theft, computer fraud, and accessing a protected computer without authorization for commercial advantage (Department of Justice, 2014). Politically, the US government went on the offensive, directly pointing the fingers at the CCP and the PLA for its role in providing support and cover for the operation. This forced American security institutions to classify the 3PLA and all the hacker organizations associated with it as advanced persistent threats (APTs) actively seeking to undermine and capture data related to US intelligence, trade secrets, and new and emerging technologies. The formal indictment of military officers from the Chinese state placed tremendous pressure on the PLA and the CCP, leading to not only political tensions between President Obama and President Xi but also fears of an American cyber-response to the 3PLA program. To curtail a potential cold-cyberwar scenario, both the United States and China agreed to a binational agreement that "neither country's government will conduct or knowingly support cyber-enabled theft of intellectual property, including trade secrets or other confidential business information, with the intent of providing competitive advantages to companies or commercial sectors" (Obama White House, 2015).

While the number of attacks directed at the United States from the PLA has decreased, they did not disappear as other non-military governmental institutions became more prominent in using their cyber-capabilities to conduct espionage and theft of American commercial sectors. The 3PLA during this period fell under a new governmental organization called the Strategic Support Force (SSF). This new body houses China's Cyber Corps (Gertz, 2018), integrating the operational units of the 3PLA with the other "general departments". The organizational restructuring around the SSF integrates the space forces, cyber forces with their hacker troops, and electronic forces to focus the state's resources on the military domain of cyber intelligence and warfare (Kania & Costello, 2018). President Xi stated in the founding ceremony that, "the Strategic Support Force is a new-type combat force to maintain national security and an important growth point of the PLA's combat capabilities" (Davidson, 2016). This enables the PLA to have more control over the operational objectives and outcomes of what many CCP officials see as the impending global cyberwar but also have absolute control over the Chinese intelligence community. Thus, while the 3PLA is still functioning under the auspices of the SSF, it no longer can set its agenda outside of the PLA–SSF organizational hierarchy as it reports directly to the Central Military Commissions (CMC) which is currently headed by President Xi Jinping.

The integration of the 3PLA in the SSF reflects the central role that cybersecurity and cyber espionage will play in the future of the PLA's military and political strategies to maintain domestic stability and active supremacy overall traditional threats and APTs. Moreover, this integration reveals that the traditional role that the 3PLA has operated around cyber intelligence is now the paradigm of all the active institutions of the PLA–SSF.

Further Reading

Chase, M.S., Engstrom, J., Cheung, T.M., Gunness, K.A., Harold, S.W., Puska, S., Berkowitz, S.K. (2015). *China's incomplete military transformation.* https://apps.dtic.mil/dtic/tr/fulltext/u2/a615374.pdf

Jian, Z. (2018). Towards a 'world class' military: Reforming the PLA under Xi Jinping. In Jane Golley, Linda Jaivin, Paul J. Farrelly and Sharon Strange, eds. "Power." Canberra: Australian National University Press.

Golley, J., L. Jaivin, P. Farrelly & S. Strange (Eds.) *China story yearbook: Power* [e-book]. 218–231. ANU Press.

Kania, EB & Costello, JK. (2018). The Strategic Support Force and the Future of Chinese Information Operations. *The Cyber Defense Review*, Spring 2018:105–121.

References

Chambers, M. (2007). Framing the problem: China's threat environment and international obligations. In R. Kamphausen & A. Scobell (Eds.) *Right sizing the people's liberation army: Exploring the contours of China's military* [e-book]. 19–68. Strategic Studies Institute.

Chase, M.S., Engstrom, J., Cheung, T.M. Gunness, K.A., Harold, S.W., Puska, S. Berkowitz, S.K. (2015). *China's incomplete military transformation.* Retrieved from https://apps.dtic.mil/dtic/tr/fulltext/u2/a615374.pdf

Davidson, L. (2016). China's Strategic Support Force: The New Home of the PLA's Cyber Operations? Retrieved February 20, 2020, from https://www.cfr.org/blog/chinas-strategic-support-force-new-home-plas-cyber-operations

Department of Justice (2014). U.S. Charges Five Chinese Military Hackers for Cyber Espionage Against U.S. Corporations and a Labor Organization for Commercial Advantage. Retrieved

February 20, 2020, from https://www.justice.gov/opa/pr/us-charges-five-chinese-military-hackers-cyber-espionage-against-us-corporations-and-labor

Finkelstein, D.M. (2007). China's military strategy: An overview of the "military strategic guidelines". In R. Kamphausen & A. Scobell (Eds.) *Right sizing the people's liberation army: Exploring the contours of China's military* [e-book]. 69–140. Strategic Studies Institute.

Gertz, B. (2014). Indictment of China Military Hackers Reveals New Details of Cyber Attack Methods. Retrieved February 20, 2020, from https://freebeacon.com/national-security/obama-administration-indictment-of-army-hackers-seeks-to-deter-cyber-attacks/

Gertz, B. (2016). Chinese Military Revamps Cyber Warfare, Intelligence Forces. Retrieved February 20, 2020, from https://freebeacon.com/national-security/chinese-military-revamps-cyber-warfare-intelligence-forces/

Gertz, B. (2018). China cyber spy chief revealed. Retrieved February 20, 2020, from https://www.washingtontimes.com/news/2018/mar/28/liu-xiaobei-heads-chinas-us-hacking-operations/

Jian, Z. (2018). Towards a 'world class' military: Reforming the PLA under Xi Jinping. In J. Golley, L. Jaivin, P. Farrelly & S. Strange (Eds.) *China story yearbook: Power* [e-book]. 218–231. ANU Press.

Kania, EB & Costello, JK. (2018). The Strategic Support Force and the Future of Chinese Information Operations. *The Cyber Defense Review*, Spring 2018:105- 121.

Obama White House. (2015). FACT SHEET: President Xi Jinping's State Visit to the United States. Retrieved February 20, 2020, from https://obamawhitehouse.archives.gov/the-press-office/2015/09/25/fact-sheet-president-xi-jinpings-state-visit-united-states

U.S. China Economic and Security Review Commission. (2016). China's intelligence services and espionage threats to the United States. In USCC (Eds.) *2016 Report to congress of the U.S.-China economic and security review commission*. 289–311. https://www.uscc.gov/sites/default/files/annual_reports/2016%20Annual%20Report%20to%20Congress.pdf

Chapter 45

US Cyber Command (USCYBERCOM)

Dominika Dziwisz
Jagiellonian University, Kraków, Poland

Scott N. Romaniuk
International Centre for Policing and Security, University of South Wales, Caerleon, United Kingdom

Contents

Introduction 305
The Evolution of USCYBERCOM 306
USCYBERCOM's Mission 307
Command Visions for USCYBERCOM 309
Conclusion 311
Further Reading 312
References 312

Introduction

According to the United States Intelligence chiefs' joint statement at a hearing on foreign cyber threats by the US Senate Armed Services Committee, protecting critical infrastructure will become an increasingly complex national security challenge since cyber threats are becoming increasingly diverse and sophisticated. There is a high probability that "adversaries equipped with similar offensive cyber capabilities could be prone to preemptive attack and rapid escalation in a future crisis because both sides would have an incentive to strike first" (Joint Statement, 2017). Taking that into consideration, it is not surprising that more than 30 countries are developing offensive potential in cyberspace (Joint Statement, 2017).

DOI: 10.4324/9781315144511-47

In the early 2000s, it became increasingly evident to the US government and military that the weapons of the past are less useful in the contemporary conflicts in which the United States is involved. In response to new security challenges, in mid-2009, Secretary of Defense Robert Gates directed the commander of US Strategic Command to establish a sub-unified Command (11th International Conference on Cyber Conflict, 2019). General James Cartwright set up a small cyber unit that in 2009, during the presidency of Barack Obama, blossomed into United States Cyber Command (USCYBERCOM), the country's first military organization that uses the Internet as a defensive and offensive weapon. Cyber Command's mission is to defend specific Department of Defense networks, as well as to attack an enemy's networks in the event of a conflict. The creation of USCYBERCOM "marked the culmination of more than a decade's worth of institutional change. DoD defensive and offensive capabilities were now firmly linked and, moreover, tied closely with the nation's cryptologic system and premier information assurance entity, the NSA" (Warner, 2015 as cited in Smeets, Lin, 2018, p. 83).

The Evolution of USCYBERCOM

Created on June 23, 2009, USCYBERCOM was not the first attempt to create such a unit, but a larger and consolidated version of pre-existing solutions. The first joint Cyber Command, Joint Task Force – Computer Network Defense (JTF-CND), was established in 1998 and was the Department of Defense's (DoD's) first organization to have authority to oversee and direct operations on individual military service and DoD networks. At first, it consisted of 23 people commanded by a two-star general. In 1999, JTF-CND evolved into Joint Task Force – Computer Network Operations (JTF-CNO) (DoD, US Cyber Command History). The unit quickly expanded, and in 2004, under the name Joint Task Force-Global Network Operations (JTF-GNO), employed 150 people responsible for both cyber offense and defense (Healey, Grindal, 2012). The same year, cyberspace was declared the fifth war domain, alongside air, land, sea, and space in National Military Strategy (National Military Strategy, 2004).

The next transformation separated the offensive (Joint Functional Component Command-Network Warfare, JFCC-NW) and defensive capabilities (Joint Task Force-Global Network Operations, JTF-GNO). As it is now acknowledged years later, offensive tasks have rarely been successful (Healey, *A Fierce Domain*). For example, one of the most compromising JFCC-NW activities was the suspension of a website which apparently recruited extremists to fight US military troops and coordinated operations in the Middle East. In fact, the CIA and Saudi intelligence cofounded this site to gather information about extremists.

On November 12, 2008, Secretary Robert Gates directed the creation of this sub-unified Command, USCYBERCOM, to operate under the authority of the United States Strategic Command (USSTRATCOM). All other cyber commands, including 24th Air Force – Air Forces Cyber (AFCYBER), 2nd Army – US Army Cyber Command (ARCYBER), US Tenth Fleet – Fleet Cyber Command (FLTCYBER), and US Marine Corps Forces Cyberspace Command (MARFORCYBER), are subject to the authority of USCYBERCOM.

After years of trial and unclear division of competences, both components, JFCC-NW and JTF-GNO, were incorporated into USCYBERCOM in June 23, 2009, which achieved Initial Operational Capability in May 21, 2010. General Keith Alexander was appointed the first USCYBERCOM commander. His duties as director of the National Security Agency (NSA) have therefore included the duties of commander of USCYBERCOM. The headquarters of both units, not accidentally, were located in Fort Meade, Maryland. As argued, the close location was not only more convenient but also necessary for the smooth operations of both units. The effectiveness of USCYBERCOM's activities depends on close cooperation with electronic intelligence. Despite objections regarding the possibility of surveilling US citizens, it has been announced that this cooperation will continue. Improved personal data security was to be ensured by restrictive internal security procedures and the supervision over NSA activities by the Department of Justice, the United States Foreign Intelligence Surveillance Court (FISA Court), and the US Congress (CSIS, 2010).

USCYBERCOM's concept for organization was approved by the Joint Staff in 2012 and called for the creation of 133 Cyber Mission Force (CMF) teams, projected to include more than 6,000 military and civilian personnel as well as contractor support from the military departments and defense components (Nakashima, 2014). Consequently, under the second USCYBERCOM's commander Navy Adm. Michael S. Rogers, the CMF evolved and is currently comprised of four types of teams:

- Cyber Protection Teams to defend DoD's information networks, protect priority missions, and prepare cyber forces for combat
- Combat Mission Teams, which support operational plans and contingency operations
- National Mission Teams providing support in case of cyberattacks of significant consequence to the nation by observing adversary activity, blocking attacks, and maneuvering to defeat them
- Support Teams to provide analytic and planning support (Nakashima, 2014; DoD, US Cyber Command History)

On October 21, 2016, all 133 teams of the CMF achieved their milestone of Initial Operating Capability (IOC), which meant, "all CMF units had reached a threshold operational capacity whereby the units could execute their fundamental missions" (US Cyber Command History).

On May 4, 2018, Adm. Michael S. Rogers relinquished command of USCYBERCOM and directorship of the NSA/Central Security Service (CSS) to Army Gen. Paul M. Nakasone. As it was announced on August 18, 2017, USCYBERCOM was elevated to the status of the nation's tenth full and independent Unified Combatant Command (CCMD) on May 4, 2018 (DoDLive). On May 17, USCYBERCOM achieved Full Operational Capability (FOC) (DoD, *Cyber Mission Force*). To reach FOC, teams had to meet a rigorous set of criteria, such as 'an approved concept of operation and a high percentage of trained, qualified and certified personnel. As part of the certification process, teams had to show they could perform their mission under stress in simulated, real-world conditions as part of specialized training events" (DoD, *Cyber Mission Force*).

USCYBERCOM's Mission

USCYBERCOM's mission is to "direct, synchronize, and coordinate cyberspace planning and operations to defend and advance national interests in collaboration with domestic and international partners" (US Cyber Command, Mission and Vision). More specifically, the Command has three main focus areas:

- Defending the DoD Information Network
- Providing support to combatant commanders for execution of their missions around the world
- Strengthening the nation's ability to withstand and respond to cyberattacks

USCYBERCOM conducts daily protection of the DoD network and is responsible for the "dot-mil" domain. Responsibility for federal civil networks – "dot-gov" – falls to the Department of Homeland Security (DHS). However, in the case of war operations, the scope of Cyber Command operations can be extended to defend the DHS's networks. Shortly after the emergence of Cyber Command, Deputy Secretary of Defense William Lynn concisely explained its mission: "We will lead the day-to-day defense of all military networks, support military and counterterrorism missions and (…) assist other government and civil authorities and industry partners." As he put it, "the key part of Cyber Command is the linking of intelligence, offense and defense under one roof" (CSIS, 2010).

Before 2018, when the White House "authorized offensive cyber operations" against US adversaries, in line with a new policy that eases the rules on the use of digital weapons to protect the nation, Cyber Command had assumed a largely defensive posture (Nakashima, 2018). Back in 2011, when the DoD released a Strategy for Operating in Cyberspace (Department of Defense Strategy for Operating in Cyberspace, 2011), one of its five strategic initiatives stated that the DoD would treat cyberspace as an operational area, but only to organize, train, and equip the United States Armed Forces so that DoD would have an advantage in cyberspace. The strategy says nothing about treating cyberspace as a domain of warfare. At that time, Gen. James Cartwright, Vice Chairman of the Joint Chiefs of Staff, was of the opinion that the approach to securing computer systems was too predictable and defense was overemphasized (Nakashima, 2011). Adam Segal, a cybersecurity expert at the Council on Foreign Relations (CFR), made similar comments. He said the strategy was devoted solely to cyber defense, and its main purpose was to change the way of thinking that the United States is militarizing cyberspace (Nakashima, 2011). James Lewis, a Center for Strategic and International Studies (CSIS) expert, was of a different opinion. He said that the fact that the DoD Strategy does not regulate offensive operations in cyberspace or during conventional warfare was not necessarily its weakness. "It's the right blend," he said (Farnsworth, 2011). The biggest difficulty of offensive and retaliatory action is to correctly detect the origin of the attack. In cyberspace, this is hardly possible. Hence, you cannot rely on the threat of retaliation to track down the aggressor. Therefore, the goal of the strategy was not to militarize cyberspace. It was assumed that denying the benefits that offensive action would bring is the best strategy to discourage the hostile use of cyberspace (Farnsworth, 2011).

Donald Trump's administration promoted a more aggressive approach and offensive actions. On September 20, 2018, Donald Trump's administration released the United States' first fully articulated cyber strategy in 15 years (National Cyber Strategy, 2018). The content of the strategy clearly indicates an interest in both military cyber defensive and offensive capabilities in areas ranging from critical infrastructure to space exploration and intellectual property protection. The strategy is structured around four pillars of priority. The third pillar, titled "Preserve Peace through Strength," states that: "Cyberspace will no longer be treated as a separate category of policy or activity disjointed from other elements of national power. The United States will integrate the employment of cyber options across every element of national power." National Security Advisor John Bolton emphasized the same: "we are going to do a lot of things offensively and I think our adversaries need to know that." "We will identify, counter, disrupt, degrade, and deter behavior in cyberspace that is destabilizing and contrary to national interests," he said (Nelson, 2018).

Bolton also announced that the strategy incorporates a new classified presidential directive, the reversal of an Obama administration directive (Presidential Policy Directive 20, PPD-20), which allows the military and other agencies to undertake cyber operations intended to protect their systems and the nation's critical networks. In short, National Security Presidential Memorandum 13 (NSPM-13) "frees the military to engage, without a lengthy approval process, in actions that fall below the 'use of force' or a level that would cause death, destruction or significant economic impacts" (Nakashima, 2018).

The strategy's provisions are reflected in the Department of Defense's Cyber Strategy, released the same year, which confirms Donald Trump's announcement of an "offensive step forward" when it comes to operations in cyberspace (Summary, DoD Cyber Strategy 2018; Weinstein, 2018). This is particularly evident in the new doctrinal concept: "defend forward" (described in the next section).

Command Visions for USCYBERCOM

USCYBERCOM's first vision statement titled "Beyond the Build. Delivering Outcomes through Cyberspace" was released in 2015. It is mainly focused on USCYBERCOM's role within the DoD; strengthening Cyber Command's partnerships across the DoD, the NSA, and the Intelligence Community; and expanding collaboration with federal agencies, industry, academia, and international partners. At the beginning of the document, it is stated that: "Our mission in cyberspace is to provide mission assurance for the operation and defense of the Department of Defense information environment, deter or defeat strategic threats to the US interests and infrastructure, and support the achievement of Joint Force Commander objectives." The main goal and challenge of Cyber Command is to "protect the things we value – freedom, liberty, prosperity, intellectual property, and personal information."

The statement identifies cyberspace as a fifth warfighting domain in which the country must have the necessary defenses. Because cyberspace is a human construct, so the broad principles of strategy and conflict still apply. What makes cyberspace different from other domains of war is the fact that "warfighting skills (…) just have to be faster and partnered." Therefore, the statement calls for "new ways of defending, fighting and partnering against learning adversaries in the contested cyber domain," which will require the need to operationalize cyberspace. However, the statement doesn't provide straight insight on how it aims to deter or defeat actors in cyberspace (Smeets, Lin, 2018).

In comparison to its first vision, the new 2018 Command vision for USCYBERCOM, titled "Achieve and Maintain Cyberspace Superiority," is a more coherent plan on how to act in cyberspace. As stated, the document "is a roadmap for USCYBERCOM to achieve and maintain superiority in cyberspace as we direct, synchronize, and coordinate cyberspace planning and operations to defend and advance national interests in collaboration with domestic and foreign partners." The document declares that the DoD is taking a more aggressive approach to protect the nation's data and networks as the document describes the notion of "continuous engagement" and "defending forward" to understand adversary weaknesses and impose "tactical friction and strategic costs." Thereby, it represents an important shift from previous thinking about cyberspace as a domain.

The key change in the Command's vision is the recognition that the majority of cyber operations purposefully remain below the threshold of an "armed aggression" and therefore it describes cyberspace as a domain of persistent contest. As written in the document: "Adversaries continuously operate against us below the threshold of armed conflict. In this "new normal," our adversaries are extending their influence without resorting to physical aggression. They provoke and intimidate our citizens and enterprises without fear of legal or military consequences." Therefore, it is very important to recognize that what is significantly dangerous to American strength is organized, sophisticated cyber campaigns that undermine American diplomatic, economic, and military power (Harknett, 2018).

The document is also skeptical that deterrence may work in cyberspace, and as a result, USCYBERCOM will prioritize offensive activity to contest an adversary's capability through persistent, integrated operations. "Continuous engagement imposes tactical friction and strategic costs on our adversaries, compelling them to shift resources to defense and reduce attacks," says the document. An approach for securing US national interests through a "strategy of persistent engagement" means that the United States is "continuously anticipating and exploiting adversaries vulnerabilities while denying their ability to exploit U.S. vulnerabilities through operations that support resiliency, defending forward, contesting and countering to achieve strategic advantage" (Fischerkeller and Harknett, 2018).

The strategy of persistent engagement is supported by the "defend forward" operational concept: "We sustain strategic advantage by increasing resiliency, defending forward, and continuously engaging our adversaries. (…) Defending forward as close as possible to the origin of adversary activity extends our reach to expose adversaries' weaknesses, learn their intentions and capabilities, and counter attacks close to their origins." It consists of three components (Kosseff, 2019):

- "Positioning" to degrade the effectiveness of adversary cyber operations
- "Warning" to obtain information about threats and the adversaries' cyber operations before they are deployed
- "Influencing" adversaries to discourage them to start cyber operations against the United States

In short, "defend forward" means "confronting threats before they reach U.S. networks" (Department of Defense Fact Sheet, 2018). Previous approaches too often dealt with adversaries inside US networks, rather than stopping them before entering

(Harknett, 2018). Therefore, the new approach will enable Cyber Command to move off of DoD networks and hunt for adversary activity on their networks. This may sound a bit similar to the intent behind developing offensive capabilities endorsed by previous documents. However, there's a fundamental difference here. According to the vision statement, Cyber Command's activities are not focused on retaliation and exercising offensive capabilities after an attack took place. They are meant to be pro-active, focused on detection of risks long before they pose any real threat to the United States or their allies. They have more in common with intelligence work and special operations than the typical tasks of armed forces.

Conclusion

In addition to the traditionally understood dimensions of war, i.e., land, sea, air, and space, cyberspace is the only dimension of war created entirely by man and, unlike the physical domains, is constantly changing. Cyber Command strives to keep up with these changes in the technological dimension, as well as developing new organizational and legal solutions. In other words, changes that take place in the cyberspace security environment are forcing the evolution of Cyber Command.

Modern wars are melting together both traditional military conflict and cyber conflict.

Therefore, the establishment of USCYBERCOM 10 years ago has opened a new area in the history of war. USCYBERCOM was created as a sub-unified Command under US Strategic Command. On May 4, 2018, it became a full-fledged Unified Combatant Command. According to the United States DoD, Cyber Command has conducted more operations in cyberspace over the past few months than in the last 10 years (Pomerleau, 2019). Cyber Command's above-average activity results primarily from the application of new legal possibilities in practice and the new vision of operation in cyberspace. Air Force Maj. Gen. Charles Moore Jr., the Command's director of operations, said that in the first year as a Unified Combatant Command, Cyber Command primarily implemented a "strategy of persistent engagement," which meant being fully engaged with adversaries in the cyber domain (Lopez, 2019).

The second area of focus for the Command is "defending forward," which means getting outside of just US networks and working with allies. As Cyber Command's mission is protecting defense networks and domestic critical infrastructure, the Command needs to continuously probe foreign networks for malicious activity to do that effectively.

Finally, the content of the above-mentioned documents and Donald Trump's security policy clearly indicate an interest in building cyber offensive capabilities. Ultimately, we can never be absolutely sure that more aggressive cyber space strategies will not switch to conventional battle domains. Therefore, the DoD should do more work to understand what types of goals or effects can accidentally lead a country into escalation of conflict.

The experience of cyberattacks in the last several years has led to effective conclusions being drawn and new and more efficient regulations have been developed. However, the new strategic concepts, such as persistent engagement and defending forward, do not only have supporters. These concepts are still in the testing phase, and it will take some time to see how effective they will be.

Further Reading

Andrues, W. R. (2010). "What U.S. Cyber Command Must Do," *Joint Force Quarterly*, *59*: 115–120. https://apps.dtic.mil/sti/pdfs/ADA536589.pdf

Borghard, E. D. and Lonergan, S. W. (2017). "The Logic of Coercion in Cyberspace," *Security Studies*, *26*(3): 452–481.

Schneider, J. (2020). "A Strategic Cyber No-First-Use Policy? Addressing the US Cyber Strategy Problem," *The Washington Quarterly*, *43*(2): 159–175.

References

11th International Conference on Cyber Conflict: Silent Battle, T. Minárik, S. Alatalu, S. Biondi, M. Signoretti, I. Tolga, G. Visky (eds.), 28 May–31 May 2019, Tallinn, Estonia, https://ccdcoe.org/uploads/2019/06/CyCon_2019_BOOK.pdf, 12.23.2019.

Achieve and Maintain Cyberspace Superiority. Command Vision for US Cyber Command, March 23, 2018, https://www.cybercom.mil/Portals/56/Documents/USCYBERCOM%20Vision%20April%202018.pdf, 12.28.2019.

Beyond the Build. Delivering Outcomes through Cyberspace, The Commander's Vision and Guidance for US Cyber Command, June 3, 2015, https://www.hsdl.org/?abstract&did=787006, 12.21.2019.

CSIS, *U.S. Cybersecurity Policy and the Role of U.S. CYBERCOM*, "CSIS Cybersecurity Policy Debate Series", Center for Strategic and International Studies, 06.03.2010, http://csis.org/files/attachments/100603csis-alexander.pdf, 12.12.2019.

Department of Defense Fact Sheet: 2018 DoD Cyber Strategy and Cyber Posture Review. Sharpening our Competitive Edge in Cyberspace, https://media.defense.gov/2018/Sep/18/2002041659/-1/-1/1/Factsheet_for_Strategy_and_CPR_FINAL.pdf, 12.21.2019.

Department of Defense Strategy for Operating in Cyberspace, July 2011, https://csrc.nist.gov/CSRC/media/Projects/ISPAB/documents/DOD-Strategy-for-Operating-in-Cyberspace.pdf, 12.21.2019.

Department of Defense, *U.S. Cyber Command History*, https://www.cybercom.mil/About/History/, 12.12.2019.

DoD, *Cyber Mission Force Achieves Full Operational Capability*, 05.17.2018, https://www.defense.gov/Explore/News/Article/Article/1524747/cyber-mission-force-achieves-full-operational-capability/, 12.12.2019.

DoDLive, *Cybercom Becomes DoD's 10th Unified Combatant Command*, https://www.dodlive.mil/2018/05/03/cybercom-to-become-dods-10th-unified-combatant-command/, 12.12.2019.

Farnsworth T., *Pentagon Issues Cyber Strategy*, "Arms and Control Today", Arms and Control Association, September 2011, http://www.armscontrol.org/2011_09/Pentagon_Issues_Cyber_Strategy, 12.10.2019.

Fischerkeller M. P., Harknett R. J., *Persistent Engagement and Tacit Bargaining: A Path Toward Constructing Norms in Cyberspace*, 11.09.2018, https://www.lawfareblog.com/persistent-engagement-and-tacit-bargaining-path-toward-constructing-norms-cyberspace, 12.27.2019.

Harknett R. J., *United States Cyber Command's New Vision: What It Entails and Why It Matters*, 03.23.2018, https://www.lawfareblog.com/united-states-cyber-commands-new-vision-what-it-entails-and-why-it-matters, 12.27.2019.

Healey J., *A Fierce Domain: Conflict in Cyberspace, 1986 to Today*, draft version, Washington, DC, August 2012, the draft of the book was made available courtesy of Jason Healey, Director of the Cyberstatecraft Initiative at the Atlantic Council.

Healey J., Grindal K., *Lessons from the First Cyber Commanders*, 03.05.2012, Atlantic Council, https://www.atlanticcouncil.org/commentary/transcript/transcript-lessons-from-our-cyber-past-the-first-military-cyber-units/, 12.21.2019.

Joint Statement for the Record to the Senate Armed Services Committee, Foreign Cyber Threats to the United States, The Honorable James R. Clapper, Director of National Intelligence, The Honorable Marcel Lettre, Undersecretary of Defense for Intelligence, Admiral Michael S. Rogers, USN, Commander, U.S. Cyber Command, Director, National Security Agency, 5 January 2017, https://www.armed-services.senate.gov/imo/media/doc/Clapper-Lettre-Rogers_01-05-16.pdf, 12.23.2019.

Kosseff J., "11th International Conference on Cyber Conflict: Silent Battle", In *The Contours of 'Defend Forward' Under International Law*, T. Minárik, S. Alatalu, S. Biondi, M. Signoretti, I. Tolga, G. Visky (eds.), 28 May–31 May 2019, Tallinn, Estonia, https://ccdcoe.org/uploads/2019/06/CyCon_2019_BOOK.pdf, 12.23.2019.

Lopez Todd C., *Persistent Engagement, Partnerships, Top Cybercom's Priorities*, 05.12.2019, https://www.defense.gov/Explore/News/Article/Article/1847823/persistent-engagement-partnerships-top-cybercoms-priorities/, 12.21.2019.

Nakashima E., *U.S. Cyber Approach 'too Predictable' for One Top General*, "The Washington Post", 07.15.2011, http://www.washingtonpost.com/national/national-security/us-cyber-approach-too-predictable-for-one-top-gener-al/2011/07/14/gIQAYJC6EI_story.html, 12.20.2019.

Nakashima E., *U.S. Cyberwarfare Force to Grow Significantly, Defense Secretary Says*, "The Washington Post", 03.28.2014, http://www.washingtonpost.com/world/national-security/us-cyberwarfare-force-to-grow-significantly-defense-secretary-says/2014/03/28/0a1fa074-b680-11e3-b84e-897d3d12b816_story.html, 12.12.2019.

Nakashima E., *White House authorizes 'offensive cyber operations' to deter foreign adversaries*, 09.21.2018, "The Washington Post", https://www.washingtonpost.com/world/national-security/trump-authorizes-offensive-cyber-operations-to-deter-foreign-adversaries-bolton-says/2018/09/20/b5880578-bd0b-11e8-b7d2-0773aa1e33da_story.html, 12.12.2019.

National Cyber Strategy of the United States of America, September 2018, https://www.whitehouse.gov/wp-content/uploads/2018/09/National-Cyber-Strategy.pdf, 12.14.2019.

National Military Strategy of the United States of America 2004: A Strategy for Today; A Vision for Tomorrow, https://history.defense.gov/Portals/70/Documents/nms/nms2004.pdf?ver=2014-06-25-123447-627, 12.20.2019.

Nelson S., *John Bolton is warning about offensive cyberattacks under a new Trump policy*, 09.21.2018, "Business Insider", https://www.businessinsider.com/john-bolton-warns-of-offensive-cyberattacks-under-a-new-trump-policy-2018-9?IR=T, 12.15.2019.

Pomerleau M., *New authorities mean lots of new missions at Cyber Command*, 05.08.2019, https://www.fifthdomain.com/dod/cybercom/2019/05/08/new-authorities-mean-lots-of-new-missions-at-cyber-command/, 12.21.2019.

Smeets M., Lin H., "A Strategic Assessment of the U.S. Cyber Command Vision", In *Bytes, Bombs, and Spies: The Strategic Dimensions of Offensive Cyber Operations*, H. Lin, A. Zegart (eds.), Brookings Institution Press, 2018, chap. 4, p. 83.

Summary, Department of Defense Cyber Strategy 2018, https://media.defense.gov/2018/Sep/18/2002041658/-1/-1/1/CYBER_STRATEGY_SUMMARY_FINAL.PDF, 12.19.2019.

US Cyber Command, Mission and Vision, https://www.cybercom.mil/About/Mission-and-Vision/, 12.12.2019.

Warner M., "U.S. Cyber Command's Road to Full Operational Capability", In *Stand Up and Fight: The Creation of U.S. Security Organizations, 1942–2005*, T. Seidule, J. E. Whitt (eds.), Carlisle, Penn.: Strategic Studies Institute and U.S. Army War College Press, 2015, chap. 7.

Weinstein D., *The Pentagon's New Cyber Strategy: Defend Forward*, 09.21.2018, https://www.lawfareblog.com/pentagons-new-cyber-strategy-defend-forward, 12.15.2019.

TERRORISM AND ASYMMETRIC THREATS

III

Zoha Waseem
King's College London, London, United Kingdom

Chapter 46

Al Qaeda in the Islamic Maghreb (AQIM)

Tavis D. Jules
Loyola University, Chicago, IL, United States

Contents

Introduction 317
Background: From GIA to GSPC 318
From GSPC to AQIM 320
A Crisis of Leadership 321
Conclusion 322
Further Reading 323
Notes 323
References 324

Introduction

Al Qaeda in the Islamic Maghreb (AQIM),[1] a Salafi-Jihadist group, is often viewed as an Al Qaeda external force operating out of the Sahel and Sahara. AQIM was founded in 1998 under the name *Groupe Salafiste pour la Prédication et le Combat* (GSPC; the Salafist Group for Preaching and Combat). Before becoming AQIM, GSPC initially emerged in 1992 out of the hardline *Groupe Islamique Armé* (GIA; the Armed Islamic Group), which was one of several[2] Islamic militant groups that participated in Algeria's *la sale guerre* (the dirty war or the Algerian Civil War) during the 1990s. Much about the history of GIA, an urban paramilitary group that called for the following of ardent Islamic principles, remains a mystery, but consensuses exist that its first *emir* (leader) was a former metal worker, Abdelhak Layada (alias Abu Adlane), who united several smaller groups fighting in the capital of Algiers. In January 1992,

DOI: 10.4324/9781315144511-49

GIA was robbed of an imminent electoral victory, after the national elections were canceled and a military coup ensued.

At the time of *la sale guerre*, GIA emerged as the biggest and most aggressive Islamist group fighting the Algerian government, while also becoming the most organized and dominant terrorist group in Algeria. GIA stated that its official duty was to create a caliphate after it overthrew the "apostate" governmental regime, using "al-Shehada" doctrine and strategy which condemned "France as the source of all evil" (Roy & Sfeir, 2007, p. 64). During its tenure, GIA's core supporters and members were the so-called foreign mujahedin fighters or "Afghan Algerians," who were militants returning home from their jihad stint in Afghanistan's training camps (Boeke, 2016). In short, it was a "radical ethno-nationalist organization [which] blended the notion of religious identity as a nationalist cause" (Smith, 2010, p. 64) of securing a Muslim homeland in Algeria.

This chapter explores and analyzes the rise of AQIM. It begins by detailing the historical background and context in which AQIM (then called GIA) arose and its fight for recognition during the Algerian Civil War. The second section discusses AQIM's metamorphosis from GSPC to its current iteration. Then, the chapter analyzes the changes that occurred in the organization's structure as it battled emerging geopolitical and ideological division within its ranks. The chapter concludes by situating AQIM within the current political climate besieged by the battle for the title of 'best' global terrorist organization.

Background: From GIA to GSPC

GIA was an extremist Salafi-Jihadist group which had a brutal and indiscriminate violence policy. GIA's motto of "no agreement, no truce, no dialogue" sums up the group's jihadi practices of vehemently targeting foreigners and *takfirs* (enemies of Islam), including Muslim women (particularly those not wearing the ***Hijab*** and in professional careers), children, and the elderly (Boeke, 2016; Kepel, 2002; Martinez, 2000). By 1993, Layada was replaced with Mourad Sid Ahmed (alias Jaafar al-Afghani), who oversaw the first instance of the murder of foreigners: two French surveyors on September 21, 1993. In 1994, GIA declared a caliphate, and *Front Islamique pour le Djihad* (FIDA; the Islamic Front for Armed Jihad), founded in 1993, and *Mouvement pour L' état Islamique* (MEI; the Movement for the Islamic State),[3] founded in 1991, pledged loyalty to GIA. However, intellectual differences soon led to tense group dynamics. In January 1995, GIA's leadership purged all Algerianists (those members who were from the "League for Da'wa and Jihad" and claimed intellectual association to Sheikh Ahmed Sahnoun, the father of the Algerian Islamic movement) and left the *takfirs* untouched (Roy & Sfeir, 2007).

GIA first began to inflict its fatwas on foreigners in Algeria and subsequently upped its ammo while gaining international notoriety. Under the Salafi emir Djamel Zitouni (alias Abou Abderrahman Amin) a series of events occurred, including the 1994 hijacking of Air France Flight 8969 in Algeria and the killing of three passengers; the 1995 France bombings that killed eight and injured 157 in the cities of Paris and Lyon, including an attack in a school in Lyon; the 1996 beheading of seven Tibherine Algerian monks; and the 1998 civilians massacre in Algerian villages surrounding Algiers (Boeke, 2016; Roy & Sfeir, 2007). From 1993 to 1998, some 100,000 civilians lost their lives, most dying at the hands of the GIA. By 1993, GIA was enlisting upwards of 500 young men per week (Vriens, 2009).

Collectively, these events led to a splintering within GIA and GSPC (the Salafist Group for Preaching and Combat). A Salafist Qur'anic interpretation backed by Osama Bin Laden and Al Qaeda was formed from its remnants with the sole purpose of waging jihad on government targets. The 1997 fatwa by Hacène Hattab (alias Abu Hamza) and Zerabib Ahmed (alias Cheikh Ahmed Abou al-Bara), calling for an end to the indiscriminate targeting of civilians was ignored and advanced the push for the creation of a new kind of organization (Smith, 2010). Hacène Hattab and Zerabib Ahmed created GSPC on April 24, 1998, by taking over the networks and phalanges (tightly knit units located in the *Wilayas* [cities] of Jijel, Sétif, Batna, El Oued, and Tebessa) of the GIA (Roy & Sfeir, 2007). The creation of GSPC initiated a new wave of Algerian ethno-nationalism (Smith, 2010). GSPC then became the principal Islamic movement and anyone working for the Algerian state was viewed as their enemy. Hattab was appointed emir of the group's eastern region, Kabyle, in Algiers and spoke against the 1995 purging of the Algerianists.

By 1997, GSPC and the fighting wing of *Suni Front Islamique du Salut's* (FIS; the Islamic Salvation Army) – *Armée Islamique du Salut* (AIS; the Islamic Salvation Army) – founded in 1994, announced a truce and other groups, such as Al Bakoun Ala El-Ahd which spun-off from FIS in 1991 and was based in the United Kingdom under the leadership of Kamereddine Kharbane and Boudjemâa Bounoua, pleaded allegiance to GSPC and became its logistical and propaganda tool. By September 1998, in addition to battling AIS, GIA began to concentrate its efforts on the toppling of the Algerian government.

As GSPC developed militarily, executing guerilla-style attacks and using small arms (mortar, rocket, and improvised explosive device), political governance structures across the Wilayas emerged. In fact, GSPC was more disciplined than other organizations and thus less susceptible to internal dysfunction and conflict. This allowed the group to expand its operations and create sleeper cells in Algeria, greater North Africa, and later in Mali. Later, the charter (el-Mithaq) of GSPC spelled out its function and structure which divided the governance of the Political Directorate and the Military Directorate. GSPC then established its own killing squads and financed itself through various legal and illegal measures ranging from the acquisition of lands, both residential and commercial, charitable donations, coercion, and smuggling. Moreover, during its tenure, GSPC managed to establish several foreign cells in Europe (Belgium, Spain, Italy, France, and the United Kingdom) and garner support from other global terrorist organizations, primarily Al Qaeda.

In the early 2000s, the Algerian government began to grant amnesty and serval GSPC fighters took it, leading to an internal upheaval. By 2003, the members of GIA who had not joined GSPC were hunted down and killed by the government. In late 2003, under Hattab, GSPC pledged an oath of fealty (*bayat*) to Osama bin Laden and Mullah Mohammed Omar (then supreme commander and spiritual leader of the Taliban and de facto leader of Afghanistan from 1996 to 2001). However, in 2004, Hattab resigned (and was later killed in an antiterrorist operation), and he was replaced by his second in command Nabil Sahraoui, until Abdelmalek Droukdel (alias Abu Musab Abdel Wadoud) took over as emir of GSPC in February 2005. Droukdel was viewed as a counterbalance to Mokhtar Belmokhtar who was the group's southern commander and future founder of Al-Mourabitoun.

From GSPC to AQIM

On September 11, 2006, 5 years after the 9/11 attacks on New York City, GSPC, under the leadership of Droukdel, was first recognized by Osama bin Laden and Ayman al-Zawahiri and then announced its full allegiance[4] to Al Qaeda and its global jihad fight, and Droukdel pleaded *bayat* to Al Qaeda's leaders. GSPC took 2 years to negotiate its merger with Al Qaeda, who argued that GSPC's agenda was too nationalist in its orientation and Al Qaeda's leaders questioned what the group could bring to the global fight against far enemies. On January 26, 2007, GSPC changed its official name from the *Islamic Jihad Base* (*Qaidat al-Jihad*) to the *Maghreb al-Islami* (QJMI) and what the West calls Al Qaeda in the Land of the Islamic Maghreb (AQIM). However, it was during this time that the AQIM's fight moved from a national struggle toward a transnational battle. Shortly after its name change, Droukdel sent GPSC/AQIM fighters to fight alongside Al-Zarqawi in Iraq, leader of Al Qaeda in Iraq (AQI), to confront their common enemy and rid the land of the American occupiers. AQIM's foray in Iraq would begin its entry into the fight for global jihad, and it is during this time, its soldiers would learn and refine their military techniques that would allow them to carry out horrific acts of violence against state and non-state actors alike. Once AQIM was rebranded, which represented a dramatic change from its earlier strategy, an upsurge in violence across Algeria began in April 2007 with the killing of 33 people from two suicide car bombs, one of which was at the prime minister's office. Later that year, a united Nations (UN) building and another government construction building were bombed, killing 60 people. By the end of the year, Ayman al-Zawahiri, AQIM's second in command, called for the cleansing of Spaniards and French by Africa's Muslim lands.

The civilian violence by AQIM only intensified in 2008 when 60 people were killed in bombings in towns outside of Algiers. Between 2008 and 2009, AQIM kidnapped several foreigners across the Sahel (including Mali, Mauritania, and Niger) and held them for ransom until this was paid in 2010. In effect, 2010 commenced the period when AQIM became highly active, and this was compounded by the fact that France's then President Nicolas Sarkozy issued a declaration of war against the group when its troops carried out a raid on the Mauritania–Mali border. AQIM responded to France's declaration with its own declaration of war against its so-called "far enemy." These pronouncements saw AQIM refocusing its efforts and intensifying the scope and pace of its violent attacks in the Saharan basin. By 2011, attacks were once again revered as four successful suicide bombings took place during a 2-month period and culminated in an attack upon Algeria's premier military academy, *Acadèmie Militaire Interarmes* (AMIA) at Cherchell, which killed 18 people (Pillar, 2011). These activities eventually led to the United Nations Security Council, the United States, and the European Union naming AQIM as a terrorist group.

In mid-2011, AQIM suffered an ideological blow when a group of its members left to form *Mouvement pour l'unicité et le jihad en Afrique de l'Ouest* (MUJAO; the Movement for Oneness and Jihad in West Africa), founded by Hamad al-Khairy[5] and Ahmed el-Tilemsi,[6] with the aim of spreading jihad across a wider section of West Africa, which was not an area that AQIM was interested in penetrating. While the split was primarily viewed as a Black-African-led one, as Algerians historically dominated AQIM, in reality, the splinter was caused over ideological jihadism, the role of religion, funding, social strategies, and insurgency tactics (Boas, 2014). The ideological crisis that AQIM suffered before the splinter was driven by an identity steeped in Black-African ethnonational and racial politics as opposed to an Algerian-driven or Arab-dominated movement. However, by 2013, parts of MUJAO, led by Ahmed al Tilemsi, would merge with the militant group al-Mulathamun (The Masked Men) Battalion (AMB) to create Al Qaeda in West Africa under the al-Moulathamoun Group (the Sentinels),[7] while the remaining faction of MUJAO, under the leadership of Sultan Ould Badi, functioned independently. More importantly, in addition to MOJWA, since its rebranding, AQIM has given rise to a number of offshoots across the region, including Boko Haram (aka the Islamic State in West Africa; inclusive of its splinter group in 2010, Al Qaeda in the Lands Beyond the Sahel [Ansaru]) (Aronson, 2014). The aim of AQIM and its various sleeper cells and factions is to attack Western targets (ranging from security forces to kidnappings to extortion). Since its allegiance to Al Qaeda, AQIM's anti-Western rhetoric has increased as it seeks to create a caliphate through the overthrowing of apostate African regimes.

A Crisis of Leadership

When the Islamic State[8] renounced its allegiance to Al Qaeda in June 2014 and set out to proclaim its own caliphate, something that was at the heart of Al Qaeda's "General Guidelines for the Work of Jihad" (Holbrook, 2017), AQIM's leadership under Droukdel began to wane as new leaders across the Sahara, with different ideologies, began jostling for power. In fact, AQIM's leadership declared the Islamic State's caliphate as illegitimate while encouraging the creed of "the Islamic Spring," which called for the greater unification of Sunni Muslims. Thus, AQIM, Al Qaeda, and the Islamic State began to compete for recruits, funding, and the alcalde of global jihadist groups. In light of its internal crisis of leadership, Porter (2011) argues that AQIM's media arm, Al Andalus Foundation, "regularly releases statements claiming responsibility for attacks and employs the vocabulary and symbolism of Salafi-jihadi thought" (p. 5), employing a Salafi-jihadi discourse grounded in the rhetoric of "*fitna* (disorder), *jahiliyya* (pre-Islamic ignorance), *fasad* (corruption), and the importance of fighting for the return of the proper way of life" (p. 7). This has become AQIM's main recruitment tool to fight the "great satan" (the West and current and former occupier of Arab lands) that governs the apostate states through its proxies (police, intelligence apparatuses, judiciary, intelligence, and elites) who aim to secularize the poor (Holbrook, 2017).

AQIM's ultimate endgame is the replacement of all apostate states and regimes with Sharia states governed by Sharia core principles and rules. Moreover, AQIM also sought to strengthen its global jihad mission by supplying several groups across the region with weapons, support, and training, including Boko Haram to carry out its 2001 attack on the UN office in Abuja, Nigeria (Aronson, 2014). In 2015, AQIM and Al-Moulathamoun merged and repledged allegiance to Al Qaeda's core leadership. Under the merger, and using the name AQIM, both groups were able to tap into each other's resources to undertake raids in Mali, Burkina Faso, and the Ivory Coast in 2015. Then, in 2017, AQIM spearheaded the merging of several local jihadist groups – AQIM's Sahara division, Al-Mourabitoun, the Islamist Tuareg organization

Ansar al-Dine (AAD; Defenders of the Faith),[9] and the Katibat Macina Liberation Front of Ansar al-Dine (MLF; the Macina Liberation Front) – to form Jamaat Nusrat al-Islam wal Muslimeen (JNIM; the Group to Support Islam and Muslims) which is led by the historical leader of Ansar al-dine, Iyad Ag Ghaly. This move also aligns with AQIM's change in its operational directions in the Sahara/Sahel region, which resulted from changing geostrategic circumstance across the region; as the organization's actions became quelled in Algeria, it began to expand in other countries. In essence, it is using its strong foundation, stemming from the Algerian Civil War, to project itself as a global terrorist organization rather than as a regional affiliate of the local terrorist branch for historical terror groups such as Al Qaeda.

In an age of anti-Islamic rhetoric and calls for more profound adherence to stricter Islamic teachings, AQIM remains a significant global terrorist threat. Since 2017, with the Libyan instability becoming unsolvable and the demise of the Islamic State's influence and territory across Syria and Iraq, as well as its subsequent banishment to the desolate landscape of Badiyat al-Sham (the Syrian Desert), which encompasses some 500,000 square kilometers spanning Southeastern Syria, Northeastern Jordan, Northern Saudi Arabia, and Western Iraq, AQIM has emerged as a regional leader in terrorism. AQIM returned to large-scale terrorism in 2017 with the killing of 77 people and the injury of dozens more in Gao, Northern Mali. AQIM poses a significant threat to regional stability and America's nationalist agenda under President Donald Trump's administration. For too long, America has ignored the rise of Islamic militantism in Africa, instead focusing on and responding to threats of greater Islamization in the Middle East. This neglect poses further danger to America's future foreign policy agenda: AQIM has emerged as a regional player by extending its terrorist networks and cells beyond Algeria to northern Africa, Europe, and soon the United States.

The 2017 emergence of JNIM, under the Malian Tuareg jihadist, Iyad Ag Ghaly, as part of AQIM's intensification process of bringing several groups under the same ideological banner, has security implications for US foreign policy in North Africa and by extension the rest of Middle East. Moreover, AQIM views JNIM as its local affiliate on the ground as it seeks to expand its global influence and recruitment. While the AQIM operational center remains in Algeria, it continues to inflict harm on its far enemies and their citizens. This new strategy of jihad expansionism is both regionally (from Algeria to the Sahara/Sahel to West Africa) and internationally (Europe) steeped in a progressive convergence of interests around global terrorism. These strategies have tremendous consequences for America's security, both foreign and domestic. AQIM, with its strong centralized Algerian leadership, is showing that it is here to play the long game as it continues to morph and adapt to the changing geopolitical circumstances. In short, Algeria should not be treated as strategic backwater country, but as a policy priority in the global fight against terrorism.

Conclusion

Today, AQIM primarily operates in Algeria, Mali, Niger, Libya, Mauritania, and Tunisia. It is responsible for the execution of frequent attacks in North and West Africa. However, the lawlessness of the southern Algerian borders and the ungoverned spaces throughout northern Niger, northern Mali, and eastern Mauritania have been incubators for cementing AQIM's strength in the region as governments have failed to undertake effective counter-terrorism measures against the group (Porter, 2011). With the rise and later banishment of Islamic States, AQIM has also had to crystallize its core mission to secure recruits as Tunisians and Moroccans accounted for a very significant portion of the foreign fighters making up the ranks of the Islamic State. Since AQIM operates and seeks to govern large swaths of territory as part of its transnational jihadist philosophy, its leadership hierarchy and allegiance are always shifting and coalescing around different groups; however, the mission remains the same: creating Sharia states based on Arabic tribal practices, cultural beliefs, and allegiance to the Prophet Muhammad in the form of the Oath of Hudaybiyyah (bay`at al-ridwân) (Guidere, 2011).

AQIM's affiliated statist with the global Al Qaeda movement is not one that penetrates at the operational level, and it is very similar to other ideological relations that other AQ-affiliates, such as AQI and Al Qaeda in the Arabian Peninsula (AQAP) have. In other words, AQIM, while affiliated with Al Qaeda, is still driven by its mission of attacking near enemies (in the Sahel and Sahara) and far enemies (France, Spain, and the United Kingdom). Thus, AQIM, should not be misconstrued as an external force of Al Qaeda but as a "complex and multi-dimensional group that combines a Salafist ideological orientation" and "pursued strategies of integration in the region based on a sophisticated reading of the local context" (Boas, 2014, pp. 1–2).

Instability across the region saw many of AQIM's fighters leaving for Libya, Syria, and Iraq. However, the international military offensive against Islamic State (IS) has meant that IS has lost its caliphate status and large cities such as Mosul, Dabiq, and Raqqa. IShas been banished to the desolate landscape of *Badiyat al-Sham* (the Syrian Desert), which encompasses some 500,000 square kilometers spanning Southeastern Syria, Northeastern Jordan, Northern Saudi Arabia, and Western Iraq, famous for its caves and rugged Mountains. The Islamic State's defeat has allowed AQIM to become the predominant Islamist insurgency in a region that holds enormous swaths of open land, frail central governments, porous institutions, and unprotected borders that are ripe for exploitation and the enactment of transnational criminal activities.

Further Reading

Chivvis, C. S. & Liepman, A. (2013). *North Africa's Menace: AQIM's Evolution and the US Policy Response*. Santa Monica, CA: RAND Corporation.

Toney, M. S. (2013). *Organizational Behavior Profile: Al Qaeda in the Islamic Maghreb*. CreateSpace Independent Publishing Platform.

Venter, Al J. (2018). *Al Qaeda in the Islamic Maghreb*. Barnsley, UK: Pen & Sword Books Limited.

Notes

1 Also called Al Qaeda in the Lands of the Islamic Maghreb (AQLIM).

2 The others were *Mouvement Islamique Armee* (MIA; the Islamic Armed Movement),and *Suni Front Islamique du Salut* (FIS; the Islamic Salvation Army) backed *Armée Islamique du Salut* (AIS; the Islamic Salvation Army). Historically, GIA fought against MIA, a mountainous group and the first post-coup group to be formed in 1992. In 1994, some of the

members of MIA, the *Mouvement pour un 'etat Islamique* (MEI; the Movement for an Islamic State), and a few other smaller groups joined together to create FIS. Some MIA members later joined the GIA.

3 MEI became a separate organization after the purges of the Algerianists.

4 Under Nabil Sahraoui's leadership, the group in 2003 pledged allegiance to bin Laden.

5 Aided in the 2008 kidnapping of the Canadian ambassador, Robert Fowler, in Niger.

6 One of the masterminds of the 2011 kidnapping of two French nationals, in Niger, in 2011.

7 Also spelt Al Murabitun, Al Moulathamoun, Al Mulathamun Battalion, and Al Mourabitoun.

8 Since 2014, when the name was changed to *al-Dawlah al-Islāmiyah* (the Islamic State). This is the current manifestation of the following: *Jama'at al-Tawhid wa-l-Jihad* (2000–2004); *Al Qaeda in the Land of Two River* (AQI; 2004–2006); *Majlis Shura al-Mujahidin* (2006); *Islamic State of Iraq* (2006–2013); and *Islamic State of Iraq and al-Sham* (2013–2014). Under Caliph Abu Bakr al-Baghdadi, the Islamic State sought to redraw colonial borders to establish a caliphate – a state based on Islamic rules of law – while at the same time attracting foreign fighters. Prior to its losing territory in 2017, the Islamic State was defined as a state in physical terms since it held physical presence, a multi-ethnic army of both foreign and regional Muslims, and several multilayered administrative structures of governments.

9 Ansar Dine was founded in 2011 by Iyad Ag Ghaly with the aim of establishing Shariah law across Mali. AQIM views Ansar Dine as its southern arm in Mali and has instructed it to act as AQIM's domestic movement in the country.

References

Aronson, S. L. (2014, April). AQIM's threat to Western interests in the Sahel. *CTC Sentinel*, 7(4), 6–10.

Boas, M. (2014, April). Guns, money and prayers: AQIM's blueprint for securing control of Northern Mali. *CTC Sentinel*, 7(4), 1–6.

Boeke, S. (2016). Al Qaeda in the Islamic Maghreb: Terrorism, insurgency, or organized crime? *Small Wars & Insurgencies*, 27(5), 914–936.

Guidere, M. (2011, February). The tribal allegiance system within AQIM. *CTC Sentinel*, 4(2), 5–10.

Holbrook, D. (2017). The Spread of its Message: Studying the Prominence of al-Qaida Materials in UK Terrorism Investigations. *Perspectives on Terrorism*, 11(6). http://www.terrorism analysts.com/pt/index.php/pot/article/view/658/htm

Kepel, G. (2002). *Jihad: The trail of political Islam*. Cambridge, MA: Belknap Press of Harvard University Press.

Lebovich, A. (2011, September). AQIM returns in force in Northern Algeria. *CTC Sentinel*, 4(9), 8–11.

Martinez, L. (2000). *The Algerian Civil War, 1990–98*. New York, NY: Columbia University Press.

Pillar, P. R. (2011, September). American perceptions of terrorism in the post-9/11 decade. *CTC Sentinel*, 4(9), 1–3.

Porter, G. D. (2011, February). AQIM's objectives in North Africa. *CTC Sentinel*, 4(2), 5–8.

Roy, O., & Sfeir, A. (2007). *The Columbia world dictionary of Islamism*. New York, NY: Columbia University Press.

Smith, G. A. (2010). Al Qaeda in the Lands of the Islamic Maghreb. *Journal of Strategic Security*, 2 (2), 53–72. http://dx.doi.org/10.5038/1944-0472.2.2.2

Vriens, L. (2009, May 27) *Armed Islamic Group (Algeria, Islamists). A profile of the Algerian terrorist organization, Armed Islamic Group (GIA)*. Council on Foreign Relations. https://www.cfr.org/backgrounder/armed-islamic-group-algeria-islamists

Chapter 47

Al Qaeda

Raphaël Leduc
Graduate Institute of International and Development Studies, Geneva, Switzerland

Contents

Introduction 325
First Generation: Al Qaeda Rises 326
Second Generation: Transcending 'The Mother' 328
Al Qaeda: The Next Generation 330
Conclusion 332
Further Reading 333
References 333

Introduction

The discussions surrounding contemporary terrorism have, for the most part, been imprisoned in a grammar of security. This has led to an analysis of Al Qaeda that characterizes it as an existential threat to Western, and particularly American, well-being. This approach has been dubbed the 'new terrorism' approach and has dominated terrorism studies since the 1990s. It has treated terrorists (mostly those stemming from Islamic groups, in particular, Al Qaeda) as actors bent on (irrational) destruction which cannot be negotiated with (Crenshaw 2007). Such an approach to analyzing these 'new' trends has not only led to a straitjacketing of the phenomenon, making for expedient policy-making in the name of the Global War on Terror (Stampnitzky, 2013) but also thin conceptualizations of core questions which led to unsatisfactory answers. If new terrorists are irrational actors who take pleasure in killing (Laqueur 2001), then any interest in their *modus operandi* is pointless and, it follows that any attempts at designing courses of actions to deal with them will be in vain, whether those strategies consist of deterrence, coercion, or negotiation.

This chapter seeks to provide an overview of the transmutations of Al Qaeda by addressing core questions of interest for security professionals and academics. It will

DOI: 10.4324/9781315144511-50

do so by stepping outside the framework of 'new terrorism' and replacing it with an inquiry based on the historical method to answer the following questions: What is Al Qaeda? What is its *modus operandi?* How did it evolve? What is likely to be its future trajectory? To answer these questions, this chapter maps Al Qaeda by contextualizing it within the three generations of members that filled both its ranks and those of its offshoots. The first generation consists of those (mostly Arab) foreign fighter veterans who fought against the Soviet Union during its invasion of Afghanistan (1979–1989), and who were catapulted into the international stage through the use of large-scale, complex transnational terrorist attacks during the 1990s and 2000s. The second generation covers the transmutation of Al Qaeda from a relatively centralized organization to an increasingly franchised network and the eventual eclipse of its brand by one of its offshoots, the Islamic State (IS). Finally, the third generation looks at the future of the foreign combatants currently in Syria and Iraq and what the end of the ongoing conflicts in these regions means for international security.

First Generation: Al Qaeda Rises

The Soviet invasion of Afghanistan was both constitutive and formative for Al Qaeda. It was constitutive because it provided Al Qaeda with its initial structure as an outwardly focused organization to fight the far enemy, but also just as importantly with its initial cadre of members: Arab foreign fighter veterans of the conflict who came from abroad to fight in Afghanistan. It was formative because it taught Al Qaeda's leadership important lessons that would become the core of the organization's strategic and operational doctrines. This section will look at the lifecycle of Al Qaeda as a corporate entity from those foundational years up to its transmutation following the Western reactions to the apoapsis of its operational success, the 2001 attacks on the United States.

Prior to the Soviet invasion, Afghanistan was already embattled in an internal conflict, but the mainstream opposition to the Afghan state did not cooperate with Islamists. It was the Soviet invasion which prompted cooperation between the opposition and Islamists as the latter could secure greater quantities of outside aid more effectively, mainly through Pakistan (Malet, 2013). The precursors for Al Qaeda were thus organizations that facilitated not only the movement of funds and material to the Afghan insurgency, but also that of transnational fighters. Maktab al-Khidamat, founded by Abdullah Azzam, was likely the most influential among them because of its vast publication network, in particular the magazine *Al Jihad* (Dorronsoro, 2005). As the conflict ended, infighting among different insurgent factions began (which included foreign fighters). The leadership of Maktab al-Khidamat bemoaned this turn of affairs and sought to redirect the group of veteran foreign fighters outwardly to defend the *ummah* (Malet, 2013), this impetus would eventually become a campaign against the far enemy – the United States and its allies.

Al Qaeda was formed in this context. As the veterans of the conflict were denied return to their home countries (Schweitzer and Shay, 2003), they could not demobilize. This gave entrepreneurial individuals like Osama bin Laden a ready cadre of veterans with which to populate Al Qaeda.

The victory against a superpower also demonstrated to the fighters the feasibility of winning, as a non-state group, against one of the leading powers of the time. The fact that states could be defeated was probably one of the most important lessons for this group. The foundation of the Al Qaeda project was constituted from the Afghanistan experience. The organization was grounded on three pillars: '(i) the relocation of authority [away from the state], (ii) circumventing of the state, and (iii) the militaristic empowerment of a non-state actor' (Ould Mohamedou 2011, 47). Al Qaeda interpreted its victory in Afghanistan as the achievement of dedicated and trained individuals who won despite what they saw as little outside support from Muslim countries. A significant level of planning and coordination in attacks executed by trained individuals would become a staple of Al Qaeda's attacks for the whole 1990s and early 2000s. The first attack attributed to Al Qaeda, a set of attacks on different hotels in Yemen (1992), validated the efficacy of their nascent doctrine as the leadership interpreted the United States' decision to not set up bases in Yemen as a victory (Scheuer 2006). In sum, the initial phase in Al Qaeda's establishment focused on the training of operatives, meticulous planning, and the cementing of a doctrine for a novel way of pressing war against states.

The 'Al Qaeda method of war' or its *modus operandi* thus took the modern applications of military power to their logical limit. If force dispersion and defense in-depth are the best means of protecting one's force against modern, highly accurate, and destructive weaponry (Biddle, 2007), then Al Qaeda arguably followed those precepts by echeloning them throughout the globe, effectively creating a battlespace that cuts through state borders, communities, and within civilian populations across the planet. The goal of this method of war would be to punish what it saw as wrongful policies, primarily the US engagement in the Middle East. The rationale for targeting civilians was twofold. First, bypassing the enemy's strong points: in this case, all the security forces of a state in order to go after the center of gravity of the state, understood to be its critical infrastructures (hence the attacks on major transportation networks, the Pentagon, and the World Trade Center). This justification is, similarly to the principle of force dispersion, taking modern methods of war to their logical extreme. The second justification for the targeting of civilians by Al Qaeda is that, according to them, individual citizens share a collective responsibility for the actions of their leaders, thus they become collectively responsible for the policies of their state (Ould Mohamedou, 2011). This rationale is eerily similar to the logic of attacking civilian morale (through strategic terror bombing) to effect changes in their government. As such, Al Qaeda's motives and rationale for their *modus operandi* are not quite out of step with traditional methods of war. It is the strategy and tactics used to achieve their goals and justified through these rationales that are novel in the scope of their application.

Al Qaeda innovated by bringing privatized violence to a transnational scale, whereas in the past, terrorism had been relatively contained within a restricted geographical area. For example, the violence in Ulster, Northern Ireland, averaged 200 deaths per year between 1968 and 1979, which is equivalent to about 230,000 deaths in the United States throughout the period. It was 'only the smallness of Ulster, its comparative remoteness within Britain and Europe, and extremely low level of outside intervention in the struggle that has kept interest in the problem in a minor key' (O'Day, 1979, 122). Unlike Irish terrorists in Ulster, Al Qaeda has specifically targeted Western metropolis using high-impact attacks. They brought the remote to the local in a way that is impossible to ignore. The September 11, 2001 attacks in New York and Washington represent the apoapsis of the Al Qaeda *modus operandi* partly because this operation brought the local (US and its allies) to the remoteness of Afghanistan (and later) Iraq on a scale that was difficult to anticipate.

The period that followed the 2001 attacks on the United States represents the beginning of the propagation of Al Qaeda from one (relatively) consolidated structure which took marching orders from the central command to a decentralized franchise system (Ould Mohamedou, 2011). This process was necessary to ensure the continuity of the organization following the intervention in Afghanistan by the United States which displaced Al Qaeda out of its haven in the country. This shift is marked by a bigger emphasis on local branches (franchises) and attacks against the allies of the United States. While the organizational structure changed, the *modus operandi* and *casus belli* did not. The demands of Al Qaeda remained consistent throughout this period and echoed the three demands from 1996: (i) that the United States ends its military presence in the Middle East, (ii) that it ends its support of Israel as it relates to its relationship with Palestine, and (iii) stops supporting Muslim and Arab regimes which were seen as corrupt by Al Qaeda (Ould Mohamedou, 2011, 97).

Whereas prior to 2003 it was possible to point to one relatively unified group, it became increasingly proper to refer to this original core as Al Qaeda al Oum ('the mother') following US interventions in Afghanistan and Iraq (Ould Mohamedou, 2017). Its franchises can be understood as distinct entities, distinguished by the regional identifiers in their names. Significantly, the mother still demanded formal allegiance from its peripheries as it leased its brand to them. This would eventually create tensions with one of the franchises, which would become known as Al Qaeda in Iraq (AQI) and then the IS, when the latter formally repudiated Al Qaeda (Holdbrook, 2017) and as the heir to the ideological movement (Ould Mohamedou, 2017) brought Al Qaeda from the transnational back to the regional.

Second Generation: Transcending 'The Mother'

Al Qaeda al Oum's association with its franchises was nebulous (Ould Mohamedou, 2017). In part, this was caused by the brand being captured for instrumental and local purposes. Al Qaeda's success meant that it was an enviable brand to imitate for any group which sought to acquire more resources or notoriety. Thus, the 'Al Qaedaziation' of groups should not be seen as a growth in power of the organization. To the contrary, it could be indicative of a loss of authority and inability to take a leading role within the transnational Islamism movement. Equating this with Al Qaeda's defeat or 'death' is misinterpreting the evidence for two main reasons. First, if groups have a will to capture the brand, which is undeniably transnational, it means that they consider their audiences to be at the very least be transnational as well. While they might have a different *modus operandi* or *casus belli* than Al Qaeda, their grievances can, but do not have to be rooted in the same historical lineage as Al Qaeda's. To have 'defeated' Al Qaeda only to be presented with a plethora of insurgencies who see themselves as their intellectual heir with their own idiosyncrasies would be the definition of a pyric victory. Secondly, and more directly *à propos* for immediate security concerns, a generation forged in the conflict of Iraq over the last decade has apparently ascended to the throne as the apparent legitimate leaders of transnational Islamic terrorism (Ould Mohamedou, 2017): they are the IS who officially broke away from Al Qaeda in 2013 and formed AQI (Lefèvre, 2018; Holdbrook, 2017).

If, for the first generation, the Afghan conflict was both formative and constitutive, the same holds true for the second one in the case of Iraq. The US invasion of Iraq taught to the future members of AQI and IS methods of warfare that they would later re-use to establish and defend their proto-state project (Ould Mohamedou, 2017). Similarly, it generated an available pool of recruits from both local and foreign sources whose total numbers, in the case of foreigners, exceeded the Afghan conflict by a whole order of magnitude. The Soviet–Afghan conflict had attracted approximately 4000 foreign fighters who went on to form the core of Islamic transnational terrorism (estimates vary significantly; Malet, 2013), while the conflict which has encompassed Syria and Iraq attracted over 35,000, with about 5,000 thousand coming from the West (Barrett, 2017).

The main innovation of Al Qaeda was to privatize violence on a transnational scale. It used violence as a communication tool to try and convince its targeted audience. It did not seek to address the elites in and out of themselves but the populations directly, thus cutting through the state. This led to several technical innovations, such as the use of complex terrorist attacks by a group of commandos that made use of local infrastructures and networks. Complimentary to that, it also included the development of a media branch which was a necessary tool in this project. The offshoots of Al Qaeda which wrestled away from its central authority around 2013 have mostly abandoned these methods in favor of ones which were adapted to their local, idiosyncratic conflicts with their home states. IS in particular stands out for blurring the distinction between the local and foreign by mixing its struggle for territorial control, its provincial expansions, and the call for terrorist activities abroad as all part of the same conflict. For IS, transnational terrorism and state-building are part of the same struggle.

Table 47.1 Comparison of the Scale of the Terrorist Attacks Conducted by Al Qaeda and IS against the West

	Al Qaeda Core Organization[1]	*Islamic State*[2]	*Islamic State (Only Successful Attacks)*
Frequency	8	91	38
Plots per year	0.47	15.67	6.33
Average deaths	470.13	4.54	11.05
Total deaths	3761	409	409

1 Data from Ould Mohamedou, 2017, p. 55.

2 Data for 2011 to June 2015 from Hegghammer (2018). Data for July 2015 to December 2017 collected by the author.

The disassociation of Al Qaeda al Oum with its franchises in US domestic security analysis should be predicated on the fact that other than IS, no other franchise of Al Qaeda, whether it be in the Maghreb (Al Qaeda in the Islamic Maghreb or AQIM), or even in Afghanistan and Pakistan, have reliably claimed attacks in the West in the past half-decade. From those claimed by IS, a clear quantitative difference can be noted which supports the idea that Al Qaeda's high-level, technical operations are no longer being used by its offshoots.

With the apparent end to the ability of Al Qaeda in conducting high-level attacks in the West and the choice of its various offshoots to focus on local conflicts, US choices in terms of foreign policy are at a critical juncture. Ayman Al-Zawahiri has largely been unable to re-centralize Al Qaeda in any meaningful form. If the grievances that gave rise to Al Qaeda are to be taken seriously, and they should be, then the United States can best hamper a potential resurgence of Al Qaeda by reducing its direct engagement on the ground in Islamic countries and instead transferring security responsibilities to local state actors (Lynch, 2013). Instead of a focus on hunting down the different offshoots of Al Qaeda al Oum's leadership, the United States would probably be better served in assessing the post-Al Qaeda situation in regions where they formerly had strong ties, a good example of that is Afghanistan which could be used as a ground for a proxy war between Pakistan and India (Lynch 2013).

Al Qaeda: The Next Generation

In trying to trace the future trajectory of Al Qaeda, there are cues, historical and otherwise, that make some alternatives more likely than others. This exercise in reducing the space of possibilities for the future of Al Qaeda is necessary in order to ensure that both research and policy-making stops being reactive when confronted with this phenomenon. This final section will enumerate the elements that are most likely to be constitutive of the next generation. First, historical cues point to the foreign fighters who joined the conflict in Syria and Iraq as likely candidates to continue the vision of Al Qaeda. As those who have the fewest local contacts, they might be the individuals who are the most susceptible to carrying on the transnational fight to the far enemy. A second likely possibility is that another of the franchises that stemmed from Al Qaeda al Oum might be able to claim the spotlight as the leader of transnational Jihad. Finally, Al Qaeda, as an organization, might itself resurface under the guise of a new leader that is better able to capture the attention of transnational Islamist movements than the post-Osama Bin Laden leadership was able to.

The grievances that gave rise to Al Qaeda's oft-repeated demands toward the United States and its allies are still present to this day. Its policy toward Israel and its involvement with governments and military presence in predominantly Muslim countries can still be interpreted by would-be supporters of Al Qaeda as problematic. Thus, Al Qaeda provides groups with an easily identifiable brand and model to use if they wish to air those grievances. This might resonate particularly strongly with those individuals who were foreign to the region but nonetheless joined territorial IS. Many will have few local roots left after the defeat of IS and are increasingly faced with governments who do not want to allow them to return to their home countries through travel restrictions and criminalization, including advocating for their killing as the only 'solution' for this group of veteran war-fighters. A similar policy by the international community in the aftermath of the Soviet–Afghan war led to a ready-made group of recruits for Al Qaeda that entrepreneurs were able to seize upon to kickstart their organization. The historical similarities are compounded by the fact that IS's territorial project is likely going to be a failure while Al Qaeda's fight against the far enemy and its methods have shown (at least to their supporters) that they can effectively change the behavior of their perceived enemies. Take for example the Madrid attacks (2004) which can be interpreted by Al Qaeda's supporters as having caused the decision of the Spanish to pull out of Iraq, a decision that was made after the attacks ahead of parliamentary elections. Another example is the 1992 attacks of hotels in Yemen which Al Qaeda credits as having pre-empted the establishment of US bases in the country.

Al Qaeda's *modus operandi* remains a powerful tool to give a sense of purpose to the transnational, stateless vagabonds which are likely to be created by a repetition of the anti-foreign fighter policies. A potential alternative to these policies could be found in the demobilization, disarmament, and reintegration policies applied in post-civil conflict zones. Some countries such as Denmark, Norway, Sweden, and Germany (Schuurman and van der Heide, 2016) have begun innovating with deradicalization programs for returnees, and security professionals should pay close attention to the results of these programs as they could be a model worth emulating in order to prevent giving Al Qaeda (or one of its successors) easy access to additional groups of fighters. From the Afghan experience, not to mention a related literature on postwar reconstruction more generally, we know that it is the fighters for which there is no room outside their military profession in the post-conflict situation (either locally or at home) who are most likely to become the next generation of transnational fighters, whether by creating for themselves a space in a fragile state or potentially where Al Qaeda's offshoots already have influence. The former would be a repetition of what Al Qaeda did by establishing its base of operations in Afghanistan.

The Islamic State was successful in establishing a network of affiliated 'provinces,' yet most of the franchises which stemmed from Al Qaeda al Oum either remained indifferent to IS or actively opposed it (Ould Mohamedou, 2017, 61). For example, AQIM is probably the franchise which most strongly fought IS influence in Northern Africa, with IS acting as a unifier for Al Qaeda's offshoots in the region (Lefèvre, 2018). However, the transfer of the torch of transnational Islamism to another Al Qaeda franchise is problematic for two reasons. First, part of what made the relationship between these franchises and Al Qaeda al Oum problematic is the fact that they welcomed the use of the brand while keeping their focus to the local, sticking to their own *modus operandi* which was different from Al Qaeda's. Unless there are significant changes in their respective situations, there are no reasons to expect them to behave differently once territorial IS collapses.

Ould Mohamedou (2017) notes that the most likely resurgence of Al Qaeda will be through bin Laden's son (Hamza bin Laden) or someone else who can claim lineage directly to Al Qaeda's leadership. The treatment of the Al Qaeda brand and organization as a hereditary title would be heavily dependent on the context. It is going to rest not only on the presence of the grievances that led to Al Qaeda in the first place but also on a romanticization of its past achievements. A good starting point to analyze such constructions by would-be leaders of Al Qaeda is through their public communications. Hamza bin Laden has made five public declarations toward the West in the past 3 years (Ould Mohamedou, 2017, 184). Contrasting those statements with IS's declaration of emancipation from Al Qaeda (2013) and their comparative reception by their respective audiences would be one way to evaluate the success of upstart entrepreneurs in capturing the Al Qaeda brand.

Conclusion

This chapter has analyzed the trajectory of Al Qaeda from its foundation to the present day. The importance of stepping outside the logic of 'new terrorism' when analyzing this phenomenon cannot be understated. Al Qaeda has clear goals and a strategy to achieve them. Those have remained quite consistent over time, even as the organization's structure shifted and waned. Importantly, their brand has proven to be fungible, with different regional insurgencies able to mimic it for their own purposes. What has changed are the tactics used by Al Qaeda and its offshoots. Al Qaeda's focus was on highly complex, high-impact commando operations, while its offshoots have focused on the use of its brand as a good to be marketed to a 'mass market' audience of potential terrorists.

Those have had very noticeable, practical impacts on what kind of terrorist attacks have targeted the West in recent years. It remains open to speculation whether this type of attacks is going to outlive IS. A possible indicator that they will not is their lowered frequency in 2017 (20 foiled and executed plots) as opposed to 2016 (29 plots); however, those numbers should be used cautiously as terrorist attacks are rare events, and the link between the development of territorial IS and attacks in the West warrants further investigation. Finally, the evolution of Al Qaida and its offshoots have had some consistent patterns, for example, the apparent cyclical switch between a focus on the regional and a focus on the transnational. When Al Qaeda was founded, its initial cadre was based on the core of a group of about 4,000 virtually stateless foreign fighters who could not be demobilized. As the intensity of the conflicts in Iraq and Syria diminishes, a pressing concern will be what to do with the over 35,000 fighters who have joined this conflict (as well as defeated local fighters who might be unable to remain in their communities).

For many countries, the concern has been on denying them return because of the perceived heightened terrorist threat they pose. However, there have been no clear empirical links between returnees and a rise in domestic terrorism or its lethality (Leduc, 2016). In the absence of such evidence, it becomes important to focus on what the failure of allowing these fighters to demobilize entails, not only for the domestic security of the countries who are denying their return but also for global security. For the case of Western foreign fighters in particular, such NIMBYism (Not In My Backyard) is passing the buck of dealing with transnational insurgents to the countries that are less able or willing to (due to a lack of resource or because they directly benefit, as Afghanistan did in the past). Thus, policies that allow those fighters to demobilize and reintegrate should be at the core of any effective strategy that seeks to deal with the future of Al Qaeda and its franchises.

Further Reading

Leduc, R. (2016). Are Returning Foreign Fighters Dangerous? Re-investigating Hegghammer's assessment of the impact of veteran foreign fighters on the operational effectiveness of terrorism in the West. *Journal of Military and Strategic Studies*, 17(1), 83–103.

Lefèvre, R. (2018). The Resurgence of Al-Qaeda in the Islamic Maghrib. *The Journal of North African Studies*, 23(1–2), 278–281.

Ould Mohamedou, M.M. (2011). *Understanding Al Qaeda: Changing War and Global Politics.* London: Pluto.

References

Barrett, R. (2017). *Beyond the Caliphate: Foreign Fighters and the Threat of Returnees.* New York: The Soufan Center.

Biddle, S. (2007). *Military Power: Explaining Victory and Defeat in Modern Battle.* Princeton: Princeton University Press.

Crenshaw, M. (2007). The Debate Over 'New' vs. 'Old' Terrorism. *American Political Science Association Annual Meeting, paper.*

Dorronsoro, G. (2005). *Revolution Unending: Afghanistan 1979 to the Present.* New York: Columbia University Press.

Hegghammer, T. (2018). Coded Data on Jihadi Plots in the West, January 2011 – June 2015. http://hegghammer.com/text.cfm?path=2176. Accessed 18 January 2018.

Holdbrook, D. (2017). *Al-Qaeda 2.0: A Critical Reader.* London: C. Hurst & Co.

Laqueur, W. (1999). *The New Terrorism: Fanaticism and the Arms of Mass Destruction.* New York: Oxford University Press.

Laqueur, Walter (2001) *The New Terrorism: Fanaticism and the Arms of Mass Destruction.* New York: Oxford University Press.

Leduc, R. (2016). Are Returning Foreign Fighters Dangerous? Re-investigating Hegghammer's assessment of the impact of veteran foreign fighters on the operational effectiveness of terrorism in the West. *Journal of Military and Strategic Studies*, 17(1), 83–103.

Lefèvre, R. (2018). The Resurgence of Al-Qaeda in the Islamic Maghrib. *The Journal of North African Studies*, 23(1–2), 278–281

Lynch, T. F. (2013). The Strategic Defeat of bin Laden's Al-Qaeda and Implications for South Asian Security. In P. Bergen and K. Tiedemann (Ed.), *Talibanistan Negotiating the Borders Between Terror, Politics, and Religion.* New York: Oxford University Press.

Malet, D. (2013). *Foreign Fighters: Transnational Identity in Civil Conflicts.* New York: Oxford University Press.

O'Day, A. (1979). Northern Ireland, Terrorism, and the British State. In Y. Alexander, D. Carlton, and P. Wilkinson (Ed.), *Terrorism: Theory and Practice.* Boulder: Westview Press Inc.

Ould Mohamedou, M.M. (2011). *Understanding Al Qaeda: Changing War and Global Politics.* London: Pluto.

Ould Mohamedou, M.M. (2017). *A Theory of ISIS: Political Violence and the Transformation of the Global Order.* London: Pluto.

Scheuer, M. (2006). *Through our Enemies' Eyes – Osama Bin Laden, Radical Islam and the Future of America.* Dulles: Potomac Books.

Schwitzer. Y., Shay, S. (2003). *The Globalization of Terror.* Piscataway: Transaction.

Schweitzer, Yorum, Shay, Shaul (2003) *The Globalization of Terror: The Challenge of Al-Qaida and the Response of the International Community*. Piscataway, NY: Transaction Publishers.
Schuurman, B., van der Heide, L. (2016). Foreign Fighter Returnees & the Reintegration Challenge. *Radicalization Awareness Network*, 1–19.
Stampnitzky, L. (2013). *Disciplining Terror: how Experts Invented Terrorism*, Cambridge: Cambridge University Press.

Chapter 48

Ansar Allah

Robert Forster
University of Edinburgh, Edinburgh, United Kingdom

Hamish Kinnear
Independent Researcher, United Kingdom

Contents

Introduction 335
Origins 336
Ideology 337
Capabilities and Tactics 338
2004–2010: The Northern Insurgency 338
2011–2014: Ansar Allah Moves South 339
2015 to Present: The Civil War 340
Threats to US Interests 341
Conclusion 342
Further Reading 343
Note 343
References 343

Introduction

Ansar Allah is the political front of the armed political and religious movement known as the Houthi Movement that has been active in Yemen since 2004. Named after its initial founder, Hussein al-Badr al-Din al-Houthi, the movement began as a splinter faction of the more moderate Zaydi revivalist organization known as *al-Shabaab al-Mu'min* (the Believing Youth) that emerged in 1992 in the northern governorate of Saada near the Yemeni–Saudi border (Freeman 2009). The Houthis became an independent faction following a political disagreement among the leadership of the

DOI: 10.4324/9781315144511-51

Believing Youth, where Hussein al-Houthi opted for political action in response to the group's grievances. Between 2004 and 2010, the movement had a limited geographic reach, fighting an insurgency against the Yemeni government from Saada and in the surrounding governorates. The events of 2011, however, granted the organization the political space to bring its grievances to the national level as one of many segments of Yemeni society in opposition to the rule of President Ali Abdullah Saleh. During the United Nations (UN) and the Gulf Cooperation Council (GCC) sponsored political transition that took place after November 23, 2011, Ansar Allah pursued a dual strategy, participating in the mandated National Dialogue and constitution-drafting process in addition to strengthening the movement's territorial control in Saada and Amran governorates by force.

In an attempt to disrupt the transition and the growing political influence of the Islamist-tribal Islah party, segments of former President Saleh's political party, the General People's Congress (GPC), assisted Ansar Allah's consolidation of territory. Citing mismanagement and the unpopular decision to remove fuel subsidies by Yemen's National Unity Government led by President Abd Rabbu Mansour Hadi, Ansar Allah aided by segments of the GPC entered the capital, Sanaa, in September 2014. Hadi's government was thrown into crisis as the GCC roadmap guiding the transition was renegotiated with the participation of UN Special Envoy to Yemen, Ismail Ould Cheikh Ahmed. A "slow coup" then began as the two sides attempted to politically outmaneuver one another with Ansar Allah taking the upper hand. The crisis intensified when a dispute over the form of Yemen's federal regions resulted in Ansar Allah kidnapping Hadi's Chief of Staff on January 15, 2015, who was on his way to submit the final draft of the Yemeni constitution. In response, the Hadi government momentarily resigned before relocating to the southern port-city of Aden. Ansar Allah's steady progression toward Aden eventually led to Hadi calling for armed intervention against them, which was answered by a Saudi-led coalition on March 23, 2015, triggering the start of the Yemeni Civil War. This chapter looks at the origins, ideology, capabilities, and threats of the Houthi Movement and its political arm Ansar Allah in Yemen.

Origins

Three primary factors led to the rise of Ansar Allah and the Houthi Movement and their emergence from the Believing Youth. Since the end of the Zaydi imamate that had ruled northern Yemen until 1962, the governorates near the Saudi border were largely neglected by the central Yemeni state. This trend intensified through the co-option of local Sheikhs into the political umbrella of the ruling GPC without any benefits transferring to the local populous (Brandt 2017, 40–74). As a result, Saada governorate was and remains chronically underdeveloped – a trend that intensified after 2004.

Second, the cultural make-up of Saada shifted following the increase of Sunni influence into the Zaydi homeland. Zaydism, adhered to by about 25 per cent of Yemenis, is a form of Fiver Shi'ism sharing greater similarities to the Sunni Shafi'ism found elsewhere in Yemen than the practices of Twelver Shiites in Iran. Nonetheless, from the 1970s, driven by an increasingly powerful Saudi Arabia to the north as well as members within the GPC, Saada came under the increased influence of Sunni (particularly Salafi) jurisprudence. To counter this influence, the Believing Youth provided instruction in Zaydi principles and traditions to young men of the region, though as a grassroots organization, it avoided party politics (Lackner 2017, 151). Instead, Zaydi political parties such as al-Haqq and the Union of Popular Forces provided representation. Indeed, one of the leaders of the Youth, Hussein al-Houthi, served as a minister of parliament for al-Haqq from 1993 to 1997. Following a political dispute with other leaders in the Believing Youth in 2001, Hussein al-Houthi opted for political action (Almasmari 2010). Initially, support for al-Houthi's movement was limited and most supporters came from areas where the youth had held their summer camps and from loyal tribes (Lackner 2017, 150). The growing activism by the movement, however, drew attention from the Saleh regime, and in June 2004, the first of six rounds of conflict between the Houthis and the Yemeni government began after the latter launched a police operation against Hussein (Brandt 2017, 153).

Ideology

Ansar Allah is defined by a flexible ideology that has allowed the movement to maneuver politically and adapt to new situations without any costs to their legitimacy. The backbone of Ansar Allah's ideology stems from the speeches of Hussein al-Houthi before he was killed in the first round of conflict on September 10, 2004. Among other aspects, the ideological framework and narrative of the Houthis draws on the Iranian revolution and Hezbollah in Lebanon, which has led many to believe that the organization is directly supported by Iran. A study of al-Houthi's speeches identifies a narrative of three interconnected items (Weissenburger 2017). Firstly, Western encroachment is a threat to Yemen, and foreign influence has led to the loss of identity and erosion of knowledge, allowing for easier divisions in Yemeni society. The West, referred to explicitly as the United States and Israel, uses the narrative of the "War on Terror" as a pretext for colonization, invasion, and the theft of natural resources. Thus, to counter this influence, it is important for Yemenis to return to Islam, unite, and take a stand against the oppressors. These tenants are summarized in the Houthi's slogan: "Death to America, Death to Israel, Damn the Jews, Victory to Islam". It is worth noting that, Hussein's speeches were externally oriented, never explicitly calling for violence and with little direct criticism of President Saleh or the Yemeni government.

Another aspect of the Houthis ideology that stems of Zaydism is the belief that *sada* (singular: *sayyid*), or those with family lineage going back to the family of the Prophet, have a right to political and religious leadership. The idea of *sada* rule and the "theological correctness" of Zaydi Islam is a direct challenge to members of government in Yemen and Saudi Arabia (Lackner 2017). When confronted on their beliefs, the Houthis claim their purpose and ideology to be motivated by Zaydi revivalism and the fight against Sunni expansionism fueled by the Yemeni government. Indeed, Ansar Allah emerges as a counter-force to Sunni Jihadist groups that operate elsewhere in Yemen such as Al-Qaeda in the Arabian Peninsula that have directly attacked Houthi followers. In fighting Sunni expansionism, Ansar Allah, from early 2014 to December 2017, joined forces with former President Saleh to pursue the followers of the Islah party, an Islamist political party that includes Salafi and Muslim Brotherhood-linked wings (Anonymous 2017). For Ansar Allah, the aim was to target the Islamist factions within Islah responsible for the proselytization of Sunni doctrine in Yemen. In addition, one of the founders of Islah, Ali Muhsin al-Ahmar, as commander of the First Armored Brigade, was responsible for carrying out most of the combat operations against the Houthis between 2004 and 2010. Meanwhile, for Saleh, the aim was to pursue the most well-established grassroots political party that agitated for, and benefited from, his removal.

Capabilities and Tactics

From 2004 to 2018, Ansar Allah transformed from an incipient group of armed followers with limited territorial reach and poor training to maintaining a military and political presence in 14 of Yemen's 21 governorates and deploying a wide range of weaponry. This section provides an overview of the expanded capabilities of Ansar Allah over three periods: the six stages of the Northern Insurgency fought between 2004 and 2010, the 2011–2014 period of revolutionary upheaval and attempted negotiated transition, and the ongoing civil war that began in 2015.

2004–2010: The Northern Insurgency

It was during six cycles of conflict between 2004 and 2010 that Ansar Allah consolidated their military capabilities. The first clashes began in June 2004, when security forces attempted to capture Hussein al-Houthi after President Saleh requested his return to Sanaa. Fighting saw 130 casualties during the first week, and by September 10, government forces using tanks and warplanes managed to track down and kill the Houthi leader, upon which they withdrew and declared the rebellion over (Freeman 2009). The first round of fighting did not end favorably for the Houthis. Given the restricted reporting environment, eyewitness detail of their tactics at the time remains unclear, but the group managed to hold out for 3 months by using the rough terrain of the Saada highlands. Access to weaponry was not an issue, given that in 2001 between six and nine million small arms were in circulation in Yemen, but with the relative surprise of the government offensive, it is unlikely that the Houthis had much preparation or major stockpiles.

The premature withdrawal of security forces in September 2004 allowed the movement time to regroup and consolidate. The second round of the conflict did not break out until April 2005. Although the Houthis had lost their first leader, Hussein's father, Badr al-Din al-Houthi, took over as the effective spiritual leader of the movement. Military operations, meanwhile, were delegated both to members of the al-Houthi family, including Hussein's younger brother Abd al-Malik, and other prominent figures within the movement. This became a key strength of the group, as from then on military operations were decentralized and not reliant on one leader. This organizational structure was optimal for the spread of the movement across mountainous areas of Saada, over which it was a challenge to maintain effective lines of communication. Instead, groups worked autonomously and were thus harder for security forces to effectively combat and track down.

The localization of separate Houthi cells also enabled the group to integrate more closely with local armed tribes outside of their traditional areas of influence. As the fighting progressed and non-Houthis were increasingly affected by the indiscriminate violence of government forces in affected areas, armed local tribes joined in the rebellion. The conflict escalated as tribes in the region re-aligned as either *for* or *against* the Houthis or the Yemeni government (Brandt 2017; Lackner 2017, 152). While these local tribes rarely subscribed to Houthi ideology, they would typically be motivated by *qisas*, a retaliation in kind for the death of a member of a tribe, or *diya*, financial compensation in lieu of kind. Houthis became increasingly effective at weaponizing these local grievances against security forces, although tribes would frequently change sides depending on the circumstance.

The periodic ceasefires of the conflict also allowed the Houthi Movement space and time to regroup and consolidate at regular intervals and significantly develop their military capabilities. According to observers in 2009, most Houthi combatants would fight in "mini platoons" of three to five people, one of whom was a sniper, and quickly withdraw after any attack. In this way, losses were kept at a minimum and the military's principal advantage –technical superiority in the possession of advanced and heavy weaponry – was minimized. Ansar Allah also learned how to construct and develop defensive systems of trenches around settlements under their control, reducing the impact of artillery fire. Toward the end of the insurgency in 2010, Houthi fighters launched larger set-piece battles. In September 2009, for example, the Houthis allegedly used 70 armored vehicles and hundreds of armed fighters in an abortive assault on the Presidential Palace in Saada city (Salmoni, Loidolt, and Wells 2010, 155). However, these kinds of attacks were the exception, not the rule.

Access to arms was not an issue in a country with one of the highest rates of gun ownership and where gun ownership is culturally associated with masculinity (Salmoni, Loidolt, and Wells 2010, 197). Indeed, this latter point is likely a driver behind the existence of a large cohort of child soldiers within Ansar Allah's ranks. As far back as 2005, the Yemeni government has claimed that the Houthis receive support from the government of Iran (Overton 2005, 8–9). However, most coverage indicates that during the insurgency, Ansar Allah was able to acquire ample supplies of equipment – including assault rifles, grenades, and other heavy weaponry – on the black market and even from corrupt elements of the Yemeni security forces (Freeman 2009, 1009).

2011–2014: Ansar Allah Moves South

In the wake of the 2011 revolutionary upheaval in Yemen and the removal of President Saleh from power, the Houthis were peripheral in the transition process and, consequently, began to move further south. There is no indication that Ansar Allah's military capabilities noticeably expanded in this period. Rather, their success in moving south and eventually capturing Sanaa was the internal chaos of the central government, which was unable to consolidate its authority amidst the ousted former President's continuing attempts to undermine it and the constant pressure from a range of Yemeni political actors energized by the revolutionary upheaval.

Resistance to Ansar Allah was primarily from the Hashid tribal confederation. Traditionally, a political stronghold for the old regime, several prominent Hashidis were also prominent politicians in the Islah party. However, the once dominant position of the confederation in the highlands north of Sanaa was weakened by declining

Saudi funds. With less money, the confederation was unable to employ the powers of patronage and less able to pursue a successful war effort. Increasingly resentful tribes that belonged to the confederation were therefore more willing to work with the battle-hardened Houthis, and the group's capabilities and geographical extent expanded further in much the same way as they had during the 2004–2010 insurgency period. In January 2014, Ansar Allah's rapidly increasing power was clear to see in its capture and destruction of the family compound of the Al-Ahmars – the leading family of the Hashid confederation. By this time, it had also become clear that Ansar Allah were working in concert with their former enemy, President Saleh and his inner circle, who did not intend to respect the new political arrangement in Yemen (Brandt 2017, 338–39).

In an attempt to influence debate during the transition, Ansar Allah also developed an extensive media presence, with affiliated pundits providing interviews with national and international media. The capture of Sanaa also allowed the Houthis to take over several state-run media outlets, including Saba News, replacing staff with loyalists. Since 2015, media repression has increased, with the Houthis ranking second worst for press freedom worldwide (Nasser 2017).

2015 to Present: The Civil War

The scope of this section will be limited to a discussion of the current military capabilities of Ansar Allah – itself a complicated topic given that many of the combatants alongside the movement are renegade elements of the Yemeni army and/or (until his assassination in December 2017) Saleh loyalists. This represents a continuation of Ansar Allah's success at securing alliances with a range of armed groups dissatisfied with the political status quo. The actual number of Houthi combatants remains subject to intense debate and, for obvious reasons, is not made clear by Houthi leadership. Discounting the contribution of allied groups, however, Houthi numbers were estimated in 2015 at being as high as 30,000 regular and semi-regular combatants.[1]

What is clear, however, is that Houthi access to and use of advanced military technology increased vastly since the seizure of Sanaa in 2014. Most fighters are armed with AK47-type assault rifles, some heavier machine guns including the DSHK 12.6mm, and improvised light cannon (Lyamin 2017). Ansar Allah has also been documented using the 9K32 Strela-2 (SA-7) man-portable, shoulder-fired, low-altitude surface-to-air missile system (MANPAD), Kornet portable anti-tank guided missiles, and heavily armed pick-up trucks, predominantly the Toyota Hilux model, known as "technicals" (see Yemen Observer 2018). Unmanned ariel vehicle (UAV) attacks have been documented with relatively unsophisticated armaments. The documented missiles in possession of Ansar Allah include the R-17 Elbrus/SS1C "Scud B", the OTR-21 Tochka/SS-21 "Scarab", the North Korean Hwasong-5, a copy of the R-17 design, S-75 surface-to-air missiles, and modified S-75s, including the "Qaher 1" and "Qaher 2" that have ranges of 250 km and 400 km, respectively. Since 2016, Houthis have also launched the Burkan series of missiles that appear to also be modified R-17s that have a maximum range of 850 km (Binnie 2017).

With the addition of new weaponry and the increased territorial scope of areas under their control, it is likely that aspects of the tactics and structural organization of Ansar Allah fighting units have undergone at least some development. However, the extent of this change is unclear, as the access of independent researchers to the movement and the country has been severely restricted by the ongoing conflict. Critically, journalists have also faced heavy pressure and violence from all sides of the conflict and most reportage is heavily biased. Ansar Allah is also reported to engage in indiscriminate attacks on civilian soft targets through the shelling of civilian neighborhoods, use of human shields, landmines, assassination of political opponents, and enforced disappearances and hostage-taking. However, attacks are usually undertaken with conventional military equipment and not vehicle-borne improvised explosive devices and, only rarely, suicide bombings. An exception is the reported suicide attack on a Saudi frigate in the Red Sea, January 2017, when Houthi fighters allegedly rammed the ship with a smaller boat, according to a statement by the Arab Coalition (Al Omran and Fitch 2017).

Nonetheless, most strategy and tactics adopted during the latter stages of the 2004–2010 insurgency and onwards will not have substantively changed. The main factor behind this is that fact that Ansar Allah fighters are fighting a mostly static war in rough, highland terrain, similar to the fighting experienced in Saada. A cursory glance at the frontlines, as of September 2018, shows that they roughly follow the borders between lowland or flat areas and the highlands, where Saudi-led coalition airpower is largely ineffective. On occasions when Ansar Allah fighters fought outside of mountainous areas, they generally performed poorly or had limited ability to protect themselves against coalition airstrikes. Fighting on the coastal plains near Hodeida and Aden, for example, has largely been in favor of forces affiliated with the UN-recognized government. In the case of Aden and its surroundings, however, the Houthi cause was also of limited salience as the region historically suffered from repeated invasions by northern counterparts and hosts a burgeoning southern independence movement. A secondary factor has been that Ansar Allah's seizure of Sanaa did not grant them lasting access to the levers of state – a useful aid in building capabilities. Access to formal revenue flows through the Central Bank was briefly acquired in 2015 but lost again when it was moved to Aden in October 2016.

Threats to US Interests

Despite their infamous slogan, there is little indication that the Houthi Movement is actively seeking to target US armed forces, civilians, or infrastructure. However, the US role in training and arming the principal member of the Arab Coalition, Saudi Arabia, embroiled in combat across Yemen, does not exclude the potential for such actions in the future. Moreover, the *New York Times* reported in March 2018 on the deployment of US Special Forces in Yemen with the mandate to track down and destroy missile sites (Cooper, Gibbons-Neff, and Schmitt 2018). These factors are still peripheral; however, opportunist attacks could still take place. Currently, the only method of an active pursuit of United States and other foreign citizens is through the tactic of kidnapping or illegally detaining civilians as hostages for financial gain or political leverage. Omani mediation has been instrumental in facilitating the release of several US and other foreign detainees since the conflict began in 2015.

There is strong rhetorical support for Ansar Allah in state-funded Iranian press outlets (see, for example, PressTV 2018), and there are credible reports that the group has received technical military assistance from Iran. However, Ansar Allah is currently predominantly motivated by domestic concerns, and there is no evidence that the group has any intent to project its power outside of Yemen and the immediate region on the Saudi border. Consequently, the principal threat to US interests are Ansar Allah's missile attacks on targets in Saudi Arabia and on shipping in the Gulf of Aden. UAV attacks on airports in the UAE have also been claimed by the movement, although Emirati officials have denied this (Trew 2018).

Since occupying Sanaa and central Yemen in 2014–2015, the Houthis have been in control of most of the Yemeni military's arsenal of missiles, predominantly Soviet-era Scud models, which it has used in strikes across the border into Saudi Arabia. Reports and rumors circulated widely in pro-Hadi and Saudi media state that missiles and missile parts are imported from Iran (see, for example, Gareth Browne 2018). Reuters has quoted Iranian officials who state that their country has provided weapons, military training, and money to the Houthis (Bayoumy and Stewart 2016). The defense information provider Jane from IHS Markit states that the import of actual missile parts is dubious, and that Iranian technical assistance in the modification of existing Scud missiles is more likely (Binnie 2017). This improving technical capability appears to be reflected in the steadily increasing range of missiles over the course of the war. Despite some casualties, most of these missiles are intercepted by Saudi air defense and actual damage has been limited. Nevertheless, reports indicate that the missiles have reached as far as Riyadh, where US diplomatic infrastructure and officials are based (Dadouch and Browning 2018). There is no indication that US facilities and personnel are specifically being targeted by Houthi-launched missiles, but collateral damage is a slim possibility. Attacks on shipping in the Gulf of Aden has taken place on multiple occasions. In July 2018, Saudi Aramco suspended shipments through the Gulf of Aden after Houthi attacks on two oil tankers (Sheppard, al-Omran, and Ravel 2018). Nonetheless, the suspension had no tangible impact on oil markets given that the route around the Cape of Good Hope does not significantly increase transit time for a fungible product like oil that is easily stored and transported.

Piracy, principally an historic issue on the Somali coastline, has been more effectively policed in recent years, but Yemen remains an important transit country for migrants fleeing conflict in Africa. With regards to arms smuggling, Ansar Allah depends to some degree on the flow of weapons into the Arabian Peninsula and, consequently, the country remains a hub for weapons smuggling. A major figure in Yemeni arms smuggling, Fares Mohammed Manaa, was governor of Saada from 2011 to 2014. Manaa is reported to have facilitated the transfer of arms to al-Shabaab, the Somali insurgent group, and is under sanction by the UN (Paraguassu 2016).

Conclusion

Ansar Allah developed considerably since their initial formation as part of a regional rebellion against the Yemeni government. Via territorial consolidation in their traditional strongholds as well as capturing Sanaa, the organization gained more formal access to revenue flows as well as maintaining some support among the population under their control. Houthi leadership has gained considerable military and strategic knowledge as well as skillfully disseminating comprehensive although crude anti-government and Saudi propaganda efforts. Nonetheless, in militarily, many recruits are young and undertrained, and there is a struggle to maintain the bureaucracy needed to pay salaries to civil servants and fighters in their areas.

The Houthi slogan and the speeches of some of its leaders would imply that the group's principal concern is attacking the United States and Israel, but beyond kidnapping US and other foreign citizens in the country, there has been little active pursuit of these aims. In the short-term, hostage-taking will likely remain an opportunistic enterprise, as in the midst of a long-lasting civil conflict, the group will maintain a regional focus. However, given their missile and drone capabilities, the group may later choose to strike directly at US targets within range as a response to US support of the Saudi-led coalition. The most likely course of action in this regard would be an attempted strike on the US Navy in the Gulf of Aden and the Red Sea. This remains highly unlikely; however, a direct strike on US armed forces would provoke a heavy US military response and increased American support for the Saudi-led coalition.

Further Reading

Brandt, Marieke. 2014. 'The Irregulars of the Sa'ada War: 'Colonel' Sheikhs and 'Tribal Militias' in Yemen's Huthi Conflict', pp. 105–122. In Helen Lackner (ed.), *Why Yemen Matters: A Society in Transition*. London: Saqi.

Day, Steven W. 2012. *Regionalism and Rebellion in Yemen: A Troubled National Union*. Cambridge: Cambridge University Press.

Yadaw, Stacey Philbrick. 2017. 'Sectarianism, Islamist Republicanism, and International Misrecognition in Yemen', pp. 185–198. In Nasser Hashemi and Danny Postel (eds.), *Sectarianization: Mapping the Neu Politics of the Middle East*. London: Hurst Publishers.

Note

1 A rough figure from 2015 provided by the Sanaa-based analyst Hisham al-Omeisy to Al Jazeera, referring specifically to followers of the Houthi movement, not sections of the Yemeni army that have defected to the rebel government (Gupta 2015).

References

Al Omran, Ahmed, and Asa Fitch. 2017. "Yemen's Houthi Rebels Launch Rare Suicide Attack on Saudi Frigate." *The Wall Street Journal*, January 30, 2017. https://www.wsj.com/articles/yemens-houthi-rebels-launch-rare-suicide-attack-on-saudi-frigate-1485816057.

Almasmari, Hakim. 2010. "Mohammed Yahya Ezan: Founder of the Believing Youth (Houthis First Movement)." *Yemen Post*, April 10, 2010. http://www.yemenpost.net/Detail123456789.aspx?ID=100&SubID=1546&MainCat=4.

Anonymous. 2017. "Dynamics of the Houthi-GPC Alliance." Yemen Peace Project. June 2, 2017. https://www.yemenpeaceproject.org/blog-x/houthi-gpc-alliance.

Bayoumy, Yara, and Phil Stewart. 2016. "Exclusive: Iran Steps up Weapons Supply to Yemen's Houthis via Oman – Officials." *Reuters*, October 20, 2016. https://www.reuters.com/article/us-yemen-security-iran/exclusive-iran-steps-up-weapons-supply-to-yemens-houthis-via-oman-officials-idUSKCN12K0CX.

Binnie, Jeremy. 2017. "Yemeni Rebels Enhance Ballistic Missiles Campaign." IHS Jane's Military & Security Assessments Intelligence Centre. IHS Markit.

Brandt, Mareike. 2017. *Tribes and Politics in Yemen: A History of the Houthi Conflict*. London, UK: Hurst & Company.

Browne, Gareth. 2018. "Arab Coalition Lays Bare Iranian Support for Houthis in Yemen." *The National*, June 19, 2018. https://www.thenational.ae/world/mena/arab-coalition-lays-bare-iranian-support-for-houthis-in-yemen-1.742032.

Cooper, Helene, Thomas Gibbons-Neff, and Eric Schmitt. 2018. "Army Special Forces Secretly Help Saudis Combat Threat From Yemen Rebels." *New York Times*, May 3, 2018. https://www.nytimes.com/2018/05/03/us/politics/green-berets-saudi-yemen-border-houthi.html.

Dadouch, Sarah, and Noah Browning. 2018. "Iran-Aligned Houthis in Yemen Fire Missiles at Saudi Capital." *Reuters*, May 9, 2018. https://uk.reuters.com/article/uk-saudi-security/iran-aligned-houthis-in-yemen-fire-missiles-at-saudi-capital-idUKKBN1IA104.

Freeman, Jack. 2009. "The Al Houthi Insurgency in the North of Yemen: An Analysis of the Shabab Al Moumineen." *Studies in Conflict & Terrorism*, 32 (11): 1008–1019.

Gupta, Priyanka. 2015. "The Child Soldiers of Yemen." *Al-Jazeera*, March 4, 2015. https://www.aljazeera.com/indepth/features/2015/03/child-soldiers-yemen-150302081855823.html.

Lackner, Helen. 2017. *Yemen in Crisis: Autocracy, Neo-Liberalism and the Disintegration of the State*. London, UK: Saqi Books.

Lyamin, Yuri. 2017. "Craft-Produced Anti-Materiel Rifles and Light Cannon in Yemen." *Armament Research Services*, September 10, 2017. http://armamentresearch.com/craft-produced-anti-materiel-rifles-and-light-cannon-in-yemen/.

Nasser, Afrah. 2017. "The Yemen War, Media, and Propaganda." *The Atlantic Council*, May 3, 2017. http://www.atlanticcouncil.org/blogs/menasource/the-yemen-war-media-and-propaganda.

Overton, Shaun. 2005. "Understanding the Second Houthi Rebellion in Yemen." *Terrorism Monitor* 3 (12).

Paraguassu, Lisandra. 2016. "Brazil's Taurus Sold Arms to Trafficker for Yemen War, Prosecutors Allege." *Reuters*, September 5, 2016. https://www.reuters.com/article/us-brazil-arms-taurus-idUSKCN11B1KM.

Salmoni, Barak A., Bruce Loidolt, and Madeleine Wells. 2010. *Regime and Periphery in Northern Yemen: The Huthi Phenomenon*. Santa Monica, CA: RAND National Defense Research Institute.

Sheppard, David, Ahmed al-Omran, and Anjli Ravel. 2018. "Saudis Suspend Red Sea Oil Shipments after Tanker Attacks." *Financial Times*, July 25, 2018. https://www.ft.com/content/f0858962-9005-11e8-b639-7680cedcc421.

Trew, Bel. 2018. "UAE Denies Houthi Rebels Attacked Dubai Airport with Armed Drone." *The Independent*, August 28, 2018. https://www.independent.co.uk/news/world/middle-east/uae-dubai-airport-drone-attack-houthi-rebels-yemen-emirates-a8510551.html.

Weissenburger, Alexander. 2017. "'Death to America, Death to Israel, Damn the Jews, Victory to Islam': The Ḥūthī Movement's Framing of Localized Grievances in Terms of International Politics." Presented at the *British Society for Middle Eastern Studies (BRISMES) Conference*, Edinburgh, UK. 7 July. https://bit.ly/2UJrgUX.

Yemen Observer Twitter Account. 2018. "Houthi Vehicle with M61 Vulcan Cannon," July 11, 2018. https://twitter.com/YemeniObserv/status/1016989559886958592.

"Yemeni Nation's Struggle for Liberty Main Reason behind Saudi-Led Aggression: Houthi." 2018. PressTV. September 20, 2018. https://bit.ly/2PBfXKO.

Chapter 49

Basque Separatists

Nell Bennett
Macquarie University, Sydney, Australia

Contents

Introduction 345
Origins of the Separatist Movement 346
The Rise of ETA 346
ETA's Operations 347
The Advent of Democracy 348
Conclusion 349
Further Reading 350
References 350

Introduction

The Basque people inhabit a region that encompasses part of northern Spain and southern France. Their unique culture, coupled with the nation-building policies of the Spanish central government, led to the development of a separatist movement at the end of the nineteenth century. Their desire for independence grew after the Spanish Civil War in response to the repressive regime of General Francisco Franco. This chapter examines the roots and trajectory of the Basque separatist movement, with a particular focus on the rise of the terrorist organisation *Euskadi Ta Askatasuna* (ETA). It will discuss the ETA's composition and operations and look at how the Spanish government's brutal attempts to put down the movement led to a spiral of violence that peaked in the late 1970s and early 1980s. The chapter concludes by discussing how Spain's transition to democracy combined with its concerted counterterrorism campaign eroded ETA's support base and operational capacities, leading to an eventual cessation of hostilities in 2011.

DOI: 10.4324/9781315144511-52

Origins of the Separatist Movement

The Basque Country is historically comprised of seven regions in the north of Spain and south of France that are populated with people who are culturally and ethnically distinct from those of the surrounding areas. The exact origins of the Basques are unknown. However, drawings discovered in the Santimamiñe caves in Guernica suggest that the Basque civilisation may be more than 20,000 years old. The Basque people managed to maintain territorial and political independence for centuries due to the inhospitable mountainous terrain of the region and their fierce resistance to foreign incursions (Clark, 1979).

Basque separatism is commonly regarded as emerging in reaction to the rapid industrialisation of the region in the nineteenth century (Medrano, 1995; Watson, 1996). The movement originated in the province of Vizcaya, which underwent a rapid transformation from a predominantly rural area to one of the world's top industrial centres (Watson, 1996). It has been argued by scholars, including Juan Díez Medrano (1995), that this change resulted in the disenfranchisement of the pre-industrial Basque elites, who formed the support base for the independence movement.

Sabino de Arana y Goiri is considered to be the father of modern Basque separatism. His early political organisation laid the foundations for the Basque Nationalist Party, the *Partido Nacionalista Vasco* (PNV). He also wrote a manifesto, *Bizcaya por su independancia*, which provided the philosophical basis for the movement. In this volume, he proclaimed the fundamental tenets of Basque separatism. These included Basque unity under Catholicism, the uniqueness of the Basque race as evidenced by their language and that autonomy should be achieved through non-violent means within the democratic system (Clark, 1979; Watson, 1996).

The separatist movement grew in the early twentieth century, and protests and strikes occurred periodically. By 1918, the nationalist party had achieved such electoral success that petitions for autonomy were presented to the central government and summarily rejected. The movement suffered a major setback in 1923 when the government of General Miguel Primo de Rivera issued a decree which illegalised all acts that could be perceived as undermining national unity (Clark, 1979).

Regionalism was further suppressed under the leadership of General Francisco Franco, and the PNV was forced to become a clandestine organisation. During the 1950s and 1960s, the Spanish government viewed a wide variety of typical Basque activities, including hiking, traditional dance and music and the use of the Basque language, to be subversive, and these acts were prohibited (Hamilton, 2006; Tejerina, 2001). Even the most casual use of the Basque language was punishable by imprisonment (Clark 1979).

The Rise of ETA

The modern Basque terrorist organisation ETA traces its origins to 1952, when a group of seven university students in Bilbao began to meet to discuss ways of advancing the Basque independence movement. This group was known as *Ekin*, which in Basque means 'to do' or 'to make' (Barros, 2003). It quickly grew in numbers and began holding meetings to discuss Basque history, culture and language (Tejerina, 2001).

Ekin merged with the youth branch of the PNV for a brief period but soon found the moderate stance of the political party to be too restrictive. In 1960, the radical members of the group split from the PNV and formed ETA.

ETA's early operations were directed towards challenging the prohibitions imposed by the Franco government on Basque cultural expression. The group rebelled by organising political and cultural gatherings, flying the Basque flag and distributing nationalist literature (Hamilton, 2006). The strongest recruitment base for ETA was the province of Guipúzcoa, which supplied nearly half of the group's members, despite the fact that it only contributed less than a quarter of the population of the Basque Country. This may be because Guipúzcoa is considered to be quintessentially Basque. Its lush mountainous geography is readily associated with the historic nation, and it has the highest proportion of native Basque speakers of the region (Reinares, 2004).

ETA did not form principally as a terrorist organisation. Indeed, the use of violence to achieve political goals was the subject of recurring controversy amongst its factions (Llera, Mata and Irvin, 1993). It was devised as a socialist working-class struggle, influenced by other left-wing revolutionary and post-colonial movements in Europe (Zabalo and Saratxo, 2015). ETA also made a strategic choice to take a broader view of Basque ethnicity than that which Arana had espoused. While Arana believed that only ethnic Basques should be allowed to populate *Euskadi*, the Basque homeland, ETA viewed the use of the Basque language *Euskera* and a sense of belonging within the nationalist community as the determinants of Basque identity (Tejerina, 2001). Accordingly, an individual's ability to identify as Basque was directly related to their involvement with the independence movement (Zabalo and Saratxo, 2015).

During the 1960s and 1970s, the core of the resistance movement consisted of several hundred activists who lived in rural and coastal villages in the south of France, near the Spanish border. This position enabled them to engage in operations in Spain and then return to seek refuge in their sanctuary. The majority of recruits joined in their early twenties and came from rural areas where a high proportion of inhabitants spoke *Euskera* (Reinares, 2004). Around 80% of members were native Basques; however, over time, an increasing number of recruits came from immigrant parents (Llera, Mata and Irvin, 1993).

ETA's Operations

By the mid-1960s, ETA had the resources to engage full-time leaders, known as *liberados*, who developed terrorist and insurgency strategies and tactics. The second rank of members were known as the *legales*, who maintained their normal life but assisted in the struggle by performing different functions. They could be either *enlaces* who ran communications for the group, *buzones* who acted as couriers, or *informativos* who collected intelligence. The third rank of operatives were not actively involved but provided logistical support and resources for the organisation (Llera, Mata and Irvin, 1993).

ETA's first serious terrorist operation occurred in 1961. It was the attempted derailment of a number of trains carrying Franco supporters to San Sebastian to celebrate the 25th anniversary of Franco's military coup (Barros, 2003). While the operation was unsuccessful, retaliation from the Spanish government was swift and brutal. More than 100 Basque citizens were arrested and tortured. Many of the detainees were sentenced to terms of 15–20 years imprisonment. The following year, ETA released a statement declaring themselves a clandestine revolutionary organisation (Clark, 1979).

The symbolic aspect of ETA violence is demonstrated through their selection of targets. ETA operations focused mostly on Spanish government targets, such as government agencies, national police stations, Guardia Civil outposts, government schools and the homes of government officials. Other targets included symbols of oppression and capitalism, including Spanish flags, financial institutions and media offices (Clark, 1979). Like most terrorist organisations, their violence usually performed both a communicative and instrumental purpose. An example of this was the 1973 assassination of the Navel Minister, Admiral Luis Carrero Blanco, a man who was generally considered to be Franco's successor. A bomb positioned beneath the street was timed to detonate just as his car drove over it on his way from morning mass to work, in accordance with his usual routine (Barros, 2003).

To finance their activities, ETA engaged in bank robberies and kidnapping and extracted what they referred to as a 'revolutionary tax' on wealthy residents. These activities took a toll on the Basque economy. Extortion has been held to be one of the factors responsible for the relative decline of the regional economy. In the 1970s, the Basque Country had the third highest GDP per capita in Spain but occupied only the sixth position by the 1990s (Abadie and Gardeazabal 2003).

In 1968, an ETA activist was killed, creating the group's first martyr. ETA responded by killing an officer of the National Police and a member of the Guardia Civil. This set off an action–reaction cycle of violence (Laitin, 1995). The Franco government laid siege to the Basque region and a 'state of exception' was instituted, which was akin to martial law. Habeas corpus was suspended and people were detained without charge or access to legal representation. Thousands of Basques were imprisoned, tortured and exiled (Clark, 1979).

The Advent of Democracy

The post-Franco era was marked by the transition to democracy in 1978. The new constitution established several autonomous communities, including the Basque Country and Catalonia. This provided them with increased political and economic autonomy, including limited control over education and taxation (Barros, 2003). This was a time during which new power-sharing agreements were being forged, and thus there was much at stake for the separatists. The years of the highest numbers of ETA casualties were 1978, the year of the referendum to approve the Spanish Constitution, 1979, the year of the Basque Autonomy Statute, and 1980 which was when the first regional elections were held in the Basque Country (Llera, Mata and Irvin, 1993). In 1978–1980, ETA was reportedly responsible for 235 deaths. These fatalities consisted of roughly 20–25% civilians and 75–80% state officials, including law enforcement personnel (De la Calle and Sánchez-Cuenca, 2006).

In the mid-1980s, France changed its tolerant stance towards ETA and began to collaborate with the Spanish government in its counterterrorism operations. As a result, ETA lost its sanctuary. In 1992, joint French-Spanish efforts resulted in the arrest of the entire leadership team of ETA. While the group recovered from this blow, it was substantially weakened (Murua, 2017).

Partly in response to this, ETA shifted its focus to obtaining a negotiated resolution with the Spanish government. The first formal negotiation with the Spanish government is commonly referred to as the *Algiers* process. However, these negotiations broke down after 3 months. In 1998, ETA engaged in what was known as the *Lizarra-Garazi* process, in which they entered into a secret pact with the moderate Basque nationalist parties. In exchange for a more robust political approach to national building, ETA agreed to lay down its arms. The ceasefire lasted 15 months but was broken after ETA decided that the moderate nationalists were not holding up their side of the bargain (Murua, 2017). Another ceasefire was called in March 2006 during negotiations with the Spanish government; however, this was terminated by the bombing of the Madrid airport, in which two people were killed. Negotiations were resumed in 2007, but the ceasefire lasted no more than 2 months.

In October 2011, ETA announced that it was ceasing its terrorist activities. Some scholars have argued that their ultimate decision to abandon this strategy in 2011 was due to a normative shift against terrorist violence. This change in public attitudes is thought to be the result of a number of factors. These include the failed attempts on the lives of Prime Ministerial candidate Jose Aznar and the popular King Juan Carlos in 1995 (Barros, 2003), the success of pacifist movements and the attack on the World Trade Center in New York (Zabalo and Saratxo, 2015).

The Spanish government's struggle with Basque separatism provides useful insights for practitioners and policymakers in the United States who are seeking to understand how to combat terrorist violence. The Franco regime's attempts to stifle the movement through the use of heavy-handed repression and indiscriminate violence merely generated more popular support for ETA and boosted terrorist recruitment. The ceasefire and ultimate disarmament of the organisation was the result of decades of negotiations. Peace would not have been achieved if the Spanish government had not demonstrated a willingness to find a peaceful political solution to the conflict. This case emphasises the limitations of military responses to political violence.

Conclusion

The unique history, culture and ethnicity of the Basque people formed the basis of the separatist movement that emerged in the late nineteenth century. The desire for independence was fuelled by policies of the Spanish government that were designed to repress regionalism and create a homogeneous Spanish state. The terrorist organisation ETA was formed in the 1960s, in part in response to the oppressive Franco government which prohibited all forms of Basque cultural expression. The government's heavy-handed response to ETA triggered a spiral of violence that reached its high point in the late 1970s, during Spain's transition to democracy. This chapter has examined the genesis, development and eventual decline of the Basque separatist movement. Legislative changes under the democratic regime granted a large measure of political autonomy to the Basque region. This, combined with a normative shift away from terrorist violence, eroded ETA's support base and resulted in their decision to lay down their arms in 2011.

Further Reading

Clark, R. P. (1979). *The Basques: The Franco years and beyond*. Reno, Nevada: University of Nevada Press.

Laitin, D. D. (1995). National Revivals and Violence. *European Journal of Sociology*. 36, 3–43.

Reinares, F. (2004). Who are the Terrorists? Analyzing Changes in Sociological Profile Among Members of ETA. *Studies in Conflict & Terrorism*. 27(6), 465–488.

References

Abadie, A. and Gardeazabal, J. (2003). The Economic Costs of Conflict: A Case Study of the Basque Country. *The American Economic Review*. 93(1), 113–132.

Barros, C. P. (2003). An Intervention Analysis of Terrorism: The Spanish ETA Case. *Defence and Peace Economics*. 14(6), 401–412.

De la Calle, L. and Sánchez-Cuenca, I. (2006). The Production of Terrorist Violence: Analyzing Target Selection Within the IRA and ETA. Estudio Working Paper 2006/230. http://epub.sub.uni-hamburg.de/epub/volltexte/2008/1870/pdf/2006_230.pdf.

Clark, R. P. (1979). *The Basques: The Franco years and beyond*. Reno, Nevada: University of Nevada Press.

Hamilton, C. (2006). The Gender Politics of Political Violence: Women Armed Activists in ETA. *Feminist Review*. 86, 132–148.

Laitin, D. D. (1995). National Revivals and Violence. *European Journal of Sociology*. 36, 3–43.

Llera, F. J., Mata, J. M. and Irvin, C. L. (1993). ETA: From Secret Army to Social Movement: The Post-Franco Schism of the Basque Nationalist Movement. *Terrorism and Political Violence*. 5(3), 106–134.

Medrano, J. D. (1995). *Divided Nations: Class, politics, and nationalism in the Basque Country and Catalonia*. Ithaca and London: Cornell University Press.

Murua, I. (2017). No More Bullets for ETA: The Loss of Internal Support as a Key Factor in the End of the Basque Group's Campaign. *Critical Studies on Terrorism*. 10(1), 93–114.

Reinares, F. (2004). Who are the Terrorists? Analyzing Changes in Sociological Profile Among Members of ETA. *Studies in Conflict & Terrorism*. 27(6), 465–488.

Tejerina, B. (2001). Protest Cycle, Political Violence and Social Movements in the Basque Country. *Nations and Nationalism*. 7(1), 39–57.

Watson, C. J. (1996). *Sacred Earth, Symbolic Blood: A cultural history of Basque political violence from Arana to Eta* (Doctoral dissertation). Reno, Nevada: University of Nevada.

Zabalo, J., and Saratxo, M. (2015). ETA ceasefire: Armed Struggle vs. Political Practice in Basque Nationalism. *Ethnicities*. 15(3), 362–384.

Chapter 50

Car Bombs

Raphaël Leduc
Graduate Institute of International and Development Studies, Geneva, Switzerland

Contents

Introduction 351
Defining Car Bombs 352
Car Ramming: The Most Credible Alternative to Car Bombs 355
Detection 355
Protection 356
US Domestic Security 357
Conclusion 358
Further Reading 358
References 359

Introduction

The use of vehicles as the medium that carries explosives to a target has a venerable history. This method of carrying attacks has been in the toolkit of different groups participating in diverse conflicts over the last century. The Irish Republican Army (IRA) made significant use of this tactic in their terror campaigns in Northern Ireland. More recently, the Islamic State (IS) has used car bombs as a military tactic in their defense of key strategic locations such as the city of Mosul (BBC, 2017b). Either as a tool of terror or as a weapon of war, little research has been done on car bombs outside of the manuals produced by military forces that seek to address specific tactical problems. This chapter seeks to provide the groundwork for researchers and non-technical experts on the topic of car bombs. This groundwork will be developed in three parts. First, it will do so by providing an operational definition of the topic. Second, it will propose a framework to help understand how and when they are used with the goal of underlining detection methods. Finally, it will discuss current force protection measures to protect against their threat in a US domestic context.

DOI: 10.4324/9781315144511-53

Defining Car Bombs

To begin with, the term car bomb is largely inadequate in capturing the universe of cases that could be classified as such. This is partly the reason why the military literature usually uses the term vehicle-borne improvised explosive device (VBIED) or suicide vehicle-borne improvised explosive device (SVBIED) in order to refer to car bombs as those terms usually better capture the cases of interest. For example, the August 19, 2003, truck bombing of the United Nations Headquarters (UNHQ) in Baghdad killed 22 people and injured over 150. The truck used was a flatbed carrying approximately 1,000 kg of explosives. A month later on September 22, it was followed by an attack using a car which was detonated when it was challenged by local police (Report of the Independent Panel on the Safety and Security of UN Personnel in Iraq, 2003). The difference between the two attacks largely rests on the difference in the size of the vehicle used, as they were otherwise similar in other attributes (intent, target, and method). Thus, car bomb as the popular term to refer to the universe of cases is inadequate. Vehicle-borne explosive device (VBED) probably better encapsulates it because it allows for vehicles of different sizes to be used as a medium and different types of ordnances which are available to would-be attackers (military grade or artisanal).

Notwithstanding this inadequacy, this chapter will continue using the term car bombs because it is widely used in popular media reports. The operational definition of car bombs will be: *any wheeled motor vehicle which replaces its ordinary cargo with explosive or incendiary materials meant to cause material and/or personnel damage through blast, thermal, or fragmentation effects to a target.* Of note is the fact that it does not matter if the vehicle is stationary or moving. It also does not matter if the target is the occupant of the car (in the case of targeted assassination), a building, security forces, or pedestrians. A problematic edge case for the definition are vehicles that routinely carry dangerous goods (such as petroleum products) which is partly covered by the concept of intent. A vehicle carrying dangerous goods that is hijacked for the purposes mentioned in the definition would be a car bomb even though its ordinary cargo has not been changed. Since the terrorist attacks of 9/11, this specific edge case has been specifically targeted by regulations under the auspice of the Federal Motor Carrier Safety Administration (FMCSA) and is closely monitored, with vehicles being tracked and an emphasis on direct communications between vehicle operators, dispatchers, and authorities (FMCSA, 2018). The operational definition of car bombs has three components which are also ways of conceptualizing their use: (i) as an attack vector (the type of vehicle), (ii) as an effect factor (the specific type of ordnance carried and desired kinetic effect), and (iii) as a specific targeting component (what is to be achieved).

To further investigate the universe of cases, the following question is asked: Why use car bombs? The conventional weapon systems of military force are used in the field to achieve specific desired effects (Cross et al., 2016). Those desired effects are themselves means of achieving specific goals. The use of car bombs can be analyzed in terms of the desired effects of the attacks and the goals they are meant to achieve in a way that is comparable to the employment of force by state security personnel. This method of analysis is particularly useful because it does not impose a narrow terrorism framework on the use of car bombs but allows for a more generalized analysis of their use. According to data from the Global Terrorism Database (GTD, START, 2017), out of the 659 attacks in the West between 1970 and 2017, only 218 happened outside of Spain and the British Isles. The comparatively low frequency of car bomb attacks outside of these regions tells us that the reason why car bombs are so popular for these groups is probably due to idiosyncratic explanations.

Grant and Stewart (2017) find that car bomb attacks in the West caused an average of 2.9 deaths per successful plot but this needs to be contextualized by the fact that it is the favored method of very specific groups who are fighting ethnic or national insurgencies. Within the West in Spain and the British Isles Outside of the West, they have been a defining characteristic of conflicts in Iraq, Algeria, and Pakistan. The use of car bombs as a tactic is thus context-specific. This can be seen in Figures 50.1 and 50.2. As a proportion of all terrorist attacks, car bombs appear to have gained in popularity since 1970, raising from about 2.5% to 7.5% in proportion. However, this trend is heavily influenced by the post-9/11 conflicts in the Middle East (Iraq, Afghanistan, Pakistan, and Syria have accounted for 77% of the car bomb attacks in the world since 2001). Focusing exclusively on the West smooths the trend considerably (Figure 50.2), but the trend is still skewed by Irish terrorism in the 1970s and Spanish terrorism in the 1990s. Removing those two specific regions yields a curve for the West that is relatively flat which indicates to us that car bombs have remained a rare event (about less than 2% of all terrorist attacks in the West) for the whole of the period where data is available (Figure 50.3).

In the context of the United States, there have been 25 car bomb attacks committed by at least 16 different groups since 1970. Thus, the rarity of car bombs and the context specificity of their use make broad generalizations based on global trends

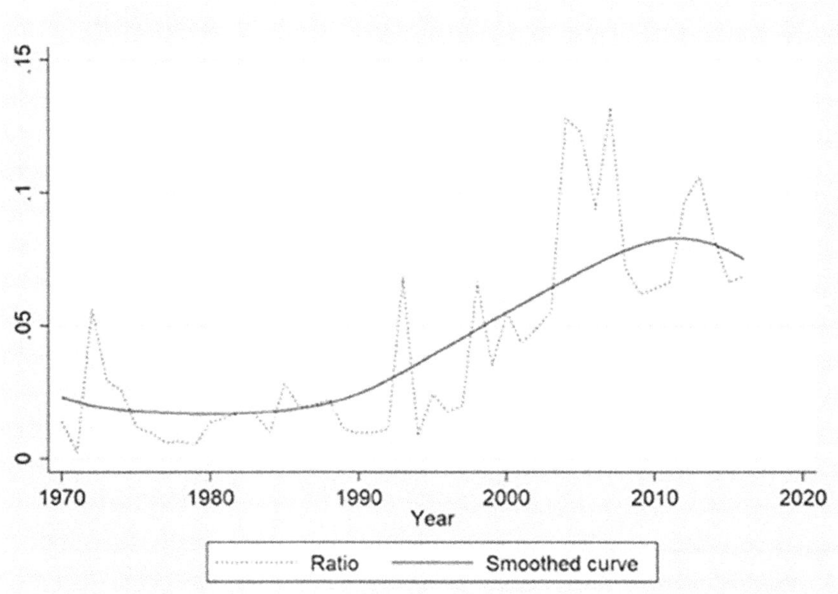

Figure 50.1 Proportion of terrorist attacks using car bombs.

Source: *GTD Dataset, START (2017).*

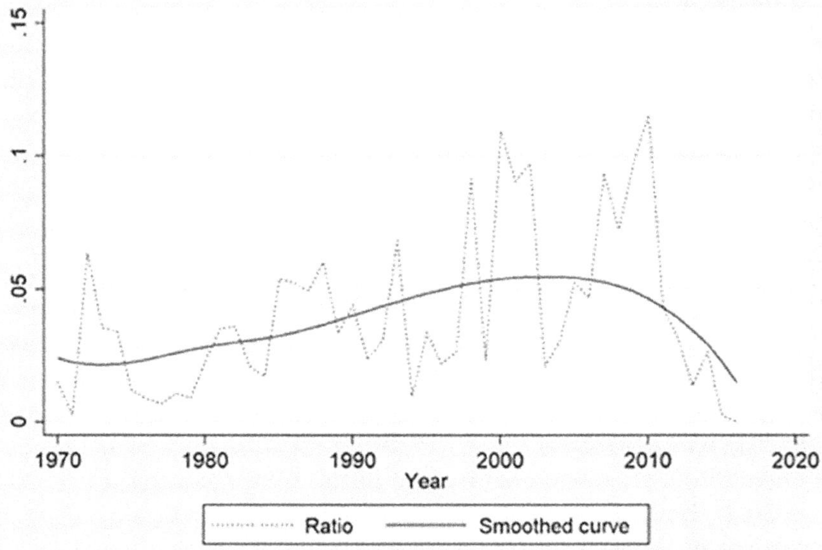

Figure 50.2 Proportion of terrorist attacks using car bombs over time in the west.

Source: *GTD Dataset, START (2017).*

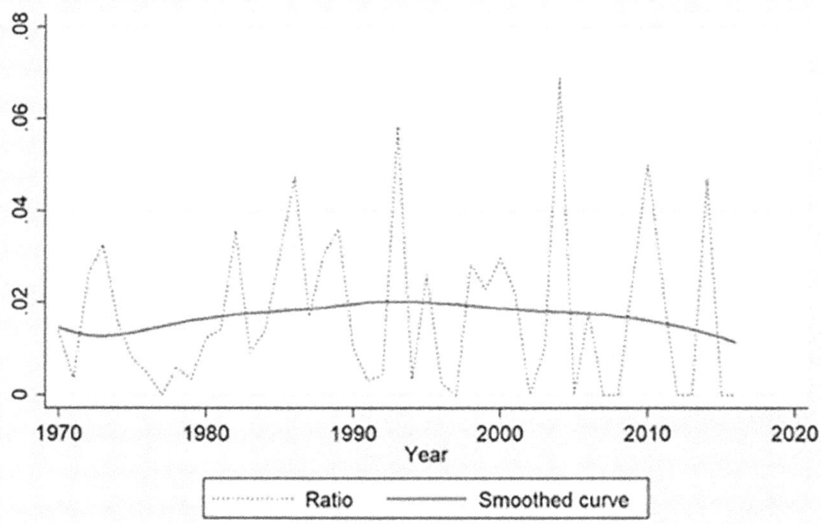

Figure 50.3 Proportion of terrorist attacks using car bombs over time in the west (excluding the british isles and spain).

Source: *GTD Dataset, START (2017).*

unhelpful in conducting trend analysis in a domestic context. What is more important is to look at the specific tactics of specific groups when trying to understand how car bombs are employed. Such an approach yields the possibility of looking at a credible alternative to car bombs that have significant overlap with the phenomenon. In this case, the apparent rise in car-ramming attacks by followers of the IS.

Car Ramming: The Most Credible Alternative to Car Bombs

Davis argues that there are several reasons why car bombs are the "poor man's air force *par excellence*," (emphasis in original, Davis 2017, p. 8). His argument for this rests on a few claims which are all rooted in the fact that it is a simple, cost-effective strategy for causing significant damage. This would explain why this tactic seems to be specifically located in the narrow context of local insurgencies who are fighting an asymmetrical conflict against state forces (Spain, Northern Ireland, Algeria, Iraq, Afghanistan, Pakistan, Syria, etc.). This explanation however fails to specify why non-state actors involved in different situations (for example, transnational terrorist groups such as Al Qaeda) have largely eschewed this specific tactic in favor of others. Al Qaeda operations have been characterized by a hitherto unprecedented level of planning and preparations which draws strong similarities to special force operations. However, none of their major operations in the West (9/11, the 2004 Madrid train bombings, or the 2005 London bus bombings) made use of car bombs. Instead, they made use of critical infrastructure either as targets or means of delivery. At the other end of the spectrum, most of the attacks inspired or claimed by the IS in the West are *ad-hoc* affairs perpetrated by one or two individuals (with a few notable exceptions like the 2015 Paris attacks). A tactic that seems to have gained in popularity seems to be the use of vehicle-ramming attacks whereby an attacker uses a vehicle to kill pedestrians by driving into them. The first instance of such attacks in the West by supporters of IS specifically targeted soldiers (May 2013 in the United Kingdom and October 2014 in Canada). Since then, they have been gaining in popularity as a means to inflict mass civilian casualties. The 2016 attack in Nice demonstrated the potential lethality of this type of attack when an attacker used a truck to kill 85 people and injure an additional 303 (*BBC*, 2016).

Detection

The potential displacement of a car bombing by car ramming should be further analyzed as it has the potential to be a more problematic type of attack for security analysts to detect. As the Nice example shows, car-ramming attacks have the potential to be just as lethal as car bombs. This is compounded by the fact that they are less expensive, require less preparation, and their direct use is not detectable; unlike car bombs which can potentially be detected through visual cues (such as a compressed suspension), visual inspection at checkpoints, or explosive detection techniques (dogs and explosive tests), there are no ways to know at the direct moment before the attack if a vehicle is 'benign' or if it is going to be used in a car-ramming attack. When it comes to preventing car bomb attacks, it is possible for security agencies to detect the plot while it is still in the planning phase through the tracking of the purchase of certain substances (such as ammonium nitrate which is commonly used in fertilizer) or the access to specific technical information that is necessary for the plotter(s) to build the bomb.

While no silver bullets, these vectors for detection of potential terrorist plots make car bomb attacks easier to detect and prevent. Furthermore, car bombs force the plotters to gather technical knowledge, acquire material, build the bomb, and find a vehicle. These activities all require more resources, more time, and preparation than a car-ramming attack which only necessitates a vehicle. This means that car bombs are not only easier to detect but also that there is more time to detect them. Thus, car-ramming attacks present would-be terrorists with a simpler, cheaper, less easily foiled, and potentially just as lethal alternative to car bombs. In the context of domestic terrorism, if the goal is to cause as many casualties as possible, car-ramming attacks should be viewed as a very viable alternative to car bombs.

Protection

As shown in the previous section, car ramming can be a more accessible, if just as lethal, alternative to car bombs. Fortuitously for security agencies, both in the United States and abroad, the protection of domestic infrastructure and individuals is very similar for both types of attacks. Essentially, protection measures are about keeping vehicles away from large groups of people through specific spatial designs of the urban landscape. Specifically, the low-cost, short-term solution is to install vehicle barriers at potential points of attacks. Those techniques, as part of a public safety framework, are already well-applied principles of urban design (Coaffee, 2008). The difference in protecting against both types of attacks rests in the standoff distance. It is not possible to study the specific effects of different improvised explosive devices (IEDs) as their designs are not consistent. However, comparing them to military-grade ordnance can give a sense of what standoff distances are necessary while keeping in mind that military explosives are often designed to maximize their lethality; so for a given explosive weight, it should be expected that the improvised device will have an equal or smaller lethal radius. Figure 50.3 shows the relationship between a given explosive weight (standardized to its equivalent in TNT, given in kilogram) and the hazardous distance of fragmentation in meters (understood as the minimum distance where fragmentation is not lethal). Noticeably, past the 200 kg mark, the manual notes that the hazardous distance flattens at around 381 m. Hazardous distance for blast effects are generally much smaller than the fragmentation effects, and this is doubly true for car bombs which tend to reduce blast effects to their targets (Champion, et al. 2009). A standoff distance of over 380 m in open space is clearly not possible in urban settings, but as a rule of thumb, more distance improves survival rates exponentially (GICHD, 2017) (Figure 50.4).

When it comes to damage to buildings, blast effects are the main threat. In this case, smaller standoff distances could protect the building and its occupants but leave pedestrians exposed. The drastic diminishing returns of bigger car bombs mean that bigger bombs are not necessarily more problematic. The more lethal scenario would involve a complex attack where attackers breach the standoff barrier and strike the target directly with the car. This can be done either through the use of

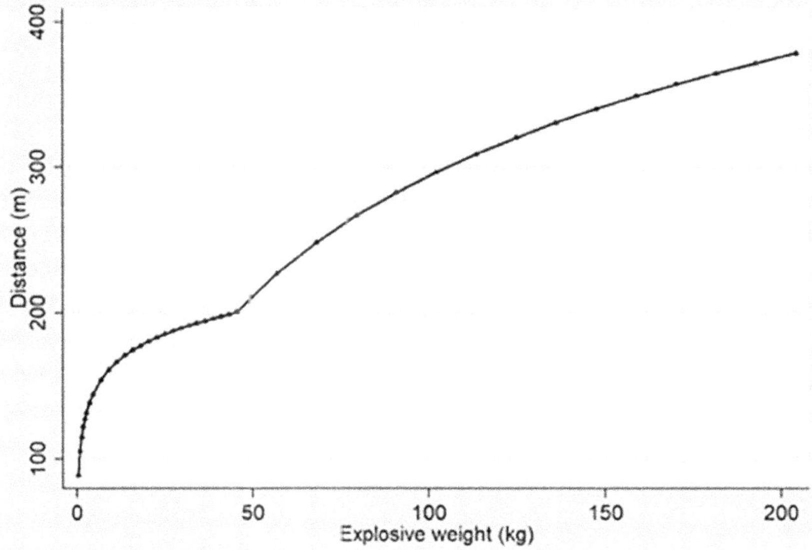

Figure 50.4 Hazardous fragmentation range as a function of explosive weight.

(Source: U.S. Department of the Army's Ammunition and Explosives Safety Standards manual (2011, p. 90)).

multiple car bombs or by using a specific vehicle which can overcome the barrier specifications (Shvetsov et al. 2017). Protecting against car bombs and car ramming can thus be seen as a potential arms race between urban planners and plotters. If car ramming is the simplest form of attack but is easily prevented by barriers, then car bombs become marginally more cost-effective. Better design against car bombs would in turn encourage more complex attacks using car bombs (or an alternative type of attack not studied here). This arms race would come at a significant cost to urban architecture, where functional spaces would be at risk of being transformed into strongholds. Thus, direct protection against car bomb attacks should be weighed against its societal costs by going beyond monetary figures. To conclude, it is important to note that a significant countermeasure against car bombs might come in the form of technologies that can detect explosive compounds through material which appear to be theoretically plausible (Tarim et al. 2015; Dunn et al. 2007) but has no practical applications as of now.

US Domestic Security

The protection of urban centers in the United States has already been spurred by major domestic and foreign attacks such as the 1995 Oklahoma and 1993 World Trade Center bombings. The hardening of public space and infrastructure is already well understood and defense mechanisms against potential car bombs and ramming attacks are becoming a feature of urban centers and US embassies abroad. While these preventive measures can help, they need to be complemented by effective crisis-response teams. For this, US agencies can look south of the border to the Mexican experience with criminal car bombings. Combining their experience with the US military's own in recent counter-insurgency (COIN) operations abroad will yield practical means for domestic first responders to prepare an adequate response to car bombs by adapting their training, equipment, and intelligence activities to this specific threat (Bunker and Sullivan, 2013). A cautionary note should however be heeded: as was the case for fortifying the city, the reconfiguration of first responders for COIN-like operations on domestic soil requires a careful cost–benefit analysis which goes beyond the scope of this chapter (and is not unique to car bombs as a threat). The costs of this potential reconfiguration based on wartime and high-intensity criminal violence operations go beyond the monetary value, and its ramifications in terms of the security discourse of society as a whole need to be critically weighted against the rarefied frequency of this type of attack in the West generally and on US soil specifically.

Conclusion

This chapter has sought to lay the foundations for an understanding of the employment of car bombs by non-state violent actors in a homeland security context. It has also provided a discussion of the detection of plots linked to car bombs and their alternatives. Finally, it exposed a short summary of trends and methods to protect potential targets. The key point that should be taken from this chapter is that car bombs are generally rare events outside of the context of insurgencies, and even then, they seem to be favored by specific groups. Thus, even though they appear to be theoretically cost-effective weapons for would-be terrorists (Davis, 2017), the likelihood of their use should not be overstated until it is empirically investigated. An empirical investigation of the use of car bombs based on quantitative work risks to hit severe limitations due to the low frequency of car bombs outside of specific regions, as such qualitative tools that focus on tracing the foiling or execution process of specific plots might yield better variables to help with detection of such attacks before they enter the execution phase.

Notwithstanding the aforesaid, it is unlikely that all plots can ever be detected and consequently foiled. Protecting likely targets (large pedestrian areas, specific infrastructure) should in this case be the contingency plan to minimize the impact of car bomb attacks (and their closest alternative, car ramming). At this point, the level of protection becomes a trade-off between a humane urban design and security. Finally, the literature on risk management and risk analysis offers ways to conceptualize those trade-offs (Steward and Mueller, 2014) in an operationalized fashion that will allow policy-makers to make informed decisions on potential threats.

Further Reading

Davis, M. (2017). *Buda's Wagon: A Brief History of the Car Bomb*. London: Verso.

Post, J. M., Ruby, K. G., and Shaw, E. D. (2007). From car bombs to logic bombs: The growing threat from information terrorism. *Terrorism and Political Violence*, 12(2): 97–122.

Wilson, C. (2007). Improvised explosive devices (IEDs) in Iraq and Afghanistan: Effects and countermeasures, CRS Report for Congress. https://apps.dtic.mil/sti/pdfs/ADA475029.pdf

References

BBC. (2016, August 19). Nice attack: What we know about the Bastille day killings. http://www.bbc.com/news/world-europe-36801671. Accessed 01 May 2018.

BBC. (2017a, 18 June). Mosul battle: Iraqi forces attack IS-held Old City. http://www.bbc.com/news/world-middle-east-40317917. Accessed 01 May 2018.

BBC. (2017b, 19 February) Mosul Assault: Iraq troops make headway against IS. http://www.bbc.com/news/world-middle-east-39018984. Accessed 01 May 2018.

Bunker, R.J., Sullivan, J.P. (2013). Cartel Car Bombings in Mexico. *The Letort Papers*, Strategic Studies Institute and U.S. Army War College Press.

Champion, H., Holcomb, J., Young, L.A. (2009). Injuries from explosions: Physics, biophysics, pathology, and required research focus. *The Journal of Trauma: Injury, Infection, and Critical Care*, 66(5), 1468–1477.

Coaffee, J. (2008). Risk, resilience, and environmentally sustainable cities. *Energy Policy*, 36 (12), 4633–4638.

Cross, K. Dullum, O., Jenzen-Jones, N.R., Garlasco, M. (2016). *Explosive Weapons in Populated Areas: Technical Considerations Relevant to Their Use and Effects*. Australia: Armament Research Services (ARES).

Davis, M. (2017). *Buda's Wagon: A Brief History of the Car Bomb*. London: Verso.

Dunn, W.L., Banerjee, K., Allen, A., van Meter, J. (2007). Feasibility of a method to identify targets that are likely to contain conventional explosives. *Nuclear Instruments and Methods in Physics Research, B*, 263, 179–182.

FMCSA, Federal Motor Carrier Safety Association (2018). How to Comply with Federal Hazardous Materials Regulations. https://www.fmcsa.dot.gov/regulations/hazardous-materials/how-comply-federal-hazardous-materials-regulations. Accessed 01 May 2018.

Geneva International Centre for Humanitarian Demining (GICHD), *Explosive Weapon Effects: Final Report*, Geneva, 2017.

Grant, M.J., Stewart M.G. (2017). Modelling improvised explosive device attacks in the West – Assessing the hazard. *Reliability Engineering and System Safety*, 165, 345–354.

National Consortium for the Study of Terrorism and Responses to Terrorism (START). (2017). Global Terrorism Database [Data file]. https://www.start.umd.edu/gtd. Accessed 15 February 2018.

Shvetsov, A.,Shvetsova S., Kozyrev, V.A., Spharov, V.A., Sheremet, N.M. (2017). The "car-bomb" as a terrorist tool at metro stations, railway terminals and airports. *Journal of Transportation Security*. 10(31), 31–43.

Tarim, U.A., Ozmutlu, E.N., Gurler, O., Yalcin, S. (2015). A possibility for standoff bomb detection. *Radiation Physics and Chemistry*, 106, 170–174.

UN (2003). Report of the Independent Panel on the Safety and Security of UN Personnel in Iraq.

U.S. Department of the Army (2011). *DA-PAM 385–64 Ammunition and Explosives Safety Standards*. Washington DC: USDA.

Chapter 51

Chemical and Biological Weapons (CBW)

James Revill and Giovanna Ferriani Madureira Pontes
University of Sussex, Falmer, United Kingdom

Contents

Introduction 361
A Short History of Chemical and Biological Terrorism in the United States 362
Factors Informing the Adoption of CBW 362
Implications for U.S. National Security 365
Conclusion 366
Further Reading 366
References 366

Introduction

Biological weapons can be understood as weapons designed to achieve their "intended target effects through the infectivity of disease-causing microorganisms and other such entities" (WHO, 2004). Such weapons can be targeted at not only humans but also animals and plants. While this definition remains useful, it is important to note that advances in biotechnology, and the convergence of biology and chemistry, are opening up greater possibilities for hostile exploitation, including, for example, the development of biological weapons for use against material targets. Chemical weapons can be seen as those weapons that achieve effects through the "toxicity" of agents and can also be used against humans, animals, and plants. With both chemical and biological weapons (CBW), the effects can be lethal, but there are cases where such weapons have been developed or used in a manner intended to be less-than-lethal.

CBW are prohibited at the international level through disarmament treaties, including the 1993 Chemical Weapons Convention (CWC) and the 1972 Biological and

DOI: 10.4324/9781315144511-54

Toxin Weapons Convention (BWC). Both these conventions were negotiated in a manner intended to prevent them from being locked into the technology of the time. Accordingly, rather than utilizing a list-based approach to defining CBW, both conventions define weapons through reference to intent. This approach ensures a prohibition on the development and use of agents such as the *Novichok* class of chemical weapons, even though specific agents within this class are not listed on the politically negotiated, illustrative schedules under the CWC. Both conventions also oblige states to transpose international prohibitions into domestic law. This has been achieved in the United States through, among other legal and regulatory measures, the Chemical Weapons Convention Implementation Act of 1998 and the Biological Weapons Anti-Terrorism Act of 1989.

A Short History of Chemical and Biological Terrorism in the United States

The United States has been exposed to acts of bioterrorism on a small number of occasions over the course of its history. In 1984, the *Rajneeshee* religious cult caused an outbreak of food poisoning in Wasco County, Oregon, incapacitating some 750 individuals in an attempt to prevent them from voting in a local election (Carus, 2000). More recently, in 2001, the "Amerithrax" attack, in which weaponized Anthrax was mailed to journalists and government officials, led to the deaths of five Americans and the sickening of some 17 others, as well as causing significant economic damage. This attack, which followed shortly after the events of 9/11, has stimulated a growing concern over the possibility of future bioterrorist attacks against the United States and its allies. Such concern has been further exacerbated by significant changes in both the capacity and geography of the life sciences, including what some see as the "democratization" of biotechnology (Gerstein, 2016).

In terms of chemical terrorism, the United States has endured a small number of chemical terrorist attacks. This includes the contamination of Tylenol capsules with cyanide in 1982 and several incidents in which letters containing crude ricin preparations have been mailed to government targets, including one case in 2013 in which a ricin preparation was mailed to then President Barack Obama (Hayden and Wadman 2013). There have also been a number of foiled chemical attacks on U.S. soil. Examples include a crude attempt by The Covenant, the Sword, and the Arm of the Lord to "poison water supplies in major U.S. cities" that was prevented by the FBI (Stern, 2000). Perhaps more significant, however, is the growing visibility of chemical weapons around the world, including the documented development and use of chemical weapons in Syria by both the Islamic State and the Syrian Regime. The continued use of chemical weapons with impunity in the region, by both state and non-state actors, risks making chemical weapons grimly fashionable and used more widely beyond the borders of the Syrian Arab Republic.

Factors Informing the Adoption of CBW

The, albeit patchy, history of CBW attacks and the growth and spread in related scientific knowledge and capacity suggest that CBW cannot be ignored from the perspective of those seeking to secure the U.S. homeland. However, the fact that CBW have been used in recent memory does not necessitate that such weapons will inevitably proliferate and become darkly fashionable in the future. Several factors will likely feed into actors' calculations over whether CBW capabilities are pursued.

The first factor is the perceived utility of CBW and the relative advantages (and relative disadvantages) of such weapons. In this regard, it is important to note that CBW have been used for a number of different utilities in the past. Furthermore, while mass killing is clearly important to some groups, such as the White Supremacist Organization, The Covenant, the Sword, and the Arm of the Lord (Stern, 2000), it is not the only function of CBW. Other utilities variously include:

- Generating media attention, as was perhaps the case with the relatively ineffective use of chlorine truck bombs in Iraq in 2006 (Garver, 2007);
- Criminal purposes, examples being the controversial case of Carol Anne Bond's use of toxic chemicals in a revenge attack;
- Sabotage, as was the objective of the early German biological weapons program during World War I;
- Incapacitation, as was the objective of the *Rajneeshee* cult's use of Salmonella on voters in Oregon, US, 1984 (Carus, 2000);
- Assassination, as was seemingly one of the objectives of the Minnesota Patriots Council foiled ricin plot, as well as a number of prominent recent cases outside the United States, such as the attack on Kim Jong Nam in Malaysia in 2017 and the use of fourth-generation nerve agents against Sergei Skripal and his daughter Yulia in Salisbury, UK, in 2018 (Sydnes, 2018).

Yet, while CBW have a number of functions beyond mass killing that may be perceived as relatively advantageous to certain actors (and yet further utilities and corresponding relative advantages for CBW may emerge in circumstances of changing warfare and violence), there are also considerable disadvantages to the pursuit of CBW when compared with other weapons, particularly small arms. CBW are often difficult to acquire, dangerous to handle, and in the process of dissemination, vulnerable to a variety of environmental factors that can weaken – or perhaps enhance – their effects. Moreover, the pursuit of even a rudimentary CBW capability will likely entail opportunity costs as resources and energy are diverted from other possible means of attack.

This leads to the second factor: complexity. Many forms of CBW, but particularly those aspiring toward mass destruction (understood here as comparable with weapons on the atomic scale), are complex and require multiple sophisticated skill sets in order to acquire, weaponize, and deliver agents to their intended targets. The same constraints do not, however, apply to the development of crude scruffy chemical weapons or indeed shabby, opportunistic bioterrorism. Arguably, the perceived "democratization" of knowledge related to chemistry and biology may undermine the extent to which complexity remains a barrier. Moreover, the United States has an active biotech community, including a growing body of so-called "DIY-bio groups" which has swollen from one group in 2008 to 42 groups located around the United States in early 2018 (DIY Bio, 2018). However, the democratization of biotechnology-related knowledge has not necessarily been extended to the complex processes of weaponizing biology; moreover, as Grushkin, Kuiken, and Millet (2013) pointed out in their 2013 survey, the DIY bio-community is largely benign and "shows a well-networked community that is aware of the risks and ethics related to biotechnology".

The third factor is the organizational structure of groups aspiring to develop and use CBW. The requirement for multiple skill sets and extensive resources for biological weapons programs aspiring to gigantic effect suggest that a degree of centralized control will likely be required for biological weapons of mass destruction (Ouagrham-Gormley, 2012), and, albeit to a lesser extent, chemical weapons of mass destruction. If the FBI (n.d.) conclusions related to the Amerithrax case are accepted and this attack was indeed perpetrated by Bruce Ivins, an experienced biodefence researcher with long-standing expertise in Anthrax weaponization, this is perhaps an exception that proves the rule. In contrast, decentralized or disaggregated forms of remotely guided CBW terrorism, yet alone so-called "lone wolf" attacks, may excel at generating ideas, but will likely perform poorly in preparing and implementing complex attacks in the absence of centralized support (Kollars and Bristert, 2014).

A further factor is the wider environmental context, specifically whether there are windows of opportunity to acquire, trial, and use such CBW. On the one hand, the United States, like many developed Western countries, offers a rich variety of possible CBW targets. Yet, on the other hand, the U.S. regulatory environment offers *comparatively* limited time and space in which the component parts of CBW can be acquired, developed, and tested without generating a response from law enforcement actors. Indeed, it is difficult to conceive of a situation in which U.S. law enforcement would passively observe indicators of an organization developing CBW, as appears to have been the case with *Aum Shinrikyo* (Danzig et al., 2012) and several past U.S. CBW plots, such as those of The Covenant, the Sword, and the Arm of the Lord (CSA) group and the Minnesota Patriots were disrupted by interventions from law enforcement agencies.

A final factor is the observability or perhaps the "fashionability" of CBW (Revill, 2017). While biological weapons are not readily observable and offer violent groups little scope for "copy-catting", "scruffy" chemical weapons – as opposed to those systematically produced for strategic purposes in the Cold War – have become grimly fashionable in parts of the Middle East with at least four documented incidents of regime use of chemical weapons and two cases in which the Islamic State was responsible for the use of sulfur mustard. The process of investigating such incidents – and attributing use with scientific certainty – remains both technically challenging and politically divisive, and notably, chemical weapons used in Syria has largely been undertaken with impunity. This has potential ramifications for the calculus over chemical weapons use beyond Syria. As was noted in the Seventh Report of the OPCW-UN Joint Investigative Mechanism (2017), "The continuing use of chemical weapons, including by non-State actors, is deeply disturbing. If such use, notwithstanding its prohibition by the international community, is not stopped now, a lack of consequences will surely encourage others to follow, not only in the Syrian Arab Republic, but also elsewhere". It is also of note that synthetic opioids such as fentanyl, which has been used as a chemical weapon in the past, appear to be increasingly used by criminal gangs in the United States in the adulteration of illicit drugs, raising the possibility of fentanyl being employed for other criminal purposes in the future.

Implications for U.S. National Security

Based on the previous analysis, the implications for homeland security are multiple. First, not all CBW are weapons of mass destruction, and those seeking to protect the U.S. homeland need to prepare for a spectrum of chemical and biological threats, ranging from sophisticated CBW of mass destruction to the use of CBW for purposes of assassination, to potentially disruptive, opportunistic attacks that, while pernicious, fall far short of mass destruction of humans and may target plants or animals with a view to causing economic sabotage.

Second, advances in science and technology cannot be ignored and there is clearly a need to guard against technological surprise from new and shiny technological advances, such as clustered regularly interspaced palindromic repeats (CRISPR), a powerful genome editing tool that enables permanent modifications to be made to the DNA of living organisms. However, there also remains a need to guard against technological surprise from the shock of old, repurposed technologies, and scruffy weapons. Many of the types of chemical weapons used in Syria remain in essence similar to the chemical weapons that stained the field of Ypres over 100 years ago. Bioterrorist attacks could potentially be sophisticated in nature, as was the case in the 2001 Amerithrax attack. However, it is also possible that bioterrorism may be opportunistically driven by actors seeking to capitalize on natural outbreaks or exploiting lapses in U.S. biosecurity systems.

Third, events believed to involve chemical and biological agents are likely to generate psycho-social effects – including panic and sociogenic illness – that exceed the casualty-causing capacity of the agent involved. As such, there needs to be effective communication strategies in place to both ensure a proportionate public response and counter the possibility of "fake news" narratives deliberately or unwittingly exacerbating the sociogenic effects of CBW incidents – real or believed.

Fourth, it will be important to ensure that the United States maintains the domestic technical capacity to both investigate – including through the development of CBW forensics and evidence handling techniques – and respond to CBW events. The process of investigation can be challenging and requires the maintenance of rather unusual skill sets that remain able to detect a range of weapons from well-characterized classical battlefield weapons to more unusual CBW variants. Related to this, the long history of dis- and misinformation surrounding CBW incidents and the propaganda value of allegations of association with chemical or biological weapons necessitate that neutral, independent international expertise will also need to be nurtured, for example, through the development of a functional network of trusted bio-related laboratories designated under the UN Secretary-General's Mechanism for Investigation of Alleged Use of Chemical and Biological Weapons (Spiez Lab, 2017).

Finally, there is much that can be – and has been – done at the domestic level to deal with the challenge of CBW and enhance chemical and biological security (and safety) through measures ranging from harder legislative and regulatory measures to softer engagement and awareness-raising strategies. However, domestic U.S. measures related to biosecurity and biosafety have come under scrutiny over the last couple of years with a number of high-profile incidents in U.S. laboratories, suggesting there is more that can be done domestically to ensure biosafety and security. Yet even then, dealing with the threat of CBW is unlikely to be achieved through national measures operating in isolation or through unilateral responses; the prevention of CBW also requires supporting other states' chemical and biological security in order to reduce the gaps in the global prohibition regimes that might be exploited as safe havens for the acquisition and development of CBW. Indeed, dealing with the challenge of CBW requires a multilateral effort to prohibit and prevent these weapons, including through diplomatic and financial support for measures such as the United Nations Security Council (UNSC) Resolution 1540, the BWC, and the CWC.

Conclusion

The category of CBW covers a range of different weapons and a spectrum of possible effects. There have been several cases where such weapons have been used in the United States by non-state actors, and many more U.S.-based CBW terrorist plots appear to have failed or been foiled. Moreover, science and technology of relevance to CBW, but particularly biological warfare (BW), is spreading and becoming much more powerful. However, this doesn't make CBW terrorism inevitable and several factors will likely have a bearing on whether non-state actors decide to pursue CBW.

From the perspective of homeland security, the above suggests a need to guard against a range of threats, including the hostile exploitation of new technology, as well as the repurposing of older technologies relevant to CBW. Dealing with CBW also requires the development of the capacity to prevent, detect, investigate, and respond to CBW, including the development of communications strategies in advance of any event believed to involve CBW and ongoing work at the national and international levels to build chemical and biological safety and security.

Further Reading

Pita, R. and Domingo, J. (2014). "The Use of Chemical Weapons in the Syrian Conflict," *Toxics*, 2(3): 391–402.

Price, R. (1995). "A Genealogy of the Chemical Weapons Taboo," *International Organization*, 49(1): 73–103.

Tucker, J. (ed). (2000). *Toxic Terror: Assessing Terrorist Use of Chemical and Biological Weapons*. Cambridge, Massachusetts: MIT Press.

References

Carus, S. "The Rajneeshees." In: Tucker, J. (ed). (2000). *Toxic Terror: Assessing Terrorist Use of Chemical and Biological Weapons*. Cambridge, Massachusetts: MIT Press.

Danzig, R., Sageman, M., Leighton, T., & Hough, L. (2012). *Aum Shinrikyo Insights Into How Terrorists Develop Biological and Chemical Weapons second edition*. Washington, DC: Center for a New American Security.

DIY Bio (2018) "local", https://diybio.org/local/

Hayden, E. C., & Wadman, M. (2013). US ricin attacks are more scary than harmful. *Nature News*, (April). https://doi.org/10.1038/nature.2013.12834

FBI. (n.d.). Amerithrax or Anthrax Investigation. Retrieved from https://www.fbi.gov/history/famous-cases/amerithrax-or-anthrax-investigation

Garver, C. (2007). Amateur Hour. *CBRNE World*, 24–27.

Gerstein, D. M. (2016). Can the bioweapons convention survive Crispr? *Bulletin of the Atomic Scientists*, (July).

Grushkin, D., Kuiken, T., & Millet, P. (2013). *Seven Myths & Realities about Do-It-Yourself Biology. Synthetic biology project.* Retrieved from http://www.synbioproject.org/site/assets/files/1292/7_myths_final-1.pdf

Kollars, N. A., & Bristert, P. D. (2014). The Terrorists that Couldn't: Seeing Terrorist Innovation as a Risky Venture. *The Homeland Security Review*, *8*(3), 199–218.

Ouagrham-Gormley, S. Ben. (2012). Barriers to Bioweapons: Intangible Obstacles to Proliferation Barriers to Bioweapons. *International Security*, *36*(4), 80–114.

OPCW-UN Joint Investigative Mechanism. (2017) *Seventh report of the Organisation for the Prohibition of Chemical Weapons-United Nations Joint Investigative Mechanism.* S/2017/904.

Revill, J (2017) "Past as Prologue? The Risk of Adoption of Chemical and Biological Weapons by Non-State Actors in the EU". *European Journal of Risk Regulation*, *8*(2), 626–642.

Sydnes, L. K. (2018) "How to curb production of chemical weapons", Nature, Comment, 13 April 2018.

Spiez. (2017). *UNSGM Designated Laboratories Workshop Report. Spiez.* Retrieved from https://www.labor-spiez.ch/pdf/en/rue/UNSGM_2017_FINAL_Report.pdf

Stern, J. E. In: Tucker, J. (ed). (2000). *Toxic Terror: Assessing Terrorist Use of Chemical and Biological Weapons.* Cambridge, MA: MIT Press.

WHO. (2004). *Public health response to biological and chemical weapons WHO guidance, Second edition.* Geneva: WHO. http://www.who.int/csr/delibepidemics/biochemguide/en/

Chapter 52

Foreign Terrorist Fighters (FTF)

Nell Bennett
Macquarie University, Sydney, Australia

Scott N. Romaniuk
International Centre for Policing and Security, University of South Wales, Caerleon, United Kingdom

Contents

Introduction 369
A History of FTFs 370
Definitional Debate 371
Why Do They Fight? 372
The Contemporary Threat 373
The Security Response 373
Conclusion 375
Further Reading 376
References 376

Introduction

Foreign terrorist fighters (FTFs), broadly understood, are individuals who travel abroad to fight in civil wars and insurgencies (Malet, 2013). In this chapter, we provide an overview of the FTF phenomenon, followed by a discussion of the difficulties that scholars have in determining just who is an FTF. Two of the key issues in this debate are the extent to which FTFs can be identified by reference to their motivations for taking part in a conflict, and whether these volunteers can be differentiated from mercenary combatants, broadly understood as those who participate in conflicts primarily for monetary compensation (Taulbee, 2007). We conclude with an

DOI: 10.4324/9781315144511-55

analysis of the potential threat posed by returning and returned FTFs and the limitations of current security responses.

A History of FTFs

The concept of the "foreign fighter" predates modern conflict, particularly 9/11. For the past quarter of a century, individuals pledging their support for terrorist and insurgent causes have participated in nearly 100 civil wars and conflicts. The Spanish Civil War (1936–1939), like other civil wars and multifaceted conflicts, emerged as a result of deep-seated feelings of injustice and outrage fueled by internal political weaknesses and foreign interference by states of all stripes. In less than 3 years, 50,000 volunteers from more than 50 countries committed to the cause of either defending or destroying Spanish democracy made their way to Spain through various channels (Renard and Coolsaet, 2018). For countries, those returning home from their time in Spain brought with them training and experience that were seen as threats to national security.

Despite the long history of international and transnational volunteerism in civil wars and conflicts, the term "foreign fighter" has only come into *common* usage over the past 30 years. As part of the "foreign terrorist fighter phenomenon," according to the United Nations Office on Drugs and Crime (UNODC, 2019), the term "foreign fighter" entered in government lexicon to refer to individuals traveling to fight for Al-Qaeda in Afghanistan. The term was eventually transposed to the Iraq theater, referring to fighters taking part in the insurgency that took root in that country following the 2003 US-led invasion. FTF researcher David Malet traced its origin to a scattering of news reports in the 1980s and found that it was not until the Siege of Kunduz in 2001 that the term "foreign fighter" gained traction in popular and policy discourses (Malet, 2009). The term gained prominence with the rise of the Islamic State (Islamic State of Iraq and the Levant, ISIL, or Da'esh), and reports that more than 30,000 people from more than 140 countries traveled to Iraq and Syria to support the insurgency (Barrett, 2017).

The lack of attention paid to FTFs could be a result of the fact that war is typically seen to be the domain of nation-states. Individuals who chose to join foreign conflicts have been largely overlooked and labeled adventurers or mercenaries. However, transnational volunteerism and the broader practice of expeditionary warfare have been common throughout history (Cilluffo, Cozzens and Ranstorp, 2010). Notable examples include the French Foreign Legion (Légion étrangère) – popularized by a wave of legion-inspired movies that followed on P.C. Wren's 1924 novel, *Beau Geste*, about the French Foreign Legion in North Africa, and which itself was the antecedent to the 1926 film under the same title – the Dutch and German volunteers who fought alongside the British in the Revolutionary and Napoleonic Wars, the European volunteers for Garibaldi, the British Auxiliary Legion (La Legión Británica or Westminster Legion) in the First Carlist War (1833–1840) (see Lawrence, 2019), and the International Brigades in the Spanish Civil War (Koller, 2013). Indeed, it can be argued that armed volunteering has been a defining characteristic of Western societies since the American and French Revolutions and the Greek War of Independence (Pécout, 2009).

In contemporary times, FTFs were notable in the Afghan civil war. During the 1980s, Texas Republican politician Charlie Wilson persuaded Congress to support Afghan mujahideen fighters in Afghanistan, turning the war into a covert Central Intelligence Agency (CIA) operation. The efforts of this one man and his impact on the course of history are presented in George Crile's 2003 book, *Charlie Wilson's War: The Extraordinary Story of How the Wildest Man in Congress and a Rogue CIA Agent Changed the History of Our Times*. Wilson's story hit the big screen in 2007 under the shortened title, "Charlie Wilson's War," directed by Mike Nichols.

FTFs played a surprisingly successful role in the Afghan civil war, ultimately pushing the Soviets out of Afghanistan entirely. It is estimated that 20,000 to 25,000 FTFs traveled to Afghanistan between 1984 and 1992 (Cragin, 2017). Some were motivated to fight the Soviet forces and protect their fellow Muslims from foreign invaders (Hegghammer, 2010/2011). Others sought to establish an Islamic caliphate, which is not dissimilar to the purported motivations of the recruits to the Islamic State (Cragin, 2017). FTFs in the Afghan conflict provided a recruitment base for Al-Qaeda, and many later traveled to the Caucasus to take part in the Russo-Chechen war in the mid-1990s (Moore and Tumelty, 2008).

Definitional Debate

Despite the popular interest in this phenomenon, researchers continue to debate exactly who is and who is not an FTF. In 2008, Cerwyn Moore and Paul Tumelty proposed a definition of FTFs that gained traction. According to them, FTFs are "non-indigenous, non-territorialized combatants who, motivated by religion, kinship, and/or ideology rather than pecuniary reward, enter a conflict zone to participate in hostilities" (Cerwyn Moore and Paul Tumelty 2008: 414). This definition is comprehensive; however, some analysts have argued that defining FTFs on the basis of their motivation raises difficulties, as people join foreign wars for a wide variety of reasons, including financial incentives (Malet, 2013; Farrelly, 2013; Moore, 2015).

In 2010, FTF researcher Thomas Hegghammer proposed a definition of a "foreign fighter" as an agent who joins an insurgency, lacks citizenship of the conflict state or kinship with its warring factions, is not directly supplied by an official military organization, and is unpaid (Hegghammer, 2010/2011). Again, this definition raises issues as it excludes participants who are remunerated. While the intention is to distinguish FTFs from mercenary soldiers, it is problematic because most FTFs are provided with some kind of provision. Indeed, leaked internal documents have revealed that recruits to the Islamic State were paid a salary and benefits (Al-Tamini, 2016). Partly with this issue in mind, in his 2015 book on the subject, David Malet adopted a looser definition of a "foreign fighter": "[a] non-citizen of a state experiencing civil conflict who arrives from an external state to join an insurgency."

Jennifer Mustapha, in her article, "The Mujahideen in Bosnia: the foreign fighter as cosmopolitan citizen and/or terrorist," considers the foreign fighters – the Mujahideen in Bosnia in this case – as cosmopolitical inquiry while showing that the "Mujahid is a decidedly unsympathetic figure in the post-9/11 war on terror context and security narrative" (Mustapha, 2013: 743). Thus, while the concept can be approached from different political angles, with the definition itself being altered by a variety of other factors, the concept has evaded a much-deserved and needed critical reflection.

Why Do They Fight?

One of the difficulties with determining who is and who is not an FTF is that it is often hard to distinguish FTFs from mercenary soldiers. While it is often argued that FTFs are driven by ideology and mercenaries are motivated by money, a closer examination of individual combatants shows that the question is more complex.

There are many reasons why people choose to become FTFs. Some choose to fight in foreign wars because they feel they have no future in their home country. Others are drawn by the promise of camaraderie, and indeed, many are encouraged to join the fight by members of their own social network (Cilluffo, Cozzens and Ranstorp, 2010). The role of networks is particularly apparent in ideological and religious conflicts, in which volunteers are often recruited through religious or political institutions (START, 2016). Motivations also change, and an individual's reasons for joining a foreign war may not be the same as his or her motivation for staying in the conflict. Some may choose to remain out of loyalty to their fellow combatants, while others may choose to do so out of ideological conviction.

Humanitarian concerns are another key motivating factor for FTFs. Many people choose to fight in foreign wars out of feelings of empathy for the civilian population of their chosen side of the conflict. In his work on FTFs in the Russo-Chechen war, Moore found that fighters from the Jordanian-Chechen diaspora in the Middle East were motivated to volunteer out of a sense of "relatedness" with, and sympathy for, the Central Asian Chechen community (Moore, 2015). Malet examined the issue of empathy from the point of view of the recruiters. He found that combatants portray the conflict in which they are engaged as a fight for the very survival of their identity group. Characterizing their struggle as an existential threat helps them to acquire recruits from diaspora communities, in cases of ethnic conflicts, and from ideological and religious sympathizers (Malet, 2013).

The desire for adventure is a strong motivator among FTFs. Because insurgents typically lack the resources of conventional forces and cannot attract recruits by offering financial incentives, they typically use the prospects of travel, adventure, and opportunities for heroism to encourage volunteers to join up. In his study of FTFs in the Burmese civil wars, Nicholas Farrelly found that economic incentives did not play an important role in the FTFs' decisions to participate because the guerrillas did not have the resources to provide volunteers with pecuniary rewards. Instead, he found the recruits to be mostly adventurers, some of whom held a genuine desire to help the local people (2013).

Fransjohan Pretorius' study of foreign volunteers in the Anglo-Boer War of 1899–1902 found that many FTFs joined the conflict out of boredom or out of a desire to visit Africa (2010). The desire for adventure has been successfully exploited by the French Foreign Legion, who have used "*change ta vie*" ("change your life") as their recruitment slogan for more than 50 years. Frank J. Cilluffo, Jeffrey B. Cozzens, and Magnus Ranstorp have similarly found that the search for meaning and adventure, the desire to alleviate boredom, and even to rebel against parents or authority figures have been motivational factors for FTFs who have traveled to Iraq and Syria (2010).

The Contemporary Threat

The rise of the Islamic State resulted in more than 30,000 people traveling to Iraq and Syria to become FTFs. It is estimated that 20% of these volunteers were from Western countries (Benmelech and Klor, 2016). The prospect of these FTFs returning to their countries of origin raises serious concerns for policymakers and law enforcement agencies. Such fears have been augmented by the 2015 attacks on the *Stade de France* as well as several Parisian restaurants and bars, which were perpetrated by a team that included former FTFs (Cragin, 2017). One difficulty with evaluating the threat of returned FTFs is that intelligence and security services are understandably reticent about foiled terror plots and returnees who are under surveillance. Another issue is that threat assessment is necessarily predictive, and terrorists often behave in ways that cannot be anticipated.

Many analysts have emphasized the risks of battle-hardened combatants carrying out terrorist attacks in their home countries. However, others have argued that the threat is over-exaggerated. This is because many FTFs die in combat, especially those who are unskilled and selected as cannon fodder or suicide bombers (Hegghammer, 2013; Byman and Shapiro, 2014). Numerous others choose not to return home but rather travel on to the next conflict (Malet, 2013). Of those who do go back to their own countries, many are disillusioned by their experiences on the front (van Zuijdewijn and Bakker, 2014). Of those who seek to perpetrate attacks in their home countries, a large number are intercepted by local security forces. Part of the reason for this is that this latest generation of FTFs is highly active on social media, which makes them easier to identify and surveille (Byman and Shapiro, 2014, 15).

An assumption that underpins security concerns is that FTFs are motivated by anti-Western sentiment. While this is true in some cases, many volunteer combatants are inspired to join foreign conflicts by events overseas rather than issues in their own countries. It is arguable that the conflict in Iraq and Syria is more focused on issues and power struggles within the Muslim world than a reaction against foreign intervention. Also, as Byman and Shapiro observed, fighting in a foreign war confers higher status than committing acts of terrorism. Domestic terrorism does not give the perpetrator the same sense of heroism as victory in a battle (Byman and Shapiro, 2014).

The Security Response

The FTF phenomenon has resulted in more than 200 American volunteers from over 100 cities in 25 states leaving their homes to fight in foreign conflicts (James, Jensen and Tinsley, 2015; START, 2016). These recruits are believed to have joined approximately 35 different militant organizations over a dozen different conflicts (James, Jensen and Tinsley, 2015). It would appear that social networks play a significant role in the recruitment of US FTFs. A recent report from the National Consortium for the Study of Terrorism and Responses to Terrorism found that more than 80% of the FTFs in the Department of Homeland Security (DHS) database were associated with people who held extreme beliefs and/or interacted with radical social networks (James, Jensen and Tinsley, 2015) and that more than 65% of recruits shared such views publicly (START, 2016). It is also notable that 87% of individuals seeking to fight with the Islamic State were aided in their journey by a travel facilitator, a number of whom were family friends or community leaders (START, 2016).

While there have been a substantial number of US FTFs, the figures are considerably lower than those recorded from European countries. Alexander Meleagrou-Hitchens, Seamus Hughes, and Bennett Clifford argue that this difference is due to the greater distance that American volunteers are required to travel to reach foreign battlefields (2018). The difference in volunteer numbers between the United States and Europe may also be due to higher rates of prosecution and conviction of US FTFs (Meleagrou-Hitchens, Hughes and Clifford, 2018). Once convicted, US FTFs typically face more severe sentences than Europeans. Traveling to a foreign country with the intention of joining a designated foreign terrorist organization is a federal offense in the United States which can be penalized with custodial sentences of up to 20 years and lifetime post-release supervision (Meleagrou-Hitchens, Hughes and Clifford, 2018).

The geographic distance between the battlefield and their home countries combined with the strict legal response to foreign fighters in the United States has meant that there have been fewer American returnees than have been seen in Europe (Meleagrou-Hitchens, Hughes and Clifford, 2018). Of those that have made it back, it has been estimated that 28% became involved in domestic terror plots (START, 2016). While proportionately small, this is nonetheless a significant number, as it only takes a few actors to inflict substantial damage.

A key issue when assessing the efficacy of security responses is understanding what causes people to fight in foreign wars. Deterrence may be effective against people who chose to join the struggle for material factors, to enhance their status, or out of a desire for adventure. However, they may be less effective against those who volunteered for humanitarian reasons, or due to emotions such as altruism or empathy for a civilian population they perceived as being unjustly victimized. A longing for justice is a common motivation for FTFs; therefore, it is important to ensure that any punishment is proportionate to the crime and that procedural fairness is observed. The mere perception of injustice can be used by recruiters and propagandists to enlist more volunteers to their side. Thus, overreaction may not only result in wasted resources but could even exacerbate the problem (Byman and Shapiro, 2014).

Disproportionately punitive responses to returnees may backfire by encouraging more people to become FTFs out of solidarity. Equally, overreliance on criminal justice responses may be insufficient as authorities are often unable to assemble sufficient proof to fully prosecute returnees. Battlefield evidence can also be extremely difficult to obtain and may face admissibility issues within courts of law, forcing prosecutors to fall back on lesser charges and causing judges to impose lighter sentences (Meleagrou-Hitchens, Hughes and Clifford, 2018).

Another important issue for law enforcement is how to deal with US volunteers who traveled to foreign conflicts but did not take part in hostilities. Are they complicit in the violence that took place? Many family groups traveled to Syria and Iraq to participate in the Islamic State project. Returning women and children may not have the same needs or pose the same risks as adult male returnees. Resocialization and deradicalization programs for children can prevent intergenerational extremism though the results of such programs have varied widely and continue to receive criticism (Radicalization Awareness Network, 2017). Many women were non-combatants; yet, still assumed active organizational roles in the conflict. These dynamics highlight the need to nuance threat assessment (Meleagrou-Hitchens, Hughes and Clifford, 2018).

Disillusioned returnees are a resource which US authorities could use to prevent future waves of FTFs. The stories of these individuals could be used as counter-propaganda to dissuade others from joining foreign conflicts or transnational terrorist movements. Tales about the realities of battle conditions could help to counteract the romantic perception that recruiters try to portray in their propaganda (Cilluffo, Cozzens and Ranstorp 2010). Disengaged returnees can also be used in targeted intervention and deradicalization programs as a condition of release or an alternative to a custodial sentence or even prosecution (Meleagrou-Hitchens, Hughes and Clifford, 2018).

For the treatment of female returnees who have taken part in terrorist acts abroad and who are considered national security threats as a result of their experiences and activities outside the country, the state generally employs the same criminal and administrative instruments that they normally would when dealing with male returnees. That said, state approaches to female returnees can vary quite a bit and range from prosecution for their direct roles in violence abroad and for the indirect support that they provide their husbands as the primary FTF actors. To analogize, the FTF wife serves as the "homefront" just as women did during World War II – remaining at home and working in the factories to support the war effort by providing essential materials and services – for their husbands (see Capone, 2019). This, however, is not a universal practice by any means and can vary from one authority to another.

Mainstream views contend that women are far less likely to engage in terrorism than men but that does not mean that women cannot take up arms and pose a serious security risk to their home country and to their destination country or countries. By traveling abroad, they can also fulfill key roles overseas that men may not otherwise fulfill, even resulting in tri-national marriages that can assist in the production of future international cooperation among terrorist and insurgent groups.

Conclusion

This chapter has provided an overview of the FTF phenomenon. Transnational volunteerism has long been a feature of civil wars and insurgencies. Yet, the term "foreign fighter" has only recently come into common parlance. Part of the reason for this may be attributed to the difficulties of distinguishing FTFs from mercenary soldiers. This is because categorizing combatants on the basis of their personal motivation is a complex undertaking. Transnational *jihadism* and the rise of the Islamic State brought the concept of FTFs to the attention of the public as well as policymakers and security agencies. While there is legitimate concern about the potential threat posed by returnees, the extent of this threat is unclear. Nuanced threat assessment and proportionate security responses are required to manage these risks.

Further Reading

Hegghammer, T. (2013). Should I Stay or Should I Go? Explaining Variation in Western Jihadists' Choice between Domestic and Foreign Fighting. *American Political Science Review*. 107(1), 1–15.

Malet, D. (2013). *Foreign Fighters: Transnational Identity in Civic Conflicts*. New York: Oxford University Press.

Meleagrou-Hitchens, A., Hughes S., and Clifford, B. (2018). The Travelers: American Jihadists in Syria and Iraq. Program on Extremism. The George Washington University. https://extremism.gwu.edu/sites/g/files/zaxdzs2191/f/TravelersAmericanJihadistsinSyriaandIraq.pdf

References

Al-Tamimi, A. J. (2016). Archive of Islamic State Administrative Documents. *Aymenn Jawad Al-Tamimi's Blog*. http://www.aymennjawad.org/2016/09/archive-of-islamic-state-administrative-documents-2

Barrett, R. (2017). Beyond the Califate: Foreign Fighters and the Threat of Returnees. *The Soufan Centre*. http://thesoufancenter.org/wp-content/uploads/2017/10/Beyond-the-Caliphate-Foreign-Fighters-and-the-Threat-of-Returnees-TSC-Report-October-2017.pdf

Benmelech, E. and Klor, E. F. (2016). What Explains the Flow of Foreign Fighters to ISIS?. NBER Working Paper No. 22190. https://www.nber.org/papers/w22190

Byman, D. and Shapiro, J. (2014). Be Afraid. Be A Little Afraid: The threat of Terrorism from Western Foreign Fighters in Syria and Iraq. Policy Paper 34. Foreign Policy at Brookings. https://www.brookings.edu/research/be-afraid-be-a-little-afraid-the-threat-of-terrorism-from-western-foreign-fighters-in-syria-andy-iraq/

Capone, F. (2019, September 23). The Children (and wives) of Foreign ISIS fighters: Which Obligations Upon the States of Nationality? *QIL*, 60, 69–97. qil-qdi.org/wp-content/uploads/2019/09/05_Child-Soldiers_CAPONE_FIN-2.pdf

Cilluffo, F. J., Cozzens, J. B., and Ranstorp, M. (2010). Foreign Fighters: Trends, Trajectories & Conflict Zones. Homeland Security Policy Institute. George Washington University. https://cchs.gwu.edu/sites/g/files/zaxdzs2371/f/downloads/HSPI_Report_16.pdf

Cragin, R. K. (2017). The Challenge of Foreign Fighter Returnees. *Journal of Contemporary Criminal Justice*, 33(3), 292–312.

Farrelly, N. (2013). Transnational Flows of Military Talent: The Contrasting Experiences of Burma and Thailand since the 1940s. In N. Arielli and B. Collins (Eds.). *Transnational Soldiers Foreign Military Enlistment in the Modern Era* (pp. 145–159). Palgrave Macmillan.

Hegghammer, T. (2010/2011). The Rise of Muslim Foreign Fighters: Islam and the Globalization of Jihad. *International Security*, 35(3), 53–94.

James, P., Jensen, M., and Tinsley, H. (2015). Understanding the Threat: What Data Tells Us about U.S. Foreign Fighters. START College Park, MD. September.

Koller, C. (2013). Recruitment Policies and Recruitment Experiences in the French Foreign Legion. In N. Arielli and B. Collins (Eds.). *Transnational Soldiers Foreign Military Enlistment in the Modern Era* (pp. 87–104). Palgrave Macmillan.

Lawrence, M. (2019). The First Carlist War (1833–40), Insurgency, Ramón Cabrera, and Expeditionary Warfare, *Small Wars & Insurgencies*, 30, 797–817. https://www.tandfonline.com/doi/abs/10.1080/09592318.2019.1638539?journalCode=fswi20

Malet, D. (2009). *Foreign fighters: Transnational Identity in Civil Conflicts*, PhD dissertation, George Washington University.

Malet, D. (2013). *Foreign Fighters: Transnational Identity in Civic Conflicts*. New York: Oxford University Press.

Meleagrou-Hitchens, A., Hughes S. and Clifford, B. (2018). The Travelers: American Jihadists in Syria and Iraq. Program on Extremism. The George Washington University. https://extremism.gwu.edu/sites/g/files/zaxdzs2191/f/TravelersAmericanJihadistsinSyriaandIraq.pdf

Moore, C. (2015). Foreign Bodies: Transnational Activism, the Insurgency in the North Caucasus and 'Beyond'. *Terrorism and Political Violence*, 27(3), 1–21.

Moore, C. and Tumelty, P. (2008). Foreign Fighters and the Case of Chechnya: A Critical Assessment. *Studies in Conflict & Terrorism*, 31(5), 412–433.

Mustapha, J. (2013). The Mujahideen in Bosnia: The Foreign Fighter as Cosmopolitan Citizen and/or Terrorist, *Citizenship Studies*, *17*(6–7), 742–755. https://www.tandfonline.com/doi/full/10.1080/13621025.2012.751718?casa_token=2ZJef3nNQm0AAAAA%3ApEr4oVs-ufL4uCQu62mqlvN_0sLIfzGtQ0rtXyzAoS3AxzHbCwJJRd99shmxT1YdyQB0pidy8Ng

Pretorius. F. (2010). Welcome but Not That Welcome: The Relations between Foreign Volunteers and the Boers in the Anglo-Boer War of 1899–1902. In C. G. Krüger and S. Levsen (Eds.). *War Volunteering: in Modern Times: From the French Revolution to the Second World War* (pp. 122–149). Hampshire: Palgrave Macmillan.

Radicalization Awareness Network. (2017). Responses to Returnees: Foreign Terrorist Fighters and Their Families. RAN Manual. https://ec.europa.eu/home-affairs/sites/homeaffairs/files/ran_br_a4_m10_en.pdf

Renard, T. and Coolsaet, R. (eds.). (2018, February). Returnees: Who are They, Why are They (not) Coming Back and How Should We Deal with Them? Assessing Policies on Returning Foreign Terrorist Fighters in Belgium, Germany and the Netherlands, Egmont Paper 101. https://aei.pitt.edu/94367/1/egmont.papers.101_online_v1-3.pdf

START. (2016). Overview: Profiles of Individual Radicalization in the United States-Foreign Fighters (PIRUS-FF). Department of Homeland Security. https://www.dhs.gov/publication/st-frg-overview-profiles-individual-radicalization-united-states-foreign-fighters-pirus

Taulbee. J. L. (2007). Reflections on the Mercenary Option. *Small Wars and Insurgencies*, 9(2), 145–163.

UNODC. (2019). Foreign Terrorist Fighters: Manual for Judicial Training Institutes South-Eastern Europe. https://www.unodc.org/pdf/terrorism/Foreign_Terrorist_Fighters_Handbook/EN_Foreign_Terrorist_Fighters_Ebook.pdf

van Zuijdewijn, J. and Bakker, E., (2014). Returning Western Foreign Fighters: The Case of Afghanistan, Bosnia and Somalia. ICCT Background Note June 2014. https://www.icct.nl/download/file/ICCT-De-Roy-van-Zuijdewijn-Bakker-Returning-Western-Foreign-Fighters-June-2014.pdf

Chapter 53

Hezbollah

Mariam Farida
Macquarie University, Sydney, Australia

Contents

Introduction 379
Historical Background 380
Hezbollah as a Regional Actor 381
Implications for US Security Concerns 383
Conclusion 384
Further Reading 384
References 385

Introduction

Since its foundation, Hezbollah has drawn considerable attention from scholars of politics and the social sciences. As such, there is a growing body of research into "the Party of God" (hereafter, the Party) (Al-Agha, 2013), especially after its involvement in the bombing of the American Embassy in Beirut in 1984 (Norton, 2007a, pp. 72–81). Consequently, many countries, including the United States in 1997, Australia in 2003, and the European Union in 2013, have included Hezbollah on their terrorist watch lists. However, the Lebanese government continues to identify Hezbollah as a legitimate resistance group with the right to fight the Israeli occupation and subsequent incursions. This chapter aims to identify how Hezbollah is transitioning from a Lebanese political party to an influential regional actor, using the Party's involvement in the Syrian conflict as a case study. This chapter then discusses the implications of this shift for US foreign policy and its homeland security interests. The discussion is framed around the general view that the emergence of non-state actors and insurgent or terrorist groups in regional conflicts, in combination with globalization and

DOI: 10.4324/9781315144511-56

technology advancements, has resulted in such conflicts being more "complex and multifaceted" than traditional inter-state warfare (Cohen, 2016, p. 7).

Historical Background

The emergence of Hezbollah not only stemmed from the Israeli invasion and subsequent occupation of Lebanon in 1982 – ostensibly to control members of the Palestine Liberation Organization (PLO) who had settled in Lebanon and were carrying out attacks against Israel (Norton, 2007) – but also because of this marginalization and the underrepresentation of the Shi'ite community in Lebanon (Traboulsi, 2007, pp. 110–130). The marginalization is claimed to be the product of neglect and political disregard in Lebanon (Saad-Ghorayeb, 2002, pp. 35–80).

According to Norton (2007, pp. 475–491), the primary catalyst in the development of Islamic militant groups in Lebanon was the Islamic revolution in Iran in 1979. However, Lebanese Shi'ites and Iran have a long history of political and religious cooperation dating back to the 17th century (Shaery-Eisenlohr, 2009). Even before Imam Ruhollah Khomeini, a religious leader and politician, took power in Iran, Lebanese Shi'ite groups had already been politically active. For example, there was the *Committee of Ulema of the Bekaa*, "Islamic Committees", and the Lebanese branch of the Iraqi Shi'ite *Al-Dawa Party* – for which Sayyid Muhammad Hussein Fadlallah was the standard-bearer in Lebanon (Al-Agha, 2011a, pp. 54–56).

In addition to this historical cooperation, the grand scale of Israeli aggression against southern Lebanon in 1978, where most of the Shi'ite population resided, gave Iran reason to support the small, emerging Shi'ite groups. Moreover, leaders of Shi'ite groups realized the need to establish a party with a well-organized structure if it was to represent the Shi'ite community in Lebanon effectively. As Qassem (2010, pp. 11–40) has explained, Shi'ite leaders agreed that Islam would be the guiding principle for Hezbollah and that it would follow Khomeini's model of *Wilayat al-Faqih* (Rule of the Clerics, initiated by Khomeini during the Iranian revolution in 1979, which constitutes the recognition of the absolute and supranational political and religious authority of the Supreme Guide, in accordance with the Wali el-Faqih theory).

As a result, the developments and events in Iran, the perceived security threat posed by Israel, and the socio-political underrepresentation of Shi'ites laid the foundation for the establishment of a party based on the principles of resistance against the Israeli occupation and the supremacy of the Supreme Guide (Ayatollah Khomeini at the time) as the descendant of the Prophet and his Imams (Qassem, 2010, pp. 11–40). Given these founding principles, leaders of Shi'ite groups drafted a proposal to establish Hezbollah, a party with a mode of operation which would ultimately combine ideological, practical, and religious dimensions to serve its political objectives (Hamzeh, 2004, pp. 15–40). A committee of nine members – comprising three senior representatives from the cells founded by the *Committee of Ulema of the Bekaa*, the Islamic Committees, and the *Islamic AMAL (Afwaj al-Mouqawma Al-Lubnaniyya)* – was responsible for submitting the proposal to the Supreme Guide for approval. Following the approval by Ayatollah Khomeini, "the different cells dissolved to form a single federating party that took the name Hezbollah" (Qassem, 2010, p. 32).

Hezbollah as a Regional Actor

As a regional actor, Hezbollah has been able to successfully merge its religious identity with its political objectives and this has allowed the Party to present itself as a role model for other jihadist movements such as Hamas. Hamas learned from Hezbollah how to avoid involvement in polemics and how to shun religious debates (Khashan & Moussawi, 2007, p. 16). This was, and remains, an important lesson for Hamas because it provides the movement with a clearer understanding of how it may best try to balance its staunch ideological base with a more pragmatic approach to achieving productive engagement from Palestinian leadership in the West Bank and the international community (Baconi, 2017). Additionally, Palestinian Islamic militants also incorporated suicide missions into their resistance strategy against Israel after interacting with Hezbollah members in Marj al-Zuhur on the Lebanon–Israel borders in 1982.

Power relationships in Lebanon are inevitably impacted by broader dynamics of international relations. Two such dynamics include the provision of finances to the March 14 Alliance (a coalition between Future Movement Party, Lebanese Forces, Phalanges, and Lebanese Socialist Party which erupted following the assassination of the former Lebanese Prime Minister Rafic Hariri) and military aid to the Lebanese government by Saudi Arabia (Gause, 2015, p. 16), and the implications of Hezbollah's alliance with Syria and Iran for its domestic and regional power base (Patrikarakos, 2012, pp. 32–46). This context reconfigures the relationships of power in Lebanon toward a sectarian balance and thus restricts and reshapes Hezbollah as a jihadist movement. This cause-and-effect relationship takes place because the sectarian divide in domestic politics and which underpins regional tensions directly impacts Hezbollah's approach to balancing its "defense of Lebanon" (p. 47) with its defense of "Arab and Islamic peoples" (p. 40) more broadly (Patrikarakos 2012). Qassem (2010) understands that it is important to improve relations with the West in order to earn legitimacy and believes that Hezbollah looks to establish such relations in the future. Hezbollah, however, is seemingly resilient enough to carry out this transformation due to its "tactical evolutions, increased public support, and resilient network of allies" (Silva, 2014, p. 2).

The transition of Hezbollah's regional identity away from the restrictive "jihadist movement" is arguably not hindered if it is not able to improve relations with the West. This is because the increasingly decisive role in regional relations that Hezbollah has achieved since 2013, both militarily (in Syria) and politically (in Lebanon), places it in a stronger position "to manipulate the local relationships between allies and foes" in the region and thus increase its capacity to act as "de-facto arbiter within the Lebanese political system" (Calculli, 2018, para. 4). Furthermore, Dionigi (2014, p. 97) emphasized the contingency of Hezbollah's foundations: "the origins and formation of Hezbollah can be understood and explained only as a result of concurrent dynamics including transnational networks, regional […] and social conditions within the Lebanese context". Therefore, Hezbollah finds itself within a dualistic ideology: one nationalistic and another "transnationally Islamist" (Dionigi, 2014, p. 97). Additionally, the extent to which systemic or domestic pressures influence the actions of non-state actors is explored by Szekely (2016) and may be applied to the case of Hezbollah. One of the key points made by the author is that the assumption that non-state actors have different priorities to state actors implies that system-level factors such as governance arrangements, technology infrastructures, and communication channels will not matter a great deal to them. It is generally assumed that the priorities of non-state actors are typically with local conflicts; namely, the "overthrow of a particular regime, control of specific territory or (in practice if not in theory) victory over rival militias" (Szekely, 2016, p. 75), As such, shifts in regional alignments – as opposed to domestic political affairs – do little to direct their behavior. Rather, the alliance behavior of the non-state actors at the local, regional, and international levels is driven primarily by an evaluation of which alliances will assist them to achieve their objectives (Szekely, 2016).

Hezbollah's actions in response to the Syrian Civil War draw attention to the Party's international agenda – that is, its relations with surrounding states and political movements – and appear to demonstrate that the Party has "other concerns that trump the 'resistance' project" (Szekely, 2016, p. 75). As such, Hezbollah is described by Szekely (2016, p. 76) as a "proto-state actor", occupying "a conceptual space somewhere between states and non-state actors". In Lebanon, the Party has a clear political presence and undertakes actions that support or challenge the elected government's authority or legitimacy, but which lacks "the authority and recognition afforded to the government" (Szekely, 2016, p. 76). In turn, the implication of Hezbollah's proto-state actor position in Lebanon of most interest is the way in which the Party uses religion as a key tool in the different state functions it assumes and in the way in which it conducts its international agenda in the region.

In terms of contemporary international relations theory and the recognition by some theorists, such as Sandler (2004), of the role of religion in international politics, the decision and actions of non-state actors such as Hezbollah, related to regional alignment particularly, take on a new perspective. Much has been written (Nasr 2007), for instance, on the ways that the Arab–Israeli conflict and the Sunni–Shi'ite division in the Middle East (typified by the Saudi–Iranian strategic rivalry) have significantly impacted the foreign policies of states in the region. This includes the extent to which they become involved in the politics of neighboring states and engage with non-state actors (Guzansky & Berti, 2014).

Regarding Hezbollah specifically, Szekely (2016, p. 76) has provided a comprehensive exploration of the way regional politics and events have impacted the Party's alliances. The author has pointed to the way the Party has clearly "benefited militarily, politically and financially from its relationship with Iran". Moreover, Hezbollah's political influence in Lebanon (and its access to arms) increased due to its alliance with Syria during the Syrian occupation of Lebanon up to 2005. More recently, Hezbollah has emerged as a crucial ally of the Assad regime in the Syrian Civil War (Guzansky & Berti, 2014). In turn, Szekely (2016) has also identified the implications of this alliance for the way Hezbollah asserts its regional agenda. As the author explained, although Hezbollah's involvement in the Syrian Civil War was framed as "necessary to preserve the 'Axis of Resistance' for the fight against Israel", another key objective was clearly to preserve the Assad regime (Szekely, 2016, p. 84). In turn, Szekely (2016) asserted that this foreign policy approach not only weakened Hezbollah's political position in Lebanon but also contributed to the destabilization of the country due to the massive influx of nearly 1.2 million Syrian refugees into Lebanon (by the end of 2015), comprising about 25% of the total population.

Irrespective of whether Hezbollah's alliance with Syria has weakened its domestic position, the Party increasingly regards itself as a regional actor rather than just a resistance group. Hezbollah's decisions regarding domestic and regional politics have become increasingly influenced by regional issues and not just resistance to Israel. Thus, the point reinforced by Szekely (2016, p. 85) is that the decision-making and strategic actions performed by the Party to strengthen its legitimacy and survival will increasingly aim to "balance a range of domestic concerns with equally complex issues of foreign policy".

Implications for US Security Concerns

Hezbollah's transformation from a resistance group to a regional actor has important implications for the United States' international security concerns which should be considered from multiple perspectives. First, being labeled by the United States as a "violent extremist organization" (Paine, 2017, p. 1), it may be argued that Hezbollah's alliance with Iran, with the latter acknowledged as "a crucial player … in the Middle East" (Bahgat, 2007, p. 6), means that the Party plays a key destabilizing role in Iran's claim for regional leadership. Indeed, the Iran–Hezbollah relationship, particularly in the context of Hezbollah's involvement in Syria, arguably strengthens Iran's claims for regional leadership as it helps to protect Iran's "closest Arab ally" (p. 34) in the region (i.e., Syria) and strengthen its borders against a hostile Sunni opposition government (Katzman, 2017).

However, given that such a leadership role by Iran includes "an ambitious nuclear program" (Bahgat, 2007, p. 6), the Iran–Hezbollah relationship arguably has the potential to hurt Iran in this regard. Any attempt by Iran to adopt a more robust leadership role in the region is bolstered by its ability to develop nuclear weapons (Nader, 2013). The key concern for the West, particularly the United States, is that an Iran with nuclear capacity will "become more aggressive in challenging US and allied interests" (Nader, 2013, p. ii). In turn, Hezbollah's emergence as a "decisive" actor in regional relations is regarded by the United States as strengthening Iran's position in the region (Nader, 2013). As such, US security concerns and its framework for peace in the region are inevitably impacted by the influence of Hezbollah's actions in the region and on the unfolding regional security relationships among allies and foes (Paine, 2017).

As a counteraction to this outcome, and the threat to US and Middle East security presented by a nuclear Iran, the United States has relied on a policy of imposing sanctions on Iran while pursuing diplomatic engagement (Cordesman, 2018). However, the recent reneging on the 2015 nuclear deal with Iran by the United States, partly in response to the Iran–Hezbollah relationship and its manifestation in Syria to support the al-Assad regime, will see US sanctions on Iran restored and even intensified. In turn, the imposition of stricter sanctions has the potential to hinder Iran's capabilities to pursue a nuclear weapons program.

Second, the Party continues to demonstrate its capabilities as an effective actor in the Middle East region, with the resulting growth in its political power base (Szekely, 2016). As such, in the (albeit unlikely) situation that the United States should engage in a military option against the Party unilaterally or in coalition with Israel or other military forces, for example, it could provoke increased support for Hezbollah among the Lebanese population. This has the potential to destabilize security relationships in the region and increase the threat to US security through a targeted response from Hezbollah or in alliance with Iran (Calculli & Legrenzi, 2016, p. 220).

The third and arguably most important implication for US security concerns associated with the continued strengthening of Hezbollah is related to the Party's presence in Latin America. Since the mid-1980s, Hezbollah has been sending operatives to the so-called tri-border area (TBA)—the nexus of the borders of Brazil, Argentina, and Paraguay – for "recruitment, training, plotting, and other terrorist-related activities" (Keshavarz, 2015, p. 1).

According to Noriega and Cárdenas (2011, p. 1), Hezbollah's proselytizing in the TBA has resulted in the establishment of several Party cells comprising around 500 operatives. Although to what extent Hezbollah (and Iran) enjoy significant religious–political influence in the TBA remains a topic of considerable debate among scholars (Keshavarz, 2015), there is general agreement that the political unpredictability in the region makes it an appealing "breeding ground for extremism" (Keshavarz, 2015, p. 2). Notably, the influence of the United States in Latin America is waning, both as a result of the United States prioritizing its strategic foreign policy interests elsewhere and due to rising anti-US sentiments (Noriega & Cárdenas, 2011). This is at a time when studies predict a likely increase in Muslim populations in new TBA countries; namely, Chile, Bolivia, and Peru by 2020 as a result of ongoing Iranian and Hezbollah proselytization (Kettani, 2010, p. 129). In turn, as Keshavarz (2015, p. 10) warns, this has implications for US security concerns as "Hezbollah will not only maintain a strong foothold in the region, but also broaden its network to unforeseen levels".

Conclusion

Hezbollah has been identified as a violent extremist organization by the United States and has subsequently been placed on its terrorist watch list. This implies that US foreign policy interest in the Party and the perception that its emergence as a non-state actor in the Middle East present genuine concerns for US security. This chapter contextualized the nature of these concerns by profiling the reasons for Hezbollah's emergence as a legitimate resistance movement and political party in Lebanon. In turn, it also explored the implications for regional and international security systems associated with the Party's growing influence as a regional actor.

Further Reading

Al-Agha, J. (2006). *The shifts in Hezbollah's ideology: Religious ideology, political ideology, and political program*. Amsterdam, Netherlands: Amsterdam University Press.

Roy, O. (2004). *Globalized Islam: The search for a new Ummah*. New York, NY: Columbia University Press.

Saade, B. (2015). Martyrology and Conceptions of Time in Hezbollah's Writing Practices. *International Journal of Middle East Studies*, *47*(2015), 723–744.

References

Al-Agha, J. (2011a). *Hezbollah's identity construction.* Amsterdam, Netherlands: Amsterdam University Press.

Al-Agha, J. (2013). *Hezbollah's DNA and the Arab Spring.* Calcutta, India: University of Calcutta Press.

Al-Agha, J. (2011b). *Hezbollah's documents: From the 1985 open letter to the 2009 manifesto.* Amsterdam, Netherlands: Amsterdam University Press.

Bahgat, G. (2007). Iran and the United States: The emerging security paradigm in the Middle East. *Parameters, 37*(2), 5–18.

Baconi, T. (2017). Why now is the time to talk to Hamas. *The Guardian.* https://www.theguardian.com/commentisfree/2017/may/02/hamas-charter-antisemitism

Calculli M. (2018). Hezbollah: From "resistance" to establishment. *OASIS Centre.* https://www.oasiscenter.eu/en/the-war-in-syria-has-transformed-hezbollah

Calculli, M., & Legrenzi, M. (2016). Middle East security: Conflict and securitization of identities'. In L. Fawcett (Ed.), *International relations of the Middle East* (pp. 218–238). London, UK: Oxford University Press.

Cohen, D. (2016). *From Resistance to Regional Involvement: Hezbollah's Changing Role Amid the Syrian Civil War* (Doctoral dissertation).

Cordesman, A. H. (2018). *Iraq: Sanctions and beyond.* New York, NY: Routledge.

Dionigi, F. (2014). *Hezbollah, Islamist politics, and international society.* New York: Palgrave Macmillan.

Guzansky, Y., & Berti, B. (2014). Is the New Middle East stuck in its sectarian past? The unspoken dimension of the "Arab Spring". *Orbis, 57*(1), 135–151.

Hamzeh, N. (2004). *In the path of Hezbollah.* New York, NY: Syracuse University Press.

Katzman, K. (2017). *Iran's foreign and defense policies* (No. CRS-7-5700, R44017). Congressional Research Service Washington United States.

Keshavarz, A. (2015). Iran and Hezbollah in the tri-border areas of Latin America: A look at the "Old TBA" and the "New TBA". *Small Wars Journal, 12*(3), 1–14.

Kettani, H. (2010). Muslim population in the Americas 1950–2020. *International Journal of Environmental Science and Development, 1*(2), 127–140.

Khashan, H. and Moussawi, I. (2007). Hezbollah's Jihad Concept. *Journal of Religion and Society, 9*(2), 1–19.

Nader A. (2013). *Iran after the bomb: How would a nuclear-armed Tehran behave?* Santa Monica, CA: Rand Corporation. Retrieved from https://www.rand.org/content/dam/rand/pubs/research_reports/RR300/RR310/RAND_RR310.pdf

Nasr, V. (2007). *The Shia revival: How conflicts within Islam will shape the future.* London: W.W. Norton & Company Ltd.

Norton, R. (2007a). *Hezbollah: A short history.* Princeton and Oxford: Princeton University Press.

Norton, R. (2007b). The role of Hezbollah in Lebanese domestic politics. *The International Spectator, 42*(4), 475–491.

Paine, A. (2017). National military strategy of the United States of America, 2017. Daniel Morgan Graduate School of National Security, 1–19.

Patrikarakos, D. (2012). State within a state. *New Statesman Ltd, 141*(5087), 36–39.

Qassem, N. (2010). *Hezbollah.* London UK: Saqi.

Saad-Ghorayeb, A. (2002). *Hezbollah: Politics and religion.* London, UK: Pluto Press.

Sandler J. (2004). *Bringing religion into international relations.* New York, NY: Palgrave Macmillan.

Silva, H. (2014). Intelligence briefing report hezbollah: The threat to the United States JUS-429 Terrorism. https://static1.squarespace.com/static/5aca4b0cb98a78beef1869ee/t/5acaaac203ce649b2a495e7e/1523231426858/Executive+Briefing+Hezbollah.pdf

Shaery-Eisenlohr, R. (2009). Territorializing piety: Genealogy, transnationalism, and Shi'ite politics in modern Lebanon. *Comparative Studies in Society and History, 51*(3), 533–562.

Szekely, O. (2016). Proto-state realignment and the Arab Spring. *Middle East Policy, 23*(1), 75–91.

Traboulsi, F. (2007). *A history of modern Lebanon*. London, UK: Pluto Press.

Chapter 54

Hijackings

Eugenio Lilli
University College Dublin, Dublin, Ireland

Contents

Introduction 387
Definition 388
Train Hijackings 388
Ship Hijackings 388
Airplane Hijackings 389
Conclusion: Terrorism, New Technologies, and Hijackings 390
Further Reading 391
References 391

Introduction

The phenomenon of hijacking is not limited to any specific geographical area; incidents of hijacking have occurred throughout the world. Similarly, hijacking is not the preserve of any particular actor; single individuals, groups, and states have all relied on hijacking for a variety of reasons. Despite hijacking's global nature, it may be argued that the United States holds a special place in the history and development of this phenomenon. In fact, the term "hijacking" seems to have originated in the early twentieth-century United States, and it was during an attack on US soil in 2001 that hijacking reached its highest level of destructiveness to this date. This chapter begins by providing a working definition of the phenomenon. It then explores the development of hijacking through examples of incidents during which hijackers alternatively seized trains, ships, and airplanes. This chapter concludes with a discussion of the relationship existing between hijacking, new technologies, and terrorism, which makes the phenomenon of hijacking an enduring threat to US national security.

DOI: 10.4324/9781315144511-57

Definition

Modern hijacking is generally defined as the illegal seizure of a land vehicle, ship, or aircraft in transit by force or the threat of force. Although the exact origin of the word "hijacking" remains unclear, the term gained popularity during the Prohibition Era in the United States (1920–1933) when rival bootleggers commandeered truckloads or shipments of illegally manufactured liquor from each other (Joyner, 1974, p. 117). Since then, there have been significant changes in the nature of the act and in the motivations of the perpetrators. To begin with, acts of hijacking have become increasingly violent. The original purpose of forcibly diverting a vehicle to a new destination has expanded to include the use of the commandeered vehicle as a lethal weapon to destroy civilian and military targets. Moreover, early hijackers overwhelmingly showed personal or private motives as justification for their actions – i.e., deserting the military, escaping political oppression, or mental disorders. However, since the late 1960s, hijacking has increasingly become the preserve of individuals and groups acting for public or political reasons – i.e., publicizing a group's grievances or making political requests (Holden, 1986). Even though since the late twentieth century, hijacking has most frequently involved the seizure of commercial aircraft, there are infamous cases of hijacking that involved other types of vehicles, some of which will be discussed below.

Train Hijackings

On the morning of May 23, 1977, nine armed Moluccans seized a rural train in the Netherlands and took around 50 passengers and the crew hostage. This was not the first time the group had resorted to hijacking. Moluccans; in fact, it had seized another Dutch train before, in December 1975. The 1977 hijackers put forward clear political demands. They wanted the Dutch government to establish an independent Republic of South Maluku on Indonesian territory, sever all diplomatic ties with the Indonesian government, and release all the Moluccan prisoners involved in the incidents of 1975. After 20 days, on June 11, Dutch special forces eventually stormed the train and ended the crisis. During the rescue operation, six of the hijackers died along with two hostages. The rest of the hijackers were arrested and convicted by Dutch authorities (Jakarta Globe, 2014). The 1977 Dutch train siege shows how hijacking had evolved into a popular tool for disaffected individuals to promote political grievances.

Ship Hijackings

On October 7, 1985, four armed men associated with the Palestine Liberation Front hijacked the Italian cruise ship *Achille Lauro* off the coast of Egypt. The hijackers demanded that Israel release 50 Palestinian prisoners and threatened to blow the ship up if a rescue mission were attempted. After it was refused permission to dock at a Syrian port, the *Achille Lauro* headed back to Egypt. Meanwhile, the hijackers decided to kill a Jewish-American passenger in a wheelchair and to toss his body overboard. Ensuing negotiations led the hijackers to agree to free the remaining hostages in exchange for a pledge of safe passage by Egyptian authorities. On October 10, the hijackers were allowed to board an airplane to leave the country. However, US fighter jets intercepted the airplane and forced it to land in the NATO air base of Sigonella, Italy. There, the hijackers were taken into custody by Italian authorities, stood trial, and eventually received prison sentences (The New York Times, 1985). The direct involvement of at least five different national governments during the 1985 seizure of the *Achille Lauro* underscores the ability of hijacking operations to draw international attention to the hijackers' cause.

Airplane Hijackings

Among all the different types of modern hijacking, airplane hijacking (also known as skyjacking or aerial hijacking) is probably the most common. Many sources identify the first reported case of airplane hijacking with an incident that occurred on February 21, 1931, in Peru (Holden, 1986, p. 880). The number of airplane hijackings per year mostly remained below double digits until the late 1960s when the frequency of such incidents increased dramatically. Airplane hijacking had its Golden Age between 1968 and 1972 (Koener, 2013). During that period, the number of reported aerial hijackings peaked at more than 300 cases worldwide (Aviation Safety Network Database). Some people resorted to acts of hijacking for transportation. They included refugees, fleeing persecution from hostile governments, and criminals, escaping prosecution from national law enforcement agencies (Holden, 1986, pp. 878–879). Other people resorted to airplane hijacking for the purpose of extortion. In a most storied case, on November 24, 1971, a man, alias "D.B. Cooper", succeeded in commandeering an aircraft in the United States. In exchange for freeing the passengers, D.B. Cooper demanded $200,000 and a parachute. After the airline company acceded to his demands, he jumped from the flying craft and disappeared with the ransom money (The New York Times, 2016).

Starting in the late 1960s, airplane hijackings increasingly became the tool of choice for radical groups seeking the satisfaction of political demands and/or a platform to publicize their views. The Palestinian group known as the Popular Front for the Liberation of Palestine (PFLP) initiated the use of aerial hijacking for political reasons in July 1968 when PFLP militants seized an aircraft en route to Israel and forced it to land in an Algerian airport instead (The New York Times, 2016). The frequency of airplane hijackings began to decrease in the mid-1970s, partly as the combined result of increased international cooperation and heightened security. The international community negotiated agreements that would make it harder for hijackers to find safe haven. These international agreements included the 1963 Tokyo Convention on Offences and Certain Other Acts Committed on Board Aircraft (1963); the 1970 Hague Convention for the Suppression of Unlawful Seizure of Aircraft; and the 1971 Montreal Convention for the Suppression of Unlawful Acts against the Safety of Civil Aviation (1971). Moreover, in 1978, at a G7 summit in Bonn, West Germany, the governments of the United States, Canada, Italy, France, Britain, West Germany, and Japan threatened to impose an aerial boycott against any country that either harbored hijackers or refused to return hijacked airplanes (Martin, 2011, p. 258). Along with legal measures, government agencies and the airlines also implemented new security measures. These included the use of metal detection and X-ray devices to search passengers and their carry-on baggage prior to boarding. Another security innovation was the Sky Marshal program whereby plain-clothes armed law enforcement officers would be aboard some flights (Dugdale-Pointon, 2005).

However, such measures did not stop 19 members of Al-Qaeda, an international extremist organization, to seize four airplanes in the United States on September 11, 2001. Al-Qaeda hijackers turned the commandeered airplanes into deadly weapons against both civilian and military targets. They flew two of the aircraft into the World Trade Center in New York, one into the Pentagon near Washington, DC, and crashed the last one onto an empty field in Pennsylvania. The final toll was around 3,000 people killed, making it by far the deadliest hijacking in human history (The Washington Post, 2011). In order to prevent similar attacks, security measures in airports were further tightened, the number of sky marshals was increased, and aircraft cockpits were reinforced and kept locked in flight (The New York Times, 2016). Legal measures were also reviewed to respond to the new circumstances. The 2010 Beijing Protocol supplemented the 1970 Hague Convention for the Suppression of Unlawful Seizure of Aircraft (1970) while the 2014 Montreal Protocol amended the 1963 Tokyo Convention on Offences and Certain Other Acts Committed on Board Aircraft. These new measures have not completely eliminated the threat of airplane hijacking but have certainly contributed to keep the number of such incidents per year extremely low. The 9/11 attacks are a telling example of the increased potential for violent and deadly effects of modern hijacking.

Conclusion: Terrorism, New Technologies, and Hijackings

In recent decades, countering terrorism has become a top priority for US policymakers. The 9/11 attacks made all too clear how preventing hijacking should be an integral part of such an effort. The link between terrorism and hijacking has therefore attracted the attention of security researchers. David Rapoport, for example, argues that each new "wave" of terrorism relies on some kind of newly available technology (Rapoport, 2003). That was as much the case of dynamites for nineteenth-century anarchists as it is today the case of cyber technologies for twenty-first-century hackers. According to Rapoport, the technology that characterized the terrorist wave of the 1970s was commercial aircraft. Two factors help to explain this. First, the 1970s witnessed a marked increase in civilian reliance on air travel, therefore increasing the number of potential targets for terrorist hijacking. Second, the international character of air travel, airplanes' ability to easily cross oceans and national borders, and the multiple nationalities of the potential hostages made airplane hijacking especially appealing to terrorists aiming at spectacular acts which, in turn, would increase the visibility of the group and their cause. Following 9/11, one could rightly add to Rapoport's list the incredible destructiveness of hijacked airplanes used as lethal weapons to destroy targets beyond the aircraft itself. More recently, means of transportation's increased reliance on Information and Communications Technologies has made them vulnerable to cyberattacks. Tellingly, in 2017, news outlets reported the successful attempt by a US Department of Homeland Security research team to remotely hack a commercial aircraft. Moreover, cyber experts working for the US government have warned that it is only "a matter of time before a cyber security breach on an airline occurs" and that the consequences of such a breach could be "catastrophic" (Motherboard, 2018). Given these ongoing developments, it is safe to say that hijacking is likely to remain a serious threat to US homeland security for the foreseeable future.

Further Reading

Philip Baum (2016), *Violence in the Skies: A History of Aircraft Hijacking and Bombing* (Chichester, UK: Summersdale Publishers Ltd).

Brendan I. Koener (2013), *The Skies Belong to Us* (New York, NY: Crown Publishers).

J. Paul de B. Taillon (2002), *Hijacking and Hostages: Government Responses to Terrorism* (Westport, USA: Praeger Publishers).

References

Aviation Safety Network Database https://aviation-safety.net/statistics/period/stats.php?cat=H2. Accessed 14 February 2018.

T. Dugdale-Pointon (14 June 2005), Hijacking, http://www.historyofwar.org/articles/concepts_hijacking.html

Hague Convention for the Suppression of Unlawful Seizure of Aircraft (1970) https://treaties.un.org/doc/db/terrorism/conv2-english.pdf

Robert T. Holden (1986) The Contagiousness of Aircraft Hijacking. *American Journal of Sociology*, Vol. 91, No. 4, 874–904.

Jakarta Globe (2014, November 05). Dutch State Sued Over 'Excessive Force' Against 1977 Moluccan Train Hijackers.

Nancy Douglas Joyner, (1974). "*Aerial Hijacking as an International Crime*", New York, NY: Oceana Publications.

Brendan I. Koener, "*The Skies Belong to Us*", New York, NY: Crown Publishers, 2013.

Gus Martin ed., "*The SAGE Encyclopedia of Terrorism*", Second Edition, Thousand Oaks, CA: SAGE Publications, 2011.

Montreal Convention for the Suppression of Unlawful Acts against the Safety of Civil Aviation (1971) https://treaties.un.org/doc/Publication/UNTS/Volume%20974/volume-974-I-14118-English.pdf

Motherboard (2018, June 6). US Government Probes Airplane Vulnerabilities, Says Airline Hack Is 'Only a Matter of Time'. https://motherboard.vice.com/en_us/article/d3kwzx/documents-us-government-hacking-planes-dhs?utm_source=mbtwitter

The New York Times (1985, October 07). Palestinian Gunmen Hijack Achille Lauro.

The New York Times (2016, March 29). Why Airline Hijackings Became Relatively Rare.

D.C. Rapoport (2003). The Four Waves of Rebel Terror and September 11. In C.W. Kegley, Jr (ed.), *The New Global Terrorism* (pp. 36–52). Hoboken, NJ: Prentice Hall.

Tokyo Convention on Offences and Certain Other Acts Committed on Board Aircraft (1963) https://treaties.un.org/doc/db/terrorism/conv1-english.pdf

The Washington Post (2011, September 8). What Was 9/11?. https://www.washingtonpost.com/lifestyle/style/what-was-911/2011/08/31/gIQAQL5RDK_story.html?noredirect=on&utm_term=.1c354041348e

Chapter 55

Improvised Explosive Devices (IEDs)

Jade Hutchinson
Macquarie University, Sydney, Australia

Contents

Introduction 393
As a Method of Violence 394
Composition and Combustion 394
Variety and Innovation 395
A Brief History and Trend of IEDs 395
Contemporary Findings in the SCP Approach 396
SCP Techniques 396
The U.S. Military Test 397
Rationality and Public Education 397
Rationality 397
Public Education 398
Conclusion 399
Further Reading 400
References 400

Introduction

Terrorists use improvised explosive devices (IEDs) because they are a successful method of terrorism; IEDs can not only be inexpensive and easily assembled but also provide an extremist with an advanced aptitude in subjugating fear. Considering this, how can terrorism prevention analysts best counter IED terrorism? The correct direction must include an acute awareness of what an IED is, why extremists utilize IEDs as a method of violence, and what anti-IED terrorist techniques are considered

DOI: 10.4324/9781315144511-58

most effective. Accordingly, this chapter aims to provide an outline of what an IED is, what are the advantages of IED terrorism as a method of violence, a brief history of IED terrorism, which situational crime prevention (SCP) techniques are favored by the United States' military, and how this information can benefit the protection of civilian targets through public education and application of SCP techniques to limit the opportunity of future IED attacks. The potentiality of IED terrorism demands attention be paid to those approaches considered most effective in the face of IED terrorism and how to educate those most vulnerable to IED terrorism.

As a Method of Violence

IEDs as a method of violence complement terrorism as a technique of punishment and coercion (Pape, 2003). IEDs provide an intimidating and destructive incendiary display, which demands the attention of expansive audiences and communicates a clear message of terror (Juergensmeyer, 2013). The IED strategically reverberates two waves of psychological perturbation upon a target audience (Yip, 2018). An initial shock of fear is induced by the destructive explosion, while the fear of anticipating another such explosive terrorist attack produces a persistent undercurrent of fear. As an operational tactic, simply constructed IEDs with publically available materials enable any unexperienced lone extremist to negotiate and influence powerful states with immense destructive power at the expense of the public (Department of Homeland Security, 2010; BBC News, 2013). This chapter focuses on those extremist individuals with resolute intention to detonate an IED as a form of punishment and coercion to attain concessions favorable to the violent extremist or their group.

Composition and Combustion

Understanding the composition and use of a common IED is instrumental to IED terrorism prevention. Although there exist many definitions, Gill, Horgan, and Lovelace (2011) coalesced 29 different definitions to suggest that an explosive device becomes:

> [An] IED when any or all of the following – explosive ingredient, initiation, triggering or detonation mechanism, delivery system – is modified in any respect from its original expressed or intended function. An IED's components may incorporate any or all of military grade munitions, commercial explosives or homemade explosives. The components and device design may vary in sophistication from simple to complex.
>
> (p. 742)

This lucid definition allows for the broad spectrum of sophistication attributed to the production of IEDs. It accounts for the large disparity of proficiency and maturity between terrorist outfits over time (Gill, Horgan, Lovelace, 2011).

But how can a relatively small device contain so much destructive power? The destructive potential of IEDs is due to the concentration and rapid release of heat and gas. This is called the "over-pressure effect" (Yip, 2018). Simply, once the explosive material is ignited within a sealed metal container, gas and heat rapidly concentrate inside and stress the metal frame (Yip, 2018). The build-up of heat and gas results in immense internal pressure which eventually exceeds the metal bonds containing it; the bonds rupture and rapidly release the thermal heat and gas, causing a shockwave-like effect (Yip, 2018; Zoltán, 2016). This emits an immense exothermic wave of turbulence that is fatal for surrounding persons (Zoltán, 2016).

Variety and Innovation

Various forms of IEDs necessitate different levels of complexity and competency to use or operate them. For instance, given the quantity of the chemical agent and environmental conditions, igniting just 2.205 pounds of high-grade explosive is sufficient to rupture a container containing toxic chemical, such as Sarin gas, to create a shockwave in tandem with nearly 3,280 square feet of poisonous gas (Yip, 2018). This is an example of an improvised explosive chemical device (IECD). The IECD needs an instructed practitioner to delicately construct and precisely ignite with the correct amounts of the correct chemicals. If clumsily constructed with incorrect measurements, the materials are not correctly chosen, and the terrain and weather conditions are not accounted for, this will significantly influence the dispersion of the toxic chemical cloud as the primary killer (Yip, S.W, 2018). A large quantity of explosive material can be ignited using a comparatively tiny amount of high-grade explosive inside a cylindrical metal tube as a form of detonator. This IED innovation has often been deployed via a street vehicle. The vehicle borne bomb (VB-IED) is the most popular method of IED terrorism, being recorded in over 40 different countries, due to its mobility and ability to carry a larger payload (Action and Armed Violence, 2017).

IEDs can be designed to function using varying types of action or trigger methods. A clock-like or digital timer releases a tremor switch to close an electrical circuit, which activates the detonator igniting the payload. This use of mechanical precision removes a portion of technical skill from the operative. A timer IED allows a terrorist to reliably predict the time it takes to plant, activate the IED, and escape (Yip, 2018). On June 15, 1996, the Provisional Irish Republican Army (PIRA) used IED terrorism as coercive violence to pressure the British government to withdraw from Northern Ireland, for example. The PIRA used a similar clock-like mechanical timer to trigger the IED and ignite 3,307 pounds of explosives within a truck in Manchester, obliterating multiple buildings on surrounding city blocks (BBC News, 2016).

A Brief History and Trend of IEDs

Since September 11, 2001, the United States has concentrated on countering new innovative, unconventional, and invasive methods of terrorism by non-state actors. Although the Irish Republication Army waged the largest, and most innovative, terrorist bombing campaign against the British rule of Northern Ireland, with 19,000 IEDs detonated against the United Kingdom between 1970 and 2005 (Oppenheimer, 2009), the Iraq War in 2003 popularized the term IED into U.S. military parlance, due to the intensity and diversity of IEDs used against U.S. military targets and local civilian populations (The National Academies, 2009).

Regarding the global landscape of IED terrorism, the United States has experienced a relatively low frequency of IEDs (LaFree and Legault, 2009). However, the most destructive IED plots have been executed by domestic organizations and lone wolves on iconic targets (Wehri, 2007). Such attacks include the Liberation Army Fifth Battalion's attempt to detonate an IED and collapse the World Trade Center in 1993 and Timothy McVeigh's VB-IED upon the Oklahoma City Murrah Federal building in 1995, killing 168 people. Since then, the use of VBIEDs and suicide IEDs has grown dramatically and become an ominous global threat in populated civilian societies (LaFree and Legault, 2009).

Statistics demonstrate how IEDs have become a global method of terror at the expense of civilians (Wehri, M.T. 2002). Recorded IED attacks between 2011 and 2016 occurred in 85 different countries and territories, with the top six countries with civilian casualties resulting from IEDs in 2016 being Iraq (with 4,851 civilian casualties), Syria (1,863), Afghanistan (1,856), Turkey (1,718), Pakistan (1,150), and Somalia (629) (Action and Armed Violence, 2017). The use of IEDs against civilians has become a major extension of international terrorist actors. Since its formation, the so-called Islamic State of Iraq and Syria (IS) has emerged as an international influence for the use of IEDs in civilian settings, with 86% of ISIS's IED attacks claiming civilian lives, and of those attacks, approximately 66% have occurred in populated areas (Action and Armed Violence, 2017). This virulent turn toward a prolific use of IEDs against civilians in populated areas has magnified the attention paid to terrorist outfits using IEDs (Wehri, 2007). The incremental increase of sophistication, civilian availability, and asymmetric destructive and psychological potential of IEDs attracts extremists toward the use of IEDs as a crude mode of terrorism, propaganda, and recruitment. Western democracies remain vulnerable and vigilant to counter the progressive and surreptitious threat of terrorism using IEDs in civilian settings (Pape, 2003, Homeland Security, 2005. Wehri, 2007).

Contemporary Findings in the SCP Approach

SCP Techniques

The SCP approach is a set of techniques that, if implemented accurately, is an efficacious terrorism prevention strategy in military operations. The SCP approach can be characterized as a practical strategy to ***harden*** potential targets of terrorism through 'opportunity reduction' (Clarke, 1980). This is done by implementing infrastructural and operational techniques which 'block' opportunities for terrorists to execute attacks on selected targets (Lasley and Guffey 2017). By constructing permanent environmental barriers and operational changes against terrorists, this is thought to 'help to either increase the costs or reduce the benefits of executing terrorist activities. This means that terrorists will be inclined to abandon their plans' (Lasley and Guffey 2017; Clarke and Newman, 2006, 2009; Morris, 2015).

The SCP approach provides comprehensive terrorism prevention strategy that is well-adaptive against IED terrorism. However, the SCP approach is an amalgam of 25 theoretical techniques (Center for Problem-Orientated Policing, 2018). Which SCP techniques prove efficacious in practice? To answer this question, we must turn to those who test SCP techniques in terrorism-prone areas.

The U.S. Military Test

The U.S. military considers the SCP approach an overall useful aid to systematically reduce the opportunity for terrorist attacks. However, a study conducted by James Lasley and James Guffey (2017) confirmed that some categories of SCP techniques practically prevail over others. Lasley and Guffey (2017) examined the opinion of 155 U.S. military personnel, from varied roles and ranks, to gauge the 'opinions of those representing the armed forces who are experienced observers' in terrorism prevention to identify which SCP techniques are most favorable. According to the study participants, U.S. military attitudes toward SCP techniques considered the following as most effective in terrorism prevention (Lasley and Guffey 2017):

- Target hardening (increase effort): Construct layers of security to the target with multiple security screenings and an increased security presence.
- Access control (increase effort): Increase defensible space surrounding the target and construct road check points to the target.
- Reducing anonymity (increase risk): Increase target surveillance with personnel and digital surveillance and block opportunities for terrorists to hide in surrounding structures.

This consensus is significant to the U.S. homeland security efforts against domestic IED terrorism and the U.S. public at large, as it narrows the selection of SCP techniques with a view to efficacy and applicability. Subsequently, this removes the probability of misallocating resources on other less successful techniques and reduces the probability of potential terrorist attacks occurring against less comprehensive SCP techniques. Additionally, these findings signal to civilians the nature and necessity of understanding IED terrorism and highlight the benefit in adopting militarily-tested SCP techniques.

Rationality and Public Education

Rationality

In addition to the above findings, Lasley and Guffey's (2017) study supports the idea that terrorists engage in a *rational* 'mental cost/benefit decision-making process' before executing acts of terrorism on a selected target (Hsu and Newman, 2011). Terrorists consistently execute attacks in constellations favorable with their spatial and environmental circumstances. Braithwaite and Johnson (2011) observed that IED terrorists in Iraq were deterred from executing attacks in areas where counterinsurgencies were present, for instance (Braithwaite and Johnson, 2011). Counterintuitively, the presence of counterinsurgents, as an opposing threat, in those areas served to reduce the perceived opportunity for a successful IED attack. This rationality highlights a vulnerable step in the terrorist's perception. Terrorists, like other criminals, need a positive evaluation of their targets' defenses and potential opportunities (Cornish and Clarke, 2002; Hsu and Newman, 2011). This suggests that adequate deterrents reduce attractive spatial opportunities for terrorists (Lasley and Guffey, 2017; Braithwaite and Johnson, 2011). Tested SCP techniques can be mobilized to target the extremist's sensitivity to limited spatial opportunities in civilian settings.

Public Education

Violent extremists wantonly exploit public life in populated areas as a resource to leverage socio-political concessions. As mentioned previously, the Action on Armed Violence IED Monitor (2017) states that between 2011 and 2016, VBIEDs have cost more lives and injuries than all other weapon launch methods combined (57%). The same report states that between 2011 and 2016, IEDs have caused injury or killed 133,317 civilian and armed actors, of which 109,696 (81%) were civilians. From those 109,696 civilian deaths and injuries, 99,060 (91%) occurred in urban populated areas (Action and Armed Violence, 2017). Therefore, if the clear majority of terrorism using IEDs occurs against civilians in populated areas, the law enforcement and public sphere must be aware of IEDs and the surreptitious actors who use them. If civilian populations are comfortably able to implement public education on IEDs in tandem with tested SCP techniques, as a form of strategy, this would illuminate society on behavior symptomatic of potential IED extremists and how to block terrorist plots (Felson and Clarke, 1997). It must be acknowledged that not every SCP technique or depth of information dissemination can be implemented or reached across every IED-prone population. Some terrorism-prone areas may harbor the necessary infrastructure or resources to adequately implement the maximum combination of SCP and education programs to protect civilian targets, while others may only be able to apply a selected few SCP on prioritized targets, in tandem with education programs for civilian personnel. Regardless, common knowledge about IED terrorism could enable anyone to detect IED extremists, foresee vulnerabilities in target security, and apply appropriate anti-IED SCP techniques to civilian institutions, and thus, help to prevent future IED attacks.

This line of thought can lead terrorism prevention authorities into a conundrum of public intelligence. What level of information and awareness should the public possess about IEDs and IED terrorism? As mentioned above, the intelligence needed to correctly design and construct an IECD is critical for its success as a method of terrorism. Hence, the emphasis on placing an opprobrium or eradicating such information from society is obvious, but unlikely to be attainable. However, in contrast, the importance of public knowledge on the various tell-tale signs, features, or functions of IEDs must be stressed. Take the case of the 1996 Manchester Bombing: a phone call warned of the bomb's existence before detonation, and the law enforcement officer who arrived at the scene confirmed the location of the IED by recognizing certain features of a VB-IED (BBC News, 2016). The application of knowledge about IEDs allowed for the evacuation of the area and reduced the death toll from thousands to zero, with only a few hundred-injured due to glass fragments from shattered window panes off nearby buildings.

Civilians have the potential to prevent terrorism; however, they lack the intelligence to identify and address target vulnerabilities with tested SCP techniques, IED characteristics, or extremist behavior. The ability to recount what features you may have seen, smelled, or heard in regard to an IED will significantly inform the response team and emergency services on what they are responding to and how to reduce the potential for further damage (Yip, 2018). To do this, the public must know what those components are to report. Additionally, the dissemination of IED intelligence enables civilian-prone areas of terrorism to collectively implement a form of anti-IED tactic through public awareness (The Express Tribune, 2017). Subsequently, this could further remove anonymity from public spaces and increase the risk of detection for clandestine agents, and thus, deter and prevent terrorism. By way of example, Singapore has implemented advanced methods in public education and intelligence to counter terrorism for nearly a decade (Yuit, 2009). For example, in 2009, following a complex military exercise called Northstar VII, Prime Minister Lee Hsien Loong commented on the utility of civilians as agents of detection against terror attacks, stating that, "[y]ou must carry on living life as normal… but at the same time always keep an eye open and be slightly suspicious and vigilant" (Yuit, 2009, p. 23).

In 2016, Singapore received targeted threats by terrorist groups which lead the Singaporean Government to launch the SGSecure Movement. The SGSecure Movement was designed to educate, sensitize, and train civilians against radicalized behavior, IED terrorism tactics, and crisis recovery, for example, through strategically placed advertisements and easily accessible online information (Yuit, 2009; Lam, 2017). Public education remains a prominent anti-IED tactic for Singapore and is increasingly adopted in observing countries.

Although there exists information in open source intelligence avenues (The Office of the NJ Regional Operations Intelligence Center Intelligence & Analysis Threat Unit, 2016), the education of such issues needs programs, teachers, and technology that represent an authority, provide knowledge, and equip civilians with anti-IED defenses. This is not to say that the effort to educate civilian audiences about IEDs is not without its courses, teachers, or security technology. For example, the Department of Homeland Security's Office for Bombing Prevention offers a Counter-IED Training Course; the International Centre for Political Violence and Terrorism Research organizes presentations on anti-IED intelligence to mixed rooms of civilian and non-civilian audiences; and Keyless Access Security is an innovation of security technology which enables civilians to remotely use non-static non-physical security systems (Department of Homeland Security, 2018. Yip, S.W, 2018. KAS, 2018). However, the U.S. military's favored SCP techniques need to be appropriately blended into these civilian programs. If advanced, the strategy of extending the public's erudition and ability through education and the application of militarily-tested SCP in civilian settings could bridge the gap between the military arena, law enforcement authorities, and civilians.

Conclusion

Counter-terrorism agencies attempt to counter IED terrorism by constantly adjusting strategies and making improvements based on past experiences and accomplishments (Yip, 2018). The need to become imaginative and interoperable in the counter-IED-terrorism community is vital to formulate tactics that deter or interdict attacks. The target population of terrorism needs to be educated on the functions of IEDs, the symptoms of different IEDs pre- and post-detonation, and how best to report that information to responding teams. It would be valuable for future research to test the efficacy of U.S. militarily–favored SCP techniques with a creative focus on IED terrorism prevention in civilian settings and understand how a program of interoperability between military forces, law enforcement bodies, and the public sphere on anti-IED intelligence would favorably benefit civilian actors in IED-prone civilian areas. Findings to these studies may provide the public with effective anti-IED techniques that do not compromise civilian life but instead improve the ability to detect and counter future IEDs attacks.

Further Reading

Clarke, R. V. and Newman, G. R. (2006). *Outsmarting the terrorists.* Westpoint, CT: Praeger Security International.

Lasley, J. and Guffey, J. (2017). A U.S. military perspective on the promise of Situational Crime Prevention for combating terrorism. *Journal of Policing, Intelligence and Counter Terrorism*, 12(2), pp. 85–104.

Wehri, M. T. (2002). *Preventing an improvised explosive device (IED) terror campaign in the United States.* Ohio, United States: University of Dayton.

References

Action and Armed Violence. (2017). Improvised Explosive Device (IED) Monitor 2017. *Government of Norway: Ministry of Foreign Affairs.* https://reliefweb.int/sites/reliefweb.int/files/resources/IED-Monitor-Report-for-web-final.pdf

BBC News. (2013). *Q&A: Pressure cooker bombs.* http://www.bbc.com/news/world-us-canada-22179102

BBC News. (2016). *When the IRA bombed Manchester.* http://www.bbc.com/news/uk-england-manchester-36474535

Braithwaite, A. and Johnson, S. (2011). Space–time modeling of insurgency and counterinsurgency in Iraq. *Journal of Quantitative Criminology*, 28(1), pp. 31–48.

Center for Problem Orientated Policing. (2018). *25 Techniques of Crime Prevention.* University of Albany; State University of New York. http://www.popcenter.org/25techniques/ [Accessed 29 Mar. 2018.]

Clarke, R. V. (1980). Situational crime prevention: Theory and practice. *British Journal of Criminology*, 20(1), pp. 136–147.

Clarke, R. V. and Newman, G. R. (2006). *Outsmarting the terrorists.* Westpoint, CT: Praeger Security International, pp. 88–94.

Clarke, R. V. and Newman, G. R. (2009). Reducing the opportunities of terrorism: Applying the principles of situational crime prevention. In W. G. Stritzke (Ed.), *Terrorism and torture: An interdisciplinary perspective.* New York, NY: Cambridge University Press, pp. 213–245.

Cornish, D. and Clarke, R. V. (2002). Analyzing organized crimes. In A. R. Piquero and S. G. Tibbetts (Eds.), *Rational choice and criminal behaviour: Recent research and future challenges.* New York: Routledge Press, pp. 41–63.

Department of Homeland Security (2010). [online] *Pressure Cookers as IED Components.* https://info.publicintelligence.net/DHSpressurecookerieds.pdf

Department of Homeland Security. (2018). [online] *Office for Bombing Prevention (OBP).* https://www.dhs.gov/obp

Felson, M. and Clarke, R. V. (1997). The ethics of situational crime prevention. In G. R. Newman, R. V. Clarke, and S. G. Shoham (Eds.), *Rational choice and situation crime prevention.* Ashgate: Aldershot, United Kingdom.

Gill, P., Horgan, J. and Lovelace, J. (2011). Improvised explosive device: The problem of definition. *Studies in Conflict & Terrorism*, 34(9), pp. 732–748.

Homeland Security. (2005). *IED Indicators.* United States. https://www.hsdl.org/homesec/docs/csis/nps21-072505-02.pdf

Hsu, H. Y. and Newman, G. R. (2011). Rational choice and terrorist target selection. In U. Kumar and M. K. Mandal (Eds.), *Countering terrorism: Psycho-social strategies.* New York: SAGE, pp. 227–249.

Juergensmeyer, M. (2013). Religious terrorism as performance violence. In Jark Juergensmeyer, Margo Kitts, and Michael Jerryson (Eds.), *The Oxford Handbook of Religion and Violence*, Oxford, UK: Oxford University Press, pp. 1–15

KAS. (2018). *Security in mobile key technology.* KAS Keyless Access Security Website. https://kas.com.au/secuirty-mobile-key-technology/

LaFree, G. and Legault, R. (2009). Empirical analysis of IED Attacks. *National Consortium for the Study of Terrorism and Responses to Terrorism.* University of Maryland. http://www.start.umd.edu/research-projects/empirical-analysis-ied-attacks

Lam, L. (2017). *Singapore under highest terror threat in recent years: 8 key points from MHA's terror report – The Straits Times.* https://www.straitstimes.com/singapore/singapore-under-highest-terror-threat-in-recent-years-8-key-points-from-mhas-terror-report

Lasley, J. and Guffey, J. (2017). A U.S. military perspective on the promise of Situational Crime Prevention for combating terrorism. *Journal of Policing, Intelligence and Counter Terrorism*, 12(2), pp. 85–104.

McCormick, G. H. (2003). Terrorist decision making. *Annual Review of Political Science*, 6, pp. 473–507.

Morris, N. A. (2015). Target suitability and terrorism events at places. *Criminology and Public Policy*, 14(2), pp. 417–426.

Nasser-Eddine, M., Garnham, B., Agostino, K. and Caluya, G. (2011). *Countering Violent Extremism (CVE) Literature Review.* Counter Terrorism and Security technology Centre. Australian Government, Department of Defence: Defence Science and Technology Organisation.

Newman, G. and Clarke, R. V. (2016). *Rational choice and situation crime prevention: Theoretical foundations.* New York, NY: Routledge Press.

Oppenheimer, A. (2009). [online] Evolution of IEDs. *Public Service Journal.* http://www.andyoppenheimer.com/wp-content/uploads/2010/07/PUBLIC-SERVICE-HA19-A-Oppenheimer-ATL.pdf

Pape, R.A. (2003). The strategic logic of suicide terrorism. *American Political Science Review*, Cambridge Press: The University of Chicago, 97(3), pp. 343–361.

The Express Tribune. (2017). *Public awareness, education on IED blasts imperative to save lives - The Express Tribune.* https://tribune.com.pk/story/1343894/public-awareness-education-ied-blasts-imperative-save-lives/

The National Academies. (2009). [online] *IED Attack: Improvised Explosive Devices.* Homeland Security. https://www.dhs.gov/xlibrary/assets/prep_ied_fact_sheet.pdf

The Office of the NJ Regional Operations Intelligence Center Intelligence & Analysis Threat Unit (2016). *Improvised explosive device awareness.* New Jersey: United States Government. https://info.publicintelligence.net/NJROIC-IED-Awareness.pdf

Yip, S. W. (31 Jan. 2018). Improvised Explosive Devices and their Effects. Presented at the *11th Terrorism Analyst Training Course, International Centre for Political Violence and Terrorism Research*, Singapore.

Yuit, G. C. H. (2009). Singapore's approach to counterterrorism. *CTC Sentinel*, 1(12), pp. 21–24. https://ctc.usma.edu/app/uploads/2010/08/CTCSentinel-Vol2Iss12-art7.pdf

Zoltán, K. (2016). Explosion of improvised explosive device effects on structures. *Hadmérnök*. http://www.hadmernok.hu/161_06_kovacsz.pdf

Chapter 56

Irish Republican Army (IRA)

Glen M. E. Duerr
Cedarville University, Cedarville, OH, United States

Contents

Introduction 403
Evolution of the IRA and Its Historical Background 404
Organizational Strategy and Leadership 405
IRA's Decline and Current Status 406
IRA's Relevance to the United States 407
Conclusion 408
Further Reading 408
References 408

Introduction

The political conflict in the British Isles is a staple of the history of the territory, undulating with vicissitudes in times of peace and war (see English 2004; Hanley 2010). From early colonial explorations by the English in Ireland, beginning with the Norman Conquest in 1169, the two countries have an intertwined history. For example, Ireland was formally brought into union with Great Britain through the 1800 Act of Union, which created the United Kingdom of Great Britain and Ireland. In the aftermath of a series of political upheavals in the late 19th and early 20th centuries, culminating in the Irish Civil War of 1919–1921, the Irish Free State was given dominion status within the British Empire in 1921 as a fulfillment of the Anglo-Irish Treaty. Full independence was granted in 1937, and then a republic was formed in 1948. Yet, the division of Ireland into Northern Ireland and the Republic of Ireland still causes political disputes among some of the peoples residing within the territory.

This chapter is split into four major sections. The first section introduces the Irish Republican Army (IRA) by providing a historical background before describing the evolution of the organization. The second section discusses the organizational

DOI: 10.4324/9781315144511-59

strategy and terrorist tactics of the IRA. In recent history, the Good Friday Agreement (GFA) is discussed with relevant impacts on the IRA. The final section describes the role of the United States as linked to the IRA, the GFA, and the British and Irish governments.

Evolution of the IRA and Its Historical Background

The term IRA has numerous meanings, depending on the time in history. For example, the IRA once referred to sets of Fenian raids—violent acts against the British in North America carried out by Irish republicans in the United States—in the 18th and 19th centuries. The IRA was also responsible for fighting the Irish War of Independence against the British, as a means of gaining dominion status within the British Empire—de facto independence at the time. Often linked with socialism, the IRA built a base of support among the political left and workers within Ireland.

The IRA opposed the 1920 Anglo-Irish Treaty dividing Ireland, in alignment with major Irish political parties like Fianna Fail but in contrast to Fine Gael—two of Ireland's prominent political parties that oppose and support the treaty, respectively. In the Irish Civil War, 1922–23, Pro-Treaty forces defeated the IRA (called the Irregulars during the conflict) and its supporting groups to maintain the new status quo of Northern Ireland as part of the United Kingdom.

The IRA, during the time of The Troubles from 1968 to 1998, split into two major factions. Both of these factions (see next paragraph) were branded terrorist organizations responsible for violence across the British Isles (McGarry and O'Leary 1995). The IRA is on the lists of formal terrorist organizations in several Western countries, especially in the aftermath of September 11, 2001. These countries include the United States and the United Kingdom. However, in some places and among some groups, the IRA is looked upon in more favorable terms as liberators and freedom fighters. No formal government lists the IRA as a group of freedom fighters, although the group retains some support among private individuals. Several governments have not designated the IRA among its list of active terrorist organizations, especially where there is no obvious geographic connection, largely in order to appear neutral on the issue or to avoid getting involved in a quarrel contained in the British Isles.

As noted in the above paragraph, the IRA has a long history, one reflected in divisions over time that have spliced the organization into a range of different groups. Most notably, the Official IRA (OIRA) and the Provisional IRA (PIRA) served as the two terrorist wings after the split of 1969 over the issue of political leadership (English 2004). By 1972, the OIRA disbanded in the aftermath of Bloody Sunday—also known as the Bogside Massacre wherein British troops fired on protesters in Derry, Northern Ireland, killing 28 people. In 1986, the Continuity IRA (CIRA) broke away from the PIRA. Then, in 1997, the Real IRA (RIRA) broke away from the PIRA (Hanley 2010). The U.S. government lists a couple of these variants of the IRA as terrorist organizations officially: RIRA in 2001 and CIRA in 2004 (U.S. State Department, 2018). These factions matter because there were severe political and strategic reasons for their splits. Over time, various splits within the IRA have eroded support for the group, both internally with rivalries between members and externally in light of the broader implications of supporting (or being perceived to support) terrorism in the aftermath of the 9/11 attacks. Put simply, there is no real tolerance of any support for terrorism, even if the root cause is national liberation; this has effectively become the official position of the U.S. government.

In 1921, when Northern Ireland was partitioned from the rest of Ireland, approximately 70 percent of the residents in the six counties of Northern Ireland were Protestant (Wallace 1971). This left a relatively small Catholic minority in what Protestants and the British government described as Ulster—nine counties in the northeast of Ireland, six of which comprise Northern Ireland. The IRA was reportedly created as a mechanism to defend this small Catholic minority in Northern Ireland in 1917 in the aftermath of the Easter Uprising in 1916. The Protestant majority in Northern Ireland feared that on the island of Ireland, the Catholic population of the Republic of Ireland coupled with their creedal brethren in Northern Ireland far outnumbered the Protestants. However, when taking the whole of the British Isles, the Protestant population including those in Great Britain was much larger than all of the Catholics in Ireland (and any Catholic minority in Great Britain). For Protestants in the United Kingdom, however, the larger Catholic population across the continent of Europe was much larger than their population. The general fear in the United Kingdom at the time was that Catholics would dominate Protestants and even attempt to forcibly change Britain. Thus, cyclically, each group feared takeover by a larger amorphous majority residing outside of their immediate borders. Effectively, no group has ever taken over another group, at least by force. Yet, both sides felt it necessary to defend themselves vehemently in the face of potential opposition. Both Catholics and Protestant in Northern Ireland therefore tried to connect their localized struggles to wider fears; Protestants to the United Kingdom, and Catholics to the wider Catholic and Irish populations of the world.

The demography has changed in the last 100 years; the Catholic population of Northern Ireland, for example, is roughly equivalent to the Protestant population now, leading to fears that a Catholic takeover is still possible. In the wake of these concerns, the GFA still holds as a mechanism to retain peaceful relations between sectarian communities. The GFA, signed in 1998, brought to an end The Troubles by creating a pathway toward a Northern Irish Assembly, in which both Catholic and Protestant groups shared power through a consociational arrangement—a mechanism of governance to share power between different groups in deeply divided societies (McGarry and O'Leary 2004).

Organizational Strategy and Leadership

The IRA was particularly active during The Troubles between 1968 and 1998. During a time of heightened conflict between the British states and the peoples of Northern Ireland, the IRA conducted hundreds of terrorist attacks. Officially, the IRA conducted 488 terrorist attacks from 1973 to 1997, killing 115 people (McGladdery 2006, 3). This led to a change in numerous areas of policy. Some were overt; others were more pragmatic. For example, most rubbish bins/garbage cans were removed from the city of London, in response to bombs being set in waste receptacles. As another example, security has been increased, especially at Conservative Party rallies and meetings in England. IRA attacks had an enormous impact on British security forces with improvements to policing and counter-terrorism activities domestically, as well as widespread international coordination with allies to better communicate about the potential for terrorist attacks.

Since the IRA conducted hundreds of terrorist attacks over the course of several decades, a comprehensive list is not possible. As a means of demonstrating the regularity with which the IRA (or offshoot groups) conducted terrorist attacks, here is a list of some of the most violent attacks resulting in high numbers of fatalities. The wave of terrorist attacks started in 1973 with a set of book bombs at the Old Bailey (Sutcliffe and Alchin 2018). Major railway hubs in London were also attacked later that year at Victoria, Kings Cross, and Euston stations. The first high-fatality attack occurred in February 1974 when 12 people were killed when a bus carrying British soldiers was attacked in northern England. Symbolic targets were also chosen by the IRA. Later in 1974, the palace of Westminster was targeted as a means of expressing conflict with all elements of the British state, including the royal family. In 1981, the Chelsea barracks and Oxford Street were both attacked, and in 1983, the high-profile department store, Harrod's was the major target—all of these are major symbolic targets across the city of London (Sutcliffe and Alchin 2018; McGladdery 2006).

The British military faced numerous attacks across the 1970s, 1980s, and 1990s. For example, in July 1982, the IRA attacked the British Horse Guards in Hyde Park. This attack killed four members of the British military alongside seven horses within the guard (Sutcliffe and Alchin 2018). In Deal, Kent, in 1989, 11 members of the British military were killed, and 30 others were injured in an attack on the Royal Marines Music School by the IRA. Some members of the IRA sought direct military confrontation with the British military, even though the attacks were conducted as coordinated acts of terrorism (the IRA directly targeted the British military, in part, to elicit a direct military response).

Other targets were chosen for a range of different reasons, such as commerce. For instance, an attack on a business in Cookstown in 1992 killed eight people. Cultural events were another reason. Eleven people were killed in Enniskillen in 1987 during a Remembrance Day celebration. Some of the targets were political in nature. For example, there were numerous other high-profile attacks such as the 1991 attacks on Number 10 Downing Street, the official residence of the British Prime Minister (McGladdery 2006). In January 1991, Prime Minister John Major was meeting with his Gulf War cabinet to discuss strategy in the Middle East when a mortar blast attacked the back of the residence. In 1984, the Conservative Party convention held in a hotel in Brighton was attacked with the goal of assassinating Prime Minister Margaret Thatcher. Thatcher obviously survived the attack, but five people were killed.

Even when the number of attacks decreased with the initiation of peace talks in the mid-1990s, the IRA maintained a presence even after the GFA in 1998. Among the most devastating of all the IRA attacks was the Omagh attack of 2001 that claimed the lives of 28 people (McGladdery 2006).

IRA's Decline and Current Status

The GFA of 1998 (also known as the Belfast Agreement) brought a formal end to the conflict—The Troubles—with a peaceful resolution (Hancock et al. 2010; Ó Dochartaigh

2015). Third-party actors like the United States, through President Bill Clinton and Senator George Mitchell (D-ME), served as non-biased outside actors, with substantial leverage and political capital to bring the parties together. Moreover, Northern Ireland was promised a devolved assembly, akin to the Scottish Parliament, and Welsh Assembly (Coakley 2003; McGarry and O'Leary 2004; Ó Dochartaigh 2015). Although there were some initial irregularities, the North Irish Assembly opened in Belfast in 2006. The unicameral body holds seats for 90 elected representatives as a mechanism of maintaining peaceful relations for the province in the aftermath of The Troubles (Coakley 2003).

In contemporary Northern Ireland, there are two major positions: unionist and republican. The unionists seek to maintain the political status quo, with Northern Ireland remaining within the United Kingdom; the republicans seek an end to the British monarchy and for Northern Ireland to join the Republic of Ireland. Politically, the IRA and its offshoots support the republican side. They have some historic connections to Sinn Féin (SF)—a political party with the second largest share of seats in the Northern Irish Assembly (in 2018). SF also has seats in the British House of Commons but refuses to occupy them as a means of protest. SF also holds seats in the Dáil Éireann and Seanad Éireann—the lower and upper houses of the Republic of Ireland's parliament. Although this is a suboptimal solution for many unionists, SF is able to fight out political debates through non-violent means, which maintains a more peaceful posture initiated since the GFA was signed (Ó Dochartaigh 2015).

The IRA is no longer a major factor in British, Irish, or Northern Irish politics. In general, even the most vehement political parties on both sides of the divide tend to debate issues rather than resort to violence. In the 2010s, some vestiges of the IRA remain, though. For example, CIRA has claimed, or been suspected of, recent terrorist attacks. Likewise, the New IRA (NIRA) is also responsible for attacks. Both groups killed one civilian in terrorist attacks in 2016 (Sutcliffe and Alchin, 2018). Despite the continuation of violence, the levels are much lower than in previous years and decades. The IRA has some staying power since sectarian issues remain, yet the power of the groups continues to decline as peaceful political normalcy grows in Northern Ireland.

IRA's Relevance to the United States

The Irish diaspora in the United States comprises a reported 40 million people, more than eight times the number of people in the Republic of Ireland. Thus, the IRA's connections to the United States is significant, especially in cities like Boston and San Francisco with particularly high Irish–American populations. Frequently, members of the IRA would "cool off" after a terrorist attack by staying in the United States. Some places have a clear political allegiance to Ireland such as the pub/restaurant in San Francisco, called "Ireland's 32," a reference to 26 counties in the Republic of Ireland in addition to six in Northern Ireland.

At times, British and American leaders were very close in their relationships. For the British, "the special relationship" with the United States is among the most important in their foreign policy. Examples include Churchill and Roosevelt around World War II, Thatcher and Reagan in the 1980s, and Blair and Bush with the Iraq War in the

2000s. Even in the midst of challenges and attacks with the IRA, the Anglo-American relationship remained pretty strong, although dependent upon those in power.

The United States, however, played a significant role in ending the violence during The Troubles. As mentioned earlier, the tandem of President Clinton and Senator Mitchell were integral to negotiating peace terms among the British and Irish governments, as well as Catholic and Protestant communities of Northern Ireland. The culmination of the negotiations was the GFA, which was signed in the wider debate surrounding devolution in the United Kingdom. When Tony Blair won the 1997 UK general election with the Labour Party, he did so with a platform to restart the failed 1979 devolution referendums in order to provide the people of Scotland, Wales, and Northern Ireland an opportunity for closer governance. This was the major catalyst for discussions on devolution, which presented a peaceful political alternative to IRA violence.

Conclusion

The IRA was predominantly active in the British Isles in the 1970s, 1980s, and 1990s. The violence perpetrated by the IRA killed hundreds and injured thousands. It took concerted efforts on the part of numerous international actors, including the United States, to bring the various sides to the negotiating table in an agreement, the GFA, that has lasted for over 20 years. There is no guarantee that IRA's violence will ever completely subside, but the aforementioned consociational structure will help in opposing Catholic and Protestant communities to maintain peaceful relations (Coakley 2003; McGarry and O'Leary, 2004).

The IRA also serves as an important case study as to how terrorism can be diminished over time and can eventually end (Cronin, 2009). Alongside Euskadi Ta Askatasuna (ETA), a major terrorist organization in the Basque Country of Spain and France, IRA is the most notorious terrorist group to have subsided in terms of violent attacks in recent decades.

Further Reading

Cronin, Audrey Kurth. *How terrorism ends: Understanding the decline and demise of terrorist campaigns*. Princeton, NJ: Princeton University Press, 2009.

Dingly, J. (2012). *The IRA: The Irish Republican Army*. Santa Barbara: Praeger.

White, R. W. (1989). "From Peaceful Protest to Guerrilla War: Micromobilization of the Provisional Irish Republican Army," *American Journal of Sociology*, 94(6). https://doi.org/10.1086/229155

References

Coakley, John. (2003). "Ethnic Conflict and its Resolution: The Northern Ireland Model," *Nationalism and Ethnic Politics*, 93(3), 25–53.

Cronin, Audrey Kurth. (2009). *How terrorism ends: Understanding the decline and demise of terrorist campaigns*. Princeton, NJ: Princeton University Press.

English, Richard. (2004). *Armed struggle: The history of the IRA*. Oxford: Oxford University Press.

Gregory, Kathryn. (2010). "Provisional Irish Republican Army (IRA)." *Council on Foreign Relations*, 16 March. https://www.cfr.org/backgrounder/provisional-irish-republican-army-ira-aka-pira-provos-oglaigh-na-heireann-uk

Hancock, Landon E., Joshua N. Weiss, and Glen M.E. Duerr. (2010). "Prospect theory and the framing of the Good Friday Agreement." *Conflict Resolution Quarterly*, 28(2), 183–203.

Hanley, Brian. (2010). *The IRA: A documentary history 1916–2005*. Dublin: Gill & Macmillan Publishing.

McGarry, John, and Brendan O'Leary. (1995). *Explaining Northern Ireland: Broken images*. London: Wiley-Blackwell.

McGarry, John, and Brendan O'Leary. (2004). *The Northern Ireland conflict: Consociational engagements*. Oxford: Oxford University Press.

McGladdery, Gary. (2006). *The provisional IRA in England: The Bombing campaign 1973–1997*. Dublin: Irish Academic Press.

Ó Dochartaigh, Niall. (2015). "The Longest Negotiation: British Policy, IRA Strategy and the Making of the Northern Ireland Peace Settlement," *Political Studies*, 63(1), 202–220.

Sutcliffe, John and Geoffrey Alchin. (2018). "Terrorism from the Troubles to Good Friday: The IRA in Northern Ireland and the British Isles". In Duerr, Glen (ed.). *Secessionism and terrorism: Bombs, blood, and independence*. London: Routledge.

U.S. State Department. "Foreign Terrorist Organizations" Accessed on October 23, 2018. https://www.state.gov/j/ct/rls/other/des/123085.htm

Wallace, Martin. (1971). *Northern Ireland: 50 Years of self-government*. New York: Barnes & Noble Inc.

Chapter 57

Lone Actor Terrorism

Raphael D. Marcus
King's College London, London, United Kingdom

Contents

Introduction 411
Definitional and Methodological Issues 412
Lone Actors? A Spectrum of Connectivity to the Group 414
Directed Attacks 415
Enabled Attacks 416
Inspired Attacks 417
Conclusion and Directions for Future Research 418
Further Reading 419
References 419

Introduction

With the prevalence of lone actor terrorist attacks in the West over the past 5 years from across the ideological spectrum, a significant amount of academic literature has emerged which attempts to better understand this phenomenon. Central issues that the literature has sought to address are the extent of these lone actors' connectivity to and direction from the terrorist group itself and the relationship between the lone actor and other likeminded individuals. In order to adequately examine these questions, this chapter first reviews the broad methodological issues which have yet to be resolved in the academic literature surrounding how to adequately define "lone actor terrorism" and highlights the most important works that have outlined a typology or profile of such individuals. Next, the chapter highlights the debates underway surrounding how "alone" such lone actors really are. Much of the academic scholarship over the last decade depicted these "lone wolves" as socially isolated loners, often with mental health issues, who lacked direct ties to a group and who are radicalized

DOI: 10.4324/9781315144511-60

and inspired to act largely due to ideological grievances. As the field of study has developed and become increasingly sophisticated, these original assertions have been challenged. Important large-scale studies have explored the extent to which these individuals actually act alone throughout the radicalization and attack planning process and highlights the varying degree of connectivity such lone actors have to a group and others in their social network. These studies place such individuals within a wider sociocultural context and highlight the importance of the lone actor's interpersonal relationships and extended network as being of critical importance for understanding the degree of "aloneness." While many of the original themes from the earlier scholarship on lone actor terrorism still hold true, additional issues have been recognized and assertions have become more nuanced.

This chapter uses illustrative examples of lone actor terrorism affiliated with the Islamic State of Iraq and Syria (ISIS) to animate the methodological discussion, while not downplaying the long history of lone actor terrorism or the significance and prevalence of other motivations and forms of lone actor terrorism, especially "right-wing" terrorism (for example, various white-supremacist attacks in the United States). An examination of recent ISIS plots in the United States and Europe demonstrates that most of these lone actors are often radicalized and inspired to carry out attacks based on interactions with small groups of likeminded individuals, either in person or online. It highlights how lone actors are not as "alone" as initially thought, that social network dynamics still have a significant explanatory power in understanding radicalization, mobilization, attack planning, and involvement in terrorist activity, and that a "spectrum of connectivity" exists between ISIS and its adherents. Overall, this chapter illustrates that while academic literature on lone actor terrorism is still in a relatively nascent stage, important strides have been made toward providing a more nuanced approach to better understanding the phenomenon.

Definitional and Methodological Issues

Despite the increased interest in the topic, academic literature on lone actor terrorism suffers from significant methodological problems in regards to quality and rigor and also lacks an accepted definition of what constitutes such an act. As in the broader field of terrorism, definitional disagreements are rampant; multiple existing definitions of lone actor terrorism exist, each with its own merit, but which vary on key points, making systematic comparisons between studies difficult and problematic (Feldman 2013; Gill 2015, p. 11; Spaaij 2010; Spaaij and Hamm 2015, p. 168–169). An important study by the Royal United Services Institute canvassed much of the existing literature and offered a working definition of a "lone actor terrorist" which is helpful for the field but will undoubtedly continue to attract criticism (Ellis et al., 2015, p. 3):

> The threat or use of violence by a single perpetrator (or small cell), not acting out of purely personal material reasons, with the aim of influencing a wider audience, and who acts without any direct support in the planning, preparation and execution of the attack, and whose decision to act is not directed by any group or other individuals.
>
> (although possibly inspired by others)

A central methodological issue that has emerged is that once a perpetrator is characterized as a lone actor terrorist, differences often arise on how to interpret connectivity to a terrorist group and the extent to which individuals are affiliated with the group or an extended network of likeminded individuals. This raises questions surrounding whether the lone actor was externally directed by the group's leadership or merely inspired to act alone or in conjunction with networked elements of the group. Notably, the answers to such questions often remain within law enforcement circles and are unavailable to academia (Spaaij and Hamm 2015, p. 174). Regarding the role of co-conspirators, several studies have grappled with whether groups of two or three individuals with no formal, direct connectivity to a terrorist group (referred to as "isolated dyads" or "triads," respectively) should be considered in the lone actor data set analyses (Gill, Horgan, and Deckert 2014, p. 426; Pantucci 2011; Pantucci et al. 2015, p. 5; Spaaij and Hamm, 2015, p. 169–170).

Significant attention in the field has been devoted toward developing a typology or profile of a lone actor terrorist, but such typologies have often been used as a tool to avoid the "definitional obstacle" (Bouhana et al. 2018). The debates surrounding the psychological profile of a lone actor terrorist are muddled and not particularly helpful, as personality traits and characteristics that apply to lone actor terrorists – isolation, trauma, military experience, anger, stifled ambition, and so forth – also apply to murderers, mass shooters, group-directed terrorists, and to those who are not terrorists at all (Corner, Bouhana, and Gill 2018; Hamm and Spaaij 2015, p. 6; Spaaij 2010, p. 862–864). Gill's important study explored the differences between group-directed and lone attackers and highlights typological and behavioral traits based on rigorous me Insufficient information to provide references for these items in the text. thodological research, although he ultimately concluded that there is no reliable profile of a lone actor terrorist (Gill 2015, p. 120). Spaaij (2012, p. 13) also illustrated that there is no typology for lone actor terrorists regarding motivating factors, grievances, and the degree of linkage to external groups.

Sociodemographic and behavioral characteristics of lone actor terrorists were analyzed from across the ideological spectrum and while it was concluded that no uniform profile existed, certain themes did arise (Hamm and Spaaij 2015). While many, but not all, lone actor terrorists were socially isolated, they also did engage in a detectable and observable range of activities within a wider group or social movement and were rarely impulsive in their decision-making. (Gill, Horgan, and Deckert 2014). Quantitative studies have categorized perpetrators by ideology and have examined jihadists, right-wing and left-wing terrorism, single issue attacks (anti-abortion, animal rights etc.), and others that may fall within a combination of several categories in order to draw conclusions about typologies of attacker personalities (Ellis et al. 2016; Gill, Horgan, and Deckert 2014; Spaaij 2010). However, as noted, standard methodological issues arise regarding assigning clear-cut motives of perpetrators, largely due to difficulty with access to data, especially with attempts to understand motives or explicit links to a terrorist organization. (Spaaij 2012, p. 44; Spaaij and Hamm 2015, p. 174).

Some have argued that ideological motivation influences attacker target selection, especially lone actors' propensity to select nongovernmental or civilian targets, while others have noted that uniformed law enforcement are now the most common target of lone actor terrorism (Becker 2014; Hamm and Spaaij 2015). Highlighting a problematic issue surrounding ideological motives, when compared to far-right actors, Islamist attackers were more likely to be depicted as criminal or violent in media reports and were often portrayed as being potentially representative of a subset of a community. Conversely, far-right actors were more likely to be labeled as mentally ill and were frequently described more individualistically (Parker et al. 2018, p. 14). Furthermore, there are lengthy disputes about which ideological motivation is more prevalent; Gill, Horgan, and Deckert (2014, p. 429) claim that since 1990, religiously inspired lone attacks are most common, while Spaaij (2012, p. 37) claims that over the last five decades, right-wing and white-supremacist lone actor terrorism is most prevalent. Regardless of which form of terrorist violence is most common, it is evident that attacks are driven by diverse ideological grievances (Bouhana et al. 2018).

Lone Actors? A Spectrum of Connectivity to the Group

While early notions that lone actors operate with little contact with formal groups or networks were popularized, there is a growing body of literature that argues that academia, the media, and government have consistently mislabeled networked attackers as lone actors. Most lone actors uphold social ties that are crucial to both their adoption and maintenance of the motivation and capability to commit an attack. They often displayed a degree of commitment to extremist movements, which may help counterterrorism practitioners in focusing their efforts to identify and investigate new individuals who have gravitated toward violent extremism (Bakker and de Graaf 2011; Schuurman et al. 2018b). Social network analysis of both Islamist and right-wing lone actor attackers has illustrated that individuals were connected with and relied on small clusters of tightly knit individuals with whom they discussed ideological concepts, relied on for support, and often signaled their intent to commit an attack (Hofman 2018, p. 15).

Lone attackers often exhibited "leakage," which is defined as communication to a third party of an intent to do harm to a target and can include in-person communication, planned or spontaneous utterances, online posts, diary entries, and so forth. Leakage is generally restricted to detectable or discoverable behavior even if the intent to be discovered is not evident by the subject (Meloy and O'Toole 2011, p. 514). In many lone actor attacks (58% according to one study), perpetrators "leaked" their intentions or involvement in potentially violent activity, as other people generally were aware of their extremist ideology or potentially violent views (Gill, Horgan, and Deckert 2014, p. 1196; Schuurman et al. 2018a). However, important findings noted that individuals labeled as lone actors who leaked their intentions to others (month or even years ahead) often turned out to have plot-relevant interpersonal ties to larger networks and were influenced by social ties and small-group dynamics, including peer pressure, leader–follower interactions, and other social–psychological processes. These findings led leading scholars in the field to proclaim that the lone wolf typology is "the typology that should not have been" (Schuurman et al. 2018b).

When examining illustrative incidents of lone actor terrorism from a practitioner-oriented perspective, it appears that group dynamics remain persistently important and that the degree to which elements within a network convey "weak signals" which will aid interdiction and counterterrorism efforts has been downplayed. Furthermore, in-person relationships appear as significant as internet and online contact when it comes to both radicalization and mobilization (Gill 2015, p. 85–100; Lindekilde et al. 2017).

Overall, the early wave of academic literature on the subject seems to have been overly rigid in its classification of lone actors, which was exacerbated by the aforementioned definitional and methodological issues. Rather than obfuscating our understanding of lone actor terrorism through rigid categories regarding the degree of control or direction by a terrorist group or network, it is more appropriate to view such ties along a spectrum or continuum of connectivity to the group itself (Schuurman et al. 2018b; Spaaij and Hamm 2015, p. 171).

Selected ISIS-linked plots clearly demonstrate that many attackers initially labeled as lone actors were actually not that "alone" and can be placed into three broad, fluid categories. Attackers were either directed, enabled, or inspired by the group, and each point on the continuum is heavily reliant on network dynamics and the attacker's interpersonal relationships, both in person or online. In fact, much of the older terrorism literature on how interactions within the group or network affect both radicalization, cell formation, planning, and attack mobilization appear more relevant than ever (for example, Sageman 2004; Silber and Bhatt 2007), though perhaps with a greater emphasis on online communications compared to prior decades. Networks, internal group dynamics, and interpersonal relationships have a significant explanatory power for understanding the degree of "aloneness" of the attacker and span of control of the group. As Schuurman et al. (2018a) highlighted, ties to online and offline extremist networks were observed in an examination of recent plots and are considered critical to a lone actor's motivation and capability to commit an attack.

Directed Attacks

The high-profile case of Mohamed Merah, who attacked a Jewish school in Toulouse, France, in 2012, killing three children and a rabbi, is a vivid example of a mislabeled lone actor. As President Nicolas Sarkozy declared in the aftermath of the attack, "There is no cell...To our knowledge, there is no network." Additionally, a French intelligence official said Merah "radicalized himself" (de Pommereau 2012). However, it was later revealed in the post-attack investigation that Merah was deeply intertwined with a large network of likeminded individuals with extensive ties to Al-Qaeda core members in Afghanistan and Pakistan. Merah was part of an elaborate network with 1,800 phone calls to 180 different people in 20 countries, including various jihadists in France and had ties to others who left France to fight overseas. He was affiliated with Forsane Alizza (Knights of Glory), a broad network of French extremists that was outlawed in France in January 2012, prior to the attack. Merah also traveled to Afghanistan, received training by Al-Qaeda in Pakistan, and had contacts with several known Al-Qaeda figures and radical preachers (BBC News, 2012). The reflexive tendency to downplay organizational ties hindered the investigation and was damaging to the credibility of the security services and the public's trust in government.

Another troubling example from the European context is Mehdi Nammouche, the perpetrator of the attack on the Belgium Jewish Museum in Brussels which killed four people. A French prosecutor at the time called Nammouche "a battle-hardened lone wolf" (Pfeffer 2014), but it was soon discovered that Nammouche was part of the broader "Molenbeek" network of extremists in Brussels. This is the same network that would reemerge with its notorious attack on the Bataclan theater, Paris, in 2015, which killed 130 people, and the 2016 Brussels airport attack, which killed 32. From a law enforcement perspective, this mislabeling of Nammouche is a nightmare scenario, as a perpetrator initially thought to be acting alone is actually only the thread, that if pulled on, would have connected to an undiscovered sprawling network of well-trained extremists. Nammouche had direct ties to Abdelhamid Abaoud, a key member of the Molenbeek cell that carried out the attacks in Belgium and France which also had extensive ties to ISIS in Syria. Nammouche himself also had traveled to Syria in 2012 and had served time in prison on drug charges. Tellingly, several months later, French politician Bernard Cazaneuve, declared: "I would like to take the opportunity to reject the term 'lone wolf' which proliferated during the attack committed by Mohammed Merah in March 2012, and which was revived in describing Mehdi Nemmouche" (JTA, 2014). This highlights, with tragic ramifications, the risks of misunderstanding the nature of the threat. Both the Merah and Nammouche attacks are extreme examples of mislabeled lone actors and resemble perpetrators with direct ties to terrorist groups and an expansive network of co-conspirators who went on to carry out larger, more lethal terrorist attacks.

Enabled Attacks

The increased use of social media and encrypted mobile applications has enabled members of terrorist groups like ISIS to direct attacks from afar or provide ongoing encouragement and motivation to lone attackers. For example, a series of disjointed ISIS attacks throughout the United States was initially assessed to have no apparent connections to the group. This notion was refuted when the role of the British ISIS facilitator Junaid Hussain came to light as a virtual plotter or "virtual entrepreneur" for the group. Hussain used social media to reach out to, correspond with, encourage, and mobilize radicalized Westerners, while offering suggestions and guidance related to attack planning. His deep and ongoing communication with at least 19 US-based individuals connected to 14 known plots highlights the degree to which these individuals were far more connected to the group than initially assessed. (Gartenstein-Ross and Barr 2016; Hughes and Meleagrou-Hitchens 2017). For example, the perpetrators of the oft-cited 2015 Garland, Texas attack on a convention center hosting a "Draw the Prophet Mohammed" cartoon contest, Elton Simpson and Nadir Soofi, had direct ties to Junaid Hussain and other virtual plotters in the days before the attack. Munir Abdul Kader in Cincinnati, Ohio, who purchased guns with plans to videotape and execute members of the armed forces and police officers, was also revealed to be in touch with Hussain, as was a Boston-based plot to behead the controversial pundit Pamela Geller, whose members were recruited by Hussain. The disparate network of US-based individuals around the country with contact to Hussain, who was considered a key member of ISIS's external operations branch, illustrates how none of these seemingly disjointed plots were in fact perpetrated by lone actors. Attacks by lone actors enabled by "virtual entrepreneurs" do not fit neatly into any category and can more aptly be placed somewhere along the spectrum of connectivity to the group, between group-directed plots and purely inspired plots (Callimachi 2017; Hughes and Meleagrou-Hitchens 2017, p. 1–2).

Germany saw a similar trend with so-called "remote controlled" attacks, in which ISIS facilitators in Syria were supporting and directing plots within Germany via online communications (usually via the encrypted application WhatsApp) and providing pre-attack instructions related to target selection and weapon choice, and even providing encouragement in the minutes and seconds leading up to the attack. Examples of such "remote controlled" attacks include the February 2016 stabbing attack at a Hanover train station by a young female perpetrator, the July 2016 Ansbach attack carried out by Mohamad Daleel outside of a bar, and the July 2016 Wurzburg stabbing on a train carried out by Riaz Khan. While all the German perpetrators attacked alone in the physical sense, "they were certainly not lone wolves in any meaningful sense" (Joscelyn 2016).

Inspired Attacks

Unlike directed or enabled attacks, attacks carried out by individuals without clear direction from a wider group and with an absence of clear command and control act as a better illustration of lone actor terrorism. This does not downplay the possibility that lone actors can be inspired by a group or motivated by its ideology. As noted, the defining element in the classification of lone actors "is an absence of direction and not an absence of links" (Pantucci et al., 2015, p. 4.). In directed and enabled attacks, a figure from ISIS itself was in close and continuing communication with the individual at various stages in the run-up to the attack. However, lone actors who lack this contact or direction with the group and are inspired to act independently often emerge from a formative, and often supportive, social and cultural environment – a so-called "radical milieu" (Malthaner and Waldmann, 2014). This milieu, where those in their supportive social environment share their perspective and objectives, approves of certain forms of violence and (at least to a certain extent) acts as an incubator for the prospective attacker (or network) both morally and logistically. This does not downplay the possibility of a lone actor who is isolated or on the periphery of a formative social network, like the well-known example of the "Unabomber" Ted Kaczynski, inspired purely by personal grievances and anarchist ideology. However, such examples should be viewed "as exceptional rather than archetypical" (Schuurman et al. 2018b, p. 2).

The 2014 shooting in Ottawa at Canada's Parliament Hill by Michael Zehaf-Bibeau, which killed one Canadian soldier, illustrates a sound example of a lone individual inspired to act by ISIS ideology. Zehaf-Bibeau, described as emotionally disturbed, a known criminal offender (mostly for drug charges), and at times homeless, had converted to Islam and espoused a radical Islamist worldview. While he did not formally belong to any religious institution in Canada, he exhibited "leakage" and signaling to co-workers and friends about his jihadist ambitions and had possibly attempted without success to travel overseas to Syria, which may have been a driver in leading him to carry out the attack. He may have also reportedly been influenced by other similar attacks that made headlines that same year. Even in this case, which appears to be a good example of an inspired lone attacker without formal ties to the group, it was revealed that the attacker was in personal contact both face-to-face and online with several known Canadian ISIS affiliates (Robertson 2014). It was ultimately concluded that while Zehaf-Bibeau acted alone, he was part of a loose ideological, operational, and communicative network whose members likely had some limited knowledge – or role contributing to – his radicalization and attack planning (Hofman 2018).

Conclusion and Directions for Future Research

While the academic literature continues to evolve and become more nuanced, it is encouraging that practitioner perceptions are aligned with academic research which suggests that small, self-organized lone actors or cells, with varying degrees of in-person or online connectivity to terrorist groups, are a uniquely difficult threat to counter. Lone actor attacks are more challenging to interdict than larger attacks organized by a group or network because of their greater social isolation and opaque online footprint (Parker et al. 2017; Spaaij 2012, p. 50–55). Lone actor terrorism is fueled by a combination of personal and political grievances which often leads the lone actor to seek out online sympathizers. In turn, this frequently results in "leakage" of terrorist intent, which culminates in a triggering event which acts as the final catalyst for the attack (Hamm and Spaaij 2015). The silver lining is that, as many of the aforementioned studies suggest, the lone actor moniker is a misnomer. Lone actor radicalization, planning, and operational activity are often (but not always) influenced by small-group and interpersonal, social dynamics or their association within a "radical milieu." Their association to this milieu or leakage both serve as possible points of vulnerability for the prospective attacker and offer opportunities for detection and interdiction by law enforcement (Hofman 2018, p. 17).

There is only a small amount of literature that systematically looks at lone actor attack planning, modus operandi, or weapon choice (Bouhana et al. 2018), and this would be a fruitful avenue for further research. New research that is methodologically rigorous and relies on sound data should continue to refine our understanding of processes of lone actors' ideological identification with others within their wider social environment and their eventual mobilization. Future studies could examine the spectrum of connectivity to a group by lone actors from different ideological categories in order to determine if, as the media has suggested, Islamist lone attackers are in fact from a defined subset of society compared to more individualistic right-wing attackers. Social network analysis may help explain how weak in-person and online links impact lone actors' trajectory toward violence and at what points leakage occurs.

For law enforcement, as illustrated in the US "virtual entrepreneur" and German "remote controlled" plots, the importance of mapping the network, both in person and online, is paramount. Exploring the relationships and personal ties between individuals and the wider social environment that comprises the radical milieu of a prospective lone attacker is critical, as is developing the ability to identify and act on instances of "leakage" and signaling by prospective attackers. For government leaders and politicians, it appears that proclaiming an assailant as a lone actor, before a thorough investigation, hurts society's faith in government and the security services, which are vital to ensure societal resilience. It also skews societal perceptions and may initially hinder law enforcement investigations. Important new research on communication during lone actor terrorist incidents highlights how the media plays a particularly important role in shaping the reactions of the general public and affected communities, and also influences possible copycat attackers (Parker et al. 2018). As for the media, the initial prevalence of the term "lone wolf" was not helpful, and the term "lone actor" should continue to be utilized wherever possible in order not to aggrandize or glorify such attacks which would be wholly counterproductive (Spaaij and Hamm, 2015, p. 168). The prevention of such attacks deserves the utmost attention, as academia's ability to contribute with rigorous and incisive research that is pertinent and relevant for practitioners should be held in high regard.

Further Reading

Brynielsson, Joel et al. (2013). Harvesting and Analysis of Weak Signals for Detecting Lone Wolf Terrorists" *Security Informatics* 2/11, 1–15.

Corner, Elizabeth and Paul Gill (2014). "A False Dichotomy? Mental Illness and Lone-Actor Terrorism" *Law and Human Behavior* 39/1, 23–34.

Ellis, Claire et al. (2015). *Lone Actor Terrorism: Analysis Paper.* Countering Lone-Actor Terrorism Series no.4, London: RUSI.

References

BBC News (2012) "Toulouse Gunman Mohamed Merah 'No Lone Wolf'", August 23.

Becker, Mark (2014) "Explaining Lone Wolf Target Selection in the United States" *Studies in Conflict & Terrorism* 37/11, 959–978.

Bouhana, Noemie, Stefan Malthaner, Bart Schuurman, Lasse Lindekilde, Amy Thorton, and Paul Gill (2018) "Lone-Actor Terrorism: Radicalization, Attack Planning, and Execution" in Andrew Silke (Ed.), *Routledge Handbook of Terrorism and Counterterrorism*. London: Routledge.

Callimachi, Rukmini (2017) "Not Lone Wolf After All: How ISIS Guides World's Terror Plots From Afar" *New York Times*, February 4.

Corner, Emily, Noemie Bouhana, and Paul Gill (2018) "The Multifinality of Vulnerability Indicators in Lone-Actor Terrorism" *Psychology, Crime, & Law*, 25(2), p. 1–22.

De Pommereau, Isabel (2012). "French Gunman the Latest of Europe's Troubling 'Lone Wolves'" *Christian Science Monitor*, March 26.

Ellis, Claire et al. (2015) *Lone Actor Terrorism: Final Report.* Countering Lone-Actor Terrorism Series no.11, London: RUSI.

Ellis, Claire et al. (2016) "Analysing the Processes of Lone-Actor Terrorism: Research Findings" *Perspectives on Terrorism* 10/2, p. 33–41.

Feldman, Mark (2013) "Comparative Lone Wolf Terrorism: Toward a Heuristic Definition" *Democracy and Security* 9/3, 270–286.

Gartenstein-Ross, Daveed and Nathaniel Barr (2016) "Bloody Ramadan: How the Islamic State Coordinated a Global Terrorist Campaign" *War on the Rocks*. July 20.

Gill, Paul (2015) *Lone-Actor Terrorists: A Behavioural Analysis*. London: Routledge.

Gill, Paul, John Horgan, and Paige Deckert (2014) "Bombing Alone: Tracing the Motivations and Antecedent Behaviors of Lone-Actor Terrorists" *Psychiatry & Behavioral Sciences* 59/2, p. 425–435

Hamm, Mark and Ramon Spaaij (2015) *Lone Wolf Terrorism in America: Using Knowledge of Radicalization Pathways to Forge Prevention Strategies*. Washington DC: National Institute of Justice.

Hofman, David C. (2018) "How 'Alone' are Lone-Actors? Exploring the Ideological, Signaling, and Support Networks of Lone-Actor Terrorists" *Studies in Conflict & Terrorism*, p. 1–22.

Hughes, Seamus and Alexander Meleagrou-Hitchens (2017) "The Threat to the United States from the Islamic State's Virtual Entrepreneurs" *CTC Sentinel* 10/3, p. 1–8.

Joscelyn, Thomas (2016) "Terror Plots in Germany, France were 'Remote-Controlled' by Islamic State Operatives" *Long War Journal*. September 24.

JTA (2014) "Brussels Jewish Museum Shooter was no 'Lone Wolf'" *Times of Israel*, June 14.

Lindekilde, Lasse et al. (2017) "Radicalization Patterns and Modes of Attach Planning and Preparation among Lone-Actor Terrorists: An Exploratory Analysis" *Behavioral Sciences of Terrorism and Political Aggression*, p. 1–21

Malthaner, Stefan and Peter Waldmann (2014) "The Radical Milieu: Conceptualizing the Supportive Social Environment of Terrorist Groups" *Studies in Conflict & Terrorism* 37/12, p. 979–998

Meloy, J. Reid and Mary Ellen O'Toole (2011) "The Concept of Leakage in Threat Assessment" *Behavioral Sciences and Law* 29/4, p. 513–527

Pantucci, Raffaello, Clare Ellis, and Lorien Chaplais (2015) *Lone-Actor Terrorism: Literature Review*. Countering Lone-Actor Terrorism Series no.1, London: RUSI.

Pantucci, Raffaello (2011) *A Typology of Lone Wolves: Preliminary Analysis of Lone Islamist Terrorists*. London: ICSR.

Parker, David et al. (2018) "Press Coverage of Lone-Actor Terrorism in the UK and Denmark: Shaping the Reactions of the Public, Affected Communities and Copycat Attackers" *Critical Studies on Terrorism* (July), 12(1), 1–22.

Parker, David et al. (2017) "Challenges for Effective Counterterrorism Communication: Practitioner Insights and Policy Implications for Preventing Radicalization, Disrupting Attack Planning, and Mitigating Terrorist Attacks" *Studies in Conflict & Terrorism*, 42(3), 1–28.

Pfeffer, Anshel (2014) "Belgium: Jewish Museum Killer Was a Lone Wolf" *Haaretz*, June 3.

Robertson, James (2014) "Exclusive: Revealed, Muslim Convert who Brought Mayhem to Canada Listened to Extremist Rants with Terror Suspect who went to Fight in Syria" *Daily Mail*, October 24.

Sageman, Marc (2004) *Understanding Terror Networks*. Philadelphia, PA: University of Pennsylvania Press.

Schuurman, Bart, Edwin Bakker, Paul Gill, and Noemie Bouhana (2018a) "Lone Actor Terrorist Attack Planning and Preparation: A Data-Drive Analysis" *Psychiatry and Behavioral Science* 63/4, 1191–1200.

Schuurman, Bart, Lasse Lindekilde, Stefan Malthaner, Francis O'Connor, Paul Gill, and Noemie Bouhana (2018b) "End of the Lone Wolf: The Typology that Should Not Have Been" *Studies in Conflict & Terrorism*, 1–8.

Silber, Mitch and Arvin Bhatt (2007) *Radicalization in the West: The Homegrown Threat*, New York, NY: New York City Police Department.

Spaaij, Ramon and Mark S. Hamm (2015) "Key Issues and Research Agendas in Lone Wolf Terrorism" *Studies in Conflict & Terrorism* 38/3, 167–178.

Spaaij, Ramon (2012) *Understanding Lone Wolf Terrorism: Global Patterns, Motivations and Prevention*. London: Springer.

Spaaij, Ramon (2010) "The Enigma of Lone Wolf Terrorism: An Assessment" *Studies in Conflict & Terrorism* 33/4, 854–870.

Chapter 58

Nationalists

Glen M. E. Duerr
Cedarville University, Cedarville, OH, United States

Contents

Introduction 421
Nationalism and Terrorism 422
Nationalism and Terrorist Groups 423
Nationalism in the US Context 425
Conclusion 426
Further Reading 426
References 427

Introduction

Nationalism, or the sense of belonging to a nation, is a modern concept with ancient roots. It gained traction in the nineteenth century, especially in Central and Eastern Europe, and across the world as the phenomenon of the nation state became the prominent vehicle of identification in the wake of declining empires. There is debate in the field of political science, of course: for some renowned scholars, such as Anthony D. Smith, nationalism is an ancient phenomenon (Smith 1991); for others, such as Eric Hobsbawm, nationalism is a much newer construct (Hobsbawm 1983). Regardless of the roots of nationalism, the recognition of nation states gained emphasis following the establishment of international organizations like the League of Nations and the United Nations (UN) in the twentieth century, which made nationalism an even more potent ideology.

In the last few centuries, nationalism developed as a means of opposing long-standing empires, and sought to provide self-determination to territorially-bound people with shared characteristics, especially language and culture. This romantic nationalism took root in Europe surrounding the French Revolution and developed

DOI: 10.4324/9781315144511-61

further in 1830 and 1848 with people demanding more rights. Nationalism served as a vehicle to protest against authoritarianism and monarchism, which were seen to be strangling economic opportunities of people, but the protests were also more broadly in favor of more localized or competing identities. Italy and Germany in part both unified around their common languages in 1861 and 1871 respectively. In the late nineteenth and early twentieth centuries, several countries gained independence partly as a result of nationalist aspirations, which then flourished with the conclusion of World War I, the "Fourteen Points" speech of American President Woodrow Wilson, and with dramatic changes to the map of Europe. In the aftermath of World War II, anti-colonial nationalism succeeded in bringing independence to many countries in the developing world. Finally, with the end of the Cold War in 1989, national reawakening in Eastern Europe led to the creation of new states with the dissolutions of Czechoslovakia, Yugoslavia, and the Soviet Union.

In most cases, nationalism was pursued through peaceful and democratic means; most nationalists are not terrorists, nor do they resort to violence when political decisions are made against them. However, in some cases, nationalism as an ideology has served as the primary reason for using terrorism as a means of fighting against what is viewed as an illegitimate and powerful empire. This chapter investigates the linkages between nationalism and terrorism in this context, then discusses particular terrorist cases across the world, before focusing on the American context. In a sense, this chapter serves as a funnel with a philosophical discussion of nationalism and terrorism at first, followed by an overview of global cases, before discussing these concepts more narrowly in the context of the United States (US).

Nationalism and Terrorism

Nationalism, the identification with a physically or ideologically defined nation or group of people, may be considered as one cause of terrorism, as it can lead an individual, or a group of people to carry out acts of terrorism as a means of trying to construct a new or different national identity for themselves. Commonly, in academic literature, the term "ethno-nationalism," or the identification with a group of people with a shared ethnic identity, is also used to connote some form of ethnic nationalist sentiments with regards to replacing the existing government, or creating a new independent state for the ethnic group in question from within the existing state structures.

One of the challenges, then, in discussing nationalism is the overlap pertaining to ethno-nationalist terrorism versus ethno-nationalist violence in civil wars. The term ethno-nationalist is useful since many contestations of the state are based on some form of ethnic identity that some sets of people feel should govern the state, or be given their own state. In some cases, especially in asymmetric conflicts where one side is more powerful than the other (militarily or otherwise), the definitional challenge is to tease out distinctions between a terrorist organization and a standing military fighting for independence. Ethno-nationalist terrorism is the use of terrorist acts by specifically ethno-nationalist groups that seek to use violence as a means to sovereignty. Technically, then, there is a difference between ethno-nationalist violence in a civil war, and ethno-nationalist terrorism in a society. The academic definitions are useful, but in practicality, the difference may mean very little to victims of violence. Nonetheless, where acts of violence fit a definition of terrorism, and a group is placed on a terrorism "watch list," this has an impact on the conflict because it generally erodes the legitimacy of the nationalist movement. In a post-9/11 environment, most governments treat ethno-nationalist terrorists as toxic to their relations with other governments affected by the terrorist group.

According to the French scholar, Ernest Gellner, "nationalism is primarily a political principle, which holds that the political and national unit should be congruent (1993, 1)." Gellner's idea here is that one group or another may contest to see which entity should have control over a state, or, in some cases, whether a new state should be created. Thus, the interconnection between nationalists and terrorism is based upon asymmetric violence to see which group controls the state. Often, terrorists target government or governmental entities as a mechanism of contesting the right to govern the state.

Nationalism and Terrorist Groups

Terrorism scholar, David Rapoport (2006), divides terrorism into three major types/groups: leftist, rightist, and ethno-nationalist. Although terrorism is typically associated with religious terrorism in the twenty-first century, the issue of ethno-nationalist terrorism was prevalent in the 1970s through the 1990s. The focus of this entry is ethno-nationalist terrorism. Groups such as Euskadi Ta Askatasuna (ETA), the Irish Republican Army (IRA), Balochistan Liberation Army (BLA), Imarat Kavkaz (IK), the Liberation Tigers of Tamil Eelam (LTTE), and Partiya Karkerên Kurdistanê (PKK) are all prominent example of ethno-nationalist terrorism with the aforementioned caveat that some of these groups also fight (or are fighting) civil wars such as the LTTE, IK, and PKK (Pokalova 2015; Romaniuk et al., 2017; Duerr 2018).

These groups operate in theatres across the world: ETA in the Basque Country between France and Spain; IRA in Northern Ireland, with contestation between the United Kingdom and the Republic of Ireland; BLA in Pakistan and Afghanistan; IK in Chechnya, an ethnic republic of Russia; the LTTE in the Tamil-majority areas of Sri Lanka; and the PKK in Kurdish majority sectors of southeastern Turkey (Romaniuk et al., 2017). Although there is overlap between nationalist and religious terrorism with some of these groups, each one has had or has the maximalist goal of creating an independent state through violence and rebellion against the existing state structures.

Of these nationalist groups, several have recently signed, or unilaterally promised, ceasefire agreements. The IRA, for example, disbanded following the Good Friday Agreement of 1998 since a peaceful pathway to conflict resolution and power-sharing was created in Northern Ireland (Cronin, 2009). ETA, in the Basque Country, formally announced a ceasefire in 2011 and announced its dissolution in 2018 (Duerr, 2018). It is not the first time that ETA called for a ceasefire, but, in the past, the group has generally reneged on the agreement within two years. Therefore, the 2011 ceasefire is much more likely to be final. Of course, this situation depends on what happens if and when ETA terrorists are released from prison.

In other cases, the LTTE and IK effectively lost their respective civil wars in Sri Lanka and Chechnya. Both groups have minimal presence in their respective regions now, and few terrorist attacks still take place. In the case of the LTTE, this group was extremely active throughout the Sri Lankan civil war from 1983 to 2009. Given the defeat of the Tamils in the conflict, terrorism is much less prominent. For a period of time, especially in the 1990s and 2000s, the LTTE were known as the most fatal terrorist organization in the world. They were also known for significant fund-raising among diaspora populations in the West, which fueled the continuation of the conflict (Bell 2005, ch.2). In the case of IK, it is plausible that the theatre of fighting has moved to Syria where jihadists associated with the Islamic State (IS) attempted to control significant swaths of Syria and Iraq (Pokalova 2015).

This form of ethno-nationalist terrorism has long been prominent in international relations. Take, for example, the Guy Fawkes plot to explode the British Houses of Parliament on November 5, 1605. The motivation, at least in part for Fawkes, was to install a Catholic Head of State, Princess Elizabeth, in place of King James I of England (also King James VI of Scotland) who unified the two kingdoms in 1603. Another example is the catalyst for the start of World War I—the assassination of Archduke Franz Ferdinand by Gavrilo Princip in 1914. Princip belonged to The Black Hand, a terror-related organization with aims to undermine the Austro-Hungarian Empire and assert independence for groups within the Balkans. The overarching goal was to create a larger homeland for South Slavs, not just build on the newly independent countries of Montenegro and Serbia (Laqueur, 1977).

As mentioned in the introduction, ethno-nationalist terrorism came to prominence in the late nineteenth century, especially in the midst of decaying empires (Austria-Hungary and Ottoman), but also with issues among the European colonial powers in the developing world. Ethno-nationalist terrorism was also a tactic used against the British Empire in India and Ireland as examples. For these nationalists, terrorism was used in their view as a mechanism to fight an asymmetric conflict against a more powerful opponent. This use of terrorism led to the oft-repeated axiom, "one person's terrorist is another person's freedom fighter." In some cases, there is a fine line between terrorism and paramilitary groups, depending on the context of a given conflict.

It is also important to present the counterclaim in the case. Of note is the fact that many nationalists also seek peaceful means to determining their political future. Short-lived terrorist movements in Quebec, Scotland, and Catalonia, for example, all disbanded within a few years of starting. In two cases, the Front de libération du Québec (FLQ) in Quebec and Terra Lluire (TL) in Catalonia disbanded soon after the first fatality, in part because public opinion turned against the cause via violent means (Crelinsten, 1987; Duerr, 2018).

In other parts of the world, some nationalists have never resorted to terrorism as a mechanism to gain support for the independence movement. This obviously depends on a robust and agreed-upon definition of terrorism, but there are regions such as Greenland (belonging to Denmark) that have never asserted a terrorist attack as a mechanism to gain de jure statehood in the UN system. At the very least in this and other cases like Veneto (Italy) or Flanders (Belgium), there has been either no violence, or very little violence not associated with an ethno-nationalist terrorist organization.

Although political contestation is high, the movements in Quebec, Scotland, and Catalonia thrive on a peaceful resolution (Crelinsten, 1987). The desire is to avoid nationalist terrorism and focus on peaceful mechanisms to obtain independence through the ballot box. This outcome requires some sophistication on the part of the government to allow secessionist parties to run for political office, whilst simultaneously making the case for national unity within their borders. For example, the Canadian and British governments have allowed for independence referendums in Quebec and Scotland as a mechanism to decide the constitutional fate of both regions.

A discussion on ethno-nationalist terrorism also has another wrinkle. Other terrorist organizations like Fuerzas Armadas Revolucionarias de Colombia (FARC) have nationalist elements despite connections to a distinct communist ideology. Although Marxism on paper is supposed to be global in nature, communism in practice often reverts to nationalist sentiments in order to complete specific political goals. Thus, FARC at times sought to rule Colombia, or at least sections of the country while imposing a brand of Marxist-Leninist governance (Romaniuk et al. 2017, ch. 12).

This discussion on Marxist ethno-nationalist terrorism also applies to many of the aforementioned cases such as ETA, IRA, FLQ, and the PKK as well as other, smaller ethno-nationalist terrorist organizations like the Armée Révolutionnaire Bretonne (ARB) in the French region of Brittany or the Fronte di Liberazione Naziunale Corsu (FLNC) in the region of Corsica in France (Laqueur, 1977; Rapoport, 2006; Duerr, 2018). Two major lessons are applicable here. First, terrorism is complex and often intertwined with ideological convictions; in many of the above cases, there has been some allegiance to Marxist thought. Second, there are dangers of radicalism that exist at the extremes of the political spectrum, and can lead to violence. Governments must seek to find mechanisms to best rule over people, especially federalism and other power-sharing models.

Nationalism in the US Context

Finally, the concept of ethno-nationalism is also slightly more nuanced in the American context. Nationalism was required to build the idea of a separate United States of America as an independent from the British Empire. In the lead-up to the Civil War, differing nationalisms in the north and south played a factor in the brutal conflict of 1861–1865. The sixteenth president, Abraham Lincoln, for example, was assassinated by John Wilkes Booth—a southern nationalist who sought revenge for the outcome of the Civil War. Southern/Confederate nationalism is an issue in specific circumstances with occasional ties to terrorism, or terror-related violent actions, especially against minorities.

Relatedly, on the issue of homeland security in the United States, the threat posed by nationalists of various stripes is significant. White nationalists and Black nationalists, for example, each seek different end goals. White nationalists typically seek to dominate the United States politically and economically via violent means. A prominent example of this is the Ku Klux Klan and their violent attacks on non-whites. Another example is southern nationalists who seek to politically dominate the south, or revitalize the Civil War end goal of secession. Black nationalists seek a range of different ends depending on the situation. This may include changes to public policy to improve the lives of African-Americans, secessionism for Black-Americans, or the promotion of the Nation of Islam. Where these protests are tied to violence, against a specific government target, or indiscriminate civilian population, there is an overlap with a definition of terrorism. Terrorism-related violence is sporadic in these cases, but also a potential menace to the society when violence is perpetrated by one ethnic group on another as a means of obtaining power, threatening others, or attempting to assert various racialized political agendas.

Finally, in the United States, there are anti-government anarchists like Timothy McVeigh, the perpetrator of the 1995 Oklahoma City bombing of the Murrah federal building. Ethno-nationalist terrorism also can have an anarchist/anti-government faction in that an individual, or small terror cell, seeks to overturn legislation or the size and scope of the government. McVeigh is a nationalist in the sense that he claims to care deeply about the country because his personal motivation for the Murrah building attack was to defend the Constitution. His reasoning and motivation were clearly flawed, and his use of violence also fit the category of terrorism. He can also be thought of as a nationalist because his motivation was to overthrow the government and create a different type of America through his attack.

For homeland security in general, the threat posed by nationalists is significant but depends on the national context. Since most states in the world are heterogeneous in nature, virtually every government faces some form of threat from an ethnonationalist minority. Yet, a peaceful working constitution can help to alleviate the threat posed in some cases.

Conclusion

Nationalist terrorism is complex with terrorist organizations across the world committing acts of terror as a means to changing political boundaries, or legislation. The threat posed by nationalists takes on different characteristics across a range of different cases, but several themes are evident. First, terrorism is still used as a vehicle for national recognition. Various groups across the world view terrorist tactics as the mode through which they can accomplish their maximalist goal of *de jure* statehood in the UN system. Second, ethno-nationalist terrorism is, in some cases, strongly intertwined with civil wars. It can be difficult to tease out distinctions between legitimate self-defense and acts of terrorism, but this is a reason why definitions as well as designations by recognized governments, can be very important to resolving conflicts, and then reducing terrorism. Finally, ethno-nationalist terrorism also overlaps with other types of terrorism, such as Marxist terrorism, religious terrorism, or anarchist terrorism. Once again, definitions are very important because the offending terrorist parties can rightly be brought to justice where there are terrorist attacks that lead to fatalities and injuries.

Further Reading

Cronin, A. K. (2003). Behind the Curve: Globalization and International Terrorism. *International Security*, 27(3), 30–58.

Hutchinson, J. (2017). *Nationalism and War*. Oxford: Oxford University Press.

Laqueur, W. (2000). *The New Terrorism: Fanaticism and the Arms of Mass Destruction*. Oxford: Oxford University Press.

References

Bell, S. (2005). *Cold Terror: How Canada Nurtures and Exports Terrorism around the World*. Mississauga: Wiley.

Crelinsten, R. D. (1987). The Internal Dynamics of the FLQ during the October Crisis of 1970. *The Journal of Strategic Studies*, 10(4), 59–89.

Cronin, A. K. (2009). *How Terrorism Ends: Understanding the Decline and Demise of Terrorist Campaigns*. Princeton, NJ: Princeton University Press.

Duerr, G. M. E. (Ed.) (2018). *Secessionism and Terrorism: Bombs, Blood, and Independence in Europe and Eurasia*. London: Routledge.

Gellner, E. (1993). *Nations and Nationalism*. Ithaca, NY: Cornell University Press.

Hobsbawm, E. J. (1983). *Nations and Nationalism since 1780: Programme, Myth, Reality*. Cambridge: Cambridge University Press.

Laqueur, W. (1977). *A History of Terrorism*. Piscataway, NJ: Transaction Publishers.

Pokalova, E. (2015). *Chechnya's Terrorist Network: The Evolution of Terrorism in Russia's North Caucasus*. Santa Barbara, CA: ABC-CLIO.

Rapoport, D. C. (Ed.) (2006). *Terrorism: The Fourth or Religious Wave*. London: Taylor & Francis.

Romaniuk, S. N., F. Grice, D. Irrera, & S. Webb (Eds.). (2017). *The Palgrave Handbook of Global Counterterrorism Policy*. London: Palgrave Macmillan.

Smith, A. D. (1991). *National Identity*. Reno, NV: University of Nevada Press.

Chapter 59

Right-Wing Extremism

Jade Hutchinson
Macquarie University, Sydney, Australia

Contents

Introduction 429
An Aside on Conceptualizations 430
Anti-'Other' Sentiment 430
Who Is the 'Other'? 431
A Brief Historical Context 432
Post-9/11 432
Post-Trump 432
Contemporary Findings 433
The Reactionary Movement 433
Recommendations 434
Conclusion 436
Further Reading 436
References 436

Introduction

Right-wing extremism (RWE) remains a significant driver of discrimination and violence in the United States (US). Like other extremist ideologies, right-wing ideology is a spectrum of conceptualizations, with no single epitome or profile. RWE ideology is, therefore, metamorphic and can be expressed through a diverse constellation of individuals and groups. Right-wing popularism has emerged into the mainstream, and delineations of extremist thought are ever-salient across its conservative audience. This chapter considers how counter-violent extremism (CVE) efforts can best conceptualize and combat RWE. An effective CVE strategy must consider how RWE acts as a motivator for violence against minority groups and how contemporary manifestations of right-wing ideology behave and adapt to social, political or ethnographic trends.

DOI: 10.4324/9781315144511-62

Accordingly, this chapter seeks to elucidate the concept of 'Otherization' which is a dominant driver of right-wing violent extremism; outline two distinct social and political eras supportive of RWE; illustrate the contemporary 'reactionary' movement, its ideological characteristics and implications; and highlight the importance of promoting multi-dimensional, interoperable programs to locate and counter RWE in the US. Through a discussion of the above, this chapter stresses the significance of the growing 'reactionary' movement for RWE groups and the necessity for multi-pronged, interoperable efforts to curb localized extreme right-wing intentions of discrimination and violence.

An Aside on Conceptualizations

The conceptualization of RWE ideology is aided by a multiplicity of intersecting right-wing themes and values. For instance, Dean et al. (2016) list six thematic values of the right-wing narrative that features in the US RWE movement: (1) anti-immigrant, (2) anti-establishment, (3) protection of Western values, (4) commitment to democratic reform, (5) traditional values, (6) strong State. Additionally, Muddle (2000) defines a right-wing movement as containing at least three of the following five right-wing ideological components, which is applicable to the US RWE movement: (1) racism, (2) xenophobia, (3) strong state advocacy (4) anti-democratic, (5) nationalism. Considered an 'ideology of ethnic exclusionism', far-right extremist ideology is an exclusivist movement motivated by various visions of social dominance, and broadly outlined by anti-democratic and authoritarian sentiment (Pedazur & Canetti-Nisim, 2004; Mudde, 2016; Carter, 2018; Campion, 2019). However, ideological genialities alone are not sufficient to view extremist groups over time. As RWE groups evolve 'these [ideological] distinctions are not so straightforward...and the lines are increasingly becoming blurred' (Ahmed & Pisoiu, 2019). Continuous analysis is required to track the ideological-evolutionary changes within and between RWE movements and groups. For example, as fragments of the RWE movement continue to adapt to sustain popularity and recognition, it is important to keep a coherent outline of its defining features and various attempts at metamorphosis. Regarding right-wing popularism, Ekström et al. (2018) conceive popularism as follows:

> as both a political discourse, or 'thin-centred ideology', representing politics and society as structured by a fundamental antagonistic relationship between 'the elite' and 'the people' ... [while styling themselves as] being one of 'the people'.
>
> (Ekström, et al., 2018, p. 2)

Anti-'Other' Sentiment

Right-wing ideology is nebulous, contextually adapted and can be applied strategically by actors, to appease a sense of injustice and prestige over the 'Other'. Right-wing ideology is broadly framed by a multiplicity of themes and values, so ideological motivations can vary wildly between right-wing extremist groups. Each group, or fragment of the movement, holds a distinctive ideological directive and is 'difficult to define' (Baysinger, 2006). However, ideological commonalities are thematic across the movement (Western traditional values and anti-'Other' sentiment, for example). Right-wing extremist groups can share individual members and at times converge in unity over commonly held goals and grievances (Kaplan, 1995). Conceived as a social movement, the RWE movement can solidify groups or encompass demographics based on shared values, identities, interests, precipitating events or threats from the 'Other' (Perry & Scrivens, 2016; Hutchinson, 2018b). Anti-'Other' sentiment aids opposing groups in a multiplicity of manners, from the formulation and maintenance of a collective identity to behavioural directives in RWE movements internationally (Snow, 2001; Hunt & Benford, 1994; Scrivens, 2017; Hutchinson, 2019a). For radical groups, anti-'Other' sentiment is an effective means of group identification, solidification and justification for violence (Taylor, 2009; Hutchinson, 2019c).

Anti-'Other' sentiment is not only reserved for street demonstrations. Extreme right-wing actors exploit the cacophonic boundaries of social media platforms to converge in discriminatory dialogue and normalize hatred against the 'Other' (Scrivens, 2017; Davey & Ebner, 2018). This has been achieved, in part, by shifting the 'Overton window'. According to right-wing facilitators, 'to shift the Overton window' is to shift the 'consensus boundaries of what constitutes acceptable public discourse' (Davey & Ebner, 2018, p. 15). As acceptability trends towards a more violent opinion of the 'Other', fringe extremists harness this shift towards moderation to execute violent extremism against the 'Other' (Davey & Ebner, 2018). This is particularly salient for right-wing extremists, given their propensity to participate in extremist online forums and utilize extremist content online, as a means of cyber-enabling indoctrination and extremist violence (Gill, et al., 2015; Gill, et al., 2017).

Who Is the 'Other'?

Champions of the anti-'Other' sentiment proclaim that the 'Other' is liable for society's economic and cultural disintegration, social paranoia, political corruption and violations of safety and security (Walsh, 2017). At times referred to as 'folk devils' (Walsh, 2017), these segregated, scapegoated identities are deemed (at least in part) 'responsible for edging society towards criminality and national collapse' (Hutchinson, 2018a). In most cases, the 'Other' is identifiable as a minority existing within the dominant culture or population. However, the practice of 'Otherization' or target for extremist violence is habitually cast over the perceived supporters or defenders of the 'Other' (pro-immigration politicians or anti-fascist activists, for example). Those identified as the 'Other' suffer a range of discriminatory tactics by radical groups, who seek to rid of them from society and avoid the associated cost. For instance, the 'Other' is often assigned with descriptive applications thematic of a 'contagion', 'savagery', 'grotesque' or illegal activity (Douglas, 1966). Extremist groups use this tactic to signify that the 'Other' is inherently 'evil, irrational' and 'perpetrating their savage customs among us' (Douglas, 1966; Stampnitzky, 2013). Additionally, inclusive descriptive applications can be conceptually leveraged by extremists to include fringe supporters, in favour of the use of targeted Otherization, as a technique to bolster extremist efforts (Hutchinson, 2019a). Descriptive applications conceptually distinguish the 'Other' from the majority and call for organized action to expel them.

A Brief Historical Context

From 2001 to mid-2018, deadly attacks as a cause of far right-wing ideology in the US have risen to 86 deaths (Bergan, et al. 2018). US history reveals a turbulent past of right-wing extremist movements, groups and personalities (Baysinger, 2006). While this is not the place for an in-depth analysis of the history of RWE, the following era-orientated summaries provide an overview for the purpose of this chapter.

Post-9/11

The Al Qaeda attacks on September 11, 2001, were transformative for the right-wing movement. In 2001, the Federal Bureau of Investigation recorded a (1618%) significant spike in anti-Islamic hate crimes (Federal Bureau of Investigation, 2001; Ser, 2016). Although this spike is not attributed exclusively to right-wing extremists and the number of anti-Islamic hate crimes dropped after 2001, anti-Islamic hate crimes remain high, compared to pre-9/11 levels (Ser, 2016). Despite minimal efforts by former US President George W. Bush (Junior) to separate Islam from its deviant counterpart, the perception of Islam was transmogrified in the eyes of right-wing groups post-9/11 (Bush, 2001. The attacks on September 11, 2001, the subsequent global war on terror and the invasion of Iraq and Afghanistan remain a historic era for shaping attitudes in the US right-wing movement. For instance, since then:

- Islam has been misinterpreted as a 'commonly held grievance' among the right-wing movement and Muslims as the 'common enemy' or 'Other' for right-wing extremist groups (Davey & Ebner, 2018);
- Right-wing extremist violence has been directed towards the Muslim identity and Middle Eastern appearance to 'protect' the 'real-American' identity; and
- An anti-Islamic sub-culture has emerged and continues to further right-wing extremism and violence (Abbas, 2017).

Post-Trump

On January 20, 2017, Donald J. Trump was inaugurated as the 45th President of the US and entered the white house adorned with the campaign slogan, 'Make America Great Again'. With its ultra-nationalistic, isolationist and right-wing undertones, President Donald Trump's political campaign revitalized RWE in North America and around the globe (Barkun, 2017; Futrell & Simi, 2017; Hutchinson, 2019c). During his political campaign and once inaugurated, President Trump's expressions of 'Otherization' caused division among many identities outside the frame of right-wing populism (Hutchinson, 2019c). In particular, it further crystallized the Muslim identity as the 'Other'. For instance, in May 2017, the US President categorized the Middle East as harbourers of 'barbaric' Islamist terrorists and presented supporters with a dichotomous perception of reality, stating that America is engaged in a 'battle between barbaric criminals who seeks to obliterate human life, and decent people…a battle between good and evil' (Friedman & Green, 2017).

The US President presented 'a choice between [only] two futures' – prosperity with 'decent' American people or face obliteration from 'barbaric' Middle Eastern 'criminals' (Friedman & Green, 2017). In July 2018, during a political engagement in the United Kingdom, President Trump conceptualized the European Union's acceptance of African and Middle Eastern refugees from Muslim populous countries, as instruments of cultural disintegration (Nguyen, 2018). The President's gestures of anti-'Other' sentiment resonate with RWE sensitivities to the socio-cultural hierarchy and confirms RWE biases of an encroaching front of immigration in general and Islamization in particular.

Partnered with gestures of 'Otherization', President Trump is celebrated and pedestaled by right-wing extremists as a political authority to engage in physical violence. In public appearances and social media publications, President Trump has condoned, and even defended, the use of physical violence against opposing entities (Baker, 2018). Effectively conditioning followers to seek violent means in defence of right-wing ideology and Donald Trump's political position as President. Scrivens (2017) highlights the impact of President Trump's political ascension on RWE in North America, stating that:

> The aftermath of Trump's electoral victory (known as the 'Trump Effect') has echoed in several ways: North America has seen an increase in hate speech and hate crimes, increased visibility of 'alt-right' commentators, and an increase in discussions on white supremacy chat forums such as *Stormfront*....
>
> (Scrivens, 2017, p. 132)

Furthermore, political support for the Republican President has featured prominently in recent instances of right-wing terrorism. For instance, in October 2018, the Floridian Cesar Sayoc Jr. was arrested and charged for sending 14 improvised explosive devices to 12 well-known critics of President Trump, and well-known critics of the US right-wing movement (Rashbaum, et al. 2018). Although Sayoc Jr. harbours an extensive criminal past and existed in a state of impecuniosity and homelessness, he affirmed his membership to the Republican party and political affinity for President Trump(Mazzei, et al. 2018; Hutchinson, 2019c). Similarly, the Proud Boys, a violent organized hate group founded by Gavin McInnes, advocate for Donald Trump's presidency and engage in street-level violence against pro-Islamic and left-leaning groups, opponents ostensibly shared by President Trump (Coaston, 2018). The President's contribution to mass-attitudinal shifts within the right-wing movement, regarding the need to radically address anti-'Other' threats to American identity and culture; has helped to revivify right-wing extremist violence and the 'reactionary movement' within the US; provides group leadership and directional influence to right-wing extremists to commit (mass)violence; and rapidly alters the national and international context which negatively effects the efficacy of CVE programs around the world.

Contemporary Findings

The Reactionary Movement

In Parker's (2018) *The Radical Right in the United States of America*, he observes the principles of RWE ideology present in the contemporary conservative movement and explicated the concept of 'conservatism'. Parker (2018) suggests that the acceptance of extreme right-wing leanings by more moderate conservatives, reveals a distinction between the 'reactionary' and 'mainstream' branches of conservatism. The demographic historically associated with reactionary movements is considered 'relatively old' or 'middle-aged', 'white, predominately male, middle-class, native-born, Christian, and heterosexual' (p. 2, 17). These phenotypical and socio-cultural components of identity do not entirely encompass the movement, yet, is suggested to have largely defined the 'true' American identity (Canaday, 2009; Devos and Banaji, 2005). By way of definition, McVeigh (2009) states that reactionary movements are:

> a social movement that acts on behalf of relatively advantaged groups with the goal of preserving, restoring, and expanding the rights and privileges of its members and constituents. These movements also attempt to deny similar rights and privileges to other groups in society.
>
> (McVeigh, 2009, pp. 32–33)

The character of reactionary movements is polarising in nature and carries an undercurrent for 'Otherization' (Parker, 2018). Reactionary movements encourage the prioritization of the dominant demographic and immediately address socio-cultural concerns of an 'Other'. In this sense, RWE principles accelerate the categorization of 'Us' and the 'Other' and effectively offer methods of strategic action. Reactionary-right movements carry an urgency to counter a perceived 'rapid decline' in ethnographic, cultural and economic status and 'rapid social change' (Parker, 2018, p. 2, 17). Such hierarchical changes render hostility and violence, justified through the lens of RWE ideology, as a necessary practice to preserve the social prestige of 'real-Americans' (Parker & Barreto, 2013; Parker, 2018).

Parker (2018) notes that the matrix of motivational factors that underpin the contemporary reactionary movement is empirically unidentifiable, due to the variable nature of ideological influence on individual or group behaviour. This chapter assumes these limitations in its examination of the potentiality of extreme right-wing actors in the contemporary reactionary movement against the 'Other'.

Recommendations

A multi-dimensional, inter-operable program, guided by geo-spatial intelligence for localized application is the recommended method of CVE for RWE. Simply removing extremist content online, or removing opportunities to express grievances, is not an adequate CVE strategy in isolation (Horton-Eddison & Cristofaro, 2017; McCann, 2018). Over-investments in the judicial or law enforcement of CVE, especially framed through the lens of a counter-terrorism approach, threatens to over-securitize and pressurize individuals to disengage or coerce individuals to accelerate their intentions of violent extremism (Dalgaard-Nielsen, 2016). This chapter acknowledges the logistical, political and economic expediency of counter-terrorism lead, nation-wide or generalized CVE programs. However, such programs are most likely inapplicable and ineffective at countering localized expressions of RWE, will quagmire resources and over-securitize individuals. The use of strict sanctions and support services to counter extreme right-wing incitements of violence is agreed upon. However, the exact nature, scope, extent and design of such a program must be tailored and evaluated against the domestic context in which it is applied (McDonald, 2018).

According to the literature, a psycho-sociologically supportive branch of CVE must be integrated, along with law enforcement, to develop community resilience to RWE (De-Goede & Simon, 2013; Dalgaard-Nielsen, 2016; Perry & Scrivens, 2017). A cumulative employment of constabulary forces, and a broad spectrum of socially supportive services, is required to suppress the presence or attraction of indoctrinating ideologies and address violent extremism (De-Goede & Simon, 2013; Dalgaard-Nielsen, 2016; Perry & Scrivens, 2017). Socially supportive services may include public education programs to expose the presence and implications of RWE, for example. It has been extensively demonstrated that anti-extremism education undermines the propogandic quality of components of RWE, such as anti-'Other' dogmas (Davies, 2009; United Nations, 2017; Ford, 2018).

Socially supportive services may also include a variation of Norway's CVE technique referred to as 'conversation intervention or empowerment conversations', which was initially shown to have encouraging results with youths involved in RWE (Bjørgo & Gjelsvik, 2015). This is not to say that social supportive services are or should be operated by individuals with generalized expertise. CVE programs must draw on the valuable resources from areas of social work and public education. However, at the practitioner level, CVE programs require individuals with specializations in CVE due to the variable circumstances of participants and the approaches required to manage their engagement in the program.

Because the locality and nature of extreme right-wing violent extremism are not equally spread across the US, publicly available geo-spatial intelligence regarding the frequency and severity of extremism must be available to the local constabulary and CVE providers. This is not to say that the US is without such public intelligence. The Anti-Defamation League (ADL) has constructed an 'interactive and customizable' virtual map, illustrating incidents of hate crimes, extremism, anti-Semitism and terrorism (HEAT) (Anti-Defamation League, 2018b). This HEAT map reveals the spread of HEAT across the US, along with the date and description of each individual incident. Geo-spatial intelligence informs local communities and CVE practitioners of the scope and presence of RWE in their vicinity.

Geo-spatial intelligence should be mapped only when using adequate supporting evidence. Depending on the intelligence used to identify areas ostensibly concentrated with right-wing extremist activity, mapping requires further evidence before allocating CVE resources to that area. For instance, geo-spatial representations of keyword searches should be considered a tentative mapping technique, because the intention of the individual who searched for those words is unclear, and so the degree of 'risk' associated with that individual is unclear. In terms of the identification and monitoring of online hate speech, the ADL produced a Cyber-Safety Action Guide to support efforts to report online hatred by civil society and private internet companies (Anti-Defamation League, 2018a). The distribution of these, or similar, resources would be invaluable to furthering CVE efforts at a local level (De-Goede & Simon, 2013; Brown & Cowls, 2015).

Conclusion

CVE agencies attempt to counter RWE using mono-framed, nation-wide initiatives and over-invest in law enforcement and judicial sanctions. The need to innovate interoperable and psycho-sociologically orientated efforts in the CVE community is vital to formulate tactics that deter or interdict right-wing violent extremism. Localized CVE efforts to educate local communities on the implications and influence of RWE and build societal resilience. The merger of mainstream conservatives with reactionary right-wing extremist attitudes will manifest familiar notions of anti-'Other' aggression. If the Muslim identity remains a hierarchical threat to the contemporary reactionary-right movement, anti-'Other' sentiment will sustain itself as a prime mover of RWE violence. It would be valuable for future studies to:

- Critically evaluate a local application of a multi-dimensional, inter-operable counter RWE initiative;
- Focus on how a cumulative program impacted the pre-and-post-hoc presence of RWE; and
- Analyse what communitive conditions set the design of the localized CVE initiative.

The findings of these studies may provide the public and CVE agencies with effective intelligence and techniques that improve the ability to detect and counter future incubations of RWE.

Further Reading

Davey, J., and Ebner, J. (2018). The Fringe Insurgency: Connectivity, Convergence and Mainstreaming of the Extreme Right. *Institute for Strategic Dialogue*, 27. http://www.isdglobal.org/wp-content/uploads/2017/10/The-Fringe-Insurgency-221017.pdf

Parker, C. (2018). The Radical Right in the United States of America. In J. Rydgren (Eds,), The *Oxford Handbook of the Radical Right* (pp. 1–23). Oxford: Oxford University Press.

Perry, B., and Scrivens, R. (2018). "A Climate for Hate? An Exploration of the Right-Wing Extremist Landscape in Canada." *Critical Criminology*, 26(2), 169–187.

References

Abbas, T. (2017). *Islamophobia is the Cause of Far-Right Extremism*. https://www.fairobserver.com/region/europe/islamophobia-far-right-terrorism-london-finsbury-park-terror-attack-british-european-news-74125/

Ahmed, R. and Pisoiu, D. (2019). What Does the 'New Right' Have to Do With the Christchurch Attack? Some Evidence from Twitter on Discursive Overlaps. *VOX-Pol*, April 17. https://www.voxpol.eu/what-does-the-new-right-have-to-do-with-the-christchurch-attack-some-evidence-from-twitter-on-discursive-overlaps/

Anti-Defamation League. (2018a). *ADL Cyber-Safety Action Guide*. https://www.adl.org/adl-cyber-safety-action-guide

Anti-Defamation League. (2018b). *ADL H.E.A.T Map*. https://www.adl.org/heat-map

Baker, N. (2018). Is Trump to Blame for 'Political Violence' in the US? *SBS News*. https://www.sbs.com.au/news/is-trump-to-blame-for-political-violence-in-the-us
Barkun, M. (2017). President Trump and the 'Fringe'. *Terrorism and Political Violence*, 29(3), 437–443.
Baysinger, T. (2006). Right-Wing Group Characteristics and Ideology. *Homeland Security Affairs*, 2(2), 1.
Bergan, P., Ford, A., Sims, A. and Sterman, D. (2018). Part IV: What is the Threat to the United States Today? *New America*. https://www.newamerica.org/in-depth/terrorism-in-america/what-threat-united-states-today/
Bjørgo, T. and Gjelsvik, I. (2015). Norwegian Research on the Prevention of Radicalisation and Violent Extremism: A Status of Knowledge. https://www.regjeringen.no/contentassets/dc64dbc441bc4a4db25f320eadd0d131/080615-norwegian-research-on-preventing-radicalisation-and-violent-extremism.pdf
Brown, I., and Cowls, J. (2015). *Check the Web: Assessing the Ethics and Politics of Policing the Internet for Extremist Material*. VOX-Pol, 42. https://www.voxpol.eu/check-the-web/
Bush, G. W. (2001). "Islam Is Peace" Says President: Remarks by the President at Islamic Center of Washington, D.C. *The White House*. Office of the Press Secretary. https://georgewbush-whitehouse.archives.gov/news/releases/2001/09/20010917-11.html
Campion, K. (2019). A 'Lunatic Fringe'? The Persistence of Right Wing Extremism in Australia. *Perspectives on Terrorism*, 13(2), 2–19.
Canaday, M. (2009). *The Straight State*. Princeton: Princeton University Press.
Carter, E. (2018). Right-Wing Extremism/Radicalism: Reconstructing the Concept. *Journal of Political Ideologies*, 23(2), 157–182. https://doi.org/10.1080/13569317.2018.1451227
Coaston, J. (2018). The Proud Boys, the Bizarre Far-right Street Fighters Behind Violence in New York, Explained. *VOX*. https://www.vox.com/2018/10/15/17978358/proud-boys-gavin-mcinnes-manhattan-gop-violence
Dalgaard-Nielsen, A. (2016). Countering Violent Extremism with Governance Networks. *Perspectives on Terrorism*, 10(6), 135–139. http://www.terrorismanalysts.com/pt/index.php/pot/article/view/564/html
Davey, J., and Ebner, J. (2018). The Fringe Insurgency: Connectivity, Convergence and Mainstreaming of the Extreme Right. *Institute for Strategic Dialogue*, 27. http://www.isdglobal.org/wp-content/uploads/2017/10/The-Fringe-Insurgency-221017.pdf
Davies, L. (2009). Education Against Terrorism. *International Review of Education*. Springer Press. https://www.jstor.org/stable/40270074?seq=1#metadata_info_tab_contents
Dean, G., Bell, P., and Vakhitova, Z. (2016). Right-wing Extremism in Australia: The Rise of the New Radical Right. *Journal of Policing, Intelligence and Counter-Terrorism Group*, 11(2), 123–125. http://dx.doi.org/10.1080/18335330.2016.1231414
De-Goede, M., and Simon, S. (2013). Governing Future Radicals in Europe. *Antipode*, 45(2), 315–335. https://onlinelibrary.wiley.com/doi/abs/10.1111/j.1467-8330.2012.01039.x
Devos, T., and Banaji, M. R. (2005). American = White? *Journal of Personality and Social Psychology*, 88(3), 447–466.
Douglas, M. (1966). *Purity and Danger*. London: Routledge and Kegan Paul.
Ekström, M., Patrona, M., and Thornborrow, J. (2018). Right-wing Popularism and the Dynamics of Style: A Discourse-analytical Perspective On Mediated Political Performances. *Palgrave Communications*, 4(83), 2. https://www.nature.com/articles/s41599-018-0132-6
Federal Bureau of Investigation. (2001). *Uniform Crime Reporting Publications: Hate Crime Statistics*. https://ucr.fbi.gov/hate-crime/2001/hatecrime01.pdf
Ford, K. (2018). A four-point plan for improving education against extremism. *British Educational Research Association*. https://www.bera.ac.uk/blog/a-four-point-plan-for-improving-education-against-extremism

Frankfurter, D. (2013). The Construction of Evil and the Violence of Purification. In M. Jerryson, M. Juergensmeyer, and M. Kitts (Eds.), *The Oxford Handbook of Religion and Violence*. New York: Oxford University Press.

Friedman, U., and Green, E. (2017). Trump's Speech on Islam, Annotated. https://www.theatlantic.com/international/archive/2017/05/trump-saudi-speech-islam/527535/#

Futrell, R., and Simi, P. (2017). The [Un]Surprising Alt-right. *Contexts*, 16(20), 76–76. https://doi.org/10.1177/1536504217714269

Gill, P., Corner, E., Conway, M., Thorton, A., Bloom, M., and Horgan, J. (2017). Terrorist Use of the Internet by the Numbers: Quantifying Behaviours, Patterns, and Processes. *Criminology & Public Policy*. 16(1), 99–117. https://onlinelibrary-wiley-com.simsrad.net.ocs.mq.edu.au/doi/pdf/10.1111/1745-9133.12249

Gill, P., Corner, E., Thornton, A., and Conway, M. (2015). *What are the roles of the Internet in terrorism? Measuring online behaviours of convicted UK terrorists*. VOX-Pol, 33, 37. https://www.voxpol.eu/download/vox-pol_publication/What-are-the-Roles-of-the-Internet-in-Terrorism.pdf

Horton-Eddison, M., and Cristofaro, M.D. (2017). *Hard Interventions and Innovation in Crypto-Drug Markets: The Escrow Example (Policy Brief 11)*. Swansea University, Wales: Global Drug and Policy observatory. https://www.swansea.ac.uk/media/Hard-Interventions-and-Innovation-in-CryptoDrug-Markets-The-escrow-example.pdf

Hunt, S. A., and Benford, R. D. (1994). Identity Talk in the Peace and Justice Movement. *Journal of Contemporary Ethnography* 22(4), 488–517. https://doi.org/10.1177/089124194022004004

Hutchinson, J. (2018a). The Australian New-Right Movement: Online and 'Others'. *VOX-Pol*. https://www.voxpol.eu/the-australian-new-right-movement-online-and-others/

Hutchinson, J. (2018b). They're Not All White, But All Alt-Patriots. *Centre for Analysis of the Radical Right*. https://www.radicalrightanalysis.com/2018/08/15/theyre-not-all-white-but-all-alt-patriots/

Hutchinson, J. (2019a). The New-Far-Right Movement in Australia. *Terrorism and Political Violence*, 1–23. https://doi.org/10.1080/09546553.2019.1629909

Hutchinson, J. (2019b). Far-Right Terrorism: The Christchurch Attack and Potential Implications on the Asia Pacific Landscape. *Counter Terrorist Trends and Analyses* 11(6), 19–28. https://www.jstor.org/stable/26662257

Hutchinson, J. (2019c). The Rise Of Radical Right Extremism In Trump's America. *Centre for Analysis of the Radical Right*. https://www.radicalrightanalysis.com/2019/01/12/the-rise-of-radical-right-extremism-in-trumps-america/

Kaplan, J. (1995). Right Wing Violence in North America. *Terrorism and Political Violence*, 7(1), 46.

Mazzei, P., Madigan, N. and Robles, F. (2018). Living in a Van Plastered With Hate, Bombing Suspect Was Filled With Right-Wing Rage. *The New York Times*. https://www.nytimes.com/2018/10/26/us/cesar-sayoc-bombing-suspect-arrested.html

McCann, C. (2018). *Simply Removing All Extremist Content Won't Stop Radicalization*. https://www.huffingtonpost.co.uk/entry/why-simply-removing-all-extremist-content-wont-stop_uk_5b55f329e4b0eb29100e5905

McDonald, K. (2018). *Is it better to 'no-platform' fascists or simply try to win the debate?* https://inews.co.uk/news/politics/should-we-no-platform-fascists-no-pasaran/

McVeigh, R. (2009). *The Rise of the Ku Klux Klan: Right-Wing Movements and National Politics*. Minneapolis: University of Minnesota Press.

Muddle, C. (2000). *The Ideology of the Extreme Right*. Manchester: Manchester University Press.

Mudde, C. (2016). *The Populist Radical Right: A Reader*. 1st ed. Routledge, Taylor & Francis Group. https://www.routledge.com/The-Populist-Radical-Right-A-Reader-1st-Edition/Mudde/p/book/9781138673878

Nguyen, T. (2018). The Far-Right Rejoices as Trump says Immigrants are Destroying European 'Culture'. https://www.vanityfair.com/news/2018/07/donald-trump-culture-wars-britain
Parker, C. (2018). The Radical Right in the United States of America. In J. Rydgren (Eds,), *The Oxford Handbook of the Radical Right* (pp. 1–23). Oxford: Oxford University Press.
Parker, C., and Barreto, M. (2013). Change They Can't Believe In Christopher S. Parker and Matt A. Barreto (Eds.). *The Tea Party and Reactionary Politics in America*. Princeton: Princeton University Press.
Pedazur, A., and Canetti-Nisim, D. (2004). Support for Right-Wing Extremist Ideology: Socio-Economic Indicators and Socio-Psychological Mechanisms of Social Identification. *International Journal of Comparative Sociology*, 3, 1–36. https://doi.org/10.1163/1569133041513756
Perry, B., and Scrivens, R. (2018). A Climate for Hate? An Exploration of the Right-Wing Extremist Landscape in Canada. *Critical Criminology*, 26(2), 169–187. https://doi.org/10.1007/s10612-018-9394-y
Perry, B., and Scrivens, R. (2017). Resisting the Right: Countering Right-Wing Extremism in Canada. *Canadian Journal of Criminology and Criminal Justice*, 59(4), 534–558.
Perry, B., and Scrivens, R. (2016). White Pride Worldwide: Constructing Global Identities Online. In J. Schweppe and M. Walters (Eds.), *The Globalization of Hate: Internationalising Hate Crime* (pp. 65–78). New York, NY: Oxford University Press.
Rashbaum, W., Feuer, A., and Goldman, A. (2018). Outspoken Trump Supporter in Florida Charged in Attempted Bombing Spree. *The New York Times*. https://www.nytimes.com/2018/10/26/nyregion/cnn-cory-booker-pipe-bombs-sent.html?action=click&module=RelatedCoverage&pgtype=Article&region=Footer
Scrivens, R. (2017). *Understanding the Collective Identity of the Radical Right Online: A Mixed Methods Approach*. (Doctoral dissertation). http://summit.sfu.ca/item/17632
Ser, K. K. K. (2016). *Data: Hate crimes against Muslims increased after 9/11*. https://www.pri.org/stories/2016-09-12/data-hate-crimes-against-muslims-increased-after-911
Snow, D. (2001). Collective identity and expressive forms. *University of California, Irvine eScholarship Repository*, http://repositories.cdlib.org/csd/01-07
Stampnitzky, L. (2013). *Disciplining Terror: How Experts Invented "Terrorism"*. Cambridge, UK: Cambridge University Press.
Taylor, K. (2009). *Cruelty: Human Evil and the Human Brain*. Oxford: Oxford University Press.
United Nations Educational, Scientific and Cultural Organization. (2017). *Preventing violent extremism through education: A guide for policy-makers*. unesdoc.unesco.org/images/0024/002477/247764e.pdf
Walsh, J. (2017). Moral Panics by Design: The Case of Terrorism. *Current Sociology*. SAGE Publications, 65(5), 643–662.

Chapter 60

State-Sponsored Terrorism

Tavis D. Jules
Loyola University Chicago, Chicago, IL, United States

Contents

Introduction 441
Forms of State-Sponsored Terrorism 442
The Continuum of State Sponsorship 442
A Brief History of State-Sponsored Terrorism 443
State Sponsorship after 9/11 444
Designations and Ramifications 445
Conclusion 447
Further Reading 447
Notes 447
References 448

Introduction

Countries involved in state-sponsored terrorism[1] and insurgencies are increasing as governments seek new avenues to curb endogenous and exogenous threats to nationhood. There is no precise definition of state-sponsored terrorism, but the concept is "inclusive of both acts of omission and commission" given "the basic disagreement over the elements of terrorism itself" (Maogoto, 2003, p. 413). State sponsorship is complex since states work in conjunction with terrorist groups for myriad reasons. It has been suggested that "one state's terrorist is another state's freedom fighter" (Pinder, 2010, p. 73), and therefore, state-sponsored terrorism "is a continuation of war by other means" (as cited in Erickson 1989, p. 26). State-sponsored terrorism then implies that one state (or sub-national groups aided or galvanized by sovereign states) intentionally arranges, originates, succors, and partakes in providing support through either direct or indirect mechanisms for terrorist acts in other countries. However, it is often problematic to identify and corroborate state support and

DOI: 10.4324/9781315144511-63

sponsorship of terrorist activities. While the designation of state sponsors of terrorism dates back to the 1970s, the concept has gained notoriety since the 9/11 attacks.

To these ends, this chapter first explores the different forms of state-sponsored terrorism. Next, the core elements of the concepts are explained followed by a brief history describing the emergence of the concept. The next section explores the unique prominence that the concept has gained in the post-9/11 period and the consequences of an event being designated a state-sponsored terrorist activity. This chapter concludes with the current perceptions of this concept.

Forms of State-Sponsored Terrorism

The current literature on state-sponsored terrorism discusses four distinct forms of state support; these ranging "from greatest to least[,] are: sponsorship, support, toleration, and inaction through inability to act" (Erickson, 1989, p. 25). These may include, but not be limited to, "politically subversive violent act or threat thereof; … an intended political outcome; and a target, whether civilian, military or material, whose death, injury or destruction can be expected to influence to some degree the desired political outcome" (Maogoto, 2003, p. 413). Across this continuum, Erickson (1989) argues that *state sponsorship* implies ownership of the terrorist actions undertaken. *State support* suggests that "capability without assuming control or direction" (p. 36), *state toleration* implies that terrorist actions are neither supported nor thwarted, and *state inaction* denotes the inability of the state to act within its borders. At the heart of state sponsorship is the employment of "tactics of terror as an extension of war to gain some advantage by the use of unconventional means" (Wiebe, 2003, p. 372). In 2001, the United Nations Security Council, led by the United States of America (US), unanimously adopted Resolution 1373 calling for "states to deny money, support, and sanctuary to terrorists" (Hoye, 2002, p. 106). This call for global recognition of an increase in terror activities was motivated by the widely emerging consensus among states that a rise in intolerance and extremism primarily drives increases in global terrorism. Moreover, numerous United Nations General Assembly Resolutions have indisputably condemned "all acts, methods and practices of terrorism as criminal and unjustifiable, wherever and by whoever committed" (UN Security Council, Security Council resolution, 1999, p. 1). This resolution not only calls for states to "refrain from providing any form of support, active or passive, to entities or persons involved in terrorist acts, including by suppressing recruitment of members of terrorist groups," but stipulates that it is in the best interest of states to share information to facilitate early terror warnings while, at the same time, "suppressing recruitment of members of terrorist groups and eliminating the supply of weapons to terrorists" (UN Security Council, Security Council resolution, 2001, p. 2). While state-sponsored terrorism is viewed as an act of war, the relationship between the state-backed proxies and surrogates and their terrorist activities is multivariate, fluid, and evolving.

The Continuum of State Sponsorship

The complex nature of state-sponsored terrorism is often viewed as a form of international terrorism while non-state-sponsored terrorism is seen as transnational terrorism

(Erickson, 1989). Sponsorship spans across a continuum ranging from active, direct, and deliberate involvement to passive support and sympathetic toleration (Byman, 2008). In this way, active support encompasses tactics based on control in the form of direct assistance, coordination of activities, and contact with terrorist organizations. Passive support then takes the form of knowing how to tolerate terrorist groups, ignoring terrorist activities, and being incapacitated to control actions within one territorial boundary. Thus, the designation of a state that sponsors terrorist activities, while not given lightly, is often promulgated after it is determined that the said state has repeatedly provided support, in various forms, to aid acts of international terrorism. State support to terrorists, according to Byman (2005), can be distilled into six categories such as "training and operations; money, arms, and logistics; diplomatic backing; organizational assistance; ideological direction; and (perhaps most importantly) sanctuary" (p. 59). Terrorist groups with state-sponsored support often have distinct advantages over self-supported terrorists. Moreover, international consensus suggests that "a broad definition of what constitutes state sponsorship—a definition that encompasses not only errors of commission, such as arming and training groups, but also errors of omission, such as unwillingness to stop terrorist fundraising and recruitment" (Byman, 2008, p. X) is warranted in today's complex geostrategic environment.

State sponsorship of terrorism is an inherently political term and is used to punish rogue nations in the interstate system. The US Department of State and its Secretary of State dictate its coinage, categorization, designation, and determination. Thus, state sponsorship ranges from military, diplomatic, political, and economic support to providing ideological directions, training facilities, sanctuary, and safe havens for terrorist groups. Pundits highlight that the term is political since a state does not give all acts and groups involved in perceived terrorism shelter for that sole reason. This is because state sponsorship can exist along a continuum ranging from a sponsor's support of a massive program to merely tolerating visible activities, such as fundraising campaigns by terrorist groups on their soil. These activities become more complex as some states may support insurgent groups that may later turn to terrorist activities to support their causes. Often state sponsorship involves the passive support of a state "knowingly allowing a terrorist group to raise money, enjoy a sanctuary, recruit, or otherwise flourish without interference from a regime that does not directly aid the group itself" (Byman, 2005, p. 222). In other words, passive support is provided when a state is aware of the alleged terrorist activities of a group and can stop all illegal activities that such group is engaged in but does not do so. As Byman (2008) poignantly asserts, states do "not actively train or arm the terrorist group, but rather [they allow] it [to] act with relative impunity—an approach that, in practice, allows the government to claim ignorance or incapacity" (p. XI). Such passive support is different from the overt support, proxy or otherwise, of a state for terror activities against other states.

A Brief History of State-Sponsored Terrorism

After the end of World War II, the 1980s had the most substantial number of terrorist attacks sanctioned and carried out by governments. State-sponsored terrorism is one of the most established forms of terrorism, and at its core, it is a "foreign policy instrument, a way to wage war using an economy of scale" (Aubrey, 2004, p. 44). A state's involvement in terrorism should be distinguished from international terrorism and transnational terrorism since state sponsors of terrorism are usually involved in one way or the other in the planning, funding, sanctioning, or undertaking of the terrorist activity.

In the 1970s, Arab states openly supported the Palestine Liberation Organization (PLO). The organization gained diplomatic recognition as it actively carried out terrorist struggles against Israel (Byman, 2005). However, there is a consensus that state sponsorship of terrorist activities extends to "a government's intentional assistance to a terrorist group to help it use violence, bolster its political activities, or sustain the organization" (Byman, 2005, p. 10). Similarly, the Bremer Commission (the National Commission on Terrorism, 2000) argues that some states "have relations with terrorists that fall short of the extensive criteria for designation as a state sponsor, but their failure to act against terrorists perpetuates terrorist activities" (p. 23). State sponsorship of terrorist activities often emerges from intrastate conflict fueled by external insurgency, the activities of rogue states, and provision and indifference of safe havens for terrorists (Kirchner, 2016).

The dawning of the Cold War saw the employment and escalation of state sponsorship tactics as the United States focused on spreading neoliberalism and the Soviet Union extolled the virtues of communism and funded communist insurgencies. In fact, state sponsorship reached its peak phase in the 1970s and 1980 as a foreign policy strategy, and it was continuously used after the end of the Cold War. During the Cold War, state-sponsored terrorist groups, such as Marxist guerrillas in Central and South America and the Middle East, were used by the Soviet Union and its Eastern European affiliates to exhort leverage and sabotage American holdings abroad (Aubrey, 2004). In this way, the Soviets used state-sponsored "terrorism as a way of avoiding the technological nightmare of nuclear war." State-sponsored terrorism was used by other states to "compensate for the preponderance of military power held by Washington and Moscow" (Sloan, 1986, p. 7). At the height of the Cold War, both the Soviet Union (assisting Palestine and other Arab states) and the United States (supporting Israel, the Contras in Nicaragua, and the Afghan Mujahideen) engaged in instances of state sponsorship. For example, by 1987, as Pakistan's fight with India over West Kashmir intensified, the Pakistani government trained jihadists groups such as Lashkar-e Tayyaba (LeT), *Jaish-e Muhammad*, and Harakat ul-Mujahedin. By the 1990s, Pakistan was instrumental in creating, recruiting, and advancing the Taliban and Osama bin Laden's global terrorist agenda. However, in the post-Cold War period, the nature of state sponsorship changed as new global terrorist networks emerged and were financed by private benefactors. Moreover, the post-Cold War period saw a shift in state sponsorship activities to states in the developing world.

State Sponsorship after 9/11

Since the 9/11 attacks, the definition of state-sponsored terrorism has been widened. Historically, state-sponsored terrorism accounted exclusively for countries who provided support to terrorists and their operations. Today, the definition includes nations that harbor terrorists or provide havens for groups. Yet, state-backers of terrorist activities still try, where possible, to limit the actions of its proxies. The United States' rhetoric of its "war on terror" doctrine in the aftermath of 9/11 attacks formed the bedrock of political and ideological objectives to overthrow other governments. In fact, state-sponsored attacks often are more lethal and more deadly than non-state-supported provocations. Nevertheless, in today's global environment, it is frequently difficult to discern if state support for a non-territorial international group is a form of indirect aggression against another state.

What is clear is that state-sponsored terrorist groups have the benefits and safeguard of statist agencies while having the ability to access state intelligence services and resources securely. For this reason, state-sponsored terrorism, which may be direct or indirect, has been categorized as a new form of "armed diplomacy" or "gunboat diplomacy" that is part of a "protracted political warfare... [which uses] a form of indirect aggression" (Sloan, 1986, pp. 7–8). In other words, it has emerged as a "tool of low-intensity conflict" (Kupperman, Van Opstal, & Williamson, 1982, p. 33), "surrogate and covert warfare" (Kirchner, 2016; Schmid & Jongman, 2017), and covert threats that can be discharged by small or large states against any perceived threat or enemy. Thus, state-sponsored terrorism is often viewed as a threat against democracy as it seeks to achieve political aims while creating a climate of fear.

Designations and Ramifications

While there are several criteria that countries take into account when designating a country as a state sponsor of terrorism, it is the US Department of State (2017) criteria of "repeatedly provid[ing] support for acts of international terrorism" (p. 303) that determines which countries fall under this definition and pursuant to three American laws (section 6(j) of the Export Administration Act, section 40 of the Arms Export Control Act, and section 620A of the Foreign Assistance Act) can be sanctioned. The United States' official list of state sponsors of terrorism dates back to 1979, under the *Export Administration Act* (EAA), commencing when Iraq, Libya, Syria, and South Yemen[2] were first placed on the list. Then, in 1982, 1984, 1988, and 1993, Cuba,[3] Iran, North Korea, and Sudan, respectively, were added to this list. Based on the designation of countries being involved in state-sponsored terrorism, currently, the US Department of State has branded Syria (designated in 1989), Sudan (named in 1993), Iran (appointed in 1980),[4] and the Democratic People's Republic of Korea (North Korea [re-designated in 2017[5]]) as having sponsored international terrorism and sanctioned them. With the label of state sponsors of terrorism comes the consequences of sanctions that take numerous forms depending on which country imposes such a designation.

Byman and Kreps (2010) suggest that state-sponsored terrorism is a kind of "principal-agent relationship," in that it has emerged as one way in which governments, if they are willing, can kill large numbers of people (Byman, 2005). Thus, governments delegate to another agent the responsibilities of carrying out terrorist acts to boost the state influence at home. While the current list of sponsors of terrorism is down to four (Syria, Sudan, Iran, and North Korea) from seven (Cuba, Iran, Iraq, Libya, North Korea, Sudan, and Syria), since the 9/11 attacks, inclusion of countries on this list has severe repercussions. Ramifications, which are usually economic and political in nature, range from the penalizing of persons and countries engaging in trade with the designated country to one of four main categories of sanctions "includ[ing] a ban on arms-related exports and sales; restrictions on exports of dual use items; prohibitions on official US Government economic assistance (except humanitarian assistance) …; and imposition of miscellaneous trade and other restrictions" (US Department of State, 2002, p. 144). Sanctions aim to punish the designated sponsor of terrorism and its affiliates so that they will be forced into submission. Of course, this does not always work, as in the case of Iran, which has thrived amid sanctions. On the flipside of this equation, many states in the Middle East argue that the United States is a sponsor of terrorism given its contained support of Israel and Israelis' activities.

Iran's designation as a state sponsor of terrorism, and "the most active state sponsor of terrorism" (US Department of State, 2002, p. 77), is grounded in its ongoing use of its Islamic Revolutionary Guard Corps-Qods Force (IRGC-QF) to cultivate terrorist activities across several groups (the Shi'i Lebanese group Hezbollah,[6] Hamas, and the Palestine Islamic Jihad) in the Middle East, as well as in Syria, Iraq, and Lebanon. It is important to note that Hezbollah is unique in that its activities are sponsored by states. These "outreach" activities range from IRGC-QF's provision of training, weapons, and financial support for cyberattacks and construction of terrorist cells. Sudan's designation is based on its affiliation and support of international terrorist groups, including the Abu Nidal Organization, Palestine Islamic Jihad, Hamas, and Hezbollah (US Department of State, 2017). Syria's designation, as the globe's most fervent sponsor of terrorism, is due to Damascus's blatant foreign policy position and geopolitical goals of openly supporting radical groups (such as As-Sa'iqa, Fatah, Popular Front for the Liberation of Palestine [PFLP], the Abu Nidal Organization [ANO], the Abu Musa group, the Democratic Front for the Liberation of Palestine, and the Popular Front for the Liberation of Palestine – General Command [PFLP-GC]) and providing a safe haven for others (the Armenian Secret Army for the Liberation of Armenia [ASALA], Hamas, the Kurdistan Workers' Party [PKK], the Palestine Islamic Jihad [PIJ], Red Army Faction [JRA], and the Pakistani group al Zulfikar) (Byman, 2005).

In the post-911 period, a new group of sympathetic states are emerging. While not officially given the designation of state sponsors of terrorism, the action of these states falls within a gray area of state sponsorship. These range from activities sanctioned in Iraqi Kurdistan by the Partiya Karkeren Kurdistan (PKK; the Kurdistan Workers' Party) and operations carried out by Iraqi jihadists in Jordan, Saudi Arabia, and elsewhere; to Eritrea's support of various guerrilla groups fighting from the Darfur region of Sudan; to Saudi Arabia's championing of jihadist causes in Chechnya, Kashmir, and Iraq; to Venezuela's arming and training of the Colombian terrorist groups Fuerzas Armadas Revolucionarias de Colombia (FARC) and Ejercito de Liberation Nacional (ELN); to Yemen's use of jihadists at home (to fight against Zaydi, a Shi'i sect) and abroad to maintain the regime's grip on power (Byman, 2008). Moreover, Syria continues to allow Iran to rearm other terrorist groups and provide weapons to Hezbollah. North Korea's re-designation is part of the Trump Administration's aim of an entire denuclearization of the Korean peninsula. New state sponsors of terrorism are more dangerous to the interstate system than the traditional sponsors of terrorism because many of the emerging sponsors of terrorism have a more complicated relationship with jihadist groups such as Islamic State and Al Qaeda and its affiliates and offshoots.

Conclusion

State support continues to be one of the deadliest and most relevant aspects of terrorism. As terrorism contains to be outsourced to nonstate actors, different agendas converge and create cataclysmic forces that are beyond the counters of the nation-state. State sponsors of terrorism are viewed as a critical impediment in the global fight against the evolving and new nature of terrorism. Since state sponsors often provide a haven to territorial and non-territorial terrorist groups, it is often difficult to penetrate these groups since one is never sure whom (a state or a group) they are fighting against. As such, every form of state-sponsored terrorism poses different challenges to counterterrorism goals, as they capitalize on the threats posed by proxy terrorist and militant organizations. Today, with the advent of globalization-supporting technological advancements, states can sponsor terrorist activities digitally with the aid of cyber-programs and cyberattacks. Modern terrorism is evolving in today's transnational era of lone wolf attacks, networking effects, and insurgencies. As such, state-sponsored terrorism, with its high leverage/low risk model, is emerging as an inexpensive alternative to conventional warfare. With the inception of network terrorism, sleeper cells, and cyber warfare, state-sponsored terrorist activities are becoming harder to discern given that there are progressions of culpability across this active two-way relationship.

Globalization has made it easy for state sponsors of terrorism to hide openly given that since the Cold War, few states blatantly support terrorism or terrorist groups; instead, they work actively behind the scenes in aiding groups and organizations in building their operations, thriving, and surviving. Cyberspace is the new frontier of state-sponsored terrorism, where cyberattacks and intrusions into another state's critical information systems are becoming the new norm. Isomorphism between states and terrorists in today's interconnected society is becoming increasingly recognized as a meaningful challenge to identifying and ascertaining state support for terrorist activities.

Further Reading

Byman, D. (2005). *Deadly Connections: States that Sponsor Terrorism.* Cambridge University Press.

O'Sullivan, M. L. (2003). *Shrewd Sanctions: Statecraft and State Sponsors of Terrorism.* The Brookings Institute.

Skuldt, A. C. (2013). *State Sponsored Terrorism? Leader Survival and the Foreign Policy of Fear.* University of Texas at Austin

Notes

1 Since the nonenforcement of the 1938 Convention for the Prevention and Punishment of Terrorism (CPPT), a global convention on terrorism has not been agreed upon. Instead, Article 1 of UN General Assembly Resolution 3314 (1957) speaks of aggression, which it defines "as use of armed force by a State against the sovereignty, territorial integrity, or political independence of another State, or in any manner inconsistent with the UN

Charter" (p. 1) and not terrorism. The lack of a precise definition of terrorism contributes to the murkiness of identifying all the core attributes of state sponsorship of terrorism.
2 South Yemen was removed from in 1990 from the US Department State's list of state sponsor of terrorism.
3 Cuba was removed from in 2015 from the US Department State's list of state sponsor of terrorism.
4 Iran was removed from in 1982 (re-added in 1984) and 2004 from the US Department State's list of state sponsor of terrorism.
5 Under the George Bush Administration and in return for limited international aid the Democratic People's Republic of Korea was removed in 2008 from the US Department State's list of state sponsor of terrorism. As a condition for its removal, North Korea agreed to move toward denuclearization of the Korean Peninsula, which did not happen.
6 Ayatollah Ali Khamenei, Iran's current Supreme Leader is deeply respected by Hezbollah leaders making the relationship one of "partner than proxy" (Byman, 2008, p.11).

References

Aubrey, S. M. (2004). *The new dimension of international terrorism*. Zürich. Switzerland: Vdf Hochschulverlag an der ETH.

Byman, D. (2005). *Deadly connections: States that sponsor terrorism*. Cambridge, UK: Cambridge University Press.

Byman, D. (2008). *The changing nature of state sponsorship of terrorism*. Washington, DC: Saban Center for Middle East Policy at the Brookings Institution.

Byman, D., & Kreps, S. E. (2010). Agents of destruction? Applying principal-agent analysis to state-sponsored terrorism. *International Studies Perspectives*, *11*(1), 1–18.

Erickson, R. J. (1989). *Legitimate use of military force against state-sponsored international terrorism*. Washington, DC: Air University Press.

General Assembly resolution 3314, Definition of Aggression, A/RES/3314 (1974), Retrieved from https://crimeofaggression.info/documents/6/General_Assembly_%20Resolution_%20 3314.pdf

Hoye, W. P. (2002). Fighting Fire With…Mire? Civil Remedies and the New War on State-Sponsored Terrorism'. *Duke Journal of Comparative & International Law*, *12*, 105–106.

Kirchner, M. (2016). *Why states rebel: Understanding state sponsorship of terrorism*. Opladen, Germany: Barbara Budrich Publishers.

Kupperman, R., Van Opstal, D., & Williamson, D. (1982). Terror, the Strategic Tool: Response and Control. *The Annals of the American Academy of Political and Social Science*, *463*, 24–38.

Maogoto, J. N. (2003). War on the Enemy: Self-Defence and State-Sponsored Terrorism. *Melbourne Journal of International Law*, *4*, 406–427.

National Commission on Terrorism (2000). *Countering the Changing Threat of International Terrorism*. Retrieved from https://www.hsdl.org/?abstract&did=992

Pinder, D. (2010). Supping with the Devil. In G. O. Faure and I. W. Zartman (Eds.), *Negotiating with terrorists: Strategy, tactics, and politics* (pp. 69–84). London, UK: Routledge.

Sloan, S. (1986). *Beating international terrorism: An action strategy for preemption and punishment*. Maxwell Air Force Base, Ala: Air University, Air University Press.

Schmid, A. P. & Jongman, A. J. (2017). *Political terrorism: A new guide to actors, authors, concepts, data bases, theories, and literature*. New York, NY: Routledge.

US Department of State. (2002). *Patterns of Global Terrorism 2001*. Retrieved from http://1.usa.gov/1aT3UDI

US Department of State. (2017). *Country reports on terrorism 2016*. Washington, DC: United States Department of State Publication.

UN Security Council, Security Council resolution 1373. (2001). [on threats to international peace and security caused by terrorist acts], 28 September 2001, S/RES/1373 (2001), Retrieved from: http://www.refworld.org/docid/3c4e94552a.html [accessed 26 October 2018.]

UN Security Council, Security Council resolution 1269, *Resolution 1269*. (1999). S/RES/1269/99 (19 October 1999), Retrieved from http://www.securitycouncilreport.org/un-documents/document/Terrorism%20S%20RES%201269.php

Wiebe, M. C. (2003). Assassination in Domestic and International Law: The Central Intelligence Agency, State-Sponsored Terrorism, and the Right of Self-Defense. *The Journal of Comparative and International Law*, *11*, 363–406.

Chapter 61

Suicide Bombers

Charlie Winter
King's College London, London, United Kingdom

Contents

Introduction 451
Pre-1980s 452
The 1980s and Beyond 452
Suicide Tactics Today 453
Explanations of Suicide Tactics 453
Conclusion 454
Further Reading 455
References 455

Introduction

Since their modern-day emergence in the early 1980s, suicide tactics have become normalized both on and off the battlefield. Today, they are witnessed regularly in the context of non-state asymmetric warfare and are considered by the insurgents who use them to be a way to make up for what they lack in terms of strategic armaments, manpower, and resources.

This chapter, which explores how and why suicide tactics are used today, has two parts. The first section is historical, providing a brief account of their use prior to the 1980s, followed by a discussion of their incidence since the 1980s, as well as an overview of how they were being used at the time of writing in the late 2010s. The second section departs from the historical perspective in order to touch on some of the key fault-lines in the academic debate regarding the causal logic of weaponizing suicide. The chapter concludes by identifying trends and implications for the future, with a particular focus on what their increasing use means for US policymakers and military practitioners deployed in theater.

DOI: 10.4324/9781315144511-64

Pre-1980s

The first modern-day suicide attack took place in Russia in 1881, when Ignacy Hryniewiecki, a member of the anarchist group Narodnya Volya, attacked a carriage carrying the then-tsar, Alexander II. While it succeeded in killing its target, Hryniewiecki's attack was ultimately unsuccessful—the revolution he and his associates had hoped to spark did not hit Russia for a further 30 years (von Borcke, 1982). Perhaps because of the operation's failure to achieve its primary outcome goal, suicide tactics were not destined to proliferate beyond Russia in any meaningful way for decades, even though anarchist terrorists continued to make use of them long after Alexander II's assassination.

During World War II, they appeared once again, this time in the form of Imperial Japan's *kamikaze* pilots. Here, suicide attacks were being used in a military context, not one that was strictly terroristic, and involved using plane-borne operatives to attack American warships in a last-ditch attempt to defend the Japanese Empire against its impending collapse (Orbell and Morikawa, 2011).

The 1980s and Beyond

While World War II's *kamikaze* operatives were by definition suicide attackers, the means by which they died are distinct from what has emerged as the suicide tactic 'norm' in more recent decades—that is, attacks perpetrated by terroristic individuals belonging to non-state insurgent groups engaged in some form of revolutionary struggle.

The Shi'ite Islamist group Hezbollah's suicide attack on a United States Marines barracks in Beirut, Lebanon, in 1983 is one of the earliest and most significant assaults of this form—though, it should be noted, it was not the first: some believe it to have been preceded two years earlier by an unrelated assault on Lebanon's Iraqi Embassy (Falk and Morgenstern, 2009: 28). In any case, the barracks bombing was a huge strategic success, something for which it is still renowned today: with just one suicide vehicle-borne bomb, Hezbollah was able to kill more than 273 people (241 of whom were serving American soldiers) and, consequently, provoke the total withdrawal of US marines from Lebanon less than six months later (Merari, 2010: 29).

In the wake of this and other successes, Hezbollah continued to use suicide tactics selectively and strategically over the coming years. Before long, on account of their demonstrable ability to win asymmetric victories against seemingly insurmountable adversaries, other groups soon began to make use of them, too, from the Sri Lankan Liberation Tigers of Tamil Eelam (LTTE, better known as the Tamil Tigers) to the Palestinian Sunni Islamist group Hamas and the Turkey-based Kurdish Workers' Party (PKK) (Schweitzer, 2000). Such was the scale of this tactical proliferation that, by the end of the 1990s, suicide attacks were already considered to be one of the foremost weapons of insurgent and terrorist groups.

The attacks of September 11, 2001, and the Global War on Terror that followed fueled this proliferation dynamic even further. First with the invasion of Afghanistan, and later in the context of Iraq, the attacks ushered in an era of monumental instability, one in which al-Qaeda and its affiliates were destined to launch thousands of suicide operations all over the world (Wright, 2016). Nowhere was the suicide attack more regularly—and dangerously—operationalized than in Iraq, where a group calling itself al-Qaeda in the Land of the Two Rivers (better known as al-Qaeda in Iraq or AQI), used men-, women-, and children-borne bombs to target infrastructure, commit massacres at holy sites, assassinate international workers, and, ultimately, spark a civil war (Hafez, 2007).

Suicide Tactics Today

Ten years on, the suicide tactic paradigm was again destined to change, this time with the 2014 rise of the Islamic State (IS), a group that emerged from the battered ashes of AQI in the 2000s. Unlike its predecessors, which had mainly confined their use of suicide operations to achieving offensive terroristic goals, IS used suicide tactics as an unconventional means with which to pursue conventional military ends. When the group was in ascendancy between 2014 and 2015, it used them offensively as a way to pierce fortifications, degrade enemy morale, and boast of resolve. As, however, its resources, manpower, and territories went into decline from mid-2016 onward, IS increasingly used suicide tactics in a defensive context, as a *kamikaze*-esque attempt to resist the immensity of the military pressure directed against it (Winter, 2017; Kaaman, 2017).

Depending on their tactical or strategic objectives, most of IS's suicide operations between 2014 and 2018 fell into one of three categories: first, there were the vehicle-borne improvised explosive devices (VBIEDs); second, there were the *inghimas* fighters, the special operatives who attacked their targets with light arms and suicide belts; and third, there were the human-borne improvised explosive device (IED) bombers, the attackers who predominantly carried out assaults on civilians using explosives-laden vests or belts (Winter, 2017).

Whatever their shape or form, other jihadist and quasi-jihadist organizations—from Hay'at Tahrir al-Sham in Syria and al-Qaeda in the Arabian Peninsula in Yemen to the Taliban in Afghanistan—adapted their use of suicide tactics to become more like that of an IS in recent years, taking to them in similar ways for both terroristic purposes *and* in order to achieve more conventional battlefield goals (Haid, 2017). It is important to note that non-jihadists continue to make sporadic use of suicide tactics too—and, indeed, this phenomenon may well accelerate in the future—but, by the beginning of 2018 at least, jihadists groups continued to enjoy ideological and technical hegemony over their implementation.

Explanations of Suicide Tactics

Seeking to make sense of this phenomenon, scholars have long debated the strategic and tactical logic of suicide attacks. While most have reached a broad consensus that they should be defined as "attacks whose success is contingent upon the death of the perpetrator," disagreements run throughout the literature (Moghadam, 2006).

Some scholars have attempted to account for the use of suicide tactics by emphasizing their communicative impact. Bloom (2004), for one, contends that they are predominantly a manifestation of political outbidding. According to her thesis, they are used chiefly in order to play to the 'home team'—that is, to compete at the intra-ideological level for support, reputation, and resources. Acosta (2016) also holds that terrorist groups use suicide tactics in order to attract supporters and rewards from larger, better-resourced organizations. While certain aspects of their theories ring true, both of these assessments are overly simplistic, applicable only in certain circumstances. Bloom and Acosta are not the only scholars to have fallen into this single-explanation trap. Pape (2003), whose original explicative theory is based on the "universe of suicide attacks worldwide from 1980 to 2001," holds that suicide tactics are used specifically in order to coerce liberal democracies into making territorial concessions to those responsible. Again, while there is truth to this explanation in certain contexts—like, say, Sri Lanka—this 'truth' is far from absolute and certainly not generalizable.

All attempts to provide a unitary explanation as to why insurgent groups make use of suicide tactics, of which there are many, are similarly flawed. Categorically speaking, there is no single explanation for their incidence—they are, as Crenshaw (2007) notes, not a "single unified method of violence," and hence, there is not a single unified reason for their occurrence.

A number of scholars, among them Hafez (2007) and Seifert and McCauley (2014), embrace this idea. For his part, Hafez examines a large collection of AQI suicide operative eulogies, noting the various contexts in which its attackers were said to have killed themselves. Focusing on their asymmetric tactical merits, he notes that suicide tactics were most often used in Iraq simply because they were deemed to be the most effective means to achieve the desired tactical and strategic ends. This is, he holds, intuitive; after all, they have a high margin of casualties per fighter lost; their human operators have a unique ability to seek out targets; they are difficult to defend against; and, as violent spectacles, they have the power to shatter enemy morale. Also appraising the various asymmetric merits of suicide operations are Seifert and McCauley. They, like Crenshaw, note that there is no single explanation, contending that all suicide attack data must be disaggregated prior to analysis. By doing this, they assert that it becomes possible to identify the causal reasons for which these tactics are used, reasons similar to those already identified by Hafez.

Suicide attacks, it seems, are best understood as a multivariate category of action, not a monolithic tool, something that can be tactical *and* strategic, communicative *and* tangible at one and the same time.

Conclusion

In recent years, the global use of suicide tactics has accelerated significantly: in 2011, an average of 17 attacks were recorded each month; 5 years later in 2016, IS alone was perpetrating more than 90 each month (GTD, 2017). This dynamic of acceleration and increasing sophistication is likely to continue to characterize the use of weaponized suicide on and off the battlefield in the coming years, as IS and its ideological associates continue to sacrifice the lives of their most fervent operatives in order to make up for their otherwise crippling asymmetric disadvantages.

For policymakers and military practitioners operating in the deconfliction and stabilization space in theater, the implications of this increasing ubiquity are significant indeed: suicide tactics already pose a potent asymmetric threat to global development and diplomatic infrastructure, and they will continue to be regarded as an effective way to spoil political settlements or reconciliation processes. It is highly likely that groups like IS will look to them even more in years to come, especially if they are attempting to make up for lost ground. With this consideration in mind, it is imperative that the international community better understands the context and circumstances within which they are deployed in order to better calibrate its response.

Besides this, the implications of their accelerating use will reach far beyond the immediate conflict theater. Indeed, suicide tactics will remain a weapon of choice for organizations seeking to perpetrate acts of terrorism abroad—in Western countries in particular, they are low-cost compared to the massive return they promise as performative acts of communication. For this reason, domestic counter-terrorism practitioners and law enforcement services must be more diligent than ever. While unsophisticated attacks using knives and vehicles as weapons have emerged as something of a "new normal" in recent years, the threat of more complex operations involving explosives is, because of groups like IS, higher than ever.

Further Reading

Crenshaw, M. 2007. Explaining Suicide Terrorism: A Review Essay. *Security Studies* 16(1). 133–162.

Moghadam, A. 2006. Suicide Terrorism, Occupation, and the Globalization of Martyrdom: A Critique of Dying to Win. *Studies in Conflict & Terrorism* 29(8). 707–729.

Pape, R.A. 2003. The Strategic Logic of Suicide Terrorism. *American Political Science Review* 97(3). 343–361.

References

Acosta, B. 2016. Dying for Survival: Why Militant Organizations Continue to Conduct Suicide Attacks. *Journal of Peace Research* 53(2). 180–196.

Bloom, M. 2004. Palestinian Suicide Bombing: Public Support, Market Share, and Outbidding. *Political Science Quarterly* 119(1). 61–88.

Crenshaw, M. 2007. Explaining Suicide Terrorism: A Review Essay. *Security Studies* 16(1). 133–162.

Falk, O. and Morgenstern, H. (Ed.). 2009. *Suicide Terror: Understanding and Confronting the Threat*. Hoboken: John Wiley and Sons.

Hafez, M. 2007. *Suicide Bombers in Iraq: The Strategy and Ideology of Martyrdom*. Washington, DC: United States Institute of Peace.

Haid, H. 2017. Al-Qaeda Shifts Back to Suicide in Syria. Chatham House. https://www.chathamhouse.org/expert/comment/al-qaeda-shifts-back-suicide-syria

Kaaman, H. 2017. The History and Adaptability of the Islamic State Car Bomb. Zaytunarjuwani. https://zaytunarjuwani.wordpress.com/2017/02/14/the-history-and-adaptability-of-the-islamic-state-car-bomb/

Merari, A. 2010. *Driven to Death: Psychological and Social Aspects of Suicide Terrorism*. Oxford: Oxford University Press.

Moghadam, A. 2006. Suicide Terrorism, Occupation, and the Globalization of Martyrdom: A Critique of Dying to Win. *Studies in Conflict & Terrorism* 29(8). 707–729.

National Consortium for the Study of Terrorism and Responses to Terrorism (START). (2016). Global Terrorism Database [201512300020 - 201101010001]. https://www.start.umd.edu/gtd

Orbell, J. and T. Morikawa. 2011. An Evolutionary Account of Suicide Attacks: The Kamikaze Case. *Political Psychology* 32(2). 297–322.

Pape, R.A. 2003. The Strategic Logic of Suicide Terrorism. *American Political Science Review* 97(3). 343–361.

Schweitzer, Y. 2000. Suicide Terrorism – Development and Characteristics. *International Conference on Countering Suicide Terrorism*. ICT Herzliya.

Seifert, K. and McCauley, C. 2014. Suicide Bombers in Iraq, 2003–2010: Disaggregating Targets Can Reveal Insurgent Motives and Priorities. *Terrorism and Political Violence* 26(5). 803–820.

von Borcke, A. 1982. Violence and Terror in Russian Revolutionary Populism: The Narodnaya Volya, 1879–83. In Mommsen, W.J. and Hirschfeld, G. (Eds.). *Social Protest, Violence and Terror in Nineteenth- and Twentieth-century Europe*. London: Palgrave Macmillan. 48–62.

Winter, C. 2017. *War by Suicide: A Statistical Analysis of the Islamic State's Suicide Industry*. The Hague: International Centre for Counter-Terrorism. https://icct.nl/wp-content/uploads/2017/02/ICCT-Winter-War-by-Suicide-Feb2017.pdf

Wright, L. 2016. *The Terror Years: From al-Qaeda to the Islamic State*. New York City: Knopf.

Chapter 62

Target Hardening

Zoha Waseem
King's College London, London, United Kingdom

Contents

Introduction 457
Conceptual Discussion and Definitions 458
Soft Targets 458
Target Hardening 460
Contemporary Developments and Lingering Concerns 461
Target Hardening and US Homeland Security 463
Conclusion 464
Further Reading 464
References 464

Introduction

In the aftermath of the attacks of September 11, 2001, and, more specifically, following the trends and patterns of lone-actor terrorism, there has been increasing interest in understanding terrorists' target selection. The tendency to attack a target to not just kill or destroy it but to generate fear, insecurity, and anxiety in a population has led to a differentiation between 'soft targets' and 'hard targets' by those seeking to understand terrorists' *modus operandi*. The trend of attacking 'soft targets' is not new and neither is the practice of 'target hardening', which, simply put, is the process by which soft targets are made less vulnerable to attacks. Indeed, the process of 'target hardening' has been recognized by criminologists long before the attacks emanating from the global war on terrorism. Essentially, target hardening is part of ongoing public and private initiatives to make civilians, state personnel, and critical infrastructure less vulnerable to attacks by terrorists.

Over the past decade, a series of internationally condemned terrorist incidents have led states to respond to threats by hardening soft targets in order to deter terrorists

DOI: 10.4324/9781315144511-65

or reduce the damage caused by attacks. These incidents include, most recently, the knife attacks that took place in London and Paris as well as vehicle-ramming attacks in both the United Kingdom and France. But long before these modes of attacks, terrorists had struck soft targets, including transportation sites (e.g. the 2007 London attacks), schools, restaurants, hotels (e.g. the 2008 Mumbai attacks), places of worship, shopping centers and commercial areas (e.g. the 2013 Westgate shopping mall attack in Nairobi), and nightclubs (e.g. the 2016 Pulse Nightclub shooting in Orlando, Florida). Hard targets, in contrast, are usually considered to include government or military buildings, such as embassies, official residences, and other well-protected facilities such as nuclear power plants. This distinction between hard targets and soft targets is usually based on the infrastructure as well as who occupies the target, but the distinction is not always clear. For example, schools and hotels are considered soft targets because they are occupied largely by civilians. However, airports can be considered both soft and hard targets depending upon the level of security deployed at individual airports. Indeed, infrastructure that is 'hardened' following an attack or threat of attack may no longer be considered a soft target.

Target hardening processes are essentially defensive measures that can include installing CCTV cameras for surveillance, militarizing critical infrastructure by deploying armed security personnel or fortifying its architecture through cement blocks, barbed wire, or metal barriers, allocating bullet-proof vehicles to politicians and other 'high-profile targets', and increasing police and/or military checkpoints on the routes leading up to critical infrastructure (such as diplomatic enclaves or financial districts). Target hardening measures usually accompany other defensive security measures and changes in police practices, such as legalizing the excessive use of force and authorizing enhanced surveillance and intelligence-gathering methods. Target hardening may also result from increased participation between sectors, such as partnerships between public and private security providers.

This chapter first examines the concept of 'soft target' and what makes them appealing before proceeding to discuss further what is meant by the 'hardening' of potential targets of terrorism. Following this conceptual discussion, I will explain how target hardening became increasingly important following the attacks of September 11, 2001, and the advent of the global war on terrorism. Before concluding, I will discuss how attacks on soft targets in the United States of America has led to target hardening in the context of US homeland security.

Conceptual Discussion and Definitions

Soft Targets

Soft targets have been defined as

> targets that lack robust security, and, therefore, are accessible to perpetrators. Soft targets, as a result, are, in relative terms, much less difficult to access and attack than their counterpart 'hard' targets, which take numerous measures to deter potential attacks by adopting a strong security posture.
> (Hersterman, 2015, p. xiii)

In other words, soft targets are those that meet the following criteria: (1) they generally have weak security measures in place and are therefore considered to be vulnerable and (2) they are easily accessible by ordinary citizens.

Attacks on soft targets are considered to be low in cost and high in impact, which makes them appealing to terrorists. They do not require an extensive amount of planning or plotting how to bypass stringent security measures in place, and, at the same time, they are fear-inducing, they can maximize casualties when they take place in crowded spaces, and they have the potential of drawing significant media attention, giving the group responsible for the attack the publicity they desire. Hersterman (2015) further details the motivations for terrorists to attack soft targets: they are cheaper and cost-efficient; there is an increased probability of success as compared to attacks on hard targets; the attack can provide the terrorist or lone actor the credibility he or she needs, which can legitimize their cause, especially when the attack is recognized by international terrorist groups such as Al Qaeda or the Islamic State.

Soft target attacks allow international groups to remain relevant and compensate for the fact that they may not have the military might to attack hard targets, especially when the group is on a decline (Ibid). Moreover, soft target attacks can make governments appear weak or illegitimate, and they have psychological impacts especially if they strike spaces frequented by civilians such as parks or transportation mechanisms (Hersterman, 2015, pp. 19–20). Others, such as Asal et al. (2009), have also maintained that ideology can play a key role in the targeting of civilians, an argument built upon the work of C. J. M. Drake (1988). For these scholars, the ideological inclinations of terrorists help justify their attacks on soft targets, such as civilians. These ideological justifications can include the non-Islamic beliefs of the civilians targeted (religious ideology) and the perceptions of civilians as the 'enemy', which often ties into the first justification.

The decision to attack soft targets also depends upon the organization and structure of the terrorist group in question. For example, groups such as the Islamic State that seek to establish an international influence and support base, but that are not necessarily capable of acquiring and holding territories because of military defeats, are more likely to encourage their supporters abroad to strike against soft targets, often indiscriminately, especially in the West. In 2016, Abu Mohammed Al-Adnani, who was one of the IS's senior leaders and former spokesman, called on international supporters to carry out 'lone wolf' attacks in the United States and Europe. In a video message, Al-Adnani appealed to his followers, 'The smallest action you do in [the US and Europe's] heartland is better and more enduring to us than what you would if you were with us' (Withnall, 2016). His message of 2016 was a reiteration of his call to violence from 2014: 'If you are not able to find an IED or a bullet, then single out the disbelieving American, Frenchman or any of their allies'. Smash his head with a rock or slaughter him with a knife or run him over with your car or throw him down from a high place of choke him or poison him' (CNN, 2018). Multiple references were made to soft target attacks in these statements to influence IS supporters who could not travel to Syria and Iraq to fight alongside the group, including knife attacks and car-ramming incidents that have taken place with increased intensity by IS-inspired terrorists in Europe and the United Kingdom between 2017 and 2018.

Soft targets are hard to defend without changing and affecting civilian life, movement, and daily activities. Defending each soft target (commercial areas, hotels, pavements, places of worship, and parks, for example) would also require an immense amount of resources (financial, technological, and human resources). At times, excessive security measures for protecting soft targets, such as hotels, can also make the businesses owning these vulnerable targets suffer, although there is always a risk that they would suffer more should a successful attack be carried out on these targets (Delafontaine, 2017). This dilemma – how stringent should 'target hardening' measures be to secure and protect potential targets – remains critical to both terrorists and those responsible for deterring and preventing terrorist attacks.

Target Hardening

The term 'target hardening' found its beginnings in the discipline of criminology as early as the 1980s. In 1984, Pay Mayhew studied the concept in relation to how law enforcement officials and agencies dealt with residential burglaries (Mayhew, 1984). In this context, target hardening referred to deterring burglars from breaking into residential spaces. However, even in the earlier periods of its conceptualization, many were skeptical about the successes of target hardening measures, arguing that criminals would simply turn to other spaces to commit crimes. This displacement of crime would later mirror the fear of 'displacement of terrorist attacks' when the concept would be applied to the field of terrorism. Despite this skepticism, in the context of crime control methods, target hardening was defined as 'an effective way of reducing criminal opportunities... to obstruct the vandal or the thief by physical barriers through the use of locks, safes, screens or reinforced materials' (Clarke, 1997, p. 17). Such 'situational crime prevention' (SCP) mechanisms, such as target hardening, were meant to increase the costs and risks associated with the committing of a particular crime, thereby deterring criminals (Freilich et al., 2018). In 1997, Ronald V. Clarke pointed out the dangers associated with SCP mechanisms, such as target hardening.

> When first introduced, the concept of situational prevention provoked fears about two unwelcome developments in society. In its more unattractive, 'target hardening' forms (barbed-wire, heavy padlocks, guard dogs and private security forces) it suggested the imminence of a 'fortress society' in which people, terrified by crime and distrustful of their fellows, barricade themselves in their homes and places of work, emerging only to conduct essential business. In its use of electronic hardware (CCTV, intruder alarms, x-ray scanning of baggage), it raised the spectre of totalitarian, 'Big Brother' forms of state control.
>
> (Clarke, 1997, p. 37)

Similar criticism would echo in the works of scholars critical of the militarization of society that results from target hardening in the aftermath of the global war on terrorism (discussed below). Nevertheless, terrorism experts drew upon SCP mechanisms and interventions to reduce terrorist attacks. Stemming from research on SCP, the concept of 'situational terrorism prevention' (STP) suggested that 'terrorists are rational actors who seek to maximize their benefits, while reducing the efforts required, risks of failure or apprehension, and other costs of committing the act' (Hsu and McDowell, 2017), which makes soft targets that much more appealing to them. And because of this, STP called for a 'systematic examination of how terrorists carry out particular attacks… and the daily arrangements of society that offer opportunities for terrorists to exploit' (Ibid). Target hardening measures would, therefore, impact these daily arrangements (movements, traffic flows, geographical clustering) within societies at risk of terrorist attacks.

The STP approach suggests that target hardening interventions prevent terrorists from carrying out attacks on specific targets, such as soft targets. This approach, and the utility of target hardening for preventing terrorism, have drawn significant attention from the academic community. Some argue that target hardening for STP can encourage terrorists to plan greater attacks, resort to the use of more lethal weaponry, or strike elsewhere on 'softer targets' (Hastings and Chan, 2013; Hsu and McDowell, 2017). A recent study by Hsu and McDowell (2017), however, has argued that target hardening has not necessarily resulted in deadlier attacks against hardened targets. However, other terrorism experts and criminologists continue to believe that target hardening can result in the 'displacement' of terrorist attacks, arguing that 'when you make it difficult for terrorists to carry out one type of attack, you increase the chance that they will start trying to carry out new types of attacks instead' (Silke, 2012, p. 64). For example, in the event that a suicide bomber cannot penetrate a heavily hardened target such as an airport, he may resort to knife attacks or vehicle-ramming attacks against soft targets such as market-goers or pedestrians.

Other research has shown that target hardening measures actually increase the value of a hardened target, and even if a group does not successfully carry out an attack on that hardened target, the mere threat of attack on it can be satisfactory for a terrorist group and provide them the publicity and attention they need (Hastings and Chan, 2013). In essence then, it can be stated that alongside the debate on whether 'terrorism works' is the debate on whether 'target hardening' works to deter terrorists and terrorism. In spite of criticisms leveled against target hardening measures, practices to secure potential targets continue to be developed as part of states' efforts to deter and prevent terrorist attacks.

Contemporary Developments and Lingering Concerns

Although 'soft targets' and 'target hardening' are not new phenomena, they did gain prominence following the attacks of September 11, 2001, in the United States. Between 2013 and 2018, some of the deadliest terrorist attacks around the world have been carried out on soft targets by a variety of terrorist groups. In September 2013, Al-Shabaab was responsible for the Westgate Mall attack in Nairobi, Kenya, which claimed over 70 lives. In December 2014, Tehreek-e-Taliban Pakistan attacked the Army Public School in Peshawar, killing almost 140 students and teachers. In November 2015, the Islamic State claimed a series of coordinated attacks in Paris, including a combination of a suicide bombing, shootings, and hostage-taking, killing over 130 people.

July 2016 was one of the deadliest months vis-à-vis attacks on soft targets around the world. On July 1, 2016, Bangladeshi supporters of the Islamic State (IS) attacked a bakery in Dhaka, killing 29 people. On July 3, the IS claimed responsibility for a suicide attack in Baghdad, Iraq, that claimed almost 300 lives. On July 12, Omar Mateen, an IS supporter, shot and killed almost 50 people at a nightclub in Orlando, Florida. And on July 14, on Bastille Day, a Tunisian IS supporter drove a truck into a crowd of people in Nice, France, killing over 80 individuals.

In 2017, a suicide bomber attacked the Manchester Arena in the United Kingdom, killing 22 concert-goers, including several children. The lone terrorist was hailed as a 'soldier' of the IS. The Manchester attack came in a series of attacks on soft targets in the United Kingdom, including attacks on Westminster Bridge, London Bridge, and a mosque in London, making 2017 one of the most challenging years for law enforcement agencies in the country, leading to several plans for target hardening (discussed below). In 2018, attacks on the Inter-Continental Hotel in Kabul, Afghanistan, a marketplace in Mubi, Nigeria, and an election rally in Balochistan, Pakistan, were similarly directed against soft targets in different locations, claimed by the Afghan Taliban, Boko Haram, and the IS.

The above mentioned attacks on soft targets exemplify an increasing trend in attacks carried out against soft targets worldwide. The frequency and scale of some of these attacks have emboldened contemporary methods of target hardening. These methods include a surge in the installations of CCTV cameras, enhanced security checks at airports, government buildings, banks, cinemas, and tourist attractions, as well as security barriers on bridges (the concrete and metal barriers installed on three bridges in London following vehicle-ramming and knife attacks are the most recent examples of such target hardening). Attacks on soft targets, especially transportation sites, have also led to urban security campaigns such as 'If you see something, say something' in the United States, or 'See It, Say It, Sorted' in the United Kingdom. These campaigns are meant to encourage better partnerships between law enforcement officials and civilians and to encourage the latter to assist security officials in preventing or investigating attacks on soft targets.

Simultaneously, such target hardening measures have also increased concerns about how these measures may be affecting societies and civilian perceptions of security. Increasing security threats to civilian spaces, especially in urban areas, may lead to securitization processes and policies that result in the militarization of urban spaces, part of which includes the hardening of infrastructure that was otherwise open and accessible to the general public. According to scholars such as Stephen Graham (2011), there is a connection between target hardening, gated communities, and the militarization of urban spaces, all of which are processes of control and othering. In fact, according to Graham, the 'hardening of urban enclaves' is part of long-established processes that pre-date the global war on terrorism – processes that are tied to the governing of urban spaces, especially those occupied by multiple ethnic, religious, and economic groups competing for control and access to resources. Those skeptical of target hardening methods believe that these measures are resulting from 'paranoia' and 'neurosis' (Graham, 2011, p. 93). This paranoia can result from a feeling of vulnerability or the perception that borders, neighborhoods, cities, nations, cyber spaces, and commercial areas are all vulnerable to security breaches and can potentially become soft targets. However, the process of target hardening does not necessarily do away with the fear and paranoia resulting from such insecurity.

Target Hardening and US Homeland Security

In 2010, Faisal Shehzad attempted to bomb the Times Square in New York City. His car bomb plot was foiled by street vendors who reported to the authorities about smoke coming out of a car at the Square. Shehzad's decision to target one of the most populated locations and the biggest tourist attraction in NYC (a soft target) was driven by an ideological motivation and the influence of al Qaeda's prominent member, Anwar Al-Awlaki (Hersterman, 2015, p. 33). Two years later, on April 15, 2013, two pressure cooker bombs were used to attack the Boston Marathon which resulted in the deaths of three people, leaving over 260 injured. The two brothers involved in the Boston Marathon attack were both influenced by al Qaeda and had allegedly drawn upon al Qaeda's literature on how to build home-made explosives.

As mentioned above, soft targets appeal to terrorists because they meet certain criteria, including the fact that 'they are frequented by many people, are easily accessible and can be surveilled without drawing too much attention to potential attackers' (Clarke and Serena, 2017). Clarke and Serena (2017) have advised that the way to prevent soft targets from terrorist attacks in the United States is to increase information sharing with other states and governments. Additionally, police departments and intelligence agencies should improve the sharing of intelligence among themselves (and across national, state, and local security departments). More resources should also be allocated to better train police and intelligence personnel and to equip them with the necessary technology needed to prevent or respond to the threat of attacks on soft targets (Ibid).

The US Department of Homeland Security has recently designed the Soft Targets and Crowded Places (ST-CPs) plan through the Office of Infrastructure Protection in the National Protection and Programs Directorate (NPPD). The Infrastructure Protection program deals with the provision and protection of critical infrastructure within the United States through partnerships between public and private sectors. Critical infrastructure includes 16 infrastructure sectors, including the transportation, water, nuclear, information technology, and communication sectors, among others. The ST-CP plan of 2018 includes soft targets, such as 'schools, sports venues, transportation systems or hubs, shopping venues, bars and restaurants, hotels, places of worship, tourist attractions, theaters, and civic spaces' (Department of Homeland Security, 2018). These targets are classified as soft targets on the basis of their accessibility to a large number of people and the limited protection and security measures that are designed for them (Ibid). DHS understands that the protection of soft targets is a shared responsibility in that ST-CP planners alongside the federal government, private sector, governments (state, local, tribal, and territorial) and the general public must work together in order to better collect, share, and communicate information. Each of these stakeholders can also play a unique role in reporting and/or responding to suspicious activities concerning soft targets. Given that the ST-CP plan has only recently been designed, its implementation has yet to be tested.

Nevertheless, the ST-CP is a comprehensive and well-rounded plan for the protection of soft targets in the United States.

Conclusion

This chapter has attempted to show why soft targets appeal to terrorists around the world and how attempts are made to secure them from potential attacks through the process of target hardening. Soft targets are increasingly an ideal choice for lone actors engaging in terrorism which, according to the Federal Bureau of Investigation in the United States, is the biggest domestic threat facing the United States at present (Hersterman, 2015, p. 82). However, target hardening measures have their downsides: they are expensive endeavors, they can disrupt everyday life, they can lead to significant changes in streetscapes and urban designs, and they do not guarantee complete protection from attacks as terrorists can chose alternative locations to carry out their strikes. Terrorist attacks can evolve in response to changes in security measures and policies pertaining to the protection of civilians and critical infrastructure. Moreover, over-securing public spaces, such as hotels, transportation sites, commercial areas, and places of worship, can result in what is known as 'security fatigue' (Hersterman, 2015, p. 114), or the idea that civilians can feel overwhelmed by increasingly securitized initiatives such as long lines at airports and multiple security checkpoints, which can result in decreased public trust in the state and a constant feeling of insecurity. Ultimately, terrorism prevention remains the most cost-effective and efficient way to reduce the likelihood of attacks against soft targets.

Further Reading

Coaffee, J., O'Hare, P., Hawkesworth, M. (2009). 'The Visibility of (In)security: The Aesthetics of Planning Urban Defences Against Terrorism', *Security Dialogue*, vol. 40(4–5), pp. 489–511.

Department of Homeland Security (2018). 'Security of Soft Targets and Crowded Places-Resource Guide', Office of Infrastructure Protection: National Protection and Programs Directorate. Available at: https://www.dhs.gov/sites/default/files/publications/Soft_Targets_Crowded%20Places_Resource_Guide_042018_508.pdf

Nilsson, M. (2018). 'Hard and Soft Targets: The Lethality of Suicide Terrorism', *Journal of International Relations and Development*, vol. 21, pp. 101–117.

References

Asal, V. H., Rethemeyer, R. K., Anderson, I., Stein, A., Rizzo, J., Rozea, M., (2009), 'The Softest of Targets: A Study on Terrorist Target Selection', *Journal of Applied Security Research*, vol. 4, pp. 258–279.

Clarke, C. P., Serena, C. C. (2017), 'How to Harden America's Soft Targets', *The National Interest*. Available at: https://nationalinterest.org/feature/how-harden-americas-soft-targets-21402

Clarke, R. V. (1997), *Situational Crime Prevention: Successful Case Studies*, Harrow and Heston Publishers: New York, USA.

CNN (2018), 'Terrorist Attacks by Vehicles Fast Facts', *CNN.com*. Available at: https://edition.cnn.com/2017/05/03/world/terrorist-attacks-by-vehicle-fast-facts/index.html
Delafontaine, A., (2017), 'Hotels as Targets of Jihadist Terror: An Empirical Analysis of the Period from 1970 to 2016', Working Paper 12, The Centre for European Peace and Security Studies at The Institute for Peace Research and Security Studies, University of Hamburg
Department of Homeland Security (2018), 'US Department of Homeland Security Soft Targets and Crowded Places Security Plan Overview'. Available at: https://www.dhs.gov/sites/default/files/publications/DHS-Soft-Target-Crowded-Place-Security-Plan-Overview-052018-508_0.pdf
Drake, C. J. M. (1988), 'The Role of Ideology in Terrorists' Target Selection', *Terrorism and Political Violence*, vol. 10(2), pp. 53–85.
Graham, S. (2011), *Cities Under Siege: The New Military Urbanism*, Verso: London.
Hastings, Justin V., Chan, Ryan J. (2013), 'Target Hardening and Terrorist Signaling: The Case of Aviation Security', *Terrorism and Political Violence*, vol. 25, pp. 777–797.
Hersterman, Jennifer (2015), *Soft Target Hardening: Protecting People from Attack*, CRC Press: Florida, USA, xiii.
Hsu, Henda Y., McDowell, David (2017), 'Does Target-Hardening Result in Deadlier Terrorist Attacks against Protected Targets? An Examination of Unintended Harmful Consequences', *Journal of Research in Crime and Delinquency*, vol. 54(5), pp. 930–957.
Mayhew, P. (1984), 'Target-Hardening: How Much of an Answer?'. In: Clark, R. and Hope, T. (eds) *Coping with Burglary*, vol. 4 pp. 29–44.
Silke, Andrew (2012), 'Chapter 4: Understanding Terrorist Target Selection', *Routledge Online Studies on the Olympic and Paralympic Games*, vol. 1(41), pp. 49–71.
Withnall, A. (2016), 'ISIS Official Calls for "Lone Wolf" Attacks in US and Europe During Ramadan', *The Independent*, May 22, 2016. Available at: https://www.independent.co.uk/news/world/middle-east/isis-official-calls-for-lone-wolf-attacks-in-us-and-europe-during-ramadan-a7042296.html

Chapter 63

Terrorism Copycat Effects

Nikita Kohli
Center for Land Warfare Studies, New Delhi, India

Contents

Introduction 467
Terrorists Copying Terrorists? 468
Copying from Terrorists – Operational and Strategic Facets 470
Copycat Attacks – A New Modus Operandi 472
Conclusion 474
Further Reading 475
References 475

Introduction

The recent Orlando and Las Vegas shootings in the United States, the mowing down of pedestrians by means of vans in urban areas, including London, Barcelona, Berlin, and Nice, and the attacks being claimed by certain international terrorist organizations, such as Islamic State of Iraq and Syria (IS), are symptomatic of bigger changes in terrorist tactics. Terrorist organizations today are not simply organizing top-down grand spectacles of violence such as the 9/11 attacks by Al-Qaeda. They are rather focused on smaller, dispersed incidents of violence, which can be easily organized, copied, and garner strong media attention. While terrorism has never fully been the domain of groups and gangs, the recent level of proliferation and mimicking of tactics and strategies typically used by larger terrorist organizations with a proper organizational structure and funding mechanism and by individuals, who mostly do not have open links to these terror organizations and are not from their trained carders, is certainly new. This new form of 'copycat terrorism' is based on the growing capacity and outreach possible via social media platforms for radicalization, organization, networking, and propaganda of the deed for the terrorist organization and

DOI: 10.4324/9781315144511-66

the 'lone-wolf' terrorists. In defining copycat terrorist attacks to be those where at least one aspect of the organizational or the strategic facet of an established terrorist group is copied for local application by an individual or a group, this chapter analyzes the impact on the way that terrorist groups now organize and operate, the way that they reach out and inspire copycat activities, and the way that states now have to respond to the unknown threat of any citizen being a terrorist sympathizer.

Basing ourselves on the understanding that the critical factor underlining the raison d'être of terrorist organization is the idea that they intentionally use violence as a tactic of terrorism to achieve a pre-determined goal, whether it be political, economic, religious, sociological, or otherwise. For this, terrorists need to ensure that the attack that they carry out goes beyond only creating terror in the minds of the targets and creates a *lasting* atmosphere of fear in the larger population. Media coverage and subsequent radicalization of others and copying of their tactics only serves to bolster the standing of the terrorist group and help them move toward achieving their goals. However, such media coverage and analysis present in the aftermath of a terrorist attack also enable violence-prone individuals and groups with ideas, strategies, and tactics that they can copy to garner greater attention to their actions, especially if it follows as a quick and subsequent action, as could be seen in patterns of mass shootings and bombing attacks (Chenoweth, 2015) by individuals and groups. With the increased media attention on in-depth analysis of any terrorist attack, it now becomes more important than ever for democratic nations to, as Margaret Thatcher argued, 'try to find ways to starve the terrorist and the hijacker of the oxygen of publicity on which they depend' (R.W. Apple, 1985). In fact, Farnham and Liem describe the copycat effect as, 'the influential power of mass communication and media to create a wave of similar behaviors amongst a given reader - or viewership' (Farnham & Liem, 2017).

The subsequent sections of this chapter detail the process of copycat terrorism and its effects. This chapter begins with defining who are the possible actors who can 'copy' the 'established' terrorist actions and structures, focusing on the different ways that groups and individuals copy terrorist tactics for their own purpose. These tactics are then divided into operational and strategic tools that can be emulated by individuals and groups. Such a differentiation of the tools and tactics being copied helps illuminate the time period that the tactics remain effective enough to be copied and the role that technological changes have in terrorist targeting, structuring, and violence methodology. This is then followed by an analysis of the effect of such copycat behavior, for the terrorists who promulgated the original tactic, for those that copy them, and for the governments and the larger public, with focus on the role of media in the process. Finally, the conclusion underlines the importance of copycat terror attacks and outlines possible response options for governments.

Terrorists Copying Terrorists?

The term 'terrorism', while having permeated itself in our everyday lives with increasing attention and news coverage of attacks worldwide, does not have a universally accepted definition. The difficulty in establishing a universally accepted definition can be best summarized by the oft-repeated phrase, "One man's terrorist is another man's freedom fighter", as mentioned in the 1947 speech of Yasser Arafat, the former

Chairman of the Palestine Liberation Organization, before the United Nations (Kolod, 2016). To fully understand and define terrorism would require states and intergovernmental organizations to give voice to the concerns and reasons of those that they label as terrorist groups, while decidedly staying away from it. However, while there is no internationally accepted definition of the term yet, Philips notes that there are three key elements of 'terrorism': "(a) intentional violence; (b) that the violence is used to spread fear in a wider audience; and (c) political motivation" (Phillips, 2015, p. 227). Terrorism can therefore be understood to be a violent, illegal act(s) conducted by an individual or a group of individuals, with or without the support of the state, against unarmed civilians and structures for a pre-determined political end goal. It is, therefore, a (violent) means to an end (political goal).

In the context of copycat terrorism, it becomes important to understand first and foremost *who* is copying *whom* and *for what end*. The simplest answer to the question of 'who' we define as a terrorist is that of an actor or a group of actors who conduct the act of violence resulting in terror creation in the minds of the people. However, with assault rifles and home-made bombs being more readily available to people, we need to step beyond the hazy contours of terrorism as being limited to non-state armed groups, which have a proper hierarchical operational structure, thought leadership, and organizational skills to effect great potential damage to the adversarial state, and must now include other categories of groups and people.

With the increase in counterterrorism efforts in recent years, and the capture and/or death of key leaders of terrorist groups, such as the demise of Osama bin Laden (former head of Al-Qaeda), we are seeing two main fallouts. The first is the demise of the old-school terrorist organizational structure, comprising of an intellectual leadership, an organizational body, and 'foot soldiers', with an established communication and command and control structure. This is now being replaced by a more dispersed, localized body of loosely tied terrorists, who are simply being monitored and motivated by the central commanding body. In his testimony before the House Armed Services Subcommittee on Terrorism, Unconventional Threats and Capabilities, Bruce Hoffman noted that:

> [t]he al Qaeda of today combines, as it always has, both a 'bottom up' approach——encouraging independent thought and action from low (or lower-) level operatives——and a 'top down' one——issuing orders and still coordinating a far-flung terrorist enterprise with both highly synchronized and autonomous moving parts.
>
> (Hoffman, 2007b)

This demise of the traditional terrorist group structure has also been hastened by an increasing intellectual leadership vacuum. In targeting the top leadership, such as Osama bin Laden, Dr Abdullah Azzam, Abu Musab al Zarqawi, and Abu Bakr al-Baghdadi, in more recent years by the United States in their long war against jihadi groups, the ideological orientations of these groups have undergone major shifts, with most of the groups unable to prop up any major intellectual leader to lead, direct, and organize major terrorist attacks. This has subsequently reduced them to copying the tactics, means, and ideology used by the previous generations of terrorist organizations to support and sustain their efforts.

The second major fallout has been the spread and open dissemination of information to the public. Counterterrorism cells after detaining or eliminating some of the biggest terrorist masterminds have wanted to discuss information about tactics and operations that enabled them to do so. Subsequently, the sharing of information across television channels and radio shows about how a terrorist group would identify people for operations and reconnaissance, for weapon system import and manufacture, their changing financial structures, etc. has enabled violent-prone and disgruntled individuals to gain access to key contact individuals like never before and copy their tactics, targeting methods, and operational factors. The multiple and ever-changing discussion of counterterrorism efforts by militaries across the world and their open discussions of merging techniques and challenges have therefore provided both *groups and individuals* access to operational and strategic facets of organizing and carrying out terror attacks. The difference between the two categories of actors remains only in terms of what they are copying, how well, and the level of its effectiveness on the aspect of creating lasting terror in the minds of the population.

Copying from Terrorists – Operational and Strategic Facets

The essence of 'copycat terrorism' lies in understanding the facets of terror attacks and plans that are being copied. There are two categories of tools of terror that can be copied and emulated by individuals and/or groups in the activities. These are often categorized as 'organizational' and 'operational tools' (Chonker, 2018). Reconceptualizing them in light of the purpose that these tools can be used for, we can categorize them as 'operational' and 'strategic'. The former category would refer to those facets of terrorism that groups and individuals look to as the basics of being able to organize and conduct a terror attack. This category would include factors such as:

- Organizational structures
- Communication
- Weapon systems
- Space of operation
- Agitational style

The second category is that of strategic facets. These factors enable group cohesion and sustain the rational for their existence and support, such as:

- Ideology
- Means and violence methodology
- Target selection
- Finance
- Publicity

While these two categories work together to define the *modus operandi* of any terrorist group and even 'lone' wolf actors, by differentiating between the two, we can observe a tangible difference in the way that they affect the thinking and organization of any attack. The former category of operational tools used by the terrorists can be copied in the short term. With the pace of technological changes and political manipulation by new and old political and social actors alike, several factors can change in a short time frame. These include the space for agitation, the weapons and communication systems that can be used, and hierarchical or dispersed organizational structures that can better target and be less susceptible to being targeted. This is observable in the almost instant carryover to encrypted messaging technology from radio and text messaging by terrorist organizations to the shift from carrying out local terrorist attacks (such as those by ethno-nationalist groups, including Front Liberation National [FLN], EOKA, and Euskadi Ta Askatasuna, i.e., ETA) to the multiple international plane hijackings (such as Entebbe, Pam Am hijacking, and Kandahar incident) made possible by the easy availability of modern aircrafts, requiring little by means of checks in the early days (Hoffman 2007a; Tan 2017).

Modern technological changes have, however, not only impacted terrorist groups and their organization, but the way that they connect. It has enabled them to carry out transnational attacks such as the Munich massacre to international attacks such as 9/11, which brought together people from varied backgrounds to carry out attacks across the world. In noting these major changes, the part of the analysis that is often missing is the number of copycat attacks that these inspired. For example, there was a quick succession of plane hijackings in the 1970s and 1980s to the organizational structure of disparate cells and inspired lone actors carrying out attacks in spired by the Al-Qaeda structure post 9/11. From the above examples, we see that the operational facets of terror attacks, while initially copied only by groups, is often also replicated by individuals. This is seen in the spate of van-mowings, mass shootouts at schools and clubs, etc., which were tactics taken up by individuals from established terrorist organizations.

The second category of strategic tools, by contrast, are more prone to be emulated over a longer period of time and are used to define not just a group, but rather a set of groups which would act in a similar manner and draw allegiance to similar causes, such as religious or economic. Due to the long-term nature of the structural facets, these are mostly copied by groups. This can be seen in the multiple left-wing organizations that were established in Europe inspired by the ideology and violence methodology and publicity garnered by the Palestine Liberation Organization, such as Baader-Meinhof group, Italian Red Brigades, and Action Directe. In the same vein, there have been multiple groups which emulate the ideology, targeting style, financing mechanism, and outreach initiatives of Al-Qaeda, such as Boko Haram, Lashkar-e-Taiba, al Shabab, Haqqani Network, Taliban, and most recently, the Islamic State. In focusing on the strategies that they use to copy the tactics of the 'original' terrorist organization, we see that issues such as ideology and financial structures are facets integral to larger terrorist organizations, who wish to copy the tactics which work, and have enabled others to sustain themselves for longer periods of time (Hoffman, 2007a; Zimmerman, 2013; Kohli, 2018).

Copying of particular tactics from established terrorist organizations, therefore, depends on two things: (1) the level of organization (i.e., whether it is an individual, a small group, or a larger group) and (2) the time frame in which they expect to attack (i.e. immediate copycat attacks focusing only on the organizational facets such as weapons and communication styles, and not ideology and financial structure).

Therefore, in understanding the way that a terrorist will function, we need to look at the number of people they are involved with and the time frame in which they hope to carry out the copycat terrorist attack.

Copycat Attacks – A New Modus Operandi

While copycat terrorism is not entirely a new phenomenon, its operationalization, the geographical dispersion of the groups copying each other, and the scale of the effect of copying terrorist tactics are certainly new. This is in part due to the expansive and unhindered capacity of traditional and social media in disseminating information about the attacks, the actors, their linkages, and possible motivations. The easy availability of information about potential targets, operational mechanisms, and information about the various terrorist organizations and who to contact where has enabled violent-prone individuals access to critical information for carrying out their own terrorist attacks. This has resulted in multiple copycat terrorist attacks, one of the most current one being the use of vans and other heavy vehicles to plow into people. Initially used by groups such as the FLN in Algeria during the freedom struggle, the tactic has gained massive popularity in recent times, especially with similar attacks being carried out in Nice, Berlin, London, and Toronto. As Anthony Cordesman (2017) writes, such attacks demonstrate that "a relatively tiny extremist minority has found that it can get vast publicity and attention with high-visibility, high-casualty attacks in a public area that have no particular political or strategic value".

Copycat terrorist attacks, therefore, have a great benefit for splinter groups, associates, and lone actors that are trying to make their mark on the screen. As the various plane hijackings previously and the recent spike in vehicular attacks show, copycat terrorist attacks allow the actors to create large-scale disruptions and high fatality rates, while requiring minimal investments from them. Continuing with the above example of the use of vans as a weapon to kill, we can see that hiring a van and using the vehicle as the weapon, with the vehicle not having any explosives in it, is a relatively inexpensive operation, especially when compared to making and deploying explosives and carrying out large-scale attacks such as 9/11. That is, the attacks being copied are those that do not require the splinter group, associate, or lone actor to invest a lot of money and can yet generate enough focus on the perpetrator(s) to be taken as serious terrorist actors, giving them credibility in the eyes of the international community as those that need to be given adequate attention and recognition. These attacks also do not require elaborate planning, extensive network development, and reconnaissance, while these are visible in grand-scale attacks being carried out by terrorist group cores. That is, a lone attacker only needs to hire a vehicle or buy a weapon from the local store, go to the location, and kill. They do not need inside information, collaboration, and get-away plans and grand-scale proclamations to be able to carry out the copycat attacks.

The potency of the ability of individuals and groups to copy the operational and strategic facets of terrorism from previous and current groups is threefold – (1) it increases the terror-creating value of the attack, (2) it increases their credibility as an important non-state actor that deserves multiple analysis and media focus, and (3) at the same time, they do not have to bear the economic brunt of organizing big terror spectacles or having to experiment with effect methods to get their desired end goal.

At the same time, copycat terrorism has had massive effects on the 'original' terrorist organizations too. With the increasing crackdowns on terrorist organizations by governments across the world, groups such as the IS and Al-Qaeda have had difficulties in mounting directed attacks from their core groups. With the increasing regulations and checks, it is now easier for governments to inhibit international travel of known terrorists and those who are associated with them, making coordinated attacks such as those in Paris and Brussels in November 2015 and March 2016 difficult, which had been "directed and facilitated by personnel specifically sent to Europe from the core of ISIL" (United Nations, 2017).

Copycat terrorist attacks remove this hurdle. What we see in these attacks being carried out by lone actors and 'associates' is that they are easier to replicate in various situations and areas and are "generally unsophisticated in nature, nevertheless causing multiple causalities, such as in Nice, Berlin, London, Stockholm, Saint Petersburg, and…Manchester" (United Nations, 2017). Thus, terrorist organizations are able to leverage communication and propaganda strategies to influence and encourage those in their local area to carry out simple attacks in their names. This can be seen in the influence exerted by the Palestine Liberation Organization on the various radical groups, including the German Red Army Faction, Italian Red Brigades, and Action Directe (Hoffman, 2007a), and the influence exerted by the Islamic State on the various lone actor attacks in Europe, where the "perpetrators often received support or resources from facilitators, and in a number of cases, were in direct contact with IS enablers online using encrypted applications before and even during the attacks" (United Nations, 2017).

Enabling copycat terrorist actors, whether as an associate or as lone actors, allows the terrorist organizations certain strategic benefits. Firstly, it allows them to mount multiple attacks from around the world without expiating their own resources or men. Secondly, by showcasing their influence over a wide audience dedicated to their cause, they demonstrate their credibility among other terrorist organizations, thus enabling their future support for mounting attacks and developing networks. Third, by enabling multiple simultaneous attacks, or backing actors who might copy their actions, they are able to create an international moment of crisis, while simultaneously removing themselves from the center of gravity. And finally, by being able to claim the credit for various international copycat attacks by various kinds of actors, they are able to create a *lasting* atmosphere of terror in the local populace, now enhanced by the extensive and unhindered use of social media.

While the development and increasing usage of copycat terror attacks has had an effect on the actors who take this up and the terrorist organizations that enable them, it has also had a major effect on the state and intergovernmental actors who have to respond to the change in tactics from large-scale attacks to small, heavy-carnage attacks conducted by even local actors. With the rise in copycat terrorist attacks, especially those that are conducted by inspired lone actors, it is now increasingly difficult for states to respond to the threat – any citizen could be a potential threat due to possibilities of online radicalization and easy access to heavy weapons which can cause large-scale disruptions. As a United Nations report on the IS notes, with the group changing its structure to resemble that of Al-Qaeda, with associated groups, inspired individuals, returnees, and 'frustrated travelers' acting on behalf of the group core around the world, "locating individuals posing a threat will become more challenging", and their integration "into already existing networks of radicalized sympathizers are major concerns for Member States" (United Nations, 2018).

The threat of violence-prone and inspired individuals carrying out terrorist attacks should not be under-estimated. Due to the lack of means in identifying a potential terrorist planning on copying a terrorist tactic in advance, increasing access to details of executing such an attack, and ready availability of small arms (especially in the United States), it would be prudent to believe that the number of such attacks would increase in the future. We are already seeing this in the increasing number of mass shootings in the United States, as well as the increasing number of small bomb explosions and vehicular-rammings in Europe.

The difference in the types of copycat attacks in the United States as opposed to Europe is based on the access to different kind of resources. With the US borders being more closely guarded, and good surveillance on the roads and major population centers, violence-prone and radicalized individuals have a lesser chance to get in sophisticated bombs and chemicals or lease a van without minimum background scrutiny. On the other hand, Europe, with its more open borders, has less defense against such attacks. However, at the same time, due to stringent gun controls in most of Europe, and heightened availability of assault rifles in the United States, mass shootings by such inspired or lone-wolf terrorists is more visible in the United States. Once again, we see that access, low price point, and methods that garner greater media attention to the attack are what determine the type of copycat attack in different geographical regions.

Conclusion

Copycat terrorism has changed the way terrorist organizations today organize their cells, plan their attacks, recruit people, target civilians, and use new weapon systems. Ideological foundations and mass appeal for causes of freedom and humanity do not resonate with the terrorist groups today. While the label 'terrorist' continues to carry negative connotations till date and continues to be a term for de-legitimizing an actor, the modern terrorist organizations wear the distinction with pride and use it to spread their 'message' to all disgruntled and violence-prone individuals to enable them to carry out attacks in their names on their own account. Copycat terrorism means that no longer are the terrorist groups themselves a threat to the state and society, but rather that they have found a way to establish 'associates' and sympathizers in far-flung areas to carry out the mission and attacks for the groups.

The combination of traditional national and international terror networks, along with 'frustrated travelers', sympathizers, foreign fighter returnees, and relocators, poses as a security threat for the people and the states around the world. Added to this is the unhindered access and reach of social media, traversing and inspiring individuals to take up the 'causes' of the terrorist organizations. This medium has been effectively used by these organizations to reach out to individuals, indoctrinate them, coordinate attacks, and get the claim for it, and subsequently, use it as a medium to inspire more copycat attacks.

The reason for the increasing popularity of copycat terrorist attacks, executed by individuals *and* groups, is the massive effect on the organization, the perpetrators, and the states. It allows the groups to create an atmosphere of terror far and wide, without having to raise or send trained terrorists from their central cadres, while at the same time allowing disgruntled individuals an avenue to re-create simple and high-visibility terrorist attacks with low investments with a group, their ideology, or for training and weapons. However, with the potential for any citizen to become a terrorist sympathizer and carry out copycat attacks, states are now finding it increasingly difficult to counter terrorism with maintaining sufficient democratic freedoms. With the media contagion effect enabling the spread of low-cost, high-visibility terror attacks, it now becomes more important than ever for states to find ways to ensure that the critical details of terrorist attacks are not available to the violent-prone individuals who might want to carry out an attack.

Understanding that terrorism is a means to an end, and that the terrorist depends on media coverage to be able to create a lasting atmosphere of terror in the minds of the people lasting beyond the physical limitations of the targets, states must now ensure that such terrorist groups get minimal attention to their actions. As with the Unabomber, if there is less attention paid to the attacks, and in-depth analysis of the terrorist organizations and their attack methodology is absent, the objective of creating terror and having a cadre of international sympathizers to carry out copycat terrorist attacks might just decrease. It is then possible to limit and contain terrorism copycat effects.

Further Reading

Farnham, N., & Liem, D. M. (2017). *Can a Copycat Effect be Observed in Terrorist Suicide Attacks?* The Hague: International Centre for Counter-Terrorism.

Jensen, T. (2007). *Terrorism, Anti-Terrorism, and the Copycat Effect.* Department of Economics, University of Copenhagen.

Nacos, B. L. (2009). Revisiting the Contagion Hypothesis: Terrorism, News Coverage, and Copycat Attacks. *Perspectives on Terrorism*, 3(3), 3–13.

References

Apple, R. W. Jr. (1985, July 16). Thatcher Urges the Press to Help 'Starve' Terrorists. *The New York Times*, p. A00003.

Chenoweth, E. (2015, December 4). Yes, mass shootings tend to produce copycats. So do terror attacks. *The Washington Post.*

Chonker, A. (2018). *Tools of Terror in Jammu and Kashmir*. New Delhi: Centre for Land Warfare Studies.

Cordesman, A. (2017, August 18). The Spain Attacks Show How Much Terrorism Is Changing. *Fortune*. http://fortune.com/2017/08/18/spain-attacks-barcelona-cambrils-terrorism/

Farnham, N., & Liem, D. M. (2017). *Can a Copycat Effect be Observed in Terrorist Suicide Attacks?* The Hague: International Centre for Counter-Terroism - The Hague.

Hoffman, B. (2007a). *Inside Terrorism*. New York: Columbia University Press.

Hoffman, B. (2007b). Written Testimony Submitted to The House Armed Services Subcommittee on Terrorism, Unconventional Threats and Capabilities. *Challenges for the U.S. special operations command posed by the global terrorist threat: Al Qaeda on the run or on the march?*

Kohli, N. (2018). *Financing Terror Enterprises: Funding Operations in Prolonged Conflicts in South Asia*. New Delhi: Centre for Land Warfare Studies.

Kolod, S. (2016, August 17). *Blog: Terrorists or Copycats? What's The Difference?* Retrieved from American Psychoanalytic Association: http://www.apsa.org/content/blog-terrorists-or-copycats-whats-difference

Phillips, B. J. (2015). What Is a Terrorist Group? Conceptual Issues and Empirical Implications. *Terrorism and Political Violence*, 27(2), 225–242.

Tan, R. (2017, June 30). *Terrorists' love for Telegram, explained: It's become ISIS's "app of choice"*. Retrieved from Vox: https://www.vox.com/world/2017/6/30/15886506/terrorism-isis-telegram-social-media-russia-pavel-durov-twitter

United Nations. (2017). *S/2017/467: Fifth report of the Secretary-General on the threat posed by ISIL (Da'esh) to international peace and security and the range of United Nation s efforts in support of Member States in countering the threat*. New York: United Nations Security Council.

United Nations. (2018). *S//2018/14/Rev.1: Twenty-first report of the Analytical Support and Sanctions Monitoring Team submitted pursuant to resolution 2368 (2017) concerning ISIL (Da'esh), Al-Qaida and associated individuals and entities*. United Nations.

Zimmerman, K. (2013). *The al Qaeda Network: A New Framework for Defining the Enemy*. Washington, DC: American Enterprise Institute.

Chapter 64

Urban Warfare

Umer Khan
University of Buckingham, Buckingham, United Kingdom

Scott N. Romaniuk
International Centre for Policing and Security, University of South Wales, Caerleon, United Kingdom

Contents

Introduction 477
The History of Urban Warfare 478
Significance of Urban Areas for US Forces 479
The Explanation of Relevant Terms 479
Complexity of Operations in Urban Terrain 480
Asymmetric Threat in Urban Areas 481
Military and Non-Military Aspects of Urban Warfare 481
US Commitment in Future Urban Wars 483
Conclusion 485
Further Reading 486
References 486

Introduction

A decade after the end of Cold War, military thinkers started to realize the prospects of urban areas as future battlegrounds. This ideology was mainly influenced by the rapidly increasing population in cities along with their political, economic, and cultural aspects (Gentile, Johnson, Saum-Manning, Cohen, Williams, Lee, Doty III, 2017: 1). According to a United Nations (UN) report, it is predicted that the world's urban population will increase by a further 2.5 billion by 2050 due to urbanization and immigration (UN DESA, 2018: 1). In 2014, the US Army Training and Doctrine

DOI: 10.4324/9781315144511-67

Command (TRADOC) highlighted in its study that as cities grow due to urbanization, many governments fail to provide adequate security, employment, infrastructure, and services. This uncertain situation can be exploited by local armed groups; consequently, urban areas become safe havens and support bases for terrorists, insurgents, or criminal organizations (US Army, 2014).

Currently, the US Army appears concerned about the operational implications in urban areas, particularly megacities. It is notable that factors like survivability, logistics, and slower pace of operations in urban areas encourage adversaries to exploit them as battlegrounds. The insurgents manipulate restricted urban spaces and presence of civilians to shield against friendly forces' superior maneuver and firepower. Living among the population and using deleterious propaganda provide opportunities to insurgents to discredit the legitimacy of friendly forces' operations. Despite these limitations, friendly forces will inevitably have to get involved in urban warfare (i.e., fighting adversaries in urban areas such as towns and cities) (Flecher, 2018).

In future, US forces may engage in urban warfare with not only irregular forces but also some regular and well-organized forces. The US and NATO envisage a scenario that Russian forces could invade Poland, Romania, and the Baltics and may reach cities such as Riga in mere 2 days. In such a case, US and NATO forces might have to engage in urban warfare against Russians to preclude a fait accompli and cost-effective success (Gentile, Johnson, Saum-Manning, Cohen, Williams, Lee, Doty III, 2017: 60). Kilcullen (2015: 262) concluded that it is time for the US to apply what it has learned through fighting in hills and valleys to "a challenging new environment of urban, networked, guerilla war in the mega-slums and mega-cities."

The History of Urban Warfare

Fighting for the cities and fighting in the cities have been a recurrent phenomenon in history. Rome has been contested multiple times by several armies from 387 BC to 1944 due to its religious, political, and military significance (FM 3-06, 2003: 1–4). Historically, combat in urban areas has always been complex and casualty intensive; however, it enabled weaker forces to fight against superior enemy. For example, in the Battle of Stalingrad, massive firepower and maneuver capabilities of Germans were neutralized by Russian's close-quarter combat (Gerwehr & Glenn, 2000: 3). Likewise, in the Battle of Hue (1968), the North Vietnamese achieved strategic success by antagonizing the American conscience with the high rate of causalities (FM 3-06, 2003: 3–10).

As an IDF brigade commander commented about their complex engagement in Beirut (1982): "Every room is a new battle. Once troops are inside a building, it is impossible for a commander to understand what his troops are confronting, the battlefield is invisible" (FM 3-06, 2003: H-7). The advantages provided by urban environment to weaker forces were evident in various operations involving US forces. For instance, in 2003, Saddam regime's paramilitary fighters (the *fidayeen*) used guerrilla tactics to confront Americans as they approached Baghdad (Gentile, Johnson, Saum-Manning, Cohen, Williams, Lee, Doty III, 2017: 41). In the Battle of Sadr City (2008), extremist elements used narrow streets of the Sadr City to restrict movement of US vehicles and carried out surprise improvised explosive device (IED) and rocket-propelled grenade (RPG) attacks. In Mosul (2016–2017), ISIS forces exploited urban infrastructure by an elaborate series of defensive works, such as fortifying buildings, blocking avenues of approach, creating obstacles, and constructing underground tunnels, to impede and delay US forces (Mosul Study Group, US Army, 2017). Similarly, in Grozny II (1999–2000), Chechens initially resisted Russian advances into the city and once the Russians entered, Chechens canalized them along narrow streets to trap and slowly reduced their strength (Billingsley, 2013).

Significance of Urban Areas for US Forces

It is critical to understand why operations in urban areas are significant for US forces despite being casualty ridden and complex. US Army Field Manual explains the following advantages of operating in urban areas (FM 3-06, 2003: 1–4):

1. Urban infrastructure, capabilities, and resources have operational or strategic value.
2. Symbolic importance of urban areas.
3. Urban areas are nodal points and dominate a region or an avenue of approach.
4. Urban areas are bitterly contested as they are the transportation, communication, and industrial hubs and hold social, financial, and political implications for any country.

Furthermore, Clausewitz explained that, 'the public opinion is won through great victories and occupation of enemy's capital - where enemy's resources are most concentrated' (von Clausewitz and Gatzke, 2003).

On the other hand, Michael Baumann highlighted the importance of urban areas from the insurgent's point of view, 'What's needed is a vanguard in the metropolis that declares its solidarity with the liberation movements of the third world. Since it lives in the head of the monster, it can do the greatest damage there' (Baumann, 1975: 46) as cited in Gerwehr & Glenn (2000: 7).

The Explanation of Relevant Terms

In 2006, the term Military Operations on Urban Terrain (MOUT) was replaced by Urban Operations (UO) (FM 3-06, 2003: ix). To understand UO, it is important to understand the characteristics of urban areas. A useful working definition of urban area as drawn from Army FM 90-10-1 is, "[a] concentration of structures, facilities, and people – that forms the economic and cultural focus for the surrounding area."

According to FM 3-06.11, "UO are operations planned and conducted in an area of operations (AO) that includes one or more urban areas." Its dominant features include human-made construction and high population (FM 3-06.11, 2002). The field manual also explains the basic necessities of UOs:

1. Assigned objective lies within the urban area.
2. Urban area is between two natural obstacles in avenue of approach and cannot be bypassed.

3. Clearance of urban area is decisive in shaping conditions for current or projected operations.
4. Political or humanitarian considerations demand control of an urban area.
5. Urban areas promise a better overall defense.

Population has been figured out as one of the most important factors in urban areas as it immensely affects the conduct of operations within it. Vygotsky related guerilla warfare to the type of population supporting it, "if guerrilla [fighters receive] support from peasantry/farmers he will prefer rural guerrilla warfare however if the support is from working-class, then urban guerrilla warfare is desired" (Vygotsky, 1896).

Complexity of Operations in Urban Terrain

Complexity of modern cities/metropolises have been identified as a major concern in recent engagements. Wolfel, Richmond, Read, and Tansey (2016) identified the complexity of operations in modern cities based on three fundamental concepts. First, modern cities are multidimensional (subterranean, surface, and vertical). Second, cities are interconnected through globalization, social media, and modern communication methods. Third, cities are uncontrollable due to inter-connectivity, rise of black market, informal economy, and lack of government control over slums. Structures inhibit maneuver, reduce application of firepower, restrict field of fire, and degrade command and control (C2) capabilities. These operations become dangerous due to cluttered three-dimensional spaces posing logistical and navigational challenges (Gerwehr & Glenn, 2000: 1). Furthermore, urban residents also create conditions for restrictive rules of engagement (ROE) which increase stress on soldiers amid terrorism and impromptu violence (Medby & Glenn, 2002: 25).

Assessing battlefield environment of cities using traditional approaches become insufficient due to the multidimensional nature of cities. The problem in the modern dense urban environment is that the operational environment (OE), including the AO, often extends much further than in the past (Wolfel, Richmond, Read & Tansey, 2016). The impact of connections and linkages, facilitated by globalization, advancement in communication technology, and media access, challenges the traditional idea of a fixed OE for analysis by an intelligence team (Kosal, 2018). Some contemporary models cover tangible and intangible variables to address these challenges. Wielhouwer (2005) suggested a topographical model that overlay the population and man-made infrastructures on natural terrain. Whereby, Harry R. Yarger suggested modeling the challenging and complicated nature of the strategic environment using US Army War College's VUCA (volatile, uncertain, complex, and ambiguous) model (Hall, 2018).

Methods of operating in urban areas will vary depending on local history, culture, climate, and state of economic development. The human dimension and its effects on UO are much more difficult to assess and understand than the dimensions of terrain. Success smiles on the side that better understands and exploits the effects of population in urban environment (FM 3-06, 2003: 2–2).

Asymmetric Threat in Urban Areas

According to US Army Field Manual, insurgents will pose asymmetrical threat in urban warfare – a threat that uses dissimilar weapons or force (e.g., sniper attacks, IEDs, ambush, insider attack, drone attack, suicide bomber, and hostage situation) to offset US superior military force and technological advantage (FM 100-6, 1996). Placing a strong opponent in a hostile territory blunts his information, surveillance, and command and control capabilities by confronting him with unfriendly and uncooperative population (Gerwehr & Glenn, 2000: 1–2). This kind of complexity of urban areas is ideal to achieve balance of power just like operations against US forces in Mogadishu and Russian forces in Grozny (Forbes, 2015).

US Army Field Manual 100-6 identifies that in future the threat to US forces will emanate from a range of individual sources (like non-state actors/sub-state actors/non-government organizations [NGOs]) to complex national organizations (foreign intelligence services/adversary military). Boundaries among these sources are indistinct, difficult to discern, and sometimes intermingled. Tracing the origins of a particular incident is cumbersome. For example, actions that appear as the work of hackers may actually involve foreign intelligence service/cyberattack teams (FM 100-6, 1996: 1–6).

In urban warfare, the adversary achieves surveillance and point targeting through cheaper asymmetric means (e.g., snipers/target-killers/armed drones) and exploits the vulnerability of urban population in markets and public places. A recent use of flying IED quad-copter by ISIS in Syria is one such case (Ball, 2017). ISIL fighters in Mosul (2017) used drones to drop 40-mm grenades and used advanced vehicle-borne IEDs to deter Iraqi forces (South, 2018).

In the case of a near-peer threat, the modern adversary possesses advance capabilities like artificial intelligence (AI), unmanned aerial platforms, swarm drones, and cyber and robotic warfare. The adversary may also covertly or overtly supply these capabilities to insurgents or use these in supporting role. These capabilities in urban areas can be employed against friendly force deployments very easily from ventilation windows, tunnels, slum rooftops, and underground terrorist dugouts. These technologies can also be used to target civilians to make them wary of friendly forces. The enemy will be planning all these asymmetric attacks behind a curtain, whereas the friendly forces will be unable to pin war crimes on a robot, swarm, or an AI system.

Military and Non-Military Aspects of Urban Warfare

In urban warfare, militaries face various challenges like problematic communications, poor command and control, and difficult target acquisition. Moreover, firepower and maneuverer are restricted due to limited fire support, field of fire, and mobility. Sustenance and logistics are also challenging due to long, dependent, and insecure supply lines. On the contrary, urban areas afford greater concealment, cover, logistic, intelligence, and storage sites of ammunition for insurgents and terrorists (FM 3-06.11, 2002: 2–33). Besides, fighting in cities provides advantage to the adversary to inflict more casualties. On the contrary, the US advantage of heavy weapons on ground and in air is restricted due to strict ROE and presence of noncombatants in urban areas (Edwards, 2000: 2). Moreover, the law of armed conflict (LOAC) imposes caution on warfighters to minimize risk of collateral damage and civilian injury (Waxman, 2000: 24).

US Joint Publication 3-06 "Joint Urban Operations" elaborates that the entire urban environment must be addressed simultaneously and systematically. "Power should be applied in a way to disable hostile elements while enabling elements that are essential to the city's functioning" (JP 3-06, 2013). A UK MOD publication emphasized that military forces have to be highly adaptable and resilient in urban warfare:

> the phenomenon of urbanization has created physically, culturally and institutionally complex cities that are challenging for military forces operating in them. Land forces have to be highly adaptable and resilient to operate successfully in these different conditions.
>
> (JDP -0-20, 2017)

Urban warfare is intelligence and surveillance intensive. Thorough knowledge of buildings, alleyways, tunnels, and rooftops may have to be acquired, through intelligence, surveillance, and reconnaissance (ISR) sources, to operate in cities (FM 3-06.11, 2002: H-13).

Contemporary military intelligence (MI) concepts like ASCOPE (areas, structures, capabilities, organizations, people, and events), PMESII (political, military, economic, social, information, and infrastructure), and SWEAT-MSO (sewage, water, electricity, academics, trash, medical, safety, and other considerations) offer some reliable intelligence and analysis tools to define OE of megacities/dense urban areas (Hall, 2018).

Mansoor (2016), in his article: "Why Can't America Win Its Wars?," appreciated American wars in Panama (1989) and Gulf (1991) as both wars precluded prolonged commitment of US forces – the Kuwaitis and Panamanians viewed coalition forces as liberators. However, Hall (2018) attributed failure of America in Iraq and Afghanistan to "poor intelligence; an imbalance of ends, ways, and means; policy-strategy mismatches; improper use of instruments of national power; deficient host-nation commitment; and a lack of popular support." He also linked failure to "too-frequent commitment of military forces without fully understanding the nature of the environment" (Hall, 2018).

According to US Army Field Manual of Urban Operations, threat forces will try to win the information war to create strategic effects. They will embark to weaken the legitimacy of US forces and make their campaign appear indigestible to domestic and world audience (FM 3-06, 2003: 3–9). Larger connectivity and smart phones provide the means to disseminate threat propaganda, misinformation, and disinformation through websites and blogs with relative ease. Mobile cameras are now as important a tool to threat actors as weapons and ammunition. Moreover, forces claiming to defend their motherland from foreign invasion enjoy popular sympathy: as evident from Stalingrad, Mogadishu, and Grozny. In future UO, attackers with effective psychological operation (PSYOPS) strategy will prevail. In Beirut, IDF experienced that the attacker must win the international propaganda battle before overwhelming an opposition (FM 3-06, 2003: H-13).

A recent research by Mercy Corps concluded that unemployment and poverty were the deciding factors whether or not young people will engage in conflict. Youth is encouraged to join insurgent camps by infuriating frustrations due to injustice, discrimination, corruption, and abuse. Just like in Nigeria, Boko Haram was able to recruit young men by widening grievances due to government failings (Keny-Guyer, 2018, para. 5). Afghan Taliban carried out a series of terrorist attacks in Kabul, killing more than 115 people, possibly in reaction to air strikes against their opium businesses (CFR, 2018 Jan). Resurgence of the Taliban insurgency and their territorial gains can only be stopped by feeding hope to Afghan nation, through visible signs of prosperity (CFR, 2018). Stable economic environments assist people in returning to normalcy and in recovering more quickly after a conflict. In Somalia, access to education and civic engagement reduced youth participation in violence (Keny-Guyer, 2018: paras. 7–10).

US Commitment in Future Urban Wars

In *Concrete Hell: Urban Warfare from Stalingrad to* Iraq, DiMarco (2012) highlighted that the trends of military history, increasing decisiveness of urban combat, and the population demographics support the idea that warfare in the 21st century will be dominated by operations in urban environment. In the future, the adversaries are likely to exploit urban areas for operational gains, and to confront them, US forces will inevitably encounter complex urban environment (Gentile, Johnson, Saum-Manning, Cohen, Williams, Lee, Doty III, 2017: 5).

US forces and commanders operating in urban environment need to be creative and adaptive. Friendly forces have proved their ability in this regard in several cases. In Fallujah, evacuation of noncombatants reduced the problem of identifying enemy and also reduced civilian causalities, which otherwise would have alienated the world opinion (Gentile, Johnson, Saum-Manning, Cohen, Williams, Lee, Doty III, 2017: xii). Similarly, in Sadr City (2008), constructing a 12-foot concrete barrier enabled the local population to feel confident of US and Iraqi soldiers and shifted momentum of operations in favor (Gentile, Johnson, Saum-Manning, Cohen, Williams, Lee, Doty III, 2017: 50). In urban warfare, creativity is also demanded in cultural, religious, and language orientation of forces. Recently in 2018, a US soldier was killed in an insider attack by an Afghan commando in Kabul due to feelings of mistrust and radicalization (Binding, 2018). Therefore, formal and informal norms of population must be respected in a manner as to win their support for friendly forces. (Gentile, Johnson, Saum-Manning, Cohen, Williams, Lee, Doty III, 2017: 30).

Mental resolve will be a battle-winning factor for US forces in any future urban conflict. On the contrary, lack of conviction, mental sickness, and psychological issues of warfighters will place a heavy bar on success of any such operation. General Peter Chiarelli, as Army vice Chief of Staff, said: "Suicide, not combat, is the leading cause of death of soldiers deployed in Middle East to fight ISIS" (*Daily Mail*, 2016).

US forces may be required to conduct multifaceted tasks in urban areas like emergency law enforcement operations (during the Battle of Panama), firefighting (during the Battle of Manila), medical evacuation and treatment, conduct of elections, running schools, institutions, and sometimes entire government (FM 3-06, 2003: 4–3). US forces may be motivated, well-trained, and amply equipped to take on new challenges, but the adversary is covert, determined, and keenly observe friendly force weaknesses. Inevitably, US forces have to allocate appropriate resources for performing these multidimensional tasks besides ensuring the safety of troops and population.

US forces in future UO need a mechanism to ensure inherent economic growth while focusing on health, education, social welfare, employment of youth, and reconstruction. Spencer (2018) referred to an estimate that over $88.2 billion was required only to rebuild the destroyed cities in Iraq. Urban warfare is coupled with urban reforms and development, or else the population may lose hope and join the alternate side.

Intelligence-based operations will be the hallmark of future urban battlefields with every section, every street, and every house becoming an intricate component of the urban combat, urban warfare environment, and battleground. Gentile, Johnson, Saum-Manning, Cohen, Williams, Lee, and Doty III (2017) pointed out that the recent trend of smart cities provides new opportunities for intelligence collection and dissemination. By 2030, some developing countries are expected to make reasonable progress in this field. Quite probably, US Army may find itself conducting operations within such a smart city (Gentile, Johnson, Saum-Manning, Cohen, Williams, Lee, and Doty, 2017: 130). In this backdrop, data collected by surveillance cameras, navigational applications, and national biometric databases can come in handy and be manipulated in favor of one's own forces.

The US must be prepared to counter threat to itself and its allies from not only the insurgents but also the near-peer adversaries. According to an assessment report by 173rd Airborne Brigade, the US Army's Rapid Reaction Force (RRF) in Europe is under-equipped, lacking personnel, and inadequately organized to confront military aggression from Russia or its high-tech proxies. The unit, during training with Ukrainian troops, learned about Russian-backed separatist using drones and electronic warfare tools to pinpoint targets for artillery barrages and employing state-of-the-art Russian antitank missiles. The unit has also identified US and NATO units' capability shortfalls in areas like air defense, electronic warfare, over-reliance on satellite communications, and GPS navigation systems. According to the report, these shortfalls got imbued due to years of fighting in Iraq and Afghanistan – where enemy had no air power or high-end technology (Wesley, 2017).

Urban warfare in Eastern Europe has not only become a hot topic for US and NATO strategists but also a defense possibility to be planned and prepared for. In November 2017, almost 4,000 combat personnel from the US, the United Kingdom (UK), Germany, Canada, Poland, Romania, Slovenia, Luxembourg, and the three Baltic States took part in the massive "Iron Sword" exercise that involved military actions in urban environment (IHLS, 2017). Given the relatively constrained environment of the Baltic States, US forces and allies, as part of NATO special operations forces in the region, could find themselves forced into conducting or supporting urban warfare against more heavily armed and outnumbered Russians. The US and its allies RRF along with local armies might need to use urban areas to attrite and delay the Russians for sufficient time to create an enabling environment for an effective counterattack (Joseph, 2018).

Finally, it is important for the US that in any future conflict, a strategic appraisal should be conducted prior to committing forces. This will help senior policymakers to better articulate strategic objectives. *Often the cost of operations is not worth achieving the political objective* (Hall, 2018). As per Sun Tzu's (Tzu, 1994[1910]) legendary words, "the victorious warrior wins before committing forces, while the defeated warrior commits forces and then seeks victory." Meilinger (2017) suggested that the US foreign policy may explore the indirect approaches of Liddell Hart to influence adversaries rather than getting stuck with the direct approaches of Carl von Clausewitz.

Conclusion

The growing trend of urbanization, population growth, and migration is increasing values of cities as hub of economy, knowledge, propaganda, and power. These cities afford great advantages for adversaries employing asymmetric capabilities to counter US forces. US forces in conflict will find themselves fighting in urban areas to evade or neutralize their adversaries from their power centers. But urban warfare is inherently prolonged, resource intensive, and heavy on men and material. Fighting urban warfare needs political resolve, strategic clarity, and well-defined end, ways, and means. Population figures out as the most decisive factor in winning the urban warfare. Winning their support is not easy as the adversary is hiding within the population; therefore, it requires extensive intelligence analysis to segregate the adversary from the population. History is replete with good and bad examples of conducting such wars. The worst of these examples used little CA and PSYOPS and were high in collateral damage.

Understanding the dynamics of urban areas is a new art of war that considers both military and non-military aspects of UO. It engages individuals, intellectuals, institutions, and leaders of the country and wins their support for the operations. Understanding the strategic nature of environment and its analysis is vital to articulate the strategic objective. All this has to be foreseen prior to committing the friendly forces. US forces in future UO need to focus on good local governance, uplifting of youth and economy to win local support and thus win wars.

The changing nature of threat calls for understanding urban warfare even better. Modern adversary will stage urban warfare in alliance with enemies within to discredit American role in international politics. They will use their in-house networks to subvert and sabotage friendly forces' peacekeeping efforts. Keeping both conventional and sub-conventional capabilities on the leading edge is not the only requirement but the just, proportionate, and ethical use of force is also being evaluated in newsrooms.

Political objectives must be selected unambiguously, international environment favorably shaped, and international opinion built before stepping into war. A wrong war at a wrong place with a wrong enemy should never be fought. Once the right conflict is selected, it must be rigorously pursued with utmost resilience. The value of objectives and political ends must justify the sacrifice of lives, money, resources, and the time spent on war.

Further Reading

Graham, S. (2008). "Imaging urban warfare: Urbanization and U.S. military technoscience," in D. Cowen and E. Gilbert (eds.), *War, citizenship, territory* (pp. 33–56). Abingdon: Routledge.

Hahn II, R. F. and Jezior, B. (1999). "Urban Warfare and the Urban Warfighter of 2025," *The US Army War College Quarterly: Parameters*, *29*(2): 74–86. https://press.armywarcollege.edu/cgi/viewcontent.cgi?article=1930&context=parameters

Rosenau, W. G. (1997). "'Every room is a new battle': The lessons of modern urban warfare," *Studies in Conflict & Terrorism*, *20*(4): 371–394.

References

Ball, R. J. (2017). *The Proliferation of Unmanned Aerial Vehicles: Terrorist Use, Capability, and Strategic Implications*. Livermore, CA: Lawrence Livermore National Lab, Livermore, United States.

Billingsley, D. (2013). *Fangs of the Lone Wolf: Chechen tactics in the Russian-Chechen War 1994–2009*. Warwick: Helion and Company.

CFR. (1999–2018). "Timeline – The U.S. War in Afghanistan." https://www.cfr.org/timeline/us-war-afghanistan

CFR. (2018, November 6). Global conflict tracker – "War in Afghanistan". https://www.cfr.org/interactives/global-conflict-tracker#!/conflict/war-in-afghanistan

Daily Mail Online. (2016, December 30). "More US troops commit suicide than die in combat in the war on ISIS." https://www.dailymail.co.uk/news/article-4074942/More-troops-commit-suicide-die-combat-war-ISIS.html

DiMarco, L. A. (2012). *Concrete Hell: Urban warfare from Stalingrad to Iraq*. London: Bloomsbury Publishing.

Edwards, S. J. (2000). *Mars unmasked: The changing face of urban operations*. Santa Monica, United States: RAND Corporation.

Flecher, M. W., (2018). *Project reaper: A Max Storm novel*. Luton: Andrews UK Limited.

FM 3-06. (2003). "Urban Operations."

FM 3-06.11. (2002). "FM 3-06.11 Combined arms operations in urban terrain."

Forbes, M. C. S. (2015). *In order to win, learn how to fight: The US Army in urban operations*. Auckland: Pickle Partners Publishing.

Fuchs, H. (2018, August 19). "It's time to end America's war in Afghanistan," *The Guardian*. https://www.theguardian.com/commentisfree/2018/aug/19/its-time-to-end-americas-war-in-afghanistan

Galula, D. (2006). *Counterinsurgency warfare: Theory and practice*. Westport: Greenwood Publishing Group.

Gentile, G., Johnson, D. E., Saum-Manning, L., Cohen, R. S., Williams, S., Lee, C., & Doty III, J. L. (2017). *Reimagining the character of urban operations for the US Army*. Santa Monica, United States: RAND Corporation.

Gerwehr, S. & Glenn, R. W. (2000). *The art of darkness: deception and urban operations*. Santa Monica, United States: RAND Corporation.

Hall, L. (2018, Nov 02) Strategic intelligence and the decision to go to war. *Modern War Institute at West Point*. https://mwi.usma.edu/strategic-intelligence-decision-go-war/

Joseph, T. (2018, March). U.S. Special ops and lithuanian reservists practiced waging Guerrilla War against Russia," *The War Zone*. http://www.thedrive.com/the-war-zone/19186/u-s-special-ops-and-lithuanian-reservists-practiced-waging-guerrilla-war-against-russia

JP 3-06. (2013). "Joint urban operations."

Kilcullen, D. (2015). *Out of the mountains: The coming age of urban Guerilla*. London: Hurst & Company.

Kosal, M. E. (ed.). (2018). *Technology and the intelligence community: Challenges and advances for the 21st century*. Cham: Springer.

Keny-Guyer, N. (2018). "Conflict is reshaping the world. Here's how we tackle it," World Economic Forum. https://www.weforum.org/agenda/2018/01/conflict-is-reshaping-the-world-mercy-corps/

Lucia, B., (2018, November 3), "US soldier killed in 'insider attack' in Afghanistan," *Sky News* https://news.sky.com/story/amp/us-soldier-killed-in-insider-attack-in-afghanistan-11543759

Mansoor, P. (2016, March 10). "Why can't America win its wars?" Howover Institution, Stanford, United States. https://www.hoover.org/research/why-cant-america-win-its-wars

Medby, J. J. & Glenn, R. W. (2002). *Street smart: Intelligence preparation of the battlefield for urban operations*. Santa Monica, United States: RAND Corporation.

MOD, UK. (2017, June). "Joint Doctrine Publication 0-20 (JDP 0-20)."

Mosul Study Group, U.S. Army. (2017). *What the battle for Mosul teaches the force*. Kansas: Army University Press.

Meilinger, P. (2017). "Basil H. Liddell Hart: His applicability to modern war," RAF CASP. https://medium.com/raf-caps/basil-h-liddell-hart-his-applicability-to-modern-war-bf4e4c9145e3

Pace. (2008). Joint Publication 3-0 Joint Operations.

Reporter. (2017, August). "NATO Preparing for Urban Warfare," *iHLS Startup Accelerator*. https://i-hls.com/archives/78315

South, T. (2018, March 6). "The future battlefield: Army, Marines Prepare for 'Massive' Fight in Megacities," *Military Times*. https://www.militarytimes.com/news/your-army/2018/03/06/the-future-battlefield-army-marines-prepare-for-massive-fight-in-megacities/

Spencer, J. (2018, November 8). *Why militaries must destroy cities to save them*. Modern War Institute, West Point, United States. https://mwi.usma.edu/militaries-must-destroy-cities-save/

Tzu, S. (1994 [1910]). *The art of war* (trans. Lionel Giles). London: The British Museum

UN DESA. (2018). "World urbanization prospects." https://population.un.org/wup/Publications/Files/WUP2018-KeyFacts.pdf

UNDP. (2016, May 31). "Preventing violent extremism through inclusive development and the promotion of tolerance and respect for diversity." https://www.undp.org/content/undp/en/home/librarypage/democratic-governance/conflict-prevention/discussion-paper--preventing-violent-extremism-through-inclusiv.html

US Army. (1996). *FM 100-6· Information operations*. Washington, DC: Headquarters, Department of the Army.

US Army. (2006). "FM 3-06 Urban operations."

US Army. (2014). "The mega city: Operational challenges for force 2025 and beyond."

von Clausewitz, C. & Gatzke, H. W. (2003). *Principles of war*. North Chelmsford: Courier Corporation.

Vygotsky, L. S. (1896). *MIA: Encyclopedia of marxism: Glossary of people*.

Wahlman, A. (2015). *Storming the city: U.S. military performance in urban warfare from WWII to Vietnam*. Denton: University of North Texas Press.

Waxman, M. C. (2000). *International law and the politics of urban air operations*. Santa Monica, United States: RAND Corporation.

Wehrey, F., Kaye, D. D., Watkins, J., Martini, J., & Guffey, R. A. (2010). The iraq effect: The middle east after the Iraq war. Santa Monica, United States: Rand Corporation.

Wesley, M. (2017). "US Army unprepared to deal with Russia in Europe," *Politico*. https://www.politico.com/story/2017/09/02/army-study-173rd-airborne-brigade-europe-russia-242273

Wielhouwer, P. W. (2005). "Preparing for future joint urban operations: The role of simulations and the urban resolve experiment," *Small Wars Journal*. https://smallwarsjournal.com/documents/urbanresolve.pdf

Wolfel, R. L., Richmond, A. K., Read, M. & Tansey, C. (2016). "It's in there: Rethinking(?) Intelligence Preparation of the Battlefield in Megacities/Dense Urban Areas," *Small Wars Journal.* https://smallwarsjournal.com/jrnl/art/it%E2%80%99s-in-there-rethinking-intelligence-preparation-of-the-battlefield-in-megacitiesdense-urb

Yarger, H. R. (2006). *Strategic theory for the 21st century: The little book on big strategy*. Darby: DIANE Publishing Co.

IV

UNITED STATES (US) DOMESTIC AND BORDER SECURITY

Erika Cornelius Smith
Nichols College, Dudley, MA, United States

Suzette A. Haughton
University of the West Indies, Kingston, Jamaica

Chapter 65

Active Shootings on College and University Campuses

Allison McDowell-Smith
Nichols College, Dudley, MA, United States

Contents

Introduction 491
History of Active Shootings on Schools 492
Active Shooters on College or University Campuses 492
Countermeasures to Active Shootings 494
Conclusion 495
Further Reading 495
References 496

Introduction

Active shooters are defined as "an individual actively engaged in killing or attempting to kill people in a confined and populated area; in most cases, active shooters use firearms(s) and there is no pattern or method to their selection of victims" (Department, 2008). This is a uniform definition agreed upon by United States governmental agencies, including the White House, Department of Justice, Federal Bureau of Investigation (FBI), US Department of Education, US Department of Homeland Security, and Federal Emergency Management Agency (Alice, 2018). According to the FBI, there have been 50 active shooter events over the course of 2016 and 2017; yet none of these active shooter events occurred in higher education institutions (Federal, 2018).

When examining active shootings on a college or university campus, the event can generally be considered a mass shooting if four or more individuals are injured or killed (Mass, 2018). Mass shooting does not have a uniform definition; yet the

DOI: 10.4324/9781315144511-69

definition of mass murderer is considered uniform with four or more fatalities in any given period of time (with no cooling-off period) (Mass, 2018). Thus, mass murders and active shooters have uniform definitions, but it's relevant to understand that a mass murder does not have to be the result of an active shooter and vice versa. However, these two have a strong correlation when active shootings are examined on college or university campuses.

History of Active Shootings on Schools

The earliest documented active shooting at a school within the United States was in 1764 and referred to as the Enoch Brown school massacre. Over the past 50 years, there have been approximately 252 school shootings, including schools ranging from K-12 (252 incidents) to colleges and universities (76 incidents) (Cato, 2018). The criteria used to classify these events as active shootings are as follows:

1. Shootings that happened on or near school campuses while classes were in session
2. Shootings where students were present, such as ones on school buses or at school-sanctioned functions, such as athletic events and dances (Cato, 2018).

There can be some discrepancy in statistics of active school shootings as some research includes different criteria, such as if a shooting occurred while school was not in session and/or anytime firearm discharges a live bullet. While the statistics can fluctuate due to the criteria utilized, school shootings in general have become more common in the United States in recent decades. In addition, the venue of these attacks has shifted, with a decrease in the percentage of attacks at elementary and middle schools and an increase in the percentage of attacks in high schools and higher education (Langman, n.d.).

Active Shooters on College or University Campuses

The top 5 deadliest active shootings on a college or university campus are as follows:

1. **Virginia Tech Shooting**: The Virginia Tech shooting occurred on April 16, 2007, and resulted in 33 deaths (including the perpetrator) and 23 injured victims (Please reference mass shootings). At approximately 7:15 am, Seung Hui Cho shot two residential assistants in a dormitory at Virginia Tech. Cho was a 23-year-old senior who also attended Virginia Tech. More than 2 hours after the initial shooting in the dormitory, Cho proceeded to a classroom building and locked various doors to prevent students from escaping. Upon securing the doors, Cho went to multiple classrooms and began shooting. In less than 10 minutes, Cho had killed 27 students, five faculty members, and himself. It was later identified that Cho had a long history of mental illness (Virginia, 2011). Critics argued that this massacre could have been prevented had university authorities obliged by

the "clear warnings of mental instability," specifically regarding social anxiety, depression, and internal rage (Osterweil, 2007). In a video sent to NBC news that was recorded by Cho between the two shootings, he stated "You had a hundred billion chances and ways to have avoided today, but you decided to spill my blood. You forced me into a corner and gave me only one option. The decision was yours. Now you have blood on your hands that will never wash off." (Osterweil, 2007).

2. **University of Texas Tower Shooting**: The University of Texas shooting occurred on August 1, 1966, in Austin, Texas, and resulted in 18 deaths (including perpetrator) and 31 injured victims. Charles Whitman was a 25-year-old former Marine who was studying architectural engineering at the University of Texas. After having lost his academic scholarship, having bad grades, and a gambling addiction, he then obtained professional help for violent impulses (Wallenfeldt, 2018).

   On July 31, Whitman wrote a note about his violent impulses, saying, "After my death, I wish an autopsy on me be performed to see if there's any mental disorders." The note then described his hatred for his family and his intent to kill them. That night, Whitman went to his mother's home, where he stabbed and shot her. Upon returning to his own home, he then stabbed his wife to death (History, 2009).

   On the next morning of August 1, Whitman carried weapons up onto the deck of the Main Building Tower at the University of Texas and began to open fire on those below him. After approximately 90 minutes, Whitman was shot dead by three police officers and an armed citizen who infiltrated the 27th floor. Upon his death, an autopsy was conducted, and it was determined that Whitman had a glioblastoma tumor that contributed to his "inability to control his emotions and actions" (Wallenfeldt, 2018).

3. **Umpqua Community College Shooting**: The Umpqua Community College (UCC) shooting occurred on October 1, 2015, in Roseburg, Oregon, and resulted in ten deaths (including the perpetrator) and eight injured victims. At approximately 10:38 am, Chris Harper-Mercer entered a writing class heavily armed and opened fire. Within 8 minutes after the initial shooting, two law enforcement officers engaged in fire with Harper-Mercer, prior to Harper-Mercer killing himself. Harper-Mercer was a 26-year old who had been enrolled in the English class where the shooting took place (Woolington, 2016). During the shooting, witnesses claimed he asked the religions of certain students, but experts maintain that Harper-Mercer was not racist, rather he was mentally ill (yet no mental health history has been released) (Theen, 2017). Furthermore, Harper-Mercer had given one student a flash drive with "a rambling and racist manifesto that complained about being a virgin and having no friends while also proclaiming that his 'success in Hell is assured'" (Theen, 2017).

4. **Oikos University Shooting**: The Oikos University Shooting occurred on April 2, 2012, in Oakland, California, and resulted in seven deaths and three injured victims. At approximately 10:30 am, One Goh ordered a nursing student within a classroom to line up against the wall where he then opened fire. Upon conducting the shooting, Goh fled the scene and turned himself into local authorities

shortly afterward. Goh was a 43-year old, prior student of this Korean Christian college. He had been upset with the administration regarding a denied payment and had gone to the college to locate that administrator but settled for random students when he found out the administrator was not present (Lee, 2014). Upon his arrest, Goh was declared mentally incompetent based upon his diagnosis of paranoid schizophrenia; yet 5 years later, he was deemed competent for trial and sentenced up to seven consecutive life terms for each victim (Ruggiero, 2017).

5. **California State University**: The California State University shooting, also referred to as the Fullerton massacre occurred on July 12, 1976, in Fullerton, California, and resulted in seven deaths and two injured victims. A shooting was conducted by the custodian at the University's library, Edward Charles Allaway. Allaway was 37-year old and used a semi-automatic rifle to open fire on both the first floor and basement of the library. Upon committing the shooting, Allaway fled the scene and then turned himself into the local authorities. Allaway was declared mentally incompetent based upon multiple diagnoses of paranoid schizophrenic on top of a history of violence and mental illness. In 2001, Allaway had petitioned to be released from state mental custody, but several doctors had deemed Allaway as still a risk to society (Luppi, 2016).

Countermeasures to Active Shootings

As a result of active shootings on college campuses and universities, the culture of societies within the United States has begun to adapt to the increased threat of active shooting. This adaptation has led to "active shooter trainings and drills, table-top exercises, emergency notification systems, and considerations of what material doors are made of and how they lock" (Langman, n.d.). Active shooter drills have become a routine for many schools, just as with fire drills. There have been increased directives to identify warning signs via a threat assessment. Increased education is necessary to effectively intervene through threat assessment. Missed warning signs can lead to active shooting scenarios. For example:

> Long before committing a sniper attack at the University of Texas, Austin, Charles Whitman talked to friends about his desire to go to the observation deck of the campus Tower and shoot people. In March, 1966, just a few months before the massacre, Whitman told the university psychiatrist that he thought about 'going up on the Tower with a deer rifle and shooting people.' No threat assessment was conducted.
>
> (Langman, n.d.)

Furthermore, policies have been updated to assist in the countermeasures to active shooters on college and university campuses. Following the Virginia Tech shooting, the Virginia Tech Review Panel examined why Cho's mental history was not provided to Virginia Tech. Virginia Tech was never provided with information regarding Cho's past, such as playing with knives, being disruptive in the classroom, or having other students fearful of him (Osterweil, 2007). The top two recommendations to universities provided by the Review Panel include:

1. Have a system that links troubled students to appropriate medical and counseling services either on or off campus and to balance the individual's rights with the rights of all others for safety.
2. Incidents of aberrant, dangerous, or threatening behavior must be documented and reported immediately to a college's threat assessment group and must be acted upon in a prompt and effective manner to protect the safety of the campus community (TriData, 2009).

Additional policies have explored zero tolerance on guns; yet the research regarding these policies is mixed. Furthermore, there continues to be great debate within our current society over how zero tolerance plays a role in active shooter scenarios.

Conclusion

While there is a uniform definition of active shooters within the United States, it is still necessary to understand that active shooter events do not always lead to mass murders and vice versa. However, based upon the top 5 deadliest active shooters on college and university campuses, these events also can be classified as being conducted by a mass murderer and being an actual mass shooting. There can also be some discrepancy in statistics with regards to active shootings based upon how an organization defines and categorizes active shootings, but the research does support that active shooters have been part of United States history since 1764.

As of 2020, the top 5 mass shootings include Virginia Tech shooting, University of Texas Tower shooting, UCC shooting, Oikos University shooting, and California State University shooting. These shootings occurred over the past decade from 1966 to 2015 and range in location from public and private to four-year and two-year educational institutions. Due to the magnitude of these active shootings, significant countermeasures have begun to be put into place to properly handle and potentially mitigate future active shootings from occurring in the higher education setting.

Further Reading

Department of Homeland Security. (2008). *Active shooter: How to respond*. https://www.dhs.gov/xlibrary/assets/active_shooter_booklet.pdf

Greenberg, S. (2007). Active shooters on college campuses: Conflicting advice, roles of the individual and first responder, and the need to maintain perspective. *Disaster Medicine and Public Health Preparedness*, *1*(1). https://www.pfw.edu/dotAsset/74ebd3f0-af76-4b35-a0e5-3a6a7b9725d3.pdf

TriData Division, System Planning Corporation. (2009). *Mass shootings at Virginia Tech: Addendum to the report of the Review Panel*. https://scholar.lib.vt.edu/prevail/docs/April16ReportRev20091204.pdf

References

Alice Training Institute. (2018). *Active shooter*. https://www.alicetraining.com/active-shooter/

Cato, J. (2018). *Here's a list of every school shooting over the past 50 years*. Trib: Total Media. https://triblive.com/news/education/safety/13313060-74/heres-a-list-of-every-school-shooting-over-the-past-50-years

Department of Homeland Security. (2008). *Active shooter: How to respond*. https://www.dhs.gov/xlibrary/assets/active_shooter_booklet.pdf

Federal Bureau of Investigation. (2018). *Active shooter incidents in the United States in 2016 and 2017*. https://www.fbi.gov/file-repository/active-shooter-incidents-us-2016-2017.pdf/view

History.com. (2009). *An ex-Marine goes on a killing spree at the University of Texas*. https://www.history.com/this-day-in-history/an-ex-marine-goes-on-a-killing-spree-at-the-university-of-texas

Langman, P. (n.d.). Warning signs of school shootings in higher education. *Campus Consortium*. https://campusconsortium.org/warning-signs-school-shootings-higher-education/

Lee, H. (2014). Details of Oikos University massacre tell of terror in Oakland. *SFGate*. https://www.sfgate.com/crime/article/Oakland-school-massacre-Jury-told-of-5-minutes-5760283.php

Luppi, K. (2016). 40 years since a 5-minute shooting spree caused a lifetime of devastation, Cal State Fullerton remembers 7 lives lost. *Los Angeles Times*. http://www.latimes.com/socal/weekend/news/tn-wknd-et-0703-cal-state-fullerton-memorial-20160702-story.html

Mass shootings: Definitions and trends. (2018). *RAND*. https://www.rand.org/research/gun-policy/analysis/supplementary/mass-shootings.html

Osterweil, N. (2007). Virginia Tech missed 'clear warnings' of shooter's mental instability. *Medpage Today*. https://www.medpagetoday.com/psychiatry/anxietystress/6546

Ruggiero, A. (2017). Oikos nursing school massacre shooter One Gog sentenced to life in prison. *East Bay Times*. https://www.eastbaytimes.com/2017/07/14/oikos-nursing-school-massacre-suspect-one-goh-to-face-life-in-prison/

Theen, A. (2017). Umpqua Community College shooting: Killer's manifesto reveals racist, satanic views. *OregonLive: The Oregonian*. https://www.oregonlive.com/pacific-northwest-news/index.ssf/2017/09/umpqua_community_college_shoot_3.html

TriData Division, System Planning Corporation. (2009). *Mass shootings at Virginia Tech: Addendum to the report of the Review Pane I*. https://scholar.lib.vt.edu/prevail/docs/April16ReportRev20091204.pdf

Virginia tech shooting leaves 32 dead. (2011). *History.com*. https://www.history.com/this-day-in-history/massacre-at-virginia-tech-leaves-32-dead

Wallenfeldt, J. (2018). Texas tower shooting of 1966. *Britannica*. https://www.britannica.com/event/Texas-Tower-shooting-of-1966

Woolington, K. (2016). Timeline of UCC shooting, aftermath: 'Somebody is outside one of the doors'. *OregonLive: The Oregonian*. https://www.oregonlive.com/roseburg-oregon-school-shooting/2016/09/umpqua_community_college_shoot.html

Chapter 66

Barrio Azteca (Los Aztecas) Mexican-American Gang

Réjeanne M. Lacroix
University of Leicester, Leicester, United Kingdom

Contents

Introduction 497
Ascent and Activities of the Barrio Azteca 498
Domestic Security Concerns 499
Difficulties in Managing the Threat 501
Conclusion 502
Further Reading 502
References 503

Introduction

The prison gang culture of the Texas correctional system facilitated the development of the Barrio Azteca in 1986. From their firmly established base in El Paso, *Los Aztecas* – as they are known in Ciudad Juárez – evolved into a Mexican–American transnational gang, utilizing their strategic location on the southwestern U.S. border to engage in transnational narcotics trafficking. Barrio Azteca's collective of Mexican and American dual citizens grants its highly organized membership the ability to cross border checkpoints so that they can conduct operations from either U.S. or Mexican jurisdictions. The interdependent relationship between narcotics trafficking and defense of acquired territory results in consequent violent crimes to maintain influence but expand as well. Subsequently, membership extends from the sister cities of El Paso and Ciudad Juárez, Mexico, into numerous American states (Federal Bureau of Investigations, 2011a). The expansion of a transnational gang synonymous

DOI: 10.4324/9781315144511-70

with large cartels, violent crime, and human insecurity by way of the drug trade signifies an identifiable domestic security concern.

Ascent and Activities of the Barrio Azteca

A key factor in understanding the domestic security threat provided by Barrio Azteca is their ascent from prison gang to transnational outfit. The dynamic environment of Mexican cartels provides opportunities for organized criminal groups to associate with more powerful players. In the case of Los Barrios, their relationships with the Vicente Carrillo Fuentes Organization, colloquially known as the Juárez Cartel, and to a lesser extent, the Beltrán-Leyva Organization, enhanced their influence in the complex world of street and prison gangs. This agreement permitted them to acquire narcotics, primarily cocaine, heroin, and marijuana, at a discounted rate and unload them in the U.S. market. Since the gang completed operations for the Juárez Cartel, the Barrio Azteca demonstrates an identifiable case where a U.S.-based gang acts as a franchise for larger Mexican drug trafficking organizations (Brackin et al., 2012, p.18). For instance, federal, state, and local law enforcement agencies accuse *Los Barrios* of criminal acts, including kidnapping, murder, extortion, firearms trafficking, money laundering, obstruction of justice, and witness retaliation, on both sides of the southwest border (FBI, 2011b). Simply put, the gang originally increased its command through its role as a proxy actor (Jackson, 2015, p.118).

Secondly, the importance of the Juárez plaza or corridor in relation to West Texas must be considered. This passageway through the Mexican state of Chihuahua is a major narcotic trafficking route into the United States. A high consumption of illicit drugs by the U.S. population provides a lucrative market and accordingly foments relationships between large cartels and local gangs (Udell, 2010, p. iii). As a result, Mexican drug trafficking organizations (DTOs) have engaged in turf wars to establish operational control over the corridor. In 2008, Barrio Azteca allied with La Línea – the armed wing of the Juárez Cartel – to counter attempts by the Sinaloa Cartel to commandeer control of the plaza. The presence of numerous members in the area as well as their cross-border relationships made it a particularly useful ally. Currently, the steady rise of the Cártel de Jalisco Nueva Generación, known as the Jalisco Cartel, and their interest in the route, further complicate the situation and partnerships. Potent criminal rivals focused on retaining command over a vital corridor instigate a continuous sense of anxiety surrounding the U.S. southern border.

John P. Sullivan notes the use of extreme violence as an instrument of control over narcotics trafficking territory (2014, p. 2). It is a logical next step that alignment with larger cartels and an entrenched presence in the illicit drug trade would propel the Barrio Azteca to gain further notoriety for violent crime. While the Juárez Cartel is infamous for its use of terror tactics (Jackson, 2015, p. 95), they commonly employed execution squads composed of *Los Aztecas* membership. The most infamous case affecting American interests occurred on March 13, 2010, when members of the gang assassinated a U.S. Consulate worker, her husband, and the husband of another U.S. official in Ciudad Juárez. These events were intrinsically linked to the drug-related violence that hampered the southern U.S. border at the time. The unequivocal reliance on violent tactics utilized by transnational criminal actors is definitely concerning.

Dynamics of regional authority have since shifted away from consolidated Juárez Cartel authority. The organization underwent a slow decline marked by the loss of experienced leadership and an inability to counter the condensed strength of the Sinaloa Cartel (Stewart, 2018). Decentralization of Mexican DTOs is evident through factions splitting from major groups and their reemergence in the criminal underworld with new leadership. This is apparent with the rise of the "Nuevo Cartel de Juárez." As a result, this power shift disturbed the relationship with the Barrio Azteca, and formerly allied factions now confront each other (Woody, 2019). Violence stemming from the devolution of once powerful DTOs and smaller transnational gangs, such as Barrio Azteca, reignited violence along the Ciudad Juárez-El Paso border to a point that the U.S. Consulate General released updated security alerts for the area (U.S. Embassy and Consulate in Mexico, 2019). Furthermore, as long as the Juárez corridor remains a lucrative narcotic trafficking passageway into the United States, it will remain disputed between rival criminal organizations. An emboldened and ascendant Barrio Azteca will seek out its niche in the criminal underworld as allegiances become indefinite. This augments the notion that Barrio Azteca contributes to border issues outside yet close to the southern U.S. border.

Domestic Security Concerns

All levels of U.S. law enforcement and homeland security are aware of the threats caused by transnational gangs. Immigration and Customs Enforcement (ICE) acknowledge that "transnational criminal street gangs represent a significant threat to public safety in communities throughout the United States" (2017). Since the Barrio Azteca are a notable model with sizable membership, it is an astute premise that the Mexican–American gang should be examined in queries related to U.S. domestic security.

While it may be a more discrete concern, *Los Barrios*' effect on U.S. human security must be considered. In an understanding of human security, it is acknowledged that the human, or population of a state, is the referent object. The well-being of citizenry is directly correlated to state security. Any criminal organization that engages in large-scale narcotics trafficking into U.S. territory triggers layers of uncertainty that span from local municipalities to the highest levels of law enforcement. For instance, the Department of Justice noted that Mexican DTOs represent the "greatest organized crime threat" to the nation, and violent street gang involvement with such superiors permits wider distribution of narcotics (United States Department of Justice, 2009, p. iii). It is widely conceded that Mexico is a major producer/supplier of heroin, methamphetamine, and marijuana, as well as transit point of cocaine, into the United States (Seelke, 2010, p. 5). This is pertinent as the Barrio Azteca is a principal well-established actor in distribution networks of narcotics who hope to expand their presence and assert dominance on their acquired turf.

Expansion of any criminal organization within U.S. borders is a conventional domestic security problem. Barrio Azteca's roots in El Paso were a natural foundation for the gang; however, the common trajectory of local affiliations and connections to more powerful cartels pose the most serious issues (Sullivan, 2014, p. 3). Transnational gangs focused on narcotics trafficking will pursue new avenues of revenue and control. This is a notable concern of law enforcement agencies as these types of criminal outfits have been migrating into the American heartland for decades (Udell, 2010, p. 4). Recent reports estimate that the Barrio Azteca claim between 1000 and 2500 members in Texas alone (Texas Department of Public Safety, 2018, p. 4). As noted, the FBI identified national reach, but within Texas, their western breadth extends to Midland County while authorities notice small-scale manifestations in Fort Bend, Galveston, Harris, and Montgomery counties (Gill, 2018).

Sizable membership, both inside and outside the prison system, becomes more problematic if a transnational gang is well organized. After decades of existence and moving around the criminal underworld, Barrio Azteca emerged as a sophisticated prison gang with the ability to undertake difficult operations. This level of cleverness is a result of the guidance as well as financial and logistical support received in their role as proxy to a larger cartel (Guerrero-Gutiérrez, 2011, p. 39). Furthermore, *Los Barrios*' usage of a strict militaristic structure, set of rankings, and violent punishment for disobedience makes them a formidable force. Within the prison system, the use of a complex coded language, based on Náhuati numerology and phrases (Guerrero-Gutiérrez, 2011, p. 40) as well as contraband cell phones, makes it difficult for gang units and intelligence to remain ahead of the threats associated with the gang.

On the other hand, the Aztecas in El Paso and *Los Aztecas* in Juárez have not been immune to decentralization and infighting (Aguilar, 2018). The more independent nature of the Mexican side of the gang places it in confrontation with its American associates when it comes to matters of territory within their hometowns and regions. Infighting between factions further spurs hints of expansion as well as the greater potential to contribute to local violence.

Due to feuds between transnational gangs and expansion into further drug trafficking territory, the Barrio Azteca is at the center of many violent crimes. The group is synonymous with its hit squads that have targeted rival drug dealers and any infringements on their territory. While the targeted killings typically occur in Juárez, the short distance to the U.S. border is a concern (Borunda, 2018a). It has been a long-standing argument at the highest levels of American governance that an increase in violent crime in Mexican border cities could theoretically overflow into cities, such as El Paso, on the U.S. periphery (Seelke, 2010, p. 7). Barrio Azteca's cross-border engagements and knowledge place them squarely in such a hostile situation. The gang has been at the center of the recent increase of homicides in Juárez; thus, such a hypothesis may not have come to fruition yet, but it is possible.

Public safety is a related concern when discussing violence surrounding *Los Barrios*. After a period of decline, authorities in Texas reinstated Barrio Azteca as a Tier 1 gang – an organization with a diverse criminal portfolio and poses the greatest security risks (Texas Department of Public Safety, p. 4). Like any other entity in the criminal underworld, Barrio Azteca has allies and rivals. Mexican cartels may conduct some oversight and direct specific actions of their affiliated gangs; however, disputes between prison or street gangs on U.S. territory develop completely domestically and for local motives. Besides their discussed cartel relationships, Barrio Azteca is reported to have recent association with individual cliques of Mara Salvatrucha (MS-13) and the Mexican Mafia (Fechter, 2016). On the other hand, gang rivals include Tango Blast, Los Mexicles, and recently, groups affiliated with the Sureños.

The situation with the Sureños is problematic as they have expanded their presence in the El Paso area and thus come in direct conflict with the interests of Barrio Azteca (Texas Department of Public Safety, 2014, p.21). Furthermore, the recent slaying of an Azteca by a Tango Blast member in a drive-by shooting, initiated by a dispute over "street taxes" collected from drug dealers (Borunda, 2018b), displays the customary use of haphazard executions conducted in public view. These are not cases of cross-border violence spilling over into the United States but rather, gang violence, spurred by the domestic drug trade, inherent in American cities. The risk of internal violent crime linked to transnational gangs with nationwide breadth is an obvious concern for those tasked with ensuring domestic security. Barrio Azteca emerges as a transnational gang that still retains a local focus which, in turn, generates concerns for public safety.

Difficulties in Managing the Threat

Combating prison and street gangs remains a difficult endeavor; however, it becomes beyond average difficulty when specific gangs are transnational and have associations with larger criminal syndicates. Management of the Barrio Azteca risk is complicated for all levels of U.S. law enforcement and federal agencies. Cooperation between federal agencies, including the FBI, Drug Enforcement Agency (DEA) and Department of Homeland Security, and local policing resulted in a decline of Barrio Azteca influence between 2010 and 2015 (Price, 2015). This weakening transpired at the same time as other gangs increased their presence in the Barrio Azteca territory. A subsequent resurgence of the gang demonstrates their resiliency and commitment to remaining a key factor in the cross-border and domestic criminal environment.

Dual Mexican–American citizenship and permanent residency statuses of Barrio Azteca membership provided them with opportunities to commit crimes in one jurisdiction and conveniently cross the border to hide out. Such an arrangement obviously complicates the ability of policing agencies to track down and detain suspects during criminal investigations. This variable was deemed beneficial by cartels and their reliance on transnational gangs to carry out execution orders or traffic drugs. For example, the *Capo*, or highest-ranking member of Barrio Azteca, Eduardo Ravelo, who remained on the FBI's Most Wanted List until his capture in June 2018, is reported to have given orders from Juárez but would routinely transit the U.S. border (InSight Crime, 2018). There may be other street and prison gangs to choose from in the contemporary criminal frameworks, but Barrio Azteca remains the most notorious for this quality.

Incarceration does not encumber operations of the Barrio Azteca, and this remains an assured difficulty in managing the threat emanating from them. At their roots, they are a potent prison gang that boasts extensive membership in the correctional system. It can be surmised that leadership and its members are as comfortable conducting business from within the constraints of prison as they are operating on the streets of El Paso. The reliance on placing gang affiliates in restrictive housing has proven constructive in neutralizing a sizable portion of institutional gang violence (Pyrooz, 2018). However, this practice does not prevent Barrio Azteca leaders from continued communication with their affiliates. Most members composing Barrio Azteca leadership positions are already incarcerated and exploit contraband cell phones, coded letters, and interactions with visitors to direct orders in the free world (InSight Crime, 2018). As a result, the gang remains challenging to gang units and gang intelligence in the domestic security framework.

Sizable membership and the typical decentralization of transnational gangs add to the complications of neutralizing the Barrio Azteca risk too. Simply put, a larger gang with associates nationwide creates a significant problem for policing. The Barrio Azteca continued to have a presence, even though their influence waned a few short years ago, because they remained one of the most active groups. These numbers remain an attractive point for Mexican DTOs seeking endless human capital to act as a franchise on American soil (Bunker, 2010, p.13). Nevertheless, large membership and changing allegiances mean that the possible decentralization of the Barrio Azteca creates an additional setback for U.S. authorities. Barrio Azteca has experienced former members exchanging loyalties and then targeting *Los Barrios* in violent crime (Borunda, 2018c). Situations such as these instigate low-level yet deadly and drawn-out violence on American streets. The unpredictable lifecycles and triggers of larger gangs like the Barrio Azteca thus require attention when discussing matters of national public safety.

Conclusion

From their origins as an El Paso-based prison gang, the Barrio Azteca steadily gained influence and a foothold in the narcotics trafficking business along the West Texas border with Mexico. They strategically aligned with larger Mexican DTOs, such as the Juárez Cartel, and expanded their criminal portfolio as a result. While their cross-border criminal enterprises attract attention from top levels of U.S. law enforcement, their impact on the destabilization of issues connected to domestic security must be paramount. Concerns over a spillover of cartel and gang-related violence in Ciudad Juárez is a plausible concern. Furthermore, feuds with rivals over territory within the United States cause an alarm as it places the general public in harm's way. As a result, Barrio Azteca exhibits a two-pronged security threat: their transnational ties and internal foothold within areas in the United States. Barrio Azteca's sophisticated membership, custom of extreme violence, and ease operating out of the prison system supports the notion that they are a problematic factor in maintaining security along the U.S. southern border.

Further Reading

Payan, T. (2016). *The Three U.S.-Mexico Border Wars: Drugs, Immigration and Homeland Security*. Santa Barbara, CA.: Praeger.

Shirk, D. (2014). A Tale of Two Mexican Border Cities: The Rise and Decline of Drug Violence in Juárez and Tijuana. *Journal of Borderlands Studies* 29(4), pp. 481–502.

Skarbek, D. (2014). *The Social Order of the Underworld: How Prison Gangs Govern the American Penal System*. Oxford, U.K.: Oxford University Press.

References

Aguilar, J. (2018, August 22). Just a Shot Away? Ciudad Juárez Residents Fear New Cartel War May Be Coming. *The Texas Tribune*. https://www.texastribune.org/2018/08/22/ciudad-juarez-residents-fear-new-cartel-war-may-be-coming/

Borunda, D. (2018a, April 24). Chuco Tango Gang Member Pleads Guilty in El Paso Shooting Murder of Barrio Azteca Rival. *El Paso Times*. https://www.elpasotimes.com/story/news/crime/2018/04/24/chuco-tango-gang-member-alejandro-leal-guilty-shooting-murder-barrio-azteca/542475002/

Borunda, D. (2018b, June 29). Juárez, Mexico, Sees Rise in Deaths as Cartel, Gang Violence Flares. *El Paso Times*. https://www.elpasotimes.com/story/news/local/juarez/2018/06/29/juarez-mexico-border-city-murders-rise-violent-crime-june-2018/743653002/

Borunda, D. (2018c, May 25). Juárez Police Arrest Alleged Gang Leader Accused of Double-Cross Fueling Mexico Violence. *El Paso Times*. https://www.elpasotimes.com/story/news/local/juarez/2018/05/25/barrio-azteca-gang-leader-double-cross-juarez-mexico-homicides-violence/641927002/

Brackin, S., Cole, J., Wesley, H., Penza-Guzman, C., Schroeder, R., Taylor, J. & Young, M. (2012). *U.S. Southwest Border Security: An Operational Approach*. Fort Leavenworth, KS: U. S. Army Command and General Staff College. https://apps.dtic.mil/docs/citations/ADA566062

Bunker, R. (2010). Strategic Threat: Narcos and Narcotics Overview. *Small Wars and Insurgencies*. 21(1), pp. 8–29.

Fechter, J. (2016). February 23) 10 Facts about the Barrio Azteca, One of the Most Dangerous Gangs in Texas. *San Antonio Express-News*. https://www.mysanantonio.com/news/us-world/border-mexico/article/Barrio-Azteca-Texas-gang-cartel-6847499.php

Federal Bureau of Investigations. (2011a) 2011 National Gang Threat Assessment. https://www.fbi.gov/stats-services/publications/2011-national-gang-threat-assessment

Federal Bureau of Investigations. (2011b, March 9) Federal, State and Local Law Enforcement Round Up Barrio Azteca Members. https://archives.fbi.gov/archives/elpaso/press-releases/2011/federal-state-and-local-law-enforcement-round-up-barrio-azteca-members

Gill, J. (2018, December 18). Barrio Azteca Makes Resurgence as Top Gang Threat in Texas. *Houston Chronicle*. https://www.chron.com/news/houston-texas/houston/article/Barrio-Azteca-makes-resurgence-as-top-gang-threat-13471487.php

Guerrero-Gutiérrez, E. (2011). *Security, Drugs and Violence in Mexico: A Survey*. Mexico City: Lantia Consultores.

InSight Crime. (2018, July 9). Barrio Azteca. *InSightCrime.org*. https://www.insightcrime.org/mexico-organized-crime-news/barrio-azteca-profile/

Jackson, S. (2015). Terror in Mexico: Why Designating Mexican Cartels as Terrorist Organizations Eases Prosecution of Drug Traffickers Under the Narcoterrorism Statute. *National Security Law Journal* 4(1), pp. 83–125.

Price, C. (2015, September 2). HSI: Barrio Azteca Presence Diminishes Due to Law Enforcement Efforts. *KFox14*. https://kfoxtv.com/news/crime-news/hsi-barrio-azteca-presence-diminishes-due-to-law-enforcement-efforts

Pyrooz, D. (2018). Using Restrictive Housing to Manage Gangs in U.S. Prisons. *Corrections Today*. July/August 2018, pp. 10–13.

Seelke, C. (2010). *Mexico-U.S. Relations: Issues for Congress*. Washington, D.C.: Congressional Research Service.

Stewart, S. (2018, September 25). What Happens When a Major Mexican Cartel Leader Falls? *Stratford*. https://worldview.stratfor.com/article/what-happens-when-major-mexican-cartel-leader-falls

Sullivan, J. (2014, March 26). Narco-Cities: Mexico and Beyond. *Small Wars Journal*. https://smallwarsjournal.com/jrnl/art/narco-cities-mexico-and-beyond

Texas Department of Public Safety. (2014, April). *Texas Gang Threat Assessment*. https://www.dps.texas.gov/director_staff/media_and_communications/2014/txGangThreatAssessment.pdf

Texas Department of Public Safety. (2018, November). *Texas Gang Threat Assessment*. https://www.dps.texas.gov/director_staff/media_and_communications/2018/txGangThreatAssessment201811.pdf

Udell, I. (2010). *Defeating the Narco-Insurgency Within the United States*. Fort Leavenworth, KS: U.S. Army Command and General Staff College. https://apps.dtic.mil/dtic/tr/fulltext/u2/a561067.pdf

United States Department of Justice. (2009). *National Drug Threat Assessment*. https://www.justice.gov/archive/ndic/pubs31/31379/31379p.pdf

United States Embassy and Consulate. (2019, January 18). *Security Alert—U.S. Consulate General Ciudad Juarez*. https://mx.usembassy.gov/security-alert-u-s-consulate-general-ciudad-juarez-3/

United States Immigration and Customs Enforcement. (2017, June 15). *National Gang Unit*. https://www.ice.gov/national-gang-unit

Woody, C. (2019, January 22). The US Has Issued a Security Alert for a Major Border City in Mexico After a Wave of Attacks on Police. *San Antonio Express-News*. https://www.mysanantonio.com/technology/businessinsider/article/The-US-has-issued-a-security-alert-for-a-major-13553606.php

Chapter 67

Beltrán-Leyva Organization (BLO)

Réjeanne M. Lacroix
University of Leicester, Leicester, United Kingdom

Contents

Introduction 505
Ascent and Decline 506
The BLO and U.S. Security 506
Decentralization and Modern Reach 508
Modern Security Threats Posed by the BLO 509
Conclusion 510
Further Reading 510
References 510

Introduction

The Beltrán-Leyva Organization (BLO) was once recognized as one of the most powerful drug trafficking organizations operating within Mexico. Effective law enforcement investigations and captures resulted in successive losses of critical leadership figures. As a result, the group decentralized and exists only in splinter groups that retain influence from their past connections and strategic alliances with powerful allies. Law enforcement and federal officials still consider these smaller operations as part of the BLO; thus, their transgressions against U.S. domestic security remain pertinent to analysis on the topic. The modern composition of the cartel continues to encroach the U.S. southern border to facilitate large-scale drug smuggling for sizable profits. It is important to analyze how the original organization, at its peak strength, achieved significant territorial reach and how newer factions benefit from this arrangement today.

DOI: 10.4324/9781315144511-71

Ascent and Decline

The BLO was founded by five brothers – Alberto, Arturo Alfredo, Carlos, and Héctor – in the Mexican state of Sinaloa. Circumstance and geography directed their immersion into drug trafficking and ascent to power. The brothers rose in the criminal subculture through originally aiding local opium producers to their later roles as violent enforcers and traffickers for leadership in other cartels. A coalition with the formidable Sinaloa Cartel and development of close familial relations with its leader, Joáquin "El Chapo" Guzmán presented advantageous opportunities to expand the clout of the BLO (InSight Crime, 2017). Access to trafficking routes into U.S. territory was one such perk.

Guzmán tasked the brothers' organization to fend off rivals, such as the Gulf Cartel, from territory and trafficking corridors held by his Sinaloa syndicate. BLO established an effective security team, with U.S. citizen Edgar "La Barbie" Valdez, commanding one faction (InSight Crime, 2017). The Beltrán-Leyva brothers proved extremely effective in infiltrating Mexican law enforcement and political officials; therefore, they augmented the influence of their cartel boss. Nevertheless, the power gained from such successful operations, as well as the wealth accumulated from the drug trade, compelled the BLO to flaunt their supremacy in the criminal underworld to the general public. This aggravated Guzmán (InSight Crime, 2017).

In 2008, the relationship between the BLO and the Sinaloa Cartel ended. The brothers believed that Guzmán provided information to Mexican law enforcement that led to the arrest of Alfredo: the BLO's leader. From this point, the two organizations engaged in a violent war. BLO subsequently formed an association with Los Zetas and the Juárez Cartel – other dangerous and powerful rivals of the Sinaloa Cartel – and benefited from their access to U.S. drug markets. This shift in power dynamics destabilized the Mexican drug trafficking environment and nature of inter-cartel relations; thus, violence erupted (Frontera NorteSur, 2010).

Mexican authorities contributed to the decline of the BLO too (Beittel, 2011, p. 18). In 2009, Arturo was killed in a shootout with Mexican Marines and Carlos was apprehended. From this point, decentralization was apparent. In an attempt to recoup the former influence of the BLO, Héctor took command of the remaining assets and called it Pacifico Sur, or South Pacific Cartel for a short while, while former enforcer Valdez took his loyalists and formed the Independent Cartel of Acapulco. The last active Beltrán-Leyva brother was subsequently arrested in 2014 and died, while incarcerated on November 18, 2018 (BBC, 2018). A leadership vacuum led Mexican authorities to deem the former powerful cartel as disbanded (Flores and Pérez, 2011); however, numerous factions remain identified as BLO to U.S. law enforcement.

The BLO and U.S. Security

Proximity to the southern border and high demand for illicit drugs in the United States present Mexican cartels with an ideal situation to engage in black market commerce. Consequently, the BLO and its activities are pertinent to U.S. domestic security assessments. At the height of their operations, they were a major supplier of illicit drugs into U.S. territory, relied on low-level street gangs in major cities for retail sales, and its membership faced repercussions from the American legal system.

The cartel actively utilized major narcotics corridors that offered deep reach into the United States. Within Arizona, the BLO moved across the Sasabe/Lukeville passage to transfer heroin, methamphetamines, and marijuana. At the same time, they shipped cocaine, heroin, and methamphetamines through the Tijuana/San Diego/Los Angeles passageway into California. The border cities of Nuevo Laredo and Laredo provided the most beneficial channel for large-scale cocaine shipments in Texas (U.S. Department of Justice, 2010, p. 9–10). Multiple accesses to U.S. points of entry and their ensuing connections to large transportation networks meant the BLO operated as a key narcotics trafficker and distributor. From this point, the organization was able to influence the volume of illicit drugs at the street level of many urban American cities. At their peak, the BLO enjoyed influence in 11 states and 30 U.S. cities (U.S. Department of Justice, p. 26).

The BLO had the connections and products to move large quantities of narcotics into the United States, but distribution and retail logistics are problematic for a group headquartered across the southern border. Other cartels created relationships with U.S. prison and street gangs to act as distribution agents as well as outsource retail sales to street level. The BLO adopted this approach and consequently expanded the reach of its distribution.

One urban area that was adversely affected by the coordinated Sinaloa and BLO cartel relationships in the mid-2000s is Chicago. The BLO was identified as a major supplier of illegal drugs in the area (U.S. Department of Justice, 2017, p. 2). While the large cartels funneled narcotics into the city, multi-layers of lower-level membership would liaise with street gangs to facilitate street-level sales. In this framework, cartel control over retail sales is limited while a clear understanding of the links between gangs and drug trafficking organizations is unclear (Woody, 2017). Such a scenario emerged in 2007 when Illinois-based Drug Enforcement Agency authorities detected a link between the Conservative Vice Lords – a street gang distinctive to the area – the BLO and Sinaloa Cartel. It was revealed through an investigation that the Vice Lords would prepare packages of millions of dollars in U.S. currency every week and transport them through Los Angeles (U.S. Department of Justice, p. 7). This scheme exhibits the national reach of the BLO but also the ease with which it operated on the U.S. mainland.

It was during this prosperous period for the BLO that U.S. authorities took note and initiated criminal cases against the Beltrán-Leyva brothers. This was an understandable outcome due to the BLO's national depth of drug trafficking network and the massive amounts of narcotics that the organization transported into U.S. territory. Héctor was indicted by Federal Grand Juries in the District of Columbia for drug trafficking in 2004 as well as the Eastern District of New York in 2009. However, the 2009 addition of the BLO, especially its then-leader Arturo, as a "kingpin," under the Foreign Narcotics Kingpin Designation Act, confirmed the domestic security issues caused by the cartel. The U.S. Treasury asserted that the BLO was at fault for smuggling multi-ton cargo, packed full of cocaine, as well as multi-kilogram packages of heroin into the United States (U.S. Treasury, 2009). These actions are important as they identify the BLO as a troublesome concern to the highest levels of U.S. governance, and thus a topic to be considered in regard to safeguarding homeland security.

The recent conviction of BLO associate Manuel Fernandez-Valencia provided insight into how large-scale smuggling ventures materialize. It was revealed that collective resources provided by the Sinaloa Cartel and BLO enabled significant amounts of narcotics to enter U.S. territory from Mexico. After a period of storage in safe houses in southern California, the illicit drugs were shipped to other parts of the country, primarily Chicago. Nevertheless, it was the scope of transportation that exhibits a vast threat for domestic security that does not necessarily evolve around the southern border. Through a sophisticated system, the trafficked drugs would be clandestinely transported by cars, buses, tractor-trailers, fishing vessels, container ships, submarines, and private aircraft (U.S. Department of Justice, 2016). Narcotics trafficking, in this case with BLO at the root, is categorically a homeland security problem encompassing land, air, and sea.

Decentralization and Modern Reach

The 2008 estrangement from the Sinaloa Cartel, and the resultant inter-cartel conflict, instigated a slow yet steady decline of the BLO. Effective Mexican law enforcement actions contributed to the death and incarceration of BLO hierarchy. A consequent leadership vacuum left an organization lacking in any sort of cohesion. Nonetheless, it is imprudent to consider the cartel as entirely defeated, as Mexican authorities publically stated. The BLO's original foundations may no longer exist as an identifiable major cartel; however, the outfit remains relevant in its contemporary formation.

Decentralization has been especially detrimental to the cartel in all its modern formats. A substantial loss of leadership personalities and experience – due to capture and assassination by law enforcement – resulted in an organization that split into numerous factions according to hierarchal loyalties. The original split between Héctor Beltrán-Leyvan and Edgar "La Barbie" Valdez Villareal caused the formation of numerous subgroups with some connection to the overall powers of the Beltrán-Leyvan Organization. These new factions often conflict with each other over territory and allegiances to new cartel bosses; however, they are still considered as part of the same BLO organization (Woody, 2017). Surviving groups continue their activities in various Mexican states, such as Guerrero, Morelos, Nayarit, and Sinaloa (U.S. Drug Enforcement Administration, 2018, p.98). For instance, organized criminal gangs La Barredora, Los Pelones (La Verdad, 2019), Los Mazatlecos (Gomez, 2017), Los Rojos (La Verdad, 2019), and Chapo Isidro Organization (FBI, 2017) are examples of BLO offshoots that remain relevant as well as entrenched in violence. It is notable to mention that Fausto Isidoro Meza, a chief drug trafficker, the namesake for Chapo Isidro, affiliated with Los Mazatlecos as well as reliable partner of Alfredo and Héctor Beltrán-Leyvan, is on the FBI's Most Wanted List. Old links to the beginnings of the BLO endure.

One BLO faction identified by U.S. officials as especially active in the cross-border narcotics trade is the Guerreros Unidos. They are a prominent force in the Mexican states of Morelos and Guerrero; however, their prior cartel connections allowed them to engage in cross-border narcotics trafficking. The Drug Enforcement Administration (DEA) asserts that this splinter of the BLO smuggles illicit drugs into U.S. territory, mainly heroin (2018, p. 98) and a large portion of the cocaine in Chicago (2017,

p. 19). Decentralization and subcontracting are apparent in this organization too. The Guerreros Unidos established their own wing – Los Tequileros – who, in turn, founded their own cell of armed special forces agents (McDonnell, 2016). Activities of numerous BLO splinter groups may be a more pressing law enforcement problem for Mexico; however, their active status validates U.S. officials' claims that the formerly strong cartel remains a hindrance to homeland security in their current arrangements.

One may question how various gangs mainly operational within Mexico can rise to the status of a domestic security concern in the United States. The ability of these smaller gangs to distribute drugs deep into the American heartland rests with their distant origins as the BLO. New-generation gangs rely on their diverse alliances with major cartels, such as Juárez, Los Zetas, and Jalisco, to gain access to drug smuggling corridors into the United States (DEA, 2018, p.98). Many of these loose coalitions were established under BLO leadership to combat the control of the Sinaloa Cartel. Linkages with these drug trafficking organizations allow the continuance of BLO-linked criminal syndicates to maintain distribution centers in Atlanta, Chicago, Los Angeles, and Phoenix. As a result, the BLO carries on its engagement with black markets across the United States from Southern California to the Gulf Coast and the Rust Belt (Woody, 2017). The cells demonstrate resiliency and the ability to network strategically to ensure their place as part of the trade of illicit drugs. Although the BLO does not operate as it did in its prior manifestation, it persists as a formidable security concern in regard to the southern U.S. border.

Modern Security Threats Posed by the BLO

It is evident that the BLO remains on the radar of U.S. law enforcement and homeland security agencies. Nevertheless, it is important to decipher in the exact ways in which it causes issues for those along the southern border and, in general, the heartland of America.

There are usually concerns that cartel-instigated violence within Mexico could potentially spillover into border cities within the United States. Factions of the BLO may be engaged in assassinations, extortion, and kidnapping in their fierce competition with rivals over territory; however, these brutalities remain strictly in specific Mexican states. As it stands in its current format, this is not a concern for those tracking the BLO. Nevertheless, BLO subgroups' complicated alliances with U.S. street gangs is precarious. As the street-level retail role in the narcotics trafficking business, retaining and gaining territory is absolute. Violence in metropolitan centers is the consequence of gangs engaged in turf wars over access to profitable points of sale. As distributors with a national reach, the BLO contributes, albeit in a distant manner, to the problems plaguing numerous American cities over illicit drugs.

A widely acknowledged domestic security concern is the narcotics trade within the United States. Human security may be a non-traditional focus of securing the homeland; however, the connection between large-scale narcotics trading and public health is evident (Swanstrom, 2007, p. 11). The use of specific narcotics, primarily opioids, has been identified as a threat to public health and safety (DEA, 2015). These threats impede on the development of community safety while draining the resources of local law enforcement agencies and those tasked with managing health care. The BLO is responsible for trafficking a significant amount of cocaine, heroin, and methamphetamines while their distribution centers have a national reach. Being sanctioned under the Kingpin Act for multi-ton and multi-kilo illicit drug shipments validates concerns that their involvement has a trickledown effect on the public health of U.S. citizens engaged in narcotics use. As such, they are one of the key contributors to the threat of human security within the United States when the effects of narcotics trafficking are analyzed.

Conclusion

The BLO once existed as a cohesive and powerful Mexican drug trafficking organization. During this period, they established their status as a major exporter of illicit drugs into U.S. territory through a variety of sophisticated means. Their nexus of distribution and storehouses in numerous U.S. cities, as well as obscure relations with street gangs, allowed their black market enterprise to attain national reach. As a result of these activities, they emerged as a perceptible threat to domestic security.

Infighting and inter-cartel rivalries that constantly plague Mexican drug trafficking organizations dealt a heavy blow to any unified interpretation of the modern BLO. Nevertheless, the factions that emerged from the original cartel have proven themselves to be just as capable to continue on the BLO's position as a major narcotic trafficking operation concentrated on the United States. New leadership and splinter groups remain just as violent and focused on financial success as their predecessors. The groups that currently represent the original perception of the BLO persist as identifiable security concerns to those agencies associated with homeland security.

It is prudent to maintain assessment of the BLO as an organization complicating security at the U.S. southern border. As long as they maintain alliances with large active cartels, such as Los Zetas and Jalisco, and they target their economic activities to north of the Mexican border, BLO splinter groups will remain relevant when scrutinizing cross-border criminal activities.

Further Reading

Buffet, H. (2019). *Our 50-State Border Crisis: How the Mexican Border Fuels the Drug Epidemic Across America*. New York, NY: Hachette.

Dickenson, M. (2014). The Impact of Leadership Removal on Mexican Drug Trafficking Organizations. *Journal of Quantitative Criminology*. 30(4), pp. 651–676.

Jones, N. (2016). *Mexico's Illicit Drug Networks and the State Reaction*. Washington, DC: Georgetown University Press.

References

'El Chapo' Rival Héctor Beltrán Leyva Dies in Jail. (2018, November 19). *BBC*. https://www.bbc.com/news/world-latin-america-46261159

Beittel, J. (2011) *Mexico's Drug Trafficking Organizations: Source and Scope of the Rising Violence*. Washington, DC: Congressional Research Service.

BLO. (2017, February 16). *InSight Crime*. https://www.insightcrime.org/mexico-organized-crime-news/beltran-leyva-organization-profile/

Cae integrante de "Los Rojos" en Morelos. (2019, January 2). *La Verdad*. https://laverdadnoticias.com/crimen/Cae-integrante-de-Los-Rojos-en-Morelos-20190102-0062.html

Federal Bureau of Investigation. (2017, September 27). *Fausto Isidro Meza Flores*. https://www.fbi.gov/wanted/cei/fausto-isidro-meza-flores

Flores, E. & Pérez, J. (2011, October 16). Cae "El Marranero", jefe de los Beltrán Leyva en Guerrero. *Proceso*. https://www.proceso.com.mx/284543

Frontera NorteSur (2010). Drug Wars in Tamaulipas: Cartels vs. Zetas vs. the Military. *Mexidata*. http://www.mexidata.info/id2570.html

Gomez, S. (2017, December 14). Los Mazatlecos Gang Hang 3 Men From Bridge In Mexico Along Message To Rivals. *Latin Times*. https://www.latintimes.com/los-mazatlecos-gang-hang-3-men-bridge-mexico-along-message-rivals-graphic-content-429230

Iban por los jefes de 'La Barredora' y 'Los Pelones' en Cancún; escaparon. (2019, January 14). *La Verdad*. https://laverdadnoticias.com/crimen/Iban-por-los-jefes-de-La-Barredora-y-Los-Pelones-en-Cancun-escaparon-20190114-0109.html

McDonnell, P. (2016, December 17). In One Small Mexican Town, the Citizens Become Armed Vigilantes to Take On a Drug Gang. *Los Angeles Times*. https://www.latimes.com/world/mexico-americas/la-fg-mexico-guerrero-standoff-20161216-story.html

Swanstrom, N. (2007). The Narcotics Trade: A Threat to Security? National and Transnational Implications. *Global Crime*. 8(1), pp. 1–25.

United States Department of Justice. (2010, May). *Mexican Drug Trafficking Organizations: Developments Impacting the United States*. https://wikileaks.org/gifiles/attach/133/133198_100521%20MX%20DTOs%20-%20Developments%20Affecting%20the%20US2010-Q0317-002.pdf

United States Department of Justice. (2016, December 1). *High-Ranking Member of Two Mexican Drug Cartels Sentenced to 27 Years in U.S. Prison for Shipping Narcotics to Chicago*. https://www.justice.gov/usao-ndil/pr/high-ranking-member-two-mexican-drug-cartels-sentenced-27-years-us-prison-shipping-0

United States Department of Justice and Police Department of Chicago. (2017, May). *Cartels and Gangs in Chicago*. https://www.dea.gov/documents/2017/06/01/cartels-and-gangs-chicago

United States Department of Justice Drug Enforcement Administration. (2015, July). *United States: Areas of Influence of Major Mexican Transnational Criminal Organizations*. https://www.dea.gov/sites/default/files/2018-07/dir06515.pdf

United States Department of Justice Drug Enforcement Administration. (2018, October). *2018 National Drug Threat Assessment*. https://www.dea.gov/sites/default/files/2018-11/DIR-032-18%202018%20NDTA%20final%20low%20resolution.pdf

United States Department of the Treasury. (2009, December 3). *Treasury Designates Individuals and Companies Tied To Beltran Leyva Organization Under the Kingpin Act*. https://www.treasury.gov/press-center/press-releases/Pages/tg426.aspx

Woody, C. (2017, October 25). Here's Where Mexican Drug Cartels Operate in the US, According to the DEA. *Business Insider*. https://www.businessinsider.com/where-do-mexican-drug-cartels-operate-in-the-us-2017-10

Chapter 68

Border Patrols and National Entry Points

Jason R. Jolicoeur
Washburn University, Topeka, KS, United States

Contents

Introduction 513
Background 514
Border Integrity 514
Border Patrols and National Entry Points 515
Border Patrols 516
Criticisms and Condemnations 519
Future Directions 521
Conclusion 522
Further Reading 523
References 523

Introduction

The events of 09/11 dramatically changed law enforcement and homeland security practices in the United States and elsewhere. As part of these changes, border patrols and national entry points took on an increasingly significant role in broader homeland security initiatives and strategies. As these strategies have evolved, border patrol agencies have increasingly been given greater authority and responsibility for monitoring and controlling national entry points and establishing national borders. However, guaranteeing the absolute integrity of national borders is a virtually impossible task that is beyond the responsibility and control of any one given agency, organization, or nation. As a result, greater cooperation and collaboration have been

DOI: 10.4324/9781315144511-72

necessitated. Efforts of this nature have conceptually contributed to a broader global coalition focused on threat identification and risk minimization. At the international level, this transition has tended to blur the concept of national borders and revised how individual nations understand domestic security threats. Within individual nations, this transition has mandated increased cooperation between agencies that have traditionally lacked a cohesive approach or common objective. Collectively, these factors have required organizational realignments, as evidenced by the creation of the Department of Homeland Security in the United States, and a revised understanding of the border protection concept, as illustrated by an increased focus on the intelligence gathering. Change is likely to become a constant in the realm of homeland security, influencing both border patrol agencies and national entry point protection efforts as contexts change, threats evolve, and protective strategies are transformed in an effort to provide greater security.

Background

Border patrols and national points of entry have become an increasingly prominent factor in American domestic security efforts during the course of the last several decades. Concerns regarding the threats associated with unprotected borders have driven broader uncertainties related to the threats posed by both terrorism and more traditional forms of criminal activity. Some (Longo, 2018) have noted that border security has become an evolving contemporary societal obsession. In spite of the relatively broad public concerns regarding issues of this nature, there is no universal agreement regarding the best means of approaching the management of border patrols and national entry points from a public policy standpoint. This lack of consensus is underscored by the growing public discord associated with national immigration policies and the related manner in which national borders are policed and those entering the country illegally are managed by immigration authorities. Given the many conflicting views associated with the management of border patrols and national points of entry, these factors will likely continue to be an important and contested public policy aspect of national security strategies well into the foreseeable future. At the same time, the manner in which they are understood and operationalized will likely continue to evolve against a backdrop of ever-increasing broader societal change.

Border Integrity

The events of 9/11 have unequivocally served to intensify the societal and governmental focus on border integrity in the United States (Brill, 2003; Longo, 2018; Riley, 2005). Perhaps more interestingly, the magnitude of these attacks has also resulted in an enhanced focus on border integrity in other countries (Karlsson 2012). Traditional assumptions have held that secure borders are necessary to maintain territorial integrity, but the events of 09/11 underscored in the minds of many their significance in regard to the preservation of national security as it relates to threats emanating from extremist groups and terrorist attacks.

The events of 09/11 are certainly not the only factors that have contributed to an increased focus on border integrity since the dawn of the 20th century. Concerns related to a variety of other factors have also contributed to this increased focus, including global conflicts (Shaw-Taylor, 2012), alcohol prohibition (Funderberg, 2014), drug distribution (Payan, 2016), criminal activity (Manaut, 2013), organized crime groups (Buscaglia & Gonzalez-Ruiz, 2006), human trafficking (Longo 2018), and illegal immigration (Roberts, Alden, & Whitley, 2013). Collectively, these factors have contributed to what some (Longo, 2018) have referred as a national obsession in the United States associated with ensuring the integrity of American borders. However, the most effective approach to securing borders remains unclear and disagreement remains concerning whether any approach will ever prove to be fully effective. Furthermore, attempts to implement revised approaches to border security have only contributed to a growing national debate regarding the development and creation of broader public policy responses associated with ensuring the sovereign integrity of national borders.

Border Patrols and National Entry Points

Any attempts to effectively secure national borders must necessarily involve the identification and prioritization of national entry points. Once this has occurred, a cohesive policy of patrolling the identified areas through which illegal entry can occur must be created. National entry points might best be defined as any location through which the integrity of national borders can be breached. Typically, the many different possible types of national entry points are divided between those that are official or recognized, such as airports, water ports, and monitored land crossings, and those that are unofficial or informal, such as unmonitored water ports or land crossings. A comprehensive border patrol strategy will attempt to incorporate strategies to control both types of entry points, albeit oftentimes by different means. Oftentimes, unofficial entry points will be protected by physical barriers and passive obstacles, such as fences or walls, whereas official entry points will make use of these devices in addition to onsite human monitoring. While technology has revolutionized homeland security efforts in general, it has been especially influential in changing how unofficial national entry points are secured. Cameras, remote sensing technologies, unmanned drones, biometric technologies, thermal imaging devices, and advanced radar systems have dramatically changed the manner in which unofficial entry points are monitored and secured (Martin, 2015). However, technology has not replaced the need for human monitoring in the form of physical border patrols as the use of technology will ultimately always occur in concert with human monitoring and response.

Borders might best be understood as marking identifiable points of departure or transition from one area or defined space to another. The border theoretically provides a manner of identifying territorial boundaries that are based primarily on political distinctions (Johnson & Jones, 2014). Oftentimes, these boundaries fall largely along preexisting geographic features, such as rivers or mountain ranges, or in relation to the racial and ethnic identities or divisions of local or regional populations. While borders are most frequently associated with marking national boundaries, the concept need not be this restrictive. Over time, additional broader ideals regarding the border concept have been envisioned and applied (Johnson & Jones, 2014). Other ways of understanding the border concept have focused on common collective interests that can transcend geographic or political boundaries, such as common economic or religious interests. However, these evolving strategies must necessarily recognize that even efforts to understand borders in the very broadest or abstract sense must ultimately be capable of recognizing the more pragmatic aspects associated with the geopolitical realities of contemporary global society. When understood from this standpoint, the significance of national borders becomes clearer, as does the necessity of border patrols as at least one possible means of ensuring the integrity and security of these national boundaries.

Border patrols were developed as a means of providing the personnel, resources, and expertise needed to monitor borders and prevent unauthorized passage through either official or unofficial points of entry. The ultimate objective of border patrol agencies or organizations around the globe is to guarantee territorial integrity while carrying out and enforcing established immigration policies. Additionally, these agencies are increasingly an instrumental part of the implementation of broader national security efforts intended to bolster homeland security initiatives.

Border Patrols

In the United States, most federal agencies involved in border security were consolidated under the Department of Homeland Security after the terrorist attack on September 11, 2001 (Koestler-Grack, 2007). Three of the highest profile domestic security agencies integrated into the Department of Homeland Security (Customs and Border Protection, Immigrations and Customs Enforcement, and the Transportation Security Administration) were collectively placed in the Directorate of Border and Transportation Security (Haddal, 2009). United States Border Patrol is the branch of Customs and Border Protection charged with the provision of uniformed law enforcement (Koestler-Grack, 2007). As the primary law enforcement agency of Customs and Border Protection, it has a definitive frontline influence on the manner in which American borders and national entry points are secured.

As of 2012, U.S. Border Patrol had more than 20,000 agents working in the field (Schroeder, 2012). While these agents are split between America's northern and southern borders and other national entry points, a vastly disproportionate number of all agents are stationed along the United States border with Mexico (Nunez-Neto, 2005). The United States Border Patrol continually faces competition from other agencies for quality employees, so it has undertaken a recruitment strategy involving perpetual outreach through advertising for employees, engaging colleges and universities, participating in career fairs, and trying to recruit transitional military employees (Homeland Security, 2015). Those individuals hired for service with the border patrol attend a residential law enforcement training academy at the Federal Law Enforcement Training Center (FLETC) in Artesia, NM. After the initial training academy, those new agents lacking requisite language skills are sent to an additional language apprehension school (Logan, 2012).

While laudable, the mandate charged to new border patrol agents in the United States and elsewhere after they complete their training is likely an intractable task for a variety of reasons (Schroeder, 2012). Perhaps most importantly, efforts to provide total border security may prove futile because nations are simply unable to provide human oversight at all possible entry points, given the reality of finite fiscal and manpower resources. While physical barriers and other target-hardening measures can complement and expand the reach of human oversight, these efforts are not totally without their own unique set of limitations. Furthermore, the task assigned to contemporary border patrol agencies is simply too broad in scope. For instance, the northern border of the United States alone extends for more than 4,000 miles and covers a vast array of different types of geography, much of which is very isolated and difficult to reach (Ward, Kiernan, & Mabrey, 2006). The mountain ranges and water features along the northern border make ensuring total border security an almost impossible task, and this is only one of two major U.S. borders. While the lack of total border security is a substantive problem in more affluent countries, such as the United States, it is an even more significant issue in countries with fewer fiscal resources given the expense associated with contemporary border security efforts.

As a result of the realization that total border security and complete territorial integrity are a virtual impossibility, most contemporary border patrol organizations have adopted an official policy that focuses of risk minimization (Schroeder, 2012). In essence, risk minimization efforts attempt to curtail the threat posed to national interests and public safety by border violations. This is a broad threat given the criminal activity, terrorism risks, and human costs that are oftentimes associated with illegal border crossings. Border patrol organizations attempt to ameliorate problems of this nature by securing the border to the greatest degree possible through a coordinated set of preventative tactics, targeted enforcement, intelligence synthesis, and general deterrence. Collectively, efforts of this nature are implemented in an effort to discourage all but the most motivated individuals or organizations from future attempts to violate the integrity of national borders. Additional tactics and measures can be associated with global risk minimization efforts, all of which are influenced by local, regional, and national priorities and preferences to a large degree.

Preventative tactics involve a variety of strategies that are commonly associated with Crime Prevention Through Environmental Design (CPTED). While CPTED principles are most strongly associated with domestic crime prevention, many can also be readily applied to ongoing border control efforts (Atlas, 2013). For instance, perceptions of the risks associated with surveillance and greater visibility can be enhanced through the use of video cameras (formal surveillance) and the removal of vegetation and shrubbery at commonly used border crossings (natural surveillance). Even the mere presence of fences and border crossing checkpoints can provide boundary definition and support territorial reinforcement which may deter some violations (Atlas, 2013). Collectively, CPTED principles are thought to contribute to reductions in targeted behaviors through the manipulation and control of the physical environment. In the case of border security, control can refer to the manipulation of the physical characteristics of natural entry points in order to make illegal entry efforts more formidable. Doing so is thought to discourage all but the most strongly motivated violators, thereby reducing the likelihood of border integrity violations.

Targeted enforcement is closely related to broader deterrence efforts and involves the use of border patrol resources to enforce immigration policies in an attempt to identify and arrest those attempting to violate them. The arrests, deportations, and potential for criminal prosecution associated with enforcement are thought to provide an example that can contribute to both general and specific deterrence. Contemporary targeted enforcement practices involve the regular assignment of border patrol representatives to common official and unofficial entry points and the sporadic application of saturation patrols at problematic locations. Targeted enforcement efforts have become a lynchpin of United States Border Patrol risk minimization efforts as evidenced by the 900,000 border apprehensions that were made by U.S. Border Patrol agents in 2003 alone (Riley, 2005).

Efforts such as the U.S. Border Patrol's Hold the Line and Operation Gatekeeper provide examples of saturation patrol that involve the use of large numbers of border patrol agents in El Paso, TX, and San Diego, CA. These operations provided a show of force that was thought to successfully reduce subsequent apprehensions for border crossing violations (Schroeder, 2012). In spite of successes of this nature with saturation patrol and targeted enforcement, displacement remains a significant concern. Simply put, displacement refers to the redistribution of a given behavior or activity from one location to another after efforts to control that behavior or activity are introduced. Displacement is an ongoing potential issue with enforcement efforts of virtually any type and it is a factor that must be accounted for across the various branches of the criminal justice system. However, given the scope, size, and nature of the American border and the broad charges assigned to border patrol agencies, displacement is perhaps a more pertinent and complicated issue in this particular setting.

Finally, intelligence synthesis is becoming an increasingly common tool used by border patrol agencies and agents as a means of identifying high-risk individuals, locations, dates, and targets. These efforts can assist with ongoing operations intended to concentrate limited resources on those individuals and locations that pose the greatest threat to border integrity and the threat from the criminal activity that is sometimes associated with border violations. Efforts of this nature have frequently involved a layered process where intelligence needs are identified and prioritized before relevant data is gathered, collected, analyzed, and disseminated (Goldman & Maret, 2016). At the conclusion of this process, intelligence information thought to be most critical can be directly applied to ongoing border patrol operations in an attempt to ensure border integrity at both official and unofficial entry points. As a part of the collection process, collaboration and information sharing involving multiple agencies is a critical consideration. This collaborative process involves creating partnerships both within a given country as well as between different nations. For instance, U.S. Customs and Border Protection has created intelligence partnerships with other federal, state, and local agencies, as well as agencies in other countries, such as Canada and Mexico (Rosas, 2006). The advent and development of fusion centers, which provide a common forum for information and intelligence sharing between federal and state governmental agencies, provides an excellent illustration of collaborative efforts of this nature.

Expanded collaboration with other countries and the relevant border patrol agencies within these countries not only benefits the intelligence-gathering process but also contributes to the process of risk minimization by increasing the efficacy of preventative efforts. As part of ongoing risk management strategies, the United States has endeavored to expand its borders outward, rather than viewing them as ending in conjunction with national territorial limits. Cooperation with other countries has allowed the United States to further immigration and national security policies outside of its national borders. In doing so, the force of U.S. police can be carried elsewhere, and individuals who pose a threat to national interests can be identified well before they attempt to enter the country. Furthermore, these partnerships have improved relationships by increasing both the quantity and quality of intelligence gathered and shared, which can in turn contribute to improving the enforcement efforts of border patrols and reducing the likelihood of unauthorized passage through national entry points.

Expanding national borders has become increasingly important as technology has dramatically increased the availability and ease of travel, allowing greater global mobility than has ever before been the case. This dramatic increase in travel and global migration has ushered in what some have referred to as a "golden age of mobility" (Elliott & Urry, 2010, p. ix). This change, when coupled with rapidly advancing technologies in other areas, has brought with it not only exceptional opportunities for growth and development but also substantive risks for previously unprecedented dangers. In terms of homeland security practice, this has necessitated in the minds of many the need for a buffer zone to allow border patrol agencies more time to adequately understand and respond to potential threats while addressing them from a great distance. This enhances the ability of border patrol agencies not only to prepare effectively for threats but also to respond to them in a timely manner. Additionally, the creation of multiple layers of review and evaluation, at the international; national, and local levels, increases the likelihood that those intending to engage in hostile acts are identified before they are able to do so.

Criticisms and Condemnations

An enhanced reliance on border patrols as a means of ensuring the integrity of national entry points is likely an inevitable consequence of contemporary global developments. However, this does not mean that there is a universal agreement regarding the manner in which enhanced border security strategies should be implemented and carried out. On the contrary, many would question both the efficacy and ethicality of the strategies currently being used in many countries. This is especially true of the immigration control strategies that are associated with American immigration policies and the related border patrol efforts to secure national entry points. As a result, conflict regarding these issues has emerged, underscoring the lack of national consensus that currently characterizes national immigration control efforts. Disagreements of this nature may well influence the future course of homeland security efforts pertaining to border security in the United States and elsewhere. As a result, it is best to view related policies as fluid and evolving rather than fixed and stagnant. Criticisms of existing strategies tend to focus on either the effectiveness of contemporary immigration control policies or the ethical nature of the manner in which those policies are implemented.

There are a number of factors that are thought to undermine the effectiveness of contemporary border security efforts. Perhaps most significantly, many have questioned the underlying efficacy of increasingly restrictive immigration policies, which necessitate more punitive systemic responses as reflected by border patrol practices at national entry points. It should be noted that not everyone agrees with the assertion that immigration policies have become increasingly more restrictive over time (Czaika & de Haas, 2016). However, research does seem to indicate that policies have become increasingly more restrictive, in at least some countries. Researchers have noted that countries like Australia, Canada, and Germany relaxed their immigration policies at the conclusion of the 20th century, while countries like Denmark, Japan, and the United States tightened theirs (Mayda & Patel, 2004; Ortega & Peri, 2009). Critics contend that if many countries are able to remain comparatively safe and secure without constrictive immigration policies, there is no real mandate for other countries to implement them. However, advocates of more restrictive policies claim that they are effective in achieving greater security and reducing illegal immigration. Research results regarding the efficacy of conservative immigration policies remain a disputed issue (Czaika & de Haas, 2013) with some evidence indicating that they are effective (Bonjour, 2011; Broeders & Engbersen, 2007) and others indicating that they have failed (Bhagwati, 2003; Cornelius, Takeyuki, Martin, & Hollifield, 2004).

Critics contend that research results indicating the general ineffectiveness of restrictive immigration policies are to be expected for a number of reasons. Perhaps most significantly, this is because they are thought to be based largely on the underlying concept of full enforcement or universal protection. In practice, this assumption is problematic given that resources are finite and cannot support all of the human and material needs (border patrol personnel and equipment, secure detention spaces for violators, etc.) required to prevent all immigration violations (Riley, 2005). Even if unlimited resources were available, a strategy focused exclusively on enforcement is problematic given that there are policy and legal limitations on the actions of enforcement agents. For instance, constitutional protections and legal precedents create safeguards that constrain the exercise of power among American law enforcement and border patrol agents. This lack of full authority undermines the ability of officers to exercise the unlimited authority that would inevitably be needed for a full enforcement strategy to be successful (Czaika & de Haas, 2016; Hollifield, 1992). Additionally, critics have noted that an enforcement focus that centers exclusively on external illegal entry is overly narrow and overlooks other important pools of individuals from whom threats may emanate. For example, it is estimated that there are approximately 400,000 orders for deportation in existence for individuals who originally entered the United States legally but then violated their conditions of entry resulting in their being in the country illegally (Riley, 2005).

Theoretical concerns regarding the implementation of restrictive immigration policies have also been voiced. Concerns of this nature are based on beliefs that enforcement-focused immigration policies will ultimately prove futile regardless of how well they are implemented because they are based on a fraudulent assumption. More specifically, they are based on the assumption that shows of force will deter those considering illegal entry. Critics contend that this orientation underestimates the influence of the causal factors motivating illegal entry attempts. Factors such as labor market deterioration, extreme poverty, religious or ethnic persecution, natural disasters, and violent conflicts generate strong motivations for migration that may not be checked by the threat of enforcement action (Burgmann, 2016). Others have theorized that once migrant communities in a given country (legal or illegal) become well established, they create a self-perpetuating cycle of migration. Familial networks, employer needs, and the requirements of the industry created to facilitate immigration create a collective sense of synergy that mandates continued immigration. To maintain the established immigrant community, and those entities and organizations that rely on this community, continual immigration must occur. This will inevitably be accomplished through illegal means if legal options are not available, regardless of the formal barriers that are put in place in an attempt to curtail it (Castles, 2004). While many criticisms have been directed at the practices of contemporary border patrol agencies, supporters contend that the future holds opportunities for dramatic growth and improvement in these agencies.

Future Directions

A number of suggestions for future directions pertaining to border patrol practices related to national entry points have been advanced. Suggestions of this nature necessarily involve the immigration policies that influence these border patrol practices. Suggestions of this nature are meant to ameliorate perceived limitations of existing strategies and tend to focus on either pragmatic or conceptual concerns or issues. Conceptually, advocates of reform believe that it is important to strive for a broader consensus regarding the limitations of a single approach to ameliorating national security threats. More specifically, many believe that reducing security threats in an increasingly global world is the collective responsibility of military, intelligence, criminal justice, and homeland security agencies (McElmurry, Kerr, Brown, & Zamora, 2016). Additionally, conceptual revisions to the manner in which "effectiveness" is operationalized and measured, as it applies to immigration policies, have been suggested (Czaika & de Haas, 2013). If countries are to implement truly effective immigration policies, they must have access to valid and reliable research results. Results of this nature cannot be obtained without high-quality research that relies on appropriate empirical approaches and accurate assessment strategies. When this type of research is obtained, it will allow for the focused distribution of available fiscal resources in the most effective manner. Perhaps more importantly, improperly framed or poorly implemented research contributes to erroneous findings that may be overly positive or pessimistic, resulting in specious public policy development (Czaika & de Haas, 2013).

Pragmatic strategies to improve the efficacy of public policy responses to illegal immigration have focused on the creation of inclusive and substantive partnerships. These efforts have included both systemic partnerships with other law enforcement, immigration, and border patrol agencies and informal partnerships with immigrant communities and local residents. Partnerships of this nature are thought to facilitate greater support, engagement, and cooperation both formally and informally, resulting in improved systemic performance. As part of this process, greater transparency and improved information dissemination channels have been suggested (McElmurry et al., 2016). These efforts are thought to provide border patrol agencies with an enhanced ability to gather necessary intelligence, improve community relations, and better engage all relevant stakeholders and partners. While suggestions for improving intervention strategies at national entry points are certainly important, advocates of reform also note that these efforts must be accompanied by a more focused attempt to understand the holistic nature of contemporary threats to national security.

To provide a more accurate depiction of all possible threats, suggestions have been advanced regarding the creation of systemic practices that will be better able to track the entry and exit of legal immigrants. It is thought that these efforts will result in an improved ability to identify those immigrants that have violated the privileges associated with their conditional entry, causing them to fall under an illegal status. At the same time that more accurate depictions of both internal and external immigrant populations are being sought, advocates of change have sought to expand legal immigration programs in an effort to reduce the broader flow of illegal immigration being driven by humanitarian crisis and economic need (McElmurry et al., 2016). This expansion is thought to be especially important in relation to temporary entry programs for workers given the influence that financial need has on the decision to violate immigration policies (Rinne, 2012). When combined with the improved tracking measures that are mentioned above, this will result in less frequent violations of national entry points and an enhanced ability to identify relevant individuals when violations do occur. Collectively, efforts of this nature, both pragmatic and conceptual, may help improve border control efforts. In doing so, it is hoped that they will also facilitate the ongoing development of immigration policies and systemic practices that are both more effective and less controversial.

Conclusion

Border patrols have become a common feature of the immigration control policies of many countries around the globe. Charged with ensuring the integrity of both official and unofficial natural entry points and protecting the national security of the countries that they represent, border patrol agencies are charged with a formidable task and face a variety of substantive challenges. Many of the challenges facing contemporary border patrols pertain to the immigration policies that they are instrumental in helping to facilitate and implement. Controversies regarding the nature of these policies necessarily encompass ongoing border patrol operations and contribute to broader societal discord. In the United States, this debate is particularly acute in relation to what many believe are overly restrictive or unnecessarily permissive immigration policies. Research has been inconclusive in regard to whether restrictive policies are able to effectively facilitate greater national security and a reduction in violations of the integrity of national borders. The resolution of this ambiguity will require additional time and resources, along with accompanying refinements in applicable research methodologies. In the meantime, there is widespread agreement that improvements in immigration policies and border patrol practices can be facilitated through a variety of conceptual, theoretical, and pragmatic efforts. Ultimately, the oversight and patrol of national entry points are likely to remain a somewhat controversial topic that is subject to a variety of broader ethical, social, religious, and political convictions and interpretations. As a result, they will likely remain quite fluid as they continue to evolve and change over time.

Further Reading

Longo, M. (2018). *The politics of borders: Sovereignty, security, and the citizen after 09/11.* New York: Cambridge University Press.

Schroeder, R. D. (2012). *Holding the line in the 21st century: 2012–2016 U.S. Border Patrol strategy.* Washington, DC: U.S. Customs and Border Protections.

Weber, L. (2015). *Rethinking border control for a globalizing world: A preferred future.* New York: Routledge.

References

Atlas, R.I. (2013). *21st century security and CPTED: Designing for critical infrastructure protection and crime prevention*, 2nd ed. Boca Raton, FL: CRC Pres.

Bhagwati, J. (2003). Borders beyond control. *Foreign Affairs*, 82(1), 98–104.

Bonjour, S. (2011). The power and morals of policy makers: Reassessing the control gap debate. *International Migration Review*, 45(1), 89–122.

Brill, S. (2003). *After: The rebuilding and defending of America in the September 12 era.* New York: Simon & Schuster.

Broeders, D. & Engbersen, G. (2007). The fight against illegal migration: Identification policies and immigrants' counterstrategies. *American Behavioral Scientist*, 50(12), 1592–1609.

Burgmann, V. (2016). *Globalization and labour in the twenty-first century.* New York: Routledge.

Buscaglia, E. & Gonzalez-Ruiz, S. (2006). The factor of trust and the importance of inter agency cooperation in the fight against transnational organized crime: The U.S.-Mexican example. In M. Caparini & O. Marenin (Eds.) *Borders and security governance: Managing borders in a globalized world* (pp. 291–302). New Brunswick, NJ: Transaction Publishers.

Castles, S. (2004). Why migration policies fail. *Ethnic and Racial Studies*, 27(2), 205–227.

Cornelius, W.A., Takeyuki, T., Martin, P.L., & Hollifield, J.F. (2004). *Controlling immigration: A global perspective.* Stanford, CA: Stanford University Press.

Czaika, M. & de Haas, H. (2013). The effectiveness of immigration policies. *Population and Development Review*, 39(3), 487–508.

Czaika, M. & de Haas, H. (2016). Evaluating migration policy effectiveness. In A. Triandafyllidou (Ed.) *Routledge handbook of immigration and refugee studies* (pp. 34–41). New York: Routledge.

Elliott, A. & Urry, J. (2010). *Mobile lives.* New York: Routledge.

Funderberg, J.A. (2014). *Bootleggers and beer barons of the prohibition era.* Jefferson, NC: McFarland and Company.

Goldman, J. & Maret, S. (2016). *Intelligence and information policy for national security: Key terms and concepts.* Lanham, MD: Rowman and Littlefield.

Haddal, C.C. (2009). *Border security: Key agencies and their missions.* Washington, DC: Congressional Research Service.

Hollifield, J. (1992). Migration and international relations: Cooperation and control in the European community. *International Migration Review*, 26(2), 568–595.

Homeland Security. (2015). *Expedited hiring plan. Fiscal year 2015 report to Congress.* Washington, DC: U.S. Customs and Border Protection.

Johnson, R. & Jones, C. (2014). Where is the border? In R. Jones and C. Johnson (Eds.) *Placing the border in everyday life* (pp. 1–14). Burlington, VT: Ashgate.

Karlsson, M. (2012). *09/11 and the design of counterterrorism institutions.* New York: Routledge.

Koestler-Grack, R.A. (2007). *The Department of Homeland Security*. New York: Chelsea House Publishers.
Logan, K.G. (2012). Border patrol. In W.R. Miller (Ed.) *The social history of crime and punishment in America: An encyclopedia* (pp. 147–150). Thousand Oaks, CA: Sage.
Longo, M. (2018). *The politics of borders: Sovereignty, security, and the citizen after 09/11*. New York: Cambridge University Press.
Manaut, R. B. (2013). The geopolitics of insecurity in Mexico-United States relations. In B. Bow & Santa-Cruz, A. (Eds.) *The state and security in Mexico: Transformation and crisis in regional perspective* (pp. 25–41). New York: Routledge.
Martin, G. (2015). *Understanding homeland security*. Los Angeles, CA: Sage.
Mayda, & Patel, (2004). OECD countries migration policy changes. In A.M. Mayda (Ed.) *International migration: A panel data analysis of economic and non-economic determinants*, Bonn, Germany: IZA.
McElmurry, S., Kerr, J., Brown, T., & Zamora, L. (2016). *Balancing priorities: Immigration, national security, and public safety*. Chicago, IL: Chicago Council on Global Affairs.
Nunez-Neto, B. (2005). *Border security: The role of the U.S. Border Patrol*. Washington, DC: Congressional Research Service.
Ortega, F. & Peri, G. (2009). *The causes and effects of international migrations: Evidence from OECD countries 1980–2005* (working paper 14833). Cambridge, MA: National Bureau of Economic Research.
Payan, T. (2016). *The three U.S.-Mexico border wars: Drugs, immigration, and homeland security*. Santa Barbara, CA: Praeger.
Riley, K.J. (2005). Border control. In D.G. Kamlen (Ed.) *The McGraw Hill handbook of homeland security* (pp. 587–612). New York: McGrw Hill.
Rinne, U. (2012). *The evaluation of immigration policies* (discussion paper 6369). Bonn, Germany: IZA.
Roberts, B., Alden, E., & Whitley, J. (2013). *Managing illegal immigration to the United States: How effective is enforcement?* New York: Council on Foreign Relations.
Rosas, M. (2006.) Canada and Mexico on the security front: A possible relationship? In J. Diez (Ed.) *Canada and Mexico security in the new North America: Challenges and prospects* (pp. 39–50). Ithaca, NY: McGill-Queen's University Press.
Schroeder, R. D. (2012). *Holding the line in the 21st century: 2012–2016 U.S. Border Patrol strategy*. Washington, DC: U.S. Customs and Border Protections.
Shaw-Taylor, Y. (2012). *Immigration, assimilation, and border security*. Lanham, MD: Government Institutes.
Ward, R.H., Kiernan, K.L., & Mabrey, D. (2006). *Homeland security: An introduction*. Cincinnati, OH: LexisNexis.

Chapter 69

Civil Liberties and Homeland Security

Suzette A. Haughton
University of the West Indies, Kingston, West Indies

Scott N. Romaniuk
International Centre for Policing and Security, University of South Wales, Caerleon, United Kingdom

Contents

Introduction 525
A Definitional Engagement of Civil Rights and Civil Liberties 526
DHS and the USA PATRIOT Act 527
The Office of Civil Rights and Civil Liberties 530
Conclusion 530
Further Reading 531
References 531

Introduction

States have to maintain a delicate balance between protecting national security and the protection of citizens' fundamental rights and freedoms. In some instances, the protection of national security may require limiting privacy rights and civil liberties. This chapter explores this concern in three ways. First, it explains the highly used terms of civil rights and civil liberties. Second, it discusses the main role of the Department of Homeland Security (DHS) in protecting the USA from disasters and terrorism. In this regard, it discusses the USA PATRIOT Act and some alleged cases of terrorism. Third, the chapter then assesses the dual role of the Office of Civil

DOI: 10.4324/9781315144511-73

Rights and Liberties in the promotion of such rights and freedoms and in the provision of redress where instances of violation have occurred. It concludes that despite exigencies posed by terrorism, civil rights and liberties are guaranteed through the USA Constitution; yet post-September 11, extraordinary measures in the form of the USA PATRIOT Act have raised questions concerning whether such rights have been curtailed through this Act or conversely if it represents a good weapon to stem terrorist activities.

A Definitional Engagement of Civil Rights and Civil Liberties

Civil rights are the basic rights that are accorded to individuals which prevent unequal treatment based on race, gender, sexual orientation, religion, or one's disability. Civil liberties on the other hand are basic freedoms which are normally guaranteed through the Constitution and/or federal law. Klarman (1996) suggested that civil rights and civil liberties are designed to protect minority rights from the excesses of the majoritarian views and actions. To him, these rights are crafted to prevent discrimination and prejudice against minority groups. The Constitution grants civil liberties to USA's citizens. The first ten Amendments to the USA's Constitution stipulate the majority of the liberties and protection guaranteed in the Constitution. These ten Amendments are known as the Bill of Rights, which was passed in 1791 and limits the powers of the Federal government.

The First Amendment guarantees the right to assemble and petition a government. It also guarantees freedom of religion, freedom of speech, and freedom of the press. The Second Amendment protects the individual right to own and bear arms. Here the possession of arms is unconnected to service in the militia, and individuals are allowed to use the arms for traditional purposes, such as self-defense within one's home. The Third Amendment forbids the housing of the military in one's private home without consent during peacetime. This Amendment is non-controversial and has never been litigated before the USA's Supreme Court. The Fourth Amendment secures freedom from unreasonable searches and seizures of one's property by the state. This Amendment protects against arbitrary arrests and forms the basis for the law concerning search warrants, stop-and-frisks, and wiretaps. The Fifth Amendment guarantees the right to due process of law. It secures the right to a grand jury and forbids double jeopardy and protects against self-incrimination. Hence, the Fifth Amendment prevents a person from being tried twice for the same crime. The Sixth Amendment guarantees the right to a trial without undue delays. It also guarantees the right to a lawyer, the right to an impartial jury, and the right to know who one's accusers are.

Terrorism cases remain one of the areas in which the Sixth Amendment is most visibly tested in the USA's Supreme Court. The Seventh Amendment guarantees the right of a trial by jury. This has supported and continued a common law practice of jury trials. The Eighth Amendment forbids cruel and unusual punishments. It also prohibits the imposition of excessive fines and bail. One area in which the issue of excessive fines has appeared in the USA's Supreme Court concerned the seizure of alleged drug cartels' properties through civil and criminal forfeiture laws. The Ninth Amendment instructs that the rights specified in the Constitution do not deny other rights retained by the people. The Tenth Amendment instructs that the powers that are not delegated to the USA by the Constitution are rights reserved to the states and/ or to the people.

DHS and the USA PATRIOT Act

DHS was established in 2002 through the Homeland Security Act. A significant part of DHS' work involves investigating and prosecuting acts of terrorism as well as contributing to counter drug interdiction efforts. Questions concerning civil liberties are often raised in the state's investigation and prosecution of terrorism. Hunter (2016) has assessed the impact of terrorism on civil liberties in varying democracies. He found that responses to acts of terrorism have weakened civil liberties as democratic states impose stringent measures to reduce such acts in order to improve citizens' safety and security.

On 26 October 2001, a month after September 11th terrorist attacks on the USA, the US Congress passed the Uniting and Strengthening America by Providing Appropriate Tools for Intercepting and Obstructing Terrorism (USA PATRIOT) Act. This Act comprised an amalgamation of many amended laws, which were previously on the books. It modified the 1968 Wiretap Act as amended in 1986 and 1994. The Wiretap Act allows the government to obtain a court order to eavesdrop on citizens' communications in the investigation of certain serious crimes. Sections 201 and 202 of the USA PATRIOT Act added cyber-related and terrorist crimes to the list of offenses by which law enforcers might procure a court order to eavesdrop on the citizens' communications for investigative purposes. Section 210 allowed the government to use a subpoena to request communication service providers to hand over credit card and bank account numbers of individuals under investigation. Trap and trace devices and pen registers are permitted through Section 216 to monitor e-mail and internet browsing communications. The USA PATRIOT Act also made amendments to the 1978 Foreign Intelligence Surveillance Act, which allowed electronic surveillance targeting foreign agents. Section 218 of the USA PATRIOT Act makes it easy for the government to apply for surveillance authority on foreign agents on the basis that the information was required for "a significant purpose" and not necessarily to collect "foreign intelligence information."

The USA PATRIOT Act was adopted without any debate or hearing due to the urgency of the situation subsequent to the September 11, 2001, attacks and the existential threat terrorism posed for the USA. To a large extent, the views of the American public were divided over the provisions of the USA PATRIOT Act. Steoff (2011) noted this level of discord and contended that the controversial provisions of the Act were tested in the judiciary, with some of the cases even appearing before the US Supreme Court. The Act created two distinct camps in the USA. First, some Americans supported the Act with the belief that it was a strong legal weapon against terrorism. Second, those who opposed the Act felt that it was the greatest threat to Americans' civil liberties since the government's actions in the 1940s over perceived communist threats. The 1940s governmental actions involved increased scrutiny of federal employees to ascertain their loyalty to the US administration. It also investigated alleged disloyal government employees and movie stars in the US film industry.

These sets of governmental actions became popularly known as the Red Square. Hence, it is felt by some people that the USA PATRIOT Act is too intrusive and infringes on personal freedoms and privacy rights by empowering law enforcers to freely use surveillance mechanisms to spy on citizens.

Martin (2002) noted that terrorism posed challenges for investigation, prosecution, and intelligence collection in accordance with the legal requirements for due process. Terrorism investigation raises concerns regarding the First and Fourth Amendments in the US Bill of Rights. Within the context of preventing and minimizing terrorism, the First Amendment is important because measures must distinguish between a terrorist who shares a particular religion, on the one hand, and law-abiding persons who also share that religion but do not engage in terrorist acts. These law-abiding persons must be guaranteed freedom of religion without being profiled as terrorists. Likewise, the Fourth Amendment secures freedom from unreasonable search of self and property. To protect this Amendment, a delicate balance must be struck between investigating and prosecuting alleged terrorists, on the one hand, and maintaining liberty from unreasonable searches, on the other.

The intent of the provisions of the USA PATRIOT Act was to create a robust mechanism designed to apprehend terrorists and make them account for their crimes. Hence, in order to conduct greater levels of terrorist arrests, the government was authorized to conduct more detailed surveillance on citizens. Sections 201 and 202 of the Act allowed law enforcers to obtain a court order to conduct eavesdropping in order to collect evidence for a number of serious offenses, including computer and terrorist crimes. Section 203 authorizes government attorneys to testify before a federal grand jury on matters concerning foreign intelligence or counter intelligence. Section 505 authorizes the issuance of Federal Bureau of Investigation (FBI) subpoenas to obtain information of relevance to investigations on foreign intelligence and international terrorism. Section 213 permits law enforcers to conduct special searches in which targets' notifications are reasonably delayed until completion of the search. Section 215, through a Foreign Intelligence Act court order, requires businesses to turn over "any tangible things," such as books, records, papers, and other documents, of a third party to government authorities, such as the FBI, to support an investigation. Further, this Section also prohibits the disclosure of the fact that the FBI is conducting an investigation and has requested such documentation. Section 216 allowed devices which recorded the sources and destination of phone calls and monitored electronic communications such as emails and internet searches.

The USA PATRIOT Act and the War on Terror were among the emergency measures the USA administration used to address terrorism. It securitized the arrest, prosecution, and treatment of terrorists in its War on Terror, which became a highly controversial matter. In the USA, cases against alleged terrorists are tried in military tribunals and civilian criminal courts. The use of military tribunals to hear cases involving alleged terrorists became a highly discussed matter as it removes the possibility of those cases being heard in the normal criminal justice system. Military tribunals were intended to be invoked during wartime and used in the trial of enemy forces. The use of these tribunals in the trial of alleged terrorists has raised some rather interesting questions about the treatment of non-state actors in conducts similar to states' military officers. Further, questions were raised about the War on Terror and whether the international legal rules on warfare applied. On the face of it, the term War on Terror suggests that alleged terrorists are accused of crimes committed in a war, yet they were not treated in accordance with the legal rules on the treatment of Prisoners of War (POW). The 1949 Geneva Convention and its 1977 Additional Protocol I stipulate the rights and the treatment of POWs. International armed conflicts form the basis by which the designation of POWs is historically used and which becomes applicable to fighters. Normally, POWs refer to a member of a state's armed force who has been captured by the enemy-state troops. The detention of POWs is to prevent them from engaging further in the conflict and hence they must be released and repatriated at the end of the hostilities. Under the Geneva Convention, POWs are protected from inhumane treatment, acts of violence, insults, and intimidation. Further, there are minimum established standards concerning the condition of their detention such as rules on their accommodation, food, clothing, hygiene, and medical care.

In the War on Terror, the USA detained many alleged terrorists and held them in Guantanamo Bay. The administration refers to these alleged terrorists as "enemy combatants", and Amnesty International argued that they were kept in conditions that violate basic human rights. Amnesty International has further contended that Guantanamo Bay is a "symbol of torture, rendition and indefinite detention without charge or trial" (Amnesty International, 2018). However, despite the War on Terror, some critics have questioned the USA government's success in the prosecution and convictions of suspected terrorists. In some of the highly publicized cases, convictions against alleged terrorists have been secured on lesser charges, such as conspiracy to commit acts of murder and not on direct acts of terrorism, because such acts are very difficult to prove. Prosecutorial misconduct has resulted in other cases being thrown out and convictions reversed. One such example involved the three Arab immigrants who were alleged to be part of a terrorist sleeper cell in Detroit. In 2004, this case was thrown out due to prosecutorial misconduct.

There have also been some noted cases in which alleged terrorists were tried in military tribunals in the USA. One prominent case is Hamdan v Rumsfeld in which Salim Hamdan challenged the legitimacy of military tribunals. Mr. Hamdan was held in July 2004 as a detainee in Guantanamo Bay and charged with attacking civilians, murder by an unprivileged belligerent, and terrorism. But by December 2005, the Detainee Treatment Act became law. This Act contends that detainees can appeal to USA courts but only after trial in a military court and if they were labeled as an enemy combatant. Given this development, the USA Supreme Court must determine whether the new law, that is the Detainee Treatment Act, would bar it from hearing Hamdan's case.

However, not all cases have been tried in military courts; there are a number of cases which were tried in civilian criminal courts and in which suspected terrorists were convicted. An instance in December 2001 involved the British citizen, popularly known as the "shoe bomber," because he hid explosives in his shoes with the intent of detonating them on an American Airlines flight. He was arrested and he pleaded guilty in a civilian criminal court. He was convicted and sentenced to life imprisonment.

Critics of the USA PATRIOT Act have also argued that the excessive powers of the Act make it open to state abuse. The Act allows secret intelligence searches, which may violate citizens' rights as it might be used to collect evidence to secure a criminal prosecution. In 2004, a Muslim lawyer from Portland, Oregon, was arrested as a "material witness" in connection with the Madrid, Spain, bombings. After two weeks, the FBI admitted to making an error with his fingerprint and another individual who was at the scene of the bombings. He was released but not before secret searches authorized for intelligence purposes were conducted at his home. He pursued a legal claim against the US Justice Department for violating his civil liberties.

Likewise, through Section 505 of the USA PATRIOT Act, national security letters or subpoenas were used to obtain records from an internet service provider. The American Civil Liberties Union (ACLU) argued that this violated the First and Fourth Amendments and hence pursued a law suit against the government on behalf of the internet service provider. However, the presiding judge found that recipients are not empowered to challenge such orders. The ACLU is nevertheless appealing this decision. The challenges that the USA PARTIOT Act might be open to abuse and that human errors can happen, which may inadvertently result in the violation of individuals civil rights and liberties, have raised the need for a specialized office with the mandate to conduct investigations and address complaints.

The Office of Civil Rights and Civil Liberties

The Office for Civil Rights and Civil Liberties (CRCL) supports the DHS by ensuring that civil rights and liberties are reflected in the documented policies of DHS. The CRCL integrates these rights and liberties by promoting them into DHS implementation policies, communicating complaint mechanisms to citizens who believe that their rights and liberties have been violated by DHS activities and through the investigation of complaints filed by aggrieved citizens concerning their civil rights and liberties.

The primary reason for the establishment of DHS was to improve USA's security and protect it from acts of terrorism on its soil, which may negatively affect the USA's critical infrastructure and harm its citizens. The Global War on Terror (GWOT) therefore was central to the protection of the USA's homeland but raised civil liberty concerns among some critics. Martin (2002) has argued that treating terrorism purely as an intelligence matter rather than a criminal matter may not be effective in the fight against terrorism. Further, he raised the notion of secret arrests without probable cause and indefinite detention as concerns for civil liberties. Hardin (2004) raises the difficulty involved in policing terrorism prior to a terrorist act and its implications for civil liberties. He argued that the judiciary is the main protector of civil liberties but it often agrees with the executive in times of crisis and emergencies. Hence, in periods of wartime, the most egregious violations of civil liberties have normally happened. Yet, in peacetime, civil liberties still face challenges.

Conclusion

Civil liberties are basic freedoms guaranteed through the US Constitution. In the War on Terror, civil liberties may have been infringed on to protect citizens from terrorist acts. The Office of Civil Rights and Liberties of the Homeland Security Department was designed to address civil rights and liberties complaints and to sensitize citizens of existing complaint mechanisms. The question of whether and of how much civil rights will have to be abrogated to provide safety for citizens against terrorism remains a controversial matter. Despite this, however, the USA PATRIOT Act remains in place, facilitating eavesdropping and greater surveillance on citizens in order to filter out those with terrorist intentions or those who have committed terrorist acts.

Further Reading

Alperen, M. (2011). *Foundations of Homeland Security: Law and Policy*, 2nd edition, Wiley Publishers.

Herman, P. (2018). *Terrorism and Literature*, Cambridge University Press.

Tankel, S. (2018). *With Us and Against Us: How America's Partners Help and Hinder the War on Terror*, Cambridge University Press.

References

Amnesty International (2018). 'Guantanamo Bay: 14 years of injustice', Amnesty International UK, accessed on: https://www.amnesty.org.uk/guantanamo-bay-human-rights

Guidance regarding the use of race by Federal Law Enforcement Agencies (2003), USA Department of Justice, Civil Rights Division, accessed on: https://www.prisonlegalnews.org/media/publications/cripa_guidance_regarding_use_of_race_by_fed_law_enforcement_agencies_2003.pdf

Hardin, R (2004). Civil Liberties in the Era of Mass Terrorism, *The Journal of Ethics*, 8:77–95.

Hunter, L (2016). Terrorism, Civil Liberties and Political Rights: A Cross-national Analysis, *Studies in Conflict and Terrorism*, 39(2):165–193.

Ip, J (2010). The Supreme Court and House of Lords in the War on Terror: Inter Arma Silent Leges, *Michigan State University College of Law: Journal of International Law*, 19 (1):1–61.

Klarman, M (1996). Re-thinking the Civil Rights and Civil Liberties Revolutions, *Virginia Law Review*, 82 (1):1–67.

Martin, K (2002). Intelligence, Terrorism and Civil Liberties, *Human Rights Magazine*, American Bar Association: Defending Liberty Pursuing Justice, 29(1) accessed on: https://www.americanbar.org/publications/human_rights_magazine_home/human_rights_vol29_2002/winter2002/irr_hr_winter02_martin.html

Steoff, R (2011), *Landmark Legislation: Patriot Act*, Marshall Cavendish Benchmark Publisher.

Sutherland, D (2014). Homeland Security and Civil Liberties: Preserving American's Way of Life, *Journal of Law, Ethics and Public Policy*, Article 13(1):289–308.

The USA Bill of Rights, accessed on: http://biblescripture.net/Bill.html

Uniting and Strengthening America by Providing Appropriate Tools Required to Intercept and Obstruct Terrorism (USA PATRIOT ACT) Act of 2001, Public Law 107-56, October 26, 2001. Accessed on: https://www.gpo.gov/fdsys/pkg/PLAW-107publ56/pdf/PLAW-107publ56.pdf

Chapter 70

Disaster Management and Assistance (DMA)

Alex D. Colvin
Texas Woman's University, Denton, TX, United States

Angela N. Bullock
Social Work Program University of the District of Columbia, Washington, DC, United States

Contents

Introduction 533
History of Disaster Management and Assistance 534
Types of Disaster Assistance and Relief 536
  Individual and Family Assistance 536
  Public Assistance 537
Risk Reduction through Disaster Management Activities, Strategy, and Coordination 537
  Mitigation 537
  Preparedness 538
  Response 538
  Recovery 539
Improving Efficiency and Effectiveness 539
Conclusion 540
Further Readings 541
References 541

Introduction

Disasters whether natural or manmade can occur rapidly, instantaneously, and indiscriminately (Khan, Vasilescu, & Khan, 2008). When a disaster strikes, the primary concerns are potential loss due to casualties (fatalities, injuries, and missing persons),

DOI: 10.4324/9781315144511-74

physical (functional) consequences on services, buildings, and infrastructure, and direct economic loss. These events can interrupt essential services, such as health care, electricity, water, sewage/garbage removal, transportation, and communications. As a result of disaster, communities are often moved to look to local, state, and national agencies for disaster management and assistance (Khan, Vasilescu, & Khan, 2008).

Disaster management and assistance encompasses dealing with all aspects of emergencies through the organization, management, and dissemination of resources. It aims to reduce or avoid the potential losses from hazards, assure the promotion of appropriate assistance to victims, and achieve rapid and effective recovery (Othman & Beydoun, 2012). This can include all activities, programs, and measures, which can be taken up before, during, and after a disaster (Khan, Vasilescu, & Khan, 2008). Additionally, it covers a wide scope, including prediction, warning, emergency relief, rehabilitation, and reconstruction (Moe & Pathranarakul, 2006).

Disaster management and assistance, often used interchangeably with emergency management, is a multidisciplinary endeavor designed to help individuals and businesses recover economically, environmentally, and socially. It may include emergency relief, often temporary in nature, in the form of financial aid and disaster loans and grants, unemployment assistance, legal services, psychological assistance, home and property assistance, and even emergency assistance for farm crops and livestock and animals. Such activities are carried out in an urgent manner when there is an onset of disaster occurrence (Moe & Pathranarakul, 2006). Disaster management and assistance typically begins as a local government function, with state and federal assistance responsibilities coming into play as the scale of event increases (Gerber, 2007). For this reason, the focus on early planning and organizing and timely mobilizing and completing to lessen the impact of the disaster is paramount (Kelly, 1995).

History of Disaster Management and Assistance

Disasters which adversely affect humans can be dated back to the origin of civilization. Consequently, societies have made several attempts to decrease exposure to the results of these disasters by developing procedures to address this initial impact and post-disaster response and recovery needs (Coppola, 2015). During the prehistoric period, individuals faced similar risks, such as starvation, harsh elements, dangerous wildlife, violence at the hands of other humans, disease, and accidental injuries, that exist today. Evidence that early inhabitants took measures to mitigate their risks can be dated back to 3200 BC to a social group known as the Asipu who lived in what is now modern-day Iraq. The risk management process entailed community members seeking advice from the Asipu when faced with difficult decisions that involved risk or danger. The Asipu utilized a methodology that is today referred to as decision analysis. The Asipu would first examine the problem, then suggest several alternatives, and provide possible outcomes for each alternative. This type of analysis is essential for any type of comprehensive risk management venture (Coppola, 2015). According to Coppola (2015), modern disaster management that encompasses global standards and organized efforts to address preparedness, mitigation, and response activities for a wide range of disasters emerged during the mid-twentieth century. In many countries, this change took place as a response to specific disaster events and evolved further due to a shift in social philosophy, in which the government played an increasing role in preventing and responding to disasters (Haddow, Bullock, & Coppola, 2017).

For instance, disaster management in the United States can be traced back to the 1800s with the enactment of the Congressional Act of 1803 (Chang, 2018; History of Federal Disaster Mitigation, 2005). This congressional act was passed to provide financial assistance to a New Hampshire town that had been devastated by fire. For the next century, ad hoc policies were initiated to respond to hurricanes, earthquakes, floods, and other natural disasters (History of Federal Disaster Mitigation, 2005). However, during this time, the federal government had very limited involvement in disaster relief efforts, and instead, neighbors, religious groups, and community organizations were primarily responsible for responding to disasters (Chang, 2018). Specifically, after the 1900 Galveston Hurricane and the 1906 San Francisco Earthquake, Congress authorized the American National Red Cross to perform emergency relief services (Olshansky & Johnson, 2014).

The passage of both the Disaster Relief Act and the Civil Defense Act in 1950 marked the shift in responsibility to the federal government. The Disaster Relief Act of 1950 gave the President authority to issue disaster declarations that allowed federal agencies to provide direct assistance to state and local governments, while the Civil Defense Act of 1950 created a nationwide system of civil defense agencies; through this legislation, defense drills became routine in schools, government agencies, and other organizations (U.S. Department of Homeland Security, n.d.). Initially, the Disaster Relief Act limited federal aid to short-term repairs of government buildings impacted by disasters. However, this Act was amended to include temporary housing and emergency shelter for disaster victims. In 1970, this Act was expanded to include the replacement of state and local public facilities, although only for reconstruction to conditions that existed immediately before the disaster struck along with providing temporary housing assistance for up to 1 year after a disaster. The Small Business Act of 1953 expanded recovery assistance to private organizations and provides loans to businesses and homeowners affected by disasters (Olshansky & Johnson, 2014). Further development of the federal system of disaster management was through the passage of the National Flood Insurance Act of 1968, which provided flood protection to homeowners, renters, and business owners (Olshansky & Johnson, 2014; History of Federal Disaster Mitigation, 2005). Both the National Flood Insurance Act and the Disaster Relief Act of 1974 marked a critical expansion of the federal role beyond simple repairing of public facilities after disasters. These Acts recognized the moral hazard associated with federal disaster assistance and promoted community responsibility to reduce the potential for disaster losses (Olshansky & Johnson, 2014).

Furthermore, an Executive Order issued in 1979 by President Jimmy Carter merged the array of federal disaster management policies and programs dispersed across a number of agencies into a new Federal Emergency Management Agency (FEMA). Agencies such as the Federal Insurance Administration, the National Fire Prevention and Control Administration, the National Weather Service Community Preparedness Program, the Federal Preparedness Agency of the General Services Administration, and the Federal Disaster Assistance Administration were transferred to FEMA. FEMA assumed most of the federal government duties outlined in the various disaster relief acts passed since 1950; however, the primary law that underlies the role of FEMA is the 1998 Robert T. Stafford Disaster Relief and Emergency Assistance Act. In 2003, FEMA lost its independent agency status and joined 22 federal agencies to form the Department of Homeland Security (DHS). FEMA is now one of the four major branches of DHS and its emphasis significantly shifted away from natural hazards to focus on the consequences of manmade disasters (Olshansky & Johnson, 2014; History of Federal Disaster Mitigation, 2005).

Types of Disaster Assistance and Relief

Disaster assistance and relief encompasses coordinated multi-agency, multi-level responses in an effort to reduce the impact of a disaster and its long-term results. Assistance is often targeted to individuals, states, territories, local governments, and businesses specifically affected by disaster (Kreiser, Mullins, & Nagel, 2018). Depending on the extent of the disaster, assistance and relief can be initiated at the local, state, national, or international levels and may be coordinated with agencies such as the FEMA, American Red Cross, and the Salvation Army, just to name a few. Assistance can include a wide range of support from operational to logistical and technical. Additionally, assistance may take the form of financial aid such as grants, loans, and loan guarantees as well as the provision of federally owned equipment and facilities (Kreiser, Mullins, & Nagel, 2018). More specifically, disaster assistance and relief activities can include rescue and relocation activities, providing food and water, action to prevent disease and disability, repairing vital services such as telecommunications and transport, and providing temporary shelter and emergency health care (World Confederation for Physical Therapy, 2016). Assistance and relief activities may occur in two main forms: 1) assistance for individuals and families and 2) assistance to the public.

Individual and Family Assistance

Individual and family assistance encompasses aid for damage to residences, businesses or personal property losses, temporary housing, disaster unemployment assistance, and disaster legal services. Individual assistance may include providing information on how to evacuate or shelter in place, seek emergency shelter, obtain food and water, handle emergency medical situations, and locate family, friends, and lost pets (FEMA, 2010). Additionally, disaster assistance may be provided as direct or indirect services. Direct services may include financial assistance to individuals and families whose property has been damaged or destroyed as a result of a federally declared disaster, and whose losses are not covered by insurance. Still more, individuals and families may seek aid with insurance claims and legal issues such as wills, powers of attorney, problems with landlords, proof of home ownership, and FEMA appeals. In other words, individual and family assistance is meant to help survivors with critical issues and expenses that cannot be covered in other ways. What is more, in some instances, the consequences of a disaster cannot be measured or quantified easily. These are referred to as intangible losses (e.g., fatalities, physical injuries, missing persons, loss of social cohesion due to disruption of community, loss of reputation, psychological consequences resulting from disaster impacts, and cultural effects). For that reason, individual, family, and community disaster assistance may be offered indirectly in the form of support resources such as crisis counseling through a crisis hotline and even online case management.

Public Assistance

Public assistance can include community disaster loans and grants to repair, replace, and restore damaged or destroyed publically owned facilities, structures, or equipment. These funds are often used for infrastructure repair, public facilities, and debris removal, and in some instances, to aid farmers and ranchers experiencing significant loss of permanent crops and livestock. This type of aid may include grants and loans to assist with recovery and can extend to include hazard mitigation grants designed to fund measures to mitigate future damage and loss from disaster. All said, disaster assistance is not intended to restore the individual, family, or damaged property to its condition before the disaster but to offer aid and comfort in the recovery process (FEMA, 2010).

Risk Reduction through Disaster Management Activities, Strategy, and Coordination

Deficiencies in planning and poor decision-making at an individual and organizational level can worsen the adverse effects of an extreme event. For this reason, it is important to work to reduce risks through disaster management activities, strategies, analysis, and coordination. Disaster risks can be reduced through systematic efforts to analyze and manage the causal factors of disasters (UNISDR, 2002). This includes the use of available information to determine the likelihood of certain events occurring and the magnitude of their possible consequences. As a process, it includes the following activities: (1) identifying the nature, extent, and risk of threat; (2) determining the existence and degree of vulnerabilities; (3) identifying the capabilities and resources available; (4) determining acceptable levels of risk, cost–benefit considerations; (5) setting priorities relative to time, resource allocation, and effectiveness of results; (6) developing methods to protect people and key resources and reduce overall losses; and (7) designing effective and appropriate management systems to implement and control (de Guzman, 2003). Risk reduction further involves analyzing the risk pre-crisis, estimating its potential effects of the crisis, and determining its importance in the scheme of things post-crisis (de Guzman, 2003; Hensgen et al., 2003; Bertrand & Lajtha, 2002). Comprehensive disaster management risk reduction is also based upon four distinct activities and/or phases: mitigation, preparedness, response, and recovery.

Mitigation

Mitigation is efforts/actions aimed to minimize the degree of risk to prevent disasters and to reduce the vulnerability of both the ecosystem and social system (Menonie &

Pergalani, 1996; Bakir, 2004; Dai et al., 2002; Mansor et al., 2004). The main functions are hazard assessment, vulnerability, and risk reduction. Mitigation seeks to "treat" the hazard such that it impacts society to a lesser degree. During the mitigation phase, structural and non-structural measures are undertaken to limit the adverse impact of natural hazards, environmental degradation, and technological hazards (Bang, 2016). Measures taken during the mitigation phase also address preventing natural or manmade events from giving rise to disasters or any emergency situations. Management activities in the mitigation phase encompass engineering techniques and hazard-resistant construction as well as improved environmental policies and public awareness, as well as hazard vulnerability and risk assessment.

Preparedness

Preparedness involves actions to prepare responders as well as the general public to pre- and post-disaster activities (Simpson, 2002). Preparedness activities are geared toward minimizing disaster damage, enhancing disaster response operations, and preparing organizations and individuals to respond. They also involve planning, organizing, training, interaction with other organizations and related agencies, resource inventory, allocation and placement, and plan testing. During the preparedness phase, measures are taken to reduce or minimize, to the maximum level possible, the loss of human life and other damage (Shreve & Kelman, 2014; van der Keur et al., 2016). This includes equipping individuals with the tools to increase their chance of survival and to minimize their financial and other losses. Preparedness activities include things such as facilitating the timely removal of people and property from a threatened location, facilitating timely and effective rescue and relief and rehabilitation. Preparedness further takes the form of practicing earthquake and fire drills along with sustained Geographic Information Science (GIS) mapping and satellite monitoring for disaster.

Response

Response consists of those actions to manage and control the various effects of disaster and minimize human and property losses. Response activities are post-activities geared toward providing emergency assistance, reducing probability injuries or damage, speeding recovery operations, and returning systems to normal levels (Haddow, Bullock, & Coppola, 2017). The main functions are evacuation (Tobin & Whiteford, 2002), sheltering (Phillips, 1993), medical care, search and rescue, property protection, and damage control. These are central considerations for taking action to reduce or eliminate the impact of disasters that have occurred or are currently occurring, in order to prevent further suffering or financial loss. Relief is one component of response.

Actions carried out in a disaster situation with the objective to save life, alleviate suffering, and reduce economic losses can include evacuation response, search and rescue, Red Cross and FEMA coordination, state police arrangement during the emergency, coordinating volunteers, hospitals, and aid agencies. The main tool in response is the implementation of plans which were prepared prior to the event.

Recovery

Once emergency needs have been met and the initial crisis is over, the people affected and the communities that support them are still vulnerable (Coppola, 2015). Recovery consists of those actions that bring the disrupted area back to an often improved normal condition (Lettieri, Masella, & Radaelli, 2009). In other words, returning victims' lives back to a normal state following the impact of disaster consequences. In the recovery phase, activities are geared toward the restoration of basic services and the beginning of the repair of physical, social, and economic damage, e.g., lifelines, health and communication facilities, as well as utility systems. Recovery activities often include such things as rebuilding infrastructure, health care, and rehabilitation (March, Kornakova, & Leon, 2017). As noted earlier, it generally begins after the immediate response has ended and can persist for months or years thereafter. The recovery phase also includes efforts to reduce disaster risk factors in the future (De Guttry, Gestri, & Venturini, 2012).

According to Moe and Pathranarakul (2006), disaster management and assistance also include a five-phase process: prediction, warning, emergency relief, rehabilitation, and reconstruction. Prediction consists of structural measures taken in advance to ensure effective response to the impact of hazards, including the issuance of timely and effective early warnings and temporary evacuation of people and property from threatened locations. Warning refers to the provision of timely and effective information, through identified institutions, that allows individuals exposed to a hazard to take action to avoid or reduce their risk and prepare effective response. Emergency relief is the provision of assistance or intervention during or immediately after a disaster to meet the life preservation and basic subsistence needs of those people affected. It can be of immediate, short-term, or protracted duration. Rehabilitation involves decisions and actions taken after a disaster with a view to restoring or improving the pre-disaster living conditions of the stricken community, while encouraging and facilitating necessary adjustments to reduce disaster risk. Lastly, reconstruction includes activities conducted to mitigate future disasters.

Improving Efficiency and Effectiveness

It is commonly agreed that there is no way of neutralizing all negative effects resulting from disaster; however, efforts can be made in order to reduce their impacts (Moe & Pathranarakul, 2006). Once emergency needs have been met and the initial crisis is over, an assessment of the efficiency and effectiveness of service provisions must occur. Lessons learned are often not incorporated into wider governance processes. Learning is often characterized as only "doing it better" as opposed to "doing it differently." Quite simply, the drive is to respond better rather than rethink the problem (O'Brien, O'Keefe, Gadema, & Swords, 2010). Based on lessons learned from managing a disaster's impact, Moe and Pathranarakul (2006) proposed comprehensive recommendations for authorities and organizations to consider including developing frameworks for effective natural disaster management, exploring an integrated approach for successfully and effectively managing disaster crisis, and providing a set of critical success factors (CSFs) for managing disaster.

Also, improving efficiency and effectiveness can include hazard mapping and employing vulnerability and risk assessment as tools for generating reliable disaster risk information which serves as a basis for making decisions on disaster reduction and response interventions (de Guzman, 2003). Efficient and effective disaster management is linked with sustainable development. Improving effectiveness of disaster management and assistance performance may also occur through the use of new technologies (Lettieri, Masella, & Radaelli, 2009). For example, social media has become central to the overall emergency management and crisis communication effort. Advances within wireless communication technologies make it easier to distribute critical and operationally relevant information. Important announcements are now commonly exchanged via social media and other digital platforms that are well suited to deliver data directly to citizens and emergency management organizations and to encourage exchanges between them (Mehta, Bruns, & Newton, 2017). For instance, multimedia information can be shared (e.g., maps, pictures, and text/audio messages) which can serve as disaster mitigation processes.

Developing an appropriate high-level knowledge structure is important. This includes increasing the transparency of the knowledge being shared along with how information is disseminated and shared with the public, including how it is distributed via the internet and online databases as well as circulated in books, libraries, newspapers, and pamphlets (Smith & Dowell, 2000). What is more, creating a high-level knowledge structure consists of effectively working with multi-level stakeholders (researchers, government or non-government agencies, community, and individuals). This multi-level stakeholder knowledge structure is a consortium designed to ensure that gaps in disaster response and needed recovery assistance to vulnerable individuals and communities are mitigated. Through knowledge sharing and data collection, all stakeholders can work together to identify specific areas that may present the most concerns during a disaster. From this, the multi-level stakeholders can create pre-disaster strategies along with plan for efficient and effective post-disaster response and recovery.

Conclusion

Effective disaster management and assistance is a key element in good governance (UNISDR, 2002). As the brief history illustrates, disaster management has continually evolved and improved over time to cover such areas as flood insurance, public facility reconstruction, housing assistance, and community and economic development. These changes were driven by the needs of government agencies as well as nongovernmental organizations to be more attentive to emergency needs of the U.S. citizenry. Although these entities have recognized the importance of improving the efficiency of the four phases of emergency management – mitigation, preparedness, response, and recovery – considerable attention should still be invested in further refining and enhancing disaster management and assistance responses in the future (Coppola, 2015).

Further Readings

Carter, W. N. (2008). *Disaster management: A disaster manager's handbook*. Mandaluyong, Philippines: Asian Development Bank.

Hodgkinson, P. E., & Stewart, M. (1991). *Coping with catastrophe: A handbook of disaster management*. New York: Taylor & Frances/Routledge.

Pearce, L. (2003). Disaster management and community planning, and public participation: how to achieve sustainable hazard mitigation. *Natural Hazards*, *28*(2–3), 211–228.

References

Bang, H. N. (2016). *30 years after the Lake Nyos disaster: What prospects for rehabilitation and reintegration in the region?* Ishpeming, MI: Book Venture Publishing LLC.

Bertrand, R. & Lajtha, C. (2002). A new approach to crisis management, *Contingencies and Crisis Management*, *10*(4), 181–191.

Chang, K. (2018). Exploring the dynamics of local emergency management collaboration in the United States – What we learned from Florida county and city emergency managers' viewpoints. *Euramerica*, 64(2), 1–71.

Coppola, D. P. (2015). *Introduction to international disaster management*. Amsterdam, Netherlands: Elsevier.

De Guttry, A., Gestri, M., & Venturini, G. (2012). *International disaster response law* (p. 774). The Hague: TMC Asser Press.

de Guzman, E. M. (2003). Towards total disaster risk management approach. *United National Office for the Coordination of Humanitarian Affairs, Asian Disaster Response Unit*.

FEMA (2010). *A citizen's guide to disaster assistance*. Washington, DC: Federal Emergency Management Agency. Createspace Independent Publishing Platform.

Gerber, B. J. (2007). Disaster management in the United States: examining key political and policy challenges. *Policy Studies Journal*, *35*(2), 227–238.

Haddow, G., Bullock, J., & Coppola, D. P. (2017). *Introduction to emergency management*. Cambridge, MA: Butterworth-Heinemann.

Hensgen, T., Desouza, K.C., & Kraft, G. D. (2003). Games, signal detection, and processing in the context of crisis management. *Journal of Contingencies and Crisis Management*, *11*(2), 67–77.

History of Federal Disaster Mitigation. (2005). Natural Disasters. *Congressional Digest*, *84*(9), 258–288.

Kelly, C. (1995). A framework for improving operational effectiveness and cost efficiency in emergency planning and response. *Disaster Prevention and Management*, *4*(3), 25–35.

Khan, H., Vasilescu, L. G., & Khan, A. (2008). Disaster management cycle-a theoretical approach. *Journal of Management and Marketing*, *6*(1), 43–50.

Kreiser, M., Mullins, M., & Nagel, J. C. (2018). Federal disaster assistance response and recovery programs: brief summaries. *Congressional Research Services*. Retrieved from: https://fas.org/sgp/crs/homesec/RL31734.pdf

Lettieri, E., Masella, C., & Radaelli, G. (2009). Disaster management: findings from a systematic review. *Disaster Prevention and Management: An International Journal*, *18*(2), 117–136.

March, A., Kornakova, M., & Leon, J. (2017). Integration and collective action: studies of urban planning and recovery after disasters. In Alan March, Maria Kornakova, Jorge Leon (Eds.), *Urban planning for disaster recovery*. Woburn, MA: Butterworth-Heinemann, (pp. 1–12).

Mehta, A. M., Bruns, A., & Newton, J. (2017). Trust, but verify: social media models for disaster management. *Disasters*, *41*(3), 549–565.

Moe, T. L., & Pathranarakul, P. (2006). An integrated approach to natural disaster management: public project management and its critical success factors. *Disaster Prevention and Management: An International Journal, 15*(3), 396–413.

O'Brien, G., O'Keefe, P., Gadema, Z., & Swords, J. (2010). Approaching disaster management through social learning. *Disaster Prevention and Management: An International Journal, 19*(4), 498–508.

Olshansky, R. B., & Johnson, L. A. (2014). The evolution of the federal role in supporting community recovery after U.S. disasters. *Journal of the American Planning Association, 80*(4), 293–304.

Othman, S. H., & Beydoun, G. (2012, September). Evaluating disaster management knowledge model by using a frequency-based selection technique. In Siti Hajar Othman and Ghassan Beydoun (Eds.), *Pacific rim knowledge acquisition workshop* (pp. 12–27). Berlin, Heidelberg: Springer.

Phillips, B. D. (1993). Cultural diversity in disasters: sheltering, housing, and long term recovery. *International Journal of Mass Emergencies and Disasters, 11*(1), 99–110.

Shreve, C. M., & Kelman, I. (2014). Does mitigation save? Reviewing cost-benefit analyses of disaster risk reduction. *International Journal of Disaster Risk Reduction, 10*, 213–235.

Simpson, D. M. (2002). Earthquake drills and simulations in community-based training and preparedness programs. *Disasters, 26*(1), 55–69.

Smith, W., & Dowell, J. (2000). A case study of co-ordinative decision-making in disaster management. *Ergonomics, 43*(8), 1153–1166.

The United Nations Office of Disaster Risk Reduction (UNISDR), (2002). *What is DRR*. Retrieved from http://www.unisdr.org/who-we-are/what-is-drr

Tobin, G. A., & Whiteford, L. M. (2002). Community resilience and volcano hazard: the eruption of Tungurahua and evacuation of the faldas in Ecuador. *Disasters, 26*(1), 28–48.

U.S. Department of Homeland Security, (n.d.). Emergency management authorities review. Retrieved from https://emilms.fema.gov/IS230c/FEM0101170text.htm

Van Der Keur, P., van Bers, C., Henriksen, H. J., Nibanupudi, H. K., Yadav, S., Wijaya, R., Subiyono, A., Mukerjee, N., Hausmann, H-J., Hare, M., van Scheltinga, C. T., Pearn, G., & Jaspers, F. (2016). Identification and analysis of uncertainty in disaster risk reduction and climate change adaptation in South and Southeast Asia. *International Journal of Disaster Risk Reduction, 16*, 208–214.

World Confederation for Physical Therapy (2016). *What is disaster*? Retrieved from https://www.wcpt.org/disaster-management/what-is-disaster-management

Chapter 71

Domestic Security

Nabil Ouassini
Prairie View A&M University, Prairie View, TX, United States

Contents

Introduction 543
Domestic Security World War II and the Cold War 544
9/11 and Homeland Security 544
Current Issues Regarding Domestic Security 545
Future Challenges 546
Further Reading 546
References 547

Introduction

Domestic security refers to the government's effort to prevent, identify, and respond to threats, attacks, or other countless dangers to the United States. Although domestic security is used interchangeably with national or homeland security, there are slight distinctions between the terms. National security tends to cover national defense, the military, and foreign relations. Homeland security developed in the aftermath of the terrorist attacks on September 11 through the creation of a government agency that directly protects the United States and coordinates between authorities in the local, state, tribal, and federal levels. Domestic security is a broader term that incorporates national and homeland security along with other non-military/law enforcement dimensions. In the United States, domestic security is of the utmost importance as government officials "solemnly swear" to "support and defend the Constitution of the United States against all enemies, foreign and domestic."

DOI: 10.4324/9781315144511-75

Domestic Security World War II and the Cold War

Since the founding of the United States, domestic security has always been one of the most imperative agendas for any administration. However, the surprise attack by the Japanese on December 7, 1941, pulled the United States into World War II and was a catalyst for establishing and reforming a wide range of domestic security policies. When the Germans, Italians, and Japanese surrendered, President Harry S. Truman restructured the nation's military and intelligence under the National Security Act of 1947. The Truman administration realized that only through the strategic collaboration between competitive government entities that a future Pearl Harbor can be averted. It was during this time that the Truman Doctrine was enacted to contain the perceived menace of communism and confront the ensuing Cold War against Stalin's Soviet Union. The decades that followed witnessed the threat of nuclear war, McCarthy's red scare, the violation of minorities' civil rights, protestors against the Vietnam War as examples of the possible threats to America's domestic security. The destruction of the Berlin Wall in 1989 and the emergence of a unipolar world implied that the United States was domestically secure from other nations and political ideologies. The events of September 11, 2001, proved that the world was on a multipolar trajectory with countless centers of power distributed among governments, corporations, non-state actors, and other entities.

9/11 and Homeland Security

Al-Qaeda's methodical terrorist attack on the Trade Towers in New York City is often referred as the Pearl Harbor of our generation. Similar to President Truman, the Bush administration announced the creation of the Office of Homeland Security (OHS) in an effort to improve American foreign and domestic intelligence. In 2002, the Homeland Security Act established the Department of Homeland Security (DHS) by incorporating dozens of agencies under the executive branch of the government. Currently, over 240,000 employees work for the DHS every day to maintain domestic security through the prevention of terrorism, the protection of the borders, the enforcement of immigration laws, the defense of cybersecurity, and the preparation of all possible emergencies through prevention, management, and recovery (Homeland Security, 2014). The Bush administration's response to the attacks on 9/11 did not avoid controversies. Along with the invasion of Iraq on the pretext that Saddam had nuclear weapons and was connected to al-Qaeda, many Americans were also wary of the Uniting and Strengthening America by Providing Appropriate Tools Required to Intercept and Obstruct Terrorism Act of 2001 (USA PATRIOT Act).

In the month after 9/11, Congress passed the Act to enhance domestic security against terrorism, border security, and money laundering and to increase surveillance. The Act has generated countless debates on its intent and use with a wide range of criticisms. These include Michael Moore's high-grossing documentary *Fahrenheit 9/11* and its claims that the USA PATRIOT Act was designed to simply induce fear in the American public to the American Civil Liberties Union's court fight against National Security Letters that allowed government officials to wiretap phone calls, emails, and other records without a warrant. Despite the relative success in the domestic fight against terrorism, there are perceptions that the USA PATRIOT Act was a trade-off between civil liberties for domestic security (Finkelstein, Mansfield, Wood, Rowe, Chay, & Ozdemir; 2017).

Current Issues Regarding Domestic Security

The United States continues to enjoy a degree of domestic security in the decade and a half after 9/11. Crime rates continue to decline according to the FBI's Uniform Crime Reports and the Bureau of Justice Statistics' National Crime Victimization Survey (Gramlich, 2018), and there haven't been any major terrorist attacks in recent years on American soil. The United States nevertheless continues to experience threats and challenges to its domestic security. Terrorism continues to be a concern, but the frequency of mass shootings has multiplied through the years with the 2016 murder of 50 in the Orlando Pulse Night Club, followed by the 2017 Las Vegas shooting of concertgoers that killed 59 and wounded 850. These mass shootings have become common on national headlines. Due to a lacking response by legislators, victims like those at a high school in Parkland, Florida, have actively advocated against gun violence: particularly those that take place in schools.

Disasters have wreaked havoc on several regions in the United States, causing great concern for domestic security. In a report on national security, the Pentagon recognized climate change as a threat multiplier that can impact America's economy and resources and initiate an instable society through hunger, famine, poverty, and other unforeseen catastrophes (Department of Defense, 2014). The Gulf Coast's Hurricane Katrina in 2005 exemplifies the harm mismanagement, lack of leadership, and delayed responses can produce for government agencies that mishandle domestic security issues. The hurricane caused 1,833 fatalities and over $108 billion in damage (Knabb, Rhome, & Brown, 2005). The widespread blame on the government forced the resignations of several officials. Recently, the British Petroleum oil spill in the Gulf, wild fires in California, and Hurricane Harvey in Houston, Texas, keep reminding the nation that disasters, both natural and man-made, will continue to be a priority in domestic security.

Transnational crimes are also a significant threat to domestic security for officials protecting the American border. There is an overall unease that Mexican drug cartels are trafficking arms, cocaine, marijuana, and heroin, especially during the opioid crisis that has become a major public health crisis. There are also concerns over human trafficking for labor and sex from many of these nefarious groups. Human smuggling and illegal immigration from these borders have been the center of political campaigns as politicians provide scenarios of possible illegal entries by international terrorists or members of Central American gangs like that of MS-13, as mentioned by President Trump.

The Trump administration has carried out a zero-tolerance approach to illegal immigration through the separation of children from their parents. The policy was halted by a federal judge who ordered the reunification of the families. The discussion of these varying domestic security concerns reveals the growing number of white supremacists in the United States. According to a report prepared for Congress by the Government Accountability Office (GAO), since September 11, 2001, domestic violent extremists were responsible for 73% of all incidents that resulted in death compared to 27% of those committed by radical Islamic extremists (GAO, 2017, p. 3). Many of these groups tend to be anti-government, call for closing the border, ending non-white immigration to America, and have a history of advocating for social change through the use of terrorism and violence.

Future Challenges

There are many future challenges to America's security that necessitate the government's full consideration. The internet and cybersecurity will be at the forefront of domestic security. Cybercrime has become widespread in recent years for three reasons. Computers have become relatively inexpensive, and cybercrime today can be committed anywhere there is an internet connection. Cybercriminals have also become more sophisticated in their strategies by making sure that their threats are severe, frequent, and difficult to track. Armed simply with a computer, a security hacker can exploit the weaknesses of computer networks in our political, economic, and security institutions. The most recent example of political cybersecurity is the allegation that Russia hacked the Democratic National Party to sway the 2016 elections. In the economic sector, the hacking of bank accounts, personal information, and the recent data breach into Equifax are reminders of how easily cybercriminals can use their skills for fraud and the disruption of the economy. The hacking of JP Morgan Chase, Sony Pictures, Ashley Madison, and the iCloud accounts are a few recent examples that made international headlines in demonstrating cybercriminals' capabilities to encroach on domestic security.

Despite the grave threats of cybercrime, the leading concern among security experts is the use of computers and networks by cyberterrorists to cause major disruption, destruction, and disorder. Terrorists have learned in recent years the numerous ways the internet can be used to fulfill their goals and objectives. Islamic State of Iraq and al-Sham (ISIS), for example, has used social media to recruit members in Western countries to their cause. In the case of cyberterrorism, there is a concern that terrorists will use computers as their *modus operandi* in carrying out attacks. Through cyberterrorism, the internet can be utilized to disrupt infrastructure. Organizations or individuals can use their hacking abilities to remotely control cars, local traffic lights, power grids, water processing plants, as well as access America's aviation network or nuclear facilities. The Department of the Treasury, the Department of Justice, and the DHS have recently taken the lead into strengthening cybersecurity and all possible threats that cybercrime/terrorism can pose to domestic security.

Further Reading

Baggett, R. K., Foster, C. S., & Simpkins, B. K. (Eds.). (2017). *Homeland Security Technologies for the 21st Century*. ABC-CLIO.

Payan, T. (2016). *The Three US-Mexico Border Wars: Drugs, Immigration, and Homeland Security: Drugs, Immigration, and Homeland Security*. ABC-CLIO.

Weimann, G. (2015). *Terrorism in Cyberspace: The Next Generation*. Columbia University Press.

References

Department of Defense. (2014). *2014 Climate Change Adaption Roadmap*. Alexandria, VA. https://www.acq.osd.mil/eie/downloads/CCARprint_wForward_e.pdf

Department of Homeland Security. (2014). *The 2014 Quadrennial Homeland Security Review*. Washington, DC. Retrieved from https://www.dhs.gov/sites/default/files/publications/2014-qhsr-final-508.pdf

Finkelstein, E. A., Mansfield, C., Wood, D., Rowe, B., Chay, J., & Ozdemir, S. (2017). Trade-off between Civil Liberties and National Security: A Discreet Choice Experiment. *Contemporary Economic Policy*, *35*(2), 292–311.

Government Accountability Office. (2017). *Countering Violent Extremism: Actions Needed to Define Strategy and Assess Progress of Federal Efforts*. GAO-17-300. Washington, DC. https://www.gao.gov/assets/690/683984.pdf

Gramlich, J. (2018). 5 Facts about Crime in the US. *Pew Research Center*. Washington, DC. http://www.pewresearch.org/fact-tank/2018/01/30/5-facts-about-crime-in-the-u-s/

Knabb, R. D., Rhome, J. R., & Brown, D. P. (2005). Tropical Cyclone Report: Hurricane Katrina, 23–30 August 2005. *National Hurricane Center*.

Chapter 72

Gangs and Law Enforcement in the United States

Tamarra Smith
Lone Star College, Houston, TX, United States

Contents

Introduction 549
The Origins 550
The Purpose 550
East Coast, West Coast, and Midwest Gangs 551
Gang Operations 553
Statistics 554
Prevention 555
Conclusion 556
Further Reading 556
References 557

Introduction

The term gang, in its original context, referred to a group of people going somewhere. The English language initially adopted the term in a negative manner in association with pirates (Howell and Moore, 2010). Street gangs in the United States seem to have originated around the late 1700s on the East Coast. The origin of gangs correlated with the end of the American Revolution. The emergence of gangs appeared to have been fueled by poverty and immigration in urban areas. Gangs formed in areas where poverty-stricken people and immigrants gathered to form support systems. European immigrants and Anglo-born natives shared a similar struggle and competitive conflict, and discrimination began to be the basis for initial gangs. The primary

DOI: 10.4324/9781315144511-76

goal of gangs is power and influence. In efforts to become more powerful, gangs have now began forming alliances.

The Department of Justice estimates about 43% of gangs have some form of alliance. They are usually segregated by territory. The biggest growth in gangs came after the Post-Industrial Era. Along with this growth came an increased need for prevention and intervention. The influx of Mexican immigrants also fueled growth in gang creation and activity. The waves of various immigrants from around the world was by far the largest influence of gangs and gang activity (Howell and Moore, 2010). Gang members predominately fall into the following categories: male, Black, Hispanic, product of single mother household, and poverty-stricken neighborhoods. Individuals continue to join existing gang groups and also form new ones in order to meet their interests and make an income as well as to have a sense of belonging. The gang groups are responsible for crimes in the places they exist, especially across the cities leading to high crime rates across the United States.

The Origins

Gang activity began for the purposes of territorial alliances and management, jobs, and entertainment for individual ethnic groups. New York was ground zero for gang origination in the United States. It then extended to the Midwest, West Coast, and much later the Southern Region. Each region had its own wave of immigrants that influenced the gang activity, bringing their own offenses. Some of the gang groups in the United States were formed as early as the eighteenth century when the nation was experiencing a rapid growth in their cities. Many were seasoned criminal groups of youth fighting for individual interests and their rights. The gangs have evolved with time to be dangerous gangs with formal structures and leadership as well as rules and regulations that govern the activities of the gang members. The gang groups are currently on a wide scale. The latest wave of gang activity is transnational gangs, which refers to gangs that incorporate multiple nationalities. They may include Russian, Asian, African, Bosnian, Jamaican, and many more. These gangs are highly organized and known by their power and influence over various government entities (Howell and Moore, 2010).

Some 33,000 violent street gangs, motorcycle gangs, and prison gangs are criminally active in the United States today. Many are sophisticated and well organized; all use violence to control neighborhoods and boost their illegal money-making activities, which include robbery, drug and gun trafficking, prostitution and human trafficking, and fraud. Many gang members continue to commit crimes even after being sent to jail. A literature review by this research of the gang groups reveals the necessity for a wide examination of existing gang member groups so that it can provide better information to the current literature in existence.

The Purpose

The gang groups establish a sense of control of the areas they operate in as they mistreat and torment the people, especially those who are against them in the society.

Many of these groups are illegal and are thus excluded in the American societies. With this kind of exclusion, the gang members afford themselves the gang groups to feel the sense of belongingness. Individuals need to belong to certain collectives that they can identify themselves with and so they end up forming or joining gang groups which they feel they are fighting for certain interests or rather their rights (Adams and Pizarro, 2009).

East Coast, West Coast, and Midwest Gangs

Researchers have established many similarities between the East Coast, West Coast, Southern, and the Midwest gang groups. First and foremost, all the gang groups require their members to follow strictly the 13 rules of conduct which among them are respecting those members who are superior of the gang (Aryan, 2011).

On top of these 13 rules of conduct, the group members are required to submit their profit returns to the group, kill the victims as demanded, and to always demonstrate their superiority. The leaders of these gang groups from different regions meet on different occasions from time to time to discuss their linked activities and how they can deal with the rival groups. These gangs from all the regions operate independently with known identities while others prefer to remain unknown. They have no alliances with each other, though some of them carry out their missions together at times depending on the magnitude of the mission and the kind of threat involved. All the gang groups noted are organized into subsets which encompass an organized set of leaders and members. Initiation processes of all the gang groups mentioned above are essentially the same as they require the initiates to beat as they kill and rob the citizens and the rival group members.

The gangs are similar in the way they carry out activities in the sense that they engage in drug trafficking, human trafficking, and murders. The groups engage in other illegal activities which include carjacking, immigration offenses, invasions, as well as daring robberies. The gangs are violent as they believe that violence is the way to make their missions successful. The gangs ensure that the victims suffer a lot or they kill them in order to hide evidence and other gangs are paid to wipe some individuals in the society or a group of people in the society (Diamond, 2005).

Most of the gang groups have spread from their activities from their home region jurisdictions to external states and cities. This is infiltrated by the movement of their members from the headquarters region to other regions as the gang members are ambitious of propagating their crimes. The families of the gang members may also shift from one region to another, forcing the members to provide their services to the gang of allegiance from wherever they are. The gang members recruited to the criminal groups usually come from those backgrounds which are poverty stricken, because the sons and daughters of the low spectrum in the society have difficulties in accessing good education and good jobs. These children end up in gangs in order to provide for themselves and their own families. Street urchins born from street families usually end up in such criminal groups. This is a major similarity of the members of these gangs from different regions.

Previous research reveals that youth are the majority members of these groups as they are energetic and more flexible. The gang leaders usually target the young individuals who have got financial challenges as they are excited by the payments offered by the group. These gangs institutionalize in that they form a very complex organization which is able to withstand the dynamic leadership changes and be able to adapt to the environmental challenges. They are organized in such a way that management at different levels and the members have their managers who organize and coordinate the crimes. Additionally, every member of the gang group has an identity, be it a tattoo of the group, a t-shirt, a way of greeting or hand signs, and many others. All these signs help them to identify with one another easily, especially when they are carrying out missions. Every group has its own code of conduct which conforms to the gang's doctrines (Diamond, 2005).

All the gangs from the East Coast, West Coast, Southern, and the Midwest fulfill the needs of the community in one way or another in order to take cover within the community as they enjoy protection. They provide the community with security from invasion by other gangs and on other cases they provide economic support to members of the community. The gangs observe certain beliefs and observe different rituals which they believe would protect them from extermination by their enemies. These rituals are performed by the senior members of the group as they are the ones ordained to do so as per the gang's set of laws and regulations.

Previous studies have found that the leaders of the gang groups display some kind of paranoid character traits. These leaders believe that paranoia trait is much needed for the enemy's invasions (Diamond, 2005). This tendency perceived by the group is exacerbated by the paranoid thinking of their commander. The leaders also portray an inspiring and charismatic personalities outwardly in order to attract more recruits. All the gangs exhibit a similar in-group dynamic in terms of their group structure with the Southern and the Midwest gangs being very fluid in structure which makes it hard for the authorities to track them down (Adams and Pizarro, 2009). The old gangs East Coast and West Coast are constructed on a rigid and institutionalized hierarchies, as they portray a strong sense of loyalty and identity on the main leader of the gang. The gang members receive instructions from their main leader who coordinates the series of criminal activities in the region.

In-group dynamic is very crucial as it helps in protecting the identity of the members so as to reduce the threat from the state. The critical thinking of the individuals related to the groups thinking. The members support each other even when one is wrong or when the leader gives insensible instructions. The gang members of each of the group simply follow the instructions since they believe that instructions are to be followed and not to be judged. This is a form of coerced-motivation phenomenon which the groups have in executing some of the biggest missions in history. There are significant differences existing between East Coast, West Coast, Southern, and the Midwest gangs. There is a psychopathological contrast between these gang groups as they differ in size and in terms of magnitude of the crimes that each group commit. Every gang commits its own kind of crimes ranging from murder, kidnapping, drug trafficking, robberies, and car hijacking among many others (Howell and Moore, 2010).

The gangs differ in terms of the activities they engage in. Taking into consideration the factors which led into their formations, research work found that the groups transact different activities. The gangs have different interests at their hearts which force them to fight for those interests regardless of being against the law. Gangs also differ in terms of resources as some have vast resources they have acquired over the years of operation, while others have relatively small resources which limits their operations. Past studies reveal that those groups with small amounts of resources which include the Midwest and the Southern have got relatively few resources but are the most daring gangs ever recorded in history (Howell and Moore, 2010).

Gang Operations

Resource is a factor which guides the operations of every gang group. The more the resources, the more the activities and vice versa is true. This research work found out that all groups are equipped with different amounts of resources. A few like the East Coast gang have more resources and thus they carry out highly intensified activities while the rest may carry the same activities but of minor magnitude, though it is always felt by the citizens who incur the losses, including the army forces and security individuals manning different places.

It is true that some gangs like the West Coast and the Midwest possess more experienced human resource as they focus on training the new recruits better than other groups as they recruit fighters who retire from other gangs. Some researches argue that the gang groups recruit their members with consideration to specific factors which they require in their operations and executions of missions. They say the gangs who engage in deadly missions always prefer retirees who have got enough experiences in their years of work.

The moral of some societies is rotten to the core as some gangs naturally emanate from within the societies. These societies nurture and provide the gangs with resources required and they give their youthful teenagers to the gang groups (Howell and Moore, 2010). The gangs differentiate in terms of size as some gangs have relatively a large number of followers and recruits while others have few members who are inexperienced. These are mostly the gangs which do not have a large following like the Southern. This is in contrast to the formation of other sophisticated gangs who have established themselves, and they can recruit individuals and use their own resources to train them without the support of the community. These are the gangs which have hidden agendas which are not known to the communities which it is reared in.

The gangs which fund themselves and are built on hidden agendas do harm the community members as required and so they disengaged themselves as their interests are different from that of the community. Those gangs which are raised and supported by the community fight for the rights of the community and support them if need be. There exists a striking difference in the environments every gang operates in. They are shaped according to the regions where they originated. Every gang adapts their activities according to the prevailing situations and the state of government security existing in the region. There are places where the government presence is high and the gangs have to devise new ways to survive, or else, they are wiped out like vermin. The kind of moral decadence witnessed in the region also dictates the way gangs differ in their ways of operation.

Race differences dominate the gangs, as different gangs recruit members of a certain race only while others recruit every member without consideration of their races. The gangs which recruit members which belong to a single race are against other races and fight against them while those which recruit all races on most cases are not against any races like the whites and non-Hispanic Europeans. The ethnic composition of the gangs varies greatly.

The researchers who have examined the extent of the delinquent activities of these gangs from the West Coast to the East Coast and the Midwest as well as the Southern have found that the rates of the offenses of the adolescents joining the gangs differ. Studies have also found that there exist differences in offending within the gangs (Survey Results, 1996). Investigations conducted by this research study found out that the gang offending is usually restricted to those gangs which are racially or ethnically homogenous in their makeup. So, ethnic differences in the offending by the gangs are an issue which dissects through the gangs differently.

Past surveys considered revealed that some gangs, like the Midwest and the Southern gangs, operate in high-risk areas compared with the East and West Coast gangs. The dominating population and the geographic diversity allow for the diversification of the gangs, and their interests of value also rely on their geographical regions. Every gang evolves according to the dynamic factors located in their region headquarters, especially the big cities. Some recent studies show a great variability as well as the complexity of the problems experienced by these gangs ranging from the East Coast, West Coast, Midwest, to the Southern gangs. It also reveals an increase in the white-power gang activities (Dun, 2017).

Modern gangs are the most dangerous ones as the Midwest gangs seemed to be deadlier in their activities and missions which resulted in massive loss of property and lives. The rules and the codes of conduct of every gang differ from one to another given every group is founded under its own rules. These codes of conduct affect the way the groups carry out their merciless activities against humanity (Howell and Moore, 2010). The gangs from the Southern, Midwest, East Coast, and the West Coasts borrow graffiti and symbols from one another and even the names. Most of the gangs operate locally and externally based on their connections and the widespread of their members. There are rival gangs who cooperate together in their criminal missions, but the mergers of small gangs are a usual phenomenon in the United States as they unite to be strong. Involvement in drugs by every member is a common phenomenon in every gang as the members depend on these hard drugs to carry out some daring activities.

Statistics

The Department of Justice estimates there may be 175k to 200k gang members in California alone. This represents more than 250% growth over a decade.

Criminal Gang Activity. The majority of gang activity is criminal in nature. The crimes are oriented toward crimes including assault, drug trafficking and smuggling, home invasions, homicide, threats, sex and weapons trafficking, and intimidation. The most prominent gang activities are street-level drug deals, assaults, threats, robbery, and major or large-scale trafficking. The most prevalently reported drugs in gang activity include cocaine, heroin, and methamphetamine (US, 2015).

The 2015 National Gang Report notes that gangs have also evolved to include financial crimes such as fraud, ID theft, prescription drug fraud, counterfeiting, social security, and tax fraud. More and more street gangs are getting involved in white-collar crimes taking advantage of leniency through the criminal justice system.

Gangs form alliances and rivalries based on territories, race, resources, and power. The goals of the alliance are to secure as much money and power as possible. Feuds form when there is an interference with the goals of the gangs. As of 2015, there are more collaborating of gangs than ever before. It is estimated that approximately 43% of gangs have formed alliances. Goals of aligning are to form hybrid gangs and deter law enforcement prevention and control efforts. They are also seeking to create mutually beneficial associations to maximize profits and drug activities.

Law enforcement officers, police officers, and judicial officials all receive threats of harm and violence. While statistically the occurrences have been stable over the last few years, each incident is troublesome and makes policing gang activity a more difficult task. In 2014, a police officer was murdered and a District Attorney's father was abducted by gang members. With the ease of widespread communication, threats are even common than decades ago. Gang members use graffiti, text messages, phone calls, emails, and social media threats prior to in-person threats and violence.

Prevention

Preventing gang violence is a priority for areas affected by gang crime. Law enforcement agencies are expected to effectively deal with crime in society. Policing gang activity requires a shift from merely apprehending offenders and holding them accountable, to being proactive and actively seeking preventative solutions based on retrospective investigations (Rojek, 2003). Traditional policing and functions of law enforcement, courts, and corrections do not always effectively resolve gang-related activities. It becomes more difficult because gangs have dedicated members who have created a huge barrier to traditional criminal justice functions. The most effective strategy to deal with gang-related crimes and activity is problem-oriented policing (Goldstein, 1979). The goal of problem-oriented policing is the practice of a variety of methods to prevent and reduce crime. Police use historical data, current trends, and evaluation of efforts to begin to formulate a plan for policing gang activity. Most departments have a gang intelligence professional researching data, about the crimes, prevention efforts, and SARA analysis. Developments in anti-gang initiatives are grounded in deterrence theories and suppression programs. Research confirms that it is beneficial for law enforcement agencies to effectively recruit members of the community as law enforcers. Also, allowing officers who have some insight into the community, the problems, and the trends, discretion to assist in the designing of the solutions can be a valuable asset to reducing gangs and gang-related crimes (Rojek, 2003).

Successful gang intervention will include the perfect mix of service and opportunities paired with accountability and supervision which will directly relate to prevalent circumstances. The National Gang Center posts helpful articles and engages in detailed research to serve as a toolkit for use by law enforcement agencies. Additionally, the Department of Justice has the Organized Crime and Gangs section established in 2010 with the primary goal of combating all forms of organized crime. The best possible outcome for gang-related intervention will require a coordinated effort of law enforcement agencies and service providers to share information. Important agencies include police, courts, schools, prosecution, and other social and community agencies. The main component of prevention is intervention through targeting and outreach to those involved in gangs. In other words, intervention starts with letting the gang members and the community know that the law enforcement agencies have knowledge of their existence and activities and have a plan to mediate the problem (Wyrick, 2006).

Another solution to preventing gang activity is informal social controls. Policing via the Broken Windows Theory to assist in deterrence and reducing opportunity will help in prevention. Additionally, community policing activities will allow law enforcement to reduce gang activity. One effective tool to problem-oriented policing is being proactive (Braga, 2008). This involves a bare minimum of researching historical data, analyzing data for patterns and trends, and creating preventative solutions based on research. Preventative solutions are implemented to deter, reduce, and eliminate the unfavorable conditions. Retrospective investigations enhance the knowledge of past crime in an effort to create preventative solutions in problem-oriented policing. Many gangs recruit students from local public schools. Community policing at the public schools helps to decrease and deter recruitment activities.

The Post-Industrial Era in the United States influenced gang growth. The Post-Industrial Era produced a more prosperous society. However, everyone did not experience the same prosperity. This disproportionate growth led to increased gang activity. Gang members targeted those that gained wealth. Resulting from these newly found targets was the formation of gang territories. Each gang desired a piece of the wealthy segment. The workforce began to create unions, and those not working created gangs.

Conclusion

Gangs are a major phenomenon in the American society dating back to 1700 when they first came to existence in the East Coast. The gangs emerged due to many reasons, but the major ones are poverty and immigration as suggested by Howell and Moore (2010). These early gangs had different interests which led to their formation: to provide their families with food and other human basic needs as well as creating a sense of belonging for the immigrants in their new countries. Gangs and gang activity are presently impacting communities across the United States without any indication of decline in membership or criminal activity. It continues to be a challenge for law enforcement to effectively mediate gangs in their activity.

Further Reading

Butler, M., Slade, G. & Dias, C. N. (2018). "Self-Governing Prisons: Prison Gangs in an International Perspective," *Trends in Organized Crime*. https://doi.org/10.1007/s12117-018-9338-7

Decker, S. & Pyrooz, D. (2011). "Gangs, Terrorism, and Radicalization," *Journal Strategic Security*, *4*(4): 151–166.
Kinnear, K. L. (2009). *Gangs: A Reference Handbook*. Santa Barbara: ABC-CLIO.

References

Adams, Jennifer J., & Jesenia M. Pizarro. (2009). MS-13 Gang Profile. *Journal of Gang Research*, Summer 2009. Web. 1 Mar. 2017.
Aryan, Brotherhood. (2011). "Aryan Brotherhood. Southern Poverty Law Center, Web. 01 Mar.
Braga, A. (2008). *Problem-oriented Policing and Crime Prevention* 2008. Problem-oriented Policing and Crime Prevention. Monsey, NY: Criminal Justice Press 2008, ISBN: 13: 978-1-881798-78-1. *Policing: An International Journal of Police Strategies & Management*, *32*(4), 806–808. https://doi.org/10.1108/13639510911000830
Diamond, Andrew J. (2005). "Gangs." Chicago Historical Society, web 01 Mar. 2017.
Dun, J. (2017). Los Angeles Crips and Bloods: Past and Present. Retrieved March 02, 2017, from https://wenstanford.edu./c;ass/e297c/poverty_prejudice/gangcolor/lacrips.htm
Goldstein, H. (1979). Improving Policing: A Problem-Oriented Approach. *Crime and Delinquency*, 25(2), 236–258.
Howell, J. A. and Moore, J.P. (2010). History of Street Gangs in the United States. *Institute For Intergovernmental Research*, *4*, 1–25.
Rojek, J. (2003). A Decade of Excellence in Problem-Oriented Policing: Characteristics of the Goldstein Award Winnera. *Police Quarterly*, *6*(4), 492–515.
Safe Streets and Gangs Unit. (2015). National Gang Report (Rep.) Washington, DC: US Government. https://www.fbi.gov/file-repository/national-gang-report-2015.pdg/view
Survey Results. (1996). Gang Member Demographics, Sex. Office of Juvenile Justice and Delinquency Prevention, 1996. Web. 13. Mar 2017.
Wyrick, P. (2006, January). Gang Prevention: How to Make the "Front End" of Your Anti-Gang Effort Work. *United States Attorney' Bulletin*, *54*(3).

Chapter 73

Improvised Explosive Devices (IEDs)

Boyd P. Brown III
Nichols College, Dudley, MA, United States

Contents

Introduction 559
A Challenge of Definitions 560
History 562
Cheap Weapons, Expensive Solutions 564
Case Study: Somalia 566
Conclusion 567
Further Reading 567
References 568

Introduction

Improvised explosive devices, more commonly referred to as IEDs, have become synonymous with the 21st century wars the United States, and many other nations, find themselves embroiled in. Since at least 2003, with the rise of the insurgency in Iraq, news stories that report on an attack while showing footage of a smoking blast crater, shattered car, and bloodied victims being rushed to the hospital have become all too common. As a consequence, for most people, the term "IED" has become linked to modern conflicts, ones in which an organized military is pitted against a violent extremist organization. For example (as of this writing), the ongoing conflict in Afghanistan in which the United States and Afghan military confront fighters from the Taliban, the Pakistani Taliban, Al-Qaeda, and the Islamic State of Iraq and al Sham (ISIS). Over 3100 US troops have been killed and more than 33,000 wounded by IEDs, including over 1600 who have lost limbs. In addition, it is estimated that as many as 360,000 other troops may have suffered concussions and mild brain injuries from blast exposure (Zorova, 2013).

DOI: 10.4324/9781315144511-77

However, the history of the IED, and its employment in both symmetrical and asymmetrical warfare, are far longer and more complex than recent coverage may imply. Even within the United States, there have been notorious attacks using weapons that, were they used today, would be referred to as IEDs. Ted Kaczynski, aka the "Unabomber", waged a nearly 20-year "IED campaign" using mostly pipe bombs to start a revolution. Similarly, Timothy McVeigh constructed a massive fertilizer bomb, in modern parlance a vehicle-borne improvised explosive device (VBIED), to carry out his devastating attack on the Alfred P. Murray Federal Building in Oklahoma City on April 19, 1995. In fact, the IED has been utilized as a tool of terror and warfare almost from the moment explosives were invented.

This chapter explores the history of the IED, discusses the challenges and opportunities it presents on the modern battlefield, and explores a case study to demonstrate why the IED has come to define 21st-century warfare.

A Challenge of Definitions

Determining a precise definition for "IED" is a difficult challenge. Marc Tranchemontagne defines an IED as "a weapon that is fabricated or emplaced in an unconventional manner incorporating destructive, lethal, noxious, pyrotechnic, or incendiary chemicals designed to kill, destroy, incapacitate, harass, deny mobility, or distract" (2016, p. 154), while the US Department of Justice defines an IED as,

> A destructive explosive device capable of causing bodily harm, great bodily harm, death or property damage; with some type of explosive material and a means of detonating the explosive material, directly, remotely, or with a timer either present or readily capable of being inserted or attached.
>
> (Gill, Horgan, & Lovelace, 2011, p. 735)

In yet another approach, Clay Wilson, in *Improvised Explosive Devices in Iraq: Effects and Countermeasures*, identifies an IED as,

> a homemade mine designed to cause death or injury by using explosives that are hidden and set off using a variety of triggering mechanisms. IEDs can utilize commercial or military explosives, or homemade explosives, and often the IED builder has had to construct them with the materials at hand. IEDs could also possibly be used in combination with toxic chemicals, biological toxins, or radiological material.
>
> (Gill, Horgan, & Lovelace, 2011, p. 736)

These three definitions represent a sample of the 29 different definitions that Gill, Horgan, and Lovelace considered in their paper, *Improvised Explosive Device: The Problem of Definition* (2011). The three authors argue that, along with "terrorism" and "extremist", IED defies easy definition. The authors found that there were seven areas along which the 29 definitions were differ:

- Degree of sophistication
- Device components

- Explosive ingredients
- Initiation/detonation type
- Delivery systems
- Perpetrator type
- What is the device designed to do?

As Bale (2009) explains, there is nothing inherently wrong with the different definitions, and many have been formulated to focus on a specific aspect of IED development and usage. However, the problem with numerous and diverse definitions of IEDs

> is that virtually any kind of explosive device that is manufactured or used by nonstate groups in more or less nonconventional ways can now be placed willy-nilly into the 'IED' category... have we simply created a trendy new buzzword covering every type of bombing carried out by guerrillas, insurgents, irregulars and terrorists?
>
> (p. 4)

Gill et al. acknowledge the concerns of Bale as they discuss the differences in the 29 definitions they considered. They then make a case for a rigorous, academic definition of IED. They argue that this is

> important for a number of reasons. First, it provides a solid foundation for the comparative study of politically violent events... Second, employing a semantically rigorous definition overcomes the kind of boundary issues that simply view all bombings (at least in terms of the end-product) as IEDs.

They argue that, if properly defined, the term "IED" "is a key term that will help future research efforts on the nature of how terrorist organizations innovate" (Gill, Horgan, & Lovelace, 2011, pp. 737–742).

The definition that is offered, and this author supports, is:

> An explosive device is considered an IED when any or all of the following – explosive ingredient, initiation, triggering or detonation mechanism, delivery system – is modified in any respect from its original expressed or intended function. An IED's components may incorporate any or all of military-grade munitions, commercial explosives, or homemade explosives. The components and device design may vary in sophistication from simple to complex, and IEDs can be used by a variety of both state and non-state actors. Non-state actors can include (but are not limited to) terrorists, insurgents, drug traffickers, criminals, and nuisance pranksters.
>
> (Gill, Horgan, & Lovelace, 2011, p. 742)

This definition has the advantage that it is specific enough to allow researchers to distinguish between attacks that use an IED and those that do not. It is also flexible enough to apply in the face of the dynamic environment in which technology and techniques are constantly changing.

History

The term "IED" dates back to at least the early 1970s in court proceedings against the Irish Republican Army as well as a 1975 book about the conflict in Palestine following World War I. In the United States, the first clear reference occurred when the US army procured a patent for a counter-IED device in 1977 (Gill, Horgan, & Lovelace, 2011, p. 733). The actual use of improvised devices goes back even further. Revill, in *Improvised Explosive Devices: The Paradigmatic Weapon of New Wars*, argues that the improvised use of explosives can be traced back at least as early as the mid-1400s, primarily in siege warfare. By the 1500s, their use had expanded to "ship-borne IEDs". Perhaps, the most well-known example of IED usage in the "gunpowder age" was the so-called "gun powder plot" against Parliament in 1605. The plot was initiated by Guy Fawkes, who had received training in explosives during the Wars of Independence. The plan was to use 36 barrels of gunpowder to blow up not only King James, but Parliament too, completely decapitating the British government. A 2003 study by the Center for Explosion Studies at the University of Wales demonstrated that, had the explosion detonated as planned, not only would Westminster Abby have been destroyed, buildings nearly a mile away would have been severely damaged as well (Revill, 2016).

On the other side of the Atlantic, the infant United States experimented with improvised explosives, particularly in the form of sea mines. However, it was the Civil War, from 1861 to 1865, that would prove a fertile laboratory for the use and development of these weapons. Initially used by Confederate forces to defend the city of Richmond, Virginia, in 1862, these types of devices were at first considered barbaric and uncivilized by many military leaders on both sides. However, as the war dragged on, both sides began to experiment with the use of explosives in novel and creative ways. In the war's aftermath, the use of IEDs expanded beyond the military arena to many of the internecine rivalries and feuds that sprung up during reconstruction and beyond. "Thus, IEDs were employed in a courtroom battle over patent rights, disagreements over property titles, anti-corruption efforts, and insurance scams" (Revill, 2016).

Improvements in technology, most notably higher quality timers and ignition devices that allowed for more precise control of explosives, and the invention and patent of dynamite by Alfred Nobel in 1867, were quickly incorporated into IED design. Through the latter half of the 19th and early 20th centuries, Irish extremists, *Narodnaya Volya* (the "People's Will") in Russia, and anarchists throughout Western Europe and the United States conducted campaigns of "dynamite terrorism". While none of these groups were ultimately successful in their goals, they were involved in some noteworthy attacks. These include the assassination of Tsar Alexander II, by *Narodnaya Volya*, on March 13, 1881 (Revill, 2016), as well as perhaps the first use of a "vehicle" borne IED at the corner of Broad and Wall Street in New York City. On September 16, 1920, anarchists used a horse-drawn cart, which they realized would blend into the everyday traffic. The red wagon was packed with 100 pounds of dynamite and hundreds of pounds of "sash weights" – heavy metal weights used to balance window curtains. The resulting explosion killed 39 people and injured hundreds and caused over $2 million in damage (King, 2011).

The political and military conflicts of the 20th century, coupled with technological improvements in both the variety and number of commercial and military-grade explosives, meant that the use of IEDs, by states and non-state actors, became a common reality. Both sides used IEDs in various forms during World War I, often in the form of booby traps to slow the advance of enemy forces and to cover the withdrawal of friendly ones. During World War II, IEDs were relegated to "second tier" weaponry for the Allied militaries; they were used by partisan and resistance groups to wage a campaign of asymmetric warfare across Europe and, to lesser extent, Asia. IEDs were in much wider use with Axis forces.

> Explosive booby traps employing grenades, mines and demolition charges were used extensively along with more novel devices, including an explosive candy bar... a Thermos flask, an army mess tin with a bomb hidden beneath the bangers and mash, and a high-explosive device concealed in a can of motor oil.
>
> (Revill, 2016, p. 37)

While the combatants in the world wars used IEDs to deadly effect, it was conflicts both in the inter-war and post-war periods that cemented the relationship between the IED and violent extremist groups. The conflicts in Palestine both between the wars and in the post-war period, as well as in Northern Ireland beginning in the 1960s, combined not only the innovative use of IEDs but also the kind of media attention that allowed these attacks to catch the attention of a global audience. This union of lightly armed guerilla fighters and IEDs is perfectly logical. These types of groups often square off against organized militaries against which they cannot hope to match up, as in Iraq or Afghanistan where the United States military had dominant military force both on the ground and in the air. The IED represents a force multiplier that enables insurgents to bring the "fight to their enemy", deny opposition forces easy access to high-speed avenues of approach, and to channelize them into ambush kill zones, while exposing the insurgent forces themselves to minimal risks.

It is therefore no surprise that, as insurgents recognized the advantage and utility of the IED, they began to employ them in a wider array of attacks, oftentimes borrowing the tactics of other groups. An example of this is provided by the LTTE – Liberation Tigers of Tamil Elam. Initially a non-violent protest movement, the LTTE formed in response to aggressive policies of the Sri Lankan government (Revill, 2016). Originally operating as urban guerillas, the LTTE was driven from their base of operations, the city of Jafna, by Indian forces. The quickly adapted and reformed as an insurgency. When they turned to violence, the LTTE embraced and perfected a little utilized form of IED attack – the suicide bomber. From 1983 to 2003, the LTTE became one of the world's most violent extremist groups and were known not only for their suicide attacks but also as the likely "inventor" of the suicide vest. The LTTE also heavily recruited women and "pioneered the use of women in suicide attacks" (FBI, 2008).

Many sources believe that, for more than a decade, the LTTE were the most prolific suicide bombers in the world. In her book *Urban Battlefields of South Asia*, C. Christine Fair notes that "the execution of suicide missions – nearly all of which are successful – has been the primary means through which the LTTE has been able to intimidate and coerce the government and the island's civilian (Tamil and non-Tamil) populations" (2004, p. 53). She goes on to observe that, "what is striking about the LTTE hits is their quality and their accuracy. To achieve these successes, the LTTE has exploited the policies of the central government. For example, during the 1989–90 and 1994–95 peace initiatives there was a relaxation of security. The LTTE seized the opportunity to infiltrate the southern parts of the island, particularly Colombo" (p.44). Not only were these attacks sophisticated and successful, the LTTE conducted a disproportionate number of IED attacks. From 1980 to 2000, the LTTE conducted more suicide IED attacks than any group with 168 attacks. In that same period, Hezbollah carried out 52 attacks, the second most, and Hamas carried out, third on the list, 22 attacks (Fair, 2004, p. 41). The LTTE's attacks seem to have provided inspiration to other groups who have embraced both their methods and materials. For example, the LTTE developed a "sea-based suicide division.... to [confront] the Sri Lankan and Indian navies. It is quite likely that their experience was adopted by Al-Qaeda in its suicide IED attack on the *USS Cole* in the harbor of Aden, Yemen in 2000" (Revill, 2016).

Prior to the war in Iraq, the United States' most searing experience with IEDs was during the Vietnam War. In that war, the United States suffered just over 58,000 deaths, of which 47,406 were the result of hostile action: either killed in action, died of wounds suffered in combat, died while missing, or died in captivity. The cause for 7450 (15.7%) of the combat deaths is listed as "other explosive device" or IED. An additional 8456 deaths (17.8%) were listed as "multiple fragmentary wounds", which may include not only both explosive booby traps and other IEDs but also injuries from mortars, grenades, and other explosive devices that were not employed as IEDs (Unknown, 2018). While the exact total is likely somewhat higher, even taken individually, the 15.7% of combat deaths caused by IEDs represents the highest casualty ratio of any conflict the United States had been involved in, up to that time. Sadly, that would not remain the case as, "by 2007, IEDs were responsible for 60 percent of military fatalities in Iraq and 25 percent of military fatalities in Afghanistan. By 2009, however, IED incidents in Afghanistan had doubled and accounted for 75 percent of casualties in some areas" (Gill, Horgan, & Lovelace, 2011, p. 732). The IED has become one of the pre-eminent weapons of the 21st-century battlefield.

Cheap Weapons, Expensive Solutions

In World War I, the most technologically sophisticated, and expensive, weapon to be developed was the tank. Ironically, this weapon was intended, at least in part, to combat one of the least technologically sophisticated and cheapest weapons of that war – barbed wire. In many regards, we see a similar dichotomy emerging around IEDs and counter-IED systems. The grim reality is that IEDs are relatively inexpensive: "The IED placed in the van and parked in the garage under the World Trade

Center [in 1993] cost less than $400. This bomb killed six people, wounded around a thousand, and caused $550 million in damages" (Hodges, 2016). They are often constructed specifically to counter equipment intended to detect them. For example, in Vietnam, many of the mines that the Viet Cong employed were made from bamboo, rendering the metal detectors used by US minesweepers ineffective.

This pattern held true when the United States became involved in wars in Afghanistan and Iraq and faced weapons they were woefully unprepared for, which forced the United States to respond: "In 2001, we lacked counter-IED doctrine.... And had to figure things out on the fly. It was a steep learning curve with a high cost in lives lost and equipment destroyed, and the United States spent billions to counter a weapon that costs only a few dollars to make" (Tranchemontagne, 2016, pp. 153–154). Included in those expenditures are new agencies within the government to help acquire IED countermeasures quickly, new countermeasures, new types of military units that focus on counter-IED operations, counter-IED laboratories, new partnerships between law enforcement, the military, and international partners, just to name a few (Tranchemontagne, 2016). Since September 11, 2001, United States, and our allies, have spent an exorbitant amount of money to combat these weapons.

The security challenges presented by IEDs are multiple and complex. According to Peter Singer, in *Brookings*, in the first nine months of 2011, there were an average of 608 IED attacks spread across 99 countries (Singer, 2012). Numbers from Action on Armed Violence paint an even grimmer picture. "Between 2011 and 2016, AOAV has recorded 124,317 deaths and injuries from IEDs, of which 81% (100,696) were civilians" (2017, p.1). And while, within the United States, the public is most likely to associate IEDs with foreign wars, the domestic threat is significant. Incidents such as the successful Boston Marathon bombing in 2013 and the serial pipe bomb attacks in Austin, Texas, in 2018 focus US population's attention on the threat for a short time, before it is diverted to other issues. However, the reality is, the attempted use of IEDs is far more common in the United States than most people appreciate. Where the United States has been fortunate is, a combination of successful law enforcement efforts and a certain amount of luck has resulted in few successful attacks.

> A good example is the Spokane, Washington plot in January 2011. Kevin Harpham, a white supremacist affiliated with the National Alliance group, recently pleaded guilty to placing a shaped charge, designed to emit a blast of shrapnel covered with rat poison (which would have kept the victim's wounds form coagulating) along a parade route for the Martin Luther King holiday. Disaster was averted when a parking lot maintenance man discovered the bomb 30 minutes before the parade.
>
> (Singer, 2012)

In fact, according to Matthew Schofield and Erika Bolstad, in the six months prior to the Boston Marathon bombing, "there were 172 IEDs reported in the United States, according to a government count" (Schofield, & Bolstad, 2013).

The emergence of the IED threat on the battlefields of Iraq and Afghanistan, and an awareness of the potential danger that it poses to the homeland, have driven spending at the Pentagon to develop counter-IED systems and tactics. While up-to-date numbers are difficult to establish, what is clear is that the US government has spent exorbitantly on systems intended to negate the impact of the IED.

> The Government Accountability Office says it's impossible to estimate the total US cost of fighting bombs over two wars. But the Pentagon has spent at least $75 billion on armored vehicles and tools for defeating the weapons...about $2 billion was spent training troops in dealing with IEDs... another $7 billion went for intelligence operations to dismantle networks and financing.
>
> (Zorova, 2013)

And while these efforts have offered limited success, insurgents have proven adept at modifying IEDs and sourcing new materials for them in order to defeat US countermeasures. Despite the exorbitant spending, the surest way for the United States to limit combat casualties from IEDs has not been to rely on countermeasures, but to change tactics. That has resulted in a heavy reliance on helicopters to avoid bomb laden roads. Another option was to limit military travel to paved roads, which are harder to place bombs on or near. And, finally, the United States has, more and more, moved US forces out of direct combat, thus limiting their exposure to these weapons. Unfortunately, the consequence of that decision, intentional or not, has been to expose our allies – particularly in Afghanistan – to face the brunt of these attacks (Zorova, 2013). Clearly, the IED threat, both domestically and internationally, is multifaceted, complex, and one for which there are no easy solutions.

Case Study: Somalia

Somalia, and specifically the militia group al-Shabaab, highlights the challenges presented by IEDs. Al-Shabaab emerged after the demise of the Islamic Courts Union in 2006 and shortly thereafter became affiliated with Al-Qaeda and Al-Qaeda in the Arabian Peninsula (AQAP). In recent years, al-Shabaab has become one of the most lethal terrorist groups in Africa, and its lethality has coincided with an increased reliance on IED attacks. "Al-Shabaab's record 395 IED attacks in Somalia in 2016 – almost 11 times the number in 2010 and nearly a 50-percent increase over 2015 – more than doubled IED-related injuries and more than tripled IED-related deaths over the previous year" (Muibu, D. & Nickels B., 2017, p. 33).

As al-Shabaab's proficiency with IEDs grew, a general assumption among security and counterterrorism experts was that the growth was linked to the influx of improved technology and expertise of foreign groups to which al-Shabaab had contracts. Indeed, until 2010, the uptick in IED strikes did seem to coincide with the flow of, in particular, Al-Qaeda-linked fighters, who were welcomed into Somalia by al-Shabaab. However, after 2010, internal disputes within al-Shabaab led to leadership changes such that "by the end of 2013, through a combination of military action and internal housecleaning, key Al-Qaeda-linked international figures in al-Shabaab... were dead, leaving the remaining foreign fighters cowed" (Muibu, D. & Nickels B., 2017, p. 34). Combined with the rise of ISIS and the Islamist campaigns in Syria and Iraq, Somalia lost its appeal to most foreign fighters and the conflict became a local one. Yet, in spite of this purge, the "destructive capacity of al-Shabaab's IED attacks significantly increased" (Muibu, D. & Nickels B., 2017), which strongly suggests that the assumptions about al-Shabaab's reliance on technical expertise and materials from foreign sources was deeply flawed.

In fact, analyses of captured al-Shabbab IEDs show that they are actually of fairly crude construction and made with local materials, such as readily available mobile phones or motorcycle alarms, and from military hardware al-Shabaab captures from government forces. While the IEDs themselves are crude, where al-Shabaab has excelled is in the adept and innovative deployment of their IEDs. In other words, al-Shabaab has refined its tactics and techniques in order to maximize the lethality of their crude IEDs. In some cases, al-Shabaab uses IEDs to disable vehicles in the lead and end of a convoy, leaving the rest of the vehicles trapped in an ambush "kill zone". They have developed tactics to target first responders and law enforcement personnel and to negate the ability of government IED detection equipment:

> In Merca for example, al-Shabaab set up a double IED trap – a small motorcycle alarm IED served as bait to lure in a bomb unit, while a second, much larger IED lay buried deeper than usual (in order to prevent detection by bomb sniffing dogs) exactly under the spot where the bomb-recovery vehicle would park while disarming the first IED.
>
> (Muibu & Nickels, 2017)

The case of al-Shabaab serves as a clear indicator of the challenges of confronting an enemy who makes widespread use of IEDs – or even the threat of using IEDs. Even in environments where technological sophistication and material may be lacking, creativity, innovation, and adaptability may enable groups to use crude devices with lethal effect.

Conclusion

The use of IEDs has a long, complex history. As innovations improved the quality of explosives, ignition systems, and timing devices, more and more diverse IEDs have evolved. In the 21st century, IEDs have become a – but not the only – weapon of choice for many insurgent groups, militias, and terrorist organizations. The low cost, low risk, and potential of high reward, both militarily and through the press, of a successful IED attack make these weapons both ideally suited for groups which are unable to confront traditional military forces toe to toe. Despite the large expenditures in counter-IED devices, nations such as the United States, insurgent innovation, and creative employment still make it possible to deploy these weapons with deadly effect.

Further Reading

Hoffman, B. (1998). *Inside Terrorism*. New York: Columbia University Press.

Revill, J. (2016). *Improvised Explosive Devices: The Paradigmatic Weapons of New Wars*. Brighton, UK: Palgrave MacMillan.

Wright, L. (2006). *The Looming Tower: Al-Qaeda and the Road to 9.11*. New York: Knopf.

References

Bale, J. (2009). *Jihadist Cells and IED Capabilities in Europe: Assessing the Present and Future Threat to the West.* Monterey: Monterey Institute of International Studies.

Fair, C. C. (2004). *Urban Battlefields of South Asia*. Santa Monica: RAND Corporation.

FBI. (2008, January 10). Taming the Tamil Tigers - From here in the US. Retrieved from The Federal Bureau of Investigation: https://archives.fbi.gov/archives/news/stories/2008/january/tamil_tigers011008

Gaskill, M. (2018, July 6). *Booby Traps of the Vietnam War*. Retrieved from War History Online : https://www.warhistoryonline.com/vietnam-war/booby-traps-vietnam-war.html

Gill, P., Horgan, J. & Lovelace, J. (2011). Improvised Explosive Device: The Problem of Definition. *Studies in Conflict and Terrorism*, 34(9), 732–748.

Hodges, R. (2016). The Improvised Explosive Device Threat to the Homeland: Americans are not prepared. Retrieved from Small Wars Journal: http://smallwarsjournal.com/jrnl/art/the-improvised-explosive-device-threat-to-the-homeland-americans-are-not-prepared

King, G. (2011, October 4). Anger and Anarchy on Wall Street. Retrieved from Smithsonian: https://www.smithsonianmag.com/history/anger-and-anarchy-on-wall-street-96057606/

Muibu, D. & Nickels, B. (2017, November). Foreign Technology or Local Expertise? Al-Shabaab's IED Capability. *CTC Sentiel*, 10(10), 33–36.

Overton, I., Dathan, J., Winter, C., & Whittaker, J. (2017). *Action on Armed Violence Improvised Explosive Device (IED) Monitor (2017)*. London: Action on Armed Violence.

Revill, J. (2016). *Improvised Explosive Devices: The Paradigmatic Weapon of New Wars*. Brighton, UK: Palgrave MacMillan.

Schofield, M. & Bolstad, E. (2013, April 16). Bombs frequent in the US; 172 'IED' incidents in last 6 months, by 1 count. McClatchy Newspapers.

Singer, P. (2012, February 7). The evolution of improvised explosive devices (IEDs). Brookings.

Tranchemontagne, M. (2016, January). The Enduring IED Problem: Why we need doctrine. *Joint Force Quarterly*, 80(1), 153–160.

Unknown. (2018). Vietnam War Casualties (1955–1975). Retrieved from Military Factory: https://www.militaryfactory.com/vietnam/casualties.asp

Zorova, G. (2013, December 19). How the IED Changed the US military. *USA Today*.

Chapter 74

Kidnappings

Megan LaMare
Nichols College, Dudley, MA, United States

Contents

Introduction 569
Further Reading 573
References 573

Introduction

A major aspect of creating a secure country is the ability to ensure that the citizens feel protected by their government. There is a lot of controversy when looking at different aspects of how to ensure the feelings of security and how the government should go about doing so while also protecting the strength of the nation overall. In recent years, there has been a rising concern in how to effectively protect American citizens from the threat of kidnapping, especially since the 9/11 attacks.

Although the threat of kidnapping is not new, over the past decade or two, there has been increasing awareness of kidnappings due to media as well as a rise in economic "thrill". There are many different kinds of kidnappings that have been reported, which led to different classifications of kidnaping as well as different recovery processes. The term kidnapping triggers the mind to think of child kidnappings or parental kidnappings. This form of kidnapping is often the most heartbreaking as it involves a child who is abducted from their family and often times live under a false name with the kidnapper acting as the child's parent. The general assumption is that these forms of kidnapping occur by a complete stranger, but in actuality, it is more common for kidnapping to be conducted by someone the child knows or even a parent. ("Kidnapping: The Basics", 2019).

In the United States, there is a federal law that prohibits parents from taking a child to another country to obstruct the other parent. Child kidnappings and missing

DOI: 10.4324/9781315144511-78

persons in the United States are often what people think of when they consider the term kidnapping, but in all actuality in the United States, there are so many resources from local police departments, sheriff's offices, state police, the FBI, and even other federal departments that kidnappings in the United States are considered less of a threat. There are no foreign laws or governments that the law enforcement needs to abide by; therefore, it is much easier to resolve in that aspect (Zannoni, n.d.).

The major concern is kidnappings that occur, or victims who are removed from the United States, where the federal government is then restricted from rescuing the victims. The most common form is kidnapping for ransom which is defined by the "criminal leveraging the hostage in order to receive a payment for their family, employer, or country in exchange for the hostage's release" ("Kidnapping: The Basics", 2019). This form of kidnapping typically receives the most attention as it usually includes a high-profile and wealthy victim in an attempt to receive a large sum of money. Kidnappers are not trying to stay hidden and go unnoticed; they want the attention of the public to persuade quick release which requires a quick payout to them. The government and high-profile victims/companies have a clear plan to resolve these forms of kidnappings ("Kidnapping: The Basics", 2019).

Other common forms of kidnapping include Tiger Kidnapping (also known as proxy bombings) where the victim of the kidnapping is forced to perform some desired action such as opening a vault, unlocking an office to provide access somewhere restricted, or planting or even detonating a bomb. There is also political and ideological kidnapping which are considered the most dangerous form of kidnappings as the victim is exposed to radical groups with a range of motives and often chose their victims for impact. Kidnappers may be looking for a ransom or some other form of redemption in their eyes, but the death or torture of these victims is also just as acceptable for them based on their motivation.

More commonly being seen are express kidnappings and virtual kidnappings. Express kidnappings are common in Latin America and parts of Africa where there is a short-term ordeal, with a quick turnaround period of the kidnapper. For example, threatening the victim to take out a specific amount of cash at an ATM, which typically ends when the kidnapper gets a quick payment. As technology continues to rise, so does the likelihood of virtual kidnapping. In this instance, a person is not physically kidnapped but resembles a scam where the criminal calls the target's family or employer claiming to have the target and promises their release upon payment of a ransom, relatively a smaller amount as kidnapping for ransom ("Kidnapping: The Basics", 2019).

Currently, in the United States, people are being forced to live among several risk factors, and kidnapping represents one of the most serious threats to the well-being of individuals, families, businesses, and states. Kidnapping poses significant traumatic physical and psychological damages but is often seen as a quick way to make a profit and is most likely to occur in countries with a strong criminal culture, corruption, social conflict, and political instability. The level of risk that American citizens have varies based on social stature, political rank, economic standing, and location (Zannoni, n.d.). For kidnappers who are looking for high-profile victims, they tend to target journalists, soldiers, high-networth individuals, and children (Boe, 2017).

In many cases, local law enforcement and security services are too ineffective to provide safe resolution to kidnapping cases in foreign countries. A major aspect of resolving kidnapping cases is preparation for kidnapping to occur and having a plan to deal with the issue. A shocking 85% of kidnappings are perpetrated by organized criminal networks, small gangs, or individuals who are looking for wealth, while only 14% of kidnappings are conducted by militant groups according to the Global Risk Consulting Control Risks report (Boe, 2017).

Due to the level of risk the kidnapping has on large companies, as of 2019, over 75% of Fortune 500 companies has kidnap and release insurance (K&R Insurance) for their employees who travel abroad to high-risk destinations (Simon, 2019). A key aspect of managing the threat of a potential kidnapping is establishing who is at risk, who is likely to commit a kidnapping, and where and when the greatest risk is. The responsibility of the mitigation falls into the hands of the companies or organizations, executives, and the families. In the best-case scenario, international intelligence is always up-to-date for their threat assessments, data profiles, and contingency plans, but in instances where it is not enough, there are things like K&R Insurance (Zannoni, n.d.).

Through K&R Insurance, companies are able to have a plan and team in place to resolve issues where employees are kidnapped in foreign nations. It allows for companies to use professional negotiators, which 97% of the time leads to the successful resolution of a kidnapping. Since the attack on 9/11, the United States has made detailed restrictions through federal law to prevent and restrict the potential ability that terrorist organizations have to get finances through criminal activity like kidnapping for ransom. New laws have made it so that citizens often do not feel comfortable going to the federal government in kidnapping cases, in the fear that they may be prosecuted if they pay ransom to get their loved ones returned home, which often leads to the use of the professional negotiators and a hidden communication between kidnappers and the victims' families (Simon, 2019).

The current law states that the United States federal jurisdiction on kidnapping extends to the following six situations:

> (1) kidnapping in which the victim is willfully transported in interstate or foreign commerce; (2) kidnapping within the special maritime and territorial jurisdiction of the United States; (3) kidnapping within the special aircraft jurisdiction of the United States; (4) kidnapping in which the victim is a foreign official, an internationally protected person, or an official guest as those terms are defined in 18 U.S.C. 1116; (5) kidnapping in which the victim is a Federal officer or employee designated in 18 U.S.C 1115; and (6) international parental kidnapping in which the victim is a child under the age of 16.
>
> (1034 Kidnapping-Federal Jurisdiction)

Since the 9/11 attacks, the USA PATRIOT Act states that financing of any kind to a terrorist organization is grounds for prosecution. That includes the payment of a ransom to a terrorist organization which has caused fear to families of kidnapping victims to reach out to the federal government for help (Simon, 2019).

Doug Milne, a British insurance broker with a focus on kidnapping and ransom insurance, stated that "by refusing to allow concessions, you drive negotiations underground, so the intelligence you might otherwise get following the case disappears.

The families feel they could potentially be prosecuted. And the government becomes the enemy" (Simon, 2019). This raises the question, is no-concession policy achieving its desired goal of preventing and deterring kidnapers from kidnapping for ransom? Does it minimize the money ending in terrorist hands? The United States and the United Kingdom are spearheading the operation and maintaining listed foreign terrorist organizations so that the public would know who those organizations are (Simon, 2019).

In 2015, former President Barack Obama released a statement about his policy change on hostage situations and kidnapping for ransom. President Obama stated that the United States government should do everything they can do to bring kidnap victims home safe. He recognized that military personnel risk their lives and safety on dangerous missions to conduct such missions, and that there are 24 steps that his executive order would implement in order for a safe and quick return of American hostages and kidnapping victims, including how to support the families of victims. He took the opportunity to ensure that each department would be involved in the need for prioritization of our national security. The National Security Council would create a hostage resource group, with senior officials responsible for ensuring the policies are consistent as well as coordinated and implemented rapidly and effectively. He stated that there would be a designated senior diplomat as a special presidential envoy for hostage affairs, focused solely on leading diplomatic efforts, as well as the creation of "Hub" for side-by-side coordination with the FBI that would incorporate the family members, thus creating one clear voice during negotiation. President Obama clearly stated that the United States would continue to enforce the no-concession law, but that families would not be indicted for paying a ransom to save their family member; there is no need to add to their hurt (Obama, 2015).

The new executive order was a huge step as far as allowing the government to be more involved and monitor kidnappings, instead of driving them underground, but clearly stated that government funds would not pay a ransom to terrorist organizations. A study by West Point's Combating Terrorism Center found that from 2000 to 2015, the Middle east had conducted 469 kidnappings of Westerners (United States and Europe), that Africa had 456 kidnappings, and Asia had 154 kidnappings. It was also reported that 79% of reported kidnappings last less than 7 days. Eighty percent of kidnappings are carried out by unaffiliated criminals; only 14% are conducted by armed groups, and only 6% are by Islamist militant groups ("Kidnapping: The Basics", 2019).

Kidnapping is a major underground criminal market with a turnover of $1.5 billion a year. To prevent massive loss to companies that are threatened with the potential of kidnapping, K&R Insurance is the only real assurance to prevent major losses to a company when it comes to paying a ransom. K&R Insurance is a viable resource under the following three conditions: (1) kidnapping should be nonviolent and denotations are short; (2) insurance premia must be affordable, $250,000 a year for multinational companies; and (3) ransom and kidnap volume must be predictable and premium income must be greater than the expected losses. If K&R Insurance providers can no longer meet these expectations, then the policies will not be worthwhile for companies (Shortland, 2016).

A major aspect of domestic security is ensuring that citizens are confident in their government to protect them. With rising concern for the threat that kidnapping poses, and whether or not the United States' current policy is effectively deterring potential kidnappers, there is currently concern as to if enough is being done. The recent policy change, that will not penalize American citizens if they are to pay a ransom, allows for a more open communication in foreign kidnapping cases. The increase in communication will provide information that was not previously being acknowledged to allow for better understanding of foreign kidnappings and how, if it all, to change policy to further protect United States citizens. A major aspect of American government safely returning kidnapping victims is the ability for entry into a country to complete rescue missions without further endangering or causing more issues; so, it will be important to have positive relationships with foreign nations as long as the government is enforcing the no-concession policy.

Further Reading

Concannon, D. M., Fain, B., Fain, D., Honeycutt, A. B. Price-Sharps, J. & Sharps, M. (2008). *Kidnapping: An Investigator's Guide to Profiling*. Amsterdam: Elsevier.

Forest, J. (2012). "Global Trends in Kidnapping by Terrorist Groups," *Global Change, Peace & Security*, *24*(3): 311–330.

Tzanelli, R. (2006). "Capitalizing on Value: Towards a Sociological Understanding of Kidnapping," *Sociology*, *40*(5): 929–947.

References

7 Kidnapping-Federal Jurisdiction. (2018, September 19). https://www.justice.gov/jm/criminal-resource-manual-1034-kidnapping-federal-jurisdiction

Boe, S. (2017, March 1). Kidnapping and the Private Sector. https://sm.asisonline.org/Pages/Kidnapping-and-the-Private-Sector.aspx

Kidnapping: The Basics. (2019, February 15). https://www.osac.gov/Pages/ContentReport Details.aspx?cid=21732

Obama, B. (2015, June 24). *Statement by the President on the U.S. Government's Hostage Policy Review*. Speech presented at Statement by the President on the U.S. Government's Hostage Policy Review in Whitehouse, Rosevelt Room, Washington, DC.

Shortland, A. (2016, November 17). Governing kidnap for ransom: Lloyd's as a "private regime". https://onlinelibrary.wiley.com/doi/epdf/10.1111/gove.12255?referrer_access_token=wvvJ1KDLSNu80L-90GpDQota6bR2k8jH0KrdpFOxC65AjejxeRLuIToOnwxp7RBWh7SZujGvGdRq-xOWs5uDICgHb22Yd5aHC_A2WULZozlyzPN_cYovS1RvlOQm5MKE

Simon, J. (2019, January 25). The business of kidnapping: Inside the secret world of hostage negotiation. https://www.theguardian.com/news/2019/jan/25/business-of-kidnapping-inside-the-secret-world-of-hostage-negotiation-ransom-insurance

Zannoni, E. (n.d.). Kidnapping: Understanding and managing the threat. http://www.home securitysa.com/article.aspx?pklarticleid=2443

Chapter 75

La Familia Michoacana (LFM) Mexican Drug Cartel

Ashley Corcoran
Nichols College, Dudley, MA, United States

Contents

Introduction 575
Further Reading 579
References 579

Introduction

Michoacán, Mexico has long been an established home for drug production and gangs. This area is subjected to impoverished farmers who cultivate marijuana and opium poppy. Many groups have reigned their power over the insecure territories in Mexico, the most powerful being the Michoacán family. It took years for La Familia Michoacana, LFM, to ingrain their dominance among the other groups and areas in the region. Nevertheless, they were able to grow and prove their dynasty while terrorizing Mexico with beheadings and attacks (Ávalos, 2017).

In the 1990s, a criminal-based organization known as El Milenio controlled the Michoacán area. They flourished by growing cannabis and opium poppy in Michoacán and then selling it to larger cartels. El Milenio ruled the area for some time until a small group of lieutenants reached out to the Gulf Cartel to overthrow their leaders. The Gulf Cartel then sent a group by the name of the Zetas to take over. The Zetas posed a threat because they were a more powerful and larger cartel. By 2003, the Zetas were the new head of the region. The locals of Michoacán resented this group because they were seen as repressive outsiders. When the drug business expanded to the methamphetamine production, the animosity increased. LFM had once worked with the Zetas to overthrow the previous and more traditional Michoacán family,

DOI: 10.4324/9781315144511-79

The Valencias. Once the Michoacán family grew more powerful, they were able to break away from their allies. They turned against the group and began to attack the dealers and addicts of the methamphetamine. LFM allied with the Sinaloa and Gulf Cartels to fight its challengers, the Zetas. They were then able to expand into new territory along the United States and Mexico border. LFM was known for their ability to corrupt local government officials mostly because of their massive profits from their methamphetamine production (Ávalos, 2017).

LFM emerged themselves as a self-styled independent vigilante group. The organization was thoroughly successful in driving the Zetas out of Michoacán. LFM was then able to expand into other states, including Guerrero, Morelos, Guanajuato, Queretaro, Jalisco, and Mexico City. The Michoacán family had its base and origins in Michoacán, specifically Sierra Madre del Su. The group's power base was located in the seven municipalities that make up "Tierra Caliente." The power base itself was located in Southwest Michoacán, about 600 miles from the United States border. Their biggest money maker continued on to be methamphetamine (Ávalos, 2017). LFM also engages in the trafficking and production of cocaine, heroin, and marijuana (Kostelnik, & Skarbek, 2013).

The Michoacán family began to control the areas of Michoacán with similar tactics from the Zetas. The underlying influence of the Zetas was visible upon the actions and beliefs of the family. Both groups made frequent use of billboard-style messages to communicate with the public. The messages would include threats of barbarous violence. LFM was notorious for the public displays of brutality, also known as "corpse messaging." The official announcement of the family's existence was through a gruesome incident that ended up making international news. LFM made their independence clear in October 2005 at Sol y Sombra, a nightclub in Uruapan, Mexico. Several men dressed in military garb marched into the bar with machine guns, and they forced the crowd to stay where they were as they tossed five human heads on to a dance floor (McKinley, 2006). There were notes attached to them which read, "Only those who should die will die. Let everyone know, this is divine justice." The message marked the existence of LFM (Kostelnik, & Skarbek, 2013).

Torture techniques such as beheadings were something that the Michoacán family were very familiar with. The threat of violence is commonly used to reduce community resistance. The use of violence also leads to promoting membership. LFM provides their members with added benefits such as money, power, a reputation, and protection. They will exclude these benefits if a member defects. Acts of defections by gang members include stealing drugs, not complying to assigned duties, and becoming involved with the government. The consequences of disobedience come in three infractions. The first is a beating, the second is a more serious beating, and the last infraction is a basis for execution. The grounds for leaving LFM are grave. Whoever leaves La Familia will die. The organization was able to grow quickly through these tactics (Kostelnik, & Skarbek, 2013). After being driven out, Zeta compared the Familia to "radical islamists" and were convinced that they were driven by "ICE" (Ávalos, 2017).

The Familia Michoacana was proudly regionalist. They claimed to have won over the public in Western Michoacán. Regional loyalties were sought because of several social projects. LFM was able to elicit cooperation from nonmembers through their generosity. The projects included building schools, roads, providing employment through the drug trade, and taking over the police's role in resolving domestic disputes. LFM was seen passing out bibles and money to the poor, only benefiting the community even more. The organization advocates a strong religious culture. The family was able to win over hundreds of recruits in just a few years (Ávalos, 2017). LFM often used the newspaper to advertise their strategies. The organization was able to excuse their actions by expressing that they are for the "good of the people." A powerful ploy that they used was punishing criminals in the community. Anyone who has committed or have been accused of acts such as rape, robbery, corrupting the youth, and engaging in other heinous crimes would be whipped or executed. LFM wanted the public to see them as an organization that is pledged to making Michoacán a better place rather than being a drug-trafficking, violent group (Kostelnik, & Skarbek, 2013).

LFM expanded rapidly and was able to grow from a small organization to one of Mexico's most powerful and brutal drug-trafficking organizations. It's been revealed that at one point, the United States Drug Enforcement Administration recovered around 33 million dollars from several LFM operations. A single subgroup within the organization has the potential to generate more than 10 million dollars in drug revenue. LFM is assumed to earn hundreds of millions of dollars annually. The organization is able to receive more than just drug-related currencies. They also own several restaurants, nightclubs, and convenience stores in Michoacán (Kostelnik, & Skarbek, 2013).

There were thought to be at least three internal factions within the LFM. They would be responsible for juggling partnerships with various cartels up until the group weakened. Each of the internal fractions reportedly was set on a degree of autonomy. One branch would be dedicated to methamphetamine production while the other would extract extortion payments, and the last would be made up of hitmen and more (Ávalos, 2017). The top structure of the organization is controlled by an executive council which consists of businessmen and drug traffickers. The inner divisions that were present within the executive council were formerly headed by the man who founded LFM, Nazario Moreno Gonzalez, "El Chayo" or "El Mas Loco." The executive council was reportedly linked to the Sinaloa Cartel. The middle management is in charge of coordinating the executive council's demands. They deal with foreign distribution cells, regional cells, and municipal cells. Middle management will perform particular tasks which include murder, extortion, and narcotics distribution. The third part of LFM's structure consists of plaza chiefs or territorial managers. The organization divides its territory and the plaza chief's control to each of the areas (Kostelnik, & Skarbek, 2013).

There were multiple leaders of the LFM from the initial start of the organization to the crippling end. Carlos Rosales Mendoza originally founded the organized crime group. Nazario Moreno Gonzalez, "El Chayo" or "El Mas Loco," was known as another leader who was dedicated to the group until he was reported killed in a shootout with police in December 2010 in Apatzingan, Michoacán. In January 2011, shortly after El Chayo's death, the group announced that it had intentions to completely diffuse. They wanted to end the suffering of the Michoacán people from the federal police. Eventually, the report of El Chayo's death proves to be wrong, but it was a rumor that continued on for years. The official death of El Chayo was reported by government officials on March 9, 2014. He was thought to be working on behalf of another drug cartel in Mexico. El Chayo was allied in a shootout with security forces in Tumbiscatio, Michoacán. They said fingerprint tests had proven his identity (Parco, 2018). El Chayo's death had triggered the split between two rival bosses in the Familia Michoacana. One of the two being, Jose de Jesus Mendez, "El Chango." He ended up being an ally to a cartel by the name of La Resistencia, but still remained with LFM until the end. The second leader who separated from LFM was Servando Gomez, "La Tuta." After leaving, he formed the Caballeros Templarios, also known as the Templar Knights. This new organization publicly announced its existence in March 2011 with the use of banners and a stage. The banner claimed that they were replacing the Familia Michoacana. The Knights then hung the bodies of two young men from bridges in a town in Tierra Caliente to create the same type of fear that LFM once did. Today, the Knights dominate Michoacán and several other regions of Mexico. They visibly influence the process of authority elections in those regions (Aranda, 2013). Mendez, the one leader who was left over of the Familia, was arrested in June 2011. He confessed to authorities that he had been forming an alliance with the hated Zetas. This alliance would result in strides against the Knights (Ávalos, 2017). Currently, Hector Garcia, "El Player," is said to be controlling Familia Michoacana and whatever operations they have left over in Guerrero and the state of Mexico.

At the height of its power, the Michoacán family was one of the most violent, potent, and powerful of Mexico's criminal organizations. The activities that they were involved in ranged from drug trafficking, kidnapping, extortion, torture, and racketeering. The group had connections inside of Mexico as well as internationally. Their worldwide contacts for methamphetamine included Holland, India, China, and Bulgaria. The Familia Michoacana also connected with criminal-based groups that were established in the United States. Groups in Chicago, Dallas, Los Angeles, and Atlanta all conspired directly with the Familia for cocaine shipments. These direct correlations shocked investigators because of the border's distance being more than 600 miles (Ávalos, 2017). Lazaro Cardenas, a major port city, served as an access spot for the Familia. The group was able to receive cocaine shipments from Colombia as well as other chemicals needed for methamphetamine that were sent and produced by Asia. The control of the port was considered very deadly. An estimated 1,500 people had died there in connection of disputes with the Familia. After drug trafficking, extortion is what provided the Familia with a reliable source of income. There was an estimated 85% of licit businesses in Michoacán making regular payments to the group (Ávalos, 2017).

In November 2011, it was reported that the government considered the Familia to be all extinct. The Knights took over much of their operations and networks. The Knights Templar had won over their colleagues in the Familia. Today, it is unclear how much power the criminal group currently holds. Authorities consider the Michoacán family to be almost extinct. With the decline of the group, some reports indicate that the group has retrenched in Guanajuato and the Mexico State. Recent news indicates that the group may be looking to gain power again after a police raid in May 2014 of an operating cell in Guerrero. There is an opportunity to gain power again in the country's southwest region following the reported weakening of the Knights Templar (Ávalos, 2017).

Further Reading

Bunker, R. J. & Sullivan, J. P. (2020). "Mexican Cartel Strategic Note No. 29: An Overview of Cartel Activities Related to COVID-19 Humanitarian Response," *Small Wars Journal*, https://smallwarsjournal.com/jrnl/art/mexican-cartel-strategic-note-no-29-overview-cartel-activities-related-covid-19

Flanigan, S. (2014). "Motivations and Implications of Community Ser ations and Implications of Community Service Pr vice Provision b vision by La Familia Michoacána / Knights Templar and other Mexican Drug Cartels," *Journal of Strategic Security*, *3*(7), 63–83. https://scholarcommons.usf.edu/cgi/viewcontent.cgi?article=1365&context=jss

Grayson, G. W. (2010). *La Familia Drug Cartel: Implications for U.S.-Mexican Security*, Washington, DC: Strategic Studies Institute, https://apps.dtic.mil/dtic/tr/fulltext/u2/a534376.pdf

References

Aranda, S. 2013, Stories of Drug Trafficking in Rural Mexico: Territories, Drugs and Cartels in Michoacán. *Revista Europea De Estudios Latinoamericanos Y Del Caribe / European Review of Latin American and Caribbean Studies*, *94*, 43–66. http://www.jstor.org/stable/23408421

Ávalos, Héctor Silva. 20 September 2017, "Familia Michoacana," *InSight Crime*. www.insightcrime.org/mexico-organized-crime-news/familia-michoacana-mexico-profile/

Kostelnik, J., & Skarbek, D. 2013, The governance institutions of a drug trafficking organization. *Public Choice*, *156*(1/2), 95–103.

McKinley, James C. 26 October 2006, "With Beheadings and Attacks, Drug Gangs Terrorize Mexico," *The New York Times*. www.nytimes.com/2006/10/26/world/americas/26mexico.html

Parco, Nicholas. 9 April 2018, "Carlos Rosales Mendoza, Founder of Mexican Drug Cartel La Familia, Shot and Killed." *Nydailynews.com*, New York Daily News. www.nydailynews.com/news/world/carlos-rosales-mendoza-founder-la-familia-cartel-killed-article-1.2479797

Chapter 76

Law Enforcement and Legal Foundations of Homeland Security

Nicholas J. Barnes
Brown University, Providence, RI, United States

Contents

Introduction 581
Statutory Law 582
Establishing the Department of Homeland Security 583
Legal Basis for Law Enforcement Against Terrorism 584
Conclusion 584
Further Reading 584
References 584

Introduction

The United States Department of Homeland Security (DHS) has a vital mission: to secure the nation from the many threats it may face. The DHS employs more than 240,000 employees in jobs that range from aviation and border security, emergency response, cybersecurity analyst to chemical facility inspector. It was created specifically to address new domestic terrorism threats that emerged in 2001 and 2002 (About DHS, 2017).

The United States came under attack in 2001 and 2002 in ways in which it had not ever experienced previously. As a response to these new threats to the country, Congress responded by passing The Patriot Act in 2001 and The Homeland Security Act of 2002, both of which were signed into law by President George W. Bush.

DOI: 10.4324/9781315144511-80

The acts created a new federal government agency to better defend the country, the DHS. The acts specifically empowered the DHS to defend the United States from acts of terrorism, as well as reorganized several existing agencies, services, and duties of the government. Despite passing through Congress with significant majorities, the acts are not without its critics; there are some contradictory regulations and what some believe is a sacrifice of personal liberty and privacy.

The terrorist attacks on September 11, 2001, were highly coordinated and had been in various stages of planning for years. Unfortunately, though various U.S. agencies had pieces of useful information that may have, in combination, helped prepare for or prevent the attack, there was insufficient infrastructure to coordinate the necessary level of intelligence sharing and cooperation (National Commission on Terrorist Attacks, 2004). In 2002, a series of attempted attacks using the toxin Anthrax further exacerbated the need for a single entity to focus on border security and domestic terrorism prevention (Ziskin & Harris, 2007).

Statutory Law

In the United States, power to propose and consider bills and enact laws lies in the Congress. Members of either the Senate or the House of Representatives may propose legislation. When a bill is introduced, it is given a number and a prefix: "H.R." signifies a House bill and "S." a Senate bill. The bill is then referred to a committee with jurisdiction over the primary issue of the legislation. A large bill, like the Homeland Security Act, will be referred to multiple committees. Within each committee, legislators will debate, collect evidence and testimony, and recommend changes. After proposed amendments are adopted or rejected, the bill will either move out of the committee or to the entire House or Senate. The full legislative body will then discuss and debate and perhaps further modify the bill. Eventually, there will be a vote to pass the "final" version. If successful, it will move to the other legislative branch and repeat the process anew. Once both the Senate and House have approved their versions of the bill, a conference between the two may be convened to reconcile any differences. It then returns to each legislative branch for a final vote, whereupon it can be signed into law by the President (NAEYC).

After the attacks on 9/11, Congress moved quickly to enact a bill that would provide additional security for the nation, as well as increased law enforcement ability to "deter and punish terrorist acts in the United States and around the world." The Act's full title is "Uniting and Strengthening America by Providing Appropriate Tools Required to Intercept and Obstruct Terrorism Act of 2001," or its ten-letter abbreviation, USA PATRIOT. To avoid using the unwieldy acronym, it is typically called the Patriot Act. The bill is a massive document, with over 300 pages of additions and modifications to U.S. law. The primary areas of focus are enhancing domestic security against terrorism, increased government surveillance ability, border security provisions, and mandated information sharing (Patriot Act, 2001).

The specific measures created by the Patriot Act would fill an entire book, but broadly speaking, they permit U.S. authorities to pursue terrorists, seize funds, and obtain information via typically extrajudicial means, like wiretapping. These amount to brand new law enforcement powers, since prior to the Patriot Act, all government officials and law enforcement agencies were restricted in their police powers by Constitutional Amendment.

U.S. citizens historically have been protected from unwarranted searches and seizures, or to be "secure in their persons," by the Fourth Amendment to the Constitution (U.S. Constitution). Furthermore, warrants may only be obtained after law enforcement demonstrates probable cause to the satisfaction of a court-appointed third party. The Patriot Act, in the effort to stop domestic terrorism, lowers the burden as long as the target is suspected of terrorist activity (Whitehead & Aden, 2001).

Perhaps the largest change was in the section of the Patriot Act titled "Removing obstacles to investigating terrorism." It establishes expanded use of National Security Letters or NSLs. An NSL is a subpoena issued by government agency, like the Federal Bureau of Investigation (FBI), Central Intelligence Agency (CIA), or National Security Agency (NSA), that permits the collection of information from a person or business. The NSL does not require probable cause, the oversight of a third party, and additionally places a gag order on the recipient, preventing them from disclosing such a letter ever being received (Patriot Act, 2001). This stands in contrast to a typical search warrant, which requires probable cause, must be approved by a court or court-appointed magistrate, and is documented. As such, the use of NSLs was eventually found to be unconstitutional in 2015 (*Doe v. Ashcroft*, 2004).

NSLs aside, many of the Patriot Act's enhanced intelligence collection and enforcement powers were given an expiration of December 31, 2005. The majority of the provisions have since been extended or reauthorized.

Establishing the Department of Homeland Security

The Homeland Security Act began its journey in the House of Representatives as bill H.R. 5005, and to give a sense of the bill's scale, it went through a whopping 13 committees before being sent to the Senate for consideration. The committees were:

- House Homeland Security (subcommittee)
- House Agriculture
- House Appropriations
- House Armed Services
- House Energy and Commerce
- House Financial Services
- House Government Reform
- House Intelligence
- House International Relations
- House Judiciary
- House Science
- House Transportation and Infrastructure
- House Ways and Means

(Creation of the DHS, 2015)

Eleven days after 9/11, the White House appointed the first ever "Director of Homeland Security" in an effort to oversee and coordinate the complicated task of safeguarding the country from further attack. It was not until the Homeland Security Act in 2002 that the DHS formally came into being (Creation of the DHS, 2015). The new DHS was a distinct new entity, which leveraged provisions already in place from the USA Patriot Act, passed the year prior. Twenty-two existing entities moved under the DHS, including the Coast Guard, Secret Service, Federal Emergency Management Agency, Immigration and Customs Enforcement, and the Transportation and Security Administration (CNN.com, 2002).

Legal Basis for Law Enforcement Against Terrorism

It is important to note that the laws protecting the liberty of American citizens do not bestow the same protections to non-citizens. This means that foreign terrorists already lack many of the same protections as Americans. Furthermore, President Bush and his administration determined that terrorists were not criminals, and thus subject to the U.S. criminal justice system, but instead to be considered foreign aggressors committing acts of war. The intense focus on prevention, rather than criminal prosecution, has led to stronger investigatory and detention powers than the government previously possessed (Whitehead & Aden, 2001). Much of this authority is granted by the Patriot Act and the Homeland Security Act.

Conclusion

The DHS, along with other federal and local law enforcement, has broad powers to detect, pursue, and prevent terrorism. These powers stem from the significant acts of Congress in the aftermath of September 11, 2001, the Patriot Act, and the Homeland Security Act. Though the scope of these powers has been challenged, they are largely intact and continue to be leveraged in the war on terror.

Further Reading

Alperen, M. J. (2017). *Foundations of Homeland Security: Law and Policy*. Hoboken: John Wiley & Sons, Inc.

Martin, G. (2019). *Understanding Homeland Security*. Thousand Oaks: Sage Publications.

Zaffar, E. (2019). *Understanding Homeland Security: Foundations of Security Policy*. Abingdon: Routledge.

References

CNN.com (Tuesday, November 26, 2002). *Bush signs Homeland Security bill*. Retrieved from http://www.cnn.com/2002/ALLPOLITICS/11/25/homeland.security/

Department of Homeland Security (September 27, 2017). *About DHS*. Retrieved from https://www.dhs.gov/about-dhs

Department of Homeland Security (September 24, 2015). *Creation of the Department of Homeland Security*. Retrieved from https://www.dhs.gov/creation-department-homeland-security

Department of Homeland Security (March 7, 2018). *Operational and Support Components*. Retrieved from https://www.dhs.gov/operational-and-support-components

Doe v. Ashcroft, 334 F. Supp. 2d 471 (2004).

Homeland Security Act of 2002, Public Law 107-296 (November 25, 2002).

National Association for the Education of Young Children (n.d.). *The Federal Legislative Process, or How a Bill Becomes a Law*. Retrieved from https://www.naeyc.org/our-work/public-policy-advocacy/federal-legislative-process-or-how-bill-becomes-law

National Commission on Terrorist Attacks upon the United States. (2004). *The 9/11 commission report: Final report of the national commission on terrorist attacks upon the United States*.

Patriot Act, or Uniting and Strengthening America by Providing Appropriate Tools Required to Intercept and Obstruct Terrorism Act of 2001, Public Law 107-56 (October 26, 2001).

U. S. Constitution, Amendment 4. n.d.

Whitehead, J. W., & Aden, S. H. (2001). Forfeiting enduring freedom for homeland security: A constitutional analysis of the USA Patriot Act and the Justice Department's anti-terrorism initiatives. *American University Law Review*, *51*, 1081.

Ziskin, L. Z., & Harris, D. A. (2007). State health policy for terrorism preparedness. *American Journal of Public Health*, *97*(9), 1583–1588. http://doi.org/10.2105/AJPH.2006.101436

Chapter 77

Los Zetas Mexican Drug Cartel

Ryan Roberts

Old Dominion University, Norfolk, VA, United States

Contents

Introduction 587
History 588
Further Reading 589
References 589

Introduction

Los Zetas (Spanish for "The Zs") is a Mexican cartel primarily concentrated in the state of Coahuila and the city of Nuevo Laredo located in the state of Tamaulipas. The name originated from the group's first commander Arturo Guzmán Decena whose Federal Judicial Police radio code was "*Z1*," a code given to high-ranking officers. Additionally, Los Zetas is considered one of the most technologically sophisticated cartels utilizing social media to coordinate their operations (Campbell, 2010; InSight Crime, 2012). Their involvement in illicit activities includes drug trafficking, gun running, protection rackets, prostitution rings, assassinations, extortion, and kidnapping (Sullivan and Logan, 2010; Grayson, 2014).

In terms of geographical presence, Los Zetas is the largest Mexican cartel. They operate in the Gulf of Mexico, in the southern Mexican states of Tabasco, Yucatán, Quintana Roo, and Chiapas, and in the Pacific Coast states of Guerrero, Oaxaca, and Michoacán, as well as in Mexico City. Outside of Mexico, their operations extend throughout the Western Hemisphere. Their continued expansion has provided Los Zetas connections in North, Central, and South America (Campbell, 2010). It has also been reported that they have expanded to Italy and begun cooperating with

DOI: 10.4324/9781315144511-81

'Ndrangheta'. In 2012, the Zetas started an alliance with Los Rastrojos, maintaining control over the drug routes between Colombia in La Guajira and the Venezuelan state of Zulia utilizing this as a gateway to the United States and Europe. In 2017, Venezuelan Vice President Tareck El Aissami was sanctioned by the United States Treasury Department under the Foreign Narcotics Kingpin Designation Act. US intelligence reports indicated that El Aissami assisted Los Zetas by facilitating drug shipments from Venezuela to Mexico and the United States (Correa-Cabrera, 2017).

The primary allies of Los Zetas are the Tijuana and Juárez Cartels in Mexico located in the Baja California region and the state of Chihuahua, respectively. Headquartered in the state of Sinaloa, the Sinaloa Cartel is the main rival of Los Zetas. After a failed alliance, the Gulf Cartel allied with the Sinaloa Cartel to combat Los Zetas (Logan, 2012). In the United States, Los Zetas has formed alliances with several Hispanic gangs, including the Sureños, MS-13, Latin Kings, and the Mexican Mafia. FBI reports also indicate that street gangs like the Bloods and Crips and the Bandidos Motorcycle Club have been known to cooperate with Los Zetas.

History

The genesis of Los Zetas emerged in the 1990s when former elite members of the Mexican Army, Grupo Aeromóvil de Fuerzas Especiales (GAFE), branched off and began working as enforcers for the Gulf Cartel. Members of GAFE received training from Israeli and US Special Forces in urban warfare which included tactics such as rapid deployment, marksmanship, counter-surveillance, and intimidation, among other skills. In 1999, Osiel Cárdenas Guillén, leader of the Gulf Cartel, recruited retired Army lieutenant Arturo Guzmán Decena, the founder of Los Zetas, who recruited other members of GAFE to assist in the fight against his rivals. Originally, they were used as bodyguards for personal protection, but eventually became the enforcement branch of the Gulf Cartel. The Zetas were used to secure smuggling routes and carry out kidnappings and executions. Over time, Cárdenas expanded the responsibilities of Los Zetas to a more operational capacity. In 2002, after the death of Guzmán Decena, Heriberto Lazcano took over Los Zetas (Skeen, 2009). Following the arrest of Cárdenas in 2003, and his eventual extradition to the United States in 2007, Los Zetas assumed a more active leadership role in the Gulf Cartel until their alliance dissolved in 2010 when the Zetas formed their own criminal organization. After the split, two major factions emerged. On one side, the Gulf Cartel allied with their former rivals, the Sinaloa Cartel and La Familia Michoacana, while Los Zetas joined forces with the Juárez Cartel, the Beltrán-Leyva Cartel, and the Tijuana Cartel. More recently, in 2016, Los Zetas Group B and Zetas Vieja Escuela formed an alliance to combat the Gulf Cartel and Cartel Del Noreste (Jones and Sullivan, 2019).

The vitriol between the Gulf Cartel and the Zetas has spilled over into the purview of the public and has been more acute in towns around the US–Mexico border. In 2010, members of the Gulf Cartel opened fire on members of Los Zetas in the state of Tamaulipas (Kellner and Pipitone, 2010). Confrontations between both groups began in Reynosa, but has since escalated, spilling over into the neighboring cities of Nuevo Laredo and Matamoros. That same year, the Gulf Cartel assassinated two members of the Zetas in Brownsville, Texas. Armed conflict between these two groups has also been reported in the Mexican states of Nuevo León and Veracruz.

Members of Los Zetas range from federal, state, and local police officers, and former US military personnel. As the number of GAFE has shrunk, the Zetas have begun recruiting former Guatemalan Special Forces, known as Kaibiles, to join, recruit, and train Zetas members (Skeen, 2009). Additionally, the rivalry that exists among the cartels has caused Los Zetas to recruit and ally with gangs in the United States to distribute their products and protect supply routes. FBI reports indicate that cartels have been strengthening their connections with US gangs. In 2010, Los Zetas allied with the Sureños in California and South Carolina. Other gangs that Los Zetas have allied with include the Latin Kings in the US, MS-13, a gang based in El Salvador which has a presence in all 50 US states, and the Mexican Mafia, a US prison gang (Sullivan and Elkus, 2012). Additionally, the Zetas continue to utilize social media to coordinate their illegal activities and as a recruitment tool. In recognition of their service, members of Los Zetas are awarded the "Los Zetas Commando Medallion."

Further Reading

Beittel, J. S. (2020, July 28). "Mexico: Organized Crime and Drug Trafficking Organizations," Congressional Research Service. https://fas.org/sgp/crs/row/R41576.pdf

Correa-Cabrera, G. (2017). *Los Zetas Inc: Criminal Corporations, Energy, and Civil War in Mexico*. Austin: University of Texas Press.

Grayson, G. W. (2012). *The Executioner's Men: Los Zetas, Rogue Soldiers, Criminal Entrepreneurs, and the Shadow State They Created*. New York: Routledge.

References

Campbell, L. J. (2010). "Los Zetas: Operational Assessment," *Small Wars & Insurgencies*, *21*(1): 55–80.

Correa-Cabrera, G. (2017). *Los Zetas Inc.: Criminal Corporations, Energy, and Civil War in Mexico*. Austin: University of Texas Press.

Grayson, G. W. (2014). "The Evolution of Los Zetas in Mexico and Central America: Sadism as an Instrument of Cartel Warfare," United States Army War College Press. https://apps.dtic.mil/sti/pdfs/ADA599872.pdf

InSight Crime. (2012, April 4). "Zetas." https://insightcrime.org/mexico-organized-crime-news/zetas-profile/

Jones, N. P. and Sullivan, J. P. (2019). "Huachicoleros: Criminal Cartels, Fuel Theft, and Violence in Mexico," *Journal of Strategic Studies*, *12*(4): 1–24.

Kellner, T. and Pipitone, F. (2010). "Inside Mexico's Drug War," *World Policy Journal*, *27*(1): 29–37.

Logan, S. (2012, February). "A Profile of Los Zetas: Mexico's Second Most Powerful Drug Cartel," Combating Terrorism Center. https://ctc.usma.edu/a-profile-of-los-zetas-mexicos-second-most-powerful-drug-cartel/

Skeen, L. (2009, October 11). "The Zetas and the Kaibiles: A Mexican Hit Squad Reconnects With Its Guatemalan Trainers," *Nacla*. https://nacla.org/news/zetas-and-kaibiles-mexican-hit-squad-reconnects-its-guatemalan-trainers

Sullivan, J. P. and Elkus, A. (2012). "Los Zetas and MS-13: Nontraditional Alliances," *CTC Sentinel*, *5*(6): 7–9. https://www.academia.edu/download/19848690/Zetas_MS-13_Sullivan_Elkus.pdf

Sullivan, J. P. and Logan, S. (2010). "Los Zetas: Massacres, Assassinations and Infantry Tactics," *Homeland1.com*. https://www.academia.edu/download/12627228/Los_Zetas-Massacres__Assassinations_and_Infantry_Tactics_%20-%20Homeland1.com.pdf

Chapter 78

Mara Salvatrucha (MS-13) International Criminal Gang

Ryan Roberts
Old Dominion University, Norfolk, VA, United States

Scott N. Romaniuk
International Centre for Policing and Security, University of South Wales, Caerleon, United Kingdom

Contents

Introduction 591
History 592
Further Reading 594
References 594

Introduction

Mara Salvatrucha, most commonly referred to as MS-13, is a street gang from El Salvador. The group has been called one of the world's largest and most violent gangs in existence (DeAmicis, 2017). Farah and Babineau (2017: 59) have recently referred to MS-13 as a group "rapidly evolving into a criminal-economic-military-political power that poses an existential threat to the states of El Salvador and Honduras." While "Mara" means "gang," "Salvatrucha" has two translations. One is slang for "Salvadoran army ant," and the other meaning is "Salvadoran peasant guerilla." The number "13" represents "M" as the 13th letter in the alphabet. Additionally, MS-13 is often categorized as a third-generation gang due to their high levels of internationalization, politicization, and sophistication. They function as a transnational gang and have become politically motivated in both their

DOI: 10.4324/9781315144511-82

country of origin and neighboring countries. Despite being designated a street gang, MS-13 self-identifies as a paramilitary political organization with paramilitary training (Smith, 2018).

Members of MS-13 can be distinguished from other gangs. One identifier they use is through symbols and tattoos. Generally, MS-13 are known to brandish several tattoos on their body, including their face (although they are beginning to move away from facial tattoos in order to be more discrete) of the number 13, the letters "M," "S," "eme," or "ese," "mara," or devil horns (a hand sign often associated with heavy metal bands), the devil's head, or pitchfork (Rose, 2017). Additional tattoos include three dots, the phrase "Mi Vida Loca," clown faces, or teardrops underneath the eye. Another method of identifying member affiliation is by the colors they wear. Colors associated with MS-13 gang members include blue, black, and white. In some sets, blue represents junior members while the color black is worn by more senior-level members (New Jersey Office of the Attorney General, n.d.). Often times, athletic apparel of teams that use these colors or jerseys with the number 13 are worn to signal membership with the gang.

Although the gang formed in Los Angeles, California, MS-13 has been identified in nearly all 50 American states. Additionally, they operate in Canada, El Salvador, Mexico, Honduras, Guatemala, and Nicaragua. Their regional presence, size, and network structure have resulted in fragmented affiliations and leadership structures, bound together by a code of honor that links members from different countries, states, and neighborhoods. Known for their brutality, the preferred weapon of choice for MS-13 is the machete. Violence serves as a means to carry out their criminal activities which include narcotics, arms, and human trafficking, smuggling, extortion, and money laundering (Arthur, 2018; US Department of Justice, 2020). Additionally, MS-13 is often hired by Mexican drug cartels as enforcers to retaliate against rival cartels or to protect drug shipments. Their main allies include the Sureños (Sur-13), another street gang, and the Mexican Mafia, a prison gang, and have been known to cooperate with both the Sinaloa Cartel and Los Zetas despite the animus between these groups. The primary rival of MS-13 is another Salvadoran gang with transnational operations, Barrio 18, also known as 18th Street.

History

MS-13 emerged in the 1980s when civil war between the Salvadoran government and leftist guerilla groups forced nearly a million refugees from their homes (International Crisis Group, 2017). A majority of the refugees fled to the United States, primarily settling in the greater Los Angeles area. Those who fled included a diverse combination of low-skilled workers, gang members, and former paramilitary guerillas of the Frente Farabundo Marti de Liberación (FMLN). Socio-economic constraints and outgroup pressures from established street gangs in Los Angeles caused Salvadoran youths to unite. What began as a means of protection from African-American, Hispanic, and white gangs, ultimately led to the formation of MS-13. As the gang began to expand, so too did their ambitions and criminal proclivities. Being of Salvadoran descent was initially a membership requirement. However, to accommodate their growth, they began permitting other nationalities such as Mexicans, Guatemalans, and Hondurans to join.

In 1996, the United States government passed the Illegal Immigration Reform and Immigration Responsibility Act. The purpose of this legislation was to combat and remove non-citizens convicted of crimes. Since a majority of the Salvadoran refugees had entered the country illegally, and members of MS-13 were involved in criminal behavior, policing targeted the gang for deportation. Once in their home country, however, members of MS-13 began recruiting within Salvadoran communities and among neighboring countries which further fueled their expansion into Central and South America (Penner, 2019).

Although mired in controversy, the Salvadoran government under President Mauricio Funes brokered a ceasefire in 2009 between MS-13 and their rival 18th Street. In exchange for reducing the gang violence and prohibiting recruitment in schools, the government paid MS-13 leaders $25 million and, in some districts, placed them on the government payroll (Farah and Babineau, 2017). During this time, they focused on gaining community support, established military training camps, and began integrating with state law enforcement agencies. Additionally, MS-13 began to strengthen their relationship with the Sinaloa Cartel and Los Zetas to train, work, and expand (Elkus and Sullivan, 2012). In the United States, Luis Gerardo Vega was invited into the inner circle of the Mexican Mafia in 2011 which facilitated their foray into distributing methamphetamines. More importantly, this alliance brought them closer to the Hispanic gangs in the southern part of California, integrating them with "la eme."

By 2014, the truce between MS-13 and 18th Street deteriorated, and their intentions became more politically motivated (Wilkinson, 2015). MS-13 leaders sought to influence political outcomes by leveraging their ties to the community. In some cases, political parties were charged a fee for the right to campaign, and in other cases, they directly financed political parties. If, however, a political party was perceived as an enemy, they prohibited them from distributing pamphlets, giving speeches, or displaying banners. Honduran President Juan Orlando Hernández, for example, was prohibited from campaigning in San Pedro Sula in 2017 (Farah and Babineau, 2017). Members of MS-13 threatened to kill anyone who chose to vote for him, forced campaign workers to quit, and prevented campaign literature supporting Hernández from circulating. They made similar threats in El Salvador against members of FMLN running for public office (Farah and Babineau, 2017).

Currently, MS-13 is one of the largest gangs in the United States and has been acknowledged and targeted by the US Justice Department. The criminal activities of MS-13 and their cooperation with Mexican cartels have become tantamount to the debate on immigration reform. In response to the emerging transnational threat, the Federal Bureau of Investigations (FBI) established the Transnational Anti-Gang (TAG) Task Force in El Salvador (2007), Guatemala (2009), and Honduras (2011). The purpose of TAG is to collaborate with host country intelligence agencies in collecting and disseminating information on MS-13 and mitigate the adverse impact their criminal activities have on public safety in the United States.

Further Reading

Farah, D. (2012). "Central American Gangs: Changing Nature and New Partners," *Journal of International Affairs*, *66*(1): 53–67.

Monteith, M. L. (2010). *Transnational gangs: The MS-13 Gang and Others*. Hauppauge: Nova Science.

Wolf, S. (2012). "Mara Salvatrucha: The Most Dangerous Street Gang in the Americas?" *Latin American Politics and Society 54*(1): 65–99.

References

Arthur, A. R. (2018, February 22). *MS-13 and Sex Trafficking*. Center for Immigration Studies, Washington, DC. https://cis.org/Arthur/MS13-and-Sex-Trafficking

DeAmicis, A. (2017, July). "Mara Salvatrucha: The Deadliest Street Gang in America," US Department of Justice, Office of Justice Programs. ojp.gov/ncjrs/virtual-library/abstracts/mara-salvatrucha-deadliest-street-gang-america

Elkus, A. and Sullivan, J. P. (2012, June). "Los Zetas and MS-13: Nontraditional Alliances," *CTC Sentinel*, *5*(6): 7–9. https://www.ctc.usma.edu/los-zetas-and-ms-13-nontraditional-alliances/

Farah, D. and Babineau, K. (2017). "The Evolution of MS 13 in El Salvador and Honduras," *PRISM*, *7*(1): 58–73. https://cco.ndu.edu/Portals/96/Documents/prism/prism_7-1/5-Farah.pdf?ver=2017-09-14-133607-060

International Crisis Group. (2017, December 19). "El Salvador's Politics of Perpetual Violence," Report No. 64. crisisgroup.org/latin-america-caribbean/central-america/el-salvador/64-el-salvadors-politics-perpetual-violence

New Jersey Office of the Attorney General. (n.d.). "Recognize the Signs." https://www.nj.gov/oag/gang-signs-bro.pdf

Penner, H. (2019). "Cultural Tactics of Salvadoran Gangs Offer Chance for US to Weaken MS-13," *Undergraduate Honors Capstone Projects. 520*. https://digitalcommons.usu.edu/honors/520

Rose, J. (2017, August 18). "Sports Jersey or Gang Symbol? Why Spotting MS-13 Recruits Is Tougher Than It Seems," *National Public Radio*. npr.org/2017/08/18/544365061/identifying-ms-13-members

Smith, C. F. (2018, May 31). "Gangs and the Military Note 2: Military-trained Gang Members as Criminal Insurgents," *Small Wars Journal*. https://smallwarsjournal.com/jrnl/art/gangs-and-military-note-2-military-trained-gang-members-criminal-insurgents

Stolpe, K. E. (2019). "MS-13 and Domestic Juvenile Sex Trafficking: Causes, Correlates, and Solutions," *Virginia Journal of Social Policy & the Law*, *21*(2): 341–372.

United States (US) Department of Justice. (2020, November 27). "More than 700 Members of Transnational Organized Crime Groups Arrested in Central America in U.S. Assisted Operation."justice.gov/opa/pr/more-700-members-transnational-organized-crime-groups-arrested-central-america-us-assisted

Wilkinson, T. (2015, April 18). "After Broken Gang Truce, El Salvador Sees Deadliest Month in 10 Years," *Los Angeles Times*. latimes.com/world/mexico-americas/la-fg-el-salvador-gangs-20150418-story.html

Chapter 79

Maritime Domain Awareness (MDA)

Allison McDowell-Smith
Nichols College, Dudley, MA, United States

Contents

Introduction 595
Importance of MDA 596
Framework of NMDAP 596
Maritime Domain Security Threats 598
Conclusion 598
Further Reading 599
References 599

Introduction

Maritime domain awareness (MDA) is the "effective understanding of anything associated with the global maritime domain that could impact the security, safety, economy or environment of the United States" (National, 2005). The maritime domain is further defined as "all areas and things of, on, under, relating to, adjacent to, or bordering on a sea, ocean, or other navigable waterway, including all maritime-related activities, infrastructure, people, cargo, and vessels and other conveyances" (National, 2005). The impact of MDA within society is great.

- 95% of the world's telecommunications travel via undersea cables.
- 90% of the world's commerce moves by sea.
- 84% of the estimated resources in the Arctic are located offshore.
- 50% of the world's oil transits seven major chokepoints.
- 44% of the world's population lives within 93 mi/150 km of a coast.

DOI: 10.4324/9781315144511-83

- Shipping is the most fuel-efficient and carbon-friendly form of commercial transport.

(Adm & White, 2014)

The initial National Maritime Domain Awareness Plan (NMDAP) was created in 2005 to outline a strategy to secure the United States, as there was not an adequate plan in place to thwart and mitigate threats to the maritime domain. The White House released an updated version of the NMDAP on December 30, 2013. The current NMDAP "supports the AUG2012 Presidential Policy Directive 18: Maritime Security (PPD-18) and merges two outdated (2005) governance documents: National Plan to Achieve Maritime Domain Awareness and Global Maritime Intelligence Integration Plan" (Gourley, 2014). When the White House issued a press release regarding the 2013 NMDAP, the National Security Council spokesperson had specifically stated "90% of the world's commerce moves by sea, making maritime security essential to the global supply chain and international trade" (The White House, 2014). The NMDAP is one of the eight plans developed as a supportive component to the National Strategy for Maritime Security, as directed by National Security Presidential Directive-41/Homeland Security Presidential Directive-13.

Importance of MDA

> The world shares a collective interest in promoting the timely and efficient flow of legitimate commerce, while protecting and securing the maritime domain from exploitation and reducing its vulnerability to disruption by either man-made or natural disasters. We recognize security as an essential element of an efficient and functioning maritime domain.
>
> (National, 2015)

When examining the significance of MDA, it is essential to recognize that MDA is both a domestic and an international collaborative process. Furthermore, MDA involves high cooperation between both the public and private sectors. In order to effectively navigate the maritime domain, there needs to be improved and integrated intelligence gathering and recognition, followed by enhancement of maritime infrastructure and the maximized legitimization of maritime use. This effective navigation is conducted through the Secretary of the Navy as the executive agent for maritime domain awareness (EAMDA), who is also responsible for the MDA actions across the Department of Defense (DOD), Navy, and Interagency (Adm & White, 2014). Maritime security operations are primarily conducted by the U.S. Navy, which is a protection force beyond our shorelines, and the U.S. Coast Guard, which is primarily responsible for securing our shorelines by providing a safer maritime trade.

Framework of NMDAP

In order to recognize and implement the importance of MDA, the NMDAP was created in 2005, followed by a long overdue update in 2013. There are core principles at the center of the framework of the NMDAP of 2013 which highlights a whole-of-nation approach with the goal of increasing collaboration among agencies. Intelligence integration is an integral part of expanding the collaboration of the intelligence community. The intelligence community has such a vast and diverse expertise within intelligence that it is necessary to utilize their expertise, in addition, to open source intelligence within society. "Crucial opportunities to prevent an incident or provide an early response can be lost without effective awareness of activities within the maritime domain. Awareness grants time and distance to detect, deter, interdict, and overcome threats" (National, 2015). The three core principles of the NMDAP of 2013 are as follows:

1. Promote unity of effort across communities of interest.
2. Foster information sharing and safeguarding through secure enterprise architectures.
3. Ensure safe and efficient flow of legitimate commerce.

(Gourley, 2014)

The plan's strategic priorities are as follows:

- Maximize maritime intelligence integration to support decision-making.
- Maximize appropriate availability of relevant maritime intelligence and information.
- Enhance international and industry partnerships, cooperation, and information sharing and safeguarding.
- Improve Global Maritime Community of Interest (GMCOI)-assured access to maritime-related threat information.
- Integrate MDA with land, air, cyberspace, and space domains to achieve integrated domain awareness.

(National, 2015)

The plan's objectives are as follows:

- *Organize stakeholders through governance*
  Proper governance to coordinate federal maritime stakeholder activities will promote an interagency shared perspective, which will acknowledge and balance the equities of federal, as well as state, local, tribal, territorial (S/L/T/T), academic, private sector, and international maritime stakeholders.
- *Continue to mitigate MDA challenges*
  This plan acknowledges previous work to identify MDA challenges, promotes the development of metrics to understand when a challenge has been addressed or mitigated, and advocates the continued development of solutions to address those challenges. The plan also recognizes that new and emerging challenges continue to present themselves, validating the requirement for a continuous reassessment process using risk management methodologies.
- *Improve domain awareness through enterprise-level access to data*
  This plan promotes maritime information sharing by transitioning from organization-centric databases to web-centric enterprise services that retrieve data

from multiple sources (e.g., clouds and databases). This shift provides authorized users more flexible access to a greater number of sources, types, and volume of data and the ability to search databases without relying on point-to-point access. Under this construct, data should be authoritative and conform to recognized standards, such as those currently employed under the National Information Exchange Model (NIEM).

- *Enhance collaboration through outreach*

> This plan encourages broad interaction to identify organizations, partnerships, best practices, and other efforts that enhance maritime security through expanded MDA collaboration between the GMCOI members. By collaborating on MDA initiatives and incorporating federal, S/L/T/T, academic, private, and international maritime partners, this plan will support and improve interagency capabilities to effectively share information on people, cargo, vessels, infrastructure, natural and manmade disasters and other potential threats within the maritime domain.
>
> (National, 2015)

Maritime Domain Security Threats

There are endless security threats which can impact the maritime domain. The main threats identified in the NMDAP are as follows: nation-state threats, terrorist threats, transnational criminal and piracy threats, and environmental and social threats. Nation-state threats refer to those regions currently engaged in "erupting, escalating, and drawing in major powers" (National, 2005). Rogue governments could be looking for ways to negatively impact the United States. Some potential methods of negative impact from the nation-states could be providing weaponry, including weapons of mass destruction, or by providing safe havens for criminals and terrorists. Furthermore, with so much shoreline around and within the United States, waterways can be utilized as exploitation measures for terrorists and criminals to attack the United States. Once again, exploitation could include the transport and/or detonation of weapons, including weapons of mass destruction and/or transporting of goods for revenue purposes. Transnational crime and piracy threats can be in relation to smuggling attempts of "people, drugs, weapons, and other contraband" (National, 2015). The other alarming maritime domain security threat is in relation to the environment and society within the United States. Examples of these threats can be either natural disasters or manmade disasters, such as hurricanes or immigration. With such a vast range of threats susceptible via maritime domain, the United States continuously works to mitigate all threats 24/7 and has to collaborate with numerous agencies to ensure the protection of the country.

Conclusion

National Security Presidential Directive-41/Homeland Security Presidential Directive-13 was issued under the Obama Administration to create the 2013 NMDAP, which is focused on securing our water borders through MDA. The maritime domain contributes 90% of the world's commerce (Adm & White, 2014) and thus is very complex when examining how to mitigate potential threats against the United States. The 2013 NMDAP works to provide a high-level strategy for all agencies, both public and private, to follow in an effort to unify our forces and expand intelligence gathering and communications in a more efficient manner. It is intended that through the implementation of the NMDAP, the United States will be able to mitigate the significant security threats.

Further Reading

Bakir, N. (2007). A Brief Analysis of Threats and Vulnerabilities in the Maritime Domain. *Non-published Research Reports, 5*. http://research.create.usc.edu/nonpublished_reports/5

Boraz, S. (2009). Maritime Domain Awareness: Myths and realities. *Naval War College Review, 62*(3). http://www.dtic.mil/dtic/tr/fulltext/u2/a519318.pdf

Jones, P. (2017). The commanders respond. *Proceedings Magazine, 143/3/1369*. https://www.usni.org/node/90093

References

Adm, R., & White, J. (2014). Advancing Maritime Domain Awareness (MDA) for the fleet and the nation. *Navy Live: The official blog of the U.S. Navy*. http://navylive.dodlive.mil/2014/01/16/advancing-maritime-domain-awareness-mda-for-the-fleet-and-the-nation/

Gourley, B. (2014). Planning for Maritime Domain Awareness: What you need to know to contribute to the effort. CTOVision. https://ctovision.com/planning-maritime-domain-awareness-need-know-contribute-effort/

National Maritime Domain Awareness Plan. (2015). http://nmio.ise.gov/Portals/16/Docs/FAQs%20NMDAP%2020131216.pdf?ver=2015-12-04-123430-287

National Plan to Achieve Maritime Domain Awareness. (2005). https://www.dhs.gov/sites/default/files/publications/HSPD_MDAPlan_0.pdf

The White House, Office of the Press Secretary. (2014, January 3). White House release National Maritime Domain Awareness Plan [Press release]. https://obamawhitehouse.archives.gov/the-press-office/2013/12/30/statement-nsc-spokesperson-caitlin-hayden-national-maritime-domain-aware

Chapter 80

Militias

Réjeanne M. Lacroix
University of Leicester, Leicester, United Kingdom

Contents

Introduction 601
Background 602
Legality and Legislation 602
Ideology 604
Foundations and the 1990s 605
The 2000s and Revival 607
Conclusion 608
Further Reading 608
References 609

Introduction

Interpretations regarding the role of militias in the United States are as dynamic as the republic's history. Distinctions between organized and unorganized militias, as well as state defense forces, are found in the Militia Act of 1903, which was later included in the U.S. Code of Laws. Later in the twentieth century, the concept of militias on U.S. territory broadened as private or citizen militias came to prominence. While the armed groups specified in Titles 10 and 32, such as National Guards of individual states' reserve forces, remain under significant federal control (Dougherty 1995, 969), private entities compose self-governing ideologies and protocols.

O'Brien and Haider-Markel (1998) offer an expansive definition of what constitutes a citizen's militia. They note it is imperative that an assembly of three or more individuals self-identify as a "militia" in order to be considered one. The stated purpose of organization must be the defense of their rights and property from an overbearing government. As well, members are required to participate in armed combat training

DOI: 10.4324/9781315144511-84

in preparation for overzealous government actions. Acknowledgment that rights to organize and train are rooted in the Second Amendment of the U.S. Constitution is another key factor (457). It is then understood that private militias are an armed ideological movement that operates outside the auspices of government supervision.

Background

The concept of militias evolved alongside United States' history and resulted in the contemporary understanding of private, or citizen, militias. These paramilitary-styled groups strongly assert the supremacy of Second Amendment constitutional rights and consider their establishment as defense against a theoretically tyrannical U.S. federal government. Militias present inconsistent grievances against the federal government, numerous motives, and a lack of unified leadership. This decentralization offers opportunity to expand general membership in the armed wing of the New Right, and as a result, state legislation specifically targets any violent or disruptive actions. Sociopolitical conditions typically influence the growth and decline of the militia movement, as witnessed in the political climate in the 1990s as well as late 2000s; thus, it is important to heed these variables. Due to their armed nature, militias will continue as an identifiable domestic security threat.

Legality and Legislation

Analysis concerning the legality of militias centers upon federal constitutional law, primarily the Second Amendment. The oft-discussed statute famously states that, "a well-regulated militia, being necessary to the security of a free state, the right of the people to keep and bear arms, shall not be infringed" (U.S. Constitution, amend. II). This decree is regularly subject to numerous interpretations, but there is little to dispute in the constitutional literalism used by militias. "Well-regulated" refers to their protocols and training while "free state" denotes a non-tyrannical government. As a result, they unquestionably believe in the legitimacy of their armed movement.

Further, private militias construe references to the "unorganized militia" in Title 10 as another supportive clause for their association. If the unorganized militia includes all able-bodied U.S. citizens unrelated to the National Guard (10 U.S.C § 246, 1956), inclined elucidation leads to acceptance of the armed patriot movement. Protections in the First Amendment permit the propagation of militia opinions in a variety of formats. As Brannan (2011) remarked, these groups are "allowed to openly disseminate their views in the name of free speech" (71).

The same applies to right of assemblage. This is especially important as ideological movements seek likeminded individuals for membership. Such political associations develop as a means to promote counterarguments to mainstream opinions, and infringement upon their rights to assemble as a group contravenes their ability to express organized free speech (Polesky 1996, 1618). Militiamen base their perceived legality on these constitutional laws and their interpretations often remain in gray areas of legitimacy.

Some legal scholars contend that the sovereign nature of citizen militias preclude them from the constitutional amendments held in high esteem. For instance, Dougherty surmises that these armed organizations have no basis to Second Amendment protections, since they are outside of the command of both state and federal governments (962). In regard to the First Amendment, the circulation of their ideological tenets faces constraint as well. The 1969 U.S. Supreme Court ruling *Brandenburg v Ohio* declared that speech leading to the incitement of violence or imminent lawless action is unprotected under the Constitution (Supreme Court of the United States, 1969). Former Pennsylvania Senator Arlen Specter referred to this decision at a 1995 judicial subcommittee hearing, which focused on the modern militia movement, by articulating, "there is a broad ambit of freedom of speech...but there is an ending point if there is violence or the imminent threat of violence" (United States Senate 1995, 2).

The establishment of citizen militias may not be federally prohibitive, but their continuance is open to legal challenge. Prohibitive legislative is more apparent at the local and state level insofar as associative criminal acts linked to the maintenance of militias are eligible for prosecution. Commentary provided by the Institute for Constitutional Advocacy and Protection at Georgetown Law notes that all 50 states have laws concerning private militias; however, their applications differ widely. Forty-eight state constitutions require the subordination of the military, and in this case, armed groups, to civil authorities (Institute for Constitutional Advocacy and Protection 2018, 3). This may be a minimalist principle, but it is important in regard to those militias of anti-government agendas, such as sovereign citizens, who act autonomously and shun the legitimacy of civic order.

The Institute of Constitutional Advocacy and Protection (ICAP) surmises that 28 states prohibit armed or military-type organizations that function without state permission (4). This proscription extends to displays of military conduct or maneuvers in public or under the patronage of state authorities. Such an edict differentiates legitimate organized or unorganized militia groups from those self-identified as citizen militia.

A key word found in relevant laws is "public." While public restrictions over organization and use of firearms are noted, militias retain the liberty to engage in combat preparedness or congregation in rural areas, without public spotlight. Consequently, private militias appear in states where legislation censures their presence. At the pre-referenced hearing, Specter expressed that, "these militias exist notwithstanding laws in some States which prohibit the formation of militias" (U.S. Senate, 1). Perception of state laws and rights afforded in the U.S. Constitution permit such growth.

Further, the ICAP report identifies laws focused on paramilitary incitement to violence and what the institute labels as "false assumption laws" (ICAP, 5 – 6). While paramilitary laws do not target militias specifically, any activities that facilitate violence or civil disorder are criminalized. This would include certain aspects of firearms training, manufacturing explosive devices, and engagement in guerilla warfare preparedness or conspiring to do so. Since these groups train in preparation to defend rights and property, they generally stockpile weapons or other materials needed for combat, and subsequently, face numerous weapons charges. Twenty-five states have enacted such legislation.

According to ICAP, "false assumption laws," currently employed in 12 states, offer yet another area to criminalize militia actions at the state level (ICAP, 6). These offenses are summarized as acts of conflation between legitimate units of armed force, such as police officers or the National Guard, and those unauthorized in such roles, primarily private militias. This may be done by engaging in deeds reserved for lawful security forces or wearing military uniforms, while not a member of a state-sanctioned organized unit. Statutes focused on the impersonation of police or peace officers are fairly straightforward; however, the issue of unsanctioned uniforms is especially pertinent to the militia movement.

Both federal and state-level statutes are important when analyzing the legality of private militias. Legitimate legal protections provided in the U.S. Constitution and the ambiguity inherent in the application of state codes permit the militia movement to subsist, as well as adapt, in a variety of situations. Subsequently, criminality intrinsic to a propensity for aggression and radical ideological frameworks present the most legal questions, as well as national security threats.

Ideology

An adherence to self-governing principles and relative independence means that militia philosophies vary across the New Right spectrum. Lack of a national umbrella organization results in variances of grievances adopting the militia banner. Chermak (2002) explained "the lack of unanimity and decentralized structure of the militia movement allow these independent groups flexibility in developing their ideological positions" (24). Nonetheless, for the sake of analytical simplicity, it is fair to classify the governing principles of the movement under two frameworks: those with a basis in constitutional concerns and those with a conspiracy theory foundation (Churchill 2011, 188).

The Federal Bureau of Investigations identified a common set of unitive beliefs that are apparent, at some degree, to both factions. These include a conviction to protect the U.S. Constitution and individual liberties, a belief that the Constitution permits citizens the right to take the government back by force, and opposition to gun control (Federal Bureau of Investigations, 2011). This set of foundational core beliefs facilitates many groups, such as tax protesters, Christian identity or far-right proponents, to move with flexibility in the militia movement. While each stream of thought promotes divergent grievances or specific agendas, concern over an overbearing federal government denotes those who decide to organize. As Brannan (2006) pinpointed, militias consider the current government order to be out of control, immoral, biased, and seeking any ruse to deprive Americans of their constitutional rights.

Gun control topics remain the foremost concern and identifiable issue linked to private militias. Baysinger (2006) determined the preservation of rights to possess and own firearms as the universal and most important issue linking diverse militias (7). Both constitutionalists and those who consider government actions as nefarious dispute any form of legislation that places restrictions on gun ownership. This is based on a generalized idea that the U.S. federal government seeks to entirely disarm the citizenry. A well-regulated militia is considered protectionary against an oppressive government with an agenda concentrated on contravening citizens' rights. The motives for such government exploits are linked to the conspiracy wing of the militia movement.

Conspiracy theorists within militias perceive various legislative acts as components of hidden agendas. They argue that the federal government plans to gradually increase its power and breadth over individual rights, and as a result, confiscate all firearms (Baysinger, 2006, 7). However, the diversity of grievances inherent in various philosophies in militias allows variations of this argument. For instance, there are numerous proponents of New World Order anxieties. It is contended that once the U.S. federal government rescinds the rights of its population and disarms them, a globalist power, such as the United Nations, will then usurp United States territory. Additionally, this theory is appended by white nationalists who label the globalist tyrants as ZOG or the Zionist Occupation Government. An absence of a well-armed militia permits this occurrence. Further, the FBI notes other conspiracies, such as the dated conception that the U.S. federal government will forcibly imprison its citizens in Federal Emergency Management Agency (FEMA) camps and force vaccinations, as customary in the militia movement (FBI, 2011).

Shifts in the sociopolitical landscape and demographics provide opportunities for undercurrents of militia philosophy to emerge as well. Since the movement is mostly aligned with conservative or right-wing philosophies, many militiamen remain in general disagreement with a liberal social climate (Baysinger, 2006, 5). For example, Churchill identified the modern men's rights movement as a beneficiary of the ongoing inclusion of concerns adopted by private militias (207). Analysts should expect further development in the various ideologies that brew in this movement as the trajectory of relevant opinions, such as gun control or globalization, differs from their core beliefs.

Foundations and the 1990s

Conservative groups focused on the U.S. Constitution and those skeptical of government involvement in personal liberties are longstanding views in the United States. In the modern era, and in protest to liberal sociopolitical developments, an identifiable patriot movement linked to the New Right entered the discourse of mainstream politics (O'Brien and Haider-Markel, 1998, 456).

One of the first groups to reach prominence was the Posse Comitatus, a Latin translation for "force of the country." While not a militia per se, the dispersed social movement provided a rudimentary model for the militia movement that materialized later. They encompassed a variety of values from distrust of government, sovereign citizenry, tax protest, Christian identity, and white nationalism. Until the 1980s, the movement capitalized on agricultural crises by extending their viewpoints to discontented Mid-Western farmers and engaged in violent acts (Baysinger, 2006, 4).

The militia movement as it is contemporarily understood manifested in the 1990s. During this period, numerous variables aligned and, thus, resulted in a consequential environment for development of militias. Economic recession had particularly detrimental effects upon blue-collar workers employed in agricultural and manufacturing sectors. Baysinger notes a correlation between an increase in membership in patriot groups and unfavorable economic conditions (6). As a result of this context, the election of Democratic President Bill Clinton brought along its own set of peculiar concerns for the constitutional and gun lobby sects.

In regard to gun rights, the Clinton administration passed the Brady Act on November 30, 1993. This act ordered federal background checks prior to the purchase of a handgun. Background checks necessitated a 5-day waiting period; however, this provision was lifted once the National Instant Criminal Background Check System (NICS) became operational in 1998. As a result of this legislation, those with firm belief in the Second Amendment and who argue the government overextended its powers were concerned.

Secondly, the militarization of all levels of police forces continued (Churchill, 2011, 190). This was explicit when Clinton modified prohibitions regarding the use of the military in domestic law enforcement and further extended the capabilities of federal agents to investigate extremist groups (Chermak, 2002, 4). A trifecta of concerns emanated from these developments. The militia movement considered this legislation as a further indication of an overbearing government persistent on infringing upon personal rights. Concurrently, adherents of New World Order (NWO) conspiracy theories deemed such laws as preparative for a globalist takeover. Lastly, higher degrees of force in altercations with armed groups usually result in more serious consequences.

Two events embodied these concerns and shaped modern militia development: the sieges at Ruby Ridge, Idaho, in 1992 and Waco, Texas, in 1993. In each case, interactions with federal officials, such as the U.S. Marshalls Service and FBI Hostage Rescue Team in Idaho, and the Bureau of Alcohol, Tobacco and Firearms (ATF) and FBI in Texas, stemmed from firearms infractions. At Ruby Ridge, Randy Weaver disputed repercussions for his failure to appear in court. The Branch Davidians in Waco faced legal ramifications for weapons stockpiling. Both of these cases have been extensively documented; thus, offering a narrative provides little for analysis.

These alarming incidents disturbed the general American populace but provoked unique anger in the patriot movement. According to Chermak, Waco and Ruby Ridge were the last straw in a political climate fueling their suspicions (36). Further, proponents recognized both incidents as state-sponsored violence authorized by a corrupt government (Churchill, 2011, 188). The combination of paramilitary-style force employed by federal agencies and corruption at subsequent legal proceedings further impelled grassroots fury. Seeking an outlet for their anger, citizens joined militias (Chermak, 2002, 37).

Militia membership grew exponentially. Churchill identifies personal discussions at meetings or venues such as gun shows, where important topics such as the Constitution, religion, or taxes, compelled locals to form armed groups (199). Such meetings provided an easily accessible platform to distribute relevant literature. Concurrently, communications developments permitted militias expanded reach for their materials and philosophies. In the late 1980s and early 1990s, easily accessible fax machines, the Internet, and e-mail mailing lists facilitated a broadened reach for militia information. The advent of conservative talk radio enabled beliefs of the New Right to reach a varied audience suitable for militia recruitment (Churchill, 2011, 196–97). A sociopolitical context, shocking events, and modern innovations greatly influenced the rise of modern militias.

April 19 emerged as a very important date to militiamen. It acknowledges the onset of the American Revolutionary War, a siege between federal agents and far-right group "The Covenant, the Sword, and the Arm of the Lord" in 1985 and Waco in

1993. As a result, the Texas Constitutional Militia purposely selected this date as their founding (Churchill, 2011, 225). The subsequent Oklahoma City bombings in 1995 firmly cemented the prominence of April 19 too.

By the late 1990s, momentum of the militia movement stalled. Firstly, the economic situation recovered. Anger over Ruby Ridge and Waco generally subsided. After several arrests of local leaders, homegrown movements disbanded. The need for armed preparedness and survivalist techniques diminished when Y2K conspiracy theories never materialized (Baysinger, 2006, 8). Committed members continued their projects, and fundamentalists pursued more relevant manifestations of action.

The 2000s and Revival

The 2000s offered the militia movement a period to regroup and evolve. A savvier, better organized movement emerged ready for public consideration in mainstream circles (Childress, 2017). The commonplace nature of conservative talk radio, polarized media, professionally developed websites, and social media pages provided abundant opportunities.

Connection between groups became more important and easier facilitated. It is unlike in the 1990s when groups remained scattered and associated mainly by similar ideologies. Social media and interest-based discussion forums let locally based groups, as well as isolated individuals, connect with others to foment shared identities (Zook 1996, 26). These linkages extend from the digital world as contemporary militias are more open to public audiences and willing to unite, with similar ideologies, nationwide. Chermak explains that even public service activities are advantageous as they provide many benefits to the community, possible recruitment, and positive public relations (49). For the modern militia, a public voice offers a chance to overhaul the unfavorable image it gained in the prior decade.

New conspiracy theories developed; however, they retained the same root suspicions as their predecessors. After the 9/11 terrorist attacks, new analytical angles of nefarious U.S. government actions, and legislation such as the Patriot Act, revived discourse on infringement of rights, as well as tyrannical regimes. NWO or globalist machinations endured with new emphasis on mass immigration patterns and the deep state. Second Amendment activists promote the concern of "false flag" operations to provoke distrust in demands for stricter gun controls after numerous mass shootings. Due to the contemporary ease of communications, these theories are available to a wide range of new adherents. The ability to create professional-looking media, as well as formats like podcasts and Internet radio shows, offers a newfound tinge of legitimacy to these fringe elements. As a result, new leadership appeared and membership in the militia movement grew (Baysinger, 2006, 8).

Survivalists, law enforcement officers, and military veterans provide important recruits in the current patriot movement. In the mid-2000s, three national groups rose in the political discourse of the New Right. The Three Percenters emerged as the first armed patriot movement in this era, while the Oath Keepers and Constitutional Sheriffs target current/former law enforcement and military for membership (Childress 2017). Further, the Oath Keepers retain links to militia history by paying homage to the date of April 19: the day of their institution.

The patriot movement profited from sociopolitical challenges, like their predecessors in the 1990s. An identifiable stream of populism resulted from economic hardships during the 2008 financial crisis and vocal anti-immigration rhetoric. Further, the election of Democratic president Barack Obama drew ire from conservatives focused on the Second Amendment and conspiracy theorists alike (Childress 2017). The militia movement once again provided an outlet for a range of suspicions and frustrations with the U.S. federal government.

During the Obama administration, legislation shifting the trajectory of civil rights and gender relations provided a setting for the existing patriot movement (Zook, 1996, 27). As conservatives and traditionalists, unity against such societal changes acts as a cohesive factor. O'Brien and Haider-Markel contend that areas with significant ideological polarity offer greater incentives for the growth of the militia movement (459). However, contemporary contexts reveal ideological polarity as a nationwide issue, and the current political landscape continues to stimulate populism.

Modern militias gained widespread national news coverage during the 2014 Bundy standoff in Bunkerville, Nevada, and the 2016 occupation of the Malheur National Wildlife Refuge in Oregon. Groups such as the Constitutional Sheriffs, Oath Keepers, and Three Percenters made an appearance in Nevada. In Oregon, the People for Constitutional Freedom and the Iowa chapter of the Three Percenters, accompanied by smaller militias, challenged the federal government's authority over public lands.

Currently, law enforcement agencies across the United States pinpoint anti-government extremists, such as the militia movement, as the most severe form of political violence (Kurzman and Schanzer 2015, 3). This is predictable due to their skilled training, unpredictable triggers, and access to weapons.

Conclusion

The strength of the militia movement fluctuates according to sociopolitical variables; however, they are likely to remain relevant in appropriate circles. A wide breadth of political and ideological grievances indicates that their positions will advance as well as gain membership from numerous likeminded citizens. Continuous access to niche media sources and ongoing fear over loss of Second Amendment rights may result in newfound stability rather than the decline of earlier manifestations. They will remain relevant to conservative political discourse and discussions over domestic security continually. Their propensity for knowledge-based armed defense, unique perceptions of U.S. political developments, and decentralization imply that these groups must remain under analytical discernment. Many militias remain peaceful; however, specific prompts for certain groupings must be identified for security purposes.

Further Reading

Jackson, S. (2017). *Conspiracy Theories in the Patriot Militia Movement*. Washington, DC: GW Program on Extremism. https://extremism.gwu.edu/sites/g/files/zaxdzs2191/f/downloads/Jackson,%20Conspiracy%20Theories%20Final.pdf

Piazza, J.A. (2015). The Determinants of Domestic Right-Wing Terrorism in the USA: Economic Grievance, Societal Change and Political Resentment. *Conflict Management and Peace Science* 34(1), pp. 52–80.

Vizzard, W.J. (2015). The Current and Future State of Gun Policy in the United States. *Journal of Criminal Law and Criminology* 104(4), pp. 879–904.

References

Baysinger, T.G. (2006). Right-Wing Group Characteristics and Ideology. *Homeland Security Affairs*, 2(2), 1–16.

Brannan, D.W. (2011). Left- and Right-wing Political Terrorism. In T.H. Tam (Ed.) *Politics of Terrorism: A Survey* (pp. 55–72). London, England: Routledge.

Chermak, S.M. (2002). *Searching for a Demon: The Media Construction of the Militia Movement.* Lebanon, NH: Northeastern University Press.

Childress, S. (2017, May 17). A Guide to the New Militia Movement. *Frontline*. Retrieved from http://apps.frontline.org/militia-movement/

Churchill, R.H. (2011). *To Shake Their Guns in the Tyrant's Face: Libertarian Political Violence and the Origins of the Militia Movement.* Ann Arbor, MI: University of Michigan Press.

Dougherty, C. (1995). The Minutemen, the National Guard and the Private Militia Movement: Will the Real Militia Please Stand Up. *John Marshall Law Review*, 28(4), 959–985.

Federal Bureau of Investigations. (2011, September 22). Domestic Terrorism: Focus on Militia Extremism. Retrieved from https://www.fbi.gov/news/stories/domestic-terrorism-focus-on-militia-extremism

Institute of Constitutional Advocacy and Protection. (2018). *Prohibiting Private Armies at Public Rallies: A Catalogue of Relevant State Constitutional and Statutory Provisions.* Washington, DC: Georgetown Law. Retrieved from https://www.law.georgetown.edu/icap/wp-content/uploads/sites/32/2018/04/Prohibiting-Private-Armies-at-Public-Rallies.pdf

Kurzman, C. & Schanzer, D. (2015). *Law Enforcement Assessment of the Violent Extremism Threat.* Durham, NC: Triangle Center on Terrorism and Homeland Security. Retrieved from https://sites.duke.edu/tcths/2015/06/25/report-law-enforcement-assessment-of-terrorist-threat/

Militia Composition and Classes. Title 10. United States Code § 246 (1956). Retrieved from https://www.law.cornell.edu/uscode/text/10/246

O'Brien, S.P. & Haider-Markel, D.P. (1998). Fueling the Fire: Social and Political Correlates of Citizen Militia Activity. *Social Science Quarterly*, 79(2), 456–465.

Polesky, J.E. (1996). The Rise of Private Militia: A First and Second Amendment Analysis of the Right to Organize and the Right to Train. *University of Pennsylvania Law Review*, 144, 1593–1642.

Supreme Court of the United States. (1969). *U.S. Reports: Brandenburg v. Ohio, 395 U.S. 444.* Retrieved from the Library of Congress, https://www.loc.gov/item/usrep395444/

The Militia Movement in the United States: Hearing Before the Subcommittee on Terrorism, Technology, and Government Information, Committee of the Judiciary of the United States Senate, 104th Cong. 1–2 (1995) (Remarks of Arlen Specter).

United States Constitution, Amendment II, n.d., Retrieved from https://www.senate.gov/civics/constitution_item/constitution.htm#amdt_3_(1791)

Zook, M. (1996). The Unorganized Militia Network: Conspiracies, Computers, and Community. *Berkeley Planning Journal*, 11(1), 26–48.

Chapter 81

National Preparedness for Natural and Human-Caused Hazards

Stephen Williams
AH Community Builders, United States Army, Harris Country Sheriff's Department, Houston, TX, United States

Scott N. Romaniuk
International Centre for Policing and Security, University of South Wales, Caerleon, United Kingdom

Contents

Introduction 611
Emergency Family Plan 612
Emergency Kit 613
Further Reading 614
References 615

Introduction

Offices of emergency management across the United States exist for the development, promotion, and implementation of planned responses to emergencies for its citizens living in both urban and rural areas. Life-threatening situations are created in emergencies caused by natural and human-caused hazards. There are hazards caused by nature like hurricanes and other tropical storms, floods, and earthquakes as well as hazards caused by humans such as terrorism, industrial accidents, and blackouts (Centers for Disease Control and Prevention, CDC, 2019). These hazards can force

DOI: 10.4324/9781315144511-85

citizens to make decisions to safely shelter-in-place or evacuate to safer locations. Among the many organizations that task themselves with emergency management, they all agree that the most fundamental preparedness begins with each individual citizen. The most important action a citizen can take is creating and developing a family emergency plan and an emergency kit (Ready, 2018).

Emergency Family Plan

An emergency plan is a course of action that is developed, practiced, and improved with the primary goal of reducing the potential of damage to life and property caused by emergency situations. The plan must effectively protect all life, including pets. Plan efficiency will depend on the inclusion of the unique needs of all members of the family or unit that is affected (Office of Emergency Management, OEM, 2018). All members, including children must familiarize themselves with the plan and ensure that they understand the significance of their actions. Plan efficiency can be maximized by practicing using mock drills, ensuring that the plan is both understood and functional.

In the United States, 90% of all presidentially declared disasters are weather related, making America the most severe weather-prone country on earth (National Weather Service, 2018). In the state of Texas for the past two decades, the urban and rural areas along the gulf coast have witnessed numerous historical storms that have caused billions of dollars in damage, record flooding, and loss of life. Beginning with Tropical Storm Allison in 2001, Hurricane Rita in 2005, Hurricane Ike in 2008, Hurricane Harvey in 2017, and three 500-year flood events in the past 3 years, emergency preparedness has become a high priority for citizens living along and near the Texas coast (National Hurricane Center, NHC 2021).

The cities of Houston, Galveston, and county governments along the coast have partnered to educate citizens on the importance of preparedness. Better resources for educating citizens in emergency planning for shelter-in-place and evacuation have been made available through community forums and an annual event in Houston that brings together every county and urban area along the Texas Gulf Coast. All of the agencies coordinate safety education with state government and national agencies such as the National Oceanic and Atmospheric Administration (NOAA), the National Hurricane Center, the Centers for Disease Control and Prevention (CDC), and the Federal Emergency Management Agency (FEMA).

All of the agencies agree that an effective emergency family plan can save lives in the event of any emergency. The family emergency plan is the first step in the response to any emergency whether it is occurring or threatening (Ready, 2018). Whether a family chooses to shelter-in-place or evacuate, a list of emergency contacts must be kept and updated. It is important to let others close to you know what you are doing in case contact is lost.

In the event that a family is not together at the time of an emergency event, it is critical that a family knows the disaster plans in place for their jobs and their children's school or daycare. As mentioned earlier, discussion of the emergency family plan is important as each member must know the importance of their role and how their actions protect them and the family unit as a whole.

An effective shelter-in-place option in an emergency family plan must be a team effort. The plan must consider the needs, understanding, and skill level of each member. If there are children, elderly, pets, or other participants with special needs, the plan must reflect these conditions. Likewise, if a family chooses or transitions from sheltering-in-place to an evacuation mode, the special needs of those same members must be considered to maintain the plan's efficiency. The family must be sure that the structure chosen is adequate when choosing to shelter-in-place. If a storm is threatening, choosing a mobile home or similar structure vulnerable to high wind is not a good decision. If there is no time to choose, educating each member on the safest locations in any structure is a benefit. Knowing escape routes in the shelter chosen is important and can save lives. Choosing meeting locations to reunite if a shelter is evacuated must be discussed and practiced if possible.

Learning first-aid for every member of the family can improve plan efficiency. Treating minor injuries in emergency situations can prevent injuries from worsening and stabilize victims until professional medical treatment can arrive. In the event, an adult is incapacitated, teaching children how to properly contact 9-1-1 services in an emergency can be life-saving. Children must also be taught their personal information such as full name, address, and parent's name when speaking to emergency responders on the phone or in person in the event of separation.

In the event of an evacuation, a family emergency plan should be one that is aware of the vulnerabilities of the family's community, that is, living in flood-prone areas, proximity to industrial plants, residing in a mobile home, or other vulnerable structure (Ready, 2018).

The family plan should be aware of local mass evacuation plans that are put in place by local government officials. The emergency plan should include copies of any maps or literature provided on this plan. The family should be aware of the location of nearby schools, community centers, emergency services, and other locations which are typically used for shelters during emergencies. Communication is always the key factor in the event of an evacuation, and the family emergency plan should include how communication will be made and maintained throughout the evacuation and returning. The travel needs of all family members, including pets, should be considered.

Emergency Kit

An emergency is defined as a situation that is serious and not expected which requires immediate attention to be managed. The emergency kit can be the best management tool when a family decides to shelter-in-place or evacuate during emergencies. The kit will have contents which reflect both basic survival needs and personal needs of each member of the family unit. Experts believe that an emergency kit should be assembled either in three parts or one multi-faceted kit with three options in mind (OEM, 2018). The three levels of an emergency kit should support staying at home, on the go, and support for a pet if needed.

Building a kit for sheltering-in-place for an emergency must include contents that support basic human needs, including first-aid, emergency lighting, non-perishable food, and water. There are many different hazards caused by emergencies, and as mentioned earlier, natural disasters are capable of crippling infrastructure, forcing citizens to endure shelters without services such as power, water, and emergency services. Once the basic survival foundation of a kit is established, the kit can be enhanced with additional items such as a fire extinguisher, rain gear, blankets, disinfectant items, bug repellant, battery-operated fans, and other items to support extensive time sheltering-in-place. These items used to enhance the kit can be chosen based on geography. Citizens who live in areas that may experience extreme temperatures, tropical areas with mosquitoes, and other nuisances should consider those environments when building the kit. The emergency kit can also be personalized for members of the family to include important documents, medication storage, emergency cash, and other items.

The second concept of an emergency kit is building one separate or a part of the larger kit that will be portable. Experts refer to it as a "go-bag", and like the name, it should be designed to have the ability to be accessed quickly and easily transported. The best type of bag used in this situation is a backpack or suitcase with wheels. The backpack has been considered one of the most effective storage vehicles for transport because it can be carried hands-free by an individual and be stored easily in most vehicle seating areas. The importance of having your hands free is that when emergency victims are evacuating, they may be moving through hazardous areas which could require their hands to be free for balance, breaking a fall, or operating a flashlight for vision. The "go-bag" or portable emergency kit can be built and stored separately or as part of the larger less portable kit, but when stored separately, the "go-bag" is more rapidly accessible.

The third concept of the emergency kit is one that can be considered for pets if applicable. Pet supplies can be basic survival, including food and water. It can also include medications, first-aid, soaps, records, leashes, and other items specific to the pet. A pet transport should also be stored with emergency supplies in the event of an evacuation.

Effective emergency management in life-threatening situations begins with the individual citizen. Life-threatening hazards caused by nature and humans, whether sudden or expected, can be minimized with a family emergency plan and an emergency kit. Each family and environment are unique, and all plans and kits will differ with varying needs of the family units. For effective emergency management to protect life, citizens must sit down, discuss, create, and practice a family emergency plan and build an emergency kit.

Further Readings

Bradley, A. T. (2011). *The Disaster Preparedness Handbook: A Guide for Families*. New York: Skyhorse Publishing.

Shojai, A. (2001). *The First-Aid Companion for Dogs & Cats*. Pennsylvania: St. Martin's Press.

Stroud, C., Altevogt, B. M., and Goldfrank, L. R. (2013). *Institute of Medicine's Forum on Medical and Public Health Preparedness for Catastrophic Events: Activities and Goals*. Cambridge: Cambridge University Press.

References

Centers for Disease Control and Prevention. (CDC). (2019). "Preparing for a Hurricane or Other Tropical Storm." https://www.cdc.gov/disasters/hurricanes/before.html

National Hurricane Center (NHC). (2021). nhc.noaa.gov

National Weather Service. (2018). "National Weather Service Safety Tips." https://www.weather.gov/safety/

Office of Emergency Management (OEM). (2018). "Preparedness." www.houstonoem.org/preparedness-are-you-ready/

Ready. (2018). "Make a Plan." https://www.ready.gov/plan

Chapter 82

Passive Surveillance

Leonard J. Samborowski
Nichols College, Dudley, MA, United States

Contents

Introduction ... 617
Knowledge, Power, and Collection ... 618
iPhone and the Galaxy of Surveillance Capabilities ... 619
Selfies and the IMINT of Facebook ... 619
Smile, You're on Facebook's Camera ... 620
Open-Source Intelligence, 280 Characters at a Time ... 620
Uploads to the Musk Mother Ship ... 621
Conclusions ... 622
Further Reading ... 622
References ... 622

Introduction

The collection of information from human sources, also called Human Intelligence (HUMINT), has been a valuable tool for hegemonic states since the *Art of War* was written around 500 BC (Pars, 2013; Schnell, 2016; Teodor, 2018). HUMINT joins other collection techniques that include signals intelligence (SIGINT), imagery intelligence (IMINT), measurements and signatures intelligence (MASINT), and open source intelligence (OSINT) as tools used to piece together diverse crumbs of data necessary to understand an adversary's intent (Clark, 2014). Within the National Intelligence Community, several organizations oversee the mining and interpretation of data by a specific technique. These organizations include the Defense Intelligence Agency (DIA and its oversight of MASINT), the National Security Agency (NSA and

DOI: 10.4324/9781315144511-86

its collection and analysis of SIGINT), the National Geospatial-Intelligence Agency (NGA: IMINT), the Central Intelligence Agency (CIA: HUMINT), and the Director of National Intelligence (DNI: OSINT) (Clark, 2016).

Knowledge, Power, and Collection

Most will accept the adage that "knowledge is power" or as Sun Tzu offered, that if you "Know your enemy and know yourself and you can fight a hundred battles without disaster" (Warner, 2006). As we seek to optimize our life position and minimize missteps, we look to information as a tool to help this process. The more information we collect and turn into knowledge or – better yet – intelligence, the better for us.

For nations, intelligence collection of enemies is the norm, embedded into statecraft and budget allocation. For individuals, data collection and analysis are increasingly implanted into our daily routines and resourced from our household budgets. We recognize that our smart device, connected to other electronic devices or networks via wireless protocols, can assist to maximize daily life, contributing to convenience, efficiency, entertainment, fitness, and financial well-being (Radziwon, Bilberg, Bogers & Madsen, 2014).

In 2020, a person's ability to access and analyze data and convert that information into actionable intelligence is remarkable. In most regards, the convenience of digits endorses the Arthur C. Clarke quote: "Any sufficiently advanced technology is indistinguishable from magic" (Curzon & McOwan, 2008). With our magic smart devices, we find ratings and directions to a restaurant, locate lost high school friends, play lullabies for our children, research and purchase stocks, face-time with grandma, laugh at emoji's, virtually decorate our office, generate our own electrocardiogram, and create "fake news" (Bakir & McStay, 2017). Our magical convenience will only get faster, more agile, and better integrated into our day. It is no longer a matter of future developments. Data access and analysis, leading to intelligence, is ubiquitous and seamlessly integrated into our "now." However, technology benefits are coupled with concerning consequences.

Integrating smart devices into our daily routine allows passive surveillance by the Internet of Things. Our new collection techniques and de facto collection agencies are embedded into how we live our days. Apple and Samsung, with over 15 billion smartphones sold, provide our passive SIGINT coverage. Facebook and Instagram provide the IMINT coverage. Amazon (with Alexa) and Google (with its internet search algorithms) are part of the HUMINT and MASINT structure. Twitter provides open-source intelligence. The beauty and danger of this passive intelligence structure is that we willingly participate in the surveillance operations conducted by these businesses. We buy the product or digital service and, through our use of that device or service, provide streams of personal data to the corporate *cloud*. Combine this passive surveillance structure with city and state collection systems (traffic cams, smart passes, ATMs, and retail store credit card readers) and the aforementioned National Intelligence systems and you have a surveillance net that provides 24/7/365 blanket coverage of American society. A ubiquitous surveillance genie is out of the bottle and she's not going back in (Rogan, 2018).

iPhone and the Galaxy of Surveillance Capabilities

In 2017, COMScore (COMScore, 2017) reported that 81% of Americans over the age of 13 years spent an average of 2 hours and 51 minutes on their smartphones each day. For an intelligence professional running a collection operation, that's 171 minutes of lucrative data streams per person. Viewed nationally, smartphone users in the United States passively supply 642 *days* of data for potential exploitation every 24 hours. Apple knows when we're sleeping (inactive smartphone), knows where we are (geo-positions, airplane mode), and knows if we're bad or good (website searches). Likewise, Samsung can identify our appetite for action movies (video searches), predict if we're left or right handed (screen swipes), and track our generosity (Uber tips).

Selfies and the IMINT of Facebook

The value of imagery interpretation has been understood since the early photographs of Joseph Niepce in 1826 (Haidar, 2020). Today, we live in a culture of image exhibitionists. Take our photojournalist-like reporting of a business trip. We travel to Las Vegas and share our selfies with family and friends. A few keystrokes and finger taps send our photos from our smartphones to the *cloud* and onto our favorite social media sites. While we trust that our smiling face is only shared with our favorite aunt or uncle, we forget that, once transmitted via the internet, our unique image is accessible to any smart hacker of the digital world. Consider the following: Facebook has 2.23 billion monthly active users (MAU), YouTube 1.9 billion MAU, WhatsApp 1.5 billion MAU, Instagram 1 billion MAU, and Tik Tok 500 million MAU (Lua, 2020). Given these social media usage rates, our innocuous digital data is potentially accessible to 7.1 billion users per month. It is unlikely that all seven billion users have our best interest at heart. Even under ideal circumstances, using strongly encrypted security techniques, and in the absence of bad intent, our picture in front of a Vegas hotel, when added to thousands of other online images, supplies lucrative data for a spy or data analyst of a global business.

In a digital world, Fred Barnard's adage, "One picture is worth a thousand words" is miserly in its estimation. Facebook alone stores over 260 billion images or over 20 petabytes of data. At peak operating cycles, Zuckerberg's company serves over one million images per second (Beaver, Kumar, Li, Sobel, and Vajgel, 2010). Using resident photo metadata, images are annotated with the creation date and location, information about the visual content, and identification of the creator (IPTC.org). But the information tsunami doesn't end there. We gleefully contribute to our passive surveillance by providing personalized commentary. Using our Vegas photo as an example, throwaway comments like, "Lost my shirt playing Blackjack" or "David Copperfield was amazing," add layers of meaning to mundane pics.

Most damaging to our privacy and the privacy of others are the unintended consequences of "tagging" our photographs. Tagging a photo with the names of our family or friends and describing our relationship (wife, daughter, father) with that person allows for the development of association nodes. You know Ted. Ted knows

Mary. Mary is married to Phil. Seems like harmless and trivia information until that information becomes intelligence that helps, as a minimum, spread marketing ads, or, more nefariously, creates personally endorsed emails designed to sway elections.

Smile, You're on Facebook's Camera

Access to the metadata of photographs helps refine facial recognition programs and the operational protocols associated with this surveillance technique. Billions of pictures, depicting billions of faces, tagged with social network context, substantially increase recognition performance (Stone, Zicker, and Darrell, 2019). Facebook is aware of the business potential of such a capability. The company has developed surveillance algorithms that use computer cameras to analyze our expressions and moods (Chinoy, 2018). By monitoring our facial expressions and scan rates, Facebook can evaluate our interest and the effectiveness of ads or social commentary (Singer, 2018). The potential of this passive surveillance is huge. We read an article online about progressive economics and frown as we scan the screen. We read an article about the wonders of capitalism and the corners of our mouth rise and our cheeks brighten. Within seconds an ad for a well-known brokerage company appears on the margins of our digital screen. We were ad targeted and likely don't mind as the intrusion was aligned with our bias (Teicher, 2018).

Facial recognition technology (FRT) as a surveillance method is not new, Bledsoe, Wolf, and Bisson worked on FRT beginning in 1964 (Bhati & Gupta, 2015). Several companies (Ever AI, FaceFirst, and Amazon Rekognition) have developed algorithms that produce a *digital print* of faces by taking measurements of 80 nodal points. These face prints require relatively small bytes of storage, so they are efficient components of identification databases (Monroe, 2009).

Facial recognition is unobtrusive to the user and passively supplied. Information is pulled by the computer software program. The subject needs only to be in proximity to a surveillance camera. As most smart devices have built-in cameras, all that is needed to begin surveillance operations is a subject and a software upgrade.

Open-Source Intelligence, 280 Characters at a Time

From the Oval Office to the streets of San Francisco, Twitter floods the *cloud* with microblog commentaries of our lives and perceptions. We self-promote with short digital bursts of our emotions, activities, wants, and needs. We message in more than 40 languages at a rate of more than 500 million daily tweets (Sayce, 2020). At upward of 280 characters per tweet that is a lucrative source of information for intelligence analysts. Tweets aggregated and analyzed with machine learning can be an invaluable resource for gaining insight into different domains of discussion and public opinion.

While short-lived (the estimated half-life of a tweet is 24 minutes), the intelligence value of the daily word equivalent of 300,000 novels is staggering (Haghighati & Sedig, 2019). Current data analytic tools can evaluate our tweets in precise granularity. The analysis goes beyond spelling and grammar; intent can be determined.

Apps that create word clouds of our tweets show word frequency. Other analytics evaluate lexical density, evaluating the structure and complexity of our word choice.

It is important to remember that we give up this information freely. No person is demanding that we tweet about our work frustrations or about our love or disdain for our president. And that self-provided data, when added with time, location, voice, and imagery, paints a comprehensive picture of who we are, our feelings, and our intent.

Uploads to the Musk Mother Ship

In 2015, a new corporation entered the passive surveillance community – Tesla. In October 2015, Tesla released software enabling Autopilot as an initial step toward self-driving technology. Since 2015, Tesla vehicles, equipped with self-driving hardware, have received over-the-air (OTA) software updates to keep the operating system current (Simons, 2020). These updates improve the functionality and safety of the self-driving technology. By November 2016, Autopilot had operated across 100,000 vehicles for 300 million active miles and 1.3 billion miles in *shadow mode* (a state where the car computer records where and when the Autopilot would have taken action in a potentially dangerous situation) (Cinti, 2017). The impact of analyzing driving data from the equivalent of 7 rounds of trips to the sun is staggering. Metadata analysis of Tesla vehicle miles could yield a plethora of useful intelligence: favorite truck stops and refueling sites, scenic road usage, accident causes (oversteering, driver fatigue, and sun glare), watt consumption by temperature conditions, average speed taken at interstate off ramps, and routine routes – all could be easily computed by a scrub of vehicle data.

Without question, the Tesla electric car is a game-changing mode of transportation. Since 2016, each model in the Tesla fleet, the S, X, Y, and 3 is equipped with Autopilot capability. This includes the Model 3, the entry-level Tesla car that provides access to the Musk ecosystem at an affordable price. Unique to the Autopilot system is the passive/autonomous updating of software that reconfigures the car. These software updates are sent via the internet and can be scheduled to activate at the discretion of the vehicle owner. The updates are seamlessly executed. The only negative is the need to park the car for 20 minutes required for the update.

A more sobering concern is the two-way flow of information from Tesla to the car and the car to Tesla. The car owner, in order to access the wonders of the cutting-edge technology, trades her/his car-driving data with Tesla. In return, Tesla provides improvements to the transportation experience culled from the fleet of Tesla vehicles. The knowledge gained by all cars in the information pool is shared with all other Tesla vehicles. The car gets safer, more comfortable, more entertaining, and more fuel efficient but in return, Tesla knows in the aggregate, the miles traveled, the average wattage rate, and the routes, times, and speeds of the trips taken. Only the user can decide if this convenience is worth the tradeoff in privacy (Acker & Beaton, 2020). For certain, it is yet another example of our passive acceptance of technological surveillance.

Our AutoINT will only grow in its blanket coverage of our road movements. By 2025, virtually every car manufacturer will have some version of an electric vehicle (Matousek, 2019). More significantly, it is safe to assume that like Tesla, the CEOs of

Audi, Ford, Mercedes, Toyota, and Volkswagen will create cars (of all fuel sources) that are capable of software upgrades that increase safety and reduce operational weaknesses. Like Tesla, if data can be downloaded, the data can be uploaded, providing petabytes of data to the auto industry.

Conclusions

The National Intelligence Community is a well-structured, richly resourced federation of agencies designed to support and defend the citizens of America. Our intelligence agencies, with the exception of the internally focused Federal Bureau of Investigation (FBI), concentrate on foreign threats and adversaries. The work of these government professionals is deliberate and dangerous, as collection operations are always conducted on unwilling antagonists. Running as a shadow intelligence community, the world of passive surveillance is a loose association of independent businesses and global entrepreneurs. Their mission is to create profit for their stakeholders. The work of these business professionals is deliberate yet stress-free. They deal with eager customers who willingly fund their own surveillance by the purchase of products and services provided by the corporations that exploit their data.

Further Reading

Bauman, Z., Bigo, D., Esteves, P., Guild, E., Jabri, V., Lyon, D. & Walker, R. B. J. (2014). "After snowden: Rethinking the impact of surveillance," *International Political Sociology*. Vol 8(2), pp. 121–144.

Dicter, A. & Byman, D. L. (2006, March). "Israel's Lessons for Fighting Terrorism and Their Implications for the United States," Analysis Paper, No. 8, The Saban Center for Middle East Policy at the Brookings Institution. https://www.brookings.edu/wp-content/uploads/2016/06/byman20060324.pdf

McLaughlin, J. (2015, November 17). "US Mass Surveillance Has No Record of Thwarting Large Terror Attacks, Regardless of Snowden Leaks," *The Intercept*.

References

Acker, A. & Beaton, B. (2020). Software update unrest: The recent happenings around Tinder and Tesla. IEEE.org. Retrieved 24 February 2020.

Bakir, V., McStay, A. (2017). Fake news and the economy of emotions: Problems, causes, solutions. *Journal of Digital Journalism*. Vol. 6(2), pp. 154–175.

Beaver, D., Kumar, S., Li, H., Sobel, J., & Vajgel, P. (2010). *Finding a needle in Haystack: Facebook's photo storage*. OSDI. Retrieved from Google Scholar 21 February 2020.

Bhati, D. & Gupta, V. (2015). Survey – A comparative analysis of face recognition technique. *International Journal of Engineering Research and General Science*, Vol. 3(2), 597–609.

Chinoy, S. (2018). *What 7 creepy patents reveal about Facebook*. New York Times.

Cinti, N. (2017). *Why is Tesla worth more than General Motors? Comprehensive analysis of the world's most captivating company*. Luiss University, Rome, Italy.

Clark, R.M. (2014). *Intelligence collection*. Sage/CQ press, Washington, DC.

Clark, R.M. (2016). *The five disciplines of intelligence collection.* CQ Press, Thousand Oaks, CA.
COMScore (2017) U.S. Cross-Platform Future in Focus report.
Curzon, P., McOwan, P. (2008). Engaging with computer science through magic shows. *ITiCSE,* June, pp. 179–183.
Haghighati, A. & Sedig, K. (2019). VARTTA: A visual analytics system for making sense of real-time Twitter data. MDPI.com. Retrieved from Google Scholar, 22 February 2020.
Haidar, R. (2020). Photoinques.com. Retrieved from Google Scholar, 22 February 2020.
IPTC.org. Retrieved from Google Scholar, 22 February 2020.
Lua, A. (2020). 21 Top social media sites to consider for your brand. *Buffer.com.* Retrieved 13 February 2020, https://buffer.com/library/social-media-sites
Matousek, M. (2019). 40 Electric cars you'll see on the road by 2025. *Business Insider.* Retrieved online 24 February 2020.
Monroe, D. (2009). *Method for incorporating facial recognition technology in a multimedia surveillance system.* U.S. Patent application, Patent No: US 7,634,662 B2.
Pars, M. (2013). Six strategy lessons from Clausewitz and Sun Tzu. *Journal of Public Affairs.* Vol. 13(3), pp. 329–334.
Radziwon, A., Bilberg, A., Bogers, M., Madsen, E. (2014). The smart factory: Exploring adaptive and flexible manufacturing solutions. *Procedia Engineering,* Vol. 69, pp. 1184–1190.
Rogan, J. (7 September, 2018). *The Joe Rogan Experience.* #1169 Elon Musk (podcast).
Sayce, D. (2020). The number of tweets per day in 2019. Dsayce.com/social-media. Retrieved 22 February 2020.
Schnell, J. (2016). Cross-cultural mis-steps by the U.S. in Iraq and their relevance for HUMINT operations. *Florida Communication Journal.* 44(1), pp. 89–95.
Simons, R.A. (2020). Driverless cars, urban parking and land use. Retrieved, Google Books, 24 February 2020.
Singer, N. (2018). *Facebook's push for facial recognition prompts privacy alarms.* New York Times.
Stone, Z., Zicker, T., & Darrell, T. (2019). Autotagging Facebook: Social network context improves photo annotation. IEEE Xplore Digital Library. Retrieved, 13 February 2020 https://ieeexplore.ieee.org.
Teicher, J. G. (2018). What do facial recognition technologies mean for our privacy? *New York Times.*
Teodor, T.O. (May, 2018). Benchmarking of information collection techniques used in HUMINT. *Scientific Research & Education in the Air Force,* pp. 89–98.
Warner, M. (2006). The divine skein: Sun Tzu on intelligence. *Intelligence & National Security.* Vol. 21(4), pp. 483–492.

Chapter 83

Radicalization Prevention and Response (RPR)

David Parker
Aarhus University, Aarhus, Denmark

David Chapot
Local Authority Counter-Radicalization Practitioner, United Kingdom

Jonathan Davis
Former Counter-Radicalization Practitioner, United Kingdom

Contents

Introduction 625
The Concept of Radicalization 626
History of Countering Violent Extremism in the United States 627
Challenges and Gaps 629
European Experiences: Central Government Leadership 629
European Experiences: Tailored Interventions for Individuals 631
European Experiences: Cognitive Consideration 632
Conclusion 632
Further Reading 633
Note 633
References 633

Introduction

In 2017, Federal Bureau of Investigations (FBI) Director Christopher Wray described terrorist threats to the United States as 'acute and persistent', with preventing terrorist attacks the number one priority for homeland security (Wray, 2017). The threat of

DOI: 10.4324/9781315144511-87

terrorism in the United States is, of course, not a new phenomenon. In the immediate post-9/11 era US agencies prioritized interdicting large-scale, usually externally orchestrated, attacks. However, while this remains important, in recent years, homegrown terrorism has become of increasing concern (Gartenstein-Ross, 2016). Much of this is a consequence of sophisticated propaganda by Islamist groups such as Islamic State of Iraq and al-Sham (ISIS), and the rise in US citizens traveling to Syria. However, a range of other ideologies contribute to the domestic threat, including individuals inspired by Sovereign Citizens and Extreme Far-Right ideologies.

Attacks in recent years by Omar Mateen in Florida (Islamist), Dylann Roof in Charleston (Extreme Far Right), and Gavin Long in Baton Rouge (Sovereign Citizens) illustrate the gravity of the threats posed by homegrown terror. Like the United States, Europe faces domestic threats from both networked groups and lone actors. However, European domestic terrorism has a much longer and more sustained history, ranging from Basque Homeland and Liberty (Euskadi Ta Askatasuna or ETA) in Spain to the Irish Republican Army (IRA) in the United Kingdom. As the United States seeks to adapt to the new security environment by addressing domestic radicalization (rather than simply interdicting attack planning), there are lessons and experiences from European approaches to preventing and responding to radicalization that can support US policymakers in their efforts. This chapter provides context to the concept of radicalization, summarizes US approaches to tackling radicalization, identifies the challenges, and provides details of European experiences that may support agencies within the US context.

Concerns about homegrown terrorism, alongside ever more sophisticated terrorist propaganda, have resulted in many countries across the West attempting to prevent (or reverse) the radicalization of citizens, as opposed to simply working to interdict attacks. To date, the United States efforts to do this have been reasonably limited and largely restricted to pilot areas. However, the nature of contemporary terrorist threats facing the United States, such as lone actor terrorism, means that US policymakers may consider more focused radicalization prevention efforts. This chapter outlines European experiences that may prove particularly useful in the US context, focusing on clear federal leadership, tailored interventions consistently available, and activities that address cognitive and ideological issues.

The Concept of Radicalization

Despite its prominence in explanations of contemporary security threats, radicalization was a term not frequently used by either academics or practitioners prior to 9/11, only becoming common following the attacks in Madrid (2004) and London (2007). Consequently, as with terrorism, there is no single definition of radicalization. For instance, some analysts focus on extremist beliefs while for others radicalization refers to the path an individual follows toward extremist, violent behavior (Neumann, 2013). Nevertheless, it is widely agreed that radicalization is a (often-gradual) process involving a variety of different factors, ranging from lack of identity to feelings of persecution. For the purposes of this chapter, it can be considered a 'change in beliefs, feelings and behaviors in directions that increasingly justify intergroup violence' (McCauley and Moskalenko, 2008: 416). Various models have been developed to explain radicalization. These range from Moghaddam's (2006) conceptual staircase, which describes radicalization using the metaphor of a narrowing staircase, starting with perceived injustice/frustration leading step-by-step to the final terrorist act on the top floor, to Sageman's (2008) Four-Prong Model which suggests the process is not necessarily so linear. Despite competing definitions and contrasting models, most scholars accept that a range of factors influence radicalization. These can stem from the individual level (e.g., isolated individuals looking for meaning in their lives), group level (e.g., peer pressure or indoctrination through social bonds), or the wider structural or socio-political context (e.g., imagery of global attacks against Muslims).

In response to the rise in domestic threats, counter-radicalization efforts have spread across the West and beyond over the past 10 years (Schmidt, 2013; Parker, Chapot & Davis, 2018), with a range of different approaches. These efforts stem from the recognition of both the difficulties and limits of interdicting domestic attacks (especially those committed by lone actors) and the financial, social, and political cost of tackling terrorism through repressive means alone. Approaches broadly cover one or more of three areas: (i) encouraging disengagement from extremist groups (whether voluntary or involuntary), (ii) reorienting ideological viewpoints and encouraging the reintegration of radicalized individuals into society, and (iii) prevention of radicalization, which has an anticipatory thrust and rests on the idea of supporting vulnerable individuals. The second two are perhaps the most challenging (and controversial) because of their focus on cognition and prioritization of the 'pre-criminal' space (i.e., focus on beliefs and behaviors that are potentially concerning and may lead to illegality but have not broken any laws at that point). It is broadly the case that European countries have placed a higher priority on addressing the early cognitive issues (based on the assumption that ideas can – although not necessarily – lead to violence) than the United States. This is in part because of strong US traditions of freedom of speech and the US government's threshold for intervention has more often been once a law has been broken. However, in the context of rising domestic terrorism and sophisticated propaganda, US policymakers may consider new options for addressing radicalization at an earlier stage. Drawing on European experiences may prove useful for those policymakers. Looking at approaches in the United Kingdom, Denmark, and Germany may be particularly helpful as these countries have long-standing programs which, according to some analysts, are also some of the most advanced (Said & Fouad, 2018; Butt & Tuck, 2014; Parker & Davis, 2017).[1]

History of Countering Violent Extremism in the United States

Having previously been handled as a local issue, efforts around countering violent extremism (CVE) gained federal backing, and some limited funding, during President Obama's administration. In August 2011, the administration unveiled its CVE strategy document, *Empowering Local Partners to Prevent Violent Extremism in the United States*, shortly followed by the December 2011 *Strategic Implementation Plan for*

Empowering Local Partners to Prevent Violent Extremism in the United States (SIP) (White House, 2011b). As indicated by the title, the approach emphasized a reliance 'on existing partnerships that communities have forged with Federal, State, and local government agencies' (White House, 2011a: 1). The SIP also emphasized interagency cooperation and involved a range of departments including the Department of Homeland Security (DHS), Department of Justice (DoJ), and the FBI (White House, 2011b). The SIP thus stood as the first federal initiative to broaden counter-terrorism initiatives beyond the realm of the military, law enforcement, and intelligence services and into the sphere of civil society, community cohesion, and community-based organizations. Following the election of President Trump federal funding was cut from the program, which appears to have had lower prioritization under the new administration (Reuters, 2017). However, in October 2018, the US government revisited CVE with the release of the *National Strategy for Counterterrorism of the United States* (White House, 2018). The document references the institutionalization of 'prevention architecture to thwart terrorism' (White House, 2018: 21), and outlines a greater role for civil society in terrorism prevention. However, the document remains high-level, discussing ambitions rather than delivery: therefore, this chapter will focus on the outputs of the SIP.

The SIP reflected the federal government's desire to enable third-sector actors through in-kind support and funding, as opposed to implementing a top-down and statutory federal program. In September 2014, Boston, Los Angeles, and Minneapolis announced they would host pilot CVE programs in partnership with the White House, DHS, and National Counterterrorism Center (NTC) (DoJ, 2014). Indicative of the localized delivery outlined in the SIP, each city fostered a unique approach to CVE. For example, the Los Angeles CVE Framework developed a three-tiered 'Prevention, Intervention and Interdiction' framework. This model, which emphasized a 'whole of community' approach, was influenced by local CVE efforts that had been ongoing since 2008 and were informed by the community cohesion approach used to reduce gang violence (City of Los Angeles, 2015). Minneapolis had distinct challenges of its own: the rise of Daesh saw a resurgence in the recruitment of young Minnesotans to fight overseas, an effort previously led by al-Shabaab recruiters (Southers and Hienz, 2015). Here, CVE funding was used to fund 'youth programmes, job training, and after-school programs…to facilitate mentorship' (Southers and Hienz, 2015). This approach, titled *Building Community Resilience*, focused on identifying causes for disenfranchisement and developing community resilience approaches to address these concerns (US Attorney's Office Minneapolis, 2015).

In Boston, seven 'Focus Areas' were identified, with an outline of how to address each. Issues included distrust of government, isolated and vulnerable youths, and the role of social media (US Attorney's Office Massachusetts, 2015). The overall goal was to 'increase the capacity of community and government as a way to protect vulnerable individuals from engagement' in violent extremism through education initiatives, support options, and raising awareness. However, concrete steps to operationalize this goal were not achieved before Obama's departure from office (US Attorney's Office Massachusetts, 2015). The White House's October 2018 strategy document provides an opportunity to once more take forward CVE efforts in the United States.

Challenges and Gaps

While these initiatives developed new and constructive relationships, there were also challenges. As Dr. Erroll Southers and Justin Heinz noted of efforts in Minneapolis, 'there are numerous organizations that secure government funding but do not achieve any measurable impact on the threat from terrorist recruiters', and that it is 'difficult to validate which programs are having a real impact based on a clearly articulated strategy' (Southers and Hienz, 2015). Furthermore, there was significant suspicion from elements of the American-Muslim community. For example, the Council of American-Islamic Relations (CAIR) Minnesota criticized CVE efforts for 'discriminatorily [targeting] the Muslim and Somali communities' (CAIR, 2016). Indeed, Bokhari (2015: 8) notes the high 'level of distrust between the authorities and American Muslims.' These challenges are not unique to US-based CVE efforts. However, the brevity of experience in these pilot sites poses a challenge when seeking to better understand the nature, quality, and impact of local CVE efforts.

Despite examples of positive work being delivered in each pilot site, the lack of continued funding makes it difficult to assess how successful (or unsuccessful) these local programs might have been. Nonetheless, several gaps and issues did clearly emerge during the period of federal funding. Three gaps, in particular, can be identified. Firstly, as noted by several researchers, CVE efforts in the United States lacked clear federal ownership, with many federal agencies initially sharing ownership of the plan (Bjelopera, 2014; CSIS, 2016). Therefore, and critically, while funding was centralized, delivery was highly localized and lacked federal strategic direction. The second closely linked issue was that, when working with individuals at risk of radicalization, US CVE efforts did not rely on the consistent use of tailored interventions, a key element of successful European programs. Instead, community-based organizations were provided with funding to deliver loosely defined programs. This left the US pilot sites with restricted experience or resources and meant that there was limited consistency across the areas delivering CVE. The third gap centers on the fact that although SIP addressed community cohesion, education, and skill development initiatives to ameliorate environmental and societal issues, it paid relatively minor attention to responding to the cognitive and ideological issues radicalization often raises. The following sections outline how European experiences may support US policymakers in addressing these three challenges.

European Experiences: Central Government Leadership

One area where the United States may be able to learn from European experiences relates to the clear leadership role shouldered by the central government, setting the strategic direction and building the framework for CVE efforts to be implemented. In the United Kingdom, a range of different government bodies are involved in the delivery of Prevent, the United Kingdom counter-radicalization strategy. The police, for instance, play a significant role through involvement in the safeguarding process, ownership of terrorism risk throughout the process, and role in drafting the Counter-Terrorism Local Profile (the report outlining terrorist-related threats within a local area) (HM Government, 2015a: 9; HM Government, 2011: 32). However, the Home Office provides the central impetus behind the strategy. The Home Office, which produced the *Prevent Strategy*, notably leads on the assessment of local Prevent delivery, provides funds for the delivery of Prevent in priority areas, and exercises oversight of the work undertaken in these areas (HM Government, 2015b: 5–7). In so doing, it creates the structures necessary for a consistent and quality-controlled national implementation of the strategy while allowing for local variance. The fact that, across England and Wales, the same form – the Vulnerability Assessment Framework – is used when assessing potential vulnerabilities to radicalization, is one example of standardized practice born of central leadership (HM Government, 2015a: 11).

In Denmark, the central government plays a key role by providing information about the nature of the terrorist threat and sharing broader expertise, notably by organizing training for relevant frontline practitioners (Vidino & Brandon, 2012: 52–53). While some of the detail of the implementation on the ground are left to municipalities, they do so by building upon, or working alongside, existing widespread multiagency networks such as SSPs (Schools, Social Services, and Police) (Vidino & Brandon, 2012: 53; Koehler, 2015: 131) and national structures such as Info-houses – frameworks for cooperation and information sharing between the police and municipalities with regards to extremism and radicalization (Hemmingsen, 2015: 27). Info-houses play a central role in Danish counter-radicalization efforts by assessing radicalization concerns and referring individuals to the most appropriate form of support (Hemmingsen, 2015: 28–29). Crucially, while the central government sets the strategic direction in Denmark, the scope for local innovation nonetheless remains and has often driven advances in Danish counter-radicalization. The municipality of Aarhus, for example, undertook local initiatives which were initially designed to supplement central government efforts but eventually influenced national delivery (Agerschou, 2014/15: 6–7). The aforementioned Info-houses, for example, were initially established as part of Aarhus' local CVE efforts but now operate nationally (Hjørnholm, 2013: 65).

The German Federal Government also plays a significant yet limited role in this domain by supporting and empowering several organizations working to address extremism concerns. For example, the German Federal Office for Immigration and Refugee Affairs (BAMF) runs a national hotline which assesses radicalization concerns, offers initial advice, answers questions raised by referrers, and redirects individuals toward the relevant local organization best able to support them (Berczyk, 2016: 48; Koehler, 2015: 132–133). In addition, the government also finances some of these organizations (Hayat). European experiences relating to central government leadership and coordination could prove particularly valuable in the US context where, as previously mentioned, federal rhetoric has not resulted in consistent leadership in practice. This point may be especially relevant considering the challenges posed by US size and the variance in CVE efforts noted on the ground. Establishing clear federal leadership could prove beneficial by ensuring that CVE efforts are informed by a robust understanding of terrorism risks, and by providing training, guidance, and support to facilitate a consistent approach built on recognized principles and adequate evidence.

European Experiences: Tailored Interventions for Individuals

Another area where the United States may benefit from European experiences is the consistent use of tailored interventions for individuals across the country when addressing radicalization concerns. In the United Kingdom, Channel – the 'multi-agency approach to identify and provide support to individuals who are at risk of being drawn into terrorism' embedded within Prevent – specifically seeks to identify individuals at risk and develop 'the most appropriate support plan for the individuals concerned' (HM Government, 2015a: 3 & 5). This support, which is tailored to the vulnerabilities of each individual, can include mentoring through an intervention provider such as a credible theological leader, diversionary activities (including activities run by local youth or sporting clubs), educational activities around topics such as critical thinking, or facilitated access to existing services (such as mental health support) (HM Government, 2015a: 17). According to Home Office figures, Channel has supported 381 individuals from April 2015 to March 2016 (HM Government, 2017: 8). As there is a Channel Panel in all areas and each Panel can access centrally approved providers, regardless of where one lives in England and Wales, an individual with vulnerabilities to radicalization can access tailored interventions and support.

Danish practitioners also offer targeted interventions provided by multiagency partners (Vidino & Brandon, 2012: 52; Hemmingsen, 2015: 7). As part of the 'Deradicalisation – targeted interventions project, these interventions can include exit talks, mentoring, assistance with seeking employment, assistance tackling drug abuse or psychological services alongside a family support group (Ministeriet for Flygtninge Indvandrere og Integration, 2011; Koehler, 2015: 132). While local variance does exist, with Info-houses functioning throughout the country such support and interventions are nonetheless available throughout Denmark. In the German context, the helpline run by the BAMF can be assessed by anyone, regardless of where they live in Germany. As previously mentioned, this helpline can then redirect individuals toward organizations which, in turn, can offer interventions. One example is Exit-Germany which works with members of far-right extremist groups who wish to distance themselves from this milieu (Exit-Germany b). Exit-Germany has supported over 500 individuals since its inception in 2000, with a recidivism rate of approximately 3% (Exit-Germany b). The support provided by the organization varies but can include practical assistance (e.g., around employment and education), psychological support, and advice on physical safety (Exit-Germany a; Exit-Germany b).

Another example is Hayat, an organization which offers counseling services and broader support to individuals linked to Islamist extremism, or their friends and relatives (Hayat). Hayat works extensively with individuals considering travel to Daesh-controlled territories to dissuade them from doing so, encourage those who have traveled to return, and assist with the reintegration of those who do return (Berczyk, 2016: 48). Through the use of its national network, Germany also makes consistent use of tailored interventions. European approaches, with their focus on the availability of tailored interventions which can be offered to vulnerable individuals, may prove beneficial in the US context where the availability of such interventions is dependent upon local initiatives. The German approach, in particular, may prove insightful by highlighting the possibility for the central government to act as an intermediary between vulnerable individuals requiring support and the relevant organizations offering such interventions.

European Experiences: Cognitive Consideration

The third area is the inclusion of cognitive, and therefore ideological, considerations within interventions. European efforts encompass both disengagements from extremist groups alongside seeking to encourage cognitive shifts (Vidino & Brandon, 2012: 1). As previously mentioned, this point may prove particularly crucial in virtue of the shift in tactics employed by groups like Daesh who now place greater emphasis on lone actor attacks. By reducing opportunities to detect such attacks (Parker et al., 2017), such tactics increase the importance of preventative efforts. In the British context, Prevent is clear that its remit includes cognition, stating that 'preventing terrorism will mean challenging extremist (and non-violent) ideas' (HM Government, 2011: 6). Ideological considerations can thus form a key part of the mentoring provided by an intervention provider which can include exploring new ideas, activities to encourage critical thinking, or the discussion of religious or political views and beliefs (HM Government, 2015a: 17).

The Danish government's approach to de-radicalization includes both disengagements from extremist groups and actions, alongside cognitive change (Ministeriet for Flygtninge Indvandrere og Integration, 2011). As such, its interventions do sometimes address ideas and beliefs (Koehler, 2015: 132). This readiness to address both behavior and ideas is also visible in Germany. Exit-Germany, for example, stresses the importance of exploring alternative worldviews and outlooks, addressing societal questions, and encouraging 'critical reflection, reassessment and successful challenge of the old ideology' as part of this process (Exit-Germany b). Hayat also claims that 'any de-radicalization process must emphasize the de-legitimization and invalidation' of the beliefs of the groups individuals ascribed to (Berczyk, 2016: 51). As such, Hayat's engagements also focus on promoting egalitarian (as opposed to discriminatory) views and stressing the difference between extremism and Islam (Berczyk, 2016: 48). This differs markedly from United States, in which a deeply enshrined commitment to freedom of speech has the potential to hinder steps taken in this direction. Nonetheless, considering cognitive change as part of counter-radicalization efforts may prove worthwhile in the US context, notably in view of the aforementioned shift toward lone actor attacks and what Gartenstein-Ross has called an 'unprecedented surge' in Daesh-inspired activity within the United States (Gartenstein-Ross, 2016: 1).

Conclusion

Increased concerns about homegrown terrorism, alongside ever more sophisticated terrorist propaganda, have resulted in many countries across the West attempting to prevent (or reverse) the radicalization of its citizens, as opposed to simply interdicting attack planning (i.e., addressing the issue at an earlier stage). To date, the United States efforts to do this have been reasonably limited and restricted to pilot areas. However, the nature of contemporary terrorist threats facing the United States, such as lone actor terrorism, means that US policymakers may consider more focused radicalization prevention efforts. This chapter has outlined European experiences that may prove particularly useful in the US context; clear federal leadership, tailored interventions consistently available, and activities that address cognitive and ideological issues.

Further Reading

Parker, D. & Davis, J. (2017). Counter-Radicalisation at the Coalface: Lessons for Europe and Beyond. *RUSI Newsbrief*, 37(1).

Said, B. T. & Fouad, H. (2018). Countering Islamist Radicalisation in Germany: A Guide to Germany's Growing Prevention Infrastructure, International Centre for Counter-Terrorism – The Hague, https://icct.nl/wp-content/uploads/2018/09/ICCT-Said-Fouad-Countering-Islamist-Radicalization-in-Germany-Sept2018.pdf

Thomas, P. et al. (2017). *Community Reporting Thresholds*. Lancaster, UK: Centre for Research and Evidence on Security Threats (CREST), https://crestresearch.ac.uk/resources/community-reporting-thresholds-full-report/

Note

1 It should be noted some scholars contest the effectiveness of such prevention strategies. For instance, see Mythen et al. (2017).

References

Agerschou, T. (2014/15). Preventing Radicalization and Discrimination in Aarhus. *Journal for Deradicalization*, 01, 5–22.

Berczyk, J. (2016). Returning from the 'Islamic State' – Experiences from the Counselling Service HAYAT-Germany. *Journal EXIT-Deutschland*, 03, 47–51.

Bjelopera, J. P. (2014). Countering Violent Extremism in the United States. https://fas.org/sgp/crs/homesec/R42553.pdf. Accessed 8 March 2018.

Bokhari, K. (2015). Occasional Paper: Countering Violent Extremism and American Muslims. https://extremism.gwu.edu/sites/extremism.gwu.edu/files/downloads/CVE%20Bokhari.pdf Accessed 11 March 2018.

Butt, R. & Tuck, H. (2014). *European Counter-Radicalisation and De-radicalisation: A Comparative Evaluation of Approaches in the Netherlands, Sweden, Denmark and German*. London: Institute for Strategic Dialogue.

CAIR (2016). Countering Violence Extremism [sic]: What you need to know about CVE. http://www.cairmn.com/civil-rights/cve-toolkit/59-cve.html. Accessed 3 March 2018.

City of Los Angeles (2015). The Los Angeles Framework for Countering Violent Extremism. https://www.dhs.gov/sites/default/files/publications/Los%20Angeles%20Framework%20for%20CVE-Full%20Report.pdf. Accessed 3 March 2018.

CSIS (2016). Turning Points. A New Comprehensive Strategy for Countering Violent Extremism. https://csis-ilab.github.io/cve/report/Turning_Point.pdf. Accessed 3 March 2018.

Department of Justice (2014). 'Attorney General Holder Announces Pilot Programme to Counter Violent Extremists'. https://www.justice.gov/opa/pr/attorney-general-holder-announces-pilot-program-counter-violent-extremists. Accessed 3 March 2018.

Exit-Germany a. Aims. http://www.exit-deutschland.de/english/?c=aims. Accessed 11 November 2017.

Exit-Germany b. EXIT-Germany: We Provide Ways Out Of Extremism. http://www.exit-deutschland.de/english/. Accessed 11 November 2017.

Gartenstein-Ross, D. (2016). Radicalization in the U.S. and the Rise of Terrorism. https://oversight.house.gov/wp-content/uploads/2016/09/Gartenstein-Ross-Statement-Radicalization-9-14.pdf. Accessed 7 March 2018.

Hayat. HAYAT-Germany. http://hayat-deutschland.de/english/. Accessed 29 December 2017.

Hemmingsen, A-S. (2015). *An Introduction to the Danish Approach to Countering and Preventing Extremism and Radicalization*. Copenhagen: Danish Institute for International Studies.

Hjørnholm, M. (2013). Militant Extremism in a Preventative Perspective. *Journal EXIT-Deutschland*, 02, 54–68.

HM Government. (2011). Prevent Strategy. https://www.gov.uk/government/uploads/system/uploads/attachment_data/file/97976/prevent-strategy-review.pdf. Accessed 08 May 2017.

HM Government. (2015a). Channel Duty Guidance: Protecting people from being drawn into terrorism: Statutory guidance for Channel panel members and partners of local panels. https://www.gov.uk/government/uploads/system/uploads/attachment_data/file/425189/Channel_Duty_Guidance_April_2015.pdf. Accessed 29 January 2018.

HM Government. (2015b). Revised Prevent Duty Guidance: for England and Wales. https://www.gov.uk/government/uploads/system/uploads/attachment_data/file/445977/3799_Revised_Prevent_Duty_Guidance__England_Wales_V2-Interactive.pdf. Accessed 29 January 2018.

HM Government. (2017). Individuals referred to and supported through the Prevent Programme, April 2015 to March 2016. https://www.gov.uk/government/uploads/system/uploads/attachment_data/file/662824/individuals-referred-supported-prevent-programme-apr2015-mar2016.pdf. Accessed 29 January 2018.

Koehler, D. (2015). 'Chapter 14 – Family Counselling, De-Radicalization and Counter-Terrorism: The Danish and German programs in context'. In S. Zeiger & A. Aly (Eds.), *Countering Violent Extremism: Developing an Evidence-base for Policy and Practice* (pp. 129–136). Perth: Curtin University.

McCauley, C. & Moskalenko, S. (2008). Mechanisms of Political Radicalization: Pathways Toward Terrorism. *Terrorism and Political Violence*, 20(3), 415–443.

Ministeriet for Flygtninge Indvandrere og Integration. (2011). Denmark's deradicalisation efforts. https://www.nyidanmark.dk/NR/rdonlyres/8A7278CB-EFAD-43CC-B6E4-EE81B8E13C6D/0/factsheetderadicalisation.pdf. Accessed 12 November 2017.

Moghaddam, F. (2006). *From the Terrorist's Point of View: What they Experience and why they come to Destroy*. Westport, CT: Praeger Security International.

Mythen, G., Walklate, S., & Peatfield, E. (2017), 'Assembling and deconstructing radicalisation in PREVENT: A case of policy-based evidence making?', *Critical Social Policy*, 37, 2: 180–201.

Neumann, P. R. (2013). The trouble with radicalization. *International Affairs*, 89(4), 873–893.

Parker, D., Chapot, D., & Davis, J. (forthcoming October 2018). Prevent and Society: An analysis of key criticisms of the Prevent Strategy's impact on social relations, with reference to two local authorities. *Feminist Dissent*.

Parker, D. & Davis, J. (2017). Counter-Radicalisation at the Coalface: Lessons for Europe and Beyond. *RUSI Newsbrief*, 37(1).

Parker, D., Pearce, J. M., Lindekilde, L. & Rogers, M. B. (2017). Challenges for Effective Counterterrorism Communication: Practitioner Insights and Policy Implications for Preventing Radicalization, Disrupting Attack Planning, and Mitigating Terrorist Attacks. *Studies in Conflict & Terrorism*, 42(3), 1–28.

Reuters (2017). White House Budget Slashes 'Countering Violent Extremism' Grants. https://www.reuters.com/article/us-usa-budget-extremism/white-house-budget-slashes-countering-violent-extremism-grants-idUSKBN18J2HJ. Accessed 3 March 2018.

Sageman, M. (2008). *Leaderless Jihad: Terror Networks in the Twenty-First Century*. Philadelphia: University of Pennsylvania Press.

Said, B. T. & Fouad, H. (2018) Countering Islamist Radicalisation in Germany: A Guide to Germany's Growing Prevention Infrastructure, International centre for Counter-Terrorism – The Hague. https://icct.nl/wp-content/uploads/2018/09/ICCT-Said-Fouad-Countering-Islamist-Radicalization-in-Germany-Sept2018.pdf

Schmidt, A. P. (2013). *Radicalisation, De-Radicalisation, Counter-Radicalisation: A Conceptual Discussion and Literature Review*. The Hague, Netherlands: International Centre for Counter-Terrorism.

Southers, E. & Hienz, J. (2015). Foreign Fighters: Terrorist Recruitment and Countering Violent Extremism (CVE) Programs in Minneapolis-St. Paul. https://priceschool.usc.edu/files/2015/05/Foreign-Fighters-Terrorist-Recruitment-and-CVE-in-Minneapolis-St-Paul.pdf. Accessed 3 March 2018.

US Attorney's Office District of Massachusetts. (2015). A Framework for Prevention and Intervention Strategies. https://www.justice.gov/sites/default/files/usao-ma/pages/attachments/2015/02/18/framework.pdf. Accessed 3 March 2018.

US Attorney's Office Minneapolis. (2015). Building Community Resilience, Minneapolis-St. Paul Pilot Program, A Community-Led Local Framework. https://www.justice.gov/usao-mn/file/642121/download. Accessed 3 March 2018.

Vidino, L. & Brandon, J. (2012). Countering Radicalization in Europe. http://icsr.info/wp-content/uploads/2012/12/ICSR-Report-Countering-Radicalization-in-Europe.pdf. Accessed 11 November 2017.

White House. (2011a). Empowering Local Partners to Prevent Violent Extremism in the United States. https://www.dhs.gov/sites/default/files/publications/empowering_local_partners.pdf. Accessed 3 March 2018.

White House. (2011b). Strategic Implementation Plan for Empowering Local Partners to Prevent Violent Extremism in the United States. https://obamawhitehouse.archives.gov/sites/default/files/sip-final.pdf. Accessed 3 March 2018.

White House. (2018). National Strategy for Counterterrorism of the United States of America. https://www.whitehouse.gov/wp-content/uploads/2018/10/NSCT.pdf Accessed 6 October 2018.

Wray, C. (2017). Statement Before the Senate Homeland Security and Government Affairs Committee: Current Threats to the Homeland, 27 September. https://www.fbi.gov/news/testimony/current-threats-to-the-homeland. Accessed 7 March 2018.

Chapter 84

Screening

Chelsea A. Brown
Prairie View A&M University, Prairie View, TX, United States

Contents

Introduction 637
Importance of Screening After Accidents 638
Homeland Security, Immigration, and Screening 638
The United States Postal Services and Screening 639
Further Reading 640
References 640

Introduction

Screening is defined as the possible identification of an unrecognized disease in a healthy, asymptomatic population utilizing tests, analyses, and any other measures that can be practiced often and efficiently to get the target subjects. Screening can be a strategy that is used in a population to identify the presence of a disease that has not yet been diagnosed and has no signs or symptoms. It includes individuals with the unrecognized symptomatic illness. Screening is designed to identify disease early with an aim to reduce mortality and to suffer from the disease to enable early intervention and management. Not all testing results in helping the person who is screened, misdiagnosis and overdiagnosis can be adverse effects of screening.

Universal screening involves screening of a particular category. The case finding often requires a smaller group based on the presence of risk factors an example is a hereditary disease in a family. Screening aims at being diagnostic, hence frequently resulting in false-positive or false-negative results. There are three categories of screening, that is, mass screening, selective screening, and multiphasic screening (Gleason, Devaska & Avery, 2012). Large-scale screening (screening of a subgroup) is offered to all regardless of the risk state of the individual. The second type of

DOI: 10.4324/9781315144511-88

testing which is selective detection is conducted for risky populations only. Finally, multiphasic screening entails the application of two or more screening tests to a large community instead of single tests for single diseases.

Importance of Screening After Accidents

Screening is essential since it is the best way of discovering medical conditions at an early stage when treatment is feasible, easy, and less expensive. Detection can prevent up to half of the breast cancer cases; this can be seen in the research done by the American Cancer Society (Cassels, 2012). Additionally, screening helps medical practitioners to discover an ailment early leading to preventive treatment that can stop diseases from developing in a person. A screening program is termed a preventive measure because it aims at determining diagnosis, influencing risk factors, and detecting abnormal changes that could develop into a disease. Additionally, screening is essential in making a final determination.

Transport Security Administration and Screening. The Transportation Security Administration (TSA) integrates impulsive security measures both noticed and unnoticed help to accomplish security in transport operations. For the airport, security begins before arriving at the airport. TSA works with the intelligence and law enforcement to share information (Gleason, Devaska & Avery, 2012). Additional measures are put in place from the point one gets to at the airport to the end of the journey. With, its aim of meeting threats that are evolving from time to time and achieving high transportation security levels, the TSA has over the years increased its security strategies.

TSA can depend on the public to be whistleblowers in any occurrence. A good instance is in the case of unattended bags, individuals who seem to be a threat to the public or individuals that tend to get into restricted areas, or even ongoing suspicious activities at airports, train stations, and ports (Screening Enrollment.docx – Helpjuice, n.d.). The TSA screening procedures' primary purpose is getting an individual safely to their destination and ensuring they travel safely. Additionally, it tends to prevent prohibited items and any other forms of threat to transportation security from getting to the sterile area of an airport. The TSA is designed to respond to information concerning threats to transportation.

Technology also plays a vital role in effective and efficient security measures. TSA created its own Innovation Task Force to improve the security technology. Automation of security has helped the TSA work better and faster with the industry and for the investors to identify and pilot advanced technology and procedures.

Homeland Security, Immigration, and Screening

The president and his senior homeland security officials in recent weeks have pulled out stops to assure the United States that the vetting process for immigrants and foreign visitors would be thorough and robust. The US Department of Homeland Security (DHS) is working to raise aviation security across the globe. Improving safety is done by implementing enhanced security measures (Cassels, 2012). The procedure is done for all the 105 departure airports around the world. In coordination with other countries, the strategy can be enacted in phases.

Enhancing aviation security worldwide is critical to keep the public safe and secure as they face the evolving threats. The Department of Homeland Security Traveler Redress Inquiry Program is a point of contact for individuals who seek solutions to difficulties they experienced during travel screening (Gleason, Devaska & Avery, 2012). An example is when crossing borders in the United States in case the travelers believe that they were poorly treated or unfairly by maybe being delayed, denied boarding, or even being identified for additional screening at the transportation hubs, they can report to the agency. The DHS Traveler Redress Inquiry Program (TRIP) is part of an effort by the Homeland Security to welcome legitimate travelers while keeping the country safe from those who want to harm its citizens.

The United States Customs and Border Protection and the TSA began the Air Cargo Advance Screening (ACAS) that required the submission of advanced air cargo information on shipments arriving in the United States from a foreign location. The process was introduced globally. However, the initiation of ACAS made the process mandatory for the airlines flying to the United States. The step aimed to raise the baseline of aviation security worldwide (Screening Enrollment.docx – Helpjuice, n.d.). The participating carriers submit the air cargo data at the earliest point before loading the cargo onto the aircraft destined to or transitioned through to the United States. ACAS has over the years employed a risk-based approach as it leverages DHS threat information.

The ACAS program is a very vital component for the US, Customs and Border Protection (CBP) to prevent illicit contraband from entering the border and ports while practicing law. The measure was built on partnership, the express and air cargo industry. This represents the private sector and the government to solve the challenging problems. The formalization of ACAS enhances and supports the security of the parcels sent and in the air cargo industry in the years to come (Gleason, Devaska & Avery, 2012). TSA and CBP aim at securing the homeland with their strong partnership. Additionally, screening of the inbound air cargo is improved with this partnership. The partnership can allow for the effective and efficient screening of a high volume of cargo imported and exported to the United States.

CBP and TSA working together employ layered security to secure inbound air cargo and various risk assessment methods that are involved in identifying high-risk cargo and finding any risks posed. Once risk cargo is identified, screening is done relative to TSA-accepted security programs. In October 2010, the global counterterrorism community stopped a potential terrorist attack when they discovered an onboard aircraft destined for the United States (Screening Enrollment.docx – Helpjuice, n.d.). The plane contained hidden explosive devices. The incident exhibited the importance of advanced information in recognizing and minimizing the efforts of terrorists.

The United States Postal Services and Screening

Mails received in the United States Postal Services are screened for suspicious items when they first arrive at the mailroom. The staff who sort mails and packages by hand are advised to test the letters as this has been proven to be the most effective way to look into the emails and the packages (Raffle & Gray, 2007). With the introduction of advanced technology mail search and security at the United States Postal Inspection Service was improved. Additionally, they came up with a mobile mail screening station to increase the speed of clearing the letters. A mobile mail screening station is a highly specialized, self-propelled facility that is designed to screen mail for explosive devices and also deter chemical, biological, radiological, and even nuclear weapons in the letter. The United States Postal Inspection Service usually operates the mobile mail screening stations. The mobile mail screening station was designed by the United States Postal Services Technical Services Division. It has a 53-foot tractor and trailer combination with eight compartment areas that house the specialized mail screening equipment. It also includes; a GID-3 ambient air monitoring system to detect chemical warfare agents and industrial toxins. HI-SCAN 7555i X-ray inspection system-scans packages and letters to detect improvised explosive devices, and Smith's Detection HazMatID to identify unknown liquids, powders, pastes, and gels. Moreover, finally, the SABRE FR air filtration table-detect toxic industrial chemicals. In addition to the technology, the mobile mail screening station is operated by a staff of five to eight people.

Further Reading

Brooks, R. A. (2011). "Muslim 'Homegrown' Terrorism in the United States: How Serious is the Threat?" *International Security*, *36*(2): 7–47.

Mullins, S. (2019, April 30). "Migration and Terrorism: The United States Can Learn from Europe's Mistakes," *War on the Rocks*. https://warontherocks.com/2019/04/migration-and-terrorism-the-united-states-can-learn-from-europes-mistakes/

Nowrasteh, A. (2019, May 7). "Terrorists by Immigration Status and Nationality: A Risk Analysis, 1975–2017," CATO Institute, Washington, DC. cato.org/publications/policy-analysis/terrorists-immigration-status-nationality-risk-analysis-1975-2017

References

3 Screening Process Philosophy - Usps. (n.d.). Retrieved from https://about.usps.com/handbooks/el312/el312c5_002.htm

Cassels, A. (2012). *Seeking sickness: Medical screening and the misguided hunt for disease.* Vancouver, British Columbia: Greystone Books.

Gleason, C. A., Devaskar, S. U., & Avery, M. E. (2012). *Avery's diseases of the newborn.* Philadelphia, PA: Elsevier/Saunders.

Odd Cast Of Characters Assaulting Statehouse Today. (n.d.). Retrieved from https://www.buckeyefirearms.org/odd-cast-characters-assaulting-statehouse-today

Overview | Homeland Security. (n.d.). Retrieved from https://www.dhs.gov/topic/overview

Raffle, A. E., & Gray, J. A. M. (2007). *Screening: Evidence and practice.* Oxford. Oxford University Press.

Screening Enrollment.docx Helpjuice. (n.d.). Retrieved from https://static.helpjuice.com/helpjuice_production/uploads/upload/image/2609/1293

Security Screening | Transportation Security Administration. (n.d.). Retrieved from https://www.tsa.gov/travel/security-screening/prohibited-items

U.S. Refugee Admissions Program - U.S. Department Of State. (n.d.). Retrieved from https://www.state.gov/j/prm/ra/admissions/

What Is Screening? | National Screening Unit - Nsu. (n.d.). Retrieved from https://www.nsu.govt.nz/about-us-national-screening-unit/what-screening

Chapter 85

The Evolution and Future of SWAT

Boyd P. Brown III
Nichols College, Dudley, MA, United States

Contents

Introduction 641
Background 642
Organizational Structure, Training, and Operations 642
The Rise and Role of SWAT 644
Conclusion 647
Further Reading 647
References 647

Introduction

Special Weapons and Tactics Teams (SWAT) have been a feature of policing in the United States since the 1970s. The intent of these teams was to provide a highly trained, heavy weapons response to patrol officers in the most-dire situations. As the "wars" on drugs, terror, and crime have been declared, the use of SWAT teams has expanded to the point that, today, most teams are used not only for tactically challenging situations but also for routine patrol and warrant service. As the use of SWAT has expanded, so to have concerns about the quality of training for SWAT officers and the seemingly heavy-handed tactics they have employed in non-violent situations. This chapter will explore the history of SWAT teams, their recommended organizational structure, and training, as well as ongoing concerns about police militarization.

DOI: 10.4324/9781315144511-89

Background

In 1965, the Watts Riots rocked Los Angeles. In 1966, Charles Whitman climbed atop the University of Texas Main Building tower and shot 48 people, killing 17 before he was shot and killed by police. In the same year, a string of violent bank robberies struck Philadelphia. These incidents, though unconnected to one another, drew attention to the inability of police officers to respond to some violent confrontations. As law enforcement professionals explored the problem, they concluded that the training, tactics, and equipment utilized by normal patrol officers were inadequate in the face of new threats. The search for a solution coalesced, by the late 1960s, into the SWAT concept. This novel idea was to train police officers in tactics and techniques often found in military units and to arm them with heavy weaponry to respond to extremely dangerous situations.

There is reasonable debate over which city formed the first "official" SWAT team; however, one undeniable fact is the man is credited as the driving force behind this revolution in the criminal justice model: a 39-year-old inspector with the Los Angeles Police Department (LAPD) – Darryl Gates. Influenced heavily by the conflict in Vietnam, Gates consulted with members of the Army and Marine Corps, and built SWAT on a military-based "squad" model. SWAT teams were armed with automatic weapons and sniper rifles and trained to breach barricaded buildings or confront armed suspects. Gates' new creation had the chance to demonstrate its effectiveness for the first time in a raid against a fortified Black Panther building in December 1969. The raid did not go according to plan from the beginning and resulted in an hours-long firefight between more than 200 police officers and half a dozen Black Panther members. Despite this, the images of police officers confronting a group most Americans saw as a radical threat, resulted in the raid being a tremendous public relations success and SWAT became a fixture of policing in the United States (Balko 2014).

Organizational Structure, Training, and Operations

It is difficult to make specific comments about the organizational structure, training, and operations of SWAT teams across the country for two related reasons. First, there is little research that has focused specifically on SWAT teams. As Kraska and Kappeler (1997) observed, during the 1980s and 1990s, as police departments embraced new "models" of policing, such as community-oriented policing (COP) or problem-oriented policing (POP), the lion's share of the research effort was spent to understand how these programs worked and if they are effective. The result, or consequence, is that a parallel trend in policing – the dramatic growth and use of SWAT teams, was largely ignored.

The second reason is that, when research has been attempted, it has been very difficult to accomplish successfully. There are several factors that contribute to this trend. For one, as Klinger and Rojek found in their unpublished 2000 report for the Department of Justice, "A Multi-method Study of Special Weapons Tactics and Teams", it can be difficult to get SWAT teams to participate in research studies. Klinger and Rojek attempted a series of surveys with 2027 police departments across the country with 50 or more sworn officers. Their first goal was to conduct phone interviews to determine if the agency had a SWAT team. They found 1183 (58%) of the agencies did. Two follow-on surveys were sent to those agencies: a SWAT operations survey (SOS) and a post-critical incident report (PCIR). The returns for those surveys were disappointing, with less than one-third participation in the SOS (N = 339) and less than 10% participation in the PCIR. These results should not be entirely surprising. Like many organizations, police departments in general and SWAT teams specifically are insular and are likely to resist scrutiny from outside agencies.

Even when research is successfully conducted, the results may not be broadly applicable. Both Kraska and Kappeler (1997) and Klinger and Rojek (2000) illustrate how diverse SWAT teams are across the country. The structure of the team and the operations they conduct are linked to factors such as the size of the municipality they serve and the size of the department, whether SWAT is a full-time or part-time duty for officers, if the team is the municipality's own or if they contribute officers to the multi-jurisdictional team, the amount of time spent on training and what the focus of that training is, and how often and for what purposes the team is deployed.

The simplest way to categorize SWAT teams is whether they are full- or part-time teams. Klinger and Rojek's research demonstrates that most departments seem to favor a part-time structure. 88% of the teams (299 out of 337) they surveyed fell in that category. An additional 8% of teams were full-time and the remaining 4% included both full- and part-time officers. The majority of teams (304 out of 337; 95%) have 30 or fewer officers; full-time teams tend to be larger than part-time ones (Klinger, David A. and Rojek, Jeff, 2000, p. 18 & 96).

While the above information is useful to help gain a broader perspective on SWAT teams around the country, it is of limited utility to ascertain the quality of the team. To better do this it is to understand how often SWAT teams train and what situations they train for most frequently. Klinger and Rojek found wide variability in these areas. Of the 337 teams surveyed, eight of them averaged ZERO hours of training per month and one averaged 80 hours. On average, teams train between 8 and 20 hours per month (Klinger, David A. and Rojek, Jeff, 2000, p. 5). The four most common skills that SWAT teams trained to accomplish were: confronting a barricaded subject (95% of teams trained for this situation), building searches (94% of teams), hostage situations (92% of teams), and serving narcotics warrants (91% of teams). At the low end of the spectrum, only 7% of teams conducted water-borne assaults, 11% conducted train assaults, and 12% aircraft assaults. It should be noted that the data Klinger and Rojek used was collected prior to the 9/11 attacks. A useful exercise might be to redo this survey and see if any of these numbers have shifted significantly, particularly as they relate to aircraft assaults.

Another informative point, relative to team training, is how few teams train in de-escalation and negotiations. 82% of the SWAT teams that were surveyed in Klinger and Rojek's study have a unit that is separate from SWAT that is responsible for conducting negotiations, whereas only 16% of teams had negotiators as part of their structure. In the current law enforcement environment, as SWAT teams train to conduct "dynamic entries" to confront active shooters, it is unlikely that this feature of SWAT will change at any point in the near future.

With this information in mind, is it possible to generalize about the structure of a "typical" SWAT team or how it trains? The simple answer is no. However, the

National Tactical Officers Association, formed in 1983, does publish a set of standards for SWAT structure and training. The National Tactical Officers Association (NTOA) "establishes SWAT Standards to serve as an efficient core set of concepts, principles, and policies to standardize and enhance the delivery of tactical law enforcement services" (2007, p. v). This chapter was developed in the post-9/11 law enforcement and national security environment, and in response to Homeland Security Presidential Directive 19, signed by George W. Bush on February 12, 2007. "HSPD-19 and the NTOA recognize that the coordination of joint response operations among bomb squads and tactical teams are critical to preparing for, deterring and defeating terrorist attacks… the NTOA believes that the development of Standards for SWAT Teams is critical" (2007, p. viii). These standards provide guidelines for the selection of personnel and designated roles, minimum training requirements, and what missions SWAT should be prepared to address.

In the NTOA Standards, all teams should have a pre-requisite 40-hour basic SWAT course training. In addition, part-time teams should spend at least 16 hours per month training to maintain critical skills, with those members assigned to "special duties" (snipers, medical support) receiving 8 more hours of training in their specific skill. For full-time teams, in addition to the 40-hour basic SWAT course, NTOA recommends that at least 25% of the on-duty time be devoted to training (2007, p. 7). Additionally, NTOA provides instruction on the number of personnel assigned to teams and the roles they fill. Their minimum structure of a SWAT team is one comprised 17 officers, in five roles:

1 SWAT Officer ➔ Designated Team Leader
4 SWAT Officers ➔ Containment
5 SWAT Officers ➔ Emergency Action
5 SWAT Officers ➔ Deliberate Action
2 SWAT Officers ➔ Precision Long Rifle Team (one spotter/one long rifle per team).

(2007, p. 13)

The NTOA Standards are non-binding guidelines that represent a proactive effort by law enforcement professionals to ensure that all SWAT teams are highly trained and skilled. These teams will be able to respond to incidents that exceed the capacity of other first responders in a manner that will "reduce the risk of injury or loss of life to citizens, police officers, and suspect" (2007, NTOA, p. 15). These standards do represent a positive step toward "professionalizing" SWAT, and an awareness of the need to do so among tactical officers. However, there is no readily available data to indicate how many SWAT teams across the country have adopted the NTOA Standards, nor how far along those teams are at implementing and achieving them.

The Rise and Role of SWAT

SWAT teams are a vital part of modern policing. They train to respond to incidents that are beyond the skill or resources of patrol officers and other first responders. It is crucial to understand the important space they fill in the law enforcement tool kit.

Nonetheless, in recent decades, a growing body of research and writing have raised concerns about both the rise in the number of SWAT teams across the nation and, perhaps more importantly, how those teams have been deployed.

When Darryl Gates developed SWAT, he envisioned it as a highly trained unit that would be the "call of last resort" for the most extreme and dangerous situations. However, as SWAT has taken hold, it has spread exponentially such that, by 2007, over 80% of police agencies serving communities of 25,000 people or more have a SWAT team (Kraska, 2007, p. 7). Along with the growth in the number of teams has been an explosion in the number of team callouts. In the late 1980s, the number of times SWAT teams across the nation responded to calls totaled around 3000, with each team, on average, conducting 13 callouts per year.

By 2007, SWAT teams were called out over 45,000 times and each team averaged more than 50 raids per year (Kraska, 2007). Furthermore, based on analysis of 1995 data "on "barricaded persons", "dangerous warrants", "civil disturbances", and "other activities". Of the total number of callouts (n = 25,201), civil disturbances accounted for 1.3% (n = 338), terrorist incidents 0.09% (n = 23), hostage situations 3.6% (n = 913), and barricaded persons 13.4% (n = 3880) (Kraska, Peter, B and Kappeler, Victor, E., 1997, p. 7). In other words, in just under 20% of situations, SWAT teams were called to respond to the kinds of incidents they were first intended to confront. In over 80% of situations, SWAT teams are called to issue warrants – low-risk police work directed at non-violent offenders, mostly people suspected of minor drug violations.

A useful example of these concerns is illustrated by Lawrence County, PA, outside of Pittsburg. In 2009, the county announced a plan to establish a part-time Emergency Response Team. "The new 15-officer unit would cost the financially strapped county $100,000 to equip and thousands of dollars more a year in training and overtime costs. The Superintendent didn't say exactly why this county needed a SWAT team or how it would be used. In Pittsburgh, a major city, the SWAT team is called out about 80 times a year. In Lawrence County, a sparely populated region with relatively low crime rates, the new paramilitary unit, if limited to high-risk assignments, will have virtually nothing to do. If these part-time officers are to be kept raid-ready, the unit will have to be called out on routine, low-risk jobs" (Fisher, 2010, p. 8).

In another example, in his book *The Rise of the Warrior Cop*, Radley Balko interviewed Stephen Downing of the LAPD. Downing's comments illustrate some of the challenges presented by the spread of SWAT teams to smaller towns and municipalities:

> Right now, I'm preparing to testify in a lawsuit stemming from a wrong-headed raid by a SWAT team in a 28-person police department. How do you even begin to select 28 people? And how do you find time to train? At LAPD, the SWAT team will spend at least half their on-duty time in training. In these smaller towns, the SWAT team is something these guys do on the side. They're patrol officers. And, so what happens is that they train by practicing on the people.
>
> (2014, p. 211)

The increased use of SWAT teams for low-risk policing has led to some eyebrow-raising raids. For example, in 2016, Margaret Holcomb, an 81-year-old grandmother living in Amherst, MA was the focus of a raid by the Massachusetts state police, supported by National Guard troops, a helicopter, and police vehicles. The raid, part of the Drug Enforcement Administration's (DEA) Cannabis Eradication Program, targeted the single marijuana plant Ms. Holcomb grew in her garden, which was cut down and hauled away by authorities (Ingraham, 2016).

A 2008 raid was immortalized when it was featured on John Oliver's *Last Week Tonight* on the HBO network. In that situation, a SWAT team raided the Contemporary Art Institute of Detroit's monthly "Funk Night". SWAT team officers stormed into the event in full body armor, weapons at the ready, all because the Institute had failed to acquire the proper liquor license (DeVito, 2014).

Officers in Spanish Fork, Utah conducted a raid on a "rave" party in August 2005. The event, which was attended by about 1500 people was relatively peaceful. The organizers had hired private security guards who were stationed around the perimeter and who searched people as they entered and confiscated any drugs they found. When the raid began, the police arrested the security guards and charged them with possession (Balko, 2014, p. 258).

These raids could almost be considered funny if the consequences for those involved were not so severe. Targets of these raids may experience significant physical damage to their property. If dogs are present, SWAT officers quite often will shoot and kill them. Family members, including young children, may be handcuffed and held at gunpoint, which may result in severe psychological and emotional stress and trauma. It is even worse when these low-risk raids escalate, or when SWAT teams raid the *wrong* address with disastrous results.

For example, on September 13, 2000, a SWAT team conducted a no-knock, forced entry raid into the home of Moises Sepulveda, as part of a coordinated effort by the Drug Enforcement Administration (DEA) and Federal Bureau of investigation (FBI) narcotics task forces. Sepulveda, his wife, and three children were ordered to face down on the floor of their home while officers pointed guns at them. Alberto, the Sepulveda's 11-year-old son, did as he was instructed. But somehow, some way, the SWAT officer covering him, Officer David Hawn, had an "unintentional discharge" – his gun fired accidentally. The bullet struck the boy in the back of the head, killing him instantly. There were no drugs found in the home of Moises Sepulveda and, as a later investigation showed, the evidence used to justify the raid into his home was "minimal" (Balko, 2014, p. 248). In July 2009, Cheye Calvo, the mayor of Berwyn Heights, Maryland, was the target of a SWAT raid over suspicion that he had received a shipment of drugs. Officers used explosives to blast open his door, stormed into his house, and shot and killed Calvo's two dogs. Calvo and his mother-in-law were held for 4 hours while officers searched his home. The police found nothing and, as it was later revealed, the SWAT team had raided the wrong house (Balko, 2014, p. 311–312).

These failed or botched raids may seem to be the "exception to the rule"; however, as Peter Kraska wrote in 2017, journalist Radley Balko received "at least two phone calls per week from journalists, lawyers, or police departments reporting a new botched raid, generally where a citizen has been killed under highly questionable circumstances" (Kraska, 2007, p. 7).

Not only are SWAT teams used to conduct more and more raids, but they have also been tasked to conduct "routine patrol". In these situations, heavily armed

SWAT officers are sent into designated "high crime" areas. Once there, they enforce a "broken windows" model of policing where even the most minor infractions are cited and often lead to an arrest. While there is little compelling evidence that these tactics actually reduce crime there is ample evidence to suggest they erode the relationship between the police and the community they serve. As Jim Fisher observes, "Ironically, funds supporting such deployments often come from federal 'community policing' grants intended to foster a friendlier, more cooperative relationship between citizens and the police" (Fisher, 2010, p. 14).

Conclusion

SWAT teams are, and will remain, a vital element in policing in the United States. When properly trained, these teams are often law enforcement's best option to respond to highly volatile and dangerous situations. At the same time, there is an important and legitimate conversation to be had, both within and outside of the law enforcement community, about how these teams are deployed and if they serve the purpose for which they were intended.

The SWAT concept was developed out of the legitimate need of law enforcement to be able to confront highly volatile situations and extremist groups. Highly trained and skilled SWAT teams have demonstrated their value time and time again across the country.

It is in the national self-interest of the United States to ensure that those departments that have SWAT teams are large enough to staff them with the highest quality officers and that they are provided adequate time to train to the peak of proficiency. Unfortunately, get tough on crime rhetoric linked first to the "war" on drugs, and more recently to the "war" on terror, has been used by many politicians and defense industry people to justify a dramatic expansion and militarization of SWAT teams. The widespread use of these teams has contributed to an erosion of the relationship between police and the communities they serve, which has led to a backlash against the militarization of the police. The outcome of that debate will undoubtedly impact the structure and direction of SWAT for years to come.

Further Reading

Balko, R. (2014). *Rise of the Warrior Cop: The Militarization of America's Police Forces*. New York: Public Affairs.

Fisher, J. (2010). *SWAT Madness and the Militarization of American Police: A National Dilemma*. Santa Barbara: Praeger.

Kraska, P. and Kappeler, V. (1997). Militarizing American Police: The Rise and Normalization of Paramilitary Units. *Social Problems*, 44(1), 1–18.

References

Balko, R. (2014). *Rise of the Warrior Cop: The Militarization of America's Police Forces*. New York: Public Affairs.

DeVito, L. (2014, October 7). *John Oliver revisits 'the funkiest shakedown in human history,' the CAID raid*. Retrieved from Detroit Metro Times: https://www.metrotimes.com/news-hits/archives/2014/10/07/john-oliver-revisits-the-funkiest-shakedown-in-human-history-the-caid-raid

Fisher, J. (2010). *SWAT Madness and the militarization of the American police: A national dilemma*. Santa Barbara: Praeger.

Fund, J. (2014, April 18). *The United States of SWAT*. Retrieved from National Review: www.nationalreview.com/2014/04/united-states-swat-john-fund/

Haberman, C. (2014, September 7). *The Rise of the SWAT Team in American Policing*. Retrieved from The New York Times: https://www.nytimes.com/2014/09/08/us/the-rise-of-the-swat-team-in-american-policing.html

Ingraham, C. (2016, October 7). *Drug cops raid an 81-year-old womans garden to take out a single marijuana plant*. Retrieved from The Washington Post: https://www.washingtonpost.com/news/wonk/wp/2016/10/07/drug-cops-raid-an-81-year-old-grandmothers-garden-to-take-out-a-single-marijuana-plant/?utm_term=.106f26fdd882

Kain, E. (2011, June 20). *The Overuse of SWAT Teams*. Retrieved from Forbes: www.forbes.com/sites/erikkain/2011/06/20/the-overuse-of-s-w-a-t-teams/#797e952dc86c

Klinger, David A. and Rojek, Jeff. (2000). *A Multi-Method Study of Special Weapons and Tactics Team: Executive Summary*. Washington DC: Unpublished DOJ Report.

Kraska, P. B. (2007). Militarizationand Policing - Its Relevance to 21st Century Police. *Policing*, 1–13.

Kraska, Peter B and Kappeler, Victor E. (1997). Militarizaing American Police: The Rise and Normalization of Paramilitary Units. *Social Problems*, 44(1), 1–18.

NTOA. (2007). *SWAT Standards for Law Enforcement Agencies*. Colorado Springs, CO: National Tactical Officers Association.

O'Brien, R. (2007, March 9). *Full-Time vs. Part-Time SWAT: Does it matter if you SWAT all of the time or just when needed*. Retrieved from Police: The Law Enforcement Magazine: www.policemag.com/blog/swat/story/2007/05/full-time-vs-part-time/

Chapter 86

The National Security Strategy (NSS) of the United States

Réjeanne M. Lacroix
University of Leicester, Leicester, United Kingdom

Contents

Introduction 649
Legal Foundation and Requirements 650
Nature and Communicative Purposes of the NSS 651
The NSS Composition Process 652
Critical Analysis 653
Conclusion 654
Further Reading 654
References 654

Introduction

The National Security Strategy (NSS) of the United States is a report that compiled by the Executive Branch that outlines national security objectives and ambitions. Published periodically, this important document provides a general framework through which a presidential administration requests resources to fulfill a successful NSS. It publicizes U.S. national security interests to lawmakers, the general public and foreign entities, as well as being a reference document for overall U.S. security policy. The creation of the NSS is a multilayered process guided by the National Security Council (NSC) that results in a report denoted by multi-agency cooperation and consensus. As a result, the NSS of the United States is intrinsically political and this leaves its conclusions open to differing interpretations.

DOI: 10.4324/9781315144511-90

The development of a NSS is a complicated and wide-ranging venture. Such a strategy must identify the objectives of a state and thus, formulate a blueprint that sets out a pathway to achievement. In this process, it is imperative that a state examines how its instruments of power – military, political, and economic – can be applied and best used to achieve established national security objectives.

This synergy between objectives, methods, and instruments of power results in a grand national strategy when it is employed to secure the vital interests of a specific state. According to Drew and Snow (1988), "grand national strategy emerges as the process by which the appropriate instruments of power are arranged and employed to accomplish the national interest (27)." An undertaking of such breadth requires a united vision that concentrates numerous threats, goals, and protocols into an indefinable source of reference. The NSS is an example of a strategy document that outlines perceptible threats to the United States and how certain administrations plan to neutralize them under the context of the preservation of U.S. interests.

Legal Foundation and Requirements

The early concept of a NSS report originated in Section 108 of the National Security Act of 1947. While this venture did not provide impetus toward the development of a unified security strategy for the United States, it offered an important legislative basis for future elaboration. In 1986, the National Security Act was amended by the Goldwater-Nichols Department of Defense Reorganization Act and the contemporary interpretation of the NSS was instituted. This action "put in place a more deliberate, structured, and formalized approach to developing an overarching national security strategy" (National War College, 2018, 2) Thus, the Reagan administration delivered the first NSS in its recognized format.

The parameters listed in Section 603 of the Goldwater-Nichols Act clearly denote the responsibilities of presidential administrations and required discussions that must be included in the NSS. In regard to obligations, the President must periodically provide Congress with a comprehensive document detailing the NSS of the United States and align that with a fiscal demand for resources. Newly inaugurated presidents are limited to 150 days to provide their administration's perception of a national strategy. The finalized NSS must be produced in two formats: classified for those with security clearances and unclassified for the general public (U.S. Congress, 1986).

Subsequently, the Act lists five significant areas of discourse and explanation that are imperative in placing the U.S. NSS in context. These include descriptions of 1) worldwide interests, goals, and objectives vital to national security; 2) foreign policy, worldwide commitments, and national defense capabilities needed to deter aggression and implement the NSS as well; 3) proposed short-term and long-term uses of political, economic, military, and other elements of national power to protect or promote U.S. interests and achieve the goals first discussed; 4) adequacy of the capabilities to carry out the NSS as well as evaluation of the balance of the elements of power in its implementation; 5) any other information that is pertinent to Congress in regard to the NSS (Goldwater-Nichols Act).

Nature and Communicative Purposes of the NSS

A treatise delving into an expansive set of themes is purposely unspecific in details and planning. The rationale for this generality is the creation of an overarching national vision rather than revealing a rigid set of tactics. As a result, a presidential administration presents a context for preserving national security but, has leeway in the numerous procedures or policies that can be employed for such a vast objective. It is then understood that a clearly written strategy would inform Congress better on the need for resources in order to implement the national security mandate (Snider, 1995, 2).

The NSS is considered to be an example of explicit strategy since it is a public declaration originating from the leadership of the U.S. government. While unequivocally stating the vision of a nation is one factor, explicit strategies include intentions as well as directions for implementation (Doyle, 2007, 624).

Further, an official document that overtly states purposes and planning operates as an act of political messaging. According to Snider, the NSS performs a series of communicative tasks that start with the communication of strategic vision to Congress, and thus legitimizes requests for resources. Consequently, that same strategic vision is conveyed to foreign constituencies and primarily focused on those not apparent on U.S. summit agendas.

At the domestic level, the NSS publicizes a general strategy to diverse subjects ranging from presidential supporters, those with niche security interests, and those seeking coherent long-term plans that can be supported by citizens.

In the context of government administration, a NSS provides the Executive Branch with an internal consensus upon which to be referred for foreign and defense policy. Lastly, the NSS aligns with and promotes a presidential agenda by its substance and presentation (5–6). While its primary function is to specify a consolidated and coherent framework for national security concerns, these examples of communicative purposes demonstrate the usefulness of the NSS as an important source of political messaging too.

The NSS is a form of reference document. It incorporates the overall NSS of the United States while imparting simplified messaging in regard to the state's security objectives and ensuing implementation. As a result, the NSS has a notable influence on subsequent security policies and ensuing proposals. Due to its scope and effect on government agencies, strategists who aid in the creation of the NSS must understand its influence on subsidiary strategies and plans (National War College, 2018, 2). Doyle suggests that other documents should be related to the overall suppositions of the NSS and other more specific texts should derive from it (625).

Since the NSS is generally released at the beginning of the year, its publication aligns with the typical timing of the Presidential State of the Union Address. While the two differ in breadth and overall substance, both present strong opportunities for presidential messaging. Each contributes to the overall vision or strategy for the improvement of the U.S. security and prosperity. Consequently, if the NSS and the State of the Union scheduling are well coordinated, strong symbiosis of a presidential agenda is perceptible (Snider, 1995, 6). This only augments the vision of a strategy with significant scope.

The NSS Composition Process

The composition of the NSS is a far-reaching enterprise that involves substantial interagency contribution and cooperation. This process is conducted by the NSC which is commanded by the national security adviser and a team of staff known as the Executive Secretariat. The NSC acts as the chief forum where the President, their national security advisers, and the cabinet can discuss and synchronize security and foreign policy topics (National War College, 2018, 3). Consequently, each administration tailors the function and roles of the NSC during the strategy-making process. Doyle contends that this is linked to the preferences of the current President and their team of national security advisers (626).

Many of the inclusions found in the NSS begin with strategies specific to certain geographical politics or general security interests. These small-scale regional and functional policies percolate in their respective agencies, departments, and services (National War College, 3). If these issues demand supplemental attention and can be identified as a U.S. objective, further stages await their clearance before being included in a larger NSS. This includes entering into the stages of interagency review and coordination processes where consensus is sought. Finally, these particular topics and approaches are examined by the NSC before a definitive review and approval (National War College, 3).

It is a substantial venture to scrutinize important objectives and possible implementation of tactics in a larger overall strategy. A format that facilitates various agendas and positions is required to impel any hint of progress rather than stagnation over disagreement. In the case of the NSS, this arrangement can be described as "an opaque and irregular set of rolling negotiations among national security principals" (Doyle, 624). Accordingly, any inclusion in the strategic vision of the United States encounters scrutiny from the Policy Coordination, Deputies, and Principals committees at the NSC.

Doyle summarized the tasks of these particular committees. The Policy Coordination Committee is defined by its interagency working group framework that is composed of senior officials or known experts. A wide breadth of geographical and policy interests gives rise to the general consensus and basic outlines that may appear in the final NSS. A step above this committee is the Deputies Committee – a collection of deputies and departmental undersecretaries that guide working groups. This committee ensures that important security issues receive adequate attention and assessment before reaching a definitive evaluation. Lastly, the Principals Committee is composed of high-level members of a presidential administration, including the Chairman of the Joint Chiefs of Staff, the Director of National Intelligence, as well as the Secretaries of State, Defense, and Treasury. They provide the final and authoritative review before the completion of the NSS (626).

The engagement of interagency cooperation and a review procedure permit the advancement of a united national vision that touches upon many areas of the security apparatus. As noted, this amalgamation of U.S. objectives and tactics provides a reference to those tasked with the development of security strategies particular to their own matters, such as foreign defense cooperation or border security. The NSS becomes a sort of "strategic touchstone" when questions arise (Doyle, 625). A U.S. security strategy reflects the consensus that emerged in the developmental stages of its maturation as well as demonstrates the values that shape the united vision found in the final publication. While layers of constructive processes and analysis warrant agreement on large-scale security ambitions, the final publication of the NSS is inherently political and thus, is liable to critique.

Critical Analysis

The purpose of the NSS is to impart national security objectives and the processes in which a particular administration plans to manage them. This document serves an important purpose; however, it is not flawless in its procedural elements or content. Since the NSS is composed of an administration in power and applies the NSC according to presidential preferences, the document essentially presents a particular understanding of national security concerns. Security policies and priorities have thus become "complicated, often ambiguous and even inconsistent" (Sarkesian, Williams & Cimbala, 2008, 3). The dimensions of national security and their progression into the final document are steeped in politics and ideological perceptions.

Important security objectives and successful frameworks must overcome numerous contested approaches in order to be considered in the NSS. While it may seem that the preparation process is controlled and streamlined, actuality presents another scenario. The compromise and consensus that appears in the final report are the products of an interagency process of interminable discussions and various working meetings. It is argued that the problem with documents like the NSS is that they "create the false impression that strategy formulation is a rational system and process" (Snider, iii). Additionally, the completion of the NSS is pressed by a predetermined amount of time and bureaucratic barriers.

Many consider the NSS as a neutral planning document but it is simply not (Snider, 5). The addition of political bargaining and differing viewpoints results in a challenging environment where presidential advisers face difficult decisions over inclusions in the final report. True compromise is elusive as advisers may agree on security priorities but later disagree on resource commitment and strategy (Sarkesian et al., 7). Vital interests may be critical to national security but, they may sometimes conflict with an administration's priorities (Doyle, 628). For example, while the ecological security topic of climate change is considered to be a modern security threat, mentioned by the Bush administration in 2002 and Obama-era security strategies, the issue is absent from the latest NSS released by the Trump administration (Nevitt, 2017).

Political influence actively continues between the Executive Branch and Congress. An analysis of the NSS process observed that the strategy formation process – within the Executive Branch as well as between the Executive Branch and Congress – is intensely political and the resulting NSS emerges only after prolonged bargaining and compromise (Snider, iii). Within the cabinet, representatives debate the importance of their portfolios and in turn, shift attention toward their priorities and demand for resources. All of these demands and outlooks must fall under the overall messaging of the NSS and thus, concessions are made. Further, once the NSS is presented to Congress, another layer of political dynamics enters the situation as partisanship determines national security assessments. The final NSS is a product of deciphering through political influence and reaching an agreement on some central security concerns. It is rightly contended that the strategy report is prepared in an atmosphere of intense, adversarial politics (Snider, 5).

Conclusion

The NSS provides a presidential administration with the opportunity to present its perception of vital security concerns, and how best to employ the instruments of power to ensure national security. From its release, a national vision concerning how the U.S. plans to secure itself at home and interact globally for a similar outcome is revealed. The concepts and strategy offered in the report provide an important benchmark that other concerned departments can reference. All subsequent proposals related to the security framework must align with the strategic vision presented in the NSS.

The development of a NSS is the product of numerous bureaucratic procedures and compromises. While it is an important document, its generality of tactics offers freedom of application as well as room for consensus. As a result, the NSS is permeated by political influence and it is essential that this does not stifle true critical analysis of vital interests. A successful security strategy is based upon foresight of crucial security issues and the ability to conjecture the proper combination of resources. Omissions from a security strategy based upon political beliefs or misjudgment of a security threat jeopardize a realistic understanding of the security environment.

Nevertheless, presidential administrations view security concerns based on the contemporary developments they face in office. The determinants of how they manage these specific issues are often correlated to their underlying political philosophies and thus, revised NSS reports shift according to transfers of power. National security is a dynamic subject and tactics are fluid and thus, the NSS of the United States must be amended for relevancy. In the conclusion, each finished NSS contributes to a greater overall understanding of the U.S. perception of national security and how it seeks to secure the homeland.

Further Reading

Stolberg, A.G. (2012). *How Nation-States Craft National Security Strategy Documents*. Washington, D.C.: Strategic Studies Institute.

United States Government. (2015, February 5). *National Security Strategy*. http://nssarchive.us/wp-content/uploads/2015/02/2015.pdf

United States Government. (2017, December 18). *National Security Strategy of the United States*. http://nssarchive.us/wp-content/uploads/2017/12/2017.pdf

References

Doyle, R.B. (2007). The U.S. National Security Strategy: Policy, Process, Problems. *Public Administration Review*, 67(4) 624–629.

Drew, D.M. & Snow, D.M. (1988). *Making Strategy: An Introduction to National Security Processes and Problems*. Montgomery, AL: Air University Press. Retrieved from http://www.dtic.mil/dtic/tr/fulltext/u2/a422016.pdf

National War College. (2018). *A National Security Strategy Primer*. Washington, D.C.: National Defense University Press. Retrieved from http://nwc.ndu.edu/Portals/71/Documents/Publications/NSS-Primer-Final-Ed.pdf?ver=2018-07-26-140012-980

Nevitt, M. (2017, December 20). Wishing Away Climate Change as a Threat to National Security. *Just Security*. Retrieved from https://www.justsecurity.org/49913/wishing-climate-change-threat-national-security/

Sarkesian, S.C., Williams, J.A., & Cimbala, S.J. (2008). *US National Security: Policymakers, Processes and Politics*. Boulder, CO: Lynne Rienner Publishers.

Snider, D.M. (1995). The National Security Strategy: Documenting Strategic Vision. *Strategic Studies Institute*. Retrieved from http //nssarchive.us/wp-content/uploads/2012/05/Snider.pdf

U.S. Congress. (1986). Goldwater-Nichols Department of Defense Reorganization Act. Retrieved from https://history.defense.gov/Portals/70/Documents/dod_reforms/Goldwater-Nichols DoDReordAct1986.pdf

Chapter 87

The Sinaloa-Tijuana Complex

Clifford Griffin
North Carolina State University, Raleigh, NC, United States

Contents

Geopolitics, Geo-economics, Geo-Narcotics, and Security: The Paradox of Border Cities 657
Geopolitics, Geo-economics, Border Security, and the Sinaloa "Cartel" 659
Geopolitics, Geo-economics, Border Security and the Tijuana "Cartel" 663
Further Reading 665
References 665

Geopolitics, Geo-economics, Geo-Narcotics, and Security: The Paradox of Border Cities

US Customs and Border Protection (CBP) is one of the Department of Homeland Security's (DHS's) largest and most complex units. Among its key responsibilities are 1) keeping terrorists and their weapons out of the US and 2) securing the border and facilitating lawful international trade and travel while enforcing hundreds of US laws and regulations, including immigration and drug laws (CBP, 2013). With a border of approximately 2,000 miles with its southern neighbor, Mexico, that incorporates numerous border towns and cities, including, but not limited to the West Texas city of El Paso, which shares a border with Ciudad Juarez in Chihuahua; Columbus, New Mexico, and Puerto Palomas in Chihuahua; San Diego, California, and Tijuana; Calexico, California, and Mexicali in Baja California; Brownsville, Texas, and Matamoros in Tamaulipas; McAllen, Texas and Reynosa in Tamaulipas; Laredo, Texas and Nuevo Laredo in Tamaulipas; and Nogales, Arizona and Nogales in Sonora, this responsibility is all the more challenging.

Border towns have long been considered safe and attractive for tourists and businesses alike, and the Mexican government instituted its Border Industrialization

DOI: 10.4324/9781315144511-91

Program in 1965, permitting foreign-owned (typically American) companies to a) establish factories on the Mexican side of the border; b) import tariff-free raw goods for manufacturing; and c) export the finished products, typically to the US.

This decision, among others, has helped to fuel the $557 billion annual or $1 million per minute trade between Mexico and the US (*UPI*, April 2019). As a result, border cities like Tijuana and Ciudad Juarez boomed. The San Diego-Tijuana region, home to some 6.8 million residents – some 40% of the entire US and Mexico border population – constitutes a $230 billion economic infrastructure engine that employs some 2 million workers and is the busiest land border crossing in the Western Hemisphere, with approximately 120,000 passenger vehicles, 63,000 pedestrians, and 6,000 trucks crossing back and forth daily (Sweeney, 2018; Williams, et al., 2017). In fact, the San Ysidro port of entry, connecting Tijuana to San Diego, is the busiest land crossing in the world through which more than 27.5 million vehicles containing 47.6 million passengers along with 16.5 million pedestrians passed through one of 26 inspection lanes in 2017 (Sweeney, 2018).

Ciudad Juarez is home to factories and business process outsourcing (BPO) centers (maquiladoras) operated by Foxconn, Eaton, Kimberly Clark, Xerox, Genpact, and Lexmark (Semuels, 2016). In fact, located along a 45-mile stretch of the US–Mexico border, the El Paso-Juarez region's six international border crossings – the world's largest urban border region – constitute a system of regional, statewide, and national significance, facilitating billions of dollars of trade, providing access to schools and businesses, and contributing to a shared regional culture and lifestyle. As El Paso's mayor noted:

> we are the 10th or 11th largest port of entry. We have $103 billion per year of trade going through this port. There are 115,000 jobs on this side of the border tied to manufacturing in Juárez. There are more than 20,000 pedestrians and 35,000 private passenger vehicles that cross each day.
>
> (*UPI*, April 2019)

But there was another side to this relationship as violence and crime have come to overshadow this perspective such that eight US border towns have been designated the most dangerous border towns in America. Common to all of these border towns is a pattern of violence instigated by drug and crime gangs and cartels vying for control of trafficking routes into the US. The coveted and highly contested trafficking routes are located in the northern states of Durango, Chihuahua, and Sinaloa – Mexico's "Golden Triangle" region. Long the epicenter of the country's drug-trafficking operations, Sinaloa is also home to the Sinaloa "cartel" and the Tijuana "cartel" – two of the country's top drug-trafficking organizations (DTOs). In 2017, for example, Tijuana (the world's busiest land crossing with over 50 million people crossing annually), with a population of 1,882,492, experienced a homicide rate of 100.7 per 100,000; Ciudad Juarez, with a population of 1,448,859, experienced a homicide rate of 56.16 per 100,000; Reynosa, with a population of 701,525, experienced a homicide rate of 41.95 per 100,000. Most drugs pass right under border guards' noses, smuggled in some of the tens of thousands of cars and trucks that pass daily through these official ports of entry (Pena & Schott 2013, 4). This drug-trafficking-related violence has been dramatically punctuated by beheadings, public hanging of corpses, car bombs, and murders of dozens of journalists and government officials. DTOs have splintered and diversified their crime activities, turning to extortion, kidnapping, auto theft, oil smuggling, human smuggling, retail drug sales, and other illicit enterprises.

The history of DTOs in Mexico dates back to the period when the US passed laws that criminalized the production, distribution, and consumption of alcohol and psychotropic substances. The 1940s witnessed a shift from the localized trafficking of homegrown marijuana and opiates grown largely in this region to the collaboration and coordination with US-organized crime to move illicit drugs through Mexicali and Tijuana (Astorga and Shirk, 2010; Astorga and Shirk, 2010). Today, according to the US Drug Enforcement Agency (DEA), some five drug-trafficking groups, including the Sinaloa and Nueva Generación Jalisco Cartel (CJNG) with bases in various parts of Mexico are operating in the Tijuana region. Tijuana has long been key to DTOs vying for control of a critical route for smuggling marijuana, cocaine, heroin, and methamphetamine by land, sea, and air into to the US, the world's largest consumer of illicit drugs. Sinaloa's capital, Culiacan, is just a 2-day drive from the US border. Understanding the geography and role of border cities in economic integration is central to understanding the illicit drugs business of the Tijuana and Sinaloa DTOs. Equally important, given the geographical propinquity of both countries, Mexico's stability is of critical importance to the US.

Geopolitics, Geo-economics, Border Security, and the Sinaloa "Cartel"

America's illegal drug market is huge. *Bloomberg Businessweek* (2014) estimates that the country spent (roughly) some $109 billion in 2010 on illicit marijuana, cocaine, methamphetamine, and heroin, and that the Sinaloa "cartel" earns at least $11 billion in annual sales to the US (Tozzi, 2014). This phenomenon has its roots in the fertile fields in Mexico's western state of Sinaloa, where huge crops of soybeans and sesame seeds, along with vast amounts of marijuana and heroin destined for US markets have long been produced. A number of individuals from this poor region have become infamous by growing and selling these narcotics and networking their way from the foothills of the Sierra Madre to become major players in Mexico's DTOs or so-called "cartels." During the 1980s, **Miguel Ángel Félix Gallardo**, a former police officer from Sinaloa, together with Rafael Caro Quintero, and Ernesto "Don Neto" Fonseca Carillo co-founded the Guadalajara "cartel." Joining this DTO were Héctor "el Güero" Luis Palma Salazar, Amado Carillo Fuentes, Ismael "el Mayo" Zambada, Manuel "Cochi Loco" Salcido Uzeta, the Arellano Félix brothers, and the now-incarcerated Joaquin "el Chapo" Guzmán – all of whom made Culiacan, Sinaloa's state capital, their hometown. Guzmán rose quickly through the ranks as a ruthless businessman and skilled networker, making key contacts with politicians and police to ensure his loads made it through without problems (*Associated Press*, February 22, 2014).

Until the end of the 1980s, the Guadalajara "cartel" composed of friends and family members from Sinaloa and, headed by Félix Gallardo, exercised near total monopoly of Mexico's illegal drugs trade. These activities were being monitored by the DEA, and undercover agent, Kiki Camarena, managed to infiltrate the "cartel," getting close to Gallardo. Acting on Camarena's information, Mexican soldiers, in 1984, launched the "Operation Godfather" raid on "Rancho Búfalo," a 1,000-hectare marijuana plantation in Chihuahua, which employed thousands of farmers, and produced some $8 billion worth of drugs annually. Camarena's intelligence threatened Félix Gallardo operation, which operated with the approval of Mexican government officials. His abduction on February 7th 1985, and subsequent torture and death on February 9, resulted in Operation Leyenda, one of the largest DEA homicide investigations ever undertaken, which identified Félix Gallardo and his two close associates, Fonseco Carillo and Caro Quintero, both of whom were promptly arrested under pressure from the US. Meanwhile, political protection enabled Félix Gallardo to remain at large until he was arrested on April 8th 1989 in Mexico City.

Félix Gallardo's arrest produced a kingmaker moment and the ushering in of a new era. In order to make it more difficult for the security forces to interrupt the drug-trafficking operations, Gallardo, reportedly with support by factions in the Mexican government, subdivided the Guadalajara "cartel" into franchises that resulted in the Sinaloa, Juarez, Tijuana, Sonora, and Gulf "cartels," respectively. Caro Quintero's Sonora "cartel" was given control of the state of Sonora; the Arellano Félix brothers' Tijuana "cartel" was given control of Tijuana; and "el Mayo" Zambada and "el Chapo" Guzmán were given control of the state of Sinaloa. What is currently known as the Sinaloa "cartel" or the Guzmán-Loera Organization, therefore, emerged from an alliance between the "el Chapo," "el Mayo," and "el Güero" groups at the beginning of the 1990s designed to control the territories of Sinaloa, Tecate, San Luis Río Colorado, and Mexicali. And since Guzmán was a nephew of the Mexican Godfather, Pedro Avilés – "El Leon de la Sierra" – founder of what would become the first significant modern Mexican DTO, he came to command a pyramid of power as a matter of heredity (as well as ruthless violence).

This restructuring resulted in the Sinaloa "cartel" becoming known as "The Federation," whose leaders recognized that its success depended upon alliances and franchises in order to reach across Mexico, the Americas, and the world. Unable – or, perhaps unwilling – to accept the division of US border smuggling plazas designated by Gallardo to heirs of the old Guadalajara "cartel," Guzmán eliminated them one-by-one, laying claim to the entire frontier. Confederates, including the Arellano Félix "cartel" in Tijuana, the Juarez "cartel," and even that of the Beltrán Leyva brothers with whom Guzmán grew up, became bitter enemies (*The Guardian*, February 13, 2019). Prior to 2008, the Beltrán Leyva Organization (BLO) was part of the Sinaloa "Federation." However, the January 2008 arrest of BLO's leader, Alfredo Beltrán Leyva, reportedly as a result of intelligence provided by Guzmán, led to the BLO's split from the Sinaloa DTO, and both organizations have remained bitter rivals since (Beittel, 2018). Another prominent example was the murder of Rodolfo Carrillo Fuentes, younger brother of Amado Carrillo, the former leader of the Juarez Cartel on September 11th 2004 while under escort by members of the state police. This event, which occurred in Culiacan, marked the separation of the Juarez and Sinaloa "cartels" (Veledíaz 2007). Once known as La Alianza de Sangre ("Blood Alliance"), this DTO reportedly has developed a presence in 17 of the 31 states in Mexico.

The prevailing view is that the Sinaloa DTOs strategy was aided elements within the Mexican state, who saw this DTO's power as guarantor of a sort of "Pax Mafiosa" that enabled it to exercise control, and go after rival – even more ruthless – newer criminal organizations like Los Zetas (Vuilamy, 2019; Kellner and Pepitone, 2010). This strategy enabled Félix Gallardo's former lieutenant, "el Chapo," to rise to the top of the DTOs. Under his leadership, the Sinaloa "cartel" grew to become one of the world's top DTOs, whose reach extended throughout the entire US, making it by far the biggest "cartel" supplier of drugs to US cities. Its operations connect manufacturers and distributors, bankers and businesses, as it extracts money at each step. By some estimates, Sinaloa had grown to control 40%-60% of Mexico's drug trade by 2012 and had annual earnings calculated to be as high as $3 billion (Beittel, 2018). This full supply chain network, including indirect distribution through third parties who bought drugs from the cartel in Mexico and carried them across the border (*The Guardian*, February 28, 2014), was facilitated in part by the organization's violent seizure of lucrative drug routes from rivals and the building of sophisticated tunnels under the US border to move its loads.

The apparent successes in the drugs war secured against the Pablo Escobar and the DTOs in Colombia resulted in a fortuitous circumstance for the DTOs in Mexico. By the mid-1980s, Sinaloa's marijuana and heroin smugglers had already turned to cocaine by providing alternate routes for Colombia's drug traffickers, who had begun to experience difficulty in shipping their product into the US market through South Florida. This relationship, however, was short-lived as the Mexicans, dissatisfied with just smuggling cocaine for a fee, began demanding payment in product and, shortly thereafter, established their own distribution networks in the US. This greater level of control resulted in much richer and much more powerful organizations and, according to Guillermo Gonzalez Calderoni, "…Now it wasn't one million or two million, it was 15, 20, 30, 40 million dollars that they could make off a single payment." In its sphere of influence, the famous Golden Triangle (where the states of Chihuahua, Durango, and Sinaloa meet), there is a criminal-type capture, and because of the role it has played in providing public services, community urbanization, and more, this "cartel" has strong local roots and is the source of the drug-trafficking culture linked to the entertainment and clothing industries, and even to religious rites and cults. With its operations ranging from Mexico's Pacific coast and along the US border – from Tijuana in the west, to Ciudad Juarez, Nuevo Laredo and Reynoso in the east, to Cancún, and other strategic points on the transportation and distribution routes – this DTO also established a presence in more than 50 countries around the world. With strong local roots, the ability to effectively use bribery at the highest political and police levels, and the constant use of violence against rival organizations (del Pilar Fuerte Celis, et al., 2019), these gangsters from Culiacan became world famous kingpins of complex criminal enterprises – many resembling multinational corporations in structure – and surpassed the Colombians by becoming the world's biggest traffickers, and the Sinaloa "cartel" becoming one of the largest criminal organizations in history.

But with time, the Sinaloa cartel's strengths became weaknesses. As the organization expanded under Guzmán, it stretched far beyond its own limits such that no one knew whom to trust. Thus, after years of uneasy co-existence, fighting between the rival groups broke out in 2005, but the violence spiraled after the Mexican President Felipe Calderón deployed tens of thousands of soldiers and federal police against the DTOs in December 2006. Estimates are that by 2009–2010, some 26,000 people had died in drug-related violence (Tuckman 2010). The Sinaloa "cartel" imploded between factions and reports suggest that Guzmán was probably shopped by Ismael "el Mayo" Zambada García, with whom he disagreed with over succession and strategy. Differences came to a head with "el Mayo's" disdain over discussions for a proposed biopic with the American movie star, Sean Penn. On the ground, Sinaloa remains a force to be reckoned with, still shipping drugs north even as the fight for local markets in Mexico sends murder rates soaring.

It comes as no surprise, therefore, when on September 24, 2016, the US Department of the Treasury's Office of Foreign Assets Control (OFAC) designated four Mexican nationals, pursuant to the Foreign Narcotics Kingpin Designation Act (Kingpin Act). Eliseo Imperial Castro, a.k.a. Cheyo Antrax, Alfonso Lira Sotelo, a.k.a. "el Atlante," Javier Lira Sotelo, a.k.a "el Hannibal" or "el Carnicero," and Alma Delia Lira Sotelo for their narcotics trafficking and money laundering in support or on behalf of the Sinaloa "cartel" and/or its high-ranking members. The Treasury argued that the narcotics trafficking and money laundering activities of these individuals served to expand the Sinaloa "cartel's" influence into California. The Southern District of California charged Eliseo Imperial Castro and Alfonso Lira Sotelo with several narcotics trafficking violations and "for materially assisting, supporting, providing services to, and/or acting for or on behalf of his uncle, Ismael Zambada Garcia, and/ or the Sinaloa "cartel."" Eliseo Imperial Castro is a high-ranking member of the Los Antrax organization, the enforcement group of the Sinaloa "cartel," and operates on behalf of Ismael Zambada García (MENA 2016). With time, however, these one-time friends would become bitter enemies, inflicting increasingly gruesome levels of violence upon one another's followers (*The Guardian*, February 13, 2016). For example, in1993, gunmen linked to the Tijuana-based Arrellano Félix organization, attempted to assassinate Guzmán at the Guadalajara airport but instead killed Roman Catholic Cardinal Juan Jesus Posadas Ocampo, outraging Mexicans (AP, 22 Feb 2014).

Despite the capture and incarceration of its founder and leader, "el Chapo" Guzmán, the Sinaloa "cartel" remains the most powerful drug organization in the world (CNN, 2019), and the US 2018 National Drug Threat Assessment states that this DTO "maintains the most expansive footprint in the US (DEA, 2018). ICE estimates that between $19 billion and $29 billion travels annually from the US to Mexico to fund DTOs and other transnational criminal activities (ICE 2019). It is the country's largest cartel, based on the volume of drugs it moves, and grew out of the coastal state of Sinaloa (Choi 2019), and one of five crime syndicates contesting a turf war across Mexico. Under "el Chapo," this DTO became a multinational, global conglomerate, through alliances, franchises and brute force, and enjoyed the services of illustrious American and British banks that embraced and cleaned their vast profits with impunity, too big to prosecute even when they were caught, blurring the line between crime and capitalism (*The Guardian*, February 13, 2019).

But the tradition continues. While Sinaloa has historically been, and still remains, Mexico's most powerful cartel, the world it came up in no longer exists. Between the early 90s and the mid-2000s, the Sinaloa, Tijuana, Juarez, and Gulf organizations were mini-monopolies, with borders that more or less stayed the same. Then, with the start of Mexico's drug war in 2006, that arrangement started to fall apart. As Mexican and American authorities took out "cartel" leaders, groups fractured and new ones emerged. And then there is the wild card of Rafael Caro Quintero. A founder of the now-defunct Guadalajara cartel, Quintero spent 28 years in jail for the 1985 murder of DEA agent Kiki Camarena, but was unexpectedly released in 2013 – to the US government's dismay (Tuckman, 2015). The DEA, in 2017 identified Quintero as one of the functioning leaders of the Sinaloa cartel "responsible for smuggling hundreds of tons of methamphetamine, marijuana, and cocaine into the United States," and is now on the list of the FBI's top 10 most wanted with a $20 million reward for information on his whereabouts

Geopolitics, Geo-economics, Border Security and the Tijuana "Cartel"

The city of Tijuana in the Mexican state of Baja California Norte is a border city to San Diego, and has long been key to DTOs vying for control of critical routes for smuggling marijuana, cocaine, heroin and methamphetamine by land, sea and air into the US, the world's largest consumer of illicit drugs. Like the Sinaloa "cartel," the roots of the Tijuana "cartel" are embedded in the state of Sinaloa, from which its founding members, including Pedro Avilés Pérez, Rafael Caro Quintero and Ernesto Fonseca hailed. These individuals all worked closely with the legendary trafficker Miguel Ángel Félix Gallardo, alias "El Padrino." who had been trafficking marijuana and heroin into the US since the 1960s. The military-led, anti-drugs campaign of the late 1970s resulted in mass arrests in Sinaloa, along with the death of Avilés Pérez. As a consequence, the group relocated to Guadalajara, formed the Guadalajara "cartel," and began collaborating with Colombian traffickers to ship large quantities of cocaine into the US.

Until the end of the 1980s, the Guadalajara "cartel" composed of friends and family members from Sinaloa, and headed by Félix Gallardo, exercised near total monopoly of Mexico's illegal drugs trade. These activities were being monitored by the DEA, and undercover agent Kiki Camarena managed to infiltrate the "cartel," getting close to Gallardo. Acting on Camarena's information, Mexican soldiers, in 1984, launched the "Operation Godfather" raid on "Rancho Búfalo," a 1,000-hectare marijuana plantation in Chihuahua, which employed thousands of farmers and produced some $8 billion worth of drugs annually. Camarena's intelligence threatened Félix Gallardo's operation, which operated with the approval of Mexican government officials. His abduction on February 7, 1985, and subsequent torture and death on February 9, resulted in Operation Leyenda, one of the largest DEA homicide investigations ever undertaken, which identified Félix Gallardo and his two close associates, Fonseco Carillo and Caro Quintero, both of whom were promptly arrested under pressure from the US. Meanwhile, political protection enabled Félix Gallardo to remain at large until he was arrested on April 8, 1989, in Mexico City. Gallardo's arrest produced a kingmaker moment and the ushering in of a new era. In order to make it more difficult for the security forces to interrupt the drug-trafficking operations, Gallardo, reportedly with support by factions in the Mexican government, subdivided the Guadalajara "cartel" into franchises that resulted in the Sinaloa, Juarez, Tijuana, Sonora, and Gulf "cartels". Five of the Arellano Félix brothers – Benjamín, Ramón, Francisco Rafael, Francisco Javier, and Eduardo – nephews of Gallardo, formed the core of the future Tijuana "cartel" which, reportedly, has developed a presence in at least 15 Mexican states.

Both Arellano Félix and "el Chapo" Guzmán had been friends, and both smuggled drugs into the US. However, the latter felt affronted when his friend refused to engage in business relationships on the grounds that Guzmán status was that of an associate of the Guadalajara "cartel" and not a "boss." Undaunted, not only did "el Chapo" proceed to smuggle drugs under the Arellano-Felix Organization's (AFO) noses but he subsequently sent his hitman Rayo Lopez to represent him at Ismael Zambada García's birthday party. Raya arrived drunk, and Arellano Félix shot him in the head, an event that initiated the war between the Sinaloa "cartel" and the Tijuana "cartel." Shortly thereafter, the AFO began their expansion when Ramón Arellano Félix killed a close associate of "el Chapo" in Sinaloa. In May 1993, the Arellano Félix brothers sent gunmen to intercept "el Chapo" at the Guadalajara airport but, instead, mistakenly struck and killed a Mexican cardinal instead. Francisco Rafael Arellano Félix was arrested by Mexican authorities in 1993, but after "el Chapo" and Palma were arrested, the Arellano Félix clan grew to unprecedented heights. They made a pact with the Caro Quintero clan in Sonora, the Milenio Cartel in Michoacán, as well as alliances in Colima, Jalisco, and Oaxaca that allowed them to dominate the trade from north to south.

Things soon began to fall apart for the AFO following the arrest of several of its leaders. In February 2002, its main enforcer, Ramón Arellano Félix, was killed in a shootout in Mazatlán; and a month later, its leader Benjamín Arellano Félix was arrested. The subsequent arrest of other mid- and lower-level operatives and the arrest in August 2006 of Eduardo Arellano, the last of the brothers, resulted in a severely crippled organization. With leadership formally passing to a nephew, Luis Fernando Sánchez Arellano, challenges began to surface from within the organization (Sabet, 2010). Traditionally, the AFO had been made up of a number of cells loyal to the Arellano Félix family, but there is also a degree of operational independence, a structure labeled by the United Nations Office on Drugs and Crime (UNODC) as a clustered hierarchy. Eduardo Teodoro García Simental, one of the "cartel's" cell leaders, challenged Sánchez Arellano's leadership, producing a major rupture in the organization. A simultaneous challenge emerged from its chief rival, the Sinaloa "cartel," which sought to take advantage of the AFO's weakness and strengthen its presence in Baja California by cultivating ties to the García Simental camp. Clearly, the conditions of the game had changed for the Arellano Félix family leadership, which had to fight off both an insurgency from within its ranks and the entrance of an outside cartel (Sabet, 2010).

The organization split into two factions following a bloody battle for control in 2008. In the vacuum left by the arrests of the AFO's key players, other DTOs in the region attempted to assert control over the profitable Tijuana/Baja California-San Diego/California border plaza. The AFO suffered another blow when Eduardo Teodoro "el Teo" García Simental, a former AFO lieutenant, aligned himself with the Sinaloa "cartel," which led to a surge of violence in Tijuana.

Fernando Sánchez Arellano maintains leadership of the diminished DTO and reportedly has worked out a deal with the dominant Sinaloa organization to pay a fee for the right to operate.

The Arellanos are said to have joined forces with the Nueva Generación Jalisco Cartel (CJNG) to oppose Sinaloa as these groups contested for street dealers or *narcomenudeo*, a development that contributed to a huge spike in homicides across Mexico in 2017. As in past years, Tijuana's homicides far outnumber those of the state's other four municipalities, Ensenada, Mexicali, Rosarito Beach, and Tecate. The city registered among the steepest increases from a total of 910 in 2016 to 1,744 in 2017 (Dibble 2018). The targets of these homicides have come largely from the city's impoverished and working-class neighborhoods, and 90% of the victims are low-level operatives. The lack of control by a single group is one key to explaining the level of violence, said David Shirk, a University of San Diego professor who tracks Mexico's trafficking groups. "There is no over-arching umbrella of control by the larger organizations that are able to establish rules of the game," he said. "There's confusion and disarray at the lower levels because there's no one to call the shots." Today, it is largely under the control of the upstart Nueva Generación Jalisco Cartel (CJNG). And the defeated Arellano Félix Tijuana "cartel" has been revived, led by the original brothers' sister, Enedina Arellano Félix, her children, nephews, and nieces, reformed as the Tijuana Cartel Nueva Generación (Vuillamy 2019). By 2018, Tijuana had become anarchic in the sense that – according to the DEA – five of the drug-trafficking groups based in various parts of Mexico have been operating in the Tijuana region. These include the Sinaloa and CJNG cartels, the BLO faction led by Fausto "Chapo" Isidro Meza; the Michoacán-based Familia Michoacana; and remnants of the group that once controlled Tijuana, the AFO, who are said to have joined forces with CJNG to oppose Sinaloa (Dibble 2018).

Further Reading

Beittel, J. S. (2011, January 7). *Mexico's Drug Trafficking Organizations: Source and Scope of the Rising Violence.* Washington, DC: Congressional Research Service.

Carpenter, T. G. (2012). *The Fire Next Door: Mexico's Drug Violence and the Danger to America.* Washington, DC: CATO Institute.

Romero Luján, G. A. and Sosa Álvarez, M. C. (2018). "Efectos De Los Costos Internos E Internacionales En El Tamaño De La Población De Las Grandes Ciudades De México, Para Los Años 1995, 2000 Y 2005" ["Effects of Internal and International Costs in Population Size of the Great Classes of Mexico"], *Revista Internacional Administracion & Finanzas, 11*(1): 25–37.

References

Associated Press. 2014. Mexico's Sinaloa Drug Chief Arrested, February 22. Available at https://www.kbtx.com/home/headlines/Mexicos-Sinaloa-Drug-Chief-Arrested-246694021.html

Astorga, Luis, Shirk, David. 2010. *Drug Trafficking Organizations and Counter-drug Strategies in the U.S.–Mexican Context.* San Diego: Center for US-Mexican Studies, University of California. Available at http://www.escholarship.org/uc/item/8j647429

Beittel, June S. 2018. Mexico: Organized Crime and Drug Trafficking Organizations, Congressional Research Service, R41576, July 3. Available at https://fas.org/sgp/crs/row/R41576.pdf

Bergman, Jake. Frontline: The Place Mexico's Drug Kingpins Call Home. Available at https://www.pbs.org/wgbh/pages/frontline/shows/drugs/business/place.html

Choi, D. 2019. A Wells Fargo Personal Banker Pleaded Guilty to Helping Launder Millions of Dollars for Drug Traffickers Like the Sinaloa Cartel. *Business Insider*. Available at https://www.businessinsider.com/wells-fargo-banker-money-laundering-drug-cartelsinaloa-mexico-2019-5 del Pilar Fuerte Celis, M., Lujan, E.P. and Ponce, R.C. 2019. Organized Crime, Violence, and Territorial Dispute in Mexico (2007–2011). *Trends Organized Crime* 22: 188. https://doi.org.prox.lib.ncsu.edu/10.1007/s12117-018-9341-z

Dell, Melissa, 2015. Trafficking Networks and the Mexican Drug War. *American Economic Review* 105(6): 1738–1779. http://dx.doi.org/10.1257/aer.20121637

Dibble, S. 2018. Control for Street Drug Trade Pushes Tijuana to Grisly New Record: 1,744 Homicides. *The San Diego Union Tribune*. https://www.sandiegouniontribune.com/news/border-baja-california/sd-me-homicidestijuana-20180102-story.html

Flannery, Nathaniel Parrish. 2017. Political Risk Analysis: Violent Crime Rising in Chihuahua, Mexico. *Forbes*, March 28. Available at https://www.forbes.com/sites/nathanielparish flannery/2017/03/28/political-risk-analysis-violent-crime-rising-in-chihuahua-mexico/#230b6e6c7f87

Kellner, Tomas, and Francisco Pepitone. 2010. *World Policy Journal* 27(1): 29–37. Available at https://muse.jhu.edu/article/379146/pdf

Loudis, Jessica. 2019. El Chapo: What the Rise and Fall of the Kingpin Reveals about the War On Drugs. *The Guardian*, June 7. Available at https://www.theguardian.com/world/2019/jun/07/el-chapo-the-last-of-the-cartel-kingpins

NBC 7 Staff. 2019. DEA Dismantles' San Diego Meth Trafficking Network Tied to Sinaloacartel. https://www.nbcsandiego.com/news/local/DEA-Dismantles-San-Diego-MethTrafficking-Network-Tied-to-Sinaloa-Cartel-510244261.html?amp=y

Pena, A. and E. Schott. 2013. Modeling El-Paso-Juarez illicit drug networks: Policy implications. *Journal of the Washington Academy of Sciences* 99(4): 1–16.

Rios, Viridiana. 2012. How Government Structure Encourages Criminal Violence: The Causes of Mexico's Drug War. PhD dissertation. Available at https://dash.harvard.edu/bitstream/handle/1/11156675/RiosContreras_gsas.harvard_0084L_10752.pdf?sequence=3

Sabet, Daniel. 2010. Confrontation, Collusion, and Tolerance: The Relationship between Law Enforcement and Organized Crime in Tijuana, *Mexican Law Review* II(2), 3–29.

Sanchez, Ray, and Sonia Moghe 2019. What the 'El Chapo' Guzmán verdict means for the powerful Sinaloa cartel, CNN online, February 13. Available at https://www.cnn.com/2019/02/12/us/el-chapo-guzman-verdict-sinaloa-cartel-future/index.html

Semuels, Alana. 2016. Upheavals in the Factories of Juarez. *The Atlantic.com*. Available at https://www.theatlantic.com/business/archive/2016/01/upheaval-in-the-factories-of-juarez/424893/

Seper, Jerry, and Ben Conery. 2010. Border Violence Threatens Americans. *the Washington Times*, April 1. Available at https://www.washingtontimes.com/news/2010/apr/01/violent-mexican-drug-gangs-pose-rising-risk-to-ame/

Sweeney, Don. 2018. 5 Things to Know About Massive San Ysidro Border Checkpoint Closed by Caravan Protest, the Sacramento Bee, November 25. Available at https://www.sacbee.com/news/state/california/article222172450.html#storylink=cpy

The Guardian. 2014. Mexican Drug Trafficking in the US: The Sinaloa Cartel's Vast Empire. February 28. Available at https://www.theguardian.com/world/interactive/2014/feb/28/mexican-drug-trafficking-sinaloa-cartel

The Guardian. 2019. The Guardian View On Drug Wars: Protect the Innocent. February 13. Available at https://www.theguardian.com/commentisfree/2019/feb/13/the-guardian-view-on-drug-wars-protect-the-innocent

Timmons, Patrick. 2019. Threat to Close Border Puts El Paso on Edge. UPI, April 2. Available at https://www.upi.com/Top_News/US/2019/04/02/Threat-to-close-border-puts-El-Paso-on-edge/8631554234827/

Tozzi, John. 2014. More Pot, Less Cocaine: Sizing Up America's Illicit Drug Market, *Bloomberg Businessweek*, March 10. Available at https://www.bloomberg.com/news/articles/2014-03-10/more-pot-less-cocaine-sizing-up-america-s-illicit-drug-market

Tuckman, Jo. 2010. Death of Drug Lord Ignacio 'Nacho' Coronel Deals Blow to Mexican Cartel. July 30. Available at https://www.theguardian.com/world/2010/jul/30/mexico-drugs-lord-shot-dead.

United States Drug Enforcement Administration. 2018. 2018 National Drug Threat Assessment. Available at https://www.dea.gov/sites/default/files/2018-11/DIR-032-18%202018%20NDTA%20final%20low%20resolution.pdf

United States Treasury Targets Tijuana-Based Cell of the Sinaloa Cartel, MENA Report, London (Sep 24, 2016).

Vuillamy, Ed. 2019. Tale of Two Drugs Lords: From Cosa Nostra to Guzmán – It's Strictly Business. *The Guardian*, February 17. Available at https://www.theguardian.com/world/2019/feb/17/tale-two-drug-lords-el-chapo-guzman-salvatore-riina-mexico-italy

Williams, Steve, Alan Bersin, Jose Larroque, and Gustavo de la Fuente. 2017. It's Time to Make the San Diego-Tijuana Border More Efficient, the San Diego Tribune, May 5. Available at https://www.sandiegouniontribune.com/opinion/commentary/sd-utbg-border-economy-tijuana-sandiego-20170501-story.html

Chapter 88

United States Citizenship and Immigration Services (USCIS)

Max Crumley-Effinger
Loyola University Chicago, Chicago, IL, United States

Content

Further Reading 673
References 673

Although the United States Citizenship and Immigration Services (USCIS) was formally created in 2002 with the establishment of the Department of Homeland Security (Homeland Security Act, 2002), USCIS immigration pursuits and policy roots date back to the late nineteenth century. As the principal United States government agency responsible for review and adjudication of petitions and applications for lawful immigration benefits, the USCIS engages in a wide variety of activities and projects to meet its stated goal of utilizing agency resources toward "identifying, addressing, and mitigating national security and fraud risks to the immigration system…" (USCIS, 2016, p. iii). Contemporary agency prerogatives reflect the steady shift of federal immigration policy from a primary focus on xenophobic labor and wage protection in the nineteenth century toward the agency's twenty-first century emphasis on national security and honoring American values (Hing, 2004; Mak, n.d.; Hing, 2006; Orchowski, 2008). Today, USCIS counts close to 20,000 employees and contractors across more than 200 offices around the globe.

Historically within the purview of state authority, the federal government assumed immigration policy and enforcement responsibilities in 1876 (Shanks, 2001; Orchowski, 2008). Gilberto Cárdenas (1975) explains that the legitimacy of federal control of immigrant admissions was justified "on-the basis of the principle of sovereign rights…" wherein the "primary aim of the legislation was to end and prevent the practice of employers of importing 'cheap' foreign labor" (p. 67). At this time,

DOI: 10.4324/9781315144511-92

federal policy focused primarily on the economic and labor impacts of immigration. For example, the passage of the Chinese Exclusion Act of 1882 and the Immigration Act of 1891 enabled pointed retardation of the importation of cheap labor from China and led to the creation of a superintendent of immigration within the Treasury Department to enforce immigration restrictions (Hing, 2004; Shanks, 2001). Such late nineteenth-century immigration acts – including the Immigration Act of 1891 and the Alien Contract Labor Law in 1885 – also placed limitations on the immigration of "undesirable individuals" who could potentially become public charges (Orth, 1907).

After the 1891 creation of the office of the superintendent of immigration in the Department of the Treasury, the Bureau of Immigration – the twentieth-century precursor to the USCIS – was later moved under the jurisdiction of the newly created Department of Commerce and Labor in 1903 (U.S. Congress, 1903a; Orchowski, 2008). The rationale for this move related to the centrality of labor and economic issues to immigration concerns of the time. Funding for the Bureau's activities came from a head tax that contributed to an "immigrant fund" (U.S. Congress, 1903b; Orchowski, 2008). Three successive changes came rather quickly: in 1906, the Bureau was renamed the Bureau of Immigration and Naturalization (U.S. Congress, 1906), then in 1913, the Bureau was divided into the Bureau of Immigration and the Bureau of Naturalization under the newly established Department of Labor, and finally, in 1933, these two bureaus were combined to create the Immigration and Naturalization Service (Orchowski, 2008; USCIS, 2012), commonly known as the INS.

The creation of this new body was accompanied by yet another relocation of these federal immigration services when the INS became part of the Department of Justice. In the early 1940s, the INS was then moved to the Justice Department, in some ways as a result of changes in immigration thinking stemming from security concerns from the conflict that was to become known as World War II (Orchowski, 2008). As Mak (n.d.) notes, for example, "government officials questioned how a department focused on the nation's employment could also handle problems related to the nation's security." Before the creation of the INS, Congress established the U.S. Border Patrol in 1924 to enhance the execution of federal immigration regulation enforcement (USCIS, 2012). These represent initial movements along the path of identifying immigration policy and enforcement as important measures for addressing national security concerns.

Federal legislative activity from the post-war period through the 1990s introduced a variety of alterations to immigration policy. The McCarren-Walter Act of 1952 perpetuated existing immigration "exclusion regimes" from the 1920s, while amendments in 1965 ended a nationality-based quota system (Hing, 2004). Further legislation provided guidance for the arbitration of refugee immigration cases, created new immigrant visa categories, "revised all grounds for exclusion and deportation" (U.S. Congress, 1990), and allowed INS administrators to "adjudicate applications for naturalization" (USCIS, 2012). Additional legislation updated regulations pertaining to naturalization and legal and illegal immigration, implemented a diversity visa program, and revised controls against unauthorized immigration (Hing, 2004; Mees, n.d.; USCIS, 2012).

With sweeping national security concerns after the terrorist attacks of September 11, 2001, the Homeland Security Act (2002) both created the Department of Homeland Security (DHS) and subsumed all previous INS functions under the new DHS.

The creation of the DHS was no small feat: according to Hing (2006), the new cabinet department affected at least 22 federal agencies and approximately 170,000 employees, "representing the biggest government reorganization in 50 years" (p. 198). The INS was abolished, and its various roles were divided between the three new immigration-related agencies under the DHS: Customs and Border Patrol (CBP), Immigration and Customs Enforcement (ICE), and the USCIS (USCIS, 2012). With the new divisions of responsibility, the USCIS was tasked primarily with handling "immigrant visa petitions, naturalization, and asylum and refugee applications" (Hing, 2006, p. 198).

Those who enter the United States without U.S. citizenship can be divided between two primary classifications – immigrant and nonimmigrant – and those who hold either visa type are generally permitted legal entry into the United States (Wasem, 2011). An immigrant visa provides the opportunity to live, work, and study with no expiration of such authorization. The nonimmigrant visa holder is one who receives legal status to remain in the United States for a specified, limited duration for a "specific purpose and whose activities... are prescribed by his or her class of admission" (Monger & Barr, 2009, pp. 1–2). USCIS provides oversight of benefits for both immigrant and nonimmigrant visa-holders, including citizenship and naturalization, employment authorization, facilitation of international adoption processes, and "civic integration" services (USCIS, 2015a).

Naturalization is the process through which individuals can gain citizenship, for example, through application or petitions based on familial connections (USCIS, 2015a). Employment permissions can be gained through applications to USCIS Service Centers, and verification of eligibility for employment occurs through E-Verify, an online system maintained by USCIS with which employers interface (USCIS, 2017d). Cultural and integration services include initiatives to support the transition of immigrants to life in the United States, for example, with employment support and the *Welcome Guide to the United States* (2015b) pamphlet. USCIS also administers databases – such as the Systematic Alien Verification for Entitlements (SAVE) program – to provide immigration status details to federal and state offices and agencies from which immigrants and nonimmigrants may request benefits or services, for example, from the Bureau of Motor Vehicles (BMV) and the Social Security Administration (Donovan, 2005).

USCIS operates five service centers throughout the United States as they review the nearly seven million applications and benefit petitions received each year (USCIS, 2016; USCIS, 2017a). These service centers are located in California, Nebraska, Texas, Vermont, and in the Washington, DC area, with each service center responsible for varying combinations of region- and case-specific services (USCIS, n.d.). Additional customer support services are available at USCIS field offices throughout the country (USCIS, 2017b). As an agency within the DHS, USCIS is headed by the Director and Deputy Director (USCIS, 2017c), with funding for its activities and its nearly 19,000 coming from a range of administrative and application fees paid by those who use USCIS services (USCIS, 2018).

Despite service-oriented responsibilities (unlike the enforcement-focused ICE and CBP), USCIS' position within the DHS may elicit hesitancy or fear for those who use their services. As Donovan (2005) explains, USCIS naturalization and immigration services take place "within a government structure whose mission is not entirely compatible with..." (p. 581) the situation of its clientele. Housed as it is within the

DHS, USCIS applicants are seeking services from an agency closely connected with those who are tasked by the federal government with national security emphases that include the arrest and deportation of some individuals seeking citizenship benefits (Donovan, 2005). This poses unique challenges for frontline USCIS staff as they work with a rightfully wary clientele and demands bravery of those who interface with an agency that has a less-than-stellar reputation for consistent adjudication of applications and petitions (Callan & Callan, 2016).

In the eyes of those who interact with USCIS, some dissonance may exist between the ostensibly supportive, service-oriented responsibilities of USCIS on the one hand and the national security focus of the DHS on the other. As Golub (2005) suggests, the post-9/11 immigration policy was inextricably linked to 9/11 exigencies: "every single piece of legislation, every activity that members of Congress look at, they do so through the lens of 9/11 and security" (p. 10). The connection between immigration and national security was concretized in the eyes of policymakers and much of the public when officials ascertained that the terrorists involved in the 9/11 attacks had entered the country through legal immigration processes and exploited loopholes in the immigration systems of the day (Donovan, 2005).

The USCIS role in immigration and homeland security responsibilities is in some ways restricted by way of the arrangements through which a body outside of the DHS issues visas. Although visa issuance regulations are within the purview of the DHS, the Department of State's (DOS) Bureau of Consular Affairs is responsible for the issuance of both immigrant and nonimmigrant visas that occurs outside of the United States (Wasem, 2011). Depending on whether the intended immigrant is outside or within the United States, immigration application procedures may be handled between both the DOS Consular Affairs and USCIS. This complicated interface between departments (DHS and DOS) and agencies (USCIS and Consular Affairs) is described by Wasem (2011):

Petitions for immigrant status are first filed with USCIS. If the prospective immigrant is already residing in the United States, the USCIS handles the entire process, which is called "adjustment of status." If the prospective LPR [legal permanent resident] does not have legal residence in the United States, the petition is forwarded to Consular Affairs in their home country after USCIS has reviewed it. The Consular Affairs officer (when the alien is coming from abroad) and USCIS adjudicator (when the alien is adjusting status in the United States) must be satisfied that the alien is entitled to the immigrant status (p. 2). This illustrates the complexity of the "frontline" role with which USCIS has been tasked in advancing immigration and naturalization services in support of U.S. homeland security efforts.

The interagency mechanism through which DHS' USCIS and DOS' Consular Affairs approve immigrant visas represents a form of "access control" (Lehrer, 2004, p. 71), one in which USCIS can exert its influence in support of its goal to mitigate "national security and fraud risks to the immigration system…" (USCIS, 2016, p. iii). In this way, USCIS and DHS play a role in the "'front line' of homeland security against terrorists" (Wasem, 2011, p. 11); however, this role is shared with the DOS Consular Affairs. Unlike its sister DHS agencies (ICE and CBP), then, USCIS' responsibilities focus less on enforcement and more on the accurate adjudication of applications and petitions for immigration benefits from those within the United States and those deemed eligible to enter the country. However, as noted, some conflicts arise within the dual role of facilitating immigration and adhering to the national security mandates of the agency and the DHS.

In fulfilling their preemptive role in protecting national security, the agency has recently "enhanced document security, strengthened the consistency of screening, and developed analytic capabilities that further strengthen our ability to make risk-informed, data-driven decisions" about such applications and petitions (USCIS, 2016, p. iv). The accompanying enforcement roles of ICE and CBP are important in terms of USCIS's national security responsibilities within the DHS because, Hing (2006) argues, "improved immigration controls and enforcement can support good anti-terrorism enforcement, but they are not enough by themselves" (p. 212).

Just as in the mid-twentieth century when the INS was moved to the Department of Justice due to security concerns, the post-9/11 inception of the USCIS and its immigration and citizenship activities and objectives reflect the continuation of immigration policy administration movement toward national security goals. Despite this, USCIS directives relating to employment benefits still reflect the bent of initial immigration policies of the nascent nation in protecting the employment of current citizens through the execution of employment access controls and eligibility programs. Freed from primary enforcement duties, the USCIS is thus charged with the additional role of supporting immigration-related cultural and integration goals.

Further Reading

DeSipio, L., & de la Garza, R. (2015). *US immigration in the twenty-first century: Making Americans, remaking America*. Boulder: Westview Press.

Chebel d'Appollonia, A. (2012) *Frontiers of fear: Immigration and insecurity in the United States and Europe*. Ithaca: Cornell University Press.

Waters, M., & Gerstein Pineau, M. (Eds.). (2015). *The integration of immigrants in American society*. Washington: National Academies Press.

References

Callan, E., & Callan, J. (2016). Peter approved my visa, but Paul denied it: An analysis of how the recent visa bulletin crisis illustrates the madness that is U.S. immigration procedure. *DePaul Journal for Social Justice*, 9(2), 1–17.

Cárdenas, G. (1975). United States immigration policy toward Mexico: An historical perspective. *Chicana/o Latina/o Law Review*, 2, 66–91.

Donovan, T. (2005). The American immigration system: A structural change with a different emphasis. *International Journal of Refugee Law*, 17(3), 574–592.

Golub, J. (2005). Immigration reform post-9/11. *United States-Mexico Law Journal*, 13(1), 9–20.

Hing, B. (2004). *Defining America through immigration policy*. Philadelphia, PA: Temple University Press.

Hing, B. (2006). Misusing immigration policies in the name of homeland security. *CR: The New Centennial Review*, 6(1), 195–224.

Homeland Security Act of 2002, Pub. L. No. 107–296, 116 Stat. 2135 (2002).

Lehrer, E. (2004). The homeland security bureaucracy. *Public Interest*, (156), 71–85.

Mak, S. (n.d.). *Immigration and Naturalization Service* in *Densho Encyclopedia*. http://encyclopedia.densho.org/Immigration%20and%20Naturalization%20Service/

Mees, K. (n.d.). In *U.S. immigration legislation online.* http://library.uwb.edu/Static/USimmigration/1986_immigration_reform_and_control_act.html

Monger, R. & Barr, M. (2009). *Nonimmigrant admissions to the United States: 2009.* Annual Flow Report. pp. 1–10. Department of Homeland Security: Office of Immigration Statistics

Orchowski, M. (2008). *Immigration and the American dream: Battling the political hype and hysteria.* Lanham, MD: Rowman and Littlefield Publishers, Inc.

Orth, S. (1907). The Alien Contract Labor Law. *Political Science Quarterly*, 22(1), 49–60.

Shanks, C. (2001). *Immigration and the politics of American sovereignty, 1890–1990.* Ann Arbor, MI: The University of Michigan Press.

U.S. Congress (1903a). *An act to establish the Department of Commerce and Labor.* 57th Congress, S. 2, Ch. 552. pp. 825–830. https://www.loc.gov/law/help/statutes-at-large/57th-congress/session-2/c57s2ch552.pdf

U.S. Congress (1903b). *An act to regulate the immigration of aliens into the United States.* 57th Congress, S. 2, Ch. 1012. pp. 1213–1222. https://www.loc.gov/law/help/statutes-at-large/57th-congress/session-2/c57s2ch1012.pdf

U.S. Congress (1906). *An act to establish a Bureau of Immigration and Naturalization, and to provide for a uniform rule for the naturalization of aliens throughout the United States.* 59th Congress, S. 2, Ch. 3592. pp. 596–607. https://www.loc.gov/law/help/statutes-at-large/59th-congress/session-1/c59s1ch3592.pdf

U.S. Congress (1990). *Immigration Act of 1990.* 101st Congress, S. 358. https://www.congress.gov/bill/101st-congress/senate-bill/358/text

USCIS (n.d.). *USCIS service and office locator.* https://egov.uscis.gov/crisgwi/go?action=offices.type&OfficeLocator.office_type=SC

USCIS (2012). *Overview of INS history.* https://www.uscis.gov/history-and-genealogy/our-history/our-history

USCIS (2015a, July 14). *What we do.* https://www.uscis.gov/about-us/what-we-do

USCIS (2015b, September 15). *Welcome to the United States: A guide for new immigrants* (USCIS Publication No. M-618). Washington, DC: U.S. Government Publishing Office.

USCIS (2016, November 16). *USCIS strategic plan.* https://www.uscis.gov/sites/default/files/USCIS/About%20Us/Budget%2C%20Planning%20and%20Performance/USCIS_2017-2021_Strategic_Plan.pdf

USCIS (2017a, April 18). *Service centers.* https://www.uscis.gov/tools/glossary/service-centers

USCIS (2017b, September 28). *Field offices.* https://www.uscis.gov/about-us/find-uscis-office/field-offices

USCIS (2017c, December 6). *Leadership.* https://www.uscis.gov/about-us/leadership

USCIS (2017d, July 20). *What is E-Verify.* https://www.uscis.gov/e-verify/what-e-verify

USCIS (2018), February 22). *About us.* Retrieved from https://www.uscis.gov/aboutus

Wasem, R. (2011). *Visa security policy: Roles of the Departments of State and Homeland Security.* Washington, DC: Congressional Research Service Publication.

Chapter 89

United States–Mexico Border Fence

Gordon Alley-Young
Kingsborough Community College – City University of New York, New York, NY, United States

Contents

Introduction ... 675
The History and Origins of the US–Mexico Border Fence ... 676
Arguments against the Fence ... 677
Arguments in Favor of the Fence ... 679
Variations in Construction and Implementation of the Fence ... 681
Current and Future Implications of the Fence ... 682
Further Reading ... 682
References ... 683

Introduction

In 1996, the Clinton administration introduced the Illegal Immigration Reform and Immigrant Responsibility Act (IIRIRA) with an initial mandate of constructing 14 miles of triple-layered fencing spanning the Tijuana–San Diego border (i.e., the first 14 miles of US border starting from the Pacific Ocean) to replace a ten-foot single-layer welded steel fence built in 1993 that had proven permeable and thus ineffective at halting undocumented border crossers. Subsequently, The Secure Fence Act of 2006 was signed into law by George W. Bush requesting extending this border fence significantly to cover other high-traffic US–Mexico border crossing points. Advocates of the fence argued that it was key in helping to control the flow of illegal drugs and the violence related to it, undocumented immigrants, and refugees fleeing violence in Latin America. Alternately, critics of the fence, some of whom have mounted legal

DOI: 10.4324/9781315144511-93

challenges to the fence, argue that it splits families and communities, damages small business and economies, and endangers the lives of refugees and undocumented immigrants as the fence makes crossing the border more difficult and dangerous. Environmentalists have questioned also the impact of the fence on the environment and wildlife. The fence is perhaps better described as fences as is not constructed uniformly meaning that different sections of the fence use different materials and construction materials; it has been constructed in sections at different times rather than as one singular fence, and areas of the fence have no fence in place. In some sections of the fence, it is not so much a physical construction as a combination of digital sensors and surveillance technology or rather a virtual fence. Different administrations have taken different perspectives on the fence, including President Donald Trump articulating his wishes to replace the border fence with an impenetrable border wall.

The History and Origins of the US–Mexico Border Fence

While the US–Mexico border was formally established in 1824, the United States did not initiate an official border patrol until 1924 with the creation of inspection and holding stations at key border crossings. In the subsequent decades following the establishment of border patrols, lengths of chain link and steel fencing topped with barbed wire were erected at high-traffic border crossings while in remote areas, landscape features like rivers or valleys and/or armed border guard patrols often served as the only barriers. In the early 1990s, increased attention to undocumented immigration and cross-border smuggling lead to the construction of more lengths of steel fencing and increased border patrols, but fence construction was not being done consistently across the border, leading to a patchwork of different fence types with varying permeability levels and vast border areas left unfenced. It was thought that more uniform and impenetrable fencing of the border would require a financing and coordination at the level of the federal government.

In 1996, the US government authorized the construction of a triple-layer fence along the US–Mexico border, first focusing on 14 miles of the Tijuana–San Diego border, under IIRIRA, to stem the tide of undocumented immigrants and illegal drugs from Mexico and Latin America. The US government allowed the property required for the fence to be acquired under eminent domain. The resulting fence thus now in some cases cuts across what once were family farms and private properties. In 2005, the House of Representatives passed Republican Congressman Duncan Hunter's amendment to the Border Protection, Antiterrorism, and Illegal Control Act (BPAICA) and expanded the originally proposed 14 miles of fence by requesting a border fence at key US–Mexico border crossing locations. The then recently created Department of Homeland Security (DHS) was charged with building the fence. By June 2009, a reported 633 miles of the originally intended 700 miles of fence had been constructed with the exception of the Rio Grande Valley. There are around 2,000 miles of shared US–Mexico border with varying estimates of around 650 miles of border fence currently existing. In wanting to expand this project, Arizona raised just over $100,000 by 2011 that grew to around $265,000 by 2013 to build its own fence. As this latter figure was not enough to build a fence, a legislative panel was convened to consider other uses for the monies, including border security.

In addition to the border fence, over 21,000 guards were patrolling US borders by 2013 (4,000 more than 2009). These guards utilized 300 surveillance towers and 10 surveillance drones in both cases double the number used in 2009. The border fence idea, as noted, was first proposed under President Clinton administration in the current era. President George W. Bush's administration continued and expanded the project while President Obama's administration did not refund the project, although the administration committed to complete work and contracts already initiated. President Trump advocates replacing the border fence with an impenetrable border wall. The United States is reported to have 7,000 miles of land border, 95,000 miles of shore, and 328 ports of entry across the country.

Arguments against the Fence

There has been a sizable opposition to the US–Mexico border fence originally proposed by Bill Clinton's administration in 1996 and sizably expanded under George W. Bush's administration 10 years later. This opposition is based on a variety of factors. Those opposed to the fence cite that it will separate families, endanger the lives of refugees and undocumented immigrants, hurt struggling economies and small businesses, violate citizens' private property rights, and harm wildlife and the environment. International opposition to the fence reportedly came from the eighth and last Premier of the USSR, Mikhail Gorbachev, who while lecturing in Texas, is reported to have referenced President Regan's opposition to The Berlin Wall and then cited the Great Wall of China and the Berlin Wall as similarly ineffectual endeavors. Arguments by others comparing the fence to The Great Wall of China and/or Berlin Wall cite not only how it will be expensive to build and maintain like these other historical barriers but also how such a structure may come to represent cultural ethnocentrism and ultimately be treated as a permeable border and not an impenetrable force as its creators might intend.

Critics of the fence complain about the lack of oversight and fairness of the land acquisition process that they argue resulted in a lack of due process. Such critics charge that the process violated individual landowners' and Native Americans' private property/land rights, that the fence divided properties on different sides of the border, and that eminent domain was practiced selectively with the most powerful landowners being the least affected. The original mandate to DHS required a consultation process with the public and other affected groups that critics say did not happen as it should have. In some cases, the DHS, responsible for building the fence, is accused of building fences within days of notifying the affected property owners and without any or enough consultation. Critics, for example, cite how the DHS held one consultation process in December 2007 as a single town meeting in Brownsville, TX, where officials entered audience comments and complaints into a computer and armed guards were present to control the audience. Critics cite lack of feedback from the officials present at the meeting and a lack of exchange in general between all those present as shortcomings of the meeting.

Critics' charges of a lack of transparency are due in part to the DHS not publishing comprehensive construction maps until summer 2009 at which time only 20 miles of fencing remained to be completed. Others argue that wealthy/politically connected landowners fared better in the eminent domain process. The River Bend Resort & Country Club in Brownsville, TX, avoided having the border fence bisect its property while private individuals living near the club had the fence cut across their property. For example, critics note how in Granjeno, TX, the fence bisected the lands of private citizens while avoiding the property of billionaire Ray L. Hunt, who was previously President George W. Bush's appointee to the Foreign Intelligence Advisory Board and a donor of $35 million toward Bush's presidential library project while private citizens who have tried to resist having the fence on their land claim publicly that government officials have characterized them negatively for their efforts.

While President Obama's administration did not extend the fence project beyond completing the previous administrations projects that were already planned and underway, they also faced criticism. Critics argued that the Obama administration followed the same practices of non-consultation and lack of transparency in their execution of the previous administration's projects. Alternately, President Trump's intended border wall, some speculate, might cut through The River Bend Resort & Country Club that managed to avoid having the border fence significantly impinging on its property, thus possibly generating criticism for the administration and border wall project from business and private interests that were not initially opposed to the border fence. Politicians from both of the major US political parties have drawn criticism for their support of the fence.

Related to the issue of land use is the environmental problems some argue the fence is causing. The fence is said to separate wildlife in the border areas from food, water, and potential breeding mates as well as interfere with seasonal migration patterns. The fence affects ecosystems like the Otay Mountain Wilderness Area and the Lower Rio Grande Valley National Wildlife Refuge areas that are a refuge for the endangered wild cat the ocelot that resemble jaguars but are of a smaller stature. The ocelot reside in Central/South America and in the US states of Arizona and Texas. The fence intersects ecosystems like the Otay Mountain Wilderness Area and the Lower Rio Grande Valley National Wildlife Refuge, a refuge for the endangered wild cat the ocelot that was at one time history hunted for its fur. Fence construction was also said to negatively affect the environment for both humans and wildlife. For instance, rock blasting done in mountainous regions resulted in waste and increased erosion that created flooding problems. Farmers on both sides of the fence claim that the fence cuts down on their opportunities to hire migrant farm workers. The fences extend into the ocean where some residents claim migrants have drowned while attempting to get around the fence.

In terms of human life, critics claim the accurate number of deaths of undocumented border crossers is not being reported. Border Patrol Statistics from 1997 to 2007 claim 7,209 lost lives at border crossings, but investigative reporters for *USA Today* claim the number is much higher. A group of reporters worked for nine months and investigating deaths in California, Arizona, New Mexico, and Texas from 2012 to 2016 to reveal how many deaths are missed, overlooked, or go unreported. Over those years, reporters claim to have found 25–300% more deaths than those reported by Border Control in three states (e.g., New Mexico's rate is 400% more than the official numbers, California's numbers were 60% more, and Arizona's were 25% more). Many of Texas jurisdictions, reporters argue, do not track migrant deaths. Often, the reporters found that migrants dying in Texas end up in unmarked graves, and DNA samples are often not taken. Border crossers on foot, sometimes called walkers, have died or faced death in the Sonoran Desert, prompting the Customs and Border Protection (CBP) to install help beacons while walkers sometimes set bush fires for warmth or to alert the authorities in order to get help.

One response to the division of families and the barrier the fence poses to migrants has come from the artistic community. In September 2017, the anonymous French artist who goes by the name JR set up an international picnic, with an eating surface emblazoned with a photo of a young child under the Deferred Action for Childhood Arrivals (DACA) program. Half the surface was on the Tecate, Mexico, side of the border, while the side was in Tecate, California. Reportedly, hundreds of people showed up on both sides of the border to break bread together in what was perceived to be a protest of the division that the fence is felt to cause.

Arguments in Favor of the Fence

Critics note that the Secure Fence Act of 2006 was signed into law by Republican President George W. Bush after being supported by both Democratic Senators like Hillary Clinton and Barrack Obama and Republican Senators like Susan Collins and John McCain, the latter of whom together with Democratic Senator Ted Kennedy sponsored legislation for guest worker status and a path to citizenship for undocumented immigrants in the United States. Those in favor of the fence claim it stems the tide of illegal drugs and undocumented immigrants from Latin America. Between 2000 and 2005, it is estimated that 850,000 undocumented immigrants entered the United States annually. In 2006, before the fence, fence supporters argue that the Yuma sector, a 118-mile section of the border in western Arizona and eastern California, was a popular crossing point for undocumented immigrants/migrants and illegal drugs and guns. CBP were challenged to stem the tide of undocumented border crossers. Now, the area has three fences, the tallest at 20 feet, floodlights, and regular patrols. Local officials reported a dramatic drop to near stoppage in the number of crossers (i.e., from 800 to 0 undocumented persons per day, from 100 to 1 undocumented persons per day) at different points along this region's border.

Some have argued, however, that one section of the border is more heavily fortified: the popular crossing points and cross-border traffic just changes its location. There is also information that suggest that by 2012 there were fewer on foot undocumented border crossers apprehended as more were said by this time to enter on tourist visas (i.e., flying or driving to the United States) and overstay their visas. The economic decline around 2012 in the United States but also worldwide might have discouraged other undocumented immigrants from crossing just as harsher state-based laws against undocumented immigrants and immigrant smugglers' fees now increased by 100% to 200%. Yet, a 2012 survey found that 70% of US-Americans wanted Obama to tighten US–Mexico border security as part of immigration reform. Some of those supporting border control via fencing point to research that argues that undocumented immigrants make up millions of workers in the US economy and that those individuals, by working for a fraction of the pay and no benefits, make it possible for employers to avoid providing the living wages and health protections that would allow US-American workers to take these jobs.

Advocates of the US–Mexico border fence also note concerns of an environmental nature. Officials have stated publicly their belief that Southern Arizona's three most destructive wildfires in 2011 occurred along major cross-border smuggling routes and that they burned over 320,000 acres of land collectively. Some point to evidence of major wildfires resulting from cross-border smuggling efforts dating back to the early 2000s (e.g., from careless use of cigarettes, matches, campfires, and/or signal/distraction fires). Fence advocates also cite the safety of citizens and property as reasons for their support. Many point to Arizona rancher Robert N. Krentz Jr., 58, who was found shot to death on March 27, 2010, while patrolling his ranch. Authorities found a hole in the nearby border fence and tracked footsteps leading 20 miles to the south in the direction of Mexico. Krentz made a radio call before his death to his brother that he was checking out someone he believed to be an illegal immigrant. Krentz's dog was critically wounded by a bullet. Similarly, drug and drug-related violence coming over the border is a major concern. In 2010, a pregnant US consular employee and her husband were murdered in Juárez while their infant was left crying in the backseat of their car; this crime was linked to cross-border drug cartels. Previous to this, Phoenix saw a spate of cross-border drug trafficking-related kidnappings in 2008. Some argue that the Mexican drug cartels' activities can be linked to crimes carried out as far away from the US–Mexico border as Anchorage, AK. In 2004, Arizona Rancher Roger Barnett was sued for allegedly violating the civil rights of undocumented individuals (accounts range from 16 to 24) whom he placed under citizen's arrest after his claims that his property had been repeatedly damaged by smugglers and undocumented immigrants using his property for passage. Barnett allegedly held a handgun at times while waiting for CBP agents to arrive. While Barnett was sued for millions for violating civil rights, he was eventually ordered to pay $87,000 in punitive damages to four of the individuals in the controversial case that was litigated in part with help from The Mexican American Legal Defense and Educational Fund.

Fence supporters point to estimates of the costs of undocumented border crossers at $74,722 per individual (with dependents $94,391), arguing that a fence or wall that prevented 200,000 single undocumented border crossers would free up almost $15 billion. As a point of comparison, estimates on the cost of President Trump's proposed border wall place construction at anywhere from $21 to $70 billion dollars. Advocates of the fence also note how more ground support is needed with the fence. Some cite how Operation Jump Start initially sent National Guard troops help fortify border fence security as well as overall border security, but that program only lasted from 2006 to 2008 when funding for it was not renewed.

Advocates of the fence also refer to Executive Order 13767 on Border Security and Immigration Enforcement Improvements that allows US government executive departments and agencies lawful means to secure the nation's southern border, prevent undocumented immigration to the United States, and to repatriate individuals with removal orders quickly and humanely. Proponents of the border fence argue that criticisms of the DHS's handling of land acquisition for the fence are due in part to the fact that their land use decisions were based on information that was too technical to be understood by the general public, thus it limited what could be disseminated in terms of information. This in turn led to a perception that the agency was not being transparent.

Variations in Construction and Implementation of the Fence

One of the most active patrol areas in the country (in terms of drugs and undocumented immigrations) is the Tucson Sector of Arizona, covering 262 miles of border. It was a testing site for the Homeland Security Department's (HSD) SBInet program, under the auspices of the Secure Border Initiative (SBI). SBI began in 2005 by DHS to further secure both physical infrastructure and digital technologies for communications/surveillance like radar, sensors, and cameras as part of SBInet. From 2005 to 2010, an estimated $800 million was spent to secure just over 5 miles of the Arizona border, leading then Homeland Security Secretary Janet Napolitano in 2010 to stay the program and call for a review. Critics have claimed publicly that the government undertook the program without first completing a cost assessment. Mobile surveillance systems (MSS) purchased under the SBInet program, with mobile sensor towers mounted on trucks, were incurred at less cost and considered to be a more successful use of technology. Some Border Patrol agents have argued that the technology, while costly, affords them more safety and effectiveness. When undocumented border crossers trip sensors, mobile cameras can surveil the individuals/groups until agents on the ground can arrive. Border Patrol also has a fleet General Atomics MQ-1, a remotely piloted aircraft (RPA) also called unmanned aerial vehicles (UAVs), and can cover vast ranges of border territory. At Sasabe, AZ, the location of a small border crossing, millions have been spent on an unsuccessful pilot project of virtual radar fence, electronic sensors, and cameras.

Often the fence is constructed of conventional construction materials such as steel, concrete, barbed wire, and combinations thereof or take the approach of having different layers of fencing (i.e., up to three) to reinforce high-traffic areas against different types of traffic (i.e., walkers, vehicles). Around 40 miles outside Ciudad Juárez, the metal fence ends about a half a mile before the Rio Grande River marks the rest of the border. Hundreds of miles in rural Texas are not fenced; for instance, Big Bend National Park through the proposed border wall could affect this area. In Tijuana, there are two border fences across the city: one made of corrugated metal and another metal fence covered in barbed or razor wire. In Nogales, the fence is better described as a wall as it is constructed out of 20-foot tall metal panels. Similarly, in El Paso, the fence is two stories of wire mesh on top of a concrete slab base. In Hidalgo, TX, the fence's construction is less cohesive and consists of a chain-link fence, a towering steel-beam fence behind the pump house with a vehicle-entry gate and an old concrete chest-high wall at the other end. In Brownsville, TX, the fence is a line of vertical spikes atop a solid concrete base. In some coastal areas, the fence extends into the ocean.

Metal portions of the fence have incurred damage and theft. In border areas like Lukeville, AZ, and Nogales, AZ, border crossers have been known to cut fences with blowtorches and place the pieces back to hide the holes so that they could be used by subsequent crossers. A former National Guardsman, Master Sgt. Robert Kelley, was convicted of stealing and selling scrap metal from the US–Mexico border fence in Arizona in 2010, was sentenced to 15 months in jail, and was required to pay over $40,000 in restitution. Between 2007 and 2008, Kelley was accused of wearing his National Guardsman uniform and using a government vehicle to steal the metal from the DHS.

Current and Future Implications of the Fence

Comparisons of the fence to The Berlin Wall cite how it too might be viewed as contrary to democracy and freedom, both values the United States has historically argued that it personifies. Businessperson and former Republican Presidential candidate Herman Cain perhaps heightened these concerns when he appeared on Meet the Press in October 2011 and suggested that his preferred border fence would be 20-feet tall and topped with electrified barbed wire. Cain later claimed the comments were made in jest and were not meant to be taken seriously. Critics charge the fence is an act of xenophobia while advocates argue it is the US exercising self-protection. Local politicians and business leaders sued DHS Secretary Michael Chertoff primarily over concerns about land acquisition to build the fence, but the Supreme Court refused to consider the case in 2009. The Supreme Court also rejected a constitutional challenge of the wall mounted by members of Congress along with environmentalists. Some individual property owners reached financial settlements with DHS in 2013 over issues relating to the eminent domain process used to places fences on and through their property.

President Donald Trump has been vocal in his desire to replace the fence with a wall. A recent Quinnipiac poll found that 64% of US-Americans oppose a wall on the border with Mexico, versus only 33% who favor it. Experts estimate the actual cost of the wall could be around $21 billion and critics in the US government argue that $21 billion would double the current federal financing of public schools or provide 6 million people with health care under Medicaid and buy school lunches for tens of millions of low-income children. Proponents of the fence argue it is helping to slow the flow of undocumented immigrants, guns, and drugs into the United States, thus keeping US-Americans safer while opponents argue that this traffic has shifted to other channels and that the financial, environmental, and human cost of the fence do not justify the possible benefits.

Further Reading

Ahmed, A., Fernandez, M., & Villegas, P. (2017, February 8). Before the wall: Life along the US-Mexico border. Retrieved from *The New York Times*. https://www.nytimes.com/interactive/2017/02/08/world/americas/before-the-wall-life-along-the-us-mexico-border.html

Dorsery, M. E. & Diaz-Barriga, M. (2010). "Beyond Surveillance and Moonscapes: An Alternative Imaginary of the U.S.–Mexico Border Wall," *Visual Anthropology Review*, *26*(2): 128–135.

Longmire, S. (2014). *Border insecurity: Why big money, fences, and drones aren't making us safer*. New York: Palgrave Macmillan.

References

Ahmed, A., Fernandez, M., & Villegas, F. (2017, February 8). Before the wall: Life along the US-Mexico border. Retrieved from *The New York Times* at https://www.nytimes.com/interactive/2017/02/08/world/americas/before-the-wall-life-along-the-us-mexico-border.html

Alter, C. (2017). Lightbox. *Time, 190*(16/17), pp. 24–25.

Congressional Digest. (2017). The pros and pons of a Mexico border wall. *Congressional Digest*, 96(8), pp. 8–29.

Drehle, D. V. (2008). A new line in the sand. *Time, 171*(26), pp. 28–35.

Dwoskin, E. (2013). Hey look, somehow the border got secured. *Bloomberg Businessweek*, (4318), pp. 21–23.

Garfield, L. (2018, June 24). 29 photos that show the US-Mexico border's evolution over 100 years. Retrieved from *Business Insider* at https://www.businessinsider.com/us-mexico-border-history-photos-2017-4

Inside Tucson Business (2011). Growing evidence says fires started by smugglers, illegal border crossers. *Inside Tucson Business, 21*(5), pp. 2–8.

Investor's Business Daily. (2010, April 8). Robert N. Krentz, border war casualty. *Investor's Business Daily*, p. A10.

Langerbein, H. (2009). Great blunders? The Great Wall of China, the Berlin Wall, and the proposed United States/Mexico border fence. *History Teacher, 43*(1), pp. 9–29.

McLeary, P. (2010). Digital defenses. *Defense Technology International, 4*(10), p. 37.

Miller, N. (2010). How property rights are affected by the Texas-Mexico Border Fence: A failure due to insufficient procedure. *Texas International Law Journal, 45*(3), pp. 631–654.

Nicol, S. (2011, February 27). Costly fence on US-Mexico border is effective – Only in hurting nature. Retrieved from *The Christian Science Monitor* at https://www.csmonitor.com/Commentary/Opinion/2011/0227/Costly-fence-on-US-Mexico-border-is-effective-only-in-hurting-nature

Nuñez-Neto, B., & Garcia, M.J. (2007, May 23). Congressional research service report for congress: Border security: The San Diego fence. Retrieved from *The Federation of American Scientists* at https://fas.org/sgp/crs/homesec/RS22026.pdf

O'Dell, R., González, D., & Castellano, J. (2017, December 27). 'Mass disaster' grows at the US-Mexico border, but Washington doesn't seem to care. Retrieved from *USA TODAY* at https://www.usatoday.com/border-wall/story/mass-disaster-grows-u-s-mexico-border/1009752001/

V

EMERGENCY PLANNING AND PREPAREDNESS AND HEALTH SECURITY

Francis Grice
McDaniel College, Westminster, MD, United States

Chapter 90

Agroterrorism

Francis Grice and Lyra Houghton
McDaniel College, Westminster, MD, United States

Contents

Introduction 687
The Threat 688
Attack Typologies 689
Disaster Potential 691
Government Legislation 692
Recommendations 694
Further Reading 695
Note 695
References 695

Introduction

Attacking the food supplies of adversaries, often with biological warfare, has long been used as a tool by states and their armies to sabotage one another. No society can function for long without adequate food supplies, and unlike soldiers and prominent members of a community, livestock and crops are generally not well guarded. The Roman Empire, for example, was known for salting and burning the fields of its enemies in order to deprive them of vital sustenance and, ultimately, starve them into submission. Similarly, during World War I, the German military reportedly sought to dramatically deplete the number of horses available to the enemy by infecting them with the disease glanders (Robbins et al., 2017, p. 17). This historical tradition continued throughout the twentieth century, with at least 13 states either having documented agricultural bioweapons programs or being widely believed to have done so.[1] While some of these have subsequently abolished these programs, others are likely to have kept them going either openly or covertly. Despite the inter-state

DOI: 10.4324/9781315144511-95

character of agricultural warfare historically, this kind of warfare today is more likely to be used by non-state actors through the medium of agroterrorism.

Agroterrorism is generally considered to stand as a subcategory of bioterrorism because the mechanism of attack involved is typically a biological agent such as a plant or animal disease (Burns, 2019). One of the most widely used definitions for the concept was provided in the early 2000s by the RAND researcher, Peter Chalk (2004), who indicated that it was "the deliberate introduction of a disease agent, either against livestock or into the food chain, to undermine socioeconomic stability and/or generate fear" (p. 1). This definition for agroterrorism has been broadly accepted within the United States government (Office of Inspector General, 2018, p. 1). An important distinction must be drawn between traditional terrorism and agroterrorism in that the former usually involves attacks on human life directly, whereas the latter typically entails a more circuitous approach in which harm is caused by infecting the animals and crops that humans depend upon for their food and, in many cases, their livelihoods.

The Threat

Agroterrorism as a method holds considerable appeal for terrorists contemplating a strike because the diseases and other substances needed to carry out such an attack are cheaper and easier to procure than many alternative biological and chemical agents. Microorganisms of the kind required can be found in naturally occurring environments around the world or can be readily created in underground laboratories by nearly anyone with experience in the field of microbiology or even just the ability to research the topic on the internet (Gill, 2015, p. 10).

Despite their ease of creation, however, agroterrorist attacks can be very difficult to detect after they have been carried out, resulting in costly delays between the time that the infection is initially transplanted into the victim crops or livestock and its eventual discovery. A good example of this can be seen in the United Kingdom, where foot and mouth was introduced (albeit unintentionally) into the bovine population of the country. A full 2 weeks passed between the moment when the first animal caught the disease and the point when the outbreak was finally identified (Gilpen et al., 2008, p. 193). This allows for the disease to grow dramatically beyond the immediate vicinity of where the attack occurred, carried by the movement and interaction of grazing animals, cross-pollination of plants, and other natural movements, as discussed below. This lag also provides the attacker with more time to distance themselves from the attack and reduces the chance that they will be identified and apprehended (Gilpen et al., 2009, p. 192). Moreover, once the attack has been detected, it has the potential to exert not only devastating agricultural and economic damage upon the country, but also cause widespread fear and panic among the population (Haralampos et al., 2013, p. 20).

Compounding the problem, America's agribusinesses are mostly organized in such a way that makes them uniquely vulnerable to an agroterrorist attack. Livestock are raised in close quarters, giving diseases the chance to thrive and spread at a rapid pace, while pathogens can be easily spread from farm to farm, as farmers often share equipment such as vehicles and medical tools to save on costs. Consequently, if a piece of equipment were to become contaminated at one farm, the contaminant could easily spread to whatever farm used it next (Olson, 2012, pp. 5-6). Obtaining and placing a disease into populations of livestock would be far easier than many would like to believe. As Grote (2007) notes in relation to food-and-mouth disease (2007), for example:

> ...can be found in as many as 60% of the countries of the world and is endemic in Africa, the Middle East, Asia and many South American nations.... Through purchase of an FMD infected animal in one of these countries, isolating the virus from one of the infected vesicles or blisters on the animal, and then transporting that virus on just about any medium, it could easily be re-introduced into the US. Simply by stopping on a highway in rural America and releasing the virus among curious livestock an outbreak could be initiated. Due to its virility, close contact or direct introduction by this simple means could produce devastating results.
>
> (pp. 7–8)

Foot-and-mouth disease would be attractive to terrorists for other reasons too, including that it does not usually pose a threat to humans, meaning that terrorists can handle it safely. It can also be transmitted through multiple mediums, including feed, the location of infected animals, equipment used to handle those animals, and of course the animals themselves. Moreover, there is no need for extensive weaponization because in a disease case like this, the animal *becomes* the weapon.

Livestock and other animals are not the only targets that are susceptible to attack. Crops, fisheries, foresting industries, and processing industries could also prove to be alluring targets due to their ease of access. Diseases and pests such as invasive insects, for example, could be quickly and quietly introduced into any plant crop. These plant infections or swarms of pests could rapidly spread through the agricultural and agribusiness sections.

Moreover, the food-processing industry is highly centralized. In many cases, a single central facility may export equipment and other resources to hundreds of farms and may receive stock from an equal number of farms in return. A single farm's contaminated stock, when sent to that facility, will therefore have the potential to contaminate hundreds of customers in turn. The step-by-step process of food production, processing, packaging, distribution, and sale, along with all of the transportation involved in between each part, provides ample opportunity for terrorists to target stock (Robbins et al., 2017, p. 19). Even the way that livestock and crops are crammed together while in transit is problematic, with overly crowded containers bringing infected and uninfected animals into close contact with one another, leading to inevitable cross-contamination (Thomas, 2018, p. 1).

Attack Typologies

While agroterrorism could theoretically be carried out by any individual or group with the right motivation and ability to manufacture, steal, or purchase diseased materials, Knowles et al. (2005) identify five main groups that are most likely to undertake such an attack. These are

> International terrorists, such as al-Qaeda, [who] pose the most probable threat for an intentional introduction of a foreign animal disease; 2. Domestic terrorists, such as anarchist or anti-government groups, [who] could be motivated to cripple the livestock industry; 3. Militant animal rights groups [who] could view an outbreak of a foreign animal disease as a positive event to promote their cause; 4. Economic opportunists [who] could financially benefit from a dramatic impact or change in market prices; and 5. Disgruntled employees [who] could attack some segment of the livestock industry for revenge.
>
> (p. 5)

While the United States has not suffered from a substantial case of international agroterrorism to date, the threat remains acute. Transnational terrorist groups such as al-Qaeda at its height often have more organization and financing than lone domestic terrorists or loosely organized animal rights extremists, meaning that an attack from one would likely be far more impactful. According to an FBI analysis, transnational groups present "the most probable threat of inflicting economic harm on the United States" via agroterrorism (Olson, 2012, p. 2). This belief was driven at least in part by the discovery by American and Allied forces report the discovery of "U.S. agricultural documents and al Qaeda training manuals targeting agriculture" in former al-Qaeda sanctuaries in Afghanistan (Olson, 2012, p. 1).

With regards to domestic agroterrorism, the United States has suffered from several notable attacks. One such attack occurred in 1970, when a domestic terrorist group poisoned the water supply of a farm in Alabama owned by a group of African American Muslims, leading to the death of 30 cows (Calum et al., 2003, p. 23). Another prominent incident occurred in 1984, when a religious cult led by Bhagwan Shree Rajneesh contaminated a range of salad bars with *Salmonella* across Dallas in Oregon, with the goal of preventing citizens from voting in the upcoming local elections, leading 751 people to become ill (Calum et al., 2003, p. 24).

Radical animal and environmental rights groups have also been known to carry out agroterrorist attacks. One notable incident involved the deliberate release of 30–40,000 minks from a Minnesota pelt farm in 2017, leading to thousands of animals dying in the world from heat stress. Those that were recaptured were placed hurriedly back into the pens, without any effort being made to maintain the same groupings as had existed before the attack. The unfamiliar social settings led the recaptured mink to then fight and kill one another. From their investigations, the FBI and other law enforcement personnel came to suspect that the perpetrator of the attack was a group of animal rights activists, with the ALF (the Animal Liberation Front) fitting the profile quite strongly (Thieme, 2017). This group and its affiliates like the Environmental Liberation Front (ELF) depend on a loose cell structure made of unaffiliated members who do not coordinate closely with one another, despite pursuing a common goal.

One example of agroterrorism by disgruntled employees in the United States happened in 1996, when a cow carcass was intentionally contaminated with the pesticide chlordane and was slipped into a supply of other carcasses intended for processing at a Wisconsin rendering plant. Chlordane, a food adulterant at the low level of 0.3 ppm, accumulates quickly in animal fat and so was an effective agent. The polluted carcasses were mixed into livestock feed and dispatched to over 4,000 farms over an area of four different states, most of which were dairy farms. After the perpetrator sent letters to customers and local officials explaining what he had done, large amounts of butter, ice cream, and cheese were recalled, and over $4 million was spent on destroying all of the food produced and all of the possibly contaminated feed. In total, the rendering facility's costs amounted to over $250 million by the end of the ordeal (Neher, 1999, pp. 181–183). The perpetrator turned out to be a disgruntled competitor whose wife had had an affair with someone at the rendering facility. A similar story happened in Wisconsin again one year later, when the owner of a food-processing plant deliberately contaminated animal grease that was to be used in feed at a rival facility. The contaminated feed, once again, had to be recalled, costing the supplier a considerable amount of money (Pate and Cameron, 2003, p. 202).

Disaster Potential

Although some agroterrorism attacks have already happened in the United States, these have been predominantly limited affairs. A better understanding of the full scope of the threat can be gleaned by considering some of the cases of accidental contamination of livestock and agriculture with diseases that have impacted both the United States and the world during the modern era. One particularly notable case occurred in Taiwan in 1997, when the country experienced an outbreak of foot-and-mouth disease in pigs and cattle that spread rapidly throughout the entire region. The damage done cost farmers $4 billion and the Taiwanese economy an estimated $15 billion in resulting trade embargoes (Agroterrorism: The Threat to America's Breadbasket, 2003, p. 2). A similar outbreak in Britain in 2001 cost the equivalent of $1.6 billion to the government in compensation to farmers, and the psychological impact on tourism rates in the country is estimated to have cost a further $4 billion (Agroterrorism: The Threat to America's Breadbasket, 2003, p. 2). The United States has not been immune to these kinds of calamity, with the exotic Newcastle disease that erupted in the poultry industry in California in 2002, resulting in a 46,000 quarantine zone being erected within the state. This outbreak was caused by an unknowingly infected rooster entering the population (Agroterrorism: The Threat to America's Breadbasket, 2003, p. 2). These outbreaks have been devastating, yet a purposely engineered bioweapon would likely be even further reaching than these accidental epidemics.

Moreover, like all types of terrorism, agroterrorism does not exist simply to destroy the amount of stock it does; the more far-reaching effects are the real intent. A quarantine of stock, culling of contaminated and potentially contaminated stock, loss in compensations, possible threat to human health, and potential international protective embargoes all contribute to massive monetary losses as well as a loss of faith and trust in the industry. Tourism numbers may decline, as seen in the 2001 UK outbreak; this too will damage the economy. All of this physical, psychological, and economic damage is massive compared to the immediate physical cost of the attack, making agroterrorism an even more attractive option for terrorists to consider.

Government Legislation

Since agroterrorism first became recognized as a security concern for the United States, the government has not been inactive. The first federal legislation to address the idea that protecting the critical infrastructure of the United States should be viewed as a national security task was the 1998 Presidential Decision Directive 63 (PDD-63), yet this did not specifically discuss food and agriculture (Monke, 2007, p21). The Farm Security and Rural Investment Act in March 2002 helped to rectify this omission by allocating funds for research and education efforts toward improving the biosecurity of the US food and agricultural system. It also placed an emphasis upon building long-term partnerships with higher education institutions to improve planning, training, outreach, and research into risk assessments, incident response, and technologies related to detection and prevention against these kinds of attack (Farm Security and Rural Investment Act, 2003, p. 321).

The mainstay of the US efforts to respond to agroterrorism as a threat was, however, not fully initiated until the passage of the Public Health Security and Bioterrorism Preparedness and Response Act in June 2002 and the Homeland Security Act in November 2002. The former aimed to regulate the possession, use, and transfer of biological agents and toxins that could threaten human, animal, and plant health (Animal and Plant Health Inspection Service, 2017). The latter created the Department of Homeland Security and included within its broad remit the monitoring and protecting of the food and agricultural systems in the United States against biological and chemical attacks (Homeland Security Act, 2002).

As a result of these two acts, all government agencies, companies, other organizations, and individuals that possess or come into contact with such substances are required to register with The Animal and Plant Health Inspection Service (APHIS), which possesses the lead responsibility for carrying out the provision of the Homeland Security Act within the US Department of Agriculture (USDA) (Animal and Plant Health Inspection Service, 2017). Veterinary Services and Plant Protection and Quarantine also play a key role by identifying and monitoring those agents and toxins that have been designated as representing a severe threat to animal or plant health and products, respectively. Agents and toxins that threaten both humans and animals ("overlap agents") are overseen jointly by APHIS and the Centers for Disease Control and Prevention (CDC), which has the primary responsibility for implementing the provisions of the Bioterrorism Response Act for the Department of Health and Human Services (HHS) (Federal Select Agent Program, 2017).

Supplementing this formal legislation are the various Homeland Security Policy Directives (HSPDs) that were enacted by the President following the Homeland Security Act. Of these, HSPD-5, HSPD-7, and HSPD-9 have proved particularly meaningful for guiding and shaping government policy relating to protecting and responding to threats against the United States food and agricultural system from agroterrorism.

HSPD-5 did not address agroterrorism specifically, but was notable in this regard for its call for the government to establish a National Incident Management System (NIMS) and a National Response Plan (NPR) (now superseded by a National Response Framework [NPF]) (Bush 2003a). These were intended to provide a coherent approach for federal, state, and local governments to work together in order to respond to any and all domestic incidents, such as natural disasters, terrorist attacks, and other emergencies, including through collaborative organization, effective training, and forward planning. (Bush 2003a). Both NIMS and the NPR/NPF have been integral in encouraging and facilitating the development of mechanisms to identify, protect against, and respond to agroterrorist incidents. In particular, following the subsequent enactment of HSPD-9, APHIS created a dedicated National Response Management Team (NRMT), which it tasked with providing leadership in the event of a national agricultural emergency, including supplying "leadership and safety; (b) guidance for disease surveillance and eradication; (c) resource identification and acquisition; (d) resolution of administrative and policy issues associated with emergency response; and (e) coordination and dissemination of information" (Gilpen et al., 2009, p. 190).

HSPD-7 addressed agroterrorism a little more directly through its establishment of a national policy for Federal departments and agencies to identify and prioritize critical infrastructure and to protect them from terrorist attacks. As part of its provisions, the Directive allocated six sector-specific agencies that would be responsible for identifying and protecting key areas of critical infrastructure. These included the Departments of Agriculture (USDA) for agriculture, meat, poultry, and eggs; the Department of Health and Human Services (DHHS) for other forms of food; and the Environmental Protection Agency (EPA) for drinking water and water treatment systems. The work of each agency was to collaborate with the Department of Homeland Secretary and all relevant government and private sector entities to conduct and facilitate vulnerability assessments and risk management strategies against attacks on this area (Bush 2003b). HSPD-7 has since been superseded by Presidential Policy Directive (PPD) 21, which lays into place a similar policy alignment, while attempting to further "strengthen and maintain secure, functioning, and resilient critical infrastructure." Of note, the Directive places the USDA and the DHHS as being co-sector-specific agencies for food and agriculture and the EPA for water and water treatment systems (The White House, 2013).

HSPD-9 honed in much more specifically on the defense of agriculture and food in the United States and begins with an explicit acknowledgement that

> The United States agriculture and food systems are vulnerable to disease, pest, or poisonous agents that occur naturally, are unintentionally introduced, or are intentionally delivered by acts of terrorism. America's agriculture and food system is an extensive, open, interconnected, diverse, and complex structure providing potential targets for terrorist attacks. We should provide the best protection possible against a successful attack on the United States agriculture and food system, which could have catastrophic health and economic effects.
>
> (Bush, 2004)

It also identified a variety of specific departments and agencies that should take responsibility for mitigating these risks as well as how these organizations should work together and what kinds of tasks that they should carry out (Bush 2004). These included the Department of Agriculture, the Department of Health and Human Services, the Department of Homeland Security, the Environmental Protection Agency, and the Central Intelligence Agency, as well as any other departments or agencies that may have relevance to a particular area (Bush 2004; Gilpen et al., 2009, p. 189). These included

> (a) identifying and prioritizing sector-critical infrastructure and key resources for establishing protection requirements; (b) developing awareness and early warning capabilities to recognize threats; (c) mitigating vulnerabilities at critical production and processing nodes; (d) enhancing screening procedures for domestic and imported products; and (e) enhancing response and recovery procedures.
>
> (Bush 2004)

Recommendations

These acts and directives demonstrate that the United States government and its agencies have at least partially recognized the magnitude of the threat posed by agroterrorism and have made a reasonably concerted effort to mitigate the risks and minimize the impact of any such attack. Their efforts to regulate and monitor the possession and use of potentially deleterious biological agents, as well as assigning responsibility for protection against agroterrorism to various agencies, are generally commendable. The absence of any major incidents of agroterrorism on American soil, beyond the comparatively minor incidents mentioned above, could be taken as proof of effectiveness.

Yet, the agricultural industry itself remains inherently vulnerable. As long as farms and related agribusinesses continue to be organized in a fashion that involves high levels of centralization, entails the widespread sharing of tools, eschews a number of key security practices, and embraces use of other practices mentioned in this chapter, they will remain at risk. A single successful attack could snowball into a major catastrophe for not only the sector, but for the country as a whole.

To forestall such a disaster, the US government will need to invest yet further energy and resources into raising awareness among individual farmers, agricultural organizations, and other players within the "farm to fork" good system of the United States about the threat of agroterrorism and how to protect against it. In particular, they should highlight the risks of certain practices, such as excessive condensing of livestock during transportation and over-centralization of food processing. They should also share more information about safer alternatives and provide incentives for adopting these other practices. Without efforts being made in this direction, the food and agricultural community is likely to remain vulnerable to a major agroterrorist attack for the foreseeable future.

Further Reading

Moats, J. B. (2007). *Agroterrorism: A Guide for First Responders*. College Station, TX: Texas A&M University Press. Retrieved from https://search.ebscohost.com/login.aspx?direct=true&db=cat01961a&AN=HLC.1570616&site=eds-live.

Seebeck, L. (2007). Responding to Systemic Crisis: The Case of Agroterrorism. *Studies in Conflict & Terrorism, 30*(8), 691–721. Retrieved from https://doi.org/10.1080/10576100701200165.

Shrivastava, A. (2016). The Rising Threat of Agroterrorism. *International Policy Digest, 3*(10), 95–96. Retrieved from https://search.ebscohost.com/login.aspx?direct=true&db=poh&AN=119558489&site=eds-live.

Note

1 The nine states with documented programs were Canada, France, Germany, Iraq, Japan, South Africa, United
Kingdom, United States, and the former USSR, while the four states that are suspected to have possessed them were Egypt, North Korea, Rhodesia, and Syria.

References

Agroterrorism: The Threat to America's Breadbasket. (2003). *Hearing before the Senate Committee on Governmental Affairs*, U. S. Senate, 108th Congress, pp. 108–491.

Animal and Plant Health Inspection Service. (2017). *Agricultural Bioterrorism Protection Act of 2002; Biennial Review and Republication of the Select Agent and Toxin List; Amendments to the Select Agent and Toxin Regulations* (RIN 0579-AE08). Retrieved from https://www.federalregister.gov/documents/2017/01/19/2017-00857/agricultural-bio terrorism-protection-act-of-2002-biennial-review-and-republication-of-the-select

Burns, B. E. (2019). Florida Law Enforcement's Role in Agroterrorism. *The Journal of the NPS Center for Homeland Defense and Security, 15*. Retrieved from https://www.hsaj.org/articles/3341.

Bush, G. W. (2003a). *Homeland Security Presidential Directive/HSPD-5: Management of Domestic Incidents*. Retrieved from https://fas.org/irp/offdocs/nspd/hspd-5.html

Bush, G. W. (2003b). *Homeland Security Presidential Directive / HSPD-7: Critical Infrastructure Identification, Prioritization, and Protection*. Retrieved from https://fas.org/irp/offdocs/nspd/hspd-7.html

Bush, G. W. (2004). *Homeland Security Presidential Directive / HSPD-9: Defense of United States Agriculture and Food*. Retrieved from https://fas.org/irp/offdocs/nspd/hspd-9.html

Chalk, P. (2004). *Agroterrorism: What Is the Threat and What Can Be Done About It?*. Santa Monica, CA: RAND Corporation.

Farm Security and Rural Investment Act of 2002. (2003). Proceedings of the 107th Congress. P. L, 107–171.

Federal Select Agent Program. (2017). *Select Agents and Toxins*. Retrieved from https://www.selectagents.gov/SelectAgentsandToxins.html

Gill, K. M. (2015). Agroterrorism: The Risks to the United States Food Supply and National Security. *U. S. Army Medical Department Journal*, 9–15. Retrieved from https://search.ebscohost.com/login.aspx?direct=true&db=cmedm&AN=25651140&site=eds-live

Gilpen, J. L., Jr., Carabin, H., Regens, J. L., & Burden, R. W., Jr. (2009). Agriculture Emergencies: A Primer for First Responders. *Biosecurity and Bioterrorism: Biodefense Strategy, Practice, and Science*, *7*(2), 187–198. Retrieved from https://search.ebscohost.com/login.aspx?direct=true&db=edsgao&AN=edsgcl.205567122&site=eds-live

Grote Jr., J. H. (2007). *Agroterrorism: Preparedness and Response Challenges for the Departments of Defense and the Army*. AEPI and USAWC Research Paper. Arlington, VA: Army Environmental Policy Institute.

Homeland Security Act of 2002. (2002). Proceedings of the 107th Congress P. L, pp. 107–296.

Keremidis, H., Appel, B., Menrath, A., Tomuzia, K., Normark, M., Roffey, R., & Knutsson, R. (2013). Historical Perspective on Agroterrorism: Lessons Learned from 1945 to 2012. *Biosecurity & Bioterrorism: Biodefense Strategy, Practice, & Science*, *11*(1), 17–24. Retrieved from https://search.ebscohost.com/login.aspx?direct=true&db=edo&AN=89926012&site=eds-live

Knowles, T., Lane, J., Bayens, G. Speer, N., Jaax, J., Carter, D., and Bannister, A. (2005). *Defining Law Enforcement's Role in Protecting American Agriculture from Agroterrorism*. Washington DC: National Institute of Justice.

Monke, J. (2007). *Agroterrorism: Threats and Preparedness* (CRS Report No. RL32521). Retrieved from https://fas.org/sgp/crs/terror/RL32521.pdf

Neher, N. J. (1999). The Need for a Coordinated Response to Food Terrorism. The Wisconsin Experience. *Annals of the New York Academy of Sciences*, *894*(1), 181–183. Retrieved from https://search.ebscohost.com/login.aspx?direct=true&db=cmedm&AN=10681988&site=eds-live

Office of Inspector General. (2018). *USDA Agency Activities for Agroterrorism Prevention, Detection, and Response* (Audit Report 50701-0001-21). Retrieved from https://www.usda.gov/oig/webdocs/50701-0001-21.pdf

Olson, D. (2012). Agroterrorism: Threats to America's Economy and Food Supply. *FBI Law Enforcement Bulletin*, *81*(2), 1–9. Retrieved from https://search.ebscohost.com/login.aspx?direct=true&db=f5h&AN=72102596&site=eds-live

Pate, J. & Cameron, G. (2003). Covert Biological Weapons Attacks against Agricultural Targets: Assessing the Impact against U. S. Agriculture. In Howitt, A. M. and Pangi, R. (Eds.), *Countering Terrorism: Dimensions for Preparedness* (195–218). Cambridge, MA: MIT Press.

Robbins, J. M., Olexa, M. T., & Grant, L. (2017). Flyover: The Potential Impact of Agroterrorism and Bioterrorism within Agricultural Aerial Application Operations. *Florida Bar Journal*, *91*(8), 16–23. Retrieved from https://search.ebscohost.com/login.aspx?direct=true&db=a9h&AN=124880501&site=eds-live

The White House. (2013). *Presidential Policy Directive -- Critical Infrastructure Security and Resilience*. Retrieveed from https://obamawhitehouse.archives.gov/the-press-office/2013/02/12/presidential-policy-directive-critical-infrastructure-security-and-resil

Thieme, N. (2017). Misguided Attempt to Free Thousands of Minks Goes Horribly Wrong. *Slate Magazine*. Retrieved from https://slate.com/technology/2017/07/thousands-of-minks-die-after-being-set-free.html

Thomas, J. (2018). *A Quick Glance at Agroterrorism Response*. Retrieved from http://dx.doi.org/10.2139/ssrn.3175579.

Turvey, C. G., Mafoua, E., Schilling, B. J., & Onyango, B. M. (2003). Economics, Hysteresis And Agroterrorism (This is Food Policy Institute Working Paper No. WP0703-011). *Paper Presented at the Canadian Agricultural Economics Society 2003 Annual Meeting Montreal, Quebec July 27-30, 2003*.

Chapter 91

Anthrax

Péter Marton
Corvinus University of Budapest, Budapest, Hungary

Contents

Introduction 697
The Nature of the Pathogen 698
The Threat of Bioaggression 700
Ease of Access 700
Difficulty of Weaponization 700
Possibility of Clandestine Dispersal 702
Uncertain Rate of Mortality in the Target Area 702
Low Probability of Onward Transmission 703
Difficulty of Decontamination 703
Conclusion 704
Further Reading 705
References 705

Introduction

This chapter consists of two parts. The first considers the nature of the anthrax pathogen, including the characteristics of its endospore form, the types of infection it may cause, the difficulties of differential diagnosis, the role of the exotoxins secreted by anthrax bacteria, and the presence and occurrence of anthrax disease worldwide. The second part provides a strategic overview of the parameters of the threat that are the most relevant to United States Homeland Security – which both prospective agents of bioaggression and those defending against them will typically consider. This is intertwined with a discussion of some of the cases of past use of the pathogen by various agents and other incidents of note, as well as with a normative discussion of the necessary measures and actions in response to the threat. The concluding section of the chapter briefly considers the impact of two developments, the ongoing

DOI: 10.4324/9781315144511-96

biotechnological revolution and the spread of antimicrobial resistance, on the threat posed by *Bacillus anthracis*.

The Nature of the Pathogen

In his 1932 novel *Brave New World*, Aldous Huxley attributed major philosophical significance to anthrax bombs (aerial bombs with anthrax spores attached to feathers around the explosive payload). This was connected by him to a broader criticism of human development as he reflected on how the liberty that enables human progress ultimately brings about scientific developments of questionable value: developments that may serve not civilization but its ultimate destruction one day. "What's the point of truth or beauty or knowledge when anthrax bombs are popping all around you?", he raises the question, at one point, through one of his story's characters. Huxley, who had contacts among British scientists with knowledge of the fledgling biological weapons programs of the era, was well-informed about the potential of anthrax as a biological weapon. To survive in the environment, *B. anthracis*, i.e., the anthrax bacterium, can reduce itself to a structural state called endospore, making it highly resistant to heat, radiation, desiccation, freezing, and to some extent even chemical disinfectants. It can even withstand some damage, thanks to DNA repair enzymes at its disposal.

It is not impossible to kill the endospores, but certainly difficult. British experiments with anthrax bombs on Gruinard Island (Northern Scotland), starting in 1941, left the area a no-go zone up till 1990. The 48 years of quarantine came to an end upon a costly decontamination effort that took 4 years to be completed, from 1986 to 1990. The quarantine did not function perfectly, and it was later admitted that on one occasion, after the carcass of an infected sheep washed ashore from the island, this led to the perishing of "seven cattle, two horses, three cats and up to 50 sheep in a nearby village" (Norton-Taylor, 1990).

The long survival of endospores was recently demonstrated in Siberia, Russia. It was reported in August 2016 that Russian authorities there suspected the carcass of a reindeer killed by anthrax 75 years ago, emerging from under a narrow layer of permafrost after a heat wave thawed the frozen soil, to have been the source of an anthrax outbreak affecting as many as 2,000 reindeer at the time. This even forced the evacuation of a number of families from the sparsely populated area (Doucleff, 2016).

The ability of the pathogen to remain a latent threat in the environment was also seen in the context of the 2001 series of anthrax mail attacks in the United States (the "Amerithrax" case by its FBI case name). The circumstances of the exposure of two victims (Kathy Nguyen and Ottilie Lundgren) to inhalation anthrax infection by the Ames strain of anthrax are not known with certainty to this day. This also poses the question of what is the minimal amount of anthrax spores required to develop an infection, given the possibility that the two victims may have been accidentally exposed to a very low number of spores only.

Three common types of clinical infection may develop once exposure to a sufficient number of spores happens. The type of infection depends on the site of exposure, with infection leading either to cutaneous anthrax (infection of the skin, being the most common and also the least deadly form of the disease if treatment is provided), to gastrointestinal anthrax (the least common but considerably more lethal), or to inhalation anthrax (affecting the lungs and the lymph nodes, being the most lethal form of infection).

The latter form of the disease, respiratory/pulmonary infection via inhalation, kills most of those affected unless antibiotic treatment is provided early. The MLD or the median lethal dose is currently estimated at around several thousand spores in the case of inhalation anthrax, with a single spore measuring one micron or 1 μm. Note that the issue of how to determine the minimum infective dose as well as the median lethal dose is subject to major conceptual and methodological debates. The cautious assessment has to be that even a single spore may cause lethal infection, if it reaches the right spot. The probability is low, but the possibility cannot be ruled out.

Timely treatment is unlikely in the initial cases due to the challenges of differential diagnosis. As long as medical personnel do not become aware of a cluster of cases showing the signature signs of an acute phase of sickness being followed by temporary improvement before relapse, or sudden death, the symptoms may be interpreted as those of a flu-like infection. Once anthrax is suspected, and testing for the presence of *B. anthracis* or antibodies occurs, the results may be available within 24 hours (Rider, 2005: 20). Chest X-rays showing characteristic changes in the tissues around the mediastinal lymph nodes may also be revealing of an anthrax infection (Rider, 2005: 19).

The first non-distinctive symptoms of inhalation anthrax may take from anywhere between 2 and 7 days (at a minimum) and up to or over 60 days to appear. Given that the first acute stage of the disease may last several days, detection may occur only weeks after the exposure incident which led to the infection of the index case. The possibility of cutaneous and other types of anthrax infections also has to be kept in mind as such infections may also result from the same exposure incident; this may be relevant with a view to detecting cases of deliberate release in acts of bioaggression, too.

Death ultimately occurs due to two toxins produced by the anthrax bacteria: these are the combinations of three protein components, a protective antigen (PA), and two other types of protein ("edema factor" and "lethal factor"). PA with the edema factor combines into "edema toxin," and PA with the lethal factor combines into "lethal toxin". These toxins are used by the bacteria to promote host infection by damaging tissues and disabling the immune response. They are secreted by live bacteria and are thus referred to as "exotoxins"(as opposed to endotoxins that are typically part of bacteria's outer membrane and are released only once a bacterium is killed by the immune system).

Due to the need for exposure to a significant number of spores for a major infection to develop, anthrax often appears as an occupational disease (note that it is traditionally referred to as "wool-sorters' disease"). If appropriate precautions are taken, infection may not result even upon handling the carcass of an animal killed by anthrax. A differential probability of infection is thus observed in regions of the world stemming from the poor veterinary supervision of the handling of carcasses (which also creates a vulnerability to agro-terrorism) as well as due to poverty and malnutrition compelling people to consume the meat of animals that have died of disease (WHO, 2018: 36-37). Only 18 cases of naturally acquired inhalation anthrax were recorded in the United States in the 20th century (WHO, 2018: 43; note that this figure does not include subclinical infections which may have gone unregistered).

Animal anthrax (affecting mostly grazing herbivores) is endemic in major parts of the world, however, including in the Middle East, equatorial Africa, parts of South America, and China, *inter alia*. The disease sporadically occurs elsewhere as well. In the United States, outbreaks among animals have been observed since the 1990s in the West, the Midwest, as well as Texas and Oklahoma (CIDRAP, 2013). As regards Texas, the strain of anthrax used in the Amerithrax attacks also came from the Lone Star State and was mistakenly named the "Ames strain" due to a misunderstanding during work with the original specimen isolated from nature.

The source of the presence of endospores in the environment is typically the hemorrhagic exudate of animals released at the time of death through the nose, mouth, and anus. Given that animal anthrax is endemic in many regions of the world, the near-worldwide natural reproduction of the threat vector is thus assured. Coming into contact with the endospores in various ways, as many as 2,000 to 20,000 human infections are estimated to result annually worldwide.

The Threat of Bioaggression

In deliberately releasing anthrax bacteria, agents of bioterrorism and biological warfare, as well as those defending against them, would typically consider the following parameters of the "process" of anthrax use: ease of access, difficulty of weaponization, possibility of clandestine dispersal, uncertain rate of mortality in the target area, low probability of onward transmission, and difficulty of decontamination. These all bear considerable relevance for United States Homeland Security.

Even as most military stocks of weaponized anthrax may have been destroyed by the countries that possessed them, the possibility of bioterrorism is underscored by Norwegian far-right lone wolf attacker Anders Breivik's references in his infamous manifesto to the use of chemical, biological, radiological, and nuclear (CBRN) weapons. He discusses the use of anthrax against whom he classifies as "category A, B and C traitors" at length (Gregg, 2011), likely leaving a legacy of heightened awareness of the potential of anthrax among far-right circles in what is an increasingly transnational far-right scene.

Ease of Access

Isolating anthrax bacteria from a deceased animal and culturing it in a laboratory may not be a cost-prohibitive challenge for a group determined to get hold of the pathogen. Attenuated strains may be available from animal vaccines, and contaminated soil may be available in some instances. Obtaining anthrax from laboratory cultured collections by theft or in a seemingly legitimate transaction is also a possibility.

Difficulty of Weaponization

Weaponization is difficult, in light of the need to provide for the aerosolization of the bacteria to maximize effectiveness for the attacker. This requires producing a powdery substance with the spores separated and concentrated sufficiently to produce particles with neutral surface charge. The smaller the particles, the greater the probability that they may reach the lower respiratory tract of a victim. At the same time, however, smaller particles of only a few spores may function less well as stable aerosols.

The process of aerosolization carries operational risks, both internal (to those involved) and external (to the site of production). With up to a hundred casualties, the April 1979 Sverdlovsk incident (in what is today the town of Yekaterinburg) is the most significant inhalation anthrax outbreak incident to date. The aerosol production process resulted in the accidental release of anthrax dust from a military compound through an exhaust pipe from which the filter was negligently removed for the course of several hours. Against a backdrop of official denial by Soviet authorities, the knowledge of wind patterns in the period of interest along with dispersion models offered the first pieces of indirect evidence pointing to the Soviet Union's biological weapons program being the real source of these anthrax infections (Meselson et al., 1994).

The Japanese doomsday cult Aum Shinrikyo never acquired a capability similar to that of the Soviet Union. They obtained anthrax bacteria for culturation from the commercially available Sterne animal vaccine, an attenuated/vaccine strain, resolving the challenge of aerosolization by the crude means of spraying a liquid suspension containing the bacteria from the rooftop of their own headquarters building in Kameido, Japan, in 1993. The attack did not pose a significant threat to human life and the odor emanating from the building apparently alerted several people nearby (Keim et al., 2001; Bleek, 2011). In the context of this attack, there was some speculation as to whether a group such as Aum may be able to synthesize a dangerous anthrax strain combining the Sterne vaccine strain with the similarly available Pasteur strain, but this remains a hypothetical discussion for now.

In another incident of note, without aiming to directly harm anyone and without attempting any form of aerosolization, the group calling itself the Dark Harvest Commando of the Scottish Citizen Army acquired soil fragments from the former biological weapons testing site Gruinard Island to then place soil fragments encased in plastic in the vicinity of several sites, including a Conservative Party conference venue in Blackpool, UK. The group executed these actions to add pressure to their demand for the decontamination of Gruinard Island (Time, 1981).

The challenge of aerosolization is the reason why some dispute whether U. S. researcher Bruce Edwards Ivins could have been solely responsible for the Amerithrax attacks, as he was a microbiologist by training, and, as such, not necessarily familiar with the physics of the process—especially if, as some reports claimed, silicon may have been added to the spores found in the mailed envelopes, although this issue remains a subject of dispute among experts. The powdery substance used in the attacks was certainly fine enough to leak from the envelopes "of an extraordinarily cheap, porous paper" in which they were sent (as described by Graysmith, 2003: 52). As Pope observes:

> Not only did the pressure of the processing machines force spores into the open air ... the routine use of blowing air to clean machines and surrounding areas spread those spores even further. The spores that escaped the envelopes in sorting centers also found their way onto other envelopes.
>
> (2011)

Possibility of Clandestine Dispersal

As discussed above, the clandestine acquisition and dispersion of anthrax is not an insurmountable challenge to a group conspiring to do this in a determined manner. Should the challenge of weaponization be resolved, the agents involved may initiate an attack whose effects the world will not be aware of for some time after the incident, leaving the perpetrators with the opportunity to cover their tracks and move to a safe location.

The U.S. postal system is by today clearly better prepared for biohazard-related contingencies than it was in 2001. It can detect and neutralize attempts to turn it into a mechanism of delivery with improved likelihood. Measures introduced include the automated screening of mail with the biohazard detection system (BDS) installed after 2002. This system, designed in cooperation between Northrop Grumman, the U.S. Army Research Institute of Infectious Disease (USARIID), the U.S. Navy Medical Research Center, the Department of Agriculture, and John Hopkins University (*inter alia*), includes an aerosol collector and a polymerase chain reaction (PCR) unit. Reportedly, it does not produce false positives, and the screening process is comparatively time efficient (Tarantola, 2013). Mail irradiation at important (mostly governmental) destination points in the postal network (rather than the irradiation of all mails, as originally envisaged in the wake of the Amerithrax attacks) is a further important measure defending against attacks using bacterial pathogens, although there are some doubts as to whether the dose of ionizing radiation used in the process can kill all anthrax spores. The procedure imposes significant costs on government, including delays in the delivery of mail and a switch to alternative delivery services in response.

This still leaves the possibility of the use of other mechanisms of attack open, including by way of dispersal from an aerial or other elevated platform, or via food distribution channels. In lieu of perfect defenses against such an attack, widespread vaccination, as proposed by some (Webb, 2003), is a dubiously effective approach, given the highly disruptive social alarm this may cause and, in the case of acting with a view to an imminent attack, the perverse incentive thereby provided to prospective attackers to re-target their attack at unvaccinated populations. A more effective response is the BioWatch program established in 2003 to monitor 30 major metropolitan areas across the United States for signs of an attack with biological agents such as anthrax or tularemia. Although it generated a large number of false alarms over the course of its operation, it is best regarded as one tool out of many for public health decision-making – one that may accelerate decision-making in the event of an actual attack, subject to confirmatory tests (Maron, 2013).

Uncertain Rate of Mortality in the Target Area

Because of the unknown and in all likelihood variable minimal infective dose and median lethal dose (variable both due to the exact site of infection in the throat or the lungs and the possibly weaker immune system of certain individuals), it is impossible to estimate with great precision the number of dead to be expected in an affected area. An oft-cited estimate anticipates anywhere between 130,000 and 3 million deaths in the case of the release of 100 kilograms of aerosolized anthrax upwind of Washington, DC (as quoted by Johari, 2002). The wind (its direction as well as its speed) introduces additional uncertainties into calculations.

Low Probability of Onward Transmission

Anthrax presents a very low risk of person-to-person transmission between humans. Under normal circumstances and with normal practices in mind, the risk is virtually non-existent in the case of inhalation anthrax and small in the case of cutaneous anthrax. From a strategic perspective, this is highly relevant, as this means that while anthrax cannot be precisely targeted as a weapon, its impact can be limited to a specific population even in the case of mass aerial dispersal, for example, in targeting the population of a city.

Difficulty of Decontamination

As noted above, decontamination is possible but costly and difficult in light of the need to achieve perfect results, there being no truly safe degree of residual contamination and the minimal infective dose being unknown. This makes the dispersal of anthrax spores, with slight exaggeration, the biological equivalent of a radiological "dirty bomb" (i.e., a bomb using radioactive substances to contaminate an area with lasting effect).

Decontamination generally has to take into account the qualities of the surfaces and materials to be decontaminated, environmental factors, and microbiological variables such as the parameters of the strain of anthrax in question (Wood and Adrion, 2019). For instance, chlorine dioxide is often used in the decontamination of buildings (Rastogi et al., 2010). Ultraviolet-C light and X-rays also play a role in various applications.

Altogether, the above-detailed parameters are not actually suitable for a highly precisely targeted attack in the United States. They are, however, suitable for a mass-casualty attack.

Weaponization may be a challenge difficult to overcome for a group of perpetrators without specialist knowledge, but the highly disruptive effect of the threat of an anthrax attack is a major incentive for hoaxes. These can tie down resources and impede or paralyze public services. Partly due to the above mentioned measures (mail irradiation and biological security screening), some of those interested in hoax attacks show in recent years a preference to simulate chemical attacks with ricin rather than anthrax mail attacks. The trouble-making potential of anthrax hoaxes persists, nonetheless, and incidents continue to be reported from around the world as of 2019.

In the meantime, the need for biopreparedness is putting a major burden on the public services affected, including on the postal and the public health system. For the U.S. postal service, the annual cost was reported to be around $15 million in 2011, a decade after the Amerithrax attacks (McElhatton, 2011). The irradiation of U.S. federal government mail in the Washington, DC area alone cost in excess of $74.7 million in the period of November 2001 to April 2008 (GAO, 2008). By one estimate, U.S. government agencies may have spent in the order of $50 billion to strengthen defenses against attacks using biological agents in the 2001–2009 period (Drogin, 2009).

This "insurance cost" is certainly significant if assessed with a view to the small fallout from actual incidents, but may be small with a view to the prospective fallout of a major attack, regarding which it is worth recalling that the Amerithrax attacks could fundamentally disrupt the operation of both the U.S. Congress and the U.S. Supreme Court, among other major consequences. In terms of overreaction, the proliferation in the post-2001 period of BSL-3 laboratories (that is, Biological Safety Level 3 laboratories) handling pathogens such as anthrax for the purposes of research may be a more concerning trend. This may be counterproductive, potentially, as our protection from the accidental or deliberate release of pathogens may only be as strong as the safety measures are in the weakest link in the network of the research laboratories concerned (Katona, Sullivan and Intriligator, 2011: 5-6).

Underscoring this point, as recently as in 2015, the U.S. Department of Defense announced that in one incident, live anthrax spores were accidentally delivered to a number of laboratories in nine U.S. federal states and a U.S. military base in South Korea. The facilities on location were unprepared for the treatment of live spores, resulting in possible exposure events and the need for preventive treatment to be administered to a number of individuals (Reardon, 2015).

Conclusion

To sum up, anthrax remains a major threat for the United States to consider as part of the biodefense agenda due to the relative ease of access to naturally occurring as well as vaccine anthrax strains, the possibility of clandestine dispersal, the low probability of onward transmission between humans (and consequently the possibility of containing the impact of the pathogen within a specific larger population), and the difficulty of decontamination (which makes the disruptive secondary effects of anthrax attacks very costly to the defender).

At the same time, anthrax cannot be highly precisely targeted and the risk of collateral damage relative to a smaller specific target is high, as the Amerithrax attacks may demonstrate. Weaponization will remain a major obstacle to prospective attackers without specialist knowledge in the near to medium term.

Counteracting these considerations in several ways, the biotechnological revolution is enhancing the threat of fully engineered advanced biological weapons (making anthrax less attractive to some prospective users, mostly state actors), at the same time, as it is contributing to the ease with which traditional biological agents, such as anthrax, can be genetically modified (e.g., via gene editing using CRISPR-Cas9, allowing users to manipulate expected implications of an anthrax outbreak or to combine vaccine and other strains). The biotechnological revolution is also making available new delivery mechanisms (e.g., nanoparticle microencapsulation technology). Furthermore, the possibility of obtaining the rapidly expanding data and knowledge regarding all of the above issues off the internet, by hacking or otherwise, may lower the capability threshold for some groups of prospective attackers, removing the need for them to possess specialist knowledge.

Another major trend to consider with a view to its impact on the threat, as well as the response to the threat, is the spread of antimicrobial resistance (AMR). Already at the time of the Amerithrax attacks, many raised concerns about the irregular and unwarranted use of the antibiotic ciprofloxacin (a.k.a. "Cipro"), with regards to how this may contribute to the spread of resistance to this antibiotic in bacteria, including anthrax. Recent research has shed light on how resistance to antibiotics may be passed on between different species of bacteria by way of horizontal gene transfer, including from commensal bacteria resident within the host system in the intestines to pathogens attacking that system (Oladeinde, 2019). In light of this knowledge, the inclination of human societies to panic upon news of anthrax outbreaks holds concerning implications in a future where antibiotics will be decreasingly useful and multidrug-resistant bacteria are on the rise.

Further Reading

CIDRAP (2013). Anthrax. Mayo, MN: University of Minnesota Center for Infectious Disease Research and Policy. http://www.cidrap.umn.edu/infectious-disease-topics/anthrax

Rider, B. (2005): Anthrax. In Croddy, E.A., Wirtz, J.J. (Eds.): *Weapons of Mass Destruction: An Encyclopedia of Worldwide Policy, Technology, and History. Volume I: Chemical and Biological Weapons.* Santa Barbara, California – Denver, Colorado – Oxford, England: ABC CLIO, 18–23.

WHO (2018): Anthrax in Humans and Animals, 4th edition. Geneva, Switzerland: World Health Organization. https://www.who.int/csr/resources/publications/AnthraxGuidelines2008/en/

References

Bleek, P.C. (2011). *Revisiting Aum Shinrikyo: New Insights into the Most Extensive Non-State Biological Weapons Program to Date.* NTI.org, 11 December 2011. https://www.nti.org/analysis/articles/revisiting-aum-shinrikyo-new-insights-most-extensive-non-state-biological-weapons-program-date-1/. Accessed 21 November 2019.

CIDRAP (2013). Anthrax. Mayo, MN: University of Minnesota Center for Infectious Disease Research and Policy. http://www.cidrap.umn.edu/infectious-disease-topics/anthrax. Accessed 20 November 2019.

Doucleff, M. (2016). *Anthrax Outbreak in Russia Thought to be Result of Thawing Permafrost.* NPR, 3 August 2016. https://www.npr.org/sections/goatsandsoda/2016/08/03/488400947/anthrax-outbreak-in-russia-thought-to-be-result-of-thawing-permafrost. Accessed 3 August 2016.

Drogin, B. (2009). Anthrax hoaxes, and costs, pile up. *Los Angeles Times*, 8 March 2009. https://www.latimes.com/archives/la-xpm-2009-mar-08-na-anthrax-threats8-story.html. Accessed 20 November 2019.

GAO (2008). *United States Postal Service: Information on the Irradiation of Federal Mail in the Washington, DC.*, Area. United States Government Accountability Office, 31 July 2008. https://www.gao.gov/assets/100/95677.pdf. Accessed 20 November 2019.

Graysmith, R. (2003). *Amerithrax: The Hunt for the Anthrax Killer.* New York: Jove Books.

Gregg, K. (2011). Norway's Anders Breivik: biological weapons. *Federation of American Scientists*, 2011. https://fas.org/blogs/fas/2011/07/norways-anders-breivik-biological-weapons/. Accessed 20 November 2019.

Johari, R. (2002). Anthrax - biological threat in the 21st century. *Malaysian Journal of Medical Science*, 9(1), 1–2.

Katona, P., Sullivan, J.P., Intriligator, M.D. (2011). *Global Biosecurity: Threats and Responses.* London and New York: Routledge.
Keim, P. (2001). Molecular Investigation of the Aum Shinrikyo anthrax release in Kameido, Japan. *Journal of Clinical Microbiology*, 2001, 39(12), 4566–4567. doi:10.1128/JCM.39.12.4566–4567.2001.
Maron, D.F. (2013). U. S. bioterror detection program comes under scrutiny. *Scientific American*, 17 June 2013. https://www.scientificamerican.com/article/us-bioterror-detection/. Accessed 20 November 2019).
McElhatton, J. (2011). Postal Service to continue post-anthrax safeguards. *Washington Times*, 9 October 2011. https://www.washingtontimes.com/news/2011/oct/9/postal-service-to-continue-post-anthrax-safeguards/. Accessed 20 November 2019.
Meselson, M. (1994). The Sverdlovsk Anthrax outbreak of 1979. *Science*, Vol. 266, 1202–1208.
Norton-Taylor, R. (1990). Anthrax bomb tests were “playing with fire”. *The Guardian*, 21 July 1999. https://www.theguardian.com/uk/1999/jul/21/richardnortontaylor. Accessed 20 November 2019.
Oladeinde, A. (2019). Horizontal gene transfer and acquired antibiotic resistance in salmonella Enterica Serovar Heidelberg following in vitro incubation in broiler ceca. *Applied Environmental Microbiology*, 5(22). e01903-19. doi: 10.1128/AEM.01903-19.
Pope, N. (2011). *The Anthrax mail attack. Pushing the Envelope – The Smithonian’s National Postal Museum*, 10 October 2011. https://postalmuseumblog.si.edu/2011/10/anthrax-mail-1.html. Accessed 20 November 2019.
Rastogi, V.K. et al. (2010). Systematic evaluation of the efficacy of chlorine dioxide in decontamination of building interior surfaces contaminated with anthrax spores. *Applied Environmental Microbiology*, 76(10), 3343–3351. doi: 10.1128/AEM.02668-09.
Reardon, S. (2015). US military accidentally ships live anthrax to labs. *Nature*, 28. https://www.nature.com/news/us-military-accidentally-ships-live-anthrax-to-labs-1.17653. Accessed 20 November 2019.
Rider, B. (2005). Anthrax. In Croddy, E.A., Wirtz, J.J. (Eds.): *Weapons of Mass Destruction: An Encyclopedia of Worldwide Policy, Technology, and History. Volume I: Chemical and Biological Weapons.* Santa Barbara, California – Denver, Colorado – Oxford, England: ABC CLIO, 18–23.
Tarantola, A. (2013). How the post office sniffs out anthrax before it hits your mailbox. *Gizmodo*, 18 April 2013. https://gizmodo.com/how-the-post-office-sniffs-out-anthrax-before-it-hits-y-5994922. Accessed 20 November 2019.
Time (1981). Biological warfare: dark harvest. *Time*, 9 November 1981. http://content.time.com/time/magazine/article/0,9171,922652,00.html. Accessed 20 November 2019.
Webb, G.F. (2003). A silent bomb: The risk of anthrax as a weapon of mass destruction. *PNAS*, 100(8), 4355–4356. https://doi.org/10.1073/pnas.0830963100.
WHO (2018). *Anthrax in Humans and Animals*, 4th edition. Geneva, Switzerland: World Health Organization. https://www.who.int/csr/resources/publications/AnthraxGuidelines2008/en/. Accessed 20 November 2019.
Wood, J.P., Adrion, A.C. (2019). Review of decontamination techniques for the inactivation of bacillus Anthracis and other spore-forming bacteria associated with building or outdoor materials. *Environmental Science and Technology*, 53(8), 4045–4062. doi: 10.1021/acs.est.8b05274.

Chapter 92

Disaster Impact on Minorities

Patrice Natalie Delevante
Independent Researcher, United States

Contents

Introduction 707
Background 708
Hurricane Katrina 708
California Wildfires 709
Conclusion 710
Further Reading 711
References 711

Introduction

Historically, disasters such as hurricanes, flooding, tornadoes, and wildfires have decimated minority communities in the United States. This has been due to a lack of community awareness and government emergency preparedness, along with minorities' distrust of government agencies and authorities, which has left such communities to fend on their own, and so resulted in numerous deaths, displacement, and injuries. For example, hurricanes and wildfires are natural disasters that damage vulnerable areas of land and consequently the victims that live there. The Great Galveston Hurricane of 1900 was the nation's deadliest hurricane ever, killing thousands of people, including minorities (National Park Service 2019). Hurricane Katrina destroyed the famed minority community of New Orleans, Louisiana, leaving thousands of people drowned or injured and displaced. Many individuals, such as onlookers and scholars, cite Hurricane Katrina as being a "man-made mega-disaster laboratory" disaster, since it was the fault of the failed levees that caused the massive and destructive floods. One can only imagine the destructive impact that California wildfires in 2018 and 2019 had on minorities living in those fire-prone

DOI: 10.4324/9781315144511-97

areas, particularly Native Americans on reservations. Disasters impacting US minority communities then are arguably social constructs, and in such cases, marginalized minority groups are victims of a failed government. As a result, disasters are sometimes known also as man-made disasters because government responses, or the lack thereof, have determined the extent of damage to communities.

Background

Disasters in the Americas long predate the existence of the modern United States. In June 1495, during Christopher Columbus's second voyage to the Americas, he experienced in this New World a "whirlwind" that "plucked by the roots." Some of the local natives termed this dangerous weather condition, a disastrous effect on settlements, "the tempest of the air…Furacanes," or the Taino peoples term for supernatural god.

Trauma studies suggest that trauma affects minorities in disaster-prone surroundings during and following a disaster, while many sociologists argue that natural disasters are socially constructed by the majority and/or government to exploit and weaken minority communities. Essentially, disasters impact minorities the most because of "unequal social relations" and a lack of preparedness, first-responders, rescue, and recovery by local agencies and the government in relation to helping them. Consequently, thousands of minorities may be killed when disasters occur. In Hurricane Katrina (discussed in more depth in the following sections), for example, such disadvantages contributed to minority communities, largely African Americans, being unable to be rescued from their homes or hospitals. A high percentage of New Orleans residents are minorities and their mistreatment has been termed racism by some scholars. Minorities are often at the bottom of the socioeconomic ladder compared to Caucasians, and some scholars have even suggested that government agencies use racism and inequality as means of control over minorities and as a way to restructure society in an oppressive, patriarchal manner. Thus, minority communities have developed a mistrust of the government. Inequality, according to Jeannie Haubert, also influences response and recovery of minorities during disasters while research by policymakers and public health officials further suggest that low-income families are disproportionately impacted by disasters and are thus most likely to experience "disaster related mental health outcomes" (Amstadter and Denielson, 2009). Poorer people are also observed as often not having access to insurance to cover damages to housing and vehicles, and many are unable to receive rescue to stadiums for evacuees.

Hurricane Katrina

Hurricane Katrina shattered communities in Louisiana, Mississippi, and Alabama and was announced as one of the deadliest and costliest hurricanes in US history. The hurricane was initially thought by meteorologists to be a less devastating disaster until Friday, August 26, but on Saturday, August 27, there was a call for evacuation from these areas from the government and local authorities on Saturday. The entire evacuation of New Orleans was then ordered on Sunday, August 28. By the end of the hurricane, a million homes had been destroyed (Plyer 2016), but the nation's crisis response system seemed unable to help the victims and to halt the looting and anarchy. Mississippi suffered the most damage to property while in Louisiana, the "poorly constructed and maintained" levees protecting New Orleans and the natural wetland barriers were breached, thus allowing the hurricane to effectively destroy the city (Squires 2006). In New Orleans, these "man-made disaster" floods caused 80% of urban New Orleans to be underwater and contributed to 1000 deaths in Southeastern Louisiana (Plyer 2016). On Tuesday, August 30, and Wednesday, August 31, the mega-disaster hurricane was rumored to have increased looting and other acts of violence, including assault. Individuals were photographed wandering the flooded streets, while other victims were trapped in homes, drowned, or at the stadium waiting for the hurricane to pass. In the days that followed, the damaged sites were visited by the government.

Hurricane Katrina is a prime example of a historical disaster being a social construct caused by a government that failed its victims. Scholars write that the victims of the disaster were mostly poor and disabled civilians who drowned, were left for dead, or were stranded. There were warning signs ahead of time, but when the hurricane struck, neither the infrastructure nor recovery system in place that would have been needed to respond to it fully occurred. Sociologists also conclude that the government's failures were a form of "corruption" due to their limited warning efforts for minority civilians to evacuate (see Belkhir and Charlemaine 2007). In sum, after Hurricane Katrina arrived, it devastated the Gulf Coast region, sending toxic waters that submerged cities, leaving 2,000 dead and millions displaced. News media captured images of civilians and hospitals awaiting rescue and recovery which became too late for many because as they waited with no food or basic supplies, causing many to perish or became ill. Since that time, there has been great public interest and fascination with the disaster and its impact on minority communities in the long recovery process.

To make matters worse, not only was the nation's response agenda lacking in recovery efforts aimed at minorities in New Orleans, dubbing what many researchers and victims termed "shameful government performance," but during the recovery afterward, domestic violence against women also increased.

California Wildfires

Ian Davies suggests that American minorities are most affected by wildfires in the country, especially Native Americans. Due to climate change, wildfires in the United States occur most frequently in the western and southern states. Davies states that these kinds of natural disasters are dangerous but adds that they become especially destructive due to socioeconomic and sociopolitical determinants, which Davies coins as "adaptive capacity." He also indicates that minorities are vulnerable to wildfires not just because they live in vulnerable zones, but because they also often lack access to transportation, such as owning a vehicle, to leave the burning area for example. Other challenges may also arise, as happened in California's Napa County, where the warning of a wildfire and the need to evacuate was spoken in English, but the town was predominantly Hispanic and conversed in Spanish. Victims of wildfires may also take longer to recover due to their poor income status. Bob Bolin summarizes this phenomenon: "The wealthy can afford losses, they have insurance, health insurance, secure jobs[...] and the poor don't." In regards to Native Americans, they are most susceptible to wildfires because the majority of their reservations are located on grasslands and other fire-prone areas" (Davies, 2016). Reservations were originally created as response to Euro-American attempts to suppress and oppress Native Americans by displacing them from their lands into reservations, following many wars, during the Trail of Tears. As a result, wildfires that kill people from these marginalized cultures and destroy their homes can be seen as a byproduct of Anglo-American racism and greed. Wildfires as disasters, like hurricanes, are man-made.

Conclusion

Jeannie Haubert suggests that sociologists should examine the conditions of social inequalities influencing disaster preparedness and recovery. She adds that future emergency preparedness should focus on civilians affected by disasters and bring advocacy and support for their recovery and rebuilding efforts. She does not see the effectiveness in naming perpetrators of disaster but rather recovery of victims. Moreover, she argues that sociological imagination and determinism are critical for sociologists to understand the relations between civilians and government during times of disaster. Haubert further describes the importance of survivor scholarship in spreading news and concerns on the state of minorities during and post-disaster. They can redefine and debunk stereotypical notions of minority representation and relations with the government and increase insight and nuanced narrations of localized suffering from the poor and their weakened and racist-filled state of recovery. Survivor scholars also contribute to increasing and representing local efforts to rebuild, and they also are survivors, which elevates their stories of diverse localized recovery, also known as "trauma pedagogical projects," to government attention (Haubert 2015). And even though Hurricane Katrina captured disturbing images of suffering and limited recovery of the poor minorities, scholars argued for the images of building and culture not taken of the disaster. There has been only limited government financial help for victims of Hurricane Katrina because the money provided has not been targeted effectively to assist them, which has furthered the problems of minority marginalization and continued poverty.

In terms of policy recommendations, the federal government should try to incorporate more socioeconomic and sociopolitical programs, such as housing and transportation services into communities with minorities, because these can lower the risks of disasters impacting heavily upon minorities when natural disasters occur. In *Crisis and Disaster Counseling: Lessons Learned from Hurricane Katrina*, researchers concluded that support for communities in the aftermath of disasters should involve healing and recommended that first-responders and relief agencies such as Federal Emergency Management Agency (FEMA) should utilize cultural sensitivity and embrace diversity within efforts aimed at the post-disaster community. They further suggest that recovery efforts should aim to nourish the healing process of the affected environment – through ideas of survival and recovery derived from that community. As a result, first-responders and relief agencies should be helped to understand that their efforts ought to be a form of social advocacy and empowerment since socioeconomic inequalities and racism reside both pre, during, and after disaster. "Support a community's national resilience and [ability] to heal itself may be the most important disaster response" (Gurwitch et al. 2002). Resilience not only grants a disaster-impacted area's healing but also ways to rethink and recover before the disaster.

Disaster outcomes can lead to comprehensive recovery efforts when communities rally together with local officials and authorities, creating truly, joint processes. The federal government should help all households located in disaster-vulnerable areas to plan ahead for disaster preparedness, while also encouraging community involvement and participation with disaster response programs and resources (Patton 2005).

Further Reading

Boin, A. & Brown, C. (2019). *Managing Hurricane Katrina: Lessons from a Mega Crisis*. Louisiana: Louisiana State University Press.

Gow, K. (2008). *The Phoenix of Natural Disasters: Community Resilience*. New York: Nova Science Publishers.

Pierre, K. (2018, November 3). "Minorities are Most Vulnerable When Wildfires Strike in U. S. Study Finds," *The New York Times*. https://www.nytimes.com/2018/11/03/climate/wildfires-minorities-risk.html

References

Amstadter, A., Denielson, C., (2009). "Factor Associated with Exposure and Response to Disasters among Marginalized Populations." In Y. Neria, S. Galea, and F. Norris (Eds), *Mental Health and Disasters* (pp. 277–290). Cambridge: Cambridge University Press.

Belkhir, J. A. and Charlemaine, C. (2007). "Race, Gender and Class Lessons from Hurricane Katrina," *Race, Gender & Class, 14*(1/2): 120–152.

Davies, I. 2016. *Recovery from Disaster: Rutledge Studies in Hazards. Disaster Risk, and Climate Change*. New York: Routledge.

Gurwitch, R, Kees, M, Becker, S. (2002). The Face of Tragedy: Placing Children's Reaction to Trauma in a New Context. *Cognitive and Behavioral Practice*. (pp. 286–295).

Haubert, J. (2015). *Rethinking Disaster Recovery: A Hurricane Katrina Retrospective*. New York: Lexington.

National Park Service (2019). *Galveston Hurricane of 1900*. https://www.nps.gov/articles/galveston-hurricane-of-1900.htm

National Research Council. 2012. *Disaster Resilience: a National Imperative*. Washington, DC: The National Academies Press. https://doi.org/10.17226/13457

Neely, W. (2016). *The Greatest and Deadliest Hurricanes of the Caribbean and the Americas*. Indiana: Universe.

Patton, J. (2005). *Pastoral Care in Context: An Introduction to Pastoral Care*. Kentucky: Knox Press.

Penuel, B. K. (2010). *Encyclopedia of Disaster Relief*. New York: SAGE.

Plyer, A. (2016). *Facts for Features: Katrina Impact*. August 26, 2016. https://www.datacenterresearch.org/data-resources/katrina/facts-for-impact/

Squires, G. (2006). *There Is No Such Thing as a Natural Disaster*. New York: Routledge.

Chapter 93

Earthquakes and US National Security

Arundhati Bhattacharyya
University of Burdwan, Bardhaman, India

Scott N. Romaniuk
International Centre for Policing and Security, University of South Wales, Caerleon, United Kingdom

Contents

Introduction 713
Silver Lining 715
Steps to Enhance National Security 716
Conclusion 717
Further Reading 718
References 718

Introduction

Earthquakes are a form of sudden and rapid shaking of the ground that are caused by shifts in the layers of rocks beneath the surface of the earth that can happen anywhere. They are one of the most dangerous and destructive among the natural calamities (Cutcliffe, 2000). The high-risk areas in the United States are California, Alaska, and the Mississippi Valley (Be Prepared for an Earthquake, 2018). In the United States, major earthquakes during the 20th century occurred in 1906 in San Francisco, in 1925 in Santa Barbara, in 1933 in Long Beach, in 1971 in San Fernando, in 1989 in Loma Prieta, and in 1994 in Northridge (Cutcliffe, 2000). The Federal Emergency Management Agency (FEMA) has sent indications that all states have some risk for earthquakes (Bailey, 2010).

DOI: 10.4324/9781315144511-98

During the aftermath of an earthquake, thousands are often found dead, with many others injured and homeless. Hospitals are frequently destroyed, so it becomes difficult for the victims to get assistance; fires often break out; and there may be cut-offs in water, gas, and electricity services. The loss is severe as found by the FEMA (Leith, 2004). On January 17, 1994, for example, the earthquake that occurred in Northridge, California, led to a loss of 44 billion dollars in insured losses (US Department of Labor, 2019). Due to substantial seismic activity, schools may collapse and lead to the death of children and teachers in large numbers. In 2005, an article published in the *Los Angeles Times* stated that more than 7,000 school buildings were at risk to the direct and indirect effects of earthquakes and seismic activity. In 2006, in a positive step, Proposition 1D was approved by the voters of California, which authorized the funding of the public school buildings in California. FEMA's Project Impact program has offered $1 million as seed money for pilot programs which would help the communities to prepare for earthquakes.

In 1997, Seattle officials took its benefit and utilized it for school retrofit project and hazard mapping. This brought the public and the private sectors together, which has resulted in national awards. President Obama's Stimulus Bill initially included rebuilding of public schools and other facilities. But there was no mention of earthquakes (Bailey, 2010). The July 2019 California earthquake was a further wake-up call for all, however. It led to gas leaks, fires, minor injuries, and some form of structural damages in the areas of habitation. President Donald Trump approved emergency declaration for assistance in the affected towns in the Ridgecrest area, which allowed the Department of Homeland Security and the FEMA to coordinate the disaster relief initiatives (CBS Los Angeles, 2019). Trump also signed an emergency declaration for Puerto Rico in January, 2020. FEMA was then authorized again to coordinate the disaster relief efforts by identifying and mobilizing equipment and resources to alleviate the effects of the earthquake (FEMA, 2020).

The destructive earthquake that occurred in October 1989 in California led to an enhancement of expenditure on public and private structure. The public attention toward greater safety and the intensification of reaction regarding security increased. In order to prepare for future earthquakes, it is necessary to insure against the damage. For that, proper research should be engaged regarding geographical distribution and the damage it caused on life and property. The damage that was caused to the public schools led to the passage of the Field Act which created standards for construction of public schools. Moreover, heavy investment was made in the field of research which has led to the need for the formation of Nuclear Regulatory Commission. This was to create earthquake-resistant design for the nuclear power plants. Furthermore, the insurance evaluation has been reassessed in order to mitigate the loss incurred due to earthquake. A group of insurance companies attempted a cooperative stance to respond to the threat of earthquake at the federal level and the Federal Earthquake Insurance and Reinsurance Corporation Act was passed. The goal of this was to help the insurance companies to offer broader and affordable residential earthquake coverage. Another step to enhance human security is the Seismic Safety Commission, which has advised the state to work with the federal government, other provinces, and the national insurance industry. This program aimed to incorporate insurance as a part of the earthquake hazard mitigation, including a tax-exempt fund from the state and assistance with earthquake insurance for homes and small businesses (Bolt, 1991). In California, the California Earthquake Authority is a privately funded and publicly managed authority, which provides coverage against earthquake. Progress has been slow, however, with the result that in 2019, only about 13.3% of the residents of California have earthquake coverage (Insurance Information Institute, 2019).

The National Earthquake Hazards Reduction Program, formed in 1977, assists the federal government to reduce losses in life and property due to earthquakes. It coordinates with FEMA, the National Institute of Standards and Technology, the National Science Foundation, the United States Geological Survey, along with other agencies, like universities, research centers, professional societies, businesses, and commissions, in doing so (FEMA, 2019). FEMA also offers earthquake-related information, guides, posters, and checklists separately for individuals, home owners, teachers, private sector, small businesses, community planners, professionals, engineers, and others.

However, there were some problems. By the 1990s, Earthquake engineers and earth scientists were complaining about reduction of federal research funds since 1985 (Bolt, 1991). This led to some improvements over time, including some agencies, like the United States Geological Survey (USGS), announcing awards for earthquake monitoring and research. Universities, state geological surveys, and private institutions can receive such grants (USGS Announces Awards for 2018 Earthquake Monitoring and Research in the United States, 2018). The 2019 budget had made provisions for mission activities. But it does not request for fund for programs that are funded by USGS partners and those engaged in research (US Geological Survey, 2019). The damage due to earthquakes would be less if designs incorporate earthquake-resistant engineering. But, in many cases, such designs are still not integrated during construction of buildings, like schools.

Silver Lining

Often times, various state and non-state actors (NSAs) come to the aid of national authorities in the wake of earthquakes and their destructive offshoots. Rescue and aid teams with relief materials are ready in many parts of the world, including the United States, to tackle the impact of earthquake. The proactive role of the media is impactful in this regard. Non-government organizations, including schools, groups, and centers, are obtaining funds from private enterprises to invest in research to enhance human security and ultimate safety goals, during the occurrence of earthquakes. The earthquake in Haiti killed 3,000,000 people and created 1 million homeless people. Within 24 hours of the earthquake, the team from the United States arrived in Haiti to support the disaster recovery engagements. President Obama called for "whole of government" approach. The US earthquake team aided earthquake victims: FEMA created incident response team and ten search and rescue groups to Haiti, while the US Citizenship and Immigration Services cleared the process for entry of 1,000 Haitian children to the United States (Givens et al., 2018). Haiti's success in tackling earthquake was also assisted by the role played by the nongovernmental organizations (Cecchine et al. 2013). Just as United States has come to the assistance of countries like Haiti, the United States is ready to tackle on any natural disaster, including earthquakes (although whether the United States would, in turn, accept foreign assistance in the event of a major domestic earthquake is debatable).

The United Nations Educational, Scientific and Cultural Organization (UNESCO) has been working in the field of disaster management since 1960. Its focus is on disaster prevention rather than on disaster relief. The Office of the UN Disaster Relief Coordinator has played the specific responsibility in disaster prevention (Nabiha Gul, Sanam Noor, 2006). Its central role has been reaffirmed. But there is a need for more sound financial support for the office. The successor body is the United Nations Office for the Coordination of Humanitarian Affairs. It coordinates humanitarian assistance and policy development (UNOCHA, 2016).

The International Decade of Natural Disaster Reduction announced by the United Nations has helped in focusing the efforts toward reduction of the risks of natural disasters, including earthquakes (Bolt, 1991). The main objective of the decade was to reduce the loss in life and property and social and economic disruption due to natural disasters (Nabiha Gul, Sanam Noor, 2006). The Hyogo Framework for Action adopted in 2005 in Kobe, Japan, has brought in the disaster-related international framework. More and more funding for research and development of technology for prediction of earthquakes are being invested. This is to predict the time, place, and the magnitude of the earthquakes. This will help in arranging for public health policies to tackle the eventualities after the earthquake takes place. Formulation of Technology Policy includes a number of stages. They are the awareness of the issue, searching for possible policy outcomes, the adoption of a particular policy by decision makers, execution of the policy, evaluation of the work done, and finally, the stage which includes continuance or termination of the policy framework. In 1973, the earthquake at Blue Mountain Lake in New York was predicted. This created a climate of optimism among the scientific community in the United States that emergency measures can not only be put in place but pre-emptive measures executed before the harmful impacts of earthquakes are realized. There is a strong hope for prediction of earthquake. This has been seconded by the USGS (W. Henry Lambright and Jane A. Heckley, 1985). The optimism about prediction of earthquakes comes from good advances in seismology and other related sciences (Geller, 1997).

Several attempts, like the passage of the California Hospital Seismic Safety Act, setting up of the Office of State wide Health Planning and Development, formation of the Earthquake Engineering Research Institute, International Association for Earthquake Engineering, creation of improved version of the computer modeling techniques, assist in building high-rise buildings in areas like Los Angeles; increase of attention for the development of the soil liquidation maps etc. was made to enhance human security (Cutcliffe, 2000). Better preparedness is required for people who are affected by natural disasters. This is one of the seven global targets of the Sendai Framework for Disaster Risk Reduction. This was adopted by the UN General Assembly in 2015 (Cazabat, 2017).

Steps to Enhance National Security

Some steps could include creation of accurate urban earthquake hazard maps, formation of seismic design provisions for new structural systems, and rehabilitation of the older ones. The Advanced National Seismic Systems and the Network of Earthquake Engineering Simulation are the efforts of the government of the United States in understanding the response of structures to earthquakes (Leith, 2004). The Advanced National Seismic System continues to analyze seismic data on earthquakes, provide reliable notifications about the occurrences, and also provide the required data for further research on earthquakes. It continues to support partnerships among the actors working at the local, regional, and national levels. It has also strengthened its infrastructure and partnerships (USGS, 2017).

Funds need to be invested more for earthquake monitoring and research, as done by Japan. Complacency should not come in the process of preparation for the eventualities caused by earthquakes. The invisibility of public safety of the imminent catastrophe that can be caused by earthquakes should be lessened. Preparation can be a cushion for dangers that can be caused by the earthquakes. It is a matter of time that the earthquake professionals understand that the next earthquake will occur. The location and the magnitude will decide on the collateral damage that will be caused. So, the false sense of security needs to be guarded against (Cutcliffe, 2000). Short- and long-term reconstruction work would add to capacity building. Donor fatigue, may at times, can be an obstacle in the path of reconstruction. Upsurges of humanitarian response should be properly channelized in proper direction. The United States has taken a positive role in humanitarian assistance operation role in the foreign countries, namely, in Pakistan. It provided relief and rehabilitation aid. It primarily provided helicopters to transport supplies to the areas affected by the earthquake (Mustafa, 2005). In 2010, in the Haiti earthquake, United States' military has provided largest international humanitarian support in the form of personnel and other capabilities. The response of the United States' military saved thousands of lives in the aftermath of the earthquake by accelerating relief efforts. The Air Force Special Operations Command was successful in re-establishing flight operations (The Military Response in the Haiti Earthquake, 2013). Such is the might of the United States military assistance in foreign countries, that it is reassuring that they do a wonderful job at home.

After the earthquake, physical and psychological health condition of the survivors is matters of concern. Major earthquakes destabilize the lifestyles of the people. There is a need to support them so that they can regain their confidence. Post-disaster employment assistance policies help in reconstruction and help in starting their new lives. Mental Rehabilitation Centers need to take the workload which falls on them suddenly. Social security reforms and resilient approach need to be visible in order to build strong relationship with the stakeholders (Ying Liang, Runxia Cao, 2015).

Earthquakes create distinct issues for insurers given the immense payouts associated with the disasters. For example, in the California earthquake of October 17, 1989, it was expected that the insurers would pay billions of dollars for the losses (Shelvor, Anderson & Cross, 1992). It also has its negative impact on the value of the firm. However, a disaster, like the earthquake, may create an increase in the demand of the consumer in order to have coverage for future eventualities (Aiuppa & Krueger, 1995). There could be a rise in demand for insurance arrangements (Reinhold P. Lamb and William F. Kennedy, 1997).

Conclusion

Earthquakes are one among the most dangerous natural calamities. The loss may be severe. In the United States, public and private expenditure has increased due to earthquakes. Group of insurance companies have come up to assist in rebuilding lives and property after the earthquake. They have a big responsibility. Whenever earthquakes take place, international support comes in. International actors, including the United Nations, have played roles in the prevention of earthquakes. The manner in which the United States has helped other countries to deal with the crises of the earthquake shows that their experience, capacity, and willingness to help others are immense. The United States should also extend its helping hand to other developing countries so that they can form teams to investigate local earthquakes and provide innovative means of emergency preparation. Transnational events today have a direct or indirect impact on the United States homeland security. This has happened more so due to globalization and advancement in technology. Transnational security challenges, like that of natural disasters, require cooperative alliance among governments and public and private partnerships (Austen D. Givens, Nathan E. Busch, Alan D. Bersin, 2018). National efforts are required in the aftermath of the earthquakes when industries or private entities fail to help the victims (Bolt, 1991). It is a holistic approach to enhance national security during times of earthquakes.

Further Reading

Greer, A. (2012, July). "Earthquake Preparedness and Response: Comparison of the United States and Japan," *Leadership and Management in Engineering*, *12*(3): 111–125.

Hough, S. E. (2010). *Predicting the Unpredictable: The Tumultuous Science of Earthquake Prediction*. Princeton: Princeton University Press.

Miles, K. (2017). *Quakeland: On the Road to America's Next Devastating Earthquake*. New York: Dutton.

References

Aiuppa, T. A. & Krueger, T. M. (1995). "Insurance Stock Prices Following the 1994 Los Angeles Earthquake," *Journal of Insurance Issues*, 23–35.

Bailey, N. E. (2010). "Earthquakes Threaten Many American Schools," *The Phi Delta Kappan*, 91(7), 35–39.

Be Prepared for an Earthquake. (2018, May). Retrieved November 23, 2019, from Department of Homeland Security: https://www.fema.gov/media-library-data/1527865427503-bbf6d7e61340e203c4607677cb83a69d/Earthquake_May2018.pdf

Bolt, B. A. (1991). "Balance of Risks and Benefits in Preparation for Earthquakes," *Science*, 251(4990), 169–174.

Cazabat, C. (2017, October 16). *Human Development Reports*. Retrieved February 5, 2020, from United Nations Development Programme. http://hdr.undp.org/en/content/human-security-and-natural-disasters

CBS Los Angeles. (2019, July 8). *'All Working Together!' Trump Approves Emergency Declaration Following Ridgecrest Earthquakes*. https://losangeles.cbslocal.com/2019/07/08/trump-emergency-declaration-ridgecrest-earthquakes/

Cecchine, G., Morgan, F. R., Wermuth, M. A., Jackson, T., Schaefer, A. G. & Stafford, M. (2013). *The U. S. Military Response to the 2010 Haiti Earthquake*. Santa Monica: RAND Corporation.

Cutcliffe, S. H. (2000). Earthquake Resistant Building Design Codes and Safety Standards: The California Experience. *GeoJournal*, 51, 259–262.

FEMA. (2019, January 14). *National Earthquake Hazards Reduction Program.* https://www.fema.gov/national-earthquake-hazards-reduction-program

FEMA. (2020, January 7). *President Donald J. Trump Signs Emergency Declaration for Puerto Rico.* https://www.fema.gov/news-release/2020/01/07/president-donald-j-trump-signs-emergency-declaration-puerto-rico

Givens, A. D., Busch, N. E., Bersin, A. D. (2018). Going Global: The International Dimensions of U. S. Homeland Security Policy. *Journal of Strategic Security*, 1–34.

Gul, N. & Noor, S. (2006). "Disasters and International Cooperation: Case Study of the October Earthquake," *Pakistan Horizon*, 59(4), 69–87.

Insurance Information Institute. (2019). *2019 Insurance Fact Book.* https://www.iii.org/sites/default/files/docs/pdf/insurance_factbook_2019.pdf

Lamb, R. P. & Kennedy, W. F. (1997). "Insurer Stock Prices and Market Efficiency Around the Los Angeles Earthquake," *Journal of Insurance Issues*, 20(1), 10–24.

Lambright, W. H. & Heckley, J. A. (1985). "Policymaking for Emerging Technology: The Case of Earthquake Prediction," *Policy Sciences*, 18, 227–240.

Leith, W. (2004). "Building for Earthquakes," *Science*, 304(5677), 1604.

Liang, Y. & Cao, R. (2015). "Employment Assistance Policies of Chinese Government Play Positive Roles! The Impact of Post Earthquake Assistance Policies on the Health-Related Quality of Life of Chinese Earthquake Populations," *Social Indicators Research*, 835–857.

Mustafa, Z. (2005). "Foreign Policy and Earthquake Diplomacy," *Pakistan Horizon*, 59(4), 29–38.

Shelvor, R. M., Anderson, D. C. & Cross, M. L. (1992). "Gaining from Loss: Property Liability Insurer Stock Values in the Aftermath of the 1989 California Earthquake," *The Journal of Risk and Insurance*, 476–488.

UNOCHA. (2016, September 29). *Our Work.* https://www.unocha.org/our-work

US Geological Survey. (2018, August 4). *USGS Announces Awards for 2018 Earthquake Monitoring and Research in the United States.* https://www.usgs.gov/news/usgs-announces-awards-2018-earthquake-monitoring-and-research-united-states

US Geological Survey. (2019). *Bureau Highlights.* https://www.doi.gov/sites/doi.gov/files/uploads/fy2019_bib_bh049.pdf

USGS. (2017, July). *Advanced National Seismic System: Current Status, Development Opportunities and Priorities for 2017–2027.* https://pubs.usgs.gov/circ/1429/circ1429.pdf

Chapter 94

Emergency Management and Response

Clifford E. Griffin
North Carolina State University, Raleigh, NC, United States

Contents

Introduction 721
Evolution of Governmental Role and Policy in Disaster Response and Management 723
Crisis Management Versus Consequence Management 725
Conceptual Confusion 726
Policy Challenges 728
Further Reading 728
References 728

Introduction

What is generally referred to as emergency management in the United States today began with the civil defense system – a federal office (Office of Civilian Defense) created by President Franklin D. Roosevelt's Executive Order 8757 in 1941 to protect civilians and address community needs during wartime (Pittman, 2011). Approximately 10 years later on September 30, 1950, Congress passed the Federal Disaster Relief Act (Public Law 81-875) authorizing the President to provide supplementary federal assistance when a Governor requested help. Prior to this law, the United States had no comprehensive disaster relief legislation in place. Instead, Congress adopted an incident-by-incident approach that resulted in a law being passed each time a community found itself in distress. For example, on January 14, 1803, the first and second readings of the bill "for the relief of the sufferers by fire, in the town of Portsmouth"

DOI: 10.4324/9781315144511-99

led ultimately to the Congressional Act of 1803, which authorized federal disaster assistance to this New Hampshire town. This bill is generally considered the first piece of disaster legislation (Library of Congress). This cumbersome, incremental approach to disaster response witnessed some 128 separate, disaster-relief-related pieces of legislation being passed between 1803 and 1950. However, it was the catalyzing hurricanes and earthquakes of the late 1960s and early 1970s that generated a consensus regarding the need for a more comprehensive system to protect citizens from non-war-time hazards and disasters. The resulting legislative responses witnessed an increasing focus on natural disasters (Pittman, 2011).

Public Law 81-875 was designed to "provide an orderly and continuing means of assistance by the Federal Government to States and local governments in carrying out their responsibilities to alleviate suffering and damage resulting from major disasters," and to "supplement the efforts and available resources of States and local governments." Subsequent disasters demonstrated the reality that effective responses were often outside of the scope of the local government's abilities; consequently, Congress passed the Disaster Relief Act of 1966, which, among other provisions, expanded federal assistance into the *recovery* arena. And on March 31, 1979, President Carter's Executive Order 12127 led to the creation of the Federal Emergency Management System (FEMA) to which all disaster-related statutory authority that then had been vested in the Presidency, as well as those invested in other federal agencies, were transferred. Today, disaster relief has evolved into a national, integrated emergency management system in the Department of Homeland Security (DHS), and FEMA operates on an incident management assistance team (IMAT) system structured around National Incident Management System/Incident Command System (ICS) compliant (management) teams that can rapidly deploy to an incident or incident-threatened venue, and become part of a Unified Command to lead a prompt, effective, and coordinated federal response in support of state, tribal, and local emergency management officials.

Emergency response structures and measures are necessary for the two broad categories of disasters – natural and man-made – although the former can exacerbate the latter due to actions that humans take or fail to take. Four broad categories of events – geophysical (earthquakes and volcanic eruptions), meteorological (tropical cyclones; winter storms; thunderstorms, tornadoes, and hail), hydrological (windstorms and floods), and climatological (forest/wildfires) – warrant the need for effective and well-coordinated emergency management systems and procedures. While floods, storms, earthquakes, droughts, forest fires, and volcanic eruptions are among the most devastating types of natural catastrophe, human-caused disasters, including explosions, major fires, aviation, shipping and railway accidents, and the release of toxic substances into the environment, can also devastate communities. Particularly important for policymakers is the realization that both natural and human-caused disasters – especially in this era of global climate change and terrorism in all of its forms and facets – are increasing in diversity and magnitude, not only in the United States but also around the world. For example, between 1980 and the first half of 2019, the United States experienced 250 weather and climate disasters for an average of 6.1 of these events; however, the average number of these events between 2014 and 2018 more than doubled to 12.6 (NOAA, 2019).

These events generate huge economic costs and human losses. When adjusted for inflation, the data indicate that the average losses over the past 30 years ranged from $140 billion to $160 billion, including average insured losses of $41 billion. That is, the United States has, since 1980, sustained 250 weather and climate disasters resulting in overall damages/costs exceeding $1 billion (including Consumer Price Index adjustment to 2019), including the year 2018, which recorded the fourth-highest total number of events only behind the years 2017, 2011, and 2016. The United States also experienced the fourth-highest total disaster costs of $91 billion in 2018, only behind the years 2017, 2005, and 2012 (NOAA, 2019). Of this amount, meteorological events accounted for 58% of insured losses; climatological 20%; hydrological 14%; and geophysical 8% (Amadeo, 2019; Löw, 2019). And, as of April 9, 2019, the United States had experienced two weather and climate disaster events with losses exceeding $1 billion each (NOAA, 2019). In light of typology, frequency, diversity, and cost, emergency management seems rather obvious. But this is where the challenge and complexity begin because each disaster, by its very nature, is unique; therefore, the different protocols, responders, and funding methods needed to address them tend to present significant challenges during all phases of emergency management (Goss and Devereaux, 2018).

Evolution of Governmental Role and Policy in Disaster Response and Management

The quintessential responsibility of government is to protect its citizens from danger, and since the establishment of FEMA in 1979, the federal government has developed a network of national, state, and local government institutions to mitigate the impact of all types of disasters. Although there is much room for improvement, this network has been relatively effective in the area of natural disaster preparedness and recovery process. However, the same is not true for man-made disasters, such as terrorist attacks or acts of mass violence, because "...the intergovernmental path is bifurcated and disjointed, making it difficult, if not impossible, for local governments to navigate" (Goss and Devereaux, 2018). What complicates this task for the United States is a federal government composed of multiple jurisdictions that share responsibility for disaster mitigation and response across an interacting network of institutions at national, state, and local levels of government. There are at least 14 federal departments and agencies responsible for the administration of dozens of recovery-related programs, many of which rely heavily on active participation by state and local governments for their implementation. Given the many different organizations that have roles in disaster preparedness, response, and recovery, it can be confusing to understand which organization or agency has which responsibilities (Goss and Devereaux, 2018).

Formally, and especially in response to the terrorist attacks of September 11, 2001, the official policy position regarding disaster mitigation and response reflects an all-hazards approach that includes the reduction of threats from natural, technological, or deliberate causes. In practice, however, modalities have not been sufficiently well-developed to achieve effective coordination within and between jurisdictions.

This has been due in part to the policy position taken by the George W. Bush Administration that identified terrorism as the primary threat to the nation and, consequently focused its efforts on the prevention of further terrorist attacks within the all-hazards approach (Comfort, 2006: 501–516). A 50-year-plus period of policy development and procedure implementation, therefore, still reveals significant shortcomings and vulnerabilities in the emergency management and response system. Attempts to understand this system and its processes require an understanding and ability to differentiate between "disaster" and "emergency;" between "crisis management" and "consequence management;" and between "general operational responsibility" and "medical responsibility."

Understanding Disaster Preparedness and Response Systems. Disaster preparedness and government response systems can be divided into two broad categories: general operational responsibility and medical responsibility. The DHS, headed by the Secretary of Homeland Security, has general operational responsibility related to federal disaster response in the United States. FEMA falls within the ambit of DHS's general operational responsibility. The Department of Health and Human Services (HHS), the Office of the Assistant Secretary for Preparedness and Response (ASPR), the Centers for Disease Control and Prevention (CDC), and the National Institutes of Health (NIH) (www.phe.gov), which falls to the Department of Health and Human Services (HHS), headed by the Secretary of Health and Human Services. Three of the key operating divisions of HHS are the ASPR, the CDC, and the NIH. ASPR was established to create a focal point or a "unity of command" by consolidating all federal non-military public health and medical preparedness and response functions in one office. Accordingly, ASPR collaborates with hospitals, healthcare coalitions, biotech firms, community members, state, local, tribal, and territorial governments, and other partners across the country to improve readiness and response capabilities. As part of its readiness program, ASPR purchases medical countermeasures, including vaccines, drugs, therapies, and diagnostic tools for public health threats or medical emergencies (www.phe.gov).

The primary purpose of FEMA is to coordinate a response to a disaster that occurs in the United States, and that overwhelms the resources of local or state authorities. And since the locus of all disasters is local, the governor of the state in which the disaster occurs must declare a state of emergency and must request from the President of the United States that FEMA and the federal government respond to the disaster. FEMA's hierarchy reflects an Administrator, Deputy Administrator, Mission Support, US Fire Administration, Regional Administration, and Office of Response and Recovery, and operates as a regional group with the regional response from the following ten regional centers: Boston, New York, Philadelphia, Atlanta, Chicago, Denton, Kansas City, Denver, Oakland, and Seattle. If a local government is unable to handle a disaster on its own, it notifies the state that it needs state and/or federal assistance. For natural disasters, the Governor's Office, in conjunction with the State Emergency Management Department or Homeland Security Department, notifies the President and FEMA of the need for federal assistance. The President, with advice from FEMA, decides whether to provide or deny federal assistance. Once a decision is made to provide assistance, the President declares the disaster site to be a "federal disaster area," a declaration that enables FEMA to provide individual assistance and aid to public entities from the National Disaster Relief Fund, as authorized by the Robert T. Stafford Disaster Relief and Emergency Assistance Act "the Stafford Act" (Goss and Devereaux, 2018). This legislation authorizes the President to issue major disaster or emergency declarations in response to incidents that overwhelm state and local governments. Either type of declaration would authorize the distribution of a wide range of federal aid to individuals and families, certain non-profit organizations, and public agencies, but major disaster and emergency classifications each trigger different kinds and amounts of assistance from the federal government (Liu, 2008).

Crisis Management Versus Consequence Management

The DHS, created in January 2004, reflects a major reorganization of US emergency management and security responses, which now incorporates the theretofore two major policy responses to major threats to the United States – the National Response Plan and the National Incident Management System – both of which had undergone extensive review (Comfort, 2006: 501–516). The National Response Plan (FEMA, 2004) was an adaptation of the former Federal Response Plan (FEMA, 2000) that identified the roles and responsibilities of the 28 federal agencies in mobilizing a response to an actual disaster. The intent of the National Response Plan was to extend the design of interagency collaboration to state, county, and municipal levels of authority in response to a disaster. It was formally adopted in November 2004 in a major effort to improve coordination among levels of governmental jurisdiction in disaster response. The National Incident Management Plan (NIMS), adapted from the earlier ICS initially developed by the US Forest Service in response to recurring wildland fires in Southern California, created a common terminology and set of standards for disaster operations that would be recognized and followed at each jurisdictional level. The intent was to develop a common method of training and practice that would allow the rapid mobilization of a response system from different organizations and jurisdictions in disaster operations for a specific incident (Comfort, 2006: 501–516).

Earlier executive orders, such as the US Intergovernmental Counterterrorism Concept of Operations Plan issued in January 2002, have also been part of the major effort to redefine governmental responsibilities to reduce the threat of disaster. This executive order first redefined the role (FEMA), making it the lead agency for consequence management, but assigning the role of Crisis Management to the Department of Justice and agencies responsible for managing security threats. This distinction of crisis from consequence management separated the major function of disaster mitigation that FEMA had developed under the leadership of James Lee Witt in the 1990s from the disaster relief-and-recovery functions that had been its traditional role (Comfort, 2006). Both functions were incorporated into the DHS when it was established in January 2004 (Comfort, 2006: 501–516).

If the disaster is a human-induced event, the disaster site is declared a crime scene by the Federal Bureau of Investigation and then handled by the Department of Justice and the DHS. The federal government's role in recovery from man-made disasters has been primarily situational, leaving impacted local communities to figure out which agency is in charge, what assistance might be available, and whom to contact for help unless the incident is of sufficient magnitude to warrant either a Presidential Declaration of Disaster or an Emergency Declaration.

Conceptual Confusion

The terms emergency, disaster, catastrophe, and hazard have been used interchangeably, often synonymously when referring to events that disrupt the normal functioning of communities, local and national. This conceptual confusion has found its way into the policy process with regard to responses to disruptive events – localized or widespread – despite the position of the scholarly community, including, and especially E. L. Quarantelli (2000), that emergencies, disasters, and catastrophes are different phenomena, and that these differences should be considered in the planning and management activities of any crisis-relevant groups (Lindell, Prater, and Perry, 2007: 2–6). A hazard is a source of danger, such as a tsunami, or an accidental release of radiological materials or toxic chemicals, that has the potential to affect people, property, and the natural environment in a given locale. Emergency is used to describe events that result in a few casualties, such as a fire or an automobile accident, or even a heart attack. Emergency is also used to describe an imminent threat such as a hurricane that is likely to strike land and which provides little time to respond. A disaster is an event that produces losses that exceed the ability of a community to handle and, which, therefore, requires support from other communities, the state.

Congress, however, seeking simplicity, speaks to the issue of emergency and the issue of a major disaster in the amended Robert T. Stafford Disaster Relief and Emergency Assistance Act, Public Law 93-288. Section 102 of this Act defines an emergency as (1988):

> ...any occasion or instance for which, in the determination of the President, Federal assistance is needed to supplement State and local efforts and capabilities to save lives and to protect property and public health and safety, or to lessen or avert the threat of a catastrophe in any part of the United States.
>
> (Public Law 93-288)

And a major disaster is defined as:

> ...any natural catastrophe (including any hurricane, tornado, storm, high water, wind driven water, tidal wave, tsunami, earthquake, volcanic eruption, landslide, mudslide, snowstorm, or drought), or, regardless of cause, any fire, flood, or explosion, in any part of the United States, which in the determination of the President causes damage of sufficient severity and magnitude to warrant major disaster assistance under this Act to supplement the efforts and available resources of States, local governments, and disaster relief organizations in alleviating the damage, loss, hardship, or suffering caused thereby.
>
> (FEMA B-761, 2017; Public Law 93-288)

With Congress having hardly clarified the conceptual confusion, FEMA, in turn, has come up with a partial resolution to the term "incident." On the one hand, FEMA describes an incident as

> ...an occurrence or event, natural or manmade, which requires a response to protect life or property. Incidents can, for example, include major disasters, emergencies, terrorist attacks, terrorist threats, civil unrest, wild land and urban fires, floods, hazardous material spills, nuclear accidents, aircraft accidents, earthquakes, hurricanes, tornadoes, tropical storms, tsunamis, war-related disasters, public health and medical emergencies, and other occurrences requiring an emergency response.
>
> (FEMA B-761, 2019)

On the other hand, FEMA defines as a catastrophic incident, "any natural or manmade incident that results in extraordinary levels of mass casualties, damage, or disruption that severely affect the populations, infrastructure, environment, economy, national morale, and/or government functions" (FEMA B-761, 2017). Accordingly, FEMA operates in accordance with the NIMS of December 2008, which articulates a set of principles that provides a systematic, proactive approach to guide government agencies at all levels, non-governmental organizations (NGOs), and the private sector. The NIMS works seamlessly to prevent, protect against, respond to, recover from, and mitigate the effects of incidents, regardless of cause, size, location, or complexity to reduce the loss of life or property and harm to the environment. FEMA, therefore, operates on an IMAT system structured around National Incident Management System/ICS compliant (management) teams that can rapidly deploy to an incident or incident-threatened venue, and become part of a Unified Command to lead a prompt, effective, and coordinated federal response in support of state, tribal, and local emergency management officials.

FEMA defines as incident management, "the level of operation of the Federal in emergency response, recovery, logistics, and mitigation." Responsibilities in incident management include the direct control and employment of resources, management of incident offices, operations, and delivery of federal assistance through all phases of emergency response (FEMA B-761, 2019). FEMA defines an ICS, "a standardized emergency management construct specifically designed to provide for the adoption of an integrated organizational structure that reflects the complexity and demands of single or multiple incidents, without being hindered by jurisdictional boundaries." ICS is a management system designed to enable effective incident management by integrating a combination of facilities, equipment, personnel, procedures, and communications operating within a common organizational structure, designed to aid in the management of resources during incidents. It is used for all kinds of emergencies and is applicable to small as well as large complex incidents. ICS is used by various jurisdictions and functional agencies, both public and private, to organize field-level incident management operations (FEMA B-761, 2019). FEMA uses three incident levels to categorize incidents based on the actual or anticipated impact, size, and complexity of the incident and the federal assistance required. Accordingly, Level I requires an extreme amount of federal assistance; Level II requires a high level of federal assistance; and Level III requires a minimum level of federal assistance (FEMA B-761, 2019). But there is still more.

Policy Challenges

A crisis occurs. How to respond? During 1995, the Oklahoma City bombing crisis, government and non-profit responders were on the scene minutes following the detonation of the massive truck bomb that destroyed the Murrah federal building. Using an ICS management, one person was appointed incident commander and was responsible for directing all other responders. But since all crises are not the same, and since a human-induced disaster site, such as a terrorist attack or cyber event, is declared a crime scene by the FBI, FEMA is challenged because of its focus on natural disasters. This aspect of emergency management is especially urgent and critical because the US economy is increasingly cyber-enabled, driven by powerful companies like Google, Apple, and Cisco. These companies are entirely reliant on the regularity and consistency in the provision of electricity for powering servers and computer networks. The advantages provided by a cyber-enabled social and economic architecture must be balanced against an overreliance on modern communications infrastructure as the post-Katrina events in New Orleans so poignantly demonstrated. The near-total collapse of landline, satellite, and cell phone communications made it practically impossible for local law enforcement and the Louisiana National Guard to coordinate response efforts. The reality is that cyber policy, regulation, and infrastructure affect society at large: private companies; private individuals; and local, state, and federal governments all – severally and jointly. Thus, a probing question for policymakers to address is this: what regulatory policies should be implemented that would simultaneously promote resiliency and security in cyber critical infrastructure such that first responders are able to react timely when that infrastructure is under threat?

Further Reading

Canton, L. G. (2019). *Emergency Management: Concepts and Strategies for Effective Programs* (2nd ed.). Hoboken: John Wiley & Sons, Inc.

Chung, J. (2013, May 7). *Counter-Terrorism and Emergency Management: Keeping a Proper Balance*, The Brookings Institution, Washington, DC. brookings.edu/opinions/counter-terrorism-and-emergency-management-keeping-a-proper-balance/

Reddick, C. (2010, August 16). "Information technology and emergency management: preparedness and planning in US states," *Disasters*, *35*(1): 45–61. https://onlinelibrary.wiley.com/doi/epdf/10.1111/j.1467-7717.2010.01192.x

References

Bailey, C. M. (2017). "Networking Emergency Response: Empowering FEMA in the Age of Convergence and Cyber Critical Infrastructure," *96 Nebraska Law Review*, 96, 509–534. https://digitalcommons.unl.edu/nlr/vol96/iss2/10

CBS News. (2018). "Natural Disasters Cost the US A Record $306 Billion Last Year," January 8. http://www.cbsnews.com/news/us-record-306-billion-natural-disasters-last-year-hurricanes-wilidfires/

Chappell, C. (2019). "Natural Disasters Cost $91 Billion in 2018, According to A Federal Report," February 6. https://www.cnbc.com/2019/02/06/natural-disasters-cost-91-billion-in-2018-federal-report.html

Comfort, L.K. (2006). Cities at risk: Hurricane Katrina and the drowning of New Orleans. *Urban Affairs Review*, 41(4), 501–516.

FEMA. (2008). *On call: disaster reserve workforce news*, September. https://www.fema.gov/pdf/dae/200809.pdf

FEMA. (2017). Incident management handbook. https://www.fema.gov/media-library-data/1511798700826-e38977943819bb12064e3144cca7c576/FnlRvwIMH20171026v1945(508).pdf

Goss, K.C. & Devereaux, G.C. (2018). *The U.S. Emergency management system: The need for intergovernmental cooperation*. https://www.napawash.org/uploads/Standing_Panels/Intergovernmental_Systems/109_APA_DISASTER.pdf

Library of Congress. *A century of lawmaking for a New Nation: US Congressional Documents and debates*. https://memory.loc.gov/cgi-bin/ampage?collId=llhb&fileName=021/llhb021.db&recNum=41

Liu, E.C. (2008). *Would an influenza pandemic qualify as a major disaster under the Stafford act? Congressional research service*, October 20. https://fas.org/sgp/crs/misc/RL34724.pdf.

Löw, P. (2019). *The natural disasters of 2018 in figures*. https://www.munichre.com/topics-online/en/climate-change-and-natural-disasters/natural-disasters/the-natural-disasters-of-2018-in-figures.html

Moynihan, D.P. (2009). The network governance of crisis response: Case studies of incident command systems, *Journal of Public Administration Research and Theory*, 19(4), 895–915.

NOAA. (2019). *US 2018 Billion-Dollar weather and climate disasters*. https://www.ncdc.noaa.gov/billions/overview

Pittman, E. (2011). How emergency management is changing (for the better). *Emergency Management*. https://www.govtech.com/em/training/How-Emergency-Management-IsChanging.html

Public Health Emergency. (2019). HHS office of the assistant secretary for preparedness and response. Available at https://www.phe.gov/about/offices/Pages/default.aspx

Robert T. (1988). Stafford Disaster Relief and Emergency Assistance Act. Public Law 93-288, as amended, 42 U.S.C. 5121 et seq., and Related Authorities, United States Code, Title 42. The Public Health and Welfare, Chapter 68. *Disaster Relief*. https://www.fema.gov/media-library-data/1519395888776-af5f95a1a9237302af7e3fd5b0d07d71/StaffordAct.pdf

U.S. Response Organizations. (2019). *Disaster Information Management Research Center*. https://sis.nlm.nih.gov/dis_courses/us_response/02-000.htm

United States Government Interagency Domestic Terrorism Concept of Operations Plan. (January, 2002). http://www.fema.gov/rrr/conplan/forword.shtm. This strategy was further developed with the enactment of the Homeland Security Act, January 22, 2002. (H.R. 5005). Federal Register. Washington, DC: February 22, 2001.

Chapter 95

Homeland Security and the Arctic

James Rogers
University of Southern Denmark, Odense, Denmark

Contents

Introduction 731
The United States and the Arctic: A Brief History 732
An Opening Arctic: 2020 Visions and Beyond 734
Arctic Drones 735
Conclusion 736
Acknowledgements 737
Further Reading 737
References 737

Introduction

Since the end of the Cold War, the mantra of "High North, low tensions" has been at the centre of scholarly and policy debate about the world's most northerly region (Lanteigne, 2019). In 1996, the Arctic Council was founded. This pioneering intergovernmental forum provided a space for "cooperation, coordination and interaction" between the eight recognised Arctic states (Arctic Council, 2015). These states – Canada, the Kingdom of Denmark, Finland, Iceland, Norway, the Russian Federation, Sweden, and the United States – have, alongside Arctic indigenous communities and Arctic inhabitants, taken action on specific "Arctic issues", including but not limited to, sustainable development, indigenous rights, and environmental protection. As the global climate emergency unfolds, this forum has never been more important. There is, however, one telling gap in the Arctic Council's remit: national security.

DOI: 10.4324/9781315144511-100

Security, when defined in a *critical* fashion as a broader human or environmental issue, has been discussed between the Arctic Council members, yet as a more traditional nation state and military focused issue, the topic has remained on the peripheries of Council discussion. In fact, despite the Arctic having long been a militarised space, dialogue on Arctic security issues has yet to find an adequate home within the international system. There is the "Arctic Security Forces Roundtable" (ASFR), a collection of 11 military leaders from nations that have an interest in the Arctic, yet with the removal of Russia from this group, it now excludes one of the Arctic's leading powers. In addition, up until 2015 the informal "Arctic's Chiefs of Defense Staff" meeting ran each year, yet this has not run for half a decade due to continued tensions between Russia and Ukraine. Thus, as Wieslander (2019) argued, "no international institution deals with hard security in the Arctic". This is perhaps surprising.

With global climate change leading to an altered melting Arctic landscape, previously unreachable resources have become accessible and new, faster, Arctic global trading routes are seeing increased levels of traffic. In 2018, shipping traffic on the Northern Sea Route (NSR) – the transit route that runs along Russia's northern Arctic coastline linking Asia and Europe – doubled compared to 2017. To be specific, the NSR surpassed "15 million tons of cargo during the first eleven months of the year" (Humpert and DeGeorge, 2019). This has led to a number of Arctic states, but also self-defined "near-Arctic" and non-Arctic actors, expressing increased interest in the region. Here, it is worth noting the growing footprint of China within Iceland and Greenland, but also collaborations between India and China with a reinvigorated Russia which is investing in new high-tech "Arctic ready" military technologies, ports, and bases. Still, these states are not alone in their Arctic interests. As Dodds and Nuttall (2019) have argued, Singapore, South Korea, and Japan have Arctic aspirations as "Asian states are noticeably investing in polar infrastructure, science, and resource development projects". Increased interest and investment does not necessarily equate in increased tension or insecurity. Much of the Arctic is already under the sovereign control of Arctic states meaning that an unregulated "gold rush" in the Arctic is unlikely.

Over the coming decades, regions of the Arctic will "open up for business" and the monitoring of state "manoeuvring" in many parts of the Arctic will be a priority for the United States and its North Atlantic Treaty Organization (NATO) allies. As the 2019 US Defence Authorisation Act outlined, the US Secretary of Defence has 6 months to report on Russian and Chinese involvement in the Arctic, particularly in regard to how military activities might "affect or threaten the interests of the United States and allies in the Arctic region" (US Congress, 2019). As an addition to this, the US Department of Defence (DoD) has released an updated "Arctic Strategy" in 2019 in which it sets out a "strategy for the Arctic region in an era of strategic competition". Building upon the 2013 and 2016 Arctic strategies, the DoD recognises the need for the United States to maintain its lethal military capabilities and a "credible deterrent for the Arctic region", while also keeping abreast of the evolving geo-strategic and political landscape in the Arctic (DoD, 2019; Pincus, 2019).

The United States and the Arctic: A Brief History

Why is the Arctic important to the United States? Looking back at the origins of US interests in the Arctic and High North, it is clear that the Arctic has often been seen as a land of economic prosperity, or strategic importance, by competing states and thus a point of contention between the United States and its rivals. For the United States, the Arctic and High North have been militarised and strategically important regions since at least the 1800s. Although it was surprising to many international leaders and political commentators that President Trump tentatively suggested the United States should purchase Greenland from the Kingdom of Denmark in 2019, it was not the first time the United States had looked to "purchase the Arctic"; most notably in terms of Alaska, but also Greenland. In regard to Greenland, the United States considered buying the vast island in 1867, 1910, and 1946. On each occasion, it was resource extraction and national security consideration that drove the proposal. Yet, as with President Trump's proposition in 2019, the suggestion was not entertained by the Danes or the Greenlandic peoples.

This being said, the Roosevelt administration and the exiled Danish government did enter an "*Agreement relating to the Defense of Greenland*" in 1941 that saw the US defend Greenland from Nazi occupation, a fate which had already befallen mainland Denmark (Sappington & Prescott, 1959). This agreement also allowed the United States to operate in Greenland as long as there was a threat to North America. Various incarnations of this earlier agreement, adjusted during the Cold War, means that today the US Air Base Thule still operates on the island, housing the US 21st Space Wing's global network of sensors. Thule provides "missile warning, space surveillance, and space control to North American Aerospace Defense Command and Air Force Space Command", while also providing an almost two-mile-long airstrip and the "northernmost deep-water port in the world" (US Air Force, 2019). Alaska, on the other hand, is a very different story.

During 1720s, the Russian Czar, Peter the Great, displayed "a keen interest" in the Alaskan coast (Office of the Historian n.d.). Over the next 100 years, Russian explorers and traders established a small foothold in the region. By 1850s, however, as the United States expanded to the West Coast and Russia sought to counter British power after defeat in Crimea, the Russian's offered to sell Alaska to the United States. This was settled with a $7.2 million price tag and completed after the Civil War in 1867. Over the next 100 years, Alaska not only became one of the 50 states that formed the union, but has become an important asset for the United States. It is a valuable land of gold and oil deposits, a home to over 700,000 people, and was a vital strategic location during the World War II, the Cold War, and through into the twenty-first century. For example, the only battle of the World War II on US soil occurred in Alaska as the Japanese occupied two of the Aleutian Islands. In addition, the lend-lease of aircraft to Russia took place across the remote Alaska–Siberia (ALSIB) route which comprised a number of new far north airfields allowing pilots to leapfrog across the top of the world "through the Canadian and Alaskan wilderness" (Garfield, 1995).

The importance of the Arctic continued during the Cold War, with the geographical "closeness" to Russia turning from being fruitful to fearful as the looming threat of a Soviet atomic attack emerged. In what was known was the "Polar Concept", US military planners recognised that the airspace over the Arctic offered the USSR the most direct and lightly-defended route to target the United States. Such fear of a vulnerable north continued through the Cold War and into the twenty-first century. Thus, for the United States, the "American Arctic" has been the frontline of defence and attack in interconnected global warfare. As the West's tense relationship with

Russia progresses through the 2020s, it will be regions such as Alaska which look over towards Russia from the North-West – but also Greenland which provides the United States with an overwatch of Russia from the North-East – that will be at the front and centre of American interests as they look up towards increased activity on the top of the world.

An Opening Arctic: 2020 Visions and Beyond

Part of what drives current US interests in the Arctic is an awareness of how technological innovation, state ambition, and climate change are altering perceptions of the world's northern most region as a space for profitable enterprise and military expedition. New commercial opportunities and evolved economic understandings of the region are emerging alongside uncomfortable security dynamics as actors compete to have power and influence. Currently, only some 15% of the Arctic Ocean has been mapped, but this is changing with unmanned vehicles developed and utilised to help track, trace, and explore uncharted waters (Depledge, Kennedy-Pipe, and Rogers, 2019). Satellites capable of covering the High North will enable not just mapping but monitoring of the region, allowing greater safety of navigation around icebergs and through sea ice, but also the monitoring of ecosystems and pollution.

These unmanned and satellites systems will also be useful for regional actors with competing security claims, helping to identify and patrol areas of sovereign rights. These technologies are also useful to for non-Arctic, or indeed "near-Arctic" states to stay informed, search for opportunities, and extend their footprint in the Arctic. In this sense, as unmanned, satellite, and remote technologies "go online" for Arctic deployment, the vast region will see an extension of the activities from non-Arctic states. Important technologies in development are earth observation and satellite programmes for the Arctic to track commercial potential and ever longer-range drone systems that will provide environmental monitoring, civil search and rescue assistance, military logistical support, surveillance, electronic warfare, and kinetic support. Put simply, the Arctic is "opening up for business", and this is both a time of opportunity for the United States and trepidation in regard to altered security dynamics.

As a recognised Arctic State, with sovereign territory rising above the 66th parallel north and into the Arctic Circle, external actor activity could give rise to positive economic opportunities and partnerships for the United States. Unavoidably, however, such activity also raises national security concerns. As President Trump's Secretary of State, Mike Pompeo, stated in May 2019:

> [t]he Arctic is at the forefront of opportunity and abundance...It houses 13 percent of the world's undiscovered oil, 30 percent of its undiscovered gas, an abundance of uranium, rare earth minerals, gold, diamonds, and millions of square miles of untapped resources, fisheries galore.
>
> (CNN, 2019b)

Pompeo's comments were to be expected. With the global climate emergency leading to the Arctic region warming almost twice the rate of the rest of the world, a number of state actors and multinational corporations have sought to harness newly accessible natural resources. A point of warning here is that "what happens in the Arctic does not stay in the Arctic". Although the Arctic is made of many diverse regional ecosystems – where climate change has a varied impact – sea ice in parts of the Arctic is still projected to all but disappear during summer months within a generation. To be specific, according to the World Wildlife Fund (*Last Ice Area – WWF Arctic*, 2022), the "average temperature of the Arctic has increased 2.3°C since the 1970s". This ice melt, along with related permafrost melting and polar wildfires, is predicted to have a severe impact on global weather patterns, sea level rise, and CO_2 emissions. This will drive more extreme weather patterns around the world, including on the US mainland. So, it is changes in the environment, exacerbated by Arctic warming, which will pose a threat to the security of communities across the United States.

Nevertheless, it appears that international business interest in the Arctic will continue, even increase, for the foreseeable, leading to additional concerns about the rise of military security issues in the region. In his May 2019 address, Pompeo was not blind to these issues and bookended his speech by asking: "[d]o we want the Arctic Ocean to transform into a new South China Sea, fraught with militarization and competing territorial claims?". These comments were aimed at China, which self-identifies as a "near-Arctic state" and has invested heavily in scientific research, logistical infrastructure, and resource extraction projects as a means to obtain influence in the region. Yet, Pompeo's comments were also pointed towards Russia which is arguably the most militarily and economically capable and prepared Arctic nation.

Arctic Drones

One of the ways Russia has sought to ensure it can effectively master its vast "Russian Arctic" territory, is through investment in remote control drone and robotic systems, with other nations quickly following suit. The mantra of "remote systems for a remote region" has been the foundation and justification for this increased investment. Russia and Canada have already invested in unmanned systems for surveying the NSR and the North West Passage (NWP), while the US Navy uses unmanned systems for research into sea ice. The US Air Force has also conducted flights of its most advanced drone, the RQ-4 Global Hawk, from its Eielson Air Force Base in Alaska. European nations also have also made their mark in the region – after all 50% of the Arctic peoples are European and 24% of the hydrocarbons consumed by Europe originate from the Arctic (Ministry of Armed Forces, 2019: 5). The British have designed and developed their new "Watchkeeper" drone for future Arctic deployment, with tests undertaken to ensure it can withstand harsh Arctic conditions (Thales n.d.). Denmark has long been using drones to patrol waters off the coast of Greenland and the latest Danish Defence Agreement (2018–2023) specifically raised concerns about "increased activity" in the Arctic and pledged to "participate in the full spectrum of military operations, including collective deterrence, assurance measures, counterterrorism, stabilisation and conflict prevention efforts as well as increased presence in the Arctic" (Danish Ministry of Defence, 2019).

To facilitate this, Denmark has prioritised its building of a drone capacity as part of its brigade structure and continues to use drones for regional surveillance.

As the Danish press reported, the Danish government also wants to harness not only drones but also satellites "to get a good overview of what is happening in the North Atlantic, from the Faroe Islands to Greenland and the sea around the North Pole, where Denmark demands ownership of the seabed" (Hannestad, 2016). Denmark is not alone in this ambition. Such remote technologies are possessed or accessible to a number of European actors – from France to Norway – and are important for broader situational awareness and monitoring of the Arctic. Yet, these European assets pale in comparison to Russian capabilities that dominate the region: when it comes to remote technologies in the Arctic, Russia leads the way. This state of affairs has been noted by the United States but requires strategic investment to adequately counter.

To be specific, Russia is in the advanced stages of establishing a remote system of border control and protection around the NSR. Since 2007, and the infamous planting of the Russian flag on the seabed of the North Pole, Russia has been seeking to re-establish its military dominance in the region. Remote technologies have helped with this. Putin's 2014 decision to set up an "Arctic Drone Squadron" was part of this push for control. With at least four airfields converted for high-tech specialised Arctic drone deployment across the mainland coastal rim of the Russian Arctic – from Naryan-Mar (Nenets) in the west, all the way to Anadyr (Chukotka) overlooking the Bering Sea in the east – Putin has gifted Russia the ability to survey and track all passage through the NSR (Boulègue, 2019). If action needed to be taken to tackle intruding or unwanted vessels in this region, new drone carrying icebreakers and ice-hardened military corvettes are being constructed to facilitate this. Fully functioning troop bases across Russia's Arctic islands also add to this monitoring and response capacity.

The "Northern Clover" on Kotelney Island has an airfield, missile-based costal defences, anti-aircraft systems, 200+ soldiers, sophisticated radar, and compliments the Anadyr drone base located just over the water on the mainland. The "Arctic Trefoil", otherwise known as Nagurskoye Air Base, is all the way on the other side of the NSR, located on Franz Joseph Land. This also has the capacity for 200+ troops, but has the added clout of advanced anti-ship missile systems with a 200-km range and a new 2,500-m runway. Russian drones and military aircraft, such as the supersonic medium-range fighter-bomber, Su-34, can now take off from this site if required (Humpert, 2019). According to a 2019 CNN report, Russia has put in place more than 470 pieces of Arctic infrastructure since 2012 alone (CNN, 2019a). All of this appears to make sense for Russia. The territory is, after all, the "Russian Arctic", and the NSR will increasingly be a vital bloodline for global trade and resource extraction. Not only this, but according to the Russian defence minister, Sergei Shoigu, 59% of the country's modern nuclear and missile arsenal will be located in the region by 2020 (Aliyev, 2019). When this is considered as a whole, it is clear to see that there has been a strategic decision made by President Putin to build-up a remote, technologically centric, "virtual net" over the Arctic.

Conclusion

There are, of course, scholars who argue Russia's new remote bases and drone technologies are dual-use, allowing for a safer SAR infrastructure around the NSR. Yet, it may be more accurate to consider these technologies as appropriate for "misuse". Russia is the world's leading Arctic military power, and the considerable Arctic technology and "drone gap" forming in the region should be of worry to Western nations, especially the United States, who wish to continue to enjoy the freedom of the Arctic Ocean, access resources, protect their populations, and monitor the climate crisis.

Acknowledgements

The author wishes to recognise the considerable contribution of Professor Caroline Kennedy-Pipe and Dr. Duncan Depledge of the University of Loughborough. Their time, advice, and points of noted critique undoubtedly added to the quality of the chapter. All points of view (for better or for worse) are, however, those of the author.

Further Reading

Depledge, D., Kennedy-Pipe, C., & Rogers J. (2019). The UK and the arctic: forward defence. *Arctic Yearbook.* https://arcticyearbook.com/arctic-yearbook/2019/2019-scholarly-papers/320-the-uk-and-the-arctic-forward-defence

Dodds, K., & Nuttall, M. (2019). *The Arctic: what everyone needs to know.* New York, NY: Oxford University Press.

Exner-Pirot, H. (2019). Between militarization and disarmament: Constructing peace in the Arctic. *Arctic Yearbook 2019.* https://arcticyearbook.com/arctic-yearbook/2019/2019-commentaries/324-between-militarization-and-disarmament-constructing-peace-in-the-arctic

References

Aliyev, N. (2019, June 25). *Russia's military capabilities in the arctic.* https://icds.ee/russias-military-capabilities-in-the-arctic/

Arctic Council. (2015, May 20). *Arctic frontiers 2020.* https://arctic-council.org/index.php/en/about-us

Boulègue, M. (2019). Russia's Military Posture in the Arctic: Managing Hard Power in a 'Low Tension' Environment, *Chatham House.* https://www.chathamhouse.org/publication/russia-s-military-posture-arctic-managing-hard-power-low-tension-environment

CNN. (2019a, April 4). *An exclusive look inside Russia's Arctic military base – CNN Video.* https://edition.cnn.com/videos/world/2019/04/04/russia-arctic-base.cnn

CNN. (2019b, May 7). *Pompeo: Melting sea ice presents 'new opportunities for trade.* cnn.com/2019/05/06/politics/pompeo-sea-ice-arctic-council/index.html

Danish Ministry of Defence. (2019). *Defence agreement 2018–2023.* https://www.fmn.dk/eng/allabout/Pages/danish-defence-agreement.aspx

Depledge, D., Kennedy-Pipe, C., & Rogers, J. (2019). The UK and the arctic: forward defence. *Arctic Yearbook.* https://arcticyearbook.com/arctic-yearbook/2019/2019-scholarly-papers/320-the-uk-and-the-arctic-forward-defence

DoD. (2019, June). Report to Congress – Department of Defense Arctic Strategy. *Office of the Under Secretary of Defense for Policy.* media.defense.gov/2019/Jun/06/2002141657/-1/-1/1/2019-DOD-ARCTIC-STRATEGY.PDF

Dodds, K., & Nuttall, M. (2019). *The Arctic: what everyone needs to know.* New York, NY: Oxford University Press.

Frank, R. *Collbohm Papers, Meetings and Correspondence. EXEC, COLL, DOC, 001.* RAND Corporation Archives.

Garfield, B. (1995). *The thousand-mile war: World War II in Alaska and the Aleutians.* Fairbanks: University of Alaska Press.

Hannestad, A. (2016, August 28). Rapport: send droner til arktis. *Politiken.* https://politiken.dk/indland/art5633958/Rapport-Send-droner-til-Arktis.

Humpert, M. (2019, December 31). New satellite images reveal extent of Russia's military and economic build-up in the arctic. *High North News.* https://www.highnorthnews.com/en/new-satellite-images-reveal-extent-russias-military-and-economic-build-arctic

Humpert, M., & DeGeorge, K. (2019, February 20). Russia's Northern Sea Route sees record cargo volume in 2018. *Arctic Today.* https://www.arctictoday.com/russias-northern-sea-route-sees-record-cargo-volume-in-2018/

Lanteigne, M. (2019, June 28). The changing shape of arctic security. *NATO Review* https://www.nato.int/docu/review/articles/2019/06/28/the-changing-shape-of-arctic-security/index.html

Last Ice Area – WWF Arctic. (2022, May 5). WWF arctic. https://arcticwwf.org/places/last-ice-area/

Ministry of Armed Forces. (2019). *France and the new strategic challenges in the Arctic. p. 5.*

Office of the Historian. (n.d.). *Purchase of Alaska, 1867.* https://history.state.gov/milestones/1866-1898/alaska-purchase

Pincus, R. (2019). Trump's new arctic policy has a familiar ring, *Defence One.* https://www.defenseone.com/ideas/2019/06/trumps-new-arctic-policy-has-familiar-ring/157622/

Sappington, N.O. & Prescott, F.C. (1959). *Foreign relations of the United States diplomatic papers*, 1941, Europe, Volume II Document 40. United States Government Printing Office: Washington, DC.

Thales. (n.d.). *Watchkeeper X.* https://www.thalesgroup.com/en/global/activities/defence/unmanned-aerial-vehicles-systems/watchkeeper-x

US Air Force. (2019). *821st Air Base Group.* https://www.peterson.af.mil/units/821st-air-base-group/

US Congress, (2019, December). *National defense authorization act for fiscal year 2020.* https://www.congress.gov/116/crpt/hrpt333/CRPT-116hrpt333.pdf

Wieslander, A. (2019, September). NATO Must engage in the arctic. *Defense One.* https://www.defenseone.com/ideas/2019/09/its-time-nato-arctic/159887/

Chapter 96

Legal Frameworks of Interstate Disaster Management

Mst Marzina Begum and Md Nurul Momen
University of Rajshahi, Rajshahi, Bangladesh

Contents

Introduction 739
Background and Context 740
Disaster or Emergencies Law in the U.S. Federal Government System 740
The U.S. Constitution 740
The Stafford Act 741
The Insurrection Act 741
Executive Orders 741
Laws at the State Level 742
Regional/Interstate Disaster Response 743
Conclusion 744
Further Reading 744
References 745

Introduction

Disaster management strategy doesn't necessarily comply with jurisdictional boundaries during the period of disaster or emergency. However, in case of a major disaster, states or local government authorities need to receive quick responses and recovery support from the federal government, along with concerted efforts between the states and local governmental entities. This might raise the question of jurisdictional boundaries and clear guidelines with respect to the division of power, and responsibilities

DOI: 10.4324/9781315144511-101

that can further worsen the situation during the disasters or emergencies (Wilson and McCreight 2012). The thrust of this chapter is to focus on some of the major legal issues between interstate disaster management in the United States.

Background and Context

It is argued that the effects of natural, man-made disasters, and even heinous terrorist attacks are not much different, as states and local government authorities require similar kinds of quick response throughout the stages of disaster management while responding to these disasters or emergencies (Henstra 2010). It is expected that after the disaster, at the very first stage, states and local government agencies provide an immediate response and support to the disaster-affected communities. As proactive measures, Henstra (2010) further added that states or local government agencies can formulate plans for deciding the future direction of measures and effective communications with the community about the catastrophic incident during the period of disaster or emergency.

After September 11, 2001, it was commonly perceived that federal disaster management strategy needed to bring new changes in the process, especially that states and local government agencies should spend more resources and effort on protecting their citizens from any form of disasters or emergencies. This may enhance their ability to properly address natural and man-made disasters and vulnerabilities in their own community (Hildebrand 2016). It is also worth noting that the Hurricane Katrina highlighted the various challenges, especially the centralized nature of the homeland security system in federal disaster management practices in the United States. In relation to Hurricane Katrina, it was found that the differences in organizational priorities had created role ambiguity within the agencies of the Department of Homeland Security (DHS) and between the actors involved at all layers of government, thus reducing the capacity for a better disaster or emergency management (Hildebrand 2016). Posner (2007) rightly observed that an absence of coordination and relations between different layers of government who are responsible for implementing disaster management, as well as delayed or poor response and recovery efforts, creates difficulties and hindrances for states and local government agencies to effectively manage disasters. Hence, the underlying reasons behind any potential gap in the disaster management process can be found in the different layers of government. However, the objective of this chapter is to examine legal issues and trends that influence how disaster management works in the federal government system in the United States.

Disaster or Emergencies Law in the U.S. Federal Government System

The U.S. Constitution

The U.S. Constitution sets out the boundaries of federal law. Under the U.S. Constitution, the Supremacy Clause is spelled out in such a way that Constitutional principles, treaties, laws, and regulations are considered as superior, and having supremacy over laws enacted by the states and local government authorities. This supremacy is termed as "the preemption doctrine" (Wilson and McCreight 2012); however, it is to be noted that the Supremacy Clause under the U.S. Constitution is apparently clear; but different aspects of the law come into conflict during their the application (Wilson and McCreight 2012). In the following section, it will be discussed how the system of disaster management as exercised in the United States is affected by the different legal frameworks.

The Stafford Act

The Robert T. Stafford Disaster Relief and Emergency Assistance Act (commonly known as Stafford Act) is a federal law. The Act authorizes the president the broad statutory power to proclaim an emergency in case of a major disaster or civil unrest. The Act says that upon receiving a governor's request through the regional Federal Emergency Management Agency (FEMA) office, the president may place a presidential declaration for a 10-day period and direct the secretary of the Department of Defense (DoD) to respond to the catastrophic incident by utilizing public or private lands or water for disaster response and recovery work, which is deemed necessary for saving lives and protecting and preserving resources (42 U.S.C. 5170b (c) (1)) ((Wilson and McCreight 2012). Hence, as statutory duty, the U.S. president may direct the DoD under Section 5170a as a "federal agency" to provide "general federal assistance" or "essential assistance" under Section 5170b. Furthermore, the Stafford Act of 1988 provided the scope of emergency power in which a presidential declaration seeks response and recovery support from FEMA (Wilson and McCreight 2012).

The Insurrection Act

On September 30, 2006, in an incident after the Hurricane Katrina, New Orleans inhabitants experienced overwhelming looting, along with poor security and protection. As a response, Congress modified the Insurrection Act of 1807 in Section 334 to authorize the president to deploy forces to disperse anyone obstructing the enforcement of order or the course of justice (Wilson and McCreight 2012). Thus, the president is now authorized to deploy the National Guard during natural or man-made disasters in order to maintain public order and uphold the course of justice in the United States. Given the context, the president determines the extent of disasters or emergencies, and whether a governor as the manager of a state is unable in maintaining safety and security of the citizens, such as civil disobedience, domestic violence, unlawful combination, or conspiracy (Wilson and McCreight 2012).

Executive Orders

Apart from the above Acts, there is a provision available for the president to respond to disasters or emergencies called "executive orders". The executive order is a type of written instruction that might be declared by the president at the federal level, a governor at the state level, or a mayor at the local government level. It is worth noting that executive orders as official directives have the full status of law, which helps to effectively manage disasters or emergencies (Wilson and McCreight 2012). For instance, Title 10 and Title 32 of the United States Code (U.S.C.) say that the National Guard is the first responder to the nation's emergencies; however, there are a number of reasons through which the president and even state governors can call up the Guard units to help respond to the catastrophic events (Wilson and McCreight 2012).

Regardless of the different Acts and executive orders, response and recovery efforts remain the first responsibility of the governor at the state level and the mayor at the local government level (Farber et al. 2010). However, if needed, a governor as a state manager may request the support of the federal government, particularly FEMA, which is needed to respond effectively and efficiently to disasters or emergencies. If, after a major disaster or calamities that overwhelms the capacities of states and local government entities, the governor may proclaim an "emergency", and request the president to help respond to catastrophic events (Wilson and McCreight 2012).

In examining the extent of a state governor's power, the American Bar Association (ABA 2006) Standing Committee on Law and National Security highlighted the various challenges regarding the application of law in their sub-committee report on the "*Hurricane Katrina Task Force*". To them, the executive authority of the states and local elected officials should be free to perform their duties at the period of emergency or disaster. However, in the United States, each state has its own constitution and statutes that have provided broad discretion to their governors to ensure human safety and protection of resources during any disaster in which there are imminent threats to lives, property, and public health (Wilson and McCreight 2012). Governors and local elected officials have special powers for the declaration of emergency so that the protection of life, health, and safety is ensured; for doing so, they may even suspend the existing legal provisions, and adopt other necessary measures to manage the disaster or emergency (ABA 2006).

Once a public health emergency declaration has been made, a governor may apply state laws within their jurisdictional boundary (Wilson and McCreight 2012). Hodge and Evan (2008) found that public health emergency laws often come into conflict with general emergency laws., For example, a governor on the state level may declare emergencies in different names, such as "general emergency", or a "disaster", or "both" (Farber et al. 2010). Furthermore, the National Emergencies Act (NEA), Sections 201 and 301, authorizes the president to declare a domestic emergency, which is also found in other federal legal frameworks. Notably, during the 2009 H1N1 influenza pandemic, the president proclaimed a national emergency under the NEA, which was made with a prior assessment by the secretary of Health and Human Resources (HHS) with respect to the extent of public health emergency conditions under Section 319 of the Public Health Service Act (PHSA).

Laws at the State Level

Federalism is the system of government that describes the shared powers between the federal and state governments. The U.S. Constitution delegates some specific enumerated powers to the federal government. At the same time, however, the Tenth Amendment of the Constitution says that any powers not delegated by the U.S. Constitution to the federal government or forbidden to states and local government authorities are reserved for them instead (Wilson and McCreight 2012). This means that unless state law is explicitly preempted by federal law or Constitutional principles, states and local authorities are free to take actions in due course. In exercising these Constitutional freedoms, states enjoy sovereignty, and many have introduced a range of disaster management laws at the state level. As a result, while the U.S. federal government system means that states require a specific Constitutional grant of emergency authority to respond effectively to disaster incidents, states also have police power within their jurisdictional boundaries to protect their own citizens from disasters or emergencies (Wilson and McCreight 2012). For instance, Indiana state law includes a broad range of legal frameworks for disaster management that cover mitigation and adaptation for all kinds of disasters or emergencies, except for those responsibilities for which federal government entities are formally legally responsible (Wilson and McCreight 2012).

Regional/Interstate Disaster Response

The existing literature on disaster management, especially on natural disasters, such as hurricanes, requires a broad examination of two key areas (LaFeber and Lind 2008). First, it focuses on the importance of intergovernmental cooperation for successful disaster management. In the United States, there are three levels of government: federal, state, and local level, and these must work together and complement each other's roles to achieve successful management of disasters or emergencies (LaFeber and Lind 2008). However, disaster management policies and practices often vary across federal, state, and local government authorities. When disasters either occur or are imminent, both horizontal and vertical coordination is emphasized between these levels of government. An emphasis is placed on the importance of "*loosely coupled*" organizations, flexible partnerships, and decentralized governance, along with the involvement of the other actors, including the private sector (Drabek 1990).

Under the FEMA, the National Disaster Recovery Framework (NDRF) has established a common platform and forum, guided by eight principles for long-term recovery efforts that enable effective recovery support to disaster-affected regional governments. NDRF includes a flexible structure that enables disaster recovery managers to prepare for recovery in a unified and collaborative manner. NDRF also provides guidance about how best to prepare in advance of a disaster with robust recovery planning (US Department of Homeland Security 2016).

Under the U.S. federal government system, states can also link together and develop interconnected relationships and coordination with other states without the prior approval or consent of the federal government (Kapucu et al. 2009). For instance, the Emergency Management Association Compact (EMAC) is a fast and flexible assistance agreement between states that aims to meet the regional needs associated with a disaster event more rapidly and readily than federal resources would otherwise allow. EMAC allows mutual aid partnerships between states who are managing a disaster and provides clear processes of implementation (Kapucu et al. 2009).

However, no emergencies require assistance from the federal government. EMAC focuses on state government cooperation "*to provide for mutual assistance… in managing any emergency or disaster that is duly declared by the governor of the affected state(s)*" (see for details-Pub. L. No. 104-321, October 19, 1966, 110 Stat. 3877 (1996) https://www.congress.gov/104/plaws/publ321/PLAW-104publ321.pdf). All 50 states, as well as the District of Columbia, Guam, Puerto Rico, and the U.S. Virgin Islands, have enacted the necessary laws and have already subscribed for EMAC membership (Wilson and McCreight 2012). Regarding the performance of the EMAC, the inquiry report of the U.S. House of Representatives regarding Hurricane Katrina suggested that the Compact had demonstrated unprecedented success in cases of mutual aid partnerships. These partnerships worked effectively fully to help manage the catastrophe (Wilson and McCreight 2012). There are also some other areas of the legal framework regarding the nature of state governor's powers that are stated in Article X of the U.S. Constitution. Under this clause, state "sovereignty" refers to applying extraordinary powers during a major disaster or emergency, in which state governors may invoke special powers that determine the extent of the catastrophic event.

As stated earlier, mutual aid agreements between states help to improve the effectiveness of responses to disasters or emergencies across the different political and jurisdictional boundaries (NGA 2019). For example, during a natural disaster, where response from one state supports neighboring states or local government agencies on a routine basis, mutual aid agreements should be strengthened. These kinds of mutual cooperation and coordination improve the nature of disaster assistance.

For successful disaster management, governors should establish legal and institutional frameworks for their jurisdiction and develop strong interstate mutual aid agreements. The National Governors Association (NGA) (2019) found that most states have experienced positive outcomes from mutual aid partnerships with other states. Moreover, governors should always be aware of the existing legal and institutional framework associated with mutual aid agreements (NGA 2019). Apart from these, governors should also focus on the other forms of mutual aid agreement and partnerships, for instance, public–private partnerships (NGA 2019).

Conclusion

Natural disasters, terrorist attacks, or other types of emergency can quickly devastate the capacities of a single jurisdictional boundary at either local or state levels. Hence, states and local government authorities need to develop mutual aid agreements between the states to complement each other by providing resources and capacities. Former President of the United States, Woodrow Wilson, pointed out that the United States as a nation needs to reflect as a system of shared government and responsibility. In this system, all layers of government should contribute to each other in order to quickly overcome any kind of national challenge.

Further Reading

Department of the Army. (2019, July 31). "ADP 3–28: Defense Support of Civil Authorities," Headquarters, Department of the Army, Washington, DC.

Kapucu, N., Augustin, M. E. & Garayev, V. (2009). "Interstate partnerships in emergency management: emergency management assistance compact in response to catastrophic disasters," *Public Administration Review*, *69*(2): 297–313. https://onlinelibrary.wiley.com/doi/epdf/10.1111/j.1540-6210.2008.01975.x

Penuel, K. B., Statler, M. & Hagen, R. (eds.). (2013). *Encyclopedia of Crisis Management* (vol. 1). Santa Barbara: Sage Publications.

References

ABA (American Bar Association). (2006). *Hurricane Katrina Task Force Subcommittee Report.* Washington, DC: ABA Standing Committee on Law and National Security, February 2006.

Drabek, T.E. (1990). *Emergency Management: Strategies for Maintaining Organizational Integrity.* New York: Springer-Verlag.

Farber, D.A. Jim, C.R.V. and Lisa S. (2010). *Disaster Law and Policy.* 2nd ed. New York: Aspen Publishers.

Henstra, D. (2010). Evaluating local government emergency management programs: what framework should public managers adopt? *Public Administration Review,* 70(2010): 236–246.

Hildebrand, S. (2016). *Controlling Disasters: Local Emergency Management Perceptions About Federal Emergency Management and Homeland Security Actions After September 11, 2001.* Paper presented at the 2016 State Politics and Policy Conference, Dallas, Texas.

Hodge, J.G. and Evan D.A. (2008). Principles and practice of legal triage during public health emergencies. *New York University. A Annual Survey of American Law,* 64(2): 264.

Kapucu, N.A. and Maria-Elena Garayev, V (2009). Interstate partnerships in emergency management: emergency management assistance compact in response to catastrophic disasters. *Public Administration Review,* 69(2): 297–313. DOI: 10.1111/j.1540-6210.2008.01975.x

LaFeber, P. and Lind, N.S. (2008). Ch. 9. Disaster management and intergovernmental relations. In *Disaster Management Handbook,* ed. J. Pinkowski, pp. 553–560. Boca Raton, FL: CRC Press, Taylor & Francis Group.

McGuire, M.D. (2012). *Martial Law Made Easy.* Nighttalker.com, June 2 21, 2012.

NGA (National Governors Association). (2019). *AGovernor's Guide to Homeland Security.* NGA Center for Best Practices, Homeland Security & Public Safety Division. February, 2019.

Posner, P. (2007). The politics of coercive federalism in the bush era. *Publius: The Journal of Federalism.* 37(2007): 390–412.

US Department of Homeland Security. (2016). *National Disaster Recovery Framework.* 2nd Edition. http://preventionweb.net/go/61906

Wilson, L.R. and McCreight, R. (2012).Public emergency laws & regulations: understanding constraints & opportunities. *Journal of Homeland Security and Emergency Management.* 9, 2, 7. DOI: 10.1515/1547-7355.2034

Chapter 97

Nuclear Threats

David Andrew Omona
Uganda Christian University, Mukono, Uganda

Contents

Introduction 747
Sources of Nuclear Threat to the United States 748
Terrorist Nuclear Threat 748
Cyber Nuclear Threat 749
Belligerent Countries' Nuclear Threat 750
Nuclear Accidents within the United States 753
Addressing Nuclear Threats 753
Conclusion 755
Further Reading 755
References 756

Introduction

Humans are unique, creative, and innovative. Through the use of the power of the mind, they have invented items that are both constructive and destructive to their own existence. The invention of nuclear technology has both eased and became a threat to humanity. John Stott and John Wyatt (2006, p. 82) in affirmation of the dangers of nuclear weapon says, "of all the global problems which confront the human race today none of them is greater than nuclear holocaust." Even though human beings have engaged in wars with devastating effects over the years, none of them can unravel the devastation that nuclear warfare can generate. This is because unlike in past wars that were fought using rudimentary weapons including sticks and stones, bows and arrows, swords and spears, muskets and riffles, or bayonets and bombs that require people to be close to the enemy for it to be effective, for nuclear weapons it is different. A nuclear weapon can be delivered using long-range missiles,

DOI: 10.4324/9781315144511-102

aircraft, drones, and even cyber technology that does not require close proximity. As the unleashed power of the atom showed at Hiroshima and Nagasaki, if a nuclear weapon is launched, it destroys not only the present but also the vestiges of old civilization, and the future pattern of life.

Kelsey Davenport and Kingston Reif (2019), in a 2019 estimates of global nuclear warheads inventories assert that, "the world's nuclear-armed states possess a combined total of nearly 14,000 nuclear warheads." Of these, roughly 90% are in the possession of Russia and the United States. The approximate warheads that are in military service are 9,500, the rest are awaiting dismantlement (Davenport and Reif, 2019). Matsui Kazumi and Taue Tomihisa (2019), the mayors of Nagasaki and Hiroshima respectively, suggest that given that the vital nuclear arms control agreements are being abandoned, and budgets for the development and production of new nuclear weapons are growing, the potential for proliferation of nuclear weapons use is evident. The nuclear threat is a reality to the United States and the world at large. Unlike during the period of the Cold War, when Russia posed the greatest nuclear threat to the United States, the growing number of countries that possess nuclear weapons, some of which are opposed to the United States, provides a formidable danger to the United States. Some of them have the capacity to lounge catastrophic attacks with weapons of mass destruction (WMD) and disruption through the use of nuclear, biological, radiological, chemical, and cyber. "They can easily attempt to deliver nuclear warheads on trucks or ships, thus eluding US tactical warning systems" (Rand Corporation, 2004).

Sources of Nuclear Threat to the United States

The nuclear threat to the United States is not a new phenomenon. It has been there from the time other powers, especially Russia, acquired nuclear technology. Now the sources of nuclear threats to the United States include (a) terrorist nuclear, (b) cyber nuclear, (c) belligerent countries' nuclear, and (d) nuclear explosions within the United States.

Terrorist Nuclear Threat

US Military Intelligence, government experts, and political leaders such as Presidents Donald Trump, Barrack Obama, and George Bush, have expressed a fear about nuclear terrorism for years (Brosnan, Semmel, Sermonis, & Reif, 2018, pp. 4–5). Of late, terrorist groups have sought to acquire nuclear weapons and, although none yet appear to have been successful, this could easily change. This is because at present, over "1,800 metric tons of weapons-usable nuclear materials-highly enriched uranium (HEU) and plutonium are stored in hundreds of sites across 25 countries. Yet, they are improperly secured and terrorists could potentially obtain access to them. If they do, they could build bombs and use them to wreak havoc upon the United States" (NTI, 2015). Terrorist nuclear attacks on US soil could come in different forms, ranging from the detonation of stolen or improvised nuclear explosive device, to the sabotage of a nuclear facility or the dispersion of radioactive material via a dirty bomb. Terrorists could easily manufacture dirty bombs by combining conventional explosives such as dynamite with radiological materials found in hospitals, research centers, and so forth. The use of such improvised nuclear explosives in a heavily populated area could be catastrophic.

Terrorist threat in the United States is a present reality. For example, over the past 25 years, there have been slightly over 20 instances of seizure of stolen weapons and usable nuclear materials (Brosnan, et al., 2018, p. 5). Probably, if those weapons and usable nuclear materials were not seized, they would have been used to attack the United States or their interest abroad. Though without success yet, terrorist groups like Aum Shinrikyo and al-Qaeda have attempted to acquire nuclear weapons. Besides, the Islamic state that once controlled more people, territory, and resources than al-Qaeda got reduced significantly but still remains a despicable menace to US security.

Although at present, no terrorist group is believed to possess nuclear weapons, several regions of the world provide conditions that could facilitate access to fissile materials, or nuclear weapons by terrorist groups. These include North Korea, South East Asia, Russia, India, Pakistan, and others. Many of these states have already suffered terrorist attacks, even on their military bases. Yet, they all continue to maintain or increase the size of their nuclear stockpiles.

The current advancement in technologies such as the manufacturing of offensive cyber tools, and artificial intelligence and machine has facilitated the diversification and increase of the potential of nuclear threat. These processes have simplified the production, manufacturing, and design of nuclear materials and weapons (Brosnan, et al., 2018, p. 5). Given this reality, President Trump urges that the United States "must prevent nuclear weapons and materials from coming into the hands of terrorists and being used against us, or anywhere in the world" (Brosnan, et al., 2018, p. 5).

Cyber Nuclear Threat

The Nuclear Command, Control, and Communications (NC3) systems of the United States and other nuclear-armed states are heavily dependent on computers and other digital processors. For example, its early warning radars launch facilities require an extended network of communication and data processing systems. The warning systems that are both ground and space-based are used to constantly watch for and analyze possible enemy missile launches, plus data on actual threats that ought to be communicated to decision-takers, also involves cyberspace operation. It is in this domain that great power rivalries seek vulnerabilities to exploit in a constant struggle for advantage (Klare, 2019, pp. 2–3). Since those systems are heavily vulnerable to cyberattacks from enemies, the security of the United States is equally at risk.

Recently, the use of cyberspace to gain an advantage over adversaries has taken many forms, and is not always aimed at nuclear systems. For example, China is accused by the United States of stealing US technical secrets, Russia is accused of interference in US elections, al-Qaeda and Islamic State are using cyberspace for recruiting terrorist groups, and criminal groups allied to belligerent states like North Korea have used it to steal money from banks. All these and others pose great threats that occupy the minds of both civilian and military cyber security personnel. Yet, for those who worry about strategic stability and the risk of nuclear escalation, it is the threat of cyberattacks on the NC3 system that exudes the greatest concern (Klare, 2019, pp. 2–3). This concern stems from the fact that, despite the immense efforts devoted to protecting NC3 systems from cyberattacks, it is very hard to ensure an enterprise that relies so extensively on computers and cyberspace is 100% invulnerable to attack. Since nuclear systems use a variety of components operating systems with differing origin dates, and various software, updates, and patches, they are open to attack from multiple vectors. Hostile actors can easily modify electronic components during production, transit, or installation and, since the whole system itself is dependent on a considerable degree on the electronic grid, it is itself vulnerable to cyberattack and far less protected from cyber weapons such as malware and computer viruses (Klare, 2019, p. 3).

Whereas activity in cyberspace is difficult to detect and attack, information exists that show that nuclear powers such as China, Russia, the United States, Iran, and North Korea, have established extensive cyber warfare capabilities. They have also engaged in offensive cyber operations on a regular basis, often aimed at critical military infrastructure. Given that cyberspace is a contested environment where no country has a monopoly, the US constant contact with adversaries (Klare, 2019, pp. 3–4) predisposes the nation to attacks. As such, the US government is under constant watch to avoid such strikes.

The path to an escalation of nuclear cyberattack in a great power crisis could "paralyze the vital command, control, and communications capabilities of an adversary, many of which serve nuclear and conventional forces" (Klare, 2019, p. 4). As Klare Matthew (2019, p. 5) notes, "The uncertainty caused by the unique character of a cyber-threat could jeopardize the credibility of the nuclear deterrent and undermine strategic stability in ways that advances in nuclear and conventional weapons do not."

Another pathway to escalation of cyberattack on the United States could arise from a cascading series of cyber strikes and counterstrikes against critical national infrastructure rather than on military targets. Unfortunately, all of the world's major powers, along with Iran and North Korea, have developed and deployed cyber weapons that are specifically designed to disrupt and destroy major elements of an enemy's key economic systems, such as power grids, financial systems, and transportation networks. As such, Russia has infiltrated the US electrical grid, and it is widely believed that the United States has done the same in Russia (Nechepurenko, July 18, 2019). Just as the Pentagon devised a plan known as, "Nitro Zeus," to immobilize the entire Iranian economy so as to force it to submit to US demands or, if that approach failed to pave the way for crippling air and missile attack (Klare, 2019, p. 6), Iran or any other enemy nuclear power could do the same in order to attack the United States.

Belligerent Countries' Nuclear Threat

Threats to the United States by belligerent countries have existed for decades and go back to the heart of the Cold War. For example, when the USSR chose to balance the nuclear power of the United States by installing nuclear warheads in Cuba, an event that came to be called the Cuban missile crisis, the presence of a nuclear arsenal that could strike the mainland United States from only 90 miles away caused considerable panic. While the settlement of the Cuban missile crisis made the US feel a bit safer in the short term, the growing number of belligerent countries with nuclear capabilities like China, North Korea, Iran, Turkey, and Russia pose a formidable threat to the United States today.

Although the Iranian nuclear initiative that Muhammed Reza Shah begun in the 1950s was rejected by Ayatollah Khamenei upon taking power, who declared a fatwa against such ambitions (NTI, 2019), later leaders of the Iranian Revolutionary forces reinstated their nuclear ambitions and turned to them for military purposes. After the inspections of the nuclear plants by a team from the International Atomic Energy Agency (IAEA), Iran was urged not to enrich uranium exceeding a certain limit. The July 1 2019 IAEA's announcement indicates that Iran had exceeded her "nuclear agreed-to limit on the volume of its stockpile of enriched uranium" (ADL, 2019). This act sent shock waves across the globe, which worsened recently when Iran proclaimed that it had enriched uranium to about 4.5% (ADL, 2019). This intensified the "tension and a series of incidents in the Persian Gulf, including attacks on US-allied tankers" (ADL, 2019). These attacks seemed to confirm the view of many United States policymakers that having nuclear weapons in the possession of the Iranian regime could present a security risk to the United States and her allies in the Middle East and Europe (ADL, 2019).

The earlier assertion by former President Mahmoud Ahmadinejad of Iran that Israel should be wiped out of the map (Kessler, 2011), and the constant threats that Iran posed to US allies in the Gulf states including Saudi Arabia, United Arab Emirates (UAE), Bahrain, and others attests to this (ADL, 2019). Such apparent threats further confirm the thinking that:

> A nuclear-armed Iran would likely further embolden Iran's aggressive foreign policy, including its deep ongoing involvement in Syria, its attacks against Israel via proxies including Hezbollah, Hamas, and other terrorist groups, and its sponsorship of rebel insurgents in Yemen. Having nuclear weapons would embolden this aggression and would likely result in great confrontation with the international community. Iran already has a conventional weapons capability to hit US and allied troops stationed in the Middle East and parts of Europe. If Tehran were allowed to develop nuclear weapons, the threat it poses would increase dramatically.
>
> (ADL, 2019)

The above assertion stems from the current saga that Iran is embroiled in within the Middle East and with its relation with the United States. The tough talk of Iran's leaders appears to confirm the widely held position that Iran is one of the world's leading sponsors of terrorism. The financial and operational sympathy support that Iran extends to groups such as Hezbollah, Hamas, and others attests to this view. It is feared that Iran has the potential to even "share its nuclear technology and know-how with extremist groups hostile to the US, Israel, and the west" (ADL, 2019).

Coupled with the above, the ongoing nuclear ambition pursued by North Korea with its belligerent rhetoric about being able to strike any part of the US exerts a great pressure upon the United States. This situation is worsened by the claim that North Korea has developed a hydrogen bomb that can be mounted on a missile (BBC, 2019). The multitude of missile tests in 2017 was a testimony to the North Korea's rapid advances in military technology for malign motives. Indeed, the Hwasong-12, 14, and 15 missiles whose firing ranges of 4,500 km, 10,000 km, and 13,000 km, respectively, puts US military bases on the Pacific Island of Guam and port cities like Pearl Harbor, San Francisco, New York, and other mainland cities within the striking range (BBC, 2019).

Whereas North Korea's nuclear threat on US defense mechanism could be rationalized by some people that it is meant to frustrate the joint US–South Korean military drills, Pyongyang's ability to develop and test fire missile capable of being launched from a submarine is indicative of its readiness to cause harm to the United States in ways difficult to detect (BBC, 2019). To show this readiness, after a successful test of its first Intercontinental Ballistic Missile (ICBM), on September 3, 2017, it tested a thermonuclear weapon (NTI, 2019). The explosive power of the warhead tested was estimated to be six times more powerful than the bomb dropped on Hiroshima in 1945. Washington has not been idle in the face of North Korea's nuclear tests, but instead has responded by installing a Terminal High Altitude Air Defense (THAAD) missile defense system at Seongju in South Korea, with the goal of countering North Korean short and medium-range missile in the event of an outbreak of war (BBC, 2019).

Another nuclear threat to the United States comes from China, which has continued "its multiyear effort to modernize its nuclear missile forces, including deploying sea-based weapons, improving its road-mobile and silo-based weapons, and testing hypersonic glide vehicles" (Coats, 2019, p. 9). These new capabilities are intended to ensure the viability of China's strategic deterrent by providing a second-strike capability and a way to overcome missile defenses. The Chinese have also publicized their intent to form a nuclear triad by developing a nuclear-capable, next-generation bomber.

The link between China and Russia adds to this threat. Of late, China and Russia are training and equipping their military space forces and fielding new anti-satellite (ASAT). These are weapons meant to hold United States and allied space services at risk, even as they push for international agreements on the non-weaponization of space. Accordingly, the People's Liberation Army (PLA) has an operational ground-based ASAT missile intended to target low-Earth-orbit satellites, and China probably intends to pursue additional ASAT weapons capable of destroying satellites up to geosynchronous Earth orbit (Coats, 2019, p. 17). These and others all provide a threat to the United States because if China dares to destroy US satellites, it can affect the operation of its monitoring systems and thereby open it for any nuclear strike.

While the nuclear threat between Russia and the United States seems to have decreased since the end of the Cold War, the March 2018 public acknowledgment by Russia President Vladimir Putin that Russia has built and is building several new weapons programs shows that Russia remains a nuclear threat to the United States. These new programs included a new ICBM designed to penetrate US missile defense systems; an intercontinental-range, hypersonic glide vehicle; a maneuverable, air-launched missile to strike regional targets; a long-range, nuclear-powered cruise missile; and a nuclear-powered, transoceanic underwater vehicle (Coats, 2019, p. 9).

Russia has also developed and fielded a ground-launched cruise missile (GLCM) that the United States has determined violates the intermediate-range nuclear forces (INF) treaty, which it has recently withdrawn from. Moscow likely "believes that the new GLCM provides sufficient military advantages to make it worth the risk of political repercussions from a violation" (Coats, 2019, p. 9).

Turkey is another country whose relationship with the United States is falling apart, as demonstrated by Turkey firing at locations in Syria in which US forces were known to be based. The United States currently has over 50 warheads in Turkey, which could be seized and used to attack the United States itself. As a result, there are some US officials who think their country should actively consider "removing American nuclear weapons from a key air base in Turkey, just 250 miles from the country's border with Syria" (Brennan, 2019).

Nuclear Accidents within the United States

While the Cold War ended over 20 years ago, the existence of thousands of nuclear weapons continues to pose a serious global threat. Russia and the United States both have set up multibillion dollars budgets to modernize their nuclear programs (Borger, June 19, 2019). Whereas the likelihood of a nuclear war between the United States and Russia has reduced after the Cold War, such a major project is indicative that the continued presence of large stockpiles makes the accidental or unauthorized use of nuclear weapons a persistent risk.

The risk of accidental nuclear explosion is not a new thing, as noted by Eric Schlosser (2013), who enumerates 32 incidents from the Pentagon's "official list of 'broken arrows' – mishaps with nuclear weapons that might threaten the public." Although dated, a 1970 study by one of US nuclear weapon laboratories, obtained through the Freedom of Information Act, is incredibly revealing. It stated that at least 1,200 weapons were involved in accidents between 1950 and 1968 (Schlosser, 2013). Even today, a plane crash, a fire, a missile explosion, lightning, human error, and dropping a weapon from an aircraft parked on a runway can be a potential risk of causing a nuclear explosion in the United States itself.

The accidents that occurred on September 15, 1980, where one of the engines on a B-52 bomber carrying four hydrogen bombs and eight short-range missiles with nuclear warheads caught fire at Grand Forks air force base in North Dakota is a particularly notable example. An accident on September 18, 1980, where a technician dropped a tool in the silo of a Titan II ICBM near Damascus, Arkansas is another. Although neither case led to a nuclear catastrophe, with the latter only being salvaged due to a heroic effort that saved the missile from exploding, there is no guarantee that this might be in the case if a similar event happened during the days to come.

Addressing Nuclear Threats

Realizing the enormity of the nuclear threat, successive US Presidents and Congress have realized the need to negotiate with countries harboring nuclear weapons. One of the most important early treaties that resulted from such talks was the Strategic Arms Limitations Talks (SALT) with the USSR in Helsinki, Finland in 1969 (Kimball, 2019, p. 1). The US chief negotiator reasoned, "The limiting of strategic arms is in the mutual interest of" both the United States and the Soviet Union (Kimball, 2019, p. 1). The SALT agreement, along with the Anti-Ballistic Missile (ABM) Treaty that followed soon after, served as initial restrictions on the superpowers' huge strategic nuclear weapons and defense systems. As a result, the two agreements helped to slow down the arms race between the two countries and thereby opened a period of US-Soviet détente that lessened the threat of nuclear war (Kimball, 2019, p. 1).

Despite this, the initial talks, agreement, and treaty opened a ray of window for more talks, agreements, and treaties between the United States and major nuclear power countries, including Russia and China, and lesser nuclear power countries like Iran and North Korea. Numerous bilateral and multilateral treaties, such as several strategic arms reduction treaties (START), the strategic offensive reduction treaty (SORT), the nonproliferation treaty (NPT), and the comprehensive test ban treaty (CTBT) resulted from these negotiations. The Honorable Thomas Countryman (2019) explains why US Presidents since Eisenhower have recognized the value of effective nuclear arms control. His arguments are provided verbatim below:

- Talking to an adversary, whether a superpower like the Soviet Union or a lesser challenger such as Iran, is not a sign of weakness, but a hardheaded and realistic means to reduce threats posed to the United States.
- Treaties provide rules that enable the United States to pursue effectively its economic and security interests. They constrain other nations' ability to act against our interests more than they constrain US freedom of action.
- Arms control agreements are not a concession made by the United States, or a favor done to another nation. It is an essential component of, and contribution to, our national security.
- In a world in which the US claims global leadership, Washington must take the lead bilaterally and multilaterally, proposing initiatives that greatly reduce the risk that WMD spread or are used.
- The pursuit of reductions of nuclear stockpiles and the eventual elimination of nuclear weapons is both a moral obligation. Since the approval by the US Senate of the Nuclear Nonproliferation Treaty in 1969, it is a legal obligation one that can and must be pursued regardless of the ups and downs of great power relations.
- There can be no winners in a nuclear war. Mutual assured destruction is not a theory, or a philosophy but rather a reality of life. Since the time the Soviet Union achieved reliable intercontinental ballistic missiles in the 1960s, neither the United States nor Russia can launch a nuclear attack on the other's homeland without the near-certain destruction of its own homeland. Arms control agreements, and associated stability mechanisms, serve to reduce the risk that a cycle of assured destruction will begin (Countryman, 2019, p. 2).

Notwithstanding such aforementioned brilliant strategy for peace at home and abroad, "due in part of a deficit of American leadership and the growing body of thought in the Administration and Congress today," many of these positive trends have been reversed and others are at risk. Countryman argues that this is because of a series of beliefs held by US political and military leaders, as provided verbatim below:

- The United States should not discuss vital national security issues, or consider compromise, with adversaries such as Russia and Iran until they have fully met US demands in all fields.
- International treaties are inherently disadvantageous to the United States, as they constrain the freedom of action of the world's leading military and economic power.
- Arms control agreements involve a degree of compromise, they grant unwarranted concessions to opponents.
- Such agreements are of no value if they do not solve EVERY problem between the parties, an all-or-nothing approach exemplified by the US decision to withdraw from the 2015 Joint Comprehensive Plan of Action (JCPOA).
- There is a way to win a nuclear war, that a numerical or technical advantage can give the United States a dominance of power that would spare our country from destruction in a nuclear exchange. Sadly, no US official today is able to repeat the obvious fact that motivated Presidents Ronald Reagan and Mikhail Gorbachev to declare: "A nuclear war can never be won and must never be fought" (Countryman, 2019, p. 3).

Given these beliefs, the United States and her allies remain under nuclear threat from all directions around the world.

In order to make some countries accept to abandon their nuclear projects, the United States either singly or with mandate from the Security Council impose targeted sanctions (Davenport and Sanders-Zakre, 2019, p. 1) or threat of attacks. North Korea and Iran are among the countries that sanctions and threat of attacks have ever been directed to.

Conclusion

In conclusion, it is clear that the United States is at a great risk from nuclear attack from multiple sources given the current urge by many states are emerging as nuclear powers. While the current increase in budget to improve US nuclear capabilities further might be a way forward for deterrence purposes, it might also end up bringing the danger it purports to fight right back to home. To avert such an outcome, the US government must engage in principled discussions with other states that have nuclear ambitions. Opting out of certain international agreements and pulling out of talks with belligerent states is not a wise option at present. Ultimately, the United States needs to understand that times are changing and there is a need to change with the times.

Further Reading

Brosnan, J, Semmel, A, Sermonis, N, & Reif, K, (2018), *Empowering congress on nuclear security: Blue prints for a new generation*, Washington DC: Arms Control Association.

Klare, T. M. (2019), *Cyber battles, nuclear outcomes? Dangerous new pathways to escalation.* https://www.armscontrol.org/act/2019-11/features/cyber-battles-nuclear-outcomes-dangerous-new-pathways-escalation

NTI. (December 31. 2015), *The nuclear threat: Despite progress, the nuclear threat is more complex and unpredictable than ever.* https://www.nti.org/learn/nuclear/

Stott, J. and Wyatt, J. (2006), *Issues facing Christians today*, 4th Ed. Roy McCloughry (reviser and updater) Grand Rapids: Zondervan.

Stoutland P. O. and Pitts-Kiefer, S. (Sept. 2018), *Nuclear Weapons in the New Cyber Age: Report of the Cyber-Nuclear Weapons Study Group*, Nuclear Threat Initiative, p. 12. https://media.nti.org/documents/Cyber_report_finalsmall.pdf

References

BBC, (9 October 2019), *North Korea's missile and nuclear program.* https://www.bbc.com/news/world-asia-41174689

Borger, J. (19 June 2019), Nuclear weapons: experts alarmed by new Pentagon 'war-fighting' doctrine, *The Guardian.* https://www.theguardian.com/world/2019/jun/19/nuclear-weapons-pentagon-us-military-doctrine

Brennan, D. (15 October 2019), *US-Turkey tensions raise fears over future of nuclear weapons near Syria*, https://www.newsweek.com/u-s-turkey-tensions-fears-future-nuclear-weapons-syria-donald-trump-erdogan-1465331

Brosnan, J, Semmel, A, Sermonis, N, and Reif, K, (2018), *Empowering congress on nuclear security: blue prints for a new generation*, Washington, DC: Arms Control Association.

Coats, D. R. (29 January 2019), *Statement for the record worldwide threat assessment of the US intelligence community*, Washington DC: US Senate.

Countryman, T. (2019), *Russia and arms control: Extending new start or starting over?* https://www.armscontrol.org/events/2019-07/russia-arms-control-extending-new-start-starting-over

Davenport, K. and Reif, K. (2019), *Nuclear weapons: who has what at a glance.* https://www.armscontrol.org/factsheets/Nuclearweaponswhohaswhat

Davenport, K. and Sanders-Zakre, A. (March 6, 2019), *Hanoi Summit ends abruptly: What's next?* North Korean Denuclearization Digest. https://www.armscontrol.org/blog/2019-03-06/hanoi-summit-ends-abruptly-whats-next-north-korean-denuclearization-digest-march-6

Heritage.Org (30 October 2019), *US Nuclear Weapons Capability.* https://www.heritage.org/sites/default/files/2019-10/2020_IndexOfUSMilitaryStrength_ASSESSMENT_POWER_NUCLEAR.pdf

History.com editors (June 2019), *Cuban missile crisis.* https://www.history.com/topics/cold-war/cuban-missile-crisis

Kessler, G. (5 October 2011), *Did Ahmadinejad really say Israel should be 'wiped off the map'?* Politics, The Washington Post- Democracy dies in darkness. www.washingtonpost.com

Kimball, G (2019), *Fifty years ago, the first strategic arms limitation talks began.* https://www.armscontrol.org/blog/2019-11-17/fifty-years-ago-first-strategic-arms-limitation-talks-began

Klare, T. M. (2019), *Cyber battles, nuclear outcomes? Dangerous new pathways to escalation*, published on arms control. https://www.armscontrol.org/act/2019-11/features/cyber-battles-nuclear-outcomes-dangerous-new-pathways-escalation

Matsui K. and Taue T. (2019), *Message from the Mayors of Hiroshima and Nagasaki*, November 2019, an email sent to me by Daryl G. Kimball, Executive Director, Arms Control Association as person on the arms control list serve, Received on 09/12/2019.

Model Diplomacy. (n.d.), *North Korean Nuclear Threat.* https://modeldiplomacy.cfr.org/preview/27

Nechepurenko, I. (18 July 2019), Kremlin warns of cyber war after report of U. S. Hacking of electrical Grid, *The New York Times*. https://www.nytimes.com/2019/06/17/world/europe/russia-us-cyberwar-grid.html

NTI (31 December 2015), *The nuclear threat: Despite progress, the nuclear threat is more complex and unpredictable than ever*. https://www.nti.org/learn/nuclear/

NTI (2019), *North Korea*. https://www.nti.org/learn/countries/north-korea/

Nuclear Threat Initiative (NTI) (2019), *Iran*. https://www.nti.org/learn/countries/iran/

Rand.org (2004), *U.S. Nuclear Weapons: Future strategy and force posture*. https://www.rand.org/pubs/research_briefs/RB111-1/index1.html

Schlosser, E. (14 September 2013), *Nuclear weapons: an accident waiting to happen*. https://www.theguardian.com/world/2013/sep/14/nuclear-weapons-accident-waiting-to-happen

Stott, J. and Wyatt, J. (2006), *Issues facing Christians today*, 4th Ed. Roy McCloughry (reviser and updater) Grand Rapids: Zondervan.

Stoutland P. O. and Pitts-Kiefer, S. (September 2018), Nuclear weapons in the new cyber age: report of the cyber-nuclear weapons study group, *Nuclear Threat Initiative*, p. 12. https://media.nti.org/documents/Cyber_report_finalsmall.pdf

The Anti-Defamation League (ADL), (2019), *The Iranian nuclear threat: why it matters*. https://www.adl.org/resources/fact-sheets/the-iranian-nuclear-threat-why-it-matters

Chapter 98

Ricin

Péter Marton
Corvinus University of Budapest, Budapest, Hungary

Contents

Introduction 759
Ricin: A Natural Chemical Weapon 759
Ricin in Weapons Programs, Terrorism, and Crime 761
Conclusion: A Note of Caution 762
Further Reading 763
References 763

Introduction

This chapter provides a brief overview of some of the key properties of the toxic chemical ricin. It then looks at the past experience regarding its use in weapons programs, terrorism, and crime, with a view to the general requirements of preparedness and the strategic lessons that may be drawn for United States Homeland Security. In the conclusion, a few critical thoughts are raised questioning the way society relates to the threat of ricin, enhancing the threat of its misuse by giving it distinguished attention.

Ricin: A Natural Chemical Weapon

Ricin is a naturally occurring, highly toxic substance (a toxic chemical) present in the seeds of the castor oil plant (*Ricinus communis*), a native plant species in India, Africa, and South America. The castor oil plant, a.k.a. ricinus or castor bean, is also a popular ornamental plant. Meanwhile, the castor oil industry is growing, with the global market forecast to be worth over $2 billion by 2025. Castor oil is used, *inter*

DOI: 10.4324/9781315144511-103

alia, in personal care products, lubricants, paper, plastics, rubber, pharmaceuticals, paints, ink, and additives (Zion Market Research, 2019). There are possible medical applications, too. Over a million tons of castor beans are processed every year (Pilch, 2005: 239).

The ricin is contained as a component in the residual "white mash" remaining upon the processing of the castor beans to extract their oil (Borowski, 2012). The Median Lethal Dose (LD_{50}) of ricin is around 22 micrograms per kilogram of body weight when ricin is inhaled or injected. Via oral exposure, the LD_{50} is higher, at around 1 mg/kg. Ricin is therefore listed as a Schedule 1 substance under the Chemical Weapons Convention and similarly as a prohibited substance under the Biological Weapons Convention, situated on the conceptual boundary between chemical and biological agents.

To produce ricin out of the waste from industrial processes, or at home, from the ornamental plant grown around the house, is not uncomplicated. Furthermore, the lethal dose is large enough to make ricin an inconvenient weapon of choice for an actor interested in mass casualties (e.g. the amount of anthrax spores required to kill the same intended number of people is a fraction of the amount of ricin required). Even so, the wide availability of conceivable sources of a Schedule 1 cytotoxic substance is of concern.

Symptoms of ricin poisoning upon ingestion include abdominal pain, inflammation of the gastrointestinal tract, and hemorrhage leading to bloody diarrhea and vomiting. The inhalation of ricin leads at first to a cough and a fever, then tightness of the chest, and difficulty breathing. The onset of symptoms occurs within 12 hours after ingestion and within 8 hours after inhalation (Audi et al., 2005). On the cellular level, ricin causes the inactivation of ribosomes in the affected cells, rendering them incapable of producing vital proteins from amino acids. This kills the affected cells (cytotoxicity). Death of the patient follows within 3–5 days of exposure upon the ingestion of a lethal dose, due to organ failure and shock, with the liver and the spleen seeing most of the damage. Death may also result from a pulmonary edema or diffuse necrotizing pneumonia developing in the lungs within 36–48 hours, if the ricin was inhaled (Moshiri et al., 2016). Injection leads directly to system-wide toxicity, manifesting progressively in weakness, swollen regional lymph nodes near the point of entry, difficulty speaking, and eventually multiple organ failure or circulatory collapse. A sub-lethal dose will evoke the production of antibodies in the person exposed, causing the emergence of immunity for the duration of several months.

Ricin on the molecular level is made up of two components, known as ricin toxin A chain and ricin toxin B chain. The toxic effect arises from the combination of these two, with the B chain making way for the A chain to enter cells. In the environment, the bond between chains A and B ultimately breaks, within 2–3 days – ricin in the environment is consequently dangerous for anyone coming into contact with it in that timeframe, while the molecule is still intact. In the form of dust, it could get into the eyes or the respiratory tract, and it may also get into the body through breaches in one's skin.

With a view to recognizing the effects of ricin, a major problem is the non-distinctiveness of the initial symptoms, especially in the case of ingestion, which might appear to medical personnel as severe food poisoning, even if multiple cases are registered in the same location and timeframe.

Ricin in Weapons Programs, Terrorism, and Crime

In weapons programs, ricin's use to coat bullets was at first contemplated, to cause poisoning in those wounded. During World War II, Britain, Canada, and the United States attempted to design a "W bomb", estimating that a 500-pound (cca. 226 kg) cluster bomb could be used to disperse ricin over 80 percent of a 100x100 yard (cca. 91.5x91.5 m) area, killing over 50 percent of those within (Pilch, 2005: 240). Notably, the challenge of effective aerosolization stood to be resolved for this purpose. In the wake of World War II, ricin was ultimately dis-preferred as a weapon of choice due to the availability of more potent agents. The 2019 Abqaiq–Khurais attack against Saudi Aramco's oil-processing facilities in Saudi Arabia involving low-flying drones and cruise missiles (with explosive payload) may show, however, that possible means of delivery for toxic chemicals are available to an increasing number of nations, including nations with relatively modest resources, as well as non-state actors, who may still find ricin to be a suitable chemical agent for their purposes.

The coating of projectiles with ricin for use in assassinations was carried out by the Soviet KGB, which used the technology (umbrellas firing miniature 1.7-mm pellets, using compressed air to launch the projectile) to provide technical assistance to the Bulgarian Communist state security service in murdering London-based dissident Georgi Markov in 1978 and in the attempted killing of another Bulgarian defector Vladimir Kostev (shortly before the attack on Markov). A number of terrorists have plotted since then to use ricin to coat building and car-door handles. The UK ricin plotters, led by Algerian Kamel Bourgass, who were arrested in 2003, were among those showing an interest in this, and while they did not produce ricin, they were in the advanced planning stage, with "no playtime recipes" according to one prosecutor (NTI, 2005), although it is worth adding that covering door handles with ricin is not necessarily an effective mode of attack. Another al-Qaida-linked group was reportedly considering poisoning food in food and salad bars (Bloomberg, 2010). A far-right U.S. group, the Minnesota Patriots Council was, however, closer to the execution of a successful attack in 1991, having extracted enough ricin from castor beans to kill up to a hundred people if effectively delivered (although their intended targets were a Deputy U.S. Marshal and a Sheriff; FAS, 1996).

The most noteworthy achievement in ricin weaponization by a group linked to the jihadi movement is Iraqi Kurdistan-based (and predominantly but not exclusively Kurdish) Islamist group Ansar al-Islam's alleged aerosolization of ricin and their alleged experiments with ricin as well as botulinum on animal (and possibly also human) subjects. The report concerning this is difficult to corroborate, however. A U.S. Tomahawk cruise missile strike destroyed the group's main training camp in Sargat, Iraq, in 2003, at the beginning of the war in Iraq. A subsequent test commissioned by MSNBC.com found traces of ricin as well as botulinum on two pieces of items from Sargat (NBC, 2003).

Criminal use of ricin commonly happens in the form of threatening mail, bordering on terrorism even when it is just a hoax, although in many instances over the last decades, such letters did contain either castor beans, or even a small amount of ricin, or both. For example, Mayor Michael Bloomberg was targeted in 2013. Some NYPD personnel displayed minor symptoms of ricin exposure after coming into contact with the letter addressed to him (Glueck, 2013), showing the need to handle all letters threatening the use of ricin with care, as hazardous material should be handled. As it ultimately transpired, the letter sent to Mayor Bloomberg was a peculiar instance of non-terrorism-related use of ricin involving Texan actress Shannon Richardson sending the ricin-laced letters to both Mayor Bloomberg and President Barack Obama, to frame her husband as the perpetrator – an ultimately unsuccessful attempt at deceiving authorities. She is now serving a prison sentence (McLaughlin, 2014).

Conclusion: A Note of Caution

One of the reasons why ricin receives as much attention as it does from U.S. Homeland Security, besides other factors (such as its objective property of being widely available and highly toxic at the same time), is cognitive in nature. As there is a large number of toxic substances that may be used in political assassinations as well as common crime, ricin stands out at least partly due to its being mentioned more often compared to other substances. This increases the chances that non-state actors will come across reference to this rather than other toxic chemicals and materials, reproducing the somewhat false reputation of ricin as a singularly toxic substance. This contributes to the threat itself. Notably, similar concerns about a fashion trend effect drove fears of attacks using nicotine-coated and nicotine-filled bullets after Norwegian terrorist Anders Breivik advertised his (eventually abandoned) plans to use nicotine-filled hollow-point ammunition in the attacks he perpetrated in 2011. Breivik even gave a detailed account of how he ordered pure nicotine online from a Chinese supplier (Diethelm and McKee, 2011).

Consider the following few examples of noteworthy cases of poisoning from history for a quick overview (Table 98.1), with which we seek to illustrate the variety available to – and already used in the past by – attackers.

In fact, many more toxic substances can be found in the environment or are produced or may be produced, with many of these available from commercial sources. The U.S. Toxic Substance Control Act (TSCA) listed 38,304 relevant substances as of 2016. The U.S. Environmental Protection Agency's Chemical Data Reporting system tracked 8,707 substances in the meantime (Chemical Safety Facts, 2019). In addition, it is worth keeping in mind that it is often the dose that makes a substance poisonous – thereby one may have an actually larger variety to consider.

As can be concluded on the basis of this, the threatened use of ricin is the scare tactic of choice for hoaxers sending threatening mail with a frequency that is out of proportion with a view to the variety of the available toxic substances. This indicates how human behavior is in general shaped by the availability heuristic. We focus on the few toxic chemicals and materials that have been used in the past in various accidents even as preparedness is needed in general against a far larger variety of chemical agents available for misuse.

To illustrate the importance of disposing of human biases: automated defensive systems, such as the Biohazard Detection Systems currently in use in mail-processing centers, test for a large number of toxins and biological agents, not just the ones made popular by discourse, whereas attackers with modest resources will still be inclined to limit search costs and seek utilization of just those substances. On the other hand,

Table 98.1 Select Historical Cases of Poisoning

Incident	*Poison Used*
399 BC death of the Greek philosopher Socrates	Toxins in the poison hemlock plant
1878–1892 murders committed by Thomas Neil Cream	Strychnine from the *Strychnos nux vomica* plant (a.k.a. strychnine tree or poison nut)
1908 Hanoi poison plot against the French colonial army	Toxins in the Datura plant
1959 assassination of Ukrainian nationalist leader Stepan Bandera	Cyanide
1997 assassination attempt against Hamas leader Khaled Mashal	An unspecified opioid
2004 poisoning of Ukrainian presidential candidate Viktor Yushchenko (non-fatal)	TCDD (a dioxin)
2006 assassination of Russian dissident Alexander Litvinenko	polonium-210 (radioactive)
2020 poisoning of Russian opposition figure and activist Alexei Navalny	Novichok (nerve agent)

Source: Author, 2020.

advanced users, such as state actors, are likely to deploy relatively unknown toxic substances in future incidents that are less likely to be detected before delivery and less likely to be treated effectively upon delivery. With regards to them, the best guiding principle for U.S. Homeland Security is to expect the unexpected.

Further Reading

Moshiri, M., Hamid, F., Etemad, L. (2016). Ricin toxicity: Clinical and molecular aspects. *Reports of Biochemistry and Molecular Biology*, 4(2), 60–65. PMCID: PMC4986263. PMID: 27536698.

Pilch, R. (2005). Ricin. In Croddy, E.A., Wirtz, J.J. (Eds.): *Weapons of Mass Destruction: An Encyclopedia of Worldwide Policy, Technology, and History. Volume I: Chemical and Biological Weapons*. ABC CLIO, Santa Barbara, California – Denver, Colorado – Oxford, England: 239–242.

Sierra, M. A. & Martínez-Álvarez, R. (2020). Ricin and Saxitoxin: Two natural products that became chemical weapons. *Journal of Chemical Education*. doi.org/10.1021/acs.jchemed.9b00841

References

Audi, J., Belson, M., Patel, M., Schier, J., Osterloh, J. (2005). Ricin poisoning: A comprehensive review. *JAMA: The Journal of the American Medical Association*, 294(18), 2342–2351.

Bloomberg. (2010). In response to Al-Qaeda's threat of ricin in the food supply. *Bloomberg*, 22 December 2010. https://www.bloomberg.com/press-releases/2010-12-22/in-response-to-al-qaeda-s-threat-of-ricin-in-the-food-supply. Accessed 6 December 2019.

Borowski, S. (2012). From beans to weapon: The discovery of ricin. American Association for the Advancement of Science (AAAS), 11 July 2012. https://www.aaas.org/beans-weapon-discovery-ricin. Accessed 6 December 2019.

Chemical Safety Facts (2019). Debunking the Myths: Are there really 84,000 chemicals? Chemical SafetyFacts.org, date not indicated (last updated in 2019). https://www.chemicalsafety facts.org/chemistry-context/debunking-myth-chemicals-testing-safety/. Accessed 6 December 2019.

Diethelm, P., McKee, M. (2011). Nicotine: Not just an unregulated poison but now a potential chemical weapon. *European Journal of Public Health*, 21(6), 681–683.

FAS (1996). Terrorism in the United States. *Federation of American Scientists, date not indicated.* https://fas.org/irp/threat/fbi_terror95/terrorin.htm. Accessed 6 December 2019.

Glueck, K. (2013). Cops: Ricin letter sent to Bloomberg. *Politico*, 29 May 2013. https://www.politico.com/story/2013/05/ricin-letter-michael-bloomberg-group-092011. Accessed 6 December 2019.

McLaughlin, E.C. (2014). Texas actress who sent Obama ricin sentenced to 18 years. *CNN*, 16 July 2014. https://edition.cnn.com/2014/07/16/justice/texas-ricin-actress-sentenced/index.html. Accessed 6 December 2019.

Moshiri, M., Hamid, F., Etemad, L. (2016). Ricin toxicity: Clinical and molecular aspects. *Reports of Biochemistry and Molecular Biology*, 4(2), 60–65.

NBC (2003). Positive test for terror toxins in Iraq. *NBC*, 4 April 2003 (date not indicated in the article at the time of writing this, established from external sources). http://www.nbcnews.com/id/3070394/ns/world_news/t/positive-test-terror-toxins-iraq/#.Xetg9JNKjIV. Accessed 6 December 2019.

NTI (2005). One suspect convicted in U.K. Ricin Plot. *NTI*, 14 April 2005. https://www.nti.org/gsn/article/one-suspect-convicted-in-uk-ricin-plot/. Accessed 6 December 2019.

Pilch, R. (2005). Ricin. In Croddy, E.A., Wirtz, J.J. (Eds.): *Weapons of Mass Destruction: An Encyclopedia of Worldwide Policy, Technology, and History. Volume I: Chemical and Biological Weapons*. ABC CLIO: Santa Barbara, California – Denver, Colorado – Oxford, England, 239–242.

Zion Market Research (2019). Global castor oil market will reach USD 1,792 million By 2026. *Zion Market Research*, 30 July 2019. https://www.globenewswire.com/news-release/2019/07/30/1893352/0/en/Global-Castor-Oil-Market-Will-Reach-USD-1-792-Million-By-2026-Zion-Market-Research.html. Accessed 6 December 2019.

Chapter 99

Sarin

Péter Marton
Corvinus University of Budapest, Budapest, Hungary

Contents

Introduction 765
The Sarin Nerve Agent 766
Homeland Security Implications of Specific Incidents 767
Muharem Kurbegovic, a Lone Wolf Attacker 768
Aum Shinrikyo's Attacks 768
The May 2004 Iraqi IED Attack Involving Sarin 769
Alleged Use of a Missile Carrying a Sarin Payload by Syrian Insurgents in 2013 769
The Alleged Use of Sarin in Chilean Secret Police Operations Under Pinochet 769
Conclusion 770
Further Reading 770
References 771

Introduction

This chapter provides a brief overview of key properties of the nerve agent sarin, including its high toxicity, the nature of the production process, the volatility of the substance, and the lethal concentration-time. It also alludes to past military and non-military users as well as some of the basic considerations regarding the necessary response to an attack on unprepared targets. The second section focuses on introducing a handful of noteworthy cases of the past use of sarin with a view to the implications of these cases for U.S. homeland security.

DOI: 10.4324/9781315144511-104

The Sarin Nerve Agent

Sarin is a non-naturally occurring (synthetic) type of organophosphorus compound of extremely high toxicity as a nerve agent, apt to be used as a chemical weapon. The nerve agent designation refers to the organ system primarily affected upon exposure, which in this case is the nervous system. Sarin is classified as a Category 1 weapon based on a Schedule 1 chemical (according to the 1993 Chemical Weapons Convention regime).

Sarin has been used as the payload in missiles, aerial bombs, and various types of artillery ammunition. Countries with militaries and other state agencies that are known or strongly suspected to have produced or obtained sarin (or sarin precursors) at one point in history include the United States, the Soviet Union/Russia, Yugoslavia, Iraq, Syria, Egypt, Libya, North Korea, Cuba, and Chile. For its part, the United States ceased the regular production of sarin in 1957. All of the above as well as a large number of sufficiently advanced other countries may be assumed to possess at least a threshold capability or just about all the pre-requisites for producing sarin. Documented use of sarin by state actors happened in Iraq (against Iran and against the Kurdish populace under Saddam Hussein) and Syria (by forces loyal to Bashar al-Assad). Past non-state users include Iraqi insurgents (post-2003) and the Aum Shinrikyo sect in Japan, among others (as will be discussed below).

The origins of the production of sarin go back to Nazi Germany where scientists working for the IG Farben firm discovered the DHMP (dimethyl hydrogen phosphate) process in 1938 (while working on developing new pesticides) to create the highly potent nerve agent, which they proceeded to name after the researchers involved, using initials and other letters from their names (regarding the production process, see Ghosh, Prelas, Viswanath and Loyalka, 2010: 341–342).

Toxic by-products emerge in the various phases of making sarin, posing a risk to both the producer and the environment, unless appropriately managed. Besides DHMP, other processes are known and have been used to make sarin. The full sarin family of nerve agents contains as many as 3652 different members. These have not all been produced by anyone so far, and, as such, many exist merely as theoretical possibilities of what may be produced (WHO, 2004: 29).

The necessary precursor materials (such as phosphorous trichloride or methanol) are dual-use substances. Acquiring them is certainly not beyond possibility even for a determined non-state actor. The sarin production process is far more difficult to master and requires expert management. Typically, sarin's final-stage precursors are stored (as this is less dangerous), and they can be applied in such a way as to mix directly before encounter with the target, e.g., in a missile warhead. Both the shelf life and the effectiveness of sarin depend on the purity of the final product. The latter is odorless and colorless, making timely detection very difficult for an unprepared target.

Given its high volatility (quickly turning into vapor from a liquid state), weaponized sarin will typically reach the skin and the respiratory system as a vapor (as a nerve gas considerably more lethal than mustard gas). It may also be injected under the skin (as a poison considerably more lethal than cyanide). As a gas, sarin's lethal concentration-time at 50% (LCt_{50}), i.e., the lethal amount of gas required to be present in a cubic meter of air for a full minute to kill 50% of all normally breathing persons staying in the affected space, is 70–100 mg.min/m³ (WHO, 2004: 175). First-responders arriving in a suspected affected area should have appropriate detection equipment, protective gear, as well as antidote auto-injection kits and the means for nerve agent decontamination.

The lethal mechanism of sarin (just like in the case of other organophosphorus nerve agents such as VX and Novichok) is the blocking of the communication pathway between the central nervous system and the muscles, by inhibiting the breakdown of the neurotransmitter acetylcholine in the nervous system, through inhibiting the enzyme acetylcholinesterase (AChE). This effect happens once a critical dose of sarin is capable of reaching the central nervous system, as a result of not being bound to red blood cell acetylcholinesterase and other esterases found in the blood (Fulco, Liverman and Sox, eds., 2000). A runny nose (rhinorrhea), tightness in the chest, and constricted/pinpoint-like pupils (miosis) are among the first signs of onset upon exposure. These are followed by the gradual loss of bodily functions (manifesting in vomiting, defecating, and urinating), twitching, convulsive spasms, and eventually, lethal asphyxia due to the loss of control over the breathing muscles – all of this potentially within 1–10 minutes upon the inhalation of a lethal concentrate.

Medical personnel have to be familiar with the symptoms to be sufficiently alert in the unlikely event when patients displaying these symptoms arrive in hospital. The SLUDGE concept, referring to the symptom-set of salivation, lacrimation, urination, defecation, gastrointestinal distress, and emesis (vomiting), may be useful to remember in the identification of a cholinergic crisis (the overstimulation of the neuromuscular junction), to then think of this as the effect of sarin (when simultaneously happening to more than one individual in the same location).

Organophosphate poisoning, which may happen as a result of exposure to pesticides, was suspected by Japanese medical staff in the wake of the sarin attacks carried out by the Aum Shinrikyo sect, making their response effective under the circumstances, faced with an attack with an unknown agent (WHO, 2004: 91). In general, the antidotes atropine, pralidoxime, and diazepam need to be administered to patients to treat the physiological symptoms. Lasting neurological impact may be expected, and the long-term monitoring of victims is advised. In the immediate aftermath of the event, there may also arise a need to address the concerns of a large number of people anxious about possible exposure.

Homeland Security Implications of Specific Incidents

The following cases of sarin use will be considered here with a view to their noteworthy implications for U.S. homeland security: the threatened use of sarin by Muharem Kurbegovic, a first-generation immigrant in the United States, in the 1970s; the attacks by the Aum Shinrikyo sect in Japan in the 1990s; the attempted use of sarin in an IED (improvised explosive device) attack by Iraqi insurgents in 2004; the alleged use of an improvised missile with sarin payload by Syrian insurgents in 2013; and – finally, and deviating from the chronological order hitherto followed – the alleged use of sarin for assassinations by Chile's DINA(the *Dirección de Inteligencia Nacional*) secret police during the time of President Augusto Pinochet.

Muharem Kurbegovic, a Lone Wolf Attacker

Kurbegovic is known as "the alphabet bomber" for having once aspired to attack targets associated with each of the letters of the name of his fictive organization, which he called "Aliens of America." An immigrant from Yugoslavia and an engineer by training, he was responsible for the bombing of LAX Airport (Los Angeles) in August 1974. The attack killed three people and injured 36. He also threatened to use sarin against government targets in Washington, DC. Beyond making the threat, he invested into building up his own library of books regarding bomb-making and chemical weapons. He acquired significant quantities of commercial chemicals necessary for making a nerve agent, amassing a large cache of precursors. These were held in a room hidden behind the medicine cabinet in his bathroom in a Los Angeles apartment (Simon, 2019: 114–115). Had he eluded capture, he may have been in a position to execute a chemical attack.

The case shows that, in spite of the difficulties of producing sarin, even lone wolf attackers may constitute a threat against the United States. Furthermore, by threatening to use chemical weapons, lone wolves can create widespread panic even without the actual capability.

Aum Shinrikyo's Attacks

The Japanese doomsday cult used sarin for mass-casualty attacks on two occasions, in Matsumoto, in June 1994, and in the Tokyo subway, in March 1995. The latter attack represented the peak of Aum Shinrikyo's operational art, with pairs of subway riders and getaway drivers placing "plastic bags of liquid sarin punctured by the pointed ends of umbrellas" on subway trains (Smith, 2005: 31). The Matsumoto and Tokyo attacks together resulted in 21 dead along with a far larger number of hospitalizations and widespread fear.

Even before these incidents, the group used sarin (as well as other nerve agents) in assassination attempts, for instance against a rival cult leader. (These earlier attempts proved to be more dangerous to the drivers tasked with delivering the sarin via an improvised vehicle-borne evaporation-dissemination system.).

The group had significant capital to invest in its subversive activities and bought land for the purpose of experimentation in Australia, allowing it to test the sarin produced before using it as a weapon. Overall, Aum Shinrikyo may have spent as much as $30 million on developing a crude chemical attack capability (WHO, 2004: 91). To make sarin, they relied on the DHMP process as they learned about it from available sources – possibly from Russian sources (Danzig et al., 2012: 29, 51).

The case demonstrates the prospective capability level that may be attained by a determined non-state actor with significant capital at its disposal, as well as the possibility of targeting confined spaces such as subway stations and subway cars for enhanced effect (even as the use of conventional explosives has so far proved far more effective for terrorists in such circumstances).

The May 2004 Iraqi IED Attack Involving Sarin

A 155-mm artillery shell containing sarin precursors, used in the construction of an IED, was found near the site of an explosion targeting a U.S. military patrol. The handling-process exposed EOD (Explosive Ordnance Disposal) personnel to the effects of the nerve agent. The precursors did not adequately mix, however, and only a small amount of sarin emerged into the environment. The EOD personnel involved experienced symptoms such as a "crushing headache", disorientation, and constricted pupils (NPR, 2017).

The case highlights the possibility that certain groups may be interested in combining bomb attacks and other tactics with the use of chemical agents.

Alleged Use of a Missile Carrying a Sarin Payload by Syrian Insurgents in 2013

The incident in question happened on March 19, 2013, in Khan al-Assal, near Aleppo, Syria. It is very hard to reach a fully conclusive assessment in attributing responsibility related to this case, as no truly independent investigation took place on the ground in a timely manner.

The combatant parties blamed each other for the attack. A number of things speak in favor of the theory of rebel use. The majority of the victims in this case were soldiers belonging to pro-government forces. There were non-independent claims that the missile used in the attack may have been an improvised missile of the kind used by rebels. There was persistent shelling of Khan al-Assal in the period concerned by rebel forces. With a view to these arguments, there is a non-infinitesimal possibility that on this exceptional occasion, sarin may have been used by the rebel forces. If they indeed managed to build a missile successfully dispersing the sarin payload upon impact, it is not impossible that the know-how related to this may be available to actors interested in attacking western countries by now, given the presence of Islamist elements among the rebel combatants in the area at the time.

A conservative assessment would nevertheless point in the direction of government responsibility for the attack, which originally may have targeted the rebel forces in a desperate move, following rebel advances. This would mean that the missile ultimately affected an area other than the intended target. Speaking in favor of this is knowledge of the significant stocks of sarin precursors the Syrian government had at the time, and the oft-seen use of sarin in aerial attacks targeting rebel-held areas in Syria, which the rebels cannot have been responsible for, as they did not have an air force.

The Alleged Use of Sarin in Chilean Secret Police Operations Under Pinochet

DINA, i.e., Chile's secret police, was established from a Chilean army intelligence unit in 1973, headed by Manuel Contreras at the time. The agency seems to have conducted a far-reaching program of assassinations up until its reorganization in 1977. Biochemists Eugenio Berríos and Francisco Oyarzún Sjöberg were the key scientists leading efforts in the framework of *Proyecto Andrea* to produce sarin, which was then reportedly used in a number of assassinations carried out by DINA. Sarin may have been tested against two unknown Peruvian detainees first, deployed at close range from a small spray tube according to one account, and conducted execution-style (González, 2013). There is speculation that in the ensuing period, the DINA considered to assassinate even regime opponent Orlando Letelier, residing in the United States, with sarin. For reasons we can only speculate about, they eventually chose to use a car bomb, killing Letelier in September 1976 in Washington, DC. Taken together with allegations that DINA operative Michael Townley (born in the United States, an agent involved in several assassinations, including the one against Letelier) may have traveled at times with a small bottle of perfume containing sarin, the case holds direct implications for U.S. homeland security.

Conclusion

Sarin remains a central element of nightmare scenarios of chemical warfare as well as chemical terrorism for the United States. However, smaller-scale acts of terrorism combining the use of sarin with other tactics – as well as assassinations – similarly have to be considered as possibilities.

Given that it is possible to successfully smuggle sarin across borders, and that prospective victims would often seem to have died of cardiac arrest, sarin may be a tool of assassinations even for actors interested in maintaining full or plausible deniability. Advantages for terrorists may lie at least occasionally in the opposite possibility: in getting publicity for their actions using a well-known and feared nerve agent such as sarin.

To underscore this point: the use of sarin in successful assassinations may have occurred in cases other than the Aum Shinrikyo and Chilean examples detailed above. For instance, the Russian Federal Security Service (FSB) killed Saudi-born Islamist commander Ibn al-Khattab, a participant of the Chechen Wars, by way of having a human asset trusted by Khattab deliver him a letter coated with a "fast-acting" nerve agent – possibly sarin or a derivative thereof (CBW Conventions Bulletin, 2002: 47). Added to this, we may also keep in mind the March 2018 poisoning of Sergei and Yulia Skripal with the Novichok nerve agent in Salisbury, UK, and the February 2017 assassination of Kim Jong-nam at Kuala Lumpur International Airport in Malaysia with the VX nerve agent, to comprehensively appreciate the danger of nerve agents being used for lethal as well as intimidating assassination campaigns in the United States.

Further Reading

Cashman, J. R. (2008). *Emergency Response Handbook for Chemical and Biological Agents and Weapons*. Boca Raton, New York, London: CRC Press, 263–268.

Ghosh, T.K., Prelas, M.A., Viswanath, D.S., Loyalka, S.K. (2010). *Science and Technology of Terrorism and Counterterrorism*, 2nd edition. Boca Raton, New York, London: CRC Press.

WHO (2004). *Public Health Response to Biological and Chemical Weapons – WHO Guidance*. Geneva: World Health Organization.

References

CBW Conventions Bulletin (2002). News Chronology – February through April 2002. *The CBW Conventions Bulletin* – Quarterly Journal of the Harvard Sussex Program on CBW Armament and Arms Limitation, 56. https://sites.fas.harvard.edu/~hsp/bulletin/cbwcb56.pdf

Danzig, R. (2012). *Aum Shinrikyo: Insights Into How Terrorists Develop Biological and Chemical Weapons*. Center for a New American Century, December 2012. https://s3.amazonaws.com/files.cnas.org/documents/CNAS_AumShinrikyo_SecondEdition_English.pdf

Fulco C.E., Liverman C.T., Sox H.C. (2000): Institute of Medicine (US) committee on health effects associated with exposures during the gulf war. In: Fulco, C.E., Liverman, C.T., Sox, H.C. (Eds.), *Gulf War and Health: Volume 1. Depleted Uranium, Sarin, Pyridostigmine Bromide, Vaccines*. Washington, DC: National Academies Press (US); 2000. 5. https://www.ncbi.nlm.nih.gov/books/NBK222849/

Ghosh, T.K., Prelas, M.A., Viswanath, D.S., Loyalka, S.K. (2010). *Science and Technology of Terrorism and Counterterrorism*, 2nd edition. Boca Raton, New York, London: CRC Press.

González, M. (2013). Las armas químicas de Pinochet, CIPER (El Centro de Investigación Periodística), 22 August 2013. https://ciperchile.cl/2013/08/22/las-armas-quimicas-de-pinochet/

NPR (2017). One Soldier's Lasting Memories Of Exposure To Sarin Gas. *NPR*, 28 April 2017. https://www.npr.org/2017/04/28/525879416/one-soldiers-lasting-memories-of-exposure-to-sarin-gas

Simon, J.D. (2019). *The Alphabet Bomber: A Lone Wolf Terrorist Ahead of His Time*. Lincoln, Nebraska: Potomac Books.

Smith, J.M. (2005). Aum Shinrikyo. In: Croddy, E.A., Wirtz, J.J. (Eds.), *Weapons of Mass Destruction: An Encyclopedia of Worldwide Policy, Technology, and History. Volume I: Chemical and Biological Weapons*. Santa Barbara, California – Denver, Colorado – Oxford, England: ABC CLIO, 29–33.

WHO (2004). *Public Health Response to Biological and Chemical Weapons – WHO Guidance*. Geneva: World Health Organization.

Chapter 100

Smallpox

Péter Marton
Corvinus University of Budapest, Budapest, Hungary

Contents

Introduction 773
The Nature of the Pathogen 773
Controversy around Variola Research, the Risk of Accidents, and the Possibility of Biohacking 776
Conclusion: Smallpox as a Biological Weapon 777
Further Reading 778
References 779

Introduction

This chapter introduces the pathogen responsible for the smallpox disease, the *variola major* virus, the various courses smallpox disease may take, the possibility and the implications of vaccination, as well as the successful eradication effort that was carried out worldwide and completed by 1977. Following this, a critical analysis is presented, which highlights the risks of continued research using the live variola virus in the laboratory environment even as such efforts may again seem warranted with a view to developments in biotechnology. The chapter concludes by considering if smallpox may be realistically viewed as a biological weapon by United States Homeland Security or by terrorists.

The Nature of the Pathogen

As long as it existed, smallpox was a grave and strongly infectious disease, taking a variety of different courses in patients. It was caused by the *variola* virus, a virulent

DOI: 10.4324/9781315144511-105

member of the *Orthopoxvirus* genus: brick-shaped, around 302–350 nm × 244–270 nm in size, with double-stranded DNA, coming in two varieties, *variola major* and *variola minor*.

Variola major is beyond doubt one of the most dangerous biological pathogens ever encountered by humanity, having killed hundreds of millions of people in the last 100 years before the eradication of the naturally occurring *variola* virus strains in the 1970s (Hopkins, 2002). Other Orthopoxviruses that can cause infections in humans include the vaccinia, cowpox, and monkeypox viruses. (Chickenpox, a disease whose symptoms may be confused with those of smallpox, is caused by the *Varicella-zoster virus*, a herpesvirus.)

The less virulent strain of the variola virus, *variola minor*, was the more widespread around the world before eradication. It outcompeted *variola major* in the process of natural selection due to leaving most of those infected in an ambulant state, capable of spreading it further, in contrast with the grave form of the disease resulting from *variola major* infection. It also left those affected immune to both variola strains upon recovery.

Variola viruses infecting humans may have originated through zoonosis from African rodent populations thousands of years ago. They have subsequently become endemic in the human population. Transmission from human to human used to happen as a result of comparatively close proximity to an infected person, via inhalation of the airborne pathogen, which reached the lungs and, from there, the regional lymph nodes – these being the primary sites of infection. As a result of viremia (the virus entering the bloodstream), other major secondary sites of infection included the spleen and the bone marrow. Upon an incubation period of around 12 days (allowing more than enough time for an infected person to fly from one continent to another) and an additional 3 or 4 days of flu-like symptoms, skin cells were targeted by the virus. The infection of the skin led to the well-known symptom of rashes appearing, at first usually on the forehead, but rapidly spreading throughout the body. In terms of differential diagnosis, it is noteworthy that the rashes appeared all over the body (including on the palms and soles), that they developed largely simultaneously, resulting in evenly developed papules and, later on, vesicles (unlike in the case of chickenpox), and that they formed more densely near the extremities of the body.

The disease then took either one of four major observed courses: ordinary, modified, malignant, or hemorrhagic. Ordinary smallpox made up as much as 90 percent of the cases, with the macules appearing on the skin developing into raised papules. Fluid accumulated in these papules, which thereby became vesicles. These stood out of the skin and could in some cases become confluent, affecting entire sheets of the skin, in which case mortality significantly worsened, up from a level of 30 percent in non-confluent cases. The modified and milder course of the disease was typically seen in people previously vaccinated. The other two forms, malignant smallpox (with no raised papules forming) and hemorrhagic smallpox (with extensive bleeding from the skin, the mucous membranes, and in the gastrointestinal tract), were usually lethal.

Several possible mechanisms could lead to a fatal outcome in patients, including increasingly severe viremia, the circulation of immune complexes (of antigens and antibodies), secondary infections, and – in the case of confluent and malignant smallpox – sepsis, as well as the loss of fluids, proteins, and electrolytes. Mostly, only supportive care could be provided (also with a view to infection control). No effective treatment was available, but vaccination proved to be at least somewhat useful after exposure, especially in the first few days following infection.

Immunization by vaccination is possible in several ways. Historically, cowpox virus has been used as well as inoculation with smallpox scabs (in powdered or other form) that have fallen off infected patients. The latter procedure resulted in a considerable number of full-fledged infections. Present-day vaccine uses the live vaccinia virus, closely related to cowpox virus, in what is still a comparatively risky form of immunization, with typically 1 out of 1000 people experiencing a major reaction and up to as many as 52 out of one million people experiencing life-threatening implications, including postvaccinal encephalitis and progressive vaccinia (people with weakened immune systems face higher risk). The vaccine is administered by the percutaneous route (skin scarification), requiring adequate barriers (such as gauze bandage) to be placed and kept over the vaccination site, to stop the vaccinia virus from spreading. The possibility of onward transmission very much exists (CDC, 2017a). Recent cases of vaccinia infection were often the result of vaccinated US military personnel coming into contact with relatives or others in their environment who may have had a history of eczema (even if they may have been asymptomatic at the time); eczema is a risk factor exposing those affected to a higher risk of infection. Meanwhile, the vaccination-provided immunity against smallpox gradually declines and is assumed fully lost within 30 years.

Eradication of the naturally occurring *variola* virus strains was completed by 1977, with the last case of *variola major* infection registered in October 1975 in Bangladesh and the last case of *variola minor* in Somalia in October 1977. As there is no knowledge of animal carriers or cases of asymptomatic human carriers (beyond the plausible incubation period), this ended the smallpox pandemic. Only one person, a medical photographer, contracted the disease since then, at the University of Birmingham Medical School. She died on September 11, 1978. This outbreak was contained through the vaccination of contacts (around 500 people). Eventually, only the victim's mother developed a mild infection. The transmission mechanism that led to the victim's infection is not known exactly, but the pathogen originated from a laboratory working with smallpox in the same building (Rimmer, 2018).

The World Health Organization's Smallpox Eradication Programme (SEP) was subsequently declared a success and closed down. Having lasted from 1966 to 1980, it involved mass vaccination campaigns in advanced countries, as well as aggressive surveillance and containment measures, including highly vigilant contact-tracing, the isolation of cases as well as contacts, and ring vaccinations (the vaccination of all likely affected contacts) in developing countries (Strassburg, 1982).

Vaccination programs also came to an end by consequence, discontinued all around the world after the passing of several years, even in the case of hospital workers and military personnel, with a view not only to the probably non-existent need for continued vaccination but also to the small but significant and possibly lethal risk of vaccination to recipients – a policy revised in the United States in the aftermath of the terrorist attacks of September 11, 2001.

Controversy around Variola Research, the Risk of Accidents, and the Possibility of Biohacking

In the aftermath of the global eradication of the smallpox virus, the World Health Organization succeeded in convincing governments to destroy most of their existing stocks of the pathogen. The number of facilities handling variola strains went from 75 in 1975 to only two by 1985. WHO advisers subsequently recommended in vain the destruction of all remaining stocks in 1990, and the World Health Assembly decided in favor of destruction to no effect in 1996. Due to suspicions raised that certain countries, such as Iran or North Korea, might also hold stocks of the virus beside the United States and Russia, and with a view to the lack of immunity of younger generations against smallpox, it was argued that research has to continue for defensive purposes, with WHO oversight (Tucker, 2006: 116–132). This proposal was ultimately accepted. Currently, the two facilities handling variola viruses are the WHO Collaborating Center on Smallpox and Other Poxvirus Infections at the US Centers for Disease Control and Prevention (CDC) in Atlanta, Georgia, and the WHO Collaborating Center for Orthopoxvirus Diagnosis and Repository for Variola Virus Strains and DNA at the Russian State Research Centre of Virology and Biotechnology (SRC VB VECTOR) in Koltsovo, Novosibirsk Region, Russian Federation (WHO, n.d.).

The WHO Advisory Committee for Variola virus Research (ACVVR) found in 2013 that research with the live variola virus was by then only needed for the development of antiviral agents; sufficient genomic sequencing had been carried out on 50 different isolates of the virus, and sufficient results were available as regards diagnostics and vaccine development. CDC nevertheless continues to list all of the three above mentioned goals (antivirals, diagnostics, and vaccines research) as important aims of ongoing work with live variola strains (CDC, 2019). Over the years, this research work included work with chimera strains (emerging in animal hosts simultaneously infected with two distinct pathogens) and the use of smallpox virus genes inserted into other poxviruses for safer research operations. The concern related to this is that some of the genetic recombination occurring as a result may actually end up increasing the emerging pathogen's lethality. To this comes added the concern that what is held in containment may find a way out into the wild as a result of accidents.

Considering the extremely destructive potential of smallpox, even a small risk of accidents is a cause for concern. In September 2019, an explosion and the resulting fire at the Russian Vector laboratory complex (mentioned above as handling smallpox) underlined the significance of those concerns even as Russian authorities denied that sources of bio-hazard would have been anywhere near the part of the building affected in the accident, where renovation works were reportedly taking place at the time. It later transpired that the explosion occurred in a decontamination room and that the one person who was reported injured had suffered burns to 45 percent of his body, suggesting that the gravity of the incident may have been downplayed (Lentzos, 2019). It is worth recalling that the only known accidental outbreak of smallpox related to biological weapons experiments occurred in the Soviet Union: the 1971 Aralsk incident, in the region of the Aral Sea, where reportedly three fatalities resulted (out of a total of ten infected persons) due to the normally uncommon hemorrhagic variant of smallpox (Croddy, 2005: 24).

Ironically, the possibility of such accidents can also be used to argue in favor of continued research, as long as more than one laboratory works with the live variola virus, in more than one country. The same argument also applies to the issue of the possibility of "leftover vials" which arose after adequately closed but forgotten vials of deep-frozen variola isolates were found in a building belonging to the National Institutes of Health in Bethesda, Maryland, in 2014 (Guardian, 2014). Some of the vials were found to contain viruses that proved viable.

Another source of concerns as to where viable variola viruses may still be available in a non-laboratory environment is an incident where an envelope containing smallpox scabs from the 19th century was found in a New Mexico university library. There existed a very small chance that these could yield live viruses, and caution was certainly warranted (USA Today, 2003).

A set of arguments about variola research and the need to retain the live virus concerns developments in biotechnology. These question the relative importance of the risks associated with laboratory legacy stocks. While the risks have to be taken seriously in any case, and the safety of laboratories has to be provided for against a host of possible dangers, we now live in a world where synthesizing the variola virus is feasible. Already in 2002, State University of New York researchers Eckard Wimmer and his colleagues reconstructed infectious poliovirus from mail-ordered synthetic DNA segments (Tucker, 2006: 117). In 2017, Noyce (2018) demonstrated the same capability in constructing a horsepox virus in a small laboratory, with little in the way of prior specialized knowledge, and a relatively small budget of $100,000 (Kupferschmidt, 2018).

This means that what some describe as "biohacking" may be a source of bioaggression capabilities in the immediate future. Against this backdrop, continued defensive research seems warranted.

Conclusion: Smallpox as a Biological Weapon

A widespread smallpox epidemic would have horrifying consequences for the United States and the world. It would certainly bring about major systemic impact on the public services, governance, and defensive capabilities of the affected countries. Moreover, the effects cannot be expected to be contained, especially when infection hits a "virgin soil population" as happened for example in Iceland in 1707–1709 (Hays, 2005: 131–133). The 12-day incubation period (during which those initially infected would typically not spread the virus) almost guarantees that the effects of the release of the virus would not be localized (due to carrier mobility).

This may be an obvious negative incentive for prospective users, including terrorists, who may need vaccination themselves to be working with smallpox in the first place. Furthermore, non-state actors are unlikely to have the capability to adequately preserve or grow the smallpox virus for use in attacks, even if they manage to obtain variola isolates from the few known possible sources (Brower, 2005: 264–265).

Arguably, it is the comparatively higher level of preparedness for a smallpox outbreak that may, with non-infinitesimal (but not great) probability, make the United States seem to be a tempting and convenient target (which may well turn out to be an erroneous belief). The attacker may act anticipating that major costs can be imposed on the defender without the risk of onward transmission outside the target population. The US Strategic National Stockpiles and CDC seek to guarantee effective containment by holding enough vaccine to mass-vaccinate the entire population of the country as a medical counter-measure (MCM) in a contingency (CDC, 2017b).

Other imaginable types of attackers may be either lashing out in desperation, using everything at their disposal to win time, or may hold beliefs that lead them to ignore the consequences, including the considerable chances of setting off a global pandemic.

The 18th-century context in North America, in which various parties have leveled accusations against each other regarding the use of smallpox as a weapon of war, is also instructive in this regard. On the one occasion when the use of smallpox is documented clearly enough to have happened, the defenders of Fort Pitt thought of this tactic as the smallpox was already spreading among them as well as among the indigenous tribes that they were fighting (Fenn, 2000: 1553–1558). In other words, they deployed smallpox in an environment where it was already present. This conforms to the general expectation that the first use of smallpox as a biological weapon may be irrational in a confrontation. The incentives may only change once the disease is endemically present, or if it is introduced to the environment by an adversary.

The 2005 Atlantic Storm tabletop decision-making exercise used a smallpox bioaggression scenario involving former decision-makers tasked to deal with a simulated emergency featuring half a dozen sites of release in as many different countries (Center for Biosecurity, 2005). The result, that within 4.5 hours, this scenario produced several thousand cases in the place of the 51 initially reported, may seem alarming. However, the assumption of an actor with the capability of weaponizing smallpox, to then release it near-simultaneously on three different continents, builds in many ways on a worst-case logic.

Ultimately, the consideration of the implications of bio-engineering and the possibility of the emergence of advanced biological weapons, along with the low probability of successful smallpox weaponization by non-state actors, may suggest the need to rethink the conventional biodefense agenda in the United States. The current concept of defense is still largely focused on a set of naturally occurring pathogens (or, in this case, one that used to occur naturally only in the past) and their comparatively well-known properties. In the future, this may not be the best way of determining what is the adequate response in terms of public policies and measures and in allocating related investments.

Further Reading

Brower, J. (2005). Smallpox. In Croddy, E.A., Wirtz, J.J. (Eds.): *Weapons of Mass Destruction: An Encyclopedia of Worldwide Policy, Technology, and History. Volume I: Chemical and Biological Weapons*. Santa Barbara, California – Denver, Colorado – Oxford, England: ABC CLIO, 261–265.

Strassburg, M.A. (1982). The global eradication of smallpox. *American Journal of Infection Control*. 10(2) 53–59.

Tucker, J.B. (2006). Preventing the misuse of biology: Lessons from the oversight of smallpox virus research. *International Security*, 31(2) 116–150.

References

Brower, J. (2005). Smallpox. In Croddy, E.A., Wirtz, J.J. (Eds.): *Weapons of Mass Destruction: An Encyclopedia of Worldwide Policy, Technology, and History. Volume I: Chemical and Biological Weapons*. Santa Barbara, California – Denver, Colorado – Oxford, England: ABC CLIO, 261–265.

CDC (2017a). Side Effects of Smallpox Vaccination. Centers for Disease Control and Prevention. Page last reviewed 12 July 2017. https://www.cdc.gov/smallpox/vaccine-basics/vaccination-effects.html

CDC (2017b). Vaccination Strategies. Centers for Disease Control and Prevention. Page last reviewed 6 January 2017. https://www.cdc.gov/smallpox/bioterrorism-response-planning/public-health/vaccination-strategies.html

CDC (2019). Smallpox – Research. Centers for Disease Control and Prevention. Page last reviewed 22 January 2019. https://www.cdc.gov/smallpox/research/index.html

Center for Biosecurity (2005). Atlantic Storm interactive. Center for Biosecurity at the University of Pittsburgh Medical Center. http://www.centerforhealthsecurity.org/our-work/events-archive/2005_atlantic_storm/flash/index.html

Croddy, E.A. (2005). Aralsk smallpox outbreak. In Croddy, E.A., Wirtz, J.J. (Eds.): *Weapons of Mass Destruction: An Encyclopedia of Worldwide Policy, Technology, and History. Volume I: Chemical and Biological Weapons*. Santa Barbara, California – Denver, Colorado – Oxford, England: ABC CLIO, 23–24.

Fenn, E.A. (2000). Biological warfare in eighteenth-century North America: beyond Jeffery Amherst. *The Journal of American History*. 86(4) 1552–1580.

Guardian (2014). Forgotten smallpox vials found in cardboard box at Maryland laboratory. *The Guardian/AP*, 8 July 2014. https://www.theguardian.com/science/2014/jul/08/smallpox-vials-found-cardboard-box-maryland-laboratory

Hays, J.N. (2005). *Epidemics and Pandemics: Their Impacts on Human History*. Santa Barbara, California – Denver, Colorado – Oxford: ABC CLIO.

Hopkins, D.R. (2002). *The Greatest Killer: Smallpox in History*. Chicago: University of Chicago Press.

Kupferschmidt, K. (2018). How Canadian researchers reconstituted an extinct poxvirus for $100,000 using mail-order DNA. *Science*, 6 July 2017. https://www.sciencemag.org/news/2017/07/how-canadian-researchers-reconstituted-extinct-poxvirus-100000-using-mail-order-dna

Lentzos, F. (2019). What happened after an explosion at a Russian disease research lab called VECTOR? *Bulletin of the Atomic Scientists*, 27 November 2019. https://thebulletin.org/2019/11/what-happened-after-an-explosion-at-a-russian-disease-research-lab-called-vector/#

Noyce, R.S. (2018). Construction of an infectious horsepox virus vaccine from chemically synthesized DNA fragments. *PLoS One*. 13(1) e0188453. doi: 10.1371/journal.pone.0188453

Rimmer, M. (2018). How smallpox claimed its final victim. *BBC*, 10 August 2018. https://www.bbc.com/news/uk-england-birmingham-45101091

Strassburg, M.A. (1982). The global eradication of smallpox. *American Journal of Infection Control*. 10(2) 53–59.

Tucker, J.B. (2006). Preventing the misuse of biology: lessons from the oversight of smallpox virus research. *International Security*, 31(2) 116–150.

USA Today (2003). Century-old smallpox scabs in N.M. envelope. *USA Today*, 26 December 2003. https://usatoday30.usatoday.com/news/health/2003-12-26-smallpox-in-envelope_x.htm

WHO (n.d.). Research using live variola virus. World Health Organization, date not indicated. https://www.who.int/csr/disease/smallpox/variola-virus-research/en/

Chapter 101

Suspicious Packages

János Kemény
National University of Public Service, Budapest, Hungary

Contents

Introduction 781
Mailed Packages 781
Public Spaces and Mass Transit Systems 782
Classification of the Threats 783
Conclusion 783
Further Reading 784
References 784

Introduction

The term suspicious package is usually used to describe two types of objects, which I define accordingly:

1. Packages received through the regular mail, which have an unusual appearance and can contain explosive devices or other hazardous materials.
2. Bags, suitcases, or other types of handheld containers (for example, bottles), which are abandoned, unusual in their appearance, placement, or other distinctiveness, are small enough to be carried by one or two people, and from which some kind of physical danger to people and surroundings is feared to emanate. In this context, the term is most often used to describe objects suspected of being explosive devices.

Mailed Packages

According to the United States Postal Inspection Service, suspicious packages received through the regular mail can include mail bombs, suspicious or harmful chemical or

DOI: 10.4324/9781315144511-106

biological substances, and also hoax devices (United States Postal Inspection Service, undated). These packages can in most cases be recognized through unusual exterior markings, such as misspellings, the absence of a return address, unusual markings, or other unusual factors, such as odor, thickness, and strange form (Safe Mail Handling Procedures, undated). In the history of politically motivated violence, devices or toxic materials sent through regular mail are a popular method of targeting public personalities and politicians or sometimes companies. But it is important to note that this way of specific targeting can be used by many different groups or individuals, not only for political but also for personal and business reasons. Domestic hate groups, disaffected workers, and vengeful romantic ex-partners can also sometimes turn to this way of attack in order to target their object of misgiving (Who Protects Your Mail, 2019, p. 15).

The possibilities for attack using suspicious packages within the United States have a wide range, including the chemical, biological, radiological, and nuclear (CBRN) spectrum. The best-known example of this is the 2001 string of attacks with letters containing anthrax. Five people were killed during this attack, 17 other were sickened, and 31 others were exposed to it and more than 10,000 people underwent procedures as the possibility for their exposure made this necessary. The attacker targeted US politicians, and in the process, 35 mail rooms and facilities were exposed to contamination. US authorities needed new technological means to complete their investigation (dubbed "Amerithrax") in order to identify the suspects (Amerithrax Investigative Summary, 2010, pp. 2–5).

Public Spaces and Mass Transit Systems

A distinction must be made between unattended and suspicious packages. Unattended packages are harmless; these items are either temporarily left unattended or are left by mistake by their owners. This however can only be determined after conducting the necessary procedures.

Depending on the location of the suspicious packages, different standard operating procedures (SOPs) were developed to deal with them. For example, on mass transit systems, the threat analysis is based on how visible the package is, whether specific threats were previously reported for the type of bag or container, were there people reported hurriedly leaving the scene, are there wires or other indications for an improvised explosive device (IED) visible, is there any indication of chemicals (such as odor, oiliness, etc.) in the package, etc. (Balog et al., 2005, pp. 7–11) In shopping centers, according to the analysis of the RAND Corporation, encouraging the public to report suspicious packages is a cost-effective way to serve as a deterrent (if the reporting works effectively) and to secure the public (LaTourrette et al., 2006, p. 37).

In countries affected by terrorism, the spotting and reporting of suspicious packages is highly important. In order to facilitate an effective cooperation with the public, during the first Intifada, Israel for example has initiated a large public awareness program, part of which focused on reporting suspicious packages (Byman, 2011, p. 332).

Suspicious packages turning out to be harmless nevertheless can be used to test security responses or procedures for example on mass transit systems (how quickly an item is recovered, how it is disposed of, etc.), which can be useful for potential perpetrators to plan attacks with explosive or other devices.

From the last two decades, the best-known example for employing unattended bags is the case of the Madrid Bombings. In the course of the attack, the perpetrators used ten backpacks filled with explosives, which they abandoned on four commuter trains. It was an attack conducted by a group sympathetic to the al-Qaeda group. As a result of the attack, 191 people were killed and more than 1700 wounded (Reuters, 2010). Less well-known cases against trains were attempted since then.

It is important to note that there is also a historical example for the use of WMD utilizing abandoned packages. The Japanese cult Aum Shinrikyo used sarin gas on March 20, 1995, targeting commuters on the Tokyo subway system. The cult had developed its own chemical weapons program, which was not military grade, but it was suitable to cause mass casualties. The attackers used plastic bags, filled with chemicals needed to develop the gas, which they placed on the subway. The attackers used umbrellas, the tips of which were sharpened in order to penetrate the bags, so the gas could fill the closed air space of the carriages. The attackers received antidotes and aimed to release the gas in a coordinated fashion. The attack killed 12 passengers and 54 people were either severely or critically injured, with more than 980 exposed to the attack, suffering mild symptoms (Smithson 2000, pp. 87–89 and 106).

Classification of the Threats

If the threat is found to be real, and some kind of device is identified, two other terms can be relied upon to classify the threat: booby traps and IEDs. JP 1-02 of the United States Defense Department defines the term improvised explosive device as "a weapon fabricated or emplaced in an unconventional manner incorporating destructive, lethal, noxious, pyrotechnic or incendiary chemicals designed to kill, destroy incapacitate harass, deny mobility or distract" (JP 1-02, 2016, p. 108). The Department of Homeland Security defines IEDs as "homemade bomb and/or destructive device to destroy, incapacitate, harass or distract" (DHS, undated). Both definitions are admittedly wide ones and ignore the issue of initiation of the charge, which can be important to better classify the threat. An older, but still used, term is booby trap, which can be viewed as a subcategory of IEDs. U.S: Army Field Manual 5-31 of September 1965 defines a booby trap as "an explosive charge cunningly contrived to be fired by an unsuspecting person who disturbs an apparently harmless object or performs a presumably safe act" (Field Manual No. 5-31, 1965, p. 3). It is rare when the threat relies on a chemical or biological component, so the categorization is less defined. Threats of this nature require highly specialist attention.

Conclusion

With the increasing public perception of terrorism as a threat to public safety and with the cases used as illustration for this entry, suspicious packages have become more concerning for United States Homeland Security. Both categories of suspicious packages identified can cause serious threats to public safety and have negative effects on the perception on security.

Regarding the use of the postal service, this method has become less popular in the last few decades for organized groups with political aims intending to attack public personalities. However, individuals and smaller groups may still find this way of operation attractive. That's why caution and adhering to the standing SOPs is important in these cases for those handling mail and calling the proper authorities when it turns out to be necessary.

Using backpacks and other smaller devices abandoned in public spaces also can represent a real threat, as the Spanish and Japanese examples have shown. The identification, threat assessment, and disposal of suspicious packages is an important part of keeping the public safe as a wide variety of possible threats can be originating from such packages and containers. Educating the public to report abandoned and suspicious packages and how to behave in such situations is essential to dealing with this type of potential threat. At the same time, it is important to keep in mind that potential offenders can use harmless bags and containers to test the response of security personnel and the authorities.

The disposal of suspicious packages can lead to disruptions in heavily used transportation hubs, such as train stations and enclosed spaces in the mass transit system, which can cause negative public responses.

Further Reading

Gerges, F. A.: *The Rise and Fall of Al-Qaeda*, Oxford University Press, 2014.

Hoffman, B.: *Inside Terrorism: Revised and* Expanded Edition, Columbia University Press, 2006.

Laqueur, W.: *A History of Terrorism* 1st Edition, Routledge, 2001.

References

Amerithrax Investigative Summary (2010, February 19), The United States Department of Justice. https://www.justice.gov/archive/amerithrax/docs/amx-investigative-summary.pdf

Balog, J. N. (2005). Public Transportation Security Volume 7 Public Transportation Emergency Mobilization and Emergency Operations Guide, Transit Cooperative Research Program Report 86, Transportation Research Board. http://onlinepubs.trb.org/onlinepubs/tcrp/tcrp_rpt_86v7.pdf

Byman, D. (2011). *A High Price: The Triumphs & Failures of Israeli Counterterrorism*, Oxford University Press.

Department of Homeland Security (undated): IED Attack: Improvised Explosive Devices, Fact Sheet from the National Academies and the Department of Homeland Security. https://www.dhs.gov/xlibrary/assets/prep_ied_fact_sheet.pdf

Field Manual No. 5-31 (1965). Booby Traps, Department of the Army.

Joint Publication 1-02 (2016). *Department of Defense Dictionary of Military and Associated Terms*, Department of Defense. https://fas.org/irp/doddir/dod/jp1_02.pdf

LaTourrette, T., Howell, D. R., Mosher, D. E., & MacDonald, J. (2006). *Reducing Terrorism Risk at Shopping Centers: An Analysis of Potential Security Options*, RAND Corporation. https://www.rand.org/content/dam/rand/pubs/technical_reports/2006/RAND_TR401.pdf

Maclean, W. (2010, January 12). *New Evidence of Qaeda tie to Madrid Blast: Expert*, Reuters. https://www.reuters.com/article/us-security-spain-qaeda/new-evidence-of-qaeda-tie-to-madrid-blast-expert-idUSTRE60B52020100112

Safe Mail Handling Procedures (undated). *National Protection and Programs Directorate*, Federal Protection Service. http://www.osec.doc.gov/osy/PDF/SafeMailing.pdf

Smithson, A. (2000). Rethinking the lessons of Tokyo, in: Smithson A. and Levy L.-A.: *Ataxia – The Chemical and Biological Terrorism Threat and the US Response*, Stimson Center, pp. 71–111. https://www.stimson.org/sites/default/files/file-attachments/atxchapter3_1.pdf

Suspicious Mail (undated). United States postal inspection service. https://www.uspis.gov/tips-prevention/suspicious-mail/

Who Protects Your Mail? (2019, October). U.S. Postal Inspection Service. https://about.usps.com/publications/pub166.pdf

Chapter 102

Urban Search and Rescue (SAR)

Scott R. DiMarco
Mansfield University of Pennsylvania, Mansfield, PA, United States

Scott N. Romaniuk
International Centre for Policing and Security, University of South Wales, Caerleon, United Kingdom

Contents

Urban SAR Operations 788
Urban SAR Operations Training 788
Urban SAR Operations Equipment 788
Use of Canines in Urban SAR Operations 789
Examples of Domestic and International Urban SAR Operations Organizations 790
Urban SAR Operation's Impact on Homeland Security – National and Local Responses 791
Further Reading 791
References 791

The need for specialized responses to rescue victims of disasters ranging from terrorist attacks to industrial accidents to natural disasters created the coordinated response of Urban Search and Rescue (SAR). These integrated and coordinated actions include the location, extraction, and initial medical stabilization of victims trapped in a structural collapse. All aspects of the process from assessment of the initial situation through the rescue phase are uniformly coordinated.

The phases of all urban SAR operations include: 1) assessing the situation; 2) The search process, and 3) the rescue phase. The safety of all victims and rescuers is paramount. Every disaster starts locally, and the local response is always the first to assess the situation and then begin the search and start the rescue process. On an escalating

DOI: 10.4324/9781315144511-107

level, if the situation warrants increased resources/specialization, local first-responders arrive and begin rescuing victims. Local emergency managers may then request assistance from the state level, who may then request Federal Assistance if the situation warrants it. If deemed necessary, Federal Emergency Management Agency (FEMA) will then activate the closest three task forces (Department of Homeland Security, FEMA National Urban Search and Rescue Response System 2016).

Urban SAR Operations

According to FEMA, when a disaster occurs that warrants national support under the National Incident Management System, FEMA will deploy the three closest task forces (or more if necessary) within 6 hours of notification to support state and local responders to "locate victims and manage recovery operations". The National Incident Management System (NIMS) is the tool that provides the coordination and the model that allows the task forces and local agencies to communicate and coordinate. The NIMS became the standard after Hurricane Katrina (FEMA 2015).

As of 2019, FEMA has activated and certified, from local responders, 28 national task forces that are staffed, equipped, and ready to participate in SAR operations in response to: hurricanes, earthquakes, tornados, aircraft accidents, hazardous material spills, and catastrophic structure collapses. Each is ready 24 hours per day to deploy if called upon (FEMA 2018). The 28 task forces are located in Arizona, California, Florida, Indiana, Maryland, Massachusetts, Nebraska, Nevada, New Jersey, New York, Ohio, Pennsylvania, Tennessee, Texas, Utah, Virginia, and Washington. Some larger states with multiple big cities have numerous task forces, like California, Virginia, and Texas.

Each task force has two 31-person teams that may include from canine teams to full equipment re-supply. SAR task force members work in four areas of specialization: search (finding victims), rescue (including getting the victims out safely from under tons of debris), technical (structural specialists who ensure safe rescues for both the victim and the rescue team), and medical (triage) (FEMA 2016).

Urban SAR Operations Training

As a matter of professionalism and in creating uniform standards, in many cases, FEMA provides hands-on-training in SAR techniques and the use of equipment, technical assistance to total agencies, and grant funding to help communities prepare for future operations. Individual members attend required monthly functional skills training often without compensation. (SUSRA) A minimum of two full "Team Level" exercises are held annually, including one 72-hour field exercise (when directed/delivered by FEMA, training is certified and the expenditure of funds is authorized) (FEMA, US&R Rescue Field Operations Guide 2006).

Urban SAR Operations Equipment

According to FEMA, each task force is expected to be self-sufficient for the first 72 hours it is deployed. The task forces, standardized by FEMA, equipment cache has

16,400 pieces and weighs approximately 60,000 pounds and is valued at around $1.4 million. Transportation for the equipment is by either tractor-trailer and/or one C-17 Globe master Aircraft or two C-130 Hercules Aircraft (FEMA, US&R Rescue Field Operations Guide 2006).

Medical equipment is designed to deal with ten critical cases, 15 moderate cases, and 25 minor cases for the victims and the rescuers. Specific medical equipment includes respirators, eye and face protection, gloves, gowns, cleaning kits, medicines, linens, needles, bandages, tourniquets, probes, cervical collars, bone saws, blood, plasma, scalpels, and everything necessary to accommodate patients from triage surgery to minor cuts and burns. After victims are medically stabilized, they are transferred to permanent local medical facilities (FEMA, US&R Rescue Field Operations Guide 2006).

SAR equipment is often necessary to extricate the victims from debris, often created by a structural collapse. Equipment of this nature includes construction equipment from jackhammers to crowbars to drills and ropes. Lifting airbags, hydraulic rescue tools, and shoring systems are also included. Other more technical tools from ground penetrating radar (GPR) to thermal (heat) sensing cameras and telescopic cameras are included in the equipment kit due to the difficult nature of these searches. Unique and sophisticated searches often call for special tools to search remotely that can penetrate cracks and crevices with gear such as camera-mounted fiberscopes and listening devices in the hope of finding a victim (FEMA 2016).

Communications for SAR operations is a bit more complicated. While all task force personnel should receive portable radios, the debris often makes reliable and uninterrupted communication problematic. Remote environments, metal, and concrete makes the transmission and reception of communications inconsistent and often adds an additional level of concern for the safety of rescuers. Additionally, generators, lighting, internet capability, cell phones, and laptops are critical (FEMA 2016).

Logistics and technical equipment is necessary for any operation ranging from a prolonged operation to a relatively simple and short one. Items include food, water, sleeping arrangements with cots, tents, and sleeping bags; kennels and sleeping pads for dogs; showers; air conditioning areas or warming tents; restroom facilities, meeting spaces, office supplies, additional clothing, decontamination stations, and maps are just a few examples (FEMA 2016).

Use of Canines in Urban SAR Operations

The use of dogs in SAR operations at the most basic level is to find a human scent and then to "alert" their human handler to the location where the victim is, despite weather, noises, or outer distractions. The two main types of notification to the human handler are based upon the specialty and training of the dog to either: "recall-find" (lead the handler back to the location of the victim or "victim loyalty" where the dogs barking leads the handler to the person) (Layton 2019).

Most SAR dogs live and train with their human handler. As these dogs often work off leash, training is critical. According to the National Disaster Search Dog Foundation, it escalates over time but averages about 600 hours of training before a dog can be considered "field ready" or able to participate in a rescue. Characteristics of a successful SAR canines include: a great willingness to hunt, boldness and a high prey drive, a strong desire to please, friendliness, attentiveness, and the two most important: obedience and focus. The training of these canines is to develop a reward system with the dogs. They will work to please, and accomplishing their task leads to being rewarded (Layton 2019). Finding and alerting their handlers of victim scent is associated by the dogs with being rewarded. Anecdotal reports of dogs becoming "depressed" when not being successful in finding live bodies have been conveyed.

FEMA considers canines critical in rescues during structural collapses. According to FEMA data, around 85% of FEMA SAR dog handlers are civilian volunteers, with the remaining 15% being members of police or fire departments (NDSDF 2019). Certification and readiness evaluations occur on the national and local levels on assessing the readiness of the dogs and their handlers.

Examples of Domestic and International Urban SAR Operations Organizations

The following is a history of select domestic and international urban SAR events and operations from the mid-1980s to the 2010s (FEMA 2016).

- 1980s Fairfax County Fire and Rescue and Miami Dade Fire Department formed urban SAR teams designed for rescue on collapsed buildings. In conjunction with the US Department of State and the Office of Foreign Disaster Aid, these teams participated in SAR operations in Mexico City, The Philippines, and Armenia after major damaging earthquakes. This was an example of early coordination at a national and international level that not only professionalized the process, but projected American influence abroad.
- 1991 – FEMA created the Federal Response plan (now the National Response Plan) and sponsored 25 national SAR task forces. This expansion of task forces allowed for geographic representation and faster response times.
- Mid-1990s – the Bombing of the Alfred P. Murrah Federal Building in Oklahoma City; Northridge Earthquake; DeBruce Grain Elevator explosion on Wichita; and Greece and Turkey Earthquakes. These incidents represented the spectrum of causes from terrorism to accident to natural disaster.
- 1999 Oklahoma Tornado Outbreak. One hundred fifty-four tornados touched down in the Midwest and Eastern United States in 2 days, with 72, including F5 rated tornados, between May 2 and 8, 1999. $1.5 billion in damage and 36 people killed.
- September 11, 2001 – The World Trade Center and the Pentagon. The terrorist attacks highlighted the response with a focus on rescue of victims.
- 2002 Utah Olympic Games. A prepositioned deployment of the task force in the event of an issue that would require deployment.
- 2010 Port-au-Prince, Haiti – a magnitude 7 earthquake. Estimates of causalities starts at 100,000 people.
- Hurricanes: Floyd; Hurricane Opal; Hurricane Iniki; and Hurricane Katrina. Hurricane seasons cause billions of dollars in damage and casualties ran into the hundreds. The 2017 season alone had over $200 billion in damage and over 3,000 people were killed.

Urban SAR Operation's Impact on Homeland Security – National and Local Responses

In the event of a major domestic (and sometimes international) incident, using the National Response Plan, FEMA-certified task forces are able to coordinate the deployment and use of first-responders in an organized and uniform method anywhere in the country to save lives. This readymade tool of national security has the ability to be used in a very short amount of time to face both natural and man-made disasters, thus mitigating the loss of life and property and projecting strength and stability home and abroad. The lessons learned have been incorporated to optimize success and became a model of local/state/federal government cooperation. For the investment in this resource, the federal government garners good will both nationally and internationally.

Further Reading

Bulanda, S. *Search and Rescue Troubleshooting: Practical Solutions to Common Search-Dog Training Problems.* (K9 Professional Training Series) Dog Training Press. 2017.

National Association for Search and Rescue. *Fundamentals of Search and Rescue.* 2nd Edition. Jones and Bartlett Learning. 2018.

Koester, R. J. *Incident Command System Field Operations Guide for Search and Rescue.* 2nd Edition. DBS Productions. 2014.

References

Department of Homeland Security. n.d. *Federal Emergency Management Agency. National Urban Search and Rescue Response System.* https://www.fema.gov/urban-search-rescue.

Federal Emergency Management Agency. n.d. https://www.fema.gov/

FEMA. n.d. *Urban Search and Rescue Task Force.* https://www.fema.gov/faq-details/Information-about-Urban-Search-and-Rescue-1370032125294

FEMA (2006) Field Operations Guide. https://www.fema.gov/pdf/emergency/usr/usr_23_20080205_rog.pdf

Layton, J. (2019). https://animals.howstuffworks.com/animal-facts/sar-dog.htm *How Search-and-Rescue Dogs Work.*

National Disaster Search Dog Foundation. n.d. https://searchdogfoundation.org/

Pennsylvania Urban Search and Rescue System. n.d. https://www.pema.pa.gov/responseandrecovery/Pages/Pennsylvania-Urban-Search-And-Rescue-System.aspx

State Urban Search and Rescue Alliance. n.d. https://www.susar.org/

Texas Task Force 1. n.d. https://texastaskforce1.org/

Urban Search and Rescue. n.d. https://en.wikipedia.org/wiki/Urban_search_and_rescue

Virginia Task Force 1 – International Urban Search and Rescue. n.d. https://www.vatf1.org/

Young, C. S. and Wehbring, J. *Urban Search and Rescue: Managing Missing Person Searches in the Urban Environment.* DBS Productions LLC. 1st Edition. 2007.

Index

Page numbers in *italic* refer to figures, those in **bold** refer to tables and those followed by “n” refer to notes.

9/11 Commission Report, 68, 115, 148; *see also* September 11 terrorist attacks

A

Acosta, B., 454
Action on Armed Violence IED Monitor, 398
active shootings on campuses, 491–495
  active shooters definition, 491
  countermeasures, 494–495
  gun tolerance debate, 495
  history, 492
  ‘leakage’ (of intentions), 494
  mass murders, 492, 495
  mass shootings, 491–492
  mental health, 494–495
  thereat assessment, 494
  troubled students as shooters, 492–495
advanced persistent threats (APTs), 56–57, 163–165, 201
Advanced Research Projects Agency Network (ARPANET), 255
Advanced Seismic System, earthquakes prediction/data, 716–717
Afghan Civil War, foreign terrorist fighters (FTFs), 371
Afghanistan
  narcotic smuggling, 131
  Soviet Union invasion, 326–327, 329, 331 371
Afghan Taliban, 483
agroterrorism, 687–694
  accidental livestock contamination, 691
  agricultural bioweapons programs, 687, 695n1
  Al Qaeda, 690
  attack typologies, 689–691
  definition, 688
  disaster potential, 691–692
  disgruntled employees, 690–691
  domestic terrorism, 690
  food-processing (centralized), 689
  foot and mouth, 688–689, 691
  government legislation, 692–694
  livestock agribusinesses (US), 688–689
  microorganisms, 688
  mink release, 690
  Newcastle disease (poultry), 691
  radical animal/environmental rights groups, 690
  recommendations, 694
  rendering plant chlordane pesticide contamination, 690–691
  Roman Empire, 687
  salad bars *Salmonella* contamination, 690
  threat, 688–689, 692
  and tourism numbers, 691
  water supply poisoning, 690
  World War I, 687
Aharoni, E., 284
Alaska, Arctic and homeland security, 733–734
Aldrich, R., 251
Alexander II, assassination, 452, 562
Alexander, K. (General), 218, 279, 306–307
Algerian Civil War, Al Qaeda in the Islamic Maghreb (AQIM), 317–319, 322, 323n2
Alien Contract Labor Law (1885), 670
Allaway, Edward Charles, 494
Alley-Young, G, 173–178, 675–682
“alphabet bomber” Kurbegovic, 768
Al Qaeda, 325–332
  agroterrorism, 690
  al Oum, 328, 330–331
  cryptocurrencies, 184
  far enemy, 326, 331
  foreign terrorist fighters (FTFs), 332, 370
  franchise system, 328, 331
  generations, 326–332
  improvised explosive devices (IEDs), 564
  Islamic State (so-called), 331
  leadership, 326, 330–332
  and lone actor terrorism, 415
  Maktab al-Khidamat, 326
  modus operandi, 325, 327–328, 331
  and Northern Ireland troubles, 327–328

nuclear materials, 132
privatized violence, 327, 329
scale of terrorist attacks, **329**
Soviet Union invasion of Afghanistan, 326–327, 329–331
suicide bombers, 454
Syrian Civil War, 329
USS Cole attack, 564
Yemen hotels attack, 327, 331
Al Qaeda in the Islamic Maghreb (AQIM), 317–324, 331
Abdelhak Layada, 317–318
Abdelmalek Droukdel, 319–321
Algerian Civil War, 317–319, 322, 323n2
allegiance with Al Qaeda, 320–321, 323
Ayman al-Zawahiri, 320
Black-African ethnonational and radical politics, 320–321
Boko Haram, 321
caliphate, 318
fatwas, 318–319
formation, 317–319, 323n2
France as "far enemy", 320
Groupe Islamique Armé (GIA), 317–318, 323n2
ideological jihadism splintering, 320–321
jihadist groups merging, 321–322, 324n9
leadership crisis, 321–322, 324n8
Mourad Sid Ahmed, 318
radical ethno-nationalism, 318–319
recruits, 319, 323
Sharia states endgame, 321, 323
sleeper cells, 319, 321
Al-Shabaab, 461
al-Shabaab al-Mu'min, 335–336, 566–567, 628
American Civil Liberties Union (ACLU), 530, 544
American National Red Cross, 535
American Recovery and Reinvestment Act (2009), 61
"Amerithrax" attack, 362, 364–365, 698, 701, 704, 782
Amini, M., 243–246
Amnesty International, Guantanamo Bay, 529
Animal and Plant Health Inspection Service (APHIS), 692–693
Animal Liberation Front (ALF), 690
Anonymous Group, 121, 178, 256
Ansar Allah, 335–343
al-Shabaab al-Mu'min, 335–337
arms smuggling, 342
assistance from Iran, 341–342
capabilities and tactics, 338–341
child soldier cohort, 339
counter-force to Sunni Jihadist groups, 337
Gulf of Aden shipping targets, 342–343
Hasid tribal confederation, 339–340
Houthi combatants, 340, 343n1
Houthi Movement, 335–336
Houthi speeches, 337, 343
Hussein al-Houthi, 335, 337–338
ideology, 337–338
and Islah party, 337–338
kidnapping, 336, 341, 343
northern insurgency (2004-2010), 338–339
origins, 336–337
pick-up trucks "technicals", 340
President Saleh, 339–340
ricin, 761
Saada government, 336–337
Saleh loyalists, 340
Somali coastline piracy, 342
southern move (2011-2014), 339–340
threats to US interests, 341–342
US Special Forces in Yemen, 341
weapons (access), 338–340, 342
Yemen Civil War, 336, 340–341
Anthem, cybersecurity, 234
anthrax, 697–705
"Amerithrax" attack, 362, 364–365, 698, 701, 704
animal anthrax, 699–700
antibiotic treatment, 699, 704–705
Aum Shinrikyo (Japanese cult), 701
biological weapons, 698
biopreparedness costs, 703–704
bioterrorism, 700–704
cutaneous anthrax, 698
decontamination difficulty, 703–704
differential diagnosis, 699
"dirty bomb" equivalency, 703
dispersal (clandestine), 702
gastrointestinal anthrax, 698–699
Gruinard Island, 698, 701
hoaxes, 703
inhalation anthrax, 699
laboratories use, 704
median lethal dose (MLD), 699
mortality, 702–703
nature of the pathogen, 698–700
onward transmission, 703
Pasture strain, 701
Sterne animal vaccine, 701
Sverdlovsk incident (1979), 701
United States Postal Services, 702
weaponization, 700–701
Anti-Arson Act (1982), 142
Anti-Ballistic Missile (ABM) Treaty, 754
Anti-Defamation League (ADL), 435
Arab Spring, 119
Arafat, Yasser, 468–469
Arctic and homeland security, 731–737
Alaska, 733–734
American interests, 732–734
"Arctic Chiefs of Defense Staff" meeting, 732
Arctic Council, 731–732
Arctic Ocean, 734–735

Arctic Security Forces Roundtable (ASFR), 732
"Arctic Strategy" (DoD), 732
Greenland, 733–734
Kotelney Island, 736
natural resources, 735
North Sea Route (NSR), 732, 735–736
North West Passage (NWP), 735
"Polar Concept", 733
Pompeo on, 734–735
Roosevelt (FDR) administration WWII, 733
"Russian Arctic", 736
seabed ownership, 736
Shoigu on, 736
surveillance drones, 735–737
surveillance satellites, 736
Trump's offer to buy Greenland, 733
warming, 734–735
Arellano-Felix Organization (AFO), Tijuana Cartel, 664–665
Armée Révolutionnaire Bretonne (ARB), 425
arson (commercial), 142
artificial intelligence (AI), cybersecurity, 245–246
Art of War (Sun Tzu), 485, 617–618
Aryan Nation, 142
Asal, V. H., 459
Ashton, K., 264
ATF (Bureau of Alcohol, Tobacco, Firearms, and Explosives), 13–16, 137–145
Achilles Program, 15
alcohol, 138–139
arson (commercial), 142
bombings, 141–142
controversial events, 142–144
counterterrorism, 15
Department of the Treasury, 13, 16
Eliot Ness, 138
enforcement responsibilities, 139–142
explosives, 141
Fast and Furious firearms investigation, 14, 144
Fire Research Laboratory, 142
firearms, 14–15, 138, 140–141, 144
function/merger review (1993), 16
Gang Intelligence Network, 16
"Guns to Mexico" project, 15
history, 138
International Programs Branch, 14
mandate overlap with other agencies' missions, 16
Oklahoma City Bombing, 143–144
organization structure, 14
Prohibition, 138
"Project Gunrunner", 15
Ruby Ridge, 142–143
Special Agents, 14
Task Forces, 141
tobacco smuggling, 15–16, 139
Waco, Texas, 143
Atlantic Storm tabletop exercise (2005), smallpox, 778
Attorney General (AG)
and Federal Bureau of Investigation (FBI), 72, 74
and National Domestic Preparedness Office (NDPO), 93–94
Aum Shinrikyo (Japanese cult)
anthrax, 701
chemical and biological weapons (CBW), 364
nuclear materials, 132, 749
sarin, 766–768, 783
AutoINT, passive surveillance, 621–622
Avian Influenza Virus (H7N9), 148–149
aviation security, screening, 638–639

B

Babineau, K., and Farah, D., 591
Bale, J., 561
Balko, R., 645
Baltic States, "Iron Sword" exercise, 484
Baluchistan Liberation Army (BLA), 423–424
Barnard, F., 619
Barnes, G. C., 219
Barnes, N. J., 581–584
Barrio Azteca (*Los Aztecas*), 497–502
ascent and activities, 498–499
Beltrán-Leyva Organization, 498
Capo Eduardo Ravelo, 501
Ciudad Juárez-El Paso border, 499
coded language, 500, 502
domestic security concerns, 499–501
extreme violence, 498, 500
gang rivals, 499–501
Juárez Cartel, 498–499
managing threat, 501–502
members/business in prison, 500–502
Mexican/American dual citizens, 497, 501
Mexican drug trafficking organizations, 498–499, 502
"Nuevo Cartel de Juárez", 499
prison gang culture (Texas), 497, 501–502
public safety concerns, 500
Sinaloa Cartel, 498–499
"street taxes", 501
Barr, W. (Attorney General), 217
Basque separatists, 345–350
Algiers process, 349
Basque Nationalist Party, 346
Ekin, 346–347
Euskadi Ta Askatasuna (ETA), 345–349, 423–424
France's stance towards ETA, 348–349
General Francisco Franco, 346, 349
General Miguel Primo de Rivera, 346
Lizarra-Garazi process, 349

Navel Minister Blanco assassination, 348
origins, 346
post-Franco era, 348–349
'revolutionary tax', 348
Sabino de Arana y Goiri, 346
Spanish Civil War, 345
terrorism diminished, 408
Bataclan theater, 416
Baumann, M., 479
Bayesian networks, 245–246
Baysinger, T. G., 604–605
Beau Geste (Wren), 370
Beck, T. J., 53–57
Begum, M. M., and Momen, M. N., 739–744
Beltrán-Leyva Organization, 505–510
ascent and decline, 506
Barrio Azteca (Los Aztecas), 498
Beltrán-Leyva brothers, 506–508
Chicago (supply to), 508
decentralization, 508–509
Drug Enforcement Agency (Illinois), 507
Foreign Narcotics Kingpin Designation Act, 507, 510
Guerreros Unidos, 508–509
Juárez Cartel, 506
leadership vacuum, 506
Los Zetas, 506, 588
Mexican drug trafficking organizations, 505
Mexican law enforcement/political officials, 506
narcotics in US, 507–508, 510
Pacifico Sur, 506
Sasabe/Lukeville passage, 507
security threats, 506–510
Sinaloa Cartel, 506, 508, 660
street-level sales, 507
subgroups, 508–509
Tijuana/San Diego/Los Angeles passageway, 507
Bennett, N., 345–350
and Romaniuk, S. N., 369–376
Berners Street Hoax (1810), 296
Bhattacharyya, A., and Romaniuk, S. N., 713–718
Bicen, H., and Cavus, N., 188
Billingslea, W., 139
Bill of Rights
civil liberties and homeland security, 526–528, 530, 583
internet service provider records, 530
bioterrorism, 698, 700–704; *see also* anthrax
Bitcoin, 182–183
blackouts, *see* electricity grid security
Blaster, 177
Bledsoe, C.
Bisson, C. and Wolf, H. C., 620
Wolf, H. C. and Bisson, C., 620
Bloom, M., 453–454
Boarder Protection, Antiterrorism, and Illegal Control Act (BPAICA), Mexico border fence, 676
body scanners, 9–11; *see also* Federal Aviation Administration
Boeing, Project (28), 126
Boko Haram, 321, 483
Bolin, B., 710
Bolstad, E., and Schofield, M., 565
Bolton, John (National Security Advisor), 309
Bomb Arson Tracking System (BATS), 142
border patrols and national entry points, 513–522
background, 514
boarder patrol strategy, 515, 518
collaboration with other countries, 518–519
constitutional protections and legal precedents, 520
criticism and condemnations, 519–521
displacement, 518
external illegal entry focus, 520
field agent numbers, 516, 518
future directions, 521–522
geographical features as boundaries, 515, 517
illegal immigration policy responses, 521
migration motivations, 520–521
national borders (significance), 516
national entry points (strategies), 522
operational "effectiveness", 521
post-9/11, 514–516
restrictive immigration polices, 519–520
risk minimization approach, 517–518
securing national borders, 515, 517
surveillance cameras, 517
targeted enforcement, 517–518
technology, 515, 519
United States Border Patrol, 516–519
Boston Marathon
improvised explosive devices (IEDs), 565
target hardening, 463
Brady Handgun Violence prevention Act (1993), 140, 606
Braithwaite, A., and Johnson, S., 397
Branch Davidians, 143
Brannan, D. W., 602, 604
Brazil, cybercrime, 223
Breivik, Anders, 700, 762
Bremer Commission, 444
Brey, P., 256–257
Broken Windows Theory, 556, 647
Brown, B. P. III, 559–567, 641–647
Bullock, A. N., and Colvin, A. D., 533–540
Bundestrojaner, 241
Bureau of Alcohol, Tobacco, Firearms, and Explosives, *see* ATF (Bureau of Alcohol, Tobacco, Firearms, and Explosives)
Bush, G. W. (President)
agroterrorism, 693–694

Mexico border fence, 675, 677, 679
National Domestic Preparedness Office (NDPO), 96
Byman, D., 443
and Kreps, S. E., 445
and Shapiro, J., 373

C

California Earthquake Authority, 714–715
California State University Shooting, 494
California wildfires (2018 and 2019), Native Americans on reservations, 709–710
Camarena, Kitt undercover DEA agent, 659–660, 662–663
car bombs, 351–358
British Isles, 353
defining, 352–355
detection/preventing, 355–356, 358
fragmentation range, *357*
frequency of, *353–354*
Global Terrorist Database, 353–354
Irish Republican Army (IRA), 351
Islamic State (so-called), 351
protection, 356–357
Spain, 353
standoff distance, 356–357, *357*
UN Headquarters Baghdad, 352
in US, 353
US domestic security, 357–358
vehicle-borne explosive device (VBED), 352
vehicle-borne improvised explosive device (VBIED), 352, 395–396, 398, 453, 550, 562–563
vehicle that carry dangerous goods, 352; *see also* improvised explosive devices; vehicle-ramming attacks
Cárdenas, G., 669
Cartel Del Noreste, Los Zetas, 588
Cartwright, James (General), 306, 308
Catino, M. S., Martin, G. and Romaniuk, S. N., xxi–xxiii
Caverly, R. J., 33
Cavus, N., and Bicen, H., 188
Center for Strategic and International Studies (CSIS), cybercrime, 219
Central Intelligence Agency (CIA), 19–23
Director of Central Intelligence Agency (D-CIA), 23
Director of Central Intelligence (DCI), 22–23
Director of National Intelligence (DNI), 23
FBI's intelligence (correlation), 22–23
genesis, 19–21
and intelligence community, 22–23
Intelligence Reform and Terrorism Prevention Act (2004), 23
National Security Act (1947), 21, 23
and National Security Council, 21–22
President's role, 22
Central Intelligence Group (CIG), 20–21
chain of custody, 167–170
definition, 167–168
evidence inadmissible, 169
Chalk, P., 688
Chapot, D., Davis, J. and Parker, D., 625–633
Charlie Hebdo attacks, 184
Charlie Wilson's War (Crile), 371
chemical and biological weapons (CBW), 361–366
"Amerithrax" attack, 362, 364–365, 698, 701, 704
assassinations, 363
Aum Shinrikyo (Japanese cult), 364
biotechnology, 363–364
bioterrorism, 698, 700–704
Bruce Ivins, 364
Carol Anne Bond, 363
The Covenant, the Sword, and the Arm of the Lord, 362–364
disarmament treaties, 361–362
Islamic State (so-called), 364
laboratories, 365
"lone wolf" attacks, 364
Minnesota Patriots Council, 363, 761
Rajneeshee religious cult, 362–363
"scruffy" chemical weapons, 364–365
Soviet weapons program, 701
sulfur mustard, 364
suspicious packages, 782–783
synthetic opioids, 364
Syrian Civil War, 362, 364–365
terrorism in US, 362
Tylenol capsules/cyanide, 362
US National Security, 365–366
White Supremacist Organization, 363; *see also* anthrax
Chemical, Biological, Radiological, Nuclear, and Explosives (CBRNE) Office, 50
Chemical Facility Anti-Terrorism Standards (CFATS), 100
Chen, P., 164
Chermak, S. M., 604, 606–607
Chertoff, M., 33, 47, 125
Chiarelli, Peter (General), 483
Chilean secret police (DINA) assassination by sarin, 769–770
China's Cyber Corps, 302–303
Chines Exclusion Act (1882), 670
Cho, Seung Hui, 492–495
Churchill, R. H., 605
CIA, *see* Central Intelligence Agency
Cilluffo, F. J., Cozzens, J. B. and Ranstorp, M., 372–373
Citizenship and Immigration Services, 41
Ciudad Juárez-El Paso border, Barrio Azteca (Los Aztecas), 499

Civil Defense Act (1950), 535
civil liberties and homeland security, 525–531
  Bill of Rights, 526–528, 530
  definitional engagement, 526–527
  Department of Homeland Security (DHS), 527–530
  Detainee Treatment Act (2005), 529
  internet service provider records, 530
  minority group discrimination, 526
  Office for Civil Rights and Civil Liberties (CRCL), 530
  religion, 528
  USA PATRIOT Act (2001), 526–530
Clapper, James Jr., 96
Clarke, Arthur C., 618
Clarke, C. P., and Serena, C. C., 463
Clarke, R. V., 460
climate change, National Security Strategy (NSS) report, 653
Colvin, A. D., and Bullock, A. N., 533–540
Community Emergency Response Team (CERT), 55
Comprehensive Crime Control Act (1984), firearms trafficking, 15
Computational Propaganda Research Project (COMPROP), Facebook, 218
computer emergency response teams (CERTS), 225, 261
Computer Fraud and Abuse Act (CFFA), 255
Computer Investigations and Infrastructure Threat Assessment Centre (CITAC), 232
Computer Security Act (1987), 209
Conficker Cabal, 178
Conficker Working Group, 178
Conficker worm, 173–178
confidential human sources (CHSe), 73
Congressional Act (1803), disaster management and assistance, 535, 722
Constitutional Sheriffs, 607–608
Continuity IRA (CIRA), 404, 407
Cooley, A., 9–11
Coppola, D. P., 534
Corcoran, A., 575–578
Cordesman, A., 472
Council of American-Islamic Relations (CAIR), 629
Council of Europe, Convention on Cybercrime, 223
Council of State Governments (CGS), National Emergency Management Association (NEMA), 154, 158
Countering Weapons of Mass Destruction (CWMD) Office, 50, 147, 150
Countryman, Thomas (Honorable), 754–755
Covenant, the Sword, and the Arm of the Lord, The, 362–364, 606
COVID-(19), 148–149
Cozzens, J. B., Cilluffo, F. J. and Ranstorp, M., 372–373
Crenshaw, M., 454
Cressey, D., 286
Crime Prevention Through Environmental Design (CPTED), 517
Criminal Justice Information Service (CJIS), 72, 75
critical infrastructure (CI), and industrial resilience, 87
critical infrastructure and key resources, 25–28, 111–116
  Customs and Border Protection (CBP), 114
  defining, 26–27
  Department of Energy (DOE), 26
  Department of Homeland Security (DHS), 25–27, 113–114
  Federal Emergency Management Agency (FEMA), 114
  Homeland Security Enterprise (HSE), 111–112
  Homeland Security Presidential Directives (HSPDs), 115
  local-level leaders, 112–113
  National Infrastructure Protection Plan (NIPP), 27–28, 113
  National Protection and Program Directorate (NPPD), 100
  9/11 Commission Report, 115
  Presidential Decision Directives (PDDs), 115
  private-sector owners/operators (collaboration), 28, 100, 114–116
  protecting, 111–116
  resilience vs. protection, 27
  state-level responsibilities, 113
  Transportation Security Administration (TSA), 114
  U.S. Coast Guard (USCG), 114
Critical Manufacturing Sector, 31–37
  current programs/plan, 34–36
  cybersecurity, 37
  Department of Homeland Security (DHS), 33
  goals and advancement, 36–37
  Government Coordinating Council, 36
  history, 33–34
  information technology, 35, 37
  National Infrastructure Protection Plan (NIPP), 31, 34–36
  production of good and resources (studies), 32–33
Critical Manufacturing Sector Coordinating Council, 32, 34, 36
Crumley-Effinger, M., 669–673
cryptocurrencies, 181–185
  altcurrencies, 184
  Bitcoin, 182
  blockchain, 182
  dark web, 184
  definition, 181
  legality and criminal activity, 183–184
  mining, 182–183

money laundering, 184
North Korea (offending), 219
precursors, 182
ransomware, 184
Silk Road, 184
terrorism issues, 184
virtual wallet, 182, 184
Cuban Missile Crisis, 276, 750–751
Customs and Border Protection (CBP)
Air Cargo Advance Screening (ACAS), 639
critical infrastructure, 114
radiation detection equipment, 46–49
Sinaloa-Tijuana region, 657
cyberattacks, 55–57
advanced persistent threats (APTs), 56–57, 163–165, 201
Anthem, 234
attack types, 206–209
baiting, 285
birthday attacks, 207
Blaster, 177
botnets, 174, 207, 244–245
bots, 206
British hospitals (Conficker B), 175
chain of custody, 167–170
Chinese hackers, 217–218, 234, 301–303
Church of Scientology's website, 121
Conficker worm, 173–178
costs in U.S., 213–214, **213**, 218
cryptocurrencies and ransomware, 184
cyber-criminals, 56
"cyber kill chain" (Lockheed Martin), 200
cyberattacks, 205–209
Darkside, 214
denial-of-service (DOS), 207, 244
distributed denial-of-service (DDOS), 207, 243–246, 261
DNS tunneling, 207
drive-by exploit, 207
hacktivism, 255–262
hacktivists, 56, 205, 257
IP fragmentation attacks, 208, 244
logical bombs, 215, 291
losses from 2015-19 in US, 198
malware, 55, 173, 206, 241, 267–271, 287
man-in-the-middle (MITM), 207, 243
Mirai worm, 178
nation-states' attacks, 56
Nigerian Prince (419 scams), 285, 287
North Korea (offending), 219, 221
organized crime, 174
password attack, 206
patient zero computer, 176
phishing, 284, 286
ping of death attack, 208, 244
ransomware, 173, 184, 205, 207, 257, 261, 271
Revil, 214
Russian hackers, 121, 176, 214, 223–224, 257, 750
Sasser worm, 174
scareware, 285
Smurf attacks, 207
social engineering (deception techniques), 283–287
spyware, 206–207
SQL injections, 206
Stuxnet worm, 178, 215–216, 289–293
TCP/SYN flood, 207–208
teardrop attack, 208, 244
telephony denial-of-service (TDoS), 208
3PLA, 301–303
Trojans, 174, 206, 261, 271
viruses, 206
Waledac, 177
WannaCry, 178, 201, 271
worms, 164, 215–216, 289–293
zero-day vulnerability exploit, 207, 240, 261, 290
cybercrime
Anonymous Group, 121, 178
Asian countries, 223
Brazil, 223
costs in U.S., 213–214, **213**, 218
defining, 214–215
democratic political discourse, 218, 226n1
dominant approaches to address, 215–217
intellectual property (IP) theft, 218
international law, 222–224
Lazarus Group, 201
national security and internet governance, 211–227
Nobelium, 214
ROSAT, 215
Russian State and cybercriminals, 220, 223–224
Russia's intelligence service, 218–219
Shanghai Cooperation Organization (SCO), 224
State-sponsored bank heists, 219
States responsible behavior, 224–226
terrorists, 56
transnational problem, 212–213, 219–220
U.S. cybersecurity framework, 220–222
U.S. Presidential Elections, 218–219, 227n2, 227n3
U.S. vulnerability, 215, 217
Cyber Mission Force (CMF), 307
cybersecurity, 231–234
artificial intelligence (AI), 245–246
attack prevention/mitigation, 177
"backdoors", 221–222, 291
computer emergency response teams (CERTS), 225, 261
Critical Manufacturing Sector, 37
Cyber Command structure (U.S.), 221
cyber governance, 216, 222
cyber sovereignty, 225–226

Cyber Storm Exercises (Homeland Security's), 201–202
Department of Homeland Security (DHS), 42, 244
digital forensics, 167–170
disaster management and assistance, 728
domestic security, 546
electricity grid security, 62
Federal and State laws on cyberattacks, 208–209
Federal Bureau of Investigation (FBI), 231, 233
FireEye, 201, 234
fixer worms, 177
grassroots crowdsourcing-like approach, 57
Homeland Security Act (2002), 208
industrial resilience, 90
"internet of things", 244
Internet "sovereign domains", 224–226
messages (don't trust), 191
MIT-IBM Watson Ai Lab, 201
MITRE ATT&CK framework, 199–201
Multi-State Information Sharing and Analysis Center, 233
National Cyberspace and Communications Integrations Centre (NCCIC), 55, 101–102, 232–233, 245, 269
National Protection and Program Directorate (NPPD), 100–103, 232
network telescope, 174
NSA Framework, 200–201
Nuclear Command, Control, and Communications (NC3), 749–750
Obama administration, 177
privacy concerns, 252
private-sector networks, 233
riots and rioting, 121
sinkhole, 175
Snowden revelations, 222, 252, 279
and social media, 187–195
State-sponsored terrorism, 446
strong passwords, 191
Supervisory Control and Data Acquisition (SCADA) system, 56
'surveillance capitalism', 252
tactics, techniques, and procedures (TTPs), 197–202
"Threat Reduction", 198
ThreatConnect, 234
United Nations (UN), 222–223
US Cyber Command (USCYBERCOM), 279–280, 305–312
US cybersecurity framework, 220–222
US Secret Service (USSS), 232
virtual private networks, 191
White House Cyber Police Review (May 2010), 56–57
worms, 164, 173–178, 206, 215–216, 289–293
Cybersecurity and Infrastructure Security Agency Act (2018), 268–269
Cybersecurity and Infrastructure Security Agency (CISA), 244–245
Cybersecurity Incident Response Teams (CSIRT), 56–57
Cybersecurity Information Sharing Act (2015), 209
Cyber Security Research and Development Act (202), 208
Cyber Threat Integration Center (CTIIC), 233
cyberweapons, 237–241
  Bundestrojaner, 241
  debates, 239–240
  definition, 238–239
  legal questions, 240
  North Atlantic Treaty Organization (NATO), 257
  Obama administration, 292
  Pentagon plan "Nitro Zeus", 750
  Stuxnet worm, 178, 215–216, 289–293
  Tallinn Manual (cyberwarfare), 225, 237–238, 257–258
  UN Charter Article (51), 224, 240
  Wassenaar Arrangement, 261

D

Dao, B., and Ouassini, A., 301–303
Davenport, K., and Reif, K., 748
Davies, I., 709
Davis, J., Chapot, D. and Parker, D., 625–633
Davis, M., 355
Dean, G., 430
defense drills, 535
Defense Intelligence Agency (DIA), measures and signatures intelligence (MASINT), 617–618
Defense Science Board Task Force on DOD Energy Strategy, 3
Delevante, P. N., 707–711
delivery pranks, 296–297
Department of Defense (DOD)
  "Arctic Strategy", 732
  assisting civilian authorities (prohibitions), 159–160
  Cyber Command, 233
  Cyber Strategy, 309–310
  electricity (blackouts and brownouts), 3
Department of Energy (DOE)
  critical infrastructure and key resources, 26
  electricity grid security, 60–61
Department of Health and Human Services, National Domestic Preparedness Office (NDPO), 95
Department of Homeland Security (DHS), 39–43
  Assistant Secretaries, 40
  border security, 41
  budget request (2020), xxii
  Chemical, Biological, Radiological, Nuclear, and Explosives (CBRNE) Office, 50

Citizenship and Immigration Services, 41
civil liberties, 527–530
Countering Weapons of Mass Destruction (CWMD) Office, 50
critical infrastructure, 25–27, 42, 113–114
Critical Manufacturing Sector, 33
cybersecurity, 42, 201–202, 244
Director of Homeland Security, 583–584
Director Perry Plummer, 159
Director Tom Ridge, xxi
disaster management and assistance, 42, 722
economic security, 42
election security, 42
establishment, 40, 96
government spending (2021), xxii
Homeland Security Act (2002), 40–41, 43
human trafficking, 42
immigration enforcement, 42–43
international engagements, 43
law enforcement partnerships, 43
Mexico border fence, 676–678, 680–682
National Cyber Security Division, 170
National Domestic Preparedness Office (NDPO), 93, 96
National Protection and Program Directorate (NPPD), 42, 99
privacy concerns, 43
roles of, 41–43
Science and Technology Directorate, 43
Secretary Chertoff, 47, 125, 682
Secretary Napolitano, 126–127, 681
Secretary Nielsen, 147, 150
Secretary of Homeland Security, 40, 43, 47, 50, 125–127, 147, 150, 681–682
Secure Border Initiative (SBI), 125, 681
September 11 terrorist attacks, 544–545
Soft Targets and Crowded Places (ST-CPs), 463–464
Special Assistant, 40
terrorism prevention, 43
transportation security, 43
Traveler Redress Inquiry Program (TRIP), 639
US-CERT program, 101–102, 233
Department of Justice (DoJ)
Broken Windows Theory, 556, 647
and Federal Bureau of Investigation (FBI), 71–72
IED definition, 560
Organized Crime and Gangs section, 555–556
Post-Industrial Era, 556
Department of the Treasury, ATF function/merger, 13, 16
Department of Transport Act (1966), Federal Aviation Administration (FAA), 66
Detainee Treatment Act (2005), USA PATRIOT Act (2001), 529
DHS, *see* Department of Homeland Security
digital forensics, chain of custody, 167–170
DiMarco, L. A., 483
DiMarco, S. R., and Romaniuk, S. N., 787–791
Director of National Intelligence (DNI), National Representative Program, 72
disaster impact on minorities, 707–711
California wildfires (2018 and 2019), 707–708
Great Galveston Hurricane (1900), 707
Hurricane Katrina, 708–710
Native Americans on reservations, 708–710
social advocacy and empowerment, 711
disaster management and assistance, 533–540, 721–728
all-hazard approach, 724
Asipu, 534
catastrophic incident term, 727
civil defense system, 721
conceptual confusion, 726–727
crisis management v consequence management, 725–726
critical success factors, 540
cybersecurity, 728
decision analysis, 534
defense drills, 535
definition, 534
"disaster" and "emergency" differentiating, 724
disaster costs (2018, US), 723
emergency term, 726
"executive orders", 535, 741–742
five-phase process, 539
Geographical Information Science (GIS) mapping, 538
gov. role and policy, 723–725
hazard assessments, 538, 540
hazard term, 726
history, 534–536
improving efficiency and effectiveness, 539–540
incident term, 727
Insurrection Act (1807), 741
legislation, 721–722, 739–744
major disaster term, 726
man-made disasters, 723, 728
mitigation, 537–538
National Disaster Recovery Framework (NDRF), 743
National Emergencies Act (NEA), 742
National Flood Insurance Act (1968), 535
National Flood Insurance Act and Disaster Relief Act (1974), 535
National Governors Association, 744
National Guard, 741–742
National Incident Management System (NIMS), 725, 727
National Response Plan (NPR), 725
preparedness, 538
President Woodrow Wilson, 744
public assistance, 537

recovery time and cost, 539
regional/interstate disaster response, 743–744
risk reduction, 537–539
Small Business Act (1953), 535
social media, 540
"Stafford Act", 724, 726, 741
Tenth Amendment, 742–744
terms in use, 726–727
terrorist attacks, 723–724
US Constitution, 740–741; *see also* Federal Emergency Management Agency; Hurricane Katrina
Disaster Relief Act (1966), 722
Dodds, K., and Nuttall, M., 732
Domestic Nuclear Detection Office (DNDO), 45–51
cargo advanced automated radiography system (CAARS), 49
Cold War, 46
and Customs and Border Protection (CBP), 46–49
DHS's Directorate of Science and Technology, 50
dismantlement of DNDO, 50
Global Nuclear Detection Architecture (GNDA), 47–48
intelligence analysis and information sharing, 49–50
Joint Analysis Centre (JAC), 49
MASINT information, 47, 50
packages under diplomatic seal, 46
radiation detection equipment, 46–49
Red Teams, 49
SAFE Port Act (2006), 47
unconventional nuclear attack (concern), 45–47
Domestic Preparedness Leadership Group (DPLG), 94
domestic security, 543–546
current issues, 545–546
cybersecurity, 546
future challenges, 546
harm mismanagement, 545
illegal immigration Trump administration, 545
kidnapping, 572–573
mass shootings, 545
Mexican drug trafficking organizations, 545
9/11 and Office of Homeland Security, 544–545
President Harry S. Truman, 544
social media, 546
World War II and Cold War, 544
domestic terrorism, 626, 690
Donovan, T, 671
Dougherty, C., 603
Douglas, R. A., 33
Doyle, R. B., 652
Drake, C. J. M., 459
Drew, D. M., and Snow, D. M., 650
drones
Arctic and homeland security, 735–737
"Arctic Drone Squadron" (Russia), 736
Federal Aviation Administration (FAA), 69–70
Mexico border fence, 677, 681
Drug Enforcement Agency (DEA)
Illinois, 507
Kiki Camarena undercover agent, 659–660, 662–663
Sinaloa-Tijuana region, 659
Duerr, G. M. E., 403–408, 421–426
Dziwisz, D., 289–293
and Romaniuk, S. N., 305–312

E

earthquakes, 713–718
Advanced Seismic System, 716–717
Blue Mountain Lake (New York, 1973), 716
California earthquake (1989), 714, 717
California earthquake (2019), 714
California Earthquake Authority, 714–715
donor fatigue, 717
Federal Earthquake Insurance and Reinsurance Corporation Act, 714
FEMA's Project Impact program, 714
Field Act, 714
Haiti earthquake, 715, 717
high-risk areas (US), 713
Hyogo Framework for Action (Kobe, Japan), 716
Mental Rehabilitation Centers, 717
National Earthquake Hazard Reduction Program, 715
and national security, 716–717
Northridge Earthquake (1994), 55, 714
Nuclear Regulatory Commission, 714
Obama administration, 714
prediction, 716–717
rescue and aid teams, 715–717
school buildings, 714
Seismic Safety Commission, 714
Trump administration, 714
UNESCO, 715–716
United States Geological Survey (USGS), 715
urban hazard maps, 716–717
Urban Search and Rescue (US&R) Task Forces, 55, 789
Echelon, 251–253, 279
Ekström, M., 430
electricity grid security, 59–63
aging infrastructure, 61
American Recovery and Reinvestment Act (2009), 61
blackouts and brownouts, 3–7
Boston Back Bay fire, 5
conventional weapons, 62
critical assets, 3

cybersecurity, 62
Department of Energy (DOE), 60–61
electromagnetic pulse, 62
Energy and Independence Security Act (2007), 61
energy security and adequacy, 62–63
grid resilience, 62
and gross domestic product (GDP), 60
increased use of electricity, 59–60
legislation, 60–61
microgrids, 63
national security, 6
Northeast blackout (2003), 5
renewable energy as distributed generation, 63
security concerns, 62
smart grids, 6, 61
unintentional outages, 4–5
Electronic Communications Privacy Act (1986), 208
electronic surveillance, signals intelligence (SIGINT), 73
emergency family plan, 612–613
emergency management, *see* disaster management and assistance
Emergency Management Accreditation Program (EMAP), 155–156
Emergency Management Assistance Compact (EMAC), 155–156, 743–744
emergency response task forces, *see* Urban Search and Rescue (US&R) Task Forces
Energy and Independence Security Act (2007), electricity grid security, 61
Enigma, 250, 253
Enoch Brown school massacre, 492
Environmental Liberation Front (ELF), 690
Environmental Protection Agency (EPA), National Domestic Preparedness Office (NDPO), 95
Erickson, R. J., 442
Estonia, Russia's cyberattack, 223–224
European Union, narcotic smuggling, 131
Euskadi Ta Askatasuna (ETA), 345–349, 408, 423–424; *see also* Basque separatists
E-Verify, 671
Explosives Control Act (1970), 141

F

Facebook
active users, 188
Computational Propaganda Research Project (COMPROP), 218, 226n1
"dark posts", 219
fake "likes", 218
imagery intelligence (IMINT), 619–620
passive surveillance, 618–620
photograph data, 619–620
U.S. Presidential Elections, 219, 227n3
Fahrenheit 9/11 (Moore), USA PATRIOT Act (2001), 544
Farah, D., and Babineau, K., 591
Farida, M., 379–384
Farm Security and Rural Investment Act (2002), agroterrorism, 692
Farnham, N., and Liem, D. M., 468
Federal Aviation Administration (FAA), 65–70
commercial space craft, 70
Computer-Assisted Passenger Prescreening System (CAPPS), 67
Department of Transport Act (1966), 66
explosive detection, 67
Federal Air Marshal Service, 66, 69, 390
Federal Aviation Act (1958), 66
hijacking, 65–66
history, 66
Next Generation Air Transportation (NextGen) System, 70
9/11 and aftermath, 67–69
Pan Am (103), 67
passenger profiling, 66–67
screening, 66–67
Transportation Security Administration (TSA), 65, 69
unmanned aerial vehicles (UAVs), 69–70
Federal Bureau of Investigation (FBI), 71–75
and ATF, 16
and Attorney General (AG), 72, 74
Counterintelligence Division (CD), 71, 73
Counterterrorism Division (CTD), 71
Criminal Investigative Division (CID), 71
cybersecurity, 71, 231, 233
and Department of Justice (DoJ), 71–72
Director Christopher Wray, 625
Director J. Edgar Hoover, 72, 74
Director Robert Mueller, 73, 75
Directorate of Intelligence (DI), 71
Disaster Squad, 74
Field Intelligence Groups (FIGs), 73
field offices (FOs), 72–73
Fingerprint Identification Division, 72
foreign intelligence, 74–75
headquarters (FBIHQ), 71–72
history, 72
Hostage Rescue Team (HRT), 74–75
human intelligence (HUMINT) squads, 73
Intelligence Branch (IB), 72–73
intelligence correlation with CIA, 22–23
Laboratory Division, 74
Legal Attaches (Legats), 73
mission overlap with other agencies, 75
National Academy Program, 72
National Domestic Preparedness Office (NDPO), 93
post-9/11 reforms, 75
pre-9/11 gaffes, 73–74
President Roosevelt (FDR), 72
resident agencies (RAs), 73

Special Intelligence Service (SIS), 73
Threat Review and Prioritization (TPR) process, 75
Transnational Anti-Gang (TAG) Task Force, 593
Weapons of Mass Destruction Directorate (WMDD), 71, 73
Federal Disaster Relief Act (1950), 721
Federal Earthquake Insurance and Reinsurance Corporation Act, 714
Federal Emergency Management Agency (FEMA)
agency's focus, 158–159
critical infrastructure, 114
disaster management and assistance, 535–536, 722–724, 727, 742
earthquakes, 714
incident levels (terms), 727
National Domestic Preparedness Office (NDPO), 93–96
National Emergency Management Association (NEMA), 158–159
Post Katrina Reform Act, 158–159
urban search and rescue (SAR), 788; *see also* Urban Search and Rescue (US&R) Task Forces
Federal Firearms Act (1938), 140
Federal Motor Carrier Safety Administration (FMCSA), 352
financial crisis (2008), 89
Financial Modernization Act (1999), 209
Firearms Owners' Protection Act (1986), 140
firearms trafficking, 14–15
FireEye, 201, 234
Fischer, E. A., 209
Fisher, J., 647
flood insurance/emergencies, 159
Ford Hunger March, 120
Foreign Intelligence Surveillance Act (1978), 73, 274, 527–528
Foreign Narcotics Kingpin Designation Act
Beltrán-Leyva Organization, 507, 510
Los Zetas, 588
Sinaloa Cartel, 662
foreign terrorist fighters (FTFs), 369–376
Afghanistan, 370–371
American volunteers, 373–375
Anglo-Boer War, 372
camaraderie, 372
Charlie Wilson, 371
contemporary threat, 373
death in combat, 373
definitional debate, 371–372
desire for adventure, 372
female terrorists, 375
French Foreign Legion, 370, 372
history, 370–371
Islamic State (so-called), 371, 373, 375
and mercenary soldiers, 371–372
Mujahedeen in Bosnia, 371
returnees, 373–375
Russo-Chechen war, 372
security response, 373–375
Siege of Kunduz, 370
social networks and recruitment, 373–374
Spanish Civil War, 370
transnational jihadism, 375
women and children (non-combatants), 375
Forsane Alizza (Knight of Glory), 415
Forster, R., and Kinnear, H., 335–343
Fortier, Michael, 143
Foucault, M., 193
Fourth Amendment, body scanners, 10
Franz Joseph Land, 736
French Foreign Legion, foreign terrorist fighters (FTFs), 370, 372
Frente Farabundo Marti de Liberación (FMLN), MS-13 (Mara Salvatrucha), 592–593
Fronte di Liberazione Naziunale Corsu (FLNC), 425
Fuchs, C., 191
Fuerzas Armadas Revolucionarias de Colombi (FARC), 425
Fukushima Daiichi Nuclear Disaster, 88
Fukuyama's 'End of History and the last Man', 251
Fullerton Massacre, 494

G

Galveston Hurricane (1900), 535
gangs and law enforcement, 549–556
active number of gangs, 550
beliefs and rituals, 552
codes of conduct, 554
delinquent activities, 554
East Coast, West Coast, Midwest Gangs, 551–553
feuds, 555
financial crimes, 555
gang operations, 553–554
gang term, 549
gangs' purpose, 550–551
in-group dynamic/coerced-motivation phenomenon, 552
leaders of gang groups, 551
leaders of gangs, 552
members per gang, 553
Mexican immigrants, 550
National Gang Center, 555
New York, 550
Organized Crime and Gangs section of DOJ, 555–556
prevention strategies, 555–556
race differences, 553–554
resources (gangs'), 553
statistics, 554–555
street gangs, 549–550

threat to law enforcement personnel, 555
Gates, Robert, 306
GCHQ (Government Communications Headquarters), 249–253
Anglo-American intelligence relationship, 250–251
Echelon, 251–253
Enigma, 250, 253
funding cuts, 251
history, 250–251
Intelligence Services Act (1994), 249
National Cyber Security Center, 199
9/11 effects, 251–252
post-Cold War world, 251
privacy concerns, 252
Second World War, 250
Snowden revelations, 252
social media, 252
'surveillance capitalism', 252
twenty-first-century issues, 252–253
Gellner, E., 423
Gentile, G., 484
Geographical Information Science (GIS) mapping, 538
Georgia, Russia's cyberattack, 224
Gill, P., 413
Horgan, J. and Lovelace, J., 394, 560–561
Gill, P. and Lovelace, J., Horgan, J., 560–561
GitHub, 245
Global Nuclear Detection Architecture (GNDA), 47–48
Global Terrorist Database, car bombs, 353
Goh, One, 493–494
Golub, J., 672
Good Friday Agreement (GFA), 405, 407–408, 423
Government Accountability Office (GAO)
IED countermeasures spend, 566
malware threat table, 269–270
Government Communications Headquarters, *see* GCHQ (Government Communications Headquarters)
Graham, S., 462
Gramm-Leach-Bliley Act (1999), 209
Grant, M. J., and Stewart, M. G., 353
Green, D., 134
Greenland
defense WWII US Air Base, 733–734
strategic value to US, 734
surveillance drones, 735
US offers to purchase, 733
Grice, F., and Houghton, L., 687–694
Griffin, C. E., 657–665, 721–728
Grote, J. H. Jr., 689
Group of Eight (G8), cybersecurity, 225
Grupo Aeromóvil de Fuerzas Especiales (GAFE), Los Zetas, 588–589
Grushkin, D., Kuiken, T. and Millet, P., 364
Guadalajara "cartel"
Sinaloa Cartel, 659–660, 662
Tijuana Cartel, 663
Guantanamo Bay, 529
Guerreros Unidos, Beltrán-Leyva Organization, 508–509
Guffey, J., and Lasley, J., 397
Guidelines for Critical Infrastructures Resilience Evaluation (document GCIE-2016), 88–90
Gulf Cartel
La Familia Michoacana (LFM), 576
Los Zetas, 588–589
Gun Control Act (1968), 140–141
gun smuggling, Fast and Furious firearms trafficking investigation, 14, 144
Guzmán-Loera Organization, Sinaloa Cartel, 660

H

hacker groups, 56
hacking, 255–262
aircraft, 390–391
amateur computer hobbyist, 255–256
Anonymous Group, 256
"black hat hacking", 256
Chinese hackers, 261
classifying the hacker, 256–258
definition, 255–256
"hacking code", 256
hacktivists, 205, 257
industrial espionage, 257
information commons, 257
Internet architecture, 258–261
Law of Armed Conflict, 261
political doxing, 257
Russian hackers, 257–258, 261
State awareness of vulnerabilities, 261–262
types of hacking, **259–260**
Ukraine's power grid, 257
"white-hat hackers", 256
Wikileaks, 256; *see also* cyberweapons
Hadzhidimova, L., 79–84, 117–122
Hafez, M., 454
Haider-Markel, D. P., and O'Brien, S. P., 601, 608
Haiti earthquake, 715, 717
Hall, L., 482
Hamas
and Hezbollah, 381, 751
improvised explosive devices (IEDs), 564
suicide bombers, 452
Hamilton, Alexander, 192
Hardin, R., 530
Harper-Mercer, Chris, 493
Hasanovic, H., 107–109
Hattiangady, P., and Romaniuk, S. N., 211–227
Haubert, J., 708, 710

Haughton, S. A., 41
and Romaniuk, S. N., 19–23, 39–43, 525–531
Healey, J., 292
Hegghammer, T., 371
Henstra, D., 740
Hersterman, J., 459
Hezbollah, 379–384
and Hamas, 381, 751
improvised explosive devices (IEDs), 564
and Iran, 383
Islamic revolution in Iran, 380
March 14 Alliance, 381
and Palestine Liberation Organization (PLO), 380
as a regional actor, 381–383
regional states foreign policies, 382
suicide missions, 381, 452
Syrian Civil War, 382
terrorist watch lists, 379, 383
tobacco smuggling, 139
tri-border area (TBA), 384
US security concerns, 383–384
HIDDEN COBRA, 270–271
High Value Detainee Interrogation Group (HIG), 73
hijacking, 387–391
Achille Lauro, 388–389
airplane hijackings, 389–391
Beijing Protocol (2010), 390
"D.B. Cooper", 389
definition, 388
Dutch train siege (1977), 388
Federal Air Marshal Service, 66, 69, 390
hacking of commercial aircraft, 390–391
Montreal Protocol (2014), 390
Palestine Liberation Front, 388–389
Peru (1931), 389
Popular Front for the Liberation of Palestine (PFLP), 389
Prohibition, 388
screening, 389
September 11 terrorist attacks, 390
ship hijackings, 388–389
term, 387
terrorism and new technologies, 390–391
Hing, B., 671, 673
Hjortdal, M., 216
Hobsbawm, E., 421
Hoffman, B., 469
Homeland Security Act (2002)
agroterrorism, 692
American Civil Liberties Union (ACLU), 544
cybersecurity, 208
Director of Homeland Security, 583–584
domestic security, 544
Secretary of Homeland Security, 40
Section (101), 41
Section (102), 40, 43
Section (103), 40
Homeland Security Consortium, 159
Homeland Security Council, National Strategy for Homeland Security (2007), xxi
Homeland Security Policy Directives (HSPDs), agroterrorism, 692–693
Homeland Security Presidential Directives (HSPDs), critical infrastructure and key resources, 115
Homeland Security Systems Engineering & Development Institute (HSSEDI), 199
Hook, Theodore, 296
Hoover, J. E., Federal Bureau of Investigation (FBI), 72, 74
HOPLIGHT, 271
Horgan, J., Gill, P. and Lovelace, J., 394, 560–561
Houghton, L., and Grice, F., 687–694
Houthi Movement, *see* Ansar Allah
Howell, J. A,, and Moore, J. P., 556
Hsu, H. Y., and McDowell, D., 461
Hughes, S., Clifford, B. and Meleagrou-Hitchens, A., 374
Human Factor Report, malware, 287
human trafficking, 42, 82–83, 133
Hunter, L., 527
Hunter, M., and Ouassini, A., 163–165
Hurricane Harvey, Urban Search and Rescue (US&R) Task Forces, 54
Hurricane Katrina
deaths, 709
harm mismanagement, 545, 709–710, 740
House of Representatives inquiry report, 744
"Hurricane Katrina Task Force", 742
Insurrection Act (1807), 741
looting, 741
racism of gov. agencies, 708–710
resident minorities, 708–709
Hutchinson, J., 393–400, 426–436
Huxley, A., 698
Hyogo Framework for Action (Kobe, Japan), 716

I

illegal immigrants
Latin Kings, 134
Mara-Salvatrucha-13 (MS-13), 134
Trump administration, 545
Illegal Immigration Reform and Immigration Responsibility Act (1996)
Mexico border fence, 675–676
removal of non-citizens convicted of crime, 593
imagery intelligence (IMINT)
Facebook, 619–620
passive surveillance, 617–620
Imarat Kavkaz (IK), 423–424

Immigration Act (1891), 670
Immigration and Customs Enforcement (ICE), 16, 79–84
budget (2018), 79
challenges and concerns, 82–83
Detention Reporting and Information Line, 80
Enforcement and Removal Operations (ERO), 79–80
Freedom of Information Act, 81–82
function of units, 80–82
Homeland Security Investigations (HSI), 79–80
human trafficking, 82–83
Immigration and Nationality Act, 80
Immigration and Naturalization Service (INS), 79
Intergovernmental Service Agreement (IGSA), 83
Management and Administration division, 81
Mexican drug trafficking organizations, 499
Office of Professional Responsibility, 82
Office of the Principal legal Advisor (OPLA), 82
sub-divisions, 80–81
U.S. Customs Service (USCS), 79
weapons of mass destruction (WMDs), 81
Immigration and Nationality Act, Immigration and Customs Enforcement (ICE), 80
Immigration and Naturalization Service (INS)
Homeland Security Act (2002), 670
Immigration and Customs Enforcement (ICE), 79
United States Citizenship and Immigration Services (USCIS), 670–671
immigration enforcement
ATF, 16
Department of Homeland Security (DHS), 42–43
immigration, nationality-based quota system, 670
improvised explosive devices (IEDs), 393–400, 559–567
Action on Armed Violence IED Monitor, 398
Afghanistan and Iraq, 395, 565
Alexander II, 562
Al Qaeda, 564
booby traps, 563, 567, 783
Boston Marathon, 565
Civil War (US), 562
civilian deaths and injuries, 398
composition and combustion, 394–395
countermeasures, 564–566
definitions, 394, 560–562
Government Accountability Office, 566
"gun powder plot" (Guy Fawkes), 562
Hamas, 564
Hezbollah, 564
history, 562–564
history and trend, 395–396
Homeland Security's Office for Bombing Prevention, 399
Irish Republican Army (IRA), 395, 562
Islamic State (so-called), 396, 481
Liberation Army Fifth Battalion, 396
Liberation Tigers of Tamil (LTTE), 563–564
method of violence, 394–395
Northstar VII, 399
"over-pressure effect", 394–395
pipe bomb attacks (Austin, Texas, 2018), 565
Provisional Irish Republican Army (PIRA), 395, 398
public education, 398–399, 782, 784
SGSecure Movement, 399
siege warfare (1400s), 562
situational crime prevention (SCP) techniques, 394, 396–397
Somalia case study, 566–567
Spokane, Washington plot, (2011), 565
suicide bombers, 453, 564
suicide missions, 396
suspicious packages, 782
toxic chemicals, 395
unmanned aerial vehicles (UAVs), 481
U.S. military test (SCP), 397
vehicle-borne improvised explosive device (VBIED), 352, 395–396, 398, 453, 560, 562–563
Vietnam War, 564–565
violent extremist groups, 563
World Trade Center bombing (1993), 564–565
World War I and II, 563; *see also* car bombs
industrial resilience, 87–91
and critical infrastructure (CI), 87
cybersecurity, 90
defining, 88
evaluating, 88–90
financial crisis (2008), 89
Fukushima Daiichi Nuclear Disaster, 88
Guidelines for Critical Infrastructures Resilience Evaluation (document GCIE-2016), 88–90
increasing resilience, 90
recovery time and cost, 89–90
self-recovery, 89
Utility Resilience Index, 89
withstanding time, 89
Information Analysis and Infrastructure Protection (IAIP) Directorate, 232
National Cyber Security Division, 101
National Infrastructure Protection Plan (NIPP), 100–101
information technology, Critical Manufacturing Sector, 35, 37
Infrastructure Analysis and Strategy Division (IASD), 101
Infrastructure Information Collection Division, 100

Infrastructure Security Compliance Division, 100
Instagram
active users, 188
passive surveillance, 618
Institute for Constitutional Advocacy and Protection (ICAP), militias, 603
Intelligence Reform and Terrorism Prevention Act (2004), 23
Interagency Board for Equipment Standardization and Interoperability, 95
Interagency Domestic Terrorism Concept of Operations Plan, 94
Intergovernmental Service Agreement (IGSA), Immigration and Customs Enforcement (ICE), 83
Intermediate-range Nuclear Forces (INF) Treaty, 753
International Association of Emergency Managers, National Emergency Management Association (NEMA), 154
International Atomic Energy Agency (IAEA), 131, 751
International Conference on International Telecommunication (WCIT-12), 224
International Organization for Migration (IOM), 133–134
International Strategy for Cyberspace (2011), 220
International Symposium on Cybercrime Response (ISCR), 223
International Telecommunication Union (ITU), 217, 224
Internet
Advanced Research Projects Agency Network (ARPANET), 255
"internet of things", 35, 244, 263–265, 618
original design/use, 217, 255
quasi-legal space, 255–256
"sovereign domains", 224–226
Internet Assigned Numbers Authority (IANA), 216–217, 226
Internet Corporation for Assigned Names and Numbers (ICANN), 178, 216–217, 226
Internet Engineering Task Force (IETF), 216
"internet of things", 35, 244, 263–265
Internet Security Threat Reports (ISTR), 223
Iran
Hamas, 751
Hezbollah, 383, 751
International Atomic Energy Agency (IAEA), 751
nuclear threats, 751
State-sponsored terrorism, 446; *see also* Stuxnet worm
Iraq War
destroyed cities, 484
improvised explosive devices (IEDs), 395
sarin, 766, 769
Irish Civil War, 403–404
Irish Republican Army (IRA), 403–408, 423–424
Act of Union (1800), 403
British "special relationship" with US and GFA, 407–408
car bombs, 351
Conservative Party Conference attack (1984), 406
Continuity IRA (CIRA), 404, 407
decline and current status, 406–407
evolution and historical background, 404–405
Good Friday Agreement (GFA), 405, 407–408, 423
improvised explosive devices (IEDs), 395, 562
Irish Civil War, 403–404
New IRA (NIRA), 407
9/11 aftermath, 328, 405
Northern Ireland, 403, 405
Northern Irish Assembly, 405, 407
Official IRA (OIRA), 404
organizational strategy and leadership, 405–406
Provisional Irish Republican Army (PIRA), 404
Real IRA (RIRA), 404
relevance to US, 407–408
Sinn Féin (SF), 407
terrorism diminished, 408
terrorist attacks, 405–406
terrorist watch lists, 404
Tony Blair and devolution, 408
The Troubles, 404–407
Islamic Revolutionary Guard Corps-Qods Force (IRGC-QF), 446
Islamic revolution in Iran, Hezbollah, 380
Islamic State (so-called)
Al Qaeda, 331
car bombs, 351
cryptocurrencies, 184
foreign terrorist fighters (FTFs), 371, 373, 375
improvised explosive devices (IEDs), 396, 481
and lone actor terrorism, 412, 415–417
Manchester Arena suicide bomber, 462
Paris attacks (2015), 461
radicalization prevention and response, 626, 628, 631–632
scale of terrorist attacks, **329**
social media, 192, 546
target hardening, 459, 461
Israel
State-sponsored terrorism, 446
suspicious packages, 782

J

Jakarta attacks (2016), 184
Johnson, S., and Braithwaite, A., 397
Joint Comprehensive Plan of Action (JCPOA), 755

Joint Task Force-Computer Network Defense (JTF-CND), 306
Joint Task Force-Computer Network Operations (JTF-CNO), 306
Joint Task Force-Global Network Operations (JTF-GNO), 306
Jolicoeur, J. R., 513–522
Journal of Digital Forensics, Security and Law, 169
Juárez Cartel
  Barrio Azteca (Los Aztecas), 498–499
  Beltrán-Leyva Organization, 506
  Los Zetas, 588
Juárez plaza, Barrio Azteca (Los Aztecas), 498
Jules, T. D., 317–324, 441–448

K

Kamien, D. G., 113–114
kamikaze pilots WWII, 452
Kappeler, V. E., and Kraska, P. B., 642–643
Kaspersky, 267
Kazumi, M., and Tomihisa, T., 748
Kelley, C., 231
Kemény, J., 781–784
  and Romaniuk, S. N., 273–280
Khan, U., and Romaniuk, S. N., 477–485
kidnapping, 569–573
  Ansar Allah, 336, 341, 343
  child kidnappings, 569–570
  domestic security, 572–573
  employees in foreign nations, 571
  express kidnaping, 570
  federal jurisdiction, 571
  Global Risk Consulting Control Risks report, 571
  high-profile/wealthy victim, 570
  K&R Insurance, 572
  Mexico border fence, 680
  militant groups, 571
  National Security Council, 572
  numbers (2000-2015), 572
  Obama statement, 572
  organized criminal networks, 571–572
  political/ideological kidnapping, 570
  risk (American citizens), 570
  terrorist organizations finances, 571–572
  Tiger kidnapping, 570
  USA PATRIOT Act (2001), 571–572
  virtual kidnapping scam, 570
Kinnear, H., and Forster, R., 335–343
Klarman, M., 526
Klinger, D. A., and Rojek, J., 642–643
Knowles, T., 690
Kobach, K., 134
Kohli, N., 467–475
Koppel, T., 56
Koresh, David, 143
Kotelney Island, 736
Kraska, P. B., 645
  and Kappeler, V. E., 642–643
Kreps, S. E., and Byman, D., 445
Ku Klux Klan, 121, 425
Kuiken, T., Grushkin, D. and Millet, P., 364

L

Lacroix, R. M., 497–502, 505–510, 601–608, 649–654
La Familia Michoacana (LFM), 575–578
  Carlos Rosales Mendoza, 577
  "corpse messaging", 576, 578
  defections, 576
  "El Chango" (Jose de Jesus Mendez), 578
  "El Chayo" (Nazario Moreno Gonzalez), 577–578
  El Milenio, 575
  "El Player" (Hector Garcia), 578
  executive council, 577
  extortion payments, 577
  Gulf Cartel, 575–576
  internal factions, 577
  Lazaro Cardenas (port for cocaine shipments), 578
  leadership splits, 578
  Los Zetas, 575, 578
  methamphetamine production, 575, 577–578
  public adverts/messages to, 576–578
  regional loyalties/nonmember cooperation, 576–577
  religious culture, 577
  Sinaloa Cartel, 576–577
  Templar Knights, 578
  "Tierra Caliente", 576
  Valencias, 576
  as vigilante group, 576
  violence/torture, 576–577
LaMare, M., 569–573
Langner, R., 290
Lasley, J., and Guffey, J., 397
Latin Kings
  illegal immigrants, 134
  Los Zetas, 589
law enforcement and DHS foundations, 581–584
  Bill of Rights, 583
  civil liberties and homeland security, 583
  Department of Homeland Security (DHS), 581
  "foreign aggressors", 584
  Homeland Security Act (2002), 581–584
  legal basis of enforcement against terrorism, 584
  National Security Letters (NSL), 583
  statutory law, 582–583
  USA PATRIOT Act (2001), 581–582

Law of Armed Conflict, 261, 482
Lazarus Group, 201
Leduc, R., 325–332, 351–358
Lee, M. T., and Martinez, R. Jr., 134
Lee, R., 131–132
legislation, post-9/11, 740
Leigh, G., 197–202, 237–241, 267–271
Lesperance, W., 147–150
Lewis, J., 308
Liberation Army Fifth Battalion, 396
Liberation Tigers of Tamil (LTTE), 423–424
  improvised explosive devices (IEDs), 563–564
  "sea-based suicide division", 564
  suicide bombers, 452
Libicki, M. C., 290–291
Liem, D. M., and Farnham, N., 468
Lilli, E., 387–391
Lincoln, Abraham, assassination by Booth, 425
lone actor terrorism, 411–419
  Abdelhamid Abaoud, 416
  Al Qaeda links, 415
  Anders Breivik, 700, 762
  Ansbach attack, 417
  anthrax, 700–701
  Bernard Cazaneuve, 416
  British ISIS facilitator Junaid Hussain, 416
  chemical and biological weapons (CBW), 364
  connections to terrorist groups, 413
  definitional and methodological issues, 412–414
  directed attacks, 415–416
  enabled attacks, 416–417
  Forsane Alizza (Knight of Glory), 415
  future research, 418–419
  Garland Texas attack, 416
  Germany "remote controlled" attacks, 417–418
  group connectivity spectrum, 414–415
  group-directed/lone (differences), 413
  inspired attacks, 417–418
  Islamic State (so-called), 412, 415–417
  "leakage" (communication of intent), 414, 417–418
  "lone wolf" term not helpful, 419
  Mehdi Nammouche, 415–416
  Michael Zehaf-Bibeau, 417–418
  Mohamed Merah, 415
  "Molenbeek" network, 416
  Munir Abdul Kader, 416
  Ottawa shooting (2014), 417–418
  Pamela Geller attack plot, 416
  quantitative studies, 413
  "radical milieu", 417–418
  Royal United Service Institute study, 412
  social network analysis, 414
  typology/profile, 413
  "Unabomber" Ted Kaczynski, 417
  "virtual entrepreneurs", 416, 418
"lone wolf", *see* lone actor terrorism
Lorenzo, R., and Romaniuk, S. N., 181–185, 263–265, 295–298
Los Zetas, 587–589
  armed conflict between groups, 588–589
  Arturo Guzmán Decena "Z1", 587–588
  Beltrán-Leyva Organization, 506, 588
  bodyguards (as), 588
  Cartel Del Noreste, 588
  Foreign Narcotics Kingpin Designation Act, 588
  Grupo Aeromóvil de Fuerzas Especiales (GAFE), 588–589
  Gulf Cartel, 588–589
  Heriberto Lazcano, 588
  Hispanic gangs, 588
  Juárez Cartel, 588
  Kaibiles (Guatemalan Special Forces), 589
  La Familia Michoacana (LFM), 575, 578
  Latin Kings, 589
  links to Venezuelan State, 588
  Los Rastrojos, 588
  Mexican Mafia, 589
  MS-13 (Mara Salvatrucha), 589, 592–593
  Sinaloa Cartel, 588
  Sureños, 589
  Tijuana Cartel, 588
  Zetas Vieja Escuela, 588
Los Zetas Group B, 588
Lovelace, J., Gill, P. and Horgan, J., 394, 560–561
Lowenthal, P., 250
Lynch, M., 192
Lynn, W., 308

M

MacCalman, M., 132
Madrid Bombings, 783
Maguire, J., 221
Mak, S., 670
Malet, D., 370–371
Malheur National Wildlife Refuge, 608
Malwarebytes, 267
Malware Trends (ICS-CERT), 270
Manchester Arena suicide bomber, 462
Manchester truck bomb (PIRA), 395, 398
Manjikian, M., 255–262
Mansoor, P., 482
Mara-Salvatrucha-13 (MS-13), undocumented immigrants, 134
maritime domain awareness (MDA), 595–599
  framework of NMDAO, 596–598
  importance of MDA, 596
  National Maritime Domain Awareness Plan (NMDAP), 596–598
  Secretary of the Navy, 596
  security threats, 598
Marrara, C. A., 31–37, 411–419

Martinez, R. Jr., and Lee, M. T., 134
Martin, G., Catino, M. S. and Romaniuk, S. N., xxi–xxiii
Martin, K., 528, 530
Marton, P., 697–705, 759–763, 765–770, 773–778
mass shootings, domestic security, 545
Matthew, K., 750
Mayhew, P., 460
McAfee, 291
McCarren-Walter Act (1952), 670
McCauley, C., and Seifert, K., 454
McDonnell, James F., 50
McDowell, D., and Hsu, H. Y., 461
McDowell-Smith, A., 491–495, 595–599
McInnes, Gavin, 433
McVeigh, Timothy, 143–144, 426, 434, 560
measures and signatures intelligence (MASINT), 74
  Defense Intelligence Agency (DIA), 617–618
Meilinger, P., 485
Meleagrou-Hitchens, A.
  Clifford, B. and Hughes, S., 374
  Hughes, S. and Clifford, B., 374
Mental Rehabilitation Centers, earthquakes, 717
Mercy Corps, 483
Merida Initiative, 131
Messenger, active users, 188
methamphetamine distribution, 593
methamphetamine production, 575, 577–578
Mexican drug trafficking organizations
  decentralization, 499, 508–509
  domestic security, 545
  federal police crackdown (2006), 661
  Immigration and Customs Enforcement (ICE), 499
  Mexican State help, 660
  prison gang culture (Texas), 497, 501–502
  Sinaloa-Tijuana region, 658–665; *see also* Barrio Azteca (Los Aztecas); Beltrán-Leyva Organization; La Familia Michoacana
Mexican Mafia
  Los Zetas, 589
  MS-13 (Mara Salvatrucha), 592–593
Mexico
  Merida Initiative, 131
  smuggling, 130–131
Mexico border fence, 675–682
  arguments against, 677–679
  arguments in favor, 679–681
  Arizona, 676–677, 681
  Arizona wildfires, 680
  Berlin Wall/Great Wall of China argument, 677, 682
  Boarder Protection, Antiterrorism, and Illegal Control Act (BPAICA), 676
  border patrols, 676–677, 681
  Brownsville (TX), 678, 681
  chain-link, 681
  Clinton administration, 675, 677
  construction variations/implementations, 681–682
  cross-political part support, 679
  cultural ethnocentrism/xenophobia, 677
  cultural ethnocentrism/xenophobia, 682
  Department of Homeland Security (DHS), 676–678, 680–682
  El Paso, 681
  environmental problems, 678, 680
  fence bisecting property, 678
  G. W. Bush administration, 675, 677, 679
  Gorbachev on, 677
  Herman Cain (Republican Presidential candidate), 682
  Hidalgo (TX), 681
  history and origins, 676–677
  Illegal Immigration Reform and Immigration Responsibility Act (1996), 675–676
  immigrant removal orders, 680
  implications current/future, 682
  international picnic (artistic response), 679
  land acquisition, 680–682
  lives lost at border crossings, 678–679
  metal portions-damage/theft, 681–682
  Nogales, 681
  Obama administration, 678
  ranchers' death/arrest, 680
  Sasabe (AZ), 681
  Secure Border Initiative (SBI), 681
  Secure Fence Act (2006), 675, 679
  Sonoran Desert, 679
  surveillance drones, 677, 681
  Tijuana, 681
  Tijuana-San Diego border, 675–676
  tourist visas, 679
  Trump wall, 676–678, 680, 682
  undocumented immigrants, 679–680, 682
  unmanned aerial vehicles (UAVs), 681
  virtual radar fence, 681
  'walkers', 679
  Yuma sector, 679
Michoacán (Mexico), drug production, 575; *see also* La Familia Michoacana
Microsoft Windows operating system, malware, 173, 175, 267–268
Middle East Respiratory Syndrome Coronavirus (MERS-CoV), 148–149
Military Operations on Urban Terrain (MOUT), urban warfare, 479
militias, 601–608
  April-19 as important date, 606–607
  background/foundations, 602, 605–607
  Brandenburg v Ohio, 603
  Bundy standoff (2014), 608
  citizen's militia, 601–603

communication technology, 606–608
conspiracy theorists, 605–607
Constitutional Sheriffs, 607–608
election of Democratic Presidents, 605–606, 608
"false flag" operations (gov.), 607
First Amendment, 602–603
gun control topics, 604–607
ideology, 604–605
Institute for Constitutional Advocacy and Protection (ICAP), 603
legality and legislation, 602–604
local and state level law, 603
Malheur National Wildlife Refuge, 608
membership growth, 606
militarization of police forces, 606
Militia Act (1903), 601
modern militia movement, 603, 608
New Right, 604, 607
Oath Keepers, 607–608
patriot movement, 607–608
People for Constitutional Freedom, 608
Posse Comitatus, 605
private militias, 603
recruits, 607
revival, 607–608
Ruby Ridge, 606–607
Second Amendment, 602–603, 607–608
Senator Arlen Specter, 603
social media, 607
Texas Constitutional Militia, 607
Three Percenters, 607–608
USA PATRIOT Act (2001), 607
Waco, Texas, 606–607
White nationalists, 605
Millet, P., Grushkin, D. and Kuiken, T., 364
Milne, D., 571
"Minaret Program", 277–278
Minnesota Patriots Council, 363, 761
Mirai worm, 178
Moe, T. L., and Pathranarakul, P., 539
Moghaddam, F., 627
"Molenbeek" network, 416
Momen, M. N., and Begum, M. M., 739–744
money laundering, cryptocurrencies, 184
Moore, C., 372
and Tumelty, P., 371
Moore, Charles. (Air Force Maj. Gen.), 311
Moore, J. P., and Howell, J. A, 556
MS-13 (Mara Salvatrucha), 591–593
distributing methamphetamines, 593
FBI Transnational Anti-Gang (TAG) Task Force, 593
Frente Farabundo Marti de Liberación (FMLN), 592–593
Los Angeles, California, 592
Los Zetas, 589, 592–593
Mexican Mafia, 592–593
removal of non-citizens convicted of crime, 593
Salvadoran Civil War, 592–593
Sinaloa Cartel, 593
Sureños, 592
tattoos, 592
Muddle, C., 430
Multi-State Information Sharing and Analysis Center, cybersecurity, 233
Mustapha, J., 371

N

Nagurskoye Air Base, 736
Nakamoto, Satoshi, 182
Nakasone, P. M. (Arm Gen.), 307
Napolitano, J., 126–127
Narodnaya Volya, suicide bombers, 452, 562
National Biosurveillance Integration Center (NBIC), 147–150
9/11 Commission Report, 148
weapons of mass destruction (WMDs), 147, 150
National Center for the Analysis of Violent Crime, 74
National Communications System (NCS), 102
National Crime Information Centre (NCIC), 72
National Critical Infrastructure Prioritization Program (NCIPP), 101
National Cyber Incident Response Plan (2016), 269
National Cyber Security Division, 101, 170
National Cybersecurity Protection Act (2014), 102
National Cyberspace and Communications Integrations Centre (NCCIC), 55, 101–102, 232–233, 245, 269
National Disaster Recovery Framework (NDRF), 743
National Disaster Search Dog Foundation, urban search and rescue (SAR), 789
National Domestic Preparedness Office (NDPO), 74, 93–96
and Attorney General (AG), 93–94
Bush, G. W., 96
criticism, 96
Department of Health and Human Services, 95
Department of Homeland Security (DHS), 93, 96
Environmental Protection Agency (EPA), 95
Federal Bureau of Investigation (FBI), 93
Federal Emergency Management Agency (FEMA), 93–96
weapons of mass destruction (WMDs), 93–95
National Earthquake Hazard Reduction Program, 715
National Emergencies Act (NEA), 742
National Emergency Management Association (NEMA), 153–160
Council of State Governments (CGS), 154, 158

Emergency Management Accreditation Program (EMAP), 155–156
Emergency Management Assistance Compact (EMAC), 155–156
Executive Director Trina Sheets, 158–159
and Federal Emergency Management Agency (FEMA), 158–159
5-year Strategic Plan, 154–156
flood insurance/emergencies, 159
International Association of Emergency Managers, 154
National Governors Association, 154
National Guard (costs), 159–160
National Incident Management System (NIMS), 154
non-governmental organization (NGO), 153
September 11 terrorist attacks, 154
National Firearms Act (1934), 140
National Flood Insurance Act (1968), 535
National Flood Insurance Act and Disaster Relief Act (1974), 535
National Governors Association
disaster management and assistance, 744
National Emergency Management Association (NEMA), 154
National Guard
costs, 159–160
disaster management and assistance, 741–742
Operation Jump Start (Mexico border fence), 680
National Incident Management System (NIMS)
agroterrorism, 693
disaster management and assistance, 725, 727
National Emergency Management Association (NEMA), 154
urban search and rescue (SAR), 788
National Infrastructure Protection Center (NIPC), 232–233
National Infrastructure Protection Centre (NIPC), 74
National Infrastructure Protection Plan (NIPP)
Annex, 31, 34, 36
critical infrastructure and key resources, 27–28, 113
Critical Infrastructure Management Framework, 35
Critical Manufacturing Sector, 31, 34–35
Information Analysis and Infrastructure Protection (IAIP) Directorate, 100–101
National Protection and Program Directorate (NPPD), 100
National Instant Criminal Background Check System (NICS), 140, 606
National Intelligence Community, passive surveillance, 622
nationalists, 421–426
anti-government anarchists (US), 426
Armée Révolutionnaire Bretonne (ARB), 425
civil wars, 422
Eastern Europe, 422
"ethno-nationalism", 422–424
Fronte di Liberazione Naziunale Corsu (FLNC), 425
Fuerzas Armadas Revolucionarias de Colombi (FARC), 425
Guy Fawkes, 424
independence referendums, 425
Ku Klux Klan, 425
Marxist ethno-nationalist terrorism, 425
Nation of Islam, 425
nationalism in US context, 425–426
Oklahoma City Bombing, 426
peaceful means to independence, 424–425
protests against authoritarianism and monarchism, 422
sanctions, 423–424
and terrorism, 422–425
terrorist watch lists, 422
US Civil War, 425
World War I-Franz Ferdinand assassination, 424
National Maritime Domain Awareness Plan (NMDAP), 596–598
national preparedness (hazards), 611–614
emergency family plan, 612–613
emergency kit, 613–614
evacuation plans, 613
first-aid/citizen education, 612–613
National Protection and Program Directorate (NPPD), 99–103
critical infrastructure and key resources, 100
cybersecurity, 100–103, 232
links with other agencies/entities, 42, 99–103
national health challenges, 148–149
National Infrastructure Protection Plan (NIPP), 100
Soft Targets and Crowded Places (ST-CPs), 463–464
National Response Framework (NPF), agroterrorism, 693
National Response Plan (NPR)
agroterrorism, 693
disaster management and assistance, 725
urban search and rescue (SAR), 791
National Security Act (1947), 274
Central Intelligence Agency (CIA), 21
Intelligence Reform and Terrorism Prevention Act (2004), 23
National Security Council, 21–22
National Security Strategy (NSS) report, 650
National Security Agency (NSA), 273–280
Armed Forces Security Agency (AFSA), 274–275
cable companies information, 277

Central Security Service (CSS), 200–201, 276
Cold War collection platforms, 277
Cold War crises, 275–276
collection authority, 274
controversies (1950s-1970s), 277–278
Cuban Missile Crisis, 276
cypher breaking, 274
Echelon, 279
Fort Meade headquarters, 275, 279
Korean War, 275
"Minaret Program", 277–278
Project Shamrock, 277
Pueblo incident, 277
Reagan years (1980s), 278
role after 9/11 and controversies, 279
Snowden revelations, 279
US Cyber Command (USCYBERCOM), 279–280, 305–312
USS Liberty attack, 277
Venona Project, 275
Vietnam War, 276–277
National Security Council
kidnapping, 572
National Security Act (1947), 21–22
National Security Strategy (NSS) report, 649–654
bureaucratic procedures, 654
climate change, 653
communicative purposes, 651
composition process, 652–653
critical analysis, 653–654
Deputies Committee, 652
Executive Secretariat, 652
legal foundation and requirements, 650
National Security Act (1947), 650
political bargaining, 653
presidential administration's explicit strategy, 650–654
Presidential State of the Union Address, 651
Principals Committee, 652
National Strategy for Homeland Security (2007), xxi
National Technical Nuclear Forensics Centre (NTNFC), 50
National Telecommunications and Information Administration (NTIA), 216
Nation of Islam, 425
Nazi Germany, sarin, 766
neural networks, 246
never agents, Novichok/VX, 770; *see also* sarin
New Information and Communication World Order (NWICO), 222
New IRA (NIRA), 407
Nichols, Terry, 143–144
Nielsen, K., 147, 150
Niepce, Joseph, 619
Non-Proliferation Treaty (NPT), 131–132
Noriega, R. F., and Cárdenas, J. R., 384
North American Aerospace Defense Command (NORAD), September 11 terrorist attacks, 68
North Atlantic Treaty Organization (NATO), 107
Tallinn Manual (cyberwarfare), 225, 237–238, 257–258; *see also* Partnership for Peace
Northern Ireland
Irish Republican Army (IRA), 403, 405–407
The Troubles, 327–328, 404–405
Northern Irish Assembly, 405, 407
North Ireland, Catholic minority/Protestant majority (NI), 405
North Korea
cybercrime, 219, 221, 271
malware (origin), 270–271
nuclear threats, 751–752
State-sponsored terrorism, 445, 448n5
North Sea Route (NSR), 732, 735–736
North West Passage (NWP), 735
Norton, R., 380
Novichok, Salisbury poising of Skripals, 770
Noyce, R. S., 777
Nuclear Command, Control, and Communications (NC3), 749–750
nuclear materials
Al Qaeda, 132, 749
Aum Shinrikyo (Japanese cult), 132, 749
dirty bomb, 132
improperly secured, 748–749
nuclear facility employees theft, 132
smuggling, 130–132
Nuclear Nonproliferation Treaty (1969), 754
Nuclear Regulatory Commission, earthquakes, 714
nuclear threats, 747–755
Anti-Ballistic Missile (ABM) Treaty, 754
anti-satellite missiles (attack warning), 752
arms control value (Countryman), 754–755
belligerent countries, 750–753
'broken arrows', 753
Cuban Missile Crisis, 276, 750–751
cybersecurity, 749–750
dirty bomb, 748–749
global warhead inventories, 748
hypersonic glide vehicle, 752
Intermediate-range Nuclear Forces (INF) Treaty, 753
International Atomic Energy Agency (IAEA), 751
Iranian nuclear initiative, 751
Joint Comprehensive Plan of Action (JCPOA), 755
mayors of Nagasaki and Hiroshima, 748
missile defense systems, 752
mutual assured destruction, 754
negotiate with nuclear weapon countries, 753–754
North Korea, 751–752

Nuclear Command, Control, and Communications (NC3), 749–750
Nuclear Nonproliferation Treaty (1969), 754
Presidents Reagan and Gorbachev "nuclear war must never be fought", 755
Russian weapons programs, 752–753
sanctions, 755
Strategic Arms Limitations Talks (SALT), 754
Terminal High Altitude Air Defense (THAAD), 752
terrorism, 748–749
Turkey, 753
weapons usable materials, 748
Nueva Generación Jalisco Cartel (CJNG), Tijuana Cartel, 664–665
Nuttall, M., and Dodds, K., 732

O

Oath Keepers, 607–608
O'Brien, S. P., and Haider-Markel, D. P., 601, 608
Office for Civil Rights and Civil Liberties (CRCL), 41, 530
Office of Biometric Identity Management (OBIM), 100, 102
Office of Cyber and Infrastructure Analysis (OCIA), 100
Office of Cybersecurity and Communication (CS&C), 100–102
Office of Emergency Communications (OEC), 42, 102
Office of Infrastructure Protection (OIP), 100–101
Office of Intelligence and Analysis (OI&A), 103
Office of State and Local Coordination, 43
Office of Strategic Services (OSS), 20
Office of the Coordinator of Information (COI), 19–20
Office of War Information (OWI), 20
Official IRA (OIRA), 404
Oikos University Shooting, 493–494
Oklahoma City Bombing, 143–144, 426
Omnibus Crime Control and Safe Streets Act (1968), 73
Omona, D. A., 747–755
Organized Crime Control Act (1970), 142
Osorio, C. P., 205–209, 283–287
Ouassini, A.
and Dao, B., 301–303
and Hunter, M., 163–165
Ouassini, N., 543–546

P

Padilla, Jose, 46
Palestine Liberation Organization (PLO), 444, 473
Pan Am (103), 67
Panetta, L., 215
Pape, R. A., 454
Parker, C., 433–434
Parker, D., Chapot, D. and Davis, J., 625–633
Partiya Karkerên Kurdistanê (PKK), 423–424, 446, 452
Partnership for Peace (PFP), 107–109
entries from former Soviet Union, 108–109
NATO Summit (1999), 108
passive surveillance, 617–622
AutoINT, 621–622
facial recognition technology (FRT), 620
Human Intelligence (HUMINT), 617
imagery intelligence (IMINT), 617–620
"internet of things", 618
National Intelligence Community, 622
photograph data, 619–620
shadow intelligence community, 622
signals intelligence (SIGINT), 617–618
smart devices, 618
smartphones, 619
social media, 618–620
Tesla, 621–622
Twitter, 618, 620–621
Pathranarakul, P., and Moe, T. L., 539
Patterson, W. R., 65–70, 129–135, 137–145
Pelton, Pelton, 278
People for Constitutional Freedom, 608
People's Liberation Army of China (PLA), 301–303
people smuggling, 133–134
Philips, B. J., 469
phishing, 284, 286
phone phreaks, 295–296
pipe bomb attacks (Austin, Texas, 2018), 565
Plummer, P., 159
Podesta, John, hacked email (Clinton campaign), 218–219, 227n2
Pompeo, Mike, 734–735
Pontes, G. F. M., and Revill, J., 361–366
Pope, N., 701
Porter, G. D., 321
Posner, P., 740
Posse Comitatus (militia), 605
Preedy, M., 249–253
Presidential Decision Directives (PDDs), critical infrastructure and key resources, 115
Presidential Elections (US)
cybercrime, 218–219, 227n2, 227n3, 257
Trump victory and social media, 219, 227n3, 257
Pretorius, F., 372
prison gang culture (Texas), 497, 501–502
Prohibition, 138, 388
Project Shamrock, 277
Protective Security Advisor (PSA) Program, 100–101
Protective Security Coordination Division (PSCD), 100

Proud Boys, 433
Provisional Irish Republican Army (PIRA), 395, 404
psychological operations (PSYOPS) strategy, urban warfare, 482, 485
Public Health Security and Bioterrorism Preparedness and Response Act (2002), agroterrorism, 692
Pueblo incident, 277

Q

Qassem, N., 380–381
Quarantelli, E. L., 726

R

radicalization prevention and response, 625–633
- *al-Shabaab al-Mu'min*, 628
- American-Muslim community, 629
- Channel (United Kingdom), 631
- cognitive considerations, 632
- Council of American-Islamic Relations (CAIR), 629
- counter-radicalization efforts, 627
- counter-violent extremism (US), 627–629
- deradicalisation project (Denmark), 631–632
- European experience of prevention strategies, 627, 629–632, 633n1
- Exit-Germany, 631–632
- FBI Director Wray, 625
- Hayat, 631–632
- homegrown terror, 626
- Info-houses (Denmark), 630
- interventions tailored for individuals, 631–632
- Islamic State (so-called), 626, 628, 631–632
- national hotline (Germany), 630–631
- Obama administration CVE strategy, 627–629
- President Trump, 628
- Prevent (United Kingdom), 629–632
- radicalization definition, 626–627
- Vulnerability Assessment Framework, 630

Radical Right in the United States, The (Parker), 433–434
Rainsy, S., 218
Rajneeshee religious cult, 362–363
Ranstorp, M., Cilluffo, F. J. and Cozzens, J. B., 372–373
Rapoport, D. C., 390, 423
Real IRA (RIRA), 404
Reif, K., and Davenport, K., 748
Revill, J., 562
- and Pontes, G. F. M., 361–366

Revolutionary Armed Forces of Colombia (FARC), smuggling, 131
RFID (radio frequency identification) chips, 264
Richardson, R. Jr., 111–116
ricin, 759–763
- Abqaiq-Khurais attack (2019), 761
- Anders Breivik, 762
- Ansar Allah, 761
- Bloomberg/Obama targets (Shannon Richardson), 761–762
- castor oil industry, 759–760
- coated bullets/projectiles, 761–762
- criminal use, 761–762
- differential diagnosis, 760
- fear and attention, 762–763
- hoaxers, 762
- laced letters, 761–762
- lethal dose (inconvenient volume), 760, 762
- median lethal dose (MLD), 760
- Minnesota Patriots Council, 761
- natural chemical weapon, 759–760
- poisoning cases, **763**
- Soviet KGB assassinations, 761
- sub-lethal dose antibodies, 760
- symptoms of poisoning, 760
- UK ricin plotters (2003), 761
- United States Postal Services, 762

Ridge, Tom (Director DHS), xxi
right-wing extremism (RWE), 426–436
- Anti-Defamation League (ADL), 435
- anti-Islamic hate crimes, 432, 436
- anti-'Other' sentiment, 430–431, 436
- counter-violent extremism (CVE), 429, 434–436
- historical context, 432–433
- incitements of violence, 435
- 'Otherization' concept, 430–431, 433
- post-9/11, 432
- post-Trump, 432–433
- reactionary movement, 433–434
- recommendations, 434–435
- thematic values/ideological components, 430

riots and rioting, 117–122
- Arab Spring, 119
- authoritarian regimes, 117–119
- civil laws, 117
- cyberattacks, 121
- definition, 118–119
- democracies, 118
- England, 121–122
- food riots, 121
- Ford Hunger March, 120
- frustrations at actions of gov., 119–120
- immigrant groups, 121
- military (in), 120
- participants, 121–122
- prison riots, 120
- public order, 117
- public space/special setting, 120
- reasons, 122
- Rousseau's theory of the social contract, 118
- types, 119–121

Riots Communities and Victims Panel, 121–122
River Bend Resort & Country Club, 678
Roberts R., 587–589, 591–593
Rogers, J., 731–737
Rogers, M., 221
Rogers, M. S. (Navy Adm.), 307
Rojek, J., and Klinger, D. A., 642–643
Romaniuk, S. N.
  and Bennett, N., 369–376
  and Bhattacharyya, A., 713–718
  Catino, M. S. and Martin, G., xxi–xxiii
  and DiMarco, S. R., 787–791
  and Dziwisz, D., 305–312
  and Hattiangady, P., 211–227
  and Haughton, S. A., 19–23, 525–531
  and Keměny, J., 273–280
  and Khan, U., 477–485
  and Lorenzo, R., 181–185, 263–265, 295–298
  and Seymour, M., 125–127
  and Williams, S., 611–614
Roosevelt, (FDR)
  Federal Bureau of Investigation (FBI), 72
  Greenland and WWII, 733
Rousseau, J. J., 118
Ruby Ridge, 142–143, 606–607
Russian Arctic islands, 736
Russian State Research Centre of Virology and Biotechnology, 776
Russia's intelligence service, cybercrime, 218–219

S

SAFE Port Act (2006), 47
Sageman, M., 627
Samborowski, L. J., 617–622
Sandler, J., 382
San Francisco Earthquake (1906), 535
sarin, 765–770
  "alphabet bomber" Kurbegovic, 768
  Aum Shinrikyo (Japanese cult), 766–768
  Chilean secret police assassinations, 769–770
  DHMP (dimethyl hydrogen phosphate) process, 766
  first-responders, 767
  homeland security implications, 767–770
  Iraq, 766, 769
  lethal concentration-time (gas), 766–767
  missile payload (alleged), 769
  Nazi Germany, 766
  organophosphate poisoning (similar), 767
  Russian Federal Security Service (FSB), 770
  state actors use, 766
  symptoms SLUDGE concept, 767
  synthetic nerve agent, 766–767
  Syrian Civil War, 769
  volatility (high), 766
Sasser worm, 174
Savage, M. D., 3–7, 25–28, 59–63, 87–91
Sayoc, Cesar Jr., 433
Schlosser, E., 753
Schmitt, M., 257
Schofield, M., and Bolstad, E., 565
Schuurman, B., 415
Science and Technology Directorate, 43
screening, 637–640
  aviation security, 66–67, 638–639
  cancer, 638
  disease, 637–638
  hijacking, 389
  Traveler Redress Inquiry Program (TRIP), 639
  United States Postal Services, 639–640; *see also* body scanners
Scrivens, R., 433
secure border initiative, 125–127
Secure Fence Act (2006), Mexico border fence, 675, 679
Segal, A., 308
Seifert, K., and McCauley, C., 454
Seismic Safety Commission, 714
September 11 terrorist attacks, 67–69, 328
  American (11), 68
  American (77), 68
  anti-Islamic hate crimes, 432
  border patrols and national entry points, 514–516
  Department of Homeland Security (DHS), 544–545
  Federal Air Marshal Service officers, 69
  Federal Aviation Administration (FAA), 68–69
  9/11 Commission Report, 68, 115, 148
  United (93), 68
  United (175), 68
  White House notification/underground bunker, 68
Serena, C. C., and Clarke, C. P., 463
Seymour, M., and Romaniuk, S. N., 125–127
SGSecure Movement, 399
Shanghai Cooperation Organization (SCO), 224
Shapiro, J., and Byman, D., 373
Sheets, T., 158–159
Shehzad, Faisal, 463
Shirk, D., 665
Shirky, C., 191
"shoe bomber", 529
Shoigu, Sergei, 736
signals intelligence (SIGINT), 249
  cypher breaking, 274
  electronic surveillance, 73
  'Five Eyes', 251
  GCHQ (Government Communications Headquarters), 199, 249–253
  history, 274–275
  National Security Agency (NSA), 273–280

passive surveillance, 617–618
US Navy vessels, 277
Sinaloa Cartel, 659–663
Barrio Azteca (Los Aztecas), 498–499
Beltrán-Leyva Organization, 506, 508, 660
Colombia drug traffickers, 661
"el Chapo" Joaquin Guzmán, 659–662
factional implosion, 661–662
federal police crackdown (2006), 661
"The Federation", 660
Foreign Narcotics Kingpin Designation Act, 662
Golden Triangle, 661
Guadalajara "cartel", 659–660, 662
Guzmán-Loera Organization, 660
Juarez Cartel, 660
Kiki Camarena DEA undercover agent, 659–660, 662–663
La Familia Michoacana (LFM), 576–577
leadership, 661
Los Antrax, 662
Los Zetas, 588
Mexican State help, 660
Miguel Ángel Félix Gallardo, 659–660
MS-13 (Mara Salvatrucha), 593
"Operation Godfather", 660
Operation Leyenda, 660
Pablo Escobar, 661
"Pax Mafiosa", 660–661
Rafael Caro Quintero, 662–663
rival group fighting, 661–662, 664
supply chain network, 661
violence, 662
Sinaloa-Tijuana region, 657–665
Border Industrialization Program (Mexican Gov. 1965), 657–658
business process outsourcing (BPO), 658
Ciudad Juárez, 658
Customs and Border Protection (CBP), 657
Drug Enforcement Agency, 659
El Paso, 657–658
Golden Triangle, 658, 661
international border crossings, 658
Mexican drug trafficking organizations, 658–665
paradox of border cities, 657–659
Reynosa, 658
San Ysidro port of entry, 658
Sinaloa Cartel, 659–663
Tijuana Cartel, 663–665
Tijuana homicides, 664–665
violence and crime, 658–659
Singer, P., 565
Sinn Féin (SF), Irish Republican Army (IRA), 407
situational crime prevention (SCP) techniques
improvised explosive devices (IEDs), 394, 396–397
target hardening, 460
situational terrorism prevention (STP), target hardening, 460–461
Skinner, D., 286
'Sky Marshals', 66, 69, 390
Small Business Act (1953), 535
smallpox, 773–778
Aralsk incident (1971), 776
Atlantic Storm tabletop exercise (2005), 778
"biohacking", 777
cowpox virus, 775
destructive potential, 776–777
eradication by WHO, 775–776
fatal outcomes, 774–775
Fort Pitt (18th-century), 778
hemorrhagic smallpox, 774
immunization (US military personnel), 775
laboratory work with virus, 775–777
live vaccine, 775
malignant smallpox, 774–775
nature of the pathogen, 773–775
smallpox scabs, 775, 777
symptoms, 774
vaccine stockpiles, 778
variola virus, 773–774
weapon potential, 777–778
"Smart Cities", 264, 484
Smith, A. D., 421
Smith, T., 549–556
smuggling, 129–135
criminal gangs, 134
definition, 129–130
diamonds (Africa), 134
EU Drugs Strategy and Action Plan, 131
Fast and Furious firearms trafficking investigation, 14, 144
insurgencies, 129–131, 139
Mexico, 130–131
money laundering, 135
narcotics, 129–131
nuclear materials, 130–132
Pakistani nuclear weapons, 132
people smuggling/human trafficking, 133–134
sanction busting, 132–133
state actors, 132
taxation avoidance, 129–130
tobacco, 139
transnational criminal organization (TCOs), 130–131
UN sanctions, 132–133
weapons of mass destruction (WMDs), 130–132
World Drug Report (2017), 130–131
Snider, D. M., 651
Snowden revelations, cybersecurity, 222
Snow, D. M., and Drew, D. M., 650
social contract (Rousseau), 118
social engineering (deception techniques)

cybersecurity, 283–287
piggybacking/tailgating, 284–285
psychology aspects, 285–286
swatting (prank SWAT call outs), 295–298
social media
APAC-favored platforms, 188
Arabic language Twitter verse, 192
disaster management and assistance, 540
domestic security, 546
editorial intervention, 193
Instagram, 188, 618
Internet-powered networked society, 191, 193
Islamic State (so-called), 192, 546
malicious actors, 189
messaging evolution, 188
Messenger, 188
militias, 607
passive surveillance, 618–620
peacebuilding "civil society", 193
personal cybersecurity, 189–191
political parties manipulation, 218, 226n1
right to privacy, 191–192
sensitive date pool, 189
State and personal power balance, 191–194
State's surveillance, 191–193, 221–222, 252
strong passwords, 191
Syrian Civil War, 192
terrorism copycat effects, 467–468
user numbers, 188, 619
virtual private networks, 191
war between states (Hamilton Paper 8), 192
WhatsApp, 188
YouTube, 188; *see also* cybersecurity; Facebook
Soft Targets and Crowded Places (ST-CPs) plan, 463–464
Somalia case study, improvised explosive devices (IEDs), 566–567
Sony, Guardians of Peace hack, 221
Spanish Civil War
Basque separatists, 345
foreign terrorist fighters (FTFs), 370
Special Weapons and Tactics Teams (SWAT), 641–647
Black Panther firefight (1969), 642
botched raid disastrous, 645–646
Broken Windows Theory, 647
"call of last resort", 645, 647
call outs to none SWAT incidents, 645–646
Darryl Gates (LAPD), 642, 645
organizational structure, training, operations, 642–644
research by Klinger and Rojek, 642–643
"routine patrol" tasks, 646–647
Stephen Downing (LAPD), 645
swatting (prank/revenge call outs), 295–298
Watts Riots, 642
Spencer, J., 484
Spokane, Washington plot, (2011), 565
"Stafford Act," disaster management and assistance, 724, 726, 741
State and Local Advisory Group (SLAG), 94
State-sponsored terrorism, 441–448
American laws, 445–446
Bremer Commission, 444
countries involved, 447n1
cyberattacks, 446
designations and ramifications, 441, 445–446
"foreign policy instrument", 443–444
forms of State support, 442
history, 443–444
Iran, 446
Israel, 446
Marxist guerrillas, 444
North Korea, 445, 448n5
official list (US), 448n5
Palestine Liberation Organization (PLO), 444
sanctions, 445–446
terrorist or freedom fighter, 441
United Nations Security Council, 442
West Kashmir, 444
Steoff, R., 527
Stewart, M. G., and Grant, M. J., 353
Stott, J., and Wyatt, J, 747
Strategic Arms Limitations Talks (SALT), 754
Strategic Services Unit (SSU), 20
Strategic Support Forces (SSF), 302-303
Student and Exchange Visitor Information System (SEVIS), 81
Stuxnet worm, 178, 215–216, 289–293
cyber war, 290–291
Obama administration, 292
United States and Israel, 164, 289–291
suicide bombers, 451–455
Al Qaeda, 454
definition, 453
Hamas, 452
Hezbollah, 452
improvised explosive devices (IEDs), 453, 564
kamikaze pilots WWII, 452
Liberation Tigers of Tamil (LTTE), 452
Narodnaya Volya, 452, 562
non-State asymmetric warfare, 451, 454–455
Partiya Karkerên Kurdistanê (PKK), 452
tactics (explanations), 453–454
vehicle-borne improvised explosive device (VBIED), 453
Sullivan, J., 498
Supervisory Control and Data Acquisition (SCADA), 56
Sureños
Los Zetas, 589
MS-13 (Mara Salvatrucha), 592
surveillance cameras, urban warfare, 482, 484

suspicious packages, 781–784
  "Amerithrax" attack, 362, 364–365, 698, 701, 704, 782
  Aum Shinrikyo (Japanese cult), 783
  booby traps, 783
  classification of threats, 783
  harmless to test security response, 782–784
  homeland security implications, 783–784
  improvised explosive devices (IEDs), 782–783
  mailed packages, 781–782, 784
  public awareness programs, 398–399, 782, 784
  public spaces/mass transit systems, 782–784
  terms in use, 781
  unattended or suspicious (distinction), 782
swatting (prank SWAT call outs), 295–298
  celebrity targets, 295–298
  deaths, 297
  delivery pranks, 296–297
  legal responses, 297–298
Syrian Civil War
  Al Qaeda, 329
  chemical and biological weapons (CBW), 362, 364–365
  Hezbollah, 382
  sarin, 769
  social media, 192
Szekely, O., 382

T

Tallinn Manual (cyberwarfare), 225, 237–238, 257–258
target hardening, 457–464
  Boston Marathon, 463
  CCTV, 458, 462
  conceptual discussion and definitions, 458–461
  contemporary developments, 461–463
  defensive measures, 458
  information sharing, 463
  Islamic State (so-called), 459, 461
  London attacks (2017), 462
  Paris attacks, 461
  residential burglaries, 460
  situational terrorism prevention (STP), 460–461
  'soft/hard targets' differentiation, 457
  'soft targets', 458–460
  Soft Targets and Crowded Places (ST-CPs) plan, 463–464
  stakeholders role, 463
  Times Square bomb plot, 463
  US Homeland Security, 463–464
  vehicle-ramming attacks, 458, 462
Tavani, H., 256
Technical Research Ships (TRSs), 277
Tehreek-e-Taliban Pakistan, 461
telephony pranks, swatting (pranking SWAT call outs), 295–298
Templar Knights, La Familia Michoacana (LFM), 578
Terminal High Altitude Air Defense (THAAD), 752
Terrill, C., 189
terrorism copycat effects, 467–475
  Al Qaeda, 474
  counterterrorism information, 470
  Islamic State (so-called), 474
  media coverage, 467–468, 470
  modus operandi, 470, 472–474
  operational and strategic facets, 470–472
  Palestine Liberation Organization (PLO), 473
  social media, 467–468
  'terrorist' label, 468–469, 474
  terrorist leadership vacuum, 469
  terrorist or freedom fighter, 468–469
  vehicle-ramming attacks, 467, 472
terrorism prevention
  Department of Homeland Security (DHS), 43
  deradicalization programs, 331
  Intelligence Reform and Terrorism Prevention Act (2004), 23
  political resolutions, 408
  situational terrorism prevention (STP), 460–461; *see also* target hardening
terrorist watch lists
  Hezbollah, 379, 383
  Irish Republican Army (IRA), 404
  kidnapping, 572
  nationalists, 422
Tesla, passive surveillance, 621–622
Texas Constitutional Militia, 607
Texas Task Force-1 (TX-TF-1), 54
Third Department of the People's Liberation Army (3PLA), 301–303
ThreatConnect, 234
Three Percenters, 607–608
Tijuana Cartel, 663–665
  Arellano Félix brothers, 663–664
  Arellano-Felix Organization (AFO), 664–665
  Avilés Pérez, 663
  Fernando Sánchez Arellano, 664
  Guadalajara "cartel", 663
  leadership splits, 664
  Los Zetas, 588
  Miguel Ángel Félix Gallardo, 663–664
  Nueva Generación Jalisco Cartel (CJNG), 664–665
  "Operation Godfather", 663
  Ramón Arellano Félix (killed), 664
  Rayo Lopez (hitman), 664
  war between Sinaloa Cartel, 664
Tijuana Cartel Nueva Generación, 665
Times Square bomb plot, 463
tobacco smuggling, 15–16, 139
Tomihisa, T., and Kazumi, M., 748
Tranchemontagne, M., 560

transnational criminal organization (TCOs), smuggling, 130–131
transportation infrastructure, Critical Manufacturing Sector, 35
Transportation Security Administration (TSA)
critical infrastructure and key resources, 114
Federal Aviation Administration (FAA), 65, 69
Transport Security Administration (TSA), screening, 638
Tromblay, D. E., 13–16, 45–51, 71–75, 93–96, 99–103, 231–234
Truman, President, Office of Strategic Services (OSS), 20
Trump administration
disaster management and assistance, 714
and hate/speech-crime, 433
illegal immigrants, 545
Mexico border fence, 676–678, 680, 682
offer to buy Greenland, 733
radicalization prevention and response, 628
right-wing extremism (RWE), 432–433
Trump victory and social media, 219, 227n3, 257
US Cyber Command (USCYBERCOM), 308–309, 311
Tumelty, P., and Moore, C., 371
Twitter
data analytic tools, 620–621
open-source intelligence, 618, 620–621
Tzu, Sun, 485

U

Ulbricht, Ross, 184
Umpqua Community College Shooting, 493
"Unabomber" Ted Kaczynski, 417, 560
United Nations (UN)
chemical and biological weapons (CBW), 365
cybersecurity, 222–223, 225
Disaster Relief Coordinator, 716
earthquakes (UNESCO), 715–716
Groups of Governmental Experts (GCE), 222–225
International Decade of Natural Disaster Reduction, 716
Office for the Coordination of Humanitarian Affairs, 716
sanctions, 132–133
State-sponsored terrorism, 442
United Nations Charter, 224, 240
United Nations General Assembly (UNGA), 222, 225
United Nations Security Council, 251–252, 365, 442
World Summits on the Information Society (WSIS), 222
United States Border Patrol, 516–519, 670; *see also* border patrols and national entry points
United States Citizenship and Immigration Services (USCIS), 669–673
applications/petitions (immigrants), 672
'cheap' foreign labor, 669
E-Verify, 671
establishment, 669
forerunner services/bureaus, 670
Homeland Security Act (2002), 670
immigrant/nonimmigrant classifications, 671
Immigration and Naturalization Service (INS), 670–671
immigration service, 671
national security/honoring American values, 669
naturalization, 671
post-9/11 immigration policy, 672
service centers, 671
sovereign rights, 669
visa issuing, 672
wary clientele, 671–672
United States Geological Survey (USGS), 715
United States Postal Services
"Amerithrax" attack, 362, 364–365, 698, 701, 704
anthrax (preparedness), 702
biohazard detection system (BDS), 702, 762
mail irradiation, 702–703
mobile mail screening station, 640
ricin, 762
screening, 639–640, 702
suspicious packages, 781–782, 784
Technical Services Division, 640
University of Texas Tower Shooting, 493–494
unmanned aerial vehicles (UAVs)
Arctic and homeland security, 735–737
"Arctic Drone Squadron" (Russia), 736
Federal Aviation Administration (FAA), 69–70
Mexico border fence, 677, 681
Urban Operations (UO), urban warfare, 479–480, 485
urban search and rescue (SAR), 787–791
dogs (use), 789–790
domestic and international operations, 790
Federal Emergency Management Agency (FEMA), 788
National Disaster Search Dog Foundation, 789
National Incident Management System (NIMS), 788
National Response Plan (NPR), 791
phases, 787–788
Urban Search and Rescue (US&R) Task Forces, 53–57
communication equipment, 789
cyberattacks, 55–57
earthquakes, 55, 789
grassroots approach, 55, 57
Hurricane Harvey, 54, 57

local emergency responders, 54
logistics and technical equipment, 789
medical equipment, 789
National Response Plan (NPR), 791
operations equipment, 788–789
operations training, 788
ordinary citizens' deployment, 54–55
Texas Task Force-1 (TX-TF-1), 54
violent extremist organizations (VEOs), 55
watershed events, 53–54
urban security campaigns, target hardening, 462
urban warfare, 477–485
Art of War (Sun Tzu), 485, 617–618
asymmetric threat, 481
Baltic States, 484
Battle of Sadr City, 478, 483
Beirut, 478, 482
collateral damage/civilian injury, 482
contemporary military intelligence concepts, 482, 484
DiMarco on, 483
and economic growth, 484
Fallujah, 483
Grozny II, 479
history, 478–479
Iraq War, 484
Law of Armed Conflict, 482
mental resolve, 483
military/non-military aspects, 481–483
Military Operations on Urban Terrain (MOUT), 479
Mosul, 478–479
psychological operations (PSYOPS) strategy, 482, 485
restrictive rules of engagement (ROE), 480, 483
surveillance cameras, 482, 484
UK MOD publication, 482
unmanned aerial vehicles (UAVs), 481
Urban Operations (UO), 479–480, 485
urban populations, 477, 480, 485
US Army Field Manual, 479, 481–485
US Army Training and Doctrine Command (TRADOC), 477–478
USA PATRIOT Act (2001)
civil liberties and homeland security, 526–530, 583
critics, 529–530
cybersecurity, 209
Detainee Treatment Act (2005), 529
"enemy combatants", 529
Fahrenheit 9/11 (Moore), 544
Foreign Intelligence Surveillance Act (1978), 527–528
Guantanamo Bay, 529
Hamdan v Rumsfeld, 529
kidnapping, 571–572
military tribunals (alleged terrorists), 528–529
militias, 607
Prisoners of War (Geneva Convention 1949), 529
"shoe bomber", 529
and statutory law, 582–583
support for, 527–529
War on Terror, 529
Wiretap Act (1968), 527
US Army Field Manual, urban warfare, 479, 481–482
US Army's Rapid Reaction Force (RRF), 484
US Army Training and Doctrine Command (TRADOC), 477–478
US Coast Guard (USCG), critical infrastructure and key resources, 114
US Computer Emergency Readiness Team (US-CERT), 101–102, 233
US Cyber Command (USCYBERCOM), 302–303, 305–312
"armed aggression" threshold, 310
Bolton (National Security Advisor), 309
command visions, 309–311
Commander Alexander, 306–307
Commander Moore, 311
Commander Rogers, 307
Cyber Mission Force (CMF), 307
"defend forward", 310–311
DOD Cyber Strategy, 309–310
domain responsibility for .mil .gov, 308
evolution (Cyber Command), 306–307, 311
Fort Meade headquarters, 307
Full Operational Capability, 307
Initial Operational Capability, 306–307
mission, 307–309
Presidential Directives, 309
Trump administration, 308–309, 311
Unified Combatant Command (CCMD), 307
USS Cole attack, 564
US Secret Service (USSS), cybersecurity, 232
USS Liberty attack, 277
US Visitor and Immigration Status Indicator Technology (US-VISIT), 102

V

Valencias, La Familia Michoacana (LFM), 576
Valiquet, J., 153–160
vehicle-borne explosive device (VBED), 352
vehicle-borne improvised explosive device (VBIED), 352, 395–396, 398, 453, 560, 562–563
vehicle-ramming attacks
car bomb alternative, 355
target hardening, 458, 462
terrorism copycat effects, 467, 472
Victims of Trafficking and Violence Protection Act (2000), 82–83

Vietnam War, improvised explosive devices (IEDs), 564
violent extremist organizations (VEOs), emergency response, 55
Virginia Tech Shootings, 492–494
Vitak, J. M., 188
Vizzard, W., 140
von Clausewitz, C., 479
VX nerve agent, Kim Jong-nam assassination, 770
Vygotsky, L. S., 480

W

Waco, Texas
  Branch Davidians, 143, 606
  and militias, 606–607
Waledac, 177
Walker, John, 278
Walter, A. T., 187–195
WannaCry, 178, 201, 271
War on Drugs, 278
Waseem, Z., 457–464
Wasem, R., 672
Waugh, W. Jr., 67
weapons of mass destruction (WMDs)
  dirty bomb, 132
  Immigration and Customs Enforcement (ICE), 81
  National Biosurveillance Integration Center (NBIC), 147, 150
  National Domestic Preparedness Office (NDPO), 93–95
  smuggling, 130–132; *see also* nuclear threats
Weaver, Randy, 142–143
Western Hemisphere Travel Initiative (WHTI), 41
West Kashmir, 444
WhatsApp, active users, 188
White Supremacist Organization, improvised explosive devices (IEDs), 565
Whitman, Charles, 493–494
Wielhouwer, P. W., 480
Wikileaks, 256
Williams, S., and Romaniuk, S. N., 611–614
Wilson, C., 560
Wilson, Charlie, 371
Wimmer, E., 777
Winter, C., 451–455
Wiretap Act (1968), 527
Wolfel, R. L., 480
Wolf, H. C., Bisson, C. and Bledsoe, C., 620
World Drug Report (2017), smuggling, 130–131
World Health Organization (WHO)
  Collaborating Center on Smallpox and Other Poxvirus Infections, 776
  Smallpox Eradication Program (SEP), 775–776
Wyatt, J, and Stott, J., 747

Y

Yarger, H. R., 480
Yemen
  Al Qaeda attacks, 327, 331
  General People's Congress (GPC), 336
  Houthi Movement, 336
Yemen Civil War, Ansar Allah, 336, 340–341
YouTube, active users, 188

Z

Zetas, *see* Los Zetas
Zetas Vieja Escuela, Los Zetas, 588

For Product Safety Concerns and Information please contact our EU
representative GPSR@taylorandfrancis.com
Taylor & Francis Verlag GmbH, Kaufingerstraße 24, 80331 München, Germany

www.ingramcontent.com/pod-product-compliance
Ingram Content Group UK Ltd.
Pitfield, Milton Keynes, MK11 3LW, UK
UKHW050233200926
475702UK00020B/3013
* 9 7 8 1 0 3 2 3 6 2 6 3 2 *